R

G O L I A

I N N E R   M O N G O L I A

oHarbin

oChangchun (Xinjing)

JILIN

oShenyang (Mukden)

LIAONING

oHohhot

oDatong   oBeijing

NORTH KOREA

HEBEI

oTianjin

oDalian (Dairen)

Taiyuan

oShujiazhuang

SHANXI

Yellow R.

SHANDONG

SOUTH KOREA

SEA OF JAPAN

oXian

HENAN

YELLOW

SEA

SHAANXI

JIANGSU

J A P A N

Han R.

A

Hefei

oNanjing

ANHUI

Suzhou
(Soochow)

oShanghai

HUBEI

oWuhan

Yangtze R.

Hangzhou

oNingbo

ZHEJIANG

EAST   CHINA

SEA

RYŪKYŪ ISLANDS

Nanchang o

HUNAN

JAINGXI

Changsha

oFuzhou

P A C I F I C

FUJIAN

oTaipei

O C E A N

TAIWAN

G X I

GUANGDONG

oGuangzhou (Canton)

Macáo

oHong Kong

oHaikou

HAINAN

Lineberger Memorial Library

Lutheran Theological Southern Seminary   Columbia, S. C.

The Cambridge Encyclopedia of China

The Cambridge Encyclopedia of
CHINA

Editor
Brian Hook
University of Leeds

Consultant Editor
Denis Twitchett
Princeton University

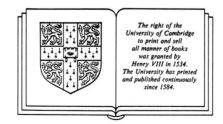

The right of the
University of Cambridge
to print and sell
all manner of books
was granted by
Henry VIII in 1534.
The University has printed
and published continuously
since 1584.

CAMBRIDGE UNIVERSITY PRESS

Cambridge

New York   Port Chester

Melbourne   Sydney

Published by the Press Syndicate of the University of Cambridge,
The Pitt Building, Trumpington Street, Cambridge, CB2 1RP
40 West 20th Street, New York, NY 10011-4211 USA
10 Stamford Road, Oakleigh, Melbourne 3166, Australia

© 1st edition Trewin Copplestone Books Limited, 1982
© Cambridge University Press, 1987
© 2nd edition Cambridge University Press, 1991

Printed in Spain by Mateu Cromo Artes Gráficas, S.A., Madrid

British Library cataloguing in publication data

The Cambridge encyclopedia of China – 2nd ed.
1. China
I   Hook, Brian
951.058
ISBN 0 521 35594 X

Library of Congress cataloguing in publication data

The Cambridge encyclopedia of China / editor, Brian Hook :
consultant editor, Denis Twitchett – 2nd edn
          p.   cm.
Includes bibliographical references and index.
ISBN 0 521 35594 X
1. China—Encyclopedias
I. Hook, Brian.   II. Twitchett, Denis Crispin.
DS705.C35 1991
951'.003—dc20   91–18600   CIP

ISBN 0 521 35594 X hardback 2nd edition
(ISBN 0 521 23099 3 hardback 1st edition)

Contributors

A.D.   **Professor Audrey Donnithorne**
            University of Hong Kong

A.G.   **Angus Graham**
            Late Emeritus Professor, School of Oriental & African Studies, University of London

A.L.   **Dr Ann Lonsdale**
            University of Oxford

B.G.H   **Brian Hook**
            University of Leeds

C.A.   **Charles Aylmer**
            University of Cambridge Library, Cambridge University

C.A.P.   **Professor Charles A. Peterson**
            Cornell University

C.A.R.   **Colin A. Ronan**
            Needham Research Institute, Cambridge

C.B.H.   **Professor Christopher B. Howe**
            School of Oriental & African Studies, University of London

C.C.   **Dr Christopher Cullen**
            School of Oriental & African Studies, University of London

C.F.   **Professor Charlotte Furth**
            California State University at Long Beach

C.M.W.   **Professor C. Martin Wilbur**
            Columbia University

D.C.T.   **Professor Denis Twitchett**
            Princeton University

D.D.L.   **Dr Donald D. Leslie**
            Canberra College of Advanced Education

D.H.   **David Hawkes**
            Emeritus Fellow, All Souls College, Oxford

D.McM.   **Professor D. McMullen**
            University of Cambridge

D.N.K.   **Professor David N. Keightley**
            University of California, Berkeley

D.P.   **Professor David Pollard**
            The Chinese University of Hong Kong

D.R.   **Don Rimmington**
            University of Leeds

D.S.   **Dr David Shambaugh**
            School of Oriental & African Studies, University of London

D.S.S.   **Professor D.S. Sutton**
            Carnegie-Mellon University

E.G.   **Professor Else Glahn**
            Formerly of University of Aarhus

E.N.A.   **Professor E.N. Anderson, Jr**
            University of California, Riverside

E.S.R.   **Professor Evelyn S. Rawski**
            University of Pittsburgh

E.T.   **Dr Ellis Tinios**
            University of Leeds

E.W.   **Elizabeth Wright**
            BBC

F.A.K.   **Professor Frank A. Kierman**
            Rider College, New Jersey

F.B.   **Dr Francesca Bray**
            University of California, Los Angeles

Contents

9 List of maps
10 Preface
11 Introduction: The Chineseness of China

LAND AND RESOURCES

16 **Geographical and Climatic Regions**
17 General geography
23 The northeast
24 The northern steppe
25 The north-central heartland
26 The inner north
27 The lower Yangtze region
28 The middle Yangtze region
29 The maritime south
30 Sichuan and the southwest
31 The high plateaux
32 The wild environments

34 **Natural Resources**
34 Energy resources
38 Metals and metallic ores
42 Other minerals
43 Cement
44 Fertilizers

45 **Communications**
45 Inland waterways
46 Maritime shipping
47 Historic routes and trade patterns
48 The modern road system
49 The railways
50 Civil aviation
51 The postal service
51 Radio and television

52 **The Economy**
52 Development
54 Agriculture
59 Industrial development
65 Hong Kong
65 Taiwan
66 Macao

PEOPLES

68 **Anthropology**
68 Origins of human culture in East Asia
72 The Mongoloid family of peoples
75 The expansion of the Han Chinese

77 **The Non-Han Cultures**
77 The national minorities
82 Scripts of the non-Han Chinese

84 **External China**
84 Historical perspective
85 Hong Kong and Macao
86 The Chinese overseas today

SOCIETY

92 **The Social Order**

92 The individual, family and community
93 The work unit
93 Hierarchy, authority and lineage
95 The status of women
96 Village society
97 Urban life
98 Social aspects of trade
99 Secret societies
99 Social aspects of communes, production brigades and teams

101 **Law**
101 Codification
101 Penal system
102 Collective punishment
103 Customary law
105 The communist legal system

107 **Education**
107 The traditional education system
109 The examination system
111 Literacy
113 Socio-political use of character reform
113 Printing
114 The introduction of Western higher education
116 Education as indoctrination: traditional and modern
117 The educational achievements of the People's Republic

120 **Health and Medicine**
120 Traditional medicine: social and philosophical background
123 Face and pulse diagnosis
124 Conduit therapies
124 Herbalism and pharmacology
127 Traditional body care
127 Traditional medical literature
129 Western and Chinese medicine combined
130 Anaesthesia
131 Medical services

132 **Games and Sports**
132 Traditional games and sports
133 Western sports

THE CONTINUITY OF CHINA

136 **Archaeology**
137 Legendary prehistory
138 Palaeolithic cultures
138 Neolithic cultures

142 **Shang: The First Historical Dynasty (c. 1554–1045 BC)**
142 The state
143 Divination
144 Religion
144 The economy
144 Bronze working

145 **The Zhou Dynasty (c. 1122–221 BC)**
145 Western Zhou: Founding and founders
146 Eastern Zhou: 'Spring and Autumn' and the Warring States

147 State of Jin
148 State of Qi
148 State of Chu
148 Wei Valley
149 Feudalism

149 **The Qin Dynasty (221–206 BC)**
149 Qin
151 Xiang Yu (d. 202 BC)
151 The Great Wall
151 Burning of the Books

151 **The Han Dynasty (202 BC–AD 220)**
151 Political ideas
151 Former Han
155 Xiongnu
155 Chang'an
155 Institutions
155 Sima Qian (145–c. 90 BC)
156 Paper
156 Xin (AD 9–23)
156 Eunuchs in Qin and Han
156 Later Han
157 Luoyang
157 Ban Gu (AD 32–92)

157 **Wei, Jin and Northern and Southern Dynasties (AD 220–581)**
157 Historical perspective
158 Cao Cao (155–220) and the state of Cao Wei (220–65)
158 State of Wu (222–80)
159 State of Shu (221–63)
159 Western Jin (265–316)
161 Eastern Jin (317–420), and southern dynasties
162 Northern Wei (387–534)
162 Power struggle in the north
163 The fall of the south

164 **The Sui Dynasty (AD 581–618)**
164 Wendi
165 Chang'an
165 Yangdi
165 The Great Wall
166 Grand Canal
166 The Turks
166 Korea

166 **The Tang Dynasty (AD 618–907)**
166 Background
167 Tang government

173 **Five Dynasties and Ten Kingdoms (AD 907–59)**
173 Background
173 Five Dynasties (north China)
174 The Ten Kingdoms
176 Tangut empire
177 Khitan empire (Liao dynasty)

177 **The Song Dynasty (AD 960–1279)**
177 Historical perspective
177 Taizu (Zhao Kuangyin) (928–76)
178 Taizong (Zhao Kuangyi) (939–97)
179 Huizong (Zhao Ji) (1082–1135) and the fall of Northern Song

Contents

179 Gaozong (1107–87) and the establishment of Southern Song
180 Government
181 The civil service and its recruitment
181 New elites
182 The commercial revolution
183 The reforms of Wang Anshi (1021–86)
184 Kaifeng
185 The Liao dynasty (904–1125)
187 Xixia (c. 990–1227)
188 The Jin dynasty (1115–1234)
188 Printing and the successful application of technology
188 Hangzhou
188 Urbanization and urban culture
189 Foreign relations
190 Neo-Confucianism

191 The Yuan Dynasty (AD 1276–1368)
191 Emperors
192 Structure of government
192 Economy
193 Factions and rebellions
194 Foreign relations
194 Religion and philosophy
194 Literature and art
194 Science and technology

195 The Ming Dynasty (AD 1368–1644)
195 Zhu Yuanzhang Rebellion (1355–67)
196 The Hongwu Emperor, 'Grand Progenitor', the Ming dynasty's founder
196 Yongle Emperor
197 Dual capitals
198 Zheng He
199 Grand Secretariat
199 Eunuchs
200 The Ming *lijia* and *baojia* systems
200 The gentry and the Ming examination system
200 Tribute and trade
201 Mongol wars
201 Japan—diplomacy, trade and piracy
202 Jiajing and Wanli reigns
202 Merchant colonization
202 Huizhou and Shanxi merchants
203 Single-whip tax reform (Yi tiao bian)
203 Jingdezhen, the ceramic centre
204 *Tiangong kaiwu*, technological encyclopedia
204 *Bencao gang mu*
204 Wang Yangming
205 Donglin Academy
205 Matteo Ricci
205 Li Zicheng Rebellion

206 The Qing Dynasty (AD 1644–1912)
206 Historical perspective
208 Nurhachi (1559–1626)
208 Abahai (1592–1643)
209 Manchu banner system
209 Shanhaiguan invasion
209 Dorgon (1612–50)
209 Manchu-Chinese dyarchy
209 Kangxi Emperor (1654–1722)
210 Rites Controversy
210 Three Feudatories Revolt
210 Tibet
211 Turkestan

212 Treaties of Nerchinsk and Kiakhta
212 Qianlong Emperor (1711–99)
213 Literary inquisition
213 Suzhou and other handicraft centres
214 Yangzhou salt merchants
214 White Lotus Rebellion (1796–1805)
215 Eight Trigrams Rebellion (1813)
215 The Canton system
216 The Macartney embassy
216 The British East India Company
216 The Napier mission
217 Lin Zexu (1785–1850)
218 The Opium War
218 The Treaty of Nanjing
218 The Taiping Rebellion
219 The Nian Rebellion
220 Muslim rebellions
220 Small Sword Society Uprising (Shanghai and vicinity, 1853–5)
220 Manchuria and Russia
222 Xinjiang
222 The Arrow War (1856–60)
223 Tongzhi Restoration
223 The Self-strengthening Movement (Ziqiang)
224 Guandu Shangban Enterprises
224 Zeng Guofan (1811–72)
224 Li Hongzhang (1823–1901)
225 *Zongli Yamen*
225 Treaty ports
225 Missionaries
226 Tianjin Massacre
226 Sino-French War (1884–5)
227 Empress Dowager Cixi (1835–1908)
227 Sino-Japanese War (1894–5)
227 The Reform Movement of 1898
229 The Boxer Uprising (1900)
230 The Russo-Japanese War (1904–5)
230 *Tongmenghui*
230 Constitutional Movement
231 Railway Protection Movement
231 Wuchang Uprising: the Republican Revolution of 1911
232 Manchu abdication (1912)

233 The Republican Period (1912–49)
233 Sun Yat-sen (1866–1925)
234 Yuan Shikai (1859–1916)
235 Parliaments
235 Warlords
236 The May Fourth Movement
237 The *Guomindang*
237 The Chinese Communist Party
238 The United Front
239 Peng Pai and the peasants' movement
240 The Northern Expedition
241 The Shanghai coup
241 Nanjing government
242 New Life Movement
243 Manchukuo
243 Jiangxi Soviet
244 The Long March
245 Marco Polo Bridge Incident
246 Anti-Japanese War and United Front
247 Chongqing
248 Joseph Stilwell
249 Yan'an
249 Rectification campaigns

250 New Fourth Army Incident
250 Civil war
252 Taiwan
252 Chiang Kai-shek

253 The People's Republic
253 Liberation
254 Mao Zedong
259 Zhou Enlai
260 New Democracy
261 Three-Anti and Five-Anti campaigns
262 Korean War
262 Land reform
263 Gao Gang
263 Agricultural cooperatives
264 Five-year Plans
265 The Hundred Flowers
265 Anti-Rightist Campaign
265 Great Leap Forward
266 The communes
267 Peng Dehuai
267 Agricultural crisis
268 Tibet
268 The Sino-Indian border dispute
269 The Sino-Soviet conflict
270 Socialist Education Movement
270 The two lines
270 Cultural Revolution
273 Ninth Party Congress
274 The Ussuri Incident
274 Anti-Confucian campaign
274 Tenth Party Congress
275 Tiananmen Incident, 1976
276 Death of Mao Zedong
276 Hua Guofeng (b. 1920)
277 'Gang of four'
277 Deng Xiaoping (b. 1904)
279 Four Modernizations
280 The opening of China to the West
280 Eleventh Party Congress
280 Zhao Ziyang (b. 1919)
281 Democracy Wall
281 Twelfth Party Congress
281 Spiritual Pollution Campaign
281 Thirteenth Party Congress
282 The Beijing massacre
284 Li Peng (b. 1928)
284 Jiang Zemin (b. 1926)
285 People's Liberation Army
285 China's nuclear capability
285 Taiwan (1949–79)

THE MIND AND SENSES OF CHINA

288 Beliefs, Customs and Folklore
288 Cosmology
288 Divination
291 Ancestor worship
294 Folk religion

296 Philosophy and Religion
296 Daoism
301 Confucianism
304 Buddhism
309 Other schools of philosophy
313 Judaism
314 Manichaeism

314 Zoroastrianism
314 Islam
317 Christianity
319 Late Qing and early 20th-century thought
321 Chinese thought since the May Fourth Movement

324 **Words and Signs**
324 Origin of the Chinese language
325 Early pronunciation
326 Chinese dialects and Modern Standard Chinese
329 The evolution of Chinese writing
329 Categories of Chinese characters
331 The Chinese writing system
333 Calligraphy
334 Metaphors, allusions and proverbial phrases
335 Personal and family names
337 Transcription
337 Dictionaries

340 **Literature**
340 Printing and publishing
342 Epigraphy and the earliest texts
343 The Confucian classics
345 Annals and histories
347 Principal poets and writers
351 Traditional fiction and popular literature
354 Dramatic narratives and oral literature
354 Western and Marxist influences in the 19th and
    20th centuries

358 **Drama, Music and Cinema**
358 The drama tradition
359 The Chinese theatre: social background
359 The dramatic form
361 The Peking Opera and the modern phase
361 Music
354 Western-style drama
365 Cinema
367 Radio and television

368 **Cuisine**
368 Historical introduction
370 The basis of Chinese cuisine today
372 Ingredients, recipes and meals
373 Beverages
374 Regional variations
376 Chinese nutritional concepts
376 Social uses of food

377 **Time and Quantities**
377 Hours
377 The traditional calendar
378 The cycle of the years
379 Coins and currencies
380 Dimensions, weights and measures

ART AND ARCHITECTURE

382 **Design and Symbol**
382 Ritual bronze vessels
385 Bronze bells
385 Stone-chimes
385 Ritual jades
386 Jade insignia
386 Ceramics
390 Bronze

390 Gold
390 Silver
391 Sculpture
393 Jade
394 Ivory
395 Symbolism in art
397 Pictorial references and emblems in Chinese art
398 Calligraphy

399 **Historical Phases and Schools**
399 Perspective
400 Neolithic period
401 Shang dynasty
401 Zhou dynasty
402 Han dynasty
404 Wei, Jin and Northern and Southern dynasties
406 Tang dynasty
409 Song dynasty
412 Yuan dynasty
414 Ming dynasty painting
416 Ming dynasty ceramics
416 Ming lacquer
416 Ming cloisonné enamel
417 Qing dynasty painting
418 Qing dynasty ceramics
418 Qing dynasty jade
419 The Republic
419 The People's Republic of China

419 **Techniques of Art Forms and Crafts**
419 Calligraphy and painting
421 Lacquer
422 Textiles
423 Furniture
424 Gold and silver

425 **Architecture**
425 Archaeological evidence
425 Available materials
426 Structural methods
427 Traditional principles of layout and planning
428 Traditional building types
431 Garden architecture

**SCIENCE AND TECHNOLOGY:
HISTORICAL PERSPECTIVE**

434 **Agriculture and Biological Sciences**
434 Agriculture
435 Botany
437 Zoology

437 **Physical Sciences**
437 Chemistry
438 Earth sciences
440 Mathematics
441 Astronomy

444 **Technology**
444 Shipbuilding
446 Salt industry and deep borehole drilling
447 Iron and steel technology
448 Mechanical engineering

451 **Mining and Civil Engineering**
451 Mining and civil engineering before 1911

452 Mining industry, 1911–49
453 Mining industry and training, 1949 onwards
454 Civil engineering, 1911–49
454 Civil engineering and training, 1949 onwards

APPENDICES
456 A: Guide for Visitors
459 B: Sources of Information
462 C: Transliteration Tables
465 D: Methods of Simplifying Characters
466 E: Chinese Communist Party Organizations
467 F: Government of the People's Republic of China
468 G: Military Organizations of the People's Republic
    of China
469 H: Major Foreign Trade Organizations of the
    People's Republic of China

470 Further reading
475 Select glossary
485 Index
504 Acknowledgements

Maps
16 General physical map
18 Temperatures: January
18 Temperatures: July
18 Annual precipitation
18 Frost-free periods
19 Soils
21 Population distribution
22 Administrative and geographical regions
32 Wild environments
37 Sources of energy
45 Inland waterways
48 Silk Road
49 Railways
68 Origins of human culture: sites
72 The Mongoloid families
79 China's minority nationalities
88 Principal places of origin in China
88 Teochiu, Hakka and Hokkien emigrant areas
88 Cantonese emigrant area
137 Distribution of major Palaeolithic sites
152 Han China 195 BC
154 Han China AD 2
159 The Three Kingdoms
160 Frontiers of Western Jin China
162 Northern Wei and Liu-Song
162 Division between Northern Wei and Southern Qi
163 North China in the early 6th century AD
163 Division between Eastern Wei, Western Wei and
    Liang
174 Five Dynasties and Ten Kingdoms
178 Song dynasty China
186 China in 1206
191 East and Central Asia under the Mongols
198 China during the Ming dynasty
199 Itinerary of Zheng He's 7th expedition
206 China in 1760
211 Tibet: early 19th century
214 White Lotus and Eight Trigrams
221 Manchuria: 19th century
226 Treaty ports
324 Sino-Tibetan languages
328 Dialects

Preface

The first edition of the *Cambridge Encyclopedia of China* was compiled at a pivotal point in the modern history of China. In 1976 the death of Mao Zedong, followed swiftly by the arrest of the so-called 'Gang of Four', brought to an end one power struggle for the right to succeed to the leadership and, ironically, marked the start of another, albeit less tempestuous, as Deng Xiaoping and his supporters sought to bring to a close the short 'interregnum' of Hua Guofeng.

In the period that has elapsed between the first and second editions of the Encyclopedia, Deng Xiaoping has led China through a period of unprecedented modernization. The change, characterized by the emancipation of private initiative in sections of the economy, the opening of China to foreign influence, the emergence of new, freer talents in literature and the arts and an upsurge in scholarly research into China's past and present, was extensive and substantial. Despite the crisis of 1989 and the intensive critical scrutiny which followed, much of the reform of the 1980s must also be seen in the context of reform in the other Marxist–Leninist systems, and appears to be part of an irreversible historical trend.

The addition of these momentous events to the historical record and their explicit or implicit integration into the text of the Encyclopedia has resulted in a major revision of the book. Accordingly, there has been substantial rewriting in the sections dealing with the political history, economy, administrative and economic geography, social organization, law, education, political philosophy and modern literature. Throughout the book the opportunity has been taken wherever possible to reflect the most recent advances in scholarly research; thus, the section dealing with archaeology has been re-written. Additions to and changes in the text have led, in turn, to a comprehensive review of the illustrations, maps, tables and charts. Many of the latter, incorporating qualitative data and other information complementing the new text, have been thoroughly revised and updated. The appendices have been thoroughly revised, and readers will also note that the process of reviewing illustration material began with the cover—which, showing the skyline of modern Beijing—aims to convey the sense of modernization through the juxtaposition of different, seemingly incongruous styles of traditional and contemporary architecture.

In addition to these changes, the opportunity has been taken to reconsider the appropriateness of the use of Wade-Giles romanization to render Chinese terms alphabetically. It was decided to reflect the adoption of *pinyin* in China, and its increasing use abroad, by converting the book to the *pinyin* form of romanization. There are some exceptions to this form of transliteration, notably the retention of certain names which, by virtue of having long since been assimilated into the English language, are used throughout the book in preference to *pinyin*. Thus, Canton, Hong Kong, Macao, Tibet, Inner Mongolia, Yangtze, Sun Yat-sen and Chiang Kai-shek have not been converted to *pinyin*.

In sum, readers will find the second edition provides an updated and substantially revised text, fresh illustrative material, and presentational and organizational changes that are intended to facilitate its use as a valuable source of information about all aspects of Chinese civilization, traditional and contemporary, as the quest for modernization continues. In its preparation, as with the first edition, I had much invaluable help and advice from Professor Denis Twitchett of Princeton University, for which I wish to record my appreciation. Thanks are also due to the Encyclopedia's commissioning editor, Ann Stonehouse, for her forbearance and wisdom, and to Callie Kendall, our editorial associate, for her energy and enthusiasm. The taxing task of converting to *pinyin* would not have been possible without the able preparation and constant surveillance of Charles Aylmer of the Cambridge University Library. Lastly, I should record my appreciation of the collective effort of all the distinguished authors whose individual contributions to knowledge have made the incomparable study of China more accessible to those who consult this book.

Brian Hook

Introduction: The Chineseness of China

The Chinese people may be expected to take their Chineseness for granted. The Chinese government may not and, with a modern constitution committed to socialist revolution, will find conscious discussion of Chineseness embarrassing unless it can define it to fit its present situation. Indeed, the subject could easily degenerate into chauvinism. Also, China today is radically different from China in 1900, and almost every aspect of Chineseness underwent considerable change during the past 3000 years. From the outside, the characteristics attributed to China are more elusive and any effort to outline them without reference to time and the processes of change before the modern era must be inadequate. Even then, the task is not straightforward.

We could, for example, say that China is a place and everything that had happened within its present boundaries was Chinese. But as a place it has had very unstable boundaries, expanding and contracting rapidly from time to time. There was even a brief period, during the Mongol conquest, when it could be said that China ceased to exist. Nor is it easier to say that China is the country of the Chinese. It begs the question, who were the Chinese? No one has ever been sure how many people did, in fact, qualify as Chinese. Figures do exist for each imperial dynasty but who were included and excluded seems to have varied considerably. Also, there were always people living outside imperial boundaries who might well be described as Chinese and in the past century the numbers of such people rose rapidly.

There is more agreement among scholars that China should be seen primarily as a civilization, although some would stress its polity as a 'Confucian' state and others the nature of its agrarian society. Yet others would rather speak of the quality of Chinese thought or the artistic genius of the Chinese. But then we would still have to take into account both place and time, because parts of the civilization spread far and, after local adaptation, would more appropriately be described as Japanese, Korean or Vietnamese, and other parts waxed and waned from dynasty to dynasty.

In short, no simple description is enough. As a society, China has been primarily agrarian and yet much of what is distinctive had been developed in Chinese cities. As a polity, a bureaucratic monarchy had lasted over 2000 years but parts of agrarian China were ruled by a nomadic tribal aristocracy for long periods and more than half of the area constituting Chinese territory today had in the past developed quite different kinds of social and political systems. When we use the broader term civilization and include in it the ideas, values and institutions that emerged and developed largely within China, we are looking at something like a complex organism that has to be understood as a whole. And what is quintessentially Chinese is the remarkable sense of continuity that seems to have made the civilization increasingly distinctive over the centuries.

I suggest that our understanding of Chineseness must recognize the following: it is living and changeable; it is also the product of a shared historical experience whose record has continually influenced its growth; it has become increasingly a self-conscious matter for China; and it should be related to what appears to be, or to have been, Chinese in the eyes of non-Chinese. In this context, the following questions may be asked. In what ways did the first Chinese feel that they were Chinese? How did that sense of Chineseness change over the centuries? How much of that sense is still relevant today? And how does this self-image compare with how others see China?

The earliest awareness of China we know of came with the rise of the Zhou dynasty at the end of the 2nd millennium BC. This happened in north China along the Yellow River valley following on the need to justify both the overthrow of the Shang dynasty and the erection of new principles of moral and political authority. Objectively, the foundations of China had already been laid by the Shang: the idea of the single ruler receiving tribute from all directions, an ideographic language, a religion of ancestor worship, capital cities of religious and political importance and an agricultural economy that could support a small aristocratic elite. This first China was not initially all that different from the states that had developed earlier in the Nile and Tigris-Euphrates valleys, but it emerged a long way away from the others and was destined to have quite a different history.

Self-awareness as a distinctive civilization, however, did not emerge until a few centuries later, with the writings of Confucius and his contemporaries (6th to 5th centuries BC). By this time the Zhou ruler was seen as having the mandate of Heaven and made to represent a cosmic order on Earth and the Chinese language was already a unique tool for education and government. A privileged elite had mastered the instruments of military and political power and begun to speculate on the moral and social basis of man's relations with man. Eventually, after continuous fighting among the leaders of this elite, the Zhou was overthrown and the Qin empire (221–207 BC) brought an extensive territory under a centralized government. Under the Qin and its successors, the civilization was to become increasingly mature and complex.

What was clearly Chinese by this time for the Chinese was their language of signs and symbols. It had overcome the limitations of speech and hearing and had united peoples who could not have understood each other otherwise. The stress on the family as a basic social unit, founded on the powerful concept of filial feeling (*xiao*), allowed it to be used to support the concept of loyalty (*zhong*) towards the emperor. Also, the facts of being the only literate polity for thousands of kilometres around and the most powerful state in a still backward neighbourhood were to lead to a sense of cosmic destiny for the Chinese Son of Heaven (*tianzi*). With the help of vast resources, strong armies, tough laws administered by central officials, and a monopoly of learning, China was promised a long period of supremacy. The length of that period and the extent that China was able to dominate the region were ultimately to confirm the superiority of that Chineseness.

There is less general agreement about how much this Chineseness developed and changed. The picture of changelessness, from the Qin empire to the mid-19th century, although strongly challenged, still survives and has been sustained by the major symbols of Chinese unity: the language, the personalized dynastic state and its cyclical fortunes, and the immense influence of Confucian rhetoric and institutions at all levels of society. But the dynastic state did not become the standard political form until after the Han dynasty (206 BC–AD 220) and similarly the cyclical view of history was confirmed only after that. Also, from the appearance of Han Confucianism in the first century BC to the state orthodoxy of neo-Confucianism in the 14th century, the changing nature and fate of Confucian ideas and values themselves refute the view of a changeless China.

There are other institutions seen as characteristically Chinese which came long after the first empire. The most important was introduced from outside China, a vital stimulus to a decaying society. This was Buddhism which, over a period of some five centuries (4th to 8th centuries AD) enriched and transformed Chinese life, thought, science and medicine, literature and fine arts to an extent that is still not adequately acknowledged. Buddhism influenced almost everything it touched and it was to touch the lives of every Chinese and reach every part of China and beyond. It stimulated the institutionalization of indigenous cults and popular practices and gave rise to the rival Daoist religion. It challenged state Confucianization and remained strong in the Chinese courts for several centuries. It was so successful that it came to be considered an integral part of Chinese civilization. Yet China cannot be described as Buddhist and this fact illuminates some features of the Chineseness we seek to identify.

For example, Buddhism enriched the common language of China, but it was also compromised and changed by its use of that language. Buddhist monks won the ear of many a Chinese ruler and dominated several courts but could offer no alternative to the bureaucratic and militaristic structure on which each dynasty depended. Buddhist temples and monasteries were built everywhere but they could not satisfy all the local and family needs of an agrarian people. Buddhist philosophy created a sense of awe among the literati, but it met resistance on two levels: it threatened the idea of the family and had to be countered; it threatened the literati monopoly of power and had to be integrated in some way into the bureaucratic system. We might add that Buddhism appealed to the universalist side of Confucianism and enhanced the idealism in Chinese thought. But because it also challenged the particularist core of Chinese state and society and questioned its supremacy under Heaven, it had to be either ejected or domesticated and absorbed. That China succeeded in the latter by the Tang dynasty (AD 618–906) underlines the inclusiveness that was a key part of Chineseness for the first thousand years of imperial history.

Another great stimulus that also came from outside China was less benevolent. The empire was subject to great pressures from tribal confederations along China's northern and western borders. During the 4th century AD the defences collapsed and hundreds of thousands of non-Chinese invaders devastated most of north China. For three centuries, the Chinese state struggled to survive, in the north by compromises with a nomadic military aristocracy and in the south by mobilizing new human and natural resources to an extent unknown before. This was a major formative period for China and by the time it was reunified, from the north, it was a very different China from that of the Han. Non-Chinese aristocratic elements in the new elites dominated the military system and the court was altogether more confident than it had ever been. Thus, the infusion of Buddhist universalism on the one hand and non-Chinese concepts of power on the other had moulded a new world-view and this world-view itself would become an essential part of Chineseness thereafter.

There were, of course, further changes during the next thousand years. A new kind of non-aristocratic literati emerged from the ruins of the Tang empire; also an expanding economy, still agrarian but strengthened by more extensive trading networks and by the larger proportion of landowners among the populace. By the end of the Song dynasty (960–1276) there had developed a rejuvenated neo-Confucianism and something of a cultural renaissance in literature and the finer arts. It has been remarked how this occurred despite the fact that the Song was militarily weak and its empire shrinking in the face of continuous Khitan, Tangut, Jurchen and Mongol threats along the northern borders. But it might have been these very pressures which further defined the acceptable limits of Chinese civilization. They were narrower and less open limits, there was less variety and more refinement, but what remained was vigorous and of high quality and showed little sign of either decadence or rigidity. The Chineseness of China was probably more clearly defined in the 12th century than at any other time.

This judgement itself is influenced by what happened soon afterwards. In 1276 the Mongols finally accomplished the total conquest of China. This was a traumatic experience for the Song Chinese and it is a wonder that it did not permanently damage the Chinese image of themselves. Two factors were important in salvaging that self-image. Millions of Chinese in north China had been living under foreign rule for over two centuries without having lost their essential Chineseness. They had confirmed that Chineseness had become so secure that it was the foreign rulers who were threatened by assimilation. Secondly, the fact that the Mongol Yuan dynasty ruled all China for only 92 years and was succeeded by a Chinese dynasty helped to erase the memory of that unprecedented humiliation. But the experience did leave its mark. The Mongol conquest was a brutalizing experience that saw a further increase of imperial power at the expense of traditional checks and balances in a Chinese court; a greater element of despotism became part of Chineseness thereafter. At the same time, Ming restoration (1368–1644) reaffirmed the supremacy of Chinese civilization and encouraged a new conservatism and an arrogance about Chinese institutions. But some of the literati themselves began to notice signs of decline and decadence in their civilization during this period.

Yet the following dynasty, the Qing, when China was once again ruled by non-Chinese (1644–1911), seemed to have confounded the pessimists. The Manchus, allied with Mongols and Chinese from outside the Great Wall, brought a new vigour to China, extended its boundaries to its furthest extent, stimulated the economy and China had a rapid rise in population during the 18th century. So confident was China once again at the beginning of the 19th century that it would be anachronistic hindsight to suggest that the seeds of destruction had already been planted in the civilization by that time. There was nothing that could convincingly show that the civilization was about to fail of its own accord.

What brought it down during the course of the 19th century was Western power, a new kind of power based on superior science and technology, political and economic organizations and a revolutionary vision of indefinite progress. Against this power, mere Chineseness, however confident, was no match. But the Chinese leaders were not to know that and could not be persuaded to re-examine the nature of that Chineseness until half a century later. And when that came, it was too late to save the Confucian imperial state.

Did that really matter? Probably not. Chineseness was surely not dependent on the empire. The Republic of 1912 was Chinese; so were the militarists, the Sun Yat-sen revolutionaries, the compradors and new bourgeoisie and the May Fourth intellectuals who worked to modernize China in order to save it. The goal was the same, the people were the same. Only the means were different and that should not have affected the Chineseness of the final product. Yet disagreements about the final product became serious and led to a polarization in the Chinese elite that was to confuse the issues. By the 1920s criticism of modern ideas had led back to Confucianism as the taproot of Chineseness; in turn, attacks on the baneful influence of Confucianism called for total Westernization as a means of revitalizing Chineseness. In 1928 the polarization unexpectedly resulted in the open and bitter struggle between the Guomindang, as guardians of the Chinese tradition, and the Chinese Communist Party, as vanguards of a new Chinese millennium. The politicization of the issues did not affect the majority of the people. The poor worked to stay alive; their Chineseness was never in question. The intellectuals argued on, but the options for those who saw no conflict between modernization and Chineseness were being reduced. The Japanese model, which might have inspired them, was closed off when Japanese aggression in China after 1931 became intolerable to the patriotic. By the end of the Second World War the choice had become one between a consciously Chinese militaristic traditionalism and a peasant-based but progressive universalism. The victory of the latter laid the foundations of a revolutionary socialist state that could hardly have been further away from the Confucian empire that had fallen only 38 years earlier.

The sense of Chineseness that, despite many changes, had cumulatively developed over the centuries was now officially set aside. In the eyes of the revolutionaries, it had been too closely identified with Confucianism in its several manifestations and that was clearly part of a corrupt and decadent past. Furthermore, this traditional conception of Chineseness was now dangerous. It was supportive of 'Great Han chauvinism' and this was inappropriate to a socialist state with many large minority peoples. Also, it encouraged familism, clannishness, localism and other kinds of particularism, all of which ran contrary to the ideals of socialism.

Indeed, the Confucian-based Chineseness was seen as elitist and for the privileged, it was inclusive, indulgent, anarchic if not libertarian, and this was contrary to the purposeful and puritanical exclusiveness that the Communist Party stood for.

The People's Republic remains, of course, Chinese, but this is to be a new kind of Chinese that it has sought to redefine. Thus for China, Chineseness since 1949 embraces all within the present borders. It is characterized by a common Marxist–Leninism with the Thought of Mao Zedong having replaced Confucianism as the dominant ideology. From this is expected to flow the main ingredients of a new Chinese civilization: socialist education, modern science and industry, popular literature and the arts, global consciousness of a fresh assessment of all of Chinese history as part of world history.

It is obvious that China cannot free itself from traditional Chineseness overnight. It might have been easier if it had a model to follow: modernization along Western lines or socialism along the way of the Soviet Union. But, having rejected the first in 1949 and the second after 1960, it had to turn to its own resources. And here it was simply not possible to chart a Chinese course without calling on the Chinese heritage and that heritage, however diluted and distorted, showed that it can turn the revolution backwards. It is in this context that the Great Proletarian Cultural Revolution foundered and that the reaction which followed seems to be affirming all three lines of development: selected parts of the Western and Soviet models bound together by viable bits of the Chinese heritage. In this way, it will start again, but differently from more traditional claims of Chineseness still being made in Taiwan, Hong Kong and among some of the larger Chinese communities in Southeast Asia and North America. It is too early to say how the rival claims will fare and whether they may one day flow into a new mainstream that all will acknowledge as unmistakably Chinese.

As long as the future Chineseness is still unclear, the world outside will continue to be ambivalent about China's traditional self-image. No one will particularly hanker for the dynastic empire, but many do admire the cultural achievements attained under that imperial framework, the fruits of three thousand years of continuous history. Will this continuity soon be broken? Or will the future China renew the key links and build afresh on the best features of that rich heritage? Despite all efforts of the People's Republic to stress its new universalist vision, the world will continue to find it hard to believe that the new Chineseness can really be so different from the old image which China says it has discarded. Whether old or new, it would be distinctively and recognizably Chinese and that may be all that matters. *W.G.*

LAND AND RESOURCES

A family team at work cultivating.

GEOGRAPHICAL AND CLIMATIC REGIONS

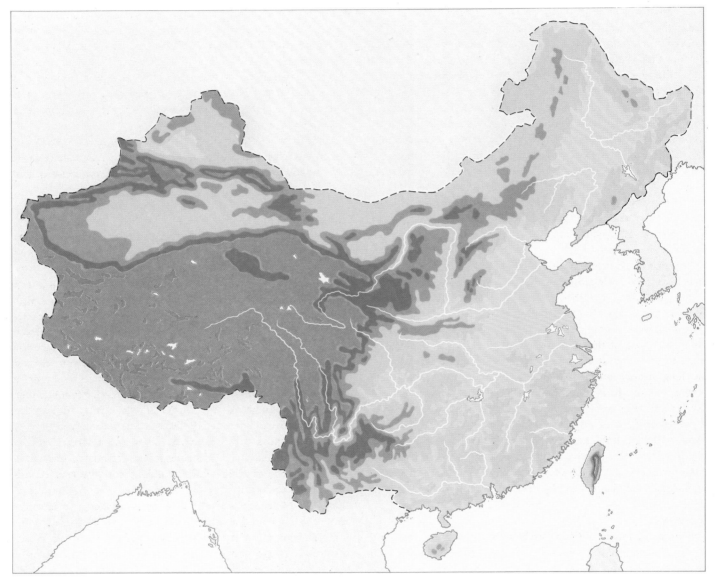

GENERAL PHYSICAL MAP

KEY

Height above sea level (metres)

0–350	1850–2500
350–1350	2500–5500
1350–1850	over 5500

General geography

With a total area of nearly 10 million sq km, China is much larger than either Western Europe or the United States mainland. Like most very large areas it also has an extremely varied geography and climate. China stretches through 49 degrees of latitude from north to south, from tropical to cool temperate conditions. Eastern China is relatively low-lying, maritime, and densely inhabited by Chinese speaking (Han) people, but western China is part of the high mountain plateau and basin country of central Asia, with scattered populations of national minorities. While constituting only 6 per cent of the total population of China, these minorities are to be found in 50–60 per cent of the country's entire area, mainly in the north, northwest, west and southwest. The 94 per cent of Chinese people who belong to the Han nationality occupy less than half the territory, but this is the eastern half, much of it richly endowed by nature and deeply humanized by dense occupation over many centuries.

The differences between eastern and western China are fundamental and have wide-ranging implications. Parts of eastern China (in Shaanxi, Shanxi, Hebei, Shandong, Henan) have been the homeland of a recognizable Chinese people and civilization since prehistoric times. Other parts of eastern China (the Yangtze provinces and those of the lowland south) have seen the spread of migrants and extension of administration at various times during the long history of the Chinese civilization. In western and northern China, however, the present extent of Chinese territory usually represents compromises of various kinds among competing territorial claims made by China and its neighbours, especially the Russian Empire, later the Soviet Union, which have been arrived at during recent centuries. Among these peripheral regions, the three provinces of the northeast (Manchuria) are exceptional in supporting a very large Han population.

Topography

The mountain ranges of China are broadly of two kinds, with different characteristics, orientations and origins. The topography of the western interior of China comprises very high ranges, with peaks of 7000–8000m, together with high plateaux and basins of an average height of 3000m in Tibet and 1000m in Xinjiang. The general orientation of these features is east–west. They assumed their modern outlines as a result of earth movements in the Caledonian and Hercynian phases of the Palaeozoic, up to 400 million years ago.

The topography of the eastern half of China, on the other hand, is dominated by mountain and plain features with a general northeast to southwest orientation. The main lines of these features were established in the Yanshan phase of Mesozoic times, up to 150 million years ago. The main topographical features of eastern China, particularly the belt of plains which extends from Hunan to Heilongjiang, and the mountain ranges of Fujian and the northeast, have taken their rise within this group of movements. Many other topographical features, such as the north China plain, the Hunan-Hubei basin, the Shandong peninsula, and the basin of Sichuan appear to derive their size and shape from the intersection of features which belong to the later Yanshan phase with others which are oriented east–west and which belong to the Hercynian movements much earlier.

In terms of elevation, the surface of China falls into three major regions—the east, mainly below 500m; the Tibetan, mainly above 2000m; and the intermediate centre and northwest, between 500 and 2000m elevation.

The climates

Climates are markedly seasonal throughout China. In winter there is extreme cooling of the continental interior of Asia, which leads to the formation of a powerful anticyclone with its centre over the Mongolian People's Republic to the north of China. Northerly winds blow out from this centre to cover all of eastern China, with the result that during winter most places have low temperatures, low humidity, low cloudiness and abundant sunshine. Snowfall is usually scarce in China, because the winds are dry. There are marked differences in average temperatures between northern and southern China in winter (January average: Beijing −4°C, Canton 14°C), but all parts of China experience a winter that is colder than other parts of the world at the same latitudes. The January mean isotherm of 0°C follows the Qinling and the western periphery of the Sichuan basin, dividing eastern China into a northern half in which winter cold is a dominating feature of human life, and a southern half in which it is not. From the point of view of agriculture, it is of the highest importance that the annual isohyet representing 750mm precipitation follows approximately the same line along the Qinling. This isohyet represents the zero line for the moistness index—to the south of this line more precipitation falls than can be evaporated; to the north potential evaporation exceeds precipitation. Taken together, these two features separate a relatively strenuous climatic environment in northern China from a relatively relaxed one in the south.

From the end of January onwards increased insolation begins to warm the Chinese landmass, and from March the Mongolian high pressure system begins to weaken. Significant instability arises in the atmosphere in northern China, due partly to warming of rock and sand surfaces in the north and west, and partly to the passage of depressions from Siberia. These conditions lead to high winds (particularly destructive to spring-sown crops in the northeast) and

TEMPERATURES: JANUARY

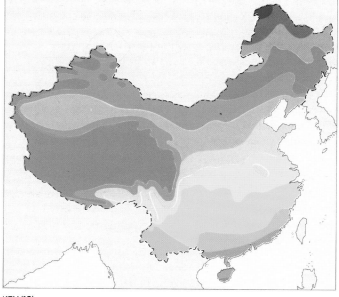

KEY (°C)

−35 to −30	−30 to −25	−25 to −20	−20 to −15	−15 to −10	−10 to −5
−5 to 0	0 to 5	5 to 10	10 to 15	15 to 20	20 to 25

TEMPERATURES: JULY

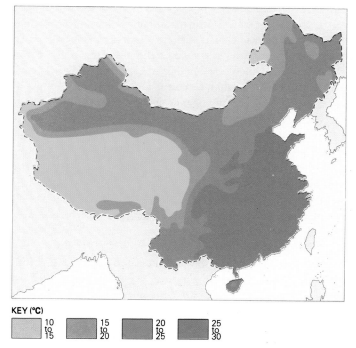

KEY (°C)

10 to 15	15 to 20	20 to 25	25 to 30

ANNUAL PRECIPITATION

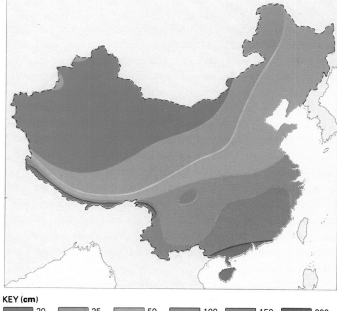

KEY (cm)

20 to 25	25 to 50	50 to 100	100 to 150	150 to 200	200 to 300

FROST-FREE PERIODS

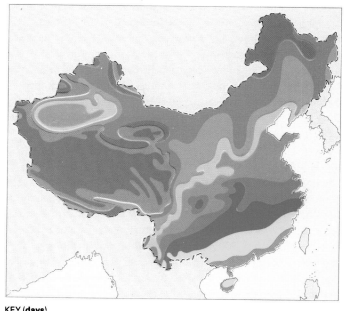

KEY (days)

30 to 60	60 to 90	90 to 120	120 to 150	150 to 180	180 to 210
210 to 240	240 to 270	270 to 300	Frost, but not every year		No frosts

duststorms in northern China, and sometimes to cold waves which penetrate as far as the Yangtze in March. Meanwhile in southern China, from March on the south coast and progressively northwards during the following months, maritime tropical air begins to return to China. Successive fronts form between underlying polar continental air and overriding maritime tropical air, and these produce the cloud and rain, cold at first but rapidly warming, of the south China spring. In April and May the zone of fronts is still in the far south, but by June the fronts and the rain ('plum rains') have reached the Yangtze; by July and August they have passed beyond the Yellow River and reached the northeast. During the summer in eastern China humidity is generally high. Summer weather consists mainly of hot, sunny phases alternating with phases of instability in the atmosphere which produce heavy rain. Towards the end of the summer (mainly July to September inclusive) typhoons, which have formed in the Philippines area, strike the coasts of south and southeastern China as far north as the Yangtze, sometimes with devastating effect.

There is little difference in monthly temperature averages in summer from place to place in eastern China (July average: Beijing 26°C, Canton 28°C). This is partly because of the invasion of tropical air; partly because the summer days, though cooler, are longer in northern China than in southern. Unlike India, there is no hot dry spring and the summer rains do not 'break' suddenly.

From September onwards the Asiatic continent begins to cool, due to the decrease in solar radiation. The high pressure centre begins once more to establish itself over Mongolia, and the southeasterly winds to slacken. Autumn is generally calm and sunny over China, and humidity falls rapidly. There are marked differences between afternoon and night temperatures. Frost appears in Beijing in November.

In terms of temperature throughout the year, and the winter weather in general, the Chinese climate behaves very predictably year to year. In terms of rainfall and the summer weather generally, it is much less predictable, particularly in the north, where average deviation from the mean of annual precipitation rises to 30 per cent. Serious drought or flood can strike almost any part of the country at any time.

Soils

The general classification and distribution of soils in China are shown on the map. There are three major soil groups: the forest

SOILS

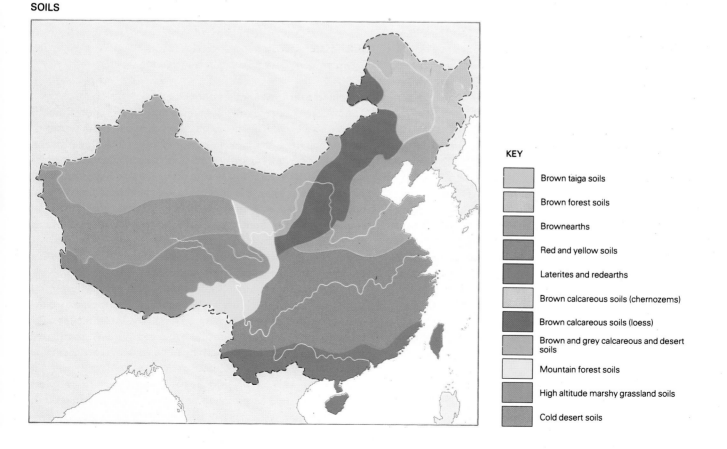

KEY

- Brown taiga soils
- Brown forest soils
- Brownearths
- Red and yellow soils
- Laterites and redearths
- Brown calcareous soils (chernozems)
- Brown calcareous soils (loess)
- Brown and grey calcareous and desert soils
- Mountain forest soils
- High altitude marshy grassland soils
- Cold desert soils

soils of eastern China, the prairie and desert soils of the north and northwest, and the high plateau soils of Tibet. The soils of Tibet and most of the northwestern area are used for farming only in small favoured localities, generally because of adverse environmental conditions, such as drought or cold, but there are two major exceptions. The first of these is the brown calcareous soils of the north. Most of these are of loess type, formed by the accumulation of material from dust storms since Ice Age times, calcareous, fertile and easily worked. These soils form the foundation of a very old arable economy in Gansu, Shaanxi and Shanxi. Deep gullying and falling water tables have greatly weakened these areas in recent centuries. The second is the black calcareous soils of the northeast, which support the important and still expanding grain farming area of Jilin and Heilongjiang.

The forest soils of the southeastern half of China display great diversity, partly because of climatic differences, partly because of human interference. In the south heavily leached red and yellow soils, and in the far south lateritic soils, predominate. In their natural form, most of these soils are thin, poor in structure, loose and unretentive of water, and lacking in humus and plant foods; but there are marked differences within local areas, depending on slope, aspect and local soil materials.

The soils of the riverine plains and deltas are usually of alluvial origin, mixed, mildly acidic and water-retentive; it is in these localities that the paddy soils have been built up. Substantial investments of labour (for levelling and water control) have usually been made in these areas; and there may also have been heavy applications of fertilizer, mainly natural. These soils are particularly important in central China.

In northern China apart from the northwest and northeast, the north China plain has mainly brownearth soils, formed in part from redeposited material (especially loess) from further inland, and much altered by cropping. These soils are generally loose in texture, calcareous and fertile, but generally dry. The poor water-retentive capacity of the soils, rather than the more northerly climate, is the main reason for the limited extent of paddy-farming in northern China. In some areas in the north China plain excessive evaporation from calcareous soils has led to difficult problems of alkalinity. In other areas extensive sand and gravel beds mark abandoned river courses.

Population and population distribution

China's population, recorded as 1 057 210 000 at the end of 1986, is by far the largest of any nation on earth. A very large population might be expected of China's great size; but in fact some population densities in the eastern half of China are among the highest on earth. Meanwhile in the generally hostile environments of western China, population (mainly of minority peoples) is very scanty. Dense populations and high population totals in eastern China depend upon a course of demographic growth which began around AD 1500 if not sooner, and which since around 1700 has been broadly continuous, although sharply interrupted in some regions and periods, as during the Taiping wars of the 19th century. Provincial populations are given in the table on p. 23, and population distributions, together with major cities, in the map on p. 21.

Discussion of China's population is inevitably dominated by considerations of policy. Rates of natural increase in population ranged from 11.7 per thousand to 23.4 per thousand between 1952 and 1979. Since 1980 it has been official policy to seek a reduction in the Chinese population, and to aim for a stable population total of around 700–800 millions, to be achieved during the 21st century. Present late-marriage regulations and the policy of one child per couple are designed to that end, but the age structure of population (46 per cent of the population were below 20 years of age in 1982) is such that China's total population is bound to rise to 1200 million at least before it begins to fall towards the target figure. The timing of such a fall will depend upon developments in the birthrate during the forthcoming decades; at present rates, it is likely to begin after about year 2040.

The figure for urban proportion of the Chinese population depends upon the definitions adopted. A conservative figure is around 20 per cent, but it is certain that in the present phase the urban proportion of population is increasing rapidly.

Provincial and local administrative units

The hierarchy of territorial administrative units used in China is complicated by various special but equivalent units with their own names, mainly in the national minority areas. This complication apart, the system has experienced quite radical change under the present central authorities, beginning in 1984 and apparently not yet completed—new lists of changes are announced from time to time. The essence of the new developments is the transfer of county-level units from the prefectures to which they formerly belonged, to the jurisdiction of neighbouring cities. The purpose of this change is said to be the expansion and opening-up of rural economies under the leadership of the cities.

The hierarchy of administrative units before 1984 had three levels—provinces and province-level units, prefectures and equivalent units, and counties and equivalent units. In the new system, many (but by no means all) rural counties have been transferred to cities at prefectural level, and the same applies to many cities at county level. In effect the older system now coexists with the newer, and the extent to which the newer has supplanted the older is extremely varied according to provinces. Thus, the table shows that in Liaoning and Jiangsu provinces all counties and all or most

POPULATION DISTRIBUTION

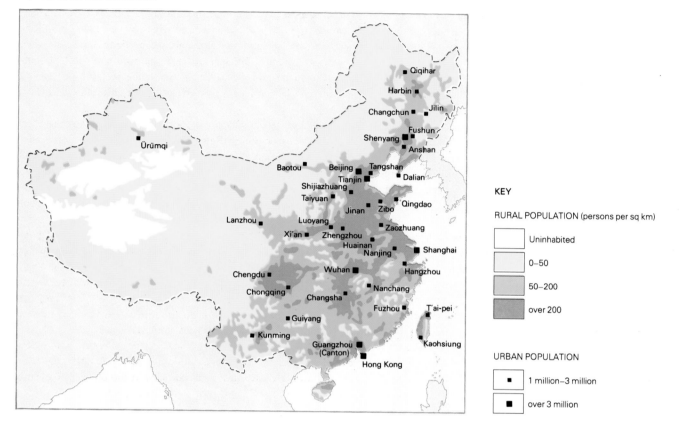

KEY

RURAL POPULATION (persons per sq km)

	Uninhabited
	0–50
	50–200
	over 200

URBAN POPULATION

▪	1 million–3 million
■	over 3 million

county-level cities are now under the leadership of prefecture-level cities; while in Hubei only 13 out of 71 county-level units have been so allocated and in Yunnan only 8 out of 123 such units. In China as a whole, 31 per cent of county-level units are now responsible to cities. Transfer to cities appears to be as much a mark of highly developed landscapes, as a means to future development.

China has 23 provinces (sheng) (apart from Taiwan but including Hainan island which was raised to that rank in 1988), 3 great cities where administration reports directly to the central government (Beijing, Shanghai, Tianjin) and 5 autonomous regions (zizhiqu) representing national minorities (Inner Mongolia, Guangxi, Ningxia, Xinjiang and Tibet). Since 1980 these first-level units have indirectly elected people's congresses with standing committees and people's governments, which replace the revolutionary committees of the Cultural Revolution era. These units are shown in the accompanying map.

The second level was, in the older system, and still is the pre-

fecture (diqu or zhuanqu), corresponding roughly to the zhou of traditional times. Prefectures in minority nationality areas may have differing names (leagues, autonomous zhou) which have equivalent status. Prefectures in their various forms are essentially organs of the provincial governments and do not have representative institutions (see table).

In the newer system the prefectures are supplemented by cities (shi) which take the same rank, and which now may have subordinate counties as all prefectures do. These cities have their own people's congresses with standing committees and local governments, of the same standing as those of the counties. In 1983, 7 major cities were separated for economic purposes from their provinces, and in these respects made directly subordinate to the central authorities. These are Chongqing, Wuhan, Shenyang, Dalian (Lüda), Canton (Guangzhou), Harbin and Xi'an.

The third-level units are either counties (xian) or cities (shi) with the rank of counties. National minority areas may use their

ADMINISTRATIVE AND GEOGRAPHICAL REGIONS

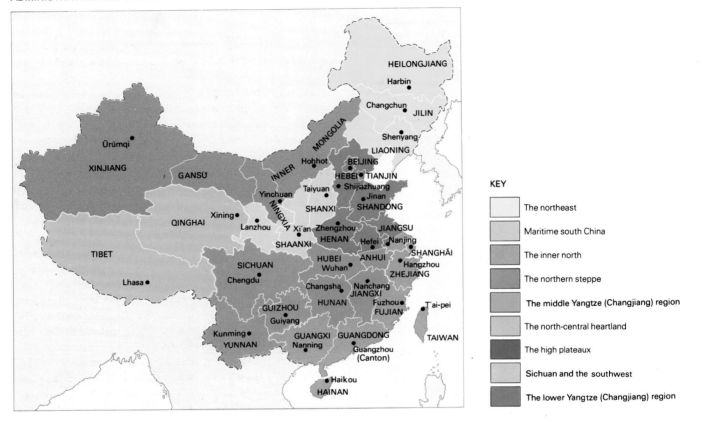

KEY

The northeast

Maritime south China

The inner north

The northern steppe

The middle Yangtze (Changjiang) region

The north-central heartland

The high plateaux

Sichuan and the southwest

The lower Yangtze (Changjiang) region

own names for these units, e.g., banners. The counties are in many ways the fundamental units of Chinese administration. An average county in a typical province, such as Henan or Anhui, is about 1200–2000 sq km in area, with a population between 600 000 and 700 000. Counties have directly elected people's congresses, with standing committees and people's governments.

Formal administration in China ends at the county level. Below this level, administration is the responsibility of local units—townships (*xiang*, at the level formerly represented by the communes) and small towns, which have their own directly elected congresses. Below these are the villages, with village committees. At the end of 1986 there were 61 766 townships, 9755 small towns, and 848 000 village committees in China. A special and recent feature of the administrative hierarchy is the Special Economic Zones. These are identified in the section on the maritime south.

Taiwan, which was under colonial administration by the Japanese from 1895 until 1945, has been administered separately since 1949 by the remnants of the Nationalist (Guomindang) regime. It has its own provincial and county hierarchies under the direct control of its own central government claiming to be the legitimate government of China. It has 5 cities and 16 counties.

Hong Kong will remain a British Crown Colony until 1997 when it will become a Special Administrative Region of China.

Macao will remain a Portuguese province until 1999 when it will become a Special Administrative Region of China.   *F.L.*

PROVINCIAL POPULATIONS (end of 1986) AND THE HIERARCHY OF
ADMINISTRATIVE UNITS (end of 1987)

Province	Units at prefectural or (equivalent) level			Units at county or (equivalent) level		
	Population (millions)	prefectures and others	cities	counties and others	cities	of which controlled by cities at prefectural level
Beijing	9.8	—	—	8	—	—
Tianjin	8.2	—	—	5	—	—
Hebei	56.2	9	9	131	9	27
Shanxi	26.6	6	5	96	5	20
Inner Mongolia	20.3	8	4	72	12	13
Liaoning	37.3	—	13	39	6	45
Jilin	23.2	2	6	33	8	24
Heilongjiang	33.3	4	10	60	9	37
Shanghai	12.3	—	—	10	—	—
Jiangsu	62.7	—	11	54	10	59
Zhejiang	40.7	2	9	58	9	49
Anhui	52.2	7	9	65	7	18
Fujian	27.5	3	6	59	5	37
Jiangxi	35.1	5	6	77	6	18
Shandong	77.8	5	10	86	15	49
Henan	78.1	5	12	111	6	47
Hubei	50.0	7	8	54	17	13
Hunan	57.0	7	6	80	18	33
Guangdong, of which	63.5	4	11	92	7	52
Hainan	5.9*	1	2	18	1	—
Guangxi	39.5	8	5	77	6	8
Sichuan	103.2	9	11	174	8	71
Guizhou	30.1	7	2	75	6	3
Yunnan	34.6	15	2	114	9	8
Tibet	2.0	6	1	76	1	7
Shaanxi	30.4	6	4	89	4	29
Qinghai	4.1	7	1	37	1	1
Gansu	20.7	9	5	67	8	12
Ningxia	4.2	2	2	16	2	5
Xinjiang	13.8	13	2	71	14	1
Total	1057.2	157	172	2004	209	686

Sources: For populations, *Zhongguo tongji nianjian 1987* (Beijing, 1987), 91, for administrative units, *Xingzhengqu huatuce* (Beijing, 1988)

*1985 figure. Source, *Guang Dongsheng tongji nianjian* (Canton, 1986)

The northeast

The three provinces of northeastern China (Liaoning, Jilin and Heilongjiang) are notable for both their environment and history, which are unparalleled elsewhere.

The distinguishing features of the environment are mainly those of climate. The summer is hot and short; the winter is long and very cold, although with little snowfall, and markedly colder in Heilongjiang than Liaoning. Typical January mean daily temperature minima are −34°C in Heilongjiang and −23°C in Jilin. Summer extends from early June to the middle or end of September; and 60 per cent or more of the precipitation takes place during June, July and August. The winter is generally clear and windy, and there are marked variations in temperature between day and night. Rainfall (about 500mm) is generally adequate.

The special features of the history of the northeast relate to its experience of Chinese colonization; and to the experience of Liaoning as a major industrial base first under the Japanese, and subsequently within the People's Republic of China. The northeast was originally the homeland of the Manchu people, whose leaders made themselves emperors of China under the Qing dynasty. Chinese settlement was not encouraged until the end of the 19th century, but immigrants poured into the northeast during the first decades of the 20th. In the same phase Japan, lacking the resources of coal and iron which are relatively plentiful in Liaoning, claimed the former Russian privileges in the northeast, extended them through railway and industrial installations, and between 1932 and 1945 effectively ruled the northeast as a satellite, as Manzhouguo (Manchukuo). By 1945 it was the most heavily industrialized region in China. Since 1949 the People's Republic has continued to invest heavily in industry in the northeast, and pioneering enterprise has extended the arable area in all three provinces. Population in the three provinces is now estimated at 100 million, nearly half of it in Liaoning, which comprises the southern 20 per cent in area. As a result of its history and relative wealth of resources, the northeast is the part of China which has most capacity to absorb increased population on the land, and at the same time it has probably the strongest heavy-industrial economy in China. In terms of development the northeast has moderate reserves of coal (Fushun and elsewhere) and oil (Daqing) and strong industrial foundations in iron and steel (Anshan), cement and machinery industries (Shenyang [Mukden]) and vehicles (Changchun). By no means all farmland has yet been taken up—in particular, the valuable black earth soils in the centre and north are not yet fully occupied. The peripheral mountains have important timber resources. The main weaknesses of the northeast are the vast distances (in spite of having the best railway network in China), winter cold (precluding double cropping), and in many areas the scarcity of labour.

F.L.

The northern steppe

The northern steppe is the loess region of China, comprising the provinces of Shaanxi and Shanxi with eastern Gansu. Today this area lies at the northwestern periphery of the cultural homeland of China, but it has been one of the most ancient and most important centres of Chinese civilization, with the imperial capital sited at Chang'an (modern Xi'an) in the Wei valley for many centuries up to Tang times. In ancient as well as modern times the Wei valley has been the main routeway from China to Central Asia, depending on access along the Yellow River route from Henan. Lanzhou now commands this route. From east and south the loess region is isolated by formidable physical barriers—the Taihang scarp which overlooks the plains of Hebei to the east, and the Qinling scarp to the south. The characteristic feature of the region is the loess soils, which have been deposited from the north by the

Part of the Great Wall, at one time the northern frontier of China.

action of the wind since glacial times. Loess soils are light, fertile and easy to work, but they are also fragile and very prone to erosion. There is no doubt that the loess environment has experienced serious degradation over a prolonged time, mainly due to gullying, which is very dramatic in the more hilly areas. Great efforts have been made to suppress gullying and check soil loss since 1949, but much remains to be done. Loess deposits vary greatly in depth, up to about 100m.

The summer climate of the steppe is hot, with July monthly averages at about 28°C, and the winter is relatively severe, with January monthly averages falling to −3°C in the south, and below −10°C at the latitude of the Great Wall. Winter climates are markedly transitional northwards. Limited rainfall is the principal constraint upon human use of the land. There is a rapid diminution of rainfall total from southeast to northwest in the region—Sian has over 500mm of rain, which is adequate to support an agrarian economy; but precipitation on the Great Wall is only about 300mm annually, sharply concentrated in summer, with only about 70 per cent reliability. This is not really adequate for agriculture. In places the Great Wall marks the frontier of desert conditions. In the northwest of the region, as in Inner Mongolia, a herding economy is traditional and still customary, especially among people of Mongol nationality. The heart of the region is in the south, in the Wei and Fen River valleys, with relatively prosperous agrarian economies based on dry grains and cotton. Some double cropping is practised.

Ambitious plans have been made at various times since 1949 for control of the loess of the northern steppe through the control of the Yellow River and its tributaries, together with afforestation.

On the loess plateau deep gullies cause soil loss, and interrupt local communications. Farmland is often terrace.

The north-central heartland

Hillside in Shaanxi Province with careful terracing to counteract both drought and flooding.

This area, basically the north China plain, comprises the provinces of Hebei, Shandong and Henan, together with northern Jiangsu and northern Anhui. Geologically, the plain extends almost to the Yangtze River, from which it is separated by local hill masses of much older rocks. Apart from some large isolated hill masses in peninsular Shandong and the mountain peripheries mainly to the west, the plain lies below 200m in elevation, and the greater part is level land with few prominent topographical features.

Structurally, the plain mainly consists of delta deposits of the Yellow River and other rivers; the Shandong peninsula was originally an island. Apart from the Yellow River, the rivers which cross the plain, particularly those in the south, are relatively insignificant except during summer storms. Even the discharge of the Yellow River is not large compared with that of the Yangtze. All the natural drainage in the eastern half of the plain has been interrupted by the cutting of the Grand Canal, which has encouraged the formation of swamps and lakes such as Zhaoyang Lake, and instability in the courses of the rivers, especially the Yellow River.

Under the government of the People's Republic of China extensive engineering works have been undertaken to stabilize drainage channels and to make provision for regulation of water flow under both flood and drought conditions—the North Jiangsu Canal and the works on the Hai River, for example. Most of the rivers of the plain flow independently of the Yellow River, and drain either the surrounding mountain areas, or the plain itself, or both. The Yellow River flows within a system of levees built of earth, in places rising 10m above the level of the plain. For many centuries to the present the Yellow River has carried a very heavy burden of sediment from the loess region. Part of this continues to be deposited in the plain section of the river's course, and so contributes to the risk of flooding.

The topography of the plain is marked by various local peculiarities. As a result of its history as the product of various phases of deposition of material from elsewhere, there are extensive patches of gravel, tracts of alkaline soil and hollows subject to waterlogging. These all create local land-use problems.

The climates of the north China plain show progression from Yangtze conditions in the south to drier and colder conditions in the north. This is especially marked in winter, when average monthly temperatures in the northern half of the plain are below freezing, and above freezing in the southern half—though in both afternoon temperatures often rise well above freezing. Frost-free days range from about 190 in the north to about 250 in the south. Snowfall is slight everywhere, and humidity very low, due to the continental winds from the north. Spring comes rapidly in March

Local achievements have been made (Dazhai, the most publicized national village model of recent years, celebrated especially for farmland construction and gully control, is in eastern Shanxi), but the area as a whole, especially the northwestern part, still has serious problems of aridity, winter cold and environmental degradation, to say nothing of poor communications, lack of opportunities to accumulate capital for development, and scarcity of labour, especially in the driest and poorest areas. The fundamental problems of the Yellow River remain unsolved. In principle, industrial opportunities are spectacular—Shaanxi and Shanxi have immense reserves of coal, and the Yellow River above Lanzhou is already harnessed for electrical power. In practice, long distances, relatively low population densities and low levels of technology restrict the major industries to those which the cities, such as Lanzhou (chemicals and textiles) and Xi'an (steel and machinery) can support. Shaanxi, Shanxi and eastern Gansu together have a total population of about 65 million.   *F.L.*

and April—frosts cease early in April even in the north of the plain. Spring, however, remains dry, with strong winds that may create dust storms, especially in the north. Summer is hot and rainy throughout, with afternoon temperatures often above 30°C away from the coasts between June and September. Annual precipitation is 400–900mm, but more in the south, and of this almost two-thirds falls in June, July or August, when humidity is also high. In September humidity falls abruptly and the rains cease. Temperatures begin to fall sharply in November. Rainfall totals everywhere, but especially in the north, are subject to marked annual fluctuations.

Most of the plain is flat and featureless, with the land everywhere under the plough, and villages, each of some hundreds of people, lying about one kilometre apart. The total population of the plain, including Beijing, Tianjin and the whole of Shandong, is estimated at 280 million, about 30 per cent of the total Chinese population. The economy of the plain is primarily agricultural, with typical gross population densities of about 400 per sq km. Local rural economies are based mainly on the continuing struggle for self-sufficiency in food, which many units have achieved even in the face of growing populations. Food crops are millet, maize (corn) and sweet potatoes, all harvested at the end of summer, and wheat, grown through the winter and harvested early in the summer. Tobacco and cotton are supplied to the state. Apart from growth in the great cities of Beijing and Tianjin, industry has been introduced in many of the cities of the plain, such as Zhengzhou (textiles), Jinan (machinery and chemicals), Luoyang (engineering), Handan (textiles), and Shijiazhuang (textiles). Oil has now been found in large quantities near the mouth of the Yellow River (Dagang and Shengli).

In terms of prospects for development the main problems of the north China plain are its vast size and population and its uniformity of resources, which limit exchangeable surpluses and diversification possibilities, especially in the central area. Its main assets are labour supply, marketable surpluses such as cotton, and some mineral resources, especially in peripheral areas, such as coal in Anhui, Henan, Hebei and Shandong. Gradual progress is also being made with the modernization of farming, but there is little opportunity to create new farmland. Where population presses so hard upon available resources, opportunities for accumulation and investment are limited, and diversification hard to achieve. Particularly in the northern half of the plain, with its problem of drought, progress is difficult.   F.L.

The inner north

The western half of China belongs geographically to Central Asia rather than to the Pacific fringe. Its northern half, lying in Xinjiang, western Gansu, Ningxia and Inner Mongolia, is mainly basin and plateau country at heights between 1000 and 2000m. In Xinjiang very extensive topographical depressions with low rainfall, such as the Tarim basin, lead to inland drainage, though on the northwestern fringe some rivers drain towards Siberia. The topographical basins such as the Tarim basin have characteristic geographical features. Encircling mountain ranges are fringed with gravel terraces which are punctuated by oases fed by melting snow in summer, while the centre of the basin is true desert, in many places with moving sand. Major routeways, ancient and modern, follow the lines of these gravel terraces and oasis chains; and farmland, villages and towns are centred on the oases. In Inner Mongolia and Ningxia, featureless plateau country, drier and poorer in the west but wetter and with good grazing in the east, extends towards the Mongolian frontier.

The climates of northwestern China display continental characteristics. Summers in the basin areas are hot, with daily maxima rising to 30°C, with thunderstorms and downpours in some years, but average precipitation less than 200mm. Winters are very dry, with daily minima in January falling below −10°C; but in the basins foehn effects (warming by air in course of descent from higher altitudes) also bring warmer winter days in most years. In Dzungaria and the Yili valley, in the extreme northwest of China, winters are colder; but precipitation, which comes from the Atlantic via Siberia, is a little more plentiful. In Inner Mongolia too, on the fringes of the northeast and the northern steppe region, rainfall is more plentiful than in Xinjiang (about 300mm) but still insufficient for arable farming.

In this region distances are immense (about 2500km from Lanzhou on the eastern fringe to Kashgar near the Soviet frontier in the west). The region is mainly populated not by Han Chinese, but by national minorities, especially Mongols, Kazakhs and Uighurs, all of whom have long histories of contact, in war and peace, with the Han Chinese in the eastern half of China. In contrast to eastern China, most of the region has very low population densities (generally less than one person per sq km); much is practically unpopulated, and cities and big towns are very few. The total population of the region is estimated at about 25 million, very low for an area of this size.

Partly due to the close proximity of the Soviet Union, the People's Republic of China has promoted the development of the northwest; but progress has been slow and limited in extent, due to vast distances and poor access, limited labour forces and the

About one-half of Chinese territory lies in central Asia, with harsh environments and low-density, mainly pastoral economies.

vast scale of the necessary projects, especially on the land. Further progress may be expected as the population grows. There are varied mineral deposits, including oil, particularly in the Yili valley area in northwestern Xinjiang. In Ningxia and Inner Mongolia, population is less scanty and access less difficult. This is mainly an animal-rearing area, but ancient irrigation works on the Yellow River have been extended, and arable farming promoted. A new steel town is in course of development at Baotou. Chronic problems of drought and communications remain.   *F.L.*

The lower Yangtze region

The lower Yangtze region, centred on Shanghai and comprising the Yangtze delta, is the most advanced and prosperous part of China. It enjoys some important advantages of environment, together with others that arise from human activity. Most of the area is an extensive and varied plain, criss-crossed by waterways and dotted with lakes. Soils, in many localities much changed by human interference, are deep and rich, usually water-retentive and suitable for paddy rice except near the coast. Here, due to recent deposition, soils are usually sandy, and many of these areas specialize in cotton. The winter is relatively short (240 frost-free days at Shanghai) and mild (mean daily minimum at Shanghai in Jan-

uary is 1°C); rainfall is plentiful (1140mm per annum). Thanks to these physical conditions and dense population (up to 1000 people per sq km) and hence plentiful labour supply, cultivation is intensive. Double cropping (using a summer crop of rice and a winter crop of wheat or beans) is practically universal, and in recent years much more varied cropping schedules have been adopted. Supplies of fodder and coarse foods such as bean foliage support dense pig populations in many areas, leading to better fertilizer supplies. Dense human populations, maintained by double cropping which in many localities yields a grain surplus, also produce valuable supplies of fertilizer. Local collective enterprise at brigade and commune levels has generated workshops and manufacturing industries in many places. The population of the whole area is estimated at about 45 million, including Shanghai.

Shanghai (population now estimated at 12.3 million, including 10 counties and a wide extent of intensively cultivated farmland) and such cities as Suzhou and Wuxi are important industrial centres with traditional industries (cotton and silk) in some cases, and industries established since 1949 (steel, machinery, shipbuilding and oil refining) in others. The lower Yangtze region is poor in minerals, but industrial growth continues to be stimulated by advantages of location, and by market, labour and technical factors.

This region continues to have good development prospects, and if China expands its overseas trade, they are bound to improve. Both the industrial and agricultural economies are in the forefront of progress in Chinese terms, and are likely to remain so.   *F.L.*

View of central Shanghai with the Wusong (Suzhou) River.

The middle Yangtze region

The middle Yangtze region comprises the provinces of Hubei, Hunan, Jiangxi and southern Anhui. Its aggregate population is estimated at about one hundred and fifteen million. Hubei, Hunan and Jiangxi are each essentially the basin of a major tributary or group of tributaries of the Yangtze, such as the Han River in Hubei (whose upper course extends the region into southern Shaanxi). Each comprises extensive plains with lakes close to the Yangtze, plus peripheral hill and mountain areas rising above 1000m eleva-

tion especially in Hubei, where settlement is concentrated in valley bottoms. Winter is cold in central China for its latitude, and the lakes may freeze, but snow is rare. By March daytime temperatures are rising rapidly; in April–July there is heavy rain, and mean daily maxima rise to 33°C. Air temperatures drop sharply in October. Flooding sometimes takes place in summer, when the level of water in the Yangtze rises dramatically, and the lakes, and some basins recently created for the purpose, act as overflow reservoirs. The Yangtze and its tributaries comprise one of the biggest navigable waterway systems in the world, and their potential for hydro-electric power generation is immense. Some large-scale works have already been undertaken, especially on the Han River; and new

Below: view of the countryside near Wuhu (Anhui Province), an area of densely settled plains with surrounding mountain environments, which are often poorly used. Bottom: the Xiang River near Xiangtan (Hunan Province) with intensive farming typical of lowland south China.

Below: village houses to the south of Changsha (Hunan Province). Bottom: landscape near Guilin (Guangxi Zhuang Autonomous Region). The area is famous for its strange and beautiful limestone peaks.

works at Jiangdu enable Yangtze water to be diverted northwards into the drier north China plain.

The plains of Hunan, Hubei and Jiangxi are all important supply areas of surplus grain to the state, and supplies of cotton are also contributed, especially from Hubei. The area as a whole is still somewhat backward compared with the Shanghai area or Guangdong, and partly for that reason development prospects for the long-term are very good. Intensification of cultivation on the land (through such measures as double cropping and more intensive use of fertilizer) still has a long way to go in this region, and there are extremely extensive tracts of wild hillside land upon which development is possible, at a price in labour. Some parts of the region, particularly in Jiangxi, are relatively thinly populated, and even in the plains population density, at 200–300 per sq km, is not particularly high, though localities vary greatly in this respect. Industrial prospects are limited for the present, though there is iron and some coal, mainly in small local fields south of the Yangtze, and great hydro-electric potential. Shortage of technical expertise and the slow growth of an industrial network in this rather old-fashioned area seem to be limiting factors, but there is one major industrial city of long standing, Wuhan, and industry is developing in others, such as Xiangtan. _F.L._

The maritime south

Maritime south China comprises Zhejiang, Fujian, Guangdong, Guangxi and the new province of Hainan, and includes Hong Kong, Macao, and Taiwan. This area is large—the sea passage from Canton to Shanghai is 1690km. It is also very diverse, including the vast delta plains around Canton and Hangzhou, the rocky mountains and local plains of the Fujian coast, and very extensive mountain and valley interiors, with extremely varied local conditions. Latitude imposes important differences in climate, especially in the winter and in spite of the neighbourhood of the sea. Frost is not experienced on the south coast, but in northern Zhejiang the frost-free period is less than 300 days. Summers are hot, and rainfall (about 1600mm in the plains) is plentiful. Most of the region is mountainous, with elevations rising to about 1000m. Human occupancy in these areas is based mainly on the limited arable land to be found in the valley bottoms—in Fujian Province only 11 per cent of the total area is arable. Great differences arise from place to place in such respects as extent of cultivable land, accessibility, degrees of commercialization of local economies, and extent of modernization. Soils over much of the area are very poor in quality, and there is risk of typhoons every summer.

The Pearl River delta plain around Canton is the most important district in this region, with population densities rising to 1000 per sq km. Much of the plain is occupied by two successive summer crops of rice, yielding a surplus of food in spite of the dense population. Hong Kong, still mainly a Cantonese city, lies at the edge of this plain, and provides an important market for vegetables and pigs. Other densely populated areas are the small plains around Shantou, sometimes called Swatow, Xiamen (called Amoy), Fuzhou and Wenzhou, and further north the extensive plains of Zhejiang, where double cropping more often takes the form of summer rice with winter wheat or beans, as at Shanghai. Inland, the mountainous areas have important resources of timber (especially in Zhejiang) and bamboo (especially in Guangxi). These and other wild resources are important wherever there are undeveloped hillsides, but their commercial importance depends on accessibility. Hillside land is also used in many areas for growing mulberry for silk, oranges and tea. Cash cropping and garden farming are now of increasing importance. In Taiwan there are similar marked differences between the rice farming of the lowlands, garden farming in the foothills, and isolated forested mountains in the interior. Hong Kong has a highly developed industrial and service economy, with an offshoot in neighbouring Macao, and in Taiwan industry has developed rapidly at Taipei and Kaohsiung. But in the rest of this area, apart from the main cities such as Canton and Hangzhou, and some others such as Foshan, industry remains limited. Hong Kong industrial investment and

The Pearl River delta near Jiujiang (Guangdong Province). Many parts of south China have excellent water communications.

employment are increasingly important in the delta. There is also significant local industry and local hydro-electricity.

A special and recent feature of the maritime south is the Special Economic Zones (SEZs). These are now five in number—Shenzhen and Zhuhai in the Pearl River delta, neighbours to Hong Kong and Macao respectively; designated areas at Shantou in eastern Guangdong and Xiamen in southern Fujian (all established in 1979); and (since 1988) the new province of Hainan island. SEZs exist to stimulate foreign investment and technological innovation from abroad—much of it coming in practice from overseas Chinese, especially in Hong Kong.

Guangdong, Guangxi, Fujian and Zhejiang have a total population estimated at 170 million. In addition, Taiwan has in excess of 18 million, Hong Kong, 5.75 million, and Macao, 250 000. The characteristic geographical advantages of the maritime southeast are its location, which before 1949 led many people from these provinces to emigrate to Southeast Asia, and many more into overseas trade, and (apart from the typhoons) its generous climates. Its characteristic weaknesses are lack of minerals, poor communications, and—in some areas, such as eastern Guangdong—extremely high local population densities, which inhibit accumulation and investment. *F.L.*

Sichuan and the southwest

The three provinces of Sichuan, Guizhou and Yunnan comprise two areas that differ greatly from each other—the Sichuan basin, and the mountains which surround it together with their plateau and mountain extension southwestwards to the frontier.

The Sichuan basin is large—270km from Chongqing to Chengdu. It is a topographical depression to which access is to be had only with difficulty—from the east by the Yangtze River through the famous gorges, through high mountain ranges from the north or through high plateau country from the south. The basin's general elevation is about 300m, and its topography is undulating and mixed. Its winter climate is peculiar and favourable. It is protected by the high Qinling mountains to the north from the cold continental winds of winter; the mean daily minimum for January at Chongqing is 6°C compared with –1°C at Wuhan. The basin's sky is very cloudy during winter, but rain, which is abundant, falls mainly in summer, from May to September.

To the south of Sichuan lies the Yunnan-Guizhou plateau, which is topographically the intermediate slopes (at about 1000–2500m elevation) lying between the high plateaux of Tibet (more

than 3000m) and the foothills of Vietnam, Laos and Burma, and further east of Guangxi and Hunan. This plateau is deeply dissected by many great rivers such as the Red River of North Vietnam, and communications are very poor, apart from the major routes. The climate of this area is sometimes called 'spring at all seasons'. Winter is cool and dry, with the extent of frost (260 frost-free days at Kunming) determined mainly by altitude. Warm days begin in March, and rain in May; the summer (June to September) is wet but not hot, with mean daily maxima around 24°C in July.

A number of features conspire to give the Yunnan-Guizhou plateau a marked 'frontier' character in China as a whole—a character which is also shared with Guangxi in some degree, and by western Sichuan beyond the basin area. One of these is the presence of national minorities recognized by the administrative system: about one-half of the total area of Yunnan-Guizhou-Sichuan comprises autonomous units representing various minorities. Yunnan alone has 23 such units, more than any other province. Another is the isolation of most of the area from the rest of China, and a third, partly dependent on the second, is the high degree of local self-sufficiency in the rural economies in the area.

The population of Sichuan is estimated at 105 million, the great majority in the basin. The population of Yunnan and Guizhou together is probably about 64 million. In the Sichuan basin settlement is dense (about 1000 per sq km), based on intensive paddy and garden cultivation; but in the mountains local environmental conditions and human adaptations display great diversity, with dependence by local communities on wild resources of various kinds (bamboo for making paper, for instance) as well as upon arable farming. There are few signs of advanced farm methods in the mountain fringes or the plateau, and in the basin itself there are perhaps more indications of stability and prosperity than of dynamism. The basin is a food surplus area, and for its needs beyond subsistence, such as steel and consumer goods, it is forced by isolation and poor communications to rely to a high degree upon what can be obtained within the region. Industrial growth, especially in Chongqing, has been stimulated partly by isolation, and now includes steel. The plateau communities are still more isolated. In terms of development, in spite of improvements in the Yangtze gorges, railways to the north and south and improved roads, isolation must continue to condition every possibility, and so must the peculiarities of the social foundations of the region, especially in a frontier zone with turbulent neighbours. There are still significant possibilities for the extension of double cropping on the land and the creation of new farmland, for the development of mountain resources such as bamboo, and for the extension of hillside cultivation for such crops as tea. Mineral resources, including coal, tin and some oil, are still grossly underexploited, and offer impressive possibilities in the longer term. *F.L.*

The high plateaux

The southern half of western China lies mostly above 3000m elevation, and comprises Tibet, Qinghai and the Tibetan autonomous *zhou* of western Sichuan. The region is that which lies above 2000m elevation. It is basically a series of vast plateaux and basins traversed by mountain ranges which lie mainly east–west but turn sharply southwards in the southeast, towards Yunnan and the Burmese frontier. The southern frontier of Tibet lies along the Himalayas, and borders with Nepal and India. The area is very extensive—about 1000km from east to west and 500km from north to south.

The climates of Tibet are mainly determined by altitude, but there are great variations due to local topography (e.g. the deep valleys of the southeast, with little rain, warm summers and mild winters) and general elevation (e.g. the plateaux of central Tibet below 5000m elevation, with mean average annual temperature between 0°C and 5°C, and a very short frost-free period).

The means of livelihood in most of Tibet depend upon local conditions, from arable farming in the southeastern valleys to pastoralism in Qinghai and large uninhabited areas in western Tibet. The government of the People's Republic of China has improved communications by road, introduced industry and extended arable farming, but these achievements are quite limited in terms of the scale of the region.

Tibet and Qinghai, with an aggregate population of about 6 million, a population density over most of the populated part of the area below one person per sq km, with vast distances and with communications greatly stretched, necessarily offer only limited prospects for development. With the exception of Xining in northwestern Qinghai, which is close to Lanzhou and shares some of its advantages, including mineral resources, there appears to be little firm prospect of substantial industrial development; and development based on the land faces difficult climatic obstacles.   *F.L.*

Livestock-farming at Painbo Farm in Tibet at an altitude of 4000m.

The wild environments

In terms of natural fauna and flora, a sharp distinction is drawn between the western interior and maritime eastern halves of China. The western interior half (which includes the inner north, the high plateaux and the western half of the northern steppe) is basically a region of high plateaux and basins with cold semi-desert climates. The vegetation cover is sparse in many areas and limited in range throughout, and belongs to the same Central Asian categories as that of southern Siberia. There is nevertheless considerable regional and local differentiation in vegetation communities— rock and sand surfaces virtually without vegetation in Inner Mongolia, gravel surfaces with woodland patches in depressions or along watercourses in the Gobi fringes, steppe grasslands graduating towards desert, coniferous forests occupying the north-facing slopes of such ranges as the Tianshan, but steppes covering the drier southern slopes of the same mountains. Everywhere in this vast region the basic environmental constraint is that of drought; and to this must be added winter cold. The effects of human occupancy are everywhere limited by the small size and wide scatter of the human populations involved; but in some areas, particularly along the Great Wall in northern Shaanxi, human use of the land has tended to intensify environmental degradation and to encourage the advance of the deserts.

In terms of its natural fauna, too, this Central Asian half of

China is dominated by its physical conditions. The wild ungulates (camels, sheep, goats, antelopes, yaks, horses) are advantaged by slight snowfall in winter, and the same is true of steppe rodents such as rabbits and gerbils. Many of the small animals are capable storers of food. Most inhabit burrows which give protection from winter cold but may stimulate soil erosion. Predators upon the grazing animals are abundant, such as wolves, foxes, vultures and eagles. Advantages are enjoyed by birds and reptiles which inhabit cracks in the rock or old burrows. Migration is a common feature of animal behaviour, stimulated by availability of grazing which depends in part upon unreliable rainfall. Rodents, unable to migrate over long distances, suffer drastic population declines during drought—but many species are able to rebuild populations very rapidly in good years.

The maritime east of China, which supports over 95 per cent of the total human population, has natural environments of a very different kind. In this half of China the natural flora is among the richest on Earth, with an exceptionally high level of endemism, or uniqueness to the region, resulting from a high rate of species survival from the Tertiary period and through Ice Age times. The maritime east of China has probably at least 30 000 native plant species (as against about 5000 in Europe)—a figure comparable with those of other floristically very rich regions such as Latin America. The natural fauna of this area is also remarkable, both in terms of vertebrates and of invertebrates such as insects and beetles. There are great differences in the species composition of plant and animal communities between the north and south of eastern China, due to great differences in climate; but in recent times areas of particularly rich diversity are found in the mountain peripheries of the northeast (Heilongjiang and Jilin) and the southwest (Yunnan and Sichuan). This is because human interference has up to now been less active in these isolated regions. Elsewhere, natural vegetation is not abundant except locally where it has similarly been protected from human interference by relative isolation—particularly in the mountains, such as those of the interfluves between the main river valleys. In such provinces as Fujian and Hubei, considerable forest stands remain in mountain areas, though those still untouched by human exploitation are rapidly diminishing in extent.

The forests of the southern mountains are very mixed in floristic composition and ecological relationships, with evergreen, deciduous and coniferous species. Considerable floristic differences result from differences in elevation, for instance rhododendron thickets and alpine meadows above the forests (about 3000m in Yunnan). Bamboos of many kinds are of special importance. Tea and oranges, among other cultivated plants, took their origin in these forests. True tropical forests occupy small and dwindling areas in the far south, especially in Hainan.

WILD ENVIRONMENTS

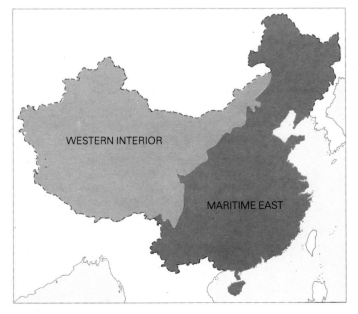

WESTERN INTERIOR

MARITIME EAST

In both traditional and modern times the immensely varied flora and fauna of China have supported a very wide range of specialist uses of these resources—animal and vegetable drugs for use in traditional medicine, bamboo for many kinds of use in construction, animals for fur and food, wild plants, fruits and fungus for food, wine, flavourings and so forth. Many specialist items of diet are of wild origin. Traditional systems of 'farming' wild resources exist, such as pond rearing of fish and the cultivation of various fungi. Many rural communities now make useful cash incomes through this kind of resource use. In the western interior and on its eastern fringes some millions of people depend for their livelihood at least in part upon the grazing of wild ranges.

However, anxiety is now being widely expressed in China about the mounting pressures upon the wild environments. Environmental damage by man is not a recent problem, but better communications, growing rural populations, rising standards and ineffective control mechanisms are together now resulting in widespread cutting of forests without adequate means to replant, leading to deforestation, destruction of dependent wild life, soil erosion and general degradation of the wild environments on a scale far greater than before.   *F.L.*

Yao women collect edible bamboo shoots, which abound in southern China.

A Giant Panda in Fengtongzhai Reserve, Baoxing County, Sichuan Province.

Environments in eastern China to the north of the Yangtze are much colder in winter than those to the south, and are generally dry. On the north China plain wild vegetation is rare due to dense human settlement and land use. The northeast is varied, with a long history of grazing use. The plains are occupied by meadow and steppe, but mixed forest is still common in the mountains. These forests are floristically rich, and contain valuable timber resources.

The fauna of eastern China is also exceptionally rich; though (as with the flora) many species which formerly occupied locations now taken up by human populations are now to be found only in the mountain forests. Elephants survive only in southern Yunnan; tigers only in the same area and parts of the northeast. Confined to the south, there are monkeys and pandas among the mammals, alligators, turtles and snakes, many kinds of frogs and toads, and a vast range of invertebrate species. More widely distributed are bears, deer, wild pigs, leopards, many rodents, wild chickens, many types of pheasant and other game birds, migrant birds from Siberia, and a further wide range of fish and insects. The food sources of most of these creatures are based upon the forest vegetation, either directly or through insect or other intermediaries; in the southern forests this food supply is much more continuous throughout the year than in those of the north.

NATURAL RESOURCES

Energy resources

Coal

Coal was one of the strange Chinese novelties that Marco Polo reported back to Europe in the 13th century. Indeed, by then coal had been mined in China for centuries. The country's first modern coal mine was built at Kaiping in northern Hebei Province in 1878.

Close to three-quarters of China's primary energy comes from coal. China possesses abundant coal reserves, estimated to be about 3.2 trillion tonnes, ranking second in the world, behind only the USSR and well ahead of the USA. In terms of verified reserves, however, China's 640 000 million tonnes (1980) follows both the USSR and the USA.

In 1987 China's coal output reached 928 million tonnes. China exported 9.6 million tonnes and imported 2.4 million tonnes of coal in 1986. The main export markets are Japan, North Korea, Hong Kong, and recently the Philippines. In recent years the open policy has led to a proliferation of small privately operated mines producing an increasing percentage of the national output.

Although some coal reserves can be found in all of China's provincial level units, the north dominates. The north and northeast economic regions together produce over half of current output, with Shanxi Province alone accounting for nearly one quarter of national output. The coal deficiency south of the Yangtze River, especially in terms of high quality coal, has created a great haulage

A large conveyor-belt moves coal from the pithead at the Xinglong-zhuang colliery in Shandong Province.

problem on the inadequate railway and coastal shipping systems. The Chinese are experimenting with the transportation of coal by pipeline. Although a great effort has been made to increase coal production in the south, only the discovery of major oil and gas reserves in the South China Sea coupled with construction of the Sanxia Dam on the Yangtze can reduce the need for these coal shipments.

Close to 70 per cent of Chinese coal is bituminous, 16 per cent anthracite and 14 per cent lignite. No less than 35 per cent of these are coking coals. Although some of these have a rather high ash content and considerable processing is needed to convert them to coke, China has had to import only small quantities since 1985.

Petroleum

References to mineral oil occur in ancient Chinese writings and it has been used in China for centuries as fuel for lamps. Modern petroleum production in China dates from the early years of the 20th century.

Estimates of China's reserves of crude oil differ widely and are supported by few facts. One foreign source estimated reserves at 2600 million tonnes in 1986 although some experts feel the figure could be as high as 4000 million tonnes. Estimates by sympathetic Westerners in the 1970s had put the reserves as high as 10 000 million tonnes. China has given estimates for total petroleum reserves at between 30 000 and 60 000 million tonnes.

China now easily ranks as one of the world's ten largest countries in oil production. Output in 1986 was reported to have been 131 million tonnes, of which about 28.5 million were exported. Roughly two-fifths of the crude exported goes to Japan, with Singapore, the USA, Brazil, and North Korea also purchasing large quantities in recent years.

Daqing, discovered in 1959 in Heilongjiang Province, is by far the largest of China's oilfields in terms of output and in 1985 produced 55.1 million tonnes or 44 per cent of China's total crude. China's other major field, Shengli in Shandong Province, near the mouth of the Yellow River, was discovered in 1962 and has been in production since 1964. It produced 27.6 million tonnes or about one-fifth of China's crude oil with production expected to double in the near future. Both Daqing and Shengli crudes have a high paraffin content and are rather heavy, but are low in sulphur and low in gasoline yield during primary distillation.

The Huabei (Renqiu) oilfield, in Hebei Province about 150km south of Beijing has developed rapidly since 1975 with production peaking in 1979. Although production dropped slightly to 10.3 million tonnes by 1985 it was still China's third largest oilfield. The Liao-He oilfield which is composed of 8 major clusters in Liaoning Province was discovered in 1967 but has had rapidly rising production since its development was completed in 1980.

ESTIMATED PRODUCTION OF RAW COAL AND CRUDE OIL IN CHINA: SELECTED YEARS, 1942–87

Year	Coal production millions of tonnes	Coal per cent of total energy production	Crude oil production millions of tonnes	Crude oil per cent of total energy production
1942 (pre-1949 coal peak)	62	—	—	—
1943 (pre-1949 oil peak)	—	—	0.3	—
1949	32	96.3	0.1	0.7
1952	66	96.7	0.4	1.3
1957	131	94.9	1.5	2.1
1962	220	91.4	5.8	4.8
1965	232	88.0	11.3	8.6
1970	354	81.6	30.7	14.1
1975	482	70.6	77.1	22.6
1980	620	69.4	106.0	23.8
1983	715	71.6	106.1	21.3
1984	789	72.4	114.6	21.0
1985	872	72.8	124.9	20.9
1986	894	72.4	130.7	21.7
1987	928	72.6	134.1	21.0

Sources: A. B. Ikonnikov, *The Coal Industry of China* (Canberra, 1977); US Central Intelligence Agency, *Chinese Coal Industry: Prospects over the Next Decade* (Washington, DC); US Congress Joint Economic Committee, *China: A Reassessment of the Economy* (Washington, DC, 1975); *Statistical Yearbook 1977* (UN, New York, 1978); Guojia tongjiju (Chinese State Statistical Bureau), ed., *Zhongguo nengyuan tongji nianjian 1986* (Chinese Energy Statistical Yearbook 1986) (Beijing, 1987); *Zhongguo jingji nianjian (1986)* (Almanac of China's Economy 1986) (Peking); *Zhongguo tongji nianjian 1988* (Almanac of Chinese Statistics) (Beijing)

In 1985 the Liao-He field produced 9 million tonnes of crude oil. Another new cluster of fields called Zhongyuan, discovered in eastern Henan and western Shandong in 1976 has been in production since 1979. By 1985 production from the Zhong yuan fields had reached 5.1 million tonnes. Southeast of Tianjin, near Bohai Bay and close to the Shengli field is the Dagang oilfield—now China's sixth largest. Production was about 3.6 million tonnes in 1985. The Karamay (Kelamayi) oilfield in Xinjiang is the largest of the inland producing oilfields and has been in production since the 1950s. But expansion of production in the northwest has been slow due to remoteness from industrial centres.

China's first oil pipeline, dating from 1958, links the Karamay (Kelamayi) oilfield in Xinjiang with the Dushanzi refinery, a distance of 147km. In 1973 a 1152km pipeline was completed from the Daqing oilfield to the port of Qinhuangdao in Hebei; later it was extended to Beijing. In 1978 the completion was announced of a pipeline from the Shengli field to the riverine oil harbour at Nanjing in Jiangsu Province. By 1979 over half of China's crude oil output was moved by pipelines. Recent pipeline developments have linked the Huabei (Renqiu) field with Beijing to the north

and Nanjing to the south, the Liao-He field with the Daqing–Lüda line, and the Zhongyuan fields from Puyang field in eastern Henan to the Shengli–Nanjing line. Currently there is approximately 9700km of petroleum and gas pipeline or about 100km of pipeline for each million tonne of crude extracted.

The Chinese industry is still too dependent on concentration at one field (Daqing) and transport-production problems. China has more than 50 oil refineries located in 21 provincial level units. Refineries tend to be concentrated in the north and northeast, the Yangtze River valley and the northwest. The main refineries are found in Beijing, Shanghai, Nanjing, Lanzhou, Dalian (Lüda), and near the Daqing and Shengli oil fields.

Considerable exploration is in hand, onshore and offshore; with the best prospects for new onshore finds in Xinjiang. New fields will be in production in the Tarim Basin in the near future. Offshore production is largely being undertaken in the form of Sino-foreign joint ventures. Besides need for foreign equipment, offshore production is facilitated by relatively efficient transport and control of foreign activities offshore is easier. Since 1985 ten coastal and southern provinces have been authorized to undertake onshore exploration and development with foreign firms.

Natural gas

Stagnating output of natural gas is indicative of only modest reserves. Onshore reserves are concentrated in Sichuan Province but discovery of natural gas off Hainan Island in 1983 by Atlantic Richfield could be just the first discovery of considerable offshore reserves. China's total production of natural gas in 1987 amounted to 13 890 million m^3, of which Sichuan accounted for 43.1 per cent. Heilongjiang, Liaoning, Shandong and Henan are the other major gas producing provinces.

Biogas (or marsh gas)—produced from fermented night soil, rubbish, grass and other organic matter—is widely used for cooking and lighting in certain parts of the countryside. Biogas reactors were first constructed on a large scale in Sichuan Province during the early 1970s. By the late 1970s there were more than 7 million family biogas reactors of $8-10$ m^3 capacity in rural China. However, the shift to family-run farms in the 1980s has led to a decrease in the popularity of biogas reactors with the total number dropping to 3.76 million by 1984. In addition to rural household cookers and gas lamp fuel generation, there are small biogas-fuelled electricity generating stations as well as pilot projects to treat urban sewage and night soil through anaerobic fermentation in reactors in Guangdong, Shandong, Shaanxi, and Jiangsu Provinces. While reactors can be used for up to 8 months in Sichuan and other southern provinces, they will operate for only 3 to 5 months north of the Yangtze River.

ESTIMATED PRODUCTION OF NATURAL GAS AND HYDRO-ELECTRIC POWER
IN CHINA: SELECTED YEARS, 1943–87

Year	Natural gas production *millions of m³*	per cent of total energy production	Hydro-electric production *millions of kw hours*	per cent of total energy production
1943 (pre-1949 oil peak)	—	—	—	—
1949	7	—	700	3.0
1952	8	—	1300	2.0
1957	70	0.1	4800	2.9
1962	1210	0.9	9000	2.9
1965	1100	0.8	10 400	2.6
1970	2870	1.2	20 500	3.1
1975	8850	2.4	47 600	4.1
1980	14 270	3.0	58 200	3.8
1983	12 210	2.3	86 400	4.8
1984	12 430	2.1	86 800	4.5
1985	12 930	2.0	92 400	4.4
1986	13 760	2.1	94 500	4.3
1987	13 890	2.0	100 000	4.4

Sources: Guojia tongjiju (Chinese State Statistical Bureau), ed., *Zhongguo nengyuan tongji nianjian 1986* (Chinese Energy Statistical Yearbook 1986) (Beijing, 1987). *Zhongguo tongji nianjian 1988* (Almanac of Chinese Statistics) (Beijing)

Hydro-electricity

At the end of 1987 hydro-electric power stations provided 100 007 million KWh, slightly over 20 per cent of China's total electric power of 497 266 million KWh. This is a lower proportion of output than expected if hydro- and thermal electricity generating capacity are compared due to restrictions on operations of hydro-electric plants because of low water levels and the demands of irrigation. Capacity utilization is only about 40 per cent.

China has about 25 per cent of world hydro-electric generating potential, with a total annual potential of 5 900 000 KW per hour. However, exploitable hydro-power potential is reckoned to be about 1 923 000 KW per hour. The Yangtze River basin accounts for approximately 53 per cent of the potential with the Yarlung Zangbo, Nu, Lancang, and Yuan Rivers of the relatively inaccessible southwest accounting for another 26.3 per cent. The high capital cost of water power has inhibited its development, but policy is now directed towards making more use of this resource. In 1985, 12 hydro-electric stations with capacity of over 500 megawatts (MW) were under construction.

Nearly one-quarter of China's current hydro-electric capacity comes from 8 hydro-electric stations of 500MW capacity and over. In additio   n there are over 130 stations with capacities ranging

A hydro-electric power station in Fujian Province.

MAJOR HYDRO-ELECTRIC STATIONS IN CHINA

Plant name (River)	Province (County)	Capacity and units *(megawatts)*	Construction period	Annual output *(KWh)*
Liujiaxia (Yellow)	Gansu (Yongjing)	1160 4 × 225 1 × 260	1958–74	5.70
Gezhouba (Yangtze)	Hubei (Yichang)	965 2 × 170 5 × 125	1970–81	5.40
Danjiangkou (Han Shui)	Hubei (Jun)	900 6 × 150	1958–73	2.88
Gongzui (Dadu)	Sichuan (Leshan)	700 7 × 100	1966–79	4.12
Shuifeng (Yalu)	Liaoning (Kuandian)	630 7 × 90	1937–41	1.90
Xin'anjiang (Xin'anjiang)	Zhejiang (Xin'anjiang)	652.5 4 × 75 5 × 72.5	1957–77	1.86
Wujiangdu (Wu)	Guizhou (Xifeng)	630 3 × 210	1970–82	3.34
Fengman (Songhua)	Jilin (Jilin)	554 5 × 72.5 1 × 70 2 × 60 1 × 1.5	1937–58	1.89

Source: V. Smil, *Energy in China's Modernization: Advances and Limitations* (Armonk, NY, 1988; Sun Jingzhi (ed.): *Zhongguo jingji dili gaikuang* (*Concise Economic Geography of China*) Beijing, 1983)

between 12MW and 500MW plus around 72 000 small stations. The small stations with below 12MW installed capacity made up slightly under 37 per cent of the total hydro-electric capacity in 1985. Many of the large hydro-electric stations are part of schemes embracing also irrigation, flood control and improved navigation. Hubei and Sichuan produce the most hydro-electric power followed by Hunan, Gansu, Guangdong, Jilin and Guangxi.

The small hydro-electric plants, frequently of about 150KW capacity or smaller are often manufactured locally with state investments generally below one third of the total cost. Their costs per kilowatt of capacity tend to be high compared with large stations, and the total number of such small stations has been declining since 1979. However, they serve local needs for irrigation and rural industry and can be designed and constructed in two to three years. The trend since 1983 has been to build slightly larger plants with about 500KW capacity.

Nuclear power

China has enough verified reserves of fissionable uranium to support an installed nuclear power capacity of 15GW for 30 years of capacity generation. Deposits have been found on the border between Jiangxi and Guangdong Provinces as well as in Xinjiang and other parts of China. Uranium is processed at Lanzhou in Gansu and Ürümqi in Xinjiang. However, it seems that domestic output may not in future be adequate for the country's requirements, as the Chinese have been showing an interest in the possibility of importing uranium.

KEY

- ● Coal-mining centres, producing over 10 million tons of coal per year.
- ○○ Principal onshore and offshore oilfields.
- ▽ Hydroelectric stations, with installed capacity of 500 MW (1985).

SOURCES OF ENERGY

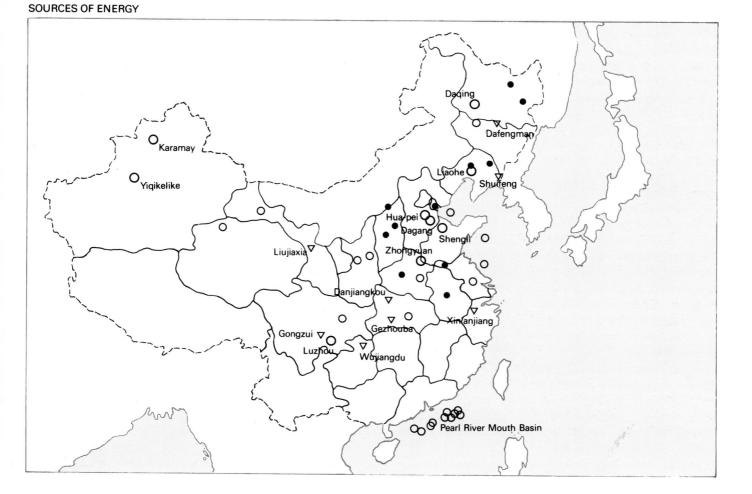

Daya Bay nuclear power plant, Guandong.

In 1982 the government announced the beginning of construction of the mainland's first nuclear power plant at Qinshan (300MW) in Zhejiang Province, 120km south of Shanghai. In 1985 China signed a contract with Framatone to build a 1800MW nuclear power plant at Daya Bay in Guangdong Province near to Hong Kong which should be completed around 1991. A 3000MW plant will be built at Changshan in Jiangsu with two reactors to be installed by 1990. It is estimated that nuclear generation may generate about 10GW or up to 5 per cent of electricity by the year 2000. Most plants will be located in coastal areas. Taiwan had 5 operating nuclear reactors by 1986.

Geothermal power

China's geothermal resources are among the world's richest. The greatest potential for development is in the southwest (Tibet and Yunnan) and the southeast (Taiwan, Fujian and Guangdong). Currently China has 7 geothermal stations with 6 of these below 1KW. Because of difficulties in drilling and other aspects of production as well as problems of controlling diffuse flow, it is unlikely that geothermal power will play more than a local role in China's energy output over the next few decades.

Traditional fuels

Wood, grass and other burnable forest biomass are still the most common domestic fuels in rural China. Estimates put total rural forest phytomass consumption during the mid-1980s at about 181.6 million tons per annum. This has contributed to massive deforestation. Forest loss since 1949 has been particularly serious in Hainan (72 per cent), Yunnan (55 per cent), and Sichuan (30 per cent) Provinces. Rural China must remain dependent on forest

biomass as a form of fuel for decades and serious shortages will continue if recently encouraged planting and forest management policies fail.

China has about 10 per cent of the world's peat reserves, about 27 000 million tonnes, found mostly in Heilongjiang Province.

A.D., R.L.E.

Metals and metallic ores

Iron and steel

Iron metallurgy was a relative latecomer in ancient China, first appearing there around 600 BC, some 800 years after it came into use in Asia Minor. However, the very early development of cast iron made large-scale production easy, and iron and steel production became flourishing by the Han dynasty. The modern iron and steel industry in China dates from the late 19th century.

China is believed to be rich in iron ore reserves. Confirmed reserves are said to be 47 200 million tonnes, placing China third in the world after the USSR and Brazil. Approximately 1000 verified deposits are found in over 600 counties in all provincial level units except the municipalities of Shanghai and Tianjin. The largest deposits are found in Liaoning Province with other major concentrations in north China (Hebei, Shanxi, Inner Mongolia and Shandong), the southwest (Sichuan and Yunnan) and central China (Anhui and Hubei). These reserves are mostly of low quality, with an iron content of about 35 per cent. Mine output of iron ore in 1986 was 141 million tonnes. The ore needs extensive beneficiation before it can be fed into iron making furnaces. The lack of facilities for this, combined with chronic bottlenecks in supply are reasons for China importing 12 million tonnes of high-grade iron ore and over 2.8 million tonnes of pig iron per annum by 1986. Most of this imported ore was used in the Shanghai area steel plants. As of 1986 China had imported over 19 million tonnes of steel products, of which plate, sheet and section steel made up close to 11 million tonnes. By 1987 China had produced 56 million tonnes of steel.

In 1986, there were 12 enterprises each with over 1 million tonne steel production capacity out of a total of 166 major iron and steel enterprises, and 1369 medium- to small-scale iron and steel works. The major iron and steel bases are Anshan and Benxi in Liaoning; Shanghai and Maanshan in Anhui; Beijing-Tianjin and Tangshan, Baotou, Wuhan, Panzhihua in Sichuan; Taiyuan and Chongqing. Special steel plants at Qiqihar, Daye in Hubei, Chengdu and Jiangyou in Sichuan, Xi'an and Xining now have

ESTIMATED PRODUCTION OF STEEL AND PIG IRON IN CHINA: SELECTED
YEARS, 1943–87

Year	Steel production millions of tonnes	Pig iron production millions of tonnes
1943 (pre-1949 steel peak)	0.9	—
1949	0.2	0.3
1952	1.4	1.9
1957	5.4	5.9
1960	18.7	27.6
1962	6.7	8.1
1965	12.2	10.8
1970	17.8	17.1
1975	23.9	24.5
1980	37.1	38.0
1983	40.0	37.4
1984	43.5	40.0
1985	46.8	43.8
1986	52.2	50.6
1987	56.3	55.0

Sources: US Congress Joint Economic Committee, *China: A Reassessment of the Economy*
(Washington, DC, 1975); US Central Intelligence Agency, *China. The Steel Industry in the 1970s
and 1980s* (Washington, DC); *Zhongguo gantie gongye nianjian (1987)* (Almanac of China's Iron
and Steel Industry 1987) (Beijing); *Zhongguo tongji nianjian 1988* (Almanac of Chinese Statistics)
(Beijing)

annual capacities of over 100 000 tonnes. Iron and steel production is now spread throughout all of China's provincial level units
with the exception of Tibet. Whereas the interior only produced
13.9 per cent of steel output in 1949 it was responsible for over 41
per cent as of 1987. However, per-tonne investment has been 3
times higher in the interior. Medium-sized enterprises with
300 000 to 500 000 tonne capacity are the backbone of the iron
and steel industry. Management of the medium-sized plants has
generally been more efficient than the smaller plants or the larger
complexes.

The plants constructed in the 1950s mainly had open-hearth
furnaces. In the mid-1960s oxygen furnaces went into operation at
the Beijing Steel Works, at Taiyuan and at Shanghai. From the late
1970s electric furnaces were installed at a number of plants. In the
1980s considerable energy savings and management changes were
made although efficiency still lags behind most Western nations.

Steel-finishing facilities have lagged behind China's production
of crude steel. Although there is a shortage of mill variety, some
large blooming and structural mills exist together with rod and bar,
plate, sheet and welded and seamless tube mills. The country is
deficient is trained personnel, tinning and galvanizing facilities,
and in wide sheet and strip mills.

Gold and silver

Small-scale production of gold, from mines and from peasant
gold-washing, occurs in at least 25 provincial level units and
output is over 2000 troy ounces a year. China is ranked fourth in
the world in gold reserves and sixth in gold production. The largest
share of gold production comes from China's 200 mines (over 50
per cent), with gold washing accounting for roughly 9 per cent and
the rest of the gold derived as a by-product from other mining
activities. Leading areas in gold mining are the Shandong peninsula, northern Heilongjiang, western Henan, northern Hebei,
eastern Jilin, Liaoning, central Inner Mongolia, western Hunan,
Hubei, northern Xinjiang, southern Shaanxi, Yunnan and Taiwan.
The largest producing area in recent years is around Mohe in
Heilongjiang Province. Between 1985 and 1988 China discovered
two major gold deposits: one along the Guizhou-Guangxi-Yunnan
border and the other along the Gansu-Sichuan-Shaanxi border as
well as deposits in Liaoning, Guangdong, Hainan, the central and
lower Yangtze valley, Yunnan and Xinjiang. Over the last decade
gold production has been going up 10 per cent per annum. A gold
refinery was opened in Zhaoyuan Xian, Shandong Province during
1986. There have been reports of inefficiencies in the gold industry
and under-reporting of finds by individuals. Exports of gold in
recent years have gone to Italy.

Silver mining is also a small-scale activity in China. Most silver
mining activity is found in Henan, Shandong, Hebei, Sichuan and
Yunnan. It is mostly mined in conjuction with other minerals.

Platinum

Traditionally China had to rely mainly on imports for its platinum
requirements. However, in 1957 a platinum deposit was discovered
in the Qilian range in Ningxia, while in 1979 the finding of a substantial deposit was reported in Yunnan. More recently the largest
reserves of platinum in China were discovered at Jinchang in Gansu
Province. New technological extraction processes have raised the
recovery rate of platinum from 49 to 75 per cent at the Jinchang
mine. Chinese imports of platinum totalled 1376 kg in 1986.

Copper

China has an estimated 50 million tonnes of copper resources.
However, the quantity of copper content in ores averages 0.4 per
cent–considerably lower than the average content in the ores of
Zaire (6 per cent) or Zambia (3.5 per cent). However, China is
still the world's ninth largest producer of copper. Mine output is
estimated to be about 185 000 tonnes of copper content per
annum.

Copper reserves are distributed in the lower reaches of the
Yangtze River valley, in Yunnan, Gansu, Shanxi and the Qamdo
area of Tibet. The 30 largest copper deposits account for 80 per

cent of the total reserves. The chief copper mines in China include the Baiyin mine in Gansu, Dongchuan, Yimen and Dayao mines in Yunnan, the Zhongtiaoshan mine at Yuanqu in Shanxi, and mines at Tongling in Anhui, at Daye in Hubei and at Dexing in Jiangxi. The Dexing mine is now given priority for development. In addition, numerous small copper mines are in operation. Because of the low grade of copper ore, costs for refining make up over 80 per cent of capital investment. Smelting of copper is done at Kunming, Baiyin, Luoyang in Henan Province, Shenyang and Shanghai. The Shanghai site smelts largely imported copper ore. Processing of copper is carried out at sites generally closer to the consumer; Shanghai, Luoyang, and Shenyang are the primary sites. Processing is also undertaken at Beijing, Tianjin, Wuhan, Canton, Chongqing and Baiyin.

Copper production has been running far short of China's requirements, and large but variable quantities have been imported. In 1986 consumption of copper was about 800 000 tonnes with imports making up 45 per cent of the total. Recent suppliers of copper ore include Canada, the Philippines and Papua New Guinea. In 1986 imports of ingots were 189 685 tonnes with those of 1985 being 346 430 tonnes. Countries supplying copper ingots vary from year to year but the UK, Japan, the USSR, Chile, Poland and the USA have been large suppliers recently. If the pace of development continues China will remain a net importer of copper at least until 2000.

Lead and zinc

China has moderately large reserves of lead, and its zinc reserves are thought to be substantial. It is the eighth largest producer of lead in the world. About 160 000 tonnes of lead, and 200 000 tonnes of zinc were estimated to have been mined in China in 1986. Lead and zinc deposits are found in the Nanling range of south China, the southwest, northwest and northeast. Old established lead-zinc mines are situated at Shuikoushan in Hunan Province and at Chaihe near Tieling in Liaoning Province. Major lead-zinc mines are found in Yunnan, Qinghai, Guangdong, Gansu and Xinjiang, as well as Hunan and Liaoning. The Fankuo mine at Shaoguan in northern Guangdong, is China's largest. Smelting is done at Changsha and Hengyang in Hunan, Shenyang in Liaoning which is the largest lead-zinc smelter, as well as the smelters established since 1949 at Zhuzhou in Hunan, Shaoguan in northern Guangdong and Kashi in Xinjiang. At Huludao in Liaoning there is a smelting facility for zinc and at Kunming there is a lead smelter.

China imported 4607 tonnes of lead ingots in 1986 which was down from 7572 tonnes in 1985. Bulgaria, Canada, Japan and Hong Kong have been major suppliers. Imports and exports of zinc have fluctuated greatly in recent years.

Tin

China was the first country to mine tin and it is a traditional export mineral. Today China is first in known tin reserves and is the world's fifth largest producer of tin. Tin is found in 13 provincial level units with close to 90 per cent of known reserves concentrated in Guangxi (37 per cent), Yunnan (37), Hunan (8), and Guangdong (7.5). It is usually mined in conjunction with copper, lead, zinc, and other minerals.

Gejiu in southern Yunnan Province is China's largest tin mining centre; production there dates back several centuries and makes up about 75 per cent of China's tin output. Gejiu tin is mined by the underground lode method. However, ore grade and hence output has been on the decline at Gejiu. In the past decade another tin base has been established at the Nandan mine in northern Guangxi. There also appear to be deposits in western Yunnan which may develop into another tin base.

China produces over 21 000 tonnes of tin annually. However, by 1986 exports of tin ores totalled less than 6000 tonnes and with increasing domestic demand it is unlikely that ore exports will rise rapidly in the near future. In 1986 China also exported slightly under 7000 tonnes of tin ingots. Tin exports have largely been to Hong Kong.

Antimony

China is the largest producer of antimony in the world. Production is estimated at about 15 000 tonnes per year. The chief antimony producing area is in Hunan Province which accounts for 80 per cent of China's total output. Xikuangshan in Hunan has the world's largest antimony mine. Antimony is also mined in Guangxi, Gansu, Yunnan, and Guizhou Provinces, often as a by-product in tin smelting operations.

China has not been an aggressive seller of antimony on the world market. The purity of Chinese antimony tends to be poorer than that of the other large producers, such as Bolivia, which lowers export demand. Chinese exports of antimony ores have fluctuated in recent years with 4031 tonnes exported in 1986. West Germany has been the leading destination. China also exports increasing amounts of antimony regulus, antimony sulphide, and antimony trioxide.

Beryllium

Little is known about China's beryllium resources except that beryl is found in Xinjiang and processing of beryl and bertrandite occurs in Xinjiang and Lanzhou. The USA has purchased beryl from China in recent years.

Nickel, cobalt and palladium

The development of one of the largest nickel deposits in the world at Jinchang in Gansu Province since 1958 has ended China's dependence on imported nickel. This mine is also the second in the world for sulphuric nickel. The grade of nickel is high and there is an abundance of associated minerals. The Jinchang mine also has China's largest reserves of cobalt as well as platinum and other minerals found there include palladium, osmium, iridium, rhodium, gold and silver. In 1986 a cobalt mine was completed on Hainan Island.

Chinese scientists are said to have developed a method of extracting nickel and cobalt from nickel phosphorous iron, a by-product in the making of calcium magnesium fertilizer. New extraction techniques have also raised the recovery rates of cobalt from 32 to 60 per cent and palladium from 3 to around 50 per cent. In 1986 China exported 2 574 tonnes of nickel ingots and imported 9 tonnes of nickel ingots and 587 tonnes of cobalt ingots. Nickel sulphate exports are also on the increase.

Mercury

Although China's reserves of mercury are of the first rank in size, they are low grade. China is a major producer of mercury, the chief mines being in Guizhou, Hunan, and Guangdong Provinces. The Wanshan mine in Guizhou accounts for 90 per cent of China's production. Other important Guizhou mines are at Tongren, Songtao, Wuchuan, and Kaiyang. Because mercury usually occurs in small pockets, mining is mostly small scale. In 1986 China exported 999 tonnes of mercury. The USA and Japan were amongst the receiving countries.

Aluminium

China has large reserves of low-grade bauxite and alumina shale. As of 1984 China was fifth in known reserves of aluminium, following Guyana, Australia, Brazil and Jamaica. China has bauxite mines in 17 provincial-level units with the largest deposits in Shanxi (30 per cent of national reserves), Henan (20 per cent), Guizhou (18 per cent), and Guangxi (14 per cent). China exports around 750 000 tonnes of bauxite annually.

China is the sixth largest producer of aluminium in the world. Most ores are first processed as aluminium oxide and then the aluminium oxide is smelted to produce aluminium. As of 1985 the industry was dominated by 8 large factories producing over 70 per cent of national output.

As production of aluminium by electrolysis consumes 18 000KWh per tonne, the industry has been hampered by shortage of electric power as well as by lack of high-grade raw material and technical resources. China's largest aluminium oxide production bases are located near bauxite mines and in electrically well-supplied areas such as Zhengzhou in Henan, Zhangtian in Shandong, Kuiyang in Guizhou, Pinguo in Guangxi, and Hejin in Shanxi. The largest aluminium plant is at Fushun, in Liaoning. However, expansion at Fushun is unlikely given local power constraints. Aluminium plants at Lanzhou and Lincheng in Gansu, and Qingdongxia in Ningxia rely on hydro-power from the Yellow River. Another major aluminium plant is at Baotou in Inner Mongolia.

Demand for aluminium, as for copper, has been rising rapidly because of the requirements of electric power transmission. This has necessitated imports of aluminium, which have fluctuated according to world market prices but generally amount to one-half of China's needs. In 1985, China imported over 480 000 tonnes, but in 1986, when prices were on average £67 (US$120) per tonne higher, only slightly under 250 000 tonnes were imported. The USSR, Switzerland, Australia and the UK have been the principal suppliers. In 1986 China also imported over 300 000 tonnes of aluminium oxide. In contrast, China exported 8679 tonnes of aluminium ingots and 6228 tonnes of aluminium products during 1986.

Manganese

China is a substantial producer of manganese ore, and the reserves are believed to be considerable. The largest deposits are in Hunan, Guangxi, Guizhou, Kuangdong, Liaoning and Jiangsu. Output is about 1.6 million tonnes of ore a year. China exports about 30 000 tonnes of manganese ore annually.

Magnesium

China's production of magnesium metal is approximately 7000 tonnes a year. China has substantial deposits of magnesite largely found in the northeast and east. Because of growing needs for magnesium, China is constructing dolomite processing plants in Liaoning and Qinghai. The largest reserves of magnesite, together with the geologically associated minerals, soapstone and talc, are at Dashiqiao in Liaoning.

Tungsten

China has threefold the rest of the world's reserves of tungsten. The largest deposit is at Xikuang in Hunan province. However, the Xikuang deposit is of low grade. China has the largest output at around 15 000 tonnes of pure tungsten. It also has the largest export volume in the world exporting 550 tonnes of low degree tungsten ore and slightly over 19 000kg of tungsten rod in 1986 accounting for about 40 per cent of the world export market. However, as processing techniques are still rather poor China imports a considerable amount of tungsten filament.

The leading province in production is Jiangxi, the chief mines there being Dajishan, Xihuashan, Guimeishan and Bangushan. Tungsten is also mined in other provinces, notably in neighbouring northern Guangdong and eastern Hunan, Zhejiang, eastern Guangxi and western Fujian. Most of these mines were in operation prior to 1949 but are now mechanized.

Molybdenum

China has extensive deposits of molybdenum. Before 1949 the only extensive area mined for molybdenum was the Yangjiazhangzi district in Liaoning. This district still has the largest annual output—about 1000 tonnes of concentrates—although the mine at Jinduicheng in Shaanxi also has significant production. A new molybdenum and tungsten mine at Xiaojiayingzi in Liaoning, was completed in 1986. Molybdenite has been found in tungsten deposits as an accompanying mineral. Estimates of output are about 9 to 11 million kilogrammes per annum. Molybdenum has been exported, in erratic quantities to Japan, the United States, Eastern Europe and other destinations. In 1986 China's molybdenum exports rose to 13 381 tonnes after a 1985 export total of 1414 tonnes.

Chromium

China has little chromium. Chromite deposits have been discovered in Hebei, Jilin and Sichuan but imports are still the mainstay for China's requirements for chromium. In recent years China has been importing 350 000–450 000 tonnes of chrome ores a year. At one time Albania supplied some two-thirds of China's imports of chromium. However, recently China has been importing chromium from other sources.

Bismuth

Bismuth has been found in Guangdong, at Shizhuyuan in Hunan and in Liaoning, in association with deposits of other minerals. China produces about 260 tonnes of bismuth a year. At times China has exported some bismuth. In 1985 a small quantity was exported to West Germany.

Titanium

Titanium has been found in Sichuan, Hebei, Liaoning, Hubei, Hainan and Yunnan with some 80 to 90 per cent of China's total reserves found at Panzhihua in southern Sichuan. The titanium concentrate grade at Panzhihua is about 45 to 48 per cent. Production levels are relatively small and foreign participation has been requested to treat slag at Panzhihua.

Rare-earth minerals

China claims that it has reserves of 36 million tonnes of rare earths or four times the reserves of the rest of the world. These deposits and their production are found largely in Inner Mongolia, the most famous being the Bayan Obo mine which produces 80 per cent of China's rare earths. Other deposits are found in Jiangxi, Guangdong, Guangxi, Hunan, and Shandong provinces. The leading rare earth for export is yttrium.

Barite

China has considerable reserves of barite and is a large producer and exporter. Deposits of barite have been found in Guizhou (60 per cent of total reserves), Hebei, Shandong, Guangxi, and Jiangxi. Annual production is estimated at about 1 million tonnes. Exports of barite have fluctuated with its demand from the petroleum drilling industry.   *A.D., R.L.E.*

Other minerals

Asbestos

China has a production capacity of about 150 000 tonnes of asbestos. Shimian in Sichuan Province is the largest producing centre and has a beneficiation mill. Shimian asbestos is of the long-fibre chrysotile type. Another major deposit exists at Peng Xian, also in Sichuan. In 1985 an asbestos dressing plant for concentrated ore with 10 000 tonne capacity began operations at Mangnai in Qinghai Province. Another 5000 to 10 000 tonne annual capacity plant is planned for Babao in northern Qinghai. Asbestos is also worked in Inner Mongolia, Shanxi, Gansu, Hebei, Jilin and Liaoning Provinces. Roughly two-thirds of asbestos is mined by open pit methods. Slightly over half of domestic consumption is of asbestos-cement products. There have been some exports of asbestos, roughly about 1000 tonnes a year, but China does not appear to have a large surplus.

Salt

Nearly 18 million tonnes in 1987, China's salt production dates back for millennia, and the salt tax was for long a major source of government revenue. China is now the second largest producer of salt in the world, after the USA.

Production is widespread with Shandong Province having the largest totals. Most of the Shandong, Liaoning, Tianjin and Beijing production comes from evaporative operations by salterns in the Bohai area. Sea salt accounts for about 75 per cent of national production, with the rest deriving from lakes and ponds (10 per cent), mines (8 per cent) and well water (7 per cent). In recent years there has been a marked increase in the proportion of salt output going to industrial purposes, particularly to the chemical industry. During 1985 many coastal salt districts were damaged and there has been a shortage of salt which has slowed production in the soda industry. Recently, large salt deposits have been discovered in Jiangsu.

Clay

China has plentiful deposits of porcelain clays in many parts of the country. China dominated the world's porcelain markets from the 8th to the 18th centuries. The most famous clay is the kaolin type from the great historic porcelain centre of Jingdezhen in Jiangxi. It is estimated that high quality, low iron content kaolin deposits are sufficient for production to continue at current levels in the Jiangxi-Anhui area for about 500 years. Important deposits of porcelain clays are also found in Jiangsu and Shandong. High-quality clays have been imported from the United Kingdom and the United States. Leading destinations for exports of clay in recent years are Japan, Hong Kong, and West Germany.

Production of porcelain wares now takes place in every provincial level unit except Tibet. In the early 1980s Guangdong, Hunan, Jiangxi, Hebei and Shandong were the leading provinces in the production of porcelain ware. About 25 per cent of the porcelain ware manufactured is exported

Talc

Large talc mines are found in Liaoning, Shandong and Guangxi. In 1986 China exported over 425 000 tonnes of talc lumps and close to 150 000 tonnes of talc powder. Japan, the United Kingdom, and Southeast Asia have been the most common destinations for talc exports. The Japanese and the Americans are involved in joint venture development of talc production.

Soda

The largest single deposit of soda discovered in China is reported to be at Wucheng mine, Henan. Very substantial deposits of soda have also been found in lakes in north Tibet. China produces over 2 million tonnes of caustic soda and close to 2 million tonnes of soda ash per annum. All provincial level units except Tibet produce caustic soda. However, production is distributed mainly in large consumer areas such as the Yangtze River delta, the Sichuan basin and the areas around Beijing and Shenyang. China exports about 3000 tonnes of caustic soda and 4000 to 5000 tonnes of soda ash per annum.

Jade

Chinese jade production has traditionally been centred in the southwest of the country. Significant finds have been reported from Liaoning and Ningxia. Hong Kong interests are involved in processing jade from Yunnan for export.

Diamonds

China is thought to have moderate reserves of diamonds, but they began to be worked only in the 1970s. The first mine, in western Hunan, began operations about 1971. In 1985 China's largest diamond deposit was found near Dalian in Liaoning Province. Finds have also been reported in Shandong and Guizhou. With the development of these deposits, and of synthetic diamond production, imports have declined. In 1986 China imported 39 000 carats of diamonds. De Beers Consolidated Mines Ltd of South Africa is involved in a diamond prospecting joint venture in Shandong. Most diamond imports and exports go through Hong Kong or Belgium-Luxemburg.

Fluorspar

China is a large producer and exporter of fluorspar. Output in 1986 is estimated to have exceeded 650 000 tonnes. The main fluorspar production districts are in Zhejiang, Fujian, Liaoning, Shandong, Hebei, Guangdong, and Hunan Provinces. Japan and West Germany are the chief export markets for Chinese fluorspar. Insignificant levels are imported via Hong Kong.   *A.D., R.L.E.*

Cement

Cement production in China began in 1889. China is now the third largest cement producing country in the world. China's output of cement has been steadily rising in recent years reaching 186 million tonnes for 1987. There are over 4500 cement plants in China with over 50 of these plants fitting the Chinese definition of medium or large scale. The medium- and large-scale plants, many of which function with equipment of 1940s or 1950s standards, account for about 30 per cent of total cement production.

The quality of cement produced by the small plants, most of which are in rural areas, is often not high. However, it is adequate for water conservancy works such as reservoirs, pumping stations and irrigation ditches. It is also used to make cement boats for freight purposes in those extensive areas of the countryside where waterways are commoner than all-weather roads.

Prior to 1949 production was largely concentrated in the northeast. Cement is now produced in every provincial level unit of China although as of 1987 only Shandong, Jiangsu, Guangdong, Sichuan, Hebei, Zhejiang, Liaoning and Henan produce more than 10 million tonnes per annum. Location of plants is influenced by availability of materials, energy and proximity to markets.

ESTIMATED PRODUCTION OF CEMENT AND CHEMICAL FERTILIZERS IN
CHINA: SELECTED YEARS, 1941–87

Year	Cement production millions of tonnes	Chemical fertilizer production millions of tonnes
1941 (pre-1949 fertilizer peak)	—	0.2
1942 (pre-1949 cement peak)	2.3	—
1949	0.7	0.01
1952	2.9	0.04
1957	6.9	0.2
1962	6.0	0.5
1965	16.3	1.7
1970	25.8	2.4
1975	46.3	5.2
1980	79.9	12.3
1983	108.3	13.8
1984	123.0	14.6
1985	146.0	13.2
1986	166.1	14.0
1987	186.3	16.7

Source: *Zhongguo tongji nianjian 1988* (Almanac of Chinese Statistics) (Beijing)

In 1986 China exported 205 930 tonnes of cement, largely to Hong Kong. At times the country also imports cement from Hong Kong and Japan plus small amounts from other countries. In recent years cement plants have been upgraded with aid from Japanese, Danish, German and French firms. *A.D., R.L.E.*

Fertilizers

China's soils are generally deficient in nitrogen, less so in phosphate and least in potash. Traditional Chinese methods of nourishing the soil were among the most effective in the pre-industrial world. All waste matter was returned to the soil, the chief fertilizers being human and animal excreta, green manure, mud from ponds and rivers, and soya bean cake. In 1974 it was estimated that the amount of nitrogen recycled from animal and human wastes was at least equal to the amount available from chemical fertilizers both made in China and imported.

China is the world's third largest producer of chemical fertilizers. Chemical fertilizers in common use in China include ammonia, ammonium bicarbonate, urea, single superphosphate, ammonium nitrate, calcium magnesium phosphate, ammonium chloride, ammonium sulphate, aqua ammonia, ammonium phosphate, potassium sulphate, calcium cyanamide and basic slag. Roughly 82.7 per cent of chemical fertilizers produced in China are nitrogenous, 16.7 per cent are phosphatic and less than one per cent are potassic. Phosphate fertilizer plants began to be built in China around 1958. There are now over 700 phosphate fertilizer plants in China. In contrast the potash fertilizer industry's development has been slow since it began in 1959 because of a lack of sylvite in convenient locations. Most production takes place in Qinghai Province. As of 1985, China had 45 fertilizer catalyst production plants dispersed in 21 provincial level units producing close to 24 000 tonnes of fertilizer catalysts.

In the mid-1980s China was importing over 9 million tonnes of chemical fertilizers (by standard contents) a year. Urea accounted for roughly half of the imports in 1986, both by volume and value. In 1986 the chief suppliers of urea were Romania and the USSR with smaller quantities coming from Hong Kong, Kuwait, Japan, Norway, West Germany and other countries. China exports very small quantities of chemical fertilizers (less than 0.9 per cent of 1986 production).

China possesses substantial reserves of raw materials for nitrogenous, phosphate and potassium fertilizers. For nitrogenous fertilizers, coal has long been the chief source of raw materials. In recent years oil, natural gas and naphtha have provided an increasing share of the raw materials for the industry. Small phosphate plants in many parts of the country have used local phosphate deposits while the large phosphate fertilizer plants have, in addition, drawn on imports. About one-half of China's phosphate resources are found in Guizhou, Hubei and Yunnan Provinces. Reserves of potassium exist in the Tarim and Qaidam Basins in Xinjiang and Qinghai respectively, while supplies have also been derived from sea salt. However, production of potassic fertilizer is far below needs.

Some 65 large and medium synthetic ammonia factories existed in China as of 1980. Prior to that date the construction of small and medium fertilizer plants was encouraged to provide for local needs, especially for nitrogenous fertilizer but also for phosphate and humic acid fertilizers. Larger state plants generally produced fertilizer for high priority state projects. In 1986, 50 per cent of China's synthetic ammonia came from small plants with large- and medium-scale plants each producing a quarter of total output. In recent years the emphasis within the industry has been on energy conservation and rise in product quality. The United States, Kuwait and Tunisia have become involved in development of China's phosphate deposits and fertilizer production since the mid-1980s. New pricing structures have meant that the margin of profit for large plants has been dropping and some small plants have begun recording losses. *A.D., R.L.E*

COMMUNICATIONS

Inland waterways

Rivers and canals were pre-modern China's primary means of communication. Because non-mechanized land transport cost several times more than shipping goods by junk, bulk commodities were moved over long distances almost solely on the waterways. The first canals were built as early as the 5th century BC. During the Han dynasty industries were mostly situated close to water transport, and metals were shipped by boat across the empire. But large-scale bulk transport dates mainly from the middle and later imperial periods when the economic heart of China in the centre and south was separated from the political capital in the north, and when regional specialization emerged with the cultivation of industrial crops. To transport grain from the Yangtze region to Chang'an and later Beijing, two grand canals were built, the first in the Sui period, the second in Yuan-Ming times, to supplement the predominantly east–west communications afforded by the rivers. Large fleets of junks carried the tribute grain north along the canals, but even greater quantities of grain were shipped commercially along the Yangtze, on which other bulk items such as coal also came from as far away as southern Hunan. In the early 19th century the Yangtze ports handled amounts of shipping equal to any in the world. Even in the 1930s Wuhu and Jiujiang, although of negligible importance for foreign trade, dealt with more shipping than any coastal port in China except Shanghai. Facility of transport has been one of the main reasons for the prosperity of the Yangtze region.

In 1936 China had around 74 000km of navigable waterways, of which 6400 were open to steamers, and a further 24 000 to steam launches. By 1987 there were 109 800km, 58 000 of which were more than one metre deep. Some of the obstacles impeding navigation in the Yangtze gorges have been blasted away, so that steamers can now safely go upstream as far as Chongqing. Rather less successful have been attempts to open more of the Yellow River to navigation, where the problem of silting has not yet been overcome.

INLAND WATERWAYS

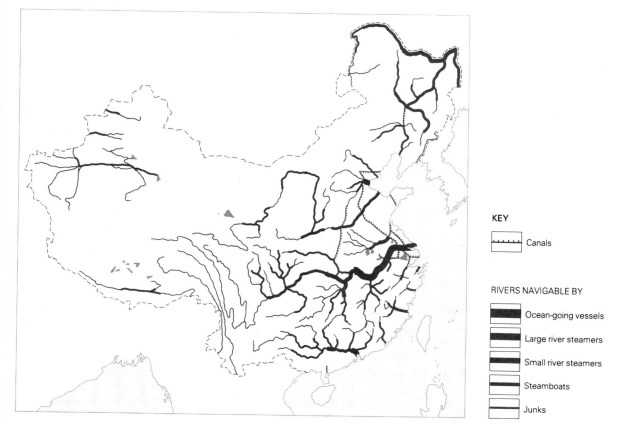

KEY

⊢⊢⊢⊢⊢ Canals

RIVERS NAVIGABLE BY

Ocean-going vessels

Large river steamers

Small river steamers

Steamboats

Junks

Traffic has also increased sharply since 1949. In 1952 motorized vessels on inland waterways accounted for 3.6 billion tonne km, in 1955 for 10.4 billion. Total modern shipping freight turnover, coastal and inland, has risen from 11.8 billion tonne km in 1952 to 292.8 billion in 1987. Part of this increase can be explained by a switch from non-motorized to motorized vessels, but even now junks remain important, especially in central and south China. After decades of neglect, a major effort to overhaul the system began in 1984.

The Yangtze has historically been China's primary transport artery and is still much the most important river system. 3638 km of the main river are navigable, and tributaries, lakes and the intricate canal system that serves east China have raised this to 18 000 km. More than one-third of all motorized river transport operates on the Yangtze, which is the chief artery of communication for the 400–500 million people who live in its watershed. Grain, coal and other materials for the steel industry account for most of the 133 million tonnes of cargo handled by the Yangtze ports in 1986.

Also important, although far behind the Yangtze, is the Songhua river system, which links the industrial areas of Harbin, Jiamusi and Qiqihar in Heilongjiang Province. About 40 per cent of the volume of cargo, which was over one million tonnes in 1957, consists of timber, and another 40 per cent is made up of coal or foodstuffs. The Xi Jiang, part of the Pearl River (Zhu Jiang) system in Guangdong, where 60 per cent of goods transported go by river, principally carries timber downstream and coal and marine products upstream.   *T.W.*

The Grand Canal in Wuxi: the canal still carries much long-distance traffic between Beijing and the lower Yangtze valley.

Maritime shipping

Archaeological evidence attests to seaborne communication from the 2nd millennium BC, and written sources to coastal trade between the Yangtze area and north China from the 5th century BC. By the 2nd century BC Chinese ships sailed along the south China coast as far as Annam. The invention of the stern-post rudder in the mid-Han dynasty stimulated the growth of shipping, but most of the still small trade with south and Southeast Asia was carried in the ships of the as yet unsinicized Yue or later in those of the Indians or Malays. Later, trade with the south and west was carried by Arab and Persian ships, although the Chinese did sail to Korea and Japan. From Song times, however, aided by the adoption of the magnetic compass for navigation, Chinese shipping greatly increased both in volume and in distances travelled. Junks now sailed to Annam, Malaya, India, the Persian Gulf, and even, in the case of the great expeditions of Zheng He (1371–1433) in the early Ming dynasty, to East Africa. Coastal shipping also took on new importance in domestic commerce and politics when in the Yuan and early Ming dynasties much of the tribute grain was sent north by the coastal route. Because of the combined dangers of bad weather and pirates inherent in pre-modern sea transport this ceased in 1415 soon after the completion of the new Grand Canal. As early as 1371 the Ming government prohibited private maritime trade, but such prohibitions were never very effective. Though renewed periodically during the Ming and early Qing, the prohibitions were sometimes relaxed and trade permitted at one or more ports. Despite the uncertainty, the junk trade with Southeast Asia flourished and the export of silk to the Philippines—and thence to the Americas—and the import of silver in return played a key part in the late traditional Chinese monetary system. Trade also continued with Korea and Japan, with copper imports from the latter in the early Qing supplying the Chinese mints and enriching the Chinese shippers.

In the mid-19th century the deterioration of the Grand Canal led to the readoption from 1848 of the coastal route for at least some of the grain transport. Though never entirely displacing junks, steamships began carrying grain from 1868. From the 1840s the growth of international and coastal shipping using Chinese ports both stimulated and was stimulated by the development of the coastal provinces. The amount of shipping, of which an increasing proportion was steam-powered, entered and cleared from Chinese ports by the Maritime Customs grew from about 25 million tonnes in the early 1890s to over 150 million in the 1930s. In the process Shanghai grew to be China's largest and one of the world's major ports.

After 1949 although Nationalist control of the Taiwan Strait compelled the development of two separate coastal fleets, north and south, coastal shipping developed steadily, and in the 1970s, with the expansion of foreign trade, China also acquired more ocean-going ships. The merchant fleet has been rapidly developed since 1974 both through construction and through purchase, to the level of about 16 million deadweight tonnes in 1986, when it was the ninth largest merchant fleet in the world. China also operates some of its ships under flags of convenience and charters a number of foreign vessels. Since 1980, the Ministry of Communications has been rapidly developing China's ports in the direction of containerization.

The fleet has primarily been used to supplement the railways in providing north–south communications—principally carrying grain to north China and coal to the Yangtze and the south; oil exports have also led to China's building up a tanker fleet. As long as Shanghai and the northeast remain China's two most important industrial areas coastal shipping will continue to play a major part. However, the policy of developing the inland provinces implies a future decline in its relative importance, which amounted to about 11 per cent of total traffic by modern transport in 1986.   *T.W.*

Camel caravan crossing a river in the far west of China, on the old silk route.

Until recently there were no roads into Tibet, and trade had to follow the old caravan routes: here a tea caravan descends from a 5000m pass near Baitang.

Historic routes and trade patterns

The high cost of traditional land transport meant that the primary items moving long distances over land were luxuries for the palace and official communications for which speed was more important than cost. The Han dynasty and its predecessors built a network of roads covering the north China plain, while great trunk routes also linked the capital with the Yangtze delta, with the southeast, with Sichuan and Yunnan, with Central Asia, and with the northern end of the Yellow River bend. This network remained the basis for those of later dynasties. In the Qing couriers carried many intra-government communications along these roads at between 150 and 400km per day. The 1200km from Nanjing to Beijing could take as little as three days, though more usually five to seven.

Although for commerce these roads were far less important than the waterways, the Han dynasty saw much trade along the famous silk road through Central Asia to Syria. This trade, which was always more important to Rome than to China, in whose economy it played only a minor role, began when gifts of silk from Chinese embassies found their way to Roman Asia. It reached a high level in the later Han and continued spasmodically for some time afterwards despite the political disunity of China. There was another route, by sea via Ceylon and Arabia, which, when political circumstances allowed, probably carried more silk to Rome than did the more famous overland road. Caravan trade in precious merchandise through Central Asia remained a feature of periods of political stability. Marco Polo's journey along these routes during the Mongol Yuan dynasty was an exception, as nearly all the traders were Asians, but from the 16th century silk was exchanged with the Russians for furs, and later tea for manufactured goods.

Overland communications between China and south Asia predated those with western Asia by several centuries. Fourth-century BC Indian sources already refer to Chinese goods, and a route up through Burma and Yunnan helped supply China with amber and other precious objects. Later, however, routes via the Tarim basin, Hotan and Kashmir became the main overland routes by which Chinese silks went to India and Buddhism came to China.   *T.W.*

The modern road system

The Beijing government built the first motor roads around the capital in about 1916, but during the 1920s private organizations such as the China International Famine Relief Commission were the main road builders. In 1932 the Nationalist government began to build a regional network centred on the lower Yangtze, work which was interrupted by the war, during which strategic highways such as the Burma Road were constructed. The system inherited in 1949 was essentially the same as that of 1937, about 120 000km of national and provincial roads, of which not all were all-weather routes and only a small proportion asphalted.

The table shows a substantial increase in the highway network, which is still small by international standards. Some 80 per cent of the network was saved by 1987, though only around 20 per cent was surfaced in asphalt. The World Bank has identified an expansion of the road network especially in rural areas as a prerequisite

for the success of China's economic targets for the year 2000. Motor truck traffic, though still very small compared to that of the railways or waterways, has increased more than commensurately with the length of highways, and China has imported trucks from Japan to keep up with demand. Non-motorized transport, such as carts and pack animals or even wheelbarrows, remains important—in terms of tonnage carried, not of freight turnover—though that importance is declining.

The economic function of non-urban highways is twofold. In the developed areas short routes serve as feeders for the railways which carry the bulk of goods transported. Average length of haul by truck is only 46km, by rail 636km. These roads connect local centres with the national transport network, reaching 90 per cent of townships in the early 1980s. Second, roads open up remote or strategic areas, sometimes being the precursors of a railway along

KEY

Mountains

Passes

Frontiers

Silk-trade routes

SILK ROAD

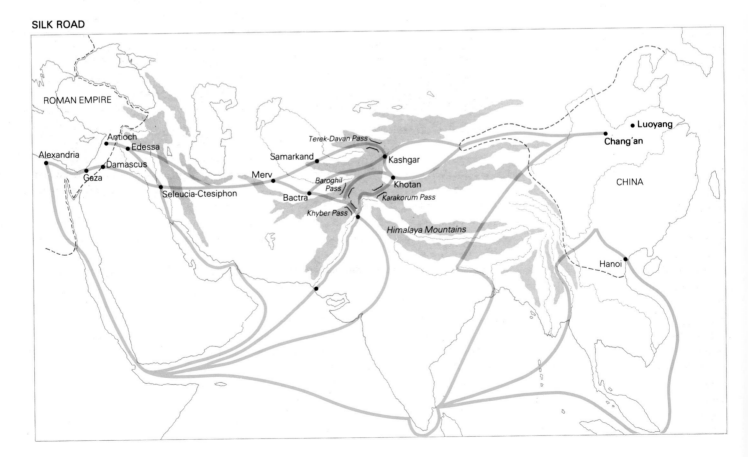

INDICATORS OF MOTOR TRAFFIC IN CHINA: SELECTED YEARS, 1936-87

Year	Length of highway network thousands of km	Motor truck traffic billions of tonne km
1936	110	*
1952	127	1.4
1957	255	4.8
1965	515	9.5
1975	784	20.3
1978	890	27.4
1982	907	94.9#
1987	982	262.1#

* Not available   # Includes non-government vehicles

the same route. From the early 1950s trunk highways such as the routes to Tibet from Qinghai, Xinjiang and Sichuan have been constructed in west China. Military considerations have also been important in road building, with all-weather highways built in sensitive areas such as Fujian, the Soviet border and the southwest. As with economic goods, however, the railways play the more important role.   T.W.

The railways

The construction of railways since 1900 has transformed the economic geography of China. Up to 1895, apart from an abortive line in Shanghai, one coal-carrying line in north China and a short line in Taiwan, the Chinese government, either because of conservatism or for fear of further imperialist encroachments, prevented the construction of railways. In the next 20 years several lines were built, mostly with foreign capital and technicians. Most were of standard gauge, though two minor lines had a 1m gauge, and the Chinese Eastern Railway built by the Russians was of a 5ft (1.5m) gauge.

Lines built before 1937 ran primarily north-south between the major cities of north and east-central China, leaving other routes to be covered mainly by waterways. In addition a relatively dense network covered the northeast, opening up the raw materials of the area to exploitation.

Since 1949, after the war-damaged network had been restored, the more important of these lines were double-tracked, while the

system has also been extended into west China. Connections with the Soviet and Vietnamese railways have been made through Mongolia and through Guangxi to add to the previous ones through the northeast and from Yunnan. The proposed link with the USSR from the line built out to western Xinjiang is now under construction. The southwest has been opened up by a number of routes connecting Kunming in Yunnan with Chengdu and with Canton. Under construction in the late 1970s were several railways presenting severe engineering problems, such as that between Qinghai and Tibet. Many new lines were built partly for military reasons; railways are the main carriers of military equipment and personnel, and most units are stationed along main lines. Most economically important of all has been the line between Sichuan and Shaanxi, which has allowed the cities of north China to tap the grain resources of Sichuan. Priorities in the late 1980s include the new Datong-Qinhuangdao line to ship coal from Shanxi and the upgrading of railways in east and south China.

Route length per capita or per square kilometre remains less not only than those of the developed countries but also, by a substantial margin, than that of India, and the heavy demands made on

RAILWAYS

INDICATORS OF RAILWAY TRANSPORT IN CHINA: SELECTED YEARS,
1915–87

Year	Route length *thousands of km*	Goods traffic *billions of tonne km*
1915	10	6
1925	12	10
1935	16	15
1952	25	60
1957	27	135
1965	36	270
1975	46	426
1978	49	535
1982	51	612
1987	53	947

Estimate

The Beijing-Yuanping line: China's railway builders have had to deal with some of the most difficult terrain in the world.

the railways and the limited capital available for their construction mean that the lines are very intensively used, with an annual load of over 10 million tonnes per kilometre route length. Only the Soviet Union matches this intensity of use, and the Chinese sources say that the network is inadequate for the needs of economic development. Although steam locomotives remain 60 per cent of the total, diesel and electric locomotives are of increasing importance, especially on key lines.

The Chinese railways have been highly vulnerable to disruption in times of social chaos. As well as the major wars of 1937–49, the conflicts of the 1920s almost stopped traffic on the north–south trunk lines, temporarily damaging industry and agriculture. The Red Guards created equally serious disorders when they monopolized railway capacity at the height of the Cultural Revolution. Unrest on the railways lingered on well into the 1970s, with many reports of worker dissatisfaction and strikes.

The railways are now the main carriers of long-haul goods in China, accounting for 60 per cent of the total volume of goods transported in 1987. Coal, by far the largest item of freight, is plentiful in the north and scarce in the south, and from about 1900 large amounts have been shipped down from Hebei and Henan to Shanghai and other industrial centres in central China. Grain transport, while of a much smaller volume, is also very important. By altering the economics of grain transport, for which water routes had previously been a necessity, the railways have made possible the growth of industrial cities in north China even where their hinterland is unable to feed them and where there is no major navigable waterway. This has been a fundamental factor in the shift of the economic centre of China back towards the north from the agricultural and water-served regions of central and south China.

T.W.

Civil aviation

Early attempts to establish air services in the 1920s were cut short by the civil wars, and regular flights began only in 1930 with a service between Shanghai and Hankou. Up to 1937 there was some small development with American and German cooperation, and six routes of a total length of 14 332km, joining Shanghai with north and south China and with the upper Yangtze, were in operation on the eve of the war. During the Sino-Japanese War the Nationalist government tried to maintain civil aviation as a link to the outside world, but by 1949 only ruined airports and a few broken-down planes remained.

Since 1949 an effort has been made to develop a civil aviation network linking the provincial capitals and other major centres, and the 1980s has seen rapid expansion. By 1986, 253 domestic routes connected 83 cities, while numbers of passengers carried have been increasing at 20 per cent a year since the 1950s, reaching 13 million in 1987. Passengers consist mainly of rapidly increasing numbers of foreign tourists and cadres on official business; leisure air travel by the Chinese people is still rare.

Internationally 27 routes are flown by the Chinese airline linking China with 25 cities throughout the world. Flights to the USSR and the Asian communist nations were started from the 1950s, while services to Africa, Europe and the Americas were started from the late 1970s. The fleet still includes some old Russian planes, but there are an increasing number of Boeings—45 by 1987—which service the most important international and domestic routes.

T.W.

The postal service

The government posts—a courier service for carrying official documents—date possibly from the 2nd millennium BC. In late imperial times express couriers handled important business, while another organization catered for local and routine documents. Concerns carrying private mail originated probably in the Ming dynasty, and by the 19th century there were several thousand offices, each quite small yet providing a highly reliable service. In the late 19th century other institutions emerged, such as the customs post and the foreign postal services in the treaty ports. In 1896 the Imperial Post Office was established under the foreign Inspector-General of Customs. Up to 1914 international mail was mainly handled by the foreign agencies, but in 1914 China adhered to the Universal Postal Union. Although at first guaranteed no monopoly by the Chinese government and therefore not profitable until the mid-1910s, the Chinese Post Office carried a rapidly increasing amount of mail, growing from 113 million items posted in 1906, to 250 million items in 1916, 588 million in 1926 and 823 million in 1936.

The number of letters handled by the post office has increased from 599 million in 1949 to 1.641 billion in 1957 and 5.479 billion in 1987. The post office has played an important part in disseminating information, as it handles subscriptions to the magazines and newspapers through which the government makes its ideas known to the masses. Therefore much effort has been put into extending regular services to all units. In 1987 96 per cent of all villages were on postal routes, while 67 per cent of all townships had post offices.

Long-distance telegraph services in China originated in 1881, and in the late Qing and Republic played a major role in political communications. Since 1949 their use, hampered as ever by the nature of the Chinese script, has been less important than that of the telephone.

The first local telephone network in Shanghai also dates from 1881. Although long-distance lines were gradually set up from the early 1900s, even in 1949 the system was limited to a few large coastal cities. Subsequently the system was rapidly developed, with the size of the system rising from 3777 channels in 1952 to 18 801 in 1978 and 53 416 in 1987. Nevertheless, many lines provided poor service and only from the 1960s were there reliable communications between the major cities. By the late 1970s about 3.5 million outlets served the basic needs of the state, and were much used in intra-government communications, with elaborate telephone conferences cutting down the need to use scarce transport. Private phones are still rare but in 1987 95 per cent of all townships and 45 per cent of villages were connected to the system. By 1986 direct satellite lines linked China with 35 other countries, and satellites had begun to be used for domestic communications.

T.W.

Radio and television

Radio was first used for internal communication within China in 1905, but broadcasting started in Shanghai in 1922. The Nationalist government established an official broadcasting service in 1928, and the number of stations continued to expand in the 1930s, but most were small and local.

After 1949 propaganda needs led to a great expansion and centralization of the service. Production of radio receivers grew sharply from the early 1970s, reaching about 40 million in 1981 before declining sharply. In the early 1970s the Central People's Broadcasting Station in Beijing was using 60 or more transmitters to beam programmes throughout the country, and there are also many local and provincial stations. A wire diffusion service enables public loudspeaker broadcasts across the nation. In 1975 there were about 106 million loudspeakers in rural China, and 92.7 per cent of production teams were linked to wired broadcasting.

The first television broadcast was made in 1957, while colour transmission began from 1973. Since the late 1970s the acquisition of a television set has become one of a number of highly priced consumer goods on which the Chinese people can spend their savings. Production of television sets increased from 2.5 million in 1980 to 19 million in 1987, while the number of stations reached 366. Since the early 1980s a small number of foreign programmes have been imported, while satellite transmissions of major sporting events such as the soccer World Cup and the Olympic Games are always very popular.

T.W.

THE ECONOMY

Development

Modern economic development before 1949

China's modern economic development was initiated in a series of industrial ventures in the last part of the 19th century. These included the establishment of companies for shipping, coal mining, a railway and textiles. Several of the companies formed at this time proved unsuccessful, either because of technical or financial misjudgements, or because the general social and political climate was unfavourable. The first successful and concerted spurt of industrial growth occurred during the First World War, during which Chinese business was protected from foreign competition.

After the war development continued, both in Shanghai, which had become a metropolitan centre of industry and commerce, and in Manchuria, where the Japanese were establishing heavy industries and consolidating the South Manchurian Railway and its associated enterprises. The Japanese seizure of Manchuria in 1931 marked the beginning of another acceleration of Japanese development which included coal and metallurgical enterprises that were later to form the basis of communist plans in the northeast region.

Outside Manchuria industrial development during the Republican period was hampered by failure to provide adequate insulation of domestic industry from foreign competition, by the inability of the government to mobilize and use state budgetary revenues for productive purposes, and by the lack of political unity and stability.

The evolution of agriculture between 1919 and 1949 was also unsatisfactory. Population density and fragmentation of land holdings in central and south China were becoming intense, and the modernization that was required was not being pursued with sufficient vigour or method. At governmental level, although some steps were taken towards the establishment of new structures of financial and technical services, no substantial sums were invested in rural capital works. The rural sector was regarded by government more as a source of revenue than as a source of wealth for the rural population. At the household level, poverty and uncertainty made investment and change all too often appear impossible or unprofitable.

The fluctuating fortunes of industry and agriculture were reflected in foreign trade. During the 1920s industrial exports (textiles) grew rapidly as did imports of industrial and related products. During the 1930s, however, the weakness of agriculture was revealed by growing imports of food and by a halting of the industrial transformation of trade.

Economic strategy 1948–60

The communist era began with the establishment of a regional economic government in northeast China in 1948. This inherited the enterprises of the defeated Japanese and administered them using Soviet planning techniques. With victory throughout China in 1949 the Party found itself responsible for the whole of the Chinese economy.

During the first few years, economic policy was primarily concerned with implementing land reform and controlling inflation. The land reform aimed at restoring production and eliminating the rural elements hostile to the Party. The anti-inflation programme relied on both stimulating output and introducing controls over the fiscal and monetary system.

By January 1953 the Party was ready to launch its First Five-Year Plan, which marked the beginning of its long-term goal to industrialize China. It was published in 1955. The Plan's strategy can be summarized as: mobilization of resources for investment on an unprecedented scale; the allocation of a high proportion of investment to heavy industry; and dependence on the Soviet bloc for imports of machinery to be paid for (after a brief breathing space) by exports of agricultural goods and raw materials. The policy of concentrating resources on heavy industry at the expense of light industry and agriculture created several strains in the economy and living standards did not rise significantly. In an attempt to speed up development in 1955 Mao Zedong called for a High Tide of Socialism. This led to the swift collectivization of agriculture followed by the socialization of industry and handicrafts. Dissatisfaction with the outcome of these campaigns, together with the emerging problems associated with rapid population growth and balance of payment difficulties, led to the adoption of the Great Leap Forward strategy in 1958. This called for even more extreme socialist measures, and included the creation of the people's communes. Socialist education became the mainspring of economic motivation. Bad policies, bad weather and the withdrawal of Soviet aid combined to bring the economy to the verge of collapse in 1960. Famine and starvation were widespread in many parts of rural China. In the thorough reappraisal of economic strategy that followed, even the future of socialism in China was brought into question.

Development strategy 1961–78

For a time China adopted a strategy that emphasized more intersectoral balance and a slower rate of growth. The planning priorities of the previous decade were reversed and became agriculture, light industry and finally heavy industry. This was a recognition of the need to raise consumption. Moreover, heavy industry was to be geared to the needs of agriculture in the form of increasing the production of chemical fertilizers, irrigation, machinery, etc.

However, once the emergency period was over and the famine had receded, political goals began to displace the new pragmatic economic strategy. In 1962 Mao launched the Socialist Education Campaign which finally led to the Cultural Revolution bringing much disruption to the Chinese economy during 1968–70. Financial incentives were downgraded and great stress was laid by Mao on both national and local self-sufficiency. From 1964 to 1972 an important element in economic strategy was to develop industry in what became designated as 'Third Front' areas—namely the relatively backward southwest and northwest provinces. This was Mao's response to what he regarded as a deteriorating international situation related to China's poor relations with India, the USSR and Taiwan, and to the Vietnam War and was so designed to redress the industrial predominance of the northeast and the coast.

Between 1970 and 1972 the Chinese economy was dislocated as a result of another 'leap' in construction, and although Zhou Enlai began to gain more control over economic policy during the period of the Fourth Five-Year Plan (1971–5) by lowering targets and putting the economy back into balance, the struggle over economic strategy with the leftist elements in the Party continued until Mao's death in 1976.

Between 1976 and 1978 Hua Guofeng, together with the newly rehabilitated Deng Xiaoping, instituted measures to stimulate agricultural production which had stagnated for many years. The Ten-Year Plan (1976–85) announced in February 1978 was overambitious and was soon scaled down. In fact, Hua was replaced by Deng, who introduced, within a few years, a new economic strategy that has remained until the present.

A modern petro-chemical plant.

Development strategy 1979–89

The basis of Deng's strategy has been a rejection of the high-speed policy of leaping forward, and of central planning as the main means of allocating resources. Deng has emphasized the need to secure balanced growth of modern industry and modern agriculture, supported by foreign trade, the import of foreign technology and the availability of foreign investment. Under Deng China has moved from being a centrally planned economy to one in which prices and markets have played an increasing role. This has been accompanied by an enormous decentralization of powers to enterprises, institutions and peasant households. For example, it has involved no less than the decollectivization of Chinese agriculture. Under Deng, consumer demand has become the main signal for the evolving structure of the Chinese economy. The importance of incentives for raising consumer welfare has been stressed by Deng and his associates. Since 1979 rural and urban income have risen much faster than in the preceding 30 years and this has been reflected in better food consumption, housing and in the availability of basic consumer goods.

However, the new strategy has stimulated many intractable problems. Such benefits of planning that previously existed have been lost, while the advantages of a market economy have been difficult to reap, bearing in mind the underdeveloped nature of China's marketing infrastructure. For example, the loss of state control in agriculture has resulted in a rapid decline in the grain sown area. Basic issues in the programme of price reform remain unresolved and with inflation at an unprecedented rate since the early 1950s, the Party announced a new period of readjustment beginning in 1988, in which economic reforms will be implemented more slowly than in the years 1978–87.

Although China achieved great success in reducing the birth-rate during the 1970s, rural population growth and its pressure on land have become major factors in China's development discussions during the mid to late 1980s. Development policy has now entered an uncertain phase. *C.B.H., K.R.W.*

Agriculture

Policy

Since 1949 the basic aims of agricultural policy have been to achieve the fastest possible growth of output so as to feed China's large and growing population, supply industrial needs and provide the necessary exports upon which the programme of industrialization depended. Until 1961 the growth of production was seen to be linked primarily to the institution of collective farms. Collectivization, it was believed, would be the means of (a) raising invest-

ment in agriculture, (b) of allowing traditional resources to be used more efficiently than in small family farms, and (c) of enabling the government to plan agriculture in the national interest.

This view was modified in the early 1960s when the government recognized the necessity of effecting a technical transformation of agriculture based on modern scientific farming. Until the early 1980s this was considered to be possible only through large-scale, socialist forms of organization. Since the early 1980s, however, the family household has been the basic organization unit in Chinese agriculture. Between the early 1950s and 1979, the government's agricultural goals were to be achieved through central planning in which physical targets existed for the output of all major products and for the sown area of major crops. Prices played a minor role. Similarly, the state controlled the marketing and distribution of all major agricultural products. Since 1979 planning and controls over production and markets have been replaced by markets and prices.

Organization

Before the collectivization of agriculture in 1955–6, agriculture was organized by 120 million individual, small family holdings, many of which were composed of scattered strips of land. Within nine years of taking control, the Communist government carried out a series of institutional reforms that replaced these family farms by very large socialist 'people's communes'. Initially, between 1950 and 1953 the government carried out a land reform programme which gave all arable land to the tillers and abolished landlords as a class. It then encouraged the formation of 'mutual-aid teams' in which families pooled their labour, draught animals and implements at peak seasons; and in 1954–5 it began to organize semi-socialist agricultural cooperatives. In 1955–6 virtually the whole of Chinese agriculture was collectivized, when full socialist cooperatives of 200–300 households were formed. All except 5 per cent of the land (retained as private plots), virtually all farm animals and implements, became the property of the collective and farm work was organized by the collective in accordance with the national plan for that area. In 1958 these collectives were merged into 'people's communes' of 5000–8000 households. These incorporated several 'communist' elements, including the abolition of private plots, private pigs and poultry and even private cooking and eating. Incomes were paid according to 'need' rather than work done. The creation of the communes led to a drastic decline in incentives and during 1959–61 they were reorganized in such a way as to restore the essential features of the collectives.

Under the new organization, communes became smaller and the basic unit for day-to-day operations and accounting became the small production team of 20–30 households. The state continued to direct what should be produced and delivered, according to the national targets. As in the collectives, the income from members was derived mainly from the work done at the team level. The state first deducted taxes, investment funds and welfare payments. The remaining revenues formed the funds out of which labour was paid. Each peasant was paid according to the number of 'labour days' he had registered during a year and the value of the labour day in that team. In addition, peasants were allowed to grow certain crops and raise livestock on the small private plots.

By 1979, Deng Xiaoping, China's new leader, concluded that the record of the communes was not good enough to warrant their retention. Farm output and incomes had stagnated for over 20 years and the lack of agricultural growth was impeding the transformation of China into a modern industrial state. Experiments during 1977-9 in Anhui, one of China's poorest provinces, showed that under household organization crop yields had risen dramatically and that a new spirit of creativity had appeared. After considerable intra-party debate, the decision was taken to decollectivize agriculture and to return to the small, family farm as the basic unit of operation. This was followed by several years of rapid growth of incomes and production, but many problems have arisen as a result of this dramatic change. For example the pattern of land use has been much more difficult to control, and the resulting structure of agricultural output has not been entirely that desired by the central government. Furthermore, peasants have spent a significant proportion of their extra income on housing rather than on productive investment. After the initial boost given to output by the abolition of the communes, it has become clear that most household farms are too small to sustain a rapid growth of output over the long term without more state control and interference. As the 1980s come to a close, the government has been anxiously striving for a form of farm organization which can combine the benefits of the household and those of some sort of 'co-operative' of a non-socialist kind. Such an institutional form has not yet been identified in China. Some hope is being placed on the enlargement of farms through the creation of a land market in which peasants may sell land leases. Such a process, however, will be very slow.

Production

One of the main tasks set by Deng Xiaoping in 1979 was the restructuring of agricultural output following the excessive concentration during the previous 30 years on a few main crops (especially grain), and the consequent neglect of many economic crops, livestock and fisheries (which are included in 'agriculture' in China). Official statistics show that this policy has achieved considerable success. Between 1978 and 1986 the share of crops in the gross value of output fell from 77 per cent to 70 per cent, while animal husbandry increased from 16 per cent to 21 per cent. Even

so, new phenomena that have appeared under the market-oriented policies include a pig cycle, and serious imbalances between supply and demand in the case of several crops. Cotton and tobacco have been in excess supply and in 1984 grain was temporarily in 'surplus' relative to effective demand. With the state no longer guaranteeing a market for all the main products offered by producers, as existed under the communes, problems relating to quality of output have also become widespread.

Grain production

In the late 1980s grain still provided 80-90 per cent of all calories in rural China and 60-70 per cent in urban China. After 40 years under Communist government, the supply of grain at stable, relatively low prices, remained one of the main concerns of the leaders. During the decade 1978-88 grain production grew at around 3 per cent per year, with sown areas declining by around one per cent and yields per hectare increasing by 4 per cent. On the demand side, at the low levels of income prevailing in many parts of the rural China, the income elasticity of demand for grain for direct consumption has been found to be high. In rural China only 4-6 per cent of calories are derived from livestock products. These facts, together with the rural population growth (over one per cent per year) mean that if rural incomes continue to rise, especially among the relative poor, the demand for grain will grow at a rapid rate. Figures for 1986 show that the provincial dispersion of grain consumption was considerable: ranging from 253kg in Jilin province to 175kg in Guizhou. By contrast, in urban China direct grain consumption had already reached saturation point, at

Wheat drying in Heilongjiang Province. This is an area where agricultural growth since 1949 has been disappointingly slow but where potential development is great.

THE COMPOSITION AND REGIONAL ORIGIN OF GRAIN OUTPUT, 1986

Grain	Output *millions of tonnes*	% of output	Regional origin of national output in 1986
Fine Grain			
Rice	172.22	44.0	NE 4.2%; N 2.8%; NW 0.5%; Centre 57.8%; SW 16.2%; South 18.5%
Wheat	90.04	23.0	NE 4.1%; N 53.6%; NW 10.3%; Centre 23.6%; SW 8.2%; South 0.2%
Soya	11.61	3.0	NE 45.2%; N 53.6%; NW 4.5%; Centre 20.0%; SW 5.0%; South 3.1%
Total	273.87	70.0	
Coarse Grain			
Maize	70.86	18.1	NE 31.8%; N 39.2%; NW 6.3%; Centre 6.7%; SW 5.0%; South 3.1%
Sorghum	5.38	1.4	NE 49.6%; N 32.5%; NW 6.5%; Centre 4.0%; SW 7.2%; South 0.1%
Millet	4.54	1.1	NE 26.0%; N 62.6%; NW 10.6%; Centre 0.6%; SW 0.1%; South negligible
Sweet potatoes	25.34	6.5	NE 3.5%; N 32.3%; NW 3.9%; Centre 26.5%; SW 24.7%; South 9.2%
Other	11.52	2.9	
Total	117.64	30.0	
All grain	391.51	100.0	NE 11.2%; N 25.2%; NW 4.7%; Centre 35.6%; SW 14.0%; South 9.2%

Regions: NE = Heilongjiang, Jilin, Liaoning.   N = Beijing, Hebei, Henan, Shaanxi, Shandong, Shanxi, Tianjin.
NW = Gansu, Inner Mongolia, Ningxia, Qinghai, Xinjiang.   Centre = Anhui, Hubei, Hunan, Jiangsu, Jiangxi, Shanghai, Zhejiang.
SW = Guizhou, Sichuan, Tibet, Yunnan.   South = Fujian, Guangdong, Hainan, Guangxi.

120–40kg per head per year, and since 1978 an increasing amount of grain has been converted into livestock products (which in 1986 accounted for 13–20 per cent of calories).

Unless the government can reverse the downward trend of the grain sown area (by raising grain prices, for example) the growth of output will continue to depend on increases in yields. This, in turn, will require more fertilizer, pesticide, water and technical skill. The trends suggest that the Chinese government's targets for grain production and consumption in the year 2000 (including the consumption of grain in the form of livestock products) will be difficult to achieve. An important problem is how to secure the right balance between food and feed grains. As far as direct consumption is concerned, the demand for fine grain (rice, wheat and soya) increases with income while the demand for coarse grain (millet, maize, sweet potatoes, sorghum) falls. As the diet changes in favour of livestock products, however, the demand for feed grain such as maize will increase.

The composition of grain production and regional origin in 1986 are given in the table above.

Industrial crops

With the exception of flue-cured tobacco, under Deng Xioaping's policy of expansion, the production of China's most important industrial crops grew between 1978 and 1986 at much faster rates than in the previous eight years. Unlike grain, the sown area of these crops increased by 43 per cent (1978–86) and in addition some impressive increases in crop yields were achieved. For example, average cotton yields per hectare fell by 0.2 per cent per year in 1970–8, but rose by 9.5 per cent per year in 1978–86. For oil seeds a downward trend of 1.3 per cent was replaced by a

Paddy fields with growing rice in south China.

growth of 6.7 per cent per year, while a negative rate of 4 per cent for sugar beet gave way to a positive rate of 8.6 per cent. An important reason for such yield rises was the appearance of a more rational distribution of production resulting from the loosening of planning controls. The accompanying table records the production of the main crops in 1986 and their growth rates 1970–8 and 1978–86.

The spurt of output since 1978 was accompanied by periods of excess supply caused by lack of purchasing power and by the low quality of output. This was particularly so for cotton, tobacco and oil seeds. A chronic shortage has persisted in the case of sugar. In striving to match supply and demand the government has relied on adjusting prices rather than imposing new controls over the sown area. Rising prices of fertilizer and diesel oil have resulted in

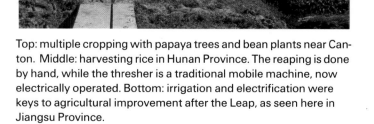

Top: multiple cropping with papaya trees and bean plants near Canton. Middle: harvesting rice in Hunan Province. The reaping is done by hand, while the thresher is a traditional mobile machine, now electrically operated. Bottom: irrigation and electrification were keys to agricultural improvement after the Leap, as seen here in Jiangsu Province.

CHINA'S MAIN INDUSTRIAL CROPS

Crop	Production in 1986 millions of tonnes	Average Rate of Growth of Output, % pa 1970–8	1978–86
Cotton	3.540	−0.4	10.4
Oil seed	14.738	2.1	13.6
Sugar beet	8.310	3.1	15.4
Sugar cane	50.280	4.6	12.8
Flue-cured tobacco	1.382	12.8	9.3

slower growth of production since 1984–5. None the less the domestic supply of raw cotton and of edible oil eased significantly under the stimuli introduced by Deng.

Livestock and fisheries

Livestock provide income, protein, fat, fertilizer and draught power in the Chinese economy. Pigs are particularly important for all except the provision of power. Since the decollectivization of agriculture in the early 1980s the raising of pigs and the production of pork has developed in classical pig cycles in which changes in the price of feed grain have been followed by drastic changes in the raising or slaughtering of pigs. The efficiency of pork production in China remains low, measured by the amount of grain required per unit of pork produced, by the carcass weight and by the time taken to raise a pig of given size. In the late 1980s lean pork production—for which there is a high income elasticity of demand—was in short supply in many parts of China, and rationing has been imposed in cities from time to time. Average pork consumption in 1986 was 12–26kg per head in urban areas, but 1–17kg in rural populations (Sichuan having the highest consumption in both rural and urban areas). In 17 provinces average rural consumption was below 10kg. Very little beef or lamb is consumed in China.

The need for draught animals remains throughout most of rural China. In 1986 only five provinces ploughed more than 50 per cent of sown area mechanically (Heilongjiang, Xinjiang, Tianjin, Liaoning and Beijing), involving 6.7 per cent of China's total sown area. In contrast, seven provinces ploughed less than 10 per cent of sown area mechanically. Mechanical sowing was even less developed. Only Xinjiang sowed more than 50 per cent of its sown area mechanically, 19 provinces mechanically sowed less than 10 per cent and nine provinces used no mechanical power for sowing. Mechanical harvesting had barely begun to affect rural China by 1986.

The Chinese government has ambitious plans to develop the pastoral livestock industry, which has considerable potential in areas such as the northwest. Technical problems relating to the creation of highly productive pastures and good breeding stock impede such development.

After a long period of neglect, China's fisheries grew at more than 10 per cent per year 1978–86, with fresh-water fish products growing faster than salt-water products. A great deal of scientific knowledge has been applied to this growing industry in order to raise yields per unit area, but the industry is still in its infancy and in 1986 only accounted for 3 per cent of the national gross value of output of agriculture. Fish consumption was minute in most provinces, even in the most prosperous urban areas. The highest estimated urban consumption was 17.6kg in Guangdong, followed by 13.5kg per head in urban Shanghai. Urban consumption in Shanxi was a mere 1.4kg per head. Rural consumption was negligible in 12 provinces. The highest was 9.1kg in Guangdong, followed by 8.2kg in Shanghai.

Land and agricultural productivity

Chinese agriculture operates under the severe constraint of a small and rapidly declining arable area. In 1986 the arable land of China was officially estimated at 96.2 million ha, but government officials believe that this may be quite a large underestimate. It is not disputed, however, that during the past 30 years the arable area has contracted continuously and that the rate of contraction has accelerated since 1978. The arable area per head of agricultural population, already small in the 1950s, declined by around 50 per cent between 1952 and 1986. Possibilities for land reclamation do exist, mainly in Heilongjiang (7.5 million ha), Xinjiang (10 million ha), Yunnan (3 million ha), and Hainan (1 million ha). Such work, however, is very costly and requires heavy earth-moving equipment, and the government does not regard reclamation as a solution to the land supply problem. Instead, since the 1950s the policy has been to compensate for the contraction of the arable area by increasing the 'multiple cropping index' (sown area divided by the arable area multiplied by 100). Under the planned economy that existed until the 1980s, this policy was very successful. But under the household with its new-found freedom of choice, the cost of multiple cropping has become the major factor determining its level, and in many areas this has resulted in a declining index. If this cannot be reversed, the only source of higher production will be increasing yields per sown area.

International comparisons suggest that this is a distinct possibility, but its success will depend on the scientific application of modern technology (using better seed, chemical fertilizers and water). China's plant-breeding programme has been highly successful, and especially since the mid-1970s chemical fertilizer applications have risen dramatically. The spread of these modern inputs, however, has been very uneven throughout China. For example, in 1986 eight provinces had less than 30 per cent of the arable area under irrigation, and these provinces accounted for 60 per cent of China's arable land. At the other end of the range, 9 provinces had more than 70 per cent of the arable land irrigated, and these together only accounted for 15 per cent of China's arable area. Under the household responsibility system it has been more and more difficult for the government to mobilize manpower and financial resources to maintain and increase the irrigated area of China. In some provinces the irrigated area has declined during the 1980s, and declining quality of irrigation has been widespread.

The provincial dispersion of fertilizer use was considerable in the late 1980s, ranging from 459kg per hectare of arable land in Shanghai to 23kg in Tibet. Fertilizer supply has not kept pace with demand, and in recent years demand has fallen because of high prices. Inappropriate fertilizer ratios (between the main plant foods) have also impeded maximizing the effectiveness of fertilizer application. Massive investment in technical advisory services is needed if the productivity and efficiency of Chinese agriculture are to be increased at rates required by rising demand. There is no evidence that such a programme is yet underway.

Agriculture and foreign trade

In 1987 the value of agricultural exports accounted for 30 per cent of total exports and agricultural imports accounted for 32 per cent of all imports. The main exports were textile fibres (excluding wool) accounting for 13 per cent of all agricultural exports, fruit and vegetables (11 per cent), meat and fish (10 per cent), and grain (5 per cent). Major imports included grain (17 per cent), sugar (12 per cent), textile fibres (8 per cent), and edible oil (5 per cent).

Under Deng Xiaoping the level and composition of China's foreign trade in agricultural products has been subject to critical examination based on economic criteria. It was decided to cut China's dependence on foreign imports of raw cotton, edible oil and sugar, even if this meant maintaining or even increasing the level of grain imports. By 1987 this policy had been partly successful. For example, between 1979 and 1987 China ceased to be a major importer of raw cotton and instead became one of the world's largest exporters. Although imports of sugar and edible oil decreased, China was not able to become self-sufficient in these products, with consumer demand rising strongly as a result of the rapid growth of personal incomes. In 1985 China was actually in surplus on its international grain account, largely as a result of very big increases in coarse grain output, but the subsequent poor performance of domestic grain output quickly reversed this position. In 1987 China exported 7.4 million tonnes, but imported 16.3 million tonnes, and such a high level of net imports is a cause of anxiety to the Chinese government. *C.B.H., K.R.W.*

Industrial development

China's industrial growth since 1949 falls into three broad phases. The turning points of these phases are the end of the First Five-year Plan and the beginning of the Great Leap Forward (1957–8), and the years 1977–8, which marked the end of Maoism and the beginning of the reform era under Deng Xiaoping. In the first of these phases, growth was exceptionally high at 15.8 per cent per annum. This pace was not a sustainable one, even had political circumstances been favourable. This was because part of this growth was attributable to post-war recovery and to the more intense utilization of pre-1949 industrial and infrastructural capital. The second and longest phase included a number of turbulent political and economic transformations during which the growth rate fluctuated wildly. The long-run rate of 9 per cent, however, was quite high, even allowing for some overstatement. It is approximately the same as the pre-war growth rate and compares favourably with the performance of other large developing economies. Since 1978, the trend of industrial output has shifted upward, rising over the whole decade 1978–88 to 14 per cent per annum. This is significantly above the long-run growth rate and is high by international standards, even including the Newly Industrializing Countries, which have distinct structural advantages over China.

Within this aggregate performance, variations through time and by sector have been considerable. Output has grown in a series of bursts—which we may measure by the growth rates achieved in successive movements from troughs to peaks. These periods and their growth rates are: 1979–80 (9.8 per cent), 1981–5 (15.9 per cent), and 1985–7 (23.3 per cent). Moreover this instability reflects even greater instability in heavy industry. For although the growth rate in this sector has been slower (12.9 per cent per annum as against 14 per cent), year-to-year variations have been

INDUSTRIAL GROWTH, 1952–57 (% pa)

Trends	
1952–1957	15.8
1957–78	9.0
1978–87	14.0
acceleration, 1979–87	
1979–80	9.8
1981–85	15.9
1985–87	23.3

Source: State Statistical Bureau

Above: the Laiyang tractor plant in Yantai prefecture, Shandong Province, has contributed to the area's mechanisation.

Below: a farmer sells melons from the back of his truck at Turfan's main free market.

Cultural Revolution posters and 'big character boards' in a factory, 1966.

40 per cent higher than for industry as a whole. The implication of these figures is that the 1980s revealed a pattern of increasing instability that could lead to a major setback in the progress of the economy. In 1988 the Chinese planners were confident that manageable growth would continue and that China's share of world industrial output would continue to increase.

The Chinese have suffered from chronic problems because of difficulties of maintaining appropriate structures and balance within the industrial sector. These difficulties are of three kinds. First are major inter-industry imbalances such as those between light and heavy industry and those between transportation, energy, infrastructure and other industrial sectors. Second, there are major imbalances within industries such as those between crude and finished steel, and those between exploration, development and production facilities in the fuel sector. Third are the smaller imbalances that arise from imperfections in central economic planning and its interaction with other resource allocating mechanisms. The impact of these latter problems on efficiency, although difficult to measure, is rather large. Rectifying imbalances at any of these levels is a difficult task and improvement of the heavy to light industry balance was a major objective of the 'readjustment' of the early 1980s. The fluctuating growth of heavy industry during the adjustment, however, shows just how intractable these problems are. The removal of other types of imbalance and especially the elimination of the costs of excessively detailed central planning, are objects of the whole reform of the industrial planning system to be discussed below.

An urban free market with colourful consumer goods, Beijing.

In spite of the difficulties in restraining heavy industry, the planners have succeeded in raising the share of light industry in total output from 43.1 per cent in 1978 to 47.9 per cent in 1987. The failure to control heavy industry, however, is reflected in the fact that while the planners intended to reduce the share of investment in national income from 37 per cent to 25 per cent, it has in practice proved impossible to reduce the rate below 30 per cent and in 1987 the rate was back at 34.4 per cent.

Ownership is another important aspect of the changing structure of industry. Before 1978 the trend was towards full public ownership of industrial assets, which was regarded as the form appropriate to the socialist stage of development. However, since 1978 there has been growing awareness that for a long time into the future, a more diversified and low-level form of ownership might be more efficient. Indeed, there has been some questioning of the proposition that fully socialist forms of ownership are best in the very long run, and as far as the current reforms are concerned, some economists argue that these will not ultimately be effective unless there is some shift away from state ownership, which has the effect of removing key responsibilities from managers and workers.

The effect of the new liberalism towards private and collective ownership has been to lower the share of industrial output under public ownership from 80.8 per cent to 68.7 per cent.

Industrial location

The location of industry has always tended to be concentrated in China. Before 1949 location was biased towards the old treaty ports (especially Shanghai and Tianjin) and towards Manchuria. Policy after 1949 was in favour of securing a more even distribution by biasing investment inland and reducing the role of the old coastal cities. This produced change, but only at a slow rate. Thus whereas east China lost 5 per cent of its share between 1952 and 1957, between 1957 and 1974 it only lost a further 0.3 per cent.

Shares of industrial output by region, 1974–87 (% pa)

	1974	1987
Northeast	19.2	14.3
North	20.2	14.0
East	35.1	39.5
Central South	14.7	21.0
Northwest	4.9	4.0
Southwest	5.9	7.5

Source: State Statistical Bureau

61

Movements in location in the 1980s have been complex. On the one hand, an important part of the new leadership had inland 'constituencies' who they wished to support by continuing the policy of redistribution. On the other hand, since 1982 decentralization and the encouragement of the coastal areas and recognition that the policy of locating industry away from potential war zones had very high costs, have combined to re-open the gap between the coastal and inland regions. Thus the Eastern Region is estimated to have recovered almost all its lost share between 1974 and 1987, in spite of the problems of Shanghai. This has been at the expense of north and northeast China. On the other hand, it is interesting to see that the southwest has significantly increased its share of industry in spite of the handicap of being inland. These trends in the distribution of output have been paralleled by those in income. Average incomes in the coastal provinces, especially Jiangsu and Guangdong, are clearly increasing in relation to inland provinces, so much so that this inequality has become a major brake on the progress of reform in the economy.

Industrial reform

Although the growth rate of industry between 1957 and 1977 was reasonably high, the output figures conceal the fact that the capital and labour costs per unit were rising. The implication of this trend in productivity was that the long-term maintenance of any constant rate of growth would require increasing levels of sacrifice by the population. This pressure on consumption would be bound to reduce incentives and hence further depress the incentives to labour productivity improvement. This kind of squeeze had clearly been at work for a number of years, which is confirmed by the fact that real, individual wages in industry were lower in 1977 than they had been in 1957.

Apart from incentives, China's industrial malaise in the 1970s was also a result of organizational confusion and decay and a failure to take advantage of the technological opportunities that were available by use of the trade sector. Problems of organization, incentive and technology interlocked with each other and the solution was therefore sought in a combination of improved incomes and income mechanisms, planning reform and the 'open door' to bring China back more fully into the world economy.

The reform of industrial planning has occurred in several stages. In the first, efforts were made to improve the quality of central planning. This involved laborious effort at the centre to improve planning norms and techniques and to lower planning targets to realistic levels. Second, early in the Deng reform, selected enterprises were allowed to develop 'within' and 'without' plan activities. Under these arrangements, after fulfilment of plan targets, enterprises were allowed to produce for allocation through non-plan channels using resources econo-

mized from the plan allocations, or acquired through liberalized arrangements for raw material allocation. This experiment was later extended to include most enterprises, although circumstances varied greatly and, in general, the scope for reforming the activities of key, large-scale enterprises was limited. Since these enterprises are by definition the most important in the economy, in this phase the reform was failing to benefit the core of the economy. Since 1984, the introduction of a contract system has reduced still further the role of central planning. In all these changes, the main incentive to change at enterprise level has been permission to retain funds that previously would have been remitted to the centre—funds which, subject to certain rules, could be allocated to personal incomes and incentives, collective welfare schemes and investment.

The main problem with the reforms is that at the stage they had reached in 1988, they had created a dual economy: part planned and part unplanned, the two parts of which did not function effectively together. Because of this duality of economic mechanisms, economic discipline collapsed and demand for capital and consumer goods got out of control. The net effect has been a rapid and accelerating growth of inflationary pressures, with rates in excess of 20 to 30 per cent for 1987–8 being reported in some cities. Although the planners have some power to restore control over enterprises by administrative measures, their difficulty has been that because the state budget is in a chronic state of deficit, the deficit has to be covered by expansion of bank money which weakens monetary control.

In September 1988 the government decided that a major halt to the reform programme in favour of stabilization had to take place. In the aftermath of this, many powers were reallocated to the central planners—especially over materials and prices. This policy implied the continuation of administrative controls over the economy to stop the misuse of the opportunities arising from the two-tier system. This policy line not only reflected the views of one important group of economists in China (strongly opposed by others), it also reflected the views of bureaucrats for whom the reform not only threatened loss of power, but also progressive loss of income relative to those gaining from the reform.

Labour system

Before 1978, urban workers were allocated to jobs, and in public sector enterprises wages were fixed by reference to fixed scales, while in the collective sector they were determined by means that left little room for the stimulation of effort or the reward of productivity.

Major changes took place in the wages system after 1978. Improvement of the average level of wages was an immediate goal of the Deng government and this was accompanied by reform of the system of wage payment. In 1978 premium and piece-work systems that had been abolished in the Cultural Revolution were restored. In this reform a limit of 10 per cent of the wage bill was imposed on the level of bonus payments. In 1981 a more general reform allowed for bonuses of up to one or two months standard wages per worker, but abuse of this system led in 1984 to the introduction of penalties for excessive overpaying of bonuses and an attempt has also been made to make a further reform under which enterprises pay a relatively small basic wage and a much larger, variable bonus component that allows the profitability of the enterprise to be reflected directly in worker incomes.

As a result of these policies the average real incomes of workers and staff in state enterprises have been rising at over 5 per cent per annum, while the rapid expansion outside the state sector has enabled average urban incomes to increase at over 7 per cent per annum between 1978 and 1986. The overall effect of the changes has probably been to provide some general incentives to work, but only in a very non-discriminatory manner, and at a high price in terms of loss of macro-economic control.

Since 1984 a major attempt has also been made to reform the system of employment administration. The key policy has been to break the 'iron rice bowl': the system whereby, in effect, employment in the state sector is permanent, and the employment system becomes a welfare system. In September 1986 the State Council announced new regulations aimed mainly at new recruits to the urban labour force, under which workers were to be hired by contracts of fixed duration and under terms that allowed dismissal. By the end of 1986 it was reported that 5.6 million workers were being engaged on a contract basis. Subsequently the implementation of a bankruptcy law allowed for entire enterprises to be closed, although little evidence of widespread occurrence of this has been noted.

The reform of the labour system and the creation of a labour market has been closely linked to the general process of reform. One element of this has been the expansion of employment in county and township enterprises whose products are sold in free or relatively free markets, and whose labour is recruited under the contract system on terms reflecting success in those markets. Thus the progress of the labour reform is likely to follow the general progress of reform.

Foreign trade and the balance of payments

Total visible trade (exports plus imports) in 1987 was $82.7 billion. There was a small deficit on visible trade of $3.7 billion. In terms of world trade, China is only a small country whose share of world trade was lower in the 1980s than it was at the end of the 1950s. This reflects the errors of past internal policies and the inward-looking approach of the Maoist period. Since 1978 trade has grown rapidly. China's share of world trade has risen and, internally, trade has risen from 9 per cent to 18 per cent of national income. But since much of this expansion represents a 'catching up' process, these shares are unlikely to rise very significantly during the next decade.

The general character of Chinese trade is indicated in the table. If we look at the balances by commodity groups we see a tendency for China to be a net exporter of primary goods and an importer of manufactures. However, the full picture is neither as clear-cut nor as simple as this. For example, manufactured goods account for two-thirds of total exports, and within these China has become a world factor in textiles. And within the raw material exports, oil and coal are predominant, reflecting natural resource endowment rather than level of development. On the import side we see that China remains a heavy net importer of plant and machinery, as would be expected in a developing economy. One feature of trade since 1978 is that China now imports significant quantities of consumer goods. On occasion, for example in 1985, this has been unplanned, but to some extent this trend is a reflection of the planners' intention to raise living standards. If domestic consumer goods are not available, they have to be imported.

China's trade partnerships reflect the market opportunities for China's exports and the availability of imports of the kind China needs. In 1987, Hong Kong/Macao were jointly China's largest partners (27 per cent of total trade), followed by Japan (20 per cent), the EEC (13 -per cent), and the US (19 per cent).

TRADE AND PAYMENTS, 1987

Trade balance	(billions US$)
Exports	39.5
Imports	43.2
Balance	−3.7
Reserves	16.2
Foreign debt	40*

Structure of Trade	imports	exports	balance
Primary products	16	34	18
food	6	22	16
mineral/oil	1	12	11
Manufactures	84	66	−18
machinery	34	4	−30
light/textiles	22	22	0

* Estimate, November 1988
Sources: State Statistical Bureau, World Bank, IMF.

China enters the electronic age: peasant children in a country factory.

The organization of trade in China was originally modelled on the Soviet system. Under this, trade decisions are monopolized by the bureaucracy. At the centre of the system was the Ministry of Foreign trade, under which were foreign trade corporations specializing in the trade of particular groups of products. Prices and the exchange rate play no significant role in allocating resources for trade and the Soviet system fails to provide the information and incentives necessary for basic level units to act rationally. These units are effectively barred from direct participation by the Ministry and the corporations.

Another aspect of this system is that it concentrates on trade in goods, and fails to develop the possibilities of trade in skills and knowledge, some of which may be available without goods. The reform of the system since 1978 has attempted to grapple with these problems. First, trade corporations have been decentralized and new ones created. Some trade corporations are attached to local government and others to ministries or even enterprises. Many appear to have only loose if any links with other parts of the economy. Further, China has created special economic zones within which economic planning is completely different from that in the rest of the economy, in an attempt to make the zones a favourable environment for foreign investment. Foreign investment, which is also a completely new phenomenon, has been structured in various forms ranging from wholly-owned foreign firms operating in China to simple processing agreements. The purpose of all these changes has been to enable China to get more benefit from the exchange of goods and the acquisition of technology through international interaction.

These reforms have led to a substantial expansion of trade, and progress has been made in foreign investment. Many problems, however, have arisen. First, relaxation of central control has produced balance of payments deficits, at times rising to crisis proportions and hence to strict corrective measures. There has thus emerged a cycle referred to by the Chinese as 'chaos after deregulation; inertia after regulation'. Apart from the cycle, China in the 1980s has moved to a position where some degree of trade deficit is normal. The planners clearly do not like this, but it is not an unreasonable position for a developing country with obvious structural bottlenecks impeding growth. More serious is the fact that the interaction of trade and domestic reform has led to a situation of chaos and irrationality. For example, foreign investment was adding uncontrollably to demand and much of the trading activity in the country reflected defects in the system, rather than China's real needs. Thus in the summer of 1988, the government decided as part of its slowing up of reform, to limit the pace of further change in trade and make some cutbacks in the freedoms relating to foreign investment. Thus while a major reversion to the policies of the closed door is unlikely, the major period of experimentation probably ended in 1987–8.

A rattan factory in the Dingzhou commune near Canton.

Hong Kong

The long-run performance of the Hong Kong economy between the 1950s and the early 1980s was very good, reflecting the success of its external orientation, resource flexibility, and internal political stability. During the 1980s, however, growth has been uneven, in response to sharply changing political and economic circumstances. In the three years 1985, 1986 and 1987, for example, annual growth rates of Domestic Product were 0, 11 per cent and 14 per cent respectively. Economically, Hong Kong's dependence on foreign trade makes it sensitive not only to world trade trends, but also to shifts in the value of the dollar to which the Hong Kong dollar was pegged in 1984. The economy thus slowed as the dollar rose in 1985 and accelerated as the dollar fell in 1986–7. Politically, the main adverse shocks occurred during the negotiations between Britain and China during 1983–5. The impact of these shocks was accentuated by their occurring at the same time as the downswing in the property cycle.

Since 1986, the colony has been operating at close to full capacity, with very low unemployment and a high level of capital utilization. Growth in the longer run will therefore depend partly on domestic factors such as the rate of investment and the policy towards labour immigration.

The dominant partners in Hong Kong's trade are the USA and China. In 1987 the USA accounted for 37 per cent of Hong Kong's exports and was easily its largest market. The role of China in Hong Kong's trade is shown particularly clearly on the import side, with China accounting for 31 per cent of Hong Kong's imports in 1987. The second largest source of Hong Kong's imports is Japan, which supplies many intermediate goods and capital goods for Hong Kong industry.

One other important feature of Hong Kong trade as it has developed in the 1980s, is the expansion of re-exports. Entrepôt trade was traditionally very important, but then declined in the 1960s and 1970s as direct exports expanded. Because of the close and expanding links between China and Hong Kong, re-exports are growing again. Hong Kong also plays an intermediary role for trade between South Korea and Taiwan and China.

The growing closeness between Hong Kong and China reflects a mixture of economic and political factors, but while these changes have been valuable to Hong Kong in the 1980s, they do also mean that the Hong Kong economy will become increasingly vulnerable to changes in the Chinese domestic situation.

Under the terms of the Joint Declaration and the Draft Basic Law, it is intended that Hong Kong keeps most of its economic characteristics after 1997 (a market economy with no exchange controls, etc.). However, the Draft Basic Law under the final version of the Law, could seriously limit the role and evolution of Hong Kong economic policy.

The growth of the Hong Kong economy in the 1990s and beyond will depend on many factors. The economy shows encouraging signs of retaining vitality and flexibility, although there are anxieties about the outflow of skilled labour and the failure of high technology industries to keep pace with progress in other parts of Asia. Increasingly, however, domestic factors will be less important than China factors. Thus although the principle of 'one country and two systems' is still the official guideline for the future of the economy, the unity of the country will count for more than the independence of two systems.   *C.B.H. K.R.W.*

Taiwan

Taiwan is one of the most densely populated islands in the world, with more than 20 million people squeezed into 36 000 sq km of land, three-quarters of which is not arable. The highest mountains in the region run through the middle, but yield few natural resources. Agriculture is the traditional main industry.

Yet since the 1950s Taiwan has had an annual real economic growth rate averaging over 8 per cent, one of the highest in the world, which it has achieved with a minimal level of price inflation, a factor that has eroded progress in many other developing areas. In 1987 Taiwan became the 13th largest trading state in the world. Imports and exports gained 37 per cent from the previous year to reach US$88 billion—slightly less than its closest competitor, South Korea, which has more than twice the population.

Per capita income in Taiwan exceeds that of South Korea. This growth in the income of the people has been spread evenly through the society with the highest 20 per cent income bracket only four times as great as the lowest 20 per cent.

The Nationalist government in Taiwan has reason to be proud of the gains its policies for economic development have brought about since taking up exile in Taipei in December 1949. The success of the Taiwan government stands in marked contrast to the corrupt and disastrous administration of the mainland economy before defeat by the Communists. The content of its policies since the early 1950s has been heavily influenced by that failure. Senior government officials, for example, feel rampant inflation in the 1940s was among the most serious factors behind the Communist victory and have zealously carried out anti-inflationary policies.

Ironically, the determination of the leadership newly entrenched in Taiwan to try to outshine the Communists on the mainland led to a series of reforms on the island that appear to be as revolutionary as those being carried out on the mainland, including a vast redistribution of land which both uprooted a landlord class which was not pro-Nationalist and extended rigid political control throughout the island.

What followed was essentially three stages of economic and social development. The first stage, 1951–60, placed emphasis on developing agriculture with the gradual establishment of import substituting light industries. This was followed by a decade of expanding foreign trade and increased sophistication of industries. In the 1970s Taiwan embarked on large-scale projects to build up a heavy industrial base and improve the basic utilities, road, rail and port facilities needed in a modern industrial state.

Since 1972 when the People's Republic of China became the representative government in the UN, Taiwan has lived increasingly in a state of diplomatic limbo. When the USA formally pulled out of Taiwan in favour of recognizing the Beijing government in January 1979, however, the unease in, and uncertainty for the future of Taiwan was largely dispelled. The US Congress gave a firm vote of support for Taiwan, and businessmen (led by the American banks) have shown renewed confidence in Taiwan's economy as a sound and profitable place both to lend money and invest.

During the 1980s Taiwan's entrepreneurs have had to contend with rising labour costs and a 40 per cent appreciation of the Taiwan dollar against the US dollar, which made their labour-intensive exports less competitive with similar exports from lower wage countries. Some entrepreneurs adjusted by shifting to technology-intensive enterprises that produce higher value-added items. As a result, electronic products have edged out textiles as Taiwan's principal export. Other entrepreneurs moved their labour-intensive operations to mainland China or to Southeast Asian countries with lower wage levels. A growing annual surplus of exports over imports since 1982 produced by 1987 foreign exchange reserves of US$76 billion, a level exceeded only by Japan and West Germany.

In 1987 the government eased exchange controls, causing a substantial rise in investment abroad, especially in the US and Southeast Asia. Exports to Japan and Europe also increased dramatically, as the government sought to decrease Taiwan's heavy dependence on the US market. Under US pressure to reduce its surplus in trade with the US, the authorities have cautiously brought down tariffs and other trade barriers. Current economic problems (1988) include an excess of idle capital that an antiquated banking system fails to direct towards productive investment, growing labour militancy and increased concern with environmental pollution.

Taiwan's economic success has placed the island in a strong position to resist Beijing's pressures to gain control over it. In a show of self-confidence, the Nationalist government in 1987 for the first time authorized trips to the mainland by Taiwan residents to visit their relatives. During the following year over 200 000 made the trip. Such travel facilitated the expansion of indirect trade between Taiwan and the mainland, which exceeded US$1 billion in 1987 and continued to grow rapidly during 1988.

The key to the economy in Taiwan and its relationship to China is that for nearly 100 years Taiwan has been independent of the mainland. The efficient Japanese established in Taiwan the foundations of a modern economy early in the 20th century. On this the Nationalists have been able to build.

The strength of the economy has bolstered the legitimacy of Nationalist rule, making possible the smooth succession of Taiwan-born Li Teng-hui (Li Denghui) to Chiang Ching-kuo (Jiang Jingquo) as president of the nation and chairman of the ruling party, after Chiang's death in January 1988. The strength of the economy has also assured the island a position in the international community, even though only 23 countries, mostly ministates, still maintain diplomatic relations with the Nationalist government.

The leadership in Taiwan, still holding fast to the principle that Taiwan is part of China, feel strongly that the developments in Taiwan, including recent democratic reforms allowing the establishment of opposition parties, should serve as a model for the mainland. The government in Beijing watches with concern growing public discussion in Taiwan of formal independence for the island, but takes encouragement from the Nationalist government's one-China position and the increasing trade and other ties between Taiwan and the mainland.   *R.C.H., R.N.C.*

Macao

The enclave economy of Macao was traditionally based on earnings from tourism, gambling, services and its gold market. In recent years, however, there has been strong growth of industry and trade in goods. This partly reflected rising labour and land costs in Hong Kong, but also the determination of Portugal, the Macao government, to improve its economic foundations before the handover of the colony to China in December 1999. Macao has also benefited from the 'open door' policies in China. It is the headquarters for many mainland companies, many of which run joint ventures there, and it has attracted new foreign investment. In a sense, Macao has been reviving its traditional function as a special intermediary between China and the outside world.

In 1987, total trade was US$2.8 billion and there was a favourable balance of trade. Among exports, textiles account for about 75 per cent, and most imports are either food or raw materials.
                    C.B.H

PEOPLES

A proud grandmother looking after her grandchild at Shajiao commune, near Canton.

ANTHROPOLOGY

Origins of human culture in East Asia

The cradle of mankind was once thought to be in Asia, but the cradle, as an eminent French prehistorian remarked, is on wheels, and it moved to Africa some 50 years ago. It is from Africa that the earliest tool-using hominids (a term which includes all humans and near-humans), as well as their probable ancestors, the Australopithecines, are known. Nearly human *Homo erectus* made its appearance in eastern Asia about 1 million years ago, and left numerous archaeological remains. Although it is possible, as evidence from molecular biology suggests, that another migration out of Africa about 200 000 years ago brought *Homo sapiens* to East Asia, fossil records strongly favour an interpretation that East Asian *Homo sapiens* evolved from the local *Homo erectus*.

Fossil apes

One important source of fossil hominoids (a term which includes humans, apes and their possible common ancestors) in China used to be the so-called 'dragons' teeth' sold as drugs in apothecaries' shops. Among the hominoids first discovered in this way was *Gigantopithecus blacki*, Black's giant ape. It was even suggested that the *Gigantopithecus* evolved into *Homo erectus* in Asia. Hundreds of *Gigantopithecus* remains have since been excavated from caves in south China, Pakistan and Vietnam. The ages of these deposits range from several million to less than 1 million years. In one of the caves in China, as well as in Vietnam, the deposits yielded *Homo erectus* remains as well. *Gigantopithecus*, it now seems, was a contemporary, not an ancestor, of *Homo erectus*.

Among other fossil hominoids found in China are *Ramapithecus* and *Sivapithecus*, recovered in Yunnan from a deposit which is probably about 8 million years old. They, too, were once thought to be the direct ancestors of humans. It was therefore argued that southern China could have been within the area where the evolution of hominids took place. A current interpretation places them in a side line, leading perhaps to Asiatic apes, not humans. Their presence in China, therefore, is not relevant to the evolution of human culture in Asia.

Australopithecines

This refers to a group of early hominids who lived from about 4 million to about 1 million years ago in East and South Africa. Out of this group emerged, by at least 2 million years ago, an early tool-using *Homo* which then evolved into *Homo erectus* and eventually into the modern humans, *Homo sapiens*. At various times, several fossil remains from China and Indonesia were said to resemble African Australopithecines. Recent re-examinations of these fossils, as well as the geological contexts in which they were found, lead us to believe that they are not as old as once thought and that the specimens should be seen as local variants of *Homo erectus*.

Homo erectus

This is an intermediate form of hominid whose remains are found in deposits dating from about 1.6 million to 200 000 years

ORIGINS OF HUMAN CULTURE: SITES

ago. It has an average cranial capacity of about 1000cc, about two-thirds that of *Homo sapiens*. The heavy browridge, receding forehead, large teeth and prognathous or protruding upper jaw give an archaic appearance to the face and head. The limb bones, however, are quite modern if rather rugged. *Homo erectus* stood and walked upright, and made and used tools with skill and precision. *Homo erectus* was the first hominid who spread out of the

homelands in Africa. It seems to have reached China and Indonesia by 1 million years ago. The greatest number of *Homo erectus* fossil remains come from eastern Asia.

A skull cap and a mandible excavated from Lantian in central China are the oldest solid evidence of *Homo erectus* presence in China. There is considerable controversy at present regarding the ages of the two specimens recovered from two different localities

EVIDENCE FOR ORIGINS OF HUMAN CULTURE IN CHINA

	Age	Glaciation	North China	South China	Kinds of evidence
HOLOCENE	10 000		Jalai Nur[2]	Xianrendong[1]	[1] pottery, bone and stone tools [2] human bones, pottery, bone and stone tools, microliths
			Xiaonanhai[3] Upper Cave[4]		[3] stone tools [4] *Homo sapiens* remains, tools and ornaments
		Dali		Laibin[5] Xiachuan[6]	[5] *Homo sapiens* skull [6] microlithic tools
UPPER PLEISTO-CENE	50 000		Shiyu[7]		[7] many specialized tools, a polished and perforated stone disc
			Xujiayao[9]	Liujiang[8] Maba[10]	[8] *Homo sapiens* skull and other bones [9] juvenile human bones, small stone tools [10] human skull cap
	100 000	Inter-glacial		Dingcun[11] Changyang[12]	[11] three juvenile teeth, large stone tools [12] left maxilla and premolar
		Lushan	Dali[13] Jinniushan[14]		[13] early *Homo sapiens*, stone tools [14] *Homo erectus/sapiens*, stone tools
	200 000			Hexian[15]	[15] *Homo erectus* remains
			Zhoukoudian[16]		[16] *Homo erectus* (45+ individuals), numerous tools, ash
MIDDLE PLEISTO-CENE	500 000				
		Dagu		Kehe[17] Yuanmou[18] Lantian[19]	[17] large stone tools [18] *Homo erectus* incisors, stone tools [19] *Homo erectus* (skull cap and mandible), stone tools
	1 000 000	Boyang	Xihoudu[20]		[20] stone tools, cut and burned bone and antlers
				Nihewan	
LOWER PLEISTO-CENE	2 000 000	Longchuan			

Source: The chronological framework based on Wu Rukang and J. W. Olsen (eds.), *Palaeoanthropology and Palaeolithic Archaeology in the People's Republic of China* Press, (London, Academic Press 1985)

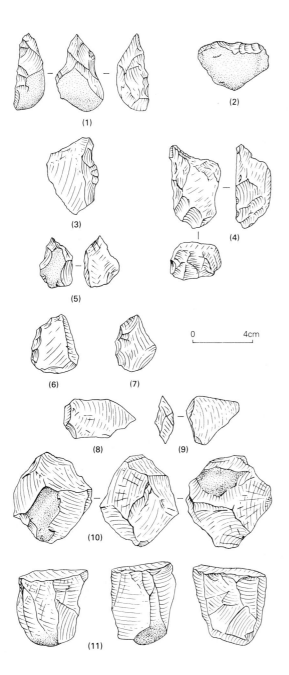

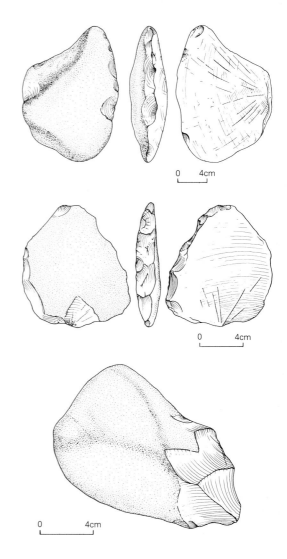

Above: tools from Xihoudu, Shanxi Province: choppers (top and centre) and a heavy triangular point of quartz (bottom). Left: tools from Xujiayao, Shanxi Province: (1) pointed tool, (2) straight-edged scraper, (3) concave scraper, (4) pointed tool with a thick scraping edge at the other end, (5) perforator, (6) and (7) engraving tools, (8) and (9) tool blanks, (10) and (11) cores from which tool blanks were made.

of the Lantian site. According to correlations with the deep sea oxygen isotope sequence, the skull cap may be as old as 1.15 million years and the mandible 650 000 years. Another opinion, based on palaeomagnetic data, places the skull cap at 750 000 and the mandible at 650 000 years. Stone tools, including a large pointed tool and flakes probably intended for cutting and scraping,

were found at Lantian as well. An assemblage of 32 stone tools, which also include a heavy pointed tool and scrapers, excavated at Xihoudu in north China could also be of a considerable antiquity, as much as 1 million years. Also recovered from this site are some animal bones and antlers, which are said to have been cut and scraped, and show signs of burning. Other evidence of early presence of *Homo erectus* in China includes stone tools collected in Kehe village in Shanxi, and two *Homo erectus* incisors and a few stone tools found at Yuanmou in Yunnan. The Yuanmou incisors are believed to have come from a level palaeomagnetically dated to about 500 000 years.

Perhaps the best-known site in China containing physical and cultural remains of *Homo erectus* is Zhoukoudian near Beijing. The 40m deep deposits at Locality 1 ('Beijing Man Locality'), now dated as 500 000 to 230 000 years old, yielded more than 45 individuals of *Homo erectus*, together with some 100 000 stone tools, ashes, and animal bones. The animals range from large and fierce ones like elephants, rhinoceros, leopards and hyenas, through deer and antelope, to small rodents. The traditional interpretation of the evidence was that this was the 'Cave Home of Beijing Man', where generations of *Homo erectus* lived, made tools, brought back the spoils of hunting, and cooked the meat over the fire to be shared with other members of the group. This interpretation, as with other interpretations of *Homo erectus* behaviour at archaeological sites in Europe and Africa, is under intense scrutiny by anthropologists. There is no question that the stone tools were intentionally manufactured and that fire was present at the site. The points of controversy are: (1) Was the fire intentionally maintained and used by *Homo erectus*? (2) Did *Homo erectus* hunt and bring back the animals? and (3) Did *Homo erectus* live here, or were the hominid bones, along with animal bones, brought into the cave fissures by either water action or carnivorous predators? A reasonable interpretation of the Zhoukoudian evidence seems to be that, over the 300 000 year period, the cave was used both by *Homo erectus* and hyenas, and that at least some of the animal remains were brought into it by *Homo erectus*, although it is not certain whether the animals were hunted and killed by *Homo erectus* or scavenged from carnivore kills. Burn marks on the bones suggest that meat was occasionally roasted over fire while it was still on the bone.

The deep deposit at Zhoukoudian records a gradual evolution both in hominid skeletal morphology and stone tools. In the upper levels of the cave the cranial capacities of the skulls tend to be larger, and the tools tend to be smaller and more carefully made. *Homo erectus* remains excavated from the Longtang Cave in Hexian, Anhui Province, in 1980 and 1981, which include the first complete skull recovered from south China, are comparable to the upper level skulls of Zhoukoudian. They are probably about 200 000 years old.

By this time, *Homo erectus* populations appear to have been distributed fairly widely in China. Tools similar to those of Zhoukoudian have been found from Liaoning in the north to Guizhou in the south. At the same time, there seems to have been little contact to the west. Acheulian hand-axes and the Levallois technique of flake production, which are common in the contemporary Palaeolithic assemblages of Africa, Europe and western Asia, are completely absent from China, and extremely rare in the surrounding regions of East Asia. It appears that in relative isolation *Homo erectus* of China developed a distinctive way of life during the Middle Pleistocene.

Homo sapiens

There is much debate at present about the origins of modern humans, *Homo sapiens*. On the one hand is a view which holds that *Homo sapiens* evolved in Africa and spread throughout the world relatively recently, perhaps about 200 000 years ago. The study of DNA molecules appears to support this theory. On the other hand, fossil evidence in East Asia suggests a continuity through time, from local *Homo erectus* through transitional forms to fossil *Homo sapiens* and finally to later prehistoric and historic populations of Asia.

In China fossils exhibiting characteristics transitional between *Homo erectus* and modern *Homo sapiens* are known from Changyang in Hubei, Maba in Guangdong, Dingcun and Xujiayao in Shanxi, Dali in Shaanxi, and Jinniushan in Liaoning. Ages obtained by various dating methods range from 200 000 years for Jinniushan to 17 000 years for Xujiayao. Fully modern *Homo sapiens* fossils have been recovered from the Upper Cave of Zhoukoudian near Beijing, as well as from Late Pleistocene deposits at several other sites. Certain features, such as shovel-shaped incisors and wide nasal bones, characteristic of Beijing Man, were also present in the archaic and modern *Homo sapiens* fossils and continue to occur among the living peoples of East Asia.

Increasing specialization of tools, more economic use of raw materials through systematic production of regularly shaped tool-blanks, and clear archaeological evidence for the use of personal ornaments and well-organized hunting and gathering activities are some of the features which characterize the Late Pleistocene assemblages of Europe and western Siberia. Similar features are found in China, too, but Chinese scientists currently interpret them as an internally generated phenomenon, the intensification of a trend towards smaller and more specialized tools already observable in the upper layers of Zhoukoudian, and culminating, according to the Chinese archaeologists' view, in the microlithic cultures found in areas of China such as the Ordos in the early Holocene. Radio-carbon dates from Jalai Nur in Heilongjiang and Xianrendong in Jiangxi suggest that pottery came into use by about 10 000 years ago; the spread of agriculture—farming and animal husbandry—seems gradually to have superseded hunting and gathering during the next few thousand years in many parts of China.

F.I.-S.

The Mongoloid family of peoples

Anthropologists would agree that there exists a vast network of contiguous peoples centring on East Asia, who form the Mongoloid population complex. They would include those considered most typical—the old 'Yellow race', of Chinese, Japanese, Koreans and peoples of the woodlands to the north of these—as well as those surrounding them in all quarters: American Indians, Polynesians, Micronesians, Indonesians (including aboriginals of Taiwan and Hainan Island), Southeast Asiatics through Burma, and many peoples of Central and Western Asia (for example Tajiks, Kirghiz, Turkomen) to the Urals (Voguls, Samoyeds) and beyond the Volga (Kalmyks). In the last regions there is interdigitation with Caucasoid peoples, and of course with Soviet colonizers in Siberia. On the borders with Afghanistan and the Indian subcontinent there is a narrower zone of mixture with the Caucasoid populations of these countries.

There are no strongly defined physical traits common to all Mongoloid peoples. Skin is medium to pale brown in colour; eyes are dark and hair is black or nearly so; body and facial hair are sparse compared with Caucasoids of either Europe or India. Cranial traits (of importance because past populations can be studied only through this source) are a flatness across the upper face, and a tendency to lateral enlargement of the middle face—'high cheekbones'. Little if anything else can be cited. If, in many people or individuals, for example American Indians, there is a sort of Mongoloid look, in some others there is simply the absence of clear resemblance to any other division of mankind.

Variation among different local populations is considerable, especially in non-cosmopolitan peoples, such as the aboriginal tribes of Taiwan. A comprehensive analysis of physical measurements for all of Asia showed a large number of regional groups among the Mongoloid peoples. A similar, more intensive study of cranial measurements, on a wider scale, groups Polynesians, American Indians, and such East Asians as Japanese and Chinese into three distinct branches hardly closer to one another than to Europeans. It has been proposed that Polynesia was originally colonized primarily from South and North America, but physical and other evidence indicates that the two major peoples, Oceanic and

THE MONGOLOID FAMILIES

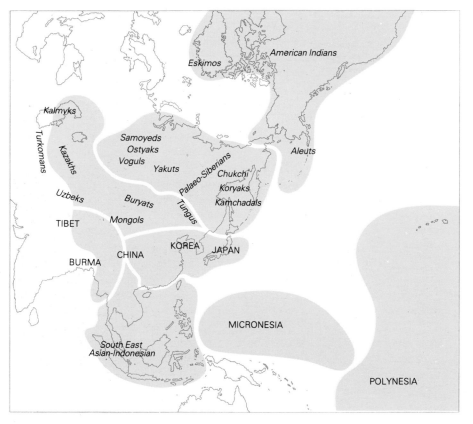

This map shows the general distribution of the Mongoloid family of peoples. There is internal differentiation as described in the text, but distinct boundaries among major population groups are hardly possible to draw, and the external boundary in Asia is also ill-defined.

Opposite, left to right: an Iban of Sarawak, Borneo; a North American Comanche; and a Goldi woman of the Soviet Far East are peoples of Mongoloid variation. The last represents the extreme or 'classic' Mongoloid. The others, though broad-faced, lack the facial flattening, typical eyefold, and retroussé nose.

American, derived independently from southern and northern Asia respectively, and are related only in this way.

Blood genetic traits have not been especially informative as to distinctions of Mongoloids from other peoples, or as to distinctions within the Mongoloids themselves. One exception is the presence of the Diego antigen of the red blood cells, commonest among American Indians, and highly variable across groups but in some reaching a frequency of 20 per cent. It occurs less frequently in Asiatic Mongoloids, is present in Chamarros of the Marianas, but is unknown in Polynesia.

A major characteristic trait of the Mongoloids is flaky, or dry cerumen, the secretion of the ear canal. It is popularly called ear 'wax' because the moist form is virtually universal outside of Mongoloids; Japanese anthropologists refer to 'honey' ear wax versus 'rice-bran' ear wax. The latter is preponderant in north Asiatics, Chinese and Japanese, and diminishes to about 50 per cent among Taiwan aboriginals, Malays and other Indonesians. It is still lower in Micronesians; Polynesians have not been examined. It is highly variable in American Indians. Outside the Mongoloid pale it is found in a modest proportion of New Guinea natives—elsewhere it is extremely rare. It has been suggested that this Mongoloid trait may result from genetic selection for resistance to ear infections, but why it should be concentrated particularly in north Asia remains unknown.

Such distinctive traits as Mongoloids possess are usually accentuated in the central populations, Chinese, Japanese, Koreans, Palaeosiberians and Eskimos. Their skin is lighter, their hair is usually straight, coarse and very black, and the flatness of the face appears accentuated, primarily by lowness of the nasal root and a burying of the eyeball within fleshy tissue of the eye socket, especially by a fold of skin over the inner end of the eye opening, cov-

ering the canthus and at least part of the upper lid itself. If one looks at such an individual in profile one can often see the eyelashes of both eyes at once because of the low upper nasal profile and the forward placement of the eye sockets. Mongoloids share a pattern of special dental variations which are rarer elsewhere, and this is accentuated in the central populations. American Indians share this accentuation, but Polynesians and other southern Mongoloids do not.

Anthropologists in the past have tended to consider these northern peoples as the 'pure' or 'classic' Mongoloids, with the corollary that other Mongoloids result from a mixture—specifically the Polynesians and American Indians, who have been said to reflect Caucasoid and other elements. The analysis of physical measurements does in fact group Koreans, Japanese and north Chinese together, separating the last somewhat from southern and western Chinese; this does not, however, constitute anything more than one group among many. It is actually likely that the supposedly 'pure' Mongoloid type was late in appearing, and is not primeval. It is suggested that certain general Mongoloid traits became emphasized by natural selection as a protection against intense cold during the last Ice Age, above all the pulling back into the face of the nose and eyeballs, in the manner already described. This is difficult to demonstrate, but it is a reasonable hypothesis. Much later the development of higher culture led to the expansion of a previously more localized group among the varied Mongoloid populations, so that it became 'typical' and homogeneous over wide areas. There is no reason to view other Mongoloid peoples as any less pure or typical.

There is very little evidence of Mongoloid origins and history. It has been proposed that this racial group derives directly from the *Homo erectus* population of Zhoukoudian (Peking Man), with an

age of about 500 000 years or less, on the basis of certain cranial and dental details common to both. This is geographically logical and acceptable, but not informative as to other problems of the later emergence of modern human populations and their differentiation. A skull, apparently of Pleistocene age but not closely dated, from Liujiang county, Guangxi, is most probably Mongoloid, of a general south Asian aboriginal affiliation. Its main significance is that it indicates the probable absence in south China of non-Mongoloid peoples in the late Pleistocene. Furthermore, the negative inference can be drawn that Mongoloids were a well differentiated division of modern man over 40 000 years ago: this is based on the knowledge that Caucasoids were appearing in Asia Minor and Europe shortly after that time, evidently displacing the Neanderthals of the area, and also by the knowledge that people indistinguishable in general form from modern Australian aboriginals had entered that continent by 40 000 years ago, and probably earlier. This same kind of population, evidently ancestral also to the Melanesians, was present at this time in Indonesia and, on the evidence of the surviving Aeta, in the Philippines, though probably not Taiwan. How far north this population extended on the present mainland of Southeast Asia is not clear, but our present state of knowledge indicates an Australo-Melanesian population complex in Indonesia (then Sundaland, the raised Sunda Shelf joining major islands), and an already varied Mongoloid complex reaching from Southeast Asia all the way north. From this, American Indian migrations from Mongoloid northeast Asia were crossing the Beringia land bridge most probably between 25 000 and 13 000 years ago.

In north China, the Upper Cave at Zhoukoudian (the cave complex which yielded Peking Man) contained several skeletons dating anywhere from 18 000 to 11 000 years ago. These have a general Mongoloid character, but close analysis does not ally them clearly with Mongoloids, as an ancestral form. The conclusion is either that the 'classic' Mongoloid form of China, Japan, and so forth, had not evolved by this time, or that it was not in occupation of one of its present main areas, north China. The latter is certainly the preferable explanation. Unfortunately, perhaps because of intensive cultivation over all of China for centuries, preservation of prehistoric skeletal remains has been extremely limited. Only in the Neolithic sites, where village cemeteries have been excavated, do such remains appear in even limited quantities. Small samples from Neolithic Yangshao and Huating settlements, as well as other scattered remains from north China, indicate populations cranially indistinguishable from living Chinese. Thus, in the gap between perhaps 16 500 BC and 7000 BC, Mongoloids of a generalized kind had been replaced by those of the 'classic' variety in north China, from the Yellow River basin westwards into Shaanxi.

By the latter date it is likely that southern China and Southeast Asia were occupied by locally varied Mongoloid populations basically similar to the north Chinese but showing less of the 'classic' stamp. At the same period, or in succeeding millennia, the fringe lands were being populated by similar people. The Jomon tribes of Japan were physically different from the present Japanese and more varied; the Ainu of Hokkaido are probably the last survivors of such aboriginals. Taiwan was settled by several archaeologically distinguishable groups ancestral to the living aboriginal tribes, whose mutual linguistic differences bear witness to long mutual isolation as a factor in preserving physical differences. In Indonesia and probably in the Philippines Mongoloid peoples were displacing Australo-Melanesian predecessors, fortified by horticulture allowing larger populations. The occupation of Micronesia and Polynesia followed once navigational skills had been developed, the arrival in western Polynesia taking place by about 1500 BC. The whole vast assembly of offshore Mongoloids, from Taiwan south and east, is connected by the network of the Austro-Melanesian languages, whose spread and apparent age of origin accord with that of the movements described.

In turn this was followed by a homogenizing on much of the mainland, as populations of the northern 'classic' form grew and spread, with the rise of Bronze Age civilization and central power. The late Shang sacrificial pits at Anyang provide many crania which collectively cannot be significantly distinguished from those of the Neolithic villages, nor from those of recent Hainan Island Chinese—unfortunately these are the only worthwhile comparisons which can be made. The Japanese proper apparently arrived about 300 BC in Kyushu from Korea, with the Yayoi culture, thereafter displacing or absorbing the Jomon inhabitants. Recent Japanese crania from the northern and southern ends of the main islands belong to a single general form, and are also close to both Bronze Age (Anyang) and recent (Hainan) Chinese. Polynesians and American Indians are well distinguished from this whole cluster, but Atayals of Taiwan, Filipinos, and even Micronesians of prehistoric Guam show greater affinities. All of this accords with historical and archaeological reconstructions of population movements.

The southwards expansion of the Han people and their culture was doubtless accompanied by assimilation of, and amalgamation with, local populations who may have been less different physically from north Chinese than other bordering peoples. While some distinctions are seen in living segments of the population, the crania from the Bronze Age of the north and recent people of the extreme south are relatively similar, and our present state of knowledge does not permit us to gauge the relative importance of Han migrants and local inhabitants in the Yangtze valley and further south.

W.W.H.

The expansion of the Han Chinese

A major problem in dealing with China's past is to define who were 'the Chinese' and what area can be considered as 'China' at any given period. The whole conception is bound up as much with a sense of cultural identity and common interest as with any hard racial reality. The commonly used term 'Han Chinese' is of course a very late one, first emerging in the 3rd and 4th centuries when 'Han', the name of the first great and enduring dynasty, also began to be used as a term for 'Chinese'—of the Chinese cultural unity.

The problem is further complicated by the fact that archaeology is making it clear that 'Chinese' culture did not derive from any single group of people, but evolved in a number of different centres. The people who identified themselves as 'Chinese' (*Xia*, or *Zhu Xia*) in the earliest surviving writings considered themselves as a group, 'the various *Xia*', with reference to a variety of non-Chinese peoples, Yi, Di, Rong, etc., who were different in race and language, but far more significantly were distinct (and *ipso facto* inferior) in culture and customs, as 'barbarians' against whose incursions 'Chinese' territory had to be protected.

Certainly as early as the 5th or 6th century BC to be 'Chinese' was a cultural rather than a racial distinction. By that period the non-Chinese groups who had lived scattered among the 'various Xia' had largely been conquered and assimilated, and the territory of the major states of the Warring States period was for the most part occupied by people who considered themselves 'Chinese'. Nevertheless, important differences remained and some parts of this area were more 'Chinese' than others; Qin in the northwest, Yan in the northeast, the Yangtze states of Chu, Wu and Yue all held a rather anomalous intermediary position with variant cultures and linguistic differences. However, by the 3rd century BC they too were permanently and fully incorporated into the Chinese cultural sphere.

With the Qin and Han the political boundaries of the newly unified empire expanded far beyond the area peopled by a recognizably Chinese population. In the south Qin advanced and occupied parts of southern and southwestern China and the north of Vietnam. Although the native peoples submitted to Chinese sovereignty and a network of administrative centres was established, very little Chinese settlement took place. The coastal zone, occupied by various peoples called Yue by the Chinese, was under effective Chinese control only around modern Canton and the Tonking delta. Here the Qin briefly established control in 221–214 BC. The area then became an independent state of Nan-yue, and was finally reconquered by the Han in 113–111 BC. The kingdom of Min-Yue—modern Fujian—was attacked by Qin, and

finally destroyed by Han in 110 BC, but the area remained outside effective Chinese control and free of Chinese settlement for centuries to come. Inland in modern Jiangxi and Hunan a skeleton administration was set up, but there was very sparse Chinese settlement, and the area remained almost entirely in the hands of its tribal Man peoples. In the southwest the Han conquered the strong and culturally advanced Dian kingdom in Yunnan in 109 BC, and subsequently pressed further into the tribal areas of western Yunnan. But here again there was virtually no Chinese settlement, and political control proved short-lived.

The expansion of the Han borders was equally spectacular in the north. Here, unlike the south, the Chinese were faced with a major environmental frontier between the region that could be exploited by settled Chinese agriculture and areas of low rainfall where a pastoral economy was the only viable way of life. In the north the Han faced the formidable Xiongnu, against whom the Qin had established a vast line of fixed defences. After a series of successful campaigns against them in 127–119 BC, the Chinese permanently occupied modern Gansu Province. Along the long frontier zone from western Gansu to the coast the Chinese garrisons set up agricultural colonies to support themselves. Huge numbers of Chinese (some say as many as 2 million) were forcibly resettled in the new northwestern districts and in northern Shaanxi. In the first century BC Chinese armies pressed west into the Tarim Basin and the Han set up a Protectorate for the Western Regions. But this was purely a military occupation established to protect the trade routes. Some small Chinese colonies were set up but no effective Chinese settlement followed. Even political control proved insecure.

In the northeast Chinese colonies were established in Liaoning and in northern Korea. Here the Chinese presence was more successful, for Chinese refugees had already set up a kingdom in the region. The Korean colonies enjoyed a high standard of culture, and survived the fall of the Han until about AD 313-16. In the Koguryŏ state that finally wrested the area from Chinese control, Chinese cultural influence remained strong, but the Han colonies were completely absorbed into the Korean population.

As the political boundaries of the Han first expanded and later shrank as Chinese military power declined, Chinese settlement of the interior provinces continued, and a significant redistribution of the Chinese population took place. The predominance of the north diminished and considerable settlement began in the Yangtze valley and in Hunan. In the 2nd century AD the northwest came under pressure from the proto-Tibetan Jiang, many of whom were settled within the Chinese borders; in the far west Chinese control of the Tarim Basin finally declined; in the northeast the Xianbi peoples in Manchuria pressed the Chinese in the frontier zone. In the southwest Chinese political domination of Yunnan was lost, and would not be re-established for over a millennium. At first in the hands of tribal peoples, from the 8th century Yunnan was the centre of stable kingdoms, first Nanzhao, later Dali, which for a while in the 9th century controlled parts of Upper Burma. It was only under the Mongols that Yunnan and Guizhou were finally to become Chinese territory. Even until the 17th century Yunnan was administered by local native governors. Chinese settlement proceeded very slowly in the southwest, and was mostly confined to the fertile valleys. Even today much of the region is inhabited by minority peoples.

In the south a gradual process of slow assimilation of native peoples by Chinese colonists took place in the post-Han period. By the 5th century the Chinese had set up an administrative network throughout the south, including for the first time Fujian. Settlement followed more slowly. The Chinese colonists faced many problems, from clearing dense forest and setting up irrigation systems to coping with a semi-tropical climate and unfamiliar diseases. Chinese and aboriginal peoples lived side by side in many areas, the Chinese farming the valley bottoms for paddy rice, the native tribes living, often by slash and burn shifting agriculture on the hill slopes; a pattern that persisted in many parts of the south and southwest until this century.

The colonization of the south, however, was slow. In 609 AD only some 10 per cent of the registered population lived south of the Yangtze. In 742 still less than a quarter of the Chinese lived in the south, and until the 10th century the south in general, and Guangdong, Guangxi and Fujian in particular were considered places on the fringe of civilization, as places of exile and banishment. Settlement was earliest in Hunan, followed by Jiangxi, and latest in Fujian, which remained sparsely peopled and backward until the 9th century.

Settlement of the south now grew rapidly. Where the south had held only a quarter of the population in 742, and was still a cultural backwater, by the 11th century 60 per cent of the Chinese lived in the south, which was rapidly becoming the dominant region in terms of culture, while the north stagnated.

From the 4th century AD onwards northern China suffered repeated invasions by various northern peoples, in particular by the Xiongnu, the Qiang and Xianbei, who set up a number of short-lived local kingdoms that were eventually unified by the Tuoba in the 5th century. During this period many non-Chinese settled in what had been Chinese territory, especially in the northwest. There was much intermarriage, and the eventual reunification of China by the Sui and Tang was carried out by a political elite of mixed blood.

During the Sui and Tang periods while the internal settlement of China proceeded, China again expanded the area under its political domination far beyond the bounds of Chinese settlement.

Of the regions controlled by the Han, Vietnam was retained. Attempted conquest of Korea and Manchuria, though briefly successful, led only to the emergence of a powerful unified Korean state, and a strong kingdom Parhae in Manchuria, both under Chinese cultural influence, but independent of Chinese control. The attempt to conquer the southwestern kingdom of Nanzhao was also a failure. The most extraordinary successes were in Central Asia, where Chinese dominance was established over the Tarim Basin and Dzungaria, and protectorate set up briefly far to the west in Afghanistan. As under the Han, this dominance was purely political. Small Chinese settlements were set up in Hami, Turfan and near Ürümqi, but after 755 the Chinese withdrew their armies to fight internal rebellions. The Central Asian outposts were cut off, and fell to the Tibetans or the Uighurs. The Tibetans occupied modern Gansu Province, and Central Asia was lost to the Chinese until the 18th century. During the 8th century many non-Chinese peoples had been settled within the northwestern border in Gansu and northern Shaanxi and Shanxi. From the 10th century the northwestern area was still partly peopled by Chinese farmers, living among Turks, Tibetans, and Tanguts, but the area was politically divided among a series of small non-Chinese principalities, which were eventually replaced by the Tangut state of Xixia (1038–1227). From the end of the 9th century parts of the northeast were in the hands first of non-Chinese warlords, then of the Khitan peoples centred in Manchuria, who set up a dynasty, the Liao (947–1125). Until the end of the Mongol period in 1367 a large population of settled Chinese farmers, and many large Chinese cities in the northeast lived under alien domination.

China finally lost control of its possessions in Vietnam in 939. In spite of attempts at reconquest in the early 15th century it would remain politically independent, though still a part of the Chinese cultural sphere.

During the Ming and Qing settlement of southern China by the Han Chinese was more or less completed, although considerable minorities especially in mountainous areas remained unassimilated and provoked occasional disturbances. In the late Song and early Ming Chinese settlement overseas began in Southeast Asia, Indonesia and the Philippines. At the end of the Ming, Chinese settlers began for the first time to colonize the western coast of Taiwan, which after various political vicissitudes finally became a part of the Qing empire in 1683, and was slowly colonized from Fujian.

The victories of the Manchu armies in the 17th and 18th centuries once again vastly extended the frontier of their empire, which by the mid-18th century had incorporated Tibet, modern Xinjiang, Mongolia and Manchuria; all of them areas with a predominantly non-Chinese population. Chinese settlement in this vast area remained minimal—a few garrison troops, convicts, banished officials and traders in Xinjiang, a few Manchu officials in

Tibet and Mongolia. Chinese farmers settled some border areas of Inner Mongolia.

Manchuria, homeland of the dominant Manchus, was theoretically banned to Chinese settlement, although many Chinese had already settled in southern Liaoning during Ming times. The ban on Chinese settlement was finally relaxed in the middle of the 19th century, after which there was a huge influx of Chinese farmers (many of them from Shandong) into the last great area of vacant land fit for permanent Chinese agriculture. This, the last of the great internal migrations, continues to the present, and in the northeast Chinese farmers long ago swamped the native population of Manchus and Tungusic peoples.

Reunification of most of the former Qing empire under the People's Republic since 1949 has been accompanied by the deliberate settlement of Han Chinese settlers in many areas formerly dominated by minority peoples. This has occurred in Tibet, in Xinjiang, Ningxia and Inner Mongolia. But in spite of these policies, in most of these areas Chinese settlers remain in the minority.

D.C.T.

THE NON-HAN CULTURES

The national minorities

Apart from the Han (the ethnic Chinese), who constitute about 94 per cent of the whole population, there are said to be over 50 other ethnic groups living in China. These national minorities, a translation of the Chinese term *shaoshu minzu*, generally have their own traditional cultures and languages. Physically the differences between these groups and the Han Chinese are not very great, the majority sharing with the Han variations of the Mongolian race-type; it is only in Xinjiang that Central-Asiatic (Turanian) and Caucasian forms are found.

The geographical distribution of the national minorities varies widely. Some, such as the Uighur, occupy compact areas, some live scattered among other groups, while others until recently led nomadic or semi-nomadic lives. Two groups deserve special mention in the context since the reason for their being classified as 'nationalities' is at variance with the criteria given above. The Hui nationality, although found in greatest concentration in the Ningxia Hui Autonomous Region, are also found scattered widely in China proper. The Hui, believers in Islam, are either the descendants of Arab soldiers who were sent to China in the 8th century to help quell the An Lushan Rebellion, and who later settled in the northwest and were rewarded with Chinese wives; or, in other cases, the descendants of Arab traders who settled in China, or of Chinese converts. Generally physically indistinguishable from the Chinese, and speaking only Chinese, their classification as a 'nationality' appears to be based largely on religious grounds. The other group are the Man (Manchu), perhaps in greatest concentration in what was formerly Manchuria, but, like the Hui, scattered throughout China proper. The Man are descended from the Manchus who conquered China in 1644, and, despite efforts by the Qing authorities to maintain Han-Manchu differences, have become completely sinicized. Although it is not clear whether Manchu still exists as a spoken language, it is evident that the great majority speak only Han Chinese. Their classification as a 'nationality' seems to rest merely on group descent, and the number of the Man in the accompanying table, suggesting as it does that these represent speakers of Manchu, is probably misleading.

The differences between the 1956 and 1980 censuses are interesting, but so far inexplicable. In harmony with the general tendency of Chinese population statistics, a significant rise in population is seen in all minority peoples, with the curious exception of two geographic areas: in the northwest, the Russian, Tartar and Uzbek populations have declined, and in the southwest, the Jingpo and Wa populations have also declined. Whether this is the result of different methods of statistic-taking, or of real changes in population-numbers, is not clear.

Although it is inappropriate to try to correlate cultural and linguistic features, the attempt is made to suggest some very broad generalizations about various aspects of the cultures of the chief linguistic groups. Leaving aside Han Chinese (whether spoken by the Han, Man or Hui), the languages spoken in China belong to eight linguistic stocks. These are genetic stocks, determined by the existence of shared cognate items in the core vocabulary within each stock. So far it has proved impossible to demonstrate a genetic relationship between any of these stocks. Moving roughly from east to west, and from north to south, the following stocks are found: Japano-Korean, Altaic, Indo-European, Tibeto-Burman, Austro-Asiatic, Dai, Miao-Yao, Malayo-Polynesian. All these stocks are also found outside China, mainly in countries adjacent to the areas where they occur in China. *G.B.D.*

Japano-Korean

The only representative in China of this stock is Korean, spoken in Jilin Province directly to the north of North Korea. Both culturally and linguistically the Korean-speaking peoples have been identical with the people of Korea.

Altaic

This is an extremely widespread stock, stretching from Siberia to

The Non-Han Cultures of China

NON-HAN ETHNIC MINORITIES OFCHINA (Grouped by linguistic affiliation)

Ethnic group	Population 1982 Census	1990 Census	Chief geographical location	Ethnic group	Population 1982 Census	1990 Census	Chief geographical location
CHINESE-SPEAKING				**TIBETO-BURMAN** (*cont.*)			
Hui	7 227 022	8 602 978	Ningxia, Gansu, Qinghai Xinjiang	Naxi (Mosɔ)	254 154	278 009	Yunnan, Sichuan
				Qiang	102 768	198 252	Sichuan
JAPANO-KOREAN				Jingpo (Kachin)	93 008	119 209	Yunnan
Korean	1 766 439	1 920 597	Jilin, Heilongjiang, Liaoning	Pumi (Primi)	24 237	29 657	Yunnan
				Achang	20 441	27 708	Yunnan
ALTAIC				Nu	23 166	27 123	Yunnan
Turkic				Moinba (Monpa)	6 248	7 475	Tibet
Uighur (Uygur)	5 962 814	7 214 431	Xinjiang	Drung (Dulong)	4 682	5 816	Yunnan
Kazak (Kazakh)	908 414	1 111 718	Xinjiang	Lhoba (Lopa)	2 065	2 312	Tibet
Kirgiz (Kirghiz)	113 999	141 549	Xinjiang, Heilongjiang	Jino	11 974	18 021	Yunnan
Salar	69 102	87 697	Qinghai	**AUSTRO-ASIATIC**			
Uzbek (Ozbek)	12 453	14 502	Xinjiang	Va (Wa, Kawa)	298 591	351 974	Yunnan
Yugur (Yellow Uighur)	10 569	12 297	Gansu	Blang (Puman)	58 476	82 280	Yunnan
Tatar	4 127	4 873	Xinjiang	De'ang (Benglong)	12 295	15 462	Yunnan
Mongolian				Jing (Gin, Vietnamese)	11 995	18 915	Guangxi
Mongolian	3 416 881	4 806 849	Inner Mongolia Hebei, NE China	**TAI (DAI)**			
Dongxiang (Santa)	279 397	373 872	Gansu	Zhuang	13 388 118	15 489 630	Guangxi
Tu (Monguor)	159 426	191 624	Qinghai, Gansu	Bouyei (Zhongjia)	2 122 389	2 545 059	Guizhou
Daur (Dagur)	94 014	121 357	Inner Mongolia, Heilongjiang	Dong (Kam)	1 426 335	2 514 014	Hunan, Guizhou, Guangxi
Bonan (Bao'an)	9 027	12 212	Gansu	Dai (Tai, Lü)	840 590	1 025 128	Yunnan
Manchu-Tungus				Li	818 255	1 110 900	Guangdong, Hainan
Manchu (Man)	4 304 160	9 821 180	Liaoning, NE China, Hebei	Shui (Sui)	286 487	345 993	Guizhou, Guangxi
Xibe (Sibo)	83 629	172 847	Xinjiang, NE China	Mulam (Mulao)	90 426	159 328	Guangxi
Ewenki (Evenki)	19 343	26 315	Inner Mongolia, Heilongjiang	Maonan	38 135	71 968	Guangxi
Orogen (Orochon)	4 132	6 965	Inner Mongolia, Heilongjiang	Gelo (Gelao)	53 802	437 997	Guizhou
Hezhen (Hoche)	1 476	4 245	Heliongjiang	**MIAO-YAO**			
TIBETO-BURMAN				Miao	5 036 377	7 398 035	Guizhou, Yunnan, Hunan, Guangxi
Yi (Lolo)	5 457 251	6 572 173	Sichuan, Yunnan, Guizhou, Guangxi	Yao	1 403 664	2 134 013	Guangxi, Hunan, Yunnan,Guangdong, Guizhou
Tibetan	3 874 035	4 593 330	Tibet, Qinghai Gansu, Sichuan	She	368 832	630 378	Fujian, Zhejiang
Bai (Minjia)	1 132 010	1 594 827	Yunnan	**AUSTRONESIAN**			
Tujia	2 834 732	5 704 223	Hunan, Hubei	Gaoshan	1 549	2 909*	Taiwan, Fujian
Hani	1 059 404	1 253 952	Yunnan	**INDO-EUROPEAN**			
Lisu	480 960	574 856	Yunnan, Sichuan	Tajik	26 503	33 538	Xinjiang
Lahu	304 174	411 476	Yunnan	Russian	2 935	13 504	Xinjiang

* Mainland only; 335 603 on Taiwan (1988).

Sources: State Statistical Bureau (*Beijing Review* 52/1990 p.30); Ma Yin (ed.), *China's Minority Nationalities* (Beijing, 1989)

C.A.

the Mediterranean. It comprises three rather distantly-related sub-stocks: Turkic, Mongolic and Tungusic, each sub-stock having several usually mutually unintelligible languages. As noted above, the Man language in Tungusic may be on the point of extinction. There is a certain correlation between these lin-guistic sub-stocks and their traditional cultures. The Turkic-speaking peoples exhibit the most variation in ways of life, ranging from the settled agricultural and home industries life of the Uighur to the nomadic sheep- and horse-herding of the Kazakhs. All are believers in Islam.

The Mongolic-speaking peoples have traditionally been nomadic, herding sheep, horses and camels across the plains, living in felt tents that were easily transportable. Their religion is generally Lamaism, a special form of Buddhism, acquired from Tibet. The Tungusic speakers are primarily huntsmen in the northern forests living a nomadic existence. Their religion is animism, with shamans who contact the spirits in cases of illness or death.

There are two features in common to all these languages. The first is that all possess what has been called a 'rigid' word order. In this context this refers to a specific language pattern in which the verb invariably comes at the end of the clause, and intra-clausal relationships are marked by elements suffixed (never prefixed) to nouns. Moreover, tense, aspect, mode and other features are indicated by suffixes to the verb. Thus, in Uighur, the sentence 'I gave this book to my younger brother' is:

bu kitapni inimge berdim: 'this-book-younger brother-give'

where the underlined elements are suffixes, -*ni* for direct object, -*ge* for indirect object and -*dim* for first person singular past. This pattern of rigid word order contrasts with the 'free' word order found in the southern stocks—Austro-Asiatic, Dai, Miao-Yao—and in Han Chinese. It is extremely widespread in Asia, and is by no means confined to the Altaic languages.

The second feature common to all the Altaic languages in China is the existence of vowel harmony. Although details vary from language to language, the general rule is that the vowels of suffixes 'harmonize' in frontness, backness and sometimes in lip-rounding with the vowel of the root. In Uighur, again, the verb roots *ber-* 'to give', *oqu-* 'to read' and *kør-* 'to look at' form the first person singular past tense with what is in fact the same suffix, but with the added feature of vowel harmony:

berdim: 'I gave'

oqudum: 'I read' (past)

kørdym: 'I looked at'

This second feature common to the Altaic languages is not nearly so widespread as the first, being found in a few languages of the Tibeto-Burman stock only. It is a very notable characteristic of the Altaic languages generally.

CHINA'S MINORITY NATIONALITIES

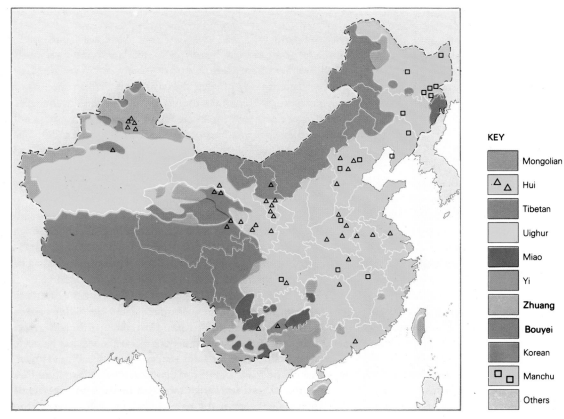

KEY

Mongolian

Hui

Tibetan

Uighur

Miao

Yi

Zhuang

Bouyei

Korean

Manchu

Others

Indo-European

There are only two nationalities of Indo-European speech in China, both found in Xinjiang. The Tajiks, speaking a language of the Iranian sub-stock, are an offshoot of the much more numerous inhabitants of the nearby Tajik Soviet Socialist Republic. The other nationality is of Russian stock, the descendants of Russian settlers of the past few centuries.

Tibeto-Burman

Unlike the language stocks already described, which are basically polysyllabic, the Tibeto-Burman languages on the whole reveal the morpheme (the smallest element capable of carrying meaning) to be monosyllabic. Although there appears to be a tendency well under way in the Tibeto-Burman languages of China for the monosyllabic morpheme to become fixed and unchanging, there is excellent evidence that this has not always been the case. To take a Tibetan example, there was the possibility of having up to four different forms for each verb in Classical Tibetan (which reflects the language of perhaps the 9th century). For example, 'to eat', following fairly regular rules, is found as:

present: *za-ba*
future: *bza*
imperative: *zo*
past: *zos*

There occurred also noun derivation such as is seen in *bzan* 'food'. Modern Lhasa Tibetan has reduced the verb forms to:

present and future: *sa*
imperative: *so*
past: *se*

and the derivation process is no longer productive, with a marked tendency towards more analytical constructions.

Along with monosyllabism, the existence of lexically distinctive tones is a widespread but not universal feature of Tibeto-Burman languages which sets them off from the northern languages, where tones are not found. This is a typical area feature of East Asia, which is nowadays widely thought to have spread over the area in relatively recent times. The spread of such a feature could only be due to language contact; where tonality may have originated is not known at all. It is confined to the basically monosyllabic languages, and may be the result of reductions of other features, such as the reduction of consonant clusters giving rise to compensatory tonality. In some languages some dialects may possess tonal distinctions, such as Lhasa in Tibet, while others, such as Amdo, may lack them. Compare, for instance, Lhasa and Amdo, with the addition of Classical Tibetan, which is also toneless:

'I, me' ŋa (rising tone) ŋa ŋa
'five' ŋa (falling tone) rŋa lŋa

where the two toneless dialects have consonant clusters which have been simplified in Lhasa, but with the tonal compensation which maintains a distinction in the words.

Unlike monosyllabism and tonality, which set off Tibeto-Burman languages from the northern stocks, a third characteristic of this stock is that word order agrees with Altaic and others to the north. Here again we find the so-called rigid word order, with the verb at the end of the sentence, and other relationships indicated by elements added always after the nouns and verbs, exactly as described for the Altaic languages. An interesting partial exception is to be seen in the language of the Bai of Yunnan, descendants of the ancient kingdom of Dali, where the typical Tibeto-Burman word order is used by older speakers, while there is a tendency among younger speakers to place the object after the verb, an aspect of the free word order—clearly the result of Han Chinese influence.

It is difficult to generalize about the way of life of such a diverse group of peoples as speak the Tibeto-Burman languages. The majority live in mountainous areas, but may be herdsmen or valley agriculturalists, while some, such as the Bai, may live in wide plains, practising wet-rice agriculture and the raising of silkworms, so that in terms of production they are indistinguishable from the Han.

Austro-Asiatic

In the far southwestern corner of Yunnan are found a relatively small number of speakers of Austro-Asiatic (often called Mon-Khmer) languages. Although living in areas of high mountains they practise dry-rice agriculture in the valleys and lower slopes. The majority of these peoples are found, in fact, not in China but in Burma, and seem to be an offshoot of the Burmese tribes. The languages, unlike Tibeto-Burman, are partly polysyllabic, and possess the free word order found in Dai.

Dai

The simple term Dai is misleading, and is not so used by specialists in the field, as it covers three markedly different although related groups of languages; Dai proper, Dong-Shui in south-central China and Li on Hainan Island. However, as only Dai proper will be discussed here, the simple term may stand.

The two chief groups of Dai dialects in China are the Northern Dai of Guangxi and Guizhou Provinces, and the Southwestern Dai of southern Yunnan Province, but these differ mainly in vocabulary and phonology, and many generalizations may be made that cover both groups. All are strongly monosyllabic, although there is a considerable number of disyllables in Southwestern Dai, in the shape of borrowed words from Sanskrit and probably some Austro-Asiatic languages. All are tonal. The feature which distinguishes them most noticeably from the Tibeto-Burman group is that all have free word order. This means that verbs precede their objects, and adverbs (in the case of Southwestern Dai) follow verbs, the direct converse of Tibeto-Burman.

A special feature of Dai which distinguishes it from other free word order groups is that there is a rule that all modifying elements follow the modified; this means that adjectives follow nouns, as do possessives, and adverbs follow verbs. For example, in Zhuang (Northern Dai):

paŋ dam (cloth black) = 'black cloth'

ran te (house he) = 'his house'.

The linguistic division between the Northern Dai and the Southwestern Dai (which is enough to make them mutually unintelligible) is reflected in their cultures. The Northern Dai, albeit in relatively recent times, have become almost identical in culture, dress and type of dwelling to the Han Chinese among whom they live. The Southwestern Dai, on the other hand, are very much a part of Southeast Asian culture. Their religion is Theravada Buddhism, their dress is almost identical to that found in Laos and Thailand, both men and women wearing a sarong-like garment, and, finally, their houses are built on top of high pilings, and not flat on the ground as among the Northern Dai.

Miao-Yao

Linguistically this stock divides into the two branches, Miao and Yao, but the differences between them are difficult to make generalizations about because of the great diversity found in Miao. All have been subject to Chinese influence, the Miao apparently in the recent past, the Yao more continuously and over a much longer period of time. This has influenced not only their vocabulary, but also to some extent their grammatical structure. Here discussion will be limited to a form of Miao often known as Green Miao, widely spoken in Guizhou and Yunnan Provinces, which appears to have been entirely uninfluenced by Han Chinese except in recent vocabulary loans, and may well represent a type of Miao once more widespread.

Miao girls from Guizhou Province.

The surprising result is that with one exception, the generalizations made for Dai apply to Miao. The Miao languages too have free word order, particularly Green Miao, all modifying elements following the modified:

ntəu kləy (cloth black) 'black cloth'.

The exception, and this feature is found in all the Miao-Yao languages, is that the possessive precedes:

ny lu tʃe (he 'classifier' house) 'his house'.

This coincidence with the Dai pattern must be regarded as fortuitous, as there is little evidence to suggest sufficient contact to have existed between the two groups for them to have exerted influence on one another.

The reason Green Miao was chosen to exemplify the Miao-Yao stock is because wherever forms of other Miao dialects, or Yao, are found to differ from Green Miao, the difference is always one in the direction of Chinese. This is most obvious in the case of Yao, where, in addition to many syntactical features clearly identical to those of Han Chinese, there are many words of Han origin which, on phonological grounds, can be shown to be of relatively ancient date.

The ways of life of the various groups of people speaking Miao-Yao languages vary greatly, as they are found in six Chinese provinces and over the borders into Vietnam, Laos and Thailand. One enduring similarity among these groups is that the majority live high on the mountain slopes, with only a few in the valleys. In China some of the villages have evidently remained in one place for a long period, but recently-established villages are to be found everywhere. The reason for this is that the prime type of agriculture carried out by these people is dry-rice farming or the growing of maize. Without fertilizer the fields quickly deteriorate, and new fields have to be found. Eventually this results in the necessity of moving the village to be sufficiently near their lands. This slow-motion nomadism is almost certainly the reason for the present wide geographical spread of the Miao and Yao peoples.

Malayo-Polynesian

Malayo-Polynesian languages are found in China only in Taiwan. They are known in Chinese as the *Gaoshan*, 'high mountain' nationality. Although now living in the mountainous areas of the east, they at one time inhabited the plains of the western part of Taiwan until the advent of the Han Chinese, after which they were either pushed out of the good agricultural land of the west by the Chinese, or were assimilated. There is a fairly large number of mutually unintelligible languages in this group, with corresponding cultural differences. These languages constitute the northernmost extension of the Malayo-Polynesian language stock, and are apparently most closely related to some of the Philippine languages.   *G.B.D.*

Scripts of the non-Han Chinese

The majority of the non-Han peoples of China have not had writing systems in their traditional cultures. However, because of culture-contact they were in some cases familiar with the notion of writing, and consequently came to employ a neighbouring language, using its script as their own written language. This happened with the Yao, who wrote their poems and hymns in a slightly modified form of Han Chinese; the Tajiks, with an Indo-European language, write in Uighur, an Altaic language. There have been other non-Han scripts in China, but only those in current use are illustrated.

Scripts such as Yi, Naxi and Zhuang (Northern Dai) which were used for only limited purposes such as prayers and songs, appear to be quickly dying out. The remainder are flourishing.

Korean is written with a combination of Han characters, used only for the many loan-words from Han Chinese in Korean, and an alphabet for the native element in the vocabulary. The alphabet was invented in the 15th century; each square block represents a syllable.

Mongol script is an adaptation of an early Uighur script, ultimately derived from Aramaic. It is written downwards, perhaps in imitation of Chinese. This script, with slight modifications, was also used by the Man (Manchu).

Uighur is a slightly modified form of the Arabic script. Their earlier script was ousted by this at the time of the conversion to Islam.

Tibetan is an adaptation of a north Indian script. It dates from the 8th century.

Yi is an indigenous script, each letter representing a syllable. It is obsolescent.

Naxi, an indigenous script apparently unrelated to any other, is an imperfect script, in that only the principal words are written. It is perhaps obsolete.

Southwestern Dai is almost identical to the scripts of northern Thailand, that of the Shans, and ultimately Burmese and Mon.

Northern Dai is based on Chinese, the characters being formed largely on Chinese principles; that is, as combinations of signific and phonetic.

Developments in the People's Republic of China

Before 1949 the Han language had already made a deep impression on many of the nationalities' languages, especially in south China. This was in spite of official dislike of too close contacts between the Han and others, and in some cases repression. Since 1949, although there have been changes in attitudes towards the national minorities in general, the general trend has been towards closer contact. Schools have been set up in all the national minority areas, and the teaching of the Han language has been positively encouraged. This is of course necessary if the nationalities' younger generation are to proceed to middle school and university. The widespread knowledge of Han Chinese will inevitably affect the other languages to an extent hitherto unknown. This, too, is encouraged as a progressive feature in the evolution of national minority languages.

On the other hand, again at various times since 1949 with varying emphases, the use of the national minority languages, especially the more widely spoken ones, has been encouraged. This has been done in several ways. There has been acknowledgement that the use of the native language in primary schools is necessary. Again, encouragement has been given to the use of existing viable scripts, especially clear in the case of Mongol, Uighur and Tibetan, for which dictionaries have been compiled, and which appear in newspapers, periodicals and some books. Another sign of this encouragement is evident in the creation of romanized scripts for some of the languages, such as Zhuang, Bouyei and Lisu, in which form some books and periodicals have appeared. Finally, there is the negative aspect of encouragement seen in not repressing or discouraging the use of the native languages in private. These two directions of official policy—on the one hand encouraging the learning of Han Chinese and increasing the influence of Han Chinese on the nationalities' languages, on the other hand, encouraging the continued use of the nationalities' languages—have the result of satisfying the nationalistic feelings of the national minorities, and at the same time helping them in the gradual process of linguistic assimilation.

The linguistic situation may serve as a general model of current policies towards the various nationalities. There has been very little attempt, especially since the end of the Cultural Revolution, to impose assimilation: instead assimilation is to be achieved through the gradual implementation of certain policies sponsored and encouraged by the Communist government. For example, Han Chinese are sent into all the areas occupied by national minorities, and native cadres are sent for training and education to the Han areas. New networks of roads connect the nationalities with the rest of China, with the result that contacts are increased, gradually leading to changes in customs, dress and indeed all aspects of life. That the changes are one-sided is due partly to the manifest mate-

An example of Naxi script.

An example of Yi script.

rial and technological superiority of the Han, and some are due to the effect of deliberate policies of the government: for example the change from nomadism in the north, and shifting agriculture in the south, to settled agriculture and a permanent village or town life, is not accompanied by any change in the Han way of life. The result is that the nationalities lead a way of life more akin to that of the Han. As with language, although coercion is rarely used, the ultimate aim appears to be a high degree of assimilation.

Nevertheless, since the Revolution of 1949 a large number of autonomous areas have been established in China, where the nationalities have a certain amount of autonomy in local affairs. The majority of these areas are autonomous counties (*xian*), but several larger areas have also been set aside as autonomous, such as the Xinjiang Uighur Autonomous Region, which includes the whole of the former Xinjiang Province; the Inner Mongolian Autonomous Region, which has replaced most of three former provinces in northern China; and the Guangxi Zhuang Autonomous Region, formerly the province of Guangxi. The establishment of the areas has taken place at various times; in 1950 Tibet was designated an Autonomous Region. *G.B.D.*

EXTERNAL CHINA

Historical perspective

The image of people from China spilling over China's borders into neighbouring territories is an old one. It originated principally from the fact that China's land borders were never firmly defined and, therefore, whenever these borders were pushed back, large numbers of Han Chinese were often left outside the China of the time. For these Chinese, there were at least three options. They could move to (or return to) China within its new borders. They could also choose to be assimilated by their new rulers, or they could stay on where they were and hope that China would expand in their direction again at some later date.

Examples of the first option of moving back were found from the earliest times in the north and northwest, along both sides of the Great Wall, but they have not been significant since the Qing empire expanded China's northern and western boundaries dramatically during the 17th and 18th centuries. The second option of assimilation was chosen usually when the Chinese settled down, but such assimilation was on a small scale and usually where there were opportunities for some upward social mobility. The best-

known example was that of Annam (Vietnam), especially before its independence in the 10th century, but there were numerous other examples, both overland and overseas, in East and Southeast Asia, notably in Korea and later in Thailand, Burma and the Philippines. As for the third option of waiting for Chinese power to return, this occurred only along China's land borders. One excellent example was the Chinese pale in the lower Liao valley in southern Manchuria. Another was the chain of Chinese settlements along the Gansu corridor leading into modern Xinjiang.

None of the examples above may be described as 'external China', but they are closely related to the phenomenon of migrant Chinese as a spillover of China's vast population and as a factor in Chinese expansion. The process had begun with the southwards movement of the Chinese during the Han dynasty. Historically, the most striking examples were the early settlements of Fujian Province, to be followed much later by the colonization of Taiwan and the sinicization of Yunnan and Guizhou, since both were gradual developments which have given rise to much speculation on how much further south China may expand.

The complex modern concept of the migrant Chinese is embodied in the term *huaqiao*, normally rendered as 'overseas Chinese' but more accurately translated as 'Chinese sojourner'. The term emerged at the beginning of the 20th century with a strong political bias. It referred to sojourners who cared enough for China to involve themselves in China's politics as well as to colonists who had the right to receive China's protection. This would have been harmless enough but for the fact that the numbers of such *huaqiao* in Southeast Asia alone had grown to over three million by 1900 and that most of them had cultivated an economic and educational advantage over the majority of the indigenous peoples of the region.

Whether the *huaqiao* were sojourners, colonists, settlers or merely refugees from a poor and chaotic China has been the subject of much debate. Whether it is still appropriate to call them all *huaqiao* is even more controversial. But that those who are recognizably Chinese are numerous and that most of them live in communities make it possible still to speak of 'external China', of 'little Chinas' or 'Chinatowns'.

There is more than one kind of 'external China'. Hong Kong and Macao stand alone, undeniably Chinese yet outside China. The Chinese communities in Southeast Asia are distinct again although there is considerable variation in each of the countries. For the rest, mainly in the larger cities of East Asia, the Americas, Oceania and Western Europe where the Chinese form well under 1 per cent of the population, a distinction may be made between those communities that are large enough to live in their 'Chinatowns' and those that are not. Only in small former colonies like Mauritius and Surinam and the territory of French Polynesia are there Chinese populations significantly more than 1 per cent of the total population.

There have also been several layers of Chinese settlement in modern times. From the 16th to the 18th century, with the exception of some notable political refugees escaping to Japan and Vietnam, traders and artisans formed the bulk of the Chinese communities overseas. Their numbers were small; they intermarried and their descendants assimilated easily except in areas under Dutch control. In the 19th century came the unskilled labourers, the 'coolies', and their numbers transformed the demographic picture in the British, Dutch and French colonies and in parts of Thailand. Since the 1920s significant numbers of well-educated Chinese teachers, journalists and political refugees have been added to the steady stream of traders and artisans who still form the backbone of all overseas Chinese communities everywhere.

W.G.

Hong Kong and Macao

Hong Kong and Macao are historical anomalies, residual European colonies on Chinese soil. A paradox has allowed the anomaly to survive: they are 'external' because they are immensely useful to China. Yet they are quite different. Hong Kong is invaluable, both to China and the East and Southeast Asian regions. Macao is necessary primarily because China does not want to change the *status quo* where Hong Kong is concerned.

Hong Kong has over five and a half million Chinese, the largest number of Chinese directly under foreign rule anywhere in the world, but the rule is not entirely foreign. The unique symbiotic relationship between British colonial officials and local Hong Kong Chinese has been stable and successful mainly because the Chinese government in Beijing needs it to be so. In some ways the British governor of Hong Kong may be seen by China as an officer performing a role comparable to that of the mayors of Shanghai and Tianjin.

But the difference is vital. Hong Kong is the nearest thing to a *laissez-faire* city-state there is, and its value to the planned economy of China lies in its continuing to be so in two of the fastest growing regions in the world. As a trading port and a financial centre, and as a training-ground for tertiary skills, Hong Kong is essential to China's modernization plans. As a centre of light industry, it has a remarkable record and may still be useful to China. As a haven for capital and for people, it is less predictable and arouses the suspicions of some of its neighbours, but this unique role is greatly appreciated among the other communities of 'external China', whether they be in Asia, America, Europe or Oceania. And, not least, the protection of property and personal freedom afforded by the British legal system has helped to minimize the negative image of colonialism for the peoples of Hong Kong.

The rapid growth of population since 1945 has greatly increased the responsibilities of the Hong Kong government, firstly in economic management, public works, law and order, and transport; then in housing and health; and then in education, welfare and the environment. Since the mid-1970s large-scale planning for new towns in the New Territories has changed the role of the government quite remarkably. The three new towns of Tsuen Wan, Tuen Mun and Sha Tin have dramatically demonstrated the flexibility and dynamism of the Sino-British partnership at a level hitherto unknown in history.

All the same, Hong Kong's efforts to live down the background of vulnerability have not brought the territory out of uncertainty. As the population rises, the margin for error has grown smaller and the possibility for tragedy and disaster for the well-established residents is still there, despite the agreement reached after detailed negotiations between China and Britain that when the lease of the New Territories runs out in 1997 all of Hong Kong will revert to China.

Two years of Sino-British talks in 1982–4 led to a formal agreement, the Joint Declaration of 1984, a comprehensive document that has been recognized as a treaty between Britain and China by the United Nations. According to the Joint Declaration a Joint Liaison Group formed by representatives of the two countries meets regularly to monitor developments until 1 January 2000. In the meantime, China established a drafting committee and a local consultative committee to produce a Basic Law which was approved in 1990, to determine the nature and structure of the Hong Kong government after it becomes a Special Administrative Region in 1997. These steps have been followed closely to enable similar arrangements to be applied to Macao two years later, in 1999.

Since the crackdown on the pro-democracy movement in Beijing on 4 June 1989, changes in policy in China have greatly increased the sense of insecurity of most Hong Kong people. Two scenarios have caught the attention of the world. The first is that most Hong Kong Chinese would try to leave to join the Chinese communities overseas and that this could spell doom for Hong Kong's future. The other is that Hong Kong's strong international position and the pull of business and profit would sooner or later overcome the fears of the people and thus restore prosperity to Hong Kong. It is generally agreed that much will depend on political conditions in China.

Even if China succeeds in continuing its open-door economic policies, the increasing dependence on China has wider regional implications. Hong Kong is a pivot between East and Southeast Asia and a link to the world beyond, a fact that was demonstrated by the controversial influx, the second in a decade, of thousands of Vietnamese refugees during 1989. China, however, can deal directly with Japan and at least North Korea, and would tend to see Hong Kong as a door to Southeast Asia. Hong Kong is likely to continue to be a key point of contact between China and various countries in Southeast Asia. And the more important the littoral states of the South China Sea become to China, the more important Hong Kong will be. In addition, if long-developed personal ties between people in Hong Kong and China and between them and those in Southeast Asia become more significant, Hong Kong's role in China's long-term relations with the region may well become indispensable. The ties Hong Kong has with some of the Chinese communities there are certainly important.   *W.G.*

The Chinese overseas today

The Chinese living outside China today are not the result of any expansionist design on the part of China. On the contrary, the vast majority of them left China because foreign invasions, civil war, political disorder and intractable economic problems made living in, or returning to, China unattractive if not impossible. The most important single factor that drew the bulk of the Chinese out of China during the 19th century was the expansion of the West into Asia, the Americas and Oceania. It was an expansion that created economic opportunities on a scale the Chinese had never experienced before.

The European entrepreneurs' demand for labour was enormous for nearly a century. When the Chinese numbers grew so large that immigration came to an end, first in Oceania and the Americas and by the 1930s in Asia, the number of Chinese overseas had risen to nearly 10 million. They were numerous enough to have become a source of alarm, especially to indigenous nationalists in the colonial territories of Southeast Asia who had begun to seek to protect the rights of their peoples. Thus it is in Southeast Asia, among China's closest neighbours, that the 'overseas Chinese' have become a major political problem for both the newly independent countries and for China. This is a problem which was compounded by the competition between the People's Republic of China and the Republic of China in Taiwan for overseas Chinese loyalties. In addition, while most Chinese settlers in the region now value their citizenship in their chosen new homes, their loyalty to these new nations is not always understood or appreciated.

Indeed, since the 1950s it has become increasingly difficult to be sure who is Chinese outside China and how many such Chinese there really are in each country. Some countries simply do not register the ethnic origins of their citizens, only of resident aliens; others try but are perplexed by those who are only part-Chinese, and make arbitrary decisions as to who are still Chinese and who have been fully assimilated into local society; few are as painstaking as Singapore and Malaysia about ethnicity. It is necessary to be very careful when speaking about the number of 'Chinese' overseas: do we mean that only those who are still nationals of China or Taiwan are the true *huaqiao*? Do we also count those who are 'stateless'? Do we adopt the principle of 'once a Chinese, always a Chinese' and try to count everyone who has one or both Chinese parents?

The table includes two kinds of counting. Only those countries in which the Chinese population is significant, either because it is large or because it is relatively successful and articulate, have been included. In most cases, the figures are rough estimates based on a variety of official and unofficial sources; they provide some idea of the dimensions of 'the Chinese problem' for some countries.

The map shows the main areas in south China from where over 90 per cent of the Chinese abroad originate. Outside the continent of Asia, the majority of Chinese are either Cantonese or Hakka. Hakka communities are few, but they are very strong in French Polynesia and Mauritius. Since 1949 North America has also attracted more diverse groups of Chinese from Taiwan and central and north China, but they are still in the minority.

The vast majority of Chinese in Southeast Asia and India come from southern China. The most notable dialect group concentrations are Hokkiens in the Philippines and Indonesia, Teochiu in Thailand and Cantonese in Vietnam. The Chinese in Malaysia and Singapore are of the most varied origins with no single dominating group. In South Korea large numbers had come from Shandong in north China, while in Japan those from Taiwan outnumber those from other provinces.

There are small communities of Chinese Muslims recorded for Saudi Arabia and Turkey. Other notable small communities are those in Réunion Island, Madagascar (Malagasy Republic) and South Africa, and in New Zealand and Papua New Guinea. There have been sizeable groups of Chinese in Cuba and Mexico, and the tiny communities in various Latin American states, notably Brazil, are now growing, as are those in Western Europe.

The rates at which the Chinese have assimilated have varied considerably. They have been rapid in Latin America and steady in some parts of Asia where they have been settling down for centuries. In other parts of Asia, however, the Chinese are numerous and relatively recent, and assimilation is minimal. In Canada, the USA and Australia there have been new influxes to revive the Chinatowns in the large cities—it will be decades before the fates of these newcomers will be known.

THE CHINESE OVERSEAS

Location	Ethnic Chinese citizens	Chinese aliens and 'stateless'	Undifferentiated
ASIA			
Southeast Asia			
Vietnam	1 400 000 (1977)	*	
Laos			25 000 (1962)
Cambodia			350 000 (1962)
Burma			400 000 (1973)
Thailand	5 600 000 (1970)	200 000 (1975)	
Malaysia	4 000 000 (1980)	*	
Singapore	2 000 000 (1982)	*	
Indonesia			3 500 000 (1986)
Philippines	1–2 000 000		
Brunei			42 500 (1977)
Elsewhere			
Korea, South			20 000 (1977)
Japan			50 000 (1962)
India			50 000 (1963)
AMERICAS			
Canada			300 000 (1980)
USA			800 000 (1980)
Jamaica	10 000 (1970)	*	
Trinidad	9 000 (1970)	*	
Guyana	4 000 (1970)	*	
Surinam			6 000 (1970)
Peru	30 000 (1959)		
OCEANIA			
Fiji			4 000 (1971)
French Polynesia	12 000 (1971)		
Australia			150 000 (1985)
AFRICA			
Mauritius			25 000 (1970)

* Not available

From the above survey it is not apparent why 'external China' should refer only to Chinese/Taiwan nationals, and those who are 'stateless', or why it should include ethnic Chinese who are citizens of dozens of different countries. The strict definition of *hua-qiao* requires that only Chinese nationals be counted and the People's Republic of China has officially kept to this definition. In this way 'external China' outside Hong Kong and Macao should refer primarily to the areas in Japan, Canada, the USA, Australia, even Great Britain, to which Chinese from China, Taiwan, Hong Kong and Macao have been migrating during the past three decades.

The narrowly legal approach, however, fails to explain the fact that Southeast Asian countries with large numbers of their own citizens of Chinese descent are obviously uneasy about China's 'overseas Chinese' policy and China's proximity, and about the loyalty of some of their own citizens. This is a problem peculiar to the region and it is the most difficult aspect of any attempt to understand the idea of 'external China'. It therefore needs separate treatment.

Mainland Southeast Asia (excluding west Malaysia)

Three of the five countries on the mainland, Vietnam, Laos and Burma, border on China and have known Chinese traders and settlers for centuries. The Chinese had come mainly overland and in small numbers until the middle of the 19th century, and most of them had long merged into the local populations. Since then, however, large numbers have arrived by sea to the southern parts of each of the countries. In the case of Laos, most of the newcomers were Cantonese and had come via Vietnam and Thailand, whereas for Burma they included Hokkiens who had come via the British Straits Settlements on the Malay peninsula. In Vietnam, especially Cochin-China in the south, the Chinese had gone directly and maintained close links with their homes in Guangdong Province and in Hong Kong.

The other two countries, Thailand and Cambodia (Kampuchea), also had large influxes of Chinese during the 19th century. Thailand received the most Chinese, almost entirely by sea, and also served as a conduit for some to reach Laos, western Cambodia, Burma and the various states of the Malay peninsula. Cambodia's Chinese had also come from China by sea, but most of them had been through Cochin-China and Thailand and maintained their trading contacts with the Chinese communities there. Thus, except for Burma, the two major points on the mainland of entry, trade and settlement were Saigon-Cholon in Vietnam and Bangkok in Thailand, and the various other communities in the four countries looked for models to the two cities.

It is, therefore, important to compare the policies adopted at the two centres and the ramifications of such policies. In Saigon-Cholon, the French colonial government had applied a policy of establishing *congregations* for the Chinese that emphasized the autonomy and separateness of the Chinese. This meant that instead of assimilating fairly quickly to a common Vietnamese identity, as might have been expected of peoples who shared many cultural and historical experiences, the Chinese tended to remain distinct and somewhat alien. In Bangkok, however, the traditional assimilationist policies, which also permitted upward social mobility for the Thai-ized Chinese, were continued even when the numbers of new immigrants grew rapidly. With the larger numbers, the policy underwent severe trials and was not always successful. But it seems clear now that intermarriage and a strong

PRINCIPAL PLACES OF ORIGIN IN CHINA

CHAOZHOU, KEJIA AND FUJIAN EMIGRANT AREAS

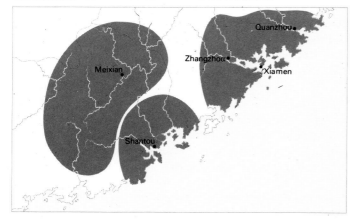

CANTONESE EMIGRANT AREA

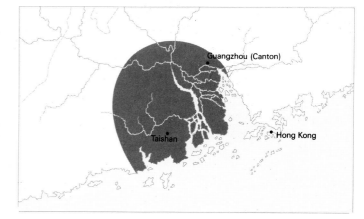

KEY

Dialect groups

Fujian (Hokkien)	Chaozhou (Teochiu)	Fuzhou
Cantonese	Hainanese	Fuqing
Kejia (Hakka)	Guangxi	Xinghua

language and religious policy have gone a long way towards ensuring the loyalty of the Sino-Thai to the Thai polity.

The contrast between the two centres has been greatly heightened by the communist victories in the three former French Indo-China states since 1975. There has been the destruction of the

Chinese communities in Cambodia. Also, the consequences of anti-China policies in Vietnam and Laos have been most severe on the remnants of the Chinese population (mostly of Vietnamese nationality) and have not spared even the highly assimilated Sino-Vietnamese in the north. This has underlined the importance of political relations with China as the major determinant even for the future of largely assimilated peoples of Chinese descent in the region.

The situation in Burma is different but seems to support the idea that continued good relations with China have made a great difference to the lives of Sino-Burmese and those of Chinese descent who have made Burma their home. Except for a brief period during the Cultural Revolution, those who are still identifiably Chinese have lived quietly and securely in the country. There have been neither the opportunities for wealth, as in Thailand, nor the pressures for re-education and relocation, as in Vietnam. Over the past three decades, a whole generation of people of Chinese descent seems to have settled down to the Burmese way of life without fear or bitterness. Everything so far suggests that Burma is unique in its special historical relation with China, but the possibility that the descendants of Chinese immigrants elsewhere in the region may ultimately evolve in similar ways cannot be ruled out.

Philippines

Chinese trading relations with most of the islands of the Philippines became important about 500 years ago, but the main settlements were in northern and central Luzon. After the Spanish conquest major communities grew up around Manila Bay and the larger Visayan Islands. By the early 19th century considerable intermarriage had taken place between Chinese men and local women and these communities grew up around rich and influential mestizo families. Most of the descendants of Chinese were Catholic and many were the patrons of later arrivals from China. But eventually they identified themselves solely with the Philippines and became an integral part of the Filipino elite.

New arrivals late in the 19th century and the first half of the 20th century encountered far greater difficulty in assimilating. There was the rise of nationalism in China at the turn of the century, and the American colonial regime imposed tough nationality laws, which were not relaxed for the Chinese until 1975, on the eve of Filipino diplomatic relations with China. And, during the period 1949–75 close relations with anti-communist Taiwan, also under American protection, made it easy for the Philippines government to leave the elaborate laws unchanged. Since 1975, however, the majority of the remaining Chinese aliens have been allowed to take Filipino nationality.

With hardly any Chinese nationals left, it would be anachronistic to speak of a Chinese problem in the Philippines or to include the ethnic Chinese there under 'external China'. The question of Chinese dominance in the Filipino economy, which has long been untrue, may soon be removed from the textbooks. All the same, historical perceptions die hard, the country's political and economic growth remains volatile, and the proximity of China and Taiwan all permit the issue of Chinese to stay alive. The older Chinese problem may become a new China problem in the future. It would be premature to suggest that the Philippines has moved away from the 'external China' orbit.

Malaysia and Brunei

Chinese traders have been regularly visiting the Malay peninsula and the north coast of Borneo for at least 500 years. The only notable settlement before modern times, however, was at Malacca. The experience of the Chinese there suggests in part the reasons why the Chinese in west Malaysia are somewhat different from elsewhere in the region. They have lived through a Malay sultanate, Portuguese and then Dutch rule, followed by British adventurism and empire and then back full circle to a modern federation of Malay sultanates. Although the Chinese population increased rapidly in the 19th century throughout the country, a sizeable proportion of the community leaders (including those in Singapore) had always come from the descendants of those with a long historical connection with the country. Thus the rise in Chinese, and then Malay, nationalism in the 20th century have both been handled with remarkable flexibility by the locally settled Chinese.

There have been relatively few intermarriages, and total assimilation to the Malay population seems unlikely because the Chinese constitute more than 35 per cent of the total population, but Chinese political loyalty to Malaysia has been achieved to some extent among the younger generation. Relations with China since 1975 have been cautious but friendly. It does seem to be in the long-term interest of both countries, and especially of those Malaysians of Chinese descent, for the relations to remain that way.

Two myths have survived to continue to endanger communal trust between Malays and Chinese: that of the wealthy Chinese and that of the lazy Malays. They have bedevilled the economic and educational developments of the country since independence in 1957. The wealthy Chinese myth has led to economic policies which appear blatantly discriminatory to the Chinese and seem to ignore the fact that the majority of Chinese are poor. The lazy Malay myth has coloured Chinese explanations of Malay failures in both education and commerce and made the Chinese discontented with the highly protectionist New Economic Policy of the government.

Communal tensions have long been present in the country and are probably unavoidable. Dire consequences have been predicted for the country since its inception, and indeed the communal riots of May 1969 were very dangerous, but there is still a strong capacity for compromise among the political leaders. If the tensions remain manageable they could even be turned to good effect to stimulate innovation and economic growth.

Brunei nearly became part of Malaysia in 1965. The percentage of its Chinese population is similar to that in Malaysia and, whether Brunei joins Malaysia or not, relations between Malays and Chinese there may have to be dealt with in similar ways.

Singapore

The history of Singapore has been inseparable from that of Malaysia, but its large Chinese population (about three-quarters of its total) has separated it politically since 1965. It continues to live in the shadow of two anachronistic features: as the former keystone of British power in Malaya and northern Borneo, and as the place continuously addressed as 'Singapore, China' and referred to as 'the third China'.

Since its independence, however, under its brilliant entrepreneurs and political leaders, the Republic of Singapore has not only survived the suspicions and jealousy of its neighbours but also won general admiration for skilful management and economic success. All the same, it remains in a delicate position between Indonesia and Malaysia, and must always be extraordinarily careful in its relations with China. It may never be able to escape the contradictory image of being the excellent example of Chinese organization and industry which would help modernize the region rapidly and, at the same time, also the reminder of the cultural and technological gap between Chinese and Malays which has long alarmed Singapore's neighbours.

Indonesia

China's relations with the ancient kingdoms of Java and Sumatra go back over a thousand years and the earliest Chinese Buddhist pilgrims to visit these islands did so 1500 years ago. After that, there were several layers of Chinese migration and settlement, including Chinese Muslims who played a role in Islamizing Java, soldiers left behind after the Mongol invasion of Java, and adventurers and traders who had been active in the declining Sri Vijayan empire of Sumatra. The process of assimilation, however, seems to have halted during the period of Dutch supremacy after 1600, especially along the north coast of Java. The Chinese population has since then been greatly enlarged by the labour migrations of the 19th and 20th centuries, and both Chinese nationalism and the new Indonesian nationalism have contributed towards a complicated 'Chinese problem'.

The most distinctive development in Indonesia was the large community of local-born (peranakan), who were partially assimilated but still identifiably Chinese. Most of them were Dutch-educated, spoke Indonesian and retained some elements of Chinese cultural and religious practices. Eventually, after 1945, most of them were reconciled to the Indonesian revolution and sought a special place as a native suku (tribe, people) in the country. But their political activities alienated many Indonesian leaders, especially the ambivalent position some peranakan took towards China. Also disastrous were the series of citizenship agreements with China that brought great confusion to them. Even more painful was the effect of these agreements on the China-born Chinese (totok) and their families. New questions arose concerning their loyalty to Communist China or Taiwan. The whole matter reached a climax when the 1965 coup destroyed all the Chinese-based organizations in the country. But the suspension of diplomatic relations with China did cool down this very sensitive issue and gradually new arrangements have been made to integrate most of the Chinese population before renewing diplomatic relations with China in 1990.

Although the distinction between totok and peranakan is less important and that between citizen and 'stateless' is now more significant, the most interesting feature of the Chinese communities in Indonesia is that of variety. The peranakan of Java are quite different from those of central and north Sumatra, and both these are different again from the local-born of west Kalimantan (western Borneo) and the Riau-Lingga archipelago close to Singapore. There are also distinctive communities in Makasar (Sulawesi), Bali, the Moluccas and Timor. It is therefore still misleading to speak of Indonesian Chinese as having a single common identity. The trend, however, is clear. Determined efforts to integrate most of the Chinese will do two things: on the one hand, draw the Chinese into the larger Indonesian nationality with indistinguishable Indonesian names and, on the other, push various Chinese groups to assimilate into the indigenous suku among whom they live.

There is also considerable variety in Chinese religious practices which seems to cut across local and regional boundaries. In conformity with government policy, all Chinese have declared their religious affiliations: traditional Chinese religion, either as Tri Dharma or an archaic Confucianism, Buddhism, Hinduism, Islam, as well as Christianity, both Protestantism and Catholicism. That this may lead to a fragmentation of the Chinese may assist their eventual integration into a secular Indonesia which encourages many different faiths.

W.G.

SOCIETY

Urban life: Shanghai's Nanjing Road.

THE SOCIAL ORDER

The individual, family and community

Chinese society under its dominant Confucian ethic long exalted the family, pressing for the proper conduct of relationships and elaborate rituals. Today under communist leadership, Chinese still recognizN the centrality of the family, although in modified form. Individualism may be an even weaker force than in other non-modernized societies, since it is rejected by both sides in the tension between families and state-supported collectives.

Although the socialist transformation, the commune system and the Cultural Revolution had reduced the family's economic functions and its role in promoting social mobility, revival of the family farm and small-scale private enterprises in the 1980s again highlighted family entrepreneurship. Individualism, which has been restricted both by traditional family demands and by state-organized collectives, continues to find little room for development. Nevertheless, as modernization accelerated in the 1980s and it became easier for Chinese to migrate and to pursue careers, the scope for individualism began to widen.

The importance given to the family helps account for a heritage of less community solidarity than in other pre-modern countries such as 17th-century Japan or Russia. To redirect loyalties, China's recent leaders created channels of mobility less subject to family control and reorganized communities to make them more responsive to outside pressures. Yet, in the rural areas, at least, communist policies suffered setbacks when they directly challenged family-centred forces. In the 1980s community power waned, as families vigorously pursued their own interests.

The traditional Chinese family, or *Jia*, ideally consisted of a father and a mother, all their sons, their unmarried daughters, their sons' wives and children, and so forth for as many generations as possible. A large, extended family was preferred, but, under conditions of high mortality and increasing pressure on available land resources, the mean household size fluctuated between 5.0 and 5.5, comparable with other pre-modern societies. When two or more sons survived to adulthood, internal family strife or finally the death of their father led to a division of property, if possible according to the accepted principle of equal inheritance among sons. The recently separated families would each begin a new family unit, striving to multiply their male offspring and to expand their property and prestige. Facing both the lineage and the outside world, the Chinese family was typically a tightly-knit unit under the unchallenged authority of its head—normally the eldest male of the eldest generation.

Historically, there were few countervailing forces to limit the role of the family. Successive dynastic legal codes reinforced family loyalties, assessing guilt and prescribing punishment according to the degree to which approved family obligations were not met, and recognizing service to one's family as a mitigating factor in crimes against outsiders. To protect officials in the bureaucracy from the temptation to place family or lineage interests above state concerns, the rule of avoidance required that appointments be at a distance from one's home administration. Imperial policies and local customary practices were based on a spirit of familism, not on a struggle to assert other priorities and not on inherited loyalties between subordinates and superiors.

Longer than other peoples—for approximately 2000 years—ordinary Chinese possessed surnames, a badge of family dignity and lineage identity. The Chinese language has a highly differentiated kinship terminology, distinguishing a greater variety of relationships than are found in other languages. The long standing tradition of private and alienable land, the prevalence of household units of production, and the widespread diffusion of aspirations for social mobility created an environment in which family solidarity could flourish.

In this context, the individual and the community each had a limited place. Normally an individual did not strike out on his own nor a community band together in such a way as to restrict family prerogatives. However, in times of dire emergency, such as banditry or war, individuals might have to fend for themselves and communities might become closed, walled and armed for self protection. Such occasions did not lead to a permanent readjustment in the ideal balance. With few exceptions, the individual's status was determined by generation, sex and age, in that order, within the family, and by the family's status. In most areas there were few organizations or activities that might offer a basis for community solidarity. The much prized acquisition of individual skills such as a high level of educational achievement or of artistic expression represented a form of family service; it did not lead to an assertion of individual rights or romantic ideals. Even during the early stages of China's modern transformation, apart from new currents within the limited urban sector, the family remained the dominant force in this triad of individual, family and community.

After 1949 the Chinese Communists took an active interest in changing this balance. The Marriage Law of 1950, coupled with the recurrent activation of small groups for political study and criticism, encouraged the individual to develop a separate identity from the family. Modernizing forces including employment opportunities beyond the household, education in community schools and migration to cities reduced family influence. Moreover, the collectivization of land as well as the diminished role of household wealth for a time undermined the family's dominance. Nevertheless, small groups had less influence than once assumed; very low divorce rates and other continuities with past practices suggest the Marriage Law had limited impact, and the majority of households still operate as units of production, earlier on private plots and lately on leased land. The eclipse of family functions in the Great Leap Forward quickly gave way to an accommodation that in many ways reinforced family solidarity, for example, through the payment of wages from the collective sector directly to the household head and through the increased importance of grandparents to child-rearing where mothers work. Restrictions on rural-urban migration and on job turnover supported a stationary family existence in which all were aware of their long-term dependence on household resources. Even in many matters encouraged by Communist ideology, such as cremation instead of traditional burial practices, rural families largely retained earlier customs or revived them in the 1980s.

As societies develop there is customarily a rise in individual decision-making—although often not a *laissez-faire* kind of individualism—and a decline in community. Communist leadership in China made some effort to reverse these effects. By transferring functions from the family to the community (the production team or the neighbourhood committee) and by denouncing the negative aspects of individualism (a 'bourgeois' phenomenon), the Chinese Communist Party sought to promote the socialist ideal of collectivity. Recently village corporate solidarity has declined, but informal associations based on the need for personal connections and sponsorship are still needed to overcome bureaucratic inertia.   *G.R.*

The work unit

Amplifying the functions of the socialist enterprise of the Soviet Union and the paternalist enterprise of East Asia, China has created the *'danwei'* or work unit with wide-ranging control over its members. Not only does it have an important role in meeting material needs from the allocation of housing to the distribution of ration quotas, it also plays a role in many life-course decision such as granting permission for marriage or divorce and evaluating political reliability. In the decentralized conditions of the Cultural Revolution, the *danwei* was strengthened as a fortress to cope with a siege of economic and political uncertainties. In the halcyon days of market experiments in the 1980s, the *danwei* lost some of its functions but remained for the conservative leadership a reassuring stronghold of genuine socialism and social control. This is the unit

that must somehow be made an efficient motivator of labour productivity if the Chinese Communists are to succeed in the 1990s in reversing the tide of private entrepreneurship that threatens to bring convergence with other modernized societies.   *G.R.*

Hierarchy, authority and lineage

Both in pre-modern times and in the communist era Chinese have professed a remarkably egalitarian ethic. Although they have acknowledged the leadership of an elite, its justification rests on dedicated preparation and individual performance rather than on privileged birth or material standing. In each period there have been exceptional limitations on the direct conversion of wealth into positions of high authority. Much conversion has been in a reverse direction; state recognition of achievement has opened the

Lingyin Temple, Hangzhou. The temple in China, traditionally the centre of lineage activities, is nowadays used for state or community organizations.

way to local power and influence. Designated from above, the officially approved elite has interacted with other local figures who are backed solely by the resources of their communities, often by organizations somewhat suspect in the eyes of the state. Until the Communist-led land reform, lineages were the principal community-based organizations that linked families as a base for aggregating power and influence. Forming a ladder between rich and poor households, lineages defended local interests while muting distinctions based on wealth or social position. Communist leaders waged a struggle against lineage organizations, seeking to substitute new associations that could form a link between households and individuals across a common social class or stratum, and could simultaneously strengthen the direct links between the leaders and the masses.

The ideal Confucian social hierarchy places the degree-holding literati at the top, acclaims the high standing and worth of the large farming population, and groups below them artisans and then merchants. Over time the character of the literati stabilized; their mediating position between the court and the populace gave them a critical role in preserving an equilibrium in the society. The literati were an elite chosen from among numerous educated aspirants, on the basis of merit through standardized examinations, and internally differentiated according to the level of academic degree awarded to each. Either as state officials, or as community leaders who performed a wide range of informal tasks of governance and social services, members of this elite simultaneously represented the interests of their lineages and localities and served the purposes of the dynasty that had honoured them.

Of course, the system of social inequalities in late imperial China was more complicated than ideal patterns might suggest. A large ruling house, ethnically distinct in the case of the Manchus, extended privilege to hundreds of thousands of people. Responsive to this group, the emperor became less accessible to the critical views of officials and of the literati in general. Local officials, serving only short stints in office with meagre resources at their disposal, found it necessary to compromise with such varied elements as powerful landowners, governmental clerks and runners, and even smugglers and bandit chiefs. As society developed commercially, merchants and their regional associations gained substantial influence. Finally, in the disorderly conditions that accompanied dynastic decline and continued through the first half of the 20th century, those who commanded superior force (the line between legitimate and illegitimate armed groups was often hard to draw) prevailed. In 1905 the abolition of the examination system which hitherto had conferred status on the elite altered irrevocably the balance between family and state interests, a balance that had proven essential to the extraordinary stability of the Chinese political order.

The lineage, or *zu*, retained its local importance after the demise of the imperial system. Indeed, as restraints on localism were relaxed, officials were no longer in a position to prevent the flexing of lineage muscle. A lineage consists of varying numbers (normally a few dozen but in noted cases as many as a few hundred) of households with the same surname and often residing in the same village. It is a patrilineal system traced back to a single male ancestor whose sons established branches and whose subsequent descendants maintained ancestral graves, tablets and halls, and usually farmed or rented out some common land. Chinese have established pervasive social values and powerful local organizations performing ritual, religious, welfare and legal roles on the basis of lineage identity. Vertically extended lineages dominated by families with wealth and high status were obvious targets for Communists eager to transform Chinese society.

The assault on lineage organizations accompanied land reform. The Chinese Communist Party reallocated lineage landholdings and collective assets, transformed their temples into public buildings, singled out their leaders as campaign targets and, during peaks of radicalism, destroyed their genealogies, graves and altars. The lineage has apparently not survived as a formal entity although it may still be a powerful informal group in some communities. Chinese are still inclined to practise surname exogamy — the surname is seen as the broadest extension of a common descent group. Whereas the lineage stands for solidarity based on kinship bonds, Communist leaders sought to structure a different kind of solidarity that would pit the majority of peasants against those whose households were prominent before the revolution, including former lineage leaders. Only after 1978 was the instrument of class struggle formally eliminated.

Mao Zedong and other leaders took a strong interest in remaking the hierarchy of Chinese society. Their analyses of class interests and struggles guided policies against particular groups and in favour of new patterns of property allocation, recruitment into desired positions and reward. They treated certain types of landlords and capitalists as enemies and gave others labels that made them continually suspect. Through the nationalization of factories and the collectivization of land, most inequalities in income became a function of state-determined wages or of work points allocated by collectives in accord with state guidelines. For more than a decade before Mao's death in 1976 policies also centred on reducing the appeal and prestige of mental labour. In contrast to the Confucian order, China's leaders opposed learning not associated with manual labour and severely hampered the training, performance and career aspirations of intellectuals. Other levelling measures adopted at least briefly during the Great Leap Forward or the Cultural Revolution include the elimination of private plots, payment with little regard for the quality of work, and advancement on the basis of class identification and group recommendation. In the late 1970s following the death of Mao and the fall of the so-called 'gang of four', many such earlier policies were repudiated. Competitive examinations open to virtually all youths were reinstated for selecting entrants to universities and to higher education in general.

Egalitarian features in the Maoist era resulted in mass poverty for the majority and misuse of power by a minority. After Mao's death mental labour regained prestige, especially when it was linked to an opportunity for living abroad. Yet, it led to modestly rewarded state jobs, which fared poorly in the inflation of the late 1980s. Rural jobs, to which urban youths had previously been assigned against their will, suddenly held out hope in coastal areas of a substantial income. After years of tight legal restrictions on migration and mobility, many farmers were shifting into other sectors of employment—some starting rural industries or moving to cities. No longer did membership in the Chinese Communist Party, service in the People's Liberation Army, and even employment in the state sector provide the automatic advantages that they had. Yet, public power could still often lead to private advantage.   *G.R.*

The status of women

Pre-modern China, in the manner of agrarian societies everywhere, asserted the superiority of men over women, supporting that perception with its ethical justifications, legal codes and customary practices. Contemporary China under Communist leadership advocates equality between the sexes, working towards that goal through exhortations in the mass media, legal reform and administrative pressures against some of the offending customary practices. The differences in ideals are pronounced and the changes in actual conditions, while not as great, are an important development of the 20th century.

Historically, there were cases of powerful or learned women and within the family elderly women often achieved an important position, but the association of males with family continuity and economic support, and of females with prescribed patterns of virtuous behaviour, contributed to many forms of differentiation between the sexes. Females suffered infanticide and the crippling effects of bound feet and inferior nurturance in early childhood that produced a biased sex ratio, confinement to the home to prevent mixing with unrelated men, opposition to the remarriage of widows among elite and aspiring families, and exclusion from the examination system, from education in general and from the direct rewards of achievement in it. These barriers have fallen, but others remain.

During the course of the struggle for women's rights over the first half of the 20th century and in the four decades of partial implementation of the Marriage Law of 1950 and its revision of 1981, attention has been drawn to the unequal state of women. Over these years the gap between urban and rural areas has widened; women have made greater gains in the cities, where there is less interference from relatives and neighbours and where more developed individual employment and schooling have transformed the conditions of life. In villages a woman still has little choice but to marry into the household of her spouse, leaving the familiarity of her own village and facing a potential conflict with her mother-in-law and the need to gain security through the birth of a son. The majority of marriages remain essentially arranged. Divorce rates are extremely low, and a woman who leaves her spouse's household is likely to be left with neither custody of her children nor ownership of property. The most humiliating conditions, such as those sometimes faced by an adopted girl with the prospect of becoming the bride of a son, were removed, but even the older age and greater earning power of today's marriageable women does not produce anything like the level of equality found in most modernized societies.

Why are there still considerable sexual inequalities in the contemporary Chinese village? One factor is the lack of sustained commitment by leaders, who coopted the women's movement and only in the 1980s permitted renewed activity. Probably more important is the weak position of women in rural life. Their level of schooling remained low in the 1980s as their labour became

Women at work transplanting rice. Agriculture has always been the basis of village life; the crop cycle dominates its organization.

It is feared the spoilt and adored 'little general' may be one result of China's single-child policy.

Village society

The rural population of China has continued to grow, doubling from an already populous 200 million in the mid-18th century to 400 million on the eve of the Taiping Rebellion and again from about 500 million at the time of the Communist Revolution in 1949 to about 900 million in 1990. The number of villages has increased much more slowly; there were perhaps one million villages on the eve of the Communist Revolution.

Among such a large number of settlements, there is, of course, considerable diversity. Japanese observers in the 1920s and 1930s found zones with average village size of a few hundred people and others with averages of 600 to 700. Within each zone, tiny mountainous hamlets contrasted with villages having as many as 2 000 inhabitants. Single lineage villages, where all households bear the same surname and share a common ancestor, are common in the southeast, while in other regions residential proximity is less likely to imply kinship ties. Walled settlements appeared in areas of recurrent banditry or inter-lineage conflict. In the north land was divided relatively equally among owner cultivators; generally higher, although varied, rates of tenancy elsewhere were increasingly accompanied by absentee ownership in the first part of the 20th century. Differences in type of farming, in access to flourishing urban markets and in long standing local traditions help account for variations in village structure and stratification.

The Chinese village is a cluster of mixed residential and agricultural compounds surrounded by fields that extend to neighbouring village nuclei. The single-storey compounds, often along both sides of a dirt road, are added to in times of household expansion or prosperity and partially rented out at other times, and they may include areas for animal shelters and storage. The largest buildings are temples or ancestral halls, now serving as public offices or schools. The land was divided into small, privately owned parcels, over which families both inside and outside the village held diverse rights. A single household might own several scattered parcels and, at the same time, rent in or out several others, depending on both its supply of labour and financial resources. Diversified household income came from selling agricultural and handicraft products, from hiring out labour or from renting out land. Villagers worked the land intensively and found other sources of income as well.

Village society was fluid and open despite the fact that residents could often find written evidence in their lineage genealogies, in grave markers, and in other monuments, that their ancestors had been in the village for as many as 10 or 20 generations. There was no fixed status order, no clear demarcation of village agricultural areas, usually not even a formal village government (despite erratic attempts in the 1920s and 1930s to create those). China did not

more valuable to the household. Moreover, there are few social settings in which informal contacts between boys and girls occur, limiting the possibility of an arrangement that avoids the payment of a substantial bride price to the girl's family.

After earlier neglect, China's leadership in the 1970s and 1980s adopted strict measures to limit population growth. The one-child policy became the norm, although rural families which gave birth to a daughter often sought permission to have another child. The rising demand for family labour after the household production responsibility system replaced communes increased the pressure against one-child limitations.   *G.R.*

have the legal barriers to migration so often observed in other pre-modern societies, but families attached ritual value to their native places and, when possible, sent resources back home or returned after sojourning elsewhere in pursuit of wealth or status. Strong intra-village organizations, especially lineages, and active inter-village communities centring on periodic marketing settlements limited village cohesion. So did the distinctive role of degree holders in forging links between local communities and the government, and the preference of the state for creating artificial groupings of households for purposes of taxation and policing. The three primary solidarities of family, lineage and village in that order gave structure to rural life.

The locality's farming cycle dictates the rhythm of village life. Despite the population density, a labour shortage is felt during peak seasons. At other times, the routine is punctuated by annual festivals and by life-cycle rituals. The Communists tried, with only partial success, to eliminate or simplify the pervasive ceremonial life of the village. Advocating policies such as birth control, individual choice of one's marriage partner and equality for women, they challenged the traditions of village society. At the same time, they have bolstered the village community as a collective within a socialist society. Yet, in the 1980s the priority shifted to economic growth. In communities with rising prosperity, rituals became more lavish. Instead of administrative measures, modernization became the major force for social change. Even the initially strict implementation of the one-child policy, which was an exception in this time of relaxed controls, was gradually yielding to popular resistance.   *G.R.*

Urban life

The cities of contemporary China demonstrate striking continuities with the past. First, the vast majority of the more than 2000 current administrative centres were likewise the seats of local government over much of the imperial era; even if few truly ancient monuments could be dated to particular periods, these sites were revered for their associations with historical events and personages. Second, despite the modern build-up of treaty ports such as Shanghai and more recently of inland industrial centres, most large cities, for example Beijing and Nanjing, also ranked among the largest cities two centuries ago when they functioned primarily as administrative and commercial centres. Third, the percentage of the Chinese population residing in cities may have only tripled over the two centuries to 1980, from a previously stable level of 5 or 6 per cent. That represents a far more modest increase (particularly if one excludes the effect of the new and exceptional urban-

ization of Manchuria) than has occurred nearly everywhere else throughout the world in the present century. In the 1980s urbanization finally accelerated.

While the earlier network of cities remains remarkably intact, the great stability in urban form characteristic of the dynastic era is less evident in very recent times. Administrative centres were long planned in partial conformity to an ancient symbolism influencing location and design of essential elements, most notably imposing city walls with prominent gates and towers. The symbolism was most evident in the capital and in northern cities in general, where gates often faced each of the cardinal directions and a largely rectangular street pattern prevailed. Over time attempts more fully to plan cities had been abandoned, particularly in the transition from Tang to Song when separately walled wards and designated marketing districts had given way to a freer street plan and to the dispersal of stores and of periodic markets to the city gates. Residential and commercial areas sprawled beyond the wall near the gates, and vegetable plots could often be found within the wall, especially at sites far from the main intersections and gates. Although cities were not highly ordered, the city wall continued to shape the form and perception of the urban environment; the closing of its gates at night increased security; at times of minor disorder it offered refuge; and, to all, the wall symbolized the administrative role of the city representing the unity of society.

New city governments in the 20th century razed some city walls (e.g., those of Canton). The People's Republic of China has carried the destruction of the city's physical heritage further, removing archways and other ornamentation and structures of the old society. The multi-storey apartment complexes and the factories erected on the urban periphery contrasted with the flat profile and ephemeral construction still dominant in much of the urban core.

Bicycle parking in Beijing.

Cities became less colourful while crowded and deteriorating public housing indicated the low priority of urban services and consumption in the competition for investment funds. The investment boom of the 1980s sparked new construction. Some Western-style hotels and many new enterprise apartment complexes near the city centre appeared along with privately funded housing in the cities and the suburbs. State housing is now being sold to those who can afford it.

The city's place both in imperial China and in the People's Republic suggests many contrasts with other societies. Historically, typically urban activities were not regarded in Chinese civilization as being as important as they were in other civilizations. There was little awareness of a distinctive urban way of life, for example, a separate corporate identity, city government, or urban elite culture. Cities were accessible to the upwardly mobile, but not so appealing that many transferred their permanent residence. When possible, urban sojourners maintained close ties with their nearest kin back home and organized native-place associations that often coincided with guilds or occupational specializations.

During the treaty port era, as foreign influences and prerogatives increased in large Chinese cities, urban and rural life diverged more noticeably. Educational and career opportunities, movements for political and cultural objectives, and prospects for prosperity became identified with the urban sector. The lure of the city persisted after 1949. In spite of efforts to reduce the rural-urban gap, socialism had more success in achieving growth in urban industry and offered more benefits to urban residents. In the 1980s this pattern changed; China's leaders learned that forced separation of urban and rural and resettlement of youths from the cities brought less benefit than stimulating growth in coastal cities and the surrounding countryside and looking for market forces to expand outward.

Urban life has undergone great change. An example can be found in the calendar. Urban residents formerly celebrated festivals of rural origin and none of their own. Now those annual festivals are largely ignored, the exceptions being the Chinese New Year, and one or two other important festivals. Once remarkable for the many common aspects of its urban and rural life, China is now remarkable for the sharp contrast between city and village living environments.   *G.R.*

Social aspects of trade

Chinese history is marked by commercial growth, especially the noted advances associated with the Tang-Song transition, the Ming and Qing late imperial era, and the modern transformation. The earliest of these milestones, the 8th to 11th centuries, does not represent a recovery from some dark period of very limited trade, as was the case in Europe, but instead shows a gradual increase in commercial activity in the already substantial administrative cities. This was accompanied by both an expansion in long-distance commerce, and all that was required for its prosperity, and the proliferation of small-scale periodic markets and towns accessible to the rural population. The 15th to 18th centuries witnessed the development of regional associations of merchants who shared a common native-place and the organization of community-wide activities based on local marketing areas. In the 20th century further reorganization of commerce took place in and around the treaty ports and in riverine and coastal areas linked to them by modern means of transportation. Under communist rule the public sector asserted control, but periodic markets were revived and led in the rising prosperity of the 1980s. Yet, there were still remote areas largely dependent on state redistribution and rationing of some items reappeared as a response to inflation.

Commercial wealth did not challenge the existing social order of imperial China. Despite the low taxes on business activities and the ease with which households could engage in commerce, merchants wielded relatively little influence. State institutions were well entrenched, remaining vigilant against organizational and ideological challenges. Moreover, merchants had to contend with a relatively open status hierarchy and educational system that gave unquestioned primacy to official service without excluding merchant households from its pursuit. They therefore kept their options open, by providing sons with a classical education and investing in land. Private business earnings were not so restricted in their use as in other pre-modern societies so long as they were not amassed in any way deemed threatening to the existing order or flaunted before officials who might find some pretext for irregular exactions.

Of all the peoples of the world, China's rural inhabitants have the longest continuous experience with regularized local exchange. Periodic markets convened every few days, contributed to the rhythm of local life. Buying and selling goods were not the only activities that took place. One also went to the market to obtain services and to participate in various types of community activities. Credit, specialized crafts, entertainment, voluntary associations, marriage go-betweens and much more were to be found.

Urban business enterprises and associations drew heavily on familial and common native-place loyalties. Operating generally on a small scale, stores and workshops used household labour and, perhaps, apprentices or hired help, closely supervised by the household head. Under the watchful eye of state officials, guilds or associations of enterprises regulated commerce within large cities. They often brought together people from the same province, who dominated in a particular trade, for example, the Shanxi bankers. In addition to their efforts to control trade for the benefit of members, these associations (some called *huiguan*) met the various needs of sojourners far from home. They offered a meeting place perhaps in a rented temple or in their own building, recreational and religious activities and, very important, various forms of social security including burial services.

In the 20th century chambers of commerce, large-scale modern enterprises and other new organizations appeared in cities, giving merchants and capitalists a powerful voice. In the 1980s the private sector quickly re-emerged, although it was restricted by lingering state controls, especially in large-scale industry and commerce.

G.R.

Secret societies

The Chinese state viewed most unofficial non-familial organizations with suspicion. Ever mindful of the danger of rebellion, it was especially intolerant of organizations such as those based on heterodox religious cults and bands of the discontented and downtrodden whose chosen names were popularly associated with uprisings that had made and broken one dynasty after another. Nevertheless, in defiance of government regulations and surveillance, such groups held clandestine meetings at which they passed on their teachings and rituals from generation to generation.

Secret societies or sworn brotherhood associations participated in every major rebellion over the nearly 2000 years of imperial rule. In times of peace, the state feared that the persistence of small bands of followers would preserve a nucleus around which others some day might rally. Consequently, even those without hostile intent were driven into conspiratorial association. However varied their ideologies, these groups voiced the aspirations of the disadvantaged, those without the full support of family and lineage, those outlawed by their inability to conform to government policies, criminal elements operating on the fringes of legality as well as others such as failed, disillusioned, dissatisfied and disgruntled scholars who were downwardly mobile. These societies frequently espoused a more egalitarian social order. Often they foresaw a utopian future, following an uprising that would create a new and just society. Usually these expectations were imbued with one form or another of Buddhist millenarianism.

These associations operated as secretive, religious fraternities. Religious cults that had evolved from the diverse traditions of Daoism and Buddhism, they offered hope of escape, for instance by claiming that members would achieve extraordinary prowess or invulnerability through reciting sutras or other teachings. Often the sect leader enhanced his own position by claiming to be the direct heir to the teachings of some major historical figure, conveyed through an unbroken line of disciples.

The need for secrecy and solidarity gave rise to such practices as initiation ceremonies, gruelling ordeals to prove fealty and worthiness, charms and passwords and sworn oaths of brotherhood. Elaborate symbolism and shared experience fostered a fraternal spirit. Through rituals imitating kinship practices and the requirement that members call each other 'brother' (their egalitarianism sometimes extended to women as well), secret societies sought to recreate the bonds of solidarity found in the Chinese family and lineage systems. Members came to each other's help in times of need; they provided mutual aid and practised the martial arts, making their group a force to be reckoned with in the local community.

Although secret societies were normally rather small groups relatively isolated one from another, certain of them had a nationwide basis. In the north the White Lotus Society, and others associated with it, gained notoriety. The White Lotus Rebellion of the late 18th and early 19th centuries forged some unity among these groups, which led to intensified and prolonged suppression. The Boxers, an offshoot of this tradition, led the anti-foreign outbursts in 1900–1. In the south various Triad societies formed loose associations of diverse groups under separate leaders. Some of these groups have been active in Hong Kong and abroad among settlements of overseas Chinese.

As the traditional political system deteriorated and gave way to warlordism and other forms of disorder, secret societies operated more openly in China. They met the need for protection and exploited the situation for their own gain. Both the Nationalists and the Communist Party had links with secret societies. After 1949 the Communists moved vigorously to suppress them. *G.R.*

Social aspects of communes, production brigades and teams

Each stage of the Communist-led transformation of rural China has left its imprint on village society. The massive redistribution and violent struggles of land reform dealt a devastating blow to traditional modes of community-wide organization and leadership and left each household with a class label that would remain as a basis for discriminatory treatment in the decades ahead. By ending absentee ownership and partially equalizing holdings, land reform also created a relatively self-contained community of independent households.

The formation of mutual aid teams and lower-state cooperatives in the early 1950s began the process of pooled land and joint management of resources. Then the sudden acceleration of collectivization in 1955 carried this process further, producing the basic features of 1970s rural social structure. Land became the property of the collective although private plots remained. Management of labour for grain production and other primary tasks was transferred from the household to the collective. In turn, the collective was a large enough entity to be subject to pressures and controls applied from above. Among the policies that strengthened the collective's hold over the household and the individual were unprecedented restrictions on movement, and on the pursuit of opportunities, such as jobs, both in rural society and within the urban sector. Out of necessity, alliances came to be forged among relatives and neighbours. They bolstered the role of the community organized around its productive activities and yet preserved an important position for separate households in all facets of life including production.

The hasty formation of large, rural communes in the late 1950s and the attempt a decade later to revive some of their radical features also had a lasting impact; they aroused fears of what might lie ahead and, because of the negative reactions they produced, caused the leadership to offer guarantees to both the household and the small-scale collective. A rough balance among the three levels of rural collectives existed for two decades before the commune system was dismantled.

In 1980 there were about 50 000 people's communes in rural China, with an average of 16 000 people per commune. During the Great Leap Forward communes covering even larger areas were given direct responsibility for allocating labour, distributing income and undertaking massive projects. However, after the retrenchment of the early 1960s, the reorganized commune became a smaller unit combining administrative functions and limited collective farm activities. It was the locus of Party and government leadership in the countryside. Its clinics, upper middle schools, small factories and service cooperatives provided facilities generally unavailable in its constituent villages. Thus, the commune's role was primarily that of a supervisory and supportive intermediate level between the full-fledged administrative centre at the county seat and the lower-level units where day-to-day decisions are made. In the new economic climate of the post-Mao Zedong era criticisms were made of excessive commune controls. For example, commune-level decisions on what could be produced on collective fields prevented the rational diversification of crops.

The production brigade resembled the commune in its primary responsibilities, but offered more elementary services that were readily accessible to virtually all villagers. There were about 700 000 of these units, some comprising a single, large village and others joining two or more, smaller villages. Among brigades, there was great diversity but they generally provided the lowest level of direct administration exercised by outsiders to the locality, a limited array of small factories and services, and minimal health and educational facilities.

Apart from a few areas in which radical measures to strengthen the brigade took hold, the production team had become the basic accounting unit and the collective focus for China's rural residents. There were close to 5 million teams in China, averaging about 30 to 40 households each. A neighbourhood in a large village or an entire small village may have constituted a team. In most respects it embodied the homogeneity of an entrenched rural community, but from time to time attention was drawn to diverse class labels such as poor peasant, middle peasant and rich peasant, as part of campaigns to generate so-called class struggle. Under the direction of local part-time leaders, the team used its considerable powers to assign daily tasks, to distribute annual earnings and to determine how to allocate funds available for community needs or welfare purposes. Dissatisfaction with economic conditions emerged repeatedly; sometimes countered by ideological campaigns, sometimes by concessions that brought minor material gains. The problem of providing adequate incentives for the collective sector persisted despite policy changes to end egalitarianism and increase incentives, and some price adjustments to increase the return on rural productivity in the late 1970s.

China's leaders promised that the rural transformation would result in substantial increases in production and in a high degree of equality. In fact, over the quarter century after collectivization, agricultural production barely out-paced population growth. Levels of personal consumption recovered from wartime dislocations in the early 1950s; yet after that, they rose marginally. The main thrust was to promote intra-team equality, while tolerating wide differentials in living standards among teams. This pattern resulted from the emphasis on team self-reliance, and the preference for payment systems within each team that did not heavily reward superior performance by individual farmers.

After a quarter of a century China's leaders reversed the collectivization of agriculture. At the beginning of the 1980s farm households rushed to take advantage of the new 'responsibility system' to obtain a long-term lease for land or to earn profits from specialization. Quickly, the lesson of China's success spread to other socialist countries: productivity could be sharply increased through the material incentives associated with family farms and a market economy. Yet, vestiges of Party control, state pricing, and uncertain ownership raised doubts about the extent of reforms while falling grain production, inadequate levels of rural investment, a reduction in sown areas and inflation posed serious problems for the advocates of reform.   G.R.

LAW

Codification

As early as 400 BC a code known as the *Fa jing* (*Canon of Laws*) was promulgated in China. It was said to have six sections: Laws on Theft, Laws on Violence, Laws on Detention, Laws on Arrest, Miscellaneous Laws, and General Laws. These sections formed the framework from which later dynasties developed their own codes.

Legal draftsmanship reached its peak with the establishment of the *Tang Code* in AD 653 during the Tang dynasty. With the promulgation of its final form in 737, the *Tang Code* consisted of 502 articles divided into 12 sections: 'Ming li' ('Terms and General Principles'), 'Wei jin' ('Imperial Guards and Prohibitions'), Zhih zhih' ('Administrative Regulations'), 'Hu hun' ('Families and Marriages'), 'Jiu ku' ('Stables and Treasures'), 'Shan xing' ('Unauthorized *Corvée* Levies'), 'Zei dao' ('Thefts and Violence'), 'Dou song' ('Conflicts and Suits'), 'Zha wei' ('Deceptions and Frauds'), 'Zalu' ('Miscellaneous Statutes'), 'Bu wang' ('Arrests and Escapes'), and 'Duan yu' ('Trial and Imprisonment'). The *Tang Code* covered most legal problems in China and as such became a monumental work, laying the foundation for the development of law not only in China but also in the neighbouring states of Japan, Korea and Vietnam.

In the codes of later dynasties it became standard practice to observe the structure and content of the *Tang Code*, the only exception being the Yuan dynasty under Mongolian domination. For example, the Song dynasty primarily followed the *Tang Code* to establish its own *Xing tong* (*Unified Code*) in 963. Moreover, the Jin authorities in 1201 promulgated the *Taihe lü* (*Taihe Statutes*) copied mainly from the *Tang Code*.

After the temporary adoption of *the Taihe lü* during the early years of the Mongolian conquest the Yuan rulers made various adjustments and innovations to the new legal order, so as to strike a proper balance between the forces of Chinese tradition, Mongolian customary law and changing social conditions. Codes having provisions of a more casuistic nature and a less unified theme than those of the *Tang Code* were from time to time established in the Yuan period, and collections of legal cases were also compiled to provide officials with established precedents on which to base their legal judgements.

After the downfall of the Yuan in 1368, the founding emperor of the Ming dynasty devoted himself to the reconstruction of the Chinese legal system along the lines of the *Tang Code,* with supplements and modifications drawn from the Yuan experience.

During the first 30 years of the dynasty several projects were undertaken to facilitate the compilation of a national code, resulting in the *Ming Code* of 1374 and its definitive version of 1397. When the Manchu rulers conquered China in 1644 to establish the Qing dynasty, the essence of the *Ming Code* was retained to serve as the basis for the establishment of the *Qing Code* in 1646, and then for the creation of the definitive version in 1740. The final version was in force until the law reform in 1905, when some Western legal principles were introduced into the Chinese system. Following the Republican Revolution in 1911 extensive reforms took place in China, particularly during the 1930s and 1940s when various new codes adopted from the Japanese and Western models were promulgated. Finally, the Communist Revolution of 1949 marked the beginning of 'socialist legality' in the People's Republic of China, although many elements of traditional Chinese law are still observed in practice.

In addition to the establishment of codes in imperial China, the authorities often supplemented the legal texts with various collections of substatutes, ordinances and other legislative measures. Official publications, such as the *Hui dian* (*Summaries of Institutions*) and the 'Xing fa zhi' (*Treatises on Punishment and Law*) of the dynastic records, also offered guidelines to deal with cases involving, especially, administrative and criminal matters. Some departments of central government issued regulations to deal with serious matters within their own jurisdiction, and provincial governments similarly published rules to control the administration of justice within their regions. These various enactments thus became important sources of law supplementing the application of codes in traditional China.

P.C.

Penal system

By the time of the *Tang Code* China had developed a sophisticated penal system, and detailed regulations were established to maintain the social order and to suppress wrongdoers. The *Tang Code* adopted the *wu xing* (five punishments) to designate the major legal penalties. Historically, the standard form of the *wu xing* was meted out in the *Sui Code* of 581–3, although the *wu xing* had existed during earlier dynasties. Through the influence of the *Tang Code* the system of the *wu xing* was employed by the law-makers of later dynasties, thus perpetuating the basic form of penalties outlined in the *Sui Code*.

The standard form of the *wu xing* consisted of: (1) *si* (death), by *jiao* (strangulation) and *zhan* (decapitation); (2) three degrees of *liu* (life exile), from a distance of 2000 *li* (1 *li* = about 500m) through 2500 *li* to 3000 *li*; (3) five degrees of *tu* (penal

Detail from the Tang woodblock *Ten Kings of Hell,* showing various punishments for wrongdoers.

servitude)—one, one and a half, two, two and a half, and three years; (4) five degrees of *zhang* (beating with a heavy stick)—60, 70, 80, 90 and 100 blows; and (5) five degrees of *chi* (beating with a light stick)—10, 20, 30, 40 and 50 blows.

Compared with death by decapitation, strangulation was considered less severe; it was commonly believed that a strangled person would still preserve his head and thus obtain his rebirth in the next world. In addition, unlike decapitation, death by strangulation kept the wholeness of the corpse and, by not damaging the body inherited from one's parents, thus lessened the degree of 'unfilial conduct' of the condemned. Strangulation was to be replaced by *lingchi* (death by slow slicing) in the Yuan period, while decapitation was retained. The practice of *lingchi* had occurred in the Liao and Song dynasties as a special measure against the offenders of very serious crimes such as treason. After having become an official degree of capital punishment in the Yuan time, the *lingchi* was adopted by the Ming and Qing codes. This mode of punishment usually inflicted on the offender eight separate cuts but, in some exceptional cases, the cuts could be extended to 24, 36 or 120 in number.

After the interruption in the Yuan period, the traditional measure of death by strangulation was restored in the Ming and the Qing. The modes of capital punishment by decapitation and strangulation were further divided into two degrees each during the Qing dynasty. They were immediate decapitation, decapitation after the assizes, immediate strangulation, and strangulation after the assizes. Unlike cases of immediate decapitation or strangulation, the other two categories of death sentence subjected the criminals to imprisonment until an execution order was actually issued. Such an order usually took place each year before the winter solstice through a final review by the emperor and, in the

meantime, every case that fell into these two categories would be examined thoroughly to determine whether the execution order should be issued in that particular year. This review system, as a token of imperial benevolence, then classified the awaiting condemned into four groups: to be executed, to be postponed until the following year, to be given a reduction in punishment, and to be allowed to live so as not to leave old or infirm parents without means of support. As a result, in the Qing period many criminals originally sentenced to death after the assizes would have their punishment commuted to banishment or deportation.

With regard to punishment by banishment or deportation, a measure *chu jun* (banishment to serve in the army) was instituted in the Yuan dynasty to supplement the traditional life-exile system. This measure was adopted in the Ming dynasty under the new name of *chong jun* and was then developed into an important punishment. During the Qing this punishment was further elaborated to include five standard degrees and one supplemental: very near (2000 *li*), nearby frontier (2500 *li*), distant frontier (3000 *li*), furthest frontier (4000 *li*), in a malarial region (4000 *li*), and the supplemental measure—deportation to serve as a slave in a Manchu or other Tartar military post.

From time to time there were also variations and modifications in regard to penal servitude and beating with a bamboo stick. For instance, instead of the traditional calculation of the number of blows in units of 10, the Yuan dynasty had six degrees of punishment with a light stick (7, 17, 27, 37, 47 and 57) and five degrees of punishment with a heavy stick (67, 77, 87, 97 and 107); but the original system was restored in the Ming period. In general, the framework of the *wu xing* became the standard form of penalty in the Chinese legal system from the Tang dynasty until the beginning of the 20th century, when various law reforms were initiated.   *P.C.*

Collective punishment

In a broad sense there were two types of 'collective punishment' in traditional China. The first was related to the so-called *baojia* organization—a local security system that grouped households into units of *pai* (10 households), *jia* (100 households), and *bao* (1000 households) so as to provide a kind of police network in the district. As it was difficult to conceal one's misdeeds from one's neighbours, the system became a deterrent to any potential wrongdoer in the local community. At the same time the law required households of the same unit to watch each other and held members of the unit responsible for failure to report a serious crime, thus forcing everyone to be on his guard. The second type was the 'collective responsibility' imposed on one's kin for the misdeeds committed by a family member. This second, more narrowly defined, variant of 'collective punishment' was the one referred to in Chinese law.

The mode of 'collective punishment' was both wide in scope and severe in degree, especially in cases of treason. According to the legal provisions governing treason in the *Qing Code,* for example, a principal offender's male relatives aged 16 or over were all liable to suffer death by decapitation; these relatives included his grandfather, father, sons, grandsons, brothers, any other male relatives living within his household (including his clansmen without mourning obligations, maternal grandfather, father-in-law and son-in-law, regardless of their family names), and paternal uncles and nephews, regardless of their places of residence. Any of the aforementioned relatives who were aged 15 or under, as well as the offender's female relatives (including his mother, daughters, wife, concubines, unmarried sisters and wives and concubines of any of his sons), were liable to become slaves to the families of meritorious officials. Thus, except in some special instances, it was almost impossible for a close relative of the traitor to escape the imposition of 'collective punishment'.

'Collective punishment' must have served as a uniquely effective warning to an individual in China, given the deep sense of family obligation and reverence. There were several reasons for imposing such harsh punishment. First, the legal penalty for the principal offender was considered inadequate in the eyes of the law, and the government had to extend the punishment to his family as a body in order to exact a maximal effect of penalty proportionate to the injury to the state. Second, it was a Chinese belief that to achieve the purpose of eradicating all 'evil seeds' of the principal offender, who was the source of evil, all his close relatives must also be destroyed. Third, the practical consideration of security undoubtedly further favoured the destruction of most of those male relatives who might be inclined to seek revenge against the government for the death of the offender. Fourth, the relatives were being punished for their own failure in educating or restraining the offender in such a way as would have prevented the grievous crime. In practice, since a disloyal act was usually the work of several collaborators, the relatives were in a position to detect what was going on and they were, therefore, punished for having failed to stop the offender or for having connived in his act.

The imposition of 'collective punishment' was, however, not extended to the offender's daughters or sisters who had been betrothed or married to other families prior to the commission of the crime. Similarly, it did not extend to the sons of the offender if they had been adopted by other families prior to the occurrence of his disloyal act, or to a woman who had only been betrothed to the offender but not yet been married and taken into his home.

Also, the offender's children who, prior to the commission of the crime, had been sold as slaves to other families or had become Buddhist monks or Daoist monks were exempted from the actual punishment. In these cases the purpose of exemptions was to protect those exempted from suffering a double jeopardy, lest they should be made responsible for the criminal acts of both the new and the former families.

The application of the principle of 'collective punishment' was made to two offences other than disloyal acts, notably, murder with intent to maim and divide the body of the deceased for magical purposes, and preparing poisons with intent to apply them to the destruction of man. In both instances the offender's wife and relatives living in the same household were liable to suffer punishment by exile. Although the mode of 'collective punishment' was less severe for these two crimes than in a case of treason, it nevertheless imposed great hardship on the family members of the offender. As a unique feature of the penal system in traditional China, the measure of 'collective punishment' became an effective means of preventing many serious crimes. It was justified by the authorities on the grounds of social order and security at the expense of 'innocent' members of the family in question.   *P.C.*

Customary law

Chinese customary law exerts its influence in at least two important areas: the informal dispute settlement at the local level of Chinese society such as clan, village and guild; and the legal process observed among members of the Chinese communities in a common law setting or in other foreign jurisdictions. The significance of Chinese customary law, however, has recently become more limited as a result of political changes and various new enactments designed to specify and define the content and procedure of law.

Historically, by the time of the Tang dynasty the Chinese authorities had developed a sophisticated legal system granting the state responsibility for the enforcement of law. Owing to the huge population and the vast territory in China, however, most communities were in practice given a high degree of freedom to exercise control over their local affairs. Clan leaders were even encouraged to settle the minor legal disputes for the villagers, provided they did not conflict with the interests of the state. In addition, traditional mistrust for, as well as fear of, the authorities prevented most Chinese from actively seeking formal legal redress. Financial considerations and the geographical distances involved also reinforced dependence upon the informal dispute settlement among members of local communities.

District court scene in Canton, about 1900.

In the realm of family law, for example, the influence of customary law has been significant, as evidenced in the Chinese concepts and institutions related to marriage, divorce and succession. Parents and household heads were sometimes entrusted with the authority to make the necessary arrangements concerning these family matters on behalf of their juniors. Whenever disputes arose, they were usually settled within the family circle according to Chinese customary law but sometimes they were presented to the clan leaders for their advice and arbitration. When the matters were too complicated or serious, only then would the cases be submitted to the authorities for adjudication or other formal settlement. The influence of customary law also extended to matters concerning contracts, transactions and other business agreements, thereby sparing the parties from the intervention of the state or formal legal process.

In a case of a misdeed or minor crime, instead of subjecting the wrongdoer to an immediate formal trial, the case was often heard and decided by the household heads or clan leaders according to usual local customs and manners. For example, a person who steals a neighbour's livestock or firewood would normally be ordered to give compensation and a public apology by means of offering a feast to the villagers or a contribution to the local temple. This kind of treatment also applied to the wrongdoer in a matter of minor injury, breach of waterway right, or even an adultery case. The public authorities interfered as little as possible in

areas where the household heads and clan leaders could prudently manage their local affairs.

By the same token, the leaders of guilds or professional bodies in traditional China were also given a wide scope of discretionary powers to settle disputes for their members according to Chinese customary law. Matters related to unfair competition, breach of contract, training of apprentices, trade protection and the like were first handled by these leaders before submission of the disputes to the public authorities for a formal hearing. For their misdeeds members were subjected to disciplinary actions and other similar punishments imposed by their own guilds or professional bodies rather than by the formal legal process, unless the gravity of the case required otherwise. Even physical harm inflicted by one member on another, or a similar assault, was sometimes within the jurisdiction of the leaders of their associations. The emphasis on the professional code of ethics and on the maintenance of harmonious relationships would be observed by all the parties concerned, thus reinforcing the dependence of members on Chinese customary law.

While abroad the Chinese under foreign jurisdiction often continue to observe Chinese customary law, especially in the realm of marriage and succession. For instance, as marriages among Chinese residents in Hong Kong or Malaysia are generally concluded and celebrated according to Chinese custom, the validity of their marriages has to be certified and established according to Chinese customary law. Similarly, with regard to adoption and inheritance, expert opinions concerning Chinese customary law are usually required when a legal dispute comes to be settled in a foreign court. Even in a case of minor crime a Chinese victim often seeks justice through the good offices of his community leaders. Although the authorities in Hong Kong, Malaysia or other jurisdictions have increasingly enacted new measures to regulate these affairs for the Chinese residents, many elements of Chinese customary law are still in force to this date, presenting an interesting dimension of the conflict of laws.   *P.C.*

The communist legal system

The triumph of the Communist Revolution in 1949 and the establishment of the People's Republic of China altered the course of legal history in China. Although various legal reforms had already taken place in the late 19th century and several modern codes were also established during the republican era, the communist regime, for the first time in China, began to formulate a new legal system based upon the foundation of 'socialist legality'.

Following the reorganization of the state structure, the Marriage Law of the People's Republic of China was promulgated on 1 May 1950 as the first major enactment of the new regime. This legislation was based upon the experience acquired from marriage regulations made during the early communist movement in the border areas. It was designed to abolish the so-called 'feudal elements' of traditional family law in China, including the institution of arranged marriages, the practice of taking foster daughters-in-law, the disregard for women and children, and the custom of concubinage. Through a vigorous campaign in 1952 to educate the public, this enactment subsequently became instrumental in social change and the reorientation of Chinese family life.

At the same time efforts were made to reallocate land through the Land Reform Act of 1950. By means of persuasion, intimidation, nationalization and confiscation, land was taken away from the owners to be redistributed among the poor peasants. Mass meetings and trials were organized by the government to implement the Land Reform Act and Party policy, resulting in the imprisonment and death of numerous landlords.

After the reconstruction of the national economy and the consolidation of Party control in the early years of the regime, a state constitution was adopted in 1954. Largely patterned on the models of the USSR and the Eastern European People's democracies, especially the USSR Constitution of 1936, it specified the National Peoples' Congress as the supreme organ of the state power and the State Council as the highest executive body. The constitution also prescribed the role and function of the judiciary and the procuracy. While the procurator's office was made independent of local political authorities to facilitate the investigation of any violations of law, the courts were expected to work more closely with people's congresses of the same levels of responsibility. A section of fundamental rights and duties of citizens was also included in the constitution to provide basic guidance for the public.

With the adoption of the constitution and other enactments, it was hoped that certain elements of the 'rule of law' and proper legal procedure would be observed. Indeed, in response to the call to 'Let a hundred flowers bloom' during the spring of 1957, a number of liberal members in the legal profession advocated the constitutional guarantees of equality before law and other fundamental human rights. They, along with the liberals of other circles, quickly became the victims of the Anti-rightist campaign that began in mid-1957. After these purges the trend to return to the 'revolutionary simplicity' of society became dominant, undermining the concepts and institutions of law. During the heyday of the Cultural Revolution of 1966−9, under the slogan of 'Politics takes command', conditions in the country made the whole legal system virtually inoperative.

In 1975 after the political upheaval of the Cultural Revolution, a new constitution was promulgated. It contained four chapters and 30 articles, much shorter and simpler than the 1954 version, and seemed to reflect compromises between contending groups in China after the downfall of Lin Biao. The political struggles among Chinese leaders intensified after the deaths of Premier Zhou Enlai and Chairman Mao Zedong in 1976. The appointment of Hua Guofeng as the new chairman and the re-emergence of Deng Xiaoping to the centre of power marked the beginning of a new era, highlighted by the arrest of the leaders of the Shanghai group known as the 'gang of four'. As a political gesture and necessity, the Fifth National People's Congress promulgated a new constitution in 1978 to regulate national affairs in the post-Mao era.

The 1978 constitution presented more similarities to the 1954 version than its immediate predecessor and sanctioned some policies to protect the right of various sectors of the population, including national minorities, factory workers, women and intellectuals. Several provisions were also included in the constitution to ensure the right of citizens (such as the rights of the accused to a defence, the right to education, and the freedom to engage in scientific research, literary and artistic creation, and other cultural activities).

Under the leadership of Deng Xiaoping a new constitution was promulgated in 1982. It consists of 138 articles and stresses the balance between the influences of Communist ideology and the need for reforms. It confirms the supremacy of the constitution and laws and provides, in Article 31, a novel theoretical ground for the establishment of a 'Special Administrative Region' to serve as the basis for implementing the 'one nation, two systems' policy with regard to the future of Hong Kong. This constitution also reflects a compromise between the political ideals and reality and thus sets a foundation for accommodating further changes as China, of necessity, modernizes. (Indeed, Articles 10 and 11 were even amended in 1988, in order to facilitate the more effective use of lands and the operation of the 'supplementary' existence of ownership by individual labourers.)

China has also taken steps to reform her legal institutions. In 1979 a set of seven enactments was adopted. They are: Organic Law of the Local People's Congresses and the Local People's Governments; Electoral Law for the National People's Congress and the Local People's Congresses; Criminal Law; Law of Criminal Procedure; Organic Law of the People's Courts; Organic Law of People's Procuracies; and Law of the People's Republic of China on Joint Ventures with Chinese and Foreign Investment. These new measures soon became a base for China to reconstruct her legal system along a more rational and reasonable framework. Other major enactments have subsequently been made to further the economic and social activities, even by modifying the orthodox

Marxist-Leninist doctrines. They include various tax laws governing individual incomes and foreign enterprises in China, Marriage Law (1980), Economic Contract Law (1981), Trademark Law (1982), Civil Procedure Law [For Trial Implementation] (1982), Rules for Implementation of the Law on Joint Ventures with Chinese and Foreign Investment (1983), Patent Law (1984), Law of Succession (1985), General Principles of the Civil Law (1986), Law on Foreign-Capital Enterprises (1986), and Law on Enterprise Bankruptcy (1986). These reforms, along with the growth of the legal profession and education, have contributed to the development of a new socialist legal system in China.

During the late spring of 1989, the government faced a series of student demonstrations advocating further political reforms. The authorities however opted for the imposition of martial law to suppress the opposition, and the confrontation led to the tragic events of Tiananmen Square on 4 June when the People's Liberation Army opened fire on the demonstrators. This incident, along with subsequent arrests and executions, met with an international outcry and has prompted the Western nations to become sceptical of China's reform movements in general and her legal developments especially. Consequently, the image of China's 'socialist legal system' as a whole has been damaged.   *P.C.*

Two convicts being paraded as part of a campaign against railway crime. The placards they are wearing proclaim them as 'thief' (left) and 'bad element' (right) and state their names and sentences.

EDUCATION

The traditional education system

Traditional Chinese belief in the importance of education derived from the teachings of Confucius and other philosophers of the middle and late Zhou periods, who held that man had a capacity for constructing a harmonious social order that would be realized only when he was both free from physical want and properly instructed. Despite his emphasis on social hierarchy, Confucius believed that almost all men had the same moral potential. He also accepted students without regard to their social status, and thus gave the Confucian educational tradition an egalitarian strand that it never completely lost.

Traditional Chinese picture map showing the ancient state of Lu in present-day Shandong and the shrines to Confucius at Qufu, the traditional site of his burial, from a history published in 1870.

Although the later Confucian classics, for example the *Mengzi* and the Zhouli (*Rites of Zhou*), describe a system of state schools existing in remote antiquity and in the early Zhou, only under the Former Han is it possible to speak with certainty of a state educational system. In 124 BC the emperor Wudi (reigned 141–87 BC) founded the Grand Academy (*Taixue*) with a quota of 50 students, and from this time on until the end of the imperial order successive dynasties maintained a central educational institution. In Han times the function of the Grand Academy was to provide instruction in the *Five Classics* of the Confucian school. Teaching was undertaken by doctors (*boshi*) of the *Five Classics*, and students took regular internal examinations before competing for selection for official service. In 8 BC the number of students was raised to 3000. Under the Later Han student numbers are said at one time to have been as high as 30 000, some of whom became involved in the violent factional struggles of the period, and even lost their lives in them. In this period the practice of making offerings to Confucius in the Grand Academy and other official schools became established, symbolizing what was from now on to be a

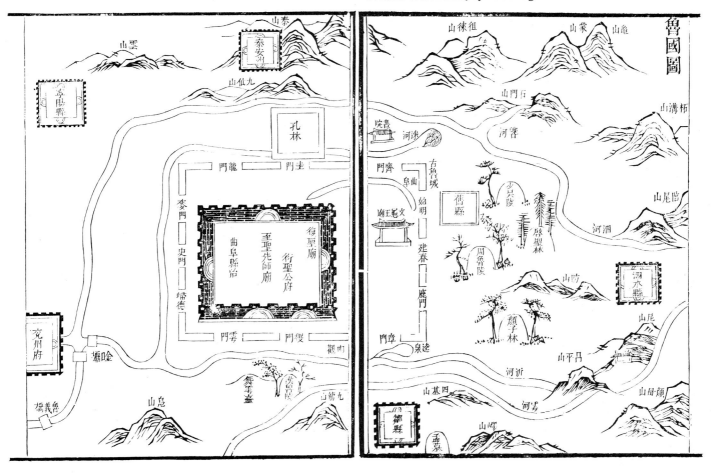

permanent connection between the cult of Confucius and the official educational system. Under the Han dynasty official provincial schools were also established and, although almost no details survive about them, in some cases at least, they are likely to have produced men who entered official service.

The period of disunity following the Han dynasty was a time when Confucian learning was in decline. Most of the dynasties, even in the 'semi-barbarian' north, set up an institution for instruction in the Confucian classics; but these suffered from the political instability of the period. Occasionally, too, independent scholars of Confucian texts are recorded as teaching, sometimes in the provinces, and attracting large numbers of students. The reunited and centralized empires of the Sui and Tang, requiring much larger numbers of officials with a common training and ideology, provided the stimulus needed to revive the official school system. The Grand Academy of the Han dynasty was re-established as one of the five directorates (*jian*), a status it was to keep until modern times. Towards the middle of the 8th century this State Academy Directorate (*Guozijian*) at the capital of Chang'an, now consisting of six schools, had a nominal enrolment of 2210 students, and there was also a smaller version in the second capital at Luoyang. After the rebellion of An Lushan in 755, financial shortages in the central government brought the enrolment down to about a quarter of this figure. The task of the State Academy Directorate in Tang times remained to prepare students for the metropolitan examinations, among which the *jinshi* degree had come to have

Traditional Chinese picture map showing the State Academy Directorate at Beijing from a historical description of the metropolis published in 1886.

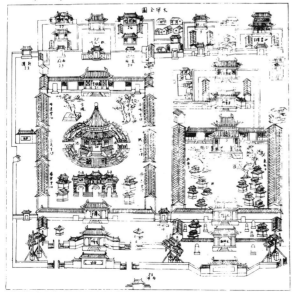

most prestige. As before, the teaching curricula consisted mainly of the Confucian classics; but three of the Directorate's six constituent schools were for mathematics, law, and calligraphy and orthography. Some of the best known literary figures of the Tang dynasty held appointments in the State Academy Directorate; yet posts in it lacked prestige. Student behaviour was often far less than exemplary, periods of residence could extend to 10 or more years, and there was at least one demonstration in 798, lasting several days and involving 265 students in an attempt to have a popular vice-president of the Directorate retained in office. Little is known about the official provincial or prefectural schools at this time, although they certainly existed, even in some cases in remoter parts of China, and prepared pupils for metropolitan examinations.

In the Song the greater wealth of society and the development of printing caused a significant expansion of the education system. The Song at first continued Tang provisions, both maintaining a State Academy Directorate that in 1079 had an enrolment of 3800 students and from 1044 decreeing the establishment of official schools at provincial and prefectural levels and for the provincial armies. But this was also a period when privately established academies flourished; it has been estimated that some 124 existed in Song times, and their scholarship, although within the Confucian tradition broadly defined, was independent of the official school curricula. Community and charity schools also appeared, and the combination of official and privately established schools that was to be characteristic of education at local level in China until the 19th century began to develop in this period.

The Mongol Yuan dynasty made it a policy to support the state education system and the cult of Confucius. A State Academy Directorate was founded in 1273, for the first time in Beijing, and it is claimed that much of the Directorate complex that still stands in the capital was completed in 1308. The Yuan also maintained an official provincial school system.

Under the Ming dynasty the connection between education and the state cult of Confucius was again reaffirmed, and the official school system benefited from government support. The State Academy Directorate was re-established in Nanjing, and, when the capital was moved to Beijing, was established there also. At the start of the dynasty it had an enrolment of several thousand divided into six hierarchically ranked Halls. Because it prepared students for the prestigious *jinshi* degree and because membership constituted a qualification for appointment, the State Academy Directorate became an important channel for official service. From 1451 onwards, however, the government allowed the purchase of student membership, and by the end of the dynasty some half of those enrolled bought their titles as students, and thereby also exemption from labour service (*corvée*) and other liabilities. For such titular students even residence in the Directorate was not required. The Ming dynasty also encouraged government schools at local level, and the number of these at the end of the 14th century has been estimated at 1200, with about 30 000 students. The government-supported system again existed alongside privately established charity and community schools and academies, although some of these last experienced difficulties as centres of unofficial Confucian learning in the autocratic climate of the late Ming.

Under the Qing dynasty the importance of the State Academy Directorate was reduced. Its student enrolment was about 300, for whom government stipends were provided, and although some famous scholars held appointments or studied there, and students from Russia also attended, it was by no means a university in the Western sense. None the less, successive Qing emperors, like their forebears, came to the Directorate and lectured in person on the Confucian classics, thus emphasizing the traditional role of the emperor as promoter of the cult of Confucius, patron of learning, and exemplar of Confucian moral values. In the face of decline, intermittent attempts were made until the close of the dynasty to reform the Directorate. Under the Qing nominal student membership was sold by the hundreds of thousands, for it continued to provide the government with revenue and purchasers with exemption from labour service and from the first rung of official examinations. The Qing government also encouraged both official and privately established provincial schools; the number of officially supported schools in 1886 has been estimated at 1810, and their total enrolment, including those who had purchased their status, about 600 000. Private academies, of which there were large numbers, came under strict state control in Qing times. Some, however, especially those directed by powerful scholar-officials, managed to continue a tradition of publishing scholarly works of a high quality, and they benefited from the support of reformers in the 19th century. None the less, by and large it was the requirements of the public examination system that determined the content of education in Qing times.

When, in 1898, the government founded the Imperial University (*Jingshi daxue*), later Peking University (*Beijing daxue*), it did not attempt to graft the modern on to the ancient institution. Efforts were, however, still made to integrate the State Academy Directorate at some level into the growing modern educational system; but when, after 1904, the traditional examinations were discontinued, it effectively lost its function. In 1905 the Directorate was amalgamated with the new Board of Education and lost all its power. A high school that it ran on its premises in this period did not survive the 1911 Republican Revolution. The traditional provincial academies fared better: in 1901 an edict ordered that they should be converted into government schools. *D.Mc.M.*

The examination system

Recruitment to the administrative service of the Chinese imperial state by means of officially conducted written examinations dates back to the Former Han. Long before this, however, in the formative middle and later Zhou periods, philosophers had provided the intellectual justification for later practice. For it was part of the polemic of almost all schools of political and ethical philosophy of this period that appointment to office should be made not on the basis of inherited privilege but on the grounds of an individual's proven abilities. Confucius himself and philosophers who followed him in the Confucian tradition may have had a hierarchical view of society, but they also believed that most men were by nature endowed with similar faculties and that they should be selected for employment according to the skills and qualities that education and moral training had given them.

In both the Former and Later Han dynasties selection for state service or promotion in rank was made mainly on the recommendation of sponsoring provincial and metropolitan officials, who nominated candidates in various categories of skill and moral worth. From 165 BC there are records of these men being ranked at the capital by their written answers to questions put to them in the name of the emperor himself. Despite official endorsement of the meritocratic principle, however, few men of really humble origin appear to have gained entry into government service in Han times.

In the period of disunity that followed the Han, the inherited centralized system gave way to one in which recommendation to

Examination cells in Canton, in which provincial examination candidates were confined, photographed in 1873.

office was made by legates who operated within prefectures, and who, even when they used written tests, made their selection from a restricted group of established aristocratic clans. It was only when the empire was reunited, first under the Sui (589–618), and then under the Tang (618–907) that the need to recruit for a greatly expanded scale of administrative institutions led to the development of a flexible and sophisticated system of centralized public examinations. Even here, however, the civil service was selected overwhelmingly from men of aristocratic background, while merchants' sons and other low status groups were excluded. Moreover, the examination system itself was only one of several routes to office, accounting for a small proportion only, perhaps at most 15 per cent, of all serving officials.

The main Tang examinations were the *jinshi* and the *mingjing*. Both were held annually at the capital, Chang'an. Competition was intense, and the success rate for the 1000 or so *jinshi* candidates was between 2 and 3 per cent, or 20 to 30 candidates a year. In the *jinshi* candidates were tested in two forms of literary composition, in knowledge of certain Confucian classics, and in ability to analyse contemporary administrative problems. In this last category an issue preoccupying the politicians of the time would often be set as a question, for example the reasons for the rise in prices or the decline in literary standards.

In the *mingjing* the main test was for rote knowledge of a limited number of the Confucian classics and their interpretation by earlier scholars. There were also separate and highly prestigious examinations announced by special decree and set, as they had been in the Han dynasty, in the name of the emperor. Other, less respected examinations were in law, calligraphy and orthography, mathematics, history, state ritual, Daoism and military skills.

In Tang times individual chief examiners were given some latitude over procedure, and candidates were expected to canvass openly and vigorously for recommendations. Nonetheless, for brief periods the principle of the anonymity or 'pasting out the name' of the candidate's script was adopted. Parallel with the highly developed examination system there emerged an articulate tradition for its criticism. Some of the leading scholars of the period held that the *jinshi* was far too literary in its emphasis and not an effective test of potential competence; others opposed the whole idea of written selection tests, preferring the principle of personal recommendation.

Under the Song dynasty the spread of printing and the increased wealth of society made education available to more people than ever before. This and the disappearance of the old Tang aristocracy in the late Tang and Five Dynasties (*Wudai*) times allowed the Song examination system to become a more important means of entry into officialdom. For although merchants' sons and other groups were still excluded, candidates from a wider social base were now admitted to the civil service through examinations. Although the *jinshi*, now by far the most prestigious examination, was conducted regularly only every three years after 1065, the annual average for successful candidates for the dynasty was 250. In the year 1256, one for which a full list survives, nearly 60 per cent of successful candidates came from families with no immediate background of official service. The range of examination subjects was similar to that of the preceding Tang dynasty, but candidates now had to pass three stages, at prefectural, departmental and, finally, palace levels. The principle of the anonymity of the candidate's script was adopted after 1033, and every script would be copied out twice and marked by two independent exam-

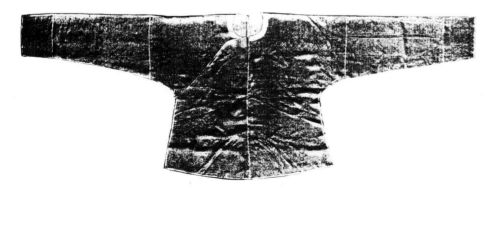

Cribbing garment (above), and detail (right), on which texts designed to help an examination candidate were written.

iners. These two marks would then be reconciled by a third examiner and converted into an order of merit. Competition was very intense, and a man might spend decades of his life as a candidate; a facilitated examination for elderly candidates was even instituted. In Song times there were still frequent complaints by leading scholars about the fairness and efficacy of the examination system, one of the main causes of discontent being the regional quotas that were imposed and that favoured culturally less developed areas, in which competition was much less severe.

The Mongol Yuan dynasty operated an examination system from the second decade of the 14th century, using for the *jinshi* separate quotas for Mongols, Chinese and other categories. Again candidates faced three successive tests, now at district, metropolitan and palace levels.

Under the Ming and Qing dynasties the examination system had overwhelming importance as the means for selection of officials. The social prestige of successful candidates at all levels was enormous, for a family or clan gained greatly in status and wealth when one of its members entered officialdom. In the Qing period particularly the demands of the system determined the content of education throughout China. As in the Song, three main stages of examination were involved. First came district and prefectural examinations, success at which gave candidates exemption from labour service (*corvée*) and corporal punishment. Secondly, there were triennial examinations at provincial capitals, success at which qualified candidates for participation in the third stage. This was the triennial metropolitan examination for the *jinshi* degree itself, the results of which were, as in Song times, confirmed by an examination in the imperial palace. In Ming and Qing times the system continued both to be ideologically important as a realization of the meritocratic ideal and to function as an efficient means of introducing fresh blood into the bureaucracy. Thus it has been estimated that under the Ming 47.5 per cent of successful *jinshi* candidates came from families with no immediate official connection, while for the Qing the estimated figure is 36.6 per cent. The numbers successful at the final stage, the *jinshi* degree itself, were smaller than their maximum under the Song, the annual average being nearly 90 for the Ming and 100 for the Qing, although again the examination was held only every three years.

Over this period, however, the content of the examinations became increasingly rigid. From 1487 onwards the *jinshi* was dominated by a stereotyped form of composition, the 'eight-legged essay', in which two lines of argument on a set subject, a citation from the Confucian classics, were developed in parallel, and which was never longer than 700 characters. Later the calligraphy of candidates itself became a criterion in the marking of papers. Corruption became common, and from 1451 the government made lower degrees, with their attendant privileges, available through purchase. Complaints against the system continued to be expressed by some of the leading scholars and satirical writers of the period.

None the less, from the 17th century onwards, the examination system was admired by Western observers. Indeed the introduction in 1855 of competitive written examinations for entry into the British civil service, and their adoption in 1883 for the United States service were very probably the indirect result of respect for an institution that had been a feature of Chinese political and cultural life for more than two millennia. But although in the course of the 19th century attempts had been made to reform and modernize the traditional system, over the final decades of the Qing it came to be realized that its classical syllabus could not be adapted to the need for modern education. The *jinshi* examinations were held for the last time in 1904, to be abolished by edict in 1905.

D.Mc.M.

Literacy

In a non-alphabetic language such as Chinese literacy cannot be acquired by memorizing a small number of symbols, but requires knowledge of many distinct characters for reading and writing. The nature of the Chinese language influences the content of basic literacy, but the Chinese did not regard this problem with any concern until the 20th century. In earlier periods they had no concept of any level of literacy below full mastery of the language and literature. This meant mastery of the Confucian classics and the large body of commentaries, histories and literary materials handed down through the centuries. This advanced literacy was attained by only a very small number of males, who studied for the civil service examinations.

Of course many Chinese could read the language at lower levels of skill. Such individuals usually had very narrowly specialized vocabularies. This was inevitable in a non-alphabetic language. Thus, a Chinese with less than 2000 characters at his disposal could read simple materials but he would not be able to read books, especially those concerning matters outside his own specialized occupation. Even at these lower levels of skill, literacy was largely, though not wholly, confined to males. Before the 20th century formal education for women was not sanctioned by Chinese society. Female literacy was discouraged by conservative attitudes and economic considerations, and the vast majority of women in China were illiterate.

By the 18th and 19th centuries China was a complex society where demand for education stemmed not merely from the lure of

The shop signs in this 19th-century Canton street exemplify the pervasiveness of writing in the urban milieu.

the civil service examinations, the key to upward social mobility, but from the rewards for literacy to be found in the market-place and in everyday life. It was a country where peasants participated in local markets and where ordinary households relied on written contracts and documents in purchases, sales, land rentals, loans, family division, and the numerous junctures at which government touched the people: tax collection, household registration, official notices of new regulations, and so forth. A network of privately financed schools, a clearly defined curriculum, and a supplementary network of charitable schools indicate that some schooling was available for many ordinary Chinese by this period.

The student would begin with the three primers that dominated Chinese elementary education from the Song dynasty: the *Trimetrical Classic (Sanzijing)*, the *Thousand Character Classic (Qianziwen)*, and the *Hundred Family Names (Baijiaxing)*. These three primers provided reading knowledge of approximately 2000 characters, the basic vocabulary acquired by boys from elite families before they enrolled in formal studies with a tutor. They could be studied in less than a year. Thereafter a student would begin to read the Four Books and Five Classics. This was the standard orthodox curriculum, adopted by a wide variety of schools throughout the empire.

The most important channel for schooling lay in the private sector. Well-to-do families hired private tutors for their sons, while ordinary families frequently banded together to hire a teacher. Sometimes a teacher would give classes in his house. Private education was thus available to villagers and city dwellers of ordinary status as well as to the rich. Boys from poor families were not necessarily barred from the classroom. There were clan schools, financed by rents from lands owned by the lineage to provide free schooling for poor members. In many regions there were charitable schools, endowed by citizens, that were often explicitly intended for boys of poor families.

If literacy can be defined as the acquisition of some functional level of reading and writing abilities, there was a scale of such skills in China by the Qing dynasty. At the top were the highly educated degree-holders and officials, as well as the failed scholar. These were the Chinese literati. Literacy was fundamental to most aspects of literati life and culture. The education of sons was mandatory in this social group, for a man's prospects rested on acquiring advanced education.

Below the literati there were men who had attended school for a few years. This group might include merchants, artisans, shopkeepers, landlords, and well-to-do peasants who tilled their own land, as well as some priests and monks. Since most elementary schools followed the standard curriculum, they studied the Confucian classics, at least in a rudimentary way. Some were forced to abandon their studies for want of funds, others were sent to work for want of talent. Whatever the cause of their interrupted education, persons in this group could read and write several thousand characters, enough either for business or for land management. Aware of the value of education, these men tried, as their means permitted, to school one or more of their sons. While the ultimate goal was success in the civil service examinations, these men used their literacy in everyday economic activities to amass wealth. Along with the failed scholars and degree-holders, they supported the market for popular literature of all kinds.

Further down the scale there were those who had attended school for shorter periods, perhaps during the slack agricultural season. Unlike the previous group these men were often not exposed to the orthodox elementary school curriculum. Their limited schooling did not provide the basis for educational advancement. Their course of study provided mastery of probably only a few hundred characters. This enabled them to keep simple accounts and cope with small market transactions but beyond such activities they most probably sought help from the more educated members of their communities.

Finally, there were many men and women who were illiterate. While their inability to read and write left them at an obvious disadvantage in Chinese society, illiterates were not cut off from their educated neighbours. Access to information contained in written materials was provided in a variety of ways, for writing was only one of several major channels of communication in Qing society. Economic and political news percolated through the market network, with the teahouse and the travelling pedlar aiding the flow of information between city and country and between the ruling elite and the ordinary citizen. Guilds, lineage organizations and secret societies were other networks disseminating information. Drama and storytelling united Chinese of different social backgrounds and transmitted a common cultural heritage.

In the 20th century Chinese reformers began to push for expanded literacy. By the standards of the industrialized world, the 30 per cent literacy rate for males in China was pitifully inadequate. One of the pioneers in adult literacy programmes was a Yale graduate named Jimmy Yen, or Yan Yangchu (1893–??). While working with illiterate Chinese labourers in France during the Second World War, Yen developed a course in basic literacy and launched a periodical using a small number of basic characters that these workers could read. He successfully tested his adult education programme in Changsha in 1922. The Mass Education Movement that he led eventually published readers, each with 1200 basic characters, for urban residents, farmers and soldiers. Graduates of the four-to-six-week literacy course could keep accounts, write letters and read simple materials.

During the 1920s and 1930s mass education movements like Jimmy Yen's became involved in carrying out broader programmes for social and economic modernization. Yen's experiment was conducted in Ding county, Hebei Province, but similar programmes existed in many other regions. Chinese Communist leaders like Mao Zedong also sponsored adult education programmes at this time.

After 1949, when the People's Republic of China was established, the attack on illiteracy resumed on two fronts. Enrolment of school-age children expanded greatly so that 96 per cent of school-age children were attending primary school in 1976. Although enrolments fell to 93 per cent in 1981, as the post-Mao economic reforms induced some parents to take their children out of school, they have subsequently climbed to over 97 per cent in 1987. China has thus finally achieved almost universal schooling. After 1949, periodic campaigns focused on providing the country's adult illiterates with a minimal education, defined in 1956 as recognition of 2000 characters for workers and 1500 characters for peasants. A 1 per cent sample survey in 1987 indicated that less than 27 per cent of Chinese aged 12 and older were semi-literate or illiterate. Tremendous regional disparities continue to exist, with literacy rates ranging from less than 30 per cent for Tibet to over 86 per cent for the northeastern province of Liaoning.

E.S.R.

Socio-political use of character reform

Character reform, also discussed on pages 331–3, is part of a broader movement for speech and writing reform that has been linked since the late 19th century with emergent Chinese nationalism and the drive for mass literacy. In contrast to the more radical proposals of the 1920s and 1930s that would have completely replaced the characters with an alphabetic writing system, the attempt to reduce the number of Chinese characters in use and to simplify characters by reducing the number of strokes needed to write them, was a moderate reform. At various periods, resistance to character reform has surfaced in political action.

The same nationalism that promotes language reform stimulates opposition to character reform. Chinese characters are closely linked in the popular mind with Chinese culture, and many Chinese are unwilling to accept a foreign alphabetic system in their place. Although the attachment to Chinese characters may be strongest amongst intellectuals, it apparently can be found even among illiterates, for whom the only meaningful literacy involves the ability to read the characters. Because character reform has been linked to speech reform and the stated goal of replacing spoken dialects with the national language, *Putonghua*, advances which emphasize the use of the phonetic alphabet have clear implications for increased political centralization and the weakening of regional loyalties. The current stagnation of language reform movements in the PRC thus reflects an unwillingness on the part of the CCP leadership to confront the regional, minority and cultural identity issues that have blocked further advances in writing reform. Incomplete though it may be, character reform has meant that Chinese educated since 1956 are cut off from pre-1949 written materials, which use the full traditional forms of the characters.

E.S.R.

Printing

Printing, invented in China, relied on the method of carving and obtaining impressions from wood blocks. Its development is intimately linked with education. Since the Song dynasty the Chinese government has been a major book publisher, financing the printing of dynastic histories, Confucian classics, commentaries, and most recently the works of Mao Zedong. The government was anxious to preserve and disseminate the approved orthodox texts, but before the 20th century major government projects produced relatively small quantities of books. In some cases only 50 or 100 copies would be printed by a government agency.

The vigorous expansion of commercial printing dates from the 13th century. By the 16th century the volume of publications from commercial printers had increased markedly while printing costs declined. From this period books seem to have been more plentiful and more inexpensive than ever before.

The advent of large-scale printing in the 16th century stimulated Chinese education. There was a large increase in the supply of the Confucian texts required for the orthodox curriculum. Books that were formerly rare were now printed in quantity at prices that many students could afford, although there were also large scholarly compilations selling for high prices. Elementary primers were also more readily available, permitting the expansion of schools. Printers brought out all kinds of educational supplements, including copies of civil service examination questions and answers. Mass printing was thus instrumental in widening the circle of potential competitors for civil service degrees. The expanded educational facilities and mass printing provided enhanced opportunities for upward social mobility.

Western printing techniques were introduced into China in the late 19th century, as Chinese began to reform the traditional curriculum. The Commercial Press, established in Shanghai at the close of the century, was a forerunner in the new educational literature, introducing new teaching methods and subjects for incorporation into the Western-style schools. Since 1949, with the establishment of the People's Republic, the Chinese have continued to rely heavily on the dissemination of printed materials in

their effort to transform values and behaviour, inside and outside the classroom. Technical, political and recreational materials covering a vast range of topics are produced and distributed by the state agencies. The Chinese government is probably the largest publisher in the world today, with the provincial and national presses printing works in the hundreds of thousands and occasionally tens of millions of copies.

E.S.R.

The introduction of Western higher education

The introduction of Western higher education was a direct consequence of the series of humiliations heaped upon China by the foreign powers from the Opium War onwards. On the one hand these resulted in the influx of Christian missionaries who, over time, set up their network of schools, colleges and universities. On the other, China's evident weakness in the face of Western military and industrial power sparked off a debate within the Chinese elite as to how it might best respond and this, inevitably, raised major questions of adaptation and adoption in educational terms. These focused on what became known as the *ti-yong* dichotomy. *Ti* (substance) represented traditional Chinese values; *yong* (use) stood for the technical skills of the West. The debate over the extent to which *ti* and *yong* could coexist with, and complement, each other was a prolonged one and, indeed, in some respects it still continues. In the late imperial period a succession of Chinese statesmen and intellectuals participated, including Zeng Guofan, Li Hongzhang, Kang Youwei, Liang Qichao, Zhang Zhidong and Yuan Shikai. All were motivated by a desire to strengthen China and, therefore, they took a very practical view of what the West had to offer, concentrating for the most part on the acquisition of linguistic and scientific skills. They differed considerably in their perceptions as to how far educational reform should go. Initially many believed that a few centres of 'Western learning' could simply be grafted on to traditional educational arrangements. As the century progressed, however, it was increasingly recognized that the whole edifice of classical learning was a major cause of China's weakness and, even before the collapse of the Qing dynasty, steps were taken to dismantle it.

The official institutions set up in the 19th century were all characterized by a heavily vocational bias. The first to be established was the *Tongwenguan*, which was founded by Prince Gong in 1862. It began as a school of foreign languages connected to the Zongli Yamen, but was actually under the direction of Robert Hart, Inspector-General of Maritime Customs. In 1866 it was granted

The Western printing press and its new type founts were most cost-effective, with enlarged volumes of printing, and testify to the expansion of the publishing industry in modern China.

college status and chairs of physics, chemistry, mathematics and astronomy were established; international law was added a little later.

By the end of the century the college provided an eight-year course of instruction. The first three were spent in learning a foreign language: English, French, German, Russian or Japanese. The students then devoted five years to studying Western science and general knowledge through the medium of the language acquired. By 1896 some 1000 had passed through the college, most of whom had received government financial support. They were subsequently employed as interpreters and secretaries to foreign embassies, as consuls and vice-consuls, or as teachers in other government schools and arsenals and, in two cases, as tutors in English to the Guangxu Emperor. In 1898 *Tongwen guan* was reorganized to become the Imperial University.

Other early institutions catered to defence needs. Prominent among these was the Fuzhou Arsenal, which in 1867 established French and English language schools to train naval officers under the management of Prosper Giquel. By 1880 some 50 students were enrolled in the English school and 40 in the French. Courses lasted for over four years and, in addition to the appropriate language, included various branches of mathematics, engineering, navigation and geography. The Imperial Naval Academy, founded at Nanjing in 1890, performed similar functions. During its first six years 120 cadets were enrolled and foreign instructors of navigation and engineering were employed. There were parallel developments in military education, with Li Hongzhang opening China's first modern Military Academy in Tianjin in 1885.

Li, as viceroy of the metropolitan province of Zhili, also developed higher education in other directions. In 1893 he founded the first government medical college and, two years later, set up the University of Tianjin. Because of the lack of candidates with 'basic' Western knowledge—a common and persistent problem—the university provided a preparatory department teaching English and mathematics as well as four schools of civil engineering, mechanical engineering, mining and law. Tianjin was also the site of the Imperial Northern Government Telegraph College, established in 1879. Specialized institutions appeared in other major cities, including a government mining and engineering college at Wuchang, opened in 1892.

Christian missions were also active. At first they had concentrated largely on providing Western education at a very basic level for the benefit of converts, seeing it somewhat as a necessary adjunct to the process of Christianization. As the century progressed, however, the Protestant missions particularly began to concentrate their educational resources at a more advanced level. American missions especially sought to set up colleges as a means of gaining access to the 'higher classes' of Chinese society and out of a belief that a Westernized elite would have an influence in national affairs out of all proportion to the numbers involved. Usually the typical syllabus of an American college was modified to meet Chinese needs by introducing Chinese literature, but the main aim of these institutions was to train Christian leaders by providing a humanistic curriculum in a strongly Christian environment.

St John's College in Shanghai, which was to become one of the most celebrated academic institutions in China with its *alumni* rising to positions at the highest levels in the Republican era, began to be built in 1879, although it did not graduate its first class until the 1890s. In 1888 the Northern Methodists established institutions in Nanjing and Beijing, both of which they termed universities. Missionaries were also active in Shandong, where steps were taken to upgrade a high school to college status in 1882. Although Catholics were generally not so interested in higher education, the Jesuits were an exception. By 1903 they had established Aurora University in Shanghai, which taught mainly in French and provided Faculties of Arts, Law, Science, Civil Engineering and Medicine.

Thus by the end of the century there were a number of institutions, both official and missionary, which claimed to offer 'Western learning' at the higher level, although it must be admitted that terms like 'college' and 'university' were sometimes used as a declaration of intent rather than a reflection of reality. And as China entered the 20th century the process accelerated considerably.

In 1902 and 1903 the first legislation for a 'modern' system of education was passed, with the Japanese pattern providing the main inspiration for implementing a 'modern' curriculum while maintaining Confucian social and familial values. In 1905 the imperial examination system was abolished and with the Revolution of 1911 such 'modern' institutions as the Imperial University, now renamed Peking University, other government higher schools and the missionary institutions came into their own. New legislation passed in 1912 under the influence of the German-educated scholar Cai Yuanpei laid the foundation for a republican system of education with specific curricular guidelines for primary, secondary and tertiary levels that were intended to inculcate republican values along with modern knowledge. The May 4th Movement of 1919, which was led by university students, gave voice to a powerful repudiation of both persisting Confucian values and Japanese aggression and led to even greater openness in the educational system.

Throughout the twenties the dominant influence was that of American progressivism, with a new set of patterns legislated for in 1922 and 1924 providing for 6 years of primary education, 3 years of lower secondary, 3 years of upper secondary and 4 of higher education. When the Nationalist government came to power in 1927, these patterns were kept and the subsequent decade saw a melding of both European and American influences within a genuinely Chinese system of modern education, which was explicitly shaped to promote Sun Yat-sen's three principles—people's rights, people's livelihood and people's nationalism.

The concrete achievements of the period between 1928 and 1949, one racked by both the eight-year Sino-Japanese War and the subsequent Civil War, were considerable. By 1949 there was a primary school enrolment of 24.4 million children in 280 930 schools, a secondary enrolment of 1.3 million in 4045 general secondary schools and 1171 specialized secondary schools, and a tertiary enrolment of 116 504 in 205 universities. While this modern educational system only touched a minority of the population, mainly those living in urban areas, it was nevertheless a substantial achievement and a valuable legacy to the Communist government which followed. *J.Ga., R.H.*

Education as indoctrination: traditional and modern

The idea that man possesses innate goodness, which can be nurtured by the proper education in order to achieve his full potential, is among the most ancient in Chinese thought. In practice, however, the imperial authorities equated 'goodness' with those attributes that were deemed desirable for the maintenance of the existing social order, with the use of education to inculcate 'correct' ideas being fully accepted as part of statecraft.

Particularly under the Ming and Qing dynasties great efforts were made to promote an official orthodoxy derived from ancient models but fully developed in the Neo-Confucianism of the Song. This 'imperial Confucianism' held that the ultimate goal was social harmony, and that this was best achieved by ascribing to each individual a clearly defined position within an extremely hierarchical family system, teaching him to accept the duties pertaining to his station, and to obey those in authority over him. All the individual's social and political relationships were defined by duty and obligation, not by rights. The family was the state in microcosm, and the qualities which defined a filial son would also make him, in the words of the Qing dynasty Yongzheng Emperor (1678–1735), 'a dutiful son and pure subject when he tills the soil, and a loyal and brave soldier when he fights on the battlefield'.

The achievement of a harmonious social order in which everyone should 'know his place' was greatly assisted by the use of a sophisticated examination system based on merit to recruit officials to the imperial bureaucracy. If he could afford the expense of the lengthy training necessary, the examination system could open a prestigious career to an aspiring young man. Success in mastering Confucian orthodoxy was well rewarded by an appropriate place in the ordered hierarchy; thus self-evidence of the system's propriety and legitimacy was rooted in the personal experience of those who had reached its summit.

The examinations also led to the indoctrination of those who obtained a formal education. For, as they had developed by Ming and Qing times, they did not really test a candidate's acumen but, rather, his ability to reproduce a rigid, conservative and officially-prescribed interpretation of the Classics, written some two millennia earlier. Orthodoxy applied not only to content but to the most minute details of form, and the slightest deviation was likely to result in failure. Thus officials, and the whole educated stratum from which they were drawn and who constituted the informal leadership at the local level, were conditioned to value conformity.

The imperial authorities were not content to leave matters there and, especially under the Qing, also actively sought to indoctrinate the masses by instituting a lecture system in every locality. Lecturers were appointed on the basis of their scholarship, age and unimpeachable character, and were required to expound imperial maxims twice a month. The emperors themselves provided edicts of a morally uplifting nature for the edification of the subjects. Attendance at the lectures was supposedly compulsory not only for 'ignorant rustics' but also young scholars.

In the 19th century the imperial system of indoctrination broke down and the examination system, which enshrined it, was abolished in 1905. Later Chiang Kai-shek attempted to inculcate Confucian principles in the New Life Movement, but it was left to the Communists to produce a new and effective system of indoctrination after 1949. In place of harmony, hierarchy and passive obedience they wished to promote self-assertiveness, struggle and a rejection of the past. The masses had to 'take the attitude of being the masters', and Marxism was their answer to imperial Confucianism. With its claim to be scientific and its record of apparently successful application in the Soviet Union, Marxism became the only source of correct thought. The Propaganda Department of the Party Central Committee assumed responsibilities throughout society and was specifically involved in the educational system.

Since 1949 ideological indoctrination has been an ever-present feature of educational life, varying in scope and intensity with the alternating phases of mobilization and relative quiescence which characterize the political process in the People's Republic.

Initially it was directed particularly towards teachers. In 1949 most of them were 'bourgeois' in both origin and attitude, and their own 'ideological transformation' was a prerequisite to their inculcation of Marxist principles in the young. Party members were appointed to key posts throughout the educational system and, under their supervision, a series of campaigns was mounted to rid the intellectuals of their 'erroneous ideas'. To 'remould' their thought they were made to study prescribed Marxist texts and to participate in 'criticism, self-criticism' sessions, which usually involved a measure of public humiliation. The indoctrination process often caused great psychological stress, and those unwilling or unable to demonstrate 'progress' might find themselves branded as 'counter-revolutionaries' or 'rightists', and even subjected to penal sanctions. On the other hand, those able to 'raise their political consciousness' to an appropriate level could aspire to join the Communist Party, in which case enhanced career opportunities would combine with Party study activities to reinforce their ideological commitment.

In schools and universities ideological indoctrination was built into the curriculum, partly as a result of wholesale borrowing from the Soviet Union. 'Politics' was a subject in its own right, beginning with moral homilies for the youngest children and progressing through the memorizing of political slogans to the actual study of Marxist texts of an increasing order of sophistication. Of perhaps greater significance was the intrusion of Marxism into 'academic' subjects. The study of Chinese literature, for example, stressed 'socialist realism' with its stereotyped presentation of 'heroes' and 'villains' in terms of the social classes they represented. Foreign literature focused on works guaranteed to show the worst features of capitalist society. The teaching of history was similarly conducted in accordance with Marxist concepts and categories, and special courses on the role of the Chinese Communist Party in ending China's weakness and promoting advance on all fronts were also introduced. It became common for peasants and workers to be invited into the classroom to recall 'past bitterness' and contrast it with the benefits of the new era. Party-controlled youth organizations reinforced the official ideology.

Until 1966 indoctrination was limited somewhat by the leadership's commitment to economic growth, which ensured that the educational system paid proper attention to the teaching of scientific, technical and other 'modern' skills. In that year, however, Mao Zedong's fears that the younger generation was insufficiently prepared to withstand the forces of 'revisionism' at home and abroad led him to launch the Cultural Revolution, and 'politics' came to dominate the curriculum to an unprecedented degree. For example, textbooks for modern language students were published which consisted of nothing but Mao's quotations in translation. A populist faith in the wisdom of the masses resulted in an attack on concepts of intellectual and scientific excellence and a xenophobic rejection of 'learning from abroad'. The level of an individual's 'political consciousness' became of the greatest importance and was measured not against the whole Marxist canon but against Mao Zedong Thought alone. It is clear that in some educational

Professor Luo Zudao, a noted academic, holding a post-graduate seminar on fracture mechanics at Jiaotong University, Shanghai.

institutions indoctrination came almost to replace teaching entirely.

After Mao's death and the arrest of the 'gang of four', China greatly reduced the emphasis on indoctrination, both in the schools and outside, and until the political crisis of 1989, the new leadership tolerated far greater intellectual diversity than at any time since 1949. One reason for this change, whose political consequences have come under critical scrutiny but which, though retarded, has not been reversed, is China's determination to modernize by relying on a technocratic model of development that has proved successful elsewhere. This model is dependent on the free exchange of ideas and information in certain fields. Related to this is the need to raise the morale of the intellectuals both by 'compensating' them for the hardships they have suffered and by emphasizing their role in China's modernization.   *J.Ga., B.G.H.*

The educational achievements of the People's Republic

The educational achievements of the People's Republic of China might be summarized by reference to three periods, each dominated by a different conception of how education should serve economic and political development.

The first period, 1950 to 1965 was a time when the Soviet model of socialist construction provided the main inspiration for educational reform.

The second period, 1966 to 1977, saw the full-blown implementation of a Maoist model of revolutionary education.

The third period, 1978 to 1988, has seen a rejection of both the Soviet patterns and their Maoist counter patterns in favour of reforms that have brought China into closer and closer relation with Western capitalist countries.

The period of socialist construction 1950–65

With the success of the Revolution of 1949, intense efforts were made to reform the education system in ways that would promote rapid development towards socialism along lines suggested by Soviet advisers, who assisted in both educational and economic restructuring. The modern educational structure of the Nationalist period was basically maintained, with 6 years of primary school, 3 years of lower secondary and 3 years of upper secondary, but curricular reforms reflected a Soviet approach to mathematics and science, as well as new content for political education. Higher education was totally reorganized along Soviet lines and extended to 5 years for many programmes. The 205 universities of the Nationalist period were transformed into a system of higher institutions with highly specialist curricular identities under the direction of such sectoral ministries as machine-building, metallurgy, agriculture, public health etc., as well as some comprehensive and technological universities directly administered by the new Ministry of Higher Education. A comprehensive socialist planning system ensured specialist graduates for all the major sectors of the economy. Complementing this highly structured formal education system were many efforts at literacy and mass education under part-time auspices, which drew their inspiration from the educational work done by the Communist Party in the Border Regions during the Liberation struggle. There were thus two tracks, one for the elite corps of experts who were to lead in socialist construction and the other to raise the general level of the masses.

Educational achievements of the period can be summarized by a look at statistics for the year 1965, when there were 116 million children in primary schools, 9.3 million in general secondary schools, 547 447 in specialist technical secondary schools and 4.4 million in agricultural and vocational secondary schools. There were 434 regular higher institutions with an enrolment of 674 426. In addition there were 8.2 million adults enrolled in primary education, 8.5 million in secondary education and 412 616 in tertiary education, all of a non-formal nature. Generally the overall educational level of the population had been raised considerably, and a group of experts had been trained for leadership roles. However, criticism of this two-track approach to socialist construction arose in the Great Leap Forward and culminated in the breaking off of all ties with the Soviet Union in the early sixties. A particular bone of contention was the very limited access

to regular higher education and the fact that the system favoured young people from good urban secondary schools, who mainly came from the families of cadres or intellectuals. The agricultural and vocational secondary schools which had developed in the expansion of the Great Leap Forward (1958) largely served less privileged groups and rural areas, and did not open the way into higher education.

The period of the Cultural Revolution 1966–77

A key concern in the revolutionary transformation of education was to eliminate the two tracks characteristic of the Soviet-inspired model of education and ensure that all young people had both the ideological and practical benefits of an education integrated with productive labour and linked to a conscious reshaping of social relations. Regular universities, as bastions of expertise and privilege, were entirely closed down for several years. The distinction between general secondary schools and agricultural-vocational ones was abolished, with all supposed to be run as open-door schools having close links with factories and farms. The whole education system was streamlined in order to eliminate what was seen as excessive academicism, with primary education reduced to 5 years, secondary to a total of 4 years and higher education to 3.

The violence and destruction of this decade have been well documented and perhaps the greatest educational losses lay in the closing of universities, the disruption of scientific research and basically a cessation in the training of personnel at a high level. Much of the energy in the subsequent decade has gone towards redressing these losses. What is often forgotten, however, is the dramatic change made in secondary level educational participation over this decade. While primary enrolments grew from 116 million to 146 million, secondary enrolments expanded from the 14 million of 1966 to 67.8 million by 1977, a remarkable achievement even though the academic standards of the better urban schools were sacrificed in the process. A concomitant change was a 10 per cent increase in female participation in secondary schools, from 30 per cent in 1966 to 40 per cent in 1977. The serious losses of the Cultural Revolution thus have to be set against this overall upgrading of the educational level of the nation, a change that may have provided some basis for the modernization efforts of the decade that has followed.

The period of four modernizations 1978–88

Considerable emphasis has been placed on education as essential for the achievement of ambitious modernization plans in the new directions introduced by Deng Xiaoping in 1978. The structure of the pre-Cultural Revolution period has been restored—6 years of primary school, 3 of lower secondary, 3 of upper secondary and 4 of higher education—but the intention has been to avoid both the two-track patterns of the fifties and the unified revolutionary patterns of the sixties in favour of a multi-track system with a kind of diversification suited to modernization needs. A major educational reform document accompanied the raising of the Ministry of Education to a State Education Commission in 1985 and laid out educational priorities for the future. A key direction is towards the popularization of 9 years of compulsory education, 6 at primary level and 3 at lower secondary level, which should constitute a common basis for all children. Yet it is recognized that in some regions it will take many years to achieve. Much of the financial support for this commitment is to be raised through local taxes, making its success dependent on both the importance local cadres give to education and the relative economic resources of different regions. Beyond this compulsory level, much stress is laid on the diversification of upper secondary and higher education, which has involved the development of a wide range of vocational and technical programmes in upper secondary schools and a great expansion of 3-year non-degree programmes in the tertiary sector. Universities, for their part, have gained increasing autonomy and been able to broaden and diversify their curricular offerings, moving beyond the narrow specialization of the fifties. The increasing involvement in academic exchange with countries of the capitalist world has resulted in 50 000 scholars and students going abroad for research and higher study between 1978 and 1987, and

a return of 20 000 by 1987. Half or more of this group have gone to the United States.

Educational statistics for 1985 give a picture of the quantitative trends and achievements of this decade. Primary enrolments were at 146.3 million, general secondary at 47 million, with another 2.3 million in vocational or agricultural schools and 1.5 million in specialized technical schools, tertiary at 1.7 million, with about one third of these in short-cycle non-degree programmes. In addition there were 87 331 graduate students working towards master's and doctoral degrees. Clearly, tertiary education has seen both an enormous expansion and a diversification over this decade, with funds from such agencies as the World Bank supplementing Chinese efforts to bring their universities up to international standards. The drop in secondary enrolments has resulted from a 'consolidation' of rural secondary schools and a renewal of emphasis on those priority schools (mainly in urban areas) preparing young people for the competitive entry examinations to higher education. Diversification, in fact, masks a revival of the two tracks so heatedly criticized during the Cultural Revolution. Nevertheless it is difficult to envisage an alternative, and the fact that secondary enrolments remain relatively high indicates the long-term success of the expansion of the seventies. Primary enrolments have been sustained, but drop-out rates are disturbingly high in rural areas where peasant families need their children's labour to meet the opportunities of the household production responsibility system.   *R.H.*

Primary-school children in Yan'an implement Mao's principle that 'education must be combined with productive labour'.

HEALTH AND MEDICINE

Traditional medicine: social and philosophical background

Traditional Chinese medicine, as practised in former centuries and even today, is based on a heterogeneous array of theories and practices that were either developed indigenously or adopted from foreign civilizations. An analysis of these theories and related practices reveals the existence of a number of distinct therapeutic systems, each characterized by its own understanding of the nature and causation of illness. The most important of these are outlined below.

Ancestral healing

The development of therapeutic theories and practices in China can be traced over 3500 years to the Shang dynasty. Archaeological evidence for an early Chinese theoretical and practical system of health care began to appear in 1899 when a vast number of inscribed tortoise shells as well as scapula-bones of ox and sheep used in divination around the 13th century BC were discovered. They indicated that at least the ruling classes of the Shang population practised what might be called 'ancestral healing'. Accordingly personal and community welfare were understood to depend, to a large extent, on a harmonious relationship between the living members of society and their non-living ancestors. Ancestral wrath, caused by human misbehaviour, resulted in crop failure, defeat in battles and similar problems affecting the entire community, as well as in toothache, headache and other illnesses affecting single individuals. Prevention and treatment of social and personal maladies required the maintenance or restoration of a friendly attitude of the ancestors towards the living, achievable through continuous offerings and prayers as well as through the accepted rules of social behaviour. The oracle inscriptions contain a few references to 'natural' causes of illness, such as wind and snow. Whether the Shang, in addition to ancestral healing, utilized drugs or employed techniques in their treatment of illness is not known.

Demonic medicine

The kingdom of the Shang was destroyed and succeeded by the Zhou. After the initial establishment of a stable order, internal strife developed at the start of the 8th century BC and resulted in what is perhaps the longest period of unrest and extreme socio-economic change hitherto known in China. It is only with this historical background in mind that one can understand the emer-

gence of demonic medicine as a new system of ideas about the causation of illness and prescribing the appropriate preventative and curative practices. With the collapse of the ancient moral order the notion of a harmonious relationship with the non-living members of society also faded. It was superseded by a concept of evil demons constantly seeking to attack man. These demons were to be repelled by the spirits inherent in man himself and also by alliances with members of the highest echelons of the spiritual hierarchy. Talismans, amulets, exorcistic spells and, in later centuries, drugs were recognized as useful in demonstrating such alliances and in directly fighting demonic intruders. Demonic medicine was widely practised up to this century; it was adhered to especially, but not exclusively, by the less privileged sections of the population for whom insecurity, caused by either socio-political or natural calamities, was a persistent reality.

In a more subtle form, demonic medicine has persisted in traditional Chinese medicine in its ontological thinking. Chinese medicine has been characterized for the past two thousand years by two fundamental approaches to an understanding of illness, including an ontological and a functional perspective. The ontological approach to illness views illnesses as results of an intrusion of foreign agents into the body. The disease is the presence of the foreign agent in the body, be it a demon, an insect, or, more recently, a bacterium or virus. Such an approach necessitates a precise knowledge of the location of the intruder in the body, and, for therapy, the elimination of it. The ontological perspective is closely associated with militaristic terminology of 'attack' and 'defence', of 'killing', 'struggle', and other such concepts, all of which abound in Chinese medical texts based on ontological perspectives. Health, in this regard, is viewed as successful defence in an ever-lasting struggle both among the individual regions or organs within the body, and between the body and possible intruders from the outside.

In contrast, the functional approach to an understanding of illness views harmony and equilibrium among the individual parts of the organism and between the organism and its natural and social environment as normal, and as a state of health. Illness reflects a malfunctioning of one or more of the subsystems within the organism. Diagnosis must take the entire organism into regard to find the causes and consequences of this malfunctioning, and therapy is to be directed at the system as a whole, not at its individual segments.

Pragmatic drug medicine and the medicine of systematic correspondence

During the turmoil of the Zhou period several philosophies emerged to explain the reasons for contemporary chaos and to advocate ways of returning to order and stability. The best known, and the ones having had the most influence on traditional medicine, were Daoism, Confucianism and Legalism.

Early Daoists saw life alternating between corporeal and non-corporeal existence, with illness and death being indicators of transition. Efforts to maintain corporeal life, and extend it to eternity, were a later development in Daoism, beginning, approximately, with the 3rd or 2nd century BC. Subsequently, a wealth of techniques for traditional body care and drugs were found to be useful in health care. In particular, knowledge of how to prepare and utilize natural and man-made substances for the prevention and cure of illness developed to become a distinct therapy system. Because it was based mainly on information gained through observation and experiments rather than on theoretical speculation this system may be called pragmatic drug medicine.

Also during the last two or three centuries of the first millennium BC, the foundations were laid for another distinct system of healing, the medicine of systematic correspondence. The theoretical foundations of this therapy system, as well as its terminology and therapeutic principles, were closely linked with the socio-political concepts of order and crisis of the Confucian ideology (especially after their modification by Xunzi (Xun Kuang) (d. 238 BC) who added Legalist notions) which were conceived and propagated at approximately the same time. As a consequence, we may assume that the rise of this healing system to a dominant position (as far as the educated elite of imperial China was concerned), its persistence until early this century, and its more recent replacement by modern Western medicine were dependent upon the fate of Confucianism and the social structure of imperial and post-imperial China.

The basic assumption underlying the medicine of systematic correspondence was that all phenomena can be grouped in either two (*yin* and *yang*) or five (the Five Phases, *wu xing*) categories. All phenomena within one category correspond to each other, being, in fact, different manifestations of one and the same principle. The various categories themselves form a complicated, but logical, system of interdependencies and mutual interactions. Thus, as day emerges from night, and as low tide follows high tide, and vice versa, the *yin* category of existence bears in it the beginnings of the *yang* category, and the *yang* category, in turn, gives way to the *yin* category. As a consequence, various subcategories of *yin* and *yang* were identified, permitting subtle gradations among phenomena associated with one or the other. For example the annual seasons correspond with the following four subcategories: *yin*-in-*yin* (or pure *yin*, i.e. winter) followed by *yang*-in-*yin* (i.e. spring), followed by *yang*-in-*yang* (or pure *yang*, i.e. summer), followed by *yin*-in-*yang* (i.e. autumn). A second system of gradation identified three *yin* and three *yang* subcategories, i.e. great-*yin*, minor-*yin* and incomplete-*yin*, and great-*yang*, minor-*yang*

and *yang*-brilliance. As the various *yin* and *yang* categories and sub-categories were known to succeed and overcome each other and, at the same time, to reproduce each other, phenomena associated with these categories were known to interact accordingly. Similarly, the Five Phases, symbolized by Water, Wood, Fire, Earth and Metal, represented five categories into which all known phenomena could be classified. In a fivefold cyclical order these categories were identified as five stages in the interaction of all phenomena. For example, just as wood produces fire, phenomena associated with the category of 'fire' were assumed to be supplied with strength by phenomena associated with the category of 'wood'; and as water subdues fire, phenomena associated with the former were believed to have control over phenomena associated with the latter. The life of an individual—in fact, the entire existence of society—is part of this system of correspondences, with every phenomenon, be it an organ, emotion, physiological function or the external means to affect these, having its definite place within this system.

Apart from this basic theoretical foundation, the medicine of systematic correspondence rested upon a peculiar understanding of the organism. The oldest Chinese medical texts preserved today, compiled approximately 1800 to 2200 years ago, depict the human body as a complicated system of tangible anatomical elements and abstract functions. For instance, the major internal organs were identified by size, colour and weight, and a rudimentary notion of blood circulating through vessels is documented. The origins of this early anatomical knowledge are unknown and—with only intermittent references to dissections—few new insights were added in later centuries; discussions documented in the medical literature focused on the functions and hierarchical order of the organs. It was not until the early 19th century, when Wang Qing-ren (1768–1831) published the treatise *Correcting Errors in Medical Literature* that a Chinese author—not yet influenced by Western medicine—reconsidered ancient knowledge on the basis of precise anatomical studies.

The medicine of systematic correspondence viewed the organism in terms of the economic structures of unified China as introduced by the Legalist administration of the Qin dynasty and continued by Confucian policy-makers of the Han era. The organism, therefore, was seen as consisting of storage and consumption systems which were linked by a system of transportation channels responsible for the transportation of resources from one place to another. These resources were conceived of as influences of subtle, dispersible matter (*qi*) emanating from a variety of external sources. After their absorption by the body, mainly through skin, mouth and nose, these influences had to be stored, transformed, transported, consumed and disposed of properly. Unbalanced exposure to external influences, as well as inadequa-

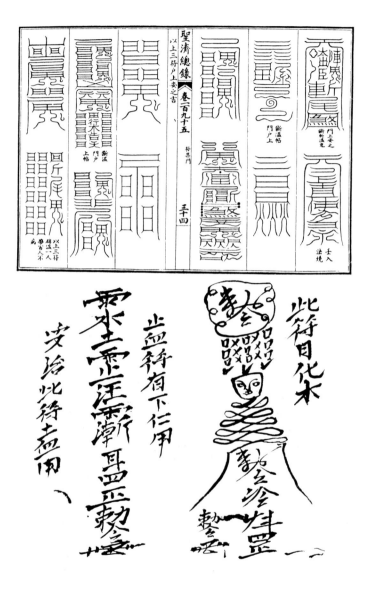

other tangible influences, but in addition required, for example, careful observation of one's emotions and of one's relationships with other members of society.

The moral component inherent in the medicine of systematic correspondence appears to have brought it into sharp contrast with the basically amoral systems of demonic medicine and pragmatic drug medicine. Belief in demonic medicine implies that adherence to ethical norms has no bearing on one's health. Similarly, the underlying notion of pragmatic drug medicine implies that there are natural or artificially produced substances available which are able to prevent or cure any health problem resulting from deviations in one's lifestyle from the correct path prescribed by nature, thereby freeing an individual from adherence to an inconvenient morality.

Furthermore, an awareness of the 'liberal' moral basis of drug medicine may have contributed to the fact that it was not until the 12th to 14th centuries that efforts were undertaken to develop a pharmacology of systematic correspondence. Up to that time the therapeutic practice of the medicine of systematic correspondence had almost exclusively relied, theoretically at least, on the conduit therapies acupuncture and moxibustion.

During the entire 2nd millennium the medicine of systematic correspondence was subjected to an increasing inner fragmentation. Stimulated by the Neo-Confucianism of the Song era to 'advance knowledge through the investigation of things', but hampered by a lack of detailed anatomical knowledge and also by the necessity of basically adhering to the fundamental notions of systematic correspondence (which happened also to be the fundamental notions of important aspects of Confucian social theory), numerous speculative schools of medical thought developed, each of which emphasized different aspects within the ancient conceptual framework while denouncing rival schools as incompetent. This situation prevailed until the early 20th century and is reflected in the antagonisms between the many different schools of so-called 'Chinese medicine' in the contemporary West.

When European and American physicians entered China in the 19th century, they did not encounter one more or less homogeneous therapy system representative of Chinese culture, but a number of partially interrelated conceptual systems including, among others, pragmatic drug medicine, the medicine of systematic correspondence and—probably strongest in terms of actual numbers of followers—demonological healing. Also, Buddhist medicine played an important part in the therapeutic spectrum of pre-modern (and modern) China. Brought to East Asia during the 1st millennium by Central Asian, Indian and, later, Chinese monks, Indian medical lore was not accepted widely in China except for certain Buddhist religious practices, i.e. prayers and

Above: a page from the notebook of an early 20th-century shaman. Top: spell drawings from a collection of prescriptions published early in the 12th century.

cies regarding any of the functions from storage to disposal, caused illness and required treatment. Consequently, prevention of illness was achieved through a certain lifestyle, exposing the individual to a balanced assortment of all essential influences and keeping the individual from depleting his resources through a variety of exhausting activities. This implied not only a regulated intake of certain foods, a regulated exposure to heat and cold and many

offerings, which continue to flourish in Chinese Buddhist communities up to the present time.

All of the conceptual therapy systems mentioned here were further fragmented by a large number of schools providing alternative and even opposing interpretations within their respective conceptual frameworks. For example, within the medicine of systematic correspondence some schools continued to propagate the ideas of a pharmacology of systematic correspondence, introduced during the Song-Jin-Yuan era, while others rejected these concepts as meaningless. Numerous opinions coexisted as to the role of demons in the human body. Some authors maintained that demons were mere illusions of one's mind, others insisted on their actual existence as distinct beings. And, as a final example, in pragmatic drug medicine a controversy was documented in Qing literature as to whether drugs discovered, and incorporated into *materia medica*, after the Han era were of any value if compared with those that had been pointed out as effective by Shennong, the legendary founder of Chinese pharmaceutics, in ancient times.

Chinese medical theory is recorded in numerous works of traditional Chinese medical literature and other references are found in marginal writings, such as historical accounts and novels. The reality of daily therapeutic practices and commonly held beliefs in pre-19th-century China is, however, difficult to assess. Only recently, through occasional observations and systematic fieldwork, has information become available on actual patterns of consultation and folk beliefs. While such research is still incomplete it suggests, first, a widespread existence of syncretic belief systems drawn from all the theoretical systems described above, and, secondly, eclectic patterns with people not adhering to a single specific medical system but varying their allegiance (now including those of modern Western medicine) so long as their problem remains unsolved.   *P.U.U.*

Face and pulse diagnosis

Traditional Chinese medicine employs four diagnostic techniques, ranked in the literature as follows: first, looking at a patient's face; second, listening to a patient's voice; third, asking a patient about his dietary preferences; and, fourth, feeling a patient's pulse. In the system of correspondence, complexion and emotional expression, the pitch of the voice and all food consumed were, among other phenomena, related, through the categories and subcategories of *yin* and *yang* and of the Five Phases, to physiological processes. Changes, for instance, in one's complexion were regarded as indicating changes in the organism.

Traditional physician in Hong Kong practising pulse diagnosis.

Likewise, each orifice of the face was considered to be linked directly to one of the internal organs, the appearance of the former reflecting the state of the latter.

During the early 2nd millennium AD pulsing became the dominant diagnostic technique. Three different pulses can be felt at each wrist; sometimes pulses at other locations are examined as well. At each pulse a large number of different pulsations is to be distinguished, like 'deep' or 'shallow', 'running' or 'pausing'. These pulsations, together with the location of the pulse, are supposed to reveal, first, the unimpeded or obstructed flow of influences through the transportation channels (or meridians) and, second, whether there are any deficiencies or over-abundancies in any of the internal storage or consumption systems of the organism, that is, whether the organs fulfil their proper functions, whether evil influences have been able to enter the organism, or whether the correct influences have been exhausted for one reason or another.

The medical literature of earlier centuries and evidence gleaned from systematic interviews with contemporary practitioners in Taiwan indicate that diagnosis on the basis of the system of correspondence is to be considered the most difficult and, therefore, seldom mastered aspect of traditional Chinese medicine. Traditional literature has, therefore, always supplied the practitioner with an alternative, that is, a mode of prescribing treatment in accordance with more obvious symptoms such as pain, diarrhoea, and so forth. Today, among traditional practitioners, a tendency exists to acknowledge and utilize diagnostic techniques and concepts of Western medicine, complemented by treatment with traditional drugs or techniques.   *P.U.U.*

Conduit therapies

Conduit therapies include acupuncture and moxibustion (usually termed together as *zhenjiu*) as well as drug therapy. In ancient times, as is suggested by some chapters of the *Huang Di neijing* (*The Yellow Emperor's Inner Classic*), acupuncture, i.e. the needling of specified points at the surface of the body, was applied to release a certain amount of blood from an artery close to an area of the body where pain or discomfort was felt by a patient. Also, as some references in early literature suggest, the technique of needling may have been employed initially to expel illness-causing demons from the body. Possibly beginning with the 3rd century BC, acupuncture and moxibustion (the burning of mugwort on the surface of the body), received a new theoretical rationale on the basis of the concepts of systematic correspondence. According to these concepts health depends, to a significant degree, on an unobstructed passage of specific influences through the organism. Treatment is required when, first, any of the 12 organic systems of the body is unable to store or transform these influences properly, resulting in deficiencies or surfeit, and, second, when the flow of these influences through the transportation channels (the conduits), which link the organic systems to each other and with the surface of the skin, is impeded. Furthermore, if 'evil' influences accumulate in the body, conduit therapies are applied to neutralize or expel them, re-establishing a dominance of 'correct' influences. The *Huang Di neijing* speaks of 365 sensitive points on the skin through which the desired effects of needling can be achieved. In subsequent centuries numerous additional acupuncture points were identified. Twelve main conduits and a number of additional secondary and tertiary 'network' conduits linked the sensitive points. All conduits and the specific organs they were associated with were classified as belonging to one of several *yin* and *yang* subcategories—i.e. the great-*yin*, minor-*yin*, incomplete-*yin*, great-*yang*, minor-*yang*, and *yang*-brilliance subcategories—and also to one of the Five Phases. Within the *yin* and *yang* subcategories the conduits were further distinguished according to their identified course either from chest to hand and from foot to chest, or from hand to head and from head to foot. As a result, each of the 12 conduits, and each of the many sensitive points linked by these conduits, were assigned a clearly defined place in a comprehensive system of correspondences. The choice of specific sensitive points to be needled in order to achieve a desired therapeutic result was suggested both by knowledge gained from experience and by theoretical considerations concerning correspondences between perceived states of illness, specific anatomical elements, desired therapeutic impact and the appropriate conduits to convey a therapeutic stimulus.

The use of drugs as an additional conduit therapy was developed in the 12th century. It was assumed that drug effects pass through specific conduits and that some drugs could guide others through specified conduits to a desired place of activity.

In recent years acupuncture has received renewed attention, supported by pragmatic and ideological considerations, not only for its traditional merits but also as a pain reliever, especially in surgical anaesthesia. Acupuncture is cheap to practise, well known to the populace and performed by vast numbers of traditional healers all over the country. However, a satisfactory explanation, on the basis of modern science, of the effects of acupuncture is not yet available.   *P.U.U.*

Ear acupuncture practised by a traditional healer in Shanghai.

Herbalism and pharmacology

The earliest known Chinese *materia medica*, listing 365 drugs, was compiled during the first or 2nd century AD; the earliest Chinese herbal, the text of which is still available, was published about the year 500. From approximately the 2nd century BC through the first millennium AD Daoists appear to have been predominant in the testing, application and compilation of knowledge on drugs. With the establishment of the Confucian teachings as the official doctrine of the empire during the Han dynasty, efforts to create an ideal society as envisaged by Daoism received a serious setback. While some Daoists continued to pursue their goals in more or less secret associations, it appears that others turned from attempts at social liberation to a preoccupation with individual liberation.

Drugs were recognized as one of several suitable media. They carried the promise of longevity, if not eternal life, and separated health from a moral order constructed by man, not by nature. Although the role of Daoism in the development of Chinese herbalism should be emphasized, contributions to its advancement came from virtually all sections of the population, including emperors and common peasants.

The accumulated knowledge is impressive. Both native and foreign substances were included in traditional Chinese *materia medica*, among them drugs from minerals, animals and plants, human substances as well as man-made chemicals. The many herbals published over the centuries not only listed individual drugs and their curative properties but were concerned also with the places of origin, secondary names, appropriate preparation techniques, contraindications and side effects, antidotes, substitutes and adulterations, storage problems as well as the synergism and antagonism among different drugs. Numerous preparation processes were developed to adapt raw drugs to specific illnesses and patients; honey, wine, brine and vinegar, among other liquids, are still widely used by traditional apothecaries to direct the effects of a drug to specific areas within the body, or to enhance or mitigate specific qualities. Similarly, different dosage forms were developed, including pills (pasted with water, honey or flour, and coated, sometimes, with wax), powders, plasters, ointments, broths, medicinal wines, distillation products, mucuses, teas, eyedrops, enemas and, most common, decoctions.

Herbs and other traditional drugs were (and still are) sold either in apothecaries' shops, which not infrequently employed their own physician, or by physicians practising independently. Until the 20th century China did not have an official pharmacopoeia, that is, a compendium defining standards for the preparation and utilization of drugs, adherence to which is strictly enforced and supervised by the government. The first such code was published in 1930.

Until the 12th century AD Chinese pharmaceutics was scarcely touched by theoretical considerations on the basis of the concepts of systematic correspondence. Drugs were described, in the herbals, as curing specific symptoms or illnesses; the problem of why a specific drug exerted a specific effect in a specific situation did not receive much explicit attention. There were some underlying notions, like magic correspondence, regarding the selection of drugs, but the sophisticated theories of systematic correspondence, that is the concepts of *yin-yang* and of the Five Phases, were applied to pharmaceutics only when Neo-Confucianism influenced medical thought. Parallel with the integration of some basic notions of Daoism into Confucianism at the time of the Song, attempts were made to integrate the use of drugs into the system of correspondence. The intended result of these efforts, known as 'Jin-Yuan Medicine', was the development of a pharmacology of systematic correspondence.

The basic principle of Jin-Yuan pharmacology consisted in associating primary drug qualities, that is, taste (pungent, bitter, sweet, salty, sour and neutral) and temperature (hot, warm, cool and cold) with secondary drug qualities, that is, intra-organic drug behaviour (ascending, descending, penetrating, draining, etc.), which, in turn, were associated with specific states of the organism. All drug qualities and organic states were therefore translated into categories of *yin* and *yang* and of the Five Phases. For example, in a particular illness identified as the result of too many *yang* influences (for instance, heat) in a *yin* organ (for instance, the liver), a physician decided that in order to eliminate this surfeit he would drain *yang* influences from another organ which was known to be supplied by the afflicted organ with *yang* influences. The latter (the 'mother-organ'), it was assumed, was then forced to send its surplus of *yang* influences to the former (the 'child-organ', in this case the heart). Such indirect draining was viewed as preferable to direct draining. The physician, then, needed to identify the *yin* or *yang* conduits leading to or from the organ to be drained and he

Illustration from a 19th-century botanical-pharmaceutical work showing the plant *Luying* (*Sambucus javanica* Reinw.) which was used to treat a wide variety of ailments.

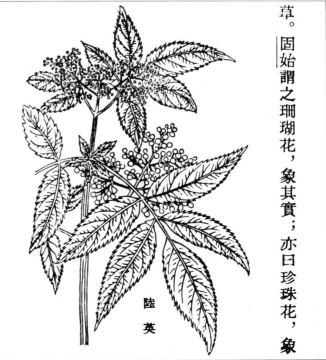

Above left: example of sympathetic magic in a 16th-century *materia medica* expressing the hope that the delivery of the drug to the appropriate part of the body might be as speedy and easy as the shooting of a crossbow bolt. Above right: traditional pharmacist in an apothecary's shop in Taipei.

had to select drugs which, in accordance with the *yin-yang* (and Five Phases) categorization of their primary and secondary qualities, were supposed to penetrate the appropriate conduit, to ascend or descend to the desired place of effectiveness and, there, to drain *yang* influences. Because the *yin* and *yang* categories were further subdivided in to *yin*-in-*yin*, *yang*-in-*yin*, *yang*-in-*yang*, and *yin*-in-*yang* as well as into great-*yin*, minor-*yin*, incomplete-*yin*, great-*yang*, minor-*yang* and *yang*-brilliance subcategories—allowing for subtle gradations of drug qualities, organic states and conduits—complicated prescriptions of numerous drugs were needed. Furthermore, specific drugs were added by Jin-Yuan pharmacologists to a prescription because they had been identified as so-called 'guiding-drugs', leading the effects of the remaining drugs of a formula through specified conduits to the desired place of action.

The Jin-Yuan pharmacology was inductive in the sense that an established body of theories was imposed, from outside, on an established body of empirical knowledge. Its merits for the practitioner of the medicine of systematic correspondence were that he was provided with a theoretical framework enabling him to understand the effects of drugs in terms and concepts similar to the notions underlying the application of needles in acupuncture, linking both of these modes of therapy with the knowledge on illness causation, treatment and prevention as provided by the paradigm of systematic correspondence. And yet, while the Jin-Yuan pharmacology appears to have been quite suitable for *post-facto*

explanations of drug effects, its predictive value seems to have been rather limited for various reasons, including the absence of objective criteria for defining primary and secondary qualities of substances. Contradictions arose as to whether a particular drug was sweet or bitter in taste, and whether it was hot or warm, a decision having important consequences for the position of this drug in the entire system of correspondence. Some authors assigned different primary qualities to one and the same drug, defining it to be, for instance, cold and warm at the same time. Such attributions were necessary to explain diverse effects of single drugs by means of the logic of systematic correspondence, that is, in order to harmonize a variety of observed drug effects with alleged primary qualities of these substances. The creative phase of the Jin-Yuan pharmacology ended with the 14th century, and no further efforts to elaborate a pharmacology were undertaken until the 20th century.

In the People's Republic of China, in Taiwan, in Hong Kong and among overseas Chinese the practice of traditional Chinese herbalism is ubiquitous. Apothecaries' shops selling herbal, mineral or animal (and even human) drugs on prescription or for self-treatment can be found in virtually all cities and larger towns.   *P.U.U.*

Traditional body care

In ancient China various techniques were developed to improve physical strength and to extend the average life-span. Breathing exercises, gymnastics (including so-called 'shadow-boxing', *taijiquan*) and massage emerged not only as methods of body care, but also as means of therapy. Possibly of an empirical origin, these techniques were, during the times of the Qin and Han, conceptualized on the basis of theories advocating the importance of a correct distribution and flow of 'subtle matter influences' (*qi*) and blood (*xue*) in the body. Since then, the cultivation of subtle matter influences essential for the organism and, equally important, the preservation or enrichment of one's primordial subtle matter, were developed as practices of mainly Daoist concern, involving not only the techniques mentioned but others, like specified sexual practices, as well. For example, the male semen (*jing*) was generally believed to be the purest manifestation of one's primordial subtle matter (*jing*) and it was known to generate new life once it had met with specific influences produced by females. As a consequence, techniques were elaborated for men not only to avoid ejaculation of semen created during repeated intercourse (preferably with different partners) but also to absorb the female component and thus reproduce life within themselves. Schools adhering to such concepts identified the right times, partner positions, frequencies and other details of sexual intercourse as distinct 'prescriptions' for the cure of illnesses.

Practising *taijiquan* in Beijing.

Buddhists came especially to appreciate respiratory techniques, and Bodhidharma, a famous Indian monk who settled in China about AD 520, is credited with the introduction of an innovative system of relaxation gymnastics. Earlier Hua Tuo, possibly a legendary figure, had invented a series of 'flowing', circular movements, supposedly enabling man to live through the entire 100 years allotted to him by heaven. In 1973 silk fragments depicting numerous phases of obviously gymnastic movements were excavated in Hunan Province from a burial site of 168 BC. In later manuals full concentration, continual exercising and its gradual intensification were recognized as important principles.

Massage was intended to be either tonifying, stimulating or sedative. Techniques employing fingertips, thumbs, the ball of the thumb or the entire palm of the hand were (and still are) applied on specified regions of the body to achieve well defined results.

P.U.U.

Traditional medical literature

More than 10 000 medical titles are known to have been published in China from the time of the Han dynasty to the end of imperial rule early this century. This vast body of literature constitutes a rich source of knowledge not only for those who are interested in the actual therapeutic value of traditional Chinese medicine but also for scholars concerned with social, cultural and medical history. Yet this material remains almost completely hidden from Western audiences despite several large collections in Europe and in the USA. There exist complete translations of traditional Chinese medical texts only a small number of which, in philological accuracy, can be compared with modern editions of ancient Greek or Latin texts.

The oldest texts extant today are fragments of manuscripts unearthed from a grave of the 2nd century BC in Hunan Province in 1973. Their contents include theoretical as well as practical considerations; drugs, gymnastics, petty surgery as well as various demonological rituals (including spells and magic movements) were recommended as major therapeutic techniques. Surprisingly, there is no reference at all to the practice of acupuncture. Authors, titles and the exact age of these texts are unknown. The body of Chinese traditional medical literature may be classified into three major groups: theoretical treatises, prescription literature and pharmaceutical literature. Apart from these, works were published on topics like medical history, veterinary medicine, specified techniques and sexual hygiene. The classics of traditional Chinese medico-theoretical literature are the *Huang Di neijing* (*The Yellow Emperor's Inner Classic*) and the *Nanjing* (*The Classic of Difficult Issues*). The *Huang Di neijing* constitutes the major source of the theoretical system of correspondence. Its authorship is largely unknown. The present version may have been compiled between the 2nd century BC and the 8th century AD; it was revised during the Song dynasty. Its content is heterogeneous and may reflect different traditions of medical thought. Throughout the centuries numerous commentaries on the *Huang Di neijing* were written, explaining or elaborating the system of correspondence. Aside from presenting the system of correspondence in general, theoretical literature was concerned, for instance, with aetiology, the oldest known specialized work on this subject being the *Zhubing yuan hou lun* (*On the Origins and Symptoms of all Diseases*) of the early 7th century. Theoretical literature was concerned further with specific health problems and their causes, like smallpox, malaria and many other illnesses, or with specific questions dealing, for instance, with diagnosis, acupuncture or moxibustion. Works focusing on the inner structure of the organism may also be counted among theoretical literature since, in the absence of systematic dissections, their contents remained basically speculative until the 19th century.

Zhang Ji (142–220?) was the author of the earliest Chinese prescription works still extant today, the best known among them being the *Shanghan lun* (*On Harm Caused by Cold*). This example of focusing on one aetiological entity was followed by only a few authors in subsequent centuries. In contrast, by the end of the Southern Song, more than 600 comprehensive collections of prescriptions had been published, listing formulae against all types of health problems. In addition, specialized works advocated specific prescriptions against children's or women's diseases while still others listed remedies against affliction of the eyes or teeth or of the mouth. Furthermore, this literary genre comprised works providing prescriptions for attaining longevity, for health maintenance through sexual practices and for therapy by means of exorcizing spells and rituals.

The third major category of traditional Chinese medical literature consists of the *bencao* works, herbals focusing on descriptions of individual drugs. Close to 400 titles are known to have been published in this category with 200 of them still being available today. The oldest *bencao* known by title is the *Shennong bencaojing* (*Shennong's Classic on* Materia Medica), supposedly compiled during the Eastern Han dynasty. It listed 365 drugs which were classified, according to their medical strength, into three groups, the 'upper' containing drugs suitable for prolonging life, the 'lower' containing drugs suitable for attacking illnesses, and a 'middle' group combining drugs of both these types. Tao Hongjing (452–536), a Daoist, was the first known author to adopt a natural order as the major principle in grouping drugs in a herbal. The first drug compendium compiled by a committee commissioned by the government was published in 659; it was also the first known to have been illustrated. The earliest printed herbal appeared in 973. During the 11th and 12th centuries the number of substances described in a single comprehensive compendium rose to approximately 1750. The only Chinese herbal widely known in the West is the *Bencao gang mu* (Materia Medica *Ordered on the Basis of Monographs and Individual Characteristics*) by Li Shizhen (1518–93). The *Bencao gang mu* is a voluminous compendium describing about 1893 substances. The author quoted 952 previously published books from various literary genres and expanded the traditional herbal to a detailed encyclopedia of medicine, pharmaceutics, mineralogy, metallurgy, botany and zoology. The *Bencao gang mu* contains not only the expert knowledge of Li Shizhen and earlier authors but also critical statements on the history of various areas of natural science. The *Bencao gang mu* represents the acme of *bencao* literature; no author in later centuries attempted to expand, or even equal, this work.

Apart from *bencao* compilations with comprehensive contents, specialized *bencao* works were written focusing on subjects including dietetics, pharmaceutical technology and the geographical location of drugs. Others were limited to the detailed description of just one drug, or were written in verse to aid the student memorizing pharmaceutical knowledge.

Chinese traditional medical literature reflects a diversity of ideas and methods. Although it was heavily influenced by the theoretical system of correspondence, the remaining conceptual systems developed in the history of Chinese medicine were

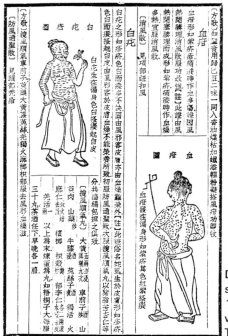

Drawings illustrating skin ailments, from an 18th-century medical work (modern Taiwanese reprint).

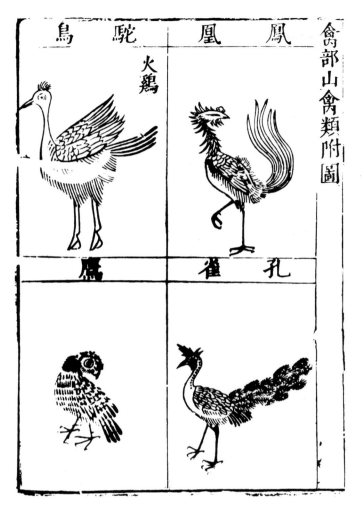

Woodblock illustrations of birds, parts of which were used as drugs, from the second edition of the *Bencao gang mu*, published in 1603.

represented in numerous works as well. Thus, pragmatic drug medicine, demonic medicine, Buddhist healing and other systems of thought had their distinct literary traditions but can also be found combined in eclectic publications. Inevitably, though, Chinese traditional medical literature mirrors the knowledge of the upper, literate sections of the population in imperial China. An exception is a treatise entitled *Chuanya* (*A String of Exceptionally Fine Prescriptions*), which resulted from interviews given by an itinerant healer in the 18th century to a medical scholar. The *Chuanya* provides its readers with a rare insight into alternative concepts and practices applied in health care by the lower strata of traditional Chinese society. The book is comprehensive in its coverage of therapeutic techniques known in pre-modern China, including,

among others, the application of needles, drugs, plasters, ointments, poultices, baths, breathing techniques and fumigation. Yet the conceptual rationale for employing these techniques appears, where discernible, to differ from the scientific paradigms documented elsewhere. For example, the application of drugs was not conceptualized in terms of the Five Phases and *yin-yang*. Drugs were described in the *Chuanya* as acting like fishing nets (affecting and cleansing the entire organism), like a cutting sword (cutting off a pathological segment from the remaining healthy organism), and, finally, like a cudgel (their effects radiating in various directions in the organism). In addition to drugs to be taken internally, numerous substances are defined and prescribed in this book as so-called spell-drugs; it is sufficient to place them at an appropriate location in or outside one's house to benefit from their particular curative and preventive effects.

P.U.U.

Western and Chinese medicine combined

When, early in the 19th century, European and American physicians began practising in China, Western medicine had not yet achieved, in daily practice, any of the remarkable breakthroughs that were to distinguish it from other medical systems in later decades. Therefore, the initial contact between Western and Chinese medical practitioners was marked by mutual interest and cooperation. Only after the discovery of antisepsis and anaesthesia, and when the potential of chemotherapy was fully realized, did Western medical men begin to look down on traditional Chinese practitioners, an attitude which was to be reinforced in the 20th century with the development of antibiotics and modern medical technology. For more than 100 years, from the middle of the 19th century through the middle of the 20th century, Western and Chinese medicine fiercely competed for patients as well as for support from government. The opposition to traditional Chinese medicine was shared, for the first four or five decades of this century, by virtually all intellectual and political groups—including Nationalists and Marxists—concerned with an adaptation of Chinese civilization to modernity and international standards. It was only after the establishment of the People's Republic of China that, for pragmatic and ideological reasons, the need to eliminate competition between Western and Chinese medicine was realized.

Cooperation or even integration of the two systems was to be attempted on a large scale in the mid-1950s. The small number of Western-trained physicians and their concentration in urban centres called for an acknowledgement of the contributions of traditional practitioners to individual and public health, and also for policies raising the standards of traditional practice. Furthermore, in 1940 the general enthusiasm of early Chinese Marxists towards Western science and medicine had been somewhat reduced by a few Marxist dogmatists pointing out the 'capitalistic, imperialistic and colonialistic context' of modern medicine. Such accusations were reinforced in the early years of the People's Republic when major difficulties arose in the Communist government's attempts politically to direct the Western-type medical establishment. Several programmes resulted from a recognition of these problems. It was assumed that traditional practitioners should be trained in modern diagnostic and therapeutic skills to fill the gap of Western-type health care in rural areas, while, at the same time, Western-type physicians were exhorted to study traditional knowledge in order to become familiar with the 'Chinese people's own heritage'.

During the 1960s programmes for an actual cooperation and combination of Western and Chinese medicine were further elaborated. In numerous clinics practitioners of the Chinese system of correspondence and of pragmatic drug medicine worked together with their Western-type colleagues in solving their patients' problems. Practitioners of demonological medicine were not included, their theories and practices being denounced as 'superstitious' by the government. The efforts to overcome the antagonism between Western and Chinese medicine led, in addition, to modern scientific research into the therapeutic principles and value of traditional drugs and techniques. Studies were designed to discover a scientific rationale, for instance, for acupuncture; likewise, hundreds of drugs recorded in the *bencao* literature were subjected to intensive pharmacognostic and pharmacological analyses. Finally, modern and traditional concepts, techniques and medications were combined in integrated treatments, especially in orthopaedics, dentistry, obstetrics, and internal medicine. The most spectacular combination of elements from modern and traditional knowledge was achieved in certain surgical operations employing acupuncture as a major analgesic and anaesthetic technique. Despite the relative success of these developments, they failed to solve all the problems arising from the continuing coexistence of Western and Chinese medicine.

In the 1970s, possibly facilitated by the ideological perspective of the Shanghai faction of the Chinese Communist Party, the so-called 'gang of four', efforts were made to achieve a dialecticalal synthesis of the two conflicting components of the Chinese health care system. Both traditional and modern practices were divested, as much as possible, of their original conceptual background and were reinterpreted on the basis of dialectic materialism as elements of what came to be called 'New Chinese Democratic Medicine'. With the downfall of the 'gang', however, renewed attention was paid to modern scientific approaches which were considered to promise the best basis of health care in China.

Abroad, in Taiwan and in Hong Kong, the combination of Western and Chinese medicine remains sporadic and depends on private initiative. There are individual physicians who have mastered and practise both types of therapy, and a few university and private institutes pursue research in traditional drugs and therapeutic techniques. *P.U.U.*

Anaesthesia

Anaesthesia in contemporary China uses identical principles as anaesthetic practice in the West. A difference has been reported in that the ratio of general anaesthesia to local or conduction anaesthesia, which is approximately 85–90 to 15–10 in Western surgery, appears to be exactly reversed in China. While Western experts have been impressed by the high degree of sophistication demonstrated by Chinese anaesthetists in applying conduction blockades, in most Chinese hospitals technical and personal prerequisites for an extensive application of modern methods of general anaesthesia seem to be unavailable. Local anaesthesia dominates, for instance, in replantation surgery. Chinese patients, fully conscious and only regionally anaesthetized, have been seen to remain quiet, without movement for up to 10 hours while undergoing micro-surgery.

During the Cultural Revolution, in particular during the 1970s, and in accordance with efforts to combine modern Western and traditional Chinese techniques, so-called acupuncture anaesthesia was forced on to Chinese surgery. This technique was developed during the past 20 years; it combined certain procedures using needles with electrostimulation, pre-medication and sometimes concurrent medication in order to achieve regional analgesia or anaesthesia for a

Preparations in a Shanghai hospital for the removal of a brain tumour while the patient is under acupuncture anaesthesia.

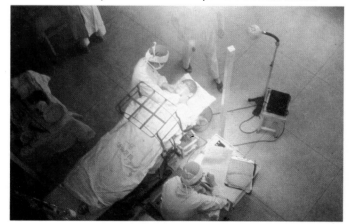

wide range of surgical interventions. The acceptance of this kind of pain relief by carefully selected patients seemed to be facilitated by their attitude of mind towards pain. Examples of surgery with acupuncture anaesthesia ranged from lens extractions in cataract patients and extirpation of cystic thyroadenoma to mitral valve surgery in mitral stenosis patients. The latter operation was performed with open pneumothorax, the patient having been taught to rely exclusively on abdominal breathing during surgery. Furthermore, acupuncture anaesthesia has been employed successfully in open heart surgery with extracorporeal circulation. Today, the role of acupuncture in surgical anaesthesia is marginal due to problems of reliability and patient acceptance.   *P.U.U.*

Medical services

The provision of medical services in the People's Republic of China has been characterized over the recent decades by: an initial extreme shortage of modern trained practitioners; an occasional antagonism between the socio-political goals of the Chinese Communist Party and the policies pursued by expert administrators advocating a Western-type health care system; the introduction of innovative programmes and unusual manpower categories; as well as the cultural legacy of the past.

In imperial China health care was greatly influenced by an antiprofessional sentiment inherent in Confucian social policy. Beginning with the 7th century, when the first known lengthy statement on professional medical ethics was published by a physician in China, a struggle ensued between a group of health care experts and Confucian dogmatists trying to prevent the emergence of a powerful professional group challenging their authority. Confucian ethics of health care, propagated for many centuries, called for an acquisition of sufficient medical knowledge by everyone, enabling any person to aid his relatives in times of need. A limited number of experts—for service at the court and in public administration—was trained, from Tang times onwards, in medical schools. In the 19th and early 20th century Western medicine was introduced on a large scale by physicians practising as Christian missionaries or working for secular philanthropic organizations. Facilities for training Chinese students in modern medicine were founded and by the 1920s and 1930s thousands of Chinese Western-type physicians practised in China, located mainly in the urbanized coastal regions. Nevertheless, when the People's Republic of China was founded in 1949, modern medical manpower resources (estimates vary between 10 000 and 40 000 physicians of widely differing qualifications) were quite inadequate to meet even the country's most urgent needs. Subsequently innovative policies, sometimes opposed by the Western-trained medical establishment, were initiated to improve the medical services available.

The primary emphasis of the health care system was directed at services for workers, peasants and soldiers. Priority in planning was given to the prevention of common and recurrent diseases. Certain widespread public and personal health problems were 'attacked' by mass-campaigns, aiming, for instance, at schistosomiasis control (and eventual eradication) and involving, at times, hundreds of thousands of people. The training of different categories of medical manpower was broadened; figures show an estimated graduation of at least 15 000 to 20 000 'regular physicians' (although of varying standards) per year from 1958 onwards. In addition, hundreds of thousands of assistant physicians, nurses, midwives and pharmacists were trained in selected areas of modern health care. To offset the lack of modern manpower in the countryside, a rotation system was begun in 1965. Physicians from urban hospitals were required to spend between three and 12 months in rural health centres, if they did not move there permanently. At times, during the Cultural Revolution, up to one-third of urban physicians were on such assignments. In addition, mobile medical teams were sent to cover remote regions without access to clinics or hospitals. These teams would spend up to three months at a given location, checking, treating and educating the local inhabitants.

So-called barefoot doctors, worker doctors and Red Guard doctors were trained until the early 1980s to perform lower-level medical services. Barefoot doctors were agricultural workers who, after attending short training courses of a few weeks' or of a few months' length, spent about half of their time with responsibilities like health education, first aid, treatment of simple ailments, immunizations and environmental sanitation. Worker doctors performed similar tasks in factories, while Red Guard doctors, mostly housewives or retired persons, staffed so-called Red Medical Posts in urban neighbourhoods, keeping statistical records, emphasizing birth control, and providing immunization, health care information and similar assistance. A referral system was set up to facilitate the provision of medical attention in accordance with the severity of each case. Payment systems varied regionally, ranging from communal or state funding to fees for service. By the mid-1980s the system of barefoot doctors, worker doctors and Red Guard doctors was superseded; medical care is provided now by hospitals or clinics, operated by various administrative units as well as by physicians in private practice.

Traditional practitioners, numbering about half a million in 1949, have increasingly been integrated into the official health care system. Their training continues both in apprenticeship settings and in medical schools. Traditional physicians practise in hospitals and clinics, sometimes cooperating with modern-trained colleagues.   *P.U.U.*

GAMES AND SPORTS

Traditional games and sports

Throughout their history the Chinese have been extremely fond of games and sports, and their weakness for gambling (*dubo*) has been an anathema to Chinese moralists as well as successive governments from ancient times to the present. Recent archaeological excavations in the People's Republic of China have yielded rich material on games in use from the Han to Tang dynasties which adds to our knowledge gathered from written sources.

Among the most ancient games mentioned are *bo* and *yi*. The former seems to have been a game of dice played by two people with six black and six white pieces each on a board of 12 squares. A similar game, using marked bamboo sticks instead of dice, was *liubo*, which became popular during the Han dynasty and is well documented by pottery tomb figurines of this period. A more complex game was *shupu* of the 4th to 6th centuries, which was played by five people using 20 pieces of five different colours and five marked bamboo sticks on a board divided into three sections of 120 squares each. Related to this was a game called *shuangliu*, invented in the 3rd century and still popular during the Song dynasty, which has survived in Japan in various forms by the name of *suguroku*. This game, corresponding to the Western game of backgammon, was played by two people using 16 pieces each and two dice on a board divided into eight sections. Original boards of several varieties of this game from the Tang dynasty have survived in Shōsōin treasure house, Nara, Japan and among archaeological finds in Chinese Turkestan.

The game of *liubo*: Han dynasty glazed pottery figurines.

The second type of ancient game mentioned above, *yi*, is usually identified with the *weiqi* of later periods. In its earliest form this game seems to have been played on boards with 17 rows of 17 squares, as shown on a Tang dynasty painting discovered in Chinese Turkestan. Specimens of boards with 18 rows of 18 squares have been preserved in China from the Sui dynasty and in the Shōsōin from the Tang dynasty, and it was not until after the latter period that the present form with 19 rows of 19 squares gradually became popular. The game, which in the West is better known by its Japanese name of *go*, is played by two people with 120 black or white pieces each, and the goal is to encircle as many pieces of the opponent as possible. More similar to chess is the Chinese *xiangqi*, which, in a somewhat altered and more complicated form, became popular in Japan by the name of *shōgi*. It is played by two people using 16 red or black pieces each on a board divided into two sections of 32 squares each. There is also an ancient version of this game for three players with a board having three rows of 32 squares based on the armies of the Three Kingdoms.

Mention should also be made of a group of racing games with dice (similar to the old European Royal Game of the Goose), the *shengguantu*, which exists in various forms and is played on a plan divided in up to 98 sections arranged in a spiral, each representing a step in the hierarchy of Chinese officialdom. The latter is also reflected in a game called *zhuangyuanchou* consisting of 63 sticks, each carrying one of the academic titles that could be gained by passing official examinations.

Among the numerous games with dice and dominoes *mahjong* (*majiang*) and dominoes (*tianjiu*) are the most popular. The former is played by four people with 136 tiles marked by suits of symbols, of which certain combinations have to be acquired. The latter seems to have developed from a game of dice and consists of 32 pieces with eyes from double one to double six, of which 11 occur twice.

Many of the games mentioned above can also be played with cards (*yezi*), the history of which can be traced back to the Tang dynasty. Unfortunately, the earliest complete packs known cannot be dated before the 17th-century literary games. These, however, already show all the characteristics of the more recent money cards (*zhipai*), i.e. four suits of 10×10 000, 10 000 strings of coins, and single coins respectively, with nine cards each plus four special cards. These were later reduced to packs of three suits only, leaving out the 10×10 000 suit.

The Chinese are also well known for their puzzles, some of the better known ones being *qiqiaoban* (which became popular in Europe by the name of Tangram) and the complicated ring filling game called *jiulianhuan*, as well as for games of skill such as throwing arrows into a pot (*touhu*).

There are numerous lottery type games of chance, such as

guessing the winners of imperial examinations (*weixing*) or the names of historical personalities (*zihua*), betting on characters from the book *Qianziwen* called *baikepiao*, etc., as well as games of social entertainment, such as guessing the numbers of fingers (*caichuan*) well known in Europe by the name of Mora.

Among the most popular children's games and toys are shuttlecock (*jianzi*), diabolo (*kongzhong*), flying the kite (*fengzheng*), windmills (*fengche*), self-righting dolls (*budaoweng*) and various other dolls made of clay, wood or straw.

In games of competition, either animals were used, as in the case of cock fighting (*douji*), bullfighting (*douniu*), or cricketfighting (*douqu*); or men were pitched against each other, as in rowing (*jingdu*), tug-of-war (*bahe*), polo (*boluoqiu*), football (*zuqiu*), a kind of hockey (*daqiu*), etc.

Some of the martial arts (*wushu*) can be traced back to the first millennium BC. Among them the different kinds of boxing (*quanfa*), have especially attracted attention in the West. Two kinds are distinguished in China: the internal (*neijia*) and the external (*waijia*) systems. The former comprises techniques based on spiritual training similar to yoga, such as *taiji*, characterized by subtle yielding, *xingyi* stressing direct confrontation, and *bagua* emphasizing circular evasion and attack. The latter includes techniques of fighting without weapons, such as the ones developed by the monks of the Shaolin many hundreds of years ago. Chinese wrestling (*xianbu*) may have been influenced by Mongol wrestling in the 13th century and was later refined into *shuaijiao*, which, together with the technique of seizing (*qinna*), may have contributed to the development of *jūdō* in Japan.   *G.P.*

Western sports

Western incursions into China during the 19th century caused some writers to compare China and Japan, noting the importance of physical fitness in Japanese culture. In 1905 the Board of Education (*Xue Bu*) stipulated that physical education, consisting mainly of military gymnastics, should be a part of the school curriculum. Western sports, as recreation rather than military training, were initially introduced by the YMCA in the treaty ports. Basketball was introduced in 1896, shortly after its invention in America, and by 1910 knowledge of track and field events, football, basketball and tennis was widespread enough for the First National Athletics Meet to be held in Nanjing.

During the Republican period the Nationalist government promoted physical education to encourage unity and to strengthen the will of the people, reasserting the earlier military slant of school sports. Meanwhile, the obvious relationship between physical fitness and the ability to fight in a guerrilla war made sports an important part of life in the 'liberated' areas. The most common sports were track and field events, and swimming was encouraged—possibly after the experiences of the Long March.

Constitutionally, sport is an integral part of Chinese cultural life and the common slogan 'Friendship first, competition second' emphasizes that sport is for the common good, not for personal glory. It has proved a major problem to achieve a satisfactory balance between 'popularization' (*puji*) and 'raising standards' (*tigao*) and sports have always been involved in the political campaigns that have surrounded this problem.

Group of men playing Western-style cards.

Jiang Jia Liang, table tennis world champion, 1985 and 1987.

A combination of popularization and the raising of standards at the opening ceremony of the Third National Games, Beijing, 1975: coloured squares make up a gigantic picture of a swimmer while children present a tableau on the ground.

Action taken to popularize sports has included 'Radio Exercises' allowing office workers and students to limber up during the day, as well as widely publicized gestures such as Mao Zedong's swim down the Yangtze in 1966. Systems of standards to be attained in sports such as running, jumping and swimming were introduced in the 'Labour Defence System' in the 1950s, and a different voluntary system in 1973. In the countryside the absence of facilities has popularized games requiring a minimum of equipment, such as basketball, volleyball and table-tennis. Card games, mainly Chinese, but including bridge (*qiaopai*) are popular at all levels of

CHINA'S PERFORMANCE AT THE OLYMPIC GAMES

Event	23rd Olympiad 1984			24th Olympiad 1988		
	Gold	Silver	Bronze	Gold	Silver	Bronze
Gymnastics	5	4	2	1	–	1
Weightlifting	4	2	–	–	1	4
Shooting	3	–	3	–	1	1
Diving	1	1	1	2	3	1
Swimming	–	–	–	–	3	1
Rowing	–	–	–	–	1	1
Fencing	1	–	–	–	–	–
Archery	–	1	–	–	–	–
Volleyball	1	–	–	–	–	1
Basketball	–	–	1	–	–	–
Handball	–	–	1	–	–	–
Athletics	–	–	1	–	–	3
Table tennis*				2	2	1

*Not an event in 1984
Sources: *Information China*, vol. 2 p.861; *China Sports*, 1989/1, p. 6

society. To raise standards, schools and institutes were established to train athletes, teachers and coaches. To spot potential athletes, a system of spare-time schools has been set up where children practise their chosen sports, while the state has sponsored some sports, such as mountaineering, which require highly specialized equipment.

China's participation in international sports began with the Far Eastern Championship Games, held 10 times between 1913 and 1934. China participated in the Olympic Games in 1932, 1936 and 1948. After 1949 arguments as to whether Beijing or Taipei should represent China led to China's withdrawal from the International Olympic Committee (IOC) in August 1959. China applied for readmission to the IOC in 1975, and by 1979 a formula was devised allowing Taiwan to participate, though not as China. Taiwan withdrew in protest, resolving the issue in favour of the People's Republic of China.

The visit of an American table tennis team to China in April 1971 was the first public signal of impending rapprochement with the USA. After the normalization of China's status by the UN in October 1971, China steadily took its place in the world sporting community, joining the Asian Games Federation and various international sports federations. Since 1981 China has participated to an ever increasing extent in regional and world competitions. Chinese teams have been pre-eminent in world table tennis, badminton, volleyball and basketball championships, and now dominate the Asian Games. China resumed full participation in the Olympic Games at the 23rd Olympiad in 1984, and has made its presence felt in several events, notably gymnastics and diving. China dominated the XIth Asian Games held in Beijing in September 1990, participation in which by 36 national teams was interpreted by the Chinese authorities as an endorsement of their actions during and after the Beijing massacre.   *N.K.M., C.A.*

THE CONTINUITY OF CHINA

Inside the Forbidden City, Beijing, looking southeast towards the Meridian Gate, the city's southern entrance.

ARCHAEOLOGY

Legendary prehistory

Chinese mythology does not constitute a unified system. Of the mythical accounts of Chinese prehistory, it is generally true that the earlier the mythical events are supposed to have taken place, the later the text in which the myth appears for the first time. For example, the often quoted myth about the creation of the world by Pangu, a deity born from the egg of chaos, is actually one of the latest (c. AD 220), and may be of foreign (Indian or Southeast Asian) origin.

A much more ancient Chinese cosmogonic myth tells of the Great Yu and his progenitor Gun, both superhuman beings who could assume the shape of various animals. Anciently the earth was covered by floods. Gun stole from heaven the magical 'ever-swelling soil' with which he constructed dams to contain the waters; when he failed and died, Yu took over the 'ever-swelling soil' and constructed channels through which the water was drained into the sea. He fashioned the land into nine islands (or 'provinces'), which he graded and distributed to humans. Yu is said to have become the founder of the first Chinese dynasty, the Xia (trad. dates: 2205–1767 BC).

Like the myth of Yu, those about the remote ancestors of the subsequent Shang and Zhou dynasties are attested relatively early (c. 800 BC). Xie, the first ancestor of the Shang royal house, was conceived when his mother swallowed an egg dropped from Heaven. Hou Ji, founder of the royal Zhou Ji clan, was likewise the issue of a miraculous union between God on High and a human mother; still a boy, he distinguished himself by inventing agriculture.

In later times, these and other figures were incorporated into a complicated genealogy of mythical figures and cultural heroes, who were gradually demythologized ('euhemerized'). Traditional Chinese historians since the Han dynasty accepted them as historical figures; a succession of Three Sovereigns and Five Emperors were said to have governed China before the founding of the Xia dynasty. Although different sources name varying sets of these, the first of the Three Sovereigns is usually taken to have been Fuxi, brother and husband of the goddess Nügua. This divine couple with human bodies and dragons' tails is usually shown intertwined and holding a set-square and compass. Nügua created the first humans by modelling figures out of clay after the Universe had been almost destroyed by the monster Gonggong. Nügua invented marriage, while Fuxi taught his subjects to fish, hunt, domesticate animals and breed silkworms. He also invented the calendar, musical instruments and the Eight Trigrams.

Also among the Three Sovereigns ranks the ox-headed Shennong, another hero credited with the invention of agriculture and the discovery of medicinal plants. He set up markets and devised a system of knotted strings to keep records, and he extended the system of the Eight Trigrams to 64 Hexagrams.

Huang Di, the 'Yellow Emperor', was the first of the Five Emperors. Huang Di suppressed a rebellion of the southern barbarian tribes and founded the Chinese empire. He invented boats and carts, pottery and armour, as well as regulating religious ceremonies and devising an agricultural calendar. He studied all natural phenomena, particularly minerals and plants, and is closely associated with alchemy and medicine.

The last two of the Five Emperors were Yao and Shun, who were idealized as model rulers in Confucian legend. Yao yielded the throne to Shun, a farmer renowned on account of his filial piety, giving him his two daughters in marriage. Shun was said to have double pupils to his eyes and to have invented the writing-brush. Shun in turn abdicated in favour of Yu of Xia, after whom the succession went from father to son; this was the beginning of dynastic rule.

Despite the patently mythical accounts surrounding its founder, there is a chance that the Xia dynasty may have really existed, though Xia archaeological remains have not yet been identified with certainty. A list of Xia kings has been transmitted. The last of them, Jie, is reported to have been corrupt and degenerate and was overthrown by Tang the Victorious, founder of the Shang dynasty.

L.v.F.

Tomb-shrine of the divine couple Nügua and Fuxi with the symbols of construction and order.

Palaeolithic cultures

Lower Pleistocene human fossils have so far not been discovered in China, but stone tool assemblages found in the Nihewan Basin in northern Shanxi testify to human activity dating back to at least 2 000 000 years ago. Differences in the nomenclature used by Chinese and Western archaeologists make comparative studies difficult, but within China there is a clear development of local technical traditions, as well as the persistence of certain physical features, from Lower Palaeolithic to modern times; this could indicate that *Homo sapiens* evolved independently in East Asia. It appears that by about 20 000 BC the populations of north China and southern and Indo-China were sufficiently differentiated to be designated respectively as Mongoloid and Oceanic Negroid.

Homo erectus

In the 1920s fossil remains of over 40 humans were found in limestone caves at Zhoukoudian near Beijing. The fossils of 'Peking Man' were tragically lost during the Japanese invasion, but more

DISTRIBUTION OF MAJOR PALAEOLITHIC SITES

Zhoukoudian, site of the discovery of the fossil remains of Peking Man.

have since been found and dated by the uranium-thorium method to 500 000(+)–210 000 BC. Similar, but in part somewhat more primitive fossils of Middle Pleistocene date have been excavated in other areas of China, e.g., Yuanmou Man in Yunnan and Lantian in Shaanxi. They all belong to a hominid of upright posture known as *Homo erectus*. Besides considerable cranial capacity (1075cc as compared to 1350cc in modern man), *Homo erectus* already has the shovel-shaped incisors characteristic of modern Mongoloids. His stone tools, chiefly made of quartz flakes, are often retouched; the principal types are scrapers, choppers, points, awls and balls. The degree of technical skill is on a par with contemporary hominid cultures elsewhere, and shows slow but marked progress over time. Peking Man was a hunter who cooked his meat over a fire and supplemented his diet with nuts and berries; there is also evidence that he practised cannibalism. The Middle Pleistocene assemblages in south and southwest China may indicate links with the hominid populations of Southeast Asia, specifically with Java Man.

Middle and Upper Palaeolithic

The gradual transition from *Homo erectus* to *Homo sapiens* during the Middle Palaeolithic (*c.* 200 000–50 000 BC) is represented by a limited number of fossils that exhibit neanderthaloid characteristics. The most suggestive tool assemblages are those of Dingcun, Shanxi. It has been proposed that the heavy tools typical of this middle Yellow River area may indicate an economy based on food gathering rather than hunting, paving the way for the later development of plant domestication and agriculture.

By 50 000 BC, modern humans were ranging widely over north and south China; for the first time, clear differences can be distinguished between regional tool-making traditions. It is reasonable to assume that these manifest adaptations to different forms of environment, but other cultural factors may also have begun to play a role. Some of the Upper Palaeolithic (*c.* 50 000–10 000 BC) cultures may be directly ancestral to later Neolithic ones in the same areas, possibly indicating continuity of population and local transition to Neolithic lifestyles.

For instance, the late Middle Palaeolithic stone industries of the Ordos region are already characterized by meticulous secondary trimming and the presence of microliths. By the time of the emergence of *Homo sapiens*, microliths were a predominant form not only of the Ordos cultures but also in nearby parts of north China, as well as Mongolia and southern Siberia. The importance of microliths (e.g., arrowheads and spear-tips) may be due partly to the shortage of stone in these areas, but it also reflects the importance of hunting in the economy. Ostrich shells and the bones of steppe animals are numerous in these sites. It has been suggested that these cultures subsequently domesticated animals and developed a pastoral economy similar to that still practised in the steppes today.

L.v.F.

Neolithic cultures

According to most Western definitions the characteristics of Neolithic culture include polished stone tools, pottery, weaving, settled habitation and a knowledge of farming. Archaeological cultures exhibiting all these features, dating back to about the sixth millennium BC (or earlier), have been identified in China. The scattered earliest remains feature roughly polished stone tools and corded or incised pottery, sometimes with signs of plant or animal domestication. Their links to later, more developed neolithic cultures in the same areas are becoming clearer as archaeological work progresses. Some archaeologists feel that early neolithic cultural assemblages throughout East and Southeast Asia show sufficient similarity to be classified as belonging to a single cultural horizon, the 'Hoabinhian' (named after a type-site in Vietnam); in their interpretation, the classic Neolithic cultures of East Asia are local developments of this widespread Mesolithic or proto-Neolithic Hoabinhian culture.

The spread of agriculture

It is thought likely that a climatic amelioration between *c.* 6000 and 2500 BC facilitated long-term experimentation with food crops and the gradual adoption of a settled lifestyle by the early inhabitants of China. Yet as early as 5000 BC a pattern of two distinct agricultural traditions was clearly established. In north China, the Neolithic economy was based on drought-resistant crops like foxtail-millet and broom-corn millet, supplemented by green vegetables and native fruits (apricot, pear and jujube). In central and southern China the climate is gentler and more humid, most Neolithic settlements were near rivers or marshes, and large quantities of wet rice of the *indica* and *japonica* varieties were grown. Fish and aquatic plants (lotus, water chestnut and caltrop) were important dietary supplements. In both areas pigs and dogs were the earliest domesticates, but by 3000 BC sheep and cattle had become important in the north, water-buffalo and cattle in the south. The distinction between dryland agriculture in the north and wet-rice cultivation in the south persists today.

Some experts claim that millet and cultivated rice are native to north and south China, respectively, and were domesticated locally. Others would say that the ancestors of both species originated further south in the tropical zone and were first domesticated in Southeast Asia, along with such crops as yams, taro and Job's tears, by Hoabinhian horticulturalists. As little is known of East Asian Mesolithic cultures it is still impossible to decide whether independent domestication or diffusion provides the more satisfactory model.

At any rate, it is no longer possible to maintain that agriculture first came to China from the West, though certain crops were eventually introduced from Southwest Asia, for example wheat and barley, which do not appear in China until the late Neolithic.

THE EMERGENCE OF NEOLITHIC CULTURES IN SOUTHEAST AND EAST ASIA

Years BC	Malaya	Thailand	Cambodia	N.Vietnam	S.E.China	S.China	N.China	N.E.China	Korea	Japan
9000						Xianrendong (9000)				Pre-Jomon Ceramic (c.14 000)
8000										Early Jomon (c.12 000)
7000		Spirit Cave (6800–5500) (possible plant domestication)		Bac Son (8000–6000) (? domestication of buffalo; ? cultivation of rice)		Zengpiyan (7000)	Peiligang (6500) (millet cultivation)			
6000										
5000	Gua Cha			Da But (6000–4000) (domestication of pig & fowl; ?cultivation of rice and fibre plants)	?			Xinle (c.5500) (incipient agriculture)		Mid-Jomon
4000			Laang Spean (4300)		Hemudu / Majiabang (c.5000)	Dapenkeng, Jinmen (c.5000) (?horticulture)	Banpo	Hongshan		
				Dau Duong (4000–3000)						
3000	Gua Kechil (3650–2050) (transitional site)	Non Nok Tha (?3740–3100) Ban Kao (c.3000)	?			Shixia (c.3000) (rice cultivation)			Ch'ulmun (c.3000) (incipient agriculture)	Late Jomon (1400) (?incipient agriculture)
2000			Samron Sen (1500) (Bronze Age)						Mumun (c.1500) (rice agriculture)	
1000										
0										Yayoi (300) (?rice and barley cultivation)

The Yellow River and the middle Yangtze through c. 3000 BC

Besides the traditional archaeological method of stratigraphy, sequences of carbon 14 (C_{14}) dates have now been established for most parts of China proper. With these new dates, the old assumption that an advanced Neolithic culture first grew up in the Yellow River region and gradually spread south and east to the rest of China is no longer tenable. It appears preferable to consider the Chinese Neolithic in terms of separate regional development of interlinked cultural traditions. The exact delineation of these traditions and the degree of interaction among them are, however, matters of debate. New evidence is constantly coming to light, and the following account should in no way be considered definitive.

The earliest known Neolithic cultures in the Yellow River valley, such as Peiligang in Henan, Laoguantai in Shaanxi, and Dadiwan I in Gansu, all date to the 6500–5000 BC range. They feature unpainted incised and cord-marked pottery; agriculture-related implements include serrated harvesting knives, large flat grinding-stones, mortars and pestles. The Peiligang farmers lived in villages clustered on loess terraces along the tributaries of the Yellow River; pigs and dogs were domesticated, and grain was stored in subterranean pits. Hemp and silk were spun and woven into cloth. The custom of burying the dead accompanied with grave goods may indicate that Peiligang villagers believed in an after-life.

Around 5000 BC these earliest cultures were succeeded by the Yangshao culture, first discovered in the 1920s. Hundreds of Yangshao sites have since been found in Henan, Shaanxi and Gansu; several local variants and sub-phases of Yangshao may now be distinguished. Banpo, near Xi'an in Shaanxi, is regarded as the type-site for the early phase of Yangshao in that area. It was a vil-

lage of semi-subterranean houses constructed of timber and wattle-and-daub, also containing activity areas such as kilns; the dwelling area was surrounded by a moat and stockade, outside of which lay the cemeteries. The relative homogeneity of grave-goods shows that the social differentiation typical of later cultures had not yet fully developed. Yangshao pottery was made without a wheel; utilitarian vessel types include the tripods and steamers typical of later Chinese cuisine. Baskets were also used.

The Yangshao culture is famous for its fine red-and-black painted pottery (including vessels as well as human figurines), which first appears in the Banpo phase (c. 5000–4000 BC) and reaches its apogee in the later Miaodigou I phase (c. 4000–3400 BC). The tradition subsequently declined and after about 3000 BC disappeared altogether from the cultures of the Yellow River plain, but it continued to flourish in Gansu and Qinghai throughout most of the 3rd millennium BC.

To the south, Yangshao-related cultures have been found in Hubei and neighbouring provinces; the earliest among these is the Daxi culture (c. 4500–3500 BC). Subsequently the highly distinctive Qujialing culture, characterized by fine eggshell-thin black ceramics, often painted red or purple, was established in this region. Qujialing farmers grew rice and kept poultry as well as pigs, sheep and dogs. Around 2500 BC Qujialing was followed, at least in the northern part of the region, by a culture similar to the contemporary Longshan cultures of north China.

The northeast

The Hongshan culture (c. 4500–2500 BC) was the northeastern neighbour of the Yangshao; its sites are distributed in the eastern part of Liaoning and adjacent regions. While its painted pottery may show some Yangshao influence, other features, such as microliths, hark back to local traditions. The beautifully carved and polished Hongshan jades are the earliest found so far in China; Hongshan sites have also yielded the earliest evidence for scapulimancy. Large monuments constructed of piled rocks doubtless had a religious function, as did clay sculptures that range in size from miniature venus figurines to the life-size statue of a goddess found at the site of Niuheliang . As yet we know little about the livelihood of the Hongshan peasants, but some Hongshan tombs display astounding wealth, suggesting a considerable amount of social differentiation.

The east coast and the lower Yangtze through c. 3000 BC

In Shandong, amazing cultural continuity may be observed from the earliest Neolithic remains, known as the Beixin phase (second half of sixth millennium BC), through the beginnings of the Bronze Age. The living conditions at Beixin and in the succeeding Dawenkou culture (c. 5000–2750 BC) of Shandong and north

Painted pottery bowl from the Banpo phase.

Jiangsu were similar to that of Peiligang and Yangshao; the two traditions were separated by a wide belt of swamps. The Shandong pottery styles are highly distinctive and of sophisticated shapes, including many types of ring-footed and tripodal vessels. Painted pottery is comparatively scarce.

Further to the south, the important riverine community of Hemudu in Zhejiang was occupied from *c*. 5000–3500 BC. The marshy site has preserved quantities of organic remains, showing that the Hemudu farmers grew rice and lived in wood-frame houses demanding a high degree of carpentry skill. Their domesticated animals included pigs, dogs, and possibly water-buffalo. Basketry and weaving were highly developed. The early pottery is handmade, low-fired and thick. Unlike the Yangshao ceramics, the principal types are jars and cauldrons, and though some painted ware is found, most is incised or cord-marked.

Many early Neolithic sites have been found along the east coast, and while there are basic similarities between the sites north and south of the Yangtze, those to the north also show affinities with the Yangshao cultures of the Yellow River plains, and those to the south with the south coast cultures. The southern branch remained centred in the Yangtze Delta. Majiabang, Songze and Liangzhu are the successive cultural phases.

The south coast
Neolithic cultures along the south China coast generally show greater affinity to Vietnamese than to other Chinese cultures, hardly surprisingly as the provinces of the south are geographically and ecologically far closer to Southeast Asia. Only a few sites in this part of China have been excavated so far. The best known from the early Neolithic is the Taiwanese site of Dapenkeng

EARLY CULTURAL SEQUENCES IN CHINA

	Gansu	Shaanxi	Henan	Hubei	Liaoning	Shandong/ N.Jiangsu	Jiangsu/ Zhejiang	Fujian/ Taiwan
BC								
6500							?	
6000	Dadiwan I	Laoguantai	Peiligang					
5500				Beixi				
5000					Xinle		Hemudu Phase 1 (5000)	Quemoy (Jinmen) (c.5300–4200)
4500	Zhongyuan Yangshao	YANGSHAO		?		Beixin	Majiabang (5000–4000)	
		Banpo (5000–4000)	Shuangmiaogou (c.5000)	Daxi	Hongshan			
4000			Hougang (4135)	?	?	EAST COAST CULTURES NORTH	EAST COAST CULTURES SOUTH	Ta-p'en-k'eng (Dapenkeng) (c.4300)
3500		Miaodigou I (4000–3400)	Dahecun (3800–3000)				Songze (4000–3000)	
3000	Majiayao (3100–2600)	Miaodigou II (3000–2500)		Qujialing	?	Dawenkou		
2500	Banshan (2400)	LONGSHAN				'Classic' Longshan (2750–2000)	Liangzhu (3300–2300)	Feng-pi-t'ou (Fengbitou)
	Machang (2300–2100)	Kexingzhuang (Shaanxi Longshan)	Henan Longshan	Qinglongquan III (Hubei Longshan)				
2000	Qijia (21500–1780)	BRONZE AGE Proto-Zhou	Erlitou ?Xia Shang		?		LATE EAST COAST NEOLITHIC	
1750					Lower Xiajiadian	Shang		Geometric

141

(c. 5000 BC), but similar sites are found along the coasts of Fujian, Guangdong and North Vietnam. They are distinguished by characteristic shouldered and stepped adzes, thick, heavily decorated cord-marked and incised pottery, and evidence that boats and fishing played an essential part in the economy.

Later evidence is scanty. Cultures similar to the Liangzhu of the Yangtze Delta developed in Fujian and Taiwan, while those further south, generally located near the sea-shore or on river-banks, often show continued economic dependence on fishing rather than farming. Others, such as Shixia in Guangdong, show evidence of extensive rice cultivation by the 3rd millennium BC, at which time rice was already well established in Vietnam.

The Longshanoid horizon (c. 3000-2000 BC)

The period from about 3000 BC onwards was one of considerable cultural contact and exchange. While the separate Neolithic cultures in each region preserved some of their own characteristics, some new, unifying features began to spread throughout most of China proper. These include certain ritual pottery vessels, as well as other high-status goods such as jades. Scapulimancy was now practised over a wide area. Moreover, walled settlements probably of military character, which enclose building foundations made of stamped earth, began to be constructed during the third millennium: the antecedents of cities. The gradual adoption of metallurgy may likewise reflect an increasing preoccupation with warfare and the production of high-status goods; the technical advances went hand in hand with organizational sophistication. Socio-economic differentiation is clearly documented by cemeteries, where tombs now fall into at least three distinct size classes, some with unprecedentedly luxurious furnishings. Evidently, access to political power became increasingly restricted to a small group of people sharing in a common elite culture, out of which eventually grew the dynastic civilization of the Shang and Zhou.

The phenomenon of cultural homogenization at the top has been termed the 'Longshanoid horizon', for most of the pottery types spreading throughout China proper in the third millennium seem to originate in Shandong, where the 'classic (Shandong) Longshan' culture succeeded the Dawenkou culture around 2750 BC. The wheel-made, often egg-shell thin, burnished black ceramics of the Longshan culture are highly distinctive.

The Liangzhu culture in the southeast is most remarkable for its sophisticated jades, which were made in the same shapes as some types of ritual jades used throughout Chinese history. Some Longshan and Liangzhu stone and jade implements bear carved animal-masks similar to those on Shang bronzes. Moreover, in contrast to the simple markers that appear on Yangshao pottery (where they may indicate ownership or the like), the markers incised on some Dawenkou, Longshan and Liangzhu pots are somewhat resemblant of Chinese characters; here may lie the sources of Shang writing.

The painted-pottery producing cultures along the western fringes of China proper were superseded at the end of the 3rd millennium BC by the Qijia, a culture of advanced farmers in whose economy herds of stock apparently played a more important part than elsewhere in China; this may show some affinity to Central Asia. The distinctive Qijia ceramic styles, however, seem to show some influence from the Longshanoid cultures to the east. Copper metallurgy was also practised.

Further east, the Yangshao tradition was heavily influenced by the east coast cultures. After some centuries of transition, by c. 2500 BC the so-called Shaanxi and Henan 'Longshan' cultures had emerged, which shared with contemporary east coast cultures such features as the potter's wheel, black burnished ceramics replacing the hitherto characteristic red ware and lime-plastered houses. In central Henan, by c. 2000 BC vessels were cast of bronze and extensive palace complexes built at the site of Erlitou (founded c. 2000–1800 BC). While some archaeologists see Erlitou as a proto-Shang site, others believe it was actually the capital of the Xia dynasty.

L.v.F.

SHANG: THE FIRST HISTORICAL DYNASTY (*c.* 1554–1045 BC)

The state

According to Zhou and Han texts the virtuous Shang (or Yin) rulers, whose family name was Zi, received Heaven's mandate to overthrow the wicked Xia dynasty. After 31 Shang emperors had occupied the throne, they in turn became dissolute, and their mandate passed to the virtuous Zhou. The reliability of the mythical and moralizing details in these accounts is uncertain, but discoveries of Shang sites and documents made since the turn of the century have confirmed the existence of a dynasty, whose 28 or 29 kings ruled for 17 generations (c. 1554–1045 BC). (The genealogical details and the dates—1766–1122 BC according to a Han chronology—are not firmly established.)

The state, which at times dominated the Yellow River plain and parts of Shandong, Shanxi and Shaanxi, was centred on a capital or cult centre similar to the one represented by the Late Shang site excavated at Xiaotun near Anyang in Henan. Most elements of Shang culture evolved from indigenous, Neolithic antecedents, although the appearance of spoke-wheeled horse chariots in the dynastic period suggests an intrusion from Central Asia. At the core of the state were groups of ritual specialists, administrators, warriors, artisans and retainers linked to the royal house by blood, belief and self-interest. Despite the existence of proto-bureaucratic administrative titles, the state was primarily patrimonial and dynastic. Authority among both living and dead depended on kinship ties and generational status. The theocrat, known while alive as *wang,* 'king', exercised a chiefdom-like power, not through an extensive administration, but through dynastic alliances, religious intercessions, and the progresses, hunts and campaigns by which he taxed outlying areas.

Important urban settlements, classified culturally as Early and Middle Shang, have been found at Yanshi and Zhengzhou in Henan, and at Panlongzheng in Hubei, but these may represent a predynastic stage. Late Shang cultural sites representing politically independent groups beyond the reach of the king's influence have been found as far away as Liaoning and Hunan.   *D.N.K.*

Divination

Shang diviners (we know the names of some 120) practised a form of divination known as scapulimancy or plastromancy. Rows of hollows were cut into cattle scapulae or turtle plastrons so that T-shaped stress cracks appeared on the front of the bone when the diviner applied a heated rod to the hollows on the back. The diviner numbered the cracks and interpreted them as auspicious, inauspicious or neutral. A record of the topic (and sometimes of the forecast and eventual outcome) was then cut into the bone. Since 1899 over 50 000 inscribed oracle-bone fragments have been unearthed from storage pits at Xiaotun. The inscriptions, with their vocabulary of 3000 plus graphs, form the earliest comprehensive body of Chinese documents we possess; they provide an invaluable record of the hopes and decisions of the last eight or nine Shang kings (*c.* 1200–1045 BC?).

In the reign of Wu Ding (*c.* 1200–1180 BC?) most aspects of life among the Shang elite were divined: rituals, ancestral curses, the luck of the 10-day week, rainfall, harvests, settlement building, sickness, dreams, and so forth. Some topics were divined in positive-negative pairs (e.g. 'We will receive millet harvest', 'We will not perhaps receive millet harvest'), with their graphs placed symmetrically on the right and left sides of the plastron. Successful divinations validated both the king's decisions and, since only the

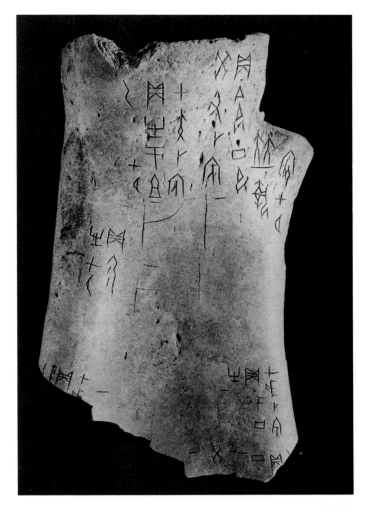

Fragment of an early Shang ox scapula used in divination, *c.* 1200 BC, containing an inscription concerning animal sacrifice to a royal ancestor.

king, styled 'I the one man', was able to prognosticate the cracks, his theocratic status. Few if any inscriptions record wrong forecasts. By their divinations the Late Shang kings laid claim to the superior wisdom, the contact with ultimate forces, that all leaders must demonstrate.

Changes in divination practice, associated with what modern scholars have called the 'New School' of ritualists (which flourished under kings Zu Jia, Di Yi and Di Xin) and involving the king's monopolization of the diviner's role, the virtual disappearance of positive-negative topic pairs, a reduction in the range of topics and in the size of the written graphs, and perfunctory, uniformly optimistic forecasts, indicate that the function and theology of divination evolved significantly.   *D.N.K.*

Religion

Late Shang ancestor worship represents a systematic ordering of beliefs, some of which had been combined with the dynasty's own religious and genealogical traditions as local groups were incorporated into the Shang polity. The ancestors, vengeful or protective, could curse, cause sickness, produce dreams, approve the king's acts, confer assistance in battle, and so forth. Ancestor worship extended to the dead, as it reinforced among the living, patrimonial conceptions of jurisdiction, hierarchy and authority.

The nine large pit tombs at Xibeigang, northwest of Xiaotun, may be those of the last Shang kings. Ritual bronzes, weapons, jades and other articles of high culture, together with the numerous retainers, buried with the lord, suggest that the Shang believed in a life after death, that status conditions of this world were projected into the next, and that religious sanctions of service and kinship, which sent the living to accompany the dead, were strong.

Many oracle inscriptions recorded prayers and rituals addressed to the royal ancestors, who were given posthumous temple names according to the 10 *gan* stems (10 labels, rather like A, B, C, D, etc.), and who generally received sacrificial offerings on their name days. 'Thus Shang Jia, the lineage founder, was worshipped on a *jia* day (*jia* being the first of the 10 stems), Da Yi, the dynasty founder, on a *yi* day (*yi* being the second of the 10 stems). Under the New School a schedule of five rituals was established and offered to the ancestors according to their generational seniority. The distribution of temple names in the king list may have been related to the transfer of power between 10 patrilineages within the royal clan; alternatively, the names may have been chosen to permit the equitable distribution of ancestral sacrifices on certain lucky days throughout the ritual week.

Di, the High God, stood at the apex of the spiritual hierarchy, having ultimate, though not exclusive, control over such matters as weather, harvest and victory. Di received no sacrificial offerings and was approachable mainly through the mediation of the Shang ancestors. The Shang also worshipped certain eminent figures like Yi Yin, the court official who served under Da Yi, and nature powers like the Yellow River or the Earth spirit.

The intensity of Shang faith is indicated by the numbers of animal victims offered. During the reign of Wu Ding, cattle, sheep and dogs were slaughtered in their hundreds. Many humans, notably captives taken from the Jiang tribe, were also sacrificed, usually in groups of 10, although as many as 300 might be immolated at one time. Hundreds of victims, frequently decapitated, have been found among the tombs and building foundations in the Xiaotun area. The violence of Shang secular culture, evident in its campaigns and hunts, was thus reflected in the theology of sacrifice; bloodshed vitalized both the living and the dead. *D.N.K.*

The economy

The dynasty's material power depended upon the efficient exploitation of a servile peasantry, particularly for agriculture and warfare. Millet agriculture, given a Late Shang climate rather wetter and warmer (mean annual temperature *c.* 2°C higher) than the present day, provided the economic base. Royal harvest-prayer rituals, directed to various places within the Shang sphere of influence, blessed the crops. Royal labour gangs farmed the land, using stone tools made in the king's workshops. Forced labourers also dug royal tombs, raised rammed-earth building foundations, and served in the royal armies, mobilized in groups of 3000 or 5000 men. An ethic of service permeated all levels of life. Although there was a fundamental social cleavage between those who worked and those who benefited from the work, a continuum of religious and political obligation required high and low alike to serve their superiors, living and dead.

The Shang kings controlled various handicraft industries, staffed perhaps by occupational clans, who produced sophisticated wood carvings, stone and jade statuettes, personal ornaments, clothes, ceramics, chariots, weapons and ritual bronzes. *D.N.K.*

Bronze working

The casting of Shang bronze vessels, thousands of which have been found, required a large labour force to mine, refine and transport copper, tin and lead ores, and to produce and transport charcoal. It required skilled technicians to make clay models, construct sectional, ceramic piece-moulds with their intricate surface patterns, manufacture clay crucibles, pour molten metal, and hand-tool the eventual product. The bronze industry, which required central coordination, was also highly labour-intensive, involving a large number of specialized operations for each object made. Ancestor dedications (e.g. 'A vessel made for Father Xin') were cast into many of the later vessels, some of which were extremely heavy; the largest yet found weighs 875kg.

Late Shang bronze decor reveals an intense interest in abstract linear pattern, in dissociated and ornamental geometric designs, such as spirals, quills and meander backgrounds, and in axial symmetry, reminiscent of the positive-negative balance of the divination inscriptions. Fantastic monster masks (called *taotie* by later scholars) with prominent eyes and gaping jaws convey a sense of mysterious animal power, abstracted, compressed and severely disciplined. Water-buffalo, sheep, tigers, birds and cicadas are among the animal-life represented. They presumably served some sacred role, perhaps as mediators between man and the ancestors, but the full meaning of the religious iconography of Late Shang is still unknown. *D.N.K.*

A Shang bronze cauldron displaying a monster mask with horns, eyes and upper jaw placed symmetrically about a central axis.

THE ZHOU DYNASTY (*c.* 1122 – 221 BC)

Western Zhou: Founding and founders

The establishment of the Zhou dynasty comes to us not really as history but as a tradition, almost a morality play peopled with archetypes. Even the date is uncertain: 1122 and 1027 BC are traditionally given, but others have been advanced. Interesting recalculations reported in *Early China* suggest 1040 or some date in the decade before that.

The Zhou were evidently a semi-nomadic clan from the northwestern fringe of the Chinese world. According to the legend of the Zhou ancestral temple, led by the 'old duke', Gugong Danfu (also called King Tai), and his brother Jili, they moved south from the upper Jing River to its confluence with the Wei (near modern Xi'an, Shaanxi). It was here that they first came into contact with the then China proper and with the Shang kings. Two generations later they displaced the Shang.

The final Shang ruler, Zouxin is depicted as a classic example: the last ruler of a sinking dynasty. Wen Wang, the 'refined', or 'literate', or 'accomplished' king (who in fact was only ennobled as 'king' after death) extended the Zhou domain, especially northwards, and became Count of the West under the Shang but later, having been falsely accused, was imprisoned. His son Wu Wang, the 'military' king, a man perhaps better suited to troubled times, conquered Shang and killed Zouxin but died soon thereafter. One of his brothers, Zhou Gong (the Duke of Zhou) consolidated the conquest (acting as regent for Wu Wang's son) and founded the feudatory state of Lu, which centuries later was to be the native state of Confucius.

The Zhou capital was at Hao, near modern Xi'an; but an eastern capital, Luoyi, was built on the Luo River (near modern Luoyang) as a stronghold from which to govern the subjugated Shang. Western Zhou rule (11th century–771 BC) was a kind of feudal monarchy, rather closely controlled among the states of the centre—*zhongguo* (the modern term for China), lying in the north China plain and the Wei valley—but less so towards the periphery. It maintained internal peace for over two centuries, until about the middle of the 9th century BC.

Socially, the Western Zhou seem to have been very similar to the Shang. The ruling class were the nobles with family names. They practised ancestor worship. Government amounted to a simple bureaucracy manned by the noble class. The army had three-man chariots as the main striking force. Divination marked every important decision or event. The rituals of the ancient religion provided the basis of social order and regulated the agricultural year. The peasants remained a separate though key element—lacking family names, taking no direct part in religious observances, involved in war as a semi-armed mob trailing after the chariots, they carried out the vital and supportive functions such as sowing and reaping.

Wen Wang (personal name: Zhang; title under the Shang: Count of the West, *Xi Bo*)

Wen Wang was given his title posthumously. His royal epithet, Wen, indicates that he was an ideal Chinese monarch, intelligent and benevolent. In theory, through these qualities alone he laid the foundation of Zhou regional power, but it seems reasonable to assume that he was also a positive, imaginative and forceful administrator and military leader. According to the literary records, which are impossible to verify, the Zhou realm included some two-thirds of China during Wen Wang's life, though he continued to recognize the political and cultural suzerainty of the Shang house and his feudal subordination to it. His title as Count of the West is presumably a recognition of his real power; but that power also produced fear and envy: slandered, allegedly by Count Hu of

Bronze ritual vessel (*fangding*) of the Western Zhou.

Chong, he was imprisoned by the Shang king, Zouxin. His sons, notably Wu Wang, gained victory over the Shang and killed Zouxin.

Wu Wang

Perhaps a mythicized opposite to his father Wen Wang, Wu Wang, the 'military' king of the Zhou founding, defeated the Shang and consolidated his victory. Wu Wang died soon after the three-year period in which that victory was won, leaving his brother, Zhou Gong, to ensure the survival of the Zhou dynasty and the orderly succession of Wu Wang's son.

Zhou Gong (Duke of Zhou; personal name, Dan)

Son of Wen Wang and brother of Wu Wang, he is famed as regent for Wu Wang's son, as builder of the 'eastern capital' of the Zhou (Luoyi), as founder of the ducal line of Lu, and as the 'familiar spirit' of Confucius. A shrewd but principled political manager, he amalgamated Shang and Zhou elements into the Zhou cultural style.   *F.A.K.*

Eastern Zhou: 'Spring and Autumn' and the Warring States

The end of Western and beginning of Eastern Zhou is generally set at 771 BC at Luoyi (near modern Luoyang). The traditional western capital, Hao, had been sacked by barbarians and dissidents, and was no longer habitable. This was the culmination of a lengthy process of disturbance and change. In 841 BC, for example, Li Wang was deposed and replaced by a collective regency until the crown prince came of age. In 771 Yu Wang was killed and two rival princes, Yijiu and Yuchen, each laid claim to the throne on his own behalf, and on that of the opposing noble cliques whose ambitions they symbolized. The kingdom was divided for 20 years, with the eastern portion under Ping Wang (the crown prince Yijiu before his accession) and the western region under the King of Hui (Yuchen). In 750 the latter was killed and the regime theoretically reunited, although the prestige of the royal house had been severely diminished. Kings Ping and Huan (who succeeded his father in 720) became pawns in the hands of powerful ministers or noble factions. King Huan tried to assert the royal power against the dominant minister, Count Zhuang of Zheng; but after a lengthy period of tension and conflict King Huan's forces were defeated and he himself was wounded at Xuge (707), largely because the forces of the nobles allied to him fled the field. This showed that the Zhou house no longer had any real power.

Despite this, the symbolic role of the dynasty, supported by the sanctions of ancient religion (ancestor worship and divination), remained important. In part this was because none of the aspirants for power was willing to see any rival replace the weak Zhou; but old loyalties also played their part. In consequence, rivalries tended to manifest themselves over the right to protect the royal house against less restrained contenders. By the 7th century BC and most clearly under dukes Huan of Qi (reigned 685–643 BC) and Wen of Jin (reigned 636–628 BC), the protective function of the states nominally subordinate to the Zhou was institutionalized for a while into a league of vassals headed by the most powerful of them, the hegemon or overlord (*ba*).

The Eastern Zhou period has two major sub-divisions: that of the 'Spring and Autumn' (*Chunqiu*), from the title of the chronicle of Lu *Spring and Autumn Annals*, which begins in 722 BC and ends in 481 BC (a period which has no significance other than the span of that book and the prestige which Confucius' alleged connection with it bestows) and that of the Warring States (*Zhanguo*), again rather arbitrarily—but variously—dated by the dissolution of the state of Jin: some begin the Warring States period at the assassination of Yao, Count of Zhi, in 453 BC, after which his holdings were divided among the three successor states of Han, Wei and Zhao; others date the new period as beginning in 403 BC, when the sovereigns of Han, Wei and Zhao were ceremonially confirmed by the Zhou king. The Warring States of the period are, as Sima Qian lists them, Zhou (the 'royal house'), Jin, Wei, Han, Zhao, Chu, Yan and Qi.

The end of the Zhou period is usually set at 221 BC, when the first emperor of Qin—Qin Shi Huangdi—unified the land on a new imperial basis. In fact, however, Qin had occupied the royal domain in 256 and stripped the last claimant of the title of Lord of Eastern Zhou in 249. The final stages of the Qin victory were an attack on Han in 231, which was destroyed the following year, followed by Zhao (228), Yan (226, although a Manchurian segment lasted until 222), Wei (225), Chu (223) and Qi (221).

The Eastern Zhou period, although politically untidy, is acknowledged as the shaping period of Chinese culture. The unique continuum of China's recorded history begins with Eastern Zhou. The *Chunqiu* and similar annals of individual states, the *Shujing* (*Classic of Documents*) and other collections of documents real or forged, the *Zuozhuan* (*Tradition of Zuo*) and other collections of anecdotes or historical romances, and of course the official collections of data upon which histories could be based—all of these works, each of which achieved canonized status and played a vital role in education, date from Eastern Zhou times or come to us through an Eastern Zhou filter.

Likewise, in the fields of philosophy, religion and literature, Eastern Zhou was either the seedbed or the essential transmitter and shaper. Eastern Zhou witnessed the decline of the ancient forms of Chinese religion and their transformation into the two major streams: Confucianism and Daoism. It was at once a period of unrest and of intense and fruitful reappraisal and inquiry. Among the various schools of thought two main strands of development are clearly discernible: one pragmatic and society-orientated, and the other personal, imaginative, mystical and salvation-orientated. Each in its own way dealt in 'self-cultivation'; each, inevitably, dealt with political philosophy, i.e. the question of how to govern China (already in Eastern Zhou times the state was an enormously unwieldy entity involving a great deal of regional variation and constantly threatening to fragment); and each strand devoted enormous energies to deriding and refuting the other.

In social organization Eastern Zhou created the framework adopted by subsequent dynasties. Legalism—a loose bundle of thinkers from different traditions rather than a proper school—offered prescriptions, structures and stratagems for handling all social problems. Military thought and technology advanced: Eastern Zhou may well have been the most dynamic military power in the world from the 8th to 3rd centuries BC, both in what it developed (e.g. the crossbow and methods of city siege and defence) and what it adapted (e.g. barbarian clothing and riding, rather than driving, horses). Economically, China was already looking towards knitting its far-flung, disparate regions into a pattern of complementary entities; the salt trade was certainly one example in this process. Moreover, the introduction of iron, and especially the capacity to mass produce iron implements, coupled with developments in agriculture, led to rapid economic growth from the 6th century BC onwards.

F.A.K.

State of Jin

According to tradition, Jin was a *guo*, a petty state, under the Xia dynasty. It was near present-day Taiyuan, Shanxi, and belonged to the Ji clan, one that was numerous and widely spread throughout China by Shang times and included the Zhou house which was to succeed the Shang. By early Eastern Zhou times, the Lord of Jin gained favour by killing the 'King of Hui' (750 BC) and thus resolving a succession dispute in favour of King Bing. Lying outside the 'central states' (*zhongguo*) along the middle Yellow River, it shared the fortune of other peripheral feudal states, growing markedly in power as Zhou declined.

By the 7th century BC Jin was strong enough to defeat Chu in the great battle of Chengpu (632 BC); and as a result Duke Wen became the second of the *ba* (overlords), succeeding Duke Huan of Qi. Unfortunately, Wen was quite old by this time and died four years later. However, his successors managed to maintain the state, despite the constant problem of internal strife among the noble clans. The state of Jin even managed to find a remedy for the menace of Chu, by creating a military challenge on the eastern flank of Chu, the state of Wu, which was Jin's ally. But by the second half of the 6th century BC, Jin's internal strife limited its capacity to conduct external affairs; and during the entire first half of the 5th century there was civil war in Jin. The climax was the assassination of the chief minister, the Count of Zhi, in 453 BC. Jin then split into three smaller states: Han, Wei and Zhao, often called the Three Jin. This break-up of Jin is usually regarded as heralding the beginning of the period of the Warring States.

F.A.K.

State of Qi

Inscriptions of Shang times indicate the existence of a principality of Chu and by the beginning of Zhou it was well established within the eastern borderlands of modern Shandong and Hebei Provinces between the Yellow River and the sea. As a plains area, Chu was suited to centralized administration. A lucrative salt trade seems to have been one economic element in the principality's wealth and power.

In the early 7th century BC the weakness and internal turbulence of the small 'central states' lying along the Yellow River tempted Chu to interfere in their affairs and they formed a protective league under Qi, then in the heyday of its power, under Duke Huan and his minister Guan Zhong (Guan Yiwu, Guanzi). Huan thus became the first *ba* (overlord) or *mengzhu* (league president), holding power from 685 to 643 BC, when he died.

Huan's death after so long and wearing a hegemony brought ruin both to the league and to Chu. For over a century and a half Qi was in turmoil and, apart from occasional surges of adventurism, isolated from the Chinese world. In 379 BC, after a lengthy struggle, the Dian family of the Gui clan replaced the Lu family of the Jiang on the throne of Qi. Unlike Jin, split into three by rival families, Qi survived by liquidating other contenders, then restricting power to the Dian family, administratively supported by adventurers from outside the state—a characteristic feature of the political administrative system of the Warring States period.

Qi was a prominent participant in the ever-shifting alliance system of the Warring States, episodes of which eventually led to the state's ruin. In 314 BC, responding to the pleas of the crown prince of Yan, Qi occupied that state but later refused to withdraw, until an uprising forced it to do so. In 285, when Qi's adventurism

had left the state vulnerable, the King of Yan allied himself with all of Qi's neighbours and took the state, except for two strongholds in the east and south. Typically the allies then disbanded, and in 279 Dian Dan was able to expel Yan and reconstitute Qi. But it was a Qi so weakened that from then on it could take no serious part in events. It was the last, anti-climactic victim in the Qin unification.

F.A.K.

State of Chu

Traditionally, the great southern state of Chu was regarded simply as the semi-barbarian arch-enemy of the Yellow River 'central states' and their larger peripheral protectors, Qi and Jin. According to tradition, Chu began turning its attention northwards at the end of the 8th century BC and by the 7th had become such a threat as to inspire an anti-Chu league under the leadership of Qi and later of Jin. The rise of the kingdom of Wu, on Zhou's eastern border, beginning in 584 BC when Qu Wuchen (a refugee from Chu acting as representative of Jin) came to Wu, effectively reduced the Chu menace. In the longer run it was internal turmoil and the vast extent and limited development of the land that contained the energies of the great southern state, especially after the demise of Wu (473) and of Wu's conqueror, Yue (333). In the final century of the Warring States period Chu—together with Qi—was regarded as the major counterbalance to the growing power of Qin. Of the victories leading up to Qin's unification of China, that over Chu (223) was probably the hardest and most decisive.

Archaeological finds and interpretations yearly are adding to knowledge of the economy and culture of Chu which occupies a particularly important place in both literature and religion. Zhuangzi, the first literary artist of China whom we know by name, was from a smaller border state near Chu and a member of the Chu court. Both he and Daoism are intimately associated with southern thought. Qü Yuan, China's first personally-known great poet, was from Chu, was a Daoist, and provided the popular model of the rhapsodic magical journey (possibly associated with drugs), which had great influence, both thematically and formally, on later poets.

F.A.K.

Wei Valley

The Wei River is a major tributary of the Yellow River. Rising in the Gansu plateau, it flows first southeast and then eastwards some

860km to its confluence with the Huang-ho (Yellow River) just at the point where that great river turns east towards the North China plain. The major tributary of the Wei is the Jing River, which joins the Wei near modern Xi'an, an area of great historical importance. The Zhou migrated down the Jing to the Wei and settled there, building their capital of Hao, two generations before the beginning of the Zhou dynasty. In later ages too the capital of China was located in the Xi'an area: Xianyang under the Qin, Chang'an under the Han and Tang. *F.A.K.*

Feudalism

Feudalism is a concept that Chinese and Western social scientists dealing with China can neither quite swallow nor quite spit out. The ancient Chinese term *fengjian* means 'to enfeoff [nobles] and so construct [the state]' and applies to an epoch in which this was Shang and especially Zhou governmental practice. Largely because of its importance to the Marxist theory of the stages through which societies have developed, feudalism is central to the vocabulary and the ideas of modern scholars. There can be little doubt that Zhou China displayed some characteristics similar to those of European feudalism: decentralized power, sub-infeudation (i.e. vassals of vassals), preponderance of the military as against other forms of vassal service, and so forth. But there are a number of important differences as well: many of the Chinese 'feudal states' were very much larger and more elaborately organized than any fief in medieval Europe; the feudal period in ancient China predates that in medieval Europe; and the preceding and succeeding periods in Marx's ladder of development both pose serious questions, since it is a moot point whether a system of production that was significantly based upon slavery ever existed in China, and certainly there has never been anything like full Chinese capitalism. *F.A.K.*

THE QIN DYNASTY (221–206 BC)

Qin

As the first imperial dynasty to be founded, Qin exercised a profound influence on the subsequent history of China. Short-lived

as it was, and subject as it has been to subsesquent criticism, Qin nonetheless bequeathed to China a heritage of imperial rule and political forms many of which were adopted by subsequent regimes in the next 2000 years. Despite protestations to the contrary, it is the institutions of the Qin empire that have largely informed China's political administration.

Shang Yang

Qin had been one of the independent kingdoms that had grown up during the Warring States period. It had existed as a small unit, in the west, since the 9th century BC, but it was during the 5th and 4th centuries BC that it acquired sufficient strength to enable it to annex or conquer its neighbours. The leaders of Qin adopted the title of king in 325 BC; and it was largely due to the ideas of Shang Yang (d. 338 BC) that the kingdom could deploy powerful armed forces and use economic resources with sufficient efficiency to achieve its final results. Shang Yang had advocated a number of measures that have subsequently been categorized as 'Legalist'. He established a system of rewards and punishments of state, and insisted that their value lay in their universal application throughout the land. He thereby induced a high degree of popular obedience, and engendered a high degree of military discipline. By other measures he sought to increase the production of grain and to facilitate its distribution. Many of Shang Yang's theories and practical measures are set out in the *Shangjunshu (Book of Lord Shang)*, which was probably compiled by his immediate followers.

Shi Huangdi (First Emperor)

Shang Yang died as a fugitive, in battle (338 BC). Shortly afterwards the kingdom of Qin took its first major step to increase its territories, by taking over areas in the present province of Sichuan, lying to the south of the original kingdom of Qin itself. This area was of particular value, owing to its rich resources of grain and timber. But it was under King Zheng of Qin, who acceded to that title in 246 BC, that the major steps were taken to form an empire in place of the seven major kingdoms, which had between them grown to occupy most of Chinese territory. Between 230 and 221 BC, Jin succeeded in conquering and annexing the six states of Han, Wei, Chu, Zhao, Yan and Qi; thereafter King Zheng assumed sovereign rule over all the territories, adopting the newly coined title *Huangdi*, or Emperor, and calling himself Shi Huangdi (First Emperor). It is from this event and its subsequent importance that the name China derives.

The government of the empire was largely influenced by Li Si, who served as chancellor to the first Qin emperor. Li Si had been a fellow-student of Han Fei, and the measures that he introduced were based on 'Legalist' principles, such as those advocated by Shang Yang. Under the overriding principle that the true purpose of government is to strengthen and enrich the state, Li Si saw that the territories of the new empire were securely held under the control of the central government. To achieve this end, the empire was divided into provincial units, whose governors were appointed directly from the centre, which could also dismiss them in cases of dereliction of duty. The wholesale introduction of this system stood in marked contrast with earlier arrangements whereby large areas of territory had been made over to a king's favourites or relatives, to be held on a hereditary basis. Li Si implemented Shang Yang's arrangements for rewards and punishments rigorously, so as to encourage service to the state and to deter criminal actions. A further measure of strong government is seen in the enforced standardization of weights and measures, and the introduction of a newly regularized script for official documents, now required in increasing multiplicity.

It cannot be said to what extent the first emperor himself took a part in introducing these measures or supervising the administration. According to the standard histories, he spent considerable time and effort in undertaking progresses in various parts of the empire, partly for religious purposes. But the main reason for these expensive and laborious expeditions was probably political, as they enabled the emperor to show himself as the living symbol of the new dispensation as widely as possible throughout his realms.

Later accounts of the Qin empire lay considerable stress on the ruthless way in which the administration was conducted and the severity of the legal punishments imposed on criminals. It was alleged that considerable popular suffering arose owing to the harsh system of conscription and the use of servicemen to fight foreign enemies (largely the Xiongnu), to build the defence-lines of the north (sometimes known as the 'Great Wall') and to construct roads, palaces and mausolea for imperial use. In addition, China is reputed to have suffered a severe blow in Li Si's measures to stamp out intellectual opposition. These included the attempt to proscribe ethical writings and scholarship, in steps described as the 'Burning of the Books', and the proscription of individual scholars.

It is probably true that in succeeding generations the severities of these measures have been somewhat exaggerated, and the permanent nature of Qin's achievements somewhat decried. The end of the Qin empire after a mere 15 years and two reigns has been ascribed in the first instance to the outbreak of rebellions in the face of popular hardship; but it is likely that there were other reasons, such as the immature state of the imperial administration and the failure of statesmen to forget their rivalries in the cause of imperial unity and strength.

The decline of the Qin dynasty

The first emperor died away from his capital city of Xianyang, while engaged in a progress in east China (210 BC). The news was kept secret for a time, while the succession was being manipulated. The chief operators in this incident were the aged statesman Li Si and Zhao Gao, a eunuch who had been serving at the court. Together, they succeeded in putting one of the emperor's younger sons, Huhai, on the throne as second emperor, and in eliminating the more appropriate heir (Fusu) and his supporter, General Meng Tian; these two were forced to commit suicide.

The second emperor was a weaker man than his father; no constructive actions are ascribed to him, and there is nothing to show that he possessed sufficient personality to impose his character upon the conduct of affairs. It is possibly for that reason that the succession had been manipulated in his favour.

The final years of Qin saw the disruption of empire, which was brought about by the outbreak of rebellions, the rivalries of statesmen and the resurrection of independent kingdoms that claimed to be the successors of those that had been abolished when the Qin empire had been formed. The final stages were marked by severe and widespread civil warfare.

The first rebellion against Qin's authority was led by Chen She, in 209 BC, and both this and several other insurrections were put down without undue difficulty. The failure of statesmen to cooperate, and their propensity to open rivalry, came to a head quite soon in a struggle between Li Si and Zhao Gao. With the execution of Li Si in 208 BC, Zhao Gao had succeeded in establishing his supremacy, but this did not last for long. In 207 BC the second emperor was driven to suicide, and Zhao Gao himself was assassinated.

By now a number of independent leaders had declared themselves masters of small areas of land. The strongest of these units was that which claimed to be the successor to the former kingdom of Chu, situated along the Yangtze River valley. In the new kingdom of Chu there soon arose two prominent leaders, whose struggle for mastery formed a theme that has featured in much of China's subsequent drama, poetry and anecdotal writing. Xiang Yu, of an aristocratic lineage, saw himself as ruler of the foremost of 18 kingdoms which were to coexist and govern China, with himself acting in the dominant role. Liu Bang envisaged the reconstruction of a single, imperial unit, to be governed centrally as Qin had been. There ensued a three cornered struggle between the remaining forces of Qin, the armies of Chu, under Xiang Yu's direction, and Liu Bang, who had become king of part of west China (since 206 BC). In the final phases of the fighting, between Xiang Yu and Liu Bang, Liu Bang eventually proved to be the victor. His successful occupation of the former metropolitan area of Qin had provided him with a natural stronghold and the records of imperial government; in 202 BC he adopted the title of emperor and the dynastic title of Han.

M.L.

Xiang Yu (d. 202 BC)

Xiang Yu was a member of one of the aristocratic families of the pre-imperial kingdom of Chu. In the civil warfare that followed the collapse of Qin from 210 BC, he became one of the chief contestants for supreme power and the main rival of Liu Bang, who defeated him in 202 BC.   *M.L.*

The Great Wall

During the Warring States period (403–221 BC) several kingdoms erected dykes or earthworks as a defence against their neighbours or potential invasion from the non-Chinese peoples of the north. It was one of the achievements of the first Qin emperor to unify a number of these walls into a single coordinated system, at a time when the newly strengthened confederacy of the Xiongnu posed a dangerous threat to Chinese security. The success of the Wall depended on effective and continuous manning, which was by no means always assured, either for the wall of Qin or for its extended successors under the Han, Tang or Ming dynasties. The latest of the walls, that of the Ming, was built of stone, and followed a quite different line from that of Qin. Remnants of the documents drawn up during the Han period to administer the garrison and control its work have been found. A serviceman's life on the Wall and its attendant hardships have formed a theme of Chinese poetry and drama.   *M.L.*

Burning of the Books

In an attempt to impose intellectual conformity, the Qin empire is alleged to have ordered the destruction of writings that advocated ethical ideals and thereby criticized the realistic and authoritarian measures of the Qin government. The success and effect of the order (213 BC), which was accompanied by the proscription of scholars, have been subject to some exaggeration. Li Si had been one of the prime forces in suggesting this measure. In doing so, he made it clear that it was only documents that were likely to be used to attack the current regime that should be banned; technical guides and manuals on, for example, divination, agriculture or medicine, were to be exempted from the order.   *M.L.*

THE HAN DYNASTY (202 BC–AD 220)

Political ideas

Han institutions and politics were influenced by ideas that may be loosely and somewhat anachronistically described as Daoist, Legalist and Confucian. At the outset of the empire, a reaction may have set in against the severely realistic and authoritarian administration of Qin, whose principles derived from the Legalist ideas of Shang Yang and Han Fei. Thus, until *c.* 135 BC, the Han government was partly influenced by a branch of Daoist thought which saw the government of man as a part of the general order of nature, and tended to deprecate excessive activity by officials as being disruptive. Thereafter a movement developed to promote and enhance the authority of the state, coordinate the use of its resources and direct the activities of the population towards imperial expansion and enrichment. Such objectives harked back to the aims of Legalist statecraft, but they were less demanding in their execution than the policies of Qin. From about 90 BC, currents of thought which had been formulated by Dong Zhongshu (179?–104? BC) sought to support imperial authority as an integral part of the universal order of *yin-yang* and as a scheme based on the ideas of Confucius, who received a radically new measure of praise. In Later Han and subsequently, imperial governments sought to show themselves as ardent believers in the orthodox Confucian view of the state, its social hierarchies and its ideal human relationships. Such protestations, however, have not inhibited the imposition of the disciplines and controls needed in the practical exercise of government, ascribed pejoratively to Legalist influence.   *M.L.*

Former Han

Three stages may be discerned in the dynastic and political history of the Former or Western Han dynasty, whose seat of government was established at Chang'an. The initial period, which lasted from 202 to *c.* 135 BC was marked by imperial consolidation, as may be illustrated in the developments of domestic policies and the avoidance of costly contacts with aliens. The stage began with the adoption by Liu Bang (256–195 BC) of the title of *Huangdi*, or emperor, following some years of fighting with rival contenders for power.

Foundation and consolidation: Gaodi

Liu Bang is first known as a local official in central China, who rose to some prominence in the reconstituted state of Chu following the weakening of the Qin empire. In 206 BC Liu Bang had accepted the title of king of Han, at a time when a number of kingdoms were being established, at the suggestion and with the support of Xiang Yu. But it soon became clear that the relations between Xiang Yu and Liu Bang would be those of rivals rather than allies, and fighting broke out between the two men and their supporters. This came to a close in 202 BC, with Xiang Yu's defeat and death, and it was in that year that the king of Han became the first emperor of the Han dynasty. Liu Bang is usually known under his posthumous title of Gaodi, and the traditional historians of China have stressed the value of his work in founding the dynasty by means of military prowess.

The re-establishment of imperial rule under the aegis of the new house was largely the work of Liu Bang's advisers, such as the famous statesman Xiao He, who served him as chancellor. His reign saw the extension of control by the central government and the elimination of all those leaders who, while supporting Liu Bang in his bid for power, could easily have turned against him as dissidents or separatists. The provincial system of the Qin empire was established in the interior of the empire, and large areas, which amounted to an arc running along the north and the east sides, were entrusted to the immediate members of Liu Bang's family as kingdoms. Successful attempts were made to collect resources of the empire by levying tax largely in kind, either as grain or as textiles. While it was claimed that the severities of the law code of Qin had been considerably reduced, the basic institutions of Qin's government were retained.

HAN CHINA 195 BC

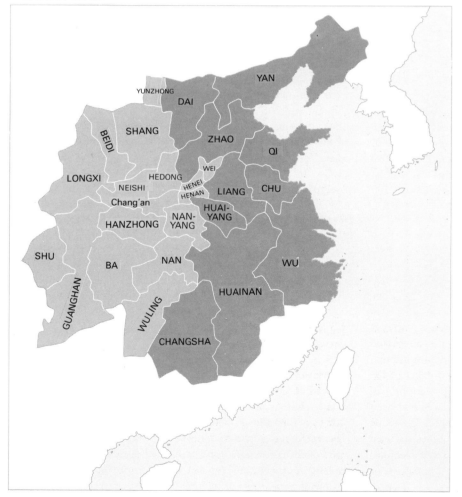

KEY

Commanderies

Kingdoms

Relations between the Han empire and foreign states or leaders were largely influenced by the chief potential enemies of China, the Xiongnu, who have sometimes been inaccurately identified with the Huns. It was the simultaneous rise of a prominent Xiongnu leader and his successful formation of a confederacy of tribesmen that had prompted the unification of defences as the Great Wall, under the Qin empire. During the first stage of the Former Han empire, Chinese foreign policies were negative rather than positive, as statesmen were anxious to avoid involvement in costly and dangerous wars. Appeasement was the order of the day rather than expansion.

Empress Lü

Gaodi was succeeded by his son, known under his posthumous title of Huidi (reigned 195–188 BC). At his death the government came under the domination of Gaodi's widow, known as the Empress Lü, who maintained the continuity of the Liu imperial house by placing infants on the throne. She also tried to place members of her own family and her immediate supporters in key positions of authority, but these attempts failed to achieve long-lasting results. At her death in 180 BC the authority of the house of Liu was firmly re-established with the accession of one of Gaodi's sons, who is known as Wendi (reigned 180–157 BC).

Wendi

Wendi is held up by Chinese historians as an example of a virtuous emperor marked by his respect for ethical ideals, his personal frugality and his determination to leave his empire richer and safer than it had been at the time when he became emperor. He continued the work started by his father in expanding the power of the central government, taking over territories that had previously been made over as kingdoms. Wendi was probably influenced by the example and advice of a young statesman named Jia Yi, who argued cogently against committing the errors that had brought the empire of Qin to ruin, that is, those of imposing excessive burdens on the population, or of exciting opposition by excessively severe punishments of state. During the reign of Wendi's successor, Jingdi (reigned 157–141 BC) imperial policies remained unchanged, with the emphasis on consolidation and the conservation of energies. By the dexterous presentation of gifts to the Xiongnu leaders China was still able to buy freedom from undue molestation by the northern tribesmen.

Expansion: Wudi

The second stage of Former Han lasted from c. 135 to c. 90 BC. China now took the initiative in foreign affairs by deliberately taking the field against the Xiongnu, in order to free the northern boundaries from the fear of invasion. Such activities were suc-cessful for a comparatively short period, as the mobility of the Xiongnu enabled them in their turn to attack the Chinese fairly effectively. Chinese initiative was also shown by the extension of the armed line of defences further west than hitherto, in order to allow Han penetration into Central Asia and the establishment of relations with some of the tribal units that were settled around the Taklamakan Desert. A further motive for extending the lines lay in the desire to protect the trading caravans that were now setting out from the interior of China, with surplus products of silk. There are signs that such a policy was actively supported by some statesmen, who were at the same time taking steps to expand and control China's economy. These steps included the foundation of state monopolies to work the iron and salt industries; the establishment of firm state control over the minting of coins; and an attempt to stabilize the production of staple goods.

Han foreign expansion also led servicemen, colonists and diplomats to the south and southwest. Large areas were incorporated into Han territory both here and in the northwest and the northeast; it was in this stage that Chinese culture began to take root in the areas to be known later as Vietnam and Korea. The policy of expansion is often associated with the age of Wudi (reigned 141–87 BC), but there is little reason to show that that emperor took any personal part in directing or implementing it. Military successes were achieved by men such as Wei Qing or Huo Qubing; the leading genius behind the plans to establish economic policies was Sang Hongyang. Diplomatic initiative had been started largely thanks to the pioneer exploration of Zhang Qian, who is the first known Chinese traveller to make a personal contact with the leaders of Central Asiatic tribes. In the course of his journeys, which took him north of India and even further west, Zhang Qian noted the possibilities for expanding Chinese trade and for forging alliances with some of the lesser peoples. It was Zhang Qian's initiative which led to the extension of the Chinese defence lines and to the establishment of the 'Silk Roads' to Central Asia.

This stage of Chinese expansion came to an end when Han strength had all too obviously been spent. By about 90 BC Chinese armies were meeting with failure rather than success in their engagements with alien forces, and the central government was finding great difficulty in maintaining their supplies. A further reason for the abandonment of expansionist policies lay in the internal dangers and weaknesses of the dynasty. A serious crisis broke out in 91 BC, in which Chang'an city formed a battleground between contending rivals. When the empress and the heir apparent were driven to their deaths by suicide, there arose the problem of who was to succeed the ageing emperor. Wudi's death in 87 BC may be said to have ushered in the third stage of dynastic and political history.

The Han Dynasty (220 BC–AD 220)

Retrenchment and decline

Zhaodi's reign (87–74 BC) witnessed plots which were directed against the emperor and the execution of Sang Hongyang (80 BC) on a charge of implication therein. Political decisions rested largely in the hands of the statesman Huo Guang, who also guided the hands of Xuandi (reigned 74–49 BC), until his death in 68 BC. During these decades a reaction set in against the deliberate policies enacted under Wudi to strengthen the government's control of the population, to increase the empire's economic resources and to extend the scope of Han influence into Central Asia. New policies, augmented in the reign of Yuandi (reigned 49–33 BC), were intended to reduce the expenditure of the palace and the government, the burdens of service imposed on the population and the severity of the state's punishments. In dynastic terms the house of Liu had lost the robust vigour which had marked some of its earlier days, and it now suffered from decadence and weakness. Effective power came more and more into the hands of the families of the emperor's consorts or those of the eunuchs, and the histories record a number of examples of intrigue that rent the court. In foreign affairs the Chinese government was now refraining from undertaking the initiative to make advances, but the visit paid by one of the leaders of the Xiongnu to Chang'an in 51 BC was acclaimed as a sign of friendly foreign relations. Retrenchment may be seen in the withdrawal of provincial units that had been established in Hainan. A successful venture undertaken by officers in the northwest in 36 BC, while disposing of one of China's enemies, received little credit from the home government.

Under the rule of Chengdi (reigned 33–7 BC) there rose to prominence a family named Wang, which was destined to alter the dynastic face of China. By acquiring effective power at the court, Wang Mang was eventually able to secure the position of regent to the last infant emperor of Former Han, before finally making an end of that dynasty and replacing it with his own house of Xin; this lasted from AD 9 to 23.

M.L.

HAN CHINA AD 2

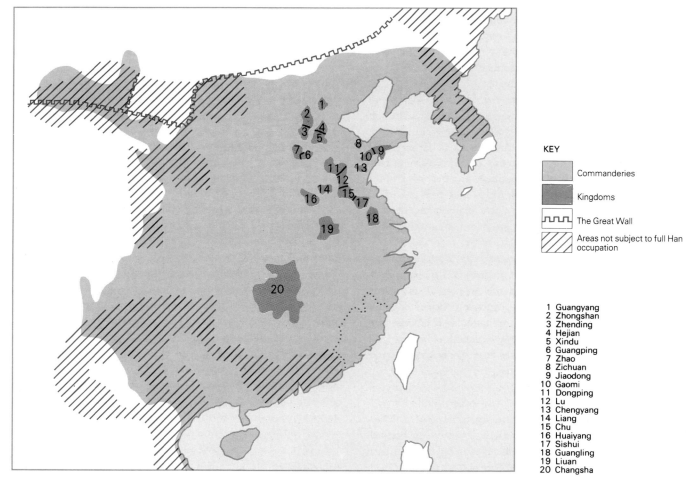

KEY

Commanderies

Kingdoms

The Great Wall

Areas not subject to full Han occupation

1 Guangyang
2 Zhongshan
3 Zhending
4 Hejian
5 Xindu
6 Guangping
7 Zhao
8 Zichuan
9 Jiaodong
10 Gaomi
11 Dongping
12 Lu
13 Chengyang
14 Liang
15 Chu
16 Huaiyang
17 Sishui
18 Guangling
19 Liuan
20 Changsha

Xiongnu

This was the name of various nomad tribal groups of Central Asia. The name is sometimes and incorrectly identified with that of the Huns. Potential intruders and despoilers of the settled farms and towns of northern China, these tribes posed especially dangerous threats when they succeeded in uniting as a confederacy, or in thwarting Chinese friendship with the small states of the Tarim Basin. It was chiefly against these enemies that the Qin and Han governments built and manned the Great Wall. The balance of power between the Xiongnu tribes and the Han empire varied considerably, with some occasions of Han victories (e.g. 119 BC), and some success at dividing the Xiongnu into separate groups; at times some of their leaders were welcomed at the Han capital.

M.L.

Chang'an

Chang'an was the ancient city in the modern province of Shaanxi which corresponds partly to modern Xi'an. It was the site of the imperial capital of the Former Han dynasty. Protected naturally by the hills to the south and the east, the city was, however, vulnerable to raids from the horsemen of the north. Quickly fortified with walls, Chang'an was laid out in a generally rectangular shape, oriented to the points of the compass, and with streets on a grid plan. The palaces were scattered at various sites, and in one case beyond the western wall. Chang'an suffered severely at the hands of the Red Eyebrows (AD 25–6). Rebuilt, sometimes at different but adjacent sites, the city served a number of dynasties, including the Tang, as a capital. Few remains of the Han city survive.

M.L.

Institutions

Originally inherited from the Qin dynasty, the Han forms of government suffered experiment and reform, as dictated by political intrigue, force of circumstance and contemporary fashions of thought. Administrative power was devolved from the emperor, and decisions were promulgated as edicts issued in his name. Statutes and ordinances provided for the general tasks of administration, which depended on the promulgation of the calendar, the annual census and regular assessment of land holdings. The central government was controlled by three senior statesmen and, at a lower level, nine ministers of state with specialist duties, who were supported by a large number of subordinate officials. These were selected, graded and appointed according to a rudimentary system of examinations, or by irregular means of nomination or privilege. By dint of good service and promotion, a junior official could make his way to become one of the senior statesmen of the empire.

Tax was collected in kind or in cash; able-bodied men were obliged to render conscript service, both in the armed forces and in the labour gangs. Punishments of state were less harsh than those of Qin, but none the less severe; rewards for service took the form of material bounties, enhanced social status or legal privileges. At the outset of the empire large areas had been made over for government as kingdoms by the emperor's sons and their descendants. By the end of the 2nd century BC most of these lands had been incorporated as commanderies, that is, administrative units governed by officials who were appointed on their individual merits.

State monopolies

State monopolies for the production of iron and salt were instituted in 119 BC as one of a number of measures which were designed to coordinate the economic effort under official control. Eighty-six commissions were established at the iron and salt mines and on the coast, with authority to work the enterprises with conscript labour and to distribute the processed goods. A tax was added to the price of sale, whose proceeds were channelled directly into the government's hands and away from private owners. Owing to persistent criticism (for example, as voiced in the formal discussions of 81 BC), impractical administration and imperial weakness, the monopolies only operated effectively for short periods in Former and Later Han. They were restored in a more sophisticated manner under the Tang dynasty.

M.L.

Sima Qian (145–*c*. 90 BC)

Sima Qian was the son of Sima Tan, with whom he was jointly responsible for compiling the *Shiji*, or *Historical Records*. As the first of China's 26 Standard, or Dynastic, Histories, this 130-chapter book established a new form for historical writing, which was adopted for successive dynastic periods. The compilers drew on older documents and archives of state, some of which were incorporated, and included their own brief comments on major events.

The *Shiji*, which covers the history of man up to *c*. 90 BC, is divided into the following groups of chapters: imperial annals, which record the actions and statements of the emperors; tables, which set out in chronological sequence the names of the kings of the states of pre-imperial China, and the noblemen and office-holders of the Han dynasty; treatises on subjects such as approved behaviour, astronomy, the workings of the economy; accounts of prominent individuals and families of the pre-imperial period; and biographical monographs of the main figures of Han history.

At the end of his career Sima Qian fell into disfavour for sponsoring the cause of a disgraced general and suffered the punishment of castration. *M.L.*

Paper

Apart from inscriptions on shells, bones, stone and bronze, the earliest writing of China was made on wood or bamboo for normal purposes, and silk for special copies of some documents. The clumsiness of wood and the high expense of silk were relieved by the development of a substance made initially from rags or wood shavings, whose form advanced from proto-paper to paper. Traditionally, the invention was presented to the court by Cai Lun in AD 105, but earlier finds suggest that some substance of this nature had been in use perhaps two centuries previously. Despite the more general introduction of paper from the 3rd or 4th centuries, wood and silk continued in use for some purposes. *M.L.*

Xin (AD 9–23)

Founded by Wang Mang (d. AD 23) at a time when the Han emperors had lost effective authority, this dynasty has traditionally been regarded as an interloper, which usurped the place of the house of Han. Wang Mang attempted to restore imperial pride, social discipline and political integrity by appealing to precepts and institutions that were ascribed to the ancient kings of Zhou. Partly as a result of his example, subsequent imperial dynasties were obliged to claim that their actions were based on such ideals and on the precepts of Confucius. However, the regime of Wang Mang failed to acquire sufficient popularity to survive for long, and the measures of reform that it tried to introduce in political and economic practice aroused resentment or inflicted hardship. In conditions of popular distress, rebel bands of peasants, known as the Red Eyebrows, rose up against Wang Mang in AD 18, and their activities played a significant part in bringing the regime to an end. In AD 23 Wang Mang was put to death by the rebels who had forced their way into Chang'an. In the following years the city was sacked, and widespread civil warfare broke out. In AD 25 the Han dynasty was formally re-established under Liu Xiu, first of the Later Han emperors (Guangwudi). The Red Eyebrows finally surrendered in AD 27. *M.L.*

Eunuchs in Qin and Han

Since the Qin empire and earlier, eunuchs had played a part in the politics of Chinese government. They had first been introduced into the palaces to serve the needs of the female occupants, and from such positions they had succeeded in acquiring a high degree of familiarity with the emperor and other members of his family, often to the discomfiture of officials serving as ministers of state. As trusted confidants of an emperor or an empress, the eunuchs acquired practical powers in government, particularly in times of emergency. It was not until the Later Han period that they feature in palace and government as the real manipulators of dynastic power. *M.L.*

Later Han

Of the rival protagonists who rose to seize control at the end of the Xin dynasty (AD 23), Liu Xiu finally succeeded in establishing the authority of an imperial regime. This was the Later, or Eastern, Han dynasty, restored after the so-called usurpation of Wang Mang. Liu Xiu claimed descent from the emperors of the Former Han dynasty; his capital was established at Luoyang.

In place of the deliberately archaic institutions adopted by Wang Mang, the Later Han emperors reverted to Former Han practice, while introducing some changes in the hierarchy and concept of officials. In dynastic terms, Later Han was at its strongest point under Guangwudi, the founding emperor, and his immediate successors. From *c.* AD 100 a process of weakening occurred. From *c.* AD 75 there had begun a series of struggles for mastery between various families of imperial consorts. Political stability depended on a balance between those families, the established officials and the eunuchs, who began to take part in these struggles from AD 92. Moreover, the situation was sometimes complicated by the enthronement of an infant as emperor. In a major crisis of AD 168 the eunuchs emerged as the victors, only to suffer eclipse and massacre in their turn, in AD 189. In the meantime a rebellion had broken out that sprang from political motives and included some elements of Messianism. The Yellow Turbans drew their strength from popular cults that were associated with the emerging Daoist religious practices. Led by Zhang Jue and others who claimed to be able to cure diseases, a religious movement gathered strength from the valleys of the Yellow River down to the Yangtze, and turned into an armed rebellion in AD 184. Although the main rebel force was suppressed, unrest from this and similar sources continued.

As a result of these disturbances and the loss of social cohesion, effective central control gave way to the rise of regional landowners who were able to set themselves up in virtual independence in the provinces. This loosening of imperial control led eventually to the division of China into the Three Kingdoms of Shu-Han in the west, Wei in the north and Wu in the south. This period began with the abdication of the last of the Han emperors, Xiandi, in AD 220.

The social and political instability of the last decades of Later Han induced some statesmen to re-assess the value of the Confucian system of state, society and individual to which the Han emperors had been heirs. Witnessing as they did the failure of the Confucian ethic to sustain the integrity and strength of empire, they favoured the adoption of disciplinary steps to restore order and eliminate corruption. Some of the measures which they advocated drew more closely from the realism ascribed to Legalist thinkers than the idealism of Confucius's followers.

In foreign affairs the Later Han dynasty saw the re-establishment of Chinese strength on the Silk Roads that led to Central Asia. Active trading conditions led to the greater export of silk to the West, but no direct contacts were established with the Roman empire.

The cultural achievements of Later Han included the institution of a major academy at Luoyang and the formation of the classical tradition and the norm of a Confucian education. The first Buddhist establishments were founded in China in the 2nd century AD, at a time when certain exercises and disciplines were being drawn together to form Daoist religion.   *M.L.*

Luoyang

Of ancient foundation and association with the kings of Zhou, this city situated in Henan Province was adopted as the capital by the Later Han emperors, from AD 25, and it served several subsequent dynasties, including the Tang, for the same purpose. The city housed half a million inhabitants in Later Han. It was laid out in rectangular shape to face the four points of the compass, and its plan was influenced by cosmological as well as practical considerations. Some of China's earliest Buddhist establishments were built in Luoyang, which was ruined by looting in AD 189–90; a new city was built to house the emperors of the Wei and later dynasties.   *M.L.*

Ban Gu (AD 32–92)

Ban Gu was the compiler, with his father Ban Biao, and his sister Ban Zhao, of the *Hanshu*, or *History of the Former Han Dynasty* in 100 chapters. Divided into four main categories of imperial annals, biographies, tables and treatises, the book covers the civil wars that preceded the foundation of the Han dynasty, and the dynastic course of Han and Xin. The work has been taken as a stylistic and literary model that has moulded much of China's subsequent historical writing. Ban Gu was also the author of other works, in prose and poetry.   *M.L.*

WEI, JIN AND NORTHERN AND SOUTHERN DYNASTIES (AD 220–581)

Historical perspective

During the four centuries between the collapse of effective Han rule and the conquest of the south by the first Sui emperor in 589 China was under a single government for only some 30 years; and even that formal unification was disrupted by rebellion and civil strife. The horrors of war were endemic throughout this long period and at times their scale and intensity rival the worst in human history, as during the mutual genocide by hostile races in which hundreds of thousands died in north China about 350. In that sense the period may be labelled a dark age, but it was not a dark age, taken as a whole, economically or culturally.

Agriculture, when left in peace, was remarkably productive, yielding a surplus to support a rich and leisured ruling class in the countryside and in the great cities, huge armies and, by the 6th century, many thousands of Buddhist monasteries and convents. The literature of these centuries had an unprecedented sophistication; in some visual arts, especially sculpture and calligraphy, the levels reached were never surpassed; much Indian and Central Asian culture was absorbed with Buddhism; and in statecraft the monarcho-bureaucratic system learned through hard experience how to improve its control and ensure its survival, although the military were never really tamed. In warfare heavy armoured horsemen, who concentrated the impetus of their charge at the tip of a lance, had a devastating impact on the battlefields of north China from 528 onwards; and in most areas of useful skills from metallurgy to medicine great advances were made. Although an outline of the events of these centuries deals mainly with upheavals and disorders, large areas enjoyed peace and prosperity for generations. Most of the achievements and the problems of the Sui and Tang in the 7th and early 8th centuries were the continuation of developments during the period of disunity.

THE DYNASTIC SUCCESSION: 220–618

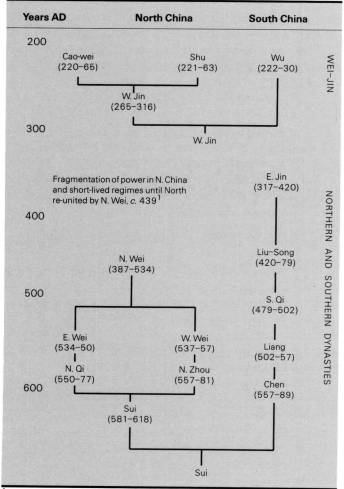

[1] See the table on p. 161

The designation for this period most often used by Chinese and Japanese historians—Wei, Jin, and Northern and Southern dynasties—covers a complicated succession of regimes in various parts of the country that are set out in the tables on this page and p. 161. The first shows in outline the most important dynasties, and the second shows the many states that rose and fell in the north in the 4th and early 5th centuries.

Certain themes are discernible throughout the period. Despite the regional rivalries, especially that between north and south, Han-Chinese and many non-Han leaders shared a belief that the Chinese world was one, united by a common high culture, and felt that disunity was inherently wrong. From the 4th century onwards it was recognized that any regime hoping to control the north had to be sufficiently multiracial to hold together the numerically pre-ponderant Han Chinese, whose agriculture created most of the wealth, and the other nationalities of the north and northwest, whose military power was much greater than their numerical importance. Throughout these centuries small groups of great Chinese hereditary rural magnates formed an elite that expected and generally received high positions under the northern and southern courts alike; but their dominance was challenged by the non-Chinese tribal leadership in the north, by the generals who were the real arbiters of power, by civilian officials of humble origins who rose on their talents and were more amenable to royal control, and by the throne itself, which was jealous of its own prerogatives. One sphere in which the interests of the state and the magnates collided was the control of land and the peasantry, and the levying of taxes and forced labour. The state, when strong enough to do so, proclaimed the ancient doctrine that all land belonged to the crown and attempted to control both its allocation and its revenues. The magnates tried to keep as many of their dependants off the state's tax-lists as possible, and, especially in times of trouble, tended to become local rulers with their own private armies of clansmen. *W.J.F.J.*

Cao Cao (155–220) and the state of Cao Wei (220–65)

The defeat of the Yellow Turbans rising of 184–96 was also the end of the real power of the Han dynasty emperors: in putting down the rebellion, the landed magnates and virtually independent military commanders grew stronger than the throne, and fought among themselves for mastery. By 205 the dictator of China north of the Yangtze was Cao Cao, whose political and military acumen more than made up for his unaristocratic origins as the grandson of a court eunuch's protégé. He recruited many surrendered Yellow Turbans into his own armies, and settled others to work as state dependants on huge public farming projects (*tuntian*) that fed and clothed his growing armies from land left waste by war. He also chose his subordinates for ability rather than birth alone. After his death his son formalized the family's dominance by forcing the abdication of the last Han emperor and founding a new dynasty, the Wei (or Cao Wei), with its capital at Luoyang, that ruled the north and in 263 conquered the southwest. *W.J.F.J.*

State of Wu (222–80)

Two rival power centres combined to prevent Cao Cao from unifying China, and created the triangular rivalry of the Three Kingdoms. In the central and lower Yangtze valley and further south,

THE THREE KINGDOMS

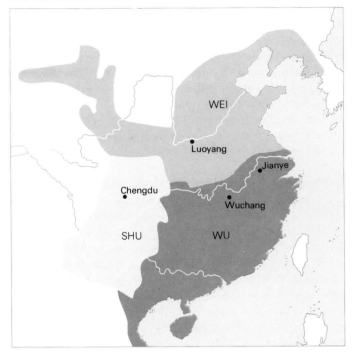

Sun Ce (175–200), followed by his brother Sun Quan (182–252), set up what was to become the state of Wu, based on the great clans that were colonizing and developing the southern frontier, a region still largely populated by non-Han peoples. It differed from the north in having an ample water supply to grow rice, a higher-yielding crop than the north's millet, and many navigable rivers and lakes that encouraged trade and were natural defences that prevented Cao Cao and his successors from bringing the full power of their much larger land-based armies to bear on their amphibious rival. *W.J.F.J.*

State of Shu (221–63)

Shu, in the southwest, was the last of the three embryonic states to form. Its natural defences were the all but impenetrable mountain ranges protecting its economic heartland, the Red River Basin, from attack. Its main political defence was the alliance with Wu achieved by Zhuge Liang (181–234), the chief minister and guiding light of a state that pretended to be the legitimate successor of the Han dynasty under the rule of Liu Pei (161–223), a distant member of the Han ruling house. Zhuge Liang made the most of its resources and extended its control in the southwest, so that even after his death it held out against unfavourable odds until it was overrun by the north in 263. *W.J.F.J.*

Western Jin (265–316)

In 265 the short-lived Wei (or Cao Wei) dynasty that had ruled the north since 220 was itself pushed off the throne by Sima Yan (236–90), a member of a family of aristocratic generals that had dominated Cao Wei politics for many years. The new regime, the Jin (or Western Jin), finally overran the isolated state of Wu in 280, bringing unification and the chance of prosperity to the Chinese world after a century of strife.

But the new state's roots were shallow, and at its outset it only had control of some 16 million people, or about a third of the registered population of the Eastern Han at its height, partly as a result of the destruction of war, and partly because it relied too heavily on the great landed families to wrest full control of the taxes and labour services of the peasantry from them. It also gave such wealth and armed forces to the princes of the blood that they were able to wage a long and devastating series of struggles for mastery from 291 to 306 (later known as the 'Troubles of the Eight Princes'), which led in turn to even greater catastrophes. Millions of non-Han Chinese, who had been resettled within the Chinese frontiers during the previous two centuries and humiliatingly mistreated by the Han aristocracy, joined in ethnic risings that led to the sacking of the capital at Luoyang by Xiongnu nationality horsemen in 311, followed in 316 by the end of such government as the Jin rulers had provided, leaving the north to be fought over for the next 150 years by rival warlords of many races.

The failure of the political system had been foreshadowed by the atmosphere of alienation and the pursuit of private satisfactions that pervaded the culture of the previous century. Ideals of public service had little influence on officials, the richest of whom vied in extravagant living, especially in the capital. In the countryside peasants often had to seek the protection of a local magnate in order to survive the times of trouble, even if this meant the loss of personal freedom and semi-servile dependency. While states rose and fell, the great rural families, ethnically Chinese and generally tracing their social and political pre-eminence back to Eastern Han times, largely survived the end of Jin rule in the north. Barbarian horsemen could loot and destroy, but if they wanted to draw permanent revenues from the rich countryside of the north China plain they needed Chinese administrative help. when members of the most distinguished Chinese families accepted high office at their courts, that encouraged the lesser clans to follow their example. As members of a conquered race, however, these families lost much of their military power, though they were still able to raise private armies in times of trouble. In these troubled times Buddhism became more deeply rooted among the whole population.

In the south, where local magnates were joined by some clans or branches of clans that had migrated *en masse* from the north in the 4th century, the aristocracy was politically and militarily dominant during the Eastern Jin. However, from the 5th century onwards their power was in decline, despite attempts in the early 6th century to revive it. Meanwhile, the process of colonization continued to force the non-Han peoples of the south, who did not have the strategic equestrian striking power of the races in the north, to submit to sinification and new masters, or to move away from their ancestral lands, or to risk annihilation.

The principal regimes that succeeded the Western Jin in the north are set out in the table. Among them the Later Zhao almost

KEY

Frontiers of Western Jin China (c. AD 290)

NON-HAN ETHNIC GROUPS IN THE NORTH AND WEST

Xiongnu and Jie

Di

Qiang

Xianbei

FRONTIERS OF WESTERN JIN CHINA

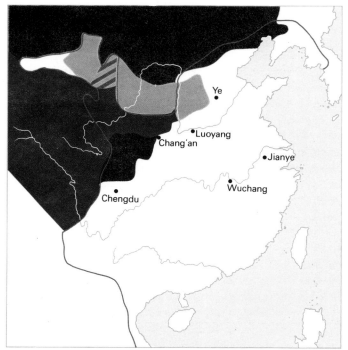

united north China, as did the Former Qin, but each of these collapsed after a generation, having failed to build a stable coalition between the minority ruling race—whose military supremacy was based largely on the mastery of mounted warfare—the other minority races, and the great Chinese clans who controlled the peasantry. It was not until the 430s that the Northern Wei rulers struck the balance that allowed the north almost a century of peace.   *W.J.F.J.*

Eastern Jin (317–420), and southern dynasties

The Eastern Jin that had been put together from the wreckage of the Western Jin to maintain Han control in the south regarded itself as the legitimate government of the whole of China; but its rulers were too suspicious of the over-powerful aristocrats and generals on whom they depended, and whose ambitions threatened the throne, to give enough support to the campaigns to reconquer the north in 313–21, 352–65, and 416–18, despite the welcome with which they were met by the Chinese populace of the north. Only when the south itself was in peril, as when the Former Qin launched the massive invasion that was stopped on the Fei River in 383, were local rivalries put aside for the sake of national survival.

The succession of four short-lived dynasties in the south that followed the overthrow of the Jin by its general Liu Yu—who became the first Liu-Song emperor in 420, and who with his nephew and successor provided 30 years of capable rule—revealed an inherent weakness in the state structure: a warlord could found a dynasty and hold it together for a generation or so, but as exceptional political and military skill are rarely inherited, his successors would be unable to preserve the throne from being seized by another general. Without a powerful ruler the state's institutions could not by themselves control too powerful a subject.

Yet despite, or perhaps because of, the weakness of the state, the 5th and 6th centuries saw economic growth in the south, with the capital Jiankang (Nanjing) becoming one of the world's great cities and a hub of waterborne trade. As smaller landowners became more important politically and economically the aristocratic principle declined. Aristocrats continued to claim the highest-ranked posts in government, but the real administrative power was often in the hands of the more humbly born, the 'cold men' who rose on their talents.   *W.J.F.J.*

Northern Wei (387–534)

During the 5th century the Northern Wei rulers, of the Tuoba branch of the Xianbei, first destroyed all their rivals in north China and then proceeded as best they could to establish direct control over the peasantry while recognizing and regulating the claims of both the Xianbei and the Chinese aristocracy to high office. During the reign of the thoroughly sinicized Xiaowendi (471–99) he and his grandmother, the Dowager Empress Feng, changed almost every aspect of state and society in a drastic reform programme. The state allocated land according to labour-power (owners of slaves and oxen receiving proportionately more than ordinary peasants) under a system somewhat misleadingly called 'equalized fields' (*juntian*); organized rural households into groups of 5, 25 and 125 with headmen responsible for delivering taxes and forced labour; enforced sinification and outlawed many of the old Xianbei ways and even the use of the Xianbei language at court; reorganized the civil service; rewrote the laws; and moved the capital to the ruined site of Luoyang, far from the barbarian influences of the old one at Pingcheng (Datong, Shanxi). Such were the resources of the reformed state that in some 20 or 30 years it had a great city of half a million people with magnificent buildings where there had been nothing but ruins before, while also maintaining hundreds of thousands of soldiers on the frontiers.

The forced pace of change and the greed and incompetence of

PRINCIPAL REGIMES IN NORTH CHINA, 316–439

Name of regime	Dates	Nationality of rulers	
1	Former Zhao	309–29	Xiongnu	Rose in Shanxi, destroyed Western Qin in 316. From 319, capital Chang'an. Ruled Hebei, Henan, Shanxi, Shaanxi. Fell to 4.
2	Cheng-Han	304–47	Ba-Di	Controlled Sichuan and parts of Yunnan and Guizhou. Destroyed by Eastern Jin.
3	Former Liang	317–76	Han	Set up by governor of far western province of Liangzhou in western Gansu and Ningxia and southern Xinjiang. Fell to 7.
4	Later Zhao	319–51	Jie	Rival then successor to 1. From 329 to 350 controlled most of north China. Fell to 5.
5	Ran-Wei	350–52	Han	Han general of 4 led rising, slaughtered Jie. Briefly controlled parts of north China. Fell to 6.
6	Former Yan	337–70	Xianbei (Murong)	State originated in late 3rd century on Liao River, moving capital to Hebei in 352. Controlled area from Shandong to Shanxi. Fell to 7.
7	Former Qin	350—94	Di	Unified north until power declined after failed invasion of south in 383. Capital: Chang'an. Destroyed by 8.
8	Later Qin	384–417	Qiang	Successor to 7. Capital: Chang'an. Controlled Shaanxi, Gansu, Henan. Destroyed by Eastern Jin.
9	Later Yan	384–407	Xianbei (Murong)	Revival of 6. Capital: Zhongshan (Ding Xian, Hebei). Controlled areas from Shandong and Shanxi to Liaoning. Fell to 13 and 19.
10	Western Yan	384–94	Xianbei (Murong)	Another successor to 6 in parts of Shanxi and Shaanxi. Destroyed by 9.
11	Western Qin	385–431	Xianbei (Qifu)	Capital: Yuanchuan (near Lanzhou). Controlled southwest Gansu until destroyed by 18.
12	Later Liang	386–403	Di	Local regime in west Gansu. Capital: Guzang (Wuwei). Fell to 8.
13	Northern Wei	386–534	Xianbei (Tuoba)	State with origins in Inner Mongolia, then capitals at Pingcheng (Datong, Shanxi) and, after 493, Luoyang. Conquered all of north China in early 5th century.
14	Southern Liang	397–414	Xianbei (Tufa)	Controlled parts of west Gansu and Qinghai. Fell to 11.
15	Northern Liang	397–439	Lushui Hu	Parts of west Gansu and of Xinjiang. Fell to 13.
16	Southern Yan	398–410	Xianbei (Murong)	Short-lived successor to 9 in parts of Shandong and Hebei until ended by Eastern Jin.
17	Western Liang	400–21	Han	In far west of Gansu with capital at Dunhuang. Destroyed by 15.
18	Xia	407–31	Xiongnu	State in northern Shaanxi and Inner Mongolia. Capital: Wancheng (Heng Shan, Shaanxi). Destroyed by 13.
19	Northern Yan	407–36	Han	Another successor to 9, in Liaoning and northeastern Hebei. Fell to 13.

'Former', 'Northern', 'Southern' and other such epithets in the names of regimes have long been conventionally used to distinguish the states that, in fact used the same title.

NORTHERN WEI AND LIU-SONG

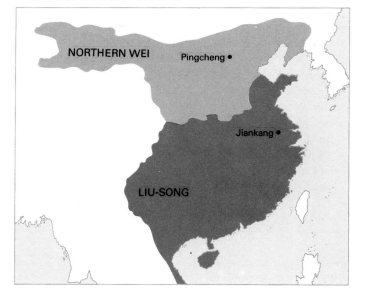

Luoyang's rulers were too much for the northern frontier, where the non-Chinese garrisons, once the honoured counter-strike forces that launched retaliatory expeditions when the steppe confederation of Rouran raided Wei territory from Mongolia, were neglected and mistreated by a remote and sinicized court. From 524 onwards they were in rebellion, and they were finally put down not by Luoyang's armies but by the heavy cavalry of the Erzhu, tribesmen of Iranian descent long settled in Shanxi. The Erzhu took and later sacked Luoyang, imposing their rule on the north, only to fall in their turn to the superior political skills of a sinicized Xianbei, Gao Huan, a former northern garrison officer and associate of theirs. In 534 he is said to have moved 2 million people from Luoyang and its environs at three days' notice to a new capital at Ye (Anyang, Henan). This was the end of the Northern Wei dynasty. *W.J.F.J.*

Power struggle in the north

The Northern Wei dynasty split into two lines, the Eastern Wei, under Gao Huan and his sons, and the Western Wei, under Gao's rival Yuwen Tai (507–56) at Chang'an. In 552 the eastern branch was dethroned, and Gao Yang made himself the first emperor of the Northern Qi, controlling most of the wealth and population of north China. Their western rivals had started off at a great disadvantage in numbers, but this forced them to go for a smaller and more efficient bureaucracy, supposedly recruited for ability and character rather than birth; to be strict in applying the regulations that kept land allocation under state control; and also to set up a soldier-peasant army that enjoyed high status. In 557 the Yuwen family ended the fiction of Western Wei rule and took the throne as the Zhou dynasty (later known as Northern Zhou). Whereas the Northern Qi regime was weakened by its own wealth, the leaner Northern Zhou state first matched it militarily and then, in 577, destroyed it. It may be that the Zhou victory can be attributed in part to the confiscation of Buddhist church property and the forced laicization of a million monks, nuns and monastic dependants in 574, who lost their exemption from tax and forced labour, whereas the Northern Qi was supporting twice that number of religious.

Zhou was, however, overthrown in 581 by one of its partly Chinese generals, Yang Jian (541–604). Having reasserted Chinese supremacy in the north as the first Sui emperor, he went on to conquer the south and reunify China.

DIVISION BETWEEN NORTHERN WEI AND SOUTHERN QI

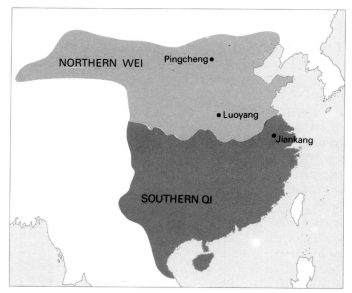

NORTH CHINA IN THE EARLY 6TH CENTURY AD

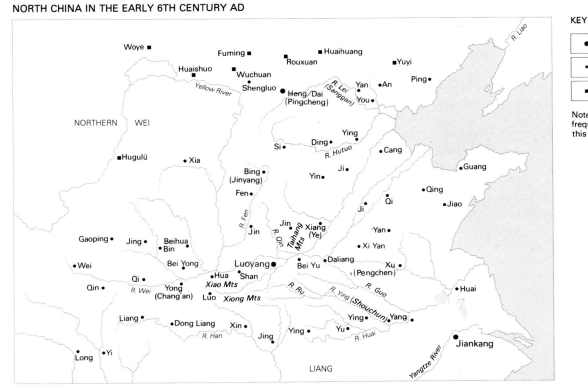

● Capital cities

· *zhou* cities

■ Garrisons

Note: place names were
frequently changed in
this period.

DIVISION BETWEEN EASTERN WEI, WESTERN WEI AND LIANG

The fall of the south

In the first half of the 6th century the south enjoyed a measure of
peace and prosperity, following the political chaos and the insistent
military pressure from the north during the second half of the 5th
century. In 502 Xiao Yan (464–549) seized the throne from the
weak Southern Qi rulers, his own kinsmen, as the first Liang
emperor, Liang Wudi (reigned 502–49). Fortunately for him no
other Northern Wei ruler was quite as determined to conquer the
south as Xiaowendi had been, and after 516, when the Wei armies
suffered catastrophically with the collapse of an embankment they
had built up on the Huai to force flood water south, Liang was no
longer under serious pressure from the north. The latter was to
become so weakened by its internal divisions that in 529 a Liang
expeditionary force of only 7000 or so men installed, briefly, a
client ruler in the Luoyang palace. But they were not reinforced,
and were soon expelled. A later attempt to get a cheap advantage
from the north's divisions brought disaster in 548, when a muti-
nous northern general, Hou Jing (503–52), was welcomed south,
only to turn his armies against the capital, which fell the next year
after a siege of five months. The great city of over a million inhab-

itants was devastated, the Emperor Wudi died soon afterwards, Hou Jing extended his ravages, and Wudi's heirs fought for the succession. As the familiar pattern of dynastic collapse repeated itself, another general, Chen Baxian, pushed them all aside and took the throne in 557, giving the new dynasty his own surname. The Chen regime was lucky to last as long as 32 years: the chaos and destruction of the Hou Jing troubles brought a revival of local power throughout the south at the expense of the centre, and only the north's own divisions enabled Chen to survive until 589, when the first Sui emperor crushed his weak southern rival.

The triumph of the north was due to political and military institutions that made the state strong, and they were largely continued during the first century and a half of Tang rule. The south was to conquer in other ways. Its culture, generally more sophisticated than that of the north, held its own against the simpler northern traditions; and the economic growth of the south continued after reunification, bringing a shift in China's economic centre of gravity from the north China plain to the lower Yangtze area.

The four centuries of disunity had been marked by many catastrophes, not least in the last 60 or so years. The civilization that developed in that troubled period was both richer and more profound than what had gone before: it was in these centuries that a melancholy sense of the impermanence of all things human began to characterize Chinese culture. *W.J.F.J.*

after launching a combined naval and land attack against the Chen Yi capital on the Yangtze, he conquered the south and reunited China. Wendi strengthened and rationalized the bureaucracy, and recentralized civil and military power on the model of the Han, at the same time laying the foundations for the great age of Tang that followed. He sensitively employed Confucianism, Daoism and, especially, Buddhism in a series of ideological measures designed to help overcome centuries of cultural and political fragmentation and reintegrate north and south China into a unified empire.

The central administrative apparatus Wendi established, the 'Three Department' (*sansheng*) system with its Six Ministries, prefigured that of the Tang. Reimposition of the 'equal-field' land tenure system of the northern dynasties and the development of a new and more efficient tax collection system swelled state coffers. He revived the civil service system, applying higher standards of merit for appointment and promotion in an effort to counter centuries of entrenched aristocratic privilege. He improved govern-

Wendi: founder of the Sui dynasty and of China's Second Empire.

THE SUI DYNASTY (AD 581–618)

Wendi

Yang Jian (AD 541–604) reigned from 581 to 604 and was canonized Wendi. His family had served the non-Chinese dynasties of the north for two centuries and had married into powerful families of the Turco-Mongol elite. In 557 Wendi married into a high-ranking non-Chinese clan, the Dugu. The eldest daughter of this union was married to the Northern Zhou crown prince, who became emperor in 578. Wendi's son-in-law proved to be a harsh and pathological ruler, and even threatened the entire Yang clan with extinction. Taking advantage of his death from a stroke in 580, Wendi liquidated 59 members of the Northern Zhou royal house and transferred imperial power into his own hands.

Made fearful and insecure by his sudden rise to eminence, Wendi was sensitive to criticism, suspicious of others and subject to outbursts of rage; he even personally beat to death some of his officials. But he was an eminently successful monarch. In 589,

mental efficiency by reducing the number of local administrative units and subjected local officials to a degree of central control unknown even in the Han; the peasant militia was similarly placed under central power. A new law code, representing a synthesis of northern and southern legal traditions, provided a direct model for the Tang code and thus for all subsequent codes of imperial China. He reinforced defences along the northern border and pursued strong diplomatic and military policies against neighbouring tribes and states. Upon his death in 604 Wendi presided over an empire unrivalled in prosperity since the Han. *H.J.W.*

Chang'an

Located slightly southeast of the old Han capital of the same name, the new Sui capital was designed by the architect Yuwen Kai along the lines of planned cities constructed on the north China plain during the disunion period. Wendi took up residence in the still incomplete city in April 583. The outer wall, made of pounded earth, extended east to west for 9721m and north to south for 8652m, making a circumference of 36.7km; its base averaged 9 to 12m in thickness and it probably stood more than 10m high. The city was divided into three zones: the palace city contained imperial residences, audience halls and pleasure pavilions; the administrative city for the first time concentrated numerous government offices in a single area; the residential city, occupying $\frac{7}{8}$ths of the total area, contained 108 rectangular walled compounds, including two large markets. The great southern gate of the city opened out on an extremely broad avenue some 155m wide, extending north to the palace city; all foreign envoys seeking audience with the Son of Heaven traversed this avenue. Intermingled in the city were hovels of the poor, mansions of the nobility, and the head metropolitan temples for Buddhism and Daoism. Chang'an was by far the largest city in the world for its day, and the largest in area of any Chinese walled capital during all of imperial times. *H.J.W.*

Yangdi

Yang Guang (569–618), was the second son of Wendi, reigned as the second and last major Sui emperor between 605 and 617, and was canonized Yangdi. His youth was dominated by his parents, the tyrannical first emperor and the jealous and meddlesome Empress Dugu. At the age of 13 he was married into the royal family of the southern house of Later Liang, thus introducing him to southern culture, for which he acquired a great love, lasting the rest of his life. After the conquest of Chen, Yangdi served for 10 years as viceroy of the south at his headquarters at Jiangdu (modern Yangzhou) on the Yangtze.

Yangdi began to have designs on the throne after his elder brother, the crown prince, became estranged from the empress. His plotting soon bore fruit, and he was proclaimed heir in 600. He may well have hastened the death of his father, who fell ill in 604, fearful that Wendi would restore the former crown prince.

As emperor, Yangdi proved to be creative, energetic and ambitious. He continued to make improvements in Sui civil administration, expanded the system of state education and civil service examinations (he introduced the famous *jinshi* degree), and presided over a revival of Confucian learning. He continued the vigorous foreign policy of his father; he extended Chinese suzerainty over some of the oases along the Silk Road and over some of the Turkish tribes to China's north, opened relations with Japan, reconquered northern Vietnam, and sent Chinese armies against the Chams further south.

In the end, a series of ruinously ambitious undertakings brought about the collapse of his dynasty, and caused traditional Chinese historians to treat him as a tyrannical and self-indulgent 'bad last' emperor. While retaining Chang'an as his centre of administration, he reconstructed an eastern capital at Luoyang in northern Henan. He reinforced the Great Wall, dredged canals, built roads and vast, lavish palaces. Countless thousands of labourers were conscripted for these and other grandiose public works projects, many of whom perished. Before the peasantry could recover from oppressive levies, Yangdi sent three massive land and sea expeditions against northern Korea. Large-scale revolts soon engulfed north China, forcing the emperor to sail into splendid isolation at his southern capital at Jiangdu. There, early in 618, he was assassinated by one of his officials. His successor was Gongdi. *H.J.W.*

The Great Wall

Since its construction by the Qin and extension by the Han, the Great Wall had been rebuilt and repaired repeatedly over the centuries, most recently during the Northern Zhou dynasty, which, one year before the founding of the Sui, had reinforced the eastern section located in the recently conquered Northern Qi state. Wendi undertook repairs in 586 and again in 587. But the most extensive work took place under Yangdi in 607, who either built or repaired a long section in northern Shanxi. More than a million men are said to have been levied for the construction, which was carried out at such a pace that it was completed in only 20 days, exacting an immense human toll. *H.J.W.*

Grand Canal

By Sui times the 'breadbasket' of China had shifted from the wheat and millet fields of the north to the lush rice paddies of the Lower Yangtze, prompting the Sui emperors to construct canals linking this productive region with their food-poor capitals. Between 584 and 589 Yuwen Kai supervised construction of a canal leading from Chang'an eastwards towards the Tong Pass. This work was continued during Yangdi's reign beginning in 605 with a canal linking Luoyang first to the Huai River and then to Jiangdu (Yangzhou) on the Yangtze. Following the canal's completion, Yangdi sailed its length leading a magnificent flotilla of boats extending in close file for some 100km. A southern extension, built in 610, reached to the region of Hangzhou. The longest portion, extending from the Yellow River to the Beijing area, and designed to supply armies defending the northern and northeastern frontiers, was built in 608–9, employing the labour of countless thousands of men and, it is said, for the first time, of women. Although portions of the canal were not new (some dated as far back as the Zhou dynasty), this integrated nationwide system, 40 paces wide and stretching almost 2000km, represented a major technological feat. It greatly facilitated the tasks of administration and defence, and increased the economic interdependence of north and south China. *H.J.W.*

The Turks

By the 550s the Tujue, descendants of the old Xiongnu enemies of the Han, had gained control of the region from the Liao in Manchuria to the borders of Persia. They were divided into a dominant eastern khanate (district governed by a khan) and a subordinate western khanate, headquartered respectively on the upper Orkhon, and on the Issyk Kul and the Talas. Fortunately for the Sui, at the very moment China was reuniting, the Turks were dividing; at the very beginning of the dynasty the western khanate shook loose of the eastern, and internal dissension further weakened the Eastern Turks. Wendi exploited Turkish rivalries, supporting khans and anti-khans to China's advantage and pressuring some tribes to acknowledge Chinese suzerainty. By the time his son took the throne, only the Eastern Turks remained a serious threat to the Sui reassertion of regional power. Yangdi vigorously pursued traditional Chinese policies of divide and conquer against the 'barbarians', but whatever gains he achieved were largely nullified by his disastrous Korean campaigns, which undermined Sui prestige in Asia. Late in 615 the Eastern Turk Khan, Shibi (reigned 609–19), signalled a renascent Turkish menace by surrounding the emperor

at the fortress of Yanmen in northwestern Shanxi and keeping him hostage there for a month before the siege was broken. During the civil wars marking the end of the Sui, the Turks resumed in full their former belligerence. *H.J.W.*

Korea

The kingdom of Koguro, which occupied modern Manchuria east of the Liao and the northern portion of the Korean peninsula, represented a serious potential military threat to the Sui, especially if it allied with other 'barbarian' peoples or helped to fan the flames of rebellion in northeastern China, where separatist feelings still ran high. In 589 Wendi attacked Koguro in response to its incursions west of the Liao. Yangdi's three unsuccessful land and sea campaigns of 611–12, 613 and 614 were much more costly in men and material. The reasons for these failures were: the formidable defences around Koguro cities, the chief military targets of the Sui; the extended Chinese supply lines, which were difficult to maintain; and the short fighting season for the Chinese invaders, which lasted only from April to the onset of rains in early summer. By 614 much of China was enveloped in civil war, precluding any further Sui attempts against the Korean kingdom. *H.J.W.*

THE TANG DYNASTY (AD 618–907)

Background

The Tang dynasty emerged from the political anarchy left by the collapse of the Sui from 616. The Tang founder, Li Yuan (566–635, reigned 618–26, posthumous title Gaozu), was a high Sui official, related by marriage to the royal families of both the Sui and Northern Zhou. When major rebellions broke out in north China he was left in charge of Taiyuan, a crucial garrison for defence against the Turks. When in 617 the Sui emperor fled to his southern capital, and it was clear that his dynasty was doomed, Li Yuan, prompted according to tradition by his son Li Shimin (the future Taizong) himself rebelled, and marched upon the Sui capital of Daxingzheng (Chang'an, as it was known under the Tang). The city fell at the end of 617, and Li Yuan installed a Sui child prince as puppet emperor. In the fifth month of 618 he took the throne for himself and proclaimed a new dynasty, the Tang, named after his own fiefdom in Shanxi.

The Tang were only one of several powerful rebel regimes which fought for the succession to the Sui, and it was not until 624 that large-scale opposition to the Tang ended, while the last recalcitrant rival rebel was not put down until 628. The Tang succeeded in this struggle thanks to their virtually impregnable northwestern base, surrounded by mountains, and to the brilliance of their generals, including Gaozu's sons. The prolonged resistance to the Tang conquest in the northeast left a legacy of disaffection that persisted throughout the dynasty. The Tang leadership was at first drawn largely from the northwestern aristocratic families of mixed Chinese and non-Han origins, and remained suspicious of the members of the northeastern elite families, who were only slowly drawn into government at its highest levels. The physical damage to the northeastern plain also had lasting effects, exacerbated by repeated droughts, floods and epidemics. Even a century later Hebei and Henan had less than three-quarters of their Sui population, and the northeast began steadily to lose its long-established preeminence as the richest and most populous region of China.

D.C.T.

Tang government

Once the initial campaigns were won, Gaozu rapidly re-established the framework of civil government, and issued a system of detailed administrative law in 624 that was to remain the basis of Tang government. The essential shape of the government remained similar to that of the Sui. The emperor ruled through two policy formulating ministries, the Chancellery (*Menxiasheng*) and Secretariat (*Zhongshusheng*), and an executive apparatus presided over by the Department of State Affairs (*Shangshusheng*). This controlled the Six Boards (*lin bu*), each responsible for policy in a specific area of government, the Nine Courts (*Jiu si*), ministries surviving from the Han period, and a variety of specialized directorates. The functioning of the government was overseen by the Censorate. During the fall of the Sui and the ensuing confusion, in order to re-establish control over the areas that submitted to the Tang, a very large number of small prefectures and counties were set up. It was not until well into the 630s that the central government once again was able to rationalize the system of local government and reintegrate it with the centralized bureaucracy. Eventually, however, the empire was divided into some 300 prefectures (*zhou*) and 1500 counties (*xian*). The prefectures were under direct central control, without any intermediate level of regional administration, so that no local unit was big enough to form a viable base for independence. Early Tang government was highly centralized, and depended on a complex system of administrative law.

The Tang, like the Sui, took over the 'equal field system' (*juntian*) of land allocation and the systems of taxation and labour service and of military organization that had been inherited from the northern dynasties of the late 5th and 6th centuries. All these systems were designed for a rather primitive society, in which money played a small role, and for a simple type of government intervening as little as possible in local affairs. Labour services were used to perform many of the functions of government at minimal cost. Specified areas of land, part of it inheritable, were allocated to all adult males, who paid tax and performed labour service (*corvée*) in return. The land grants envisaged were generous, but it is doubtful how far the system was enforced, especially in southern China. The actual land-holdings of farmers seem to have been much less than the law provided for. But the government very carefully registered both land and people, and strictly limited land holdings and controlled the acquisition of landed property. Taxation, almost entirely levied in grain and cloth, fell almost exclusively on the rural population.

The military organization, which took its final form in the 630s, was based on some 600 militia units (*fubing*) most of which were stationed in the loyal northern and northwestern centres of Tang influence. The troops of these units were farmers who supported themselves, but had the obligation of regular military training, and of either annually performing two months' service in rotation with one of the guards' units at the capital or to serve for a term in a frontier garrison. The Tang armies also included some long-service troops. Many of these, especially in the cavalry essential for border warfare, were Turks, Tanguts, Khitans or other non-Chinese tribesmen, led by their own chieftains.

Taizong (Li Shimin)

Li Shimin (600–49, reigned 626–49) was Gaozu's second son, and was an important general during the Tang pacification of the eastern plain. He was rivalled, however, by his elder brother Li Jianzheng, who was made heir apparent. In 626, after a long series of intrigues, Li Shimin engineered a *coup d'état*, the so-called Xuanwu Gate Incident, in which his brothers were murdered and he seized control of the government. Shortly thereafter Gaozu was forced to abdicate.

Taizong's reign is famous as an era of exemplary 'good government'. He was able to appoint an excellent group of ministers with whom he established close rapport. Although always unquestioned ruler of his court, his advisers enjoyed great freedom to express both advice and criticism. In later years he became increasingly dictatorial and his reign was marred by disputes over the succession, but he deserves credit for consolidating the regime set up by his father and for inculcating a fine *esprit de corps* among his officials. He was an extremely active ruler, personally involved in every major decision, and his style of government could only be followed by an emperor cast in the same heroic mould, and possessing his sure instinct for choosing talented and harmonious advisers.

His reign was equally important in the military sphere. In 630 he finally crushed the Turks who had threatened north China constantly for half a century. With the northern frontier secure, Taizong embarked on a series of campaigns against the peoples of the Tibetan borderlands, westwards into the Tarim Basin to secure control of the silk routes, and finally against the Korean kingdom of Koguryŏ. Strong resistance to Chinese invasions had been a major factor in the downfall of the Sui. By the end of Taizong's reign, although the Korean campaigns were again costly failures, Chinese control was established into the Tarim and Dzungaria, and the Tang were firmly established as a great Eurasian power, with diplomatic ties with Byzantium, the doomed Sassanian empire in Iran, the newly emergent Tibetan kingdom and with a huge range of tribal peoples all over Asia.

Cosmopolitan contacts

With these wide contacts, the Tang empire became a more open and cosmopolitan society than China has ever been before or since. Trading communities of Iranians from Central Asia, caravan traders from the steppes, Persians, Arabs, Uighurs and Jews settled in the two capital cities, Luoyang and Chang'an, in ports like Canton and Yangzhou, and in many other trading towns. They brought with them their own religions—Islam, Judaism, Nestorian Christianity, Zoroastrianism and Manichaeism. They were allowed to live in their own communities, controlled by their own headmen according to their own customs and law. They brought with them new forms of entertainment; Tang popular music and dance was deeply influenced by Central Asia. New forms of poetry based on foreign tunes came into vogue. They influenced Chinese taste, fashions and cuisine. They provided models for new styles in ceramics and metalwork. Foreign traders, monks, even physicians settled and worked freely in China.

Until the 760s many of these foreign contacts came via the Central Asian caravan routes. After that date the overland routes were disrupted and the sea routes to India and the Persian Gulf from Canton and Yangzhou predominated. Foreign shipping carried Chinese goods to Malaysia, the Indonesian islands, India, Ceylon and the Middle East. At first Arab shipping dominated this long distance trade, while Korean and Japanese ships also carried on a lively trade with China. But in the 9th century Chinese ships also began to range into the Indian Ocean, carrying cargoes of Chinese silks and ceramics. In the 8th and 9th centuries both Yangzhou and Canton were said to have had foreign populations of over 100 000.

Besides trade, China also exported its cultural influence. During the Tang, hostage princes from many of the surrounding peoples were educated at the Tang court, and returned to their countries imbued with Chinese culture. Japan, Korea and Parhae (a state which grew up in Manchuria in the 8th and 9th centuries) became states organized on the Tang model, employing the Chinese written language. So, to a lesser degree, did the state of Nanzhao in Yunnan. By the end of the Tang the Chinese influence in East Asia, in which Chinese culture played the same role as Graeco-Roman culture in the west, was firmly established.

Buddhism

The most all-pervading of all foreign influences was Buddhism. By the 7th century it influenced every section of Chinese society. Under the Tang Chinese pilgrims such as Xuanzang travelled to India to renew scriptural knowledge, incidentally broadening Chinese knowledge of India, while many foreign monks visited China. Until the mid-8th century Chinese Buddhism was constantly renewed from India. Thereafter, when the links were cut, Buddhism became an almost entirely native religion following paths of its own. Meanwhile Buddhism had a wide appeal, not only to the educated, for whom it was the most lively mode of thought, but also to the common people.

With this broad support the Buddhist communities became extremely wealthy and influential. Successive Tang emperors (who claimed to be descended from Laozi, founder of Daoism) tried to bring the monasteries and their monks under firm control, but with little lasting success until the suppression of the monasteries in the 9th century.

D.C.T.

Xuanzang

Xuanzang (602–64) was the most successful Chinese Buddhist pilgrim to undertake the arduous journey to India. Unlike pilgrims of other faiths and countries, Chinese Buddhists were eager not only to visit holy places but also to obtain scriptures in India which could be taken back to China for translation.

Born in 602, Xuanzang was ordained at an early age. He soon became dissatisfied with existing translations of Buddhist texts and in 629 set out for India across Central Asia, alone and without official permission. He reached India after several years of hazardous journeying and studied at the Buddhist University of Nālandā, where he became proficient in Sanskrit. He also travelled within India itself, and was well received by local rulers.

In the intervening period the Tang empire had expanded into Central Asia, so the emperor Taizong personally welcomed him, seeing him as a valuable source of information on the lands to the west. Xuanzang provided the emperor with a written account of these, the *Xiyuji* (*Record of the Western Regions*), but insisted also on being allowed to translate the Buddhist literature he had brought back. Taizong, who eventually became more interested in Buddhism through Xuanzang's influence, authorized the provision of a team of assistants.

By the time of Xuanzang's death in 664 he had only translated about 75 texts, but these included several very lengthy ones. Buddhist literature in Chinese was increased by about one-quarter through his efforts, and his translations set new standards of accuracy. His criticisms of earlier translators, with whom he differed in philosophical beliefs also, caused controversy, but his retranslations of texts already available in many cases did not supplant the existing versions in popularity. Moreover, his main philosophical treatise, the *Chengweishi lun* or *Vijñaptimātratā-siddhi*, though intensively studied in China for a while, had little influence on the development of Buddhist thought there. This was because although it was always respected as a systematic statement of the 'Idealist' position in Buddhist philosophy, it denied that all men possessed the potentiality of enlightenment, a key idea for Chinese Buddhists. Its transmission to Japan by the monk Dōshō in 653 secured a more important place for it in early Japanese Buddhism prior to the introduction of schools representing the mainstream of Chinese Buddhist thought, but otherwise it was not until the rise of modern Indology in Europe that the value of this and other translations came to be fully appreciated.

Xuanzang himself has, nonetheless, always been a popular figure in China if only because of the heroic scale of his achievements. There is evidence that his exploits had entered popular legend long before the publication of the novel *Xiyouji* (*Journey to the West, or Monkey*), in 1592, fixed his present-day image in the Chinese popular consciousness. *T.B.*

Chan and Pure Land Buddhism

The Chan school of Buddhism (*Zen* in Japanese) arose in China in reaction to the complexities of Buddhist doctrine as it was introduced from India and further elaborated by Chinese monks. The school stressed that it maintained a separate tradition of Buddhist truth bypassing all elaborate doctrinal systems, that its truths went beyond what could be expressed by the written word, and that enlightenment was to be found through an insight into one's own true nature rather than through doctrinal study.

This separate tradition was said to have been brought to China in the early 6th century by Bodhidharma, last of a line of Indian patriarchs to have transmitted it from the time of the Buddha and initiator of a line of Chinese patriarchs of whom the sixth, Huineng, may be seen as particularly embodying the ideas of non-reliance on the written word and seeing into one's own nature.

Huineng lived in obscurity in south China, dying in the early 8th century, and although he was reputedly illiterate and unordained at the time of his enlightenment, he was put forward posthumously by his followers as the true Sixth Patriarch against an established northern claimant, Shenxiu (606?–706).

The iconoclastic influence of Chan spread rapidly from the 8th century onwards and by the end of the 9th century two major schools had emerged: Linqi (Japanese *Rinzai*), which emphasized *gongan* (Japanese *kōan*), paradoxical problems designed to jolt the disciple out of conventional thinking into enlightenment, and Caodong (Japanese *Sōtō*), which emphasized meditation. Chinese monastic Buddhism has remained principally Chan Buddhism to this day.

Pure Land Buddhism takes its name from the common Buddhist idea of the Pure Land, *qingtu*, a paradise presided over by a Buddha. The school is only concerned however with the Western Paradise of 'Buddha, since in the *Sukhāvatī - vyūha sūtra* (*Larger Sukhāvatī vyūha Sūtra*) translated into Chinese as the *Wuliang-shou jing*, it is asserted that anyone who calls on the name of Amitābha may through his assistance be reborn there. Though rebirth in the Western Paradise was already important to early Chinese Buddhists such as Huiyuan (344–416), Tanluan (*c.* 476–542) first identified this as an 'easy' form of Buddhism appropriate to the degenerate age in which he lived. In the 7th century, by which time Amitābha and his attendant Avalokiteśvara (Chinese Guanyin) had become popular objects of devotion, Daochuo (562–645) took up this idea, controverting other Buddhist thinkers who for doctrinal reasons were reluctant to concede that an ordinary unenlightened person might enter paradise. In doing so, he legitimized such popular devotional practices as counting with beans the number of times Amitābha was invoked, a custom which also gave rise to the Chinese use of the rosary. Daochuo's work was continued by his disciple Shandao (613–81), who is regarded as an incarnation of Amitābha in Japan, and by others during the Tang dynasty who propagated faith in Amitābha through songs and illustrations so that Pure Land became from that time onwards the most influential form of Buddhism in Chinese society as a whole. *T.B.*

Gaozong

Taizong's successor, Gaozong (628–83, reigned 649–83) came to the throne as a young man presiding over a court of elder statesmen who had held power under his father, and proved unable to provide the needed leadership. After a few years he began to suffer recurrent bouts of incapacitating illness, and came under the complete dominance of his second empress Wu Zhao. His reign, nevertheless, was far from a mere anti-climax after

Taizong. At home state institutions were further strengthened, and a wide range of cultural projects undertaken. Abroad, the Chinese armies pushed ever deeper into Central Asia until, following the collapse of Sassanian power, Chinese protectorates were set up in what is now Afghanistan and Russian Central Asia, and Chinese power was extended further westwards than at any other time in history. These protectorates were short-lived. Islam conquered Iran and pressed on into Afghanistan and the region around Bukhara and Samarkand, while the Tibetans threatened the Chinese supply lines. But China remained unchallenged master of Central Asia as far west as Ferghana, and exerted influence in the Pamirs. In the east Gaozong's troops finally conquered Korea. But it proved impossible to hold the conquered territory, and as the Chinese withdrew Korea was for the first time unified by the state of Silla, which remained totally independent of the Tang, although deeply influenced by Chinese culture.

These constant wars of expansion came to an end in the 670s, and China was forced on the defensive, first by threats from Tibet, and second by the resurgence of Turkish power to the north, where a tribal confederation controlled the steppe from Manchuria to Lake Balkhash. The Tang were forced to set up an ever larger and ever more costly defence system of permanent armies which by the early 8th century comprised over half a million troops.

Gaozong's reign ended in a crisis. The huge financial burden of distant conquests and the new defence establishment, a growing bureaucracy, and the failure of the state to keep up with changes in the population and land-holding, and consequent shortage of revenues combined with repeated years of natural disasters to restrict tightly the state's activities.

The Empress Wu (Wu Zhao)

Empress Wu (627?–705) is said to have been in the harem of Taizong, later becoming a nun and then a secondary consort of Gaozong, about 652. After vicious palace intrigues involving rival court factions, she ousted the legitimate Empress Wang in late 655 and had her brutally done to death, and then achieved total dominance over the emperor, consolidating her power during periods when he was too ill to rule. From 660 onwards she exerted increasing influence at court, and proved a most adept political manipulator, handling court factions with consummate skill.

When Gaozong died he was succeeded by Zhongzong, but when he showed signs of an independent spirit Empress Wu deposed him, and installed his brother, Ruizong, as nominal emperor, with all power concentrated in her own hands. In 688 her ever growing pretensions caused some princes of the Tang royal family to rebel. Their rising was easily crushed, and was followed by a series of bloody purges, in which very many of the royal family and of the officials were killed. A reign of terror lasted for several years, the Empress's secret agents being given a free hand to root out all opposition.

In 690 the Empress, having prepared the way with a series of ceremonial and ritual acts, usurped the throne herself, and thus became monarch of a new dynasty, the Zhou, and the only female ruler in Chinese history.

Her rise to supreme power took place during a period when women played an important role in public life, a feature rooted perhaps in the semi-alien origins of many of the great clans which dominated Tang court life. But Tang women in general enjoyed far greater personal freedom, and far more influence over events than would be the case in any later period. The Empress Wu's reign was followed by the two short reigns of the restored emperors Zhongzong and Ruizong, both of whom were overshadowed by their womenfolk.

Although Empress Wu came from an aristocratic family, it was not one of the dominant northwestern elite. She tried to break their political dominance by recruiting, through the state examinations system, an elite group of court officials, selected purely on the grounds of ability. First established under the Sui, the examinations only very slowly replaced hereditary privilege and personal recommendation as means of entry into official life. In the late 7th century, more and more high officials began their careers by taking the annual examinations which tested both their knowledge of the conventional curriculum of classical texts and their grasp of public affairs. Even though examination candidates never accounted for more than about 10 per cent of Tang officials, the system did produce an intellectual elite within the bureaucracy, filling many of the key posts at court. The Empress selected many fine officials who set the tone of political life during the first quarter of the 8th century.

However, her arbitrary methods of government finally destroyed the close relation between ministers and the throne that had existed in Taizong's time. Her ministers' tenure of office was insecure, and their influence rivalled by a succession of worthless favourites, while court affairs were subject to the unpredictable whims of the Empress.

A major crisis was caused by the invasion of Hebei by the Khitan tribes, and by renewed warfare with the Turks, who were bought off by the marriage of one of the Empress's nephews to the Turkish Qaghan's daughter. The Empress now decided that after her death the succession should revert to the Tang royal house, not to her own family, and the deposed Zhongzong was made heir apparent.

After about 700 the Empress, now very aged, gave more and more power to her latest favourites, whose frivolous excesses finally provoked her ministers first to impeach them, and when that failed, to organize a coup which deposed the Empress and restored Zhongzong to the throne.

Zhongzong and Ruizong

Zhongzong's short reign was dominated by his Empress Wei, and by ministers who had served Empress Wu. It was a period of severe natural disasters and economic strain. The Empress and her entourage unleashed a regime of unprecedented corruption, with offices blatantly sold and public business neglected. In 710 the Empress Wei, fearing the loss of her power, poisoned Zhongzong and set a young prince on the throne with herself as regent. A counter coup was organized by the future Xuanzong, which placed the former Ruizong on the throne. His brief reign was dominated by a struggle for power between his third son, the future Xuanzong, and the formidable Taiping, daughter of the Empress Wu. In 713 Xuanzong led another coup that eliminated the princess and her faction, and established himself firmly on the throne.

Xuanzong

Commonly known by his title Minghuang, 'the Brilliant Emperor', Xuanzong's (685–761) reign (712–56) was a high point of Tang power, and one of the most splendid epochs of Chinese culture. Himself a great patron of the arts, poetry, music and the dance, a profound scholar of Daoism and Esoteric Buddhism, his capital was alive with cultural activity and his court included many great scholars and writers of distinction. His reign began with a period of reform. The corruption of the preceding decade was ended. Steps were taken to reform the administration and restore the morale of its officials, to bolster the state's finances and strengthen the border defences. These reforms left the chief ministers far more powerful than they had been before, and posed the threat that a powerful chief minister could become virtual dictator.

The defence measures were successful. The Turks were defeated and weakened by internal strife, the Tibetans defeated. The huge permanent armies along the frontier were given a new and more effective command structure. The governors of these frontier command zones controlled armies far exceeding in size and efficiency the troops under the direct control of the central government.

To pay for these armies Xuanzong employed a succession of financial experts to restore the state revenues. The registration of population was gradually restored to a new degree of efficiency, producing great numbers of new taxpayers. The canal and grain transport system, neglected during the 20 years when Empress Wu had transferred her capital to Luoyang, was reorganized to provide adequate grain supplies in Chang'an, thus obviating the need to move the seat of government periodically, as had been the case

since the seventh century. The coinage was supplemented, and new taxes introduced to levy revenue from the prosperous urban population as well as the peasants.

These reforms were largely the work of members of the old aristocratic families, who again began to rival the men chosen by examination during Empress Wu's time. From 720 onwards there was constant tension between the two groups, which finally ended in 737 with the total victory of the aristocrats and the rise to supreme power of Li Linfu (?–752). An extremely able administrator, Li Linfu's dictatorial authority was based on the powers granted to chief ministers early in Xuanzong's reign, and aided by the emperor's gradual withdrawal from active participation in government as he became ever more engrossed in his studies of Daoism and Tantric Buddhism.

Li Linfu held on to his power until his death in 752, the later years being marred by repeated purges of factional rivals. In the mid-740s the emperor became infatuated with one of his minor consorts, the gifted Yang Guifei, and gave high office to some of her relatives, notably to her cousin Yang Guozhong, who began to rival Li Linfu in court intrigue, and who succeeded him as chief minister. Meanwhile the power of the border governors, who had won remarkable victories in foreign campaigns, continued to grow. Since some generals had become involved in intrigue at court, it was decided to place these extremely powerful and sensitive commands under foreign generals rather than Chinese civil officials who might have political ambitions.

An Lushan's rebellion

By 750 one of the generals, An Lushan, half Sogdian and half Turk, had acquired control of the whole northeastern frontier.

An Lushan was both loyal to Xuanzong and in awe of the administrator Li Linfu. When the latter died, and was replaced by Yang Guozhong who strove to build up a rival military power base in the northwest and Sichuan, conflict between An Lushan and the court was only a matter of time. In 755 he invaded Hebei. His seasoned troops quickly drove south and took Luoyang where he enthroned himself emperor of a new Xia dynasty. The court reacted very slowly, but eventually halted An Lushan's armies at Tong Pass, and slowly regained the initiative in Hebei. In mid-756, however, Yang Guozhong persuaded the emperor to make a frontal attack on the rebels, using the armies withdrawn from the northwest frontier. They were routed and the rebels took Chang'an. Xuanzong fled to Sichuan. On the way, at Mawei, his troops mutinied and forced him to have his beloved Yang Guifei executed along with Yang Guozhong—an incident that became a well-known theme in literature and drama. Meanwhile the heir apparent had gone to Lingwu in the west, where he usurped the throne, being known by his posthumous title Suzong.

The rebellion dragged on, under a succession of leaders until 763. Although fighting was spasmodic, much of the richest region of China in Henan and Hebei was repeatedly ravaged and the canal system was disrupted. Probably millions died, and millions more fled to the comparative safety and prosperity of the south.

Provincial autonomy

One of the ways in which the central government managed to retain control during the rebellion was by extending the system of provincial government used on the northern frontier to the whole country. In Hebei, as the rebel generals surrendered many were confirmed in command of their territory as Tang military governors. Some of these governors in Hebei and Henan became virtually independent of central control, even claiming the right of hereditary succession to their posts. Provincial autonomy was not confined to Hebei. The military governors throughout northern China enjoyed great freedom, and the army played a major role in their administrations. Even in southern China, where provincial governors were mostly civil officials, the provinces enjoyed a new degree of autonomy.

The central government found itself denied any tax revenues from most of the northern provinces, and came to depend heavily on taxes from the south. It also sought to levy revenues indirectly from areas not under close control by collecting a monopoly tax on salt. In 780 the newly enthroned Emperor Dezong (reigned 780–805) determined to wrest power back from the provinces. As a first step, he enacted a tax reform, known as the two tax system (*liangshuifa*). This rationalized the complex taxes and surcharges that had evolved since 755 into two levies made in summer and autumn, after the wheat and rice harvests. Based on an assessment of cultivated acreage and household wealth, part of the tax was also taxed in money. The system remained in force until the 16th century. The rates were not universal, as had formerly been the case. Each province was assessed a tax quota, and was allowed to raise this as they wished.

The provincial governors in Hebei saw this reform as a threat, and when it was followed by attempts to curtail their right to hereditary succession and to cut down their armies, they rebelled. A series of risings lasted until 785, and again came near to destroying Tang power. The end was a compromise, which left Hebei semi-independent. Further attempts at military conquest in the early 9th century also failed. But elsewhere the authority of the provinces was by degrees whittled away, and central power gradually restored.

Eunuch power

Under Dezong and Xianzong (reigned 805–20) various rebellious provinces were conquered and their territories brought under central control or divided up, until only the hard core of Hebei Province remained. The key to government success was the building up of very powerful palace armies under their own control. In an effort to ensure that these armies were free of involvement in court politics, their command was given to eunuch generals. Until the An Lushan Rebellion eunuchs had played only a minor role; from the 780s, largely because of their commands of the empire's best troops, they gradually infiltrated every level of central government. In the 9th century they formed a eunuch council of imperial advisers, controlled the emperor's access to information, became involved in court factions, and frequently interfered in the succession to the throne. In 835 the civil officials, abetted by Emperor Wenzong, attempted to purge them, in the so-called Sweet Dew Incident. But their coup miscarried, and the eunuchs carried out a massive purge of the bureaucracy. Thereafter eunuchs were ensured a permanent place in the conduct of the government

Economic and social changes

The late 8th and 9th centuries were the beginning of a long period of sweeping changes in China's economy. The movement of population to the south meant that the Yangtze valley rapidly began to replace the great plain of Hebei-Henan as China's most populated and richest region. The agriculture of the south was more productive than the north, and the economy produced larger surpluses leading to greatly increased trade, circulation of goods, new industries, more market towns and a more powerful class of merchants. The regime in Chang'an became entirely dependent on the Yangtze and Huai valleys for grain supplies, and also for revenues.

Society too changed. The old aristocratic clans had long since become a metropolitan elite, their fortunes inextricably tied to those of the dynasty. They were replaced in provincial society by a broader based educated elite, with access to office through the examinations. The provincial governments brought office and wealth to many men of lowly origins who served in their armies. The old strict bar on men of merchant background gaining office began to be relaxed. Such people could more easily acquire status as rural landowners since the *juntian* land allocation was abandoned and a free land market developed. Many of the displaced persons uprooted in the rebellions of the 8th century became tenant farmers on their estates.

Until this time the south had generally been peaceful and prosperous. In the 830s the Yangtze valley began to suffer a long series of natural disasters, including floods, droughts and a great pestilence. The heavy tax burden in the region also engendered discontent.

Foreign affairs

The An Lushan Rebellion had forced the Tang to withdraw their garrisons from the northwest. In 763 the Tibetans overran the weakened border defences and seized the modern province of Gansu. The Tang outposts in the Tarim were cut off and one by one fell either to the Tibetans or to the Uighurs, who had replaced the Turks as the main power in the steppes. The Uighurs remained generally on good terms with the Tang, being mainly interested in the trade in horses which they conducted on their own exorbitant terms. The main preoccupation remained the Tibetans, until their kingdom suddenly collapsed around 840. Another powerful new enemy was Nanzhao, the kingdom in Yunnan which in the early 9th century expanded into upper Burma, and repeatedly invaded Sichuan and the Chinese province of Annam (Tonking). In the 850s and 860s there was constant warfare in the far south, which put great strain on the Chinese military machine, organized to defend the northern frontiers.

Huang Zhao's rebellion

The 860s and 870s saw a number of minor rebellions in the Yangtze region and Zhejiang, followed by the spread of endemic banditry and social disorder, and by mutinies in the provincial armies. In the late 870s this came to a climax with the activities of Huang Zhao, the leader of a confederation of bandit gangs which roamed over south China in 878–9 and then marched north, taking Chang'an in 880, and driving the emperor into exile in Sichuan. He was so tyrannical, however, that he rapidly lost all support, and in 883 he was dislodged from the capital and fled to the east, where he was killed in 884.

The emperor returned to the devastated capital, but the rebellion had caused such havoc that the Tang regime could not be effectively restored. The dynasty dragged on until 907, but for the last 20 years China was gradually divided up among regional regimes, and the dynastic government was the pawn of generals.

D.C.T.

FIVE DYNASTIES AND TEN KINGDOMS (AD 907–59)

Background

The period officially begins in 907 and ends in 959. But it would be better understood if it is seen as one that began with the fall of the Tang capital Chang'an to Huang Chao's rebel forces in 880 and which did not really come to an end until the submission of the kingdom of Southern Tang to the Song empire in 975. The 95 years would then be recognized as a period during which a great empire collapsed and several rival groups attempted to unify China before the Song founder Zhao Kuangyin finally succeeded. During this time great social changes occurred. The aristocratic families of north China were largely destroyed. New clans with military and merchant backgrounds emerged with political power and acquired enough learning to become part of the literati-gentry groups that came to dominate the Chinese state for the next 10 centuries. The fragmentation of the area of the former Tang empire encouraged the rapid economic development of south and central China, but the northern defences were permanently weakened and this enfeebled the Song that followed after 960.

The Five Dynasties were all in north China and their power base was Henan Province. All but one of the Ten Kingdoms were in central and south China. The exception was Northern Han (951–79), which considered itself a successor of the fourth dynasty, the Han (947–50), but really owed its survival to military aid from the Khitan empire.

W.G.

Five Dynasties (north China)

The Five Dynasties in chronological order are Liang (907–23), Tang (923–36), Jin (936–46), Han (947–50) and Zhou (951–9).

Liang

There were three emperors: Taizu (907–12), usurper Zhu Yougui (912–13) and Modi (913–23).

The founder, Zhu Wen, was one of Huang Chao's rebel officers, who betrayed his leader and became the military governor of a key province on the Grand Canal. He retained his plebeian dislike for an aristocratic government dominated by eunuch courtiers, and his dynasty initiated a new-style government employing the secretaries and officers of his provincial *yamen*. His ambition to be the emperor of all China, however, overtaxed the dynasty's resources and most of his reforms came to nothing.

Tang

There were four emperors: Zhuangzong (923–6), usurper Mingzong (926–33), Mindi (933–4) and usurper Feidi (934–6).

Son of the Shatuo Turk mercenary, Li Keyong, who was Zhu Wen's great rival from the 880s, Li (originally Zhuxie) Cunxu tried to restore the Tang structure of government but failed. His successor, one of his father's retainers, was more practical and adopted a provincial structure more like that of the Liang. But he was too old to establish a strong dynasty.

Jin

There were two emperors: Gaozu (936–42), Chudi (942–6).

The accession of the founder, another Shatuo Turk officer, Shi Jing-tang marked a major turning point in the history of north China. The price he paid for Khitan support was to give up 16 prefectures south of the Great Wall and thus destroy the traditional defence system which had ensured the security of the Han and Tang empires. Indeed, the Khitans were so strengthened by the cession that they could have conquered north China in 946 if they had been prepared to garrison their troops there.

Han

There were two emperors: Gaozu (947–8) and Yindi (948–50).

The shortest dynasty officially recognized in Chinese history, its founder was also a Shatuo Turk officer. His brother refused to surrender when the dynasty fell and founded the Northern Han, the last of the Ten Kingdoms.

Zhou

There were three emperors: Taizu (951–4), Shizong (954–9), Gongdi (959).

The founder, Guo Wei, led a Chinese revolt against the Turkic leadership, but it was his adopted son Chai Rong who laid the foundations for the Song unification. Unfortunately, Chai Rong died when only 38 years old and it was left to one of his officers to seize the throne from Chai's baby son and finish the task. With this dynasty a modified version of the provincial structure first adopted by the Liang in 907 was used successfully to build up a strong central military government.   *W.G.*

The Ten Kingdoms

Of the Ten Kingdoms during this period, seven could be described as Yangtze states: Wu (902–37), Southern Tang (937–75), Wuyue (908–78) in the delta area (at least Wu and Southern Tang with imperial ambitions); the little states of Jingnan (913–63) and Chu (907–51) in the middle Yangtze; and Former Shu (908–25) and Later Shu (934–65) in the rich Sichuan basin of the upper Yangtze. The remaining three were the Min (909–45) at Fuzhou in Fujian; the Southern Han (907–71) in Guangdong and Guangxi, with its capital at Canton; and the Northern Han (951–79) in northern Shanxi.

The middle Yangtze states had no pretensions to be anything but superior military provinces. The Gao and Ma families who ruled Jingnan and Chu as long as they did are the best reminders there are of the extent of the fragmentation of the Tang empire and of the fundamental weakness of all aspirants to inherit the Tang mandate of Heaven.

FIVE DYNASTIES AND TEN KINGDOMS

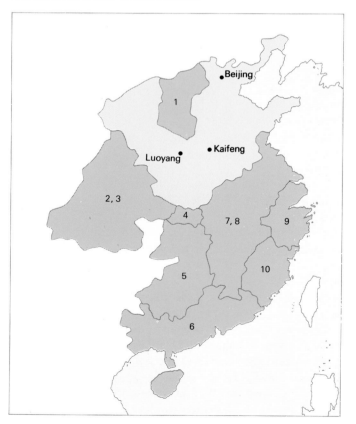

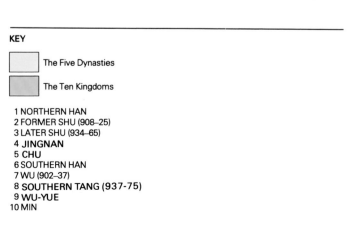

KEY

☐ The Five Dynasties

▨ The Ten Kingdoms

1 NORTHERN HAN
2 FORMER SHU (908–25)
3 LATER SHU (934–65)
4 JINGNAN
5 CHU
6 SOUTHERN HAN
7 WU (902–37)
8 SOUTHERN TANG (937–75)
9 WU-YUE
10 MIN

Two general points need to be stressed. First, while north China was culturally impoverished during this period, the Yangtze states were the main repositories of what remained of the flower of Tang civilization. In particular, Southern Tang, Wuyue and the two Shu kingdoms had just enough wealth and stability to keep some cultural and intellectual activities flourishing. Second, during this long period of division, there had revived some of the practices and forms of inter-state relations which came close to resembling aspects of modern diplomacy.

Wu and Southern Tang Kingdoms

The four rulers of Wu were Yang Xingmi (902–5) and his three sons, of whom only the third, Yang Pu (also the last ruler, 920–37), actually declared himself an emperor in 927. The state's original power base was the great Tang province of Huainan and the city of Yangchow (Yangzhou) on the Grand Canal. But with the break-up of the Tang empire, Huainan lost its key economic role for north China. It is significant that the capital was moved to Jinling (modern Nanjing) just before Yang Pu became emperor. For most of Wu's 35 years of existence, the Yangtze delta area was in turmoil and real power was in any case in the hands of Xu Wen and his family. It was Xu Wen rather than the Wu rulers who had ambitions to succeed the Tang. It was, therefore, not surprising that when Xu Wen's adopted son, Xu Zhigao (real name Li Sheng) usurped the Wu throne, he called his dynasty Tang.

The three rulers of Southern Tang were remarkably learned and cultured for their times. The founder reverted to the Tang imperial surname of Li to give him a dubious claim to the Tang heritage. But his experience in government gave the dynasty the peace and prosperity to make a good start. Under his son, Li Jing (943–60), Southern Tang expanded south to take the Min Kingdom and west to absorb the Chu state. These successes in the south and west did not help it in the north when the Zhou emperor Chai Rong marched south to take all of its lands north of the Yangtze. After that, Southern Tang totally lost its capacity to assert its imperial claims. The third ruler Li Yu (961–75), a very fine poet famous for his tragic verses, could do little except wait for the new Song empire to falter. When Song did not, but grew from strength to strength, the end of Southern Tang was merely a matter of time.

The Shu Kingdoms

Former Shu and Later Shu were not successor states. The former had been founded by the late Tang guards officer, Wang Jian (908–18), who, despite his plebeian origins, built his empire on the model of the Tang. But it was no match for the troops of the Shatuo Turk claimant who won power in north China in 923 and

'restored' the Tang. Shu was taken and formed part of the Tang empire for nine years until the military governor, Meng Zhixiang (934), declared his independence. His son, Meng Chang (934–65), ruled for 31 years and was the only other ruler. Although Later Shu had all the trappings of the Tang, it was secure in the wealth and strategic position of the Sichuan basin and does not seem to have had ambitions to unify China and claim the Tang mandate. But its prosperity and rich cultural life could not save it when the Song armies arrived in 965.

Wuyue Kingdom

Qian Liu (902–31), his son and three grandsons ruled the kingdom for over 70 years, the longest surviving of all the states of the whole Five Dynasties and Ten Kingdoms period. Qian Liu started as a common soldier but rose to become an able and shrewd Tang military governor. He was territorially ambitious for his kingdom and adopted the trappings of empire for some 20 years. He died when he was 80, the most long-lived ruler of the period, and one of the very few Chinese rulers to have attained such a ripe old age. Meanwhile, he laid firm foundations for a stable and prosperous kingdom and a cultivated dynastic house. His successors wisely gave up his empire building plans and concentrated instead on developing a network of commercial, diplomatic and cultural relations which enriched the kingdom and ensured its survival despite its small size and relatively limited natural resources.

Min Kingdom

This was a southern kingdom (modern Fujian) founded by a rebel army from Henan in north China. After the death of its leader in 897, his brother, Wang Shenzhi, took over as a Tang military governor, and in 909 he became King of Min and ruled for 17 years. These were Min's only stable years. The next four rulers, two sons, a grandson and then another son of Wang Shenzhi, were all assassinated after brief periods on the throne. The last ruler, yet another son, defied his brother and established an even smaller Kingdom of Yin in 943. Within three years the continuous disorder in the kingdom attracted the attention of Southern Tang and the subsequent invasion led to the fall of Min in 945. Thus, although prosperous because of the development of sea-going trade (including trade with north China, Korea, the southern coasts of China and Southeast Asia), Min was one of the most unstable kingdoms in a troubled period.

Southern Han Kingdom

The area covering most of modern Guangdong and Guangxi Provinces remained under direct imperial administration longer than any other part of Tang China and it was not until 905 that a local commander seized power as military governor. This was Liu Yin

(905–11), who was soon followed by his half-brother Liu Yan (911–41). By 917 Liu Yan had proclaimed the empire of Da Yue and then renamed it Southern Han. As the area had remained loyal to Tang, it had attracted a large number of senior Tang officials and their families and they had provided the Southern Han court with impressive talents and genuine Tang imperial institutions. The spirit of the Tang, however, was soon lost as the kingdom developed its commercial potential, especially as a port for the Southeast Asian trade. Being furthest from north China, it was relatively secure from the imperial designs of the northern dynasties. At the same time, it did try to expand its territory northwards into Hunan and Jiangxi and southwards into Annam (northern Vietnam). Of special interest was the opportunity in the 930s for Southern Han to incorporate Annam into its empire. Failing to take it marked a historic delimitation of the boundaries of southernmost China. *W.G.*

Tangut empire

The Tanguts (Dangxiang) were Tibetan tribes whose service to the last Tang emperors earned them the imperial surname Li, and official control of the lands between the Helan mountains and the Ordos in modern Ningxia. They kept that control through the Five Dynasties, while their leaders accepted appointments as hereditary military governors as well as other high court titles. They continued to acknowledge the sovereignty of the first two Song emperors and adopted the imperial Zhao surname but some of the more independent tribal leaders under Li Jiqian (963–1004) refused to submit and sought the support of the Khitans. From 986 onwards the group that paid tribute to the Khitans (Li Jiqian married a Khitan princess and was recognized as the King of Xia) became stronger and, with diplomatic skill and Khitan military aid, laid the foundations of a large empire, the third power in 11th century China. The Xixia empire came into being in 1038 with Li Yuanhao (1003–48), declaring his independence and proclaiming himself emperor of Da Xia.

From 1038 until its destruction by the Mongols in 1227, the Tangut empire had 10 emperors: Jingzong (1032–48), Yizong (1048–67), Huizong (1067–86), Chongzong (1086–1139), Renzong (1139–93), Huanzong (1193–1206), Xiangzong (1206–11), Shenzong (1211–22), Xianzong (1223–6) and Li Xian (1226–7).

Apart from Jingzong or Li Yuanhao, the most notable reigns were the two that spanned 107 years, those of Chongzong and Renzong. During their reigns the empire became a considerable cultural centre. The Xixia script was used not only to translate the Confucian classics and numerous Buddhist sutras but also to com-

pose original treatises on law and administration, medicine and military affairs, literature and phonetics and other subjects. Unfortunately the empire's capital was so badly destroyed by the Mongols that only a very small portion of Tangut artefacts has survived. The bulk of these artefacts is now preserved in the Soviet Union, while other fragments are also to be found in China and Japan. *W.G.*

Example of Xixia script, used during the Tangut Empire not only for Confucian classics and Buddhist sutras, but also to compose original treatises on many subjects.

Khitan empire (Liao dynasty)

The Khitans (Qidan) were a confederation of largely proto-Mongol tribes from the Inner Mongolia area and parts of the three provinces of western Manchuria. Tribes by that name had been an occasional threat to the Tang empire since the 8th century, but it was not until the rise of Yelü Abaoji in 901 that a powerful confederation emerged to carve out a large north Asian empire. In 907 the empire was formally established, and in 916 Chinese-style reign-titles began to be used. Later, after 936, the empire was chiefly known as Liao.

The Liao dynasty had nine emperors: Taizu (907–26), Taizong (926–47), Shizong (947–51), Muzong (951–69), Jingzong (969–82), Shengzong (982–1031), Xingzong (1031–55) Daozong (1055–1101) and Tianzuodi (1101–25).

The first two were clearly the most remarkable. They successfully combined the Tang system of government with tribal ways, ruling the largely Chinese population in the south through a southern court modelled on the Tang while establishing a northern court to deal with the various nomadic tribes. The key feature of the empire, however, was its efficient and original military organization which enabled it not only to subdue most of the tribes in north and central Asia and over-awe the Song Chinese, but also to conquer various Manchurian states and thereafter confine the Koreans to the peninsula.

Yelü Abaoji devised a Khitan script, taught his tribes to preserve their ways and resist being sinicized, and developed an economy that was based on Chinese agricultural skills and tribal pastoralism. Although Tang imperial conventions were freely adopted and, in particular, Tang methods and rhetoric on foreign relations were successfully applied to Chinese and non-Chinese alike, he and his successors were able to keep the Khitan way of life essentially untouched by Chinese civilization. Only in Buddhist practices and institutions did the nomads come to live more like the Chinese in their empire.

Khitan Liao's most decisive contribution to Chinese history lies in the power balance it created first between itself and the Song and then, through the help it gave the Tanguts at critical moments, between itself, the Xixia and the Song in the three-way balance that established a new basis for peace in north Asia for almost a century. Also worth noting is that when the dynasty fell in 1125 a member of the imperial house escaped west and restored a new 'Khitan' empire (better known as the Kara-Khitay) in Central Asia. This helped to confirm the use of Kitai for China in Russian and to promote the use of the somewhat exotic 'Cathay' in other languages.

W.G.

THE SONG DYNASTY (AD 960–1279)

Historical perspective

The history of the Song falls into two distinct periods, Northern Song, 960–1126, and Southern Song, 1127–1279. During the former the country was unified and ruled from the Song capital at Kaifeng. During the latter, while the Jurchen Jin dynasty ruled over the north, Song held sway only over the territory south of the Huai River, with its capital located at Hangzhou. Song history is inextricably linked with those of the alien dynasties of Liao (Khitan), Xixia (Tangut), Jin (Jurchen) and the Mongol Yuan, all of which occupied parts of former Chinese domain and the last of which conquered the whole of it. Though somewhat unjustly considered weak in the face of these powerful rivals, Song featured remarkable economic, technological, intellectual and artistic growth and is often taken as the truly formative period for the late imperial era enduring down to 1911.

C.A.P.

Taizu (Zhao Kuangyin) (928–76)

The founder of the Song, Zhao Kuangyin (reigned 960–76), claims a special page in history not only because he achieved virtual reunification of the country following the division of the Five Dynasties, but also because he brought to an end the militarism which characterized China during that period. Zhao himself issued from a northeastern Chinese military family, of the sort that had dominated politics since the late ninth century. Large of stature and an able warrior, he rose to become commander of the Palace Corps in 959 under the energetic Emperor Shizong of the Later Zhou dynasty, whose death the following year left a seven-year-old child on the throne. In an episode provoked by invasion from the north and reminiscent of the Roman Praetorian Guard, the Corps mutinied and placed their 32-year-old commander on the throne. There is no evidence to confirm suspicions of Zhao's initial complicity.

The new regime which Zhao Kuangyin, or Taizu, now attempted to consolidate was faced by three major problems. First the empire was divided into a dozen small, competing kingdoms, none wholly secure from the other. Second, power in these individual states, especially in north China, lay largely in the hands of the military, firmly entrenched territorially and a standing challenge to central authority. Third, the Khitan state of Liao based in Manchuria but already in possession of northern Hebei, stood poised to exploit any weakness shown by its neighbours to the south. Fortunately for Song, a passive monarch occupied the Liao throne during these years, undertaking no new initiatives in north China, while Taizu, for his part, wisely avoided any confrontation until he had eliminated his rivals in China. It is indeed in successfully tackling the first two of these problems that Taizu's achievement as a monarch lay. Through war and diplomacy he had brought all but two of the regional kingdoms under his sway by the time of his death in 976. Equally striking was his success in defusing the power of the provincial military, which he accomplished by adroit manipulation of commanders and troops and persistent application of centralizing measures.

Taizu was subsequently given a strong Confucian image by Chinese historians who applauded his harnessing of the military and restoration of the civil service examination system. Yet, he was essentially a military man with a shrewd, practical grasp of power and politics whose policies were not only brought to fruition but were also given a new, civilian direction by his brother and successor, Taizong.

C.A.P.

Taizong (Zhao Kuangyi) (939–97)

The younger brother and successor to Taizu was the real consolidator of the Song empire. Zhao Kuangyi (reigned 976–97), despite early literary predilections, followed a military career like his father and brother before him. Holding several sensitive positions including Commander of the Palace Corps during Taizu's reign, he was well placed to seize the succession in 976. Taizong first addressed himself to the task of completing reunification. The state of Wuyue fell without a struggle in 978, as did the state of Northern Han in 979. Of traditionally Chinese lands only those occupied by the Khitan remained outside the empire. Taizong's vigorous but costly military efforts at recovery were repeatedly frustrated by the Khitan. This territory never in fact came under Song control.

Taizong's greatness as a monarch lay in his consolidation of Song central authority and his establishment of civilian primacy at all levels of government. These results were achieved through the implementation of several key policies. Expanding Taizu's efforts, he dismantled the structure of large provincial administrative and military units which had been the foundation of the militarists' power. Administrative posts were progressively filled by civil officials, many of whom qualified for office through the civil service examinations, used on a large scale for the first time in this reign. Measures achieving greater centralized control over fiscal management and the armed forces were also adopted. As a result, the Song state under Taizong became more centralized and had a more effective institutional structure. Taizong himself was a prolific writer, a good calligrapher and a sponsor of scholarship.

C.A.P.

SONG DYNASTY CHINA

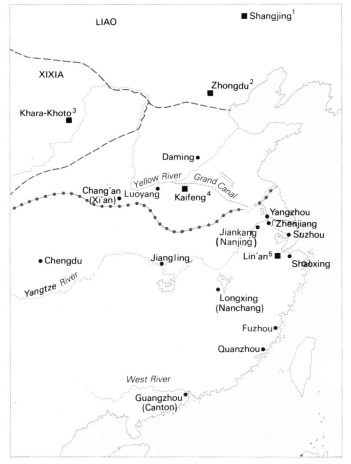

KEY

■	Capitals	
●	Major cities	
---	Boundaries between Northern Song, Liao and Xixia	
-●-●-	Southern Song boundary with Jin and, after 1234, with Yuan (Mongols)	

[1] Liao capital

[2] Jin capital (Peking)

[3] Xixia capital

[4] Northern Song capital

[5] Southern Song capital (Hangzhou)

Huizong (Zhao Ji) (1082–1135) and the fall of Northern Song

As the last emperor of Northern Song, Huizong (reigned 1101–25) has been held mainly to blame for the collapse of the dynasty. Indeed, evidence of misrule and mistaken policies is not hard to find. Coming down heavily on the side of the reformers (heirs of Wang Anshi), he further polarized Song politics by proscribing 120 of the most prominent conservatives. Not a good judge of men, he put his trust wholly in the opportunist Cai Jing (1047–1126) and in several eunuchs, the most prominent of whom was Tong Guan (d. 1126), who provided him with unreliable intelligence as well as poor counsel. Mounting financial problems were exacerbated by Huizong's taste for luxury and led to special levies which fell heavily on certain sectors of the population. A revised land tax

The refinement and grace of Emperor Huizong's art are evident in his *White goose and red polygonum.*

system was especially onerous for the people of north China. The outbreak of rebellions in Zhejiang in 1120 and in Shandong in 1121 indicated that popular support for the regime was waning.

Having concluded an offensive alliance with Song against the common enemy Liao in 1120, the Jurchen Jin dynasty crushed the latter in 1123, without significant Song aid. For its part, seeking to exploit the alliance to recover Liao-occupied northern Hebei, Song provoked a conflict with the Jurchen and at the same time exposed its own military weakness. An initial attack on and blockade of Kaifeng by the Jurchen in 1126 resulted in Huizong's abdication in favour of Qinzong (1100–61) and a humiliating treaty for Song. Further friction over the implementation of treaty terms led to renewed hostilities and the Jurchen conquest of north China, including Kaifeng, the following year. Taken captive with Qinzong and the entire court, Huizong spent the rest of his life in captivity, dying in 1135.

Yet, although he failed against the Jurchen, Huizong has to his credit some enlightened policies. He promoted the expansion of educational facilities, the establishing of hospitals and relief homes for the needy, land reclamation and flood control measures. He was also one of China's most famous patrons of art. An accomplished painter, calligrapher and poet, he raised the status of painting, founded an academy at court, and attempted to bring together and catalogue all the great paintings then known (many of which, alas, perished in the ensuing disaster).   *C.A.P.*

Gaozong (1107–87) and the establishment of Southern Song

A curiously underrated monarch, Gaozong (reigned 1127–62), played the central role in preserving the dynasty and establishing a new power base in the south. The ninth son of Huizong, the then Prince of Kang was absent on a mission from the capital when it fell to the Jurchen Jin dynasty in the winter of 1126–7 and soon fled south to restore the dynasty. Jurchen pressure, forcing him to abandon his initial headquarters at Zhenjiang and temporarily even his second one, and subsequent capital, at Hangzhou, in combination with a general breakdown of law and order culminated in 1129 in a military *putsch* that forced him to abdicate for a few weeks.

In face of those adversities Gaozong sought to re-establish the foundations of imperial rule. His government gradually erected an integrated set of controls in the lower Yangtze region and extended them into Sichuan and other regions. This brought a steady increase in revenue, although the high tax rates stimulated some bitter resistance.

The war between the Jurchen Jin and Song, punctuated by some bitter campaigns, persisted for more than a dozen years, until it became clear that neither side could break the stalemate. Judging by his diplomatic initiatives, Gaozong was among the first to realize this, relatively early on abandoning any hopes of recovering the north in his lifetime. His architect of peace was Chief Councillor Qin Gui (1090–1155), who in 1141 negotiated a peace treaty with the Jurchen Jin. The agreement brought peace but at a heavy cost in reparations, in an annual subsidy, and in Song pride. Moreover, either as a condition for negotiations or out of mistrust of its own army, the Song court ordered a withdrawal and stripped the powerful commanders of their authority. The most popular general and leader of the revanchist groups, Yue Fei (1103–41), was falsely accused of treason, imprisoned and then executed. These events began the process of turning Yue Fei into a national hero, Qin Gui into an arch villain and Southern Song politics into a lasting state of polarization between the pragmatists, who accepted coexistence with Jin, and the revanchists, who found it intolerable. But, however controversial, Gaozong's policies brought a peace that, apart from a brief interruption by an unsuccessful Jin attempt at conquest of the south in 1161, proved fairly stable.

Having seen many of his policies succeed but weary of facing the demands of rule, Gaozong abdicated in favour of a nephew in 1162 and spent the next quarter of a century in happy and cultivated retirement. *C.A.P.*

Government

Like all Chinese imperial regimes, Song government was absolutist in principle, hierarchical in organization and, relative to the size of the country, thin in its governing apparatus. It differed from its predecessors in achieving a new degree of centralization and of civilian control over the military. And in comparison with both earlier and later governments it provided an open forum for discussion and criticism; it was least threatened by internal rebellions; and it was most moved by the spirit of Confucianism. Its sins were weakness in external defence—although no other Chinese government ever faced such powerful enemies for so long—and underadministration in the face of growing social problems.

Though at the pinnacle of power, Song emperors after Taizu and Taizong were not strong, dominating personalities. Some like Shenzong and Huizong in Northern Song or Gaozong and Lizong in Southern Song were intelligent and for the most part committed rulers. But the characteristic posture of the Song monarch was perhaps analogous to the chairman of a board, accepting and approving the board's (his ministers') recommendations. This

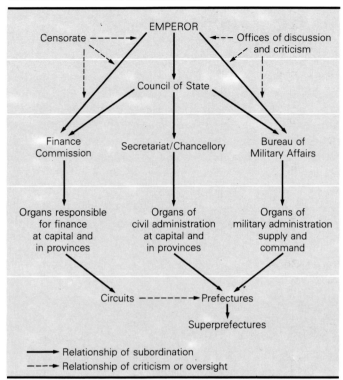

STRUCTURE OF SONG GOVERNMENT

opened the way for dominance by individual ministers such as Wang Anshi and Cai Jing in Northern Song and Qin Gui (1090–1155) and Shi Miyuan (d. 1233) in Southern Song who enjoyed virtually dictatorial powers.

Song central government, which evolved directly out of preceding Five Dynasties regimes, featured at the highest level a tripartite division of authority between general administration, finance and military affairs. The responsible organs were the Secretariat-Chancellery, the Finance Commission and the Bureau of Military Affairs. They were both policy-making and executive in function. Senior officials of the first and third qualified as members of a Council of State consulting directly with the emperor. The Secretariat-Chancellery was responsible for the widest range of administrative units and activities, most importantly those concerned with personnel and justice. The Bureau of Military Affairs was wholly civilian in composition and assured civil dominance over the military at all levels above the tactical. The highest degree of specialization existed in the Finance Commission, which usually was staffed by financial experts. A feature of the Song system was the provision of channels through which criticisms, complaints and proposals could be made. These began with the Censorate and Bureau of Policy Criticism but included several other organs as well. Bureaucratic wrongdoing was the most frequent target, but Song records burgeon too with protests against imperial decisions.

The basic unit of administration in the provinces was the subprefecture (or county), which numbered something over 1200 under Northern Song. Its staff included regular officials, but its work depended on services exacted from headmen and other local personnel who were recruited to deal with taxes, police activities, public works, etc. Above the subprefecture was the prefecture. These numbered about 315 and were directly subordinate to the central government. Awareness of the late Tang-Five Dynasties experience with strong provincial forces was the reason for not establishing high-level offices with comprehensive powers for the provinces. As some higher authorities were needed for supervision, the Song solution was to appoint intendants, responsible for so-called circuits several prefectures in size but to limit their authority to one sphere of activity, such as fiscal, judicial, transport and monopolies, or military. Eventually the number of such circuits reached 26. All officials in the provincial administration were centrally appointed. *C.A.P.*

The civil service and its recruitment

The Song civil service consisted, depending on the period, of 10 000–18 000 formally qualified officials who provided a personnel pool from which some 10 000 established government positions were filled. It excluded the vast majority of people actually working for the government–military officers, a huge clerical sub-bureaucracy, and local servicemen of various sorts. All officials were ranked initially by a system of titular offices, established by strict protocol, and after 1080 by a system of classification titles numbered from 1 to 40. In general, appointments were made to posts commensurate in importance and responsibility with the rank of the official. Promotion hinged on a variety of factors: method of entry into the service; seniority and experience; merit ratings; and success at special examinations. An additional factor was recommendation by a superior, which in this dynasty became highly institutionalized as a system of sponsorship. Remuneration took the form of a salary, regular grants of cloth and grain, a pension on retirement and, for some officials, the possibility of obtaining admission into the civil service for a family member, a practice known as 'protection'. As in other dynasties, the official occupied a privileged position before the law, the penalties for virtually all offences being reduced at least one degree. A particularly severe punishment, inflicted, for example, for extreme venality or flagrant maladministration, was loss of official status.

Because membership in the civil service conferred the highest status society had to offer, entrance to it was obviously a crucial matter. There were three modes of entry: examination, protection and transfer from military and clerical services. The last of these was the least significant numerically. Protection, the only practice in Song government other than the imperial succession which rested on the hereditary principle, permitted officials of high rank or those specially designated for this privilege to nominate a son for civil service status. Very widely used, this mode of entry rivalled and in most periods exceeded the examination system in producing officials. Yet the latter had greater impact because high office was largely dominated by officials with degrees and because this was the device which introduced new blood into the government and elite ranks.

The examinations were held at three levels—success at the lower being a qualification for the next—the prefectural, the departmental (held at the capital) and the palace. While a variety of fields of study leading to different degrees was available in the examinations, the literary examination which conferred the *jinshi* degree (the so-called doctorate) was the most prestigious. Based on humanistic knowledge and literary skills and producing over 200 *jinshi* degrees a year once in full operation, the Song examinations were the first to be used as a major means of official recruitment. They provided perhaps 40 per cent of all officials and the majority of the higher ranking. Their impact, whether on the civil service, political life, or the social structure can hardly be exaggerated.

Unlike later dynastic systems, success in a lower examination did not qualify one for office. Moreover, sale of degrees was unknown. However, a special examination, the 'facilitated examination', gave the government considerable flexibility in enlarging or narrowing access to service. Held irregularly for those who had failed the *jinshi* a given number of times, this examination was used frequently in Southern Song to recruit personnel for the lower bureaucratic ranks. *C.A.P.*

New elites

The turbulent conditions of the 10th century, increased access to the civil service, expanded educational opportunities, rapid economic growth and the Jurchen conquest of north China in 1127 all combined to shape new elites under the Song. A political elite, of diverse origins and consisting of barely three dozen lineages, emerged to dominate national politics throughout the 11th century. It enjoyed a strong local foundation as well, in this respect resembling a much larger group of local elites. Locally, the position of these elites rested on wealth, lineage, marriage ties, learning and frequently official status, and seems to have been even stronger under Southern than under Northern Song. No counterpart to the earlier national elite appears in the later period, however.

Entry into the civil service, especially by examination, unquestionably opened up elite ranks to new social elements throughout the dynasty. However, current opinion holds that it more commonly simply increased mobility *within* those elite ranks. The most significant 'motor' of social change, therefore, was probably the rapid economic development of the period. At a time when government service had always conferred special prestige in China, the disappearance of groups of ascribed status, such as the early Tang aristocracy, opened the way for wealth to play a new role. Moreover, at a time when agriculture was providing greater profits than ever before (because of its partial commercialization combined with an expanding market, because of its greater productivity and because of freer labour conditions), the government's *laissez-faire* land policy permitted significant land accumulation and fostered the emergence of a new landlord class. The expansion of commerce and of urban centres encouraged the investment of land profits in these sectors, while, vice versa, entrepreneurial profits

were often used to acquire the much coveted land. Despite the prejudice against merchants, the rich social documentation of the time suggests that many lived very well indeed and enjoyed *de facto* status as members of the elite.

In contrast to earlier times, military service provided only a very limited avenue of upward mobility, anti-military attitudes first hardening in this period.

C.A.P.

The commercial revolution

The 'commercial revolution' had its origins in late Tang times and ran its course until the Mongol conquest of the 13th century. It was an outcome of the fundamental change in the human geography and demography of China which saw the first intensive development of the Yangtze River valley and of the southeastern littoral and the first economic integration of the country (excluding only the far southwest). Specifically, it was the product of a dramatic increase in agricultural production, a steadily growing market and numerous improvements in the means of exchange and distribution.

Agricultural growth resulted from an increase both in the amount of land under cultivation and in productivity. The former was achieved by expansion into new areas, including widespread land reclamation, the latter by a variety of means—the adoption of rice strains with higher yields, more effective treatment of the soil, improved farming implements, the spread of double-cropping, specialization of production and the systematic diffusion of up-to-date agricultural information. An increase in the population, which grew to exceed 100 million under Song, was sustained by this agricultural growth, which in turn was further stimulated by the increase in demand. By Northern Song the bulk of the population lived south of the Huai River (the traditional line of division between north and south), and this southwards movement entailed growing settlement and exploitation of precisely those regions with the greatest economic potential.

Rising commercial activity was closely linked to changes in three allied sectors—transport, marketing structure and means of exchange. The existing network of roads and canals was improved and expanded. Water transport, being several times cheaper than land and enjoying almost limitless possibilities in the water-rich south, achieved a new level of importance. Under the old structure of marketing, relatively few goods moved beyond the local market town and those that did circulated in government-supervised markets in established administrative centres. From late Tang a rising volume and new patterns of trade upset this order; new marketing centres developed and existing administrative centres became hubs of commerce too. The government's efforts were mainly confined

This detail from *A Literary Gathering*, attributed to Emperor Huizong, exemplifies the cultural and social life of the learned Song elite.

to the levying of commercial taxes, both on transit and on sales (though in the case of international trade it actually undertook to dispose of the goods). The search for adequate means of exchange was long and difficult. Despite a tremendous increase in the production of the principal metal, copper, and of silver, the economy consistently out ran its money supply. But private traders and bankers, followed in time by the government, worked out a wide range of devices such as bills of exchange, promissory notes and finally paper money. Monetization of a major part of the economy occurred as a result.

As rice (above all), cloth, tea, vegetables, timber and other agricultural products and a wide variety of handicraft goods moved in volume along the trade routes, the economy and human geography of the country assumed a new shape. Along the main lines of communication and much of the littoral, an advanced sector developed, geared to trade, often specialized in production, and containing a host of urban centres. In essential ways it stood apart from those areas less accessible to such changes, where the economic pace was slower and traditional patterns dominant. *C.A.P.*

Water transport played a central role in the life of the Song capital, as demonstrated in the scroll by Zhang Zeduan, *Spring Festival on the River.*

The reforms of Wang Anshi (1021–86)

Perhaps the most famous and controversial reform attempt in Chinese history, this episode occurred in the years 1069–76. Background conditions were severe budgetary shortages facing the state, a declining tax base, the ineffectiveness of a bloated army, a malaise among officials, growing disparity between rich and poor, and the actual impoverishment of some segments of the peasantry. An activist emperor, Shenzong (1048–85), ascended the throne in 1067 and two years later summoned to court Wang Anshi, who had already established a glowing reputation as an innovating administrator. Apart from his impact on contemporary events, Wang Anshi is significant for the three following reasons: for his deep belief in institutional reform (as distinct from the Confucian emphasis on reform of the individual); for his clear recognition of the socio-economic foundations of a strong state; and for his grasp of the importance of economic growth. He was by no means original in these respects as a thinker, but no thinker ever enjoyed the power he did.

Wang's reforms fell into three broad categories, financial and economic, military and educational. Measures directly pertinent to

agriculture included a national land survey, aimed at bringing order and precision to the tax registers, and state loans to peasants at relatively low rates of interest. Government finances were given new flexibility by adoption of a system of local or regional disposal of tax goods according to market conditions. If this were in part intended to counter the monopolistic practices of the large traders, the same concern was revealed in the measure providing for direct government purchases from small traders, bypassing the intermediary of the merchant guilds, and also for state loans to small traders. An altogether new tax was created to pay for local government services, replacing the old service obligation that was both inefficient and ruinous to some households. Military measures included the creation of a militia, intended to serve both national defence and local security functions, the rather ill-advised adoption of a system of horse-breeding by peasant families (most of whom were totally inexperienced) and the establishment of a new central arsenal. His principal educational reform was a revision of the civil service examinations, giving new emphasis to analysis of political problems and to law at the expense of literary achievement and replacing former interpretations of the Classics with his own.

An evaluation of Wang's reform programme is impossible, both because of the lack of sources and because the programme was short-lived. Wang had the satisfaction of seeing an improvement in state finances, in the army and in local services. However, following Shenzong's death in 1085, the conservatives led by the great historian Sima Guang (1019–85) gained power and scrapped the reforms. When reformists regained power in 1093, conditions were much less favourable for effective action and many of the reforms themselves were perverted. The reform programme had not only antagonized the conservatives, but because of its controversial nature it did not get the support and cooperation essential for its implementation from the average careerist-minded bureaucrat.

C.A.P.

Kaifeng

The capital of Northern Song and the last imperial capital (following Chang'an and Luoyang) to be located in the Yellow River valley was Kaifeng. In Song times it was usually known either as Bianjing or Dongjing. The adoption of Kaifeng as capital, dating first from the Five Dynasties period, signifies the economic and political reorientation of the country which had been underway since mid-Tang. While Kaifeng's position on the north China plain gave it a productive hinterland on which to draw, it was equally important for any national capital to have direct links with the rapidly developing southeast. Located at the head of the Grand

Access to Kaifeng was by one of twelve gates, as shown in this detail from the celebrated scroll by Zhang Zeduan.

Canal, the principal north–south artery, Kaifeng met this need admirably. Yet events were fated to pose the question whether or not the advantages adequately compensated for the striking drawback of this location, its military indefensibility.

A product mainly of economic growth, Kaifeng lacked the symmetry and order of the great Tang capital, Chang'an. By the mid-10th century the city had so far outgrown its earlier walls as to require a new outer perimeter, this running 28km in circumference. But markets and suburban settlements soon engulfed this as well. Estimates set the population at one million or more.

Kaifeng's days of glory came to an end with the Jin conquest of 1127. No longer an imperial capital (save for a short period during the Mongol conquest) and its role as a centre of national communications eliminated, it steadily declined. It lived on in the minds of Song people to the south, for whom it remained the true capital.

C.A.P.

The Liao dynasty (904–1125)

The Khitan dynasty of Liao at the height of its power occupied Manchuria, Inner Mongolia and the northern prefectures of Hebei and Hedong in China proper. Such was the impression the Khitan made on their age that their own name was taken into Slavic and Middle Eastern tongues as the standard name for China (and into English as a secondary one—'Cathay'). Speaking an Altaic but not yet precisely identified language, this nomadic nation began its ascent to power under the chieftain Yelü Abaoji (872–926), who, in the process of unifying the Khitan and related tribes, declared himself emperor in 907. The young state developed without interference from the south because of China's divided condition in this period. On the contrary, itself interfering in Chinese affairs, it gained possession of northern Hebei in 936. Efforts at recovering this area by the Song resulted in a series of wars, which were only ended by the Treaty of Shanyuan in 1005. Giving Liao diplomatic parity with Song, the treaty also assured it an annual income of 100 000oz (2835kg) of silver and 200 000 bolts of silk—in 1042 raised to 200 000 and 300 000, respectively—in the form of a subsidy. These funds played an important part in the Khitan economy which according to region was partly agricultural and partly pastoral. However, because of growing demand for Song goods, much of the silver and silk flowed back south across the border. While a state of peaceful coexistence was maintained with Song, Liao enjoyed the status of suzerain in respect of Xixia, the Korean kingdom of Koryo, and other states.

The Khitan constituted a ruling minority of less than a million in a state estimated at five million. Their military superiority rested on their cavalry organization and tactics which in many ways anticipated those of the Mongols. Despite (or because of) strong Chinese cultural influence, the Khitan took a number of steps to preserve their native culture and separate cultural identity. This included the creation of an alphabetic and an ideographic script, which remain indecipherable and appear not to have inspired any significant body of literature. The multinational character of the Liao empire is reflected in its political system. This featured native style rule from the Supreme Capital in southern Jehol over the tribes to the north and Chinese style rule from the Southern Capital at modern Beijing over the sedentary Chinese population to the south.

In view of the strength of Liao throughout the 11th century, its rapid collapse under the attacks of its former Jurchen vassals from 1115 is surprising. Divisions in the leadership appear to have played an important part in this collapse. A remnant of the Khitan aristocracy and army fled westwards and successfully established a state in Central Asia (Kara or Black Khitay) which endured until the Mongol conquest a century later. *C.A.P.*

Xixia (*c.* 990–1227)

Strategic factors go a long way to explain the success and durability of Xixia, a thinly populated kingdom occupying the territory of modern Ningxia and western Gansu in northwest China. On the caravan routes linking East with Central and Western Asia, it enjoyed a steady source of revenue in its role as middleman. At the same time its security in the face of the immensely greater Song

was guaranteed by the Liao empire in the northeast which, while recognized as overlord by Xixia, shared a common interest in preventing any Song advance northwards. In addition to trade, the economy was based on oasis agriculture and pastoralism, horses providing the major export to Song China.

The dominant ethnic element in the state were the Tanguts, a Tibetan-related people. Information on the Tanguts has come mainly from Chinese sources. Few traces of their capital at Kara-Khoto survived the Mongol destruction in 1227, and the ideographic Tangut script has, until recently, defied deciphering. Chinese influence was strong, Tang nomenclature and institutions in particular being taken as models. But the polity seems to have been in the form of a confederation. Buddhism was manifestly the dominant religion.

Despite serious gaps in our knowledge of Tangut political history, it is clear that Xixia rose as a Chinese client state in the 10th century, achieving independent status late in the century. There were periodic attempts at expansion, initially to consolidate control over the trade routes and subsequently to gain advantage from Song. The latter effort was engineered by the ruler Li Yuanhao (d. 1048), who fought against Song in the 1030s, styled himself emperor in 1038, and extorted a highly advantageous treaty from Song in 1044. In return for peace and Li's acknowledgement of himself as a Song vassal, he and his kingdom received an annual stipend of 50 000oz (1417kg) of silver, 130 000 bolts of silk, and 30 000 catties of tea (plus further amounts under a special 'gift' arrangement). The treaty served its purpose for the next several years, but sporadic conflicts began in 1068 and persisted until the end of the century. The payment in tea, a valuable commodity for the western trade, was eventually raised to 225 000 catties.

Amid the turmoil in the northern borderlands accompanying the Jurchen Jin destruction of Liao, Song launched a series of attacks on Xixia in 1115–19 but met with little success. After the Jurchen triumph in north China, direct contact between Xixia and Southern Song was broken off, while Xixia–Jin relations were on the whole amicable. Tangut resistance to Mongol pressure, which began in earnest in 1209, was by no means negligible, but unable to withstand the harshly punitive Mongol campaign of 1225–7, the dynasty was destroyed. *C.A.P.*

The Jin dynasty (1115–1234)

The dynasty that has come to be known as Jin was founded in 1115 by Aguda, tribal leader of the Jurchen, a Tungusic people in Manchuria who had been subjects of the Khitan state of Liao. The dynastic name of Jin ('gold') reflects its geographical origin (the 'Gold River' in Manchuria was the home of the imperial clan Wanyan). Together with the Song, the Jin overthrew the Liao, who then turned against the Song and conquered their capital of Kaifeng in 1126–7. After protracted warfare Jin and Song concluded a peace in 1141. A period of coexistence, interrupted by brief warfare, followed until the Mongol attacks of 1214–15 reduced Jin to a buffer-state, and finally annihilated it in 1234.

In the early years the Jurchen had adopted Liao institutions in addition to their native tribal system. After 1140 the system of government was more closely modelled on the Chinese Tang and Song patterns. Some earlier traditions survived, however, such as the system of five capitals inherited from Liao. Administration was

multilingual, with documents in Chinese, Khitan and Jurchen. (In 1119 and 1138 special scripts for the Jurchen language had been invented and introduced.) Positions of political power were largely in the hands of Jurchen aristocrats, but on the whole there was not much racial discrimination. The legal system was based on the Tang code.

The population in c. 1200 was over 50 million, mostly Chinese. Other nationalities besides the ruling Jurchen minority included Bohai, Khitans and other nomad tribes. The Jurchen were organized in military agricultural colonies distributed over the conquered territories. Agriculture was the economic basis of the state. Slavery was quite common (chiefly prisoners of war). The state

CHINA IN 1206

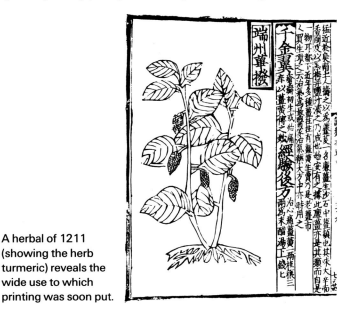

Manuscript fragment in Jurchen script discovered in Khara Khoto (Inner Mongolia).

was economically self-sufficient. An important source of revenue were the annual payments from Song (silver and textiles). Trade with neighbouring states (Song and Xixia) was state-controlled.

Internal stability was endangered by factionalism among the Jurchen aristocracy. The Khitans in the northeast of the state frequently rebelled. Among the Chinese population, however, organized rebellions rarely occurred until the early 13th century when Chinese insurgents rose in Shandong, but without lasting success.

Foreign relations with Song, Xixia and Korea were formalized (routine embassies). Jin regarded not only Xixia and Korea but for some time (1141–65) Song, too, as vassal states. The greatest danger came from the Mongols, who finally defeated the Jin despite the latter's military valour.

Philosophers under the Jin were cut off from the development of Song Neo-Confucianism. In religion the court favoured Buddhism and sponsored the printing of Buddhist scriptures. An important development was the emergence of the Daoist movement Quanzhen ('Complete Realization'), which combined asceticism with an attempt to combine Daoism with Confucian and

Buddhist ideas and attracted many followers among Chinese intellectuals.

The educated Jurchen elite soon amalgamated with the Chinese, and had lost their national traditions by 1200. Some Jin writers achieved fame, e.g. Yuan Haowen (1190–1257), who also compiled an anthology of Jin poetry. In the towns drama (vaudeville, burlesque) began to flourish. In painting, the Jin achievements were respectable but not outstanding. Altogether, conservatism may be regarded as a dominant characteristic of Jin culture. *H.F.*

Printing and the successful application of technology

While Song shows no less creativity than other periods in making original inventions and discoveries, it was in the sphere of application that the Chinese of this age made their primary and remarkable technological contribution. The best example of the Song genius at application is provided by printing.

Known from the end of the 8th century, woodblock printing developed rapidly from the 11th century. Technological innovation as such played little part in this growth. While, for example, movable type was invented about 1040, the standard technique remained the carving of an entire page on a single block of wood. The explanation lies, rather, in a combination of other factors: the increased demand once printed books began to circulate; the availability of skilled craftsmen; the government's willingness to sponsor printings; and private entrepreneurs' willingness to invest.

A herbal of 1211 (showing the herb turmeric) reveals the wide use to which printing was soon put.

Printing was by official and private presses, the latter both for trade and for private circulation. Recognized centres of printing emerged at Kaifeng, Chengdu, Hangzhou and Fuzhou, but by Southern Song the industry had spread throughout the realm, 173 locations having been identified. Books on every conceivable subject were printed: the Classics and their commentaries, the histories, poetry, Buddhist and Daoist works, popular fiction, local histories and reference works.

The availability of cheaper and a vastly increased number of reading materials was a boon to education and brought about a significant increase in literacy. With more candidates preparing for the civil service examinations, manuals and reference works as well as schools and teachers were needed and printing contributed to the institution becoming a truly national one. The government found in printing an efficient tool for the propagation of laws, information and ideas. A much greater familiarity with the Classics and with literature in general provided the basis for the revival of Confucianism in the Song period.   *C.A.P.*

Hangzhou

The adoption as Southern Song capital of this beautiful city, once the capital of the Five Dynasties state of Wuyue, came about *faute de mieux*. Gaozong, a refugee from the conquering Jurchen Jin, attempted to set up a new government in the south, initially preferring to settle his court on the banks of the Yangtze at Zhenjiang. But Jurchen pressure pushed him further south to this site, which became known as his 'temporary residence' (*xingzai*). The name stuck, so that at the end of the Song Marco Polo regarded 'Qinsai' as the proper name of the city. Between the beautiful West Lake and the Zhe River and surrounded on all but the eastern side by green-clad hills, the city took on a narrow, oblong shape along a north–south axis. As with Kaifeng, growth overtook the city walls (some 20km in circumference), creating new neighbourhoods and markets to the north, east and south. Hangzhou's political role helped account for its reaching a population of about 1.5 million and thus becoming a huge centre of consumption. However, as it was located in the heart of the country's most rapidly developing region and benefited from excellent communications, it was destined to become an important commercial hub in its own right.   *C.A.P.*

Urbanization and urban culture

It is possible to speak of a distinct urban culture in China only from Song times. One consequence of the commercial revolution was widespread urbanization, resulting in concentrations of population in unprecedented numbers. This phenomenon was most dramatically illustrated in the growth of large cities, which reached a million and more residents in the cases of Kaifeng and Hangzhou, and exceeded 100 000 in another dozen cities. However, the growth of small towns into large ones and of villages and markets into towns was equally important. These cities and towns evolved along new and less ordered lines than earlier times when significant clusters of population occurred around administrative centres. Gone were the old inner walls separating ward from ward and, in the absence of a military threat (save on the frontier), the population spilled beyond the outer walls to form new settlements. Nourished by commerce, these cities and towns served primarily as centres of exchange; as they grew, they became centres of consumption and investment as well. A huge service industry developed, not only catering to the demands of the wealthy, but also supplying the daily needs of the commoner. The multitude of handicrafts were in many cases part of this service industry but in others were geared to larger-scale production and export to distant markets.

The urban population was as diverse in composition as the activities and occupations it pursued. The officials and intellectual elite enjoyed highest status, but the new social and economic environment favoured successful businessmen and enabled them to rival their betters in living standards. Town life drew many of the well-to-do from the land and the phenomenon of absentee landlordism began to appear. It was the ability of the towns to attract brains and money that gave them an influence in the country quite out of proportion to the population they contained (surely not over 10 per cent). Below the elite and the wealthy, an urban middle class of unknown dimensions existed, including shopkeepers, successful craftsmen, scribes, petty officials and the like. Labourers and menials formed the bulk of the population, which was periodically swelled by hardship in the countryside.

The new urban culture distinguished itself by the character of its social life, its higher level of literacy, its educational facilities and the wealth and variety of its entertainment. Life in the towns was enriched by frequent festivals, many of Buddhist and Daoist origin, others marking important seasonal changes. These were popular events in which residents from all walks of life participated. Associations of many sorts brought together smaller groups to pursue specific interests and purposes, for example, religious and literary societies. Merchant and craft guilds, though mainly professional bodies, served a social function as well. A veritable entertainment industry was called into existence, located in restaurants, teahouses, amusement parks, theatres, brothels and the streets and including singers, musicians, dancers, actors, playwrights, jugglers, magicians, acrobats, prostitutes and others. Of

The bustle of urban life is vividly portrayed in the *Spring Festival on the River* scroll of Zhang Zeduan.

most lasting interest is the theatre, many of whose products crossed the fine line from mere entertainment into art. There were many kinds of theatre—puppet plays, shadow plays, a northern type variety show including drama and a somewhat purer form of drama of southern origin. Little of this literature has survived, but the plots are known to have dealt with historical romances, supernatural episodes and realistic themes and characters of the day. Another form of 'theatre' enjoyed tremendous success and fortunately is well known to us, the tales of professional storytellers. Many of the scripts used by the storytellers, which became the basis of the colloquial short story in China, survive and reveal aspects of Song life and psychology unknown to us in any other way. *C.A.P.*

Foreign relations

No major Chinese dynasty found its fortunes so closely interwoven as did Song with those of neighbouring states, whose impact, both externally and internally, was deep and unremitting. By the same token Song alone among major dynasties never enjoyed a truly expansionist phase. Brought to a halt in 979, unification fell short of recovering important areas in the northeast and northwest. Former Chinese territory was held by the Khitan empire of Liao and by the Tangut kingdom of Xixia, Northern Song's two powerful rivals.

The 12th century brought dramatic changes. When former Manchurian vassals of Liao, the Jurchen, rebelled in 1115 and sought an alliance, Song saw a golden opportunity to withdraw from the Shanyuan Treaty of 1005 and reassert itself in the north. Although the alliance was made, the Jurchen, now the Jin dynasty, overcame Liao virtually without Song assistance and induced Song to accept them as Liao's successors in the treaty arrangements. Song's military efforts against Xixia in 1115–19 also failed. Growing friction between the new treaty partners in the northeast led to open conflict in 1125 and then to the Jurchen capture of Kaifeng and conquest of all of north China in 1127. Only after years of fighting following the establishment of (Southern) Song at Hangzhou did it become clear that total conquest by either side was unlikely. A new treaty was signed with the Jin in 1141, providing for the payment of the customary Song subsidy. Despite renewed attacks by the Jin in 1161 and by the Song in 1206, the agreement served to maintain generally peaceful relations down to the Mongol invasion. Cut off from direct contact, Xixia, remaining independent but in vassal status in regard to Jin, was no longer of concern to Song.

For more than 200 years after the conclusion of the first Song treaty with a 'barbarian' in 1005, compromise on the principle of Chinese political and cultural supremacy had on the whole brought peace. The entry of the almost unknown Mongols into north China beginning in 1209 met with only a passive response from Song, content at the spectacle of barbarians destroying each other. The Mongol conquest of the north interrupted by Genghis Khan's great westward expedition against Khwarezm and his death in 1227, was achieved slowly and only with great effort. Save for short-term cooperation in 1233–4 to destroy the tottering Jin court, Song stayed clear of involvement with the new barbarians. Then in 1234, under fresh leadership, it did a turnabout and launched an attack to recover the territory south of the Yellow River. This violation of the existing truce, failing disastrously, provoked the hostilities that 40 years later brought down the dynasty. While the Mongol victory in 1276–9 has an air of inevitability about it, Song resistance was stiff and prolonged. Moreover, the Mongol effort, time and again interrupted by changes of leadership and political divisions, was only brought to successful conclusion by an exceptional monarch, Khubilai Khan (1215–94).

C.A.P.

Neo-Confucianism

Original, diverse and even inconsistent, Neo-Confucianism in its formative stage during the Song must be distinguished from the later philosophical system and intellectual orthodoxy of Ming and Qing times. It emerged in a period of intellectual excitement and inquiry when the best minds suddenly rediscovered ancient Confucianism. But, if the spirit of revival was central to the phe-

nomenon, Song thinkers from their vantage point, a millennium and more removed, reinterpreted the old texts and cast Confucian thought in quite a different light. The secularization of thought was reflected, among the intelligentsia at least, in a sharp reaction against Buddhism and the new importance attached to the temporal world. This change in attitude was manifest in the lively interest in political and social reform; in the construction of a metaphysical system wholly based on the Chinese secular tradition; in the emergence of a remarkably sophisticated historiography; and in the appearance of new aesthetic values in prose, poetry and painting.

While signs of a Confucian revival can be found in late Tang, the movement really dates from the 10th century. It issued above all from a growing awareness of classical doctrine fostered by the civil service examinations and the increasing availability of Confucian texts which the rapid advance in printing made possible. From the beginning, Neo-Confucianism evolved along two rather distinct lines, self-cultivation and institutional reform. Both, rejecting Buddhist indifference towards the world, sought to create the good society. But while the former assumed the need first to perfect man (or at least individual men), the latter aimed at the positive use of a government imbued with Confucianism to achieve the accepted ideals. Inevitably, Confucian reform became mired in the practical measures designed to meet urgent political and social problems as demonstrated by the reforms of Wang Anshi. With the apparent perversion of the reform programme in late Northern Song followed by the loss of north China to the Jurchen Jin in 1127, a decisive shift towards self-cultivation and metaphysical speculation occurred, characteristic of Southern Song thinkers. Indeed, obsession with the external problem virtually extinguished the impulse for reform.

Until recently conventional wisdom in China saw a direct line of transmission of *true* Neo-Confucian doctrine from Cheng Yi (1032–1107), to Zhu Xi (1130–1200), the acknowledged great syncretist of the school. However, there were many contributors to the debate: the founder of the important Idealist school, Cheng Hao (1031–85); the materialist Zhang Zai (1020–77); such figures primarily concerned with the application of ideas as Wang Anshi and Ye Shi (d. 1224); the great historiographer Sima Guang, whose history was infused with new political theory; and the literary figure and historian Ouyang Xiu (1007–72). Their achievement was not only to breathe new life into Confucianism but also to create a more comprehensive and fully reasoned conception of man, the world and the cosmos, meeting questions posed in the areas of politics, ethics, metaphysics and epistemology, than had ever existed in the Chinese tradition. Ironically, the imprint of Buddhism (and even Daoism) on this revived Confucianism, albeit unconscious and unintentional, was far from insignificant.

C.A.P.

THE YUAN DYNASTY (AD 1276–1368)

Emperors

The Mongol emperors of the Yuan dynasty were the descendants of Genghis Khan, who had united the tribes of the steppe in 1206 and conquered a part of north China in 1215. The conquest of China as a whole was completed by his grandson Khubilai Khan (reigned 1260–94, canonized as Shizu) in 1276–80, but the state name Yuan ('Origin') was adopted as early as 1271. Khubilai was concurrently emperor of China and the Great Khan of the Mongol world empire, even though his rule of the latter was long disputed by other Mongol princes. Under Khubilai the imperial court was transferred from Mongolia to the south. The Yuan emperors had two capitals, the winter capital of Dadu (now Beijing) and the summer capital of Shangdu (now Dolonnur,

Khubilai Khan, most famous of the Yuan emperors, completed the Mongol conquest of China.

KEY

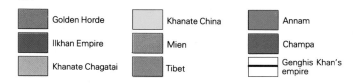

Golden Horde	Khanate China	Annam
Ilkhan Empire	Mien	Champa
Khanate Chagatai	Tibet	Genghis Khan's empire

EAST AND CENTRAL ASIA UNDER THE MONGOLS

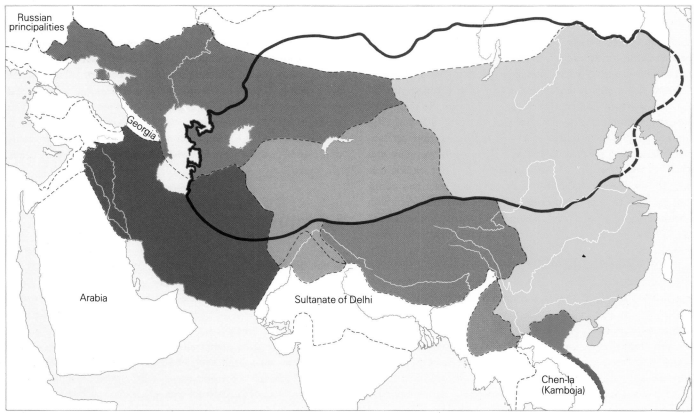

Inner Mongolia). While still crown prince, Khubilai was under the influence of Chinese advisers whose importance is shown by his adoption of Chinese institutions at all levels during his reign. He was a powerful personality, his fame as a stern and sometimes benevolent ruler spreading beyond China proper.

An inherent weakness of Mongol imperial rule was the absence of fixed procedures for succession. This lead to dissension and struggle among the imperial princes, particularly from 1321 onwards. More than once two pretenders competed for the throne, each backed by a group of Mongol nobles and Chinese followers. None of Khubilai's successors had his stature, and imperial power declined as a consequence. Several emperors were put on the throne at a young age, to be little more than figureheads. The last emperor was Toghon Temür (reigned 1333–68, canonized as Shundi). He too became emperor while still a child. His education had been Chinese and under his rule Chinese civilization made progress at court. He lost his throne to Zhu Yuanzhang, who in 1368 founded the Ming dynasty. Toghon Temür fled to Mongolia from where he tried in vain to reconquer China (d. 1370). *H.F.*

Structure of government

Many features distinguish the Mongol Yuan government from that of the Chinese dynasties. The traditional reliance on scholar-bureaucrats selected through literary examinations was replaced by a form of military government where original Mongol institutions and ways of administration coexisted with Chinese-type institutions. Administration was bilingual (Mongolian and Chinese, the latter frequently not in classical but in vernacular language). This was made possible by attaching interpreters and translators to offices at all levels. In contrast to the leading role of civilian authorities under the Song, the Yuan state was dominated by the military. Tribal or ethnic affiliations interfered with traditional Chinese lines of command. All these factors tended to impair the efficiency of government control in times of crisis.

Central government was remodelled after Khubilai's accession. The most important civilian office was the Central Secretariat which supervised the subordinate traditional Six Ministries (finance, war, official appointments, rites, punishments and public works). The highest military office was the Military Council, which may be regarded as a kind of General Staff. Both organizations had already existed under the previous dynasties of Song and Jin, but their function differed under the Yuan. The third of the three highest central authorities had no precedent in China. It was the Xuanzhengyuan, which served concurrently as a provincial government of Tibet and a supervising agency for the Buddhist clergy in the empire. Its head was, as a rule, a Tibetan lama. Important posts in the central government were mostly filled by Mongols or their allies, whereas few Chinese rose to positions of power. Only in cultural affairs could Chinese officials exercise some control (historiography, the Hanlin Academy, etc.).

Local government at the lower echelons was modelled on Chinese precedents (counties, prefectures, etc.), with, however, Mongol administrators attached to many offices (*darughachi*, 'seal-bearers'). The provincial administrations were regional branches of the Central Secretariat, so that at least in theory the central government could directly control the provinces. Some regional territories had been given as fiefs to Mongol princes and generals after the conquest; these fiefs enjoyed a certain degree of independence from the general administration.

Yuan law was only imperfectly codified. At first the code of the Jin was used in northern China. It was abolished in 1271 but no new comprehensive code was compiled; instead the legal system used case-law. Important decisions were collated and published so that a minimum of jurisdictional unity could be maintained. Yuan penal law was characterized by ethnic discrimination: some laws applied only to foreigners. For administrative and legal purposes China's population was divided into four classes: Mongols; *semuren* 'people of special category', i.e. Central Asian allies of the Mongols, mostly Uighurs and other Turks; *Hanren* (northern Chinese and former non-Chinese subjects of the Jin like Jurchen and Khitans); and *Nanren* ('Southerners', the inhabitants of the former Song state). Mongols and, to a lesser degree, *semuren* enjoyed legal and fiscal privileges. Buddhist monks and nuns were in principle subjected to the jurisdiction of the *Hsüan-zheng yüan*. Although the basic concepts of Mongol law reflected earlier Chinese traditions, some features were influenced by Mongol customs. *H.F.*

Economy

Population figures for the Yuan are difficult to interpret. The registered population in the 1340s was about 60 million, but this only comprised those who were taxed. Moreover, a considerable part of the Chinese, chiefly in the north, was probably not included in the census because they paid their taxes to Mongol fief-holders. A figure of 80 million might be a more accurate estimate for the total population of China.

Agriculture was the economic basis of the state. The most productive and densely populated regions were in southeast China (in present-day Zhejiang Province). As with earlier regimes the Chinese peasant continued to maintain the state, and the ruling minority of Mongols and their allies. As a rule the Mongols left private agricultural property intact, but after the conquest they gave some state-owned fields to their aristocracy as fiefs.

The reunification of China after 1276 had far-reaching effects on the economy. Interregional trade began to flourish. This was partly due to the repair of transportation facilities such as the Grand Canal. The metropolitan region of Dadu was dependent on grain transports from southeast China. A state-controlled network of postal stations provided fast communication between the capital and the regions, including Mongolia, Manchuria and parts of Central Asia.

The Yuan government did not share the traditional Chinese mistrust of private enterprise. Domestic trade became remarkably free; the same is also true for artisan and proto-industrial entrepreneurship, which coexisted with state-controlled industries. The result was urban growth and even prosperity. Maritime trade between China and ports in Southeast Asia and the Indian Ocean remained subject to state supervision but flourished considerably. This is also true of the caravan trade to Central and Western Asia. Chinese goods (chiefly silk) even reached Europe. Imports consisted mostly of luxury goods (jewellery, drugs, perfumes) and slaves.

Taxation followed, on the whole, Chinese precedents. The peasantry paid taxes in kind (grain, textiles) and in money (poll-tax). Merchants were taxed according to turnover. In addition many *ad hoc* taxes were levied on the population. Also the *corvée* supplied manpower for the building of canals, dams, bridges and public buildings. The Mongols and *semuren* were exempt from all taxes, as were the clergy of all religions, whose monastery fields were also exempt from the usual land tax. State revenues were considerable but the requirements of the imperial court were enormous, and the maintenance of garrisons throughout the country costly.

The currency system was unique. Under earlier dynasties (Song and Jin) paper money had played a subsidiary role in addition to bronze coins. The Mongols realized that the production of copper was insufficient to provide enough coinage for a country the size of China and therefore made paper money the only legal tender, with bronze coins (cash) as a subsidiary. Silver in ingots was also used for larger transactions. It was also possible and even obligatory to pay taxes in paper money. This system functioned as long as the economy remained productive. A fatal inflation occurred during the last years of the Yuan, when the country was disintegrating as a result of rebellions and domestic wars. *H.F.*

Factions and rebellions

A distinction should be made between factionalism within the Mongol ruling class and rebellions of the Chinese population. There were two sources of factionalism among the Mongols. One was the struggle for succession as Great Khan. After the death of Möngke in 1259, his brother Khubilai was proclaimed successor by his followers, but at the same time Khubilai's younger brother, Arigh Böge, held a meeting of tribal leaders in Mongolia which elected him as Möngke's successor. Khubilai and Arigh Böge fought each other for several years until the latter submitted in 1264. Khubilai's rule was also threatened from Mongolia by the pretender Khaidu, who was a descendant of Ögödei. Despite having the resources of China at his disposal Khubilai was unable to subdue Khaidu. Khaidu died in 1301 and it was not until 1303 that Khaidu's son submitted to the Yuan emperor Temür. Similar struggles were to recur.

The second source of dissent among the Mongol aristocracy was the antagonism between those who wished to preserve their traditional nomadic way of life, and those who tried to build up a working relationship with their Chinese subjects.

After the extinction of the Song state there were no organized loyalist movements fighting against the Mongol overlords. The population acquiesced in the new regime. Loyalist feelings for the defunct Song were, however, widespread among the intellectuals. Nostalgia for the past splendour of the Song was frequently expressed in writings, which were seldom censored by the Mongol government. During the first decades of the 14th century there occurred some minor local rebellions, all without lasting effect. Only under the last emperor did popular rebellions weaken Mongol rule, chiefly after the disastrous floods of the Yellow and Huai Rivers which displaced many peasants. The attempts of the government to repair the dams using forced labour created further unrest and discontent. At the same time local rebellions broke out in the densely populated regions of southeast China, some of them led by messianic Buddhist sects. In the 1350s large parts of China were fragmented into virtually independent local regimes and satrapies. At first rebellion was against the upper classes. Later the expulsion of the Mongols became a major aim. One of the rebel leaders, Zhu Yuanzhang, succeeded in eliminating rival movements and in conquering Dadu, thus bringing Mongol rule to an end. *H.F.*

Foreign relations

Relations with foreign nations were dominated by the view that the Mongol Khans were the legitimate rulers over the world. Under Khubilai there were several military expeditions outside China, each to be regarded as an attempt to remind other states of the supreme rulership of the Khan. Two naval expeditions against Japan (1274, 1281) failed, as did two attacks on Java (1281, 1292). Also, the expeditions against Champa, Annam and northern Burma did not result in lasting territorial gains. Relations between the Mongols in China and the other Mongol states in Asia were loose. The Ilkhan state in Persia remained an ally of Khubilai and his successors, whereas other descendants of Genghis Khan disputed their overlordship. The Mongol rulers in China saw themselves in the same position as Chinese emperors of the past, as rulers of all-under-heaven who regarded other nations as tribute-bearing vassals.

Informal relations between the outside world and Yuan China were quite numerous. Franciscan missionaries found their way to China to establish Roman Catholic hierarchies. The first recorded arrival of Europeans in medieval China seems to have been a visit of northern European traders at Khubilai's court in 1261. In 1342 a papal legate, John of Marignola, was received in Shangdu by the emperor. The travels of Marco Polo (c. 1271–92) and his book also contributed to knowledge about China in the West. *H.F.*

Religion and philosophy

Chinese religions continued to exist under the Mongols, who did not try to impose their native religion upon their subjects. At first Daoism was favoured by the Mongol rulers, but from the middle of the 13th century onwards Buddhist influence increased. Some of Khubilai's advisers were or had been monks. After Tibet had come under Mongol rule, Buddhist lamas became prominent at the court and converted the imperial family and some aristocrats to Lamaism. The Tibetan lamas enjoyed many privileges, and their arrogance caused much resentment among the Chinese. In 1281 religious Daoism was partly outlawed and some texts were proscribed as apocryphal, but Daoism as an organized religion of the Chinese continued to exist alongside Chinese Buddhism. Monasteries of both religions remained centres of Chinese culture.

Foreign religions in China benefited from the generally liberal religious policies of the Mongols. Nestorian Christian communities mostly of Turkic or other Central Asian origin existed in many towns. There were also Muslims and Jews who had migrated to China, but as yet no Chinese seem to have been converted to these creeds. Manichaeism, which had already spread to China under the Tang, merged with Buddhist sectarianism.

Philosophy in China became influenced strongly by Neo-Confucianism, and the school of Zhu Xi and his followers gained prominence after the reunification of China. It dominated the official interpretation of the Confucian classics. In the later years of the Yuan a revival of legalistic, state-oriented thinking took place; it influenced thought under the early Ming. *H.F.*

Literature and art

Chinese literature of the Yuan period was, on the whole, traditional in so far as productions in the literary language were concerned. At the same time literature in the vernacular flourished in the cities (novels, stories and dramas). The theatrical literature of the Yuan was of remarkable creativity and vitality, and the collection known as Yuanquxuan (*100 plays*) was later regarded as the most important achievement of the period. Some foreigners, chiefly Uighurs and other Turks, distinguished themselves in traditional Chinese genres.

Chinese painters continued to work in the tradition of the Song. Many Yuan painters, chiefly in the 14th century, excelled in landscape painting. The court and academy painters were of less importance than the literati artists. Figures like Zhao Mengfu (1254–1322) and Ni Zan (1301–74) are among the greatest of Chinese artists. Chinese calligraphy also flourished. Imperial patronage was important in the promotion of Buddhist painting, sculpture and architecture, sometimes involving Tibetan and Nepalese artists. The printed editions of the Buddhist canon in Chinese and Tangut ordered by the court were beautiful specimens of book-printing with woodcut illustrations. Secular book-printing also maintained the high standard already reached under the Song. *H.F.*

Science and technology

Among the technological achievements the use of gunpowder must be mentioned. It is possible that this led to the introduction of gunpowder to Europe in the late 14th century. Astronomical instruments were built according to Islamic methods (observatory in Dadu, 1279). In hydraulic engineering too, some Near Eastern experts were active. Many medical handbooks and treatises were written. One of them was translated into Persian in 1313. An atlas of China produced 1311–20 is evidence of the sophistication of cartography under the Yuan. The overall technological level of Yuan China was on a par with, if not superior to that of, contemporary Europe. *H.F.*

THE MING DYNASTY (1368–1644)

Zhu Yuanzhang Rebellion (1355–67)

By the second quarter of the 14th century China was torn by rebellions against the Mongol Yuan dynasty. The most widespread were the Red Turban revolts that by the 1340s had fanned out from the middle Yangtze to Shandong. These revolts drew upon such diverse doctrines as the Maitreya cult in popular Buddhism, Manichaean elements, and on Confucian and Daoist values and symbols.

In 1352 Zhu Yuanzhang, an orphan and Buddhist novice, joined the private guard of Guo Zixing, a minor local military leader who acknowledged the overlordship of Han Liner, the Red Turban 'Little Prince of Radiance', and claimant to the throne of a so-called restored Song dynasty. When Guo died in 1355, Zhu became effectively the rebel leader. His military fortunes quickly prospered. He crossed the Yangtze and in 1356, at the second attempt, captured Nanjing and turned it into his base. His rebellion continued to acknowledge the remote Song dynastic claims of Han Liner the Red Turban figurehead, until Han was drowned in suspicious circumstances while in Zhu's custody in 1367. In 1361 Zhu had taken the title Duke of Wu, in 1364 the Prince of Wu, and clearly had dynastic aspirations of his own.

The major turning point in Zhu Yuanzhang's rebellion occurred in 1363, when he managed to defeat his militarily stronger rival Chen Youliang (1320–63), who controlled the entire central Yangtze region and claimed hegemony over the southern half of the Red Turban movement. The decisive defeat came in the great naval battle of Poyang Lake in Jiangxi, which Zhu then followed up in campaigns to consolidate all of central China, west to the Yangtze gorges. Then he turned his attention to the destruction of other rivals, especially Zhang Shicheng based down river at Suzhou, which finally fell to his armies in 1367.

Throughout the 1360s Zhu built an orderly and expanding government administering territories that stretched across the middle of China. He proclaimed his new Ming dynasty on New Year's Day (23 January 1368), using the name—Ming, 'radiance'—as a final gesture towards the Manichaean elements in the Red Turban doctrines that had sustained his rebel beginnings. *F.W.M.*

EMPERORS OF THE MING DYNASTY

Name	Temple Name	Born	Died	Enthroned	Reign title and dates in effect
Zhu Yuanzhang	Taizu	1328	1398	1368	Hongwu (1368–99)
Zhu Yunwen	(Huizong)	1377	1402?	1398	Jianwen (1399–1402)
Zhu Di	Taizong	1360	1424	1402	Yongle (1403–25)
	Chengzu (conferred 1538)				
Zhu Gaozhi	Renzong	1378	1425	1424	Hongxi (1425–6)
Zhu Zhanji	Xuanzong	1399	1435	1425	Xuande (1426–36)
Zhu Qizhen	Yingzong	1427	1464	1435	Zhengtong (1436–50)
	(captive 1449–50)			restored 1457	Tianshun (1457–65)
Zhu Qiyu	Daizong	1428	1457	1449	Jingtai (1450–7)
Zhu Jianshen	Xianzong	1447	1487	1464	Chenghua (1465–88)
Zhu Youtang	Xiaozong	1470	1505	1487	Hongzhi (1488–1506)
Zhu Houzhao	Wuzong	1491	1521	1505	Zhengde (1506–22)
Zhu Houcong	Shizong	1507	1567	1521	Jiajing (1522–67)
Zhu Zaihou	Muzong	1537	1572	1567	Longqing (1567–72)
Zhu Yijun	Shenzong	1563	1620	1572	Wanli (1572–1620)
Zhu Changluo	Guangzong	1582	1620	1620	Taichang (1620)
Zhu Youjiao	Xizong	1605	1627	1620	Tianqi (1620–7)
Zhu Youjian	Sizong	1611	1644	1627	Chongzhen (1628–45)
Zhu Yousong	Anzong	1607	1646	1644	Hongguang (1645)
Zhu Yujian	Shaozong	1602	1646	1645	Longwu (1646)
Zhu Youlang		1623	1662	1646	Yongli (1647–61)

Source: Goodrich and Fang, *Dictionary of Ming Biography* (New York, 1976); p.. xxi

The Hongwu Emperor, 'Grand Progenitor', the Ming dynasty's founder

Zhu Yuanzhang took the reign-title 'Hongwu', meaning 'vast military achievement'. The Hongwu reign is marked by vigorous consolidation of power and of institutional foundations of the Chinese state that, in essential form, lasted through the Ming and the subsequent Qing dynasties. Zhu proved to be a hard-working, conscientious, if ruthless, ruler; his reign exhibited both shrewd statesmanship and uninhibited cruelty, particularly towards the scholar-officialdom who served his government at the higher levels. He was both dependent on the literati to fill those roles and unendingly suspicious of them. Two great purges (1380 and 1393) and many smaller ones eliminated tens of thousands of officials and their entire families, and maintained an atmosphere of intimidation that characterized the Ming conduct of government in many succeeding reigns.

Zhu Yuanzhang, the Hung-wu Emperor; a flattering portrait of the Ming dynasty founder, c. 1377.

The purge of 1380 was conducted to curb the ostensibly over-ambitious activities of the chief minister of the court, the senior chancellor, Hu Weiyong (d. 1380). As a result the civil and military power bloc he had formed was removed, the offices of senior and junior chancellor and the unified command over the military were abolished. Consequently, leadership over the executive organs of government, the Outer Court, shifted to the emperor himself, that is the Inner Court.

The Hongwu reign can be seen as a high point in Chinese imperial history. Effective, honest local government was stressed, rehabilitation of the rural economy began to take place after more than a century of destructive stresses, the conquest of Yunnan filled out the boundaries of 'China proper', and the Ming tribute system brought a China-dominated international order to much of East Asia. The population of China, probably close to 130 million in the early 13th century may have been as low as 70 million at the beginning of Ming, and probably exceeded 200 million again at the end of the Ming dynasty in 1644. *F.W.M.*

Yongle Emperor

When Zhu Yuanzhang died in 1398 his eldest son, Zhu Biao, had predeceased him. Zhu Biao's eldest surviving son therefore succeeded the founder in 1398, completely in accordance with the Ancestral Admonition, the dynasty's house law. His name was Zhu Yunwen (1377–1402); he is usually known to history by his reign-title as the Jianwen Emperor. This young man reigned for less than four years through which a long civil war was fought. He was overthrown by his uncle, Zhu Di (1360–1424), who usurped the throne to reign as the Yongle Emperor.

The Yongle Emperor possessed many of his father's qualities: he was intellectually and physically vigorous, capable in war, and a shrewd manager of the machinery of state. Fourth among the founder's 26 sons, he had been enfeoffed Prince of Yan and based at the former Yuan dynasty capital city of Dadu, renamed Beiping (modern Beijing). Preferring that city to Nanjing and confronted incessantly by the problems of defending the nearby northern borders against resurgent Mongol power, he transferred the national capital there in 1420, after largely reconstructing the city and renaming it Beijing ('northern capital').

Chinese historians have sometimes looked upon the Yongle reign (1402–24) as the 'second founding' of the Ming dynasty, so important were the institutional adjustments and further consolidation accomplished then. The usurper was bound by the house law set out by his father to maintain the institutional form of the state; none the less he guided a transition from the founder's often extreme ways, to more stable, somewhat more practical ways of conducting government. Yet certain of the abuses of the Ming system also are blamed upon him, especially the ever more important roles subsequently assumed by eunuchs, the increasing power of the Inner Court Grand Secretaries, the weaknesses of the northern border defence system, and the degeneration of learning encouraged by the digests of 'safe' classical learning, (the *Daquan*) and the rigidly formalized eight-legged essay system of the civil service examinations.

As a sponsor of learning, the Yongle Emperor is best known for the *Yongle dadian*, an immense manuscript compilation of what his scholar advisers held to be the essential core of all Chinese learning, in 22 877 'chapters' (*juan*), completed in 1408 by a team of over 2000 scholars. Never printed, it existed in one, later two manuscript copies, the first of which disappeared in Ming times, and the second of which was dispersed in the 19th century.   *F.W.M.*

Dual capitals

Some earlier dynasties, notably the Han and the Tang, had designated two or more capitals at which the court resided at different times. From the beginning of the Ming dynasty there was uncertainty about having the capital of a united China for the first time located south of the Yangtze, away from the ancient heartland of the civilization. But the eventual Ming system of dual capitals emerged quite apart from those precedents and considerations; its two capitals functioned simultaneously as complementary centres of somewhat different installations and activities.

At first Nanjing (then called 'Yingtian', 'in response to heaven's mandate') was enlarged and greatly reconstructed, in the 1360s and 1370s. Its population grew from about 100 000 in the 1350s to about a million by 1400, forming probably the largest city in the world at that time (as Chinese capitals were through most of the imperial era).

After the usurpation in 1402 the Yongle Emperor determined to create a new capital at modern Beijing, on the base of the Yuan dynasty capital city at that site. In size only slightly smaller than Nanjing, the new capital was, however, more sumptuous. He called his new capital 'Shuntian' ('in compliance with heaven's commands'), and Beijing ('northern capital') in relation to Nanjing ('southern capital').

From 1420, when Beijing was first designated the principal capital, until 1441 the intent of successive emperors remained uncertain; after that date Beijing was unambiguously the principal capital and Nanjing the secondary capital. Late Ming writers regarded Beijing as the residence of the court, and of the executive agencies and, with the Mongol Wars, as the seat of military power; while Nanjing supervised the fiscal resources of the state and sup-

plied the poorer north with the wealth produced in the lower Yangtze basin.   *F.W.M.*

Zheng He

Zheng He (1371–*c*. 1433), from Yunnan, was a Muslim of at least partially non-Han race, of a family that had been prominent in Yunnan under the Yuan dynasty. At about the age of 10 he was recruited for palace service, castrated and sent to Nanjing by the Chinese armies then conquering the southwest for the Ming founder, the Hongwu Emperor. Trained for military service, he followed the future Yongle Emperor in campaigns in defence of the Great Wall in the 1390s and in the Civil War of 1398–1402, completely winning the ruler's confidence and esteem. He briefly became chief eunuch in the palace, then was given command of the overseas expeditions that the emperors sponsored for three decades in the early 15th century.

During the years 1405 to 1433 China became an important maritime nation, sending successively seven immense fleets under Zheng He's command on expeditions to Southeast Asia, the Indian ports, the Persian Gulf and even to the east coast of Africa.

After the Yongle Emperor's death in 1424 Chinese court officials began to attack the expeditions as wasteful and essentially inconsequential for a great agrarian nation that recognized no state interest in the sponsorship of overseas trade or the extension of diplomatic influence to far regions. A seventh and final expedition was launched in 1430; it went as far as the Arabian Peninsula and Africa, having renewed diplomatic contacts all along the way, and returned in 1433. No further official expeditions were launched. The busy maritime activity of the Chinese, mainly the southwest coastal carrying trade, was carried on by private merchants without any further benefit from the state's presence and sponsorship, indeed, at times in spite of the state's efforts to deny Chinese merchants a legitimate role in it.   *F.W.M.*

Grand Secretariat

Ming emperors were deprived, by the reorganization of the central government decreed in 1380 by the Hongwu Emperor and made binding on all successors, of the traditional assistance provided by chancellors, chief counsellors or prime ministers heading the Outer Court. On the one hand, the heads of the Six Ministries (of Personnel, Revenues, Rites, War, Justice and Works) and of other implementing agencies were made responsible directly to the emperor (and no longer, as previously, to a Central Secretariat headed by chancellors, and so forth), and thus their responsibilities

CHINA DURING THE MING DYNASTY

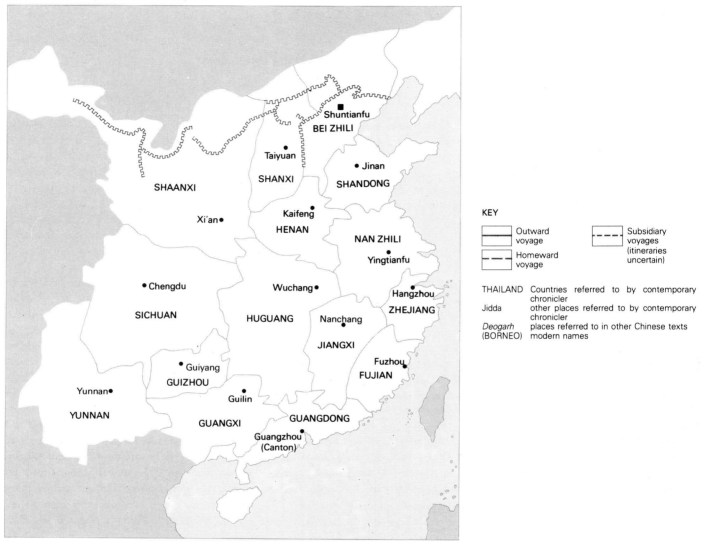

KEY

Outward voyage

Homeward voyage

Subsidiary voyages (itineraries uncertain)

THAILAND — Countries referred to by contemporary chronicler

Jidda — other places referred to by contemporary chronicler

Deogarh (BORNEO) — places referred to in other Chinese texts / modern names

were increased. Simultaneously, however, the supervisory and coordinating functions fell to the ruler himself, or to his secretaries, eunuchs and others of his Inner Court. Few emperors after the founder (Hongwu) and the usurper (Yongle) had the energies, the talent or the will to perform conscientiously.

Scholar-officials attached to the five, later six, halls of the palace compound were the logical candidates for the bigger roles; as secretarial assistants for such routine tasks as drafting edicts, they could readily become advisers. These 'Inner Halls' (*Neige*) were staffed by young scholars who were placed high in the palace examination. The head of each Hall bore the title of

'Grand Secretary' for the Hall, and as the Halls were ranked in precedence, the head of the highest ranked Hall was the Chief Grand Secretary. The Grand Secretaries formed in time a kind of pseudo-cabinet, headed by their Chief Grand Secretary. Yet even when, as became customary, they were given concurrent posts in the Outer Court, for example, as heads of the Six Ministries, they did not have the legitimate, institutional base as heads of a Central Secretariat and coordinators of administration that prime ministers of previous dynasties had enjoyed. Thus the Grand Secretariat in Ming times evolved into an indispensable but weak organ of government.

F.W.M.

ITINERARY OF ZHENG HE'S 7TH EXPEDITION

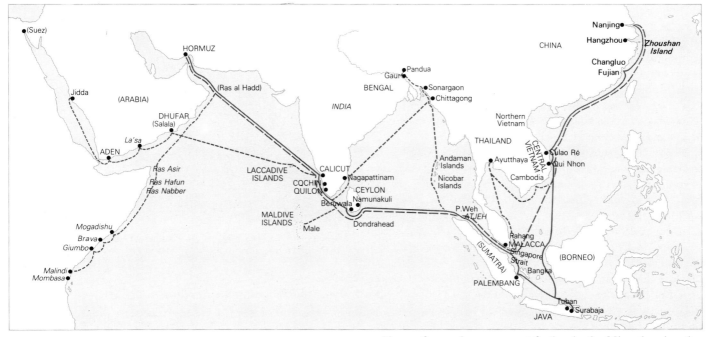

Eunuchs

The Inner Palace City, or Forbidden City, in which Ming emperors resided was divided into the front halls where government was conducted, and a very extensive complex of rear palaces and courts in which the emperor, his consorts and harem resided with thousands of women and eunuchs to serve them. Other adult males (including the emperor's own sons after puberty) were not allowed to reside in, scarcely even to visit, those parts of the palace city.

The palace eunuch organization was set up like the civil bureaucracy, with a structure of offices, ranks and titles. It included 12 bureaux, functionally specific (for example, for utensils, granaries and storehouses, imperial clothing, food and drink, ceremonial equipment, music, the imperial writing implements and official seals and, most important, a Bureau of Ceremonial responsible for constant attendance on the emperor and all arrangements for his meetings with others). The director of the Bureau of Ceremonial was the most powerful of the eunuchs, the undisputed manager of the palace city and of all eunuchs posted throughout the realm on special assignment. When the reigning emperor allowed it, this chief eunuch could become a kind of chief minister of the realm, even a wilful dictator who could browbeat officialdom, control finances, appointments and policy and, as an extension of the imperial person, virtually rule the empire.

Abuse of eunuch power went further in the Ming than in other dynastic eras. The following notorious eunuch dictators dominated Ming government: Wang Zhen, who was killed in 1449, at Tumu, during an ill-fated campaign against the Mongols when the Emperor Yingzong (reigned 1436-50, and again 1457-65) was captured; Wang Zhi, who controlled the government and the northern border defences from about 1477 to 1481; Liu Jin, who directed the Zhengde Emperor's debaucheries while manipulating the government between 1506 and 1510; and Wei Zhongxian, the most hated of all eunuch dictators, who virtually ruled China during the Tianqi Emperor's reign, 1620-7.

The Ming court recruited eunuchs in large numbers from the mid-15th century onwards, and had as many as 70 000 regularly in service throughout most of the last century of Ming rule. Most eunuchs were castrated as children before the age of 10, usually younger sons of poor families who 'volunteered' them for palace service, or children taken from non-Han frontier peoples.

Despite notorious examples of abuse of power, there are many examples in Ming times of eunuchs in the highest positions who were honoured by the scholar-officials for their responsible conduct, personal probity and expert assistance in government. A palace school to educate young eunuchs existed from the early 15th century, many became experts in documentary forms, institutional intricacies and bureaucratic procedures. Many pursued military careers in the imperial guard units or at the Great Wall defence bastions, and were formidable fighters.   *F.W.M.*

The Ming *lijia* and *baojia* systems

The Ming founder, the Hongwu Emperor, understood the problems of rural society and strove to achieve better government for the common people. He is seen by most scholars as having restored stability to local society by improving local government and bringing a greater equity into the lives of poor farmers. For many regions throughout most of the dynasty, rural society was secure and prosperous.

The Ming structure of sub-county local government contributed to the stability of peasant society. The *lijia* represents the extension of governing below the county (*xian*) level, responsible for levying and collecting taxes and services. It was operated by private individuals in village society. The *li* was a group of 110 households, subdivided into 10 *jia*; the 10 households that paid the largest land tax served in a 10-year rotation as its heads, and cooperated with the *liangzhang*, chiefs of grain tax collection. It was responsible for the decennial census registration recorded in the Yellow Registers, for maintaining maps of landholdings in the so-called 'Fish-scale Register' (from the resemblance of a map to the pattern of scales on a fish), and for levying and collecting taxes and labour services on the basis of those. This system was a Ming innovation. It established a norm that has persisted in some measure into the present century.

The *baojia* system, in contrast, was not effectively implemented during the Ming. It was a system for organizing groups of households in decimal units, loosely analogous to the *lijia* in structure, but for other than fiscal responsibilities. Based on ancient texts, the idea had been given new reality in the Song dynasty innovations associated with the great statesman Wang Anshi. The Ming founder, Hongwu, evidently wished to establish a genuine village community government in which the *baojia* system would provide mutual responsibility, surveillance, police and militia services. If efforts had been made to establish a *baojia* system throughout rural society in the early Ming, it did not endure. Nonetheless, the concept, the name and a variant form of its realization were transmitted to the succeeding Qing dynasty, and was important then as a functioning counterpart to the Qing *lijia* system.   *F.W.M.*

The gentry and the Ming examination system

The elite of late imperial Chinese society were the holders of privileged status achieved through the civil service examinations. Called *shenshi* or *shenjin*, meaning variously degree-holders, lite-

Detail from *Spring Dawn at the Palaces of Han* by Qiu Ying (died *c.* 1552), giving a picture of upper-class life in Ming times.

rati, scholar-bureaucrats or officials, they are loosely known in English as the Chinese gentry.

Restored to full functioning early in the Ming, the civil service examination system soon held a virtual monopoly on access to higher office-holding; an unofficial elite of wealth existed alongside the examination degree-holding gentry, to some extent overlapping with it, imitating it in values and life-styles. The lowest level degrees, unimportant for office-holding and of much less prestige, were open to purchase after the mid-15th century. Openness of society and fluidity of status appear to have been more characteristic of Ming than of any other dynastic era. P.T. Ho's study (1962) shows that in each of the 17 triennial examinations for the highest degree (the *jinshi*) between 1371 and 1610 for which full data exist (out of a dynastic total of 90 such examination years) between 44 and 84 per cent were from families in which no ancestor for three generations had held any degree status whatsoever, while no more than 8 per cent in any of those examinations came from a family that had produced a *jinshi*, or highest degree-holder, in the three preceding generations. This would indicate a society more open to upward mobility than any other pre-modern society hitherto known.   *F.W.M.*

Tribute and trade

During the 10th to 14th centuries, when China was locked in struggle with the dynasties of conquest from the steppe, its relations with the non-Chinese world depended heavily on treaties, on reciprocity among states, and on China's buying off its enemies to obtain peaceful relations. With the reassertion of Chinese supremacy late in the 14th century, procedures based on ancient concepts but somewhat new in practice were invoked. The Tribute System, managed by the Ministry of Rites, dominant from the founding of the Ming until the early 19th century, linked foreign trade and other aspects of the relations between the Chinese state and the rest of the world to China's culturocentric world-view which assumed China not only to be the largest and oldest among the states of the world, but also the source of their civilization. The tribute offered was of no more value, and usually much less, than the gifts bestowed by the Chinese throne upon the tribute bearers; the Chinese state had no profit motive in fostering the tribute system, and perceived no advantage to China in fostering foreign trade.

The tribute relationship was allowed to mask the true significance of the system for the states voluntarily bringing tribute to the Chinese court. For them, the trade conducted under its aegis was its crucial component. In Ming China, foreign trade was managed by the imperial household, subsidiary to the palace procurement offices staffed by eunuchs; goods for sale in China were stopped at a border crossing point, either a coastal port city or a land crossing barrier. Such trade was open to eunuch peculation and official corruption. The unending friction this generated contributed to the problems of piracy at sea and to raids, warfare and hostility towards the Chinese in the steppe. The Ming state never solved these problems. *F.W.M.*

Mongol mounted archer in a Chinese painting of the 15th or 16th century. The Mongols threatened China's security throughout most of the Ming dynasty.

Mongol wars

After expelling the remnants of the Yuan dynasty from north China in 1368, the armies of the Ming founder (the Hongwu Emperor) had to campaign in the Mongol steppe throughout most of his reign.

By the late 14th century the Inner Asian steppe had been transformed into one Mongol cultural world sharing the heritage of Genghis Khan; the Ming state was forced to accept its existence—a new circumstance in the long history of China's relations with the steppe—and to defend China against the ever-threatening resurgence of Mongol military might. That was seen as the primary threat to China's security.

The Ming founder reinforced the Great Wall as a fall-back defence position, the Wall as we see it today being largely a Ming structure. He enfeoffed his elder sons at strong garrison commands placed along it.

Successive Ming rulers led armies against the Mongols, but without significant achievement. Much of the hostility between Chinese and Mongols turned on the penetration of the nearer

steppe by Chinese traders and usurers, later by Chinese farmer-settlers, and on the unsatisfactory conduct of the tribute-trade relationship. The Chinese were slowly displacing the Mongols in the nearer border territories, and the Mongols themselves, especially after their 16th-century conversion to Tibetan Buddhism and adoption of its monastic institutions, were slowly retreating from pure nomadism, thus losing their comparative advantage in warfare over the Chinese. *F.W.M.*

Japan—diplomacy, trade and piracy

At the time of the Ming founding, Japan had long been split by civil war. Once the power of Ashikaga Yoshimitsu was well established in 1392, relations between the two countries flourished. The Japanese cooperated in the suppression of piracy, and the Chinese emperors in the early 15th century sent friendly embassies with lavish gifts and high praise for Japan.

Trade was of great importance to the Shogunate, which shipped sulphur, swords, and other materials and products to be exchanged for Chinese copper coins (which became the standard currency in

Japan), silks, ceramics, Buddhist books, art objects and other goods. Nominally restricted to a decennial tribute mission to China, in practice this trade was constant and flourishing, and had to be controlled through a 'tally system' (*kanhe*; Japanese *kangō*), a licensing system that identified authorized trading delegations and ensured orderly procedures at designated Chinese ports. That system functioned well through the 15th century, but became inoperative as Ashikaga power declined in the 16th. The growth of unlicensed trade, or smuggling, gave rise to competition among carriers and ultimately to renewed piracy which was not reduced until a fresh policy committed to the relaxing of an ill-advised Chinese embargo on all coastal trade and suppressive measures had effect from the 1560s onwards. Coastal commerce and the carrying trade, in which Europeans now became active, flourished at the end of the Ming.

Relations between the two countries were interrupted by the Japanese invasions of Korea under Hideyoshi Toyotomi in 1592–3 and 1597–8. He proclaimed his continental campaign was aimed at the conquest of China. As it, in any event, guaranteed the security of Korea, China was compelled to send large forces to support its ally. That costly effort exhausted Chinese fiscal resources. With the death of Hideyoshi in 1598 and the establishment of the Tokugawa Shogunate in 1603, Japan came under a stable government that, until the end of the Ming, encouraged orderly foreign trade. Nagasaki had a large Chinese resident merchant community; the trading links between it and Fujian ports flourished as never before, now greatly enriched by the immense flow of New World silver from Acapulco via Manila. At the end of the Ming, however, concurrent with the Japanese exclusion policy adopted in the 1640s, Chinese–Japanese relations entered a new and more subdued era. *F.W.M.*

Jiajing and Wanli reigns

After the death of the fifth Ming ruler, Emperor Xuanzong, in 1435, and until the end of the dynasty (1644), the subsequent rulers were at best mediocre. Nevertheless, the quality of government was well maintained by the scholar-bureaucracy until late in the 16th century. Two long reigns of mid- and late Ming deserve special mention.

The Jiajing Emperor, who reigned 1522–67, came to the throne unexpectedly, after the death of his childless cousin, the Zhengde Emperor, who had one of the most disorderly reigns in all of Chinese history. In contrast, the young Jiajing Emperor displayed great seriousness and, for the first half of his long reign, a perceptive attentiveness to governing. After that he turned his attention almost exclusively to Daoist religious practices, allowing powerful

Grand Secretaries to dominate the government while he secluded himself, cut off from the realities of the day. He was sternly rebuked for that in 1565 by a minor official Hai Rui (1513–87).

Despite the Jiajing Emperor's degeneration as a ruler, his reign is looked upon as an age of great general prosperity throughout society. In foreign affairs his reign was marred by Japanese piracy and Mongol invasion. Also, during his reign the Portuguese were given permission to settle and trade in the Pearl River estuary, leading to their acquisition of Macao around 1565.

His grandson, the Wanli Emperor, reigned for 48 years (1572–1620). In its first decade his reign was marked by the notable reforms carried out by the vigorous Chief Grand Secretary Zhang Juzheng. After that, his principal delights seem to have been ignoring his court and frustrating his high court officials. The Wanli Emperor's refusal to rule created great difficulties for administration; the conduct of government seriously declined. Many historians have traced the decline in the dynasty's fortunes to the start of his reign. *F.W.M.*

Merchant colonization

Merchant colonies (*shangtun*), like soldier and civilian colonies, were a form of agricultural colony (*tuntian*) developed in early Ming times to support frontier garrisons. When it proved impractical for the frontier garrisons to become self-sufficient in food, and the administration had found transportation by convict labour unsatisfactory, merchants were induced to transport supplies in return for access to the government's lucrative salt monopoly. To reduce costs, the merchants in turn recruited settlers and developed civilian agricultural stations, a system that worked well until the mid-15th century. Gradually, however, because of inflation, manipulation of the salt-for-grain ratios, corruption and bureaucracy, it became less attractive to merchants.

Finally, the government's permitting merchants to deliver silver to the frontier to purchase supplies locally created an inflated grain market and led to weakened frontier defences on account of inadequate provisions, and the system which had some success for a century fell into abeyance. *F.W.M.*

Huizhou and Shanxi merchants

Huizhou is a poor mountain prefecture of southern Anhui Province; Shanxi is a province of agriculturally-marginal north China. The economic limitations of these poorer interior regions encouraged the emergence of entrepreneurial activities as an alternative to dependence upon agriculture. People went forth from Huizhou as pedlars of local products—especially inksticks, inkstones, paper and brushes—and as they succeeded in business, formed guilds of merchants that came to specialize in pawnshops, money shops and other enterprises extending far beyond southern Anhui. The guilds of Shanxi merchants specialized in money shops and in transfers of funds, papers of credit and other banking services needed by the growing commercial sector of mid- and late-Ming society. Both groups continued to flourish through the Qing period. The Shanxi banks still represented the major element in native banking in China in the early 20th century.   *F.W.M.*

Single-whip tax reform (Yi tiao bian)

The early Ming government continued the twice yearly land tax system (*liangshuifa*) that had been in use since the great tax reform of 780, in the late Tang dynasty. Thus the Ming agrarian taxes were collected in a Summer Tax and an Autumn Tax plus a variety of labour services, some levied on households and some on adult males. These were managed and collected by the *lijia*. By mid-Ming times some of the tax-in-kind of agricultural production (grains, textiles and fibres) and most of the service levies were regularly commuted to payment in silver, although they would be collected in copper cash, at a manipulated ratio of copper to silver. The system of levies, of delivery, of rates of commutation, and extraordinary levies, had become immensely complex, and ridden within equities and abuses. Collection became ever more difficult, and many counties were in arrears.

To deal with this crisis some district magistracies began experimenting with new ways of apportioning their counties' quotas related to acreage and grade of registered land and number of adult males, merging all the former separate levies into one combined annual tax, to be paid in silver. 'Single-whip' is a pun on the term meaning 'consolidated', or 'combined in one register', 'one whip' and 'one register' being homophones. As the new experiments proved workable, they were modified and their application broadened. By the end of the 16th century the shift to it was complete and the new procedures more or less uniformly applied.   *F.W.M.*

Jingdezhen, the ceramic centre

Centres for making ceramics of the highest artistic quality, in addition to the ubiquitous small kilns firing daily use wares for local consumption, had long existed in many places throughout China.

By the early Ming the rapidly growing ceramics works at Jing-

dezhen had become the largest centre of ceramics production in the world. The Jiangxi site possessed ready access to limitless supplies of the highest quality kaolin and other mineral materials, an abundance of wood fuel and was served by water transport connecting north to the Yangtze, and south to the passes leading to the ports of Fujian and Guangdong. By Ming times it was said to have several hundred thousand skilled craftsmen. There were 300 kiln complexes, each with certain firing specializations. The division of labour in the intricate processes of porcelain manufacture had gone so far that a Ming source states that a piece might be worked on by up to 80 pairs of hands performing separate tasks, one after another.

Jingdezhen wares were bought by the Ming court, had a national market and were exported to Korea, Japan and throughout East and Inner Asia. By the late 16th century they had become important in European trade. Plain white wares were shipped to Canton, then painted and refired specially for the foreign market; these became the famous 'export wares' that were a staple of foreign trade in the Qing period.   *F.W.M.*

Wood-block illustration from the Ming technological encyclopedia *Tiangong kaiwu:* the use of the potter's wheel for trimming and shaping.

Tiangong kaiwu, technological encyclopedia

The *Tiangong kaiwu* by Song Yingxing (*c.* 1600–60), first published in 1637, is an important source for the history of China's industrial technology. An excellent translation and study of the work in English, reprinting many of its finely-executed original wood-block illustrations, was prepared by E-tu Zen Sun and Shiou-chuan Sun, published under the title: *T'ien-kung k'ai-wu (Tiangong kaiwu) Chinese Technology in the Seventeenth Century*, Pennsylvania State University Press, University Park and London, 1966).   *F.W.M.*

Bencao gang mu

Bencao gang mu (*Materia Medica Ordered on the Basis of Monographs and Individual Characteristics*), China's most important compendium of pharmacological knowledge, builds on a long tradition of knowledge in that field. It was compiled by an obscure scholar, naturalist and practising physician of Hubei Province, Li Shizhen, whose dates have been established in recent Chinese scholarship as 1518–95.   *F.W.M.*

Wang Yangming

The philosopher Wang Shouren (1472–1529) is best known in China and abroad by his courtesy name, Wang Yangming. Son of an eminent scholar-official, Wang prepared for and strove to achieve a career in public office; he passed the *jinshi* examinations in 1499 after several attempts, he assiduously studied military matters, and he submitted recommendations on statecraft to the throne. He alternately served in office and took long leaves for philosophical study.

His philosophy is best known by the slogans developed to characterize its major tenets: the extension of innate knowledge, (*zhi liangzhi*) the identity of mind (*xin*) and principle (*li*); the unity of knowledge and action (*zhi xing heyi*). These idealist concepts lie at the basis of his important challenge to Neo-Confucian orthodoxy.

Wang's philosophy had a profound impact on Chinese society, challenging the norms of behaviour as well as the orthodox tenets of philosophy and classical learning. His many important followers tended to split into various groups after his death. Wang's emphasis on the innate goodness, hence worth, of all persons regardless of learning or cultivation is credited with having aroused

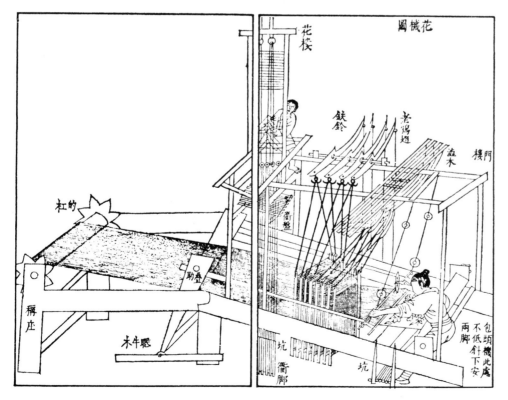

Illustration from the *Tiangong kaiwu* showing a drawloom for figure weaving.

populist movements, of extending education more broadly to the masses and increasing literacy in late Ming society, and in greatly stimulating altruistic and philanthropic commitment. At the same time, his later followers' unconventional behaviour (in contrast to Wang's own observance of the proprieties) that his emphasis on intuitive ethics permitted, was credited by some 17th-century thinkers with having undermined government and society, leading to the collapse of the Ming dynasty. Strongly anti-Wang School movements had developed by the late 16th century.   *F.W.M.*

Donglin Academy

The Donglin or 'Eastern Grove' Academy was an old centre of Confucian studies re-established in late Ming times, at Wuxi, Jiangsu Province, by a league of scholars active from the last quarter of the 16th century, committed to combating the 'degenerate' influences of Wang Yangming's teachings and to promoting a conservative, reformist political programme for the recovery of a strong, upright society.

Its founding leaders were Gu Xianzheng (1550–1612) and Gao Panlong (1562–1626), both natives of Wusih. As young men, both had been active, in association with a 'pure critics' (*qingyi*) faction in public life, in attacking the improper behaviour of high officials. In 1603 the two joined forces to rebuild the long-defunct Academy, to be used as a site for their study and teaching, and for gatherings of the politically-committed. It soon attracted the support and association of scholars and officials throughout the lower Yangtze valley.

As a political faction with an active role in government, the Donglin adherents first came to dominate but not to control the government in Beijing. After the accession of the Tianqi Emperor in 1620 they ran foul of the hated eunuch-dictator Wei Zhongxian and were purged in 1625. Many were arrested, tortured and killed on his orders in 1625 and 1626. Gao, who had been purged from a high post in Beijing, returned to the Academy at Wuxi, and only avoided that fate by committing suicide in 1626. The Donglin group were rehabilitated in 1629, after a change of emperors and the fall of Wei Zhongxian. Many remained important in government to the end of the dynasty.   *F.W.M.*

Matteo Ricci

Matteo Ricci (1552–1610), an Italian Jesuit, well educated in theology, science and the humanities at Rome, was the most important figure in the early phase of Jesuit missionary activity in China. Ricci reached Macao via the mission base at Goa, in 1582. At Macao he studied Chinese. He entered China in 1583, one of the first small group permitted to reside in the country, and served at four new mission stations he helped to open. He finally reached Beijing with permission to stay in 1602, such permission having been refused earlier. He became a stipendiary of the court, and helped other Jesuits later to achieve official status as employees of the Bureau of Astronomy.

Ricci was a remarkable linguist; he devised his own romanization for Chinese, compiled his own dictionary, and thoroughly mastered spoken and classical Chinese. His memory was the wonder of his Chinese associates, who also valued his learning in mathematics and astronomy, geography and physics, but who responded less enthusiastically to his religious teaching. His importance stems not from the few important converts he made but from his remarkable intellect and personal qualities, and his having used those effectively in promoting the mission policy of cultural adaptation. He and his Jesuit colleagues were accepted as literati from abroad, and admired for their learning. Although that was the basis of their success at the Ming court, the policy of accommodation was strongly criticized by other religious orders. The resulting dispute led to the Rites Controversy that deeply stirred European intellectual life in the 17th and 18th centuries, and which jeopardized the Jesuit relationship with the Qing emperors.   *F.W.M.*

Li Zicheng Rebellion

The rebellion of Li Zicheng, a native of Mizhi, northern Shaanxi (*c*. 1605–45), formally ended the Ming dynasty. The forces he led had their origin in a popular uprising caused by economic deprivation and government neglect in the far northwest. Their progress was facilitated by the government's preoccupation with the challenge from the Manchus and by its own ineptitude. When the rebel army somewhat fortuitously surrounded and entered an undefended Beijing, and the hapless Chongzhen Emperor hanged himself, on 25 April 1644, the Manchu army poised at the Great Wall, in concert with the main Ming defence army under General Wu Sangui (1612–78), who was blocking them just inside the Wall, could see a common cause in pursuing the despised ruffian mob within China. This allowed the Manchu chieftain, Dorgon (1612–50) to invade Beijing on 5 June without having met any Ming defenders, and to proclaim a new dynasty, the Qing (established since 1636 in Mukden), as successor to a Ming dynasty that heaven and circumstances, not they, had destroyed.   *F.W.M.*

THE QING DYNASTY (1644–1912)

Historical perspective

Although the founding of the Qing dynasty is usually dated from the seizure of Beijing by Manchu forces in June 1644, the state's origins can be traced back to the late 16th century when a dynamic young Jurchen (Manchu) tribal leader named Nurhachi began to organize his people into a political and military force which was to play a significant role in the affairs of East Asia for the next three centuries. The process of organization was a protracted one, however, and despite the valiant efforts of Nurhachi and his talented son Abahai, it was not until the Ming dynasty had experienced a series of economic and military disasters during the late 1630s and early 1640s that the Manchu armies were able to push south of the Great Wall through the strategically important Shanhaiguan—literally 'Mountain-Sea Pass'—to stay. Even then the road to Beijing was actually opened for them by a large-scale peasant uprising in north China, which caused the last Ming emperor to commit suicide as his capital was being overrun by rebel forces in April 1644.

Nor did Dorgon and other Manchu leaders have an easy time of it once they had established themselves in Beijing and proclaimed their dynasty to be the legitimate successor to the Ming. Indeed, for the next four decades much of their time was taken up trying to pacify the southern half of the country in the face of widespread economic dislocation and of stubborn resistance from so-called 'Ming loyalists' who were hopeful of staging a restoration or using that as an excuse to seize the Dragon Throne for themselves. In fact, it was not until after the defeat of the 'Three Feudatories' in 1681 and the annexation of Taiwan in 1683 that China once again enjoyed an extended period of domestic peace.

This period was a remarkable one, however, lasting for more than a century and encompassing what many believe to have been the most glorious era in pre-modern Chinese history. The main part of the credit belongs to three extraordinary descendants of

CHINA IN 1760

Nurhachi who between them ruled the Qing empire for 138 consecutive years. The first of these was Kangxi (reigned 1661–1722), who became emperor at the age of six, assumed actual control of the government at 15, and proved to be a shrewd and extremely able administrator for most of his 61 years on the throne. He was also an astute politician who succeeded brilliantly in the difficult and delicate task of projecting an imperial image which was acceptable to his Manchu and Chinese subjects alike.

In December 1722 Kangxi was succeeded under rather mysterious circumstances by his fourth son, Yinzhen (1678–1735), who reigned for the next 13 years as the Yongzheng Emperor. A perceptive, talented and mature man of 44 when he came to power, the Yongzheng Emperor wasted little time placing his stamp on Qing governmental operations. Moving to correct abuses that had developed during his father's last few years on the throne and to check potential threats to his own power, the Yongzheng Emperor brought the dynasty's military establishment under tighter central control and reduced the influence of both the Manchu aristocracy and the Chinese-dominated civil service. At the same time he instituted a series of bureaucratic reforms which made his administration probably one of the most efficient and least corrupt in all of Chinese history.

Perhaps the main beneficiary of that administration's efficiency was the Yongzheng Emperor's fourth son, Hongli (1711–99), who, as the Qianlong Emperor, succeeded to the throne in 1735 and dominated the politics of his realm until his death in 1799. During his long reign the Qing empire experienced what some writers have termed a 'golden age' as its armies subdued one outclassed opponent after another and its economy expanded with a vigour not seen since the late 16th century. In 1750 China was probably the strongest, wealthiest and most populous nation on Earth, with a rich and diverse domestic and international trade and a rapidly growing population which was already well in excess of 200 million. That rapid demographic expansion continued into the 19th century; the economic growth which had accompanied it did not.

Following his mission to the Qing court for the British government in 1792–3, Lord Macartney wrote that 'The empire of China is an old, crazy, first-rate Man of War, which a succession of able and vigilant officers have contrived to keep afloat for these hundred and fifty years past. ... But whenever an insufficient man happens to have the command on deck, adieu to the discipline and safety of the ship.' Even as Macartney was offering this opinion, the ship was beginning to experience some rough seas. And while it is of course unwise to pin the blame for this solely on the quality of imperial leadership, part of the problem clearly was that during the last few years of his six decades on the throne, the Qianlong Emperor began to overlook levels of governmental corruption and inefficiency which he would not have tolerated in his younger days.

This, in turn, contributed to a swelling tide of anti-dynastic sentiment which broke into open hostility with the White Lotus Rebellion in the 1790s.

Despite the efforts of the conscientious and perhaps underrated Jiaqing (reigned 1796–1820) and Daoguang (reigned 1821–50) emperors, conditions in China continued to deteriorate during the early 19th century. This was particularly true during the late 1820s and early 1830s when the country's long-standing balance of trade surplus with foreign nations came to an end and silver began flowing out of China in ever increasing quantities to finance the purchase of opium. Since the Qing empire's monetary system was based to a large extent on unminted silver traded by weight and copper coins issued by the government, this development had an extremely adverse effect on the Chinese economy (and on government finances), as the resulting sharp increase in the value of silver meant that many people were unable to pay their taxes and debts and that unemployment increased dramatically in both urban and rural areas. At the same time the generally favourable climatic conditions which prevailed throughout most of the 18th century appear to have given way to more unsettled ones, with the result that floods, droughts and other natural disasters are recorded with terrible regularity in the historical writings of the period. The situation was not helped by the fact that governmental corruption and declining resources meant that many canals and dikes were not properly maintained and that public relief programmes frequently appear to have benefited the administrators more than those they were designed to help.

It was under these conditions that the Qing authorities had to confront an increasingly confident and aggressive foreign presence in East Asian waters during the 1830s. And although they successfully resisted the demands made by Lord Napier in 1834, their attempts to control the opium trade and to stem the outflow of silver inevitably brought them into direct conflict with those Westerners whose profits were adversely affected by their actions. Cultural and diplomatic misunderstandings added to the tension, and in 1840 the complicated and protracted struggle known as the Opium War began. It ended with the Treaty of Nanjing in 1842, in which the defeated Chinese agreed, among other things, to pay Britain a large indemnity and to permit more free trade between the two countries. A supplementary pact signed the following year allowed the British extraterritoriality and granted them most-favoured-nation status. Similar treaties were soon agreed with the USA and France as well, and what some writers have called China's 'century of humiliation' had begun.

Although Sino-Western relations once again became strained in the late 1840s and erupted into violence in 1856, the most serious threats to the Qing dynasty's survival during this period were internal ones, in particular the great mid-century rebellions, the

Taiping, the Nian, Muslim and the Small Sword Society Uprising, which devastated huge sections of the country. The best known of these rebellions, the Taiping, began in the southern province of Guangxi in 1850 and over the next few years grew into one of the great anti-government uprisings in human history. At its height the Taiping movement controlled much of south-central China, including the rich lower Yangtze region, and its founder, Hong Xiuquan (1813–64) seemed destined to topple the Qing and establish his own dynasty. He was prevented from doing so, however, by internal dissension in the Taiping ranks and by the emergence of talented military commanders on the Qing side. Hong died in his 'palace' at Nanjing shortly before the city was retaken by Qing forces in July 1864.

Three years earlier the sickly and harassed Xianfeng Emperor (reigned 1851–61) had died and was succeeded by his five-year-old son, Zaichun, who 'reigned' for the next 13 years as the Tongzhi Emperor. In fact, during much of this time imperial power actually was in the hands of various regents, the most important of whom were Prince Gong (1833–98) and the emperor's mother, who is perhaps best known as the Empress Dowager Cixi. Even before Zaichun's accession, the experience of the Arrow War and particularly of the Anglo-French occupation of Beijing in 1860 had convinced Prince Gong and others in positions of influence that the dynasty needed to learn from the West if it were to have any chance of survival. With the support of military heroes such as Zeng Guofan, Li Hongzhang and others, the next several decades saw the central and provincial governments implement a number of modernization projects which were designed above all to improve the Qing's military position. The failure of the dynasty's forces in both the Sino-French and Sino-Japanese Wars is perhaps some indication that the results achieved by this Self-strengthening Movement were considerably less than its promoters had hoped.

Nor were the dynasty's fortunes aided by the fact that for much of its last half century of existence, politics in Beijing were dominated by the Empress Dowager Cixi, who, following the death of her own son in 1875, manipulated the imperial succession to put a three-year-old nephew on the throne as the Guangxu Emperor (reigned 1875–1908). Even when the Emperor assumed personal rule as a teenager in the late 1880s, the Empress Dowager continued to wield considerable influence from her 'retirement' home at the Summer Palace. Indeed, when the Guangxu Emperor decided to support the Reform Movement espoused by Kang Youwei, Liang Qichao, and others in 1898, she saw to it that the 'movement' and its leaders were crushed and that the Emperor was stripped of power and placed under house arrest. Shortly thereafter she gave her tacit support to the so-called Boxer Movement, which ended disastrously with the foreign occupation of Beijing in 1900

and the Boxer Protocol of 1901. Among other things, the Protocol obliged the Qing government to pay huge indemnities to the allied powers as well as to punish those officials who had been guilty of encouraging anti-foreign activities. Although the Empress Dowager managed to retain her influence through all of this, even she apparently was shaken by these developments and agreed to implement some of the reform proposals which she had so ruthlessly suppressed only a few years earlier.

Other reforms soon followed, but they proved to be too little too late, and during the first decade of the 20th century revolutionaries associated with the Tongmenghui and other groups staged a series of anti-government uprisings which culminated in that at Wuchang in October 1911. Four months later the last Qing emperor, who had been selected by the Empress Dowager just before her death in 1908, abdicated and more than 2000 years of imperial rule came quietly to an end. *W.S.A.*

Nurhachi (1559–1626)

Nurhachi was the Jurchen (Manchu) leader credited with laying the foundations for the establishment of the Qing dynasty. The son of a tribal chieftain who was killed in battle in 1582, Nurhachi spent the next several decades consolidating his power in modern Manchuria through military campaigns and skilful diplomacy. As his strength grew in the early 17th century, he became more and more hostile towards the Ming dynasty, and in 1616 he proclaimed himself emperor of a new state, which he called the Later Jin. In 1618 he declared open war on the Chinese, and during the next few years his forces captured virtually all the territory formerly held by the Ming east of the Liao. However, after 1622 his offensive bogged down, and in early 1626 he was defeated in an attack on the Chinese stronghold of Ningyuan. Nurhachi was wounded in this engagement, and although the extent of his injuries is unknown, he died in September of that year with the conquest of China still nearly two decades away. *W.S.A.*

Abahai (1592–1643)

The eighth son of Nurhachi, Abahai became the second emperor of the Later Jin dynasty on his father's death in 1626. Although Nurhachi had intended power to be shared among a number of princes including Abahai, by the early 1630s the latter had emerged as the undisputed leader of the Jurchen (Manchu) peoples.

In 1636 Abahai changed the name of his dynasty to Qing and proclaimed himself emperor. A talented military commander, he personally led a series of successful campaigns against the Chinese, Koreans and Mongolians, and, bolstered by defections from the Chinese side, by the early 1640s he controlled much of the territory north of the Great Wall. He was also instrumental in establishing the bureaucratic machinery necessary for administering China, the conquest of which began in earnest the year after his death. *W.S.A.*

Manchu banner system

With its origins in traditional Jurchen (Manchu) clan and village organization, this 'system' began to assume definitive shape in 1601 when Nurhachi grouped virtually every tribesman under his control into four administrative units which he called banners (*gusai* in Manchu). These units, which took their names from the different coloured (yellow, white, blue or red) banners assigned to them, were responsible not only for providing warriors for Nurhachi's campaigns but also for governing the 'civilian' populations left behind. As Manchu power increased, so did the number of banners. In 1615 four more Manchu banners were established and by the early 1640s there were eight Mongol and eight Chinese banners as well. Following the conquest of China many bannermen were stationed in and around Beijing while others were placed in strategic locations throughout the empire. However, as time went by their military prowess declined, and by the mid-19th century they were incapable of dealing with either internal rebellion or foreign invasion. *W.S.A.*

Shanhaiguan invasion

Shanhaiguan (literally 'Mountain-Sea Pass') is a strategic pass at the eastern terminus of the Great Wall approximately 300km east-northeast of Beijing. During the late Ming period Shanhaiguan was an important Chinese military stronghold against the Manchus, and it was through this pass in the spring of 1644 that the latter launched their final and ultimately successful invasion of China. However, the circumstances surrounding the beginnings of this invasion are not entirely clear. Tradition has it that the Manchus were invited through Shanhaiguan by the Ming general Wu Sangui (1612–78) to help him defeat a rebel who had sacked Beijing. Nevertheless, recent research suggests that the Manchus took advantage of the chaos in north China caused by a large-scale uprising to push through the pass themselves and that presented with a *fait accompli*, Wu decided to surrender and serve the Manchu cause. *W.S.A.*

Dorgon (1612–50)

The 14th son of Nurhachi, Dorgon had a distinguished military career during the reign of his half-brother Abahai. At Abahai's death in 1643 some elements at the Manchu court wanted Dorgon to become the next emperor, but he is said to have refused out of loyalty to the late ruler. Ultimately, Abahai's young son Fulin (1638–61; reigned 1644–61) was placed on the throne and Dorgon was chosen as one of two co-regents. In 1644 Dorgon personally led the final invasion of China and soon emerged as the most powerful figure in the Qing government. During the next few years he directed the conquest of central and southern China, eliminated many of his enemies in the Manchu aristocracy, and imposed his will on the imperial bureaucracy. Following his death in December 1650, Dorgon's political opponents began a campaign to discredit him, and his family and supporters suffered in the years that followed. It was not until the late 18th century that the Qianlong Emperor officially rehabilitated him and restored his deserved reputation as one of the outstanding early Qing leaders. *W.S.A.*

Manchu–Chinese dyarchy

This term is sometimes used to describe the system whereby Qing rulers tried to protect their interests by placing roughly equal numbers of Manchus and Chinese in the major offices in Beijing and by ensuring that Manchus were well represented in high provincial posts as well. Recently, the applicability of the term for the early Qing period has been questioned because it tends to obscure the important role played by Chinese bannermen in representing the Manchus at the provincial level. *W.S.A.*

Kangxi Emperor (1654–1722)

As one of the great rulers in Chinese history, the Kangxi Emperor (reigned 1661–1722) assumed absolute control of the Qing government in 1669 at the age of 15. For the next three decades he spent much time consolidating the dynasty's position militarily, overcoming a variety of internal and external threats. The Kangxi Emperor realized, however, that the agrarian sections of his empire could not be ruled 'on horseback', and he worked assiduously to improve his administration and to cultivate his image as Confucian emperor *par excellence*. He made a series of personal tours to investigate local conditions, held special examinations to attract scholars to his government, sponsored scholarly projects, patronized the arts, and became a staunch supporter of Confucian morality. For much of his reign the empire appears to have been very well governed, although he lost his grip somewhat in the last few years of his life, which were marred by bitter struggles among various princes over who would succeed him. The circumstances surrounding his death and the succession of the Yongzheng Emperor (1678–1735; reigned 1722–35) are still a source of controversy. *W.S.A.*

Rites Controversy

This term refers to a disagreement between rival groups of Catholic missionaries in 17th- and 18th-century China over whether Chinese converts should be allowed to continue ceremonial rites such as those honouring Confucius and their own ancestors. The Jesuits, who worked among the sophisticated upper classes, said yes on the grounds that the rites in question had ethical and philosophical significance, but were not religious in nature. The Dominicans and Franciscans, who ministered to the poorer and more superstitious elements in society, strongly disagreed and appealed to Rome for a decision in the matter. In 1704 it was decided in their favour, much to the displeasure of the Kangxi Emperor, who supported the Jesuit position. When the Vatican tried to enforce its decision, relations between Rome and Beijing quickly deteriorated and Catholic missionaries never again acquired the favoured treatment that the Jesuits had enjoyed during the early Kangxi reign. *W.S.A.*

Three Feudatories Revolt

During their conquest of China in the mid-17th century the Manchus placed large areas of southern and southwestern China in the hands of Chinese collaborators. The three most powerful of these were Wu Sangui (1612–78) in Yunnan and Guizhou, Shang Kexi (d. 1676) in Guangdong and Geng Jingzhong (d. 1681) in Fujian. Alarmed by the threat these men eventually posed to the central government, in 1673 the young Kangxi Emperor attempted to strip them of their power, thus touching off a major civil war that at times appears to have come close to toppling the dynasty. When the so-called 'Three Feudatories Revolt' ended in 1681, however, Wu, Shang, Geng and many of their supporters were dead, and the Qing government was in firm control of the territories they had once ruled. *W.S.A.*

Tibet

Within a few decades after their accession to power, the Qing rulers recognized that control over Tibet would facilitate the subjugation of the Mongol peoples. Lama Buddhism spread from Tibet to Mongolia, and the 17th-century Mongols respected, if not revered, the Dalai Lama. In 1577 the third Dalai Lama had converted the Altan Khan, the most powerful Mongol ruler of his time, to Buddhism. The Mongol nobility and eventually the ordinary Mongols followed their leader's example. Having converted to Tibetan Buddhism, the Mongols became embroiled in Tibetan affairs. As late as the 17th century the Dalai Lamas, who were the heads of the Yellow Sect (Ge lugs pa) of Buddhism (a sect founded by Tsong-kha-pa (d. 1419) to restore monastic discipline, i.e. by enforcing celibacy, the wearing of yellow robes, and by imposing other restrictions and routines to regulate monastic life), still faced competition from other Tibetan sects. It was only with the military assistance of a Mongol, the Guushi Khan, that the Dalai Lama in 1643 crushed the older Red Sect, his principal opponent, and became the undisputed spiritual leader of Tibet.

Owing their authority, in part, to the Mongols, the Dalai Lamas of the 17th and 18th centuries often supported influential Mongol khans in their conflicts with China. The fifth Dalai Lama, who rebuilt the Potala palace as his residence in Lhasa and centralized political control over much of Tibet, was invited to Beijing in 1652 where he was accorded a magnificent reception. Yet he remained until his death in 1682 a staunch supporter of the Mongols, some of whom were deadly enemies of the Qing. His successor and, in particular, his successor's regent bolstered the Dzungar Mongol Galdan in his struggles with China. Even after the Qing finally defeated Galdan in 1696, the sixth Dalai Lama and his regent continued to be implacably hostile to China. Lha-bza Khan, whose ancestor Guushi Khan had helped to install the Dalai Lama as the supreme spiritual ruler in Tibet, despised the regent and in 1705 had him assassinated. He sought to impose his own candidate as the reincarnation of the Dalai Lama, an act that prompted Tsewang Rabtan, Galdan's successor as head of the Dzungars, to move against him. In 1717 Tsewang, who feared an alliance of Lha-bza Khan with the Qing, stormed the Tibetan capital, killed Lha-bza Khan, and installed a new Dalai Lama.

The Qing court believed that it could not allow the Dzungar Mongols, its dreaded enemies, to control the Dalai Lama. In 1720 Qing forces ousted the Dzungars from Lhasa and imposed a new ruler. The Qing sent several other expeditions, and by the middle of the 18th century, it had established a protectorate in Tibet. It appointed resident commissioners (ambans) who collaborated

TIBET: EARLY 19TH CENTURY

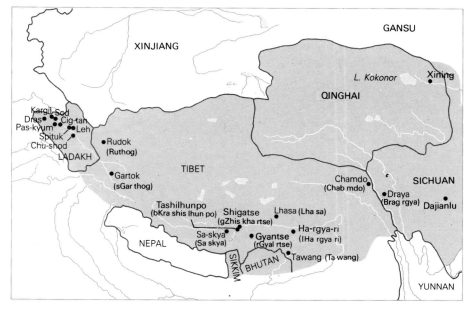

with the Dalai Lamas in ruling Tibet. In 1792 it even intervened in Tibetan affairs by sending forces to protect Tibet from a Nepalese invasion.

This expedition proved to be the last successful venture for the Qing in Tibet. In the 19th century its rival for influence in Lhasa was Britain, a far more formidable foe than the Mongols. Britain eagerly sought to trade for Tibetan shawl wool and to block Russian expansion from Central Asia into Tibet. From 1816 onwards Britain gradually became more influential in Tibet. Since the Manchu garrisons in Tibet had, by this time, deteriorated, the Qing could not help its Tibetan subjects prevent British penetration. In 1903 a British expedition led by Colonel Francis Younghusband forced its way into Lhasa, compelled the Dalai Lama to flee, and imposed a treaty on Tibet. By 1906 the Qing had signed a protocol with the British which recognized China's sovereignty in Tibet but also confirmed British trading and diplomatic privileges. In effect, the Qing no longer had exclusive control over Tibet.   *M.R.*

Turkestan

The history of Turkestan and Dzungaria in the 17th and 18th centuries was shaped by the vicissitudes in the fortunes of the Dzungar Mongols, who established the last empire of the steppes. Under the leadership of their chief Kharakhula and his son Galdan, the Dzungars had embraced Buddhism, built a capital city, and initiated an expansionist policy. Turkestan offered rich possibilities for expansion, for it was inhabited by sedentary Uighurs and nomadic Kazakh and Kirghiz tribesmen, who could not cooperate to stave off potentially troublesome foreigners. Their most influential leaders were the Black Mountain Khoja and the White Mountain Khoja, heads of the principal Sufi orders in Central Asia. Both of these Muslim leaders had coveted and obtained political power, making them the most important potentates in Turkestan. Each fought to be supreme in the region, and their constant conflicts enabled their enemies to impinge on their territories. In the late 1670s the White Mountain Khoja, who had been expelled from his land by his rival, called upon the Dzungars for assistance, and in 1679 Galdan took advantage of this request to invade and conquer Hami, Turfan and most of the rest of East Turkestan.

Fearful of the growth of the Dzungar empire in Western Mongolia and Turkestan, the Qing became embroiled in a 70-year struggle to oust the Dzungars from its northwestern frontiers. Many of the battles took place in Dzungaria and Turkestan, and the Muslims in these regions were often pawns in the Qing-Dzungar struggle. Though the Qing defeated Galdan in 1696, his descendants continued the war and often sought a base in East Turkestan from which to make incursions on China. In 1713 his nephew Tsewang Rabtan captured the town of Hami, from which he was dislodged by a superior Qing force, and in the 1720s he attacked the Kazakhs west of Dzungaria, compelling these nomadic peoples to become vassals of the Tsar in return for Russian protection. The raids of Tsewang Rabtan and his successors, however, led nowhere because the Dzungars were unable to unify their fellow Mongols or the Turkic peoples of Central Asia in an anti-Qing coalition. Capitalizing on the disunity of the Dzungars and of the Muslims in Turkestan, the Qing sent an expedition in 1754 to eliminate once and for all the Dzungar menace. Zhaohui, the leader of the expedition, was so brutal in his suppression of the Dzungars that by 1756 they no longer survived as a people.

The Muslims of Turkestan, who had been either under attack or dominated by the Dzungars for almost a century, now attempted to assert their independence. When envoys from China arrived in Turkestan to demand tribute, the local rulers had them killed. The Qianlong Emperor immediately dispatched Zhaohui to deal with what he perceived to be 'rebellious subjects'. By 1758 Zhaohui had pacified Dzungaria and East Turkestan, and the Qing now ruled a vast domain (to be known eventually as 'Xinjiang'), inhabited by different peoples who were not always loyal and were, in fact, often hostile to China. *M.R.*

Treaties of Nerchinsk and Kiakhta

The Treaties of Nerchinsk (1689) and Kiakhta (1728) defined the commercial and diplomatic relations of China and Russia for more than a century. Before the signing of these treaties Chinese and Russian forces had, on several occasions, clashed in Manchuria, and the outbreak of a full-scale war between the Tsarist court and the Qing court seemed a strong possibility. These clashes resulted from Russia's eastwards expansion. Attracted by the furs and minerals of Siberia and by the reputedly fabulous wealth of the Chinese empire, Russian adventurers and merchants had begun to move into Siberia in the late 16th century. By 1647 they had established towns and forts across Siberia to the shores of the Pacific.

As they ventured southwards, they reached China's northern frontiers. They demanded tribute from the tribes who dwelled in the Amur River region and who owed allegiance to the Qing court; they built the fortified town of Albazin within the Qing borders; and they encouraged the vassals of the Qing to defect. In 1683 the Qing Emperor complained in a letter to the Tsar that '[Russians] have without a reason, invaded our ... frontier, disturbed and injured our hunters, boldly engaged in robbery, and repeatedly harboured our fugitives ...'. Two years later Qing forces attacked and destroyed Albazin. War seemed imminent, but neither side

relished the thought of combat.

Their conflict was, in fact, reconcilable. The Russians, who feared an alliance of the Qing, the Mongols and the frontier tribes of the Amur region against their territory in Siberia, realized that they could not defend both Siberia and the Amur area and were willing to renounce their bases in the Amur in return for security for Siberia. They would be even more compliant if they were permitted to trade with China. The Qing rulers, who in turn feared an alliance of the Mongols and the Russians, were eager for a settlement. They would allow the Russians to send trading caravans to China in return for territorial concessions in the Amur region.

In 1689 the Russian envoy, Fedor Golovin, met Qing officials in the town of Nerchinsk on the Russian side of the border to negotiate a settlement. With the assistance of Tomás Pereira and Jean-François Gerbillon, two Jesuits who had been stationed in China and who could serve as interpreters for the negotiators, Golovin and his Manchu counterparts concluded the Treaty of Nerchinsk late that summer. The treaty did not delineate the precise boundaries between China and Russia in Manchuria and Mongolia, but it provided for Qing control of the Amur River region and called upon the Russians to withdraw from Albazin. (The repercussions of the Treaty of Nerchinsk are still felt in contemporary Sino-Soviet relations: the ceded territories form part of the areas under dispute between the two countries, the Ussuri Incident of 1969 being an example of its extent.) The Russians also agreed to return fugitives and deserters to the Qing. The Manchu court recompensed the Tsarist court for these concessions by allowing the Russians to send trading caravans periodically to Beijing. By signing the treaty the Qing conceded that Russia was an independent state, not a vassal of the Qing empire—an important concession for a government that perceived itself to be superior to all other states.

The Treaty of Kiakhta offered commercial privileges and other special benefits to the Russians. Russian merchants were permitted to trade for Chinese goods in markets at Kiakhta, a town north of Mongolia, and at Tsurukhaitu, a town north of the Manchurian frontier. They did not need to accompany official state caravans all the way to Beijing in order to trade. The Russian court did not, in fact, send any state caravans after 1755, and most Sino-Russian trade was conducted at Kiakhta (as Tsurukhaitu did not become a flourishing centre for commerce). The treaty also accorded Russians a hostel (*Eluosi guan*), which might be considered the first permanent foreign embassy in Chinese history, grounds on which to build an Orthodox Church, and a Chinese language school (*Eluosi wenguan*) for Russian students.

The treaties were satisfactory to both the Tsarist and Qing courts and governed their relations until the middle of the 19th century. *M.R.*

Qianlong Emperor (1711–99)

Inheriting a bulging treasury and an efficient administration from his very capable father (the Yongzheng Emperor), the Qianlong Emperor (reigned 1736–96) presided over one of the most glorious periods in pre-modern Chinese history. During this period, which lasted for much of the Qianlong reign, the economy expanded vigorously, the arts flourished, and the Qing military establishment scored a series of victories over hopelessly outclassed enemies on various frontiers. Like his grandfather (the Kangxi Emperor), the Qianlong Emperor was deeply concerned about his imperial image and at times seems to have been obsessed with the idea of being recognized as the greatest ruler in all of Chinese history. To this end he studied painting and calligraphy, wrote (or had written in his name) vast collections of

Occupying the Qing throne for 60 years, the Qianlong Emperor is widely regarded as one of the greatest rulers in Chinese history.

poetry, became a generous patron of the arts, sponsored scholarly projects, made inspection tours of the empire, and boasted shamelessly about his armies' accomplishments.

The Qing bureaucracy appears to have performed quite well for most of his reign, but official corruption is said to have increased markedly following the Emperor's appointment of the Manchu Heshen (1750–99) as one of his chief advisers in the late 1770s. This corruption eventually helped give rise to widespread popular unrest, which culminated in the famous White Lotus Rebellion. By the time this rebellion began, the Qianlong Emperor had abdicated his throne, although he and Heshen continued to wield actual power until the former's death in 1799. Shortly thereafter Heshen was arrested and permitted to commit suicide, but the dynasty was never again to enjoy the peace and prosperity that had marked the middle decades of the 18th century.   *W.S.A.*

Literary inquisition

Although censorship of one type or another has been known throughout Chinese history, the term 'literary inquisition' usually refers to the 16-year (1772–88) campaign by the Qianlong Emperor and his advisers to eliminate works or parts of works they considered to be objectionable on political or moral grounds. Particular targets were writings thought to be anti-Manchu either in tone or content and those which dealt with sensitive strategic matters such as border defence. The precise effects of the inquisition are difficult to gauge, but well over 2000 works were ordered destroyed. Although many of these somehow survived, the total loss for the study of Ming and Qing history is thought to have been great, a fact that casts a considerable shadow over the Qianlong Emperor's reputation as a patron of learning.   *W.S.A.*

Suzhou and other handicraft centres

For centuries prior to the Manchu conquest of China, Suzhou, the largest city in the world in the 15th and 16th centuries, had been a handicraft and commercial centre of national and even international importance, a position which the city maintained during the early Qing period. Although its craftsmen produced a wide range of goods, Suzhou was most famous for its high-quality silk and cotton textiles. These were sold not only throughout China, but also found their way into the markets of Japan, the New World and Europe. Other early Qing textile centres that deserve mention include Nanjing, Hangzhou, Huzhou,

Songjiang, Shanghai, Chengdu, and Canton. During this period the Chinese also made the finest porcelain in the world, with that of Jingdezhen in Jiangxi Province being particularly famous. Excellent porcelain was also produced at Yixing in Jiangsu and Dehua in Fujian.   W.S.A.

Yangzhou salt merchants

For centuries prior to the Manchu conquest the city of Yangzhou on the Grand Canal just north of the Yangtze River had been a political, commercial and cultural centre of great importance. Much of the city's prosperity in Qing times was based on the fact that it served as headquarters for the so-called Liang-Huai Salt Administration, which was responsible for the manufacture and distribution of salt in a vast region of eastern and central China. During the Qing period, and particularly during the 18th century, government-licensed salt merchants in Yangzhou, many of whom were aggressive and industrious natives of other provinces, amassed enormous private fortunes which must have ranked among the largest in the world at that time. Considerable amounts of this wealth were spent in vulgar display, but it was also used to sponsor scholarly and artistic projects as well as to provide education and to purchase official degrees for members of the merchant families themselves.   W.S.A.

White Lotus Rebellion (1796–1805)

In the last decades of the 18th century White Lotus sects in north China became frequently characterized by millenarian visions that prompted believers to rise in rebellion against the established order. These religious groups, loosely organized through master-disciple ties around itinerant teachers who performed cures, gave instruction in ethics and in special arts of meditation and physical fitness, and led devotional rituals for their congregations, holding out a promise of salvation through their deity, the Eternal Venerable Mother. Predictions about the imminent arrival of a millennium ushered in by the Maitreya Buddha sent by the Eternal Mother, long a part of sectarian eschatology, became increasingly common.

These beliefs gained wide acceptance among an extensive network of believers in Henan and Hubei in the 1780s. Intensive investigations by local officials into this heterodox sect in 1794–5 resulted in hundreds of arrests. A pair of sect leaders named Liu Song (1715?–94) and Wang Faseng (1760–1805) became correspondingly specific in their millennial predictions. Two relatives

were designated the religious teacher and the restoration emperor of the new era. Believers began to make plans for surviving the terrifying catastrophes that would accompany the transition, a time when 'a black whirlwind would rise and blow all day and all night, killing countless people, and leaving mountains of bones and oceans of blood'. The date for the general rising was fixed for the third lunar month (April) of 1796.

Miao uprisings in Hunan-Guizhou had already necessitated the movement of troops through Hubei, and in the early spring of 1796 believers in the western part of that province, provoked into action by their fear of arrest, rose up ahead of schedule, and thousands of others soon joined them. The rebels attacked small cities, but pressed by government soldiers, held them only temporarily and gradually moved westward into the mountainous border between Hubei, Henan, Shaanxi and Sichuan. There they found safety in the inaccessibility of the terrain and continuing support among the poor and immigrant people of the region, and there they were able to hold out, with diminishing vigour, for 10 years.

For the first four years government campaigns conducted by ill-coordinated army units failed to defeat these guerrilla opponents. Although 1796 was technically the first year of the reign of the Jiaqing Emperor (reigned 1796–1820), it was in fact his 85-year-old father, the Qianlong Emperor who, although 'retired', still held the reins of power. Qianlong in turn relied on his chief minister and notorious favourite, Heshen, and on the latter's bureaucratic fac-

WHITE LOTUS AND EIGHT TRIGRAMS

Areas affected by the Eight Trigrams uprising, 1813

• Beijing

Area affected by the White Lotus uprising, 1796–1805

tion. Misleadingly optimistic reports from the field (accompanied by extensive corruption) masked the stalemate and misled the ageing emperor.

It was not until Jiaqing took power in 1799 (upon his father's death) that new policies could be implemented. Heshen and his associates were removed; fresh soldiers were brought in from Manchuria and the southwest; a single overall commander was appointed; and a strategic hamlet policy (known as 'strengthening the walls and clearing the countryside') that had already been devised by local gentry and officials as their own solution to the rebel problem, was authorized. Progress was slow but sure, and by 1805 the rebellion was over. The experience was a formative one for the reform-minded Jiaqing Emperor and the men who served him well in these efforts. But the difficulties of coping with guerrilla warfare waged by religious believers foreshadowed problems that would continue to tax the ingenuity of Qing rulers, as did the dangers of using militia organizations that relied on gentry networks for controlling local disorder.   *S.N.*

Eight Trigrams Rebellion (1813)

In the 1810s there was a revival of White Lotus millenarianism on the north China plain. In 1811 a former apothecary, salesman and day labourer, Lin Qing (1770–1813), now a sect teacher, made contact with another religious leader named Li Wencheng (c. 1770–1813). Li Wencheng cemented contacts between his and other sect congregations in southern Zhili, northern Henan, and western Shandong, soliciting contributions and promising high positions and great benefits in a coming millennium. Lin Qing did likewise among men and women in and around Beijing. The two men called their new confederation the 'Eight Trigrams'. Lin Qing declared himself the reincarnation of Maitreya Buddha, and said that Li Wencheng would rule as 'King of Men'. The time of calamities prior to the era of 'endless blessings' was predicted from sect scriptures to begin on the 15th day of the ninth lunar month (8 October) of the year 1813. Believers prepared knives, distributed white cloth sashes, and learned magical formulae that would serve for both identification and protection.

Lin Qing's ambitious goal was the seizure of the Forbidden City. He then intended to wait for the arrival of colleagues from the south, occupy Beijing, kill the Jiaqing Emperor (reigned 1796–1820) (at that moment en route to the capital from Manchuria), and begin to institutionalize their 'heavenly doctrine'. Remaining at home to await the outcome, Lin Qing sent 250 men into the capital on schedule and by the appointed hour most were waiting nervously outside the palace. Eunuch pupils of Lin's led the way, but in a combination of over-eagerness and uncontrolled panic no

more than 80 rebels entered the Forbidden City complex. The rebels were armed only with knives and the conviction that cosmic forces would assist them. These proved no match for the muskets, bows and arrows of the palace staff, aided by the future Daoguang Emperor (reigned 1821–50) and other imperial princes. Within 24 hours the Trigram rebels had been seized or killed, and within two days Lin Qing himself had been arrested.

In the meantime, uprisings on the southern plain had begun nearly 10 days ahead of schedule, precipitated by the unexpected arrest and torture of Li Wencheng. Magistrates had been murdered, several cities attacked, and a rebel headquarters set up at Hua city in northern Henan. For the next few months several thousand sect members recruited thousands more new followers, and roamed a corridor 100km wide. A Qing army was slowly assembled, commanded by generals who had served the Jiaqing Emperor a decade before against other sectarian rebels, and the Eight Trigrams were gradually encircled. As rebel bands took refuge in Hua city, government armies (assisted in minor ways by local militia) regained control of the countryside. By late November the siege of Hua had begun. In order to prolong the life of the movement Li Wencheng escaped with one thousand supporters, only to be trapped by pursuing soldiers in the foothills west of Hua. On 1 January 1814 Hua city was invaded by 15 000 soldiers, and the rebel occupation ended.

The Jiaqing Emperor, although affronted by the audacity of a group that dared invade his very residence, was justly pleased at the relative speed and efficiency with which order was restored. The rebellion had little impact on the stability of the dynasty and once again popular millenarian hopes were dashed, but the ideology that generated the uprising and the social and economic conditions that fermented it remained.   *S.N.*

The Canton system

The Canton system, which regulated all legitimate Western trade with China from 1760 to 1842, was based upon the premise that this trade was a boon benevolently granted by the Son of Heaven to barbarians from afar. If submissive and obedient, Western merchants were permitted to conduct their business in Canton under the close supervision of native guarantors. The Chinese merchants who served this function belonged to a monopolistic guild known as the Cohong. All aspects of the trade as well as the foreigners' well-being and good conduct were the responsibility of the Cohong. As the upholder of Confucian anti-commercial values, the Qing state could not acknowledge the importance of this trade. Nevertheless, the court and bureaucracy applied themselves with unremitting energy to plundering it through official and unofficial exactions imposed on the Cohong.

Foreign merchants had to endure many irksome restrictions and regulations. While resident in Canton they were confined to the '13 factories', the river-bank area, denied the company of their wives and discouraged from studying Chinese. During the off-season they had to withdraw from Canton to Macao, a nearby Portuguese possession. Further, they could only communicate with officials through the Cohong. However, such were the profits of the China trade that few of those engaged in it—least of all the members of the British East India Company—were prepared to put it at risk by challenging the terms under which the Chinese deigned to permit it. *E.T.*

The Macartney embassy

In 1792 King George III of England sent Lord Macartney, Baron of Lissanoure, to China as a special ambassador to the Qing court. Macartney's instructions were to negotiate with the Qianlong Emperor concerning the regularization of diplomatic and commercial relations between the two countries. Arriving in China in June 1793, Macartney was granted several audiences with the Emperor at his summer residence north of Beijing. As a mark of special favour, albeit one granted after some diplomatic wrangling, the ambassador was even permitted to dispense with the customary kowtow ('three kneelings and nine prostrations') when greeting the emperor. However, all of Britain's substantive requests were rejected and the embassy returned home with little more than a slightly improved understanding of China and Chinese ways, and two condescending edicts from the Emperor to George III in which the latter was warned not to attempt to contravene Chinese laws and customs. *W.S.A.*

The British East India Company

By the end of the 18th century the British East India Company dominated Western trade with China and served as the foreign counterpart to the Cohong in the Canton system. Tea formed the basis of the China trade; the British market for it seemed insatiable. However, no commodity commanded a comparable market in China. The deficit had to be met by carrying silver to China.

In India the East India Company had grown into a government that relied on its monopoly over the production and distribution of opium for an increasing share of its revenue. After the Qing renewed its ban on the importation of opium (1796), the Company ceased importing and distributing the drug so as not to endanger its privileged position in the tea trade. Instead, it sold its opium at public auctions in India to country traders (private merchants licensed by the Company) who then disposed of it off the China coast.

In 1819 the volume of the opium trade suddenly began to increase. Demand rose as a direct consequence of the lowering of prices, brought about by international competition. In the first two decades of the 19th century the trade averaged 4000 chests a year but by 1830 it had risen to nearly 19 000 chests. China's trade surplus soon became a deficit and silver began to drain out of the country.

The sudden increase in the demand for opium in China in the 1820s excited the private merchants engaged in the China trade. They grew increasingly dissatisfied with the restrictions of the Canton system and with the comfortable cooperation that existed between the Cohong and the East India Company. They were also displeased with the Chinese ban on opium, which forced them to rely upon irregular means to carry on their business. Their agitation, strengthened by the arguments of British manufacturers who wanted to see China opened to their products, finally succeeded in bringing about the abolition of the East India Company's monopoly of the China trade in 1833. From the British point of view free trade had triumphed. *E.T.*

The Napier mission

In response to the Chinese request that Britain appoint a headman to take the place of the Select Committee of the East India Company at Canton when the latter's monopoly on trade with China ended in 1833, the foreign secretary, Lord Palmerston, dispatched Lord William John Napier (1786–1834). As the Superintendent of Trade at Canton, Napier was expected to protect British interests. At the same time, as an official of His Majesty's Government, he was to communicate directly and as an equal with Chinese officials. Henceforth Anglo-Chinese relations were to be conducted 'on a permanent and honourable basis'. From the Chinese point of view Napier, as a representative of a foreign ruler, could aspire to nothing more than the status of a tribute bearer. Equality was out of the question. It soon became evident that Napier could not press the case for equal intercourse and at the same time protect British commercial interests. His arrival in Canton without proper clearance, his persistence in attempting to communicate directly with the governor-general and his audacity in taking his grievances against the governor-general to the people of Canton through printed broad-sheets brought a swift and sharp response. All foreign trade was halted and Napier held hostage in the factories until he agreed to leave Canton. He was determined to hold out, but his own failing health combined with the growing disaffection among the British merchants at the suspension of trade forced him to withdraw. Napier's mission like those of Lord Amherst (1816) and Lord Macartney (1793) failed to move the Chinese officials, whose assumptions of superiority remained unshaken.   *E.T.*

Lin Zexu (1785–1850)

Lin Zexu, the son of a teacher, began his career as an administrative official in 1820 and soon gained a reputation for just administration. He entered the debate on the opium question with a detailed memorial (10 June 1838) recommending rehabilitation of addicts as well as strict suppression of the opium trade. The Daoguang Emperor (reigned 1821–50) summoned him to Beijing in late 1838 and, after questioning him closely, appointed him high commissioner with plenipotentiary powers to deal with the opium problem at Canton.

Remembering how quickly Lord Napier had yielded to the suspension of trade in 1834, Lin felt confident that the same weapon could be used to block imports of the drug. He arrived in Canton on 10 March 1839 and almost at once demanded all of the opium in the possession of the foreign merchants. He also made it known that in future all foreign merchants would have to sign a bond promising never again to import the drug. At the same time, he struck at native dealers and users. The foreigners did not take Lin seriously. On 24 March, therefore, he ordered the suspension of all trade and blockaded the factories. In all some 350 foreigners, including the British Superintendent of Trade, Captain Charles Elliot (1801–75), were held hostage. Elliot commanded all British subjects in Canton to surrender to him all of the opium belonging to them or under their control. He issued receipts to the merchants and assumed full responsibility on behalf of the British government for its full value. He then handed over the 20 283 chests of opium thus collected to Lin for systematic destruction. Lin permitted the resumption of trade on 4 May and the next day lifted the blockade of the factories. Elliot did not depart at once but when he did leave Canton for Macao on 24 May 1839, he took the entire British community with him. The late summer and autumn of 1839 saw skirmishes between the Chinese and British but Lin felt confident that he held the upper hand. He even obtained an imperial edict terminating trade between China and England (13 December 1839).

The court was pleased with Lin's apparent success and early in 1840 promoted him. Britain, in the meantime, had decided that war was the only fit response to Chinese presumptuousness and harassment. When war came and the court was faced by the challenge of a British fleet in northern waters, its estimation of Lin plummeted. He was dismissed from office and exiled to Central

Asia. By 1845, however, he had been rehabilitated and in 1850 he was again made an imperial high commissioner, this time to assist in the suppression of the Taiping rebels. He died a natural death en route to his new posting.

Lin's policies were bound to fail for he did not understand the importance of opium to the tea trade, the government of India or the British exchequer.   *E.T.*

A 19th-century Chinese view of Lin Zexu supervising the destruction of the opium surrendered by Captain Elliot, Canton, June 1839.

The Opium War

The British government found cause for war with China in the unreasonable behaviour of Commissioner Lin Zexu at Canton. Lin was accused of seeking to suppress without due warning a system of trade (in opium) in which British merchants and Chinese officials had long connived to their mutual profit. Towards this end he had held British subjects hostage and seized British property. He had then pursued and harassed those same subjects. To the British government of the day such acts could not go unpunished.

The British expeditionary force assembled off Macao in June 1840 but instead of striking at Canton it moved northwards and by late August was at the mouth of the Beihe. Skilful negotiating by the Qing persuaded the British to return to Canton, where after delays, aggravation and skirmishes, Captain Elliot and the Qing envoy concluded the Chuenpi (Chuanbi) Convention (20 January 1841). Both governments rejected this agreement: the British because it did not go far enough, the Chinese because it conceded too much.

In the course of renewed fighting in the vicinity of Canton in May 1841, British forces were involved in the celebrated incident at Sanyuanli. Although the incident was of no military significance, it revealed the degree to which the peasantry around Canton had become politicized. The combination of anti-foreignism and anti-official sentiment manifested by these rural masses was to spread and pose a grave threat to the Qing.

Sir Henry Pottinger (1789–1856) replaced Elliot as plenipotentiary leading the expeditionary force in August 1841. Pottinger easily captured four coastal cities and then settled in for the winter to await reinforcements for a campaign up the Yangtze. The Yangtze campaign began in May 1842 and by 20 July the British forces had captured the junction of the Grand Canal and the Yangtze River. With the way to Nanjing open to the British, the Qing finally accepted the hopelessness of its position and agreed to binding negotiations. *E.T.*

The Treaty of Nanjing

The Treaty of Nanjing, which brought the Opium War to a close, was signed by the British and Chinese on 29 August 1842. It contained the following provisions: (1) an indemnity of $Mexican 21 000 000; (2) four ports, in addition to Canton, opened to foreign trade; (3) equal relations between Britain and China, with British consuls in each of the ports opened to trade and residence; (4) the abolition of the Cohong monopoly; (5) fixed tariffs on exports and imports; and (6) the surrender of Hong Kong to Britain in perpetuity. Opium was not legalized. The Treaty of Nanjing established the framework within which British trade with China could expand. It also marked the beginning of China's century of unequal treaties. *E.T.*

The Taiping Rebellion

The founder of the *Taiping tianguo*, or Heavenly Kingdom of Great Peace, was Hong Xiuquan (1813–64), of Hua County, Guangdong. He was of the Hakka (*Kejia*) linguistic group, an ethnic minority from which all the important leaders of the rebellion were drawn. Disappointed in the government examinations, Hong had hallucinations of ascending to Heaven and being commissioned by Jehovah to exterminate 'demons', which in Hong's mind were first understood to be the spirits of China's traditional folk religion. Under the influence of a Christian tract written by the convert Liang Fa (1789–1855), Hong believed he was the second son of Jehovah and younger brother of Jesus.

Proselytizing among Hakkas in Guangxi Province gave Hong's religious conversion a political twist. Oppressed by culturally distinct neighbouring groups, the Guangxi Hakkas formed a God Worshipping Society under the leadership of Hong's cousin, Feng Yunshan (1822–52). The society was a militarized self-defence league of religious congregations. Under the influence of Feng and local leaders such as Yang Xiuqing (d. 1856), Hakka ethnic consciousness developed national political ambitions, with anti-Manchu aims probably derived from the local secret society tradition. The 'demons' of Hong's dream now became identified in the Hakka mind with the Manchu regime.

Now began a long exodus from Guangxi towards the Yangtze valley, during which time Taiping doctrines and institutions were defined more explicitly. A more complex political structure was developed. Power was divided among 'kings' (*wang*), each with a regional designation plus an 'Assistant King'. Feng Yunshan was designated 'Southern King', and Hong himself remained 'Heavenly King', though with reduced executive authority. The real chief of staff and political leader was the Eastern King, Yang Xiuqing, who now entered trances and spoke as the Holy Ghost.

The Taipings fought northwards to the Yangtze at Wuchang, then descended to Nanjing, the seat of the Liangjiang governor-general. They captured the city in March 1853, and renamed it 'Heavenly Capital'. A northern expedition was launched towards the Qing capital at Beijing, which, however, was turned back near Tianjin. The rebellion was now in effect a regional regime, with military control extending over broad sections of the central and lower Yangtze, the richest region in China.

Institutions included prohibitions against opium, wine and tobacco; a strict segregation of the sexes (later abandoned); and a utopian 'land system' (apparently conceived on the northwards march), which defined a socio-political order based on state ownership of property (in trust for God), a hierarchy of residential producer groups based on congregations of 25 families, and a merging of political and military command at all levels. The system was based partly on the *Rites of Zhou*, a utopian text of late antiquity. The precarious military situation and the necessity of leaving local elites in place in order to collect taxes efficiently meant that this system was never effectively installed. Civil service examinations were instituted, however, based on Christian rather than Confucian themes.

Taiping religion, originally based on Hong's revelation, was enriched by a Chinese translation of the Bible (Gutzlaff version). Commentaries and tracts were issued by the theocrats themselves, principally Hong and the Eastern King, Yang Xiuqing.

Taiping military domination of the central Yangtze was shaken by internal dissension among the kings. Yang aimed at supreme power and sought to place himself on the same level of honour as Hong himself. Hong sought the aid of Wei Changhui, the Northern King, who killed Yang in September 1856, then was killed in turn by Hong, who feared his ambitions too. Shi Dakai (d. 1863), the Assistant King, was in turn suspected by Hong, and left the Heavenly Capital on a long, independent campaign which ended in his defeat and capture in 1863. The Taiping military position was rebuilt by Li Xiucheng (d. 1864)—named 'Loyal King'-and Chen Yucheng (d. 1862)—named 'Brave King'. In 1859 and 1860 Li campaigned eastward towards the Yangtze delta and established Taiping garrisons in the major cities of eastern Jiangsu and Zhejiang.

Opposing the Taipings, in addition to the Qing regular army under such commanders as Xiang Rong (1801–56), Zhang Guoliang (1823–60) and He Chun (d. 1860), were the new irregular armies of Zeng Guofan (1811–72) and his protégés, such as Li Hongzhang (1823–1901) and Zuo Zongtang (1812–85). These forces, organized on personalistic principles and indoctrinated with Confucian teachings, eventually assumed the major burden of suppressing the rebellion. Zeng, appointed Governor-general of the Liangjiang provinces, along with his brother Zeng Guoquan (1824–90), led his Hunan army in recapturing Anching (1861) and other Taiping strongholds. Li Hongzhang raised a mercenary force in his native Anhui, which fought the Taipings from the delta region, aided by the 'Ever-victorious Army', a foreign-led and armed auxiliary force which came under the command eventually of Charles Gordon, a British officer. In addition to this important foreign component, Li's forces were aided by British and French advisers and munitions, and briefly by troops from these countries

as well. The main burden of suppression, however, was borne by the Chinese forces of Zeng and Li. Nanjing was taken by Zeng Guoquan on 19 July 1864. Hong Xiuquan had himself died of illness during the siege, and most of his adherents were killed.

The Taiping world-view was in some respects quite traditional, despite their radical social aims. It appears that the Taipings were even less intellectually prepared than their Qing antagonists to cope with foreign intercourse, or to profit from it. The single exception was Hong's cousin Hong Ren'gan (1822–64), who was missionary-trained and as 'Shield King' sought unsuccessfully to institute Western-influenced economic and political reforms. Taiping Christianity, which seems to have died out as a spiritual force after 1864, was sufficiently eclectic to horrify Western missionaries and diplomats, and alien enough to repel most of China's literate Confucian elite.   *P.A.K.*

The Nian Rebellion

A regional rebellion of the Huaibei area (north of the Huai River) of diverse forms, the Nian movement, properly so-called, lasted from 1852 to 1868. Armed bandit gangs called *nian* (a band or group) existed as early as 1814. Some members of the White Lotus sect were among them, although salt-smuggling gangs and ordinary bandits were more prominent. Flooding of the Yellow River in 1853 and the militarization of Huaibei in response to the Taiping invasion allowed the *nian* to gain a foothold in settled society. Earth-walled communities were taken over by bandit chieftains, and 'Nian' became a proper name designating a league of semi-militarized communities. Whole villages would set forth on seasonal plundering expeditions, bringing back loot to their walled fortresses.

An early leader, Zhang Luoxing (d. 1863) declared himself leader of a large Nian confederacy in 1852, grouping his adherents into a military system based on 'banners'. Nian imagery now included Ming restorationist and White Lotus symbolism, although the ideology of the movement remained eclectic. No dynastic regime was ever constructed.

A new phase of the movement began in 1864, with the absorption of some Taiping forces under Lai Wenguang (d. 1868), and a reliance on mobile cavalry forces wholly separated from the old community bases. The movement was suppressed by 1868 by forces of Zeng Guofan and Li Hongzhang, which relied on a systematic effort to control the earth-wall settlements and a blockade strategy to encircle and destroy the mounted Nian armies.

P.A.K.

Muslim rebellions

The 'Panthay Rebellion'—or uprising of followers of Islam in Yunnan Province—broke out in 1856, a product of ethnic-religious hatred between local Muslims and Han Chinese. Its leaders were the Grand Priest, Ma Dexin (d. 1874), Ma Rulong (d. 1891), and Du Wenxiu (d. 1872). Du established a capital at Dali, where his kingdom survived for 15 years. Ma Rulong defected to the Qing in 1860, which turned the tide against the rebels. Dali fell in 1873 in a campaign led by Ma and the Qing general Cen Yuying (1829–89).

The Muslim Rebellion in the northwest (1862–75) was a response to official discrimination against Muslim subjects in Shaanxi and Gansu Provinces. It was also fuelled by conflict between adherents of the 'New Teaching' and orthodox Muslims. Covering wide areas of Shaanxi and Gansu, and headed by a 'New Teaching' leader, Ma Hualong (d. 1871), the revolt was ultimately suppressed by Governor-general Zuo Zongtang.

Both these devastating ethnic-religious uprisings demonstrate that although the Qing dynasty had had unprecedented success in subjugating the peoples of the inner Asian frontier, its policies for management of internal ethnic minorities were relatively unsuccessful.

P.A.K.

Small Sword Society Uprising (Shanghai and vicinity, 1853–5)

A branch of the secret society of the Triads, or Heaven and Earth Society (Tiandihui), the Small Sword Society is thought to have been founded in Xiamen about 1850. The society established a branch in Shanghai, with unemployed sailors and artisans as its principal members. Ultimately it comprised seven branches with a membership drawn from Fujian, Guangdong, Zhejiang and Shanghai. Its leader was Liu Lichuan (d. 1855), a Cantonese. Some members infiltrated local militia corps raised to defend Shanghai against the Taiping Rebellion in 1853. The uprising can be seen as a product of the economic dislocation caused by the opening of foreign trade at Shanghai, popular outrage at corruption in the Jiangnan grain tribute tax, and the inspiration of the Taipings.

The society sparked a successful attack on nearby Jiading, on 5 September 1853, with slogans denouncing corrupt officials and onerous surtaxes. On 7 September they attacked and soon captured the walled city of Shanghai, and shortly afterwards the cities of Chuansha and Qingpu. The society founded a regime called 'The Great Ming' (*Da Mingguo*, a standard Triad restorationist

symbol). Later this was dropped, as the society claimed affiliation with the Taiping government in Nanjing. There was, however, no actual military cooperation between the two groups. Consultation between Qing officials and the consuls of Great Britain, France and the USA led to a joint Chinese-French attack on the walled city of Shanghai, which was quickly taken. Liu Lichuan was killed as his forces retreated from the city.

P.A.K.

Manchuria and Russia

The Manchu rulers of China had, since the earliest years of the Qing dynasty, attempted to exclude foreigners from Manchuria. They wished first to have Manchuria available as a haven if they were expelled from China. They also sought to maintain their monopoly on furs, ginseng, gold and other valuable products of Manchuria. Above all, they were anxious to preserve the purity of Manchu culture and traditions. The Qing emperors therefore prohibited their Chinese subjects from settling in Manchuria, which at that time comprised the three provinces of Fengtian, Jilin and Heilongjiang. By the Sino-Russian Treaty of Nerchinsk (1689), they succeeded in laying claim to the Amur River region, thus blocking Russian penetration into Manchuria. At the height of its power in the 17th and 18th centuries the Qing court preserved the three northeastern provinces for the Manchus.

As the Qing declined, however, it could not enforce its policy of exclusion. Starting in the late 18th century Chinese farmers, merchants and craftsmen, who were attracted by the fertile land and the abundant natural resources of Manchuria, began to migrate illegally into the Manchus' ancestral homeland. Even more ominous was Russian expansion along China's northeastern frontier. The Tsarist court had, as a result of the treaties of Nerchinsk and Kiakhta (1728), established a regular and profitable overland trade with China. In the 19th century it began to face competition from the less costly and less precarious seaborne trade with China initiated by the Europeans and by the Americans. The British victory over the Chinese in the Opium War opened up more Chinese ports to Western trade, further undercutting Russia's overland commerce. The Opium War also exposed China's military weakness. Seeking to stave off Western commercial competition and to profit from China's distress, the Russians ignored the Treaties of Nerchinsk and Kiakhta and advanced into northeastern Manchuria.

Nikolai Muraviev, the Russian governor-general of eastern Siberia, was the most forceful advocate of an aggressive policy in Manchuria. He believed that Russian control of the lower Amur River would lead to an expansion of trade between Siberia and Manchuria, encourage more Russian colonists to settle in Siberia, enable Russia to compete with the Western powers for the China seacoast trade, and create a buffer zone in case of a Western, principally British, attack on Siberia. From 1849 to 1856 he dispatched three expeditions to explore the Amur and to colonize northeast Manchuria. His forces founded such new towns as Nikolaevsk (named for Tsar Nicholas I), Mikhailovsk and Bogorodsk along the northern banks of the Amur.

The Qing court protested against these violations of the treaties it had signed with Russia, but its officials, beset by the Taiping Rebellion and by military threats from Britain and France, could not prevent Muraviev's incursions. In 1858 the court, hoping to

gain Russian support against the British and French, ordered Yishan, the military governor of Heilongjiang, to negotiate with Muraviev. Within a few weeks, Muraviev and Yishan had signed the Treaty of Aigun which virtually granted Russia jurisdiction over the northern banks of the Amur and provided for joint Qing-Russian control over the land east of the Ussuri River to the sea. The Qing court, fearful of further Russian encroachments in the northeast, did not ratify the treaty. The joint British-French attack against Beijing in 1860, however, forced the court to make concessions not only to the two Western powers but also to the Russians. In 1860 the Qing reluctantly signed the Treaty of Beijing, and in

MANCHURIA: 19TH CENTURY

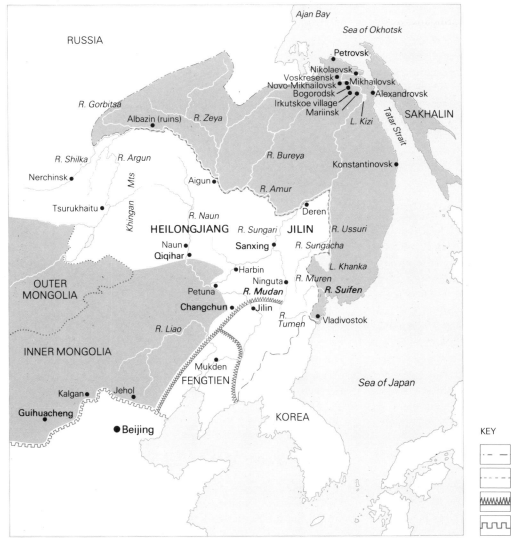

KEY

– · –	Border between Russia and Qing China in 1689
– – –	Border between Russia and Qing China from 1860
⋀⋀⋀⋀	Willow Palisades
⊓⊔⊓⊔	The Great Wall

the following year its officials and their Russian counterparts negotiated a supplementary agreement which delineated the boundary
in Manchuria. The Russians obtained the northern banks of the
Amur and sole jurisdiction over the maritime territories east of the
Ussuri as well as exclusive commercial and diplomatic privileges
in Manchuria.

Despite these gains, the Russians did not, in the late 19th century, fulfil their expectations. They were unable to overcome
British supremacy in the China coast trade. The population of
Siberia increased but not as dramatically as the Russians had
hoped. Similarly, the overland trade via Siberia and Manchuria
expanded, but Russia's imports from China outstripped its exports
to China. Moreover, the Russian pressure in Manchuria caused the
Qing to reconsider its policy of exclusion. To counteract Russian
influence and to save Manchuria for China, the Qing began to
encourage Chinese colonization. In the middle of the 19th century
the population of Manchuria was about 3 million, but by 1895–
1900 it had grown to 9 million, most of whom were recent Chinese
migrants. This dramatic rise in population eventually permitted
China to control Manchuria despite Russian and Japanese aggression in the late 19th and early 20th centuries. Neither the Russians
nor the Japanese could persuade enough of their own people to
settle in Manchuria so that they could wrest control of the area

M.R.

Xinjiang

Xinjiang became a province of China in 1884. The Qing, however, had controlled the region since the 1750s and had established a military administration. Qing garrisons and military
governors were stationed in Dzungaria, the area north of the
Tianshan Mountains which was characterized by a nomadic pastoral economy, and East Turkestan, the area south of the Tianshan which supported a mixed economy of oasis agriculture,
trade and some pastoralism. The Qing court rarely interfered in
local affairs and, in theory, granted self-rule to the local leaders.
It did not proscribe the practice of Islam in its newly-conquered
lands nor did it prohibit domestic or foreign commerce. As long
as Xinjiang remained peaceful and paid the required taxes, the
Qing rulers would not impose new religious or cultural patterns.
Qing policy would seem to have been benevolent and not overly
exploitative. Yet Xinjiang in the 19th century was to become the
most rebellious territory in the Qing empire.

Rebellions broke out, in part, because the Qing could not control its own officials and people and the corrupt native rulers. The
officials sent by the Qing often exploited the local populations—
the Uighurs, Kazakhs and Kirghiz—in Xinjiang. Similarly, the

Manchu banner troops, on occasion, took advantage of the local
peoples. Chinese Muslims (known as '*Tungans*') and Han Chinese
from China proper, whom the Qing court encouraged to settle in
Xinjiang, grated on the sensibilities of the non-Chinese, who must
have feared that they would be swamped by Chinese colonists.
The local rulers often cooperated with corrupt Qing officials in
exploiting their own people. The Muslims, believing themselves to
be oppressed, were thus more receptive to the New Teachings
(*Xinjiao*), which vigorously called for a pure form of Islam
untainted by Chinese influences.

The unrest caused by official exploitation and by the development of a resurgent Islamic order erupted into several rebellions
or holy wars (*Jihad*) in the 19th century. The khanate of Kokand
was one of the main sources of support for the rebels. Kokand,
which had initiated a profitable trade with China's northwest in
1760, bridled at Qing regulations on commerce and used the rebellions to extract concessions from the court. Diyā 'ali-Dīn in 1815,
Jahangir from 1820 to 1828, and Walī Khan in 1857 led unsuccessful holy wars against the Qing. In 1830 Kokand itself launched
a more successful attack on Xinjiang which compelled the Qing to
grant extraordinary commercial and diplomatic privileges to that
khanate. These outbreaks culminated in the full-scale Muslim
rebellions which plagued China's northwest from 1862 to 1878.

Russia capitalized on the unrest to acquire more territory and
concessions from the Qing. In 1851 Russian merchants were
empowered to trade in Yili and Tarbagatai, and the Russian government was permitted to set up consulates in the same towns. In
1860 Kashgar was opened to Russian trade and, in 1864, the Tsarist and Qing courts signed the Treaty of Tarbagatai, by which
China turned over most of the lands north of Lake Issyk-kul to
Russia. The Treaty of St Petersburg of 1881 granted Russia the
right to establish consulates in Suzhou and Turfan and offered the
Tsarist court control of Dzungaria west of the town of Yili.

Fearful of additional Muslim rebellions and of further Russian
incursions, the Qing changed the status of Xinjiang from a military
colony to an integral part of China. In 1884 Xinjiang became a
province and was accorded a civil administration of its own. This
transformation did not deter the Muslims of Xinjiang from rebel-
ling against Qing authority for the remaining 25 years or so of the
dynasty.

M.R.

The Arrow War (1856–60)

The Arrow War climaxed the controversies between China and
the West in the post-Opium War period, such as the British right
to enter the city of Canton, the extension of trade beyond the five

ports, the legalization of opium, and the diplomatic residence in Beijing. The pent-up dissatisfaction exploded over a minor incident in Canton involving a Chinese-owned, Hong Kong-registered *lorcha* (a Chinese–Western hybrid vessel), the *Arrow*. On 8 October 1856 Chinese police boarded the *Arrow* to arrest 12 Chinese crewmen on suspicion of piracy and smuggling, and during the turmoil, the British flag was torn. Harry Parkes, British consul at Canton, demanded an apology to the flag and the release of the crew. The Chinese did release the crew but refused to apologize, so Parkes had the British navy bombard Canton. The Chinese retaliated by burning the foreign 'factories'.

Britain was reluctant to be dragged into war by a petty consul but felt duty-bound to defend its honour, and sent an expedition under Lord Elgin. France sent another under Baron Gros on the pretext of avenging the murder of a Catholic priest. The Anglo-French forces overran Canton, captured Governor-general Ye Mingchen (1807–59), and created a puppet government under Parkes. They moved northwards to Tianjin and forced on the Chinese the Treaties of Tianjin in June 1858, which provided for diplomatic residence in Beijing, the opening of 10 new ports and the payment of indemnities. Russia and the USA obtained similar treaties by virtue of their most-favoured-nation status.

In 1859 Elgin's brother, Frederick Bruce, arrived to exchange the ratifications. Insisting on exchanging them in Beijing rather than in Shanghai as the Chinese wanted, Bruce ignored their warnings and sailed north. He ran into a blockade at Dagu, where the Chinese defeated him. After this 'Dagu Repulse', Britain and France sent Elgin and Gros back to China and the Anglo-French

Prince Gong, head of the *Zongli yamen* (Foreign Office).

forces occupied Beijing, burned the Summer Palace and drove the Emperor into exile. Prince Gong, the Emperor's younger brother, accepted the Conventions of Beijing (1860), which re-affirmed diplomatic residence in Beijing, increased the indemnities, and ceded the Kowloon Peninsula to Britain. China was now tightly bound by unequal treaties from which it was not entirely freed until 1943. *I.C.Y.H.*

Tongzhi Restoration

The Tongzhi Restoration refers to a period of dynastic revival during the reign of Emperor Tongzhi (1862–74), when China was able to maintain peace with foreign powers and suppress internal rebellions. The Self-strengthening Movement, the revival of Confucian morality, the reorganization of the civil and military administrations, and the rehabilitation of the economy all pointed towards a second blossoming of the dynasty. These efforts were made under the co-regency (*tongzhi* means 'ruling together') of the two Empresses Dowager, Cixi and Cian, with the support of Prince Gong and provincial leaders Zeng Guofan, Zuo Zongtang (1812–85), and Li Hongzhang. The spirit of restoring strength and reviving the old order prompted contemporaries and historians to refer to the period as the 'Tongzhi Restoration'. In fact, it was merely a temporary recovery. *I.C.Y.H.*

The Self-strengthening Movement (Ziqiang)

The movement 'To make oneself strong' was promoted in the early 1860s by Feng Guifen (1809–74), who invoked the words of the scholar Wei Yuan (1795–1856) that China should 'learn the superior barbarian techniques to control the barbarians'. The idea won the support of Prince Gong and Wenxiang in the capital and Zeng Guofan, Zuo Zongtang (1812–85) and Li Hongzhang in the provinces. From 1861 to 1895 a number of diplomatic and military modernization projects were launched, of which the more salient ones were: the *Zongli yamen* (foreign office) in 1861 and its language school, *Tongwen guan*, in 1862; the Jiangnan Arsenal, 1865; the Fuzhou Dockyard, 1866; the Nanjing Arsenal, 1867; the Tianjin Machine Factory, 1870; the dispatch of Chinese students to the USA, 1872; the Chinese Merchants Steam Navigation Company, 1872; the Kaiping Coal Mines, 1877; and the Beiyang Fleet in 1888.

Although the list looks impressive, it represents only a superficial attempt at modernization, hardly scratching the surface of Western civilization. There was no plan to remake China into a modern state; the objective was to strengthen the existing order, not replace it. China's defeat by Japan in 1895 after 30 years of 'Self-strengthening' exposed the limitations of the movement.

The Yangwu Movement was virtually the same as the Self-strengthening Movement, referring to gun-making, ship-building, mining, shipping, telegraph, etc.—generally items of foreign origin. *Yangwu* is frequently translated as 'foreign matters', as distinguished from foreign or diplomatic affairs. *I.C.Y.H.*

Guandu Shangban Enterprises

This term refers to a type of merchant operation under government supervision during the Self-strengthening period, such as the China Merchants Steam Navigation Company, the Kaiping and the Shanghai Cotton Cloth Mills. Capital came from private investors, who were responsible for the profits or losses without involving the government. But the latter, as patron, might provide loans and frequently appointed officials or approved merchants to head these enterprises; hence they smacked of bureaucracy and nepotism. *I.C.Y.H.*

Li Hongzhang with W.E. Gladstone at Hawarden Castle.

Zeng Guofan (1811–72)

Born on 28 November 1811 in Xiangxiang, Hunan, Zeng Guofan was a scholar, general and statesman best known for suppressing the Taiping Rebellion. Obtaining the *jinshi* degree in 1838, he entered the Hanlin Academy and rose to be the junior vice-president of the Board of Rites in 1849. In late 1852, while mourning his deceased mother, he was urged by the court to organize a defence against the high-riding Taipings. Reluctantly, he cut short the mourning period, studied military strategy and trained a temporary army called the 'Hunan Braves' or the 'Hunan Army' (*Xiangjun*) along with a small navy to fight the Taipings. Persevering through early failure, Zeng gradually turned the tide. By 1864 his brother broke into Nanjing and toppled the Taiping kingdom. Zeng became the most powerful and admired scholar-official-general in the country. He remained at Nanjing as governor-general of Liangjiang, disbanded most of his Hunan Army to avoid Manchu suspicion and promoted the reprinting of classical works destroyed during the civil war.

Zeng exemplified the traditional Confucian virtues and many viewed him as a model official while his critics condemned him as 'traitor and executioner'. Although a traditionalist, he realized China's need for change in the new international situation and supported the programmes of the Self-strengthening Movement.

Zeng was probably the greatest statesman of his time but he left a legacy of military regionalism based on personal loyalty, which many believe was the seed of later warlordism. *I.C.Y.H.*

Li Hongzhang (1823–1901)

The scholar, statesman and leading modernizer Li Hongzhang was born on 15 February 1823 in Hefei, Anhui. He received the *jinshi* degree in 1847, worked on the staff of Zeng Guofan, and rose to eminence during the Taiping and Nian campaigns. Appointed governor-general of Zhili and superintendent of trade for the Three Northern Ports in 1870, and enjoying the favour of Empress Dowager Cixi, Li was virtually China's 'prime minister' until 1895. He frequently overshadowed the *Zongli yamen* (foreign office) by negotiating foreign treaties and settling disputes.

It was Li who cried out that China must change in order to meet the unprecedented foreign challenge. He promoted the modernization programmes of the Self-strengthening Movement, and was instrumental in creating or sponsoring the Jiangnan Arsenal, the Nanjing Arsenal, the Tianjin Machine Factory, the China Merchants Steam Navigation Company, the Chinese educational mission to the USA, the Imperial Telegraph Bureau and the Beiyang

Fleet. Yet for all this apparent achievement, Li was unable to prevent China's defeat by Japan in 1895, and was severely criticized by his countrymen. He survived, however, and the court relied on him to negotiate a peace settlement with Japan in 1895, a secret alliance with Russia against Japan in 1896 and the Peace Protocol of 1901 after the Boxer Uprising. On 7 November 1901 the exhausted 'Bismarck of China' died, a frustrated man. His attempts to save China by piecemeal modernization without corresponding institutional reform was superficial at best. His integrity was also questionable at times. Yet without him the twilight of the dynasty would have been much dimmer. *I.C.Y.H.*

Zongli yamen

This term is the abbreviation of *Zongli geguo shiwu yamen* (Office for the General Administration of the Affairs of the Different Nations), or foreign office, established in 1861. Heretofore China, the Middle Kingdom or Celestial Empire, had not maintained a foreign office. The Treaties of Tianjin (1858) and the Conventions of Beijing (1860) gave foreign powers the right to diplomatic residence in Beijing, and foreign legations were established in 1861. Foreign representatives, therefore, demanded a centralized foreign affairs organ in the Chinese government and the need clearly existed for the creation of a new foreign office.

The *Zongli yamen* was governed by a Controlling Board appointed by the emperor, with a prince of the blood serving as its head and a number of ministers as its members (from 3 in 1861 to 13 in 1884), who were all concurrent high metropolitan officials. Below them were 16 secretaries, half of them Manchu and half Chinese. It maintained five bureaux: Russian, British, French, American and Coastal Defence. In addition, the Inspectorate-general of Customs and the *Tongwen guan* (language school) were attached to it.

Conceived of as a temporary office with no power to create policy (such power belonged to the emperor and the Grand Council) but only the obligation to execute it, the influence of the *Yamen* depended on that of its political advocates. Since Prince Gong, the long-time presiding officer, and Wenxiang, the chief minister, were both grand councillors, their recommendations were usually approved. But after Wenxiang's death in 1876 and Prince Gong's dismissal in 1884, the *Yamen*'s influence waned steadily in direct proportion to the rise of Li Hongzhang, whom the Empress Dowager Cixi entrusted increasingly with foreign matters. In 1901 the *Zongli yamen* passed out of existence in favour of a new Ministry of Foreign Affairs (*Waiwubu*). *I.C.Y.H.*

Treaty ports

These were places designated by China's treaties with foreign powers as open to foreign residence and trade. Under the Treaty of Nanjing (1842) Canton, Xiamen, Fuzhou, Ningbo and Shanghai were the first to be opened. The Treaties of Tianjin (1858) and the Conventions of Beijing (1860) opened 11 additional ports—Niuzhuang, Hankou, Zhenjiang, Jiujiang, Danshui (Tamsui), Tainan, Shantou (Swatow), Zhifu (Chefoo), Jiongzhou, Nanjing and Tianjin (1860). By the end of the Qing dynasty (1912), there were approximately 50 treaty ports.

These ports were symbols of foreign imperialism and a constant reminder of China's semi-colonial status. On the other hand, they nurtured a hybrid culture and a cosmopolitan atmosphere, with an urban-commercial orientation that served as a source of Western influence and led China towards modernization, reform and revolution. The 'treaty port intellectuals and mandarins' played an important role in the Self-strengthening Movement, while the merchants and compradores provided a good portion of the needed capital and managerial skills. *I.C.Y.H.*

Missionaries

Many early missionaries were said to have behaved with an attitude of self-righteousness, racial arrogance and cultural superiority. They won a privileged position through the unequal treaties and forcefully interceded between their converts and local Chinese officials. The gentry, in particular, viewed them as a disruptive threat to Chinese orthodoxy and incited mobs against them with ridiculous stories and false charges (e.g. the Tianjin Massacre).

However, from the 1880s Timothy Richard, W. A. P. Martin, Young J. Allen and other like-minded missionaries grew sympathetic to Chinese culture and customs, and decided to 'secularize' their work through the promotion of Western knowledge. From 'saving the heathen from the sufferings of hell', they moved to 'saving the heathen from the hell of suffering in this world'. They sponsored schools, libraries, hospitals, newspapers and magazines to promote Western culture and progress. With their Society for the Diffusion of Christian and General Knowledge among the Chinese, they reached a wider public and touched such important personages as Wang Tao (1828–97?), Li Hongzhang, Kang Youwei, Liang Qichao, and Sun Yat-sen. By disseminating the idea of national salvation through reform and revolution, the missionaries played an important role in the modern transformation of China. *I.C.Y.H.*

TREATY PORTS

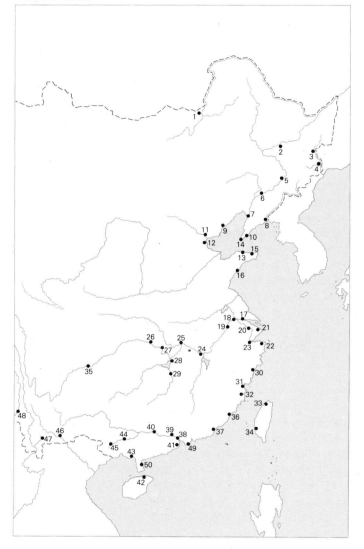

KEY

1 Manzhouli	18 Nanjing (Tiangning)	35 Chongqing
2 Harbin	19 Wuhu	36 Xiamen
3 Suifenhe	20 Suzhou	37 Shantou
4 Hunchun	21 Shanghai	38 Guangzhou
5 Jilin	22 Ningbo	39 Sanshui
6 Mukden (Shenyang)	23 Hangzhou	40 Wuzhou
7 Niuzhuang (Yingkou)	24 Jiujiang	41 Jiangmen
8 Andong	25 Hankou	42 Qiongzhou
9 Qinwangdao	26 Shashi	43 Beihai
10 Dalian	27 Shashi	44 Nanning
11 Tianjin	28 Yuezhou	45 Longzhou
12 Dagu	29 Changsha	46 Mengzi
13 Zhifu (Yantai)	30 Wenzhou	47 Simao
14 Port Arthur (Lüshun)	31 Sanduao	48 Tengyue (Momein)
15 Weihaiwei	32 Fuzhou	49 Hong Kong
16 Qingdao	33 Danshui	50 Guangzhouwan
17 Zhenjiang	34 Tainan	(Zhanjian)

Tianjin Massacre

This refers to a major anti-foreign and anti-Christian riot in 1870. It was a typical 'missionary case' (*jiaoan*) grown out of Chinese xenophobia, suspicion and superstition, and foreign arrogance and insensitivity to Chinese feelings. Christianity, in Chinese eyes, was a heterodox sect and a disturbing influence. Tianjin was particularly vulnerable to anti-foreign sentiment since it had been occupied by Anglo-French forces in 1858 and 1860. In 1869 a French Catholic church with an orphanage was built on the site of a razed Buddhist temple. It offered payment for orphans, thereby giving rascals an incentive to kidnap children. Rumour became rife that the missionaries extracted the hearts and eyes of the children to make medicine. With gentry agitation, the incensed public gathered to demand justice. The truculent French consul, Henri Fontanier, fired a pistol and killed a Chinese. The mob fell on him and killed 10 nuns, two priests and several other foreigners. When foreigners demanded reprisal, the court asked Zeng Guofan to investigate. His conciliatory approach provoked a barrage of criticism and drew accusations of appeasement, and he was replaced by Li Hongzhang. Li settled the case by agreeing to punish the culprits heavily, pay 400 000 silver tales (a unit of weight used in China for silver bullion) for the loss of lives and properties, and send an apology mission to France.

I.C.Y.H.

Sino-French War (1884–5)

As France extended its influence northwards over Annam (northern Vietnam) and acquired the right to navigate the Red River by the Treaty of 'Peace and Alliance' (1874), the government of Annam asked for Chinese protection. Initially China sent only the irregular 'Black Flag Army', remnants of the Taipings, but after 1883 regular troops were dispatched.

Chinese officialdom was divided between Li Hongzhang's espousal of a peace settlement and the *Qingliu* (Purists) group's clamour for war to defend China's honour and uphold its obligations to a tributary state. The court vacillated. When the Li–Fournier agreement of 11 May 1884 specifying Chinese withdrawal and recognition of French interests in Vietnam was rejected by both governments, fighting resumed. The French navy attacked Keelung (Jilong) in Taiwan and also destroyed the Fuzhou Dockyard, which was built with French aid in the 1860s. A preliminary treaty was arranged in Paris on 4 April 1885 by James D. Campbell, the London agent of Sir Robert Hart, and in June a formal treaty was signed. France won complete control of Vietnam, dealing a shattering blow to the Qing tributary system and revealing the ineffectiveness of the Self-strengthening Movement. *I.C.Y.H.*

Empress Dowager Cixi (1835–1908)

Cixi, the woman who ruled China from 1861 to 1908, was born on 29 November 1835, to a minor Manchu family, Yehonala. A concubine of the Emperor Xianfeng (1851–61), she bore him a son while the Empress, Cian, was childless. When the Emperor died in 1861, Cixi, Cian and Prince Gong staged a successful *coup d'état* and Cixi became the real power as Empress Dowager, although she shared the title of regent with Cian and Prince Gong. The two dowagers sat behind a screen to receive ministerial reports, but it was Cixi who dominated important decisions. She was a narrow-minded, selfish and uneducated woman, whose primary consideration was to keep herself in power as long as possible. She patronized corrupt eunuch politicians, misused public funds, obstructed reform and manipulated the imperial succession. When Emperor Tongzhi died in 1874, she managed to install another boy emperor, Guangxu, to ensure her continued regency. Politically, she was astute and decisive, a master at the game of 'balance of weakness'. She must be held largely responsible for the failure of dynastic regeneration and modernization. Yet her powerful personality lent a certain stability to government. Three years after her death in 1908, the Qing dynasty was overthrown. *I.C.Y.H.*

The Empress Dowager Cixi in 1903.

Sino-Japanese War (1894–5)

This war between China and Japan was fought over Korea, against whom Japan had long clamoured for a punitive expedition. Japan's activities were intensified after its annexation of Liuqiu in 1879. China, although caught up in conflicts with foreign powers, sought to defend its most important tributary and buffer state. In the early 1880s Beijing urged Korea to open up to Western trade and diplomacy as a means of checkmating the Japanese. Li Hongzhang was put in charge of Korean affairs, while Yuan Shikai was installed as Chinese Resident in Korea.

The immediate causes of conflict were the assassination in 1894 of a pro-Japanese Korean politician, Kim Ok-kyun, in Shanghai and the Tonghak Uprising in Korea, which gave Japan an excuse to send troops. The insurrection had been suppressed by Yuan, but the Japanese troops would not evacuate. Li tried diplomacy to avoid a military confrontation, but to no avail. On 1 August 1894 war was declared and China, after 30 years of Self-strengthening, was soundly beaten on land and at sea. The Qing court sent Li to Japan to negotiate a peace. The Treaty of Shimonoseki of April 1895 required that China recognize the independence of Korea, cede Taiwan, the Pescadores and the Liaodong Peninsula, pay an indemnity of 200 million silver tales, open four ports and allow Japanese to manufacture locally in China. The Liaodong Peninsula was retroceded by Japan under the Triple Intervention of Russia, France and Germany, at a cost of 30 million tales to China. The defeat sealed the fate of the Qing dynasty by totally exposing the weakness of the regime. Externally, it invited further encroachment in the 'scramble for concessions', and internally it encouraged movements for reform and revolution. *I.C.Y.H.*

The Reform Movement of 1898

The Reform Movement of 1898 was the culmination of efforts by the scholar-official class to improve China's lot within the existing system. It ran parallel with the revolutionary movement which aimed at overthrowing the dynasty and replacing it with a new kind of government, which had found expression in the Taiping Rebellion, and later in the revolutionary activities of Sun Yat-sen and the final eruption of the Wuchang Uprising.

Sporadic proposals for reform by scholar-officials predated the Opium Wars, but the subsequent encroachment by foreign powers and the internal unrest associated with it had given added urgency and impetus to the need for reform. Over a period of some 30 years disconnected efforts were made by various provincial authorities to introduce Western machinery and weapons to enrich and strengthen the nation in what has become known as the 'Self-strengthening Movement'. The philosophy behind this effort was best expressed by the now famous maxim that 'Chinese learning provided the basis' and 'Western learning was for practical use.' But long before China's defeat by Japan in the Sino-Japanese War (1894–5) had proved the inadequacy of this policy, a new group of literati emerged who urged that China should go further in its reforms and learn from the West. Among these were Kang Youwei and a group of young scholars who had gathered round him. The crisis following the Sino-Japanese War, and the so-called 'scramble for concessions', which threatened to break up China, finally won the Emperor's patronage for the persistent Kang Youwei. His followers were admitted into the government's inner cabinet and for some 100 days, from the middle of June to the third week of September 1898 (hence the name 'Hundred-Day Reform'), reform edicts were issued in profusion in the name of the Emperor. For the first time a reformist policy had been adopted by the government and a propaganda machine resembling that of a modern political party had been set in motion.

The conservative majority, however, both at court and in the provinces, felt their very existence threatened by the proposed reform measures, and rallied round the Empress Dowager Cixi, the Emperor's aunt to whom he owed the throne. Although ostensibly in retirement, she still retained the ultimate authority on important issues of state, and kept her hold through numerous court officials and eunuchs who owed her their sole loyalty. Realizing the Empress Dowager was a powerful opponent, the reformers sought to enlist the support of Yuan Shikai, the commander of the new Chinese army. However, Yuan betrayed them to Cixi, who, on 21 September, with the ruthlessness that characterized her nearly 50 year *de facto* rule over China, staged a coup which put an end to the reform movement within a matter of hours. The Emperor was made a prisoner in his own palace and all the reform edicts were rescinded. Six prominent reformers, including the younger brother of Kang Youwei, were put to death, and many others dismissed, imprisoned or exiled.

Kang Youwei (1858–1927)

A scholar of the Confucian classics and leader of the Reform Movement of 1898, Kang first came to public notice through a controversial work in which he portrayed Confucius as a reformer. This interpretation was considered by conservatives as so outrageously revolutionary that it had to be officially suppressed. Like many enlightened intellectuals of his day, Kang saw change in China's institutions and education system as the only way to overcome internal crises greatly aggravated by foreign aggression. He resorted to memorializing the throne, urging various reform measures, and succeeded in gaining support among

metropolitan and provincial officials. After Germany's seizure of Jiaozhou, his proposals finally gained imperial approval. With his inspiration and advice and that of his supporters now controlling the inner cabinet of the government, reform by decree was launched. It had lasted barely three months, however, when the Empress Dowager Cixi staged a coup.

With British help, Kang managed to avoid arrest. He lived in exile for 15 years in various parts of the world continuing his campaign. During this time radical changes took place in China, and Kang's path and those of his fellow-countrymen became more and more divergent. After the Boxer Uprising, as China drifted towards revolution through belated and ineffectual reforms, including, ironically, nearly all those measures Kang had advocated, Kang the constitutional reformer became a die-hard monarchist. Upon returning to China in 1913, he became an indefatigable monarchist campaigner and a fierce critic of Sun Yat-sen and of the Republic. He devoted himself to the restoration of Manchu imperial rule and played a conspicuous part in Zhang Xun's (1854–1923) imperial restoration attempt of 1917. But these efforts came to nothing and he is chiefly remembered for his role in the 1898 Reform Movement.

Liang Qichao (1873–1939)

For some 30 years China's leading publicist, Liang Qichao came first into prominence during the Reform Movement of 1898. A follower of Kang Youwei, he emerged as a leading light of the movement when in Beijing in 1895 he helped to draft the reform memorial jointly presented to the Throne by the candidates for metropolitan examination then gathered in the capital. Thereafter, he devoted himself to the cause of reform by lecturing and especially by writing. With the aid of the Japanese legation in Beijing, he narrowly escaped arrest when the Empress Dowager Cixi staged the 1898 palace coup, and continued to campaign for reform in Japan through the journal he established there. A prolific writer with a brilliant, lucid and appealing style, Liang came to exercise a great influence on the Chinese intelligentsia. Because of this, his cooperation was eagerly sought by Sun Yat-sen and his revolutionary colleagues who also had their headquarters at that time in Tokyo. However, instead of cooperation there arose a fierce rivalry between Sun's camp who contended it was essential to overthrow the dynasty and establish a republic, and Liang's who advocated constitutional monarchy. Liang meanwhile had become estranged from the position adopted by his former teacher Kang Youwei, who by now was fast becoming a die-hard monarchist.

After the Manchu regime was overthrown, Liang participated actively in Republican politics, serving in various capacities in Yuan Shikai's and subsequent governments. He also played a prominent role in the campaign against Yuan's monarchical attempt and later against the short-lived Restoration of 1917 in which Kang Youwei was involved. A purveyor of knowledge of Western history and institutions, Liang, like some of his contemporaries lost his admiration for the West after his European tour following the First World War. He also became a critic of Marxism, which had begun to make an impact in Chinese intellectual circles in the wake of the May Fourth Movement. By then, however, he had been overtaken by a new generation of intellectual leaders, although his more scholarly works continued to attract some attention.

H.-M.L.

The Boxer Uprising (1900)

The Boxer Uprising was a popular protest movement by the peasants of northern China directed against Manchu misrule and foreign encroachment. Originating in Shandong Province with links going back to the anti-dynastic White Lotus Society, the movement was formed to oppose oppression and extortion by local officials. Seen as the spearhead of foreign influence in the interior of China, the Christian missionaries along with their converts became ready targets for the deprived and discontented. Germany's seizure of Jiaozhou, coming at a time of worsening rural economic depression, accelerated the movement which spread rapidly, attracting various dissident elements to its ranks. With no binding ideology and insufficient weaponry, it fell back on ancient popular beliefs, and its adherents practised martial exercises known as 'Harmony Fists', hence the name 'Boxer'. The bravery of the Boxers in the face of overwhelming weaponry, believing that they were impervious to the foreigners' bullets, also won for them the attribute of fanaticism.

When the movement eventually spilled over from Shandong into the metropolitan province of Zhili, in which Beijing was situated, the Manchu government with the conservative extremists now in control, wedged between threats from within and threats from the powers without, tried to neutralize them by diverting the internal fury against the foreign aggressors. Finally, with the approval of Empress Dowager Cixi, who blamed foreign influence for the recently suppressed Reform Movement and who resented foreign intervention on the Emperor's behalf following the coup of 1898, the discontented peasants, supported by government troops, laid siege to the foreign legations in Beijing.

In retaliation, the foreign powers sent expeditionary forces to China and ended the siege by occupying the Chinese capital on 14 August 1900. With efficient organization, which the Boxers lacked, the foreign armies added to the devastation wreaked by the Boxers. Beijing was stripped bare and the surrounding countryside and villages laid to waste at the slightest suspicion of anti-foreign feeling. The missionaries and their converts, whose bullying behaviour had earlier made them the main target of the hostile mob, now emerged to take revenge. Meanwhile, the Empress Dowager and the Emperor had fled to Xi'an whence the court did not return until January 1902, leaving Li Hongzhang to save the situation.

An outcome of the negotiations was that the powers, by the Peace Protocol of 7 September 1901, extorted a crippling indemnity from China. So outrageously excessive was the indemnity that some foreign governments, notably the USA and Great Britain, volunteered to rechannel some of it to finance the education of students abroad (who were known as Boxer Indemnity Scholars). By the same protocol foreign troops remained in occupation of important lines of communication as well as at many strategic points, including a large area of the Inner City of Beijing, which became known as the Legation Quarter. Russia, ostensibly prompted by fear of a general rising, took to the wholesale massacring of the Chinese in the territory ceded by China to Russia in 1860, and also seized the whole of Manchuria. The continued occupation of Manchuria in disregard of treaty commitments, was to become one of the causes of the Russo-Japanese War (1904–5).

The events of 1900 had far-reaching consequences. While the tenacity and fanaticism with which the Chinese peasants fought, coupled with the rivalry and jealousy among the powers, helped to avert the partition of the country, the economic burden, the humiliation accompanying further infringements on sovereignty and interference in China's internal affairs in the provisions of the Boxer Protocol sealed the fate of Manchu rule and the pulse of revolution quickened.

H.-M.L.

Armed 'Boxers' near Tianjin, 1900.

The Russo-Japanese War (1904–5)

The Russo-Japanese War, triggered off by the surprise attack by Japanese submarines on the Russian fleet in Port Arthur during the night of 7–8 February 1904, was the result of conflict between two opposing expansionist powers: Russia, who drove eastwards into Siberia, the Chinese maritime provinces and Manchuria, and Japan, who tried to gain a foothold in continental Asia via Korea. The clash was accelerated by China's defeat at the hands of Japan in 1895 and by the scramble for concessions when Russia gained possession of the Liaodong Peninsula. Japan had claimed this territory, where Port Arthur is situated, as a prize of victory after the Sino-Japanese War (1894–5), but was forced by the combined pressure of Russia, Germany and France to return it to China. The Boxer Uprising afforded Russia an opportunity to consolidate its position. Japan was now faced with the choice of either forsaking its continental ambitions or seizing the chance to dislodge its opponent by force. The decision in favour of war was made possible by an alliance with Great Britain in 1902, who then felt the need of an ally to safeguard its interests in Asia in face of the threat from other European powers acting in concert.

From the beginning the war went in Japan's favour, and after storming the supposedly impregnable fortress of Port Arthur, and all but eliminating the Russian fleet in the Battle of Tsushima Japan was able to drive deep into Manchuria in the knowledge that the line of communication was secure. These successes demoralized the Russians and caused disquiet among the great powers, since here was a European giant being completely humiliated by a small Asian nation. The USA, recognizing a potential threat to its Pacific interests, was prompted to intervene. With the good offices of President Theodore Roosevelt, a treaty signed at Portsmouth, New Hampshire in September 1905, by which Russia was forced to surrender rights in Manchuria to Japan, whose paramount interests in Korea were recognized, brought peace. The débâcle had repercussions within Russia. Japan had to forgo a war indemnity, but was amply compensated. As for China, the victim on whose territory the struggle had been conducted, the war stirred up unprecedented nationalist sentiment, which exploded into the anti-dynastic and anti-imperialist activities that helped bring about the collapse of the Manchu regime. *H.-M.L.*

Tongmenghui

The *Tongmenghui*, or Alliance Society, was the Chinese revolutionary party founded under the leadership of Sun Yat-sen in Tokyo in July 1905 with the aim of overthrowing the Manchu rule. It was an amalgamation of various Chinese revolutionary groups then based in Japan. With its propaganda organ *Min Bao* (*The People's Journal*), it coordinated revolutionary activities that led to the Wuchang Uprising of 10 October 1911. Its members dominated the Provisional Republican Government set up in Nanjing in 1912. After Sun Yat-sen resigned the provisional presidency in favour of Yuan Shikai through a compromise which led to the abdication of the Manchu emperor, the *Tongmenghui* absorbed four splinter parties with three other parties to form the *Guomindang* (Nationalist Party). Following the failure of the so-called Second Revolution in 1913, and the subsequent forced dissolution of parliament by Yuan, the remnants of the old *Tongmenghui* who took refuge in Japan regrouped to form the *Zhonghua gemingdang* (Chinese Revolutionary Party) in 1914. The party was reorganized yet again in 1919 and renamed the *Zhongguo guomindang* (Chinese Nationalist Party). Although the new party bore little resemblance to the old *Tongmenghui* and ex-membership of that society was rarely accompanied by privilege and power, it has remained prestigious for a member of the present-day *Guomindang* (in Taiwan and elsewhere) to claim a connection with the old *Tongmenghui*, to which the present party likes to trace its ancestry. *H.-M.L.*

Constitutional Movement

The Constitutional Movement was begun by the class of gentry-entrepreneurs to gain a greater say in government through reforms aimed at achieving a constitutional monarchy. Growing increasingly vocal in the aftermath of the Boxer Uprising, this movement was really a continuation of the 1898 Reform Movement. In the face of persistent clamouring, the Manchu court, which had been forced to introduce reforms in the education and examination systems after its return to Beijing in 1901 following its flight to Xi'an in 1900, finally responded by dispatching various missions abroad to study the constitutional question. The reports from these missions, however, merely enabled the court to procrastinate. The government's attitude was mainly due to its feeling of insecurity after the 1900 débâcle, which had left it substantially weakened and humiliated, and thus subject to increasing threats posed by anti-dynastic activities. Although staunchly monarchist, the protagonists in the movement were almost exclusively Han Chinese, who stood to gain only at the expense of the ruling Manchu clique.

In the agitation that followed the Russo-Japanese War, in which Japan's victory was seen as a triumph of constitutional monarchy over absolute autocracy, the government was pressed into declaring its intended constitutional reforms in September 1906. However, when the draft constitution, heavily weighted in favour of the throne, was published two years later, nine years had been set aside as a preparatory period for its introduction. This aroused widespread protest and the government was inundated with petitions urging the convening of a national parliament. When provincial assemblies were introduced in October 1909 and the national consultative council a year later, the protests intensified. Neither of these organs had more than the right to criticize, suggest and discuss matters referred to it, decision-making and policy-formulation remaining the prerogative of the provincial and national governments.

With the death of the Empress Dowager Cixi in November 1908 and removal of the firm hand that had guided it for so long, the Manchu court sought to conciliate the increasing belligerence of the Constitutional Movement by reiterating its determination to introduce reforms and by agreeing to shorten the preparatory period to six years. But time was not on its side. In May 1911 as a step towards the introduction of a constitutional monarchical government it established what was intended to be a responsible cabinet. But by allocating nine of its 13 posts to the Manchus, mostly imperial clansmen and nobles, the court only increased the already heightened ethnic tension. Highly-charged emotional protests, followed by the revolt of the Railway Protection Movement, helped create the situation in which at Wuchang in October 1911 Manchu rule was pushed to the point of no return.   H.-M.L.

Railway Protection Movement

The Railway Protection Movement, which contributed to bringing down the Qing dynasty, was both a forceful dramatization of China's struggle for modernization and a popular demonstration against the encroachment of imperialism and the misrule of government. Introduced into China in 1866, railway building had a chequered career. In the 30 years to the outbreak of the first Sino-Japanese War in 1894, a total of 364km were built—some 286km with British money and under British control. Railway building became of foremost priority in attempts at modernization following China's defeat at the hands of Japan in 1895, and since China was too impoverished to finance such ventures itself, struggles for the rights developed among the powers during the 'scramble for concessions'. Each power claimed rights in what it regarded as its sphere of influence: Russia in Manchuria and northern China; Germany in Shandong; Britain, the Yangtze Valley down to the Burma frontier; Japan, Fujian; and France in the provinces bordering on Indo-China. Railways were at once spearheads of modernization and spearheads of foreign encroach-

ment; each railway concession was accompanied by claims for mining and other rights in the territory along the way. Hence railways were likened by Zhang Zhidong (1837–1909), the viceroy at Wuchang who figured so prominently in China's railway programme, to scissors, by means of which China ran the danger of being cut up by the powers.

Resentment against foreign scheming gave rise to a railway rights recovery movement. The local gentry, from whose ranks now rose commercial and industrial entrepreneurs, aware of the profits that this new foreign enterprise would bring, succeeded in persuading the government to build the lines in their respective provinces with local resources. Starting in Sichuan Province in 1903, this merchant finance and construction of railways was extended to other provinces including Hubei, Hunan and Guangdong.

However, because of insufficient capital and incompetence, the plan did not succeed. When the able, pragmatic, but later much maligned Sheng Xuanhuai (1844–1916) became minister of communications in 1910, he saw that the only way to have the railways built quickly and economically was to resort to foreign loans and outside technical assistance. This he set out to do in May 1911 by nationalizing all the trunk lines and leaving the branch lines for the provincial 'merchants'. In venturing upon this otherwise sound nationalization plan Sheng had greatly underestimated the strength of the gentry-entrepreneur interests that dominated the newly-created provincial assemblies. Disguising their self-interest as patriotism, they stirred up a government boycott movement, refusing to pay taxes and other levies. The killing and arrest of demonstrators and local gentry leaders by the panicking provincial authorities on 7 September 1911 threw the whole of Sichuan into ferment. This unrest, exploited by revolutionaries and other dissidents alike, quickly extended to other provinces, unleashing latent anti-dynastic sentiments. In the process the resistance of the gentry-entrepreneurs, most of whom were constitutional monarchists, and the actions of the revolutionaries overlapped. The withdrawal of troops from Wuchang to control the unrest in Sichuan left that city more vulnerable when the revolutionaries made their move on 10 October 1911.   H.-M.L.

Wuchang Uprising: the Republican Revolution of 1911

The Wuchang Uprising was an anti-dynastic revolt that took place on 10 October 1911 at the seat of the Huguang Viceroyalty and centre of a planned national railway network on the middle reaches of the Yangtze River. The climax of a long series of anti-

EMPERORS OF THE QING DYNASTY

Personal name and lifespan	Temple name	Posthumous name	Enthroned	Reign title and dates
Nurhaci (1559–1626)	Taizu	Gao (Wu) Huangdi	—	Tianming (1616–26)
Abahai (Khungtaiji) 1592–1643	Taizong	Wen Huangdi	—	Tiancong (1627–36)
				Chongde (1636–43)
Fulin (1638–61)	Shizu	Zhang Huangdi	1643	Shunzhi (1644–61)
Xuanye (1645–1722)	Shengzu	Ren Huangdi	1661	Kangxi (1662–1722)
Yinzhen (1678–1735)	Shizong	Xian Huangdi	1722	Yongzheng (1723–35)
Hongli (1711–99)	Gaozong	Chun Huangdi	1735	Qianlong (1736–95)
Yongyan (1760–1820)	Renzong	Rui Huangdi	1796	Jiaqing (1796–1820)
Minning (1782–1850)	Xuanzong	Cheng Huangdi	1820	Daoguang (1821–50)
Yizhu (1831–61)	Wenzong	Xian Huangdi	1850	Xianfeng (1851–61)
Zaichun (1856–75)	Muzong	Yi Huangdi	1861	Tongzhi (1862–74)
Zaitian (1871–1908)	Dezong	Jing Huangdi	1875	Guangxu (1875–1908)
Puyi (1906–67)	—	—	1909	Xuantong (1909–11)

Note: The family name of the imperial clan was Aisin Gioro. The dynastic name was changed from (Later) Jin to Qing in 1636.

C.A.

Puyi, the last Manchu emperor, seen here when he was head of the Manchukuo government.

dynastic revolts, it owed its success not so much to the strength and organization of the main plotters, the disaffected military personnel, the *Tongmenghui* and secret societies, but rather to the unrest caused by the government's railway nationalization scheme in the Yangtze provinces, particularly in Sichuan where the Railway Protection Movement had broken out into large-scale open armed rebellion. The uprising took place as the result of the accidental exploding of a bomb on 9 October in the revolutionary headquarters in the Russian Concession of Hankou. Police investigations and arrests forced the revolutionaries to advance their plans and army units who had been won over seized control of Wuchang on 10 October 1911, their task having been made easier by the transfer of part of the garrison to Sichuan.

The sentiments manifested in the Railway Protection Movement and the Constitutional Movement enabled provinces and strategic towns and cities to rise to the republican cause. Within two months representatives from 17 provinces had gathered together and set up in Nanjing the Provisional Republic Government under Sun Yat-sen and Li Yuanhong (1864–1928), a local military commander in Wuchang. The Provisional Government, however, although dominated by the *Tongmenghui*, was only a fragile coalition of divergent political elements and its power was more nominal than real. The conservative forces, on the other hand, proved to be much more tenacious than the dynasty they supported and quickly filled the place the Manchus had vacated. In the face of overwhelming odds Sun Yat-sen, in order to secure the Manchu abdication, was obliged to give way to Yuan Shikai, the very man the Manchu government had called to its aid on the outbreak of the Wuchang Uprising. Under him and the warlords who succeeded him, China was to remain a republic in name only. However, what took place in 1911, and what the date 10 October or 'Double Tenth' has come to symbolize, unleashed a series of events, of which the establishment of the People's Republic of China in 1949 may be seen as the culmination.

H.-M.L.

Manchu abdication (1912)

On 12 February 1912 the last Manchu emperor, Puyi (1906–67), was forced to abdicate by the revolutionary government which came into being in Nanjing after the Wuchang Uprising. Yuan Shikai, to whom the Qing government had entrusted the handling of the crisis, succeeded by a series of manoeuvres, including treachery and manipulation, in orchestrating the abdication and gaining the provisional presidency of the Republic for himself in place of Sun Yat-sen, who resigned in favour of Yuan. The abdication not only brought to an end the 268 years of Manchu rule, but also marked the formal break with over 2000 years of continuous imperial tradition.

Puyi, under the reign-title Xuantong, was six years old when forced to abdicate. He had been named as the Guangxu Emperor's successor by his great aunt, the notorious Empress Dowager Cixi, in November 1908 upon the death of the Emperor, allegedly just a day prior to her own. Continuing to live in the Forbidden City under the title of Manchu Emperor with all the privileges granted him by the abdication agreement, Puyi became a rallying point for monarchists. In July 1917 he was restored to the throne for 12 days by General Zhang Xun's (1854–1923) dramatic but short-lived coup. Then in 1924, forced out of the Beijing palace by the Christian General Feng Yuxiang (1882–1948), he was given protection by the Japanese. After the Japanese seizure of Manchuria in 1932, Puyi was made head of the puppet government of Manchukuo, which came to an end with Japan's defeat in 1945. Captured by the Russian army, Puyi was later handed over to the Chinese government. After a term of imprisonment, he was made a citizen of the Communist state and worked *inter alia* as gardener and librarian. He died in the former imperial capital, where he had abdicated some 55 years earlier, so ending a life whose course had been largely dictated by others. The autobiography attributed to him (entitled in translation *From Emperor to Citizen*), but actually composed by many hands and 'polished' by the famous author of *Rickshaw Boy*, Lao She (1899–1966), is in spite of its many mistakes an interesting piece of historical documentation of the China of Puyi's time.   *H.-M.L.*

THE REPUBLICAN PERIOD (1912–49)

Sun Yat-sen (1866–1925)

Revolutionary and founder of the *Guomindang* (Chinese Nationalist Party), Sun Yat-sen (Yixian) is honoured even by his enemies as 'father of the nation', although his tenacious struggles for political power did not bring success during his lifetime.

Sun's early life made him a marginal figure in Chinese society. Born into a Guangdong farming family near the Portuguese colony of Macao, he lived for a time with his brother in Hawaii, and was educated in missionary and medical schools there and in Hong

Kong, becoming one of the earliest Western-trained intellectuals. By 1895, convinced of China's desperate need for reform, he was a full-time rebel. Forced into exile after an abortive plot in Canton, he became an international figure after imperial officials briefly imprisoned him in 1896 at the Chinese legation in London, and for over a decade toured Chinese settlements overseas, raising money to finance mutinies and secret society risings in China. Although all of these came to nothing, Sun made himself the preeminent republican opponent of Manchu rule, and in 1905 he was elected by radical students in Tokyo to head the umbrella organization known as the Revolutionary Alliance (*Tongmenghui*), precursor of the *Guomindang*. With the fall of the Manchus in 1911 he was the obvious candidate for president.

Perpetual exile and seeker of foreign solutions, Sun Yat-sen usually had himself photographed in foreign dress.

But Sun was soon a political outsider again. In the new environment neither his skill at inspiring opposition for a common cause nor his much publicized contacts overseas were effective. He resigned in favour of the northerner, Yuan Shikai, but when Yuan in 1913 suppressed the *Guomindang*, Sun again threw himself into revolutionary politics; successively, he attempted to build a Chinese Revolutionary Party out of old party members willing to swear personal allegiance to him, wheedled subsidies from Japan in 1915 and Germany in 1917, and endeavoured by sheer force of personality at Canton (1917–18, and 1921–2) to make local warlords fight his wars against the north.

Expelled temporarily from Canton, Sun once again sought solutions abroad, and in 1923 accepted a Russian offer of help, agreeing to admit Chinese Communist Party members into the party. With the enthusiastic support of the patriotic youth of the May Fourth generation, he introduced unprecedented discipline, a specific platform, mass organization and anti-imperialist and anti-warlord propaganda, and set up the Whampoa Military Academy to train the nucleus of a party army. Although Guangdong remained under warlord control until after his death in March 1925, Sun had radicalized the party and laid the groundwork for its subsequent expansion.

Sun Yat-sen's influential writings reflected a thoroughly Westernized cast of mind. Besides ambitious plans to develop railways, roads, mines, harbours and even department stores with foreign capital, he optimistically proposed a time-table for a three-stage transition from military through party tutelage to full constitutional rule, and drew up a five-power constitution which supposedly improved on the checks and balances of Western democracies by adding censorial and examination branches. Neither these schemes nor his *Three People's Principles*—Nationalism, Democracy and People's Livelihood—supplied the *Guomindang* with a workable guide after his death. Sun's achievement was, rather, to personify defiance against bureaucrats, warlords and (in his last, radical years) foreign imperialism, at a dismal time when China resembled, as he said, a 'dish of sand'. He found the words and gestures to inspire those Chinese who sought at once unity, national dignity and Westernization.   *D.S.S.*

Yuan Shikai (1859–1916)

Yuan Shikai—imperial reformer, Republican president, would-be emperor and so-called father of the warlords—came from a Henan family of civil and military officials. Having twice failed the *juren* civil service examination, he acquired a staff position through family connections and went with his patron to Korea, where China's suzerainty was under challenge from Japan.

Yuan's competence as military organizer and skill in politics and diplomacy soon made him the leading Chinese official in Korea. When after 12 years he returned to China, he devoted his attention to military reform; by 1899 his New Army was the best in China. Becoming a favourite of the all-powerful Empress Dowager Cixi, Yuan kept himself and his troops intact through both the aborted 100 Days of Reform and the Boxer Rebellion. By 1902, as Beiyang (Northern) commissioner, he was the chief military and diplomatic official in north China. His military reforms were extended to six Beiyang divisions, and then to the whole country. Although his star waned with the consolidation of

Unprepossessing despite his medals, Yuan Shikai looks less China's indispensable man than the 'emperor' who over-reached himself.

Manchu control in 1906 and with the death of the Empress Dowager in 1908, personal ties cultivated with military subordinates like Duan Qirui (1865–1936) and Feng Guozhang (1859–1919) were as strong as ever, and the court was obliged to turn to him during the 1911 revolution. His negotiations for the Qing abdication gave him charge of all imperial forces; subsequent negotiations with the republican provinces which had declared their independence brought him the office of president in the new Republic.

Confident of his rightful authority, Yuan set about re-establishing central control. In this he made no attempt to rally the support of the gentry/merchant social elite in the provinces or to cultivate republican sentiment or a nascent sense of nationalism, but depended instead on his carefully created civil/military bureaucratic machine, with the help of a cosy relationship with Britain and other powers who sought a 'strong man' to protect their manifold rights in China. Having subordinated the cabinet to his will, he secured a 'Reorganization Loan' in exchange for foreign supervision of the salt revenues, dissolved parliament which had opposed him, revised the constitution to make himself life president, and suppressed the *Guomindang*. By 1915, 12 of China's provinces were firmly administered by Beijing and the remainder acquiescent. To strengthen his authority further, Yuan resorted to an imperial restoration and proclaimed himself Hongxian Emperor. The reaction to this was public denunciation by the respected intellectual Liang Qichao (1873–1929), the secession of Yunnan Province, and a two-month war led by Republican officers under the Hunanese Cai E (1882–1916). Not only were Yuan's coffers emptied and many divisions tied down, but Yunnan won the support of Guizhou, Guangxi and other southern provinces. Pressed by Japan and other powers, and criticized by some of his oldest followers, Yuan restored the Republic. He died before resistance had been quelled. His death inaugurated the grim era of warlords, many of whom had made their careers in his Beiyang army.   *D.S.S.*

Parliaments

Constitutions and representative assemblies, even Qing officials agreed by 1906, marked all strong modern nations. When elections were permitted at the provincial level in 1907 the Confucian-educated scholar gentry flocked to participate. The National Assembly of 1910, elected from the Provincial Assemblies, exercised strong pressure for rapid constitutional rule. The elections of 1913 were probably the most democratic in liberal terms, but franchise was limited to males over 25 paying 2 *yuan* in taxes and owning landed property worth 500 *yuan*, and the campaign was marred by the government-instigated assassination of the *Guomindang*'s chief parliamentary liberal, Song Jiaoren (1882–1913). The new house of representatives and senate were dominated by *Guomindang* members determined to control President Yuan Shikai's cabinet through the Provisional Constitution of 1912, but Yuan bypassed and ignored legislative prerogatives and eventually dissolved parliament and banned the party. The reconvened parliament came into a similar conflict with Yuan's strong-man successor, Premier Duan Qirui (1865–1936), notably over the issue of war with Germany and plans for foreign loans. In 1917 a majority of assemblymen left Beijing, but failed to mobilize behind Sun Yat-sen or win the support of Guangxi warlords at Canton. Meanwhile, a rival parliament pliable to Duan's wishes had been elected in the north under a specially contrived law. In spite of the dubious legality, by this time, even of the 1912 parliament, efforts to solve political problems by 'constitutional means' persisted, the most notorious being the wholesale bribery, at 5000 *yuan* a vote, in the presidential election of the warlord Cao Kun (1862–1938).

The parliamentary system had failed not just because of military repression but because men of power thought more of orthodoxy and morality than constitutional legality, and because no strong party had been created outside parliament to transcend provincial and personal attachments. The very idea of parliament was discredited by the members' extreme factionalism and avarice. In the 1920s most educated Chinese turned towards party government in the search for unification and civil hegemony.   *D.S.S.*

Warlords

The term 'warlord' is applied to sub-national politicians who enjoyed virtual territorial autonomy because of military forces owing them personal allegiance. In the so-called warlord period (1916–28) hundreds of such men dominated China, bringing insecurity and arbitrary exactions to the people, negating civil authority, and reducing the Beijing government to impotence.

The origins of warlords were diverse; while some had been bandits, soldiers in the imperial forces or Confucian scholars, many had received some modern military education in the late Qing reforms. In the North most armies derived from Yuan Shikai's New Army; in the South from the province-based armies created between 1906 and 1911 in imitation of them. All possessed modern weapons and the rudiments of modern organization. Ideologically and socially, warlords were hybrids, speaking of republicanism and national unity, but couching their telegrams in Confucian moral terms and collaborating with traditional civil elites.

Warlord power was unstable, being personal in nature and based on imperfect financial control of loosely demarcated territorial bases. Petty warlords tapped the revenues of market towns, river valleys or provinces to feed their troops, often relying upon control of the domestic opium traffic. The more successful warlords held well-defended peripheral regions—Zhang Zuolin (1873–1928) of Manchuria, Yan Xishan (1883–1960) of Shanxi, Tang Jiyao (1886?–1927) of Yunnan—or built up exceptionally loyal and effective armies as did Feng Yuxiang (1882–1948), the so-called Christian general. They fought each other for wealthy regions and especially for Beijing, whose capture promised foreign recognition and access to the surplus from the foreign-supervised Maritime Customs and the Salt Administration. The largest civil wars (between the Zhili and Anhui warlord cliques in 1922 and 1924) mobilized two or three hundred thousand troops, perhaps 5 per cent of whom became casualties.

The Nanjing government (1928–37) obliged the great war-lords to submit to party authority, but failed to root out personalism and localism from the military. In the western periphery warlordism flourished until the 1940s.   *D.S.S.*

The May Fourth Movement

This was an intellectual and political movement aimed at modernizing and strengthening the nation. It took its name from a demonstration in Beijing on 4 May 1919, when students protested against the decision of the Great Powers at Versailles to assign defeated Germany's rights in Shandong to Japan instead of returning them to China. Police suppression and arrests brought on supporting demonstrations and strikes in other cities, intensified the spirit of nationalism, and popularized a 'new culture' movement already under way.

By 1919 Beijing was an important intellectual centre. Under the dynamic leadership of Cai Yuanpei (1868–1940), Beijing University had a brilliant faculty, most of whose members such as Hu Shi (1891–1962) and Chen Duxiu (1879–1942), had received advanced education abroad. They inspired their students with liberal reformist ideals. The *New Youth Magazine* (*Xinqingnian*), founded by Chen and edited by some of the professors, emphasized intellectual inquiry and instilled a sense of iconoclasm towards traditional Chinese culture. Intellectuals searched for the underlying causes of China's backwardness; many concluded that the culture itself needed drastic reform.

Interest in anarchism and socialism revived, and revolutionary Russia became very popular with its promise to give up all special privileges won by the tsarist regime from China. In a number of cities young intellectuals created new anarchist and socialist study groups, started reformist journals, and began to 'go among the

Cai Yuanpei (1868–1940): classical scholar, revolutionary leader, student in Europe, Cai revitalized Peking University during his presidency (1916–26).

people' to spread knowledge and create workers' organizations. Thus, the May Fourth Movement inspired a new generation of leaders in many fields. It led to a revival of support for the *Guomindang* and to the founding of the Chinese Communist Party.

C.M.W.

The *Guomindang*

As the revolutionary party led by Dr Sun Yat-sen, and after his death under the leadership of Chiang Kai-shek, the *Guomindang* became the ruling party of China from 1928 to 1949, and thereafter in Taiwan. The *Guomindang*, or Chinese Nationalist Party, traces its history through several short-lived predecessor organizations beginning in 1894. These were the Society to Restore

China's Prosperity (*Xingzhonghui*), founded in Hawaii and Hong Kong, 1894–5; the Revolutionary Alliance (*Tongmenghui*), set up in Tokyo in 1905; the National People's Party (*Guomindang*), established in 1912 as a parliamentary party in China; and the Chinese Revolutionary Party (*Zhongguo gemingdang*), started in Tokyo in 1914. Most were amalgams of other organizations, and all were short-lived. In 1920 Dr Sun established the *Zhongguo guomindang* (Chinese People's Party) in Shanghai, to aid his return to Canton. After being driven from Canton by General Chen Jiongming (1878–1933) and back in Shanghai in August 1922, he set about reviving the *Guomindang* and agreed to admit Communists. He also conferred with Dr Adolf Joffe (1883–1937), sent by the USSR to negotiate a treaty with Beijing. Their meeting presaged Soviet assistance to the *Guomindang*, the next stage of the party's history.

In February 1923 Dr Sun returned to Canton with the help of mercenary troops financed through his party. In October Michael Borodin (1884–1953) arrived as the agent of the USSR and the Comintern to assist Sun Yat-sen and the Nationalist Party. The two set about creating a centralized and disciplined party similar in structure to the Communist Party of the USSR. The *Zhongguo guomindang* held its First National Congress in January 1924, adopting a constitution with a new five-level structure in which power descended from the ruling Central Executive Committee elected by an annual congress of delegates. The congress adopted a reformist programme to improve the life of all classes and now strove to become a mass-based party, although led by an elite. Its propaganda took on a strongly nationalistic and anti-imperialist tone. Dr Sun's lectures on 'The Three Principles of the People' (*sanmin zhuyi*) became the party's official ideology. He also issued his 'Fundamentals of National Reconstruction for the National Government of China', which stated that, after a successful military reunification of the country, the new government should prepare the people for self-government during a period of tutelage. This document did not mention the *Guomindang*; but later the party took upon itself the role of tutelage—in fact, dictatorship.

The *Guomindang* established the Whampoa Military Academy in June 1924 to train and indoctrinate officers for an army under its direct control. At first the USSR financed the academy and provided Soviet military instructors and arms. Dr Sun selected Chiang Kai-shek to be the academy's commandant, from which position he rose to prominence in the party. Gradually, the 'Party Army' became an effective fighting force, while other loyal units in Guangdong were retrained and rearmed with Russian help. In several campaigns the renamed National Revolutionary Army secured Guangdong and by the middle of 1926, six corps and several independent divisions made up an army numbering about 100 000 officers and men.

The *Guomindang* established branches in cities throughout China and its membership grew to about 200 000 by January 1926 when the Second National Congress met in Canton after Dr Sun's death. General Chiang Kai-shek, now an important figure in the party, soon began to dominate it.   *C.M.W.*

The Chinese Communist Party

Two leaders of the May Fourth Movement, Chen Duxiu (1879–1942) and Li Dazhao (1888–1927), founded the party and most of its early members were active in the movement. Li and Chen were attracted to Marxism and Bolshevism by the successful Russian Revolution, Lenin's anti-imperialist stand and the Soviet promise to restore China's lost rights. The Communist International, or Comintern, founded by Lenin in 1919, sent agents to provide some financing and policy guidance. Early in 1920 a Comintern agent, Gregory Voitinsky, met Li in Beijing and Chen Duxiu in Shanghai, and Chen Duxiu undertook to organize a Communist party. He and others recruited patriotic intellectuals to set up Socialist Youth Corps and Communist cells in several cities. Towards the end of July 1921 representatives of six such cells, with a total membership less than 60, met in Shanghai for the First Congress of the Chinese Communist Party (*Zhongguo gongchandang*). Mao Zedong later became the most famous of the delegates. The Congress resolved to organize the proletariat in

Below left: Chen Duxiu (1879–1942), founding editor of New Youth Magazine, dean of Peking University, and head of the Chinese Communist Party, 1921–7. Below right: Li Dazhao (1889–1927), librarian and professor at Peking University, a popularizer of Marxism and co-founder of the Chinese Communist Party. Executed in April 1927.

unions and oppose all other political organizations. They did not yet appreciate Comintern policy.

In August 1920 the Second Congress of the Comintern adopted Lenin's theses on revolution in colonial and backward countries, which, with elaboration and refinement over the years, guided the Comintern in its relations with Asian revolutions, including that of China. Lenin postulated that the first revolutionary stage, a national liberation struggle, would be led by the bourgeoisie. Native Communist parties should actively support this struggle but must maintain their autonomy and organize the proletariat. A crucial task was emancipation of the peasantry from tenancy and feudal bondage. After liberation the native Communist party, having organized the toiling masses, must move to the second stage, the struggle against capitalism and the bourgeoisie, and the seizure of power in a socialist revolution. The Comintern should aid and guide all anti-imperialist and national liberation struggles to forge a single world revolution led by the USSR. Comintern strategists, ill-acquainted with China, had still to identify the national revolutionary group or party worthy of its support. Hendricus Sneevliet (1883–1942), a Dutch Communist, who used the pseudonym H. Maring, was the broker who brought the Chinese Communist Party to the *Guomindang*.

Sent to China by the Comintern in 1921, Maring became convinced the Chinese Communist Party would fare best if it worked within the *Guomindang*. After clearing this with Moscow, he saw Sun Yat-sen in Shanghai in August 1922. Sun agreed to admit Communists to his party, which, in his view, should enrol all revolutionaries. Maring then imposed his plan on the reluctant Chinese Communist leaders, according to their account. Thus, in September a few, including Li Dazhao (1888–1927) and Chen Duxiu (1879–1942), joined the *Guomindang*.

The Chinese Communist Party held its Third Congress in Canton in June 1923, with Maring attending and insisting that members work within the *Guomindang*. Obediently, the congress resolved to focus the party's activities on development of a national revolutionary movement with the *Guomindang* as its leader. Communists should all join the other party, help reorganize it into a party of the masses, and strengthen its influence among workers and peasants. The Chinese Communist Party would retain its independence and should try to absorb all truly class-conscious revolutionaries from existing labour organizations and from the *Guomindang* left wing. The Comintern's Executive Committee sent a directive to this congress, which argued for broadening the national revolution by aggressively preparing for agrarian revolt, and for changing the *Guomindang* into the leader of a democratic anti-imperialist and anti-feudal front. Such plans would not be easy for a young party, made up mostly of intellectuals and having only some 400 members, to carry out.

Several of the leaders opposed the requirement to work within the *Guomindang* and to strengthen it, but they bowed to Comintern discipline. *C.M.W*

The United Front

There was opposition on both sides to Communists joining the *Guomindang*. At the First *Guomindang* Congress a conservative group tried to amend the new constitution to prohibit dual party membership. Li Dazhao (1888–1927), a delegate, explained the Chinese Communist Party's purpose in having its members join the senior party—it was entirely to serve the national revolution and had no sinister aim. However, his prepared statement was decided upon by the communist 'fraction' among the delegates—'the bloc within'. Each party, schooled by Michael Borodin (1884–1951), had the strategy of gaining control of every organization in which it had members. Already beginning to receive Soviet aid, Sun Yat-sen quelled the opposition and nominated three Communists to the 24-man *Guomindang* Central Executive Committee and seven to be among the 17 reserve members; this the congress duly approved.

Michael Borodin (1884-1951), original surname, Gruzenberg: agent of Soviet Russia and the Communist International in China, 1923-7.

Both parties grew in political influence and sophistication during this United Front period. After Dr Sun's death, the anti-imperialist movement made great strides due to the May 30th and the June 23rd Incidents in 1925, in which police in the International Settlement in Shanghai and foreign troops in Canton killed many demonstrating Chinese. By aggressively leading patriotic protest strikes, the Chinese Communist Party attracted many new members, but still had only a fraction of the *Guomindang*'s growing membership. It was particularly effective in dominating the labour movement.

A group of *Guomindang* veterans, led by Dai Jitao (1891–1949) on the theoretical plane, agitated for the separation of the two parties. In November 1925 nearly half the members of the *Guomindang* Central Executive Committee met near Beijing in the 'Western Hills Conference' and resolved to expel the Communists, dismiss Borodin and punish Wang Jingwei (1883–1944), the leader of the *Guomindang* left wing, centred in Canton. The Communist Party's Central Committee held a plenary meeting in December, and Chen Duxiu (1879–1942)—faced with this conservative opposition and never satisfied with the restraints on Communists in the other party—proposed withdrawal and a cooperative alliance between the parties for the national revolution—that is, 'a bloc without'. Again the Comintern opposed: Communist influence was growing in the *Guomindang*, which was gaining national stature as the leader of the revolutionary movement supported by the USSR.

At the Second National Congress of the *Guomindang* in January 1926 about a third of the delegates were Communists. The congress excluded the 'Western Hills Clique', which had set up a rival party headquarters in Shanghai, reconfirmed the admission of Communists, praised Borodin's guidance and thanked the USSR for its help. It elected an enlarged Central Executive Committee, increasing the number of Communists to seven with the same number among the alternates. The Central Executive Committee then elected a nine-man Standing Committee with three leftists headed by Wang Jingwei; three Communists; General Chiang Kai-shek, Tan Yankai (1879–1930), a veteran of great prestige, and Hu Hanmin (1879–1936), a conservative who had been sent off to Moscow.

This congress marked the high point of the United Front, for in March Chiang Kai-shek curbed Communists in the National Revolutionary Army, in which Zhou Enlai was a principal political officer; arranged the dismissal of several Russian advisers whom he suspected of conspiring against himself; and caused the departure of his rival, Wang Jingwei. A plenary session of the Central Executive Committee in May installed Chiang's supporters in key party positions, and took other measures to curtail Communist influence in the *Guomindang*.

C.M.W.

Peng Pai and the peasants' movement

Peng Pai (1896–1929) was a product of the May Fourth Movement, influenced while a student in Japan to a concern for rural poverty. Having joined the Chinese Communist Party he returned in 1921 to his native Haifeng in southeast Guangdong determined to spread the 'new culture'. Coming from a wealthy landlord lineage, he undertook to organize tenant peasants and win them fairer treatment. At first quite successful, the Haifeng Peasants' Association was crushed in March 1924 by Chen Jiongming, earlier patron of Peng. Peng fled to Canton, where he soon became the most active leader in the *Guomindang*'s hesitant move towards the rural population. The *Guomindang* established a Peasants' Bureau in its central headquarters, with Peng Pai as its secretary; and it sanctioned the creation of a Peasants' Movement Training Institute to prepare cadres to organize peasants' associations. (Mao Zedong directed the Institute's final session in mid-1926.) Communists dominated the Institute and directed the movement from the beginning, while insisting that peasants' associations be autonomous, controlled neither by the government nor the *Guomindang*.

Peasants in Guangdong had many grievances. Because of land shortage there was a high proportion of tenants heavily burdened by rents. Hired farm labourers in some areas were virtual serfs. Taxes for landowning peasants were arbitrary and unpredictable. After a slow start, the leaders of the peasants' movement succeeded in organizing many village and inter-village associations designed to improve the peasants' lot and draw them into the national revolution. The Guangdong Peasants' Association, set up in May 1925, claimed about 200 000 members in 22 counties. A year later the claim was 626 457 members in 66 counties, for by then most of Guangdong was under *Guomindang* control. Some organizing had also begun in neighbouring provinces.

Encouraging rent- and tax-reduction struggles, the activists brought on conflicts with local power structures. Tenants won some battles and lost many. The spreading rural conflict added to the tensions within the United Front and posed a fundamental issue: was violent social revolution to be part of the national revolution? This was the underlying disagreement between the Chinese Communist Party and conservative and centrist elements in the *Guomindang*. When the Northern Expedition set out, Peng Pai stayed in Canton as head of the *Guomindang* Peasants' Bureau; the fundamental issue remained unresolved. He was executed by National government authorities in August 1929, a martyr to his beliefs.

C.M.W.

The Northern Expedition

The National Revolutionary Army began this campaign north-wards from Guangdong in June 1926 and ended its drive in Beijing two years later.

Chiang Kai-shek was commander-in-chief, General Vasily K. Blyucher (1889–1938?), who used the pseudonym Galin, was a principal strategist, and the major units had Russian military advisers. The well-disciplined Army had a political department to propagandize against the enemy and win support from the population in conquered areas. Bribery assured much defection from the enemy. There were four main phases to the campaign.

The first drive through Hunan was directed against armies under Wu Peifu (1874–1939), with the Wuhan cities on the Yangtze as the target. Hankou and Hanyang were taken by early September and Wuchang, the capital of Hubei, invested. Chiang Kai-shek then struck at Jiangxi to the east; it was defended by troops of Sun Chuanfang (1884–1929). Nanchang, the provincial capital, and Jiujiang on the Yangtze fell in early November. Along most routes of march political workers spread nationalistic propaganda and set up mass organizations in cities and peasants' associations in the countryside. In October General He Yingqin (b. 1890) launched a coastal campaign through Fujian and by the end of 1926 was on the borders of Zhejiang.

At this point there was a pause for consolidation, for the National Revolutionary Army had suffered heavy casualties and had absorbed many enemy units that had to be regrouped and indoctrinated. The anti-imperialist movement exploded early in January 1927 when angry Chinese crowds seized the British concessions in Hankou and Jiujiang, a triumph for the Nationalists but a warning to the powers. The revolutionary camp now had rival centres, one at the Wuhan cities, dominated by leftists and Communists, and advised by Michael Borodin (1884–1953); the other at Nanchang, where Chiang Kai-shek had gathered conservative supporters. Borodin hoped to form an alliance of military forces against Chiang, who now hated the Russian political adviser. The Wuhan centre held a plenum of the Central Executive Committee in early March, which Chiang refused to attend. Its object was to reduce his authority and prepare for the return of his exiled rival Wang Jingwei (1883–1944).

Chiang was planning a campaign to capture the lower Yangtze provinces from a coalition headed by the Manchurian general, Zhang Zuolin (1873–1928). This was the second military phase. Shanghai fell on 22 March and Nanjing on the 24th. In Nanjing some entering Nationalist troops attacked foreign residents and the British, American and Japanese consulates, killing seven persons and looting foreign property. To effect a rescue, British and American gunboats laid down a barrage, which killed some 15 Chinese troops and four civilians. The 'Nanjing Incident' aroused great fears among foreigners in China, and the powers now had some 16 000 troops in Shanghai to protect that citadel of imperialism. General Chiang arrived in Shanghai on 26 March and set about allaying foreign fears and curbing the militant mass movement that had liberated the city before his army arrived.

In May the third military phase began when each centre launched a drive northwards. About 1 June their forces arrived at Zhengzhou and Xuzhou respectively, where the two north-south railways crossed the east to west Long-Hai Railway. Feng Yuxiang (1882–1948) and his *Guominjun* (National People's Army), which had been equipped by the USSR, joined the attack by driving east-wards out of Shaanxi. General Feng now held the balance of power and he played a decisive political role.

After conferring separately with Wang Jingwei and Chiang Kai-shek, he cast his lot with the richer and ordered the Wuhan centre to purge itself of Communists and dismiss Borodin. Hunanese commanders had already begun to suppress Communist-led peasants' associations, and the leftist leaders of the *Guomindang* had seen a telegram from Stalin ordering a Communist effort to seize control of the *Guomindang*. Hence in July the Wuhan leadership insisted that Communists withdraw from the *Guomindang*. Borodin departed for Russia, his mission unfulfilled. However, under Stalin's orders, the Chinese Communist Party launched a series of revolts in August. All were defeated by superior military power, but thereafter the two parties fought a 10-year war.

The last phase of the Northern Expedition came in the spring of 1928 after the rival factions had come together under Chiang's leadership and Wang Jingwei had been driven into exile once more. Feng Yuxiang led the attack north from Zhengzhou, while Chiang, again the commander-in-chief, directed the attack north-wards from Xuzhou. There were now no Soviet advisers. The eastern drive against Tianjin was temporarily halted by a clash with Japanese troops sent to Jinan to protect Japanese nationals—the 'Jinan Incident' of early May 1928. The Shanxi Army of Yan Xishan (1883–1960) reinforced the western drive on Beijing. Knowing he could no longer hold the capital, and 'advised' by Japan to withdraw to Manchuria peacefully, Zhang Zuolin pulled back in such a way that his old enemy, Feng Yuxiang, was unable to take Beijing, which fell to Yan Xishan's troops on 8 June. Soon thereafter the main Nationalist commanders met before Sun Yat-sen's bier in a temple in the Western Hills to announce the completion of the Northern Expedition.   *C.M.W.*

The Shanghai coup

This was the decisive action taken by Chiang Kai-shek and his conservative supporters to break the Chinese Communist Party's control of the mass movement in Shanghai and to disarm that party's military force, the Workers' Inspection Corps. The coup was part of a broader conflict in many cities during April 1927 between conservative and radical groups in the National Revolution.

The Communist Party was well entrenched in Shanghai. It controlled most of the modern labour unions, was influential in the students' associations, and had many front groups. Communist leaders in Shanghai (Zhou Enlai was one) had created a paramilitary force to discipline the labour movement—that is, to enforce strikes—and had used assassins to terrorize foremen in Chinese and foreign-owned enterprises. Together with their leftist allies, the Communist leaders had carried out two abortive uprisings in Shanghai. Just as the National Revolutionary Army was approaching, the third mass uprising succeeded in liberating the city from northern military control and in disarming the Chinese police. Various workers' inspection corps gathered quantities of arms and enrolled defeated northern troops. The radicals then tried to organize a municipal government of their choice that would be linked to the Nationalist government in Wuhan.

There was also strong opposition. Shanghai was the centre of the Guomindang's most conservative wing. A number of Nationalist generals were now strongly anti-Communist. The Chinese and foreign business communities had experienced disruptive strikes mounted by the General Labour Union. The Western authorities did not intend to permit the foreign settlements to be seized, as had happened in Hankou. The Nanjing Incident intensified foreign fears; it was readily believed to have been Communist-inspired. These groups supported Chiang Kai-shek's determination to bring the radicals under control, a course urged on him by the Japanese Consul-General and by Chinese business leaders, who provided millions to finance the enterprise. Chiang's principal military subordinate at Shanghai, General Bai Chongxi (1893–1966), ordered all irregulars to surrender their arms and he suppressed a number of such groups that resisted. Some three thousand members of the Workers' Inspection Corps defied his orders; they were well armed and controlled a number of strongpoints. Stalin telegraphed to advise them to bury their arms, but they did not.

On 1 April Wang Jingwei (1883–1944) arrived in Shanghai from France, via Moscow. He tried to dissuade his conservative colleagues from their planned action, while they urged him to join them. Wang met with Chen Duxiu (1879–1942), the secretary-general of the Communist Party, and they issued a joint statement which emphasized the need for unity in the revolutionary camp and tried to dispel two 'rumours' current in Shanghai—that the Communist Party intended to organize a workers' government, invade the foreign concessions, subvert the Nationalist Army, and overthrow the Guomindang; and that the Guomindang leaders planned to expel the Chinese Communist Party and suppress the labour unions and their inspection corps. Then Wang left for Hankou, urging that the Communist problem be settled at a Central Executive Committee plenum on 15 April.

The suppression plans were already well advanced. Chiang Kai-shek had engaged Du Yuesheng (1888–1951), a powerful gangster leader who lived in the French Concession, to carry out the purge. Du hired several hundred gunmen, who, together with units of General Bai's troops, were disguised as workmen. By arrangement with the foreign authorities, these units passed through the barricades into the Chinese sections of the city before dawn on 12 April. They suppressed the various inspection corps, sending captured leaders off to General Bai's headquarters, where some hundreds were executed. Zhou Enlai, although captured, escaped. Thereafter various radical unions and other organizations were shut down, and the Chinese Communist Party moved its headquarters to Hankou. Chiang Kai-shek was not in Shanghai on the day of the coup; he had gone to Nanjing to supervise a similar operation in preparation for establishing a new Nationalist government there, dominated by conservatives.   *C.M.W.*

Nanjing government

The Nanjing government usually refers to the government of the Guomindang (Nationalist Party), established in Nanjing in 1927 and ousted by the advancing Japanese in December 1937, although a Nationalist administration also operated at Nanjing from 1945 to 1949. The first Nationalist government at Nanjing was established on 18 April 1927, by Chiang Kai-shek following a purge of Chinese Communists, a new government with a wider range of Nationalist factions but without Chiang in September 1927, a further one with Chiang in January 1928, and on 10 October 1928 this Nationalist government was formally declared as the National Government of China, with Chiang as president.

In practice the Nanjing government controlled only a portion of eastern central China in 1928, relying upon the cooperation of warlord allies established in the remainder of China. In a series of wars the Nanjing government gradually extended its direct authority, but even by 1937 large areas remained outside its direct authority and the land tax, China's major fiscal resource, was assigned to the provinces, not to the centre. Major wars were fought against the Guangxi clique of militarists and Feng Yuxiang

(1882–1948) in 1929, against Feng Yuxiang, Yan Xishan (1883–1960) and Chiang's chief Nationalist rival Wang Jingwei (1883–1944) in 1930, against a separatist nationalist government at Canton with its northern ally Shi Yousan in 1931, against the 19th Route Army in Fujian in 1933 and against the southwest in 1936. Concurrently campaigns were launched against the Communists, both militarily in rural areas, especially in Jiangxi, and by the intelligence services in the cities. Japan began to occupy Manchuria from 18 September 1931. The Nanjing government's response was to seek redress, not by military means but through diplomatic channels, although fighting occurred at Shanghai from January 1932 involving the 19th Route Army, resolved by a truce in May 1932. Thereafter the central government stressed internal pacification before external resistance, allowing the Japanese to advance gradually in north China, until a firmer Chinese policy developed after the Xi'an Incident of December 1936, when Chiang Kai-shek was arrested by Zhang Xueliang (b. 1898), former ruler of Manchuria.

The Nanjing government under the *Guomindang*, which claimed to be providing political tutelage for the Chinese, had two forms: strongly presidential under Chiang up to 1931, and, from 1932, a weak presidency with power shared between the executive under Wang Jingwei and the military under Chiang. Throughout, government was confronted by factional struggles, among the CC Clique (commonly so called because it was led by two brothers, Chen Guofu and Chen Lifu), the Whampoa or Military Clique, the Political Study Clique and, after 1932, the Reorganization Clique, and Chiang's leadership was needed to ensure government activity. The government succeeded in regaining tariff autonomy for China, but although gaining the return of a few foreign concession areas, did not remove all foreign privileges and treaty port rights. The government sponsored financial reform, seeking to develop a uniform silver dollar and then in November 1935 a managed paper currency, which became well established by 1937, despite government budget problems from high military and debt service costs. The communications network, roads, rail and airlines were developed and opportunities for education were expanded, although much more was planned on paper than could be achieved in practice. The government failed to make any serious change to benefit the peasants, laws on rent reduction not being carried through, while its reliance upon customs and urban taxes impeded modernization.

Opinion remains sharply divided upon the overall merits of the Nanjing government, some arguing that by 1937 the basis of a successful regime had been laid, only to be destroyed by the Anti-Japanese War, while others argue that its rural failure and militaristic style were the sources of its weakness, leading to its replacement by more revolutionary forces.   *R.T.P.*

New Life Movement

The New Life Movement was inaugurated on 19 February 1934 by Chiang Kai-shek in Jiangxi Province where he was engaged in his Fifth Encirclement Campaign against the Chinese Communist Party in the south of the province. Between 19 February and 26 March Chiang gave five speeches on the movement and its ideology, and in March the movement spread from the Jiangxi capital, Nanchang, where its first public demonstrations were held, to other provinces; there were New Life promotional associations in nine provinces by the end of April 1934 and in 19 provinces by the end of 1935. Leadership lay with Chiang and the military from 1934 to 1936, its daily work often entrusted to the police, the military police and the boy scouts, but from 1936 Madame Chiang Kai-shek (Soong Mei-ling) and the more Christian and American-oriented parts of the *Guomindang* came to dominate, with the New Zealander George Shepherd (b. 1894) as a director from 1935.

The initial reason for the movement was to fight the Communists politically in Jiangxi, by a Nationalist-led mobilization of the population. The movement proceeded in two phases, mass demonstrations to publicize its aims, followed by more regular leadership to promote these aims. The movement sought to remedy the lack of public morale which Chiang had identified as a cause of China's inability to achieve equality with other nations, and its chief slogans were 'from self to others' and 'from simple to complex', implying reform of the simple behavioural patterns of the individual as the basic requirement, stressing orderliness, cleanliness, simplicity and frugality. The movement's leaders saw the traditional Chinese values of propriety, righteousness, integrity and sense of shame as reinforcing the New Life morality, and opposed both the Communist stress on class struggle and the May Fourth Movement's stress on individualism as expressions of selfish interests. In practice the movement laid stress on public health and disciplined behaviour, with very little activity in tackling welfare problems except in Jiangxi, thereby earning a reputation for triviality. The movement was beset with contradictions, seeking to be a mass movement while rejecting popular initiative, and as it failed to arouse people to create a totally organized society, it sought to achieve this by organizational methods, resulting in giving itself a militaristic image. The movement sought to use the language of social revolution to promote harmony within the existing *status quo* and therefore is open to accusations of being traditionalist in its use of Confucian virtues as a way to harmony, and of being fascist. The movement was principally active between 1934 and 1937, but its results were seen as unsatisfactory by outside observers and its founders. It lost force during the Anti-Japanese War (1937–45).   *R.T.P.*

Manchukuo (Manzhouguo)

Manchukuo was the name formally adopted by the Japanese in March 1932 to designate the new state formed from China's three northeastern provinces (Manchuria) under Japanese control. In 1933 the Japanese army advanced into Jehol and this province was annexed to Manchukuo. The Japanese invasion of Manchuria began on 18 September 1931 from the Japanese-controlled south Manchurian railway zone and proceeded smoothly with limited Chinese military resistance except in the far north. China appealed to the League of Nations to bring pressure on Japan, but despite a commission of inquiry under Lord Lytton (1876–1947) the League was unwilling to act positively for China, although Japan withdrew from the League in protest against the commission's report (February 1933). Having conquered Manchuria, Japan carried out extensive propaganda for its independence from China, which was declared on 18 February 1932. On 9 March Henry Puyi (1906–67), the last Qing emperor, was installed as chief executive of a republic, and Zheng Xiaoxu (1860–1938) as premier. Changchun was designated the capital, and renamed Xinjing. Japan extended formal recognition to Manchukuo by the September 1932 Protocol of Alliance, and the form of the state became an empire in March 1934. Although there was a State Council and a system of ministries headed by Chinese, real power lay with the Japanese vice-ministers and advisers who pervaded the government. The senior Japanese military officer in Manchukuo also acted as Japan's ambassador. In 1935 Zhang Jinghui (b. 1871), a former Manchurian military man, became premier, but gradually the Japanese turned to younger Japan-educated Chinese to staff the bureaucracy.

Japan's intention in conquering Manchuria was to obtain economic advantages from its raw materials and to consolidate Japan's security position against the USSR. Economically Japan gained an increasing stranglehold by hindering other foreign enterprises: in 1935 this was reinforced by the purchase of the Soviet-owned Chinese Eastern Railway in north Manchuria. Investment was poured into the development of railways and transport facilities, and industry and mining developed rapidly, even if the costs were sometimes uneconomic in peacetime terms. The Japanese army sought to prevent large-scale capitalist penetration of the Manchurian economy and therefore relied on newer, smaller financial companies in Japan as the source of private capital. Even with this limitation Japan created an industrial potential that was by far the greatest in China, and which was to form the basis for communist advance after 1949, despite Soviet depredations in 1945–6.

Japan had envisaged large-scale emigration programmes to Manchuria but the difficulties of the terrain and the continued presence of Chinese bandits reduced this programme almost to nothing. Hence Japanese security was provided by the Japanese army and units of the Manchukuo army, without a large rural presence by the Japanese. Throughout its existence Manchukuo was affected by rural insurgency, but very little of this was effectively harnessed by the Chinese Communist Party, in contrast to the rest of China.

Manchukuo remained diplomatically isolated until the Manchukuo-German Trade Agreement of April 1936, and the recognition of Manchukuo by Italy in November 1937 and by Germany in May 1938. Nationalist China never formally recognized Manchukuo, which Japan regarded through the 1930s as evidence of the anti-Japanese stance of China, but trade between Manchukuo and China continued and postal and transport links were resumed. It required the Japanese conquest of eastern China before a Chinese puppet regime would recognize Manchukuo. Manchukuo ceased to exist with the Japanese surrender at the end of the Second World War in August 1945, when troops from the USSR occupied the area.

R.T.P.

Jiangxi Soviet

The Jiangxi Soviet was the most important of the rural areas governed by the Chinese Communist Party between the break-up of the United Front between Communists and Nationalists in 1927 and the Long March, which started in October 1934. In 1927, as Communist forces were dispersed under Nationalist attacks, most Communists retired to remote mountainous areas throughout China, while seeking to retain an underground urban organization intact. The group under Mao Zedong established itself in the Jinggang Mountains on the Hunan-Jianxi border in September and October 1927, using guerrilla warfare techniques and developing an army based on more egalitarian principles of command and better behaviour towards the local population. During 1928 Mao's group, although reinforced by others under Zhu De (1886–1976) and Peng Dehuai, faced grave difficulties, including peasant apathy even with a very radical policy on land redistribution. In January 1929 its forces moved to south-central Jiangxi, where rapid growth in numbers and controlled area occurred, with the development of the application of 'mass line' techniques for mobilizing and channelling popular grievances, and the April 1929 adoption of the policy of confiscating landlord land only. In areas controlled by Communist forces, now called units of the Red Army, local governments were established in the soviet style, Communist Party branches relying on poor peasants and hired labourers to supervise the soviets, which were defined as representative councils of workers, peasants and soldiers. On 7 February 1930 Mao's forces created a Southwestern Jiangxi Government and the Party's urban leaders began to plan a national soviet government, holding congresses of soviet delegates in May and July 1930.

Meanwhile the urban activities of the Communist Party had failed to flourish and under the leadership of Li Lisan (b.c. 1899) the rurally developed Red Army was ordered to take Changsha, the capital of Hunan, in July 1930, and then Wuhan. Although Changsha was briefly captured, lost and then threatened again, the Red Army without adequately organized urban support could not face the Nationalist armies in positional warfare. Thereafter the Red Army withdrew to the countryside, while the urban organization of the Communist Party gradually fell into the control of Communists trained in Moscow, often called the '28 Bolsheviks', including Chen Shaoyu (1904–74), Qin Bangxian (1907–46) and Zhang Wentian (b.c. 1898). In November and December 1930 the First Encirclement Campaign by Nationalist forces began in south Jiangxi, but was defeated by guerrilla tactics, as was the second campaign of February to June 1931. The third campaign led by Chiang Kai-shek in the summer of 1931 petered out as Japan invaded Manchuria in September 1931, and in this lull the first National Congress of the Chinese Soviet Republic convened on 7 November 1931 in Ruijin, Jiangxi, creating a provisional central soviet government at Ruijin with Mao as chairman. By this time there were five soviets in Jiangxi: the Central Soviet based on Ruijin, and smaller ones on the northeast, northwest, southwest and southeast borders of the province, the latter adjoining the territory of the Central Soviet. Two in Hubei, on the southwest and northeast borders (the latter under Zhang Guotao's leadership (b. 1897) called E-Yu-Wan) were almost as strong as the Central Soviet in 1931. Although wild claims exist, it seems likely that a maximum of 9 million people lived in these soviets, with up to 3 million in the Central Soviet. The Fourth Encirclement Campaign of 1932 was defeated in Jiangxi by early 1933, but the fifth campaign, beginning in October 1933 with 750 000 Nationalist troops and new tactics, proved too powerful, leading to the Communists' Long March. During 1932 and 1933 the urban-based Party leadership gradually moved to Ruijin and began to dominate Party life in Jiangxi, while Mao retained some power in the administrative sphere. The urban leaders demanded a more radical land policy and the full protection of Communist-administered territory which reduced the opportunities for guerrilla warfare. Both policies were later criticized by Mao as reasons for the loss of Jiangxi.

The Jiangxi period was very important for the Chinese Communist Party, with the appearance of the Party army, the opportunity for administrative experience, the development of the mass line, the growth of a rural strategy and the appearance of new leaders, including Mao. Although ultimately a failure, it provided vital lessons for the future.

R.T.P.

The Long March

Although several different Chinese Communist groups were forced to march long distances in the mid-1930s to avoid military pressure from government forces, the term 'Long March' is usually reserved for the wanderings of the Communist forces that abandoned Soviet

Nationalist soldiers during the Encirclement Campaigns in the 1930s.

areas south of the Yangtze River in the latter part of 1934, in particular the First Front Army, which left the Jiangxi Soviet in mid-October. The success of the Nationalist government's Fifth Encirclement Campaign, including major victories in April and July 1934, forced the Communist decision to evacuate the Jiangxi Soviet, and in October 90–100 000 men and 35 women began to march westwards, leaving behind over 20 000 activists, as well as the severely wounded. Although beginning as a retreat, the march gradually developed a destination, north China, closer to the USSR and to the advancing line of Japanese invasion. To reach the small Communist base in north Shaanxi the marchers had to pass through much of southwest and west China, the group with Mao Zedong covering some 9600km in 11 provinces at an average of 27km a day. The marchers were under almost continuous attack from Nationalist forces, and although some provincial forces allowed them to pass unscathed, the overall deprivations of the march and the numerous battles meant that only about one-tenth of the Communists who set out from the various parts of central China reached Shaanxi. The first marchers reached north Shaanxi in September 1935, the group with Mao in October 1935, and the last groups with Zhang Guotao (b. 1897) and Zhu De (1886–1976) in October 1936.

Politically, the Long March saw the re-emergence of Mao Zedong as a senior leader at the Zunyi Conference in January 1935, where he was elected to the Standing Committee of the Politburo of the Communist Party and made director of the Central Committee's Military Affairs Committee. The conference criticized the military errors of the final period of the Jiangxi Soviet and of the early part of the march, including the transport of too much equipment, but did not attack the general party political line. A decision was reached that the First Front Army should seek to join the Fourth Front Army under Zhang Guotao in Sichuan, and the slogan 'Go north to fight the Japanese' was adopted. In June 1935 the two armies met and a stormy Politburo conference followed, Zhang seeking greater representation for his stronger forces. Further conferences occurred in late June 1935 at Lianghekou, where Zhang sought in vain to challenge the Zunyi reorganization of the leadership, and in August at Maoergai, where Mao argued for continuing north to Shaanxi while Zhang proposed to remain in Sichuan or, if necessary, to march west to Tibet or Xinjiang. On 1 August the Party also issued an appeal for a united front against Japan and the cessation of civil war. After a redistribution of men, the Communist forces divided into an eastern column under Mao, which advanced northeastwards, and a western column under Zhang and Zhu De, which initially remained in Sichuan. However, it was driven westwards by the Nationalists, where despite reinforcement by the Second Front Army under He Long (1896–1977) their position was precarious. Zhang's units finally marched into north Shaanxi in October 1936, but Zhang sought again in November and December 1936 to move westwards.

Soldiers of the Chinese Red Army, after arrival in northern Shaanxi at the end of the Long March.

This move failed disastrously and Zhang was tried for his errors by the Central Committee in January 1937.

The Long March, a major dividing line in the history of the Chinese Communist Party, ensured the survival of the Party's veterans into the Anti-Japanese War (1937–45) and created a heroic epic for the Party. The march showed the strength and value of Party discipline and ideological commitment, developed the guerrilla warfare skills of the Communists, began the consolidation of Mao's leadership and broke the Party's reliance on advice and legitimation from Moscow.   *R.T.P.*

Marco Polo Bridge Incident

The Marco Polo Bridge Incident began shortly after 10pm on 7 July 1937 at Lugouqiao near the city of Wanping southwest of Beijing, when a Japanese soldier went missing during night manoeuvres by the Japanese army. The Japanese army was entitled to station 1350 troops in the Beijing-Tianjin area by the Peace Protocol of 1901 after the Boxer Uprising, to ensure security of passage from Beijing to the sea, but by July 1937 Japan had some 7000 troops in the area and was conducting manoeuvres in areas and at times beyond the Protocol limits. Two railway routes led south from Beijing; in 1936 the Japanese moved troops into Fengtai on the more easterly line, an area not in the Protocol, and then forced the Chinese to sanction this in September 1936. Thereafter the Japanese sought to buy land between Fengtai and Wanping on the more westerly rail route, but met resistance from the magistrate in Wanping. The Japanese tried in vain to have the Chinese garrison at Wanping removed and also conducted six sets of manoeuvres over the land they sought. On the 7 July manoeuvre, when a soldier was missing after a bullet was fired at the Japanese, they demanded entry into Wanping for a search, and when this was refused, they bombarded the town, even though the missing soldier had returned. The *de facto* Japanese commander in north China (his superior having recently suffered a heart attack) ordered the local commander to avoid operations pending an inquiry, since the deployment of Japanese troops was inappropriate for a major action at Wanping and the General Staff in Tokyo had ordered that there should be no incidents in north China in order to avoid international complications, on condition that Nationalist Chinese troops did not enter north China. On 9 July the local Japanese commander unsuccessfully attacked Wanping and a local settlement was agreed on 11 July between the military officers in north China.

The Chinese government at Nanjing regarded the incident as of more than local importance, and while reserving the right to review any local settlement, dispatched troops northwards. The Japanese government in response permitted the mobilization of three divisions in Japan on 10 July and began to send reinforcements to north China from 12 July. On 16 July Chiang Kai-shek, the Chinese leader, demanded the withdrawal of the reinforcements and on 19 July stated that the incident had been engineered by Japan. On 20 July Song Zheyuan (1885–1940), commander of the 29th Chinese Army in north China, began Chinese withdrawals after apologizing to the Japanese. However, clashes began again on 25 July, leading to an ultimatum to Song by the Japanese. Song refused to retire as the Japanese demanded and fighting flared on the 27th, leading to the occupation of Beijing and Tianjin by the end of July. The Japanese government then proposed a new agreement with Nanjing on the basis of a demilitarized zone around Beijing and Tianjin, a Nationalist administration of north China led by a Japanophile and negotiations for a general China-Japan treaty. This proposal was not answered as the tense situation at Shanghai in central China developed into war, and China attacked Japanese naval installations and forces from 14 August.

The Marco Polo Bridge Incident is now considered the start of the Anti-Japanese War (1937–45), but it is doubtful whether general war had been the intention of the local Japanese command in north China. Full-scale hostilities developed from China's desire to end local settlements and risk a war of resistance, and from Japan's wish to keep the Nationalist armies out of north China.   *R.T.P.*

Anti-Japanese War and United Front

The Anti-Japanese War (1937–45) is dated from the Marco Polo Bridge Incident (7 July 1937) near Beijing, although heavy fighting in north China began in late July, resulting in the loss of Beijing and Tianjin to Japan. A second front was opened in Shanghai in mid-August, where a three-month battle developed, resulting in the loss of Shanghai in November and then Nanjing, China's capital, on 12 December 1937. By the end of 1937 Japan had also advanced to the Yellow River in north China and by October 1938 Japan had overrun Hankou and Canton. In February 1939 Japan took Hainan Island, and in March, Nanchang. Thereafter the war front was relatively stable until 1944, with the Japanese occupying the cities and railways of eastern China, and the Free China government based in Chongqing ruling western China.

In eastern China between the Japanese-controlled lines of communication, new local governments developed, relying on guerrilla warfare to ward off Japanese marauding. Communists played important roles in many of these liberated areas, where the whole population was mobilized for war activity through mass organizations. In the Japanese zone a number of puppet governments were established, the most important being the Provisional Government in Beijing (December 1937), the Reformed Government in Nanjing (March 1938) and the Reorganized National Government in Nanjing (March 1940), but none of these governments was able to stand independently of Japanese power.

Foreign military aid to China came initially from the USSR, with some financial aid from Britain and the USA, but in December 1941 China joined the Allies by formal war declarations against Japan and Germany, thereby gaining access to American military aid. The USA began to develop airfields in China for the bombing of Japan, which provoked Japanese campaigns in 1942 and much more forcefully in 1944, when the Ichigo campaign pushed Japanese power into much of southwest China. The Japanese army was still firmly entrenched in China at Japan's surrender in August 1945.

Chinese resistance to the Japanese was organized initially on the basis of a united front of all patriotic elements. The front was formalized by the agreement of the *Guomindang* and the Chinese Communist Party on 22 September 1937, whereby the Communist soldiers were reorganized as the Eighth Route Army (later the 18th) of the National Revolutionary Army, and the Communist Party abolished its soviet areas and its policy of land confiscation. The Communist Party had been calling for an anti-Japanese united front before 1937, but Chiang Kai-shek, the *Guomindang* leader, had rejected these calls until his arrest at Xi'an on 12 December 1936 by Zhang Xueliang (b. 1898), who, as commander of China's Northeastern Army, wished to resist Japan rather than fight the Communists. In the latter part of 1937 Communist soldiers joined in the defence of Shanxi and in 1938 members of the Eighth Route Army spread across north China organizing resistance. The National government allowed a Communist Party office to be set up at its capital, began to pay a subsidy to the Communist government at Yan'an and in October 1937 authorized the creation of the New Fourth Army, from Communist remnants south of the Yangtze River. A People's Political Council was convened in July 1938 with representatives of all political parties, as a body to advise the government. Nevertheless, tension gradually mounted between the Communists into Nationalists over the expansion of Communist forces into areas beyond those prescribed by Chiang, resulting in the reimposition of the Nationalist blockade on Communist areas and in military incidents, culminating in the New Fourth Army Incident in January 1941. Thereafter political and military cooperation virtually ceased at the national level, but the Communist Party still used the United Front as the basis of its political strategy in the liberated areas. The war period saw a rapid expansion of Communist strength, while the Nationalist government, beset with inflationary worries and far from its coastal base, weakened despite a numerical increase in its armies.   *R.T.P.*

Chongqing

Chongqing is a city in Sichuan at the confluence of the Yangtze and Jialing Rivers. It was the seat of government of Free China during the Anti-Japanese War (1937–45), with all the offices of government transferred to it by October 1938; it suffered extensively from Japanese bombing from mid-1939. Chongqing was isolated by the Japanese occupation of eastern China and its overseas links were through Yunnan Province, from Indo-China (up to 1940), Burma (up to 1941) and by air over the 'Hump' of high mountains from India from 1942.

The Chongqing government under Chiang Kai-shek mobilized some 14 million soldiers for the war against Japan, suffered over 3 million casualties, and received recognition as one of the Great

Top: Chongqing, Free China's capital, under attack by Japanese bombers. Middle: a steel factory near Chongqing during the Anti-Japanese War. It manufactured steel from materials supplied by Sichuan Province. Bottom: a view of Chongqing and the Yangtze River.

Powers by Britain and the USA, with Chiang attending the Cairo conference in late November 1943. In January 1943 the unequal treaties imposed upon China in the 19th century were terminated, restoring full rights to China. The Chongqing government, although dominated by the *Guomindang* (Nationalist Party), did allow some activities by other political groups, including the Chinese Communists, whose principal representative in Chongqing was Zhou Enlai. Economically the government was at a disadvantage, having lost the coastal cities, and although some 120 000 tonnes of industrial equipment was moved into the interior, there were production difficulties, resulting in shortages and hoarding. Military expenditures were largely financed through the issue of paper currency, given the limited fiscal resources available. This resulted in rapid inflation, which damaged morale and alienated much of the population. To try to alleviate these problems industrial cooperatives were promoted and there was a return to central government collection of land tax. Foreign financial assistance to the Chongqing government included a variety of currency stabilization loans, the support of Free Chinese activities in Shanghai until December 1941, and loans by the USA after December 1941, including gold for sale to soak up excessive liquidity. Military aid came from the USSR up to 1941 and from the USA from 1942, with Joseph Stilwell as commander of US forces until his replacement by General Albert Wedemeyer (b. 1897) in late 1944. Militarily, the Chongqing government commanded the Chinese army through a system of war zones, relying mostly on positional warfare and an extensive no-man's-land between Chinese and Japanese troops, but its authority was limited in the liberated areas behind Japanese lines where guerrilla warfare was predominant. By 1945 Chongqing controlled a large army, with 39 of its divisions fully equipped by the USA, but wartime tensions and difficulties had reduced the ability of the government to tackle efficiently the problems of post-war reconstruction.   *R.T.P.*

Joseph Stilwell

Joseph Warren Stilwell (1883–1946), nicknamed Vinegar Joe, an officer of the US Army, visited China briefly in 1911 and served in Beijing, 1920–3, and in Tianjin, 1926–9. He was a US military attaché to China from 1935 to 1939. In January 1942 Lieutenant-general Stilwell was appointed Commanding General of the US Army Forces in the China-Burma-India theatre, Chief of Staff to the Supreme Commander China Theatre, Chiang Kai-shek, and supervisor of US Lend-Lease aid to China.

Reaching China in March 1942, Stilwell joined the Chinese army in Burma, which retreated into India by May 1942. He returned to Free China's capital, Chongqing, where friction developed between Stilwell and Chiang Kai-shek over Free China's war effort, which Stilwell regarded as inadequate. He also clashed with General Claire Chennault (1890–1958) of the China-based US 14th Air Force over the relative merits of infantry development and aerial bombing for the defence of Free China. From December 1943 to July 1944 Stilwell devoted much effort to the recapture of north Burma and the opening of the Ledo Road, but as Japan penetrated further into China during the Ichigo campaign against US air-bases in China, President F.D. Roosevelt (1882–1945) suggested to Chiang in July 1944 that Stilwell should take command of the Chinese army. Chiang attached certain conditions, including no independent command of Chinese Communist troops by Stilwell. In September 1944 Patrick Hurley (1883–1963), Roosevelt's presidential emissary to Chongqing, secured Chiang's consent to Stilwell's command over Chinese troops, but when Stilwell demanded unrestricted command, Chiang asked for Stilwell's recall, which occurred on 19 October 1944. Stilwell left immediately, refusing Chiang's offer of Chinese military decoration, and ended the war as commander of the US 10th Army.

R.T.P.

General Joseph Stillwell (left), with General Frank Merrill.

Yan'an

Yan'an is a city in north Shaanxi, which from January 1937 to March 1947 acted as the seat of the Central Committee of the Chinese Communist Party and as the capital of the Communist-controlled areas of China. After 1947 Yan'an came to symbolize the whole revolutionary approach to Communist development, stressing self-reliance, the mass line, simpler administration, and rectification of the Party through study and persuasion.

The Communist leadership moved its headquarters to Yan'an from the more northerly Baoan at the end of 1936, and from there led a rapid expansion of Communist power once the Anti-Japanese War began in July 1937. The Party grew from c. 20 000 members in 1936, to 200 000 in 1938, 800 000 in 1940 and to 1 200 000 in April 1945. Its armed forces, the Red Army, grew from some 22 000 in early 1936 to over 180 000 by the end of 1938, to 500 000 in 1940 and to 880 000 in March 1945, with a comparable growth in supporting militia. As the war spread, Japanese inability to control the countryside fully, while seeking to exploit it economically, led to the development of liberated areas behind the Japanese lines, in which Communist Party skills in government organization and guerrilla warfare gave it a leading role: 19 such areas were claimed by the Communists in 1945, with a population of 96 million.

In 1937 the Nationalist government recognized the Yan'an area as a special region of the national government, called the Shaan-Gan-Ning Border Region. It provided a subsidy of some 100 000 Chinese dollars per month, and the Communists ruled this area, fluctuating from 15 complete counties in mid-1937, to about 24 in 1938, to about 18 in 1939–41, and expanding to 29 counties with 1.5 million population after 1941. In mid-1939 the Nationalists imposed a blockade on the region, cutting the subsidy in 1940, and maintaining some 500 000 troops to enforce a blockade in the 1940s. Communist policy between 1937 and 1941 stressed the United Front, class harmony and moderate reform, directed by a growing bureaucracy, but from 1941 a series of campaigns were launched to change the governmental style. These included the rectification (*zhengfeng*) campaigns to strengthen the quality of party personnel and to promote the Maoist interpretation of Marxism, a campaign for 'crack troops and simple administration' (1941–3), a 'to the village' campaign to involve Party officials in rural service (the first one in 1941–2), a campaign to reduce rent and interest (1942–4), a cooperative movement to reorganize the village economy (1942–4), a production movement (1943) to involve Party officials in production and to promote labour heroes, and an education movement (1944) to promote literacy. These campaigns served to develop the mass line as a key Maoist strategy,

Mao Zedong's cave at Yan'an.

involving mobilization of the masses as the means to solve problems, not mere reliance on party leadership.

Politically the Yan'an period saw the emergence of Mao Zedong as Party leader and theoretician fully confirmed. Mao's views on the sinification of Marxism and his definition of the historical stage of 'New Democracy' were accepted by the Party Congress of April 1945, when Liu Shaoqi emerged as Mao's right-hand man. Political consciousness and the level of education in the Party were raised by the large number of schools established in Yan'an, the most famous of which were the Central Party School and Kangda, the anti-Japanese Military and Political Academy.

Internationally Yan'an was in radio contact with Moscow from late 1937, but Western presence was limited to the occasional journalist, until the American military and diplomatic visits of 1944. The Japanese army never seriously threatened Yan'an itself, but the city was bombed.   *R.T.P.*

Rectification campaigns

The first large-scale rectification (*zhengfeng*) campaign of the Chinese Communist Party occurred during the Anti-Japanese War and is usually dated 1942–4, although Mao Zedong spoke of 1942–mid-1945. The campaign followed the rapid growth in Party membership from about 20 000 in 1936 to 800 000 in 1940 and the lack of sufficient progress in Party education work from 1938. Although foreshadowed by Party directives during 1941 and the December 1941 Drive to Reduce Bureaucracy, the campaign began in earnest after two speeches by Mao in early February 1942, when he attacked subjectivism in study, sectarianism in Party work and formalism in propaganda and literary work, and stressed that dogmatism of the intellectuals was a graver danger than the empiricism of practical workers. In a speech in May 1942 he further outlined Party policy on artistic issues at the Yan'an Forum.

The campaign developed initially in northern Shaanxi with meetings of officials in Yan'an and the study of at first 18 and later 22 documents by Mao, Liu Shaoqi, Chen Yun (b. 1905) and various Russian leaders (but including no documents by those close to Wang Ming (Chen Shaoyu (1904–74) one of the '28 Bolsheviks'). The aim of the campaign was to spread the methodology of the mass line to the Party membership and to develop a flexible understanding of Marxism-Leninism among new members, but as the campaign spread geographically it increasingly stressed Party purification and anti-subversion. By 1944 the stress had shifted to the study of Party history and the campaign revealed the triumph of Mao over the '28 Bolsheviks' faction around Wang Ming, whose dogmatic approach had been criticized. Although a few were purged from the Party, the campaign aimed at consolidation, which then allowed further expansion to 1 210 000 members by April 1945.

A further Party rectification campaign was held in 1947–8 and since 1949, under the People's Republic of China, they have been launched periodically on a nationwide scale to serve political and ideological ends, for example during the various agrarian reforms, the Hundred Flowers and Anti-rightist movements (1956–8) and the Cultural Revolution. *R.T.P.*

New Fourth Army Incident

The New Fourth Army Incident occurred at Maolin, Anhui Province, south of the Yangtze River, where the headquarters force of the Communist New Fourth Army—comprising 4000 soldiers, 2000 wounded and 3000 political and medical workers—was surrounded on 4 January 1941 by the 40th Division of the Nationalist Army, and largely destroyed in a 10-day battle.

The New Fourth Army had been created in October 1937 with the approval of the Nationalist government from Communist remnants in central China, with an authorized strength of 12 000 men under Commander Ye Ting (1897–1946) and his deputy, Xiang Ying (1898–1941). It was supposed to operate only south of the Yangtze River, but by late 1938 three of its detachments were operating north of the Yangtze. During 1939 several clashes occurred

between New Fourth Army units and Nationalist units, as the New Fourth Army spread beyond the limits set by the Nationalist government, the earliest publicized one occurring on 12 June. In late 1939 units began to move into northern Jiangsu and during 1940 the bulk of the New Fourth Army troops, now totalling over 100 000 men, moved north of the Yangtze, ousting Nationalist units in Jiangsu.

In June 1940 at Chongqing, the wartime capital, a general understanding was reached between Communist and Nationalist negotiators, whereby the Communists were to be free to operate in most areas north of the Yellow River, while withdrawing the New Fourth Army from central China. To implement this from 19 October 1940 the Nationalists sent a series of telegrams to Ye Ting ordering him to move the remainder of the New Fourth Army troops, including the headquarters force, north of the Yangtze. The telegram of 9 December imposed a deadline of 31 December for the move. Ye protested at the suggested routes for crossing the Yangtze, and after the deadline expired, his headquarters force began to march southwestwards, whereupon it was attacked and defeated, Xiang being killed and Ye taken prisoner.

The incident marked the end of the United Front at the national level. The Nationalists accused the Communists of insubordination, and dissolved the New Fourth Army on 17 January; the Communists accused the Nationalists of an attack on patriotic soldiers and proceeded to develop the New Fourth Army north of the Yangtze under new leaders. The whole incident greatly enhanced Communist prestige. It also ended the policies of Xiang Ying, particularly that of mobile warfare based on class accommodation and harmony with the Nationalists—a policy favoured by Wang Ming (Chen Shaoyu (1904–74) one of the '28 Bolsheviks') Mao Zedong's leading opponent within the Chinese Communist Party. *R.T.P.*

Civil war

The civil war between the Chinese Communist Party and the *Guomindang* (Nationalist Party) was openly fought in China from mid-1946 until the final victory of the Communists in 1949–50, preliminary conflicts having erupted after Japan's surrender, at the end of the Second World War in August 1945. The civil war marked the culmination of political and military rivalry of the parties, which had begun in 1927 and been somewhat muted during the Anti-Japanese War. Between August and October 1945 the leaders of the two parties, Mao Zedong and Chiang Kai-shek, met in Chongqing to discuss their parties' future activities, while their armies sought to reoccupy Japanese-held areas of China, the Nationalists with American transport assistance.

The two leaders agreed to the convening of a political consultative conference, which was held in January 1946 with the encouragement of the American presidential ambassador General Marshall (1880–1959), who arrived in mid-December 1945. Marshall also organized a ceasefire on 10 January, supervised by teams consisting of an American, a Nationalist and a Communist, and on 25 February 1946 reached an agreement to cut back Communist and Nationalist armed forces on a 1:5 ratio and to integrate both into a national army.

Despite these signs of cooperation, the situation was militarily tense, especially in Manchuria, where the presence of troops of the USSR proved an added complication. Large-scale fighting developed in April 1946, especially at the Manchurian city of Changchun, retaken by the Nationalists in May. Marshall organized a further 15-day truce on 6 June, but thereafter fighting developed rapidly. The Nationalists, enjoying at least 3:1 superiority in numbers and great advantages in equipment, proved very successful during the first year of the war, claiming to have gained 191 000sq km by June 1947, including the Communist capital Yan'an in March 1947. Politically, the Nationalists in July 1946 announced plans for a National Assembly to be held in November 1946, contrary to the timetable agreed in January 1946. This Assembly adopted a constitution, which the Communists rejected as illegal.

From mid-1947 the fighting entered a critical stage for the Nationalists, as garrison duties occupied increasing numbers while the Communists harassed over-extended positions with their expanding army. A general Communist offensive developed in the second half of 1947, winning victories in Henan and north Hebei. During 1948 as Communist forces approached and, in November, surpassed Nationalist numbers, the Communists took over major cities in Manchuria, and at Jinan, with large numbers of Nationalist troops surrendering to the Communists. The major battle of Huai-Hai between October 1948 and January 1949 resulted in a Nationalist defeat in positional warfare around the town of Xuzhou. The Nationalist armies in Beijing and Tianjin surrendered in January 1949 and the Communists crossed the Yangtze River on 21 April. Their advancing armies forced the Nationalist government to Canton, then to Chongqing (13 October), and finally to Taiwan, and the People's Republic was proclaimed on 1 October.

The Nationalists' defeat ultimately came by military means, thereby exposing military weakness, including the failure of Nationalist generals to cooperate, the problems of intervention by Chiang Kai-shek and the effects of the garrison, defensive mentality. The Communists also earned their victory by the quality of their soldiers and generals, by their mobilization of the population through social policies, including renewed land reform in north China, and by the absence of widespread corruption in government. The Nationalists also suffered from the hyperinflation arising from over-issue of paper currency, which eroded urban support. During the civil war the USA provided arms and finance, although not to the extent that the Nationalists requested. However, the Nationalists never lost battles for lack of arms, and suggestions that the USA 'lost China' should be viewed in terms of the overall situation.   *R.T.P.*

Mao Zedong, with his wife Jiang Qing behind, evacuating Yan'an in March 1947 during the Civil War.

Hyper-inflation: a clerk counts huge numbers of banknotes to be paid out in salaries.

Taiwan

Taiwan, an island of about 33 600 sq km, off the coast of Fujian Province, was incorporated into the Qing empire in 1683 as a prefecture of Fujian, becoming a full province in 1887. It suffered invasions by Japan (1874) and France (1884), before being lost to Japan in 1895 by the Treaty of Shimonoseki concluding the Sino-Japanese War (1894–5). Local leaders declared a republic rather than obeying the order to surrender, but this resistance was quickly quashed by the Japanese, who ruled Taiwan as part of their empire for 50 years (1895–1945), carrying out a wide range of economic developments as sugar and rice production were expanded for the Japanese market. The Japanese language was promoted for administrative and educational purposes, while public health work and Japanese migration helped the population to grow from about 3 million (1905) to 5.9 million (1940).

During the Second World War Taiwan was subjected to bombing by US planes from late 1943 until 1945, but the island was not recaptured by force of arms. The return of Taiwan to Chinese control was envisaged in the Cairo Declaration (1 December 1943); following the Japanese surrender, the Chinese government

in Chongqing proclaimed sovereignty over Taiwan on 30 August 1945, naming Chen Yi (1883–1950) as governor. Arriving in Taiwan in October 1945, Chen Yi soon alienated the population by his discrimination against Taiwanese as colonials and by his staff's corrupt misuse of Japanese properties. Public indignation at the maladministration by mainland Chinese and at the ambiguous attitude towards Taiwan by the mainland government finally boiled over in Taipei in late February 1947. Chen Yi appealed for order and discussed reforms with local representatives, while awaiting military reinforcements from the mainland. He then declared martial law and ruthlessly suppressed the Taiwanese; the official casualty list on 29 March was 1860 civilians. Chen Yi was dismissed by the mainland government, and replaced by Wei Daoming (b.c. 1899). During 1948, as the civil war turned against the *Guomindang* of Chiang Kai-shek, preparations were made for a withdrawal to Taiwan and a senior Nationalist general Chen Cheng (1897–1965) was appointed governor of Taiwan. The mainland exodus increased through 1949, swelling the mainlander population from 47 551 (1945) to some 2 million in 1950. Taiwan became the base of the Nationalist government of the Republic of China with Taipei as its capital, on 8 December 1949.   *R.T.P.*

Chiang Kai-shek

Chiang Kai-shek (1887–1975), a native of Fenghua district, Zhejiang, received his military training at Baoding Military School (1907–8) and in Tokyo (1908–10). There he joined the anti-Manchu Revolutionary Alliance Society (*Tongmenghui*) in 1908 and met Sun Yat-sen in 1910. He fought at Shanghai during the Republican Revolution of 1911 and during the 1910s worked to promote the revolutionary activities of Sun Yat-sen by military service and commercial activities. By 1923 he was chief of staff in Sun's headquarters in Canton and was selected by Sun to visit the USSR in September–November to study military organization. On his return he was elected to the Military Council of the *Guomindang*, the Nationalist Party, and after some hesitation became the head of the Whampoa Military Academy, where with Soviet help he built up a Party army for the *Guomindang*.

After Sun's death in March 1925 Chiang's position in the *Guomindang* improved with the growing role of the Party army, and he was elected to the *Guomindang*'s Central Executive Committee in early 1926. He showed great political skill after the 20 March 1926 incident, reducing Communist penetration of the *Guomindang*, while keeping Soviet cooperation, and as supreme commander led the successful Northern Expedition of the *Guomindang*, resulting in the capture of the lower Yangtze valley by March 1927. In April 1927 he split the *Guomindang* by attacking the Communists in Shanghai and setting up a government in Nanjing.

In August 1927 he retired for political reasons and, after a visit to Japan, returned to Shanghai to marry Soong Mei-ling, the American-educated and Christian sister-in-law of Sun Yat-sen. In 1928 he returned to politics as chairman of the National Military Council and commander-in-chief of the second stage of the Northern Expedition, which resulted in the capture of Beijing. In October 1928 he became chairman of the National government based in Nanjing and acted as principal coordinator of the various groups which backed that government, consolidating his power by successful wars against party dissidents during 1929 and 1930. Following the Japanese invasion of Manchuria in 1931 and the subsequent reorganization of the government and Party, Chiang lost his government chairmanship and was given a military role.

Chiang Kai-shek (right), Mme Chiang, and Lord Mountbatten at a training base in India for Chinese soldiers, *c.* 1943.

This he rapidly exploited by the development of Bandit Suppression Headquarters, which subsumed all authority under a military guise. At this time Chiang sought to revitalize the *Guomindang* by the development of the Blue Shirts, a youth corps of devoted followers, and to strengthen the populace by the New Life Movement. In December 1935 Chiang was appointed president of the Executive Yuan, equivalent to prime minister, after the attempted assassination of his chief party rival, Wang Jingwei (1883–1944), by an anti-Japanese patriot. During the Nanjing decade (1928–37) Chiang was well-known for his anti-Communism and for his wish to strengthen China economically and militarily before facing the aggression of Japan directly. However, after his arrest at Xi'an in December 1936 by the former Manchurian warlord Zhang Xueliang, he gradually turned to a policy of opposing the Japanese and reducing the confrontation with the Communists. In 1938 he was elected party leader (*zongcai*) of the *Guomindang* and in 1943 as chief of state attended the Cairo conference with US President F.D. Roosevelt (1882–1945) and British Prime Minister Winston Churchill (1874–1965). In 1945 he held six weeks of talks with the Communist leader Mao Zedong, but on failing to reach agreement on a coalition, Chiang pursued civil war with the Communists. The war resulted in Chiang's defeat and withdrawal to Taiwan in 1949, where he remained as president until his death, overseeing the modernization of the island with American help and forever speaking of a return to the Chinese mainland.   *R.T.P.*

THE PEOPLE'S REPUBLIC

Liberation

'Liberation' indicates the founding of the Chinese People's Republic on 1 October 1949. The new government faced five problems: the establishment of its authority; control of hyperinflation; restoration of the war-wrecked economy; redistribution of land to the peasants; and the definition of its international position.

Six military regions were created at this time, representing the areas occupied by individual Communist armies, to provide military government until the last Nationalist units on the mainland (still a million strong) had been eliminated. People's Liberation Army units took the initiative in bringing together, at each administrative level (province, prefecture and county), an alliance of local representatives, delegates of the mass organizations, and members of the existing Nationalist local authorities, to create a new structure of government. In Beijing, a Chinese People's Political Consultative Conference was called in September 1949; it represented all groups and parties expected to support 'New Democracy'.

Inflation was brought to an end by price controls, which the new government was able to enforce because it was already, as the inheritor of industries formerly controlled by Japanese or Nationalist interests, in a position of economic dominance. Control of inflation was also assisted by an index-linked guarantee of the value of wages and savings.

Economic recovery was given priority over immediate social changes: private industry and commerce were encouraged, and protected from excessive demands on the part of the newly established trade unions, while the commercialized sector of agriculture was similarly protected against the effects of land reform. By 1952 the economy had in most respects been restored to the best prewar levels of production.

Mao Zedong, Chairman of the Communist Party of China, proclaims the establishment of the People's Republic of China from the rostrum of Tiananmen Square on 1 October 1949.

Land reform had already commenced during the civil war. It was regarded by the Communist Party not only as necessary in principle, but as an immediate means of gaining peasant loyalty.

The Common Programme of the New Democracy had resolved on friendship with the USSR, in accord with Mao Zedong's advocacy of a policy of 'leaning to one side'. This was not seen to preclude normal relations with the USA, from which China would at that time have been willing to accept economic assistance. The rejection of discreet Chinese overtures, however, left China little alternative to exclusive reliance on the Soviet Union. With regard to Taiwan, the US government changed its position and said that its status remained to be determined; and at the outbreak of the Korean War, it effectively separated Taiwan from China. China signed a Treaty of Friendship, Alliance and Mutual Assistance with the USSR on 14 February 1950, directed against the possible military revival of Japan under US influence. The Treaty gave the USSR the use of Dairen and Port Arthur and a share in the control of the railways of Manchuria. It was followed by a Soviet credit of US $300 000 000.

J.G.

Mao Zedong

Mao (26 December 1893–9 September 1976) was born in the village of Shaoshan, Hunan Province. He was the son of a poor peasant who had become affluent as a farmer and grain dealer. Though schooled in the Confucian classics from the age of eight, Mao early rebelled against paternal authority, leaving home to attend a secondary school in the provincial capital, Changsha. There he came in contact with new ideas from the West.

In October 1911, when the uprising against the Manchus spread to Hunan, Mao enlisted in the revolutionary army, and spent six months as a soldier. This gesture may or may not have been inspired by his boyhood admiration for military heroes, including Napoleon and George Washington, as well as the great warrior-emperors of the Chinese past.

After graduating in 1918 from the First Provincial Normal School in Changsha, Mao spent a half year at Peking University as a library assistant. There, during the months leading up to the May Fourth student demonstrations, he came under the influence of the two founders of the Chinese Communist Party: Li Dazhao and Chen Duxiu.

Returning to Changsha, Mao Zedong organized a number of demonstrations aimed at forcing the government to oppose Japan. His writings at the time are filled with references to the 'army of the red flag' throughout the world and to the victory of the Russian Revolution, but it was only in January 1921 that he finally embraced Marxism.

Right to left: Mao Zedong with his uncle, father and younger brother Zetan, c. 1919.

Mao's wife Yang Kaihui (executed in 1930), with his infant sons Anying (standing), killed in the Korean War, and Anqing; c. 1923.

In July 1921, he attended the First Congress of the Chinese Communist Party. When, in 1923, the young Party entered into an alliance with Sun Yat-sen's *Guomindang* (Nationalist Party), Mao was one of the first Communists to join the *Guomindang* and to work within it. In 1924, he was a leading member of the *Guomindang* Executive Bureau in Shanghai.

In the winter of 1924–5, Mao returned to his native village of Shaoshan for a rest. There, witnessing the reaction of the peasants to the shooting of several dozen Chinese by foreign police in Shanghai (May and June 1925), he suddenly became conscious of the revolutionary potential inherent in the countryside. Despite his origins, Mao had, in the course of his student years, adopted the Chinese intellectual's patronizing view of the workers and peasants. His conversion to Marxism had forced him to revise his estimate of the urban proletariat, and now he turned back to the world of his youth, seeking to channel the protest movements of the peasants into organized political action.

Pursued by the military governor of Hunan, Mao fled to Canton, the main bastion of the *Guomindang*, led by Chiang Kaishek since the death of Sun Yat-sen in March 1925. Apart from serving as Acting Head of the Propaganda Department of the *Guomindang*, and attending the Second *Guomindang* Congress in January 1926, Mao headed the *Guomindang*'s Peasant Movement Training Institute from May to September 1926.

When, in the spring of 1927, Chiang Kai-shek turned on his communist allies and utterly destroyed the workers' movement in the cities, it was obvious that in the immediate future the revolu-

tion could survive only in the villages. For most communists this was a regrettable necessity, an aberration to be surmounted as rapidly as possible. Mao Zedong, on the other hand, was now fully at home with this idea.

Mao grasped at a stroke, in the autumn of 1927, the decisive importance of organized military force, as distinguished from spontaneous mass violence, in standing up to armed repression. It took him several years to understand a second basic point, namely that victory would not finally come all at once, in a great nationwide revolutionary conflagration, but would be won only at the end of a prolonged and bitter struggle in which the *Guomindang*-held cities would be gradually surrounded by the revolutionary countryside.

When a few thousand troops who had survived the perils of the Long March arrived in the northwest in the autumn of 1935, events were already moving towards a renewed united front with the *Guomindang* against Japan. In August 1935 the Comintern at its Seventh Congress in Moscow called for an anti-Fascist united front, and the Chinese Communists gradually came to accept that such a united front must include Chiang Kai-shek himself. The Xi'an incident of December 1936, in which Chiang was kidnapped by military leaders from northeastern China who wanted to fight Japan, accelerated the evolution towards unity. By the time the Japanese began their attempt to subjugate all of China in July 1937, the terms of an accord between the Communists and the *Guomindang* had been virtually settled, and the formal agreement was signed in September 1937.

In the new circumstances of the Anti-Japanese War, the guerrilla tactics which Mao Zedong and Zhu De (1886–1976) had developed earlier in the struggles against the *Guomindang* enabled them to lay the foundations of their future triumph by expanding into the vast unoccupied areas of the Chinese countryside behind the

Mao Zedong in 1938, lecturing at the Anti-Japanese Military and Political University in Yan'an.

Japanese lines. Mao did not, of course, have primary responsibility for the military aspect of these tactics. His contribution lay partly in fusing war and politics into a coherent strategy, but it lay even more in the impact which his overwhelming sense of identification with the destiny of China produced on his compatriots.

Though Mao Zedong soon came to be regarded by many Chinese as a natural leader in the war against Japan, unchallenged supremacy in the Chinese Communist Party itself did not automatically follow. Mao had neither the first-hand knowledge of the Soviet Union possessed by some of his rivals, nor their ability to read Marx or Lenin in the original. He did claim, however, to know and understand China. The differences between him and the Soviet-oriented faction in the Party came to a head at the time of the Rectification Campaign of 1942. This movement aimed to give a basic grounding in Leninist principles to the thousands of new members who had been recruited since 1937. But an equally important goal was the elimination of what Mao called 'foreign dogmatism'—blind imitation of Soviet experience and obedience to Soviet directives. The study of Mao's own thought, as the quintessential expression of what he had called in 1938 'sinified Marxism', was a key instrument in this struggle, and led inevitably to a cult of his person.

In March 1943, Mao became for the first time chairman of the Secretariat and of the Politburo. At about the same time, the Rectification Campaign assumed the form of a harsh purge of elements insufficiently loyal to Mao, run by Kang Sheng (one of Mao's key supporters in the Cultural Revolution). Many Party members were tortured, and some were driven to suicide. Soviet spokesmen have denounced the Rectification Campaign of 1942–3 as an attempt to eliminate all those genuinely imbued with 'proletarian internationalism' (i.e., devotion to Moscow). It is therefore not surprising that as the civil war with the *Guomindang* approached its climax, Stalin's lack of enthusiasm for a Chinese Communist victory became increasingly evident.

When the Communists did take power in China, both Mao and Stalin had to make the best of the situation. In December 1949 Mao travelled to Moscow, where, after two months of arduous negotiations, he persuaded Stalin to sign a treaty of mutual assistance accompanied by limited economic aid. Before the Chinese had time to profit from the resources thus made available, they found themselves dragged into the Korean War in support of the Moscow-oriented regime in Pyongyang. Only after this baptism of fire did Stalin, according to Mao, begin to have confidence in him and believe he was not a 'Tito'.

Despite these tensions with Moscow, the policies of the Chinese People's Republic in its early years were based in many respects, as Mao later said, on 'copying from the Soviets'. While Mao and his comrades had experience of guerrilla warfare in the countryside, they had no first-hand knowledge either of running a state, or of large-scale economic development. A five-year plan was therefore drawn up under Soviet guidance, and put into effect beginning in 1953, with Soviet technical assistance. Yet within two years, Mao took steps that led to the breakdown of the alliance with Moscow.

Mao proclaimed in 1949 that while previously the Chinese revolution had taken the form of 'encircling the cities from the countryside', it would in future follow the orthodox road of the cities leading and guiding the countryside. He therefore accepted in 1950 that collectivization would be possible only when China's heavy industry had provided the necessary equipment for mechanization. In July 1955, he reversed this position, arguing that in China, the social transformation could run ahead of the technical transformation. Deeply impressed by the exploits of certain cooperatives which claimed to have radically improved their conditions without any outside assistance, he came to believe in the limitless capacity of the Chinese people to transform at will both nature and their own social relations when mobilized for revolutionary goals. Those in the leadership who did not share this vision he denounced as 'old women with bound feet'.

Mao's new policies from the mid-1950s onwards, while building in many respects on Lenin's theories and Stalin's practice, also involved conceptions inspired by his experience during the struggle for power. The political methods developed at that time are frequently summed up under the term 'the mass line'. This has generally been accounted one of the positive attributes of the Chi-

nese Communist movement, but it should not be imagined that this slogan meant for Mao giving the people their heads and doing whatever they wanted. On the contrary, he repeatedly made it clear that the duty of the Party leadership was to listen to opinion at the grass roots, and then to put forward and impose ideas and policies which the masses were incapable of conceiving for themselves.

Even before Khrushchev's secret speech of February 1956 denouncing Stalin's crimes, Mao Zedong and his colleagues had been discussing measures for improving the morale of the intellectuals, in order to secure their willing participation in building a new China. At the end of April 1956, Mao proclaimed the policy of 'letting a hundred flowers bloom'—that is, the freedom to express many diverse ideas. Stalin, he said, had been 'too leftist' in dealing with opposition.

Despite the disorders called forth by de-Stalinization in Poland and Hungary, Mao pressed boldly forward with this policy, against the advice of senior colleagues. When the resulting 'great blooming and contending' got out of hand, and called into question the axiom of Party rule, Mao turned savagely against the educated elite which had betrayed his confidence. Henceforth, he would rely on the creativity of the rank and file as the agent of modernization.

During the winter of 1957–8, Mao worked out the policies characterizing the 'Great Leap Forward', formally launched in May 1958. While his economic strategy was not so one-sided and simplistic as commonly believed in the 1960s and 1970s, and though he still proclaimed industrialization and a 'technical revolution' as

Mao Zedong and Chiang Kai-shek toast one another at a banquet during the abortive negotiations held in Chongqing in the autumn of 1945 about arrangements for post-war collaboration between the Communists and the Kuomintang.

his goals, Mao displayed great anxiety regarding the corrupting influence of the fruits of technical progress, and an acute nostalgia for the purity and egalitarianism which had marked the world of the Jingganshan and Yan'an eras.

Thus it was logical that he should endorse the establishment of 'people's communes' as part of the Great Leap strategy. As a result, the peasants, who had been organized in cooperatives in 1955–6, and then in fully-socialist collectives in 1956–7, found their world turned upside down once again in 1958. Chaos ensued, and by the winter of 1958–9, Mao himself had come to recognize that some adjustments were necessary. He insisted, however, that in broad outline his new Chinese road to socialism, inspired by the conviction that China, though 'poor and blank', could leap ahead of other countries, was basically sound.

At the Lushan meeting of the Central Committee in July–August 1959, Peng Dehuai, the Minister of Defence, denounced the excesses of the Great Leap and the economic losses they had caused. He was removed from all his party and state posts, and detained until his death during the Cultural Revolution. From this time forward, Mao regarded any criticism of his policies as a crime of *lèse-majesté*, meriting exemplary punishment. Almost immediately, he began building an alternative power base in the People's Liberation Army, which the new Defence Minister, Lin Biao, had set out to turn into a 'great school of Mao Zedong Thought'.

Mao attends a special session of the Supreme Soviet in Moscow in November 1957 on the occasion of the 40th anniversary of the October Revolution. Left to right: Khrushchev, Mao, Song Qingling (Mme Sun Yat-sen), and Voroshilov.

The disorganization and waste created by the Great Leap, compounded by the impact of natural disasters and of the termination of Soviet economic aid, led to widespread famine, in which, according to recent official Chinese accounts, millions of people died. The response to this situation of Liu Shaoqi (who had succeeded Mao as Chairman of the Chinese People's Republic in 1959) and the economic planners was to make use of material incentives, and to strengthen the role of individual households in agricultural production. At first, Mao reluctantly agreed, but he soon came to see these methods as implying the repudiation of the whole Great Leap strategy. Moreover, he was persuaded that 'new bourgeois elements' were emerging among the bureaucratic, technical and artistic elite. At the 10th Plenary Session of the Central Committee in September 1962, he responded with the call 'Never forget the class struggle!'

At the end of 1964, when Liu Shaoqi refused to accept Mao's demand to direct the spearhead of class struggle against 'capitalist roaders' in the party, Mao decided that 'Liu had to go', and shortly launched against Liu and like-minded figures in the Party the root-and-branch attack known as the 'Great Proletarian Cultural Revolution'. During the first phase of this movement, the onslaught on authority in all its forms which Mao Zedong promoted under the slogan 'To rebel is justified!' went beyond anti-bureaucratism to something in appearance very much like anarchism. Mao was, however, no anarchist, but a believer in a 'strong socialist state'. When the Shanghai leftists Zhang Chunqiao and Yao Wenyuan (who were later to make up half the 'gang of four') came to see him in February 1967, after setting up the Shanghai Commune, Mao asserted that the demand for the abolition of 'heads' which had been heard in their city was 'extreme anarchism' and 'most reactionary'; in fact there would 'always be heads'. Communes, he added, were 'too weak when it came to suppressing counter-revolution'. He therefore ordered them to dissolve theirs, and replace it by a 'revolutionary committee'.

Such organs, based on an alliance of former Party cadres, young activists, and representatives of the People's Liberation Army, were largely controlled by the People's Liberation Army, and it was to Lin Biao and the army that Mao turned in 1968 to restore order when the Red Guards persisted in challenging every form of authority, and in waging bloody struggles among themselves, instead of concentrating their fire on the 'capitalist roaders' in the Party.

By 1969 it was possible to hold the 9th Party Congress, but it took more than two years thereafter to rebuild the shattered Party apparatus. Lin Biao was unenthusiastic about handing power back to the discredited Party bureaucrats; his death, in circumstances which remain obscure, diminished, though it by no means eliminated, the army's role.

Mao and Lin probably also differed on relations with the super-powers. In 1970–1, the Chinese government, thoroughly alarmed by Soviet intervention in Czechoslovakia, sought an accommodation with the USA as after all a less dangerous enemy than the USSR. At the time of President Nixon's first visit, in February 1972, some argued that Zhou Enlai was the author of this initiative. In fact, this strategy was Mao's very own, as he confirmed in early 1976 by inviting former-President Nixon to China as his personal guest.

Apart from Lin Biao, this policy was widely supported within the leadership. No similar consensus obtained in domestic politics. In the early 1970s, a compromise was sketched out, involving the reassertion of the need for unified Party leadership, tempered by the anti-bureaucratic spirit of the Cultural Revolution. Even before the death of Zhou Enlai, who was its principal architect, this compromise was overturned. All recognition of the importance of professional skills was swallowed up in an orgy of political rhetoric, and all things foreign were regarded as counter-revolutionary. Mao's last decade, which had opened with manifestos in favour of the Paris Commune model of mass democracy, closed with paeans of praise to that most implacable of centralizing despots, the first Qin emperor.

Some of the excesses of 1973–6 must be attributed to Mao's incapacity, old and ill as he was, to control the actions of his wife Jiang Qing and her associates. The fact remains, however, that in many respects he *did* share their values, and must be presumed willingly to have sanctioned their policies. In particular, though he believed in the need for unity (which he proclaimed once again as a goal at the 10th Party Congress in 1973, as he had in 1969 at the 9th), unity could, in his view, be achieved only through struggle. In one of his very last directives, in May 1976, Mao stressed that revolutions would continue to break out in future because 'junior officials, students, workers, peasants and soldiers don't like big shots oppressing them'.

Mao Zedong devoted himself to the pursuit of social revolution, economic modernization and national resurgence in China. In the last of these three directions, he achieved a very considerable measure of success. Before he was 60, he had unified China as it had not been unified since the heyday of the Qing empire, and at the end of his life, the President of the United States made the pilgrimage to the Forbidden City. The government he led likewise presided over the liberation of the peasantry from the domination of the landlords, and over the liberation of Chinese women by marriage reform, thereby effecting radical changes in the fabric of Chinese society. In the economic domain, substantial growth was achieved in the two decades from the mid-1950s to the mid-1970s, but the human cost in violence and starvation probably exceeded even that of Stalin's forced industrialization in the 1930s.

Mao in 1967, receives the adulation of 'revolutionary teachers and students' brandishing their 'little red books' of his sayings, in a scene typical of the spirit and style of Chinese politics during the 'Great Proletarian Cultural Revolution'

In the end, economic reality and human nature proved to be more intractable adversaries than either the *Guomindang* or the foreign powers. The millenarian hopes of the Great Leap Forward could not be realized, and a decade after Mao's death, the Cultural Revolution had been 'completely negated' in China. Thus the ultimate verdict of history on Mao's work as a whole remains very much open, but his role as the architect of the Communist victory, and the founder of the People's Republic, will assuredly not be forgotten.

S.R.S.

Zhou Enlai

Zhou Enlai was born in 1899 to a family of minor gentry in Shaoxing. His father was a traditional graduate but had never held office; he died early, and Zhou Enlai was brought up by relatives, first in Huaian and then in Shenyang.

His early education and experience were typical of his generation. He went to Nankai Middle School in Tianjin, where he studied the Chinese classics in association with modern subjects, and especially the works of the 17th-century patriot philosophers Gu Yanwu and Wang Fuzhi. He went to Japan to study, first at Waseda, home of the Japanese New Village Movement (which also influenced the creators of the peasant movement in China, Li

Dazhao and Peng Pai), and then at Kyoto. He returned to China in 1919 to join in the May Fourth Movement. Like the young Mao, he became deeply involved in student journalism; he helped to organize in Tianjin a student group called the Awakening Society, similar to Mao's New People's Study Society; and like Mao he participated in Li Dazhao's new Marxist Study Group. In 1920 he went to France, where he became a Marxist. He helped to organize, in association with members of Mao's New People's Study Society who were also in Paris, a European branch of the new Chinese Communist Party.

Returning to China in 1924, he occupied a key position in the new united front of Nationalists and Communists as deputy political commissar of the Nationalist military academy at Whampoa. He played a major role in organizing the workers' militia, which opened Shanghai to the advancing revolutionary army in 1927, and narrowly escaped execution in the right-wing *coup d'état* which followed. He helped to organize the Nanchang Uprising. He joined the Jiangxi Soviet in 1931 and played a leading part in its administration.

When under the threat of Japanese invasion in 1936 the alliance between Nationalists and Communists was renewed, Zhou was the chief negotiator first in discussions between Chiang Kai-shek and his captors responsible for the Xi'an incident, and then in early 1937 in the negotiations in Nanjing on the united front against Japan. The Nationalists having retreated to Chongqing, Zhou was director of the Communist Party Office there from 1940 to 1945. As the deputy director of the political department of the Military Affairs Commission of the alliance forces in Chongqing, he found himself serving under Chiang Kai-shek in the same relationship as at the Whampoa Academy almost twenty years before. The second united front, however, was even more riven by internal suspicion and hostility than the first, and when the New Fourth Army Incident occurred in 1941 Zhou Enlai withdrew from Chongqing to Yan'an; but by his persuasiveness and personal charm he had already vastly enhanced the reputation of the Chinese Communist Party among both foreign observers and Chinese intellectuals. He was able to detach a significant number of the latter to form the China Democratic League, which later supported the Communist regime.

He returned to Chongqing in 1944 and subsequently represented the Chinese Communist Party in the negotiations with Patrick Hurley and George Marshall. When these negotiations failed to remove the threat of civil war, he returned to Yan'an on 19 November 1946.

On the establishment of the People's Republic of China, Zhou Enlai became premier and held that post until his death. He also served as foreign minister until 1958, and retained the general direction of China's foreign relations thereafter. He played a key part in the Geneva settlement of Indo-China in 1954. In April 1955 at the Bandung Conference of Asian and African Peoples he established China's prestige in the third world. In 1956 during the troubles in Poland and Hungary which followed Khrushchev's condemnation of Stalin, Zhou visited these countries and exerted China's influence in re-uniting the shaken Communist bloc.

It was events at home, however, which were to tax Zhou Enlai's skills as a mediator to their utmost. When the Cultural Revolution threatened to engulf China in civil war, the responsibility for preventing the total breakdown of government fell to him as premier, while the task of preventing the destruction of the Party by internecine strife fell to him as the only major Party leader who was respected by virtually all factions and interest groups but identified with none. By 1974, however, he had earned the enmity of the 'gang of four', and he came under a bitter and prolonged political attack in the disguise of a campaign against Confucianism. This hostility lasted until his death on 8 January 1976.

Zhou Enlai has left behind him in China a posthumous reputation almost equal to that of Mao. He had his own charisma, and he was much more visible than the remote Chairman. Where Mao is remembered with respect, Zhou is remembered with warmth, as the peacemaker who always sought to achieve the widest possible measure of agreement consistent with principle.

Zhou Enlai and Jiang Qing in Beijing, May 1973.

The strength of his reputation was shown in the demonstrations held in Tiananmen Square and in major cities at the Qingming Festival of 1976, in his memory and in support of Deng Xiaoping, whom many Chinese regarded as Zhou's most appropriate successor.   *J.G.*

New Democracy

The Communist Party of China, following the Leninist theory of the nature of revolution in pre-capitalist countries, divided the future development of Chinese society into two successive phases: the bourgeois-democratic revolution, followed by the socialist revolution. New Democracy described the first phase, its policies and its institutions; the name is derived from an essay by Mao Zedong published in 1940.

On the attainment of national power the Communist Party of China convened a Chinese People's Political Consultative Conference, representing various political parties, geographical regions, mass organizations, minority nationalities, religious groups, the overseas Chinese, and various intellectual and professional circles. This Conference acted as a provisional national assembly. Its composition reflected the Communist view that there was support for the 'bourgeois-democratic' phase of the revolution from four classes: workers, peasants, petty bourgeoisie and national bour-

geoisie; and that opposition could be expected only from the landlords, the 'bureaucratic capitalists' associated with Nationalist control of the economy, and the 'comprador' class comprising those Chinese industrialists and traders deemed to be dependent on foreign economic interests.

The Chinese People's Political Consultative Conference resolved on a Common Programme, which included the abolition of imperialist privileges, the redistribution of land, and friendship with the USSR (the three main policies to which Sun Yat-sen had committed the reorganized Nationalist Party in 1924), as well as a policy of economic development through industrialization.

During the New Democratic phase private enterprise would be encouraged, and the non-Communist parties would be represented in a coalition government led by the Communist Party. The length of the phase was not stipulated. A fairly long period seemed implicit in the programme, but it was effectively brought to an end within six or seven years by the socialization of agriculture, commerce and industry in 1955–6 in the course of the implementation of the First Five-year Plan. During the Hundred Flowers Movement there were many bitter complaints from members of the non-Communist parties and from non-Communist public figures generally that the democratic aspects of New Democracy had been in practice nugatory, even after the promulgation of the Constitution of 1954.   *J.G.*

Three-Anti and Five-Anti Campaigns

The Three-Anti Campaign (August 1951) was directed against cadres (party and state functionaries), and the evils of corruption, waste and bureaucracy. The subsequent Five-Anti Campaign (January 1952) was directed against private industry and commerce, and the evils of bribery, tax evasion, theft of state property, abuse of state economic information and cheating on government contracts.

The Communist Party of China, exceptional among Communist Parties in power for its rich experience of rural life, by the same token lacked experience of urban industrial conditions. The problems of continued tolerance of capitalist commerce and industry proved less tractable than had been anticipated. The ambiguous and uneasy relationships created, complicated by controversy within the Party leadership over the interpretation of the role of the private sector, gave immense scope for abuses. Characteristically, the Communist Party of China attempted to solve these problems by cleaning out its own house first, rather than by blaming and attacking private business. It was only when exami-

nation of cadres during the Three-Anti Campaign had revealed the extent of collusion deemed to be corrupt between public servants and private employers that the attack was swung around to the business community.

The Five-Anti Campaign was carried on by methods analogous to those used in the land reform, with in this case employees being mobilized to accuse their employers. The more serious accusations eventually came to the courts, but in a witch-hunt atmosphere. By the end of the campaigns in June 1952 about 4.5 per cent of cadres were said to have been found guilty, and 1 per cent of businessmen to have been given custodial sentences, though it is probable that several times this proportion were subjected to crippling fines. Some of the accused committed suicide under the intense psychological pressure imposed.

J.G.

Korean War

Hostilities between North and South Korea broke out on 25 June 1950, after a long escalation of mutual provocation. North Korea was then firmly under Soviet influence, and it is unlikely that China was a party to the commencement of hostilities. The response of the Chinese press was so hesitant and ambiguous as to suggest that China had formulated no policy until American troops representing the United Nations crossed the 38th Parallel. This act was regarded in Beijing as a vital threat to Manchuria, where almost all of China's modern industrial capacity was concentrated. When warnings to the USA not to approach the Chinese border had been ignored, China sent 180 000 'volunteers' to Korea in October 1950. After initial setbacks, by December 1950 the Chinese and the North Koreans succeeded in driving the South Korean and United Nations forces back to the 38th Parallel. Peace negotiations then began, but dragged on until July 1953.

The effects of the war on Chinese internal affairs were considerable. Hitherto the policies of the Communist Party of China had been based on confidence in the support of most of the Chinese people, and were not on the whole marked by harshness. This was apparent in policy towards the urban private sector, landlords, the intellectuals, and even the remaining functionaries and representatives of the defeated Nationalist regime. The Korean War, however, led to a swing to severity. From the point of view of Communists in Beijing, the American operations in North Korea had all the appearance of the anticipated 'war of intervention'. The Communist Party of China found evidence of revived hopes among those classes, such as landlords, who were suffering from the revolution, and of rumours among them that Chiang Kai-shek

would 'be back in time to eat his moon-cakes'. At the same time, considerable forces of Nationalist troops still existed in many parts of China. As a result, land reform was now carried out more ruthlessly. A bitter campaign against Counter-revolutionaries was launched. Intellectuals came under new pressure. Policy generally was radicalized. The level of mutual confidence between Party and non-Party people, so manifest in the first months after Liberation, was never regained.

J.G.

Land reform

The maldistribution of land ownership in China was regarded by all parties as a gross social injustice and a main cause of rural economic stagnation. The Communist Party of China believed that their past success in dealing with the land tenure problem was the decisive factor in their successful rise to power; and rapid completion of the redistribution of land was regarded as a necessity for the consolidation of the authority of the new regime in the countryside.

In a pre-history extending back to the time of the Jiangxi Soviet, Chinese Communist land reform policy had been moderated in order to secure the maximum of effective redistribution with the minimum of economic and political dislocation. This moderation, however, was not easy to maintain in a party of which perhaps 50 per cent of members were categorized as poor peasants. In October 1947 Liu Shaoqi drew up a programme of a very egalitarian kind. Mao Zedong condemned it in April 1948, reviving the moderate programme of 1933. In spite of this, left-wing pressures in the villages were so strong that in 1949 land reform had to be halted in Henan Province until excesses could be brought under

A land reform struggle meeting near Beijing, 1950.

control. As areas with different social and economic conditions were conquered, new problems appeared; in particular, the relatively commercialized agriculture of the lower Yangtze could not easily be regarded as merely 'feudal', while to treat it as such might wreck the food supplies of half a dozen great Yangtze cities. An intra-Party debate arose as to whether Yangtze farming was 'feudal' or 'capitalist'. It was decided in theory that it was feudal, but in practice the commercial farmers—the 'rich peasants'—were protected. This protection was made general by the moderate Agrarian Reform Law of June 1951. Land reform had been begun in 1947 in areas where the Communists were in control; it was complete by 1952; the late date of the law indicates how long controversy continued.

In comparison with land reforms elsewhere, the Chinese reform chose, basically, to abolish tenure on existing farms rather than to redistribute in a new egalitarian pattern; to take the natural village as the unit of redistribution, while confiscating land without compensation; to leave former landlords with enough land for subsistence and with their commercial or industrial assets intact; and to organize the movement from the bottom, rather than to impose reform from above. Attempts were made to maintain legality and to avoid unjustified force, but the mobilization of the poor in 'speak-bitterness' meetings was in conflict with these attempts and—especially during the Korean War—there was considerable arbitrary violence. On the whole, however, considering that the Chinese land reform was the greatest single act of expropriation in human history, it was surprisingly well conducted.

It did not create equality in the village; some peasants after the reform still retained twice as much land as their poorest neighbours, so that among the poor there remained a strong incentive for the further redistribution of wealth which would be entailed in the collectivization of agriculture.   *J.G.*

Gao Gang

One of the few Communist Party of China leaders of peasant origin, Gao Gang created and successfully defended a small rural soviet in Shanxi in the late 1920s and early 1930s. It was there that the remnants of the Red Army found refuge at the end of the Long March. Thereafter Gao Gang rose to the central leadership of the Communist Party, and by 1949 controlled Manchuria. The three provinces of the northeast contained almost all China's heavy industries, mostly built during the long Japanese occupation. Soviet troops had stripped the factories of equipment before Liberation, however, and Manchuria was dependent upon Russian willingness to replace it. Gao Gang was, therefore,

at the same time the master of China's only effectively industrialized area, and dependent upon the USSR for its effective restoration. His policies were characterized by the very rapid imposition of Soviet-type centralized planning and management, and by a close special relationship with the Soviet Union. The system of the division of China into six military regions, of which the northeast was one, facilitated a high degree of independence from Beijing, which—among other developments—allowed Gao Gang to create a strict separation of government, Party, army and economic administration, through which he could maintain a degree of personal power unrivalled elsewhere in China.

In 1952, when preparations were being made for the First Five-year Plan, Gao Gang was brought to Beijing to head the State Planning Commission. He made an ally of Rao Shushi, who was identified with China's only other large industrial centre, Shanghai. The alliance quickly met with hostility. The circumstances have never been revealed, but they can be surmised with reasonable probability: Gao Gang's excessive bias towards the development of heavy industry, his uncompromising acceptance of Stalinist centralism, his manipulations to strengthen his own personal power, and his exceptionally close relations with the USSR, could all be expected to alarm many of his colleagues in Beijing. His position was probably weakened by the death of Stalin in 1953, within months of which he was under attack. He is said to have committed suicide just before his disgrace, and that of Rao Shushi, were publicly announced in early 1955. Rao Shushi disappeared at the same time.   *J.G.*

Agricultural cooperatives

It was widely assumed in China that the redistribution of land to the peasants would have to be succeeded by some form of cooperative organization of agriculture, in order to provide better marketing, supply and credit arrangements, and to facilitate the consolidation of scattered holdings, the development of irrigation and flood control, the use of machinery, and in general the dissemination of innovation. In Communist Party hands, the model of cooperative chosen was, inevitably at that time, the Russian *kolkhoz*.

The Chinese Communist Party, however, being aware of the disastrous results of Soviet collectivization in 1928–9, and having themselves considerable experience in organizing various types of rural cooperative during the Yan'an period, initiated a gradualist process by which it was hoped that agriculture could be collectivized without disruption and loss. Collectives were to be developed in three stages: the mutual-aid team in which farmers still operated on their own account, but joined in cooperative labour at the busy seasons and in the creations of new infrastructure; the first-stage cooperative in which the land was worked on common account, but a dividend paid on the land submitted to the cooperative; and finally the full collective, in which the dividend on land was abolished and the net production of the cooperative entirely divided on the basis of individual labour inputs. Within these stages, the acquisition of common assets was encouraged to ease the transition from one phase to the next. Richer peasants were paid in instalments for tools and beasts submitted to cooperative ownership. It was anticipated that steadily increasing production would prevent individual loss of income.

The campaign was begun, experimentally, in 1951 and made general in 1953. Controversy soon arose, however, with many Party leaders asserting that, as the success of large-scale farming would depend mainly on the introduction of machinery, and as machines were not yet available, there was no point in pushing collectivization. Mao Zedong, in return, argued that only if Chinese peasants first pooled their surplus labour and their savings in a collective effort, could they improve production to the point at which they could afford machinery and other modern inputs. In 1955 he circumvented a reluctant Central Committee by convening a conference of local representatives, who reported favourably on the progress of collectivization; and on this basis Mao secured a speeding-up of the process. With Mao's authority behind them, however, local cadres pushed the process on by means little short of outright coercion, so that in the course of little over a year the vast majority of the peasants, with no experience of cooperation beyond the mutual-aid team, found themselves in fully collective farms. Most of the advantage of the carefully designed gradualist process was thus lost; but enough preparation had been done to ensure that, in spite of some resistance and disruption, production and incomes after collectivization rose rather than fell. On the other hand, it is now admitted that increased collective production and incomes have not been enough to overcome the disincentive effects of collective working, except in the most prosperous areas of the country. Between 1978 and 1982 the collectives were superseded by a return to individual farming, carried out under contracts between the farmers and the state authorities.   *J.G.*

Five-year Plans

Although China, in common with most Communist countries, formally follows a system of quinquennial planning, these Five-year Plans, except for the first, 1953–7, have not in practice played a primary role in guiding production. Sudden changes of economic strategy, accompanied by controversies within the Party leadership, have deprived them of reality. Planning in periods of five years has not proved very appropriate in Chinese conditions; with industrial production still dependent on the harvest, and the harvest still liable to substantial fluctuations, operational planning has to be done by the year, on the basis of the previous year's harvest. Longer perspective planning has to be over ten or twelve years so that future harvests can be averaged out with confidence. Moreover, the course of events in China has been such that centralized, material balance planning on the Soviet model has frequently been in abeyance: it was fully implemented 1955–6, decentralized in 1957, virtually abandoned 1958–60, painfully and only partly restored 1961–5, minimized 1966–76, and then replaced to a significant degree by a managed market.

The first plan, however, was a reality. Worked out largely before the death of Stalin and the beginnings of economic reform in the USSR and Eastern Europe, it closely followed the Soviet model. The plan consisted of a balance sheet of existing resources, which were allocated from the centre to sectors and enterprises. Enterprise operations were controlled by a set of targets which left little room for self-management, and no scope for market operation. In content as well as in structure, the plan was orthodox, based on the two prevailing assumptions of the early 1950s: that the most rapid economic development would be achieved by putting the maximum of resources into heavy industry, from the growth of which the spread effects would stimulate light industry and agriculture; and that the most effective way to provide employment for surplus rural labour was to build modern industries in the cities.

In its own terms the first plan was a success. The rate of growth in industry was a remarkable 14 per cent per annum, and the development of heavy industry was especially impressive. However, even before the plan period had ended there was general dissatisfaction with it among Chinese leaders. The anticipated spread effects from heavy industry had not materialized. The rapid growth of urban industry had done virtually nothing to diminish the rural labour surplus. Agriculture, although its growth had been satisfactory in comparison with that in comparable developing countries in the same years, was still growing too slowly to sustain a continued process of industrialization at the pace set in the First Five-year Plan. Finally, the Hundred Flowers Movement had revealed the serious discontent which the bureaucratic nature of economic management had created, while Khrushchev's condemnation of Stalin had made the populations of all socialist countries, including China, less tolerant of rigid authoritarianism.

By the end of the First Five-year Plan the Communist Party of China was ready to rethink its strategy.

J.G.

The Hundred Flowers

The Hundred Flowers refers to two developments that were distinct and significantly different, although related. The first was an offer by the Communist Party of China of greater freedom of discussion for intellectuals, and wider tolerance in the fields of art and literature, science, academic issues and religion. The second was the positive encouragement of greater freedom of debate in political matters, which briefly allowed unprecedented tolerance of criticism of the Communist Party.

The original Hundred Flowers Movement followed criticism by Premier Zhou Enlai of the demoralizing political pressures under which China's intellectual and scientific establishment had been compelled to work. It was initiated in a speech in May 1956 by Lu Dingyi, who referred to the ancient adage, 'let a hundred flowers bloom, and a hundred schools [of thought] contend'. The new policy did not have immediately obvious results, but the condemnation of Stalin by Khrushchev in February 1956, and the consequent disturbances in the Communist world, culminating in the Hungarian Rising, caused the leadership of the Communist Party of China to begin an intensive process of rethinking in both the economic and political fields. In particular, Mao Zedong in February 1957 made a speech, *On the Correct Handling of Contradictions Among the People* which offered a theoretical justification for greater freedom of political discussion and criticism. In this, Mao rejected the Soviet theory that socialist society is conflict-free, and asserted on the contrary that conflicts among the people, and between the people and the state, inevitably continue under socialism. He further asserted that it is precisely these conflicts that stimulate progress. It indicates the opposition he faced within the Communist Party that this speech was not made to any Party meeting, but to the Supreme State Conference; Mao thus made his appeal for greater freedom over the heads of the Party leaders.

In the course of three months his colleagues were won round to a reluctant acceptance of Mao's demand for freedom. On this ambiguous basis the Chinese people were invited to criticize the regime and its policies, and the Communist Party instructed to accept the criticisms made. After much hesitation, criticisms poured forth. They were many and various, but all tended to show resentment of the Communist Party monopoly of political power and economic management, the high-handed way in which this monopolistic authority was exercised, and the absence of the human rights theoretically guaranteed by the Constitution of 1954. Criticism was frequently backed up by strikes, demonstrations and occasionally riots. Mao was prepared to tolerate these, but his fellow leaders were not. An attack on the critics was launched in early June 1957 through the *People's Daily*, and this developed into the Anti-Rightist Campaign.   *J.G.*

Anti-Rightist Campaign

During the Hundred Flowers Movement demands were made for more democratic government: freedom for the non-Communist parties which ostensibly formed part of a coalition government, independence of the judiciary and the procuratorate, freer trade unions, and greater freedom from Soviet influence. Against the wishes of Mao Zedong, the Communist Party reacted to these criticisms by condemning the critics, many of whom were dismissed from their posts and exiled to the rural areas. Some were imprisoned. The period of free criticism thus ended in June 1957. Mao's speech *On the Correct Handling of Contradictions Among the People*, originally delivered in February 1957, was only then published, and in this version included specified limits to discussion: it must be such as to unite the population, benefit socialism, strengthen the state, consolidate social institutions, especially the Communist Party, and strengthen international Communism.

The event was not, however, without its long-term consequences, and these were paradoxical. First, the evidence of the violent unpopularity of the centralized and bureaucratic system which the regime had created could still not be ignored. It became a factor in the post-Stalinist reappraisal in which the Communist Party of China was then engaged, and along with various economic considerations led Mao Zedong to attempt to create a decentralized and non-bureaucratic alternative in the Great Leap Forward and the communes. Second, when this new alternative failed melodramatically, China's intellectuals made common cause with the Party's right wing, who then sought to rehabilitate those they had themselves persecuted, while Mao opposed their rehabilitation. On the next occasion when he attempted to subject the Communist Party to public criticism, during the Cultural Revolution, the intellectuals were equally made the target, while freedom to criticize was given this time to students and young people. *J.G.*

Great Leap Forward

Discontent with the methods and results of the First Five-year Plan, concern with the problems (and the possibilities) of 'de-Stalinization', as well as the experience of popular hostility to centralized bureaucracy shown during the Hundred Flowers Movement, led the Communist Party of China to consider substantial changes in strategy and organization. The first result was a cautious decentralization, accompanied by some reduction in the level of capital accumulation. In late 1957, however, Mao Zedong succeeded in winning the support of a majority of the Central Committee for a radical alternative to the orthodox

Soviet organization of production and investment. This was foreshadowed in his speech *On the Correct Handling of Contradictions Among the People*, in which it was proposed to encourage and assist the peasant communities to build their own industries and to carry out their own farmland construction. It was decided to limit taxation and procurement so as to leave them with greater means to do so. Mao meanwhile systematized his own critique of Stalinism, in a number of documents not published at that time and beginning with *On the Ten Great Relationships*. The major points made in this were: Stalin set the level of accumulation of capital out of the peasants' surplus too high, and so 'drained the pond to catch the fish'; he gave too high a priority to heavy industry, and so by severely injuring light industry and agriculture, actually limited the possible growth of heavy industry itself; he overstressed collective incentives and neglected individual incentives; he gave no opportunity for the mass of the people to participate in development and social change, of which they were merely the passive recipients. Mao's most trenchant criticism, however, was that in agriculture the Soviets 'in thirty years have failed to create a true collective system; all they have done is to perpetuate the counter-productive exploitation of the landlords', with the state as universal landlord.

This critique expresses the spirit in which the Great Leap was launched. Behind it was also the earlier experience of the Communist Party of China in the Border Regions, where lack of capital had induced them to develop labour-intensive methods of construction, siege conditions had forced them to develop intermediate technologies, and the scattered nature of their territories had compelled them to depend on community development rather than on central planning.

Briefly, the peasant communities were to be encouraged to transform their own lives by using their own surplus labour, savings and local resources. Surplus rural labour would be used in water-conservancy construction, and to set up small industrial establishments to process crops, manufacture farm tools and provide consumer goods. The profits of these would create, for the transformation of agriculture, the funds which agriculture itself was not sufficiently productive to generate.

The Great Leap was a disastrous failure. Its major premise was that it should be conducted by democratic persuasion, but in spite of elaborate preparations it was carried on largely by coercion. The authoritarian Communist Party inevitably proved to be a poor instrument with which to conduct a vast democratic movement. Instead of economic development through community self-management, what happened was that the centralized, authoritarian allocation of resources was thrust right down to the grass roots, where local cadres reallocated peasant resources as freely as if they were state property. These abuses might have been checked in more normal circumstances, but such unrealistic expectations of a rapid revolution in productivity were created during the movement, that local cadres were put under pressure to raise targets repeatedly, until only by the most severe coercion could they hope to deliver what they had been forced to promise. The economic result was a gross waste of investment. The political result was an irreversible disillusionment. Ironically, all the dangers had been foreseen, but nevertheless could not be avoided. Finally, in 1959 unusually bad weather struck the over-extended, exhausted and demoralized rural labour force. The experiment was brought to an end.   *J.G.*

The communes

The communes were created as the institutional framework for the Great Leap Forward. The existing agricultural producers' cooperatives (full collectives) were combined in groups to form a new large farming unit coterminous with the *xiang*, the lowest level of public administration, usually embracing a population of about 20 000. The commune was given the responsibility not only for the conduct of farming, but for agricultural construction and the development of local industry. It was also merged with the *xiang* political administration to become an all-embracing social unit, whose provisions included education, welfare and health services and the militia. It was also the unit of capital accumulation and investment.

From a practical point of view, the commune was designed to be a unit large enough for the effective deployment of local resources, but small enough to be responsive to democratic control. From a theoretical point of view, its significance is indicated by its Chinese name, *gongshe*, which was a 20th-century neologism created to refer specifically to the Paris Commune of 1871. The implication is that the Chinese commune was an alternative to the 'bourgeois state' which had survived the revolution in the form of state capitalism. Chinese socialism was henceforward to be based on 'autonomous communities, voluntarily united for the defence of the whole', thus realizing Lenin's vision in *State and Revolution*.

The first commune (called Sputnik) was created in Henan in the spring of 1958; Mao gave it his blessing; the movement spread, and in August 1958 the Central Committee accepted it and laid down guidelines.

The commune was, however, discredited along with the Great Leap Forward. It became the directing centre of the unintended but widespread practice of coercive reallocation of peasant resources. It ceased to be an autonomous community organization—a collective—and became, in effect, an organ of the state. It was far too large for the conduct of farming, and although its constituent brigades and teams were from the beginning intended to be the main units of farm-management and of distribution of farm income, they soon lost their powers to the commune level. The commune area usually included richer and poorer villages; its leaders sought to put the surplus of the richer at the service of the poorer, and this proved intolerable, as Mao Zedong himself was the first to see. By 1959 it had been necessary to assert firmly that the production team must continue to be the main unit of ownership and of income distribution, and the commune administration thereafter confined itself to tasks appropriate to its higher level, that is, to its political responsibilities, investment in infrastructure, and the development of such local industries as had survived the débâcle of the end of the Great Leap Forward.

In 1982 in the course of the reform of the rural economy the communes were abolished; their political responsibilities were handed over to revived local government, while their economic powers were inherited by purely economic bodies, differently named in different places. In practice, however, the division of function was less distinct. The local governments retained considerable commune-style economic control and initiative. Politics remained to some extent in command. *J.G.*

Peng Dehuai

Born in 1900 in the same area of Hunan as Mao Zedong, Peng Dehuai held a commission in the Nationalist army, but deserted to join the Communist Party of China in the crisis of 1927. After taking part in the Long March, he rose to high command. He led the Chinese 'volunteers' in Korea, and signed the armistice at Panmunjom on 27 July 1953. In 1954 he became Minister of Defence and a member of the Politburo.

Peng's opposition to the Great Leap Forward was based on general grounds, but his main personal concern was with the military implications of the policies of 1958 and 1959. The communes consisted of citizens in arms, Paris-Commune style. In this aspect they represented preparation for a guerrilla defence, made necessary perhaps by the fact that the recently proposed Soviet terms for assistance in the defence of China were unacceptable, as they would have involved in practice Soviet control of the Chinese coast and of Chinese air-space. Peng, identified since 1940 with a preference for conventional military operations, was probably reluctant to accept resort to a form of people's war. There is circumstantial evidence that he was deviously prevented from influencing the critical decision on stepping up the militia.

At the enlarged Politburo Conference which met at Lushan from 2 July to I August 1959, Peng Dehuai presented his severe criticisms of the Great Leap Forward in a Letter of Opinion addressed to Mao Zedong; unfortunately this was circulated before Mao himself had received it. Mao admitted the difficulties and accepted personal responsibility for them, but refused to accept so sweeping a condemnation of his policies. Peng was dismissed from office.

The situation, however, was more complicated than such an account suggests. Later evidence shows that the majority of the Chinese Communist Party leadership concurred in Peng's criticism, and might have been expected to support him at Lushan. That they failed to do so was certainly due to their suspicion of his relations with Khrushchev, whom he had met abroad shortly before the conference. Khrushchev had received him with a degree of amity unexpected at a time when Sino-Soviet relations were under strain, and Peng's criticisms at Lushan on 16 July were followed on the 18th by Khrushchev's speech condemning Chinese policy in broadly similar terms; both diagnosed Mao's policies as an expression of 'petit bourgeois fanaticism'. It is a reasonable conclusion that the failure of Peng's colleagues to support him at Lushan expressed resentment at this apparent collusion. Peng was replaced as Minister of Defence by Lin Biao, while Luo Ruiqing became Chief of Staff. He was not subjected to punishment, but permitted to move freely in China on prolonged inspection tours during which he continued to accumulate material on the consequences of the Great Leap policies. During the Cultural Revolution, however, he was subjected to severe persecution by Red Guards.

A nationwide movement in his support began immediately after his dismissal in 1959. Peng, at Lushan, is said to have exclaimed, 'I will play Hai Rui!', thus identifying himself with a famous imperial official of that name who had courageously sided with the people against the authorities. His supporters therefore used the Hai Rui story as a parable, in plays and in historical writings. It was by an attack on one such play, Wu Han's *The Dismissal of Hai Rui*, that Mao Zedong later launched the Cultural Revolution. *J.G.*

Agricultural crisis

From 1959 to 1961 bad harvests reversed the hitherto steady rise of Chinese agricultural production. In 1957 the grain harvest had been about 195 050 000 tonnes. It had risen further in 1958 to 200 million tonnes, but by no means to the level extravagantly claimed under the influence of Great Leap Forward euphoria. In 1959, however, according to the best estimates, it fell to 170 million tonnes, and in 1960 to 143 million tonnes.

Supplies of industrial raw materials also fell sharply as efforts were made to make up the deficiencies of food supplies, while a substantial part of the urban workforce returned to the villages to find subsistence. Consequently, the level of industrial activity diminished sharply.

This serious situation was partly the result of weather conditions, which remained adverse for three years, with almost half of China's arable area severely affected.

It seems to have been the general opinion in China, however, that the adverse weather, as a factor in economic decline, was less important than the disruption caused by the Great Leap Forward and the communes. The general view was that disorganization accounted for 70 per cent, and the weather for only 30 per cent, of the losses. Among the reasons given for the crisis were the disincentive effects of the 'free supply system', by which a basic income was paid to all members without reference to their labour contribution; the excessive withdrawal of farm labour for participation in local industry or farmland construction; the ineptitude of farm management at the commune level; the ill-informed interference of the higher levels in farm operations; the abolition of private plots and the private sector; and the disincentive effects of coercive reallocation of resources from richer to poorer villages.

In 1962 there was a recovery in agricultural production, but at a heavy ideological price. During the crisis Party authorities had turned a blind eye to practices which might increase food supplies, even if they undermined collective agriculture. Private land reclamation spread, and in many areas family farming was resurrected. The subsequent Socialist Education Movement was in origin an attempt to deal with this problem.   *J.G.*

Tibet

In October 1950 the People's Liberation Army marched into Tibet. An agreement was signed with the ruler, the Dalai Lama, in 1951 allowing the existing system dominated by a theocratic elite to continue but under Chinese control. The Chinese claimed to observe the agreement but the traditional system was being eroded. In 1956 the Chinese formed a Preparatory Committee for the establishment of the Tibet Autonomous Region, and the local government, nominally under the Dalai Lama, came under pressure to introduce reforms. The traditional elite, joined by discontented Khambas from the east and, it is alleged, marginally helped by American and Taiwan sources, rebelled in March 1959. The rebellion was easily suppressed. The Dalai Lama and several tens of thousands of Tibetans fled to India from where they continued to constitute a challenge to the legitimacy and acceptability of Chinese rule.

After the rebellion Tibet was rapidly reformed along Chinese Communist economic, social and political lines. Although it became one of the most heavily subsidized regions of China, evidence has since shown that the material conditions of the 1.8 million Tibetans in the region did not improve. In the countryside they were forced to abandon their traditional barley for other grains not suited to the conditions of the high plateau. In the urban areas economic and social conditions were skewed heavily in favour of the Han Chinese. The Cultural Revolution was an unmitigated disaster for Tibet. The religion which is the heart of Tibetan culture and society was desecrated. Some 4000 monasteries were totally destroyed. The 10-year ban on religious practices was not lifted until 1976. Conditions were slow to improve and in May 1980 the then General Secretary of the Chinese Communist Party, Hu Yaobang, on a visit to Lhasa apologized to the Tibetan people for their maltreatment. Despite some improvements, evidence from Western tourists and journalists who have been able to visit selected places in the region suggests continued discrimination against Tibetans and their culture. In September 1987 and in March 1988 demonstrations in Lhasa were bloodily suppressed.

Although China has problems with other national minorities, Tibet is unique as the only region inhabited by an overwhelming majority of a single nationality with a wholly non-Chinese culture and a tradition of virtual independence stretching back more than 700 years. The Chinese Communists, like the Nationalists before them, have always insisted that Tibetan independence is not negotiable. Thus, in 1988 the government refused to open negotiations with the Dalai Lama about autonomy after he had indicated that he would no longer insist upon sovereign independence.

The international community, which in the 1950s challenged the legality of the Chinese occupation of Tibet, has long since accepted its integration into the People's Republic. However, beginning in 1988 Western governments have raised formally the question of human rights violations in Tibet.   *M.Y.*

The Sino-Indian border dispute

The basis of the Indian position is that the borders with China were clearly established by the British Raj and that the Indian government has inherited these from the British. The Chinese government insists that the borders established by the former imperial powers should be renegotiated by independent national governments. Moreover, the Chinese also dispute the legality, clarity and observance of the boundary lines which the Indians claim were established by the British. The dispute between the two states focused in the West on the Aksai-Chin plateau claimed by India as part of Ladakh, and in the Northeast Frontier Agency area over the McMahon Line.

Before the Tibetan revolt of 1959 the Chinese, unbeknown to the Indians, had built a road through western Tibet across the Aksai-Chin plateau. After the revolt Indian troops were sent into the disputed border areas. Chinese forces near these areas had already been reinforced. Incidents became more serious and the first major clash occurred in the summer of 1959. Although it did not then escalate into a war, all attempts at negotiating a settlement failed. In 1960–1 China settled the boundary questions with Burma and Nepal, and began border negotiations with Pakistan. The latter included the border with Pakistan-held Kashmir. Indian nationalist sentiments, which had already been aroused, now became even further inflamed. The Indian government took a negotiating position which called upon the Chinese to accept India's claims. In 1962 India began a 'forward policy' by which its troops pushed beyond the line of actual Chinese control. After repeated warnings they struck back in force on 20 October. Within a month the Chinese troops had scored an overwhelming victory. China then announced a ceasefire and unilaterally withdrew its forces 20km from what it called 'the line of actual control' as of 7 November 1959. It was not until 1980 that a working party was established by both sides to resolve the problem. Many rounds of talks have been held and not even the visit to China in December 1988 by India's Prime Minister Rajiv Gandhi brought about a breakthrough in the deadlock. *M.Y.*

The Sino-Soviet conflict

Following what on the surface had appeared to be a close alliance, China and the Soviet Union began a bitter dispute in the late 1950s, which within a few years transformed their relationship into one of the most significant great power conflicts since the Second World War. In 1982 relations began to improve and they were normalized again in 1989.

The treaty of alliance signed by Mao in Moscow on 14 February 1949 provided the nascent People's Republic with a degree of security against possible American attack. Although the treaty allowed the Soviet Union special rights in Xinjiang and the northeast (Manchuria) these were ended in 1954 and throughout the 1950s the Chinese benefited greatly from the alliance. In addition to the greater security the Soviet Union provided during China's confrontations with the United States, Soviet assistance facilitated the building of China's heavy industrial base. Moreover the Chinese chose to model much of the administration of the state, the economy, the armed forces, education, social welfare and science upon the Soviet experience.

By the end of the 1950s the alliance began to break down as a result of the Soviet pursuit of peaceful coexistence with the United States while Sino-American relations were still extremely hostile. This was compounded by Mao's growing doubts about the

'socialist' quality of the Soviet economic and political system. Mao objected to Khrushchev's 1956 de-Stalinization speech and he resented the Soviet leader's attempt to lay down the law to others without even consulting them. Khrushchev made no secret of his contempt for the Great Leap Forward and Mao angrily rejected Khrushchev's proposal for a joint Pacific fleet and the idea that China should allow the Russians to build and man a communications complex for this purpose on China's east coast. He described it as an attempt to control China. In 1959 Khrushchev withdrew his promise to provide China with a sample atomic bomb and indicated his support for India in the Sino-Indian border skirmishes. In April 1960 the Chinese publicly criticized the Soviet leadership as revisionist and in June the thousands of Soviet experts in China were suddenly withdrawn and all aid was stopped. This was a massive blow to an economy already disrupted by the terrible economic consequences of the Great Leap Forward. The final parting of the ways came in 1963 when the Russians signed the Test-ban Treaty, thereby in Chinese eyes joining with the Americans to obstruct China's path to becoming an independent nuclear power.

By 1962 Mao had dismissed the Soviet leadership as not only revisionist, but also as a right-wing dictatorship. In Mao's view, a capitalist restoration had taken place in the Soviet Union and it was with this example in mind that he launched the Cultural Revolution ostensibly to prevent his country from 'changing colour' too.

The Vietnam War exacerbated relations, and once the Soviet Union was deemed to have reached the state of aggressive imperialism by its invasion of Czechoslovakia in 1968 Mao Zedong and Premier Zhou Enlai designated it as China's most dangerous enemy. This was confirmed by the massive Soviet military build up near China's northern borders including the Mongolian People's Republic. This in turn paved the way for the Sino-American rapprochement in 1971–2. For the next 10 years the Sino-Soviet conflict dominated Asian-Pacific international relations and affected the global balance between the Soviet Union and the United States. As the Soviet Union perceived a deepening alignment between China and the West, China's leaders in turn felt threatened by Soviet strategic encirclement. In particular they were concerned firstly by Soviet assistance which alone enabled Vietnam in December 1978 to invade and occupy Cambodia; secondly, by the Soviet invasion of Afghanistan a year later; and thirdly by the persistent military threat of Soviet forces present to the north coupled by the newly deployed Soviet Pacific Fleet. Meanwhile Mao's death and the new policies of reform in China had removed the principal ideological objections of the Chinese to the Soviet Union.

In 1982 with an American Administration determined to restore military superiority over the Soviet Union and with the Russians bogged down in Afghanistan and elsewhere against the backcloth of a declining Soviet economy the Chinese felt less threatened. They shifted the foreign policy towards a greater balance between the two superpowers and responded positively to Soviet initiatives to improve relations. Trade began to expand. After Gorbachev in 1986 indicated a new Soviet approach to the Asia-Pacific in the context of restructuring the Soviet system, relations improved still further. By February 1989 Soviet troops were withdrawn from Afghanistan, there was evidence of Soviet pressure on Vietnam to withdraw from Cambodia and Soviet forces were being reduced in the Far East. The stage was set for the normalization of Sino-Soviet relations as symbolized by a Sino-Soviet summit in May 1989, the impact of which was eclipsed by the student movement calling for democracy, less bureaucracy and an end to official corruption. To some extent the student movement had itself drawn inspiration from *glasnost* and *perestroika* in the USSR.   *M.Y.*

Socialist Education Movement

Because the prime objective of this campaign was to root out corruption among grass-roots officials with respect to accounts, granaries, property and work-points (the basis of peasant remuneration) the Socialist Education Movement is also known as the 'four clean-ups'. Formally launched by a Central Committee draft resolution on rural work in May 1963, it constituted the Chinese Communist Party's response to the widespread demoralization in the countryside, caused in large part by the 'three bitter years' of economic setbacks (1959–61) resulting from the Great Leap Forward. A feature of the campaign was the injunction to senior officials to make on-the-spot investigations for periods of up to six months; the most notorious example of such 'squatting at a point' was performed by Wang Guangmei, the wife of head of state Liu Shaoqi, who spent five months incognito in a commune near Beijing. During the Cultural Revolution, with which the Socialist Education Movement was officially merged in December 1966, the changes of policy during the movement were ascribed to the 'two-line' struggle between Mao Zedong and Liu Shaoqi.   *R.MacF., D.S.*

The two lines

These are also known as the two roads, the proletarian and the capitalist. According to the Central Committee decision of 8 August 1966 on the Cultural revolution, this movement's main target was 'those Party persons in power taking the capitalist road'. The capitalist road, it was revealed in subsequent months, was the route taken over previous decades by those Chinese leaders who had opposed Mao Zedong on issues like collectivization, mechanization of agriculture, the management of industry and the content of education.   *R.MacF.*

Cultural Revolution

More precisely known as the 'Great Proletarian Cultural Revolution', it represented Mao Zedong's attempt to prevent the Chinese revolution from degenerating in the way he believed the Soviet one had done. As a result of Khrushchev's alleged 'appeasement' of America and his peaceful coexistence policy, Mao set out to discover why Leninist principles of foreign policy had been abandoned in the homeland of the revolution. His findings, published in nine polemics in 1963–4, were that the Soviet Union had suffered a capitalist restoration encouraged by the emergence of a 'privileged stratum' and a revisionist ruling clique. To prevent China, too, from taking the 'revisionist road to capitalist restoration', Mao argued that it was crucial to train a new generation of totally dedicated revolutionary successors, whose *weltanschauung* (world-view) would be genuinely Marxist-Leninist (and by implication, Maoist)—hence the need for a *cultural* revolution.

But in the face of the grim economic realities of the mid-1960s, Mao evidently decided that most of his long-time colleagues, who increasingly ignored him, were themselves becoming a Khrushchevist 'privileged stratum' and must be replaced by younger, 'redder' successors. The Cultural Revolution was thus a double operation: the purging of the older generation of Chinese leaders and their replacement by a new generation whose revolutionary zeal would be enhanced by the very act of toppling the 'power holders'. As Mao put it: 'You learn to swim by swimming, you learn to make revolution by making revolution.'

The first salvo of the Cultural Revolution was fired in November 1965, the first major victims were revealed in May 1966, the most turbulent phase of Red Guard activity continued until autumn 1967 and an initial balance sheet was drawn at the Party's Ninth Congress in the spring of 1969. But the Cultural Revolution was not officially declared terminated until after the death of Mao Zedong in September 1976.

Liu Shaoqi (1898–1969)

As Mao's heir apparent for the Party Chairmanship from the late 1940s until the Central Committee plenum in August 1966, Liu Shaoqi was designated during the Cultural Revolution as the 'top Party person in authority taking the capitalist road'. His whole revolutionary career—as a leader of the labour movement in the

1920s, underground party boss in the 1930s, theoretician of party organization and discipline in the 1940s, head of state from 1959—was minutely re-examined and found to be irretrievably flawed.

After the foundation of the People's Republic in 1949, Mao and Liu sometimes disagreed on major policy issues, but when Mao decided that a successor had to be groomed if China were to avoid a Soviet-style, post-Stalin struggle for power, it was to Liu that he passed on his state chairmanship. Although both men were advocates of the 1958 Great Leap Forward, they drew differing conclusions from the subsequent economic débâcle. Liu sought China's recovery through pragmatism and discipline; whereas Mao, increasingly obsessed with the fear of revolutionary degeneration, became convinced of the need for a new wave of revolutionary dynamism.

After his initial demotion within the Party hierarchy in August 1966, Liu gradually disappeared from public view. Vilification of his views and career gradually intensified until he became known as 'China's Khrushchev'. Liu and his urbane wife Wang Guangmei were subjected to repeated 'struggle sessions' at the hands of the Red Guards during August 1967. Liu himself was severely beaten

Reviewing the May Day parade in 1952, Liu Shaoqi stands between Zhou Enlai and Mao Zedong.

until he reportedly lost the use of one leg, put under house arrest (while his wife was sent to the notorious Qincheng prison outside Beijing), and finally consigned to a cell in Kaifeng where he contracted pneumonia and died an ignominious death in 1969. He was the last major victim of the Cultural Revolution to be posthumously rehabilitated in 1980.

Peng Zhen (b. 1902)

First secretary of the Beijing Municipal Party from 1949 and mayor of the capital from 1951, Peng Zhen was the first Politburo member to fall victim, in May 1966, to the Cultural Revolution. The dismissal of Peng and his Beijing *apparat* enabled Mao to

After the purge of Peng Zhen and the Beijing Party in 1966, Maoist Red Guards held triumphant rallies in the Chinese capital.

direct the Cultural Revolution from the capital; hitherto, he had had to rely on supporters within the Shanghai Municipal Party because of the tight grip Peng had maintained on Beijing affairs.

Peng's fall cast a shadow on Liu Shaoqi, whose close colleague he had been from the mid-1930s as his lieutenant in the Party's North China Bureau. Peng's skill as an organizer—he had been imprisoned for some six years in the 1920s and 1930s for his activities among urban workers—won him at various times the leadership of the Party's organization department, the Party School and, from 1956, the second-ranking post (under Deng Xiaoping) in the Party secretariat.

During the early years of the regime Beijing was often the pacesetter for national campaigns—against counter-revolutionaries, against corruption, for the take-over of private industry and commerce—and Peng figured prominently; he appeared to stand an outside chance of being Chairman Mao's successor. But he clashed with the Chairman on a number of occasions, and his fate was probably sealed when in the mid-1960s he was contemptuous about Mme Mao's (Jiang Qing's) attempts to revolutionize Peking opera. While the first to go, Peng Zhen was almost the last surviving major victim of the 1966–7 purge to be rehabilitated, emerging from the shadows in early 1979. During the 1980s Peng again became an influential member of the Party elite, becoming Chairman of the National People's Congress and playing a leading role in legal reform and public security.

Red Guards

Although Peng Zhen's fall gave Mao and his associates control of the capital, the Chairman still needed an instrument to use against the senior Party officials in Beijing and the provinces whom he wished to purge. Mao turned to the students, whose predecessors' activities during the Hundred Flowers period a decade earlier convinced him that they would be ardently anti-bureaucrat.

First they were encouraged to turn on their teachers. Then on 18 August 1966 at the first of eight, million-plus rallies in Beijing, Mao donned the arm-band of a Qinghua University group calling itself the *Hongweibing* or Red Guards. This sparked the formation of Red Guard units at universities and schools up and down the country. At first the Red Guards, brandishing the little red book of Mao quotations distributed by the army, confined themselves to destroying or desecrating the remnant symbols of bourgeois society: cultural relics, churches and temples, and 'superfluous' private property like musical instruments, jewellery and books.

The momentum of Red Guard activity was maintained by mutual encouragement as free railway passes enabled millions of youngsters to travel the length and breadth of China exchanging experiences with their brethren elsewhere. Thus emboldened they

began to follow Mao's injunctions 'To rebel is justified' and 'Bombard the headquarters', and began to drag Party leaders from their offices, parade them through the streets in dunce hats, and subject them to mass 'trials'. Much of their activity was spontaneous but the Red Guards looked for guidance and anti-revisionist ammunition from the new Cultural Revolution Group, headed by Mao's former political secretary, Chen Boda, with Mao's wife, Jiang Qing, as his most prestigious assistant.

The January Storm

Red Guard activities in the streets of China's cities inflamed the workers, some with envy, others with hostility. In Shanghai an abdicating municipal Party leadership and widespread economic grievances formed an explosive combination. Even before Mao at the end of 1966 ordered the Cultural Revolution extended to factories and farms, Shanghai's economy had come to a halt as rival workers' organizations fought each other and demanded new (and different) deals from the municipal leaders. In an attempt to restore order, the *People's Daily* (the official Party newspaper) on 26 December authorized managers to pay back wages to workers who had been laid off, an instruction that triggered a further rash of economic demands and a buying spree. Shanghai was now paralysed and Zhang Chunqiao, deputy head of the Cultural Revolution Group and himself a former Shanghai official, flew to the city on 4 January to attempt to get the city moving. With the widespread use of troops and public security personnel and with Mao's overt support for his leadership, Zhang brought Shanghai back to life by March.

The Wuhan Incident

Mao's order to army commanders to support the revolutionary left in Shanghai and elsewhere, issued on 23 January, was to prove a fateful one. Initially it helped inexperienced Red Guards in their struggles against entrenched and experienced Party officials, though the latter staged a brief comeback during what was known as the 'February counter-current'. This led in turn to a renewed leftist upsurge and subsequently, with the army ordered on 6 April not to restrain the revolutionaries, to internecine and bloody feuding among the Red Guard and similar organizations.

One of the worst trouble spots was the central Chinese industrial city of Wuhan. When the heads of public security and propaganda visited Wuhan in July 1967 on a provincial tour to try to settle some of the major factional disputes they unhappily designated as true Maoists a faction previously rejected by the local military commander. Infuriated, he arrested them and Zhou Enlai extricated them and dismissed the Wuhan military leadership only with difficulty. The whiff of warlordism conveyed by the Wuhan Incident shook the leftists in Beijing, and though their initial reaction was to tighten military discipline and distribute weapons to the Red Guard units, by the early autumn of 1967 extremist members of the Cultural Revolution Group had been purged and the army had been authorized to restore order and send the Red Guards back to their schools and universities.

Revolutionary committees

As part of his strategy to persuade Shanghai workers that the city was getting a new deal, Zhang Chunqiao proclaimed the creation of a Shanghai 'Commune' in place of the old municipal government. Mao disapproved of the idea and soon Shanghai followed the pattern of other provinces in setting up a 'revolutionary committee', the hallmark of which was supposed to be a three-way revolutionary. alliance between Party cadres acceptable to the Maoists, the army and representatives of revolutionary mass organizations, like the Red Guards, composed of students or workers. Due to the considerable variations in the level of violence and degree of chaos in different provinces, the formation of such revolutionary committees lasted from 31 January 1967 until September 1968. After the Wuhan Incident the percentage of military men in the leading organs of the revolutionary committees rose from less than a third to almost one-half (19 of the total of 29 such committees were virtually created by the army), thus signalling the significantly enhanced power of the People's Liberation Army in domestic politics.   *R.MacF., D.S.*

Ninth Party Congress

Held between 1 and 24 April 1969 the Ninth Party Congress marked the end of the turbulent phase of the Cultural Revolution, the beginning of the reconstruction of the Party, and the apogee of the power of Defence Minister Lin Biao—enshrined as Mao Zedong's successor in the new Party constitution passed at the Congress—and the military. Less than a quarter of the Eighth Central Committee survived in its much enlarged successor, evidence of the swathe which the Cultural Revolution had cut through Mao's old comrades. But the proportion of soldiers (41 per cent) to cultural revolutionaries (possibly 28 per cent) confirmed the suppression of the left that had taken place since the Wuhan Incident; the 25-man Politburo contained nine serving soldiers and three former marshals.

The terseness of the new Party constitution reflected the anti-bureaucratic thrust of the Cultural Revolution and it dispensed with the one-time powerful secretariat. Lin Biao's political report, the only Congress speech to be published, analysed the genesis and development of the Cultural Revolution, and held out an olive

branch to those of its victims who had raised their political consciousness. If bad people went wild again, the masses would have to be aroused again to strike them down—presumably in one of the series of cultural revolutions that Mao had always predicted would be necessary to keep China revolutionary. In a long section on foreign affairs, Lin breathed fiery defiance at both American imperialism and Soviet revisionism.

Lin Biao (1907–71)

Lin Biao, who was commissioned at 18, was the youngest and arguably the most brilliant of all the Communist generals during the Long March, the Anti-Japanese War and the civil war. His defeat of the Japanese at the Pingxing Pass, and his capture of Manchuria from the Nationalists after the war followed by a rapid and victorious march to the far south of the country are among the most notable achievements in the annals of the People's Liberation Army.

Lin's career was punctuated by long bouts of illness—he spent three years in a Soviet hospital from about 1939 until February 1942—and he was relatively inactive during the early years of the

Mao and Lin Biao in 1969 at the time of the latter's formal designation in the party constitution as Mao's successor.

Communist regime. But he had been a close adherent of Mao's from the early 1930s and presumably it was Mao who ensured that he was regularly promoted within the Party, joining the ruling Politburo Standing Committee in 1958. When Defence Minister Peng Dehuai challenged Mao over the communes in 1959 and lost, Lin Biao replaced him.

Taking his cue from Mao, Lin the primacy of politics in the moulding of the People's Liberation Army, though he did not neglect military training. In the mid-1960s when China's leaders were worried about the state of morale in the country the army was held up as a model of political rectitude. When the Cultural Revolution was launched, Lin Biao soon emerged as Mao's successor. It may never be known whether Mao really wanted Lin to succeed him or used this manoeuvre to ensure that the army was on his side against the Party bureaucrats—or both. Lin Biao's constituency was a narrow one and the upshot was that by the Party's Ninth Congress the Party machine was dominated by serving soldiers. Mao's famous dictum on the need for the Party to command the gun and not vice versa seemed threatened. Over the next two and a half years Mao and Premier Zhou Enlai worked to reverse this situation, and Lin apparently reacted by attempting a *coup d'état* in September 1971. Lin's daughter is reported to have betrayed him, and he and his wife and fellow conspirators allegedly died while fleeing to the Soviet Union when their plane crashed in Mongolia. The opportunity was used to eliminate a number of serving soldiers from the Politburo who may or may not have been co-conspirators. *R.MacF., D.S.*

The Ussuri Incident

The two battles between Soviet and Chinese border forces on 2 and 15 March 1969 for the occupation of a small island in the Ussuri River, which along with the Amur River (or Heilongjiang), constitutes the main border between northeast China and the Soviet Union, set in motion a crisis that nearly brought the two giants to the point of war. The battles took place after a marked deterioration in Sino-Soviet relations. Tension remained high especially after a Soviet incursion into Xinjiang in the west in August against the background of barely concealed Soviet nuclear threats. The crisis was diffused when Soviet Premier Kosygin flew to Beijing, where he and Premier Zhou Enlai agreed to hold border talks.

The incidents arose from a long-standing Sino-Russian dispute about the riverine borders. The Soviet government argued that by the Treaty of 1860 (whose relevant map has never been published) the border ran on the Chinese bank whereas the Chinese maintained that it ran along the centre of the main channel of the river

(the Thalweg Principle). At stake was not only control of the rivers but also several hundred islands. The disputed island (Zhenbao in Chinese or Damansky in Russian) was one of these and stood as a test case for the rest. The battles grew out of more vigorous border patrols by both sides. Their respective versions of the battles differ but both admit to several hundred casualties. The incidents did not, however, expand in military terms beyond border skirmishes.

In July 1986 the border issue was resolved in principle when Gorbachev conceded in his speech at Vladivostok that the border did indeed follow the main channel of the rivers. *M.Y.*

Anti-Confucian campaign

Ever since the creation of the People's Republic in 1949 Communist propagandists have denounced Confucianism as the source of most of the values of the society which they sought to remould. But the anti-Confucian campaign, launched with an article by a philosophy professor in August 1973 on the eve of the Party's Tenth Congress, had a more particular political motive. The article clearly reflected the disquiet of the remaining radicals in the Politburo, the future 'gang of four', at threats to the 'socialist new things' introduced in the Cultural Revolution, notably in education, and at the return to public life of a number of senior officials disgraced during the Cultural Revolution, most notably Deng Xiaoping, once denounced as the 'No. 2 powerholder taking the capitalist road'. 'Confucius', it was clear, was represented by Premier Zhou Enlai who had sponsored Deng's re-emergence from the shadows. As a result of compromises hammered out at the Tenth Congress, the anti-Confucian campaign was redirected, with Lin Biao explicitly linked with the sage. *R.MacF., D.S.*

Tenth Party Congress

Held between 24 and 28 August 1973, the 10th Congress witnessed the official excoriation of Lin Biao, the expulsion of his remaining followers from the Central Committee, and the emergence of Wang Hongwen, a young Shanghai workers' leader who had first distinguished himself during the January Storm, as the prime candidate for the succession after the deaths of Mao Zedong and Zhou Enlai. Wang Hongwen and other radicals within the Politburo had to accept the return to the Central Committee of former leaders like Deng Xiaoping; in return Premier Zhou backed such Cultural Revolution innovations as the abandonment of examinations, which was designed to make it easier for peasant and worker children to obtain higher education. Despite this compromise on domestic affairs there was clear evidence of disagreement over foreign policy in the political report made by Zhou Enlai and the report on the new Party constitution by the more revolutionary Wang Hongwen as the opening to the United States was questioned.   *R.MacF., D.S.*

Tiananmen Incident, 1976

The death of the 77-year-old Premier Zhou Enlai on 8 January 1976, after a three-year struggle with cancer, caused widespread grief in China but went unmarked by the leadership. Zhou, who had been a member of the Chinese Politburo even longer than Mao Zedong and had been premier ever since the founding of the People's Republic in 1949, was respected for his tireless devotion to duty and his modest air. During the Cultural Revolution he had attempted to protect individuals and the nation from its worst excesses. With Zhou gone, only the rehabilitated Deng

Xiaoping appeared to stand in the way of a new wave of radicalism, and by now it was clear that he was in trouble as a result of his criticism of Cultural Revolution policies in general and educational and science policies in particular.

The grassroots mood of concern expressed itself in an unprecedented demonstration in the principal public place in the capital, Tiananmen Square. The Qingming Festival, the traditional time for the paying of respects at the graves of parents and ancestors, was on 4 April and by that day in 1976 the monument to revolutionary martyrs in the square was festooned with and surrounded by thousands of wreaths for, poems to and portraits of the late premier. It was a striking demonstration that the Chinese people believed that the communist revolution had produced more than one heroic leader; it was also implicitly a demonstration of support for Deng, and the heir to Zhou's moderation. Among the wreaths were some placards supporting Deng and others denouncing Mme Mao (Jiang Qing).

In April 1976 Beijing citizens erected wreaths in Tiananmen Square in memory of the recently dead Premier Zhou Enlai.

The announcement of Mao's death stressed his achievements in struggling against erroneous lines, devising the rural base area strategy that brought the Communists to power, and pinpointing the need to continue class struggle within the Communist Party even after it had achieved power (i.e., by cultural revolution). Hailing him as the 'greatest Marxist of the contemporary era', the announcement also praised his struggle against revisionism within the international Communist movement led by the Soviet Union. *R.MacF., D.S.*

Hua Guofeng (b. 1920)

Hua Guofeng succeeded Mao Zedong in the key posts of Chairman of the Communist Party's Central Committee and Chairman of the Party's Military Affairs Committee while retaining the premiership he had assumed after Zhou Enlai's death. He also was appointed editor of Mao's works, thus becoming custodian of the Chairman's intellectual legacy. His first act was to encompass the disgrace of the remaining Cultural Revolution radicals within the Politburo who were officially denounced as the 'gang of four'.

Hua was a beneficiary rather than a major protagonist of the Cultural Revolution. At its outset in 1966 Hua was a provincial Party secretary and vice-governor in Hunan with wide bureaucratic experience. Despite Red Guard criticism, he was the leading provincial official to survive the Cultural Revolution, emerging as vice-chairman of the provincial revolutionary committee in 1968 and a member of the Central Committee at the Party's Ninth Congress in 1969. When a new post-Cultural Revolution Party committee was established in Hunan in December 1970, Hua became its first secretary. In 1971–3 Hua worked also in Beijing, his duties apparently including the investigation of the Lin Biao affair, an assignment which helped to obtain him entry to the Politburo at the Party's Tenth Congress in 1973. At the January 1975 meeting of the National People's Congress, he became a vice-premier and Minister of Public Security, while later that year he gave the main speech at the National Agricultural Conference to promote the campaign to learn from Dazhai.

Though not responsible for the purge of the Party during the Cultural Revolution, Hua's words and deeds after his entry into the Politburo probably provoked ambivalent reactions among rehabilitated old cadres. His claim to be Mao's chosen successor rested on a note to him from the Chairman which simply said: 'With you in charge, I am at ease.' His energetic personal involvement in the rescue operations after the massive Tangshan earthquake in the summer of 1976 would have helped his reputation, but at the same time he participated in the second disgrace of

The 'gang of four' and their allies had the wreaths erected by Beijing citizens to Premier Zhou Enlai removed. This sparked a day of rioting at the end of which soldiers guarded Tiananmen Square.

The message embarrassed China's leaders and overnight all the wreaths were removed. The result was a massive demonstration of anger in the square on 5 April, when there were clashes between members of the 100 000 crowd and security personnel which continued sporadically until 9.30 pm when the square was cleared by tens of thousands of militiamen, police and soldiers. On 7 April the Politburo met and dismissed Deng Xiaoping from his posts, though not from the Party; Hua Guofeng, who had been acting premier since Zhou's death, became premier and first deputy chairman of the Party. There ensued a nationwide anti-Deng campaign in which the deputy premier was denounced by name in the official media. *R.MacF.*

Death of Mao Zedong

This occurred on 9 September 1976, but due to Parkinson's disease the Chairman's powers had been failing for some time. Mao's body lay in state in the Great Hall of the People from the 11th to the 17th during which time over 300 000 people were said to have paid their respects. A memorial rally was held in Tiananmen Square on the 18th. During the next six months a memorial hall was built in the centre of Tiananmen Square on the traditional imperial north–south axis between the Forbidden City and Qianmen Gate, where Mao's body rests in a crystal sarcophagus.

Hua Guofeng held all the major positions of power after Mao's death but his authority was gradually eroded, and he lost his party chair and the premiership to allies of Deng Xiaoping.

which was the first step in the undermining of the Peking Party apparatus. Zhang Chunqiao was a vice-chairman of the Cultural Revolution Group and took over Shanghai on its behalf during the 'January Revolution' of 1967. Like Yao and Mme Mao, he entered the Politburo at the Ninth Congress, but he achieved a further promotion to the Politburo standing committee at the Tenth.

Both Zhang and Yao had years of work in the Shanghai Party propaganda apparatus prior to the Cultural Revolution. The third member of the so-called 'Shanghai mafia', Wang Hongwen, sprang into prominence during the January Revolution as a workers' leader. He entered the Central Committee at the Ninth Congress and then, for reasons which are still unclear, was catapulted into national leadership when he emerged from the Tenth Congress third in the Politburo after Mao Zedong and Zhou Enlai.

Whether Wang, Yao or even the undoubtedly able organizer Zhang Chunqiao would have risen so high without the patronage of Mme Mao (Jiang Qing) is uncertain, though it is known that Mao had noted approvingly the views of Zhang and Yao in the late 1950s. What is clear is that Mme Mao herself was elevated into the top leadership by her husband at the start of the Cultural Revolution because she was one of the few people whom he could trust in his struggle against the Party.

After their fall the 'gang of four' were accused of a wide variety of crimes including forgery of Mao's instructions, opposition to Zhou Enlai, attempting to use the militia to usurp power and defaming Hua Guofeng. Mme Mao, who apparently had not lived with her husband since 1973, was the most strongly criticized, being accused, among other things, of playing poker while Mao was ill, enjoying a bourgeois life style and seeking to be an empress. Mao was said to have denounced her for wanting to take over as Chairman of the Party. *R.MacF.*

Deng Xiaoping whom he personally denounced. The ambiguity of Hua's position was therefore heightened when Deng was again rehabilitated in 1977, and there was much circumstantial evidence to suggest that while he retained his offices, much real power accrued to his nominal deputy, Deng Xiaoping. At the 1980 National People's Congress Hua gave up his premiership to Zhao Ziyang. *R.MacF.*

'Gang of four'

This epithet was coined by Mao to describe his wife and her three 'radical' associates, Wang Hongwen, Zhang Chunqiao and Yao Wenyuan, the rump of the Cultural Revolutionaries remaining in the Politburo after the Tenth Congress. Yao had written the original polemic in November 1965, against a Beijing historian,

Deng Xiaoping (b. 1904)

Deng Xiaoping was the most important beneficiary of the fall of the 'gang of four'. After an interval of some nine months, perhaps accounted for by the need for the terms of his return to power to be worked out, he re-emerged at a Central Committee plenum in July 1977 as a deputy Chairman of the Party and a vice-premier. Whatever agreement had been worked out between him and Hua Guofeng, it soon became clear that the 73-year-old Deng was the decisive figure in the formulation of policy, perhaps a not surprising development in view of his long revolutionary experience.

Deng was a worker/student in France, with Zhou Enlai, for six years in the 1920s, leaving in 1926 for some months study in

Left: The fall of the 'gang of four' unleashed a flood of satirical cartoons in revenge for the death and destruction that occurred during the Cultural Revolution, but when Mme Mao (Jiang Qing) appeared in the dock at the end of 1980, her defiant attitude drew grudging admiration from some Chinese. Below: The 'gang of four' occupied prominent places within the immediate post-Mao collective leadership, but when they were summarily purged they were painted out of official photographs.

Moscow before returning to China. Back home he worked for the Party in north China and in Shanghai and was then sent as a political commissar to a short-lived soviet on the Vietnam border. By 1930 Deng had joined Mao Zedong in Jiangxi and became a member of his inner circle. During the civil and Anti-Japanese wars Deng gradually rose to prominence as a political commissar with the Communist forces, entering the Central Committee in 1945.

In the early years of the People's Republic, Deng was the leading party official in southwest China, based in his native province of Sichuan. He was transferred to Beijing in 1952 becoming successively a vice-premier, finance minister, secretary general of the Party, member of the Politburo and, at the Party's Eighth Congress in 1956, general secretary of the Party and a member of the Politburo's six-man standing committee. The evidence suggests that Deng's rapid rise was due in part to his long association with Mao.

But after the collapse of the Great Leap Forward, Deng, unlike Mao, was more interested in pragmatic solutions to China's economic problems than in worrying about revolutionary degeneracy; Mao complained later that Deng never reported to him in the 1960s. Deng became an early and, after Liu Shaoqi, the most important victim of the Cultural Revolution, although unlike Liu he was never criticized by name in the official media, only being alluded to as the 'No. 2 power holder taking the capitalist road'. Deng's first rehabilitation occurred in 1973 and it was soon apparent that he had been brought back to take over the reins of government from the ailing Zhou Enlai. Deng was clearly a threat

to any hopes that Mme Mao and her collaborators might have of inheriting Mao's mantle. They used Deng's advocacy of a reshaping of educational policy to undermine his position even before the death of Zhou Enlai, and they secured his dismissal after the Tiananmen incident. Since his second coming Deng has dedicated himself to the rapid development of the Chinese economy and to a rapprochement with the West in general and the United States in particular.   *R.MacF.*

Four Modernizations

The 'Four Modernizations', namely agriculture, industry, national defence and science and technology, are the framework for the Chinese development programme. They derive from a statement by Mao in 1963: 'If in the decades to come we don't completely change the situation in which our economy and technology lag far behind those of imperialist countries, it will be impossible for us to avoid being pushed around again.' On the basis of Mao's injunction, Premier Zhou Enlai put forward the proposal for all-round modernization in the four sectors by the end of the century at the Third (1964–5) and Fourth (1975) National People's Congress sessions. The programme speeded up after the fall of the 'gang of four' and the rehabilitation of Deng Xiaoping, and at the Fifth National People's Congress (1978) an ambitious 10-year plan was announced by Chairman Hua Guofeng. China rapidly increased its purchases of industrial equipment from Japan and the West. However, by 1979, possibly as a result of the return to power of senior economic specialists, the Chinese realized that they were in danger of over-extending themselves and a slow-down was announced.   *R.MacF.*

Opposite: Deng Xiaoping was to be the most important beneficiary of the fall of the 'gang of four'.

Hua Guofeng (far left) still outranked a rehabilitated Deng Xiaoping (centre) at the first post-Mao Party Congress in 1977.

The opening of China to the West

The main opening to the West began with the policy of 'reform and openness' in December 1978. Some of China's leaders had earlier tried to develop a closer relationship but without much success. In 1963 and 1964 a window was opened to the medium capitalist countries as a source for foods and imports of technology. It came to a rapid end as China first became absorbed in the issues of the Vietnam War and then in the turmoils of the Cultural Revolution. However, the key turning point was the rapprochement between China and the United States in 1971 and 1972 when for strategic reasons both sought each other as a counterweight to the Soviet Union. The high point was the visit by President Nixon in February 1972 and the signing of the joint communiqué in Shanghai. This paved the way for extensive Sino-Western cooperation. The Japanese government soon normalized relations as did those few other Western countries who had not already done so.

Although the principal impulse for the rapprochement was strategic, foreign trade expanded rapidly. The total value of that trade trebled from US $4.6 billion in 1971 to US $14.5 billion in 1975. Major turnkey plants were imported from Western countries. But the opening to the West was limited by a domestic conflict between those who stressed the priorities of modernization headed initially by Zhou Enlai and then by Deng Xiaoping and those who stressed the revolutionary values of the Cultural Revolution headed by what were later called 'the gang of four' backed by the declining Mao. It was not until the Third Party Plenum of December 1978 that China became committed to the policy of reform and openness with modernization given the overriding priority. This paved the way not only for the still further expansion of foreign trade which by 1988 reached the value of US $102.9 billion, but also for the opening of the Chinese economy to an interdependent relationship with the global economy. In 1980 China joined the International Monetary Fund and the World Bank. It established four special economic zones to attract Western investment and a variety of joint ventures with Western companies. Loans were obtained from Western governments and institutions. In 1984 14 cities were granted the right to deal directly with foreign companies. A whole series of legislation was introduced to facilitate more extensive foreign economic relations. In 1985 and 1986 provinces and regions were delegated the rights within limits to engage directly in foreign economic relations. Meanwhile trusts and corporations were established to deal in trade and investment. Tens of thousands of students were sent to Western countries, notably the United States.

As a result of the new foreign policy of 'independence' enunciated in 1982 China began to develop multi-faceted foreign eco-nomic relations throughout the world. But there is no doubt that access to the advanced technology available only in the capitalist countries is vital to China's long-term aspirations for modernity. However, the growing interchange with the West poses ideological challenges to China's leaders who are determined to retain the monopoly of power of the Communist Party. *M.Y.*

Eleventh Party Congress

Convened on 19 August 1977, the 11th Congress officially reinstated Deng Xiaoping as Party vice-chairman, State Council vice-premier and vice-chairman of the Military Affairs Commission. A then-obscure provincial official Zhao Ziyang First Party Secretary of Sichuan province, was also elected as an alternate member of the Central Committee. In his typical style, Deng gave a no-nonsense closing address to the Congress calling for 'less empty talk and more hard work'.

While the Congress restored Deng's portfolios, it was not until the pivotal 3rd Plenum of the 11th Central Committee in December 1978 that he outmanoeuvred Hua Guofeng, garnering real power and setting the political agenda. The 6th Plenum of 27–9 June 1981 was also significant in that Hua Guofeng was demoted and replaced by Hu Yaobang as Party Chairman, and the Central Committee officially adopted the 'Resolution on Certain Questions on the History of Our Party Since the Founding of the PRC'. This Resolution, among other subjects, undertook to re-evaluate the legacy of 'Comrade' Mao Zedong and found that despite 'great contributions' Mao had erred repeatedly in a 'leftist' direction beginning with the Great Leap Forward in 1958. The Resolution judged Mao to have been 70 per cent good, 30 per cent bad. *D.S.*

Zhao Ziyang (b. 1919)

Born in 1919 to a landlord family in Henan Province, Zhao joined the Party at the age of 19 and fought with the CCP guerrilla forces against the Japanese in his native province. After 1949 Zhao served as a leading Party cadre in the southern province of Guangdong. It was there that he got his first taste of the effect of material incentive systems in boosting agricultural and industrial production. This policy cost him dearly during the Cultural Revolution, but his efforts also caught the eye of Deng Xiaoping—who would later groom Zhao as his successor, only to purge him in 1989.

Zhao Ziyang made his reputation in Sichuan. There he engineered the 'Sichuan miracle' by halting famine and, through the experimental introduction of the agricultural responsibility system, restored the province's role as 'China's rice bowl'. Zhao also experimented with a variety of incentive systems designed to stimulate the industrial, commercial and financial sectors of the economy. These efforts earned him widespread fame, a place on the 11th Central Committee, and—in 1980—as Hua Guofeng's successor as Premier of the State Council. In 1987 Zhao succeeded Hu Yaobang as General Secretary of the Communist Party, as well as becoming first vice-chairman of the Military Affairs Commission, only to be purged following the May–June 1989 pro-democracy demonstrations and subsequent massacre. Zhao was stripped of all his posts for his role in supporting the 'counter-revolutionary rebellion'. *D.S.*

Democracy Wall

During the autumn of 1978 big-character posters began to appear on public walls in the Hsidan District of Beijing that called for a 'fifth modernization'—democracy. The posters drew great public attention and quickly spread to college campuses and other cities in China. They criticized the authoritarianism of the Maoist period and openly called for the institution of a multiparty system, an independent judiciary, free elections, freedom of information and publishing, and the establishment of a democratic polity. Scores of underground journals appeared simultaneously that expressed a broad spectrum of views.

This was initially tolerated by the leadership, even used by Deng Xiaoping and his allies in their competition with Hua Guofeng and the 'whateverists' (those who held to the view that whatever Chairman Mao said was correct), but was brought to an abrupt halt in spring 1979. After the wall posters were removed, several of the more outspoken critics (notably Wei Jing-shen) were arrested and imprisoned. *D.S.*

Twelfth Party Congress

The 12th Party Congress, held from 1–11 September 1982, signalled the consolidation of Deng's power and the dawning of the post-Mao reform era. Presided over by the new Party General Secretary and Deng Xiaoping's protégé Hu Yaobang, the 12th Congress designated 'economic construction' as the central task of the nation, promulgated a new Party constitution launched a three-year 'rectification' campaign aimed at weeding out deviant Party members, re-established a Party Secretariat responsible for coordinating day-to-day affairs and centralizing policy, created a Central Advisory Commission for retired Party elders and a Cen-

tral Commission for Discipline Inspection to monitor corruption and nepotism within the Party, and elected a new Central Committee and Central Military Commission. The new leadership that emerged from the 12th Congress was packed with Deng supporters. *D.S.*

Spiritual Pollution Campaign

Concerned that the 'Open Door Policy' was responsible for the introduction of 'unhealthy Western tendencies', conservatives launched a campaign against 'spiritual pollution' in the autumn of 1983. This began as a criticism of intellectuals applying the theories of 'humanism' and 'alienation' to question socialist society. The scope of this campaign was widened to include ordinary citizens for such activities as dancing, growing long hair, being concerned with fashion, interest in modernist art forms, even the 'bourgeois' pursuit of growing house plants. Chinese intellectuals in particular began to protect themselves from this new 'cold wind'. The campaign lost momentum in the spring of 1984, only to re-emerge in 1987 and 1989 in the form of the campaign to 'Combat Bourgeois Liberalism'. *D.S.*

Thirteenth Party Congress

In the wake of widespread student demonstrations in January 1987, which resulted in the downfall of Hu Yaobang as CCP General Secretary, the Party convened its 13th Congress from 25 October to 1 November 1987. Zhao Ziyang was confirmed as Hu's successor and Li Peng succeeded Zhao as Premier of the State Council. The Congress had been delayed by many months of inner-party wrangling over personnel appointments. Party elders and more conservative elements within the leadership who were discontented with the Hu-Zhao reforms were temporarily successful in restricting further decentralization of the economy and devolution of political authority. In the ideological sphere, General Secretary Zhao announced at the Congress the theory of the 'primary stage of socialism' which held that China must establish a 'commodity economy' before it could move further along the 'socialist road'. This, Zhao claimed, was totally in keeping with the 'universal principles of Marxism'. *D.S.*

Premier Zhao Ziyang with Communist Party General Secretary Hu
Yaobang at the 12th Party Congress, September 1982.

The Beijing massacre

Hu Yaobang's death on 15 April 1989 triggered the most extraordinary public demonstrations and indictment of Communist Party malfeasance witnessed in the 40 years of the People's Republic. What began as several hundred students from universities throughout the capital marching to protest against corruption in the party quickly mushroomed into widespread prodemocracy demonstrations in the heart of Tiananmen Square.

For several weeks during May 1989 the Square was filled with hundreds of thousands of demonstrators. Aside from calls for democracy and criticisms of the party for its corruption, press freedom became a central theme. The student demonstrators were joined first by a small contingent of journalists from the New China News Agency, and then by people from many walks of life: industrial workers, doctors and hospital staff, scholars from the Academy of Sciences and Academy of Social Sciences, service sector personnel, cadres, even members of the People's Armed Police.

The demonstrations gained added impetus from the 70th anniversary of the May 4th Movement and the three-day visit of Soviet leader Mikhail Gorbachev to attend the Sino-Soviet Summit. Gorbachev's schedule was repeatedly interrupted by the crowds of demonstrators—at this point numbering in the millions—and the

Chinese leadership was deeply embarrassed by this fact. Following Gorbachev's departure from Beijing for Shanghai, the central leaders began to contemplate serious action to bring the demonstration to a halt.

Premier Li Peng first made the gesture of meeting student representatives but proceeded to warn them to disperse. Some students went on hunger strike and many were taken to hospital, where Zhao Ziyang, Li Peng and other Politburo members visited them. On 26 May Zhao Ziyang made a last-ditch attempt to persuade the students to leave the Square. He had just lost a vote in the standing committee of the Politburo which had decided to impose martial law and to suppress the demonstrations by force. This was the last time Zhao was seen in public. The imposition of martial law was formally announced on 27 May. Over the next week, under the eye of international television, several attempts were made to move troops into the centre of Beijing, only to be repeatedly blocked by human barricades, which prevented the occupation of the city centre for a week.

Deng Xiaoping, frustrated, flew south to Wuhan where he convened an emergency meeting of commanders of China's 7 military regions. Upon Deng's return to the capital, a complete news blackout was imposed on the foreign media on 2 June and approximately 350 000 troops were deployed around the capital.

In the early hours of 4 June units of the 27th Army Corps from

Above: Students demonstrating in Tiananmen Square, Beijing, for political reforms. Left: Tiananmen Square, 4 June 1989. Hundreds of students in the Square were killed or injured in a pre-dawn assault by government troops and tanks.

the Beijing Military Region began an assault on the city centre. Armoured personnel carriers and infantry units entered from the east and the south of Tiananmen Square, killing many of those still remaining in and around and around the square. It is estimated that hundreds were killed in and around the Square itself, while several thousand others lost their lives in other parts of the city. Several hundred soldiers also perished. Hundreds more died in Chengdu, the capital of Sichuan Province, where, as in numerous other provincial capitals, massive demonstrations had also taken place.

Following the massacre, the authorities began a nation-wide round-up of 'counter-revolutionary elements'. Thousands were arrested and some were executed. Some student leaders and dissident intellectuals fled the country. Abroad, some Chinese diplomats sought political asylum, and numbers of students and scholars studying overseas declined to return. A purge of Party ranks ensued, concentrating on Zhao Ziyang and his reformist followers.   *D.S.*

demonstrated an avid interest in new technologies. In the field of foreign affairs he has specialized in relations with the Soviet Union and Eastern Europe. Premier Li's political career had been relatively undistinguished before 1989. He announced the imposition of martial law and was a member of the faction that ordered the suppression of the pro-democracy demonstrations.   *D.S.*

Li Peng (b. 1928)

Li Peng was orphaned at the age of three when his father was executed by the *Guomindang* for participating in the revolutionary Nanchang Uprising. He subsequently became an adopted son of Zhou Enlai. In 1948 Li was sent to Moscow to train for a career as a hydro-electric engineer. He returned to China in 1954 and worked in the power industry at the local, regional and central levels until 1983 when he became involved in central politics. He became Premier of the State Council in 1988.

Li is thought to be an advocate of heavy industry, price controls and central planning. With his engineering background, Li has

Jiang Zemin (b. 1926)

Jiang Zemin succeeded Zhao Ziyang as General Secretary of the Chinese Communist Party on 24 June 1989 following Zhao's dismissal and the suppression of pro-democracy demonstrations. He was subsequently confirmed at the Fourth Plenum of the 13th Congress of the CCP.

Jiang Zemin and Li Peng attending the 4th plenary session of the 13th Central Committee of the Communist Party, 27 June 1989.

Jiang joined the party in 1946, a year before he graduated from Shanghai's Jiaotong University, as an electrical engineer. In 1955 he spent a year in Moscow. From then until the 1980s he held a number of managerial party positions related to heavy industry and electronics, serving as Minister of the Electronics Industry in the early 1980s, before becoming the mayor of Shanghai. As mayor, Jiang helped open Shanghai's door to foreign investment.

Jiang relinquished the post of mayor of Shanghai in 1988, but retained the position of municipal party secretary, earning Deng Xiaoping's support when he closed down the liberal newspaper *World Economic Herald* immediately after martial law was declared.   *D.S.*

People's Liberation Army

The People's Liberation Army traces its origins to an abortive uprising by Communist-led troops at Nanchang, Jiangxi, on 1 August 1927, against pro-Nationalist forces. The fundamentals of the Maoist strategy, the creation of base areas defended by peasant armies which was the foundation of the Communists' victory 21 years later, had been established. During these two decades, which witnessed such epic achievements of what was later called the People's Liberation Army as the Long March, resistance to Japan and victory in the civil war, the role of the army and its leaders assumed critical importance within the Chinese Communist Party.

The victorious Communist forces settled down after 1949 as garrisons in the areas of China which they had conquered, loyal to Mao's dictum that the Party should command the gun, until the rise of Lin Biao gave their commanders a new role in China's polity. In the meanwhile, Chinese troops distinguished themselves in the Korean War (1950–3), suppressed a rebellion in Tibet (1959), gained a convincing victory over Indian troops in the Himalayas in 1962, but suffered serious if local defeats on the Sino-Soviet border in 1969.

China's brief invasion of Vietnam in 1979 underlined what Beijing generals had long been arguing: that despite a total strength of almost 4 million men, the People's Liberation Army's equipment was 20 years out of date and its whole strategy and structure needed radical overhauling. Subsequently China sought modern military equipment from the West, and concentrated on becoming a professional fighting force.

During the 1980s the political leadership has sought to streamline and modernize the PLA. One million servicemen were demobilized; ranks were reinstituted on 1 October 1988 after a more than 20-year hiatus; the 11 Military Regions were merged into 7

force structures and made more integrated and flexible in order to contend with a broad range of contingencies; some advanced weapon systems and defence technologies were imported from the West; military education was improved, including the establishment of a National Defence University and the training of officers abroad; and the Maoist doctrine of 'people's war' has—for all ostensible purposes—been jettisoned. The withdrawal of the PLA from the domestic political arena engineered by Deng Xiaoping during the decade of the 80s was suddenly reversed by their use in suppressing the pro-democracy demonstrations in Tiananmen Square.   *R.MacF., D.S.*

China's nuclear capability

As early as the mid-1950s while still a close ally of the Soviet Union and sheltered by its nuclear umbrella, Mao determined that China should have its own nuclear capability. A Sino-Soviet agreement on nuclear matters, the precise details of which are still unclear, was unilaterally abrogated by the Russians in 1959, but the Chinese went on to explode their first A-bomb in October 1964 and their first H-bomb in June 1967.

With the exacerbation of Sino-Soviet hostility during the 1970s, the Chinese evidently decided that a regional capability was the priority for their nuclear forces. By the end of 1978 China had conducted 24 nuclear tests and stockpiled hundreds of nuclear weapons, suitable for either strategic or tactical use.

Chinese advances in the field of rocketry were demonstrated when the country's first satellite was launched in 1970. In December 1975 China became only the third country to launch and recover a satellite.

China's nuclear programme accelerated throughout the post-Mao era. To supplement its ageing bomber and medium-range ballistic missile (MRBM) forces, Beijing successfully tested a solid-fuelled, full-range (13 000 km) ICBM in 1980, a submarine-launched ballistic missile (SLBM) in 1982 and an ICBM with multiple independently-targeted (MIRV) warheads in 1985. Technical problems have plagued these breakthroughs, and these systems have not been fully deployed. None the less, China possesses a minimal, second-strike nuclear deterrent capable of inflicting significant damage on any regional aggressor.   *R.MacF., D.S.*

Taiwan (1949–79)

Following their defeat in the civil war Chiang Kai-shek and his remnant forces in the course of 1949 withdrew to the island province of Taiwan. There he resumed the presidency of the Republic of China and declared his determination to return one day to the mainland and overthrow the Communist rulers whom he claimed were bandit usurpers. The system of government was patterned on the one which Chiang had led on the mainland. Taiwan itself was officially regarded as just one of the provinces belonging to the Republic of China. Effective power was therefore in the hands of Chiang, the Nationalist Party and the one million mainlanders who largely made up the armed forces and the police, and who dominated the main positions of the Party and the state. In addition to Taiwan itself Chiang's forces also occupied several islands near the Chinese coast which technically belonged to the adjacent provinces. The most noteworthy are Quemoy and Matsu, which are part of Fujian Province. These symbolized that the Republic of China was more than Taiwan island itself and they also symbolized the determination of Chiang to return to the mainland.

With the outbreak of the Korean War in June 1950 the US President Truman interposed the 7th Fleet between Taiwan and the mainland thus saving it from imminent attack from across the 193km-wide Taiwan Straits. The Chiang Kai-shek regime was regarded as the legitimate government of China and it was not until 1971 that it lost the UN seat to the People's Republic of China and the overwhelming majority of states came to recognize the latter as the sole legitimate representative of China. In December 1978 the USA finally normalized relations with the People's Republic leaving Taiwan recognized as the Republic of China by a declining rump of 20 states. Nevertheless by the Congressional Taiwan Relations Act of that time the USA retained certain commitments towards the island and the people. These were partially acknowledged in the 1982 Joint Communiqué with the People's Republic that formally allowed the USA to continue to supply arms to the island at a continually reducing long-term rate.

Meanwhile as the result of new economic policies begun in the early 1960s Taiwan began to develop at a remarkable rate so that by the 1980s it was regarded as one of the few Newly Industrialized Countries with a per capita income in 1988 of US $6000—higher even than some of the OECD countries. By the 1980s this economic 'miracle' was accompanied by political changes under the astute leadership of Chiang Ching-Kuo (whose father Chiang Kai-shek had died in 1975). As more Western-educated younger men were given managerial responsibilities and as more local Taiwanese were inducted into politics the stage was reached in 1987 when Martial Law was lifted and an opposition party allowed to stand and win seats in open elections. After Chiang Ching-Kuo's death in 1988 his nominee, the local-born Li Teng-hui, was elected president.

Beginning in 1979 Beijing leaders have sought to induce reunification with the island on the basis of a formula of 'one country two systems' by which Taiwan would retain its existing system but under the sovereignty of the PRC. While resisting these blandishments the Taiwan government has allowed economic relations to develop with the mainland that in 1988 reached the value of US $2.5 billion and it has also permitted tens of thousands of its citizens to visit the mainland in non-official capacities. *M.Y.*

THE MIND AND SENSES
OF CHINA

One of the stone statues of warriors and mythological beasts that line the ceremonial 'Way of the Mings'.

BELIEFS, CUSTOMS AND FOLKLORE

Cosmology

Until the Communist Revolution in 1949 China had one of the most highly developed cosmological systems in the world. It was so complex, in fact, that ordinary people could not hope to understand more than a fraction of the system. Instead the peasantry, and to some extent members of the literate elite, relied on trained specialists. The services of cosmological interpreters (fortune tellers and geomancers) were required for any event or venture that might involve an element of risk—from the selection of an auspicious date for a wedding to the siting of a new building. From the client's point of view the interpreter's primary task was to guard against disaster. The specialists themselves might have a more complicated vision of their own role in society but this was beyond the comprehension, or interest, of ordinary people.

Perhaps the most important of the many elements in the Chinese cosmological system was the *yin-yang* dichotomy.

Yin was normally seen as the collective representation of all forces in the universe that emanate from darkness, while *yang* was the representation of light. It followed from this basic division that aspects of human experience were often conceptualized as opposites: for example, day-night, life-death, good-evil and male-female. The sexual dichotomy, with its unambiguous connotation of male supremacy, was often used to justify the suppression of women. In the traditional view women are thought to be weak, emotional and untrustworthy—characteristics that relate to their *yin* nature. At a higher, more philosophical level the ideas about *yin* and *yang* were less concrete and, rather than a distinct dichotomy, the forces were seen as complementary. In the esoteric literature of Daoism, for example, *yin* and *yang* were inseparable and interacted in a dialectical relationship.

It is in the realm of ancestor worship and funerary ritual that most Chinese encountered ideas about *yin* and *yang*, as well as other cosmological elements. It is worth noting here that the spirit, or soul, of every deceased person was divided into several parts, all of which had to be dealt with in an appropriate manner before the deceased could 'settle in' as an ancestor. The bones of the ancestors, and with them the grave, constituted a very powerful repository of *yin* forces. Not surprisingly the bones had to be treated with the greatest of care lest disaster strike the family. In many parts of China, notably in the south, the bones of important ancestors were exhumed after approximately seven years and transferred from coffins to ceramic pots, which were, in turn, reburied in specially selected places.

Here another set of cosmological ideas came into play; the siting of graves is governed by the forces of 'wind and water', or *fengshui*. 'Wind and water' was the disarming term that the Chinese used for the art—some would call it a science—of geomancy. This particular form of geomancy involves the manipulation of the Earth's natural forces for the benefit of knowledgeable people, or those able to pay for this service. Every hill, field and body of water was said to affect the course of 'wind and water' influences as they passed through the landscape. Some locations, notably on the sides of hills which had gently flowing streams or ponds below, were ideal for graves; others could be ruinous. The same applied for important buildings such as houses, temples and ancestral halls.

Most peasants had some knowledge of 'wind and water', but few would be so bold as to proceed with the burial of their own father or the siting of their own house without consulting experts. These men, called *fengshui xiansheng* or 'wind and water gentlemen', were treated with great respect because they were thought to hold the key to prosperity and happiness. If the grave of one's ancestor were located in an auspicious spot, the good influences (*yang*) of the landscape were transmitted through the ancestor's bones (*yin*) to his descendants. Even the slightest shift in the skull's location or the excavation for a rival grave nearby could adversely affect this delicate relationship between living and dead (and between *yin* and *yang* influences). Changes in 'wind and water' were often cited as causal factors when discussing success and failure in the real world. Whole lineages were said to have declined or even disappeared because of interference with the ancestral bones. Even today in modern Hong Kong, 'wind and water' disputes are a regular feature of local-level politics. Complaints about the location of buildings or graves are a convenient way to carry on long-standing feuds. It is also thought to be more legitimate to complain about disruptions in one's 'wind and water' than to speak openly about a rival's political actions. 'Wind and water' thus becomes an acceptable language for the pursuit of otherwise taboo topics, notably political and economic rivalry.

J.L.W.

Divination

Divination was practised in China from about 1700 BC or earlier. Initially, it was intended to discover the answers of occult powers to simple questions that concerned matters of everyday life or the immediate outcome of a proposed action (for example the chances of a good harvest, the choice of times for religious services, the likely success in the hunt or in battle). With the growth of Chinese science and philosophy from about 500 BC, divination took its place among

Ancestral graves, the last stage in the burial cycle. Here the bones catch and transmit the influences of 'wind and water'.

a number of means whereby the Chinese tried to organize their lives and control their actions so that they could best conform with what they believed to be the major truths and patterns of the universe; it was felt that only by taking such precautions could it be ensured that the outcome of a proposed plan, or the choice of several possibilities (for example the choice of an heir or of a site for a building) would be successful. The chief characteristics of divination are the importance attached to linear configurations, the combination of intuitive insight with intellectual prowess, and the process of standardization.

Initially, the seers who pronounced the results of divination drew on their intuitive powers of perceiving and interpreting signs in the cracks deliberately formed on bones and shells (scapulimancy), in the linear patterns created by manipulating a plant's stalks (milfoil), and the natural but invisible lines on the earth (geomancy). Intellectual considerations entered in when it was attempted to explain or interpret those patterns in the light of scientific observations and rational explanations of the workings of heaven and earth. When, with the passage of time, the intuitive powers of a seer were eclipsed or mistrusted, rules for procedure were instituted, perhaps to ensure that a less gifted diviner would take the steps that were prescribed. Schemes were written down to provide a guide or authority for the interpretation of signs that had been produced by random processes with shells or with stalks, or to supplement the intuitive appreciation of certain features of the earth; reason and rules were replacing insight. Divination by means of stalks (or coins) and the *Book of Changes*, and geomancy with a magnetic compass have formed a highly significant part of religious activity until modern times.

Scapulimancy

The earliest method of divination was to apply fire or heat to the shoulder bones (*scapulae*) of animals or the shells (*plastra*) of turtles to induce random cracks in the material. It was believed that a diviner could determine the outcome of a proposed plan of action or the likelihood of an occurrence—for example, rain—from the shape, frequency or other circumstances of the cracks. During the Shang dynasty this method of divination was practised regularly for the kings, who wished to ascertain their immediate future or answers to practical problems. As a by-product, the procedure has provided the earliest known examples of writing, for a record of each act of divination was inscribed on the bone or shell. The choice of turtles for the practice was later explained as being due to the magical properties of the creature; it was the longest-lived animal known to man, and was regarded as a repository of eternal truths. Material remains reveal how a method that started as a random process became standardized: the bones or shells were used several times, with the heat applied in neat rows; the questions were put and interpretations given according to set formulae. Divination by turtle shell was practised at least until the beginning of the 1st century AD.

Milfoil

The origins of divination by means of the yarrow plant, or milfoil, are unknown. Probably, diviners somehow brought into being a written line of one of two forms, either whole or broken; and it has been suggested that a whole line signified a favourable, positive answer, and a broken line an unfavourable, negative answer. By the 8th century BC, or perhaps earlier, a procedure had developed for forming a figure of six such lines in parallel (the total number of possible hexagrams was 64), and the answers to questions put to divination depended on the particular combination of broken and unbroken lines.

Whatever the original methods may have been, by the beginning of the first century AD at least diviners were forming a hexagram by manipulating 50 stalks of the yarrow, whose manifold stems were believed to show that it possessed magical properties. One of the 50 stalks was discarded, and the rest were divided into two groups at random. The diviner separated the stalks in each group, removing them in batches of four. Depending on the number of stalks remaining in his hand at the end of the procedure (0, 1, 2 or 3) he inscribed either a complete or a broken line. After six applications of the procedure the complete hexagram was formed. A further complication was introduced by the numerical combinations of the process, which determined whether each line was regarded as fixed or moving. A hexagram which included one or more moving lines was itself thought to be in a state of motion, changing towards another.

Yijing (*The Book of Changes*)

From the pattern of the hexagram or hexagrams a seer could determine the answer to a given problem intuitively. But there soon followed a need for explicit guidance and authority for the less gifted diviners. Probably from this need there arose one of the oldest, most highly revered and widely circulated books of Chinese literature, the *Yijing* or *Book of Changes*. Associated with this book and deriving therefrom arose a wholly symbolical scheme of universal philosophy that linked intuitive divination with China's intellectual development. The earliest parts of the *Book of Changes*, which are known as the *Zhouyi* or *Changes of Zhou*, form only one of several guides that were made to assist in the interpretation of the hexagrams. The text provides a title for each of the 64 figures, together with a guide to its general character and to the particular significance of each line.

The book soon acquired a new character and purpose, when the hexagrams came to be taken not only as a series of answers to particular problems, but also as the symbols of 64 situations that occur in the universe and repeat in cyclical fashion. Divination with the stalks and the *Zhouyi* moved from an attempt to answer a specific problem to a means of ascertaining in which one of the 64 situations the inquirer chanced to be placed; for with such information he could choose from alternative decisions and regulate his life. Simultaneously the *Changes of Zhou* was being extended by a number of commentaries which sought to explain

Two of the possible arrangements of the 64 hexagrams of the *Yijing*.

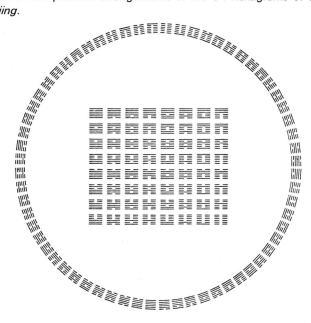

the hexagrams within a general philosophy and according to the observed cycles of change in heaven and earth. The enlarged *Book of Changes*, which reached its present form at about the start of the first century AD, was invoked both by diviners who intuitively sought clarification to problems from its highly esoteric text, and by metaphysicians and scientists, who saw in it a universal scheme of being and a means of comprehending the mysteries of creation. It is highly significant that some of the most brilliant minds of the Han and Song periods had no difficulty in combining the two principles inherent in this tradition: a belief in the power of the stalks to reveal truths by random and irrational processes, and an understanding of the world on rational grounds.

Geomancy

Geomancy, or *fengshui*, is a means of divination intended to find the most suitable sites for establishing a city, house or tomb. Practised for many centuries either in its present or its antecedent forms, it has exercised a profound influence on the face of China's landscape and on city plans.

Since at least the 2nd century BC the Chinese have regarded the earth as a living organism, comparable with other organisms such as the human body. Just as the human body incorporates channels along which its life blood pulsates, so it was thought that the earth included similar channels, sometimes described as 'the veins of the earth' or 'the veins of the dragon'. Parts of the earth which are favourably sited lie at points where such channels converge, bringing with them the natural blessings that enrich a living body. Such benefits are described as *qi*, or natural energies, and the channels along which they pass are invariably winding. Forces of an evil nature (*sha*), may make a direct approach to a site along a straight, man-made line, such as a ditch or roadway. The geomancer possesses intuitive powers of discrimination which enable him to detect how far a site lies open to beneficial or pernicious influences. Such powers disclose forces that are otherwise unperceived; but a large number of printed manuals have been drawn up in order to explain the features that control the presence of these forces, and to define a site's fortunate or unfortunate properties in terms of the physical lie of the land or the incidence of hill, valley or river. Dependence on such manuals has tended to standardize the process and detract from its spontaneity.

Like other forms of divination, geomancy has depended on combining intuition with sophisticated intellectual theories. The intellectual elements spring from the belief that man's fortune depends on accommodating himself to his natural surroundings and to the eternal rhythms that regulate the movements of heaven, earth and man. A site will be suitable for an inhabitant, alive or dead, whose nature conforms with the spatial relationship of the site to the whole of earth and with the temporal relationship

Geomantic compass from China, probably made in the 18th century.

efited. However, should the descendants neglect the spirit of an ancestor by failing to make regular offerings at his grave, the ancestor would be cut adrift in the other-world and seek nourishment (and attention) elsewhere. Ancestors abandoned in this way became 'hungry ghosts', a general term for spirits of dead people who did not have any reciprocal relationships with the living. It was not uncommon for an ancestor to make the transition from a benevolent, cooperative spirit into a vengeful, dangerous ghost. Ancestors also look out for their own; among peasants it was well understood that 'my ancestor is your ghost'.

The ancestral cult thus played an integral part in the Chinese kinship system and, as a cult, its membership (both living and dead) was restricted to people who shared the same patriline. There were two sides to Chinese ancestor worship: the domestic cult and the lineage cult. The domestic side, also known as the

imposed by the heavenly bodies. In assessing the value or quality of a site, a geomancer uses a highly intricate compass, which shows how an individual's circumstances (for example, date and time of birth) coincide with such relationships and their influences. By such means a city, home or tomb may be sited to suit the major rhythms of earth and heaven, and the universal cycle of the 64 hexagrams used in divination with milfoil.

Since the 11th century geomancers have used a compass fitted with a magnetic needle, but antecedents of these instruments without such a device date from the 2nd century BC, as do certain manuals. Geomancy differs from the other major forms of divination in one major respect: whereas scapulimancy and the use of milfoil stalks depend on the human induction of random patterns, in geomancy the qualities of a site are seen as springing from natural lines that already inform the earth.   *M.L.*

Ancestor worship

The ancestor worship cult, for which the southern Chinese were particularly noted prior to the Communist Revolution of 1949, draws together many of the elements of cosmology and geomancy. Reciprocity between living and dead was the key to this system of beliefs. For instance, the flow of good 'wind and water' (*fengshui*) influences through the bones of the ancestor was thought to bring prosperity to his descendants. The living, in turn, had the awesome responsibility of sustaining the spirits of the ancestors and protecting their graves. As long as this reciprocal relationship was maintained both the living and dead ben-

Representation, at a Ghost Festival in Kowloon, of the 'God of the Underworld', ruler of ghosts.

'family cult', was concerned with immediate ancestors, usually those who had died in the past five or six generations. The names of these people were written on a large paper sheet which was kept on the family altar. This list of names was the centre of all ritual activity in the household. (In some parts of China individual wooden tablets were used instead of the paper sheet.) With each death in the family the sheet was burned and a new one produced with the most recent ancestor taking the place of a remote predecessor. The latter was, in effect, dropped from the domestic cult and in a few generations might have been forgotten altogether. The only way for an ancestor to escape this fate was to make provision during his lifetime to be included in the lineage cult. He did this either by buying a 'seat' for his spirit on the altar of an ancestral

hall or by becoming rich enough for his sons to build a hall in his honour.

The lineage cult did, of course, have much in common with the domestic cult; both were founded on the same set of ideas and both depended on reciprocity between living and dead. Yet they must not be confused, because the principles of organization were quite different. The lineage cult focused on a group of generalized ancestors, most of whom were no longer included on the domestic altars. The ancestors in question went back to the foundation of the lineage, which, in many parts of south China, meant upwards

Domestic ancestral altar with the names of individual ancestors written on a sheet of paper.

Below: ancestral altar, with wooden tablets, inside an ancestral hall. Each tablet represents a male ancestor, arranged in rows according to generation. Founding ancestors are on the top row. Bottom: wooden ancestral tablets showing the generation numbers, full names and surnames of wives.

of 40 generations. Each ancestor was commemorated by a carved wooden tablet (usually about 30cm high), which stood on a large altar together with other tablets at one end of the ancestral hall. The tablet normally bore the ancestor's full name, generation number, titles and wives' surnames. Ancestral halls were often magnificent buildings, ideally with three large chambers and elaborate decorations. These ancestral halls were the most visible symbol of lineage wealth and prestige.

Ancestral tablets were the focus of many lineage rituals, including regular worship ceremonies during which all elders assembled to pay their respects before the altar. Elders (men aged 61 and over) played a central role in all lineage cults and the oldest surviving member of the most senior generation was deemed the ritual leader of the whole lineage. The 'lineage master' as he was called, rarely had any real political power but he often wielded considerable moral authority. His seal of approval, along with that of other elders, was required for any activity or enterprise that involved the lineage as a corporate group. Elders were seen as the living link between the ancestors and the younger generations. One must not, however, confuse this form of ancestor worship and filial respect with a system of gerontocracy; the political and economic leadership of the lineage was controlled by men in their prime, irrespective of generation or age.

The ancestral halls, with their rows of tablets, were also the social centres of the lineage. Here banquets were held as well as

Below: ancestral hall with public notice of a wedding. Bottom: division of sacrificial pork in an ancestral hall, one share going to each surviving descendant of the founding ancestor.

Elders presenting offerings, including roast pigs, to an ancestor at a major grave.

assemblages and informal meetings. Primary schools for lineage children were located in most halls, with pupils literally studying under the watchful eyes of the ancestors. Ancestors, in their tablet embodiment, were kept informed of all decisions affecting the lineage. For example, the marriage of every male descendant was dutifully reported before the ancestral altar; it was this act, along with the banquet inside the hall, that sealed the marriage and made it legitimate. The lineage cult thus stressed continuity of the descent line and constant interaction between living and dead. Ancestors and their descendants were equally responsible for the maintenance of the lineage as a viable organization.

Even though descendants were expected to treat their ancestors with respect, this was by no means automatic. As in any reciprocal relationship, the ancestors had to earn this respect. In most parts of China the expenses of ancestor worship (which could be considerable) were underwritten by the ancestors themselves through the institution of landed estates. A man could either set aside property for this purpose during his lifetime or rely upon his sons to establish an estate in his name after death. The rent produced from the ancestral estates paid for all worship paraphernalia and, if money were left over, the remainder was divided among living descendants—an additional bonus for maintaining the ancestral cult. Ancestors who left a large enough estate were never forgotten because their graves were visited every year by a procession of descendants who presented their forebear with roast pigs, a prestigious and expensive offering. The graves of ancestors who did not leave land were eventually forgotten. And, unless they or their sons were prosperous enough to buy a 'seat' for their tablets in an ancestral hall, these unfortunates ceased to be recognized as ancestors.

Ancestor worship, therefore, was not based on sheer benevolence or filial piety. It was practical in the extreme. There was no reason, at least after a few generations, to respect impoverished ancestors; they had done little to earn this respect. There were cases in which descendants had taken ancestral tablets out of their hall and burned them unceremoniously. A reason frequently given for doing this was that the ancestors had broken their covenant with the living: 'Why should we bother to worship them? They left us with little land and they cannot even protect us from our enemies. They will be equally useless as ghosts.'

The full lineage cult, with its elaborate rituals and halls, was usually associated with the wealthiest lineages in the southern regions of China. The ancestors of these lineages were fortunate enough to have been pioneers when the southern frontier was opening and, as a consequence, they left large estates. Ancestral cults of the type described were rare in the north and, even in the south, only the most powerful kinship groups were able to maintain them. Thus, for the majority of people throughout the Chi-

nese Empire, ancestor worship was restricted to the domestic cult. After a few generations most Chinese had little reason to be concerned with predecessors who had left only their memory. *J.L.W.*

Folk religion

'Folk religion', as practised in China prior to the Communist Revolution of 1949, is usually defined as those sets of beliefs held by ordinary people; it must be distinguished from the religious traditions of the old elite. Folk religion was not, as is commonly believed, an unsophisticated amalgamation of the Three Great Traditions (Confucianism, Daoism and Buddhism). Nor was it simply a pale imitation of the more philosophically-inclined state

'Chanting fellow' operating at a wedding ritual.

religion. There were, of course, important elements and themes that reappeared in nearly all manifestations of religious belief in China. One was the *yin-yang* dichotomy; another was the tripartite division of supernatural beings into gods, ghosts and ancestors. It is quite another thing, however, to argue that there was *a* Chinese religion or one set of beliefs that together constituted the *core* of China's religious tradition. Most anthropologists who have worked on this problem would no doubt agree that it is best to speak of local traditions and local cults which relate, in turn, to specific communities or regional alliances. 'Folk religion', therefore, must be understood as a generalized term used as a form of shorthand to represent these local traditions.

As with ancestral cults, religious cults were based very largely on reciprocity and pragmatism. The major difference between the two systems was that one was confined to lineal predecessors while the other related primarily to gods who might not have had a kinship link with the supplicant. In both cases, however, the worshipper concentrated on establishing a personal relationship with the supernatural being. Gods, like ancestors, were expected to look after their living devotees and, if results were not forthcoming after reasonable effort, one god could be abandoned for another. In this sense folk religion offered much more scope for choice than did the ancestral cult.

Local gods were often the spirits of virtuous historical figures who either lived in the region or who were thought to have had a special relationship with the people. Every region of China had an enormous pantheon of gods, some with Daoist or Buddhist connections and others with purely local or animistic origins. Cults developed around deities who were thought to be particularly effective. The most popular had temples built for them, with resident priests to look after spiritual needs and lay committees to manage the social affairs of the cult. Temple cults sometimes grew into major enterprises that united thousands of devotees and controlled vast resources.

Attendance at the festival of one god need not preclude joining a procession for another god. Ideas regarding the exclusive devotion to a single deity were not unknown in China but such intolerance applied to only a minority. In most communities it was the women who interceded with the gods on behalf of the family. Their pragmatism in the pursuit of family protection was legendary. It was not unknown, for instance, for idols to be broken when a god failed to fulfil its side of a relationship. Contracts between devotee and deity were initiated by offering special foods, incense and 'spirit money' (which was transmitted to the other-world by burning). If the relationship were to continue the deity had to reciprocate in some fashion, usually by giving instructions (through some form of divination) which solved the supplicant's problem.

Company of 'chanting fellows' at a village ritual.

For ordinary people, both in the countryside and in cities, the religious system was a reflection of their vision of the world. For instance, the afterlife was normally seen as an extension of the present life—which meant that bureaucratic harassment, political intrigue and economic worries would not cease upon death. If anything, life after death became more complicated. Much of what has come to be called 'folk religion' involved the protection of deceased family members in the other-world. Souls of the dead had to pass through a series of hells before they were allowed to rest and settle in as proper ancestors. The passage required passports, visas, guides, equipment and money to bribe the bureaucratic guardians of hell. It will come as no surprise that this vision of hell was a reflection of most people's experiences in the real world.

Perhaps the most common type of religious practitioner in China was the so-called 'chanting fellow' who acted as the ritual leader at funerals and mourning rites. These men claimed to be 'Daoist', in the sense that they often employed Daoist texts as part of their ritual paraphernalia. However, a high percentage were barely literate and had had no formal training in the interpretation of Daoist or any other texts. In addition to their role in funeral rites, 'chanting fellows' were treated as general religious consultants by their clients. On occasion, they worked with nuns who were attached to Buddhist convents; these women had severed all family ties and earned their living by chanting sutras at funerals. The *mingjing* of Buddhist and Daoist traditions was not considered to be unusual or unnatural by anyone involved.

Mediums and diviners operated within a more limited domain than 'chanting fellows' and normally specialized in one set of problems—often relating to personal well-being or family harmony. There were, of course, nearly as many styles of divination as there were local cults in China. Some mediums, usually women, claimed to be able to dispatch part of their own spirit into the other-world where it visited the deceased relatives of paying clients. Others placed themselves in trance during which they were thought to be possessed by gods who communicated through them (in either speech or writing). Mediums of the latter type tended to be male and often played the leading role in large temple cults.

There were many other categories of religious specialists in China: monks, fortune tellers, temple keepers, masters of esoteric arts and educated priests who devoted themselves to the study of classic texts. The religious beliefs that these practitioners represented are so complicated and so heterogeneous that they defy attempts to make sense of them as a unified system of thought.

J.L.W.

PHILOSOPHY AND RELIGION

Daoism

Concepts

Daoism is the name given to a tradition of Chinese thought that has been seen as standing in opposition to Confucianism, although both have much in common. Where Confucianism excludes much from its concerns, concentrating on maintaining good order in human society through the preservation of cultural values, Daoism includes in its scope a variety of topics deliberately ignored by Confucians, and also questions the values that Confucians promote.

Most all-inclusive of Daoist concepts is that of *Tao*, the Way, which means not any particular path to be followed, but rather the sole unseen reality lying behind appearances. Regarding the standards Confucians sought to impose as artificial, Daoists stressed *wuwei* or 'action without contrivance', *ziran*, 'that which is spontaneous'. As for the cultural achievements which Confucians deemed to have been introduced by their sages, the Daoists considered them inferior to the primitive simplicity of earlier times.

Ideas such as these are prominent in the writings of Daoist philosophers of the pre-imperial period, but it is probable that their highly articulate arguments against the Confucians and other schools of thought also reflect the existence of less articulate groups at this time who were also involved in very un-Confucian pursuits, and who in later ages named as their patron sage not Confucius but Laozi, who was considered to be the principal Daoist philosopher. Thus there were many who were involved in the pursuit of immortality, which meant becoming a *xian* or transcendent being with a physical undying existence, who came to consider themselves as being Daoist, and who certainly would not have been accepted as Confucians, since the latter explicitly rejected any concern with the occult.

Methods of achieving immortality varied considerably. An underlying idea is that steps should be taken to preserve or enrich one's *qi*, which literally means 'breath', but which also has cosmological significance, since it refers to the ether or energy out of which the world is formed. At first breathing exercises were recommended to absorb *qi* from outside the body, but during the Tang dynasty the emphasis was changed to exercises designed to preserve the portion of primal *qi* present in the body from birth. At about the same time a similar process of internalization can be seen taking place in the development of ideas concerning alchemy, a popular alternative path to immortality. From the Han dynasty onwards alchemy was primarily conceived of as an attempt to produce a pill, *dan*, through the refining of cinnabar, which would confer immortality on anyone who ingested it. By the Song dynasty the whole alchemical process of refining was more often thought of as a physiological process aimed at creating an immortality-conferring substance within the body. This was termed the *neidan* or 'internal pill', as opposed to the *waidan* or 'external pill'. One reason for the loss of popularity of the latter was probably that most alchemical concoctions were highly poisonous and had by the Song claimed the lives of many victims, including a fair number of emperors.

The tendency to see the pursuit of immortality as an internal process also had a long history. Even in very ancient texts, dating back perhaps to the late Han, the gods who could give instructions concerning immortality were seen as existing simultaneously in the macrocosm of the outside world and in the microcosm of the human body, and a system of meditations was employed to visualize the gods within. These meditations are still employed by Daoist priests in Taiwan today; for since the 2nd century AD the practices for adepts so far described have coexisted with a communal religious tradition giving much more emphasis to external matters. In the course of time this tradition came to absorb many elements from Buddhism and also from folk religion. Here immortality was seen as dependent in the first instance on correct moral behaviour, although one's merits or demerits in this respect could be reported to the god in charge of human destinies both by an external god of the stove, who resided in every home, or by the malevolent 'three worms' (*san shi*), who dwelt within the human body: belief in the latter spread outside China as far as Japan. A whole panorama of heavens and hells was envisaged in the afterlife, and mighty spiritual beings such as the *Tianzun* or 'Heavenly Honoured Ones' rivalled in their cosmic magnificence the Buddhas, whose worship was introduced from India. Yet such developments, though often contrary to the spirit of the earliest Daoist philosophers, did not entirely obscure their initial insights. Even the most exalted of *Tianzun* were seen as but mere emanations from the Absolute, the unseen *Dao*.

Rituals

The performance of ritual is not only the most visible aspect of Daoism: it has also been throughout the centuries the main means by which Daoist priests have earned their living. Daoist texts show that over a millennium ago a large number of different types of ritual were performed, and some of these involved quite spectacular displays of frenzied religiosity, such as the *tutanzhai* or 'retreat of mud and soot', a collective rite of penitence so called because the participants smeared their faces with ashes and wallowed in mud to beg the gods' forgiveness of their sins. But such rituals attracted strong criticism from Buddhists, who always vied with the Daoists for popular and imperial patronage, with the result that today these rituals have completely disappeared. The main rituals for which Daoist priests are required in traditional Chinese communities are public sacrifices for communal prosperity and rites for the dead, and even in the latter case Buddhist practitioners are ready to provide alternative rites.

The most important task that the Daoist priest is called upon to perform is to officiate in the *jiao* or community festival. Such festivals are held in Taiwan and Hong Kong at regular intervals, although the most elaborate *jiao*, connected with the renewal of the community temple, may be a once in a lifetime event, since more than a full cycle of 60 years is allowed to elapse before it is deemed necessary to go to the expense of organizing a fresh one.

The *jiao* is a lengthy and costly event which takes place over three days at the very least and is extended to five, seven or even more days if the community can afford it. Three- and five-day *jiao* are, however, the most common, and the basic structure is always the same in any case. This is because the *jiao* includes different types of ritual, some of which are considered optional. All the rituals usually take place at the community temple, but there is a clear distinction between those which are conducted within the temple itself, which are not open to the public, and those which take place in full view of the populace outside the temple.

Daoist priest from Hua Shan, the sacred mountain in western China, photographed during the 1930s.

The presence of the Daoist priest and his assistants is necessary for the former type of ritual, which includes traditional Daoist practices such as the burning of written memorials in Classical Chinese script so as to convey messages and requests to the gods. Daoist priests may also take part in the public rituals, but these often include rituals from the tradition of Chinese folk religion which may be performed by priests from that tradition who are quite ignorant of the rubrics in Classical Chinese used by the Daoists. There is a tendency towards the deliberately spectacular here: climbing a ladder of 36 sword blades is but one example. It is the inclusion of more peripheral rituals of this sort which may make the *jiao* longer.

Some rituals, such as those for the feeding of hungry ghosts, are closely connected with Buddhist beliefs and may even be performed by Buddhists. The Daoist priest may also delegate other parts of the *jiao*, such as the ritual recitation of religious texts, to his assistants, but the overall conduct of the *jiao* remains under his direction from start to finish, and he bears the responsibility for the ritual meditations he conducts on behalf of the community, which are conceived of as creating a mystical incense burner within his body paralleling the use of actual incense going up to heaven in the rituals. These meditations, which are only mastered after long training, are dispensed with in some Chinese communities, resulting in a one- or two-day festival.

Apart from the important *jiao* festival the Daoist priest also makes his living from day to day through performing rituals for individuals. These include rites of exorcism for dealing with illness and other types of misfortune brought about by spiritual forces. Although such services are by no means the monopoly of the Daoist, since practitioners from the folk religion tradition also have similar rituals, the greater knowledge of the Daoist commands respect, and Daoist ritual remains distinct, since communication with the gods is effected through the burning of written documents, whereas in folk religion practices, spirit mediums are used. The Daoist also has at his disposal a knowledge of rituals for the use of magic power such as the power of thunder. Thunder magic has been used by Daoists in their battles with spiritual powers for about 1000 years.

Sages

Although different groups of Daoists throughout history have looked to very different leaders for inspiration there has been without a doubt but one sage whose position in Daoism rivals that of Confucius in Confucianism, namely Laozi, the reputed author of the *Daodejing* (*The Way and Power Classic*). First mentioned in writings attributed to Zhuangzi (*c.*300 BC) as an older contemporary of Confucius, traditions about him in the first century BC were already so vague and contradictory that modern scholars have despaired of identifying him with any historical figure. His biography, nevertheless, grew increasingly impressive with the passing of time. By the 2nd century AD he was conceived of as a superhuman figure, merged with cosmic processes, who had entered history not once but several times. At about the same time the Chinese were presented with a new sage, the Buddha, from lands to the west of China. Since Laozi was supposed to have disappeared westwards after writing the *Daodejing*, speculation soon arose that the Buddha was either Laozi himself in Indian guise or one of his disciples. Although the earliest Chinese Buddhists may have been glad of the attention which this speculation brought them, a debate soon developed over the relative merits of Buddhist and Daoist teachings in which the Daoists claimed that Laozi had only transmitted to the barbarians a diluted version of his doctrines and produced accounts of his travels to the west elaborating on this theme. These stimulated vigorous polemical disputes with the Buddhists, which only ceased when the Mongol emperor Khubilai Khan decided against the Daoists in 1281 and ordered the burning of all literature prop-

The Daoist sage Lao Zi riding an ox: illustration from a Ming work of reference.

agating the story. Meanwhile the worship of Laozi had become firmly established, and had even during the Tang dynasty received extensive state support, since the emperors of the ruling house fancied themselves to be descended from him.

No such honours were ever accorded any of the other Daoist sages who are mentioned in the pages of Zhuangzi, including Zhuangzi himself, and the only other figure who assumes a truly patriarchal importance in Daoist belief was clearly a historical personality, albeit a shadowy one. Zhang Daoling lived in the 2nd century AD in what is now Sichuan, leading a movement which came to be known as the Way of the Celestial Masters (*Tianshidao*), and which was based on a revelation to Zhang by the deified Laozi. Both this movement and a similar movement in east China calling itself the *Taipingdao*, but better known as the 'Yellow Turbans', eventually came into violent conflict with the central government. But whereas the latter group was effectively suppressed, Zhang Daoling's grandson, Zhang Lu, negotiated a surrender to the government in AD 215 which preserved his organization intact. Although later generations of the Zhang family did not manage to maintain a unified control over the movement, all subsequent organized Daoist groups tended to look back to Zhang Daoling as their founder, even if their actual links with the *Tianshidao* were often tenuous. The Zhang family (or persons claiming descent from Zhang Daoling) emerged once more to a position of prominence during the Song, and even managed to establish themselves as officially recognized leaders of the Daoist church. This caused Western observers in the 19th century to refer to members of their line as 'Daoist Popes', but despite the respect with which the current Celestial Master, the 64th, is still held in Taiwan, neither he nor any of his forebears since the Han dynasty has exercised any real unifying influence over the various groups claiming descent from Zhang Daoling's movement.

During the Tang dynasty, indeed, more official recognition was given to a quite different succession of leaders, a chain of masters and disciples who were connected with Mount Mao in Jiangsu. Foremost among these had been Tao Hongjing (456–536), heir to a revelation traced back to Yang Xi in the 4th century. Yet despite Dao's pre-eminence in the Daoist church, his patrician approach to religion, concerned with the editing of texts and such adjuncts to the pursuit of immortality as alchemy and pharmacology, may also be traced back to Ge Hong (283–343), whose main work, the *Baopuzi* (*The Master Who Embraces Simplicity*) typifies the concerns of the individual gentleman interested in the occult but not in mass movements.

Such movements erupted once again in Daoism after the collapse of the Northern Song in 1127, although the only one of these to survive to the present has been the Quanzhen school founded by Wang Chongyang in 1163. But although Wang's teachings, much influenced by Buddhism, had a widespread impact, especially on monastic Daoism, the typical sage revered by the common people is a more mysterious figure similar to Laozi, such as the immortal Lu Dongbin, once a hermit of the Tang dynasty, to whom many poems are attributed.

Writings

Daoist literature has for the most part been preserved until the present day as part of the Daoist canon, *Daozang*, a collection of over 1400 texts gathered together and printed under imperial auspices in 1445. Earlier editions had been printed from 1116 onwards, but none of these has survived, still less earlier versions of the canon which had been compiled and circulated in manuscript from the 8th century AD until that time. It is possible to discern, however, that the basic principles of organization of the canon go back even further than this: different groups of Daoists

seem to have first conceived of their various scriptures as constituting a single collection from about the beginning of the 5th century, probably under the influence of Buddhists, who were already accustomed to thinking in this way. At this time scriptures were divided into three groups. The first of these was the Shangqing (Supreme Purity) group, consisting of texts revealed to the visionary Yang Xi between AD 364 and 370, which included new versions of texts already in existence, such as the *Huangtingjing* (*Classic of the Yellow Court*), a classic of interior meditations. The second was the *Lingbao* (Sacred Jewel) group, a similarly revealed corpus of texts, and the third was based on the *Sanhuangwen* or *Writings of the Three August Ones*, a somewhat older type of text ascribed to figures of remote antiquity.

Although this tripartite division may have reflected a certain feeling of common identity among the three schools whose texts were included, it ignored other writings which could be considered as part of the Daoist tradition, and so about a century later four supplementary sections were added to accommodate these. The first contained the *Daodejing* of Laozi, and similar texts. The second was devoted to the *Taipingjing* (*Classic of the Great Peace*), a lengthy scripture which had once served as an inspiration to the Yellow Turban rebels of the Later Han dynasty. The third gathered together various works on alchemy and the fourth consisted of scriptures belonging to the *Zhengyi* school, another name for the Way of the Celestial Masters, the other main religious movement of the Later Han. These supplementary sections have no internal subdivisions, unlike the first three groupings, which are each divided according to genre into 12 categories, again under the probable influence of Buddhist schemes of classification. Thus basic texts are followed by talismans associated with them, and then by commentaries, diagrams and so forth.

A glance at the canon of 1445 shows that in the course of time various anomalies have crept into the scheme of organization, with the result that often texts are not at all in the section where one might expect to find them. Thus the *Daodejing*, together with the writings of Zhuangzi and three other similar works, is included in the section for the *Sanhuangwen*, while in the section to which it was originally allocated we find one of the most influential treatises on alchemy, the *Cantongqi* (*The Kinship of the Three*) attributed to Wei Boyang of the 2nd century AD. In the section supposedly devoted to alchemy are several works dating back to the pre-imperial period whose authors had no obvious connection with any sort of Daoism whatsoever, such as the *Sunzi* (*Master Sun*), a military treatise.

It is no wonder, therefore, that scholars have gone to other sources to help supplement the materials found in the canon. Daoist priests in Taiwan for example use manuscript copies of ritual texts which give far fuller descriptions of ritual performance than the versions in the canon. Daoist texts also are included among the Dunhuang manuscripts discovered at the beginning of this century. (A unique collection of paintings, books and manuscripts in Chinese, Tibetan, Uighur and other languages was sealed for safe-keeping in rock-hewn temples at Dunhuang near the western extremity of the Gansu corridor about 1035; it was discovered and reopened in 1900.) These, for the most part, date back to the Tang dynasty and include not only full versions of texts in the canon but also other works which had been completely lost by 1445. Even more remarkable has been the recent archaeological discovery in China of lost texts from the 2nd century BC, together with a version of the *Daodejing* dating from that period.

The *Daodejing* was probably always the most widely circulated of Daoist scriptures: an emperor of the mid-8th century even ordered that every household should keep a copy. But several other types of Daoist literature also achieved a wide influence. The scriptures transcribed by Yang Xi, for instance, were widely admired for their fine calligraphy. Daoist writings on the techniques for obtaining immortality through drugs fostered the growth of writings on protochemistry and pharmacology, while collections of biographies of the immortals, the earliest of which is the *Liexianzhuan* (*Biographies of the Immortals*) of the Later Han, exerted a strong influence on the development of Chinese tales of the supernatural.

T.B.

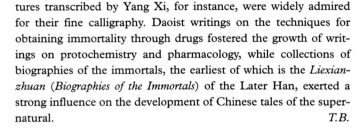

The *San qing* or Three Pure Ones, the highest divinities of Daoism. Taken from the frontispiece made in 1445 for the Daoist Canon, prepared by the Ming dynasty.

Confucianism

Confucianism is the philosophy of the school that acknowledged Confucius (551–479 BC)—the name is a latinization of the Chinese *Kongfuzi*, 'venerable master Kung'—as its founder, and provided the social and political ethos which remained dominant for the major part of the history of imperial China. It constituted the framework within which almost all non-Buddhist philosophical speculation took place from the Song until modern times.

Background to Confucius

By the time Confucius was born the Zhou dynasty, established some 500 years earlier, was in decline, and its political, economic and social structure was undergoing changes which called its basic values into question. The feudal lords of the states, who theoretically owed allegiance to the Zhou sovereign, the source of political and religious authority, in practice ruled autonomously. Moreover, within the states the feudal lords were also finding their control increasingly undermined by their leading ministers and the more powerful clans. Such was the case in Confucius's native state of Lu (in present-day Shandong), where the ruler had become a mere figurehead while the leaders of three clans, the Meng, Shu and Ji wielded the real power. Perhaps the most significant social phenomenon of the late Zhou period was the emergence of the class of *shi* or minor aristocrats, who took up positions as administrative officials, advisers, clerks, or mercenaries, and who did not necessarily confine themselves to serving in their native states. It was from this class that Confucius emerged to become the first Chinese philosopher.

Life and disciples

The facts of Confucius's life, in themselves rather sparse, are almost inextricably interwoven with a mass of myth and legend fabricated or fostered by later Confucians in order to increase the master's prestige. Nothing is really known about his ancestry or the status of his family—although one tradition would make the Kong descendants of the Shang royal house who had arrived in Lu from Song. The same is true of his upbringing and, despite the tradition that he was at one time Minister of Crime in Lu, all one can say of his official career is that he was probably a minor court official there.

Confucius certainly regarded himself as a failure. He saw it as his mission to restore the Way (*Dao*) of the ancients; to revive the moral values of an idealized past and preserve the elaborate structure of ceremony and ritual in which, he believed, those values

found their expression. The ceremonies and rituals known as *li* regulated all human conduct whether it be within the family, in the context of the feudal relationships between superiors and inferiors, governors and governed, or in religious observances. Indeed the various *li* constituted the code of behaviour which would ensure the harmonious operation of what was seen as forming an integral whole. For Confucius, the individual's observance of these *li* was a positive contribution to the harmony of society—which was implicitly equated with the state or the group of states which made up the civilized Zhou world, but for those whom he taught and for himself, government office and the influence it brought with it afforded the ideal means of restoring the Way. His teaching was very much a training for potential office-holders, and several of his immediate followers were appointed to important positions in Lu and in other states (where they continued to regard themselves as his disciples). Confucius himself, having failed to gain any satisfactory appointment in his native Lu by the time he was approaching 60, set out to try to convince the rulers of other states that they should practise his Way. Although he travelled for several years, he returned to Lu with his mission unaccomplished, and resumed his teaching.

For the manner and content of Confucius's teaching the only reliable source is the *Lunyu* (*Analects*), a compilation of his conversations and sayings transcribed—often with little or no indication of their context—by his disciples. While the thread running through his teaching is obviously a concern with moral conduct as the basis of social and political harmony, there is an absence of any sustained argument or development of theory. In dialogue the master appears as one convinced of the truth of his doctrine, responding to the questions of individual disciples with their particular needs in mind. His general pronouncements tend to be uncompromisingly bald. He is notably reluctant to define what is for him the cardinal virtue of *ren*, variously translated 'benevolence', 'goodness', 'human-heartedness's and 'love'. A homophone of the Chinese for 'man', the character as used by Confucius combined all the moral qualities of the perfect man and included loyalty, reciprocity, dutifulness, filial and fraternal affection, courtesy, friendship and good faith. The assumption was that the ancient social order corresponded to a natural moral order, and that man fully realized himself in the perfect fulfilment of his roles as subject, father, son, friend, husband, etc.

Confucius's teaching was clearly a humanistic system of ethics, but there is some disagreement among scholars as to whether his reluctance to discuss religious or supernatural matters denoted scepticism or awe. The material which Confucius used for teaching included versions of texts which subsequently became Confucian 'classics' or *jing*. Paramount among these was the *Book of Odes* or *Shijing*, a collection which contains poems from early

Zhou times. A thorough knowledge of the *Shi* was an essential element in the culture of members of the official class. As Confucius himself once said to his disciples, 'The *Shi* will enable you to arouse people's emotions, observe their feelings, establish social relationships, and express any sense of injustice. At home it enables you to serve your father, and abroad to serve your prince.' In fact, since the poems of the *Shi* served as a regular source of

Stone-rubbing of Confucius.

allegorical reference in the diplomatic exchanges between states, officials had to be familiar with their interpretation and able to seize allusions to them. Confucius may have contributed in some way to rearranging the 300 poems which make up the collection, but his work certainly fell short of the 'editing' traditionally attributed to him. Similarly, traditions that he edited the *Book of Documents* (*Shangshu* or *Shujing*) and the *Ritual* (*Li*) and that he composed the *Spring and Autumn Annals* (*Chunqiu*) and a commentary on the *Book of Changes* (*Zhouyi* or *Yijing*) are not justified on the evidence available. It would appear that in this respect he was, as he described himself, 'a transmitter and not a creator', his concern with the examples of history and with the *li* notwithstanding.

Twenty-two disciples are mentioned by name in the *Lunyu*, and while he doubtless had more, the 72 accorded him by tradition is, suspiciously, a sacred calendrical number. The most famous of them was perhaps Yan Hui. He was a disciple who never gained office, but he remained uncomplainingly poor and unswervingly faithful to his principles. His virtue and intelligence won him the admiration of his fellows, and Confucius was heartbroken when he died. In many respects Yan Hui exemplified the concept of the true gentleman or *junzi* (literally 'lord's son'), which Confucius constantly held out to his disciples. The gentleman may be of humble origins and poor: the essential is that his heart be sincerely set on the Way. He is modest, polite and deferential, avoiding unseemly contention with his fellows. Steadfast in success and failure alike, his concern is always with what is morally right, and his education is an unending refinement and affirmation of the moral sense as opposed to the acquisition of practical accomplishments.

Official cult

Although Confucius had expressed his disapproval of sacrificing to the spirits of any ancestors but one's own, during the Han dynasty a regular cult of Confucius developed under the impetus of the growing prestige and influence of the scholar classes and the espousal of Confucianism by the Han emperors (and Wang Mang) as the orthodox state ideology.

In AD 59 the Han emperor decreed that sacrifice should be made to Confucius and the Duke of Zhou—the statesman who presided over the foundation of the Zhou dynasty, and whom Confucius had venerated—in schools throughout the empire. In so doing he inaugurated the practice which, despite vicissitudes and modifications, persisted until modern times. In the 7th century the Tang emperors established temples to Confucius in both the capital and the provinces, and whereas previously only the tablets of the Duke of Zhou and Confucius had figured in the temple, henceforth Yan Hui displaced the Duke of Zhou and the tablets of other disciples were introduced. From this time on the Confucian temple became a kind of national hall of fame where the tablets of men of out-standing literary achievement were placed after their deaths. In the Ming dynasty, by a decree of 1530, the custom of placing images of Confucius and other worthies in the Confucian temple (it is uncertain for how long this had been the rule) was brought to an end and the tablets alone sanctioned. This remained the accepted form up to the present century.

Development and role of Confucianism in Chinese civilization

After the death of Confucius, Confucianism remained for over 300 years merely one (albeit a major one) of a number of schools which contended for recognition and adoption by the rulers of the various Warring States (Zhanguo), who were themselves struggling for overall control of the Chinese world. The philosophy of the period consists to a large extent of a series of conflicting concepts of man and society, alternative diagnoses of the existing situation, and rival proposals for dealing with it which were peddled from state to state by their advocates. Eventually it was the state of Qin, which had relied on the policies of the Legalist School, that achieved domination and unified China in 221 BC. But it fell in 206 BC, and within a century its Han successors had turned to a form of Confucianism. The two great Confucian philosophers of the Warring States period, Mencius (a latinization of Mengzi 'Master Meng') (c. 370–290 BC) and Xunzi (c. 298–238 BC), both stated unequivocally that a ruler who employed Confucians in his administration and put Confucian ideas into practice would be bound to rule all China. By Mencius' time, although a Zhou king still survived, it had become generally recognized that a new unifier of the states would emerge from elsewhere, and Mencius travelled from court to court in search of such a ruler.

In arguing that a truly moral ruler would receive the spontaneous support of the people in all the states who would then unite under his rule, Mencius appeals to two theories which subsequently became central to Confucian thought. The first is that of the Mandate of Heaven (tianming), a theory which the Zhou rulers had used to justify their overthrow of the Shang. According to this theory when the rulers of a dynasty cease to be virtuous they lose the support of Heaven, a phenomenon manifested in the revolt of their subjects, who then rally to the man whom Heaven has designated as the approved successor. The second theory, implicit perhaps in the pronouncements of Confucius, but elaborated by Mencius, is that human nature is fundamentally good: that all men have an innate predisposition to goodness. Mencius adduced as evidence of this the instinctive reaction of anyone who sees a child about to fall into a well. He insisted that the moral nature, like any plant, required proper cultivation in order to grow and function as

it should. To create the conditions of such cultivation was the responsibility of the individual and a fortiori of the ruler.

Both Mencius and Xunzi, in the books which bear their names, provide a much fuller exposition of Confucian ideas than can be found in the Lunyu. Xunzi, however, refused to accept the Mencian thesis that human nature is good, arguing that Heaven is neutral and that man must create his own morality. He laid great stress on ritual and education as the means to bring order to society, but unlike Mencius was prepared to judge moral argument by utilitarian criteria. In the long term he proved less influential than Mencius, whose doctrine became regarded as orthodox by Confucians from the Song onwards.

It was under the Han that Confucianism first became recognized as the state orthodoxy, but it was the Confucianism of Dong Zhongshu (179–104 BC). This was an amalgamation of Confucian morality with elements culled from cosmology and other superstitious beliefs within a framework which correlated the human, natural and supernatural spheres and emphasized portents and numerology. Natural disasters for example were regarded as manifestations of Heaven's displeasure with events in the human sphere. Dong became adviser to the Han emperor and was instrumental in achieving the recognition of Confucianism as state orthodoxy, but one may already observe the often uneasy compromise which resulted from the community of interest between the scholar classes and the imperial house. 'Subject the people to the ruler, and subject the ruler to Heaven', declared Dong. In exchange for their assistance in controlling the people the emperor had to accept the counsels and even rebukes of his Confucian advisers—but the balance of power was a constantly shifting one.

Confucianism was to a large extent eclipsed by Mahāyāna Buddhism and to a lesser extent by Daoism in the minds of the ruling elite from the 5th century onwards, while more popular forms of Buddhism exerted a strong influence over the masses, and continued to do so until the Neo-Confucian revival in the 11th century. The advocates of Neo-Confucianism (a vague Western term used to describe developments in Confucianism from the Song revival onwards, and for which the Chinese equivalent is Daoxue (The Learning of the Way)) aimed at the moral regeneration of the entire country, and to this end they made a determined effort to restore Confucian authority over a society infiltrated by Buddhism at every level from the court to the countryside. Han Yu (768–824) was an early precursor, but his attacks on Buddhism were resumed and amplified by Song Confucians, who rejected it as an erroneous theory which had had disastrous social and political consequences. Buddhist teaching, which denied the reality of personality, maintained that existence was an illusion, and advocated such unfilial practices as celibacy and mortification of the body, was anathema to these anthropocentric, life-affirming Confucian moralists because it undermined the very foundations of their Way.

The Neo-Confucian movement was characterized by a reaffirmation and revitalization of classical Confucian ethics, the advocacy of political and social reforms, a new historical consciousness, and a heightened awareness of the political role of the bureaucracy and its moral responsibilities. On a purely philosophical level, it had to meet the challenge of Buddhist metaphysics. The new Confucian metaphysics which emerged from this confrontation with Buddhism was, however, in some respects indebted to it. At its heart, for example, lay the concept, borrowed from Mahāyanā that immanent in all universal phenomena is a unifying principle or noumenon which is present in man as his moral nature. Zhang Zai (1020–77), however, set this concept firmly in the world of reality in his description of all existence as a material flux informed by this principle. The metaphysical system was completed by the interpretations which Cheng Yi (1033–1107) and Zhu Xi (1130–1200) gave to classical works such as the *Daxue* or *Great Learning*, the *Zhongyong* or *The Mean*, and the *Mengzi*, and the writings of Zhou Dunyi (1012–73). The *Daxue, Zhongyong*, and *Mengzi*, together with the *Lunyu* made up the famous *Four Books* which were subsequently studied in all Chinese schools.

Neo-Confucianism

From its beginnings Neo-Confucianism tended to take one of two philosophical directions. The Rationalist School of Cheng Yi (1033–1107) and Zhu Xi (1130–1200) sought for the unifying principle or *li*, identified with the Way, in the external phenomena in which they believed it to be immanent as moral as well as natural principles. Thus, for Cheng and Zhu moral action entailed the investigation of the various principles, all of which were aspects of the one great principle or Way, which were inherent in the world around them and exemplified in the Confucian classics. This attitude inspired re-examination of these classics both in terms of textual exegesis and philosophical interpretation. It also lay behind Neo-Confucian interest in historical scholarship and in political institutions past and present. Moreover, as the Confucian bureaucracy saw its political role as a contemporary counterpart to that of Confucius and Mencius, providing the moral counsel and the check on the ruler's actions necessary to good government, Neo-Confucianism became in effect the ideology of the scholar-official class. The examination system reinforced this trend, and from 1315 onwards Zhu Xi's interpretations of the Confucian classics—and hence the philosophical doctrines of the Cheng-Zhu School—were officially recognized as orthodox in assessing the papers of civil service candidates. Cheng-Zhu Confucianism was inherently conservative and paternalistically authoritarian. The individual's duty, indeed his fulfilment, lay in harmonious conformity with, and honest service of the pyramidal socio-political structure over which the emperor presided.

The other great branch of Neo-Confucianism, the School of Mind, however, stressed that the one great principle lay in oneself, in the principles of one's own nature (recalling Mencius' doctrine of the nature's innate goodness), and consequently advocated a form of moral intuitionism, which, as developed by such thinkers as Wang Ji (1498–1583), Wang Gen (1483–1541) and Li Zhi (1527–1602) became strongly individualistic and even iconoclastic. Lu Xiangshan (1139–92) was the leading exponent of this school in Song times, and proclaimed 'The universe is my mind, and my mind is the universe', but it was Wang Yangming (1472–1529) who brought its doctrines to their full fruition.

Wang endorsed Lu's saying, but this signified no retreat into quiescent subjectivity. An important government official, who himself led a vigorous public life, he emphasized the unifying aspect of a self-cultivation whose ultimate goal affirmed both the sagehood of the individual and the reality of the universe. He regarded effort as vital to the development of one's innate moral wisdom (*liangzhi*), and taught the unity of knowledge and action—conceived as one process beginning with intention and only completed, or made 'sincere' (*cheng*) in the realization of that intention.

Prior to the introduction of European philosophical ideas, all subsequent Chinese thinkers tended to adopt positions somewhere between the extremes of these two schools, but by the end of the Qing dynasty scholars such as Tan Sitong (1865–98) and Kang Youwei (1858–1927) were trying to adapt Confucianism to take account of foreign religious and philosophical influences.

I.McM.

Buddhism

Introduction and assimilation

Buddhism first reached Chinese soil about the time of Christ as a religion of foreign merchants who plied the trade routes linking China with the Western world. Although these foreign Buddhists did not actively engage in proselytization, knowledge of their religion gradually spread among the Chinese. By the year AD 166 the Buddhist religion had already penetrated the imperial court and counted among its devotees Emperor Huan, who established within the palace a shrine honouring both the Buddha and the Daoist deity Huanglao.

Despite these early, impressive gains, Buddhism remained a religion that was practised primarily within foreign settlements until the beginning of the 4th century, when it suddenly began to attract large numbers of devotees from the upper levels of Chinese society. Under the Eastern Jin dynasty there emerged as the representative figure of Chinese Buddhism the gentleman-monk, who had access to the imperial court, the homes of the powerful families and the salons of the literati. Usually coming from a prestigious family, the gentleman-monk was well educated in both the secular literature and the Buddhist scriptures, expounding both with equal enthusiasm. He was at once a classical scholar, a court chaplain, a literary critic, a confidant of the power elite, and often an artist and a calligrapher as well.

During this period the literati were fascinated by Buddhist ideas, which, superficially at least, resembled Daoist concepts. Already in the first century AD some Chinese believed that Laozi, the legendary founder of Daoism, had moved to India before his death, where he subsequently became the Buddha. Viewing Buddhism as being essentially an Indian manifestation of Daoism, which at the time was undergoing a major revival, the literati and their gentleman-monk friends studied the voluminous Buddhist literature in the hope of finding clues that might help elucidate the *Zhuangzi* and *Laozi*, the two major classics of Daoism.

The apparent similarity between Buddhism and Daoism was in large measure attributable to the practice adopted by the translators of the scripture, who deliberately selected Daoist terms to represent Buddhist concepts in order to make Buddhism more palatable to the Chinese. Thus, even such commonplace Buddhist words as 'Buddha', 'Nirvāna', 'non-substantiality', 'śūyatā' and 'karma' were rendered into Chinese by such Daoist concepts as 'The Immortal' (*xian*), 'non-activity' (*wuwei*), 'non-being' (*wu*), and 'natural allotment' (*fen*).

A proper understanding of Buddhism was first achieved through the efforts of Daoan (314–85) and Kumārajīva (350–409). One of the most learned and venerated monks of his day, Daoan denounced the prevailing Buddhist-Daoist syncretism, pointing out that Buddhism must be approached in its own terms and not those of Daoism, even if this should mean some diminution of its popularity. Assigning much of the confusion to the haphazard methods of translation, Daoan laid down guidelines for future translators stressing the importance of philologically accurate translations. After hearing reports of the reputed linguistic skills of a Central Asian monk named Kumārajīva, Daoan persuaded the ruler of north China to invite the monk to settle in Zhang'an in order to work on new translations under imperial sponsorship.

Although Kumārajīva was active in Chang'an for only eight years, he made an enormous contribution to the popularization of Buddhism through the high quality of his translations, which were widely read and admired. Among the 35 texts that he translated will be found many of the most important scriptures of Chi-

Large seated Buddha with standing Bodhisattva at the Yungang caves. Northern Wei dynasty, *c*. AD 460–70.

nese Buddhism. Kumārajīva enabled his contemporaries to acquire a firm grasp of basic Buddhist ideas by lecturing on his translations before large assemblies of Chinese monks, often numbering in the thousands, who then produced definitive commentaries.

By the end of the 5th century Buddhism had swept across China. The size of the Buddhist church in the north is reported to have reached 6478 temples and 77 258 monks and nuns by the year 477; the statistics for south China for the same period show 2015 temples with a clergy of 32 500. Successive rulers vied with one another to demonstrate their support for Buddhism by constructing new temples, donating estates for their upkeep, authorizing mass ordinations of monks and nuns, holding elaborate vegetarian banquets for thousands of members of the clergy, and sponsoring literary activities such as the translation of scripture, the production of commentaries, and the compilation of historical works, biographies of eminent monks and nuns, and catalogues of the canon.

This lavish patronage of Buddhism provoked resentment among followers of both Daoism and Confucianism, who criticized Buddhism from a variety of standpoints. Clerical practices such as shaving the head, wearing free-flowing robes, and cremation of the body were denounced as un-Chinese and hence uncivilized. Joining the clergy was called an anti-social act because of the vow of celibacy, which was seen as a threat to the continuity of the family. Confucian bureaucrats in particular decried the refusal of the clergy to render homage to the secular ruler, asserting that Buddhism would ultimately bring about the collapse of the state because of its ever-expanding clergy that generated no wealth through its own labour, paid no taxes and, worst of all, squandered

Buddha preaching under the Bodhi tree with Bodhisattvas, monks and a donor in a late 7th or 8th century Tang dynasty painting.

the precious resources of the nation by constructing magnificent temples and casting colossal images.

Although such criticisms occasionally resulted in harsh persecutions, particularly in the periods 446–52 and 574–9 in north China, and 842–5 throughout the whole of the empire, Buddhism had so thoroughly permeated Chinese society that it could not be eliminated in a short-lived attempt at suppression, no matter how severe. By the Tang dynasty the state had established at least nominal control over the church by bringing the clergy under the jurisdiction of the secular legal codes and appointing a layman to oversee church affairs, while within the temples, prayers for the well-being of the imperial family and the stability of the empire became as much a part of the daily religious routine as the devotional exercises and meditations.

Chinese Buddhist schools

The Chinese word *zong*, usually translated as 'school' or 'sect', is used by Buddhists in three different senses: to signify the doctrine of a particular scripture; to refer to a master-disciple lineage through which a particular doctrine is transmitted; and to denote a religious organization whose members adhere to a specific doctrine or interpretation of scripture. It should be remembered, therefore, that when we speak of Chinese Buddhist 'schools', we are in fact referring to *zong*, a term that has a broader meaning than is conveyed by its English equivalents. The problem is further complicated by the fact that some of the 14 'schools' mentioned below fit only one of the three meanings of *zong*, whereas others cover all three.

The first group of schools to appear were the so-called six exegetical schools that flourished in the 5th and 6th centuries, each centring around a particular text or group of closely related texts. The names of the schools, which are identical with the titles of the texts on which they focus, are in approximate order of their appearance: (1) the Pitan, which was concerned with the study of the *abhidharma*; (2) the Chengshi, named after an *abhidharma*-type treatise called the *Satyasiddhi*; (3) the San-lun, literally 'Three Treatises', which was devoted to the study of three works belonging to the Mādhyamika, a school of Indian Mahāyāna; (4) the Niepan, which expounded the doctrines of the *Mahāparinirvāna Sūtra*, a scripture emphasizing the ultimate attainment of enlightenment by all beings and the eternal nature of the Buddha; (5) the Dilun, which was based on the *Daśabhūmivyākhyāna*, a treatise belonging to the Yogācāra, the other major school of Indian Mahāyāna; and (6) the Shelun, which studied the *Mahāyānasamgraha*, also a Yogācāra treatise.

The six exegetical schools may in a sense be viewed as a Chinese extension of Indian Buddhism, since their exponents were concerned primarily with explaining through lectures and commentaries specific Indian texts. The first distinctively Chinese school of Buddhist philosophy was the Tiantai, which appeared during the Sui dynasty. Founded by Zhiyi (538–97), Tiantai attempted a grand synthesis of Buddhist thought around the *Lotus Sūtra*. In order to reconcile the seemingly contradictory doctrines expounded by the six exegetical schools, Zhiyi advanced the idea that the Buddha, sensing the intellectual and spiritual limitations of unenlightened men, revealed his teachings gradually, beginning with the simplest ones and then progressing by stages until reaching what Zhiyi deemed to be the supreme utterance of the Buddha, the *Lotus Sūtra*. In this way each scripture within the canon was seen as pointing the way towards the final message of the Buddha as revealed in the *Lotus*.

The other major philosophical school was the Huayan, whose doctrines were systematized by Fazang (643–712). Like the Tiantai, the Huayan accepted the notion of a progressive revelation of scripture, but differed from the former in its assertion that the *Avatamsaka Sūtra* (*Huayan jing*), not the *Lotus*, represented the highest teaching of the Buddha. The central doctrine of the *Avatamsaka* was the interrelatedness of all things, which signified on the religious plane that there was ultimately no distinction between the unenlightened man and the Buddha.

Two other schools of considerable importance that might be classified as philosophical are the Faxiang and the Lü. The former, brought to China by Xuanzang, is based on the *Vijñaptimātratāsiddhi* of Dharmapāla (flourished mid-6th century), a major Yogācāra thinker. Although the Faxiang is more Indian than Chinese in its character, its detailed analysis of the mind and its doctrine that external objects do not exist apart from the mind have exerted a continuing influence on Chinese thought. The Lü school, which was systematized by Daoxuan (596–667), was concerned solely with defining and interpreting ecclesiastical law (*vinaya*), which it did from the standpoint of Faxiang idealism. Ordination ceremonies have traditionally been entrusted to monks of this school.

Whereas the philosophical schools tend to be preoccupied with metaphysical questions, the four religious schools—the Three Stages (Sanjie), Esoteric (Mi), Pure Land (Qingtu) and Chan—deal with the practical goals of Buddhism: alleviation of suffering and realization of enlightenment. The Three Stages school, founded by Xinxing (540–94), taught that the world passed through three stages, in the course of which man's spiritual and moral character progressively declined. Since Xinxing believed that by the 6th century the world had entered the third, final stage in which man was no longer capable of good deeds, he urged his contemporaries to avoid the exclusive worship of any single Buddha and instead pay homage to all Buddhas equally. The Three Stages school was eventually suppressed because of its refusal to recognize any government as benevolent.

The Esoteric was another school that did not outlive the Tang dynasty as an independent tradition. Although *tantras* (manuals for Esoteric rituals) were translated into Chinese as early as the 3rd century AD, it was not until the 8th century that Esoteric rituals were regularly performed at the court for the protection of the emperor and prosperity of the nation. Despite the disappearance of Esoteric Buddhism as a school after the suppression of 842–5, specific Esoteric rites, such as the use of secret hand signs (*mudrās*) and incantations (*mantras*), are practised even today at masses for the dead.

The two most important religious schools in China today are the Pure Land and the Chan. The former, which originated in the early 5th century and eventually became the most popular religious movement in China, stresses faith in Amitābha Buddha, who has vowed to deliver to his Pure Land all beings who invoke his name. The other major religious movement was the Chan, supposedly transmitted to China by the semi-legendary Bodhidharma (died *c.* 528). Basically an indigenous Chinese school that arose as a reaction against the intellectualization of Buddhism, Chan emphasized the practice of meditation as the principal means of realizing one's inherent Buddha-nature and cautioned against over-reliance on such external exercises as scriptural study, sutra chanting and image worship.

A unique form of Buddhism, known to Westerners as Lamaism, evolved in Tibet. The word *lama* (Sanskrit *guru*) signifies a religious teacher or monk of high standing. Buddhism is said to have first reached Tibet simultaneously from India and China during the reign of King Srong btsan sgam po (620?–9), who supported the new faith and ordered the creation of a system of writing in order to make possible the translation of the Buddhist scriptures into Tibetan. Despite some initial reverses, Buddhism became by the 12th century the national faith of the Tibetan people, which it remained until the absorption of Tibet into the People's Republic of China in the 1950s.

Lamaism is basically an amalgamation of Indian esoteric Buddhism, popularly referred to in the West as Tantrism, with Bon, the indigenous shamanistic religion of Tibet that centres around exorcistic rituals and the worship of various benevolent or demonic spirits. Of the seven major schools of Lamaism, the most important is the dGe lugs pa (called Yellow Hats in China), a reform movement founded by Tsong kha pa (1357–1410), which requires a high standard of morality for the clergy and strict adherence to the precepts. The successive Dalai Lamas, who until 1959 had been both the spiritual and temporal rulers of Tibet, served as the hereditary heads of the Gelupka church.

Although Lamaism was first introduced into the Mongol court in the 13th century and received the enthusiastic patronage of

The Tianningsi pagoda outside the walls of Beijing, with its 13 superimposed roofs. A temple once stood beside this pagoda, which dates from the 11th or early 12th century.

Khubilai Khan, who appointed the Tibetan Grand Lama 'Pags pa (1235–80) as his religious preceptor, it was only in the 17th century that Lamaism emerged as the dominant creed of the Mongols, a position that it enjoyed until its suppression in the anti-religious campaigns of the 1930s. The Manchus, who had been converted to Lamaism before their conquest of China in 1644, supported Lamaist institutions throughout the Qing dynasty in the hope of retaining the good will of the Dalai Lamas whose allegiance to the throne was deemed essential for exercising effective political control over the Tibetan and Mongol peoples.

Literature

The Taishō edition of the Chinese Buddhist scriptures, which was published in Japan between 1924 and 1928 and is recognized as the standard version, consists of 1692 works translated from Indian and, occasionally, Central Asian languages. This vast corpus of sacred literature, commonly known as the Buddhist Canon, fills some 32 000 large, closely-printed pages.

Following a long-established Buddhist custom, the Chinese divided their canon into three sections. The first consists of the sutras (*jing*), which purport to be the discourses of the Buddha. Typically, a sutra will open with the words: 'Thus have I heard. One time when the Buddha was staying at such-and-such a place, accompanied by such-and-such disciples, the Brahman so-and-so put the following question to him. ...' This stereotyped introduction is then followed by a dialogue between the Buddha, his questioner and sometimes their respective disciples. Of the 1692 works in the Taishō canon, 1420 are classified as sutras.

The second section is made up of *vinayas* (*lü*) and *vinaya*-related texts. *Vinayas* are codes of ecclesiastical law that regulate every aspect of the life of the monk and nun. They deal with such questions as how the monk's (or nun's) robe is to be made, what kind of food he may eat, the size and layout of his cell, etc. The *vinayas* also contain the text of the precepts that are administered to monks and nuns at the time of their ordination. Eighty-four works belong to the category of *vinaya*.

The last section of the canon, called simply *lun* (treatises) in Chinese, consists of commentaries on sutras, systematic expositions of Buddhist teachings (*abhidharma*), doctrinal works of the Indian Buddhist philosophical schools, and texts on logic. The 188 works in this section of the canon are all of Indian authorship.

The translation of Buddhist texts into Chinese was a massive endeavour spanning almost 11 centuries and involving hundreds of translators. The first translations of Buddhist scripture, made in the middle of the 2nd century AD, were the work of An Shigao, a missionary from Parthia (present-day Iran), who singlehandedly managed to translate 35 texts, of which 21 still survive. The translation of the scripture was undertaken by both monks and laymen who had emigrated to China from virtually every Buddhist land: India, Parthia, the Yuezhi kingdom (in the region of present-day Afghanistan and Kashmir), Vietnam, Tibet and especially the city-states of Central Asia.

The early translators faced great difficulties in their efforts to put Buddhist texts with their highly specialized vocabulary and multi-syllabled names into Chinese, a monosyllabic language

that had no ready-made equivalents to express the technical terminology of Indian Buddhism. To make matters worse, few of
the early translators had a knowledge of written Chinese. Thus,
they were compelled to make oral translations, which were then
converted into the literary language by their Chinese collaborators whose understanding of Buddhism was often tainted with
Daoist preconceptions. Since a translator tended to work independently of other translators, often numerous translations of the
same work appeared, each with its own newly-coined Chinese
terminology.

In 364 Daoan compiled the first comprehensive catalogue of the
611 Buddhist scriptures then available in Chinese translation. For
each scripture Daoan supplied the name of the translator, if
known, gave an account of the circumstances of the translation,
questioned the authenticity of the text where appropriate and,
most importantly, indicated the different Chinese translations of a
single Indian work. Daoan's catalogue became a model for later
Buddhist bibliographers. In all 15 catalogues of the canon have
been issued, the last major pre-modern one having been completed in 1285.

The quality of the translations improved markedly after the
arrival of Kumārajīva in 401. Completely at home in both Chinese
and various languages of India and Central Asia, Kumārajīva not
only produced elegant translations but also coined much of the terminology that became standard for later generations of Chinese
Buddhists.

Another great translator deserving of mention is Xuanzang, a
Chinese monk who spent 15 years in India, where he acquired a
profound knowledge of Sanskrit. After returning to China in 645
he devoted himself to translating new texts that he had acquired
during his travels abroad and retranslating older ones that he felt
were inadequate. The 75 texts that he translated fill 1330 fascicles,
which in volume represents 21 per cent of the entire canon extant
today.

Despite the size of its scripture, Chinese Buddhism developed
around a relatively small number of texts. Among the most prominent are the *Lotus Sūtra* the three Pure Land sutras, the *Diamond
Sūtra*, the *Heart Sūtra* and the *Vimalakīrti Sūtra*, all of which are
available in English translation. The *Lotus Sūtra* is one of the
most popular works of Mahāyāna ('Great Vehicle'), the lay-ori-
ented branch of Buddhism practised in China, Vietnam, Korea
and Japan, as opposed to the Theravāda ('School of the Elders')
followed in Sri Lanka, Burma, Thailand, Laos and Cambodia,
which is the sole surviving school of the conservative monk-ori-
ented wing of Buddhism pejoratively termed Hīnayāna ('Little
Vehicle') by Mahāyānists. The *Lotus* stresses the essential harmony of Buddhism, taking the position that the multitude of
seemingly conflicting doctrines within Buddhism are merely

expedients devised by the Buddha to lead people of differing
intellectual and spiritual capacities to the ultimate teaching of
Buddhism as embodied in the *Lotus*, namely all beings—whether
good or evil, male or female, high or low—will ultimately achieve
enlightenment if they put their faith in the Buddha and venerate
him, not simply as a wise teacher, but as an eternal, transcendent
being who has appeared in the world solely to help all humanity
escape from suffering.

The three Pure Land sutras refer to the *Larger Sukhāvativyūha
Sūtra* (*Wuliangshoujing*), the *Shorter Sukhāvativyūha Sūtra* (*Emi-
tuojing*), and the *Sūtra for Contemplating the Buddha Amitāyus*
(*Guan wuliangshoujing*). The *Larger Sukhāvativyūha* gives an
account of the enlightenment of Amitābha (Amitāyus) Buddha
and sets forth his vows to create a Pure Land called Sukhāvatī
(Paradise) to serve as a haven for all tormented beings; the *Shorter
Sukhvativyūha* describes the glories of Amitābha's Paradise; and
the *Sūtra for Contemplating the Buddha Amitāyus* explains the various meditation practices that will enable one to view the Buddha
Amitābha and his Pure Land.

The *Diamond Sūtra* and *Heart Sūtra* are particularly popular
within the Chan (Japanese: Zen) tradition. The former appealed
to Chan masters because of its insistence that enlightenment can
be realized only through an intuitive religious experience and not
through the formalistic study of scriptures. The *Heart Sūtra*, which
is one of the shortest works in the Buddhist canon and hence easily
memorized by laymen, stresses the non-substantiality of all
things—a key Mahāyānist concept. Also popular with laymen is
the *Vimalakīrti Sūtra* whose central figure is Vimalakīrti, an idealized layman who, despite his family responsibilities and worldly
commitments, surpasses the learned monk-disciples of the
Buddha in his spiritual insights and attainments.   *S.W.*

Other schools of philosophy

Between the 5th and 3rd centuries BC a variety of philosophical
schools flourished; afterwards all were either defeated by or
absorbed into Confucianism and Daoism. The grouping of the
thinkers into schools, which to some extent was retrospective,
became systematized in the bibliography of the *History of the
Former Han Dynasty* by Ban Gu (AD 32–92). This work also laid
down what was to remain the official attitude towards these her-
etics: they are one-sided, but their works should be read for their
strong points, without forgetting their errors from the Confucian
standpoint.

Mohism

The earliest rival of Confucius (551–479 BC) was Mo Di (Mozi). The little reported of him in *Mozi*, the corpus of the writings of his school, implies that he lived in the late 5th century BC and was of humble origins, probably a carpenter. The Mohists survived until the 3rd century BC as an organized community apparently based on the artisan class. They were committed to 10 curiously heterogeneous doctrines which are defended one by one in the 10 triads of chapters (8–37) that form the core of the *Mozi*.

These essays are the earliest Chinese attempts at the reasoned defence of ideas. Unlike Confucius, who accepted and refined the moral tradition he inherited, the Mohists proposed novel doctrines; and although they quoted the classics to show that long ago the sages thought the same, they also recognized the value of innovation, and derided the Confucians for thinking that 'the gentleman follows and does not originate'.

Their fundamental ethical principle was an equal concern for the benefit of all, without favour to oneself or one's own kin. This is the doctrine of 'Love for everyone' (*jian'ai*), highly offensive to Confucians who placed family loyalties first. As a corollary they preached 'rejection of aggression', treating the offensive wars of states (as distinct from defensive wars to the techniques of which the community applied its skills in the crafts) as no different from private crimes of violence. They submitted current practices to the utilitarian test of whether they benefited rather than harmed the people, and in particular condemned useless luxuries, the prolongation of mourning to three years demanded by Confucians, and the extravagance of the great court orchestras, under the slogans 'thrift in expenditure', 'thrift in funerals' and 'rejection of music'. They supported the new bureaucratized states that emerged with the decay of Zhou institutions, and recommended promotion to office purely on grounds of merit, even from the peasant, artisan and merchant classes ('elevation of worth'). They also advocated a unification of standards by universal conformity to immediate superiors in the political hierarchy, and in the case of the ruler, conformity to the will of Heaven ('conforming to superiors').

They condemned the Confucian's tranquil acceptance of destiny whether he succeeds or fails, on the grounds that it undermined the faith that efforts will be rewarded ('rejection of fatalism'). They also differed from Confucians in seeing Heaven as a personal power who loves the good and hates the wicked. They regarded reward and punishment by Heaven and the spirits as the ultimate sanction of morality, and therefore maintained the goodwill of Heaven towards man and the existence of spirits ('the will of Heaven' and 'explaining the spirits').

Yangism

An ideal of health and longevity achieved by living in accordance with one's nature is expounded in certain chapters of the eclectic encyclopedia *Lüshi chunqiu* (*c.* 240 BC) and in a block of non-Daoist chapters (28–31) in *Zhuangzi* (*c.* 200 BC). Its fundamental principle is that all external possessions are replaceable, but the life and health of the body are not; as personal property even a single hair of one's own is more valuable than the empire itself. The thinker whose name was used by other schools to label this doctrine was Yang Zhu (*c.* 350 BC), who, however, is not known to have left any writings and was never cited as an authority by its advocates.

Yangism provides the earliest theoretical justification for preferring the comforts of private life to the risks of a career in office, a function later served by Daoism and Buddhism. Its proponents thought of themselves as renouncing wealth and power in order to protect their 'genuineness' (*zhen*) and avoid being tied to worldly things. However, refusal of power is also the refusal to benefit the people by good government; the Confucian Mencius (372?–289? BC), for example, saw Yang Zhu as an egoist who would not give a hair of his body to benefit the whole empire. Mozi's chief disciple, Qin Guli, is said to have embarrassed Yang Zhu by asking 'If you could help the whole world at the cost of one hair of your body, would you do it?', and to have been embarrassed in his turn by a Yangist who re-joined 'If you could gain a state by cutting off one of your limbs, would you do it?'; neither side quibbled over the point that what the Yangist calls *gaining* a state is for the Mohist an opportunity to help it.

For Yangism the supreme goal is to last out one's term of life in good health, and therefore the desires may be indulged only in moderation. Six hundred years later, however, Yang Zhu was turned into the spokesman of a philosophy that preferred the intense enjoyment of an hour to length of life, in the hedonist chapter of the Daoist book *Liezi* (*c.* AD 300).

The Tillers

Throughout the literature of the 3rd and 2nd centuries BC, accounts of the Golden Age of Shennong ('Divine Farmer'), the legendary inventor of the plough, reflect a political ideal foreign to any of the major schools and suggestive of peasant Utopianism. Shennong was an emperor who taught his people how to farm but did not issue decrees or reward or punish, his realm was decentralized in small fiefs, war was still unknown, each individual supported himself by his own manual labour; Shennong worked his own grain-field while his empress worked her mulberry field. There were no laws and the only function of government mentioned was to ensure a constant supply of grain and steady prices by storing in good years and distributing in bad.

To the 'Tillers' (*Nongjia*, 'Farmers' School') this was the ideal society. Their lost books on agriculture (the first of them entitled *Shennong*) are listed in the bibliography of the *History of the Former Han Dynasty*, with the comment that some of the school thought that there was no point in serving a sage king, wished to make the ruler plough side by side with his subjects, and upset the degrees of superior and inferior. The only Tiller known by name is Xu Xing, described by Mencius as a preacher of the words of Shennong, who, about 315 BC, at the head of a small community of farmers and craftsmen, taught that instead of taxing his subjects the ruler should be supporting himself by working with his own hands.

The Sophists or 'School of Names'

In the late 4th century BC the Sophists Hui Shi and Gongsun Long were the first to study logical puzzles for their own sake. They proposed paradoxes arising from the 'infinite' and the 'dimensionless', from the relativity of 'the similar and the different', and from the distinguishing of the 'mutually pervasive'. A number of theses of the Sophists are listed in the final chapter of the Daoist *Zhuangzi*, but without explanation. The series of 10 ascribed to Hui Shi consists largely of spatio-temporal paradoxes on the themes of the infinite and the dimensionless (the point), such as 'The dimensionless cannot be accumulated but its circumference is 1000 miles', 'The sun is simultaneously at noon and declining, a thing is simultaneously alive and dead', 'The South is infinite yet is finite.' There is also one on the theme of similarity and difference: 'While being similar on the large scale they are different from the similar on the small scale, this I call "Similarity and difference on the small scale"; the myriad things are all similar and all different, this I call "Similarity and difference on the large scale".' The series was apparently designed to prove that to divide up space, time and the things within them leads to contradiction and therefore everything is one, for the last thesis is 'Love the myriad things indiscriminately, heaven and earth are one unit.'

A forged *Gongsun Long Zi* ascribed to Gongsun Long contains some old stories about him (Chapter 1) and two genuine essays of the Sophists (Chapters 2 and 3). Of these, the 'Essay on the White Horse' explores the theme of mutual pervasives, Gongsun Long's speciality; it argues at length that a white horse is not a horse, on the grounds that the shape named 'horse' and the colour named 'white' although mutually pervasive are distinct, therefore what is called a 'horse' cannot be what is called 'white'. The other, the 'Essay on Pointings and Things', is very problematic; on one interpretation, still controversial, it first expounds and then resolves a paradox which, since names serve to 'point out' (*zhi*) one thing from another, is involved in applying the name 'world': 'When no thing is not what is being pointed out, it is what is pointed out which is not what is pointed out.'

The Sophists were derided as frivolous wordmongers by the other schools, and ignored after 200 BC. About AD 300 interest revived among Daoists, but already their remains were as sparse as today. Between AD 300 and 600 the *Gongsun Long Zi* was forged, with three new essays (Chapters 4–6) including an *Essay on the Hard and the White* in which the old theme of the 'mutually pervasive' (*jian bai*, literally 'hard and white') is misunderstood as a particular Sophism, that the hard stone one touches is not the white stone one sees.

The Yin-Yang School

Early Chinese thought is primarily moral and political, and for a long time philosophers showed no interest in the cosmological schemes current among such specialists as diviners, astronomers and physicians. But late in the 3rd century BC the Yin-Yang school led by Zou Yan used cosmology as a theoretical basis both for the political and moral order and for explanation and prediction of the rise and fall of dynasties. The writings of Zou Yan and his followers disappeared except for a few fragments, but their cosmology filled so obvious a gap that it was incorporated whole into Confucianism and Daoism. It provided the cosmological framework of the sciences for some 2000 years.

The fundamental concepts are the pair 'Yin' and 'Yang' and the 'Five Agencies' (*wu xing*). The latter term is commonly translated 'Five Elements', but the *wu xing* were conceived (as also were the Yin and Yang) as energetic fluids patterning the correspondences and recurrences of the cosmos rather than as elements of which it is composed. The active Yang and passive Yin cooperate as male and female, high and low, heaven and earth, or take turns to grow and diminish in the alternations of motion and rest, light and dark, hot and cold. The Five Agencies, which are earth, wood, metal, fire and water, activate all groups of five such as the Five Colours (yellow, green, white, red and black), and take turns, each conquered by the next, in sequences such as the rise and fall of dynasties. Thus the dying Zhou dynasty reigned by the agency of fire and had the colour red, and the coming dynasty was expected to belong to water and to black. The conqueror Shi Huangdi (246–210 BC) did find it expedient to act out his role in this scheme, honouring water and choosing black as the emblematic colour of the new Qin dynasty. Zou Yan is also credited with geographical speculations which failed to take root in the tradition. He claimed that just as China is composed of nine regions, so the continent in which it is the Middle Kingdom is only one of nine separated by impassable seas.

The appeal from the 2nd century BC onwards of this kind of cosmology to Confucians is easily understood; it assures the harmony of man and nature, the unity of the cosmic and the moral orders, by entitling us, for example, to class ruler and subject with heaven and earth as Yang and Yin, and fit the Five Norms (the Confucian cardinal virtues) with the Five Colours to the Five Agencies.

Later Mohism

The Mohists of the 3rd century BC, who learned from the Sophists but progressed beyond their games with paradoxes, were the only Chinese school with a full commitment to rationality comparable with that of the Greeks. Impressed by the changes of the times and the declining authority of the sages, they sought a new basis for certainty in the logically and the causally 'necessary' (*bi*): 'The judgements of sages, employ but do not treat as necessary: the 'necessary', accept and do not doubt'.

The *Canons* and other writings in the dialectical chapters of *Mozi* (Chapters 40–45) discuss logic (for which they are a much richer source than the scanty remains of the Sophists), ethics, geometry, optics and mechanics, on the basis of a nominalist theory of the common name as extended from one to other particular objects on the grounds of their similarity, together with a fourfold classification of knowledge as knowledge of names, of objects, of how to relate them, and of how to act. The *Canons* begin with 75 definitions and 12 analyses of ambiguous words, and use chains of definitions to show that the circle is knowable and the moral virtues are desirable 'beforehand' (*xian*), without appeal to experience. Logical and verbal puzzles are solved, sometimes by analysis and deduction from the definitions, sometimes by presenting series of parallel propositions to show how the meaning of a word has changed in context. As an example of the latter, in idiomatic usage *sha dao* 'killing robbers' is executing them while *sha ren* 'killing people' is murder, so that 'Although robbers are people, killing robbers is not killing people;', the point is clarified by a string of parallel instances of the type of English 'Although a goose is a bird, cooking one's goose is not cooking a bird'.

The later Mohist ethics, the most highly rationalized in Chinese philosophy, systematizes the practical utilitarianism of early Mozi by building up a structure of definitions of moral terms from the undefined term 'desire', to show that they are what 'the sage desires "beforehand" on behalf of men'. In the sciences the *Canons* offer explanations solely in terms of *gu* 'causes', ignoring or repudiating such current explanatory concepts as the Yin and Yang, the Five Agencies, and the symbols of the *Book of Changes*.

The Mohist school died out about 200 BC, and the technical terminology of the dialectical chapters, and their many textual problems, raised difficulties which did not begin to be solved until the 19th century. About AD 300 the Daoist interest in the Sophists revived the study of the *Canons* (misunderstood scraps of which

were used in the forged *Gongsun Long Zi*), but it is probable that by then most of them were already unintelligible.

Legalism

There is a considerable literature of practical statecraft, scornful of the moralism of Confucians and Mohists. In most of it, though not in all, the concept of law is central, so that it came to be classed under the heading 'Legalist'. The greatest of the Legalists was Han Fei (d.233 BC), whose *Han Fei Zi* is among the surviving texts. The other writings, apart from the fragments ascribed to Shen Dao (flourished 310 BC), carry the names of famous ministers in certain of the states, *Guan Zi* (Guan Zhong of Qi, d.645 BC), *Shang Zi* (Shang Yang of Qin, d.338 BC), and the fragments ascribed to Shen Buhai of Han (d.337 BC). For the most part they seem to represent traditions of political thought in the administrations of the respective states in the 3rd century BC.

Shen Buhai (or the tradition of his state which went under his name) emphasizes the 'techniques' (*shu*) of ruling, in particular the comparison of 'performance and title' (*xing ming*), the control of officials by checking their deeds against their precisely formulated responsibilities. 'Power' (*shi*) was stressed by Shen Dao, and 'law' (*fa*) by the Qin tradition of *Shang Zi*. Han Fei gave the first place to law but recognized all three as essentials of government. In spite of all differences between those who came to be classed as 'Legalist', it is common ground to them that good government depends, not on the moral goodness of administrators, as Confucians and Mohists supposed, but on the functioning of sound institutions.

In the classic Legalism of Han Fei the ruler rewards and punishes in strict accordance with his own laws, without favour to rank or person, comparing the deed with the verbal prescription as impersonally as a carpenter checks a square or circle against his L-square or compasses. Moral goodness is not merely irrelevant but disruptive, since in a system of rewards and punishments adapted to ordinary human selfishness there can be no place for people too noble to be tempted by the promise of wealth and power, or with moral scruples stronger than their fear of penalties. (*Shang Zi* is especially notorious for its scorn of morality.) Whereas Confucians distrust reliance on penal law, and maintain that in the last resort society is held together by the cement of a traditional code of 'manners' (*li*), Legalists think of the social order as imposed by force from above. Not, however, as a mere instrument serving the desires of the despot: the ruler, although absolute in power, has his place within the automatically functioning system, and acts without regard for his own preferences, as neutrally as the beam of a balance which rises on the lighter side and goes down on the heavier. Legalist didactic verse extols this objectivity in the mystic-sounding language of Daoism: the absence of wishes and preferences is the sage's 'emptiness' (*xu*), the abstention from interfering in the system is his 'Doing Nothing' (*wu wei*), the course which the system follows independent of his will is the Way, the *Dao*.

According to Han Fei, the reason why government must depend not on moral appeals but on reward and punishment is that it has to take account of the behaviour of the majority, and only a few are capable of preferring morality to their own interests. But although Han Fei studied at one time under the Confucian *Xun Zi*, who maintained that human nature is evil, he does not make the point in terms of the Confucian issue of the goodness of human nature. He takes it for granted that men will look after their own interests first of all, but thinks that whether there are conflicts of interest depends on such factors as the pressure of population on resources. In the underpopulated world of the past, morality was sufficient to harmonize interests, but population has been growing in geometrical progression and, with intensifying competition for resources moral constraints become ineffective.

Both *Shang Zi* and *Han Fei Zi* are remarkable in advancing beyond the abstract recognition of changing times and the irrelevance of past models which Legalists share with Daoists and Later Mohists to an understanding of specific connections between historical conditions and changing institutions.

The Legalist state is above all a machine for making war, in which every occupation is judged by whether or not it contributes to the strength of the state, and scarcely anyone passes the test except the farmer and the soldier. Teachers of the classics, hermits, merchants, soldiers of fortune are seen as so many parasites of which it must be rid. The state of Qin put the Legalist policies into practice and confirmed their effectiveness by completing the conquest of the rest of China in 221 BC. With the quick collapse of the Qin dynasty in 209 BC Legalism came to be credited with responsibility both for its brutal harshness and for the speed of its fall. But even after the final victory of Confucianism in the last century BC, this heresy was not so much destroyed as submerged. As moralists the Confucians hated Legalism, in particular the blatant amoralism of *Shang Zi*, but they could not quite dispense with the only available manuals of practical statecraft. The quantity of Legalist literature which survives, vast compared with that of any other heterodox school except the Daoist, is itself a testimony to its lasting influence.   *A.G.*

Judaism

Origins

The earliest evidence for the existence of Judaism in China comes from the Tang dynasty, when in AD 878 in Khanfu (Canton) Jews were said to have been slaughtered. Jews and Muslims were forbidden by the Mongols to circumcise, slaughter ritually, or marry paternal cousins. Marco Polo, Ibn Battutta, etc., mention Jews in Hangzhou, Beijing and Quanzhou. But it was only in Kaifeng that Jews left any records.

Kaifeng

Founded in the Song dynasty, with a synagogue (*qingzhensi*) in 1163, by immigrants probably from Iran (although whether by sea or by land is not determined), the Kaifeng community flourished until the 18th century, surviving into the 20th. Jews were on good terms with the authorities, both in the Ming and early Qing, becoming officials, physicians and army officers. Zhao Yingcheng (1619–57), who helped rebuild the synagogue destroyed in the 1642 flood, was a *jinshi* of 1646, vice-commissioner and special Imperial envoy.

The community took in non-Jewish women, assimilated Confucianism, but survived remarkably. They were Rabbanites, followers of Maimonides. The Chinese called them *tiaojinjiao* (the religion that extracts the sinews). The final decline was probably due to isolation from Western co-religionists from the 16th century, abetted by floods, and possibly the ravages of the Taiping Rebellion. In 1850 the synagogue was still standing, but in a dilapidated state; in 1866 it no longer existed. By the 20th century Judaism was virtually extinct, although the Jewish label lingered on until 1940 and even later, preserved by the inertia of Chinese bureaucracy and family traditions.

Our main sources are: Chinese inscriptions of 1489, 1512, 1663 and 1679 (rubbings and copies, Vatican, Bibliothèque Nationale); Jesuit letters by Ricci (who met Ai Tian in Beijing in 1605), and Gozani, Domenge and Gaubil (1704, 1712 and 1721–5 descriptions); Torah scrolls (Cambridge, Oxford, etc.); Torah section-books, prayer books, including Haggadah (with some Judaeo-Persian rubrics); and a Chinese-Hebrew Memorial Book of the Dead (mostly obtained in 1850–1 by Protestant delegates, now in Hebrew Union College, Cincinnati).

Western communities

From the 1840s Jews from Baghdad and elsewhere settled in Shanghai (and Hong Kong), coming mainly as traders. The Sassoon family was the most successful. After 1917 the small Russian Jewish community of Harbin grew to 10 000, others going to

Tianjin and Shanghai. From 1933 to 1941 German and Austrian refugees swelled the numbers, especially in Shanghai. Synagogues and community life flourished.

In the 1930s the Japanese had a scheme, the Fugu plan, to encourage German refugees to help develop Manchuria, but the Japanese attitude was ambivalent, and the Jews preferred Shanghai. In 1939 there were communities in several cities, with 20 000 Jews in Shanghai, 3000 in Harbin, 2000 in Tianjin.

From 1949 there has been a steady exodus to Israel, USA and elsewhere. By 1959 only 300 were left, and by 1970 no community life as such existed, with few if any individuals remaining (apart from the synagogue and community of Hong Kong).   *D.D.L.*

Manichaeism

The influence of Mani (*Moni*), *c* AD 216–74, and of Manichaeism (*Monijiao*, later *Mingjiao*), on both Chinese religion and society was greater than that of the other Persian religions, and Nestorianism, but the accepted date of arrival is later, 694, although some scholars find an earlier influence on Daoism.

In 694 the *Erzongjing* 'Scripture of the two principles', demonstrably Manichaean, was brought to China by a *Fuduodan* 'complete initiate'(?) of Persia. According to the 17th-century *Min shu*, a *mushe* (master) propagated the religion in the reign of Gaozong (650–83), but this has been doubted by some scholars. In 719 a great *mushe* arrived from Tokharistan.

In 732 a limited antireligious proscript attempted to stop the Manichaeans from influencing the Chinese and making converts, but allowed the foreigners themselves to carry out their ceremonies. However, with the conversion of the powerful Uighurs in *c.* 762 and their help against An Lushan, Manichaeism flourished again among the Chinese too.

There may have been temples earlier (there is a confused reference for 631; and a more acceptable one for *c.* 719 in the *Minshu*), but certainly a Manichaean (*Dayun huangming*) temple was built in 768 in Chang'an, and others in *c.* 771 in Jing, Yang, Hong (Nanchang) and Yue (Shaoxing); and in 807 in Luoyang and Taiyuan. The entry was clearly overland, spreading to the East.

In 842 and 843, with the Uighur decline, a renewed and heavier persecution occurred. Nevertheless, the religion survived underground, to influence thereafter the secret societies, especially in Fujian and Zhejiang, until the Yuan and Ming dynasties. Marco Polo mentions a sect in Fujian, now thought to be Manichaean. It is also thought that Zhu Yuanzhang, founder of the Ming, was influenced by Manichaeism. But the religion was proscribed in 1370.

Manichaean texts in Chinese have been found in Dunhuang, Quanzhou, and elsewhere.   *D.D.L.*

Zoroastrianism

Zoroastrianism entered north China with the Persian embassies of *c.* 516–9, influencing particularly the Empress Dowager Ling. During the Sui, or earlier, tent leaders (*sabao*) were appointed in Chang'an and the provinces to rule over the believers, with a miniature extra-territoriality imposed by the Chinese authorities.

In 621 a *xianci*, 'Zoroastrian shrine', for *hu*, 'Central Asian or Iranian foreigners', was established in Chang'an; in 631 a *muhu* (Magi) priest was accepted at court.

With the Arab conquest of Iran from *c.* 652, Iranians of various religious denominations (not always distinguished by Chinese scholars) fled to China, were accepted by the Tang rulers, and established themselves as Jewellers, magicians, courtesans and traders of various sorts. By the 8th century, there were four (or five) Zoroastrian shrines in Chang'an, two (or three) in Luoyang, one (or two or even three) in Kaifeng, and others in Yangzhou, Dunhuang, Taiyuan, Wuwei, Liangzhou, Yizhou. These names suggest an overland entry, as one would expect. Magians were slaughtered in Khanfu (Canton) in 878; and Hongzhou is also mentioned.

There was a religious persecution and proscription of Buddhism and foreign religions including Zoroastrianism in 843–5, and less is known about it thereafter. Song references mention fire worship and the *xian* god in Kaifeng and Zhenjiang. Zoroastrianism is not thought to have survived into the Yuan or Ming dynasties.

Zoroastrianism (as opposed to Nestorianism and Manichaeism) was not a proselytizing religion, its scriptures were not translated into Chinese, and possibly no Chinese were converted. However, Chinese surely patronized these 'magicians'. During the Tang the *huoxian*, 'fire *xian*', was worshipped twice a year, but native Chinese were forbidden to participate in prayers and sacrificial ceremonies. Clearly the authorities were worried about possible political influence.   *D.D.L.*

Islam

Historical background

Islam came to China as early as the Tang dynasty, probably during the 8th century AD. The first Muslim settlers in China were Arab and Persian merchants who travelled via the sea routes around India, and who soon found the Chinese trade remunerative enough to justify their permanent presence in Chinese coastal cities. Large Muslim communities grew up in Yangzhou, Canton and later in the ports of Fujian. In those days the Muslims were permitted to live apart in separate quarters and to maintain their own way of life and systems of laws, their seclusion facilitated by the virtual extraterritorial rights that they enjoyed. They preserved their Arabic names, their original dress, their Persian and Arabic tongues, and conducted their religious and social life independently of the Chinese. Moreover, many of them married Chinese women or bought Chinese children in times of famine, thus not only consciously contributing to the numerical growth of the Muslim community, but also unwittingly injecting into their midst the first germ of their ultimate ethnic assimilation.

The Yuan rule considerably boosted Muslim existence in China inasmuch as the Muslims, together with other non-Chinese groups (*semu*) were superimposed on the Chinese by the Mongol conquerors. Indeed, the Muslims, both those who had settled in China in previous centuries and the newly-arrived allies of the Mongols from the Muslim sultanates of Central Asia, wielded a great deal of power, the most prominent example being Seyyid Edjell who conquered Yunnan for the Yuan and was nominated by the Khan as the first governor of that province. The borders of Central Asia being wide open for trade and ideas during the Mongol rule, large numbers of Muslims settled in the north-western and southwestern provinces of China, and strong ties were established between the Muslims of China and the lands of Islam.

The retrenchment of the Ming and the self-imposed isolation that came as a reaction to the rule of the Mongol Yuan dynasty over China, constituted a major watershed in the fortunes of Chinese Muslims. From then on one could indeed speak of 'Chinese Muslims' and no longer about 'Muslims in China'. For the Muslims adopted Chinese names, became fluent in Chinese and in most cases, at least as far as China proper was concerned, became outwardly indistinguishable from Chinese. This same trend continued in the Qing dynasty until the end of the Qianlong reign (1796).

The decline of the Qing dynasty, characterized by a sharp rise in population, a scarcity of resources, together with the weakening of centralized power, and the rise of anti-establishment groups such as secret societies, was, in this instance, also accompanied by a strong Muslim revivalist movement in China. This movement, which gathered momentum during the 19th century, was contemporaneous with a similar outburst of Muslim fundamentalism in India, and was generated by the spread of the Naqshbandi Sufi Order from Central Asia into China one century earlier. The most dramatic result was the *avant-garde* role that the 'New Teaching' faction of Chinese Islam played in Muslim rebellions during the final years of the Qing. Indeed, the Muslim revolts of the mid-19th century, which threw most of China's northwest and southwest into chaos, were partly inspired by the fanaticism of the 'New Teaching' faction.

The Muslim revolts were in the main initiated in provinces where the Muslims constituted a high proportion of the total population. In Gansu, a rebellion was led by the messianic figure of

Interior of a mosque in Canton.

Ma Hualong (d. 1871), who attempted to establish a Muslim state, but it ended in failure. In Yunnan, Du Wenxiu (d. 1872) proclaimed himself 'Sultan Suleiman' and governed a secessionist Muslim state for about 15 years before he was defeated by imperial forces. The same fate awaited the revolt of the Muslims in Xinjiang. But although these rebellions of the 19th century were quelled, with great bloodshed, the Muslims never abandoned their separate identity and their craving for a schism from the Chinese polity.

Since 1949 the policy of the People's Republic of China has been shaped by a desire to demonstrate to the Muslim world China's fair treatment of the Muslims within her borders while at the same time seeking to maintain national security in the strategically important border areas populated by national minorities including the Muslims. Events have determined which of the two aspects of the policy has been dominant at any one time. In the early 1950s internal considerations dominated and the Muslims were oppressed to the point of causing unrest and open rebellion. Following the Korean War and the relaxation of domestic and external policies of the People's Republic of China, prominent Muslim leaders were encouraged to advance the cause of China's foreign policy. After the Hundred Flowers campaign, domestic considerations again prevailed, while Chinese relations with the outside Muslim world reached their lowest ebb. The attempts at reconciliation with the outside world in the early 1960s were brought to an end by the Cultural Revolution, which resulted in a wave of intimidation against the Muslims. President Nixon's visit to China and the ensuing thaw in USA-Chinese relations and Chinese acceptance into the community of nations again provided for China's relaxation of its domestic policies towards its national minorities. In the post 'gang-of-four' era, a conscious effort has been made to integrate the national minorities peacefully, to contribute to their development economically, and to pay lip-service to their autonomy culturally in order to ensure stability in the border areas which are inhabited by Muslims and other national minorities. China's conflict with the USSR encourages it to abide by the policy of pacification, in the face of the enhanced importance of the border areas and the perceived Soviet menace.

The people and their creed

Compared to the core-lands of Islam in the Middle East, or even to the major countries of peripheral Islam in Asia, much less is known of the Muslim community in China today. China for the better part of a millennium has been relatively isolated from the rest of the world, and accordingly Chinese Muslims have been

An Iman outside his mosque in Urumqi, Xinjiang Uighur Autonomous Region.

cut off from the wider Muslim community. This has had a remarkable impact upon the development of Chinese Islam, as far as the forms of coexistence between the Confucian (and then the Communist) host culture and the guest culture of the Muslims are concerned.

Another peculiarity of Chinese Islam lies in the difficulty of defining who is a Chinese Muslim. Apart from the Muslims who are scattered throughout the eastern population-belt of China, where they constitute a noticeable minority in virtually all large cities, there are large concentrations of Muslims in the less 'Chinese' provinces of the northwest and the southwest, where the Muslim presence is comparable to that of other national minorities. While the Muslims of the large urban centres have been more thoroughly sinicized, at least as far as their ethnic appearance and their material culture are concerned, there are clear characteristics distinguishing the Tungans and Uighur-Turkic Muslims of the northwest. Whereas in the large cities the Chinese-Muslim community has been divided up into local congregations headed by Ahongs (mullahs), which for the most part lack supra-local or supra-provincial organization, the Muslims of the Chinese periphery maintain a much more communal-ethnic existence facilitated by their territorial attachment to extensive areas.

This pattern of distribution of the Chinese Muslims has resulted in a dual response on the part of the Muslim community to the host culture. While the urban Muslims tend to be more 'docile'—perhaps because of their awareness of their insignificant weight within their environment, the ethnic Muslims who constitute the majority or a sizeable minority in the western provinces, tend to evince much more self-confidence, assertiveness and even a rebellious spirit.

Since no reliable statistics are available, it is very difficult to give exact figures of Muslims belonging to either group. Estimates suggest that the total Muslim population of China today is around 35 million, perhaps 10–15 million of whom are 'ethnic Muslims', while the rest are urban. In traditional China all Muslims were lumped together under the term 'Hui', and under the Chinese Republic they were recognized as one of the five constituent groups of the Chinese people. But under the Chinese Communist government they have been subdivided into smaller groupings: Uighurs in Xinjiang and Hui in Ningxia, both enjoying an 'autonomous' status, while others, especially those residing in the urban centres, have been omitted from official statistics of the Hui. Thus, while some Chinese might refer to '40 million Muslims' in China, statistics would indicate the existence of only six million Uighurs and some five to six million Hui in the 'autonomous' regions excluding the majority of Chinese Muslims who reside in the cities or in the large Muslim communities of Shanxi, Gansu, Yunnan and Sichuan.

Islam being a totalistic way of life, which knows no distinction between the political and the social, the religious and the cultural, and the secular and the holy, is bound to seek the attainment of an Islamic polity as the only way to carry out in practice the word of Allah. Thus, while Muslims are required to live under Islamic rule, those who suffer under minority status in non-Muslim lands endure a permanent strain between loyalty to their country of residence and the requirements of the universal *umma* of Islam. As long as their Islamic creed and religious practice are not jeopardized by the non-Muslim ruler, they can submit to the authority of their host country, even while entertaining messianic cravings as to their ultimate entry into the Abode of Islam. But when the degree of oppression becomes unbearable, as was the case in China during the 19th century, or when relatively liberal policies allow the Muslims to express their religio-political concerns, as during the Hundred Flowers campaign in China, they are likely to voice secessionist desires. The current revival of Islam throughout the world has drawn renewed attention to the large Muslim population of China.   *R.I.*

Christianity

Nestorians

Nestorius (flourished 428–36), the heretical bishop of Constantinople, taught that Christ had two persons, human and divine. His church in Persia and Baghdad sent missionaries to India and China from the 6th to the 10th centuries. In 1623 Jesuits discovered the 'Nestorian Tablet' at Xi'an, recording in Syriac and Chinese a Nestorian mission to the Tang capital in 635, to teach the religion of Daqin or Syria, which was well received by the Emperor Taizong (reigned 626–49). The authenticity of this tablet was suspect until the discovery in 1908 of a Chinese Christian *Hymn to the Trinity* and a list of Chinese Christian books among the manuscripts of Dunhuang, and identification of references to Syrian Christians in Imperial Edicts of 683, 745 and 845. A Metropolitan, David, was consecrated in China before 823. Nestorians emphasized monastic Christianity and suffered severely from the Edict of 845 proscribing Buddhism and ordering the secularization of monasteries; 3000 'foreign monks' were returned to lay life. A sharp decline followed, and a Nestorian mission of 987 found no Christian communities in China, but remnants of Nestorian belief were noted by 14th-century missions from the West.

Friars

Genghis Khan (1162–1227) and his grandson Khubilai (1214–94), emperor of China, 1260–94, both requested the Pope to

The 'Nestorian Tablet', the oldest relic of Christianity in China.

send priests to teach Christianity. In 1246 John of Piano Carpini (1180–1252), a Franciscan, reached the Mongol court in Asia, followed in 1253 by William of Rubruck (flourished 1250), a Dominican. In 1287 Rabban Sauma (1250–94), a Nestorian Christian from Beijing, reached Rome; his visit persuaded the Pope to send John of Monte Corvino (1246–1328), a Franciscan, to China. He reached Beijing in 1294, built a church, taught choristers and bible-clerks Greek and Latin and claimed 6000 converts by 1305. In 1308 he was consecrated the first Archbishop of the Catholic Church in China. After his death the See declined. A further Papal embassy under John Marignolli (flourished 1340) remained in China from 1338–46. There were now two bishoprics, Beijing and Quanzhou (Zaitun). The last bishop of Zaitun was murdered in 1326 in Chinese revolts against Mongol rule, and in 1369 the Archbishop was expelled from Beijing. No further Western missions were sent for 200 years.

Jesuits

St Francis Xavier (1506–52) died on the point of entering China, but in 1583 another Jesuit, Matteo Ricci (1552–1610), reached China from Macao, receiving permission to live in Beijing in 1600 and winning imperial favour by his skill in regulating clocks and making maps. He devoted himself to teaching the language and understanding Chinese civilization, and adapted Catholic rites for Chinese converts, a process known as 'accommodation'. By 1610 the Jesuits claimed 2 000 converts, but many were infants who died young. Three Chinese converts led missions to Hangzhou and Shanghai. In 1602 Benedict de Goes (1562–1607) travelled overland from India, first identifying China with 'Cathay'. In 1622 the Congregation for the Propagation of the Faith (Propaganda) was founded in Rome and Ricci's 'accommodations' were upheld. In 1622 Adam Schall von Bell (1591–1666) succeeded Ricci in Beijing. Because he correctly predicted the eclipse of 1624 he was appointed to the Board for Calendar Regulation. In 1644 Qing forces occupied Beijing but Schall retained the new emperor's favour, becoming president of the Board in 1645. By 1650 there were said to be 150 000 Christians in China.

Christians won favour from 1667 because of Kangxi's respect for Schall's colleague, Ferdinand Verbiest (1617–88), and the first Chinese bishop, Luo Wenzao (1617–91), was consecrated in 1685. In 1692 an imperial Edict tolerating Christianity brought Franciscan and Dominican missions also to China. They rejected Jesuit 'accommodations', particularly for funerals, ancestor-worship and titles for God, and the controversy, the Rites Issue, raged from 1693 to 1705. The Jesuits obtained an imperial ruling upholding their view that Chinese rites had no heretical religious significance, but the Catholic Church ruled against Jesuit practice in 1704. The Emperor thereupon expelled all priests who refused to accept Ricci's 'accommodations' and official toleration for Christianity ended abruptly. Missionaries of other orders continued to enter China, and learned Jesuits remained at court as mathematicians and astronomers. Meanwhile, Russian Orthodox priests settled in Beijing as part of the Russian mission accepted under the Treaty of Nerchinsk (1689) and subsequently under the Yongzheng Emperor (1727).

Protestant missions

Robert Morrison (1782–1834), of the London Missionary Society, arrived in China in 1807. Official hostility made preaching impossible but he published his translation of the Bible in 1819, baptized 11 converts in Canton and Macao between 1807 and 1834, and founded the Anglo-Chinese College at Malacca in 1818. After the Treaty of Nanjing (1842) ended the First Opium War, British and American missions of all denominations arrived, their diversity making conversion more difficult. In 1846, when the Taiping rebels, whose ideology was partly Christian, swept central China, the Western powers briefly considered supporting them but sided with the Qing emperor. In 1850 St Paul's College was established in Hong Kong to train Chinese for the ministry. In 1865 James Hudson Taylor (1832–1905) founded the China Inland Mission, sending interdenominational missionaries, male and female, into the interior. By 1895 they had reached Xinjiang and Tibet and were resident in the other provinces. Mission schools and hospitals were established with considerable success, and five universities had been founded by 1893, but there was also a growth in popular hostility to Christianity, culminating in the Boxer Rebellion (1900–1) in which many thousands of Chinese Christians, some 200 Protestant missionaries and a larger number of Catholics were killed.

Missions returned soon after and Chinese Christians played a significant part in the Republican Revolution of 1911. Sun Yat-sen was a Christian and Chiang Kai-shek was baptized in 1930.

At the founding of the People's Republic in 1949 there were over 8000 Christian missionaries in China. In 1951 they were encouraged to leave and few remained by 1953, but Chinese Christians were not openly attacked until 1958. The freedom of worship and belief was even guaranteed by the constitution of 1954. Between 1955 and 1966 the churches were increasingly criticized as unpatriotic imperialist relics. The Protestant Churches formed the Three-Self Patriotic Movement (self-governing, self-supporting, self-proselytising) in 1954. The Catholic Churches united in the Chinese Patriotic Catholic Association in 1957; church property was absorbed by the state and links with churches overseas were

The Shandong Christian University Hospital with the hospital advisory board in the 1920s.

Anti-Christian poster from the time of the Boxer Rebellion (1900–1): Jesus is represented as a pig and Westerners as goats.

broken. Many individual Christians faced self-criticism and imprisonment. In the Cultural Revolution most churches and temples were closed and many destroyed, the greatest freedom of worship being allowed to Chinese Muslims. After the fall of the 'gang of four' some freedom of worship was once again tolerated for believers in Christianity, Buddhism and Daoism alike.   *A.L.*

Late Qing and early 20th-century thought

During the last two imperial dynasties, the Neo-Confucianism originally developed by the masters of the Song dynasty dominated philosophy and guided the moral and spiritual life of most Chinese. Its hegemony was aided by the support of the imperial government, which identified Cheng Yi (1032–1107) and Zhu Xi's (1130–1200) Rationalist School with the orthodox transmission of the Confucian Way, and set Zhu Xi's own commentaries on the *Four Books* and the *Five Classics* as texts for the imperial civil service examinations. Indeed, with the Ming–Qing consolidation of autocracy in politics and the spread of literacy in society below, Neo-Confucian values achieved a new level of codification in law, morality books, clan genealogies, encyclopedias and educational literature. The 'three bonds' (three of Mencius' five relationships, namely, those between emperor and official, father and son, husband and wife) and the 'five relationships' (the 'three bonds' plus the relationships between elder and younger brother and between friend and friend) were taught as absolute norms underpinning social relationships, political authority and cosmic order.

However, beneath this façade of an unchanging ritual order were complex and creative cross-currents in metaphysics, ethics, moral psychology and classical studies. Zhu Xi's Neo-Confucian synthesis was challenged in the Ming by the 'Idealist' School of Wang Yangming (1472–1529), and in the Qing by the empiricist school of 'evidentiary research'. Wang Yangming criticized Zhu Xi for a dualistic metaphysic that encouraged the search for 'principle' in an ultimately ungraspable outer universe. His moral metaphysic of inner experience led his followers to intuitionist interpretations of truth and anti-scholastic moral activism. The school of 'evidentiary research', reacting against the centrality of self-cultivation in the teachings of both Wang Yangming and Zhu Xi, sought factual understanding of classical texts, which led to new historical and linguistic perspectives.

None the less, though Neo-Confucianism accommodated both doctrinal tensions and a diversity of personal styles of faith, the system was fundamentally challenged only in the late 19th century, when the imperial political order was waning. Philosophically, the impact of Western thought can be compared to that of the foreign religion of Buddhism 1500 years before. However, where Buddhism had revolutionized Chinese religious consciousness, the democratic and scientific ideas of the 19th-century West pointed to the secularization of all values, and the transformation of China into a modern nation committed to the goal of an industrial revolution. Ironically, an ultimately secularist message was first transmitted to reform intellectuals of the 1880s and 1890s by Protestant missionaries, in the form of a natural theology not lacking metaphysical presuppositions of its own. This, plus the richness of the symbolic resources the tradition afforded, helped the first generation of intellectual 'Westernizers' to see their task as a radical revision, but not a total repudiation, of the core values of the Confucian tradition. In keeping with scholar-official ideals, they also saw themselves as 'superior men' (*junzi*) with a mission to save society by combining moral and political leadership.

First among them was Kang Youwei, a visionary scholar from the Canton delta area, where the Western presence had been entrenched since the Opium War. By the late 1880s Kang had moved beyond the assumptions of the then dominant 'Self-strengthening' movement, which taught resistance to foreign encroachment through technological development while preserving a Chinese 'essence' in values. The 19th-century expansion of Chinese cultural awareness to include peoples both powerful and civilized from outside the boundaries of the old sinocentric world system implied for Kang a relativization of the concept of civilization itself in both time and space. He found support for such a break with Confucian canon in Western science, which he interpreted as a new cosmological truth and as a method of verification. A few years later, under the influence of Social Darwinism, Kang decided that a long submerged prophetic tradition of Confucianism—the 'new text' school—in fact taught a fully fledged evolutionary theory of progress, in light of which the struggles between China and the West would result in a syncretic world civilization, realizing the old utopian Confucian vision of Great Unity (*datong*).

Kang and his followers emerged as leaders of the 'one hundred days' reform' of 1898, an ill-fated effort to graft constitutionalism onto the imperial monarchy. Although the reformers, including Kang, were exiled, and Kang's most brilliant associate Tan Sitong (1865–98) was executed, the movement for institutional change proved irreversible. Reform proposals for industrialization projects, administrative restructuring and Western-style education became official policies after 1902. However, by calling on the Emperor to share power with an enlightened public opinion, the reformers had challenged the sacred basis of imperial autocracy. Further, their goal of moral progress was linked to a fundamental challenge to the system of ritual relationships, foretelling the eventual replacement of hierarchical and particularistic social values (*li*) with universal, egalitarian ones.

As a Confucianist, Kang Youwei tried to reconcile his spiritual faith with his commitment to social change by distinguishing the Confucian cosmic-moral principle of Goodness (*ren*), from any of its relative historical manifestations in social practice (*li*). This opened the way for a separation of sacred value from secular morality, severing the unity of 'Heaven, Earth and Humanity' which had made traditional Confucianism an organic system. In an effort to adjust to such a severance, Kang proposed that Confucianism be institutionalized as a state religion in a secularized society.

In spite of the context of dynastic crisis, the 1898 reformers were largely optimists, for whom evolution appeared as a benign unfolding of progress, with an internal logic which made its manifest and latent aspects interdependent. Spurred by the introduction of modern schooling and by the abolition of the classical civil service examination system, effective from 1906, youth flocked to the treaty ports, to Japan and to Western countries to study the new secrets of 'wealth and power' for China. A modern periodical press mushroomed, and people joined new forms of voluntary association such as study societies and political parties. Through the influential translations of Yan Fu (1854–1921), the ideas of Adam Smith, J.S. Mill and T.H. Huxley were made available in Chinese. French Enlightenment thought and 19th-century socialism became accessible through adaptations from the Japa-

nese and through journals published abroad. During the next 15 years of intensive exploration of Western thought, the evolutionism of Herbert Spencer, T.H. Huxley or P.A. Kropotkin provided a conceptual framework for analysing the relationship between Chinese and Western history and cultures. However, controversy arose when evolutionists doubted China's ability to be found 'fit' in the evolutionary struggle unless the core values of Confucianism were abandoned.

Within this framework Liang Qichao, an influential journalist and advocate of constitutionalism, argued that the Darwinian competition between peoples rewarded those with a powerful capacity for social 'grouping', with the lesson that China should model itself on the parliamentary democracies. However, because Liang thought democracy was based on a collective sentiment rather than legal rights, he believed that psychological renewal rather than institutional reform was the most basic requirement for Chinese progress. And, because he could not envisage a transformed Chinese psychology divorced from China's historical morality, he became an evolutionary gradualist who taught the modernity of those Confucian ritual relationships which could be seen as based on distinctions of biology or natural ability, or on the 'concern for posterity'.

Evolutionary thought facilitated the acceptance of Western liberalism as the socio-political value system of historically advanced peoples, and at the same time forced intellectuals to question the possibility of maintaining a linkage between the Confucian cosmic-spiritual order and changing socio-political values. When the political instability which followed the overthrow of the monarchy created a national mood of disillusionment with parliamentary institutions, opinion soon polarized around neo-traditional and socially revolutionary alternatives. Conservatives, such as the scholars of the 'national essence' clique and a new generation of Confucian philosophers now familiar with Western metaphysics, contrasted the 'materialist West', marked by a spirit of competition, materialism and aggression, with the 'spiritual East'. Rejecting Kang Youwei's Confucian church and Liang Qichao's reformed ritual ethics as utilitarian compromises, they did not so much seek to block the social change seen necessary for China's survival as to elevate the core value of Goodness (*ren*) to a spiritual principle independent of the secular social process. In the hands of the Peking University philosophy professor Liang Shuming (1893–1988), Confucianism was reinterpreted as an 'inner' faith, offering an alternative to that sense of the meaninglessness of existence which no amount of social improvement relieves. Following his lead, Confucianists turned away from debates on social ethics to a revival of Wang Yangming's metaphysic of moral experience. However, in the post-traditional context of 1920 this neo-Confucian philosophy of 'mind' was associated with the thought of

Western 19th-century idealists like Rudolf Eucken and Henri Bergson—i.e. with an intuitionist defence of religious value against the secularizing forces of scientific rationalism.

Although early Republican controversy over the future of Confucianism did lead to a viable modernist defence of faith, neo-traditionalists found themselves in the minority among intellectuals. The climactic May Fourth Movement of 1919 was the creation of a radical 'new youth' who rejected both Confucius and evolutionary gradualism. Originally nurtured on the republicanism of the *Tongmenghui* (Alliance Society) or on an anarcho-communism adapted from Kropotkin, the radical movement came of age with the 1919 'May Fourth' demonstrations against the European betrayal of Chinese rights of self-determination at the conference of Versailles. This anti-imperialist protest not only toppled the Beijing government cabinet, but became the symbol for the younger generation's intellectual rebellion against the entire traditional heritage. The magazine *New Youth* took from the liberal West the slogans of 'science' and 'democracy'. From the utopianism of the reform evolutionists it took the call for the psychological renewal of the Chinese people, and their emancipation from all ritual relationships. However, it made all of these the immediate goals of a 'cultural revolution', associated with practical campaigns for the emancipation of women, freedom from arranged marriage, a new scholarship and art, and for the substitution of the vernacular for the classical written language. These reforms were rationalized by a reductionistic attack on Confucianism as no more than a corrupt system of social ethics underpinning the feudal order, whose cosmic-moral claims were invalidated by scientific reasoning. Finally, faith in elite enlightenment gave way to faith in class struggle for those 'new youth' who followed the May Fourth leaders Chen Duxiu (1879–1942) and Li Dazhao (1889–1927) in their conversion from anarchism to Marxism after 1919.

Ironically, in turning towards revolutionary socialism May Fourth radicals showed that they shared with modern Confucian conservatives a common disillusionment with Western liberal ideologies. However, in spite of communist affinities with collectivist and populist aspects of the traditional culture, and the tenacity—even among intellectuals—of Confucian social ethics at the level of inarticulated assumption, the May Fourth Movement left the Confucian ritual system fatally weakened. It had lost its philosophical underpinnings in a unitary cosmic order of interdependent natural, human and metaphysical realms. Although Confucianism has been noted among world religions for its this-worldly orientation, the break of the linkage between social ethics and the sacred caused that final 'decay of ritual' Confucianists had often feared but never experienced.   *C.F.*

Chinese thought since the May Fourth Movement

During China's first cultural revolution, the May Fourth Movement, it appeared that the future could only belong to one of the two anti-traditional currents then dominating the intellectual debate: liberalism and pragmatism on the one hand, or the more radical ideas of Marxism and anarchism on the other. Most participants in these events saw Confucianism as not merely pernicious, but irrelevant, and the partisans of tradition were altogether on the defensive. Half a century later, the influence of pre-modern Chinese thought was both pervasive and deep, and it would not be wholly frivolous to argue that the most significant and forceful promoter of traditional values within the People's Republic of China was none other than Mao Zedong. After Mao's death, ideas and values of foreign origin became once again more influential than they had been since the 1930s, but at the same time the prestige of Chinese culture remained high.

In the initial stages of its effective introduction into China, Marxism was beyond question a vehicle of Westernization. However debatable its claims to scientific validity, it encouraged the attempt to discover the objective laws of social development, thus giving further impetus to the process of secularization. It also fostered the quintessentially Western value of struggle. Both the Promethean struggle for the mastery of man over nature, and class struggle to transform the foundations of the existing society, were profoundly subversive of the Confucian ideal of cosmic and social harmony. The first, and to some extent the second of these ideas of struggle had been introduced in the late 19th century with the theory of evolution and other Western currents of thought, but were to be carried by the Communists to levels previously unknown. The Marxists also introduced categories of analysis, such as definitions of social classes, which long remained so foreign that as late as the mid-1930s key terms like 'proletariat' and 'bourgeoisie' were often transcribed phonetically, rather than translated into their Chinese equivalents, in order to make explicit the assumption that such terms were derived from a foreign rather than from a Chinese matrix.

In the early 1920s many of the founding members of the Chinese Communist Party wrote about the prospects for 'proletarian' revolution with no serious attention to the differences in social structure and state of historical development between China and capitalist countries. The Leninist interpretation of Marxism, to which they had been introduced by the time the Comintern pushed them into the first United Front with the *Guomindang* in 1923–4, brought a more realistic appreciation of the differences between China and the West, as well as theoretical justification for collaboration with the bourgeoisie in a substantially pre-capitalist society. It also opened the door to more drastic adaptations of Marxism to the Chinese environment, such as those advocated by Mao Zedong in 1938 under the slogan of the 'Sinification of Marxism', which were regarded in Moscow as nationalist heresies.

Meanwhile, less radical conceptions of reform were encouraged by the visits to China, in 1920–1, of Bertrand Russell (1872–1970) and John Dewey (1859–1952). The former, who came fresh from a sojourn in the Soviet Union, advocated a version of communism without dictatorship which Mao Zedong, who attended one of his lectures, found rather naive. Though Russell retained some disciples, Dewey was undoubtedly more influential, largely because of the activities of his student, Hu Shi (1891–1962). Hu was the only liberal intellectual of the May Fourth period whose prestige continued to rival that of the radicals, such as Chen Duxiu and Li Dazhao, who had gravitated towards Communism. At the moment of the decisive parting of the ways between the liberal and Marxist wings of the May Fourth intellectuals, he launched the famous controversy about 'problems' and 'isms' in 1919, and played the central role in it. In a word, Hu proposed a 'social engineering' approach to the problems facing China, which would involve dealing with the country's weaknesses one by one, while not allowing the minds of the Chinese to become fettered by 'isms', i.e., by rigid doctrines. Li Dazhao, Hu's most important antagonist on this occasion, defended the crucial role of 'isms' or ideologies, which he perceived rather in the terms suggested by the literal meaning of the Chinese expression zhuyi: 'leading idea'. Without the guidance of such a structured ideology, argued Li and other future Communists, one would go astray and be unable to solve particular problems.

Throughout the ensuing decades Hu Shi maintained a similar stance. For their part, the Communists took, of course, Marxist ideology as their guide. None the less, it is worth noting Hu Shi's undeniable influence on Mao Zedong during the early stages of the May Fourth Movement, for Mao continued to have (or to profess) until the end of his life an abhorrence for those who dealt only in abstract theories, without coming to grips with reality. It was Mao who put into circulation in the early 1940s the slogan 'shishi qiushi', or 'Seek the truth from facts', and it has been argued that there is more of Dewey than of Marx in his essay 'On Practice'.

The adherents of liberalism in its various guises continued to defend their point of view down to 1949, but for the most part, this 'third force' was so ground between the upper and nether millstones of Marxism, or Marxism-Leninism, and the nationalist ideology of the Guomindang, as to be incapable of playing a significant role in shaping events.

A remarkable feature of Guomindang ideology was the contribution to its elaboration by students of Marx, and even by former members of the Chinese Communist Party. In 1919 Sun Yat-sen's close adviser Hu Hanmin (1879–1936) possessed as subtle an understanding of Marxism as any Chinese, an understanding acquired in the course of the polemics about the nature of socialism which he had conducted against Liang Qichao on Sun's behalf during the first decade of the 20th century. Sun Yat-sen himself, in his Three People's Principles, nationalism, democracy, and people's livelihood, characterized the third principle as a practical method for implementing communism, and added that all supporters of the Guomindang should regard the Communist Party as a good friend. After Sun's death in 1925 and the break with the Communists, Hu Hanmin continued to the end, while rejecting class struggle and Soviet domination, to show regard for Marxism as a method of analysis.

It might have been assumed that, when the Guomindang under Chiang Kai-shek's leadership moved decisively to the right in the 1930s, such Marxist influences would disappear. In fact, Tao Xisheng (b. 1899), who is commonly thought to have ghost-written Chiang's China's Destiny, was himself a Marxist, though a somewhat singular one. In particular, he made the assumption that in China the ruling elite, both in imperial times and to some extent in his own day, was superimposed on society without being organically related to it, so that pre-revolutionary China was a 'proto-capitalist society dominated by a feudal ideology'. What brought his approach into convergence with that of Chiang Kai-shek (and also, in some ways, with that of Mao Zedong) was his insistence on the uniqueness of Chinese history, and the continuing relevance both of the experience and of the culture of the past.

Chiang Kai-shek, for his part, drew little from Marxism, save for Lenin's elitist and hierarchical approach to political work. Sun Yat-sen's heritage in fact tended in a similar direction; not only had he stressed his own personal authority as leader of the Guomindang, but his interpretation of 'democracy' in the Three People's Principles, while recognizing the people as the ultimate repository of sovereignty, stressed that they should not meddle in politics, but allow the experts to get on with the job of government.

In the mid-1930s, in the context of the New Life Movement, Chiang Kai-shek carried this tendency much further, explicitly declaring his admiration for, and adhesion to, the 'leadership principle' of Fascism, in its German and Italian forms. At the same time, he stressed the continuing value and relevance of Confucian moral and social principles. Thus he equated Sun Yat-sen's maxim 'Action is easy, knowledge is difficult' with the famous sentence from the Confucian Lunyu, 'The people may be made to follow a course of action, but they cannot be made to understand it.'

China's uniqueness, and the continuing value of Chinese culture, was also, of course, a theme of neo-Confucian conservatives such as Liang Shuming (1893–1988), who continued to enjoy considerable prestige in intellectual and academic circles even after 1949, until he fell victim to the Anti-Rightist Campaign which succeeded the Hundred Flowers in 1957. Liang himself, though he did not participate actively in the major controversy of 1923 on 'science and the philosophy of life', shared the scepticism of leading protagonists of this debate, such as Zhang Junmai (Carson Chang) (1887–1969), regarding the claims of science as a panacea for the world's ills. This view could only bring him into conflict in the end with the claims of 'scientific socialism', despite the many areas of agreement between him and Mao Zedong regarding the virtues of the peasantry and the countryside.

Following the establishment of the People's Republic of China, philosophers naturally debated topics which exercised Marxists elsewhere, such as the relation between thought and existence, and between the superstructure and the economic basis of society. Particular importance was attached, from the mid-1950s onwards, to the problem of the nature of contradictions in society, which loomed so large in Mao's own thought. Side by side with these Marxist themes, there was continuing and lively discussion about the nature and historical role of figures in traditional Chinese thought such as Confucius, Laozi, and Zhuangzi.

It was assuredly no accident that precisely in 1964, the year when the Sino-Soviet split became open and irreconcilable, Mao Zedong wrote and spoke at greater length about a wide range of traditional Chinese thinkers than at any other time in his career. Not only did he refer in the process to 'Buddhist and Daoist materialism', but his evaluation of Confucius was by no means wholly negative. While naturally rejecting Confucianism as an answer to China's problems in the 20th century, Mao praised Confucius's contribution as an educationalist, and even said that he was of 'poor peasant origin' and had, in his youth, been close to the people.

Mao Zedong's support for the harsh and one-sided attacks on Confucius published during the Anti-Confucius Campaign of 1973–5 was thus not in keeping with his own previous statements, and must be explained by his political aims at the time. The fact that in Mao's last years, this campaign, focusing on traditional Chinese thought, and the 'Campaign to Study the Theory of the Proletarian Dictatorship', which took its texts from Marx, Lenin and Stalin, were going on simultaneously, symbolized the dual nature of Chinese thought and culture during his 27 years as the ruler of China. It may also be seen as a reflection of Mao's failure to forge a true synthesis between Marxism and the Chinese tradition.

One factor hampering the development of Chinese thought during the era of Mao Zedong lay in the fact that Marxism was

taken to mean Leninism, and indeed Leninism coloured by Soviet ideas and practices under Stalin. Mao said, at the time of the campaign in 1956 to promote 'a hundred flowers and a hundred schools', that in China a hundred schools really meant *two* schools, the bourgeois school and the proletarian school. Apart from work on traditional Chinese thought, philosophical discussion was therefore limited to debates among 'Marxist-Leninists', and doctrinaire polemics against every form of 'bourgeois ideology', including Western interpretations of Marxism.

For more than a decade after the inauguration of Deng Xiaoping's programme of reform in 1978, the situation was radically different. Stalin's doctrinal authority was widely rejected, and some bold thinkers explicitly criticized Lenin for stressing dictatorship rather than democracy, and the role of the Party rather than that of the people. Virtually every current of thought abroad in the world, from the Frankfurt School to ideas about the 'third wave' and the 'information society', was discussed critically, but in reasonably objective fashion, and many important works of the most varied tendencies were translated.

Some of the Marxist controversies of the 1950s continued to be pursued in similar terms, but most Chinese philosophers were more interested in devising new answers to new problems. Indeed the Party leadership, headed by Hu Yaobang and then by Zhao Ziyang, appeared to encourage the view that Marxism could only maintain its vitality if it was developed and adapted, not dogmatically reasserted. At the same time, the proclaimed goal was 'Chinese-style modernization', and this was taken to include the preservation and assimilation of elements in the heritage of old China (including Chinese philosophy) judged to be still of value today. In this perspective, the writings of philosophers in Taiwan, including those of the Confucian persuasion, were likewise an object of attention.

In the intellectual realm, as in that of concrete economic and political reform, the central thrust was the effort to adapt China to the 'era of the entrepreneur'. This quest led, both in thought and in policy, to uncertainty and confusion regarding the ultimate parameters of reform, but it also lent an element of excitement and open-endedness to Chinese thought which had scarcely been in evidence since the May Fourth era. These developments ultimately proved unacceptable to the old men of the Long March and Yan'an generation, and the students' attempt to summon up from the May Fourth heritage not only democracy and science, but basic human freedoms as well, led to Stalinist repression and the resurgence of obscurantist thinking. Before the 4 June 1989 massacre, however, the consciousness at least of the urban population had been raised to a degree which makes it extremely unlikely that the present reactionary phase can long endure.

S.R.S.

WORDS AND SIGNS

Origin of the Chinese language

Chinese is the general name for a wide range of dialects whose historical and descriptive classification as variants of a single language is based primarily upon social considerations: the characteristics unifying the speakers of the dialects are more easily found in the economic, political and cultural conditions (the last of the three being reflected most expressively in the distinctive script and the momentous written tradition using the script as its vehicle) shared by them for several millennia, rather than in common linguistic features. These can be specified only in very broad terms as the occurrence of tones (patterns of pitch, loudness and duration which signal the differences in meaning of elements otherwise identical in their sound) in the phonological system, the prevalence of monosyllabic morphemes (the smallest elements capable of carrying meaning) and monomorphemic words, and the tendency to employ syntactical rather than morphological devices in grammar, i.e. to indicate grammatical rela-

tionships of words by their order and by using special relation-marking words, not by changing the form of the words.

The shared linguistic features place Chinese in the Sino-Tibetan language stock, of which it is by far the largest member (the total number of speakers of Sino-Tibetan languages can only be estimated at about one billion, which makes them the second largest group in the world after Indo-European languages). However, the way in which Chinese modified these features sets it distinctly apart from the other Sino-Tibetan languages, and suggests that Chinese developed in an idiosyncratic direction away from the linguistic centre of gravity represented by the other languages in the stock, possibly under the influence of a language or languages of another type.

The question of the origin and historical affiliation of Chinese is further complicated by the profound and lasting influence Chinese culture had exerted for many centuries upon diverse language communities in its vicinity. This influence was mediated by the Chinese script which several of these communities adopted (the morphemic nature of the script made this possible in a way similar to that in which Arabic numerals and road signs can be used by speakers of different languages), and together with it also a large

SINO-TIBETAN LANGUAGES

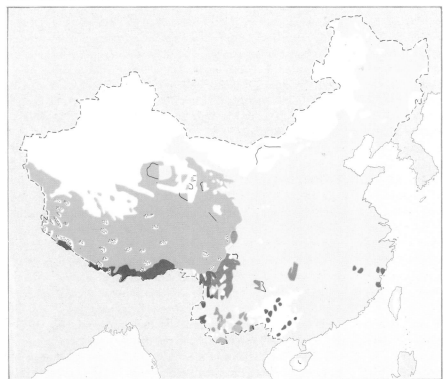

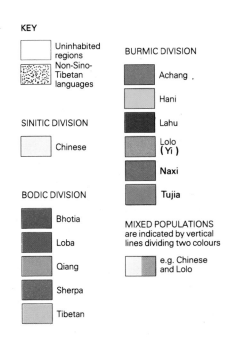

KEY

Uninhabited regions

Non-Sino-Tibetan languages

SINITIC DIVISION

Chinese

BODIC DIVISION

Bhotia

Loba

Qiang

Sherpa

Tibetan

BURMIC DIVISION

Achang

Hani

Lahu

Lolo (Yi)

Naxi

Tujia

MIXED POPULATIONS are indicated by vertical lines dividing two colours

e.g. Chinese and Lolo

amount of Chinese lexical elements and grammatical patterns. Because of this, such languages as Japanese, Korean and Vietnamese show a great deal of superficial similarity to Chinese, although they are not related to it by origin: none of these three languages actually belongs to the Sino-Tibetan stock.   *P.K.*

Early pronunciation

The Chinese writing system is not based on the phonemic principle, and it reflects speech sounds only in an abstract manner without much system. Partly because of this, and partly because of the heavy textual bias of traditional native Chinese scholarship, no substantial interest in the concrete early pronunciation of Chinese appeared until the latter half of the 19th century, when the Western linguistic approach was first applied to the study of Chinese on a large scale.

The foundation upon which the study is based is almost entirely the work of the Swedish scholar Bernhard Karlgren (1889–1978), who designed the method of investigating the early pronunciation of Chinese, and whose writings established the basic framework of its development.

Karlgren's method, similarly to the generally accepted techniques of comparative linguistics and internal reconstruction, refers to modern dialects for concrete phonetic values, but it departs from the techniques by relying much more on indirect evidence in reconstructing the phonological patterns characterizing the earlier stages of Chinese. This was made necessary because sufficient and reliable information on modern Chinese dialects was lacking at the time of the reconstruction (to some degree it still is), and it was made possible because there happens to be much more varied evidence of this indirect kind available for Chinese than in the case of other languages, mainly Indo-European, the investigation of which led to developing the comparative techniques.

In the first place, there exists a number of Chinese works whose aim was to elucidate systematically those aspects of earlier texts which had to do with pronunciation, in particular with rhyming. The most prominent among these is the *Qieyun* compiled by Lu Fayan in the beginning of the 7th century AD. Rhyme dictionaries of this kind present an especially clear picture of the phonological patterning in what Karlgren assumed to be a standard dialect of Chinese in the period ending at about AD 600.

Another source of information was found in the sphere where Chinese came into contact with other languages at different points in its history. On the one hand, there was the plethora of Chinese loan-words in Korean, Vietnamese and especially Japanese which had been exposed to Chinese influence in identifiable stages. By

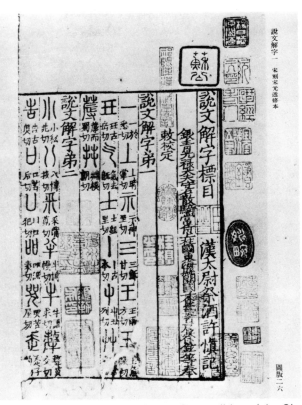

A facsimile of the first page from a Song edition of the *Shuowenjiezi*.

careful comparison, it became possible to trace down the regular reflection of sound features which characterized the Chinese models. On the other hand, it proved useful to examine how Chinese itself reflected the influence of foreign languages, in particular those written in a phonemic script, the approximate phonetic values of which at the time of the borrowing were known. This was mainly in the case of Sanskrit, from which technical terms and proper names were borrowed extensively in the middle of the 7th century AD, when Buddhism flourished in China. Old literary texts themselves became a source of evidence where they could be shown to have employed the features of speech sounds, such as in rhymed poetry. Of particular importance in this sense became the classic collection of rhymes known as *Shijing*, dating from 800 to 600 BC. Finally, the character script as such was used as indirect evidence. Even though it had not been designed to represent either phonemic classes of sounds or their phonetic values systematically, it made use of the association between speech sound and written symbol as a device for eliminating ambiguities and for generating new symbols. The association which could be extracted from the patterning of the characters and their parts then became the basis for setting up classes of speech sound properties at the time when the script was formed. Early Chinese works listing characters according to their structure, such as the *Shuowenjiezi*, published about AD 100, came to assume special importance in this respect.

By using indirect evidence from these varied sources, and by comparing it with the data from modern Chinese dialects, three stages were established as a convenient frame of reference: Ancient Chinese, representing a variant of the language as it was pronounced about AD 600; Archaic Chinese, reconstructed for the more loosely delimited period of about 1200–800 BC; Modern Chinese, as it is reflected in contemporary dialects.

Despite the work of Karlgren and many other Western and Chinese scholars, much still remains unknown or controversial not only about the various parts of the frame delimited by the three stages, but also about the relationship of the three stages to each other. This is mainly because the complex network of the lines of Chinese dialectal descent can no longer be retraced with any precision, and it cannot be ascertained how the stages fit into the network. Moreover, most of the research in reconstructing the early pronunciation of Chinese has been concentrating on segmental phonology (i.e. the vowel and consonant structure of syllables), and although some advance has been made by the more recent generation of Chinese linguists in the historical study of tones, very little is still understood about early Chinese prosodic features (all sound features which are not segmental, such as tone, stress and intonation), in particular the crucial area where segmental and prosodic features influence each other. Nevertheless, it is generally agreed that certain broad trends in the development from Archaic through Ancient to Modern Chinese can be identified, and that individual modern Chinese dialectal groups preserve some features of earlier pronunciation while departing from others. Thus, it is taken that Archaic Chinese had a rich system of consonants and simple vowels which generally became reduced, with earlier contrasts having shifted to the tonal area, the development of complex vowels, etc. Among modern dialects, those spoken in the coastal region of southern China are said to have preserved most faithfully earlier final consonants and tonal classes, and those of central and eastern China initial consonants. Northern Chinese dialects, especially the dialect spoken in Beijing and vicinity, which has become the basis of Modern Standard Chinese, are thought to have departed the furthest from the phonological features of Archaic and Ancient Chinese, their characteristic property being very simple segmental and prosodic syllable structure.   *P.K.*

Chinese dialects and Modern Standard Chinese

Modern Chinese dialects are distributed geographically in two zones. One is the southeastern part of China delimited roughly by the Yangtze River in the north, the sea in the south and the east, and a line running generally in the northeasterly direction towards the Yangtze from the border between China and Vietnam. The other zone is the rest of the country or rather that part of it where Chinese or *Han* (as opposed to the languages spoken by national minorities, such as Tibetan, Mongolian, etc.) is spoken, i.e. the whole of the area north of the Yangtze, and the region south of the Yangtze in the southwest.

The southeastern zone is characterized by great dialectal diversity. Although it is much the smaller of the two zones, it is very densely populated and, in view of its coastal nature, it is the cradle of most members of the Chinese communities which became established outside China proper, especially in Southeast Asia. Six large groups of dialects are recognized in this zone, spoken by about 30 per cent of the *Han* population of China proper (the total number of *Han* speakers is not known; when the last dialectal survey was completed in 1958, it was estimated at over 540 million), and also by the majority of overseas Chinese:

Wu dialects (9 per cent) spoken mainly in southern Jiangsu and in Zhejiang, further sub-divided into Northern (most prominently represented by Shanghai dialect) and Southern;
Xiang dialects (5 per cent), largely of Hunan, further divided into Old and New (including the dialect of Changsha);
Gan dialects (3 per cent) spoken mainly in Jiangxi;
Kejia or Hakka dialects (4 per cent) spoken in large scattered areas in Guangxi and Guangdong;
Yüe or Cantonese dialects (5 per cent), mainly of Guangdong, and including the dialects spoken in Canton and Hong Kong;
Min or Fujianese dialects (4 per cent), further divided into Northern and Southern, spoken mainly in Fujian, and by the indigenous Chinese population of the islands close to China's mainland, including Hainan and Taiwan.

The vast northern and southwestern zone is linguistically much more cohesive, and mainly because the centre of China's political power has shifted to its northern part, it has become the base area of the emerging standard language. The dialects of this zone are generally referred to as Northern Chinese or Mandarin dialects, and they are spoken by about 70 per cent of the *Han* population. They are further divided into four sub-groups: the Northern sub-group of the dialects of Hebei (including Beijing), Shandong,

Henan, and the whole northeastern part of China; the North-western sub-group spoken in Shanxi, Shaanxi and the rest of the country to the west of these two provinces; the Southwestern sub-group of the dialects of Sichuan, Hubei, Yunnan, Guizhou and the remaining area to the west; and the *Xiajiang* sub-group of dialects spoken mainly in Anhui and Jiangsu.

The degree of difference between Chinese dialects is more like that between the languages belonging to one of the Indo-European groups (such as, for example, the Romance languages), rather than between the dialects of any one of them. The differences are basically of three kinds. The most striking is that of pronouncing differently what are by their origin syllables representing the same morphemes. For example, the word for 'difficult' is pronounced *nan* in Beijing, *le* in Yangzhou (a *Xiajiang* Mandarin dialect), *lan* in Changsha, and *ne* in Suzhou (a Northern *Wu* dialect); they are all derived from the same Ancient Chinese word which was probably pronounced *nan*, and they are written with the same character. This provides Chinese dialects with the most significant kind of superficial distinction, but also one which is most easily overcome when communication between speakers of different dialects is attempted. The second kind of difference is that of the choice between different related items in the lexical stock characterizing an earlier historical stage of the language. For example, the most common word for 'to fear' is *pa* in Beijing, and *kiang* (corresponding to the Modern Standard Chinese pronunciation *jing*) in Fuzhou (a *Min* dialect of the Northern sub-group); both words are contained in the lexical stock of Ancient Chinese, and although the speakers of each of the two modern dialects prefer their respective word, they recognize the other as a rare synonym. Thirdly, there are differences in grammar, that is, differences in the arrangement of words within sentences, and the way in which the relationship between the words is indicated. Even though the last two kinds of differences are not as obvious as the first, they are more difficult to overcome, and they constitute the most substantial obstacle in communicating over dialectal boundaries.

Apart from this, there are differences of stylistic level rather than of kind. In the manner of languages such as those of the Romance group, where there are not only the specific differences between the individual languages as they developed from Vulgar Latin, but also those brought about in each of them by the continued influence of Classical Latin, in Chinese there are also dialectal differences related to the level of the early normative style of writing, besides differences in dialectal speech forms. The normative style, loosely corresponding to Classical Latin in the case of Romance languages, which is called *wenyan*, or Classical Chinese, was employed in most Chinese writing until 1919 (in some styles of writing, elements of it are still used now), and it was also taken as the source of the educated dialectal variants of style: the same

wenyan sentence has as many pronunciation variants as there are dialects. These variants are known as 'reading pronunciations', and they are often quite different from the corresponding speech forms (written in the same characters) in the same dialect. Apart from the 'horizontal' differences between dialects on each corresponding level of style, there are thus the 'vertical' differences of stylistic level within each dialect. The actual differences between dialects are then placed in points of intersection of these two dimensions. For example, the word for 'to fall' is pronounced *lao* (tones are disregarded in this example) in normal speech in Beijing dialect but it becomes *luo* in the 'reading pronunciation' of this dialect. In the dialect spoken in Taiyuan, which belongs to the North-western sub-group of Mandarin dialects, the pronunciation of this word has two variants, *lue* and *lua*, and there is no 'reading pronunciation'. In *Xiamen* dialect, which is one of the Southern *Min* dialects, the word is pronounced *lak* in the 'reading pronunciation', and either *lo* or *liok* otherwise. In Fuzhou, where a dialect of the Northern *Min* sub-group is spoken, the word is *lo* colloquially, and *lou* in the 'reading pronunciation'. Any conclusion about the difference between the dialects in the pronunciation of this word will obviously depend on which of the variants in each dialect is chosen for comparison. All are written with the same character.

In order to appreciate fully the complex relationship between modern Chinese dialects, it is further necessary to take into account the strong but uneven influence of prestigious local dialectal variants, such as the influence of Shanghai dialect on other dialects in the *Wu* group, and, finally, the growing influence of Modern Standard Chinese. These influences contribute to the relative ease with which educated speakers of different Chinese dialects, especially those who come into contact with a broad variety of people in their life, communicate with each other. However, the ease disappears progressively in indirect proportion to received education and social mobility: people of different dialectal groups at the other end of the range have as much difficulty in oral communication as uneducated speakers of, say, different Romance languages.

One of the reasons why the educated reading pronunciation variants developed in Chinese dialects is that there had not existed in China until the 1920s a standard form of oral communication corresponding to the written standard *wenyan*. Although it gradually became the accepted requirement for officials during the past few centuries of imperial China to use the language of the court, that is, the polite variant of Beijing dialect, in formal oral contact throughout the country, this was obviously a standard in a very limited sense. Nevertheless, this ill-defined variant of Beijing dialect known as *guanhua* or Mandarin (both the Chinese and English terms are at times still used to refer to Modern Standard Chinese outside China), became the forerunner of the modern standard.

This, however, emerged gradually in China only under the influence of the concept of European standard languages and the importance of their role in modern society, which was imported into China after the Western impact in the middle of the 19th century. With the demise of the imperial rule, the formation, definition and application of Modern Standard Chinese became part of the larger political and cultural movement aimed at emancipating and modernizing China.

The concept of Modern Standard Chinese was, in the first place, linked closely with the rejection in 1919 of the *wenyan* written standard and its replacement by *baihua*, the vernacular written style, which had a similar background to the oral standard: it was based on earlier traditions of the style of popular fiction but primarily inspired by the models of European literary languages. *Baihua* became one of the foundations of Modern Standard Chinese, and the new literature using it as its vehicle is still referred to when the oral standard is defined. The history of Modern Standard Chinese is also closely connected with the movement for the

DIALECTS

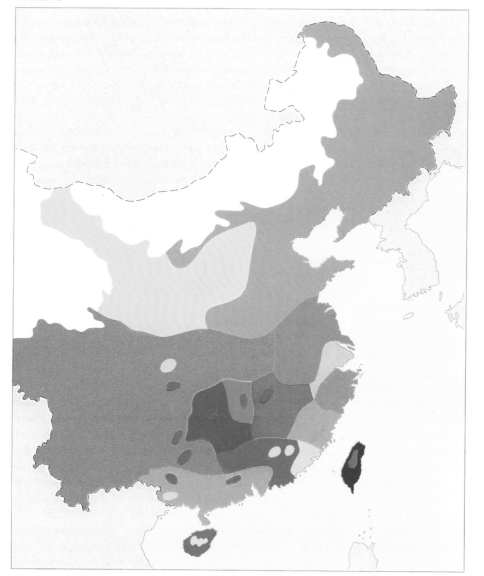

KEY

Northern Mandarin

Northwestern Mandarin

Southwestern Mandarin

Xia-Jiang Mandarin

Northern Wu dialects

Southern Wu dialects

Gan dialects

Old Xiang dialects

New Xiang dialects

Cantonese Yue dialects

Southern Min dialects

Northern Min dialects

Hakka (Kejia) dialects

Other languages

reform of the script and national enlightenment in general, since the widespread use of the oral standard was seen from the beginning of the movement in the early years of this century as the necessary condition of its success.

The immediate predecessor of Modern Standard Chinese as it is understood today was *guoyu* or National Language (the term is still used in Taiwan and often also outside China), first launched in 1919. It was based on Beijing dialect, and its relatively sophisticated concept, together with the lack of a sufficiently strong centralized state machinery necessary to implement it thoroughly, were responsible for its failing to become a generally accepted oral standard. Another reason why it did not succeed fully was that it became associated with right-wing political groups, and it was consequently opposed by many prominent intellectuals. The movement for the oral standard was interrupted by the civil war and the war against Japan, and not revived until after 1949. In its present form, Modern Standard Chinese or *putonghua* is the result of a compromise between *guoyu* aims and earlier left-wing views on language issues. It is firmly based on Beijing dialect but it tends to embrace a wider variety of dialectal features, and it is seen as anchored in the whole of post-1919 literature. Since its promulgation is viewed as the basic condition for achieving the success of the language policies of the People's Republic of China, which themselves constitute an important part of the general political programme, it has had the full support of the state, and it is now very close to reaching the status and application corresponding to those of a European oral standard, in all aspects of life in China. *P.K.*

The evolution of Chinese writing

Recent archaeological finds have shown that Chinese writing existed as far back as 4000 or 5000 BC which seems to add more weight to the claim that Chinese is the world's oldest written language.

Since the mid-1950s a number of Neolithic sites have been discovered in north China. Among the Neolithic pottery wares found are some bearing the signs and symbols of the two main types of early writing, both of which are closely linked with later writings on oracle bones and bronze wares. The earliest known examples of Chinese writing are ideographic signs found on Neolithic pottery wares unearthed in Banpo, near Xi'an in Shaanxi. The pottery has been established by the radiocarbon method of dating as belonging to the Yangshao culture, which existed between 8000 and 5000 BC, and the writing closely resembles signs inscribed on bronze wares of the Shang-Yin and Zhou periods. The other main type of early writing—pictorial signs—was found on Neolithic pottery vessels unearthed at Quxian in Shandong. Radiocarbon dating

has established that these wares belong to the Dawenkou culture, which probably coexisted with the Yangshao. The particular examples discovered are dated about 3000–4000 BC.

In the absence of commonly accepted terms these two earliest types of writing may be referred to as Early Proto-Characters and Late Proto-Characters respectively, and can be regarded as the forerunners of Chinese ideograms as we know them. The evolution of Chinese writing is summarized in the table overleaf, and from this it is evident that both the primitive types of Chinese writing are closely linked with *guwen*, or Archaic Characters (2690–827 BC), and the later forms of writing.

The development of Chinese writing has always followed a cycle of elaboration and specialization followed by simplification and standardization, and then elaboration and standardization. What seems to be unique about the Chinese script is the extremely long period of total stabilization of the *kaishu*, or Standard Characters, which have remained unchanged from AD 220 to the present.

R.S.W.H.

Categories of Chinese characters

Traditionally Chinese characters have been classified into the following categories known as *liushu*, Six Types of Writing. These categories were first introduced by Xu Shen (AD 58?–147?), the compiler of the first Chinese dictionary (*Shuowenjiezi*), in AD 121.

Xiangxing, pictograms
These are pictures of natural and artificial objects, animals, plants, human forms and parts of the human body. Some of the earlier forms were quite elaborate and realistic, but have since become highly stylized. However, a fair number of pictograms are still discernible even in their present forms.

Zhishi, simple ideograms
Some of these are pure signs in logical or abstracted terms, for example, *san* (three) consists of three horizontal lines and *zhong* (middle) is indicated by a vertical line going through the middle of a rectangle. Others are pictograms modified by signs, for example, *ren* (the sharp edge of a knife) is represented by a picture of a knife with an indicator pointing to that particular part of the object, and *ben* (root, basis) is a picture of a tree with an indicator pointing to the bottom part.

Huiyi, compound ideograms
These are combinations of two or more ideograms denoting abstract concepts. For example, *dan*, which means 'dawn', is indicated by the sun above the horizon; *kan* which means 'to

look', is represented by 'a hand over the eye' and is considered one of the most expressive ideographs. *Xiu*, 'to rest', is represented by a man reclining against a tree; when two trees are put together it is *lin*, 'grove', and three trees make *sen*, 'forest'.

Xingsheng, phonograms

These consist of one or more semantic elements of which one is the radical indicating the general category of meaning, and one phonetic element which may contain two or more parts, giving the sound (sometimes just the final vowel without the initial consonant). It is the combination of the semantic and the phonetic elements that indicates the precise meaning. For example, *jian*, to fry, and *ao*, to stew, share the semantic element *huo*, 'fire', and denote different ways of cooking. *Yuan*, garden, and *pu*, vegetable garden, share the semantic element *wei*, an enclosed piece of land, and are differentiated by the phonetic elements *yuan* and *fu*—the former retaining both the initial consonant and the final vowel of the original and the latter retaining only the final vowel.

EVOLUTION OF CHINESE WRITING

Description	Period	Examples
		meaning: five / seven / eight / sun / mountain / moon / cloud / horse / listen / shut / fly / protect / dust
Early proto-characters (*Banpo taowen*)	4000–5000BC[1]	five, seven, eight
Late proto-characters (*Dawenkou taowen*)	3000–4000BC[1]	sun, mountain
Archaic characters (*Guwen*)	2690–827BC	five, seven, eight, sun, mountain, moon, cloud, horse, listen, shut, fly
Great Seal characters (*Dazhuan*)	827–221BC	five, seven, eight, sun, mountain, moon, cloud, horse, listen, shut, fly, protect
Small Seal characters (*Xiaozhuan*)	213–206BC	five, seven, eight, sun, mountain, moon, cloud, horse, listen, shut, fly, protect, dust
Scribe characters (*Lishu*)	206BC–AD353	五 七 八 日 山 月 雲 馬 聽 關 飛 護 塵
Standard characters (*Kaishu*)	AD220–present	五 七 八 日 山 月 雲 馬 聽 關 飛 護 塵
Cursive script (*Caoshu*)	46BC–present	五 七 八 日 山 月 雲 馬 聽 關 飛 護 塵
Running script (*Xingshu*)	AD353–present	五 七 八 日 山 月 雲 馬 聽 關 飛 護 塵
Unorthodox characters (*Sutizi*)	c. AD1000–present	云 馬 听 関 孫 護
Modern simplified characters (*Jiantizi*)	1956–present[2]	云 马 听 关 飞 护 尘

[1]Range   [2]Mainland China only

The phonetic element *tong* is used in both *tong*, 'paulownia', and *tong*, 'copper', which sound identical, but whose meanings are differentiated by the semantic elements *mu*—'tree, wood', and *jin*—'gold, metal'.

The making of the phonograms represents the most productive method of coining new characters out of existing components, and 90 per cent of Chinese characters belong to this category, including a large number of entirely new characters created since the 19th century, such as those denoting chemical elements.

Jiajie, phonetic loans

These are extended uses of existing characters. The borrowed characters usually retain their original sounds but are sometimes given slightly modified pronunciation. For example, *ling*, 'to give an order', is extended to mean 'the person who gives orders' and then 'a county magistrate', but the same meaning can also be imparted to an unrelated character *chang*, 'long, lasting', of which the pronunciation is changed to *zhang* in the new use.

Zhuanzhu, derivative characters

These are synonymous characters that are used as mutually interpretative items in dictionary entries. Most are closely associated both semantically and phonetically and some even share the same radicals. For example, both *kao* and *lao* mean 'old' and are listed under the *lao* radical. But *kao* later acquired the extended meaning 'to examine', (derived from its original meaning 'old' because in ancient times youngsters were usually examined by their elders). As a result, *kao* has been used exclusively to mean 'to examine' in the modern language. The membership of this category is very small, but the Six Types of Writing would be incomplete without it.   *R.S.W.H.*

The Chinese writing system

The components of characters

The great majority of Chinese characters consist of two elements: the radical, which gives an idea of the meaning, and the phonetic, which gives some clue to the sound. The radical provides semantic information of the classificatory kind. For instance, the water radical denotes a form of liquid, the gold radical denotes gold or metal, and the heart radical refers to emotions. In conventional Chinese dictionaries characters are grouped according to these radicals.

The term 'phonetic' needs some qualification, as it does not always give the pronunciation of a full syllable but sometimes merely a final vowel without an initial consonant.

Most radicals can no longer function as full characters. Those which can often have their graphic form slightly modified when serving as mere components. Some radicals can also serve as phonetics either singly or combined. The precise meaning of a character is determined by the combination of its semantic and phonetic elements.

The graphic structure of characters

Chinese writing is almost entirely based on the brush, which because of its sharp point can effect thick and thin strokes and thus dictates the entire process in writing Chinese characters. The basic strokes in Chinese writing, and the basic constructions of Chinese characters are summarized in the tables overleaf. There has always been a difference between the standard written form, which is executed with a brush, and the standard printed form, which is done by engraving, although the Beijing government has been trying to reduce the difference since 1956. The traditional way of writing Chinese characters has been in vertical columns from right to left, but since 1956 in mainland China the practice in writing and printing has changed to the Western manner of horizontally from left to right.

Modern writing reforms

The first systematic effort to simplify the characters in modern times was made by a group of linguists led by Qian Xuantong (1887–1939) in 1934 when a proposal was drafted for the adoption of some 2400 simplified characters. In 1936 the Nationalist Ministry of Education officially approved the first list of 324 simplified characters. However, this was not consolidated upon because of conservative opposition and due to the outbreak of the Sino-Japanese War of 1937–45.

After the establishment of the People's Republic in 1949 the government in Beijing saw the need to eliminate illiteracy. It was apparent that the traditional characters, the use of which had been confined to the intelligentsia who could afford to spend the necessary years to master them, were too numerous and too complex for the majority of people to learn. In an effort to make written Chinese accessible to everyone, a Committee for Reforming the Chinese Written Language was set up in 1954. In the following year, three important decisions were made: to simplify the Chinese characters; to propagate the Common Speech (*putonghua*), and to implement the Scheme for a Chinese Phonetic Alphabet, or *Hanyu pinyin*. Under the first measure a total of about 2200 simplified characters has been introduced since 1956. Some of these were further modified in 1964 and in 1986. In developing these simplified characters, the seven different methods shown in Appendix D were used.

They are: (1) reviving a simpler ancient form of an existing character; (2) standardizing characters with more than one form by

BASIC STROKES IN CHINESE WRITING

Description	Stroke and its variations	Examples
Horizontal stroke	一	一 十 上
Vertical stroke	丨	十 工 下
Downstroke to the left	ノ ノ ノ	千 人 月 六
Downstroke to the right	ヽ ﹨	人 又 這
A dot	ヽ ゝ ⺌	主 心 黑 以
A tick	ノ ⼂	河 地 把
A hook	亅 ⺆ ㇆	小 衣 成 狗
Horizontal with a hook	㇖	字 常 皮
Angle open to the left	⊓ フ フ フ ㇉ ㇓ ㇌ ㇎ ㇐	五 口 又 刀 月 乙 風 奶 陣
Angle open to the right	㇄ ㇄ ㇄ ㇄ ㇄ ㇄ く	七 山 元 弟 毋 公 女

BASIC CONSTRUCTIONS OF CHINESE CHARACTERS

Horizontal combinations			Vertical combinations			Total or partial enclosures		
	朵	忠		北	林		疾	康
	官	究		濃	披		勻	匍
	黑	墾		劉	都		建	遵
	荒	鼻		腳	謝		起	題
	茄	霜		騎	脂		區	匾
	替	怒		部	魏		聞	鳳
							凶	幽
							圍	圈

endorsing that which is easiest to write and in some cases further simplifying it; (3) giving official status to a large number of hitherto non-standard characters including those in *caoshu*, or cursive script, *xingshu*, or running script, and *sutizi*, or unorthodox characters (see under Calligraphy); (4) abbreviating the components (the radicals, or semantic elements, and the phonetic elements) of existing characters; (5) deleting a part or parts, sometimes substantial, of existing characters; (6) assigning one character to the roles of two or more homophonous ones and in some cases further simplifying it; and (7) creating new characters by altering the basic principles of the construction of existing characters.

There have been criticisms of some characters created by several of these methods on the grounds that their simplification has been achieved at the expense of distinctiveness. Indeed, their creators were so anxious to lessen the effort to acquire and produce them that they overlooked other equally important factors: their reception and discrimination. As a consequence, redundancy is reduced to zero or below zero and this causes communication failures to occur. *R.S.W.H.*

Calligraphy

Chinese calligraphy is the way of the brush, a most responsive and versatile instrument with an almost limitless range of stylistic expression. The Chinese brush is made of animal hairs attached to a stem usually of bamboo or wood. The distinctive feature of the Chinese brush is that the tuft always culminates in a sharp point, in contrast to the spread brush used by Western painters. This enables the infinite range of thick and thin strokes on which Chinese calligraphy is based.

The various styles of Chinese calligraphy are discussed in chronological order, as listed in the table on p. 330 on the evolution of Chinese writing.

Guwen, Archaic Characters

This is a collective name for the so-called *Jiaguwen*, or Shell-and-bone Characters, inscribed on tortoise shells and oracle bones of the Shang-Yin period, as well as those found on bronze wares, stone drums and pottery wares of the Zhou period up to 827 BC. They are mainly pictorial and ideographic.

Dazhuan, Great Seal Characters

This style, sometimes called *Zhouwen*, was devised during the Zhou period by a court recorder named Zhou, who codified the then existing writing systems into a standard vocabulary of some 9000 characters. Examples are found in the inscriptions on bronze wares, stone tablets and pottery wares of this period.

Xiaozhuan, Small Seal Characters

The first emperor of the Qin dynasty, who unified China under a strong central government in 221 BC, had his prime minister Li Si devise a single writing system to be used throughout the empire. It was to be the first uniform script for all China. There are three main features of this revolutionary move: first, variant forms of characters, which existed before the Qin period and which could amount to several dozen in number, were abolished and only one form was adopted as the standard; second, the sizes and shapes of characters were made to conform to a uniform size in an upright position; third, characters were made to adhere strictly to symmetry and geometric forms and the strokes were evenly executed. The Small Seal Characters represent an important step in the evolution of Chinese writing in marking a clear move towards formalism.

Lishu, Clerical Characters

With the establishment of a central government and with the extension of the empire's frontiers, the Small Seal Characters proved to be too cumbersome for administrative efficiency and a script with more easily and quickly executed characters was perfected by Cheng Miao. This was the first script to use the brush to full advantage. The strokes of the characters are deliberately uneven and wavy with terminations ending in a decided flick. Little if any effort is directed towards balance and symmetry while distortions and exaggerations are deliberately introduced to enhance the formal appeal of the characters. The complex strokework of the *lishu* belies appearances and cannot be fully appreciated by the uninitiated. It is undoubtedly the most elaborate and most difficult of all styles of Chinese calligraphy to execute.

Caoshu, Cursive Script

The *caoshu* was born of the need for a 'quick version' of the *lishu*, due to its being highly time-consuming and thus unsuitable for everyday purposes. There have been many types of cursive script devised under different names for both practical and artistic reasons, which are collectively described as *caoshu*. The most common and most representative variety is known as *jincao*, or Modern Cursive Script. The principle of *caoshu* in general and *jincao* in particular is that in its execution the size of individual characters can be enlarged or reduced and the strokes freely modified or eliminated altogether. Furthermore, the strokes within each character and in neighbouring characters, which are normally independent of one another, may be joined together. As a result, a whole line composed of many characters may be written with one continuous application of the brush. A criticism of the cursive script, particularly the erratic types, is that the characters are often illegible to the layman, and sometimes to experts. It therefore defeats its primary purpose of saving writing time, and calligraphers practise it mainly as a means of artistic expression. Readers appreciate it in the same way as they may look at an abstract painting, for its practical value has virtually been lost.

Kaishu, the Standard Characters

Though it was a great leap forward, *caoshu* went too far to answer everyday needs; some way had to be found to bridge the gap. In the third quarter of the 1st century AD *kaishu*, which began as a modification of the *lishu* with an eye to its general adaptability to ordinary requirements, came into being. It is reputedly the work of Wang Cizhong, a man of whose life and career we know nothing. This somewhat modest scheme gradually developed into a script embodying all the aesthetic qualities of a long tradition while shedding the excessive ornateness and complexity of its predecessors. Being easy to execute, the script also suited everyday purposes. It therefore rose to be *the* script of the Chinese written language and has remained the norm. It has been alternatively called *kaishu* (Standard Characters), *zhenshu* (Regular Characters) and *zhengshu* (Orthodox Characters).

Xingshu, Running Script

Xingshu was reputedly devised by Liu Desheng of the Later Han period and is a cross between the Standard Characters and the near-abstract, sometimes erratic Cursive Script. Generally, the characters in the Running Script style are more or less uniform in size and there is less variation in the thickness of individual strokes. The strokes within each character are sometimes joined together, but individual characters remain independent of one another. As a result, although the strokes have been simplified to some extent, they are still discernible to the reader. This happy compromise enables characters to be written at a fair speed with no loss of legibility. Furthermore, in executing the characters the calligrapher is still allowed sufficient freedom for personal expression. *Xingshu* has therefore become the most popular style, and is widely used in writing manuscripts, personal letters and other informal papers.

Sutizi, Unorthodox Characters

Although *kaishu* has been the norm for all formal uses since AD 200, since about AD 1000 simplified forms have existed for most of the frequently used characters, some of which are drastically abbreviated. These Unorthodox Characters resulted from the need to produce a large number of characters within a short space of time. Although these simplified characters had never been officially approved, they had been widely adopted for less formal uses, such as wood-block printing of popular novels, for nearly a thousand years. In 1956 the government in Beijing decided to adopt a large number of Unorthodox Characters in their original or modified forms as one measure to reform the Chinese written language. Consequently, what were regarded as unorthodox forms have become, along with some newly introduced ones, the standard forms in mainland China.

The *sutizi*, usually not mentioned in works on Chinese writing and calligraphy, represent an important link between the *kaishu* and the Modern Simplified Characters, without which some of the new simplified forms cannot be properly explained.

Jiantizi, Modern Simplified Characters

Jiantzi normally refers to a group of 2200 abbreviated characters of different origins which were officially introduced by the Beijing government from 1956. Their use is largely confined to mainland China and, to some extent, Singapore and Malaysia.

Metaphors, allusions and proverbial phrases

The Chinese language is immensely rich in metaphors, allusions and proverbial phrases, which have become a natural and indispensable part of everyday language.

The great majority of these expressions are in the classical style, which is highly suitable for the purpose because of its terseness. Many of them can be traced back to the time of Confucius and even those in colloquial style have been in existence for hundreds of years. All the examples given below are in current use and have a relatively high frequency.

Metaphors and allusions

The majority of Chinese idiomatic expressions falls into this category, and this also includes similes for the simple reason that they cannot be easily differentiated from the rest in the frequent absence of words equivalent to *like*, *as* or *such* in English. Over nine-tenths of these expressions are in four syllables, and this has proved to be the optimum size and therefore the most productive pattern for such idioms, which range from a normal phrase to a complete sentence. Some Chinese metaphorical expressions may seem novel to Western people because of cultural differences, while others will seem familiar:

Qīng chū yú lán, ér shèng yú lán: indigo blue is extracted from the indigo plant (yet is bluer than the plant it comes from)—the pupil surpasses the teacher.

Xian rù wéi zhŭ: he who enters first becomes the master—first impressions stick.

Yī zhēn jiàn xuě draw blood with one prick of the needle—hit the nail on the head.

Gé xuē sāo yǎng: scratch an itch from outside one's boot—attempt an ineffective solution.

Proverbial phrases

Chinese proverbial expressions, which are normally full sentences, consist of five or more syllables, although they are not always quoted in full. On the whole, they may strike the Western reader as being less original than the metaphorical expressions, for many of them resemble existing proverbs in English and other European languages so closely that they may read like literal translations. This is because they refer to the same universal truths. The examples given below are chosen to reflect the Chinese way of thinking in presentation, if not in content.

Qiǎo fù nán wéi wú mǐ zhī chuī: even a clever housewife cannot cook without rice—you can't make bricks without straw.

Zhǐ bāo bu zhù huǒ: you cannot wrap fire in paper—there is no concealing the truth; the truth will out.

Yī ge bā zhang pai bu xiang: you cannot clap with one hand—it takes two to make a quarrel.

Wǔ shí bù xiào bǎi bù: one retreating 50 paces mocks one retreating 100—the pot calling the kettle black.

Xiehouyu

Xiehouyu is roughly equivalent to aposiopesis in English. It is a two-part allegorical saying of which the first part, always stated, is descriptive while the second part, sometimes unstated, carries the message. These highly expressive sayings, of which some are based on puns, add colour and humour to the language although their use is strictly confined to everyday conversation.

Hé shang dǎ sǎn, wú fǎ wú tiān: like a Buddhist monk holding an umbrella, no hair (law) nor Heaven. Since a Buddhist monk must have a shaven head, he is without hair (which is homophonous with the word 'law'), and since he is sheltered from the weather he is immune from Heaven's law: defy laws human and divine; be absolutely lawless; run wild.

Xiázi chī húntun, xīnli yǒu shù: like a blind man eating a bowl of dumplings who knows exactly how many he has eaten (as he is free from distractions, a blind man counts better than one who can see)—be perfectly clear in one's own mind about the real situation.

Yǎba chī huánglián, yǒu kǔ shuō buchū: like a mute eating gentian [a bitter herb]—be unable to tell one's bitter experience; be compelled to suffer in silence.

Newly coined idioms

Newly coined idioms, which came into being during the past three decades, should not be ignored as their use is extensive in mainland China. Most of them are modified versions of conventional idiomatic expressions, classical or otherwise, and new uses for old words, but some are highly colloquial. A large number of these have been attributed to Mao Zedong.

Yī qióng èr bái: both poor and blank; economically poor and culturally blank (a phrase used by Mao in 1958 to indicate that China is not developed economically and is like a blank paper on which the new can be written).

Gǔ wèi jīn yòng, yáng wèi Zhong yòng: make the past serve the present; make foreign things serve China.

Liǎng tiáo tuǐ zǒu lù: walking on two legs (referring to a series of policies for balancing the relations between industry and agriculture, heavy and light industry, enterprises run by the central government and those run by local authorities, etc.).

Mǎyǐ kěn gútou: ants gnawing at a bone—use a concentration of small machine tools to make huge machines; plod away at a large task little by little.

Bù pò bù lì: no destruction, no creation—no omelette without breaking eggs.

R.S.W.H.

Personal and family names

The names by which a Chinese is known are various and complex. The *xing*, or surname, is that of the family into which one is born or adopted; it usually consists of one syllable represented by one character, though there are some surnames composed of two characters. The *ming*, or personal name, is usually in two characters but may be only one. Together they make up the name by which a Chinese is formally known, and the compound *xing-ming* is used to refer to one's full name. But it is normally impolite for anyone except a person's elders or superiors to address him by his *ming*, so for social purposes the *zi*, or 'style', is used in its place. In addition to these names many Chinese have a *hao*, or sobriquet, which is acquired later in life, either chosen by the person or conferred upon him by others. In Chinese the surname is written or spoken first. Normal Chinese names of Han origin have a minimum of two and a maximum of four characters, but the great majority of them consist of a monosyllabic surname and a dissyllabic personal nam.-

The earliest family names can be traced back some 4700 years to Huang Di, the Yellow Emperor, who gave 12 different names to his sons. From these 12 names, clan and family names developed and there have been about 6000 such names in Chinese history. According to a recent handbook published by the Chinese Post Office, there exists today a total of 5730 Chinese surnames of which 3470 are monosyllabic (mostly of Han nationality) and 2260 are polysyllabic (chiefly of minority nationalities). However, the most common ones amount to only about 400 and the following five major surnames constitute approximately one-fifth of the total Han population in North China: *Zhang, Wang, Li, Zhao* and *Liu*. The origins of these surnames were mainly symbols of clans or their leaders, which were associated with certain virtues, events or achievements, places, official positions held by individuals and natural objects worshipped.

Given names, which can be in either one or two characters (two being much more common), can in theory be freely chosen from the Chinese lexicon of over 56 000 items, although there are certain guiding rules which are sometimes followed, e.g. the differentiation of male and female names, the indication of ranks in a clan, the seniority among brothers and sisters in a family, and trends or vogues associated with particular periods or regions. Consequently, Chinese given names are much more informative than Western ones. Individual characters in Chinese given names can have meaning at three different levels: first, their original meanings as monosyllabic words; second, their combined meanings in the dissyllabic compound if consisting of two characters; and third, in some cases where the monosyllabic or dissyllabic surname can be joined together to form a phrase, clause or sentence, this can carry some special meaning or meanings.

Mao Zedong

Mao Zedong was both his original and official name. The monosyllabic surname Mao means 'hair, fur', and the dissyllabic given name Zedong means 'watery place' or 'blessing' and 'east' separately, and either 'east of the watery place' or 'a blessing for the east' jointly. He also had a *zi*, or 'style', Runzhi, which is derived from the given name and which means 'to moisten, to enrich' and 'it, them, subordinative particle' separately, and 'to enrich it (or them)' jointly. The latter name was used only by his seniors and close friends.

Zhou Enlai

Zhou Enlai was both his original and official name. The monosyllabic surname Zhou, apart from being the name of a dynasty, also means 'circuit, circumference, vicinity', and the dissyllabic given name Enlai means 'grace, favour' and 'to come, to arrive' separately and 'favour forthcoming' jointly. He had a *zi*, or style, Xiangyu, which means 'hover in the universe'.

Deng Xiaoping

Deng Xiaoping was originally named Deng Xiansheng according to his family register and his three brothers and three sisters have the same character *xian* as the first element of their given names. At school he was called Deng Xixian and also known as Deng Bin, but his official name has been Deng Xiaoping in adult life.

According to the Chinese tradition dating back thousands of years, although a man can have a great number of alternative given names, he would never change his family name except under extraordinary circumstances, such as being ordered to do so by imperial decree or being married into a wealthy family without a male heir on condition that he carry on the name of his future wife's family.

However, a new trend has developed in Communist China. It is now fairly common for a Communist Party member to have a number of pseudonyms and later use one of them as his official name, abandoning his original family name and given name completely; and parents and children do not always share the same family name. In both cases the purpose seems to be the concealment of the real identities of individuals:

Hua Guofeng

According to unofficial reports, his original name was Su Zhu. The monosyllabic surname Su means 'to revive; the name of an ancient state in north China', and the monosyllabic given name Zhu means 'casting, founding'. His official name Hua Guofeng is said to have been chosen by him in the late 1930s on joining the Chinese Communist Party. The monosyllabic surname Hua means 'China, flower; ostentation', and the dissyllabic given name Guofeng means 'nation, national' and 'the sharp point or cutting edge; van' separately, and 'national vanguard' jointly. It is supposed to be an abbreviation of Zhonghua Kang Ri Jiuguo Xianfengdui (Chinese Vanguards in Resisting Japanese Aggression and Saving the Country), of which he was a member. His four children are understood to have retained his original family name Su.   *R.S.W.H.*

Transcription

The earliest attempt to transcribe Chinese with a Western script was made in 1605 by the Italian Jesuit missionary Matteo Ricci (1552–1610). Since then more than 50 different systems have been devised, including several created by the Chinese themselves. Today there are no less than 21 international and European systems in current use.

The first and only non-Latin system of transcription officially adopted by the Chinese Government was called *Zhuyin Zimu* or

'Pronunciation Alphabet' (later changed to *Zhuyin Fuhao* or 'Pronunciation Symols'). It was introduced in 1918 using a set of simple, ancient forms of characters instead of letters of the Latin script. This became the standard system for marking pronunciation in dictionaries and textbooks in China until 1958 when it was replaced by the government of the People's Republic with a Latin system called *Hanyu Pinyin*, which literally means 'Chinese Spelling' or 'Chinese Spelled', and which has been generally known in the West simply as *pinyin*. *Zhuyin Fuhao* is still used in Taiwan and some other areas.

However, the most widely used system for over 100 years has been the Wade-Giles System. It was first devised by Sir Thomas Francis Wade (1818–95) in 1859 and later revised by Herbert Allen Giles (1845–1935) in 1892. Despite its many technical shortcomings it has been the only truly 'international' system adopted by both the Chinese and people in the West. Although Beijing officially abolished the deep-rooted Wade-Giles System even for 'external' use in 1979, it is still being used in Taiwan, Hong Kong and many other parts of the world. Furthermore, it has also been the system used in virtually all the published materials on China in English, and in the catalogues and indexes in many libraries, museums and other institutions.

The application of the Wade-Giles System is complicated by the existence of another form, known as the Postal System, which has been used exclusively for spelling Chinese geographical names. It was first introduced by the Chinese Postal Administration in 1906 and officially abolished by the People's Republic of China for external use in 1979, but it is still retained in Taiwan and some other areas. The Postal Romanization System differs from the Wade-Giles System in two main aspects: 1) that all hyphens, aspirates, diacritical marks, etc., have been abolished, and 2) that a Southern pronunciation, which is called the Nanjing syllabary by the Giles' Dictionary, is used to substitute the original Northern pronunciation, such as 'k' and 'ts' for 'ch'. As a result, it has produced some very wide discrepancies in spelling.

The existence of some well-established irregular forms of transliteration also adds to the confusion. They include the anglicized forms of loan-words, such as kowtow instead of *ketou*; the latinized forms of a small number of Chinese personal names in many European languages, such as Confucius instead of Kongfuzi; and the dialect readings of certain names in English, such as Sun Yat-sen instead of Sun Yixian.

In addition to these systems, two other systems which were used primarily for teaching purposes are worth mentioning. The first, *Guoyu Luomazi* (or GR)—alternatively spelled *Gwoyeu Romatzyh*—was devised by the Chinese and first introduced in 1928 as the Second Form of the National Phonetic Alphabet. It is the only system that incorporates tonal spelling, thereby doing away with diacritical marks. However, because of its complicated rules of spelling, it has never been very popular in China or abroad. Even in Taiwan, where it still has the nominal status of an alternative system of national transcription, the authorities felt it necessary to simplify it by abolishing its distinctive tonal spelling in 1984. It was used by some linguists in Britain and the United States for teaching spoken Chinese with some success from the late 1940s to the 1960s, but has now almost completely died out. The second system, the Yale University System, was introduced in 1943 and was widely used in the United States until the late 1960s, when it was gradually replaced by *Hanyu pinyin*.

Today a student of Chinese needs to know at least two major systems of romanization: *Hanyu pinyin* for current materials, especially those from mainland China, and Wade-Giles for words and names used in older and sometimes even current references, including those found in catalogues and indexes. Knowledge is also needed of the Postal System for Chinese geographical names that deviate from the Wade-Giles System. (See also Appendix C.)

R.S.W.H.

Dictionaries

There are about 56 000 Chinese characters in existence, of which fewer than 10 000 are still in use. A desk dictionary lists some 11 000 items and a Chinese intellectual uses between 6000 and 7000 characters. A learner of the language needs to know a minimum of 1200 to 1500 characters in order to read non-classical texts.

Words do not always coincide with characters, for over 50 per cent of the 'words' in Modern Standard Chinese consist of two or more characters or syllables, and there are no less than 450 000 words and idiomatic phrases in the classical language and some 50 000 in Modern Standard Chinese, although one can get by in everyday conversation with a vocabulary of merely 3500 words.

Chinese-Chinese dictionaries

The first Chinese dictionary, entitled *Shuowen Jiezi* (*Simple and Compound Characters Explained*), was compiled by the great etymologist Xu Shen (AD 58?–147?) and published in AD 121. It contains 9353 characters under 540 radicals. This method of classifying Chinese characters under radicals has since become the standard practice in most Chinese dictionaries, although many diversified systems have been developed.

Other major dictionaries of characters include the *Kangxi zidian* of 1716, compiled by Zhang Yushu, Chen Tingjing and others, with 49 174 entries. An important feature of this dictionary is that all characters listed are in *kaishu*, or Standard Characters, in the first dictionary; consequently, the 540 radicals were reduced to 214.

The *Zhonghua da zidian* of 1915, compiled by Ouyang Pucun and others, has 46 867 entries. It still is one of the authoritative sources on single characters although it will be superseded by the new *Hanyu da zidian*. For everyday purposes, however, the standard work on single characters is the *Xinhua zidian* (1st pub. Beijing, 1953; 6th rev. edn, 1987) which contains some 11 000 single characters and 35 000 compounds.

The most comprehensive encyclopedic dictionary of Chinese in conventional characters is *Zhongwen dacidian* compiled by Zhang Qiyun and others (Taipei, 1962–9, 40 vols.). It contains some 50 000 single characters and 370 000 compounds, including both classical and colloquial expressions. The most up-to-date encyclopedic dictionary of Chinese in simplified characters is the new version of *Cihai,* compiled by Xia Zhengnong and others (Shanghai, 1979, 3 vols.), with some 15 000 single characters and over 90 000 compounds. A supplementary volume has been added later (Shanghai, 1983). Another notable addition to this category is *Dacidian* published by the San Min Book Co. (Taipei, 1985, 3 vols.) with 15 106 single characters and 127 430 compounds.

The first dictionary of spoken Chinese was compiled by Li Jinxi and others, and entitled *Guoyu cidian* (Shanghai, 1943–75, 8 vols.). It has some 100 000 entries. It has been revised and enlarged by He Rong, Wang Xiyuan and others to represent the Taiwan and overseas norm (Taipei, 1981, 6 vols.). The mainland norm is represented by *Xiandai Hanyu cidian*, compiled by the Institute of Linguistics of the Chinese Academy of Sciences (Beijing, 1965; rev. edn, 1978). It contains about 53 000 entries. The latest and the most ambitious one of its kind is *Hanyu dacidian*, compiled under Luo Zhufeng (13 vols., vols. 1–2, Shanghai, 1986–7). The project began in 1975 and is expected to be completed in 1990. It will contain some 370 000 lexical items, both classical and modern.

One of the major dictionaries of classical Chinese is *Ciyuan* (1st pub., Shanghai, 1915; rev. edn, Beijing, 1979–81, 4 vols.). The most exhaustive dictionary of Chinese characters is the projected *Hanyu da zidian* (10 vols., vols. 1–6, Wuhan, 1986–9) which, when completed, will contain some 56 000 single characters, the largest collection to date.

Chinese-English dictionaries

The earliest work was Robert Morrison's *A Dictionary of the Chinese Language* (London and Macao, 1815–23, 6 vols.). It consists of three parts: Part 1 Chinese-English arranged according to radicals, Part 2 Chinese-English arranged alphabetically, and Part 3 English-Chinese. This was followed by Samuel Wells Williams' *An English-Chinese Vocabulary in the Court Language* (Shanghai, 1844) and *A Syllabic Dictionary of the Chinese Language* (Shanghai, 1874). In 1892 Herbert Allen Giles published *A Chinese-English Dictionary*

(Shanghai, 1892) in which he adopted a modified system of romanization devised by Sir Thomas Francis Wade, and since known as the Wade-Giles System.

The first Chinese dictionary based on analytical principles was Frederick Williams Baller's *An Analytical Chinese-English Dictionary* (Shanghai, 1900). It was later supplemented by Bernhard Karlgren's *Analytic Dictionary of Chinese and Sino-Japanese* (Paris, 1923).

The earliest works compiled by the Chinese are *A New Chinese-English Dictionary* (Shanghai, 1918) by Li Youwen, and *A Complete Chinese-English Dictionary* (Shanghai, 1920) by O.Z. Tzang. The latter in its revised and enlarged form (Shanghai, 1937) contains about 8000 single characters and some 20 0 00 compounds arranged in the traditional radical system and was the most comprehensive work at the time. But a later one, *A Chinese-English Dictionary* by Robert Henry Mathews (Shanghai, 1931), proved to be more popular, especially its revised American edition renamed *Mathews' Chinese-English Dictionary* (Cambridge, Mass., 1943) with 7785 characters and 10 400 compounds arranged according to the Wade-Giles romanization. For the next three decades the Mathews *'Chinese English Dictionary* was the standard comprehensive reference work for students of Chinese even though it was rendered obsolete after the late 1950s by the drastic changes in the Chinese language on the mainland. *The Concise Dictionary of Spoken Chinese* by Chao Yuen Ren (Zhao Yuanren) and Yang Lien-sheng (Yang Liansheng) (Cambridge, Mass., 1947) lists only a small number of single characters arranged according to the radicals together with a few essential compounds under each character. It is significant in that it is the first dictionary that indicates: whether a listed character can function as an independent monosyllabic word in Modern Standard Chinese or is merely a 'bound morpheme' that is always attached to another element; the grammatical function or functions of each item or its combination; and its stylistic class.

The Dictionary of Spoken Chinese compiled by the staff of the Institute of Far Eastern Languages of Yale University (New Haven, 1966), which is based partly on the above, consists of two parts, Chinese-English and English-Chinese, and lists compounds as well as single characters totalling 10 000 items arranged according to the Yale romanization. It gives detailed information on the grammatical functions of all listed items with an elaborate system of description, and illustrates usage with many sample sentences. As it covers only expressions that are actually spoken it is inadequate for reading normal texts.

In 1963 the US Joint Publications Research Service published the *Chinese-English Dictionary of Modern Communist Usage* (Washington, DC, 1963), which is an English translation of a Chinese-German dictionary first published in Beijing in 1959. It contains some 35 000 words arranged according to the *pinyin* romanization

A page from Matthews'
Chinese-English
Dictionary (1966).

and was the first such dictionary to cover new expressions created in mainland China after 1949.

The 1970s saw a good crop of more up-to-date dictionaries, for example *A New Practical Chinese-English Dictionary* compiled by Liang Shih-ch'iu (Liang Shiqiu) and others (Taipei, 1971) contains just over 7000 characters and some 80 000 compounds. Lin Yutang's *Chinese-English Dictionary of Modern Usage* (Hong Kong, 1972) started out as a highly ambitious project but the end product, though brilliant in some parts, is sadly disappointing. Both of these dictionaries fail to take into account current terms used on the mainland.

The Chinese-English Dictionary of Contemporary Usage (Berkeley, 1977) by Chi Wen-shun (Ji Wenxun) and others, fully justifies its title. The most comprehensive work of its kind, however, is *A Chinese-English Dictionary* compiled by the staff of the Department of English at the Beijing Institute of Foreign Languages (Beijing, 1978), with some 120 00 entries under 6000 character headings arranged according to *pinyin* romanization.

English-Chinese dictionaries

The earliest work in this field is also Robert Morrison's *A Dictionary of the Chinese Language* (Part 3 English-Chinese) (London and Macao, 1822). The first such work compiled by a Chinese is *An English and Chinese Lexicon* by Kwong Ki Chiu (Kuang Qizhao) (Hong Kong, 1868), containing only about 8000 entries. A full-sized one did not appear until 1908, when *An English and Chinese Standard Dictionary* compiled by Yen Hui-ching (Yan Huiqing) was published (Shanghai, 1908). This was followed by *Webster's Collegiate Dictionary in Chinese Translation* by Kuo Ping-wen (Guo Bingwen) and others (Shanghai, 1923) with over 100 000 entries, and *A Comprehensive Chinese-English Dictionary* by Huang Shih-fu (Huang Shifu) and others (Shanghai, 1928) with 130 000 words and 74 000 idiomatic phrases.

A New English-Chinese Dictionary by Cheng I-Ii (Zheng Yili) and others (Shanghai, 1950) marked a new era in providing completely fresh translations in the modern colloquial instead of the literary or semi-literary style as used in previous works. It also has an exhaustive Chinese index. In a second edition (Beijing and Hong Kong, 1984) entries have been increased to more than 120 000, simplified characters have replaced regular characters, but the original Chinese index has been omitted.

A New English-Chinese Dictionary (Shanghai, 1974) with over 80 000 entries was compiled during the Cultural Revolution. Even in its second edition (Shanghai and Hong Kong, 1987), it suffers from an overabundance of political jargon.

The Far East English-Chinese Dictionary compiled by Liang Shih-ch'iu (Liang Shiqiu) and others (Taipei, 1977) has over 16 000 entries. It uses regular characters and a style of language that follows the Taiwan and overseas norm in its Chinese translations and explanations.

R.S.W.H.

LITERATURE

Printing and publishing

Paper and printing are two Chinese inventions that have had an immeasurable effect upon Western culture, for without them the cheap and widespread circulation of books and knowledge that was one of the preconditions for the development of the modern world would have been impossible.

Paper, without which printing would hardly have been practicable, was probably invented in western China in the first century AD. Originally made from mulberry bark, hemp, worn-out fishing nets and a variety of other fibres, the technique of papermaking was rapidly perfected. By the 4th century it had largely replaced the older writing materials, silk, bamboo and wooden strips. By AD 500 it was also in use throughout Central Asia, and by 800 was being manufactured in Baghdad. In China a wide variety of paper was freely available, and by the Tang period papermaking was both a large industry and a fine art. It was produced on a vast scale: the Board of Finance alone used more than half a million sheets a year in preparing the tax assessments.

Books were normally prepared in scrolls; sheets of paper were pasted together to form a continuous roll, mounted on a wooden roller, with a sheet of heavier paper or silk forming a cover. The scroll commonly carried the text of a 'chapter' of a book. *Juan*, the word for a scroll, remained the standard term for a chapter long after this form for books and manuscripts had been abandoned.

The precise origins of printing are obscure. The Chinese used seals since long before the Han period, and later used large seals carved from hard wood to reproduce Daoist charms in large numbers. Rubbings were also made from texts carved in stone. Later small wooden stamps were used to print textile designs, and similar stamps were used for the reduplication of images of the Buddha; many examples of this kind dating from the 6th century have been found in Gansu and Xinjiang.

The first surviving examples of the printed word come from Japan; Buddhist charms (*dharani*) printed in great numbers under the Empress Shōtoku in about 770 to celebrate the end of a period of civil war. These were printed from copper blocks roughly 460 × 50mm, cast from clay models. The technique was almost certainly taken from China, where from the 8th century we have ample evidence that printing from wooden and sometimes metal blocks was widespread. In 835 the Chinese government attempted to prevent the sale of crudely printed calendars that had been flooding the market all over the country. In 848 we read of the printing of a hagiography of a famous Daoist alchemist. Some printed books were very long; the printed monastic rules of Luoyang's Buddhist monasteries ran to over 800 pages, and we know of the printing of such large items as dictionaries and other reference books, one dictionary running to 30 scrolls, as well as many books on divination, geomancy and interpretation of dreams. Large blocks, each forming roughly a page, were used for early printed books. The pages were simply pasted together to form a continuous scroll, just as manuscripts were. Such a scroll is the earliest surviving Chinese printed book, the copy of the Diamond Sutra discovered by Sir Aurel Stein in Dunhuang and now in the British Museum. This fine scroll, 16 feet long, was printed from seven separate wooden blocks, and with a finely drawn illustration as frontispiece. It is sometimes claimed, though with little firm evidence, that it was printed in Sichuan. This region was most important in the history of printing. Other very early printed charms discovered in Dunhuang certainly come from there, as do various fragments of printed dictionaries from the late 9th or 10th centuries. Other items were printed in the capital Chang'an, some in the Dunhuang region itself. By the 10th century printing had also spread to the lower Yangtze valley.

So far printing had been largely either of Buddhist charms and sutras, or of practical texts with a large potential sale. The literary evidence from the 9th century suggests that printed books were generally of poor quality, often printed on coarse paper with many illegible passages. Printing provided only a marginal part of the production of books, which largely continued to be reproduced in manuscript. A flourishing book trade existed: there were bookshops in Luoyang in the first century AD, and in the 9th century we know of book markets in Chang'an, Luoyang, Chengdu, Yangzhou and other cities.

In the 10th century printing developed still further. The techniques of block printing were rapidly perfected. Large-scale printing projects were undertaken in Sichuan, where the *Wenxuan* anthology and the entire Confucian canonical scriptures were printed before 952, while a rival edition was printed in Luoyang. Printing of the canonical literature made possible the wider dissemination of the standard texts and helped spread education. It also became an instrument of state control: printing of the classics privately was forbidden, and the state was able to ensure that all copies in circulation were identical with the orthodox text.

A vast spread of printing, much of it of superb quality, took place during the Song. The Confucian classics were followed by all the standard dynastic histories, a project which took 70 years to complete. The entire Buddhist canon, the Tripitaka (an enterprise which entailed the cutting of 130 000 blocks), was first published in 971–83 and several other editions followed. The entire Daoist religious canon, was printed three times between 1019 and the end of the 13th century, and a vast number of literary works, practical handbooks, works on medicine and agriculture were produced.

Not all printing was the work of government agencies; many private scholars printed their own works, or reprinted rare books for distribution. But commercial printing for a mass public also began on a large scale. Mass-production of cheap books was a speciality of two areas of Fujian, Masha and Shufang. Masha later became famous in Ming times for poorly printed books taken from blocks of soft banyan wood, easy to cut but giving bad impressions, and also for the production of cheap pirated abridgements of books. Some of the printing families in Shufang remained in existence from Song times until the Qing period. The Song was a truly great period for fine printing with wood-blocks; the style, calligraphy and design of Song books was outstanding. The most famous centres of fine printing were Hangzhou, the capital Kaifeng and Sichuan.

During the Song, too, printed books were generally no longer produced in scroll form, apart from the first edition of the Buddhist canon. The printing block was used for the impression of a double page divided by a central panel along which it was folded. The paper was very thin and printed on one side only, with the blank side folded in. The doubled sheets were sewn together at the outer margin to form a volume (ce). A large book would comprise several such volumes, which were held together in a stiff cover, rather like a slipcase, called a tao.

Wood-block printing remained standard until the introduction of Western printing techniques at the end of the 19th century. Block printing was a very flexible form of book production; it could be used to reproduce any type of calligraphy, any number of different sizes of characters, and any of the innumerable variant forms and rare characters that exist. It could equally well be used to reproduce graphics, illustrations or even non-Chinese scripts. The block could be corrected or amended by inserting wooden plugs in the surface. A block made of good fine-grained hard-wood—usually jujube or pear, could produce a few thousand impressions before wear became serious. Paper was laid on the inked surface and rubbed by hand—no press was used. Once cut, the block could be stored and impressions taken as required. A book could remain 'in print' for a century or more.

The huge publishing projects of the early Song required the cutting of tens of thousands of large blocks: those for the Buddhist canon, for example, had to be housed in a specially-built storehouse. During the Song, therefore, the Chinese also experimented with movable type printing. This was first invented about 1040 by a man called Bi Sheng, who used movable type made of ceramic material. These were set on an iron forme in a mixture of wax and resin, and could easily be reused. In the early 14th century Wang Zhen, a local official in Anhui, tells us that type made from a tin alloy had also been used; he himself printed using a font of wooden movable type.

The basic problem for Chinese movable-type printing was, as it remains today, the enormous number of characters required. Although movable type is ideal for printing in an alphabetic language, a Chinese printer needed to hold type for a constant stock of between 8000 and 10 000 characters, and had constantly to cut special type for rare characters. Wang Zhen's font had some 60 000 type. His compositor sat between two huge revolving tables with a framework of compartments for the type: one held the commonly used characters, the other rarer characters arranged by rhyme. The set-up type was wedged in a wooden frame, using bamboo strips for margins, and an impression taken as from a wood-block.

Neither ceramic type nor wooden type could be made to very accurate dimensions. Moreover, every character had to be cut individually. Although metal type of copper and lead was used quite widely in the lower Yangtze area in the 15th and 16th centuries, it was very expensive, and all movable type printing had a poor reputation because of the number of errors in setting, a problem which did not at all affect block printing.

Movable metal type was extensively used for government printing in Korea from the 13th century onwards, and particularly after 1392, using fine copper type cast in sand which made duplication relatively simple. In China metal type normally was not cast but was cut individually, as with wooden type. The greatest feat of metal movable type printing in China was the production early in the 18th century of the enormous imperial encyclopedia *Tushu jicheng*, which comprised 800 000 pages. The type-face used was very large, and the font was cast in copper, using ceramic moulds formed from wooden models. It entailed the manufacture of a quarter of a million characters taking nine years to complete. After the encyclopedia was printed, however, the font was melted down to make copper coin, and when later in the 18th century the government undertook a huge programme of reprinting rare books, the government printers reverted to the use of movable wooden type.

Apart from such government projects, where cost was not important, block printing remained the norm. The technical virtuosity of Chinese wood-block printing reached a peak late in the 16th century, when illustrated books of fine quality and even multicoloured editions were produced. The ready availability of many highly skilled block-cutters made the further development of movable type uneconomical for the ordinary printer.

By the late Ming period publishing and printing were a large and varied industry producing everything from fine editions of literary works, through a huge range of practical books down to school primers and crudely printed ephemera for popular reading, not to speak of government forms and, during the Song, Yuan and Ming periods, paper money. There was a nation-wide distribution of books, with the commercial printers of Fujian printing large editions for sale in the great cities of Jiangnan.

In the 19th century the adaptation of Western printing techniques for Chinese led to a further revolution in printing and publishing, centred mainly in Shanghai. By the 1930s the Commercial Press claimed to be the world's largest publishing house. Traditional printing still continues as a fine handicraft, but for general use was gradually abandoned early in this century. The role of the wood-block print has also been filled by various photographic methods of reproduction in facsimile. 	*D.C.T.*

Epigraphy and the earliest texts

The earliest Chinese writings are the Shang dynasty inscriptions on animal bone and turtle shell, the records of royal divinations performed during the reigns of the last nine kings from Wu Ding (*c.* 1200–1180 BC) to the infamously evil Zhou, a period of uncertain length which corresponds to roughly the last third of the dynasty and is dated, by traditional, orthodox literary sources, to 1324–1123 BC. The corpus, known commonly as the oracle bone inscriptions, consists of approximately 100 000 fragments of engraved bone and shell excavated, often under unscientific conditions, in the Anyang area of northern Henan Province, from 1899 until the present.

All matters involving the ritual activities of the Shang king and members of his family, the governing of the state, relations with friendly and hostile neighbours, the welfare and health of the royal family, as well as many other subjects of minor and major importance, were announced to the ancestors by the king or other diviners in the form of predictions, often stated in the positive and negative mode, about the near future: 'We shall receive the harvest of millet / We shall not obtain a (good) harvest of millet'; 'We shall destroy Zhou / We shall not destroy Zhou'; 'Dun will have sickness / Dun will not have sickness.' Upon this announcement, a flaming brand was touched to a hole chiselled into the surface of a bovid scapula or a turtle plastron carefully cleaned and polished to a high lustre reminiscent of jade, bronze and other 'bright utensils'—*mingqi*—used in the ancestor cult. With a popping sound the shell or bone would crack and the ancestor's response, thus voiced through the mouth prepared for him, would be interpreted as 'highly happy', 'amply happy', 'slightly happy', or 'unhappy'. If the ancestor's joyful agreement were not expressed, sacrifices, sometimes of shockingly excessive proportions, would be made and the ritual repeated in an attempt to obtain it. Later a prognostication, based on the answer of the spirit, would be offered by the king.

Shang scribes, using sophisticated bone and jade carving techniques known in the coastal area of China from at least the 5th millennium BC, engraved a written account of the divination on the bone or shell used. These texts, like later Chinese documents, were written in columns, but, unlike later manuscripts, they might on occasion be read left to right instead of the more usual right to left. A typical inscription on a turtle shell from the reign of Wu Ding reads:

Divining on the day bingshen, *the Diviner Ke tested the proposition, 'On the coming day* yisi *we shall make a wine libation to Xia Yi [an earlier Shang king].' The king, prognosticating, said, 'To offer a libation would mean to have a calamity. We should perhaps have flaming torches.' [Later it turned out that] on the day* yisi *we offered the wine libation and at the dawn of the next day it rained. We beheaded a victim and this brought the rains to their fullest. We beheaded a victim for Xian [i.e. Tang, the founder of the Shang house] and it rained more. [In an effort to stop the rain(?)] we performed a ritual expulsion and axed sacrificial victims to the Bird Star [α Hydrae].*

Writings such as this make the Shang the earliest literate people east of the Indus. For the Shang ruler these records, especially ones marked with a large number of 'happy' ancestral responses and confirmed by subsequent events, served as effective symbols of his power and ability to communicate with spiritual forces and thus to govern and maintain his state and protect himself and his people from adversaries. In this we may see the seed of the profound, indeed religious, awe with which later Chinese regarded written documents even to the point of using them as talismans against evil influences. But the oracle bone inscriptions also serve as an archive of the day-by-day activities of the Shang king comparable in form to the later state annals of the Zhou, such as the *Chunqiu* or *Spring and Autumn Annals* of Confucius's native state of Lu and the imperial annals which occur in all of the dynastic histories.

The writing system employed by the Shang is the earliest known ancestor of modern Chinese graphs. Over 3000 Shang graphs are known, of which 800 can be interpreted and identified with modern characters. They appear more pictographic than their later counterparts and more of them are polyphonic and polysemic, that is, one graph may stand for two or more different words that are neither homophonous nor synonymous. Moreover, unlike his successors, the Shang scribe would fairly often invert characters. Thus we find graphs and their mirror images in the inscriptions. For example, the Shang ancestor to the modern graph 明 appears as ☽, written with the left and right sides as in the modern graph, and as ☾, its mirror image and the form given in the inscription translated above. Nevertheless, Shang osteoglyphs exhibit such features of later Chinese graphs as being composed of a semantic and phonetic component and the overwhelming majority of them are already identified with a fixed sound and limited cluster of semantic associations. Most of the principles used by the Han dynasty lexicographer Xu Shen (AD 30–124) to describe the Chinese script can be applied to Shang graphs. Such a fully mature writing system begs for antecedents but archaeologists have found none. (The symbols on pottery sherds unearthed at a number of Chinese Neolithic sites cannot be considered attempts at representing language and are rather comparable to the owner's marks found on ancient Near Eastern ceramics.)

Although the Shang may have written on silk, wood and bamboo, such texts have not been found. We do possess, however, records not related to divination preserved on pottery, jade, stone and bronze. Of these, the bronze inscriptions, which appear relatively late in the Shang, are most numerous. Bronze inscriptions, carved first into the clay mould used in the casting, are brief accounts of the provenance of the vessel. They ordinarily reveal the name of the maker, the name of the ancestor to whom it is dedicated, the name of the vessel, and a mark or emblem which, because of its ornateness and pictorial qualities, is not thought to be an ordinary graph in the writing system.

The Zhou, after their conquest of the Shang, continued and greatly expanded the practice of inscribing bronze vessels while at the same time apparently placing much less emphasis on recording divinations. Western Zhou bronzes were cast to mark important military and political activities, very often the occasion of enfeoffment of a nobleman or the presentation of gifts by a superior and their inscriptions record the event. The inscriptions are lengthy. The longest—over 500 graphs—is on the famous Maogong ding (dated to about 827 BC); at least 50 other bronzes have inscriptions of 100 or more characters. But even an inscription of average length—50 to 100 graphs—is filled with information. An inscription on a wine vessel unearthed in late 1976 in western Shaanxi is a 56-character record of royal gift-giving to a vassal named Xing:

On the day wu yin in the first quarter of the ninth month of the 13th year, the King was in residence in Chengzhou at the temple-palace of Hu, the Superintendent of Lands. He went to the great hall and assumed his position. Father Zhi stood to the right of Xing. The King proclaimed, 'Let the Recorder of Documents and the Manager of Documents bestow on Xing painted breast-trappings for horses, hempen sandals, and scarlet slippers'. Xing, doing obeisance and knocking his head to the ground, responded, 'I shall praise the King's grace [by casting a vessel].' Xing hopes that for 10 000 years it will be ceaselessly treasured.

Bronze commemorations extolling the generosity and kindness of the Zhou dynasty kings are, both in content and form, reminis-

cent of the genuinely early chapters of the canonical *Book of Documents* and the hymns of praise found at the end of the *Book of Odes*. Recent discoveries of inscribed bronzes from the late Spring and Autumn and Warring States periods of the Eastern Zhou dynasty promise to supplement the historical narratives of the *Zuozhuan* (*Tradition of Zuo*) and *Zhanguoce* (*Intrigues of the Warring States*).   *J.K.R.*

The Confucian classics

The Confucian classics make up a corpus of texts accepted from the Former Han as the ultimate sanction for the ideas of the Confucian school of cosmology, ethics and government. This corpus, diverse in its content, was at first quite small; but as time went on more texts were included.

The *Five Classics*

Early Han sources speak of the *Five Classics* (*Wu jing*), and this original group already spans a wide range of subject-matter. The first in the traditional order, the *Book of Changes* (*Zhouyi*, or *Yijing*) is primarily a divination manual, a series of brief texts for a sequence of 64 hexagrams, groups of six broken and unbroken lines. The earliest part of the *Book of Changes* may be of early Zhou date, but there are later accretions and appendices, some probably as late as the Han. The text as a whole has served as much more than a manual for divination, however, for it has supplied many of the concepts and much of the terminology of philosophical and cosmological speculation for successive intellectual movements in China.

The second classic, the *Book of Documents* (*Shangshu* or *Shujing*) is a collection of documents, mostly in the form of homilies in direct speech with a minimum of narrative introduction. Some of these, attributed to the sage kings of remote antiquity, are in fact late Zhou idealizations. A number are concerned with the foundation and first two reigns of the Zhou, and are particularly important for their formulation of early Chinese ideals of the right to rule and the moral laws of government. The latest events referred to in the collection took place in 626 BC.

The *Book of Odes* (*Maoshi* or *Shijing*) is a collection of song texts that are believed to date from between the early Zhou and about 600 BC. The collection contains edited versions of just over 300 folk songs from the different states of the Zhou period, on the themes of courtship, marriage and military campaigns, and also more formal and solemn hymns celebrating the greatness of the Zhou and its various ceremonial occasions, such as feasts, sacrifices and hunts. The *Book of Odes* is the one Confucian classic that may be said with certainty to have been used extensively in his teaching by the historical Confucius. As a result of the interest of Confucian scholars, from late Zhou times, many of the *Odes*, and especially the more straightforward folk songs, were given highly moralistic allegorical interpretations. The *Odes* have been important in Chinese literary history partly for the influence of their style and subject-matter on later poetry, but especially because early and lasting ideas on the nature and function of poetry were developed in connection with them.

The fourth of the *Five Classics* was given the general title of the *Ritual* (*Li*). Since Han times, however, there have been three officially recognized ritual classics. The *Ritual Prescriptions* (*Yili*) is a collection of ritual rubrics governing rites of passage, banquets, archery contests and other observances, the composition of which is not likely to date from earlier than late Zhou. The *Ritual of Zhou* (*Zhouli*) or *Offices of Zhou* (*Zhouguan*), an account of the early Zhou as an ideal state, listing its officials and their functions in detail, is also accepted as being of late date. Its idealized formulation of an official hierarchy has been used as a blueprint by successive reformers in Han, Tang and Song times, and again more recently by the Taiping rebels of the mid-19th century. Finally, there is the *Record of Ritual* (*Liji*), a collection of treatises on ritual matters brought together in the Former Han period. Some of these treatises were attributed to early figures in the Confucian tradition, notably the *Great Learning* (*Daxue*), which was ascribed by some early scholars to Confucius's disciple Zeng Shen and by others to Confucius's grandson Kong Ji, and the *Doctrine of the Mean* (*Zhongyong*), believed also to have been by Kong Ji. These two works, which emphasize that it is the duty of individuals to pursue a path of introspection and self-correction as a prerequisite to good social and political order, were particularly influential from Song times onwards.

The last of the *Five Classics* of the early Han series was the *Spring and Autumn Annals* (*Chunqiu*), a very terse chronicle of events in the state of Lu (in modern Shandong) from 722–481 BC. The great importance of the *Spring and Autumn Annals* derived from the late Zhou tradition that Confucius himself had edited it and written into it in cryptic language his judgements on the behaviour of figures in the chronicle. In late Zhou and early Han, interpretation of what ideas Confucius had invested in the chronicle grew more and more speculative. The texts of three main traditions of exposition, all of which later became Confucian classics, survive: the *Gongyang Tradition* (*Gongyangzhuan*), the most speculative of the three; the *Ku-liang Tradition* (*Guliangzhuan*); and the best known but last to be officially recognized, the *Tradition of Zuo* (*Zuozhuan*), attributed to Zuoqin Ming, believed to be a contemporary of Confucius. This was a long and discursive narrative of events in the Spring and Autumn period. With the *Book of Documents*, the *Spring and Autumn Annals* and the *Tradition of Zuo* greatly influenced early Chinese attitudes to the compilation of histories, not least because they exemplified traditional Confucian stress on the moralistic and didactic purpose of history writing.

Later inclusions

By the Later Han dynasty, two more texts had been accepted into the corpus of Confucian classics. The *Lunyu* (*Analects*), which is probably mostly of an early date, is a collection of the sayings of Confucius himself and his disciples. They concern principally Confucius's emphasis on education and the meritocratic principle, his stress on the social function and value of ritual and on goodness (*lien*), caution towards the supernatural, and belief in the social and political order of the early Zhou. The *Classic of Filial Piety* (*Xiaojing*), traditionally held to be by Zeng Shen, is a brief text now believed to be of late Zhou or early Han date. In it the principle of filial piety, or reverence and obedience towards one's parents, is formulated as a rule to be followed by all levels of society and as a law of the universe itself.

By the start of the Tang dynasty, another book, a glossary of words in the Confucian classics, the *Erya*, was also included among the classics. A final work, making the total 13 from Song times, was the *Mengzi* (*Mencius*). This was a record of the teachings of Mencius, an influential late Zhou exponent of the Confucian tradition. The *Mengzi* became important in the Song period for two main reasons: its rebuttal of the rival philosophies of its day was especially appreciated by Song Confucians engaged in formulating a philosophical system intended to make redundant the rival traditions of their own time, Buddhism and Daoism, and Mencius' belief in the innate moral goodness of all human beings became central to their view of man.

The *Four Books*

In the Song period four texts from within the full corpus of 13 classics received special attention. This short series comprised the *Lunyu*, the *Mengzi*, the *Great Learning* and the *Doctrine of the Mean*. Known as the *Four Books* (*Sishu*), these were promoted as a conveniently brief formulation of Confucian moral teaching. They played an important role in education, and, from 1314 until late Qing times, formed part of the curriculum for public examinations.

Commentaries

Commentaries to the Confucian classics were produced continuously from Han times, for there was always an assumption from the 'Burning of the Books' in 213 BC that critical study would yield a more accurate text and a fuller and more refined understanding. When in the post-Han period of dis-union all literature except

Buddhist and Daoist material was divided for classification purposes into four categories, the Confucian classics and commentaries formed a single category.

Four main stages in the interpretation of the classics may be distinguished: the period of primary commentaries, which explained the texts themselves of the classics, and which lasted from Han times to about AD 420; the age of sub-commentaries, which explained both the texts and the primary commentaries, from about 420 to the early Song; the period of Neo-Confucian exegesis, in which scholars returned to the texts of the classics themselves, and read a more sophisticated philosophical system into them; and, finally, under the Qing a period of renewed and rigorous empirical research into the philology, phonology and textual history of the corpus. The sum of this activity was considerable: in 1782 an official, but not comprehensive, catalogue for the imperial collection, the *General Catalogue for the Complete Collection in Four Treasuries* (*Siku quanshu zongmu*), gave notices for no fewer than 1776 works of classical scholarship. The state from time to time approved as orthodox existing texts and commentaries, particularly with a view to their use in public examinations. From late Han times onwards it also had the texts of the classics inscribed in stone and set up in the Grand Academy (*Taixue*) or State Academy Directorate (*Guozijian*). This was done, for example, in AD 175, 837, 1177 and 1793–1819. Some of the engraving of 837 may still be seen in the Forest of Stele (*Beilin*) at Xi'an, while that of 1793, completed after revision in 1819, is still in the State Academy Directorate in Beijing. *D.L.M.*

Annals and histories

China's written historical records, extending back nearly three thousand years, form the longest uninterrupted tradition of historical documentation of any civilization. No other pre-modern society was so aware of the past or evolved such careful provision for recording what it considered important among the events of its own time. Although many of the states of the Zhou period (*c.* 1122–249 BC), probably kept chronicles, the earliest extant historical works are the *Book of Documents* (*Shangshu* or *Shujing*), comprising in part early and middle Zhou documents, and the *Spring and Autumn Annals* (*Chunqiu*), the chronicle covering the period 722–481 BC for the state of Lu (in present day Shandong), where Confucius lived. By the Former Han (206 BC–AD 25), both these works were considered Confucian classics, and they, with the *Tradition of Zuo* (*Zuozhuan*), a lengthy narrative for the Chunqiu period, also accepted as a classic, exerted great influence on the later practice of history writing.

In the course of the Former and Later Han dynasties two no less influential models were produced. The first was the *Historical Records* (*Shiji*) by Sima Qian, a history of China from early times to the beginning of the first century BC. A number of important innovations in this great work were adopted by later practice: Sima Qian divided his history into four parts, first 'basic annals', modelled loosely on the *Chunqiu;* then tables or charts, tabulating events that occurred in states in different parts of the China of the Zhou period; then two particularly influential sections, one for monographs or treatises on specific topics, such as the calendar, state ritual, irrigation and economic developments, and one for the biographies of individual figures and descriptions of foreign peoples. In the Later Han, Ban Gu made use of this model, but restricted the coverage of his *History of the Han* (*Hanshu*) to the dynasty itself. One of his most significant departures from the *Historical Records* was the extension of the monograph section to cover topics such as the administrative geography of China, penal legislation, administrative institutions and portents. He also included a catalogue of book titles.

Histories on the plan of these two outstanding Han dynasty works were compiled in the period of disunity that followed the

An imaginary likeness of Sima Qian (*c.* 145–*c.* 86 BC), the great Han dynasty historian, from a Japanese reprint dated 1651 of a Ming dynasty book of portraits of famous men.

Han. The chronicle form of history, in which, on the model of the *Chunqiu*, events were integrated into a single chronological sequence, was also used, and other works classified as history, in such areas as topographical description, genealogy and biographies, were compiled.

The reign of Taizong, from 626–49, at the start of the Tang dynasty was a key period in Chinese historical scholarship. Five histories of the preceding period of disunity, compiled by imperial command, were completed in 636, and three more were added shortly afterwards. All these works followed the models of the *Shiji* and the *Hanshu*, for they comprised 'basic annals' and biographies, and in some cases monographs also. The bibliography monograph compiled in conjunction with the first five of these histories shows that history as a class of writing was now considered one of the four divisions into which all written works, except Buddhist and religious Daoist material, were divided, the other three being the Confucian classics and commentaries, philosophical works and literary anthologies. The history division contained 13 sub-divisions, of which the most important were for 'standard histories' on the Han models; chronicle form works; court diaries; collections of documents; works on penal law; administrative geography; biographies, genealogies and bibliographies. The total number of titles listed in this bibliography, including those of works lost when it was compiled, was 874. This classification was to be followed, with slight amplification only, to modern times, and works in all the sub-divisions of the history division were produced in increasing quantities.

The reign of Taizong also saw the setting up of a sophisticated official apparatus for the compilation of a record of the Tang dynasty itself. To the History Office (*Shiguan*), established as a separate institution for the first time in 629, were sent records of court events and discussions, documents from central and provincial administrations, and biographies of deceased senior officials. These the official historian compilers eventually worked into a 'dynastic history'. The ultimate purpose of this continuous process was to produce a work for the entire dynasty on the model of the *Hanshu*. The operation was directed by a chief minister and run as a department of government. The technique the historians used was usually to abbreviate or condense primary documents; their own comments and assessments were added only in brief and separate paragraphs. This approach has given a deceptively objective tenor to much Chinese historical writing, disguising the fact that it almost always embodies Confucian moral prejudices and often conceals more specific sectional and factional loyalties as well. Only in recording certain categories of technical information, for example in the monographs on official institutions or administrative geography, were historians objective.

Later dynasties followed the Tang in maintaining a History Office, in completing the histories of the dynasties that had preceded them and in compiling an official record of their own times. The result of this activity is a series of 25 'standard histories', starting with the *Historical Records* of Sima Qian and ending with a history of the Qing dynasty in draft form that was published only in 1928. This series, compiled over two millennia, does not exactly correlate with the sequence of dynasties. For the Tang dynasty, for example, there are two histories, the second commissioned to improve on the first, and for the Five Dynasties (*Wu dai*), the brief period between the Tang and the Song, there are again two. For the Mongol Yuan dynasty, dissatisfaction with the history produced in the early Ming led to the completion and printing of a new version as late as 1922. The series is naturally not uniform in quality and reliability; the later works tend to be longer than the early ones, and there is a consistent trend towards the inclusion of more secular rather than religious material. Despite its unevenness, however, this impressive monument to the durability of the form Sima Qian had pioneered provides scholars with a repository of clearly organized and accessible information.

The historical outline furnished by the 25 'standard histories' has been supplemented by many more, often privately undertaken, specialist works. Among these *Zizhi tongjian (Comprehensive Mirror for Aid in Government)*, a chronicle style history by the Song scholar and statesman Sima Guang, which spans the period 403 BC to AD 959 in 354 chapters, is especially famous. Sima Guang carried the critical sense that has informed the best Chinese historical scholarship to new lengths in assessing the reliability of the 322 books he used as sources for his chronicle, and has moreover, in his 30 final chapters, left notes on the reasoning he followed in many cases. Another remarkable tradition in the field of historical scholarship was that of compendia describing the history and evolution of the administrative institutions of the imperial state and including much primary documentary evidence. The first extant example of this kind of historical compilation dates from AD 801, and the final examples were produced under the Qing.

At a local level, from Song times onwards provinces, prefectures, counties and even in some cases villages kept gazetteers, which typically were published in successive and amplified editions through Ming and Qing times. Again these histories, of which a recent catalogue lists 7413, though often limited by the same Confucian outlook that characterized the dynastic histories, have preserved a vast amount of information, about local economic conditions, trade, social structure, prominent figures and even buildings.

The 'standard histories', chronicle histories, institutional compendia and local gazetteers mentioned above are, however, only specific examples within the broad range of writing that Chinese scholars classified as history. A catalogue of the imperial library completed in 1782, the *General Catalogue for the Complete Collection in Four Treasuries* (*Siku quanshu zongmu*), gave descriptive notices of historical works in 15 categories, for in the course of time two subdivisions, one of which was for works criticizing historical scholarly method itself, had been added to the early Tang official scheme referred to above. The total number of historical works in this catalogue, which was acknowledged as not comprehensive and which omitted the many local records, was 2136. One of the tasks modern Chinese scholars have embarked on is to prepare critical, punctuated editions of some of these works, to replace the sometimes superbly printed but unpunctuated texts of traditional Chinese book production. *D.L.M.*

Principal poets and writers

Early Chinese poetry 850 BC–first century AD

The earliest Chinese poetry is anonymous. It is preserved in a collection of some 300 songs (*Shijing—Book of Odes*) most of which appear to date from the two and a half centuries between 850 and 600 BC. Most of them are stanzaic, rhymed (as is all Chinese verse) and in lines of four syllables. A characteristic feature is the *xing* or opening line of natural imagery with implied but often uncertain reference to the subject. Of the heterogeneous contents—work-songs, ballads, love-songs, dance-songs, nuptial songs, hymns, complaints and songs of praise for victorious warriors—all but one or two of the last-mentioned are anonymous, and even the one or two names tell us nothing about the status of the singer. The songs appear to have been collected by musicians at the courts of the Zhou kings and their princely feudatories as a repertoire for use at feasts and ceremonies, and familiarity with their words came to be expected as a knightly accomplishment. Their use as teaching material by Confucius in the training of young noblemen for employment at the princely courts ensured their survival in the Confucian canon and the perpetuation of the allegorizing interpretation of them favoured by his disciples.

The first nameable Chinese poet belonged to a cultural tradition far removed from that which produced the songs. Qu Yuan wasa kinsman of King Huai of Chu (reigned 328–299 BC), a kingdom situated to the south of the old Zhou states having its capital on the central Yangtze near Lake Dongting. Chu preserved intact the old shamanism (a primitive religion in which all good and evil is thought to be brought about by spirits which can be influenced by the priest-doctors, the shamans) which in the north was by now sinking to the status of a village religion, and it was the chants and ecstatic invocations of the shamans, or *wu* as the Chinese called them, which inspired Qu Yuan's rhapsodic verses. *Chuci* (*Songs of the South*), the collection in which they are found, was compiled more than two centuries after his death and contains the work of other Chu poets and much that is of uncertain authorship, but there is no question of the shamanistic ancestry of these poems or of the presence in the collection of a great and original poet. Qu Yuan's best-known poem, the *Lisao*, 'On Encountering Sorrow' is an allegory in which beautiful women and flowers represent statesmen and their virtues. It tells the story of Qu Yuan's estrangement from his king, whom he had served loyally, and describes his journeys in a flying chariot through a supernatural world peopled by gods and spirits. The poem is interspersed with moralizing reflections on legendary history and ends on a note of despair. Qu Yuan is believed to have drowned himself while an exile in southern Chu.

The role of the loyal courtier disgraced by jealous rivals and rejected by a misguided prince was one with which later generations of courtier poets could easily identify, and Qu Yuan had many imitators. The lamentations of the rejected and the unsuccessful could not, however, have much appeal for the leaders of an expansive, self-confident age like the Han, and Sima Xiangru (d. 117 BC), the greatest of all the Han courtier-poets, used the *fu* or 'rhyme-prose'—a development of the rhapsodic style of verse invented by Qu Yuan—to glorify his imperial master. His '*Fu* of the Great Man' has a celestial journey like *Lisao*, but is more in the nature of a triumphal progress for the emperor become a god, while his *Shanglinfu* contains a hyperbolical account of an imperial hunt, after which, as an additional flattery, the emperor is shown regretting the wastefulness of the hunt and turning to the intellectual pleasures of philosophy and art. In even longer, more elaborate *fu* characterized by the same hyperbole and lexical exuberance later writers such as the historian Ban Gu (AD 32–92) and the astronomer-poet Zhang Heng (AD 78–139) attempted descriptions of whole cities and their environs. *Fu* were written on every conceivable subject and could be of any length, but the long, panoramic *fu* requiring much research and sometimes years of labour is most typical of the period.

Chinese poetry, 2nd to 6th centuries AD

By the end of the 2nd century a completely different kind of poetry based on contemporary song-forms—short lyrics having regular pentasyllabic lines—was beginning to appear. Some of the best early examples are anonymous. Cao Zhi (AD 192–232), son of the great warlord Cao Cao, the first well-known poet to use it is equally famous for his *fu*. Cao Cao himself wrote drinking-songs in the four-syllable *Shijing* verse, which continued to be used intermittently for another century or so.

The 3rd century, politically a period of darkness and dissolution, saw a revival of philosophical Daoism and was intellectually a period of great distinction. Ruan Ji (210–63), its most distinguished poet, is known for a sequence of 82 poems in five-syllable verse, most of them 10 or a dozen lines long, called *Yunghuaishi* or *The Heart Unburdened*. They are written in a language at once simple, beautiful and impenetrably obscure. Ruan Ji's best friend, the amiably eccentric Xi Kang (223–62), was executed for no worse a crime than too independent an attitude, and Ruan Ji survived in the midst of a murderous court by assuming a drunken buffoonery totally at odds with the pervasive melancholy of his poems.

With the growing diversity of literary forms the beginnings of literary criticism appear. The most notable essay in criticism dating from this period is by the poet Lu Ji (261–303) and is itself in the form of a *fu*. With its studied cadences, metrical regularity and elaborate diction it foreshadows the Parallel Prose or Four-Six Style which, throughout the period of disunity during the Wei, Jin and Northern and Southern dynasties, came to be used in more and more kinds of written communication. The densely allusive *fu* of Yu Xin (513–81), a southern exile at one of the northern courts, are perhaps the most extreme example of this elaboration of the medium at the expense of the message it conveys.

Not all poets and writers of these centuries were euphuists, however. Tao Qian, or Tao Yuanming as he is more often called (365–427), one of the greatest Chinese poets of any age, was as much an original in his verse as in his life-style. Disillusioned with the constraints of office, he retired to a life of poverty on his smallholding, which he cultivated himself. His affectionate but unsentimental descriptions of cottage life and stoical, good-humoured acceptance of its hardships, even of death itself, have impressed a wide variety of readers. He also wrote what is still one of the best-known Chinese stories, 'The Peach Blossom Stream', about a fisherman who accidentally stumbled into a terrestrial paradise but was afterwards unable to rediscover it.

Xie Lingyun (385–433) is often described as China's first nature poet. He was an aristocrat, a devout believer in Buddhism and an enthusiastic mountaineer. He was also wealthy enough to be able to practise landscape gardening on a vast scale on his large estate. The best of his poems communicate the sense of mystery experienced in the high mountains and in the beautiful lake and river scenery of the south.

Two works of great importance to the future advancement of Chinese letters appeared in the 6th century. One is the *Wenxin diaolong* (*The Dragon-carving of the Literary Mind*) by Liu Xie (465–521), a minor functionary of the Liang dynasty who ended his days as a Buddhist monk. It is a masterly survey of literature and systematic examination of the principles underlying its composition which at the same time is itself a work of great literary distinction. The other is the *Wen xuan* (*A Select Anthology of Liter-*

ature) compiled by Liu Xie's contemporary, the Crown Prince Xiao Tong (501–31). It was an inexhaustible inspiration to poets and writers in the centuries which followed and our principal source for much of the literature of the Han-North/South dynasties period which is still extant.

Chinese poetry of the Tang dynasty

The Tang dynasty is regarded as the Golden Age of Chinese poetry. Among explanations advanced for its explosion of poetic talent are the emergence of new forms, particularly the perfection of the so-called New Style Verse or Regulated Verse (in which poems containing a fixed number of five- or seven-syllable lines were made to conform to elaborate rules governing the tonality of the syllables), the important place accorded to poetic talent by the administration in its recruitment of the bureaucracy, and the cultural distinction of the unfortunate Emperor Xuanzong's court, of which a number of the greatest Tang poets were at one time or another members. The greatest of them—perhaps the greatest Chinese poet—Du Fu (712–70), made a homeless refugee by the An Lushan rebellion, looked back with nostalgia, through his years of wandering, at his brief, blissful days at Xuanzong's court. Conscientious, humane, sensitive and generally ill, Du Fu recommends himself to us not only as a consummate and constantly developing artist, but as a man who clung passionately to what we should call civilized values at a time when they were collapsing all around him.

Du Fu's friend and contemporary Li Bai (701–62) is in every respect a contrast. A Daoist, wine-bibber and bohemian, he seriously compromised himself during the An Lushan rebellion by his convivial and probably harmless involvement with a rebel fleet and was at one time imprisoned and very nearly executed. A mercurial, dashing personality manifests itself in his poems, many of which are in irregular old-style ballad metres. Sometimes his imagination reaches rhapsodic heights as in the famous Tianmu poem in which he visits the Tianmu ('Heavenly Mother') Mountain in a dream and momentarily glimpses the hidden fairy world inside it.

Another contemporary, Wang Wei, was also compromised during the rebellion, through no fault of his own. Wang Wei was a devout Buddhist and a distinguished landscape painter. Though in office through most of his life, he spent as much time as he could at his rural retreat. He has a mystic, quietist attitude to nature which lends a profound, mysterious quality to his simple poems.

Among the poets of the 9th century Bai Juyi (772–846) was the first Chinese poet to have an international reputation. His popular ballad 'The Everlasting Wrong' was sung in tea-houses all over the empire and his works were eagerly sought after in Korea and Japan. Bai Juyi endeavoured to write in a simple diction that even the uneducated could understand. His friend Yuan Zhen (779–831), with whom he frequently collaborated, was the author of a short story based on an amorous intrigue of his own youth, which, in a much romanticized version, was immortalized centuries later in a well-known play, *Xixiangji* (*The Western Pavilion*).

The contemporary vogue for short stories told in succinct, unadorned prose as far removed as possible from the florid, ornamental Four-Six style is connected with a movement, part literary, part-philosophical, led by the great Confucian Han Yu (768–824), a fine, if at times eccentric, poet and a great essayist. His *guwen* or 'ancient style' movement was a deliberate attempt to write a simpler, more direct prose, free of the allusions and metrical encumbrances of Parallel Prose, by basing himself on Han and pre-Han models. Unfortunately the archaism of style and grammar which the movement inspired often made for greater rather than less obscurity. The development of written Chinese into a sort of clerk's Latin wholly different from the spoken language may be said to date from this period. Liu Zongyuan (773–819), another of the movement's leaders, is equally well-known for his prose and poetry. Among his prose writings the descriptive pieces about places he visited in his travels are particularly fine.

Of Han Yu's numerous protégés Li He (790–816) deserves special mention for the strange and exciting imagist type of poetry which so puzzled his contemporaries and still seems strangely modern.

Li Shangyin (813–58), particularly in his 'Untitled' poems in seven-syllable Regulated Verse, uses a mysterious, opaquely rich, sensual imagery whose erotic melancholy has a faintly *fin de siècle* air about it. His is a poetry which deliberately exploits ambiguity but even at its most obscure exercises a compelling fascination. It was imitated, 200 years later, by Song poets of the Xikun School.

Nearly all the Tang poetry so far mentioned was of the metrically regular kind known as *shi*, in which the lines are of equal length. Just as five-syllable poetry had developed out of a popular song style at the end of the Han period, so a new kind of lyric verse called *ci*, in which lines of irregular length were combined in fixed stanza-patterns, evolved out of the popular song styles of the Tang period. During the Five Dynasties period which followed the break-up of the Tang, some of the finest poetry was written in this new form. The best-known poet in this new style was Li Yu (937–78), last ruler of the short-lived Southern Tang dynasty, who lost his kingdom and died in captivity. His lyrics have a delicacy and haunting melancholy, enhanced in the popular imagination by the tragic and romantic circumstances of his life. A few of his poems are still very widely known.

Chinese poetry of the Song

Ci, for all their delicate charm and sensibility, were at first greatly restricted in subject-matter. Although written by men, they were, like the popular songs from which they originated, in great part concerned with the boudoir repinings of courtesans and court ladies. During the Song dynasty, when many more poets made use of this medium, the range of subject-matter as well as the variety of stanza-patterns was greatly extended.

Many of the best-known Song poets and writers were distinguished politicians or administrators. Versatility is a Song characteristic. Ouyang Xiu (1007–72) is equally distinguished as statesman, philosopher and poet and almost as well-known for his delightful essays as for his *ci*. The reforming Prime Minister Wang Anshi (1021–86) was himself a sensitive poet. It is a sign of the greater tolerance of this age that the great poet Su Shi', or Su Dongpo as he is more often called (1036–1101), though Wang's political enemy and forced to spend many years in semi-exile, retained his respect and admiration as a poet and exchanged courtesies with him during his retirement.

Su Dongpo more than any other writer represents the urbanity, good humour, freedom and elegant refinement of Song culture at its best. His prodigious output of poetry, if a little short on passion and a little inclined to facileness, is always enjoyable. Like several other Song poets he was an excellent calligrapher. His beautiful calligraphy, of which many examples have survived, is at once elegant and manly, free yet controlled.

The poets of the Southern Song were often patriots in whose consciousness the national disgrace of an empire half under barbarian occupation was an ever-present shadow. Lu You (1125–1210), who lived to be 85 and whose staggering output amounts to some 10 000 poems, reverts again and again to his desire to ride sword in hand against the barbarian foe and sweep them back into the desert. The slightly fustian quality of these heroics, in contrast to the bitter antiwar poetry of Du Fu, whom Lu You deeply admired and in other respects often imitated, is perhaps due to the fact that the Southern Song policy towards the north was mainly a pacific one.

Lu You's contemporary Fan Chengda (1126–93) is particularly well known for the idyllic, somewhat idealized picture of rural life he gives in a sequence of poems called 'The Farmer's Year'.

No account of Song lyric poetry would be complete without some mention of Li Qingzhao (b. 1084), the only Chinese woman poet whose poems are still widely read. Li Qingzhao shared the interests of her antiquarian husband and has left a charming picture of their life together in a colophon she wrote for his book on inscriptions, but they were made refugees by the Tartar invasion, and when he died suddenly she was condemned to a rootless, lonely life without him.

Chinese poetry of the Yuan, Ming and Qing dynasties

Yuan Haowen (1190–1257), who served under the Jurchen Tartar rulers but refused to continue in office when they in turn were conquered by the Mongols, wrote a strong, simple kind of verse that is sometimes almost conversational in tone. His 30 quatrains 'On Poetry' make a valuable contribution to Chinese criticism. Under the Yuan dynasty Chinese literary culture languished and Chinese men of letters often turned to the world of entertainment for a livelihood, but many of the Yuan playwrights also wrote excellent lyrics for their own or their friends' amusement. The robustly humorous verses of Guan Hanqing and the more melancholy humour of Ma Zhiyuan's songs in the 13th century deserve a special mention.

The Ming poet Gao Qi (1336–74) was executed at the age of 38 by the monstrous founder of the dynasty by being cut in two at the waist. His crime was to have written a harmless poem in praise of someone who had innocently incurred the emperor's displeasure. The painfully unoriginal quality of most Ming verse is perhaps not surprising after such a beginning. During the 276 years of Ming rule, and to a large extent during the 268 years of Qing rule which followed, Chinese creative genius in the field of literature found its outlet mainly in the unofficial, private, safely anonymous worlds of drama and fiction. In the 'official' fields of formal verse and classical prose a frigid archaism was the rule. Factionalism, now lethal in politics, found a safe place in literary criticism-pedantic quibbling, for the most part, about which ancient models were to be imitated and literary history, with a few eccentric exceptions like the painter Tang Yin (1470–1523), became a matter of schools and movements rather than of individual names. Towards the end of the dynasty a freer, anti-archaizing spirit begins to manifest itself in the person of Li Zhi (1527–1602) and the so-called Gong'an School led by the brothers Yuan Songdao (1560–1600), Yuan Hongdao (1568–1610) and Yuan Zhongdao (1575–1630). The Qing poet Yuan Mei (1716–97) was greatly indebted to Gong'an ideas in his own somewhat shallow contributions to literary criticism.

The simple but strong and supple form of classical Chinese favoured by these later Ming writers was used to great effect by the virtually unknown Shen Fu (flourished 1786) in his *Six Chapters of a Floating Life* which contains one of the most enchanting accounts of married love written in any language and in the delightful ghost stories of Pu Songling (1640–1715) in his *Strange Stories from the Liao Studio (Liaozhai Zhiyi)*. It was made successful use of by writers like Yan Fu (1853–1921) and Lin Shu (1882–1924) in early translations of European philosophical and scientific works and works of fiction.

Many of the greatest intellects of the Qing dynasty devoted their energies to the philological study of ancient texts. Wang Guowei

Yan Fu: his translations introduced Western writers to China.

Wang Guowei, writer and scholar of the later Qing.

(b. 1877), a profoundly learned scholar, steeped not only in every kind of Chinese traditional learning, but Kant and Schopenhauer as well, drowned himself as the Revolutionary Republican Army approached Beijing in 1927, a loyal subject of the defunct Qing empire. He makes a convenient place to end at, but classical prose and classical poetry are still very far from dead.   *D.H.*

Traditional fiction and popular literature

The short story in classical language

During the centuries that followed the Han period China developed a tradition of anecdotal literature recording personal memorabilia, strange and anomalous events, and miracle stories of a religious character. Against this background, and gaining strength and colour from historical moralists and narrative poets, writers of the 8th and 9th centuries created a short-story literature which has inspired the Chinese imagination ever since. Among the works which stand the test of time are 'The Tale of Yingying', a study of passionate love unfulfilled, 'The Tale of Li Wa', in which a courtesan redeems baseness with loyalty, 'The Tale of Liu Yi', based on dragon-maiden legends, and 'Inside the Pillow', a fable on the theme of 'life's a dream'.

Stories in this style and tradition appeared through the succeeding centuries and reached a new climax in the 17th century with the collection *Liaozhai Zhiyi* by Pu Songling (1640–1715). His stories explore dealings between the real and the spirit world in a style whose allusive elegance has remained the toast of discriminating readers.

The short story in vernacular language

Two late-Ming editors, Hong Pian (flourished 1560s) and Feng Menglong (1574–1646) have left us a rich corpus of stories in the vernacular idiom. The stories are virtually all anonymous and difficult to date reliably: recent research suggests a range of dates from *c.*1300 to the 1620s. In content, they cover folk-tale, romance, law-court cases, domestic dramas, ghost and demon adventures, historical episodes and picaresque heroics. They combine a prosaic, even humdrum narrative manner with brief interludes of verse description or proverbial wisdom. And they affect the mannerisms of a narrator addressing a live audience. Feng's impressive collection of 120 pieces in all stimulated the 17th century to write more, most successfully in two books of stories by Ling Mengchu (1580–1644). But the genre did not outlive the century.

Religious ballads

Among the contents of the remarkable sealed library found in the caves of Dunhuang are manuscripts of narrative works (*bianwen*) mostly dating from the 10th century AD. They treat subjects from Buddhist scripture and mythology, sometimes from history and lay folklore, expanding and developing a canonical text or a story-line through a mixture of prose narrative and metrical passages designed for intonation. The precise function of these texts is still debated, but they were ancestral to a long tradition of similar works in later centuries. One of the most prolific forms has been the *baojuan* or 'precious scroll': texts for liturgical use or edifying reading, current in manuscript or in print at least from the 16th century until recent times. Here again the themes cover theology, religious mythology and lay folklore, often with reference to the teachings of heterodox and esoteric religious sects.

Pinghua and *Cihua*

A small cluster of surviving texts allows us to glimpse the ephemeral narrative forms favoured by less sophisticated readers before the great developments of the 16th century. From the early 14th century we have a series of popularized narratives (*pinghua*) covering the more adventurous and spectacular periods of China's early history. In a rough and ready prose they develop a characteristically heroic vision of the past, enriched with themes from folklore.

A more recently discovered cache of 15th-century texts entitled *Cihua* (*Verse Tales*) shows us a secular form corresponding to the *baojuan*. The mixture of prose and balladic verse is similar, and seems designed for performance as well as reading. The themes are taken from history, law-court cases, ghost- and demon-lore.

Sanguozhi yanyi (*Romance of the Three Kingdoms*)

The events and issues of the Three Kingdoms period (AD 184–280) have long engrossed the Chinese. The official record, *Sanguozhi yanyi* (late 3rd century) endorsed the legitimacy of the Wei kingdom, but later tradition, enriched by heroic legends and folklore, increasingly favoured the Shu. This vigorous and partisan celebration of a past age was refashioned into an extended prose narrative by (so tradition has it) Luo Guanzhong, a dramatist of the 14th century. We know for certain that the book existed before 1500. It was revised into a final and enduringly popular form by Mao Zonggang in the 17th century.

The *Sanguozhi yanyi* encloses the Three Kingdoms in a classic historical cycle, within which division and unity follow inevitably upon one another. A nation divided and at war with itself gives a setting uniquely apt for probing men's motives and allegiances, and this is one of the book's chief concerns. It affirms the Confucian values of loyalty in social relationships; it celebrates the qualities of courage and sagacity. Its supreme heroes are Liu Bei, the ruler of Shu, and his sworn brothers Guan Yu and Zhang Fei, whose 'Peach Orchard' oath of loyalty even to the death stands as exemplary of its kind. The dauntless ferocity of these warriors is balanced by the insight and imagination of Zhuge Liang, the famous strategist of Shu, and by the political resourcefulness of Cao Cao, his principal enemy in Wei.

The action of the book, which largely respects known historical facts, ranges with equal effect from large-scale strategic battles to striking tactical gambits, acts of individual heroism and moments of tense personal challenge and decision. The study of great men struggling against fate, the use of memorable action to reveal character, and a clear, accessible prose have together made this one of the most popular and widely read of all Chinese books.

Shuihuzhuan (*The Water Margin*)

The minor rebellion led by Song Jiang in the last years of the Northern Song (1120–1) had little effect upon the course of Chinese history, and yet in popular tradition it became the most powerful and lasting symbol of rebel values in the Chinese world. Song Jiang became a central figure around whom gathered legends of other bandits and rebels. The complex of stories circulated in many forms: we still have remnants of a primitive prose version and a number of plays from the 13th and 14th centuries. Eventually they were formed into one huge, organic structure, the *Shuihuzhuan*, and this, in various revised forms, has become one of China's major prose epics. Tradition associates the names of Shi Naian and Luo Guanzhong with its creation. But we lack even the original text and can know nothing useful about its author. What does survive is a mass of revised editions, varying greatly in length and textual character, from the 16th and 17th centuries. This free abundance was cut short in 1644, when Jin Shengtan (d. 1661) published a truncated version, stylishly rewritten, which won universal popularity until modern times.

These complexities seriously affect the *Shuihuzhuan's* integrity. As originally conceived, it tells the story of a brotherhood of 108 rebel heroes built up through many individual adventures and personal tragedies to a point of final and complete solidarity—a point at which the band turns collectively from fighting the forces of government to fighting its enemies. In the last of their loyal campaigns the heroes fall in death one by one until the cycle of their rise and decline is complete. Jin Shengtan would not allow rebels the dignity of belated loyalty to a legitimate government and swept away all but the first 70 chapters of a book which by then ran to 120. The book's challenging political implications have continued to exercise theorists in China even in recent times.

The *Shuihuzhuan* develops an ideal of rude manhood which

prizes physical valour and resourcefulness, unwavering loyalty between comrades, spontaneous (even brutal) antagonism to political power abused and to perfidious womanhood. To protect these values the heroes inflict bloodshed and terror without concern. Their deeds are described in prose which, though informal and vernacular in idiom, has a tense and compelling eloquence. And their personalities, despite those deeds which subvert many of China's most valued institutions, emerge with a larger-than-life distinctness that has won them an honoured place in Chinese cultural tradition.

Xiyouji (*The Journey to the West*)

This huge prose narrative of the 16th century ultimately derives from a real journey made by the great Buddhist translator Xuanzang (596?–664) between AD 629 and 645. He left his own account of the lands of India and Central Asia he visited, but in the course of time the journey was overlaid with folklore and fable, and came to be seen more as a journey of the spirit through hardship and danger to Paradise. The Xuanzang of popular tradition dedicated himself to the goal of collecting sacred texts from the Buddha's own hands. He was protected and guided by grotesque spirit-guardians—a monkey, a pig and a dark spirit of the sands—and his journey was extended into a sequence of adventurous episodes in which the guardians and their battles became the centre of interest. Late in the 16th century an author (some say Wu Cheng'en, 1506?–82?) took up the rich inheritance of traditional versions of the story and developed them into a large-scale prose work in the fashion of his time.

The result, entitled *Xiyouji*, is the comic masterpiece of Chinese literature. It succeeds in combining a sense of the grandeur of the pilgrim's divine mission with a merciless exposure of human fallibility in its participants. The most brilliant realization is the character of the monkey, who ranges at will through the heights and depths of the universe, at once passionate and mocking, as he sets about his task as guardian and guide. His fellow pilgrim, the pig, is ruled by coarser human appetites, and the cheerful friction between the two at every stage and level of their enterprise is one of the book's chief delights.

The narrative contents are deeply indebted to folklore and popular religion. So clearly do the universal themes of mythology show through the book's transparent texture that, from the time of its first publication, editors and commentators have been drawn irresistibly to erect upon it layer after layer of allegorical significance—a process which continues unabated in our own time. The appeal of the book does not in the end rest upon such grave exegesis, and it has long been established as a favourite with readers young and old.

Jin Ping Mei (*The Golden Lotus*)

In the late 16th century, an age which refashioned traditional themes into large narrative structures and cultivated all manner of popular literary and dramatic forms, the *Jin Ping Mei* came as a bold experiment. Its unknown author adopted the hundred-chapter scope of more traditional fiction, borrowed an episode from the *Shuihuzhuan* for his subject, freely drew upon the popular songs and stories of his time, and made from all this a powerful, forward-looking novel of provincial life.

The borrowed materials do not conceal the newness of his enterprise. The action takes place almost entirely within the private household of a Shandong merchant, Ximen Qing. While he grows in wealth and influence, contemptuously manipulating the officers of local government, his six wives and their servants contrive a deadly network of social and sexual rivalry, jealousy, revenge and degradation. Their struggle for survival brings about their destruction: Ximen Qing's own relentless debauchery finally kills him, and his household, without his central support, collapses and scatters its members in all directions. A scene of macabre vengeance reappears from the *Shuihuzhuan*, and history itself completes the invited disaster as barbarian conquerors sweep into northern China.

Much of the *Jin Ping Mei* deals with petty details and incidents of domestic life and with the ferocious passions engendered by them. The author profoundly understood the society of women and conveys in his narrative the character of their life, their dialogue and relationships as convincingly as any modern realist. He also conveys an awareness of the pleasures of life, and luxuriates in descriptions of female beauty, of food, clothes, music, spectacle and erotic adventures of all kinds. His unabashed freedom of sexual reference, so essential to this study of bedroom politics, has earned the book both misconceived censure and prurient notoriety. In fact it is grimly moralistic: popular notions of retribution and reincarnation thinly disguise a view of mankind that is uncompromisingly black.

The text is rich in dialect expressions, editorially imperfect and often corrupt—features which still await the attention of a serious modern editor.

Rulin waishi (*The Scholars*)

Wu Jingzi (1701–54) worked on this, his famous satirical novel, in the 1730s and 1740s, at a time when he passed from the inherited security of an eminent landed family in east China to a state of penury in Nanjing. On a personal level, the book presents an apologia for the attitudes and style of life which led him to turn away from seeking distinction in official examinations and devote himself to unbridled public and private generosity. The gesture which finished with his fortune was the restoration of a Nanjing temple to the legendary founder of Wu. And this quixotic act of family piety claims a proud place in *Rulin waishi*, where we also find a shrewd and candid portrait of the author himself. Around him are clustered the spongers and confidence men attracted by this easy prey, but also the more sympathetic, though no less sharply observed, members of his family and staff.

The *Rulin waishi* is a string of episodes linked more by theme than by plot. Individually, they mostly derive from the experiences and anecdotes of his family and friends, some with only perfunctory fictional disguise. But the *Rulin waishi* amounts to more than a personal scrapbook: it sustains an intense and wide-ranging critique of a whole class in Chinese society—the men who pursued learning with their eyes on examination success and official distinction. Wu saw the examination system of his time as an abuse of true learning, stultifying talent and rewarding ineptitude. He found truly civilized values only outside the official academic institutions, and gave his book an outer frame of exemplary culture, beginning with Wang Mian (1287–1359), the herd-boy turned hermit-painter, and ending with four plebeian exponents of gentlemanly arts.

The book is written in a light, subtle, truly vernacular prose; its narrative moves restlessly, within very few pages darting from end to end of China and from top to bottom of the social system. It shows men not always as fixed, static characters, but as changing, often profoundly, under the influence of circumstances and new social relationships. The satire is harsh, at times grotesque. More than most, this book gains resonance and significance in proportion to the reader's own experience of Chinese life.

Hongloumeng (*Dream of the Red Chamber*)

Cao Xueqin (1715?–63), the author of this most beloved of Chinese books, was born into a family which had served as personal bond-servants to the Kangxi Emperor. As a child he lived in patrician splendour in Nanjing until the family suffered disgrace and ruin, when they moved to Beijing. There, in impoverished middle age, he eventually embarked upon the novel in which the family memories, bitter and sweet, were painfully relived. The book never reached a settled and final condition. Scholars still struggle to disentangle the manuscripts and editions in which 80, probably original, and 40 revised (or supplied?) chapters are severally or jointly preserved. And connoisseurs are fascinated by the implications of early manuscript commentaries from the hands of people very close to the author.

The book takes us into the sumptuous private world of a patrician family, and within that into the world of the pampered adolescents who inhabit a symbolically enclosed garden inside the family compound. Their tiny society, with its exquisite sensibilities, its tenderness, reproach, tears, longing and regret, is a fairyland in fact as well as in metaphor. For the author has placed the whole sublunary action within a framework of divine predestination, and to his hero, the boy Baoyu, he gives privileged knowledge of the destinies awaiting the girls among whom he lives. As violence and tragedy overtake them individually and collectively Baoyu detaches himself from the world and stalks off into a wintry landscape.

For millions of Chinese readers *Hongloumeng* grips the heart with the pangs of first love. But it also surrounds the young people at its centre with a complex and undeniably real society of mature men and women hardened by age, greed, lust, ambition or bitter experience. All internal and external calamities which befall them are the fruits of adult responsibilities ignored or betrayed, and the formal reliance on a surrounding mythical framework never dispels this unpleasant reality.

The story is written with an intoxicating sweetness and euphony. It develops the novelistic skills first tried in the *Jin Ping Mei* and gains poetic intensity from the tradition of lyrical drama.

Jinghuayuan (Flowers in the Mirror)

Li Ruzhen (1763–1830?), the author of this colourful, encyclopedic novel, was a successful scholar but did not rise to high government office. His *Jinghuayuan* was in print by 1828. It offers an imaginative extravaganza in praise of women and denounces the discrimination suffered by them in traditional society. The conceit implied in the title (flower-spirits exiled from heaven become women on earth), the picturesque and tendentious voyagings imagined in the early chapters and the elaborate moral allegory in the last are the most attractive features of this otherwise unwieldy book.

Lao Can youji (The Travels of Lao Can)

This short novel, which appeared between 1904 and 1907, chronicles an imagined journey through parts of north China. Lao Can, a wandering philanthropist who lives by healing the sick, embodies many ideas and sympathies of the author, Liu E (1857–1909), an active but often misunderstood campaigner for reform in the dying years of the Chinese empire. The book is episodic and formless, but full of varied and vivid scenes of contemporary life and landscape. Liu's sympathy for the victims of a harsh and corrupt judicial system and for those of the inadequately controlled floodwaters of the Yellow River underlies much of the narrative content. His vernacular prose descriptions are renowned for their eloquence and exactness of observation. *G.D.*

Dramatic narratives and oral literature

Dramatic narratives

This heading represents the Chinese term *zhugongdiao*, a form of narration developed during the Song period. Its outstanding characteristic was the alternation of prose narrative with interludes of song organized in tiny suites of tunes, each suite set in a distinctive musical mode and key. This musical versatility gives the form its conventional name, literally 'all the modes'. A performance possibly of this type is described in Chapter 51 of *Shuihuzhuan*. Only two complete texts, perhaps from the 13th century, remain as survivors of the genre: *Xixiangji* by Master Dong, retelling the story of Yingying from the Tang tale, and *Liu Zhiyuan*, a heroic tale of the founder of the Han dynasty. A third, on the romance of the Tang emperor, Xuanzong, and his favourite Yang Guifei is fragmentary.

Storytelling

Literary sources from the 12th century to recent times describe a flourishing storytelling profession in the society of traditional China, best documented for urban centres. It has now all but died out. The limited opportunities for first-hand study reveal a wide variety of styles and performance techniques, always with a strongly local character. The long prose sagas of Yangzhou contrast with the rhythmical 'southern ditties' (*nanyin*) of Guangdong and the drum songs of the north. The profession was tightly organized in schools and guilds, with specialized traditions passed down through long apprenticeships to new generations of performers. Oral skills gained by experience took precedence over written texts, and some forms were indeed the preserve of blind artists. Subject-matter ranged as widely as drama and fiction through history, folklore, romance and domestic affairs. A more or less close relationship has generally been assumed to exist between oral and written narrative. *G.D.*

Western and Marxist influences in the 19th and 20th centuries

In the 19th century the Chinese intelligentsia were forced to take notice of the West because of its military prowess; their attention then turned to Western political and social systems as the source of that strength; only lastly did they show interest in Western culture. In fact it was with reluctance that they acknowledged that the West had a culture worthy of the name. The first translations of

Western literature were made in the 1870s, but were of little account. It was not until the 1900s that translations appeared in any appreciable numbers. Among the first British authors represented were Rider Haggard, Walter Scott, Charles Lamb (*Tales from Shakespeare*) and Charles Dickens. Dumas, *père* and *fils*, and Victor Hugo were foremost of the French. Harriet B. Stowe's *Uncle Tom's Cabin* was the most popular American work. Pushkin was the first Russian on the Chinese scene, followed by Lermontov and Tolstoy. Crime stories also flourished, Sherlock Holmes becoming almost a household name. High adventure, romance and a powerful tug at the heartstrings were evidently at a premium. At the same time there was also interest in the way of life and especially the moral code and spiritual goals of Westerners that these works revealed: by the turn of the century these too had come to be taken seriously. Lin Shu (1852–1924), the most famous and prolific of Chinese translators, had the highest regard for Dickens's compassion and a gingerly admiration for Haggard's questing imperial adventurers. Byron, one of the few foreign poets introduced in this first phase, was similarly valued for virtues the Chinese felt they lacked, namely devotion to love and liberty. Yet native Chinese writing showed few visible signs of being affected by foreign example. Traditional literary forms still survived the strain and agitation attending the collapse of the Chinese state. Huang Zunxian (1848–1905), for example, is considered to have been the great innovator of his day, and his impassioned poems on current events did brush aside conventions of composition and diction, but he did not break the mould of the old verse forms.

The traditional style of literature was challenged in the second decade of this century by the New Literature Movement associated with the political upheavals of the May Fourth Movement. This 'literary revolution', which was announced in 1917, developed and put into effect the ideas of the previous generation, but a vital difference was that its practitioners, through having studied abroad, had fed on Western literature at a formative stage. They were ready to accept in its totality the notion that the written word should follow the spoken word, to discard the classical heritage, and to experiment with the great variety of exotic forms they had discovered in their reading. Indeed, they were obliged to turn to Western models, as they could not create a new literature out of thin air. At the same time as creating their own works, they carried out a greatly expanded programme of translation, both to educate their fellow countrymen and as individual acts of homage. By the end of the 1920s almost all the foreign literary giants had been represented. The degree of influence they exercised in China, however, was not in proportion to their stature; it was related to the social concerns and emotional needs of the younger section of the educated class, who were the pace-setters. Some European authors of unquestionable eminence did make a tremendous impact because of their ideas, but their works proved to be beyond imitation in China. Ibsen was a case in point. 'Ibsenism' dominated public discussion after a special issue of the *New Youth* magazine on Ibsen was published in 1918, and the self-emancipation of Nora in *A Doll's House* remained a burning issue for several years, but Chinese playwrights did not seem to learn much from his dramatic art. Similarly, Tolstoy's 'What is Art' (trans. 1921), which connected good art with the transmission of uplifting emotions, was eagerly seized upon, but his great novels were made less welcome than *Resurrection* and his parables. Still, practically all contributors to the New Literature either had their declared foreign mentors (sometimes multiple), or located themselves in a framework of theory imported from the West. In the latter respect, Realism and neo-Romanticism initially disputed the territory; at the end of the 1920s 'proletarian literature' made its challenge, followed by 'mass literature', which arose out of the Soviet Union but eventually found itself living a changed life in the Chinese countryside under Communist control during the war against Japan. Politically less committed writers, for their part, acquired in the 1930s the sophistication and confidence to find their own individual way. Since most of the more prominent among them had studied abroad, however, they continued to take some colouring from the literature of their host countries. The onset of war blurred the picture considerably: hitherto different paths now converged in response to the call of patriotism or the urgent need to write of the things at hand.

Fiction under the Republic

The strongest foreign influence on fiction in the first decade of the New Literature came from pre-revolutionary Russia, which had closer affinities with China than the industrialized democracies of the West. Russian idealism also appealed to young Chinese eager to construct a new society, and the link was doubly forged when they found themselves subject to the same frustrations and despair as the Russian intellectuals who had gone before them; Chinese fiction in the 1920s abounds with characters who identified themselves with Russian fictional heroes, and often shared the same fate. Lu Xun (1881–1936), the author of the first modern short story to be published in China (in 1918), took his title, 'The Diary of a Madman', and his basic design, from Gogol, and others of his stories were either prompted by, or borrowed from, Russian ones. But Lu Xun's debt was more in terms of technique than of content, with the influence coming above all from Andreyev and Artzybashev, and also the Pole, Sienkiewicz. To some extent he was describing the same phenomena, an ignorant peasantry and, later, lapsed or renegade revolutionaries. At the same time Yu Dafu was picturing the alienated intellectual who is so ineffectual that he does not get as far as declaring himself—essentially the 'superfluous man' of Turgenev. In the late 1920s and early 1930s, following the involvement of many young political activists in the Northern Expedition, which was to sweep away the warlords, and the subsequent coup against the left by Chiang Kai-shek, the revolutionary with fire in his belly (in some cases the dead fire of nihilism) appeared in the work of Ba Jin (b. 1904) and Mao Dun (1896–1981). They in their turn found Russian writers helpful in constructing the typology of characters and setting up telling scenes, as well as drawing lines of conflict and contradiction. To the names of Turgenev, Andreyev and Artzybashev was added that of Ropshin for his *Pale Horse*. By about 1930 the writings of the literary left in China were being directly influenced by developments in the Soviet Union. Its influence made itself felt diffusely in the entry of the proletariat into Chinese fiction, in the theme of class conflict, and the stress on economic factors. Only occasionally was a particular work obviously used as a model, one example being Fadeyev's *The Rout* for Xiao Jun's *Village in August* (1934), which was about a band of guerrillas in Manchuria.

The influence of other European countries on fiction in China is less tangible. Certain books were extremely popular in the early stages of the New Literature, including Goethe's *Die Leiden des jungen Werther* (trans. 1921) and Romain Rolland's *Jean-Christophe* (trans. 1926), but the variety of foreign literature to which people were exposed was so diverse and the discussion of it ranged so widely that the threads cannot be neatly disentangled. One major writer who did freely acknowledge his debts was Lao She (1898–1966), who taught in London in the 1920s. Starting with Dickens, whose weakness for demented characters is clearly in evidence in his early novels and stories, Lao She passed quickly over Conrad, and then turned to Swift's *Gulliver's Travels* for a framework for his own *Cat City*, an allegory of the parlous state of China. But for *Rickshaw Boy* (1937) he needed no props, and thereafter the sense of place in his books was overriding.

Poetry under the Republic

The preponderance of East European over West European and American influence noticeable in fiction was reversed in poetry. Initially the Anglo-American school of Imagism and the phenomenon of Whitmanism appealed in their different ways as example and inspiration to budding Chinese poets seeking to rid the medium of stale custom and breathe some life into the weakly infant New Verse. Imagism was introduced and demonstrated by Hu Shi (1891–1962) to give clarity and point to the shapeless free verse that was adopted as much for moral as artistic reasons. Guo Moruo (1892–1978) was inspired by Whitman to celebrate manifestations of life and strength in the world about him, and the indomitable spirit of great men of all times. In the mid-1920s the

'Crescent' school came together to promote two aims: to impose some discipline by composing in regular stanzas, and to enrich the texture of contemporary verse by reference above all to English romantic poetry. Keats was the master to whom both Wen Yiduo (1899–1946) and Xu Zhimo (1895–1931) paid homage, though Wen also drew on classical Chinese poetry and Xu had too a fondness for Hardy. Again, both experimented with the dramatic monologue and dialogue, probably with Browning and Hardy in mind. About the same time 19th-century French poetry made itself felt, first through the impenetrable symbolism of Li Jinfa (1900–76), whose collections were published between 1925 and 1927, and then in the melancholy, dreamlike, impressionistic poems of Dai Wangshu (1905–50), which took their cue from Verlaine's 'rien que la nuance'. Ai Qing (b. 1910) sojourned in France like Li and Dai, but he was more intent on grim reality than aesthetics; his leaning was towards Verhaeren and Apollinaire. The lean, gaunt style he developed was nevertheless his own. With Germany, the most successful transaction in poetic terms was undoubtedly that between Rilke and Feng Zhi (b.1905): Feng's *Sonnets* (1941) blended several of the themes and intimations of the ninth Duino Elegy into his own perspective with remarkable ease and fluency. Of Russian poets the only one to attract much of a following was Mayakovsky; to the left wing in China he was the great trail-blazer, a poet of stunning novelty and explosiveness who swept the language of the street into his verse. He left his mark on Ai Qing, but the man most closely identified with him was Tian Jian (1914–1985), the 'drumbeat' poet of the war against Japan, mainly on account of his pulsating rhythm, common language and rapid ringing of changes in length of line. The radical

Lu Xun (extreme right of group), at the height of his fame in 1933 with Bernard Shaw in Shanghai.

poets who migrated to the Communist stronghold of Yan'an during the war, however, were encouraged to learn from indigenous folksong.

Drama under the Republic

Since Chinese drama had previously been built around song sequences, the new spoken play when it came to China was entirely dependent on foreign models. As with other branches of literature, pre-May Fourth productions had little connection with what came after, though in both phases there was a shortage of home products and therefore frequent recourse was had to adaptations of foreign plays. Appreciable audiences were not attracted to the spoken drama until the mid-1930s, and when they did come they wanted to be entertained, hence the popularity, either at first or second hand, of Oscar Wilde and the French masters of the 'well-made play'. More daring or more intellectual Western playwrights exerted their influence on closet drama or student productions. Ibsenist motifs abounded (the idea in *Ghosts* of the sins of the father being visited on the son lasted well, for example), but Eugene O'Neill stands out as a dramatist who made a direct contribution to more than one well-known Chinese play: besides more subtle effects, the device he used in *The Emperor Jones* of staging episodes from the fugitive's past in the form of hallucinations reappeared in Hong Shen's (1894–1955) *Zhao Yanwang* (1922) and Cao Yu's (b. 1910) *The Wild* (1937). Shaw was well known, but generally considered too wordy; a Shavian style of debate was nevertheless employed in the comedies of Ding Xilin (1893–1974) and Xu Yu (1908–80). Even Molière found a pupil, an able one at that, in Li Jianwu (1907–1982) in the late 1930s; Li also found sufficient cause in China to justify the passage there of Schiller's *Die Räuber* (in 1946). Despite his eclecticism, Li was typical in that his best plays owed least to others.

Developments since 1949

After the People's Republic of China was founded in 1949 all the arts came under the sway of Marxism. By this time Western forms of literature had become natural to Chinese writers, and the approved source of inspiration was not very inspirational, so it was mainly to conform to doctrine that they shaped their works, the doctrine of Socialist Realism, with certain Maoist refinements. The Socialist Realism promulgated in the 1950s in China was in essence the same as that laid down in the 1930s in the Soviet Union. It required that subject-matter should be so selected as to confirm the Marxist-Leninist view of the world. Socialism was to be shown as ever growing in strength and moulding society in the way intended, with capitalism in all its manifestations going to the wall. Men and women were to be portrayed as overcoming all difficulties, whether those of the physical world or of human relationships. Writers were to show 'the typical in the individual'. As the 1950s were the great decade of the 'production struggle' there was in fact every opportunity to feature the toiler as hero, and the doctrine did not generally act as a constraint on production.

With the Great Leap Forward of 1958–9 the literary sights were raised to take in Revolutionary Romanticism, at the instigation of Mao Zedong, whose own poetry is marked by the hyperbole and imaginative vigour that the term implies; nevertheless, Revolutionary Romanticism was not the invention of Mao: it was already twinned with Socialist Realism in the Soviet programme in 1934. Amateur poets responded immediately to the new call, but prose fiction could not so comfortably accommodate itself. In the following short phase, which coincided with a downturn in the economy, the Chinese establishment fought a rearguard action against revisionism in literature, the chief target being the Yugoslav line of 'active coexistence', which threatened to re-admit humanism, 'eternal values', and so on. At the same time there was enough support at home for a literature of wide range and broad appeal to allow some satirical and controversial works to appear.

Ideological rectitude reasserted itself with a vengeance in the Cultural Revolution, the age of the 'revolutionary model operas'. Appropriate scraps from Engels and Lenin were adduced, but the real authority derived from Mao Zedong, particularly that section of his 'Yan'an Talks' (1942) which decreed that art should be 'higher, more intense, more concentrated, more typical and more ideal' than real life. The net result was to create a pyramid structure with the invulnerable revolutionary hero standing on top.

After the 'gang of four' fell in 1976, it took writers some years to find their own voice. The first genuinely new notes were sounded by the 'misty' (*menglong*) poets led by Bei Dao, Gu Cheng and Shu Ting, so called because of their veiled references and private imagery. They were more reacting against conventional Chinese verse than responding to external influence, from which they were in any case mostly cut off. In time the barriers against the outside world were dismantled, but as knowledge of foreign languages was lacking, it was themes and techniques rather than individual quality that attracted the more receptive younger generation of writers when 20th-century world literature became available to them through translations and commentaries. 'Alienation' and 'stream of consciousness' were two of the most popular talking points, and in the theatre 'absurdity' appeared in Gao Xingjian's (b. 1940) *Bus stop*, a Chinese version of Beckett's *Waiting for Godot*. Alarmed by the interest in such 'unhealthy' tendencies, the Party launched a campaign against 'spiritual pollution' in 1983–4, targeted at Western Modernism, and made a further attempt to combat 'bourgeois liberalism' in 1986–7, but in both cases the inhibitory effect was short-lived. The guidelines once insisted on that writers should support socialism and the leadership of the

Communist Party were, until the influence of the events of the summer of 1989, generally ignored. Sex, violence and anomie have re-entered Chinese literature, due in no small measure to foreign example.

In Taiwan by contrast, the literary world has always kept abreast of current trends in the West. The 1960s was the great decade for graduates of university foreign literature departments to show their paces. The 1970s saw the more sturdy growth of native-born novelists who dig down to the very roots of society for their materials. Poets have deliberately fractured the language in their pursuit of modernism. For some time, but largely unnoticed, literature in Taiwan has been part of world literature.   *D.P.*

DRAMA, MUSIC AND CINEMA

The drama tradition

Chinese drama, as we know it today, has a continuous history of some 900 years. The first record of the performance of a play dates back to the early part of the Northern Song period. This performance took place in the entertainments quarter of the capital Kaifeng and is evidence that the vast and prosperous Song cities with their countless forms of public entertainment created the milieu in which Chinese drama took shape.

This highly distinctive theatre was made up of various elements—music, song, recitation and movement—some of which as individual items had existed in China for over 1000 years before the Song, but the final formation of the drama appears to have resulted from the merging of two existing forms of entertainment, ballad medleys and comic sketches.

These developments in the theatre were not restricted to northern China since there is evidence of similar evolution of style elsewhere—in particular, in Zhejiang and Fujian—but it was the northern style that was to emerge as the dominant form. The period of the Yuan dynasty, in fact, saw a remarkable flowering of the northern style of plays, which had become known as *zaju* , 'variety plays' or 'miscellany plays'. Not only was there a wide range of themes—historical, picaresque, religious, courtroom and military, as well as love stories—but the poetry written as librettos for the arias was recognized as being of the highest standard. The obvious reason for this surge in quality was the interest shown in the theatre by literary men, who were denied access to official careers under the Mongol rule of the Yuan dynasty.

The most celebrated and prolific of the *zaju* writers was Guan Hanqing, whose life spans roughly the last 70 years of the 13th century and who is regarded by many as China's most outstanding playwright. He is credited with having written over 60 plays, of which 17 have survived. His lively personality is reflected in his work, but his concern about injustice and corruption in society can be seen in what is perhaps his best known work, *Injustice Suffered by Dou E*. It is a tragic piece about a widow who is falsely accused of murder and is executed following a forced confession under torture, but whose name is cleared in the final act when she reappears in a ghostly form. If the story of Dou E is a tragedy, then Wang Shifu's *The Western Chamber* is the archetypal love story in which the handsome scholar and beautiful girl, after various adventures, are eventually united.

In the course of the Ming dynasty the *zaju* began to decline, and by the second half of the 16th century it had been replaced as the major theatrical style by a form of drama from south China. This style was called the *chuanqi* and could be distinguished from its northern predecessor by its music, the extended length of its plays and by its recognizably gentler tone.

A scholar, Gao Ming, who wrote in the second half of the 14th century, was one of the playwrights who developed this style and his famous play *The Story of the Lute* was thought to be the best of the early *chuanqi* pieces. It explores a theme familiar in popular Chinese writing—the complex problems of loyalty and responsibility that arise when a scholar leaves his home and family and achieves success, position and a second and advantageous marriage in the capital.

From the middle of the 16th century southern drama moved into a more refined phase as dramatists began to use the music of the *Kunqu* (literally, 'Kun tunes'; named after the city Kun-shan), a form of drama popular in the Suzhou area, the economic and cultural centre of the Lower Yangtze region. It soon spread, and by the 17th century it was the supreme style of theatre in the country. A number of outstanding plays were written in this style, of which the most notable were Tang Xianzu's (1550–1617) *The Peony Pavilion*, a love-story, linking dream and reality; Kong Shangren's (1648–1718) *The Peach Blossom Fan*, which gives a vivid portrayal of the disastrous events when the Ming dynasty fell to the Manchus; and Hong Sheng's (c. 1645–1704) *The Palace of Eternal Youth*, which is a powerful presentation of the famous story of the Tang Emperor Xuanzong, and his love for the concubine Yang Guifei.

The sophisticated *Kunqu* began to lose ground in the course of the Qing dynasty and virtually disappeared in the middle of the 19th century when the Taiping wars brought destruction to the Suzhou area. By then, however, a new form of theatre, the Peking Opera, was already in the ascendancy.   *D.R.*

The Chinese theatre: social background

The theatre world produced masterpieces of drama literature in the form of *zaju* (during the Yuan period) and *Kunqu* (in the 16th and 17th centuries). However, these sophisticated styles were based upon only a small section of the vast array of popular theatrical forms that developed in China from Song times onwards. This popular theatre was largely ignored or unacknowledged by the educated classes and was left almost exclusively in the hands of the professional actors and drama troupes. Players' theatres like this have existed elsewhere in the world (e.g. the *commedia dell'arte*) but nowhere have they matched the scale and variety of the popular theatre in China.

The popular theatre also came to be integrated closely into the framework of Chinese society and became institutionalized to the point where it was an indispensable feature of the social and religious life of the community. It existed as a medium for popular entertainment from the 10th century and there are detailed descriptions of theatre buildings in the Song cities. It is known that there were over 50 theatres in the Northern Song capital at Kaifeng and even more in Hangzhou, the capital of the Southern Song. However, it seems that most performances did not take place in theatres as such, but were given either on the permanent stages to be found in village temples and wealthy residences or, more likely, on temporary stages which the drama companies themselves would set up. The travelling theatre companies would perform as a matter of course at all kinds of public occasions, such as local New Year celebrations and other festivals. Influential families would regularly hire the companies to put on plays to accompany the ceremonials of ancestor worship, and any rich patron could engage actors to perform for family celebrations, such as weddings and birthdays.

Theatricals were thus all-pervasive in Chinese life, but none the less the acting profession as such had the lowest social status. Actors were ranked with prostitutes and slaves, and it was government policy to deny them social advancement, since they and their children were officially banned from the civil service examinations. The drama world does seem to have been associated with prostitution from the earliest times and the theatres of the Yuan period may in many cases have been little more than brothels. The travelling life of most actors inevitably led the settled population to view them as vagabonds. In addition, the practice which forbade men and women to appear on the stage together led to further complications. The companies were necessarily all-male (or, to a lesser extent, all-female) and the homosexual background to much of the female impersonation expertise in the all-male companies did nothing to raise the moral status of the profession in the eyes of most of the community. It was not until modern times that actors and actresses were able to gain a respectable position in Chinese society.

D.R.

The dramatic form

The most important of the elements that constitute a Chinese play is the music. It is therefore reasonable to refer to the plays as 'operas', although they have little resemblance to opera as it is known in the West. It is the musical element that distinguishes one form of Chinese drama from another. Each style of drama has its own repertoire of melodies, which are entirely familiar to the audience, and the writer of a play is therefore a librettist rather than a composer. The small orchestra which accompanied the plays, and traditionally was visible to the audience on the side of the stage, would vary in its range of instruments according to the style of drama. The orchestra would consist of strings, wind instruments and percussion, and the percussion—drums, gongs, cymbals and the distinctive clapperboards—in many styles held a dominant position. The strings were either bowed, as in the case of the two-stringed fiddle or *huqin*, or plucked, as with the lute or *pipa*. The best-known of the wind instruments was the transverse flute or *dizi*. On the whole, the strings were used more in northern styles and the wind instruments in the south, with the *dizi* being an important element, for example, in the *Kunqu*, a form of drama popular in the Suzhou area.

A performance by a travelling theatre company.

The plays were presented on a bare stage with minimum props, so that attention was focused entirely on the performance of the actors, whose costume and make-up would range from the virtually plain to the highly exotic. The actors would perform their parts within specific role categories, which would be immediately recognizable to the audience. These role categories, reminiscent to some extent of the *commedia dell'arte*, were, with slight variations, common to all styles of drama in China and normally consisted of four main types: the male role or *sheng*, the female role or *dan*, the painted face or *jing* (which included particular male characters such as warriors, gods, etc.) and the clown or *chou*. An actor would specialize in one, or possibly, two of these role categories. Symbolic gestures and movements, familiar to the audience, would be used to signify riding a horse, stepping over a threshold, etc. and objects like whips or oars could be carried to make the symbolism more explicit. The whole performance was an elaborate and stylized presentation of emotions and action.

The original Yuan *zaju* or 'variety plays' were composed within strict limits, with normally only four acts and restrictions on the use of singers and music within the acts. The later southern plays were much longer and more diffuse and, from the *Kunqu* style onwards, the habit grew of performing only particular sections or acts. This supports the view that the Chinese were more interested in presenting intensity of feeling surrounding one incident rather than analysing emotions or action over a protracted sequence, and it may help to explain the absence in the Chinese theatre of tragedies of the type known in the West.   *D.R.*

The Peking Opera and the modern phase

Above: character roles from Peking Opera: (1) *Laosheng* (old man), (2) *Jing* (warrior, god, etc.), (3) *Wenchou* ('civilian' comic role).

Far left: actress in battle costume (playing a male role). Left: Mei Lanfang as Yang Guifei.

The Peking Opera emerged in the capital as a distinctive theatrical form in the first part of the 19th century. It was a fusion of two musical styles, the *xipi* and *erhuang*. The origins of these musical styles are not clear, but their blending into one new form of theatre seems to have occurred among drama troupes in Anhui Province. It was a visit of an Anhui company to Beijing in 1790 for the Qianlong Emperor's 80th birthday celebrations that introduced the new style to the capital.

In the first half of the 19th century, as the popularity of the new Peking Opera increased, four 'Great Anhui Companies' dominated the Beijing stage. They introduced an altogether more vigorous style of stage presentation, and their emphasis on acrobatics has been a feature of the Peking Opera ever since. This 'military' phase continued in the second half of the century and the most popular performers of the period were the exponents of the *laosheng* or older male roles (usually generals). The greatest of these performers was Cheng Zhanggeng (1812–80) who was thought by many to have been the outstanding Peking Opera actor of the 19th century. Another exponent of *laosheng* roles was Tan Xinpei (1847–1917), whose career stretched into this century and who helped in the training of the best-known of all Peking Opera actors, Mei Lanfang (1894–1961). Mei was an exponent of the *dan* (female) roles and his fame spread all over China and beyond. His supreme position as an interpreter of female roles indicates that the content of the Peking Opera widened considerably this century, and the respect paid to him confirmed the rise in the status of the Chinese acting profession. (Mei was one of the last female impersonators or *dan* since these roles have now been taken over entirely by actresses.)

The Peking Opera is a popular form of theatre and is not credited with any great literary quality. The structure of the plays is generally loose and they draw their material mainly from earlier plays and traditional novels and stories. The music is relatively simple with a limited number of aria sequences and the dominant instruments are the percussion and *huqin*, the two-string fiddle.

During the 20th century proponents of modernization in China have looked critically at the traditional theatre. Radicals in the May Fourth period wanted to see it abolished altogether, but a more considered approach has been to introduce reforms. The theatre buildings have been made more Western in style and there have been many attempts to modify the form of the dramas. Mei Lanfang himself experimented with plays on contemporary themes presented in a partially realistic way. The government of the People's Republic of China, on assuming power in 1949, was uneasy about the political and social content of some of the traditional repertoire and, as a result, some plays were banned or revised. However, traditional theatre continued without major disturbance until the Cultural Revolution in the mid-1960s.

The Cultural Revolution deemed all traditional drama to be the propaganda of the old 'feudal' classes and the Chinese stage was occupied exclusively from 1966 to 1971 by the eight so-called model operas (in fact, five Peking Operas, two ballet-dramas and one symphonic work). The model operas were not without interest stylistically despite their unambiguous political message and the heroic posturing that went with it. The musical innovations and the use of realistic settings and contemporary themes may, in the long term, be seen as part of the development of the traditional theatre.

The new leadership which came to power following the death of Mao Zedong has positively encouraged the revival of the Peking Opera and all the regional forms of traditional theatre. However, there are indications that the authorities will wish to see that the theatre reflects the new spirit of modernization, and there are signs that experiments with the content and the form of the traditional plays will continue.   *D.R.*

Music

A Chinese child singing a folksong might well be supposed, by a casual Western listener, to be singing a Scottish (or for that matter, Irish or English) folksong. This is because the most typical Chinese melodies make use of an octave of five notes only: *do, re, mi, so, la, (do')*. Even though sets of seven notes (*do, re, mi, fa, so, la, ti (do')*) were extensively used at one time in China (and their influence persists), the skeleton of Chinese melody is always conspicuously one of five notes. But if the *scalar* structure of a Chinese tune reminds us of the five-note structure of many Western folksongs, the *melodic* structure is different. Chinese melody tends to flow on without repetition, whereas Western tunes tend to build up by repetition.

These five notes—*do, re, mi, so, la*—are also a harmonically agreeable chord; and the Chinese were aware of this harmony well over 2 000 years ago. The music of Confucian ritual (today almost vanished) laid great stress on the perfection of harmonious interrelationships between notes. There is evidence from song lyrics that the Chinese were playing free-reed mouth-organs as early as the 7th century BC, and such instruments—today to be heard in China, Japan, northeast Thailand, the Mekong Basin and Borneo—are usually played in simple harmonies of parallel fifths, fourths and octaves, with or without drones. This harmonic thickening of a melodic line—like the *organum* of medieval Western music—is still to be heard in certain kinds of Chinese opera and in village bands, and owes nothing to Western influence.

The most ancient Chinese music (the music of Confucian ritual) must originally have sounded somewhat like that of Bali or

Java today, for example, being played by an orchestra in which bell-chimes and stone-chimes were an important component, together with large zithers and mouth-organs. However, the instruments most commonly to be heard in China now have almost all been imported over the centuries from Central Asia. This applies in particular to the lutes, both plucked and bowed, and to the oboes and transverse flutes. Notwithstanding this importation of instruments, Chinese music has its own highly distinctive character. A musical broadcast from Beijing is likely to be confused only with the music of close neighbours such as Mongolia or Tibet. *L.E.R.P.*

Modes and scales

At least by the 3rd century BC the Chinese had developed—and in this development they were alone—an arithmetical procedure by which, theoretically, all possible notes of a (12 + 1)-note chromatic octave could be generated from a single fundamental note. The ordered mystery of this process fascinated not only generation after generation of Chinese musical scholars throughout the centuries, but also the Jesuits when they first made contact with the Middle Kingdom. To link music into the complex system of Chinese cosmology, the first note into the cycle, *huangzhong* (Yellow Bell), had to be of fixed pitch. Eleven further notes were produced by blowing on bamboo tubes of standard diameter, each either one-third shorter or longer than the previous tube. The invention of this process of cutting bamboo tubes to produce specific pitches is attributed to Ling Lun, mythical music-master to the mythical emperor Huang Di. By this process the following series is created: c-g-d-a-e-b-$f\sharp$-$c\sharp$-$g\sharp$-$d\sharp$-$a\sharp$-$e\sharp$ ($=f\natural$), (c being chosen here as the first note for convenience). This series was not regarded as a functional chromatic scale, but served to establish the fundamental notes for a complex system of scales and modes.

Scales are sequences of a limited number of pitches from the possible set of twelve generated in this way on a mathematical basis; the different modes can be regarded as created by shifting the final of such a scale from one note to another. The most typical Chinese scale is the five-note scale ('five sounds', *wu sheng*), without semitones, namely *do-re-mi-so-la*; but already in Zhou times seven-note scales are mentioned. The two additional notes are called *bian* ('becoming') and introduce the semitones *ti* (*biangong*) and *fa* (*bianzhi*).

From early times Chinese theoreticians attempted to resolve the problem of what is known in the West as the Pythagorean comma, that is, the slight sharpness of octaves produced by a generating process using blown fifths. A well-tempered scale, identical with the European, was established in theory in the writings of the Ming prince Zhu Zaiyu (AD 1596). In practice, however, Chinese musi-

cians of all periods adjusted pitches by ear in performance. Most probably, musical theory provided mathematical justification for established practice.

Musical notations

Although the twelve absolute pitches of the ancient musical system of China had definite names, it appears that at first they were not used to write down musical melodies. The earliest known musical notation from China is a tablature for zither, said to date from the 6th century AD. A tablature is a system of notation that describes how a note is to be produced, where the fingers are to be placed, rather than defining an absolute pitch. The latter is determined by the construction and tuning of an instrument. During the Tang dynasty musical tablatures are frequently mentioned in textual sources and in contemporary catalogues of libraries. Some of these notations survive in Japanese copies, for instance, a fragment of a modal prelude for the 4-stringed lute, *pipa* (AD 746), and a copy of a lute-tutor, presented in 838 to the Japanese official Fujiwara Sadatoshi by the Chinese *pipa*, master Lian Chengwu. Notations in tablature for about 120 suites and single-movement pieces, many of which can be traced by title in Chinese sources of the Tang period, are preserved in Japanese compilations from the 9th to the 13th centuries. A manuscript fragment, probably of late Tang or Five Dynasties date, and containing lute-tablatures closely related to those surviving in Japan, was discovered in the hidden library at Dunhuang (Cave of a Thousand Buddhas) in northwestern China.

A number of musical notations, both tablatures and pitch-notations (relative and absolute) survive from the Song period; for instance, tablatures for drum, zither, etc. are to be found in the popular encyclopedia *Shilin guangji*. Ritual melodies from the Tang dynasty are recorded in an absolute pitch-notation in the works of the Song philosopher Zhu Xi, and 29 songs of the poet-composer Jiang Kui also survive. From the Ming period, in addition to an abundance of zither tablatures, two different notations in the Daoist canonic collection, *Daozang*, have survived. One is as yet undeciphered, but from appearance is clearly an intermediate step between Tibetan liturgical notations and the notation of Japanese Buddhist chant. The other is in *gongche* notation, known from earlier Song sources and similar to Western sol-fa. The earliest notations for Chinese opera date from the Qing period. Notations for *Kunqu* (an operatic form originating in Ming times) and Peking Opera texts use only *gongche* notation, and only the vocal part is notated.

Since the 1920s an originally French numerical system of notation (1, 2, 3, 4, 5, 6, 7, for *do, re, mi, fa, so, la, ti*), first used by the Japanese, has been adopted, and is now the most commonly used notation in China.

Musical instruments

The earliest Chinese bone inscriptions dating from about 1300–1050 BC contain characters for musical instruments. They provide evidence for the use of drums played with drumsticks, stone-chimes (lithophones), and flutes. Excavations at the Shang sites at Anyang have yielded stone-chimes and vessel flutes.

During the Zhou period there is textual evidence for a considerable increase in the number of instrumental types. Percussion clappers, wooden scrapers ('tigers'), stringed instruments, flutes, and free-reed mouth-organs are all mentioned. During this period the classification of musical instruments into eight classes ('the eight sounds', *ba yin*) took place. A traditional list would include:

Class	Instrument
Stone	stone-chime (lithophone)
Metal	bell
Silk	zither
Bamboo	flute
Wood	pestle-and-mortar
Skin	drum
Gourd	mouth-organ
Earth	vessel-flute

Of the instruments used in Zhou times, the zither *qin*—originally probably five-stringed but later seven-stringed—has become the most refined musical instrument of China. The 26-stringed zither *se* is no longer in use, but its smaller version, the 13-stringed zither *zheng* (an ancestor of the Japanese *koto*) survives and is particularly popular in southern and southwestern China. The mouth-organ *sheng*, perhaps ancestral to the Western instrument

of the same name, although different in shape, consists of 13 or so slender bamboo-pipes of different sounding lengths opening into a wind-chest. The lower end of each pipe, concealed in the wind-chest, is covered by a free-reed of bronze. When a small hole near the reed is stopped, the pipe will sound.

The unification of China, and the ensuing dynasty of the Han, saw extensive contacts with the nomadic tribes of Central Asia, and, as a result, new instruments appeared on the Chinese musical scene. The most important of these was the four-stringed, short lute, *pipa*. In late Wei times, a vertical harp, *konghou*, came to China, to be seen in the frescos at Dunhuang, on a stele of the 6th century AD, and as fragments in the Japanese Imperial Storehouse at Nara. It never established itself in Chinese music, however, and its use was restricted to foreign orchestras at the Sui and Tang courts. In Tang times other lutes were introduced, such as the *yueqin*, a four-stringed flat lute, and the *sanxian*, a three-stringed flat lute played with a plectrum.

Bowed instruments probably originated in Central Asia sometime during the Tang period, and by Song times were used in China for popular folk music. Their collective name is *huqin*, 'barbarian *qin*'. The best known instrument of the family is the *erhu* with its beautiful veiled timbre. In Chinese opera bowed instruments are prominently represented, for example, the *jinghu* of Peking Opera.

Contact with Western music and with Western musical instruments has led to the development of a range of bowed instruments, based on the *huqin*, but ranging in size from double-bass to violin. These instruments have been developed to suit new compositional styles strongly influenced by Western writing.   *R.F.W.*

The seven-stringed zither *qin*.

The mouth organ *sheng*.

The *erhu*, one of the many varieties of two-stringed fiddles.

Western-style drama

The history of the modern drama movement in China goes back to the beginning of this century. The first major attempt to stage a Chinese play resembling a Western-style drama was in 1907 by Chinese students studying in Tokyo. They had come under the influence of the developing modern theatre in Japan. The main achievement of their curiously hybrid presentations of an excerpt from *La Dame aux Camelias* and a version of *Uncle Tom's Cabin* was that they won the warm approval of the Japanese drama critics. This student success gave inspiration to a modern theatre movement which was developing in Shanghai and which became known as 'the civilized drama' or *wenmingxi*. The *wenmingxi* was a mixed form, half Chinese, half Western. It was given great impetus by the Republican Revolution of 1911 and vied in popularity at that time with the traditional theatre in Shanghai and the cities of the lower Yangtze Valley. However, its popularity and prestige soon began to wane and it was condemned as backward in the May Fourth period.

The May Fourth Movement prompted a serious study of the Western theatre; European and American plays began to be translated. The performance of plays was organized largely by student drama clubs and the modern theatre became very much the interest of the educated, urban classes. This section of the community has remained the audience for the modern drama to this day. Enthusiasts like Tian Han (1898–1968) and Hong Shen (1894–1955), who brought back ideas on the theatre from their experiences studying abroad, made a major contribution to the establishment of a modern theatre and by the 1930s fully professional standards of writing and performance had been achieved. The work of Cao Yu (b.c. 1905) and his early plays, *Thunderstorm* (1933) and *Sunrise* (1935), are a measure of this achievement.

The Anti-Japanese War gave some stimulus to the modern theatre, which was able to make a positive propaganda contribution to the war effort and at the same time reach a wider public. After 1949 the new leadership gave support to the modern theatre as a realistic stage form and professional companies were set up throughout the country. Official policies placed constraints on the choice of subject-matter and of the established playwrights, Lao She (1899–1966), who wrote a number of plays after 1949, seems to have adjusted most easily to the new standards.

The whole modern theatre world was subjected to violent attack during the Cultural Revolution and virtually no plays were performed for 10 years. There has since been a major revival including the staging of plays by Cao Yu and Lao She, and numerous productions of foreign plays, including Shakespeare (there was a Shakespeare festival in 1986), Brecht's *Life of Galileo* and Arthur Miller's *Death of a Salesman*. Some young dramatists with experimental approaches to the theatre have also emerged. The most notable perhaps is Gao Xingjian, whose play *Bus Stop* with its similarity to *Waiting for Godot* caused some controversy. There seems to remain some uncertainty, however, in the minds of the young playwrights as they search for a form of modern theatre which will be both modern and Chinese. The official clampdown following the Tiananmen Square events in 1989 has inevitably placed further restraints on these experiments.

The 1979 Beijing production of Brecht's *Life of Galileo*, a play reflecting an emphasis on 'seeking truth through facts'.

In addition to the straight plays, another foreign import has been a new form of opera in the Western mould, called *geju*. Although it retains a distinctly Chinese flavour, it has taken over the stage conventions and the realistic settings and costumes of Western opera, and the instruments in the orchestra are largely Western. The best known example of these operas is *The White-haired Girl*, which was first performed in 1945. There have been many others since then and the ease with which contemporary subjects can be handled suggests a continuing interest in this form.   *D.R.*

Cinema

Film-making in China goes back to the beginning of this century, but those early activities were largely in the hands of foreigners, and it was not until the beginning of the 1920s that a Chinese film industry began to take shape. As public interest grew, and with it the prospect of commercial profit, small film companies appeared in large numbers in the major Chinese cities and by the mid-1920s, Shanghai, already recognized as the film capital of China, had no fewer than 300 such companies.

In the pre-Second World War years the Hollywood influence was all-pervasive and the majority of films shown in China were American. The Hollywood studio structure, with its star system, became the basis for Chinese film-making and much of the film equipment used was made in the USA.

The Chinese studios were highly productive and over 1 000 Chinese films were made before the Second World War. Stock adventure and romance themes, often adapted from traditional stories and plays, were dominant in the early period and production standards were not impressive. The personnel of the film world was drawn from the modern theatre and, in particular, from its early popular form. Later, dramatists with a more thorough background in the Western theatre became involved in cinema work and people like Hong Shen, Ouyang Yuqian, Tian Han and Xia Yan attempted to raise standards. They also brought a greater emphasis on contemporary, social themes, and because of this often found themselves at odds with government censors.

Of the many pre-war films mention should be made of *The Orphan Saves his Grandfather* (*Guer jiu zu ji*), made by the Star Company in 1923 and the first Chinese film to have wide success in China; *Singsong Girl Red Peony* (*Genü Hongmudan*), the first Chinese 'talkie', made in 1931 by the Star Company, and scripted by Hong Shen; and *Song of the Fishermen* (*Yu guang qu*), which was completed by the Lianhua Company in 1934 and which was perhaps the most widely successful of the more serious social criticism films, winning acclaim at the 1935 Moscow International Film Festival.

During the Anti-Japanese War much of the film industry was dispersed and, where possible, patriotic films were made in support of the war effort. Some companies, however, did carry on working in occupied Shanghai. Production was resumed after the war and a number of successful films appeared in the 1945–8 period.

With the establishment of the People's Republic of China in 1949 film-making was brought under the control of the Ministry of Culture. All feature films, together with the increasing number of documentary and educational films, were expected to support the new government and its policies. American films disappeared and the 1950s saw a flood of films from the USSR and Eastern Europe.

Since 1949 there have been periods of great activity in the Chinese cinema, for instance in the mid-1950s and early 1960s, and also after the fall of the 'gang of four'. At other times the cinema has been subjected to political attacks and restrictions, as with the 1951 controversy over the film, *Life of Wu Xun* (*Wu Xun zhuan*) (Kunlun Company, 1950), and in particular, during the late 1960s, when the Cultural Revolution saw leading cinema personalities persecuted and most filming brought to a halt.

Much of the film work in China after 1949 was disappointing by Western standards. There was a persistent tendency to employ static, theatrical production techniques. The emotional impact was over-sentimental or melodramatic, with predictable plots and stereotyped characterization. However, a considerable number of films reached a good standard, including the Zhejiang opera *Liang Shanbo and Zhu Yingtai* (*Liang Shanbo yu Zhu Yingtai*), one of the first colour films made in China (Shanghai, 1953) and much admired when shown in the West in 1955; the *Kunqu* opera *Fifteen Strings of Cash* (*Shiwu guan*) (Shanghai, 1956); and *New Year Sacrifice* (*Zhufu*), an adaptation of a story by Lu Xun filmed in Beijing in 1955.

The major revival in film activity after 1976 prompted much critical comment on the need to raise standards. Audiences welcomed the opportunity to see a wide range of films from the 1950s and 1960s, which were banished from the screen during the Cultural Revolution, but critics still called for new films of better quality. The cinema remains a widely popular form of entertainment in China and the achievements of film-makers in the coming years should measure the success of the new cultural policies.

The studios responded and films appeared which demonstrated a more sophisticated use of the medium. *Rickshaw Boy* made in 1984 by the veteran director, Ling Zifeng, as an adaptation of the famous novel by Lao She, recreated accurately and sensitively pictures of life in pre-war Beijing. However, the young directors have been innovators and they have managed to bring film-making in China to world attention. The impetus has come from a group of

Still from *Fifteen Strings of Cash* (1956)

students who attended the Beijing Film Academy when courses resumed after the Cultural Revolution and who graduated in 1982. This so-called 'Fifth Generation' of graduates from the Academy includes Chen Kaige, Zhang Yimou, Wu Ziniu and Tian Zhuang-zhuang. Chen and Zhang, as director and cameraman respectively, combined to produce *Yellow Earth*, in which, through a simple plot of a PLA man coming to collect folksongs in war-time Shaanxi, they created a series of haunting images of the poverty of life and the persistence of traditional practices in that arid region. They followed this with *The Big Parade* in which they explored the relationship between the individual and society in symbolic terms through army selection and training for a National Day parade. Tian Zhuangzhuang with his individual and wide-angled perspectives has looked towards more remote regions and obscure themes. His *On the Hunting Ground* explores the rituals of Mongol hunters and *The Horse Thief* depicts traditional religious practices in Tibet, including 'sky burials' where corpses are exposed for vultures to eat.

Many of these young film-makers were given their chance to direct in regional studios outside the main centres. Prime among these has been the Xi'an Studio, headed by Wu Tianming. *The Horse Thief* was made there, as was *The Black Cannon Incident*, a political satire, directed by Huang Jianxin, in which a ludicrous misunderstanding about a missing chess piece produces a whole series of costly repercussions. In 1988 two Xi'an Studio films, *The Old Well*, directed by Wu Tianming himself, and *Red Sor-*

ghum, directed by the versatile Zhang Yimou (who also played a leading role in *The Old Well*) received top awards at the Tokyo and Berlin International Film Festivals. *The Old Well* describes the painful struggles of Shaanxi villagers trying to dig a well and *Red Sorghum*, against the background of the Sino-Japanese War, depicts the lusty relationship between a widow and the labourer she marries.

The new directors had their problems. In some cases films did not meet with official approval and were withdrawn. *The Horse Thief* suffered this fate, as did *Dove Tree*, directed by Wu Ziniu, which showed itself too sympathetic to the Vietnamese side in its story about the Sino-Vietnamese border war. Quality films were also not necessarily money-spinners at the box office and studios had to bolster their income with receipts from more popular entertainment films, mostly of the *gongfu* (kung-fu) variety. In addition, there was the rapidly growing presence of television which almost certainly explains the 30 per cent decline in cinema attendance in the last 5 years. Chinese cinema, however, through the work of the new generation of directors did manage to leave behind its theatrical and didactic past and establish itself as an independent art form, achieving the international recognition it deserved. Sadly, since the 1989 Tiananmen incident, the authorities have imposed stricter political contols on the cinema, and the innovatory films of the 'Fifth Generation', as well as the popular *gongfu* (kung-fu) productions, have given way to films which express a more orthodox ideology.'

After 1949 the old Shanghai film world in style, and, to some extent, in personnel, moved to Hong Kong. Hong Kong had developed a sizeable film industry in the 1930s, which specialized in Cantonese language films, but in the 1950s the emphasis switched to films in the main northern dialect (Mandarin).

Well over 100 films are produced in Hong Kong each year and the dominant companies have been the huge Shaw Brothers enterprise and Golden Harvest, and more recently Cinema City and D and B Films. Films are aimed not simply at Hong Kong, but also at Taiwan, Southeast Asia and, increasingly, China, with co-productions set up with Chinese studios.

The themes of Hong Kong films have been generally escapist—adventure, mystery and romance—often in a historical setting, and in the mid-1970s the industry gained a Western following with a series of popular *kung-fu* films. The problems of modern life in Hong Kong, however, attracted the attention of young directors, and films like Allen Fong's *Father and Son* and *Ah Ying* and Ann Hui's *The Boat People* appeared to herald a new, more serious movement in the Hong Kong film world. Unfortunately commercial pressures seem to have made it difficult to sustain this development.

The cinema in Taiwan has been very much under the shadow of the Hong Kong film industry and it is only recently that Taiwan films have begun to achieve wider recognition. None the less, there have been over the years a number of films made in Taiwan for home consumption, some of which, while not matching recent standards in China itself, have achieved a realism of plot and setting superior to some of the more commercialized Hong Kong productions. Hou Hsiao-hsien's (Hou Xiaoxian) depictions of life in the Taiwan countryside in *Summer at Grandpa's* and *The Time to Live and the Time to Die* and Edward Yang's *Taipei Story* are perhaps the most impressive, but later films by young directors like Hou and Yang have not been so popular with Taiwanese audiences.   *D.R.*

Radio and television

Radio transmissions began in China in the 1920s and in the years before the Second World War radio stations were set up all over the country. The *Guomindang* appreciated the importance of radio and brought it under official government control. Short-wave transmissions were developed to reach more remote areas.

In 1949 the Chinese Communist Party placed radio under the centralized authority of its Propaganda Department. The Central People's Broadcasting Station in Beijing became the controlling agency for all stations throughout the country. Many of its programmes are relayed by local stations and it also transmits broadcasts overseas in many languages.

Programmes consist of news and commentary, education (science, technology and, more recently, foreign languages) and general entertainment such as music, operas and plays. The relaxation of cultural controls after 1976 allowed for a wider range of entertainment programmes including increased time for Western music.

Television was first seen in Beijing in 1958 and, in spite of the loss of technical assistance from the USSR, use of the medium grew rapidly and this growth has accelerated in recent years. It is estimated that there are now 120 million television sets in China, that is one for every 10 people, and that almost 50 per cent of Chinese families have sets compared with only 2 per cent in 1978. The national television company in Beijing, China Central Television, transmits on two channels and in addition there are nearly 400 local stations throughout the country which transmit their own programmes as well as relaying one of the Central Television channels. The marked increase in local television, often using local dialects, can be seen from the fact that in 1983 there were only 51 television stations outside Beijing. Most stations reserve time for education programmes but in 1988 a new national station, China Educational Television, was set up exclusively for educational transmissions. Central Television transmits by microwave and Chinese satellite, but China Educational Television uses the international satellite, Intelsat, and it is calculated there are now about 6000 satellite dishes throughout China. Transmission reception is generally good, though there are still problems in the central mountainous regions.

Transmissions are now day-long. They include extensive news coverage with Central Television carrying 5 news programmes in a day including one in English and another devoted exclusively to economic matters. Feature films, both Chinese and foreign, are regularly shown and recent years have seen major developments in the production of television dramas. These have included serialized adaptations of traditional works, such as *The Journey to the West* and *Dream of the Red Chamber* and the works of modern writers like Lao She and Ba Jin. These drama series have proved extremely popular, as have imported series from Japan, the USA and Britain.

Advertising, both public service and commercial, was introduced on Chinese television from 1979, but transmission time for this purpose remains limited, compared with commercial television elsewhere. Television in China is funded by the government and there is no charge or licence for viewing. Income from advertising is used for investment in equipment.

The major expansion in television services in recent years marks it out as the most important cultural and educational medium in the country.   *D.R.*

CUISINE

Historical introduction

China has satisfied the three classic requirements generally accepted as necessary for the development of a great cuisine: geographical variety; a peasantry forced by millennia of necessity to use every reasonable means of getting and conserving food; and a long-established elite, which typically sought to enhance its status and consolidate its political position by showing off the quantity of food and the skills of the cooks at its command. In addition to (or because of) this, the Chinese from earliest recorded times have regarded food as one of the most important subjects for social regulation and symbolic structuring. This is shown by the incredibly detailed sections on food in ancient books of rites such as the *Zhou li* and *Liji*; the writings of Confucius, Mencius and other philosophers; and both folk and classical poetry.

By 5000 BC in what is now known as China, millet, rice and Chinese cabbages (or similar plants) were cultivated, dogs, pigs and chickens were raised, and game, fish and wild vegetable foods were abundant. The pottery vessels of the Chinese Neolithic period (*c.* 6000–1700 BC) show that boiling and steaming became the dominant methods of cookery. By the end of that period wheat and (probably) barley were grown, and sheep, cattle and water-buffaloes were raised. Archaeology, as well as the above-mentioned texts, show that from earliest times Chinese cuisine was based on grain, with fresh or pickled vegetables as the standard side dish, and meats—usually stewed—for the elite or for special occasions such as sacrifices for the ancestors. In other words, the distinction already existed between *fan* 'grain food' (especially rice) and *song* 'food to eat on or with the *fan*', or *cai* 'vegetables or dishes to eat with the *fan*'. Fruits, nuts, etc. are served as extra snacks. *Fan* was either millet (*Setaria italica* and *Panicum miliaceum*) or rice; wheat and barley were rare and sorghum (*gaoliang*), contrary to frequently published but inaccurate claims, did not reach China until much later. Chopsticks were apparently in use by the dawn of history in the Shang dynasty, as were most items of the traditional Chinese *batterie de cuisine*. Stir-frying gradually became the major method for cooking meat and over the centuries virtually replaced both roasting and grilling. At this time meat was often pickled and soya beans became important.

From the Han dynasty through the Yuan and later China was strongly influenced by south and west Asia via Central Asia, the degree of influence increasing northwestwards. Most of the common foods of India and the Near East were introduced, but principally those that could survive and grow in Central Asia and north China. Periods of particularly strong influence were during the Wei and other dynasties established by Central Asian peoples (including, later, the Yuan) and the outward-looking middle Tang period. As a result, Chinese food was transformed, especially in the north. There Muslim influence led to the abandonment of dogs, snakes and the like as food, and brought Central Asian specialities such as filled meat dumplings (ancestral to *jiaozi*) and wonton (in Cantonese dialect *wonton*; in Mandarin *huntun*), sesame seed pocket bread (ancestral to *shao-ping*), and many other products with a wheat base. Sheep and goat became more popular; crops ranging from coriander and alfalfa (the *muxu* of *muxu* pork, originally served with alfalfa sprouts) to sorghum and broad beans modified Chinese cuisine. Perhaps noodles and other pasta foods came via this route, though noodles are usually considered a Chinese invention. (Incidentally, Marco Polo did not bring pasta to Italy, though he may well have introduced some special forms of pasta. Such foods were well known in Italy before his time.) Wheat increased in popularity partly because it usually could be winter-grown in rotation with summer-grown millet. Increasing maritime contact with Southeast and south Asia, especially from mid-Tang on, brought significant results of which the introduction of high-yield, quick-maturing rice from Champa (southern Vietnam) in the Song dynasty, which launched a real 'Green Revolution' in China, is the most important.

After the Yuan period overland influences declined; milk products, for example, retreated, although Chinese in much of west China continue to use yoghurt and milk, and the western minority groups still depend very heavily on dairy foods. From the 16th century onwards most new foods came by sea. By far the most important were the New World foods introduced by the Spanish and Portuguese. The Spanish Philippines, politically and economically administered as a part of Mexico, served as an important contact. Maize and sweet potatoes revolutionized China by providing crops that would produce enormously heavy yields on steep rainy slopes, sandy coastal soils and other areas previously almost worthless. Maize has tended to replace millet and sorghum as the summer crop. Peanuts provided more oil and protein. Chilli peppers provided a superb source of vitamins A and C and of some minerals, especially in Hunan, where they were quickly incorporated into the traditionally spicy food of that area, subsequently expanding all over southwest China. (The spiciness of cuisine there does not primarily derive from contact with India.) White potatoes became locally important from the middle Qing dynasty.

Within the past 150 years Western influences have increased; beer, sodas, coffee, bread, candies and cakes are all consumed. Vegetables such as tomatoes, broccoli and asparagus have become popular.

COMMON PLANT FOODS NATIVE TO CHINA

Rice (*Oryza sativa*)

Millets (*Panicum* spp.).

Winter melon/hairy gourd (same species, *Benincasa cerifera*)

Soyabeans (*Glycine max*)

Red beans (red-seeded *Vigna* spp.)

Chinese chives (*Allium tuberosum*)

Chinese leeks (*A. chinensis*)

Chinese green onion (*A. Fistulosum*)

Chinese cabbages and mustards
(*Brassica alboglabra, B. pekinensis,*
B. chinensis, B. juncea)

White radish (*Raphanus sativus*)

Mallow leaves (*Malva* spp., anciently
common, now rarely used)

Common yellow day lily (for buds) (*Hemerocallis* spp.)

Water spinach (*Ipomoea aquatica*)

Jujube or 'dates' (*Zizyphus* spp.)

Orange (*Citrus sinensis*)

Tangerine and mandarin orange (*Citrus reticulata*)

Peach (*Prunus persica*)

Mei (*Prunus mume*, usually mistranslated plum, actually a
species of apricot)

Oriental plum (*Li, Prunus salicina*)

Arbutus fruit

Mihoutao or Chinese gooseberry, or 'kiwi fruit' (*Actinidia
chinensis*)

Chinese pear (*Pyrus* spp.)

Chinese chestnut (*Castanea mollissima*)

Chinese hazelnut (*Corylus chinensis*)

Gingko nut (Gingko biloba)

Sichuan pepper (= brown pepper, fagara; *Zanthoxylon*
spp.)

Star anise (*Illicium verum*)

Cassia (*Cinnamomum cassia*)

COMMON PLANT FOODS INTRODUCED TO CHINA

Native to West and South Asia	Native to Africa, spreading via West Asia	Native to Americas	Native to Southeast Asia
Wheat	Sorghum	Maize	Ginger (also China?)
Barley	Watermelon	Sweet potato	Yard-long bean (also China?)
Oats		White potato	Sugar cane
Broad bean		Manioc (tapioca)	Banana
Pea		Peanut	Pepper
Sesame		Tomato	True yam (also China?)
Mung (green) bean		Red and green pepper	Taro (also China?)
Large-heading onion		Squash	Clove
Garlic		Pineapple	
Melon		Guava	
Cucumber		Papaya	
Carrot			
Spinach			
Aubergine (eggplant)			
Alfalfa			
Lettuce			
Coriander			
Apple			

The history of Chinese cuisine has thus been one of borrowing from abroad, but with the borrowings incorporated into a native framework of Neolithic and early historical origin. However most Chinese foods, especially the vast range of vegetables and fruits, have remained native to China.   *E.N.A.*

The basis of Chinese cuisine today

In spite of great regional variation, Chinese cuisine has several features that unify it into a single tradition. Among the most basic are those noted above: contrast of *fan*, *song* and '*dimsum* (*dianxin*)' or 'dot-the-hearts' (snacks); stress on boiling, steaming and stir-frying (in that order); use of chopsticks. Together they serve to separate Chinese food from all but the similar and heavily Chinese-influenced cuisines of Japan and Korea.

Until recently, the vast majority of Chinese derived 85 to 95 per cent of their calories from grain. The rest came mainly from vegetables; these included many that were high in otherwise scarce vitamins and minerals. Soya beans and other beans, cabbages, mustard greens, chillies and carrots were notably important for this. Potatoes, mostly sweet potatoes, were the only really large calorie source apart from grain; usually they were taken as *fan* rather than *song*. The caloric dominance of *fan* derives partly from the low caloric values of many of the commonest vegetables, such as Chinese cabbages, bamboo shoots, cucumbers, melons and other gourds, and many of the leaf crops. Fats and animal proteins were rare everywhere, and often even the lesser elites tasted meat only

Drying fresh noodles on a frame in Sichuan in 1944. Wind-drying and wind-curing of many foods is still a widespread and effective practice in China today.

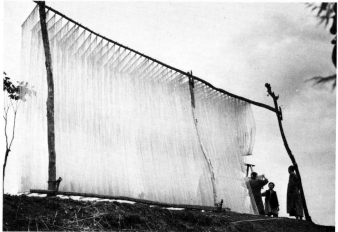

on special occasions. Only in areas with rich aquatic resources could ordinary folk expect much animal protein. *Fan* remains a staple food, forming part of everyday life. A typical Chinese greeting is 'Have you eaten *fan*?' In southern China *fan* means boiled rice; in the north it may also refer locally to millet porridge, wheat goods, or other products. The classic method of preparing *fan* is simple boiling, producing a range of textures from dry and fluffy to thin and watery, depending on the amount of water used. Wheat, however, is made into noodles, steamed breads, filled steamed dumplings, baked products, etc. rather than boiled directly, and most other foreign grains are usually made into noodles, dumplings, flat cakes, though in several areas various grains are made into rice-like form and boiled. Most wheat flour in China today is brown whole wheat; white flour is reserved for special foods. Outside China, however, highly-milled white flour has prevailed among all Chinese.

Many Chinese consider vegetables to be their favourite food. Greens, green beans and tender squash-like gourds are especially widely loved. Even more characteristically Chinese, and almost as important nutritionally, are the many products of the soya bean, which itself may be eaten boiled, but which is usually ground with water, the liquid being boiled and drunk, or precipitated (with gypsum or other coagulant) to make bean curd, which occurs in many forms and styles. Buddhists create imitation meats of all sorts from bean curd and from wheat gluten. The other standard use of soya beans is in making fermented preparations, usually with flour added: soya sauce (soya protein hydrolysate in water with salt), many highly-flavoured pastes, fermented beans and bean curd. Various fungi and moulds serve as the fermenting agents. Fermentation renders the nutrients in the bean more digestible and available. Indeed, there are few more nutritious foods than the soya preparations.

Animal protein comes primarily from pigs and, where available, fish and other aquatic life. Poultry is saved for special occasions. Other meats are rare. Many people avoid beef, since cattle work for people. This avoidance is believed to derive from India via Buddhist transmission. Sheep and goat meat is eaten locally. Almost everything that can provide protein, from elm seeds to silkworms and rats, is used in time of need. Non-Chinese tend to think of Chinese food in terms of snakes, dogs and the like, but such foods are eaten only in the south and even there, seldom. In general, aquatic foods are preferred to land animal products; even far inland, dried specialities such as shark fins and sea cucumbers command premium prices and high prestige. The well-known Chinese avoidance of all dairy products is apparently due to economics—soya beans produce equivalent products cheaper, and dairy goods would have been procured in large measure from the Central Asian and Tibetan peoples traditionally hostile to Chinese. However, in west and south China dairy products are eaten a good deal. Most Chinese adults are unable to digest lactose (milk sugar) and thus may feel sick after consuming much fresh milk, but this would be no obstacle to consuming dairy products soured or otherwise processed—such foods are the main animal protein source of the equally lactose intolerant Central Asians and Indians.

Chinese cuisine today is uniquely efficient in its use of resources. The basic foods of a given region are in general those which can be grown and produce most nutrients per acre. Labour is lavished on tiny plots of land, that they may produce the maximum amount of grain, soya beans or animals. The most widely used foods—rice, wheat, sweet potatoes, soya beans, Chinese cabbages, pigs, poultry, pond-reared fish, to name the dominant foods in various categories—are those that give the maximum quantity for the least expenditure of everything except human labour. In cooking them the same general principle applies. Boiling and steaming often go together: the rice is boiled in a closed pot; on it are put small dishes of fish and vegetables, which steam as the rice boils. Stir-frying uses minimum fuel and oil; foods are cut fine and cooked very quickly (which, like steaming, has the added advantage of pre-serving vitamins). Fuel-consuming and oil-consuming methods such as baking and deep-frying are rare. Slow-cooking—by boiling in stock—is common but typically done in large quantities. Cooking water is not discarded; boiled vegetables make soup. It would be hard to find a more cost-effective and efficient cuisine than the Chinese. Of course, there are exceptions—such as the elaborate wedding and other banquets that have come under heavy censure recently for wasteful, conspicuous consumption. But even

feast foods are often economical; e.g. pigs and poultry, the favoured meat animals, are more efficient converters of feed to meat than are cattle or sheep, and easier to raise on household and agricultural wastes. Together with attention to efficiency there is a concern that ingredients should be the best, freshest and best-kept possible. Waste through transport or spoilage is avoided. Chinese cuisine is known for its stress on bringing out the flavours of fine ingredients, as by cooking them quickly and adding a minimum of heavy sauces or flavourings.   *E.N.A.*

Below: salt fish on sale in a traditional shop-house. The better-quality fish are hung up or arranged in neat patterns. Paper over the head protects this most vulnerable part from damage, moisture and insects. Bottom: rice for sale in a shop dealing in rice and other bulk staples. The bins contain rice of different grades and origins.

Production of soyabean foods in a modern plant in Changsha, Hunan Province. The large earthenware jars are used as fermentation and settling vats. The net bags serve to drain excess liquids from products.

Ingredients, recipes and meals

Chinese cuisine has definite rules for the appropriate combining of the ingredients into various dishes, and of dishes into an appropriate meal. Certain ingredients are thought to harmonize better than others; specific cooking methods are appropriate to specific combinations. Complicated dishes often involve marinating the diced meat before cooking. Typical liquid ingredients such as *jiu* (fermented grain beverage), soya sauce, sesame oil, with ginger and garlic are used to enhance the desired flavours, cancel undesired ones and blend all in harmony. Texture, almost as important as flavour, is carefully managed; crisp yet succulent textures as of fresh vegetables are generally the most favoured, but other textures are needed in a meal for variety. Cornstarch is used to thicken the cooking liquid; before maize came to China, and even today in some areas, Chinese arrowroot or lotus-rhizome starch were used. A complex feast dish will have meat, vegetables, spices, fermented bean-flour preparations and flavouring liquids in combination, and two or more different cooking methods used at various stages of preparation. However, Chinese cooking is seen at its best and purest in uncomplicated dishes in which two or three main ingredients are combined in a simple and quick preparation, which may then be further flavoured at the table, where dip sauces, vinegar, oil and pepper are provided for the purpose. This principle of allowing the diner to participate in the culinary creation reaches its highest development in several styles of chafing dish; raw ingredients, thinly sliced, are provided around a boiling pot, and the diners boil their own foods and then flavour them with sauces to individual taste. Here the cook's skill lies in the thickness and evenness of slicing, and the quality of the sauces provided.

General principles for combining dishes into a meal include, above all, rules for maintaining variety. A typical home meal might include boiled rice, soup, steamed fish and stir-fried pork with vegetables. Thus, each dish is in a separate category—the cooking method, appearance, texture and main ingredients are all different. At a feast it is harder to maintain such a level of diversity—several stir-fried dishes may occur, for instance—but still a high level of diversity is maintained. As in individual dishes, flavours, textures and ingredients should complement and harmonize each other, rather than being the same or (at the other extreme) so different as to clash.

PRINCIPLES OF CHINESE CUISINE

BASIC METHODS (several may be combined in one dish)

Boiling

Steaming

Stir-frying

Roasting

METHODS RARELY USED

Baking	Drying
Grilling	Pickling
Deep-frying	Salting
Smoking	

BASIC MEAL STRUCTURE

Fan with flavouring, from a dash of soy sauce to a variety of mixed dishes

Soup and/or drink

SOME TRADITIONAL AIMS

To preserve flavours of ingredients (accompanied, therefore, by a demand for freshness and high quality of the same)

To harmonize different flavours in any dish (things are rarely served by themselves, except, for example., fruit as snacks)

To cook quickly (except for some simmered dishes)

SOME CHARACTERISTICS

Extreme stress on variety and quality of vegetables, especially onion types, gourds, greens; low regard for starchy roots

Use of fermented soyabean products as the principal seasoning or flavouring; pepper, Sichuan pepper, star anise, ginger in secondary place

Preference for pork and aquatic products among meat foods; fish and shellfish especially

Importance of thin soups with many vegetables as food, drink and medication

Lack of interest in sweets (even fruit eaten semi-ripe and sour flavoured); this characteristic is changing fast

Avoidance of dairy foods, except in west China

Great concern over effects of food on body, especially 'heating' and 'cooling' effects (a major point of difference from Korea and Japan)

Cutting food into manageable pieces before cooking

Use of chopsticks

Economizing on meat by cutting fine and mixing with vegetables

Opposite: Stir-frying in a wok. The kitchen is relatively modern – note the frame window – but traditionally furnished. It would probably have, in addition to what is shown, some 'sand pots' for stewing and various small dishes for steaming, as well as knives and a few other implements.

A peasant household at mealtime. Most Chinese families are fond of eating outdoors: it is preferable to eating in the often-cramped housing, and when outdoors, one can watch the world go by and invite friends to join in the meal. Even though such invitations are usually and politely declined, they maintain the *gan-qing* – the friendly and relaxed feeling – of the neighbourhood.

Last, but by no means unimportant, is the appearance of the dish. The Chinese are less concerned with food as visual art than are some other cultures, and are usually (not always) unwilling to sacrifice flavour or texture for appearance, but, especially at feasts, food is expected to be visually striking and attractive.   *E.N.A.*

Beverages

The commonest beverage in China is soup; this often serves as the chief source of liquid, and is often made quite watery in consequence. Thin soup traditionally ends the meal; when water is short, bowls may be 'washed' only by having this final soup eaten from them. The classic and traditional drink of China is fermented grain beverage, made from malted millet, rice or sorghum. It is known as *jiu*, like all alcoholic drinks and even tinctures (tincture of iodine is iodine *jiu*). *Jiu* is almost invariably translated 'wine' in English, but 'wine' correctly refers to drinks made from fermented fruit juice—fermented, undistilled grain drinks are correctly 'beer' or 'ale'. The *jiu* of the Chinese classics was apparently a thick, non-carbonated ale. Distilling came to China during the medieval period, and distilled liquors, generally known as *Shaojiu* ('burned' or 'roasted' *jiu*), became popular. These are also miscalled 'wine' in most English sources, but are technically vodkas—distilled, unflavoured, unaged, white (i.e. clear) alcoholic drinks made from grain and/or potatoes. The Chinese have always drunk a good deal of *jiu*, whenever possible, and drinking became a serious problem in some circles at various times in China's history; even the fall of dynasties has been attributed to it. However, such reports are probably exaggerated, and the Chinese are much better known today for their exceedingly low incidence of alcoholism, apparently a result of the unwritten but very firm social codes concerning drinking. Such codes to some extent go back to the written codes of the Zhou dynasty, which were established—the *Shiji* (*Book of History*) tells us—because drink had ruined the two preceding dynasties and the Zhou hoped to protect their own from such a fate!

Tea became widely known during the Tang dynasty; its use increased slowly, due primarily to its high cost. Even today it is too expensive to be the universal drink that non-Chinese suppose it to be. Tea arrived from the Indian border country, and was later ascribed to the Indian Buddhist missionary Bodhidharma, who was so annoyed at falling asleep while meditating that he cut off his eyelids and threw them on the ground, where they became tea bushes. This story is significant in illustrating early awareness of the sleep-preventing value of tea and the usefulness of that quality in religion; coffee was winning its way through the Near East at the same time for similar reasons.

Traditional Chinese drinks are now experiencing severe competition from those recently introduced. Coffee has displaced tea in many overseas Chinese households and communities; beer and wine are gaining fast against native *jiu*; sodas and soft drinks are displacing soya bean 'milk', herb teas, crabapple and hawthorn juices, and other traditional equivalents. Children are drinking more and more cow's milk. Drinks have become westernized more than have foods. However, the finest *jiu* survive and flourish, notably the Shaoxing 'wine' so indispensable for cooking (and not much like the sherry that often replaces it in the West). The best teas, such as *Longjing* and Taiwan *wulong* (oolong), also seem in no danger of being forgotten, though coffee is now grown in China, notably in Yunnan.

E.N.A.

Regional variations

Everyone agrees that China has regional culinary styles: few seem to agree on what they are. Classic formulations always list five, perhaps only because of the great concern with the 'fiveness' characteristic of systematics in classical Chinese culture. Naturally the five are associated with compass points (or with major cities or provinces at these compass points): north (Beijing or Hebei), east

SOME NATIONAL MINORITIES' VARIATIONS

Style	Staples	Some typical ingredients	Special characteristics	Substyles
UIGHUR	Wheat	Cheese, yoghurt, grapes, apricots, melons, mutton	Similar to food in Afghanistan, northeast Iran. Large, flat wheat bread baked in sunken ovens is staple. Melons often considered the finest in the world. Filled dumplings cooked in stew or soup, etc., common; also pilaffs of rice.	
MONGOL	Traditionally supposed to be dairy foods, but grain always important	Yoghurt, mutton, fermented mares' milk (kumiss), butter	Simple cuisine; grain foods derived from China and Central Asia.	
TIBETAN	Barley, buckwheat	Butter, mutton and yak meat, tea, white radish	Staple food, barley roasted and then ground to meal, thus producing an 'instant' food typically mixed into buttered tea. Rancid yak butter especially common. Hybrid of yak and cattle gives much milk. Vegetables and fruits only in lower, warmer areas. Feast dishes simple, northwest China types. Tibetan food is broadly similar to that of several other southwestern highland peoples.	East, west and south/central cuisines different; several peripheral groups have other variants.
KOREAN	Barley, buckwheat, sorghum, rice (but not much in China)	Cabbages, onions, garlic	Meat typically grilled. Many soups. Commonest food is pickled vegetables, often with meat added; *kim chi* (pickled cabbage with garlic, red peppers, and often many other things) especially famous, Markedly simpler, less high calorie, saltier, spicier than Han Chinese food.	

(Shandong, or Hangzhou, for example,), south (Canton or some comparable unit), west (Hunan, Sichuan), centre (usually Henan). There are reasonable grounds for regarding any or all of these as distinct culinary styles. However, a far better systematization is that which divides China into four main regions, north, south, east and west. Within these regional divisions each province and major city has its own sub-style, and areas near the borders of regions have transitional cuisines that may be markedly distinct: for example, the Chaozhou cuisine of northern Guangdong Province, which draws on both Fujian and Cantonese traditions and adds a good deal of its own, or the almost unclassifiable cuisine of the Hakka people, which can be loosely included in the south but is really not much like any other Chinese style. Furthermore, highly spiced food is very popular in west China, particularly in Hunan. The reason for the Hunanese love of spiced dishes is unknown, but is attested in the earliest poems we have from there—the *Chuci*

REGIONAL VARIATIONS

Region	Staples	Some typical ingredients	Special characteristics	Substyles
NORTH	Wheat Millet Maize	Onions, Beijing white cabbage, lamb, pears, chestnuts, aubergines (eggplant), green pepper	Great stress on steamed wheat rolls and dumplings with or without filling. Many stir-fried dishes. Fairly simple, straightforward cuisine. Special sweet-sour fish from Yellow River. Peking duck and other Beijing dishes show special refinement of capital city.	Beijing, Henan (especially diverse and famous), Shandong, Shanxi, Shaanxi, Manchuria (the North East)
WEST	Rice Maize	Soyabean curd, broad beans, cabbage, red peppers, garlic, bamboo shoots, Sichuan pepper, dried mushrooms	Famous for highly spiced food, with garlic, ginger, chilli pepper, Sichuan pepper, and fermented soyabean and soyabean-flour preparations all important. Many foods from mountain forests, and a wide variety of freshwater fish from rivers and lakes. Yoghurt common in parts of Yunnan. Famous duck dishes.	Jiangxi, Hunan, Hubei, Sichuan, Yunnan
EAST	Rice Sweet potatoes	Sea foods, cabbages, gourds, bean curd, mushrooms, leaf vegetables, aquatic plants	Great stress on soup and stews, including red-cooking (stewing in stock with soya sauce, star anise, etc.); an incredible variety of soups, often several at one meal. Use of *jiu* and its sediment in cooking. Very wide variety and high quality of both freshwater and saltwater fish and shellfish, including famous crabs; these aquatic foods typically cooked simply, bringing out pure flavours. Most varied of Chinese regions. A common feature is heavy use of lard and peanut oil; food quite oily compared to other regions.	Lower Yangtze (many styles—each city has its own); Fujian; Taiwan (Japanese influenced); Hainan Island (a distinctive outlier); Chaozhou (Teochiu) (Cantonese-influenced Fujian style)
SOUTH	Rice	Sea foods, mustard greens, many other leaf vegetables, tomatoes (recently)	Very quick cooking, including a lot of stir-frying at high temperature. Sea foods especially important and choice. Stress on bringing out simple flavours of ingredients, but also many complex mixed dishes. Contrary to frequent impressions based on overseas restaurants, sweet-sour dishes and chop suey are not typical. (And fortune cookies were invented in California.) Wide variety of rich and filling snacks (*dianxin*). Hakka is distinctive, simple, with excellent fowl and pork dishes; a mountain cuisine using less oil or aquatic products.	Cantonese (with many local variations); Hakka

375

(*Songs of the South*) (*c.* 250 BC)—and tomb finds of a comparable period. The popularity of this cuisine spread west and southwest during the Qing dynasty. Therefore, when in the 16th century the chilli pepper first came to China, it was added to an already spicy style.   *E.N.A.*

Chinese nutritional concepts

An important factor in determining Chinese diet is traditional dietary lore. China possesses an ancient and still widely believed nutritional science, not always in accord with modern scientific findings but at least as sophisticated and accurate as any culture's traditional beliefs about food as medicine. The most important concept is the 'heating–cooling' continuum; foods are arranged according to how 'hot' or 'heating to the body' they are, the heat being of spirit rather than of temperature. Rich, high-calorie, spicy foods, and foods subjected to high heat in cooking, are the most heating; these may cause or aggravate fevers, constipation, rashes and sores, and other hot, tight or red symptoms. Low-calorie, cool-coloured, bland foods, notably vegetables such as watercress and white or green radish, are cooling; these may lead to weakness, low body temperature, pallor, shivering and other symptoms of cold. Easily digestible protein foods such as chicken are slightly heating. Most other foods are neutral or balanced such as staple grains (unless baked or otherwise processed in an especially heating way), many fish, many fruits and vegetables. Part of the same system, less important but widely found, is a 'wet–dry' continuum. Much home treatment and prevention of disease is carried out by varying diet according to this system. The system was borrowed (in Han times?) from the Near East—it is basically the same as the Galenic or Hippocratic humoral system of Europe—and assimilated to the Chinese *yin/yang* dichotomy, already influential in classification of flavours and foods before the arrival of the humoral theory.

In addition to the hot–cold continuum, there is a continuum from safe to poisonous; many foods not poisonous in themselves are poisonous in some combinations and situations, or to individual eaters. Other foods are specific for clearing away 'wetness', for cleaning and harmonizing the body, and for building strength or building blood (*buxue*). These last foods tend to be either nourishing, digestible protein foods or—in the case of the blood-builders—red-coloured, a kind of sympathetic magic also found in other parts of the world. For similar reasons of appearance, walnuts are thought to strengthen the brain. Unusual and expensive foods are especially prone to be classed as building up the body. Many of these foods are called 'aphrodisiacs' in the (prurient?) West, but their aphrodisiac quality comes (in Chinese thought and

in reality) only from their strengthening or tonic effects on the body in general. Sexual activity is one of the first things affected by malnutrition, and the frequent undernourishment of the Chinese people gave the protein foods of the better-off a real and obvious value in this, as in other aspects of vital energy.

In these and other ways, medical beliefs have greatly influenced the diets of many Chinese, but families and individuals have always varied in how seriously they took this lore; even the codifying of food lore in the famous *Bencao gangmu* (*Materia Medica Ordered on the Basis of Monographs and Individual Characteristics*) failed to impose uniformity, though it evidently increased consensus.   *E.N.A.*

Social uses of food

A greater influence on food was and is its use to communicate social messages. The Chinese have taken food 'language' to a pitch of complexity probably unrivalled elsewhere. Foods are used to mark group affiliation, occasion, status, respect and other social factors. At many a feast, the talk is confined to polite and relatively empty phrases, while the real messages communicated are expressed in the choice of foods, the seating arrangements, the giving of particularly fine morsels to particular guests, the structure and order of toasts and drinking contests, etc. Food choice may indicate or disguise ethnic affiliation as the diner chooses. Of course every occasion—a visit by relatives, a festival, a holiday, a wedding, a birthday—has its special food or foods. Chinese New Year is particularly rich in special occasion-making foods. Some foods are high prestige (shark fins and bear's paws), some are for special occasions but within reach of most people (chicken and good fish), some are ordinary everyday foods appropriate almost anywhere (Chinese cabbages and staple grains), some are low status (sweet potatoes and wild greens). Business is typically conducted over food, and it is traditionally appropriate to close any deal or agreement at a special meal.

A special case of the social use of foods is in religious sacrifices. Some foods, notably pork, poultry and fruit (especially bright-coloured fruit like citrus), are regarded as appropriate or even obligatory at particular sacrifices. The more important the rite, the more food and especially meat there will be. While the actual foods offered and the actual rites have changed greatly since the Shang and Zhou dynasties, these generalizations have held since then. Always, sacrifices are similar to feasts, but differ in detail—of sequence, foods emphasized, ways of serving—so that the religious sphere is marked off from the secular, but not marked off too sharply. Customs of food preparation for sacrificial rites vary considerably by region and even village.

In an ancient and elaborate society, with a varied geographical setting, the use of food as a major mode of social communication contributed further to an already complex cuisine. The Zhou dynasty ritual texts show that this had been accomplished long ago. Today Western food and the social needs of a new age are being assimilated into the great heritage of Chinese cuisine—changing it and enriching it rather than endangering its survival.

E.N.A.

TIME AND QUANTITIES

Hours

The need for regulating the ceremonial and administrative activities of the imperial bureaucracy led to an early interest in time measurement and the precise division of day and night. In Shang times rough indications such as 'dawn' or 'noon' were sufficient, but by the time of the Western Han the use of water-clocks enabled the day to be divided into 100 equal *ke* of 14.4 minutes each. Careful attention was paid to the seasonal variation in the lengths of day and night. In parallel with this system, common usage divided the day into 12 *shi*, 'double-hours', each of which was correlated with one of the 12 cyclical characters, the *dizhi*, 'earthly branches'. Each double-hour was also correlated with one of 12 animals, so that we have the Rat (11pm–1am), Ox (1–3am), Tiger (3–5am), Hare (5–7am), Dragon (7–9am), Snake (9–11am), Horse (11am—1pm), Sheep (1–3pm), Monkey (3–5pm), Cock (5–7pm), Dog (7–9pm), and Boar (9–11pm). In the latitude of the ancient capital cities Luoyang and Chang'an (approximately 35° N) the sun never sets later than about 7.15 pm. Therefore, the five double-hours Monkey to Dragon always fall during the night; they are known as the *wu geng*, five 'shifts' or 'watches'. *C.C.*

The traditional calendar

The Chinese calendar was of the lunisolar type. In addition to attempting to keep the civil year in step with the Sun (as in the West), it tried to keep its months in step with the phases of the Moon. Its three basic periods were the day, the lunar month (the interval between new moons) and the tropical year (the interval between successive spring equinoxes). For the needs of a simple agricultural community it is sufficient to note that the length of the lunar month (or 'moon') varies between 29 and 30 days, and that there are about 12 moons in a year.

It was the ruler's duty to declare to the people the beginning of a new month and to regulate the seasons of agricultural work. Precision in this became linked with imperial prestige, and by the end of the 1st millennium BC official almanacs were being published giving rules for the calculation of solar, lunar and planetary positions to much greater accuracy than was required for practical timekeeping. Throughout the next 2000 years official efforts to improve the methods of calendrical mathematical astronomy continued, and came to include such matters as the prediction of eclipses of the Sun and Moon. The basic difficulties remained that neither the lunar month (mean 29.53059 days) nor the tropical year (365.24219 days) contained a whole number of days, and there was not a whole number of lunar months to the year. The first difficulty was dealt with by alternating long and short months of 29 and 30 days, giving an average of 29.5 days. The periodic insertion of a pair of successive long months brought this average closer to the true mean month-length. There was still the problem that 12 lunar months fell almost 11 days short of a full year. Thus

THE TWENTY-FOUR SOLAR SEASONS

Approximate dates	The solar seasons
5 February	Spring begins
19 February	Rain water
5 March	Excited insects
20 March	Vernal equinox
5 April	Clear and bright
20 April	Grain rains
5 May	Summer begins
21 May	Grain fills
6 June	Grain in ear
21 June	Summer solstice
7 July	Slight heat
23 July	Great heat
7 August	Autumn begins
23 August	Limit of heat
8 September	White dew
23 September	Autumnal equinox
8 October	Cold dew
23 October	Hoar frost descends
7 November	Winter begins
22 November	Little snow
7 December	Heavy snow
21 December	Winter solstice
6 January	Little cold
21 January	Severe cold

every few years it was necessary to add an extra ('intercalary') month so that a given season always fell in the same numbered lunar month. Complex rules for this were evolved, although about 1000 BC a month was simply added whenever the need became apparent. The precise dates of the summer and winter solstices were checked by observations of the shortest and longest shadows cast by a standard upright pole at noon. In addition to the division into lunar months, the year was also divided into 24 *qi*, 'solar seasons', whose names were descriptive of the phenomena which occurred during them.

Although the Gregorian calendar has been in official use since 1911, most Chinese are still aware of the lunar calendar, and traditional festivals continue to be celebrated as it lays down. The first day of the first lunar month (the Chinese New Year) usually falls in early February or late January.   *C.C.*

The 'ox of spring', which symbolizes the beginning of the agricultural year, from a 1981 almanac.

The cycle of the years

A year can be specified in two ways in Chinese usage. The first is independent of political events, and makes use of the 60 possible combinations in pairs of 10 characters known as the *tiangan*, 'celestial stems', with the 12 *dizhi*, 'earthly branches'. Thus the first year

A GROUP OF FOUR CYCLES: AD 1804–2043

The table shows the number of each year within the 60-year cycle and the animals traditionally taken as corresponding to the 12 'earthly branches'

Shu	Rat	1	1804 1864 1924 1984	13	1816 1876 1936 1996	25	1828 1888 1948 2008	37	1840 1900 1960 2020	49	1852 1912 1972 2032
Niu	Ox	2	1805 1865 1925 1985	14	1817 1877 1937 1997	26	1829 1889 1949 2009	38	1841 1901 1961 2021	50	1853 1913 1973 2033
Hu	Tiger	3	1806 1866 1926 1986	15	1818 1878 1938 1998	27	1830 1890 1950 2010	39	1842 1902 1962 2022	51	1854 1914 1974 2034
Tu	Hare	4	1807 1867 1927 1987	16	1819 1879 1939 1999	28	1831 1891 1951 2011	40	1843 1903 1963 2023	52	1855 1915 1975 2035
Long	Dragon	5	1808 1868 1928 1988	17	1820 1880 1940 2000	29	1832 1892 1952 2012	41	1844 1904 1964 2024	53	1856 1916 1976 2036
She	Serpent	6	1809 1869 1929 1989	18	1821 1881 1941 2001	30	1833 1893 1953 2013	42	1845 1905 1965 2025	54	1857 1917 1977 2037
Ma	Horse	7	1810 1870 1930 1990	19	1822 1882 1942 2002	31	1834 1894 1954 2014	43	1846 1906 1966 2026	55	1858 1918 1978 2038
Yang	Sheep	8	1811 1871 1931 1991	20	1823 1883 1943 2003	32	1835 1895 1955 2015	44	1847 1907 1967 2027	56	1859 1919 1979 2039
Hou	Monkey	9	1812 1872 1932 1992	21	1824 1884 1944 2004	33	1836 1896 1956 2016	45	1848 1908 1968 2028	57	1860 1920 1980 2040
Ji	Cock	10	1813 1873 1933 1993	22	1825 1885 1945 2005	34	1837 1897 1957 2017	46	1849 1909 1969 2029	58	1861 1921 1981 2041
Gou	Dog	11	1814 1874 1934 1994	23	1826 1886 1946 2006	35	1838 1898 1958 2018	47	1850 1910 1970 2030	59	1862 1922 1982 2042
Zhu	Boar	12	1815 1875 1935 1995	24	1827 1887 1947 2007	36	1839 1899 1959 2019	48	1851 1911 1971 2031	60	1863 1923 1983 2043

Source: C. Goodrich, *A Pocket Dictionary Chinese-English* (reprinted Hong Kong, 1965)

of the 60-year cycle is designated *jiazi*, the second *yichou*, and so on, the cycle of stems repeating every 10 years and the branches every 12. The combination *jiazi* recurs after 60 years and the cycle starts again; thus 1980 is a *gengshen* year, and so were 1920 and 1860. The 'branch' allotted to a year also determines the symbolic animal associated with it.

The second system specifies a year uniquely and makes use of *nianhao*, reign-periods. Before the 2nd century BC no more is involved than the name of the ruler on the throne and the relevant year of his reign. From 163 BC onwards it became customary to adopt reign-period titles, often of an optimistic or auspicious kind, and an emperor might have as many as a dozen different ones in succession during his reign. Thus Emperor Xuanzong of the Tang dynasty began his reign with the *Kaiyuan*, 'Beginning Epoch', period, of which the first year was AD 713. The next of his reign titles was *Tianbao*, 'Heavenly Treasure', of which 'year one' was 742. Emperors of the Ming and Qing dynasties used only one reign title each, and it is by this title that they are commonly known to Westerners. Thus Qianlong is the reign title of the emperor who reigned from 1736 to 1795, not his personal name. AD 1912 was designated as the first year of the Republic, *Minguo*, and years were counted on this basis until the adoption of the Western system by the People's Republic in 1949. The *Minguo* year-count is still used in Taiwan.

C.C.

Coins and currencies

In the 2nd millennium BC the small shell of the cowrie (brought from outside China) seems to have played a limited role as a token of value. When bronze came into general use (*c.* 1500 BC) ingots of the metal formed a convenient medium of exchange with intrinsic value as material for tools and weapons. The official casting of standard ingots in the outline of such tools as spades or knives (*c.* 7th century BC) marked the introduction of coinage, and the disc coin was in use by the 4th and 3rd centuries BC. This was the *qian*, or 'cash', pierced with a square hole and carried in strings of 1000, which remained the standard medium of small transactions for 2000 years. Metal shortages (as from *c.* AD 200–700) led to coin scarcities as currency was melted down, and governments caused economic dislocation by debasement such as that carried out under Wudi, the Han emperor who reigned 141–87 BC. Larger transactions were made using silver ingots of a standard weight of one *liang* (approximately 37g); this unit is commonly called a tael (a Malay word) outside China. From the 16th century AD onwards the Spanish silver peso ('Mexican dollar') became a current coin and remained so into the present century.

Spade money, Zhou dynasty.

Round coins of the Qing (above) and Tang (below) dynasties.

Knife money, Zhou dynasty.

Gold was rarely minted in China, but paper money is a Chinese invention. Wudi made compulsory sales of 'deerskin certificates' to the nobility for large sums, but true banknotes did not circulate until the growth of a cash economy under the Tang and Song. In AD 811 the government issued 'flying cash' certificates reimbursable at the capital for making payments in outlying regions. Private bankers issued certificates of deposit which functioned as cash and were redeemable on demand at a 3 per cent service charge. The issue of these was nationalized under the Song in AD 1024; the system worked well at first but was later ruined by over-issue without adequate backing reserves, causing loss of confidence. Subsequent issues tended to meet the same fate, and silver remained the principal medium of exchange for large sums

C.C.

Dimensions, weights and measures

From ancient times the standardization of weights and measures was regarded as one of the important ritual functions of the imperial government, and the derivation of the units used was often given a metaphysical significance. Standardization was to a large extent achieved after the unification of China by the Qin dynasty in 221 BC, including the introduction of a standard gauge for the axles of carts to facilitate travel over deeply rutted roads. From time to time the dimensions of ritual objects and imperial regalia were laid down with great precision. The practical significance of standardization for a centralized bureaucratic state collecting taxes in kind is obvious.

Attempts by tax-collectors to 'squeeze' extra revenue by using oversize measures gave rise to a tendency for the size of official standards to be increased. This eventually resulted in a situation described by an imperial edict of AD 721, which defined a 'short' system based on the old standards for ritual purposes, and legitimized an inflated 'long' system for general use. Chinese units are usually related by factors of 10, a fact which facilitated the introduction of the metric system after 1928. Approximate equivalents (valid for recent centuries) of units likely to be encountered by the Western reader are:

Length: the 'inch' (*cun*), about 30mm,
the 'foot' (*chi*), about 300mm (10 *cun*),
the *li*, about 500m
Area: the mow (*mu*), about 0.06 hectares
Weight: the common names used by Westerners are Malay words: the tael (*liang*), about 37g; as a weight of silver, the tael also served as a unit of accounting; the catty (*jin*), of 16 *liang*, about 600g; the picul (*dan*), of 100 catties, about 60kg.

C.C.

ART AND ARCHITECTURE

Wall painting of courtly ladies and attendants, from the tomb of Princess Yangtai at Qian Xian, near Sian; Tang dynasty.

DESIGN AND SYMBOL

Ritual bronze vessels

From Shang times onwards ritual vessels for sacrificial and cere-monial purposes are numbered in some quantity among the cast bronze objects. The vessels can be divided into three groups: food vessels, of which three were intended for the preparation of food and a possible five for the service or presentation of food; wine vessels, of which six or seven were for the storage or carrying of wine, and five or six were for pouring or drinking; and water vessels.

Vessels for preparing food

There were three types of vessel cast, with either three or four legs so that they could be placed over the fire.

Li: a three-legged vessel with two upstanding handles, and hollow legs. Dated from the Shang and early Zhou periods only.

Ding: a three- or four-legged vessel with two upstanding handles, and columnar legs. If the vessel has four legs, it is rectangular. Later examples of the late Zhou or Warring States period are rounder and dumpier, with three cabriole legs and often a lid.

Yan: a steamer made in one or two parts, the lower section resembling the *li*. The upper part may have a grid across the bottom, and this is normal when the vessel is made in two parts. The rim is sur-mounted by two handles.

Vessels for serving food

Gui: a deep circular vessel with spreading lip and foot-ring. It normally has two handles, occasionally four, and very rarely none; handles are usually sur-mounted by animal heads. A few examples of middle Zhou are raised on three small feet and may have lids. Some are fixed to massive cubic plinths. Common to all stylistic periods of the Bronze Age, it is less numerous in the later centuries.

Fu: a rectangular vessel with four angular feet at the corners and a matching cover; a vessel intro-duced in the middle Zhou.

Ding

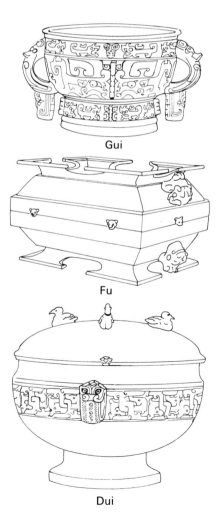

Gui

Fu

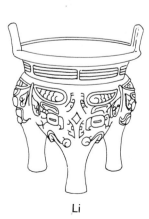

Li

Yan

Dui

Dui: a roughly spherical vessel made in two almost identical halves with lugs and rings; introduced in the middle Zhou.

Dou: a wide bowl on a high spreading foot, common to all periods, but only in the 5th to 4th centuries BC does it acquire a lid.

Fangyi: a rectangular casket with a lid resembling a hipped roof. It is generally regarded as a vessel for storing grain, but one modern Chinese authority believes it should be included among the wine vessels. It is confined to the Shang and early Zhou periods.

Vessels for storing and carrying wine

You: a wine bucket with a swing handle and a lid; the lower part of the body is usually bellied and the vessel stands on a high slightly spreading foot or on four bird feet. Where it meets the body, the handle is surmounted by animal heads. Shang and early Zhou in date, those of early Zhou may be extravagant in form and decoration.

Zun: a massive vessel generally with a broad body, straight sloping shoulders and widely flared mouth; the foot spreading. Some examples have a rounded bulb body and a rather high foot. Variant forms are in the shape of birds or animals. Most date from the Shang and early Zhou.

Hu: a storage vessel, usually elliptical in horizontal cross-section, slightly bellied and provided with tubular lugs at the neck for the passage of a cord; later examples may have ring handles fitted to animal mask escutcheons. Commonly thought to date from the Bronze Age, continuing into Han.

Lei: a wine, or perhaps water, vessel, either rectangular or circular in cross-section, and provided with a lid. The shoulders are wide and the body tapers to the foot. Ring handles on the shoulder are fitted to masked lugs, and on the lower part of the body on one side is a similar handle and mount. Shang and early Zhou in date, but it may also occur in the round-bodied form in middle Zhou.

Dou

You

Hu

Fangyi

Zun

Lei

Jia: a tripod vessel with rounded body spreading at the lip, which is surmounted by two capped columns. On one side of the body is a loop handle. A few are recorded with four legs and with rectangular body, the capped columns occurring on the short sides and the handle on one long side. It is confined to the Shang and early Zhou periods.

Bu: a large round vessel contracting to a plain rim and mouth; the foot slightly splayed. Datable mainly to the Shang and early Zhou periods.

Yu: a rather elegantly proportioned wine or water vessel with a spreading lip and spreading foot; it has two handles, springing from well below the rim, that are bent upwards. It seems confined in date to the early Zhou.

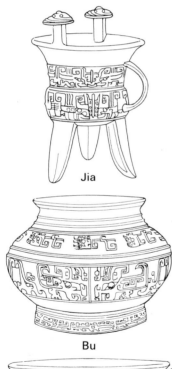

Jia

Bu

Yu

Vessels for pouring wine or from which to drink

There is some doubt as to both name and function of the *Zhi* and the *Gu.*

Guang: a jug-shaped vessel, elliptical or rectangular in section, on a slightly spreading foot. The spout is wide and the cover, with an animal head, overhangs the edge. The handle may be elaborate. Some examples have a division across the middle separating front from back, and may be provided with a ladle that fits through a slot at the back of the lid. Such examples are believed to have been intended for the mixing of wine as well as its service. The type occurs only in the Shang and early Zhou periods.

He: a wine kettle on three or four legs, with a lid linked to the body with chain. Opposite the straight spout is a loop handle surmounted by an animal head. The vessel occurs throughout the Bronze Age, but later examples have a curving spout, cabriole legs and a handle arched over the body.

Jue: a vessel with a narrow elliptical or circular body standing on three triangular-section splayed legs. It has a large open spout, opposite which is a flattened and extended lip; a loop handle is on the side of the body. At the root of the spout two capped columns spring from the rim. It appears in the earliest Shang finds and seems to have died out quite early in the Zhou period.

Zhi: a drinking vessel with a wide belly and flaring lip, some times provided with a lid. It is usually circular in section, but occasionally oval. Most are datable to Shang and early Zhou. The name was first applied to this vessel in the Song period and it is not certain whether it is correct.

Gu: a tall, slender trumpet-mouthed vessel with a small narrow body and high spreading foot. It is thought to be a drinking vessel, but it is uncertain whether it is correctly named.

Water vessels

Water vessels for ceremonial and ritual purposes number only three certainly—the

Guang

He

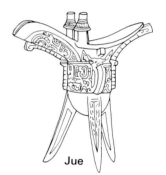

Jue

Zhi

Gu

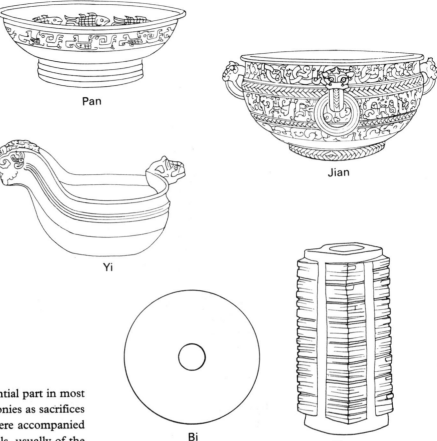

Pan

Yi

Jian

Bi

Zong

pan, yi, and *jian*—with possibly two others which are normally included among the wine vessels: *bu,* and *yu.*

Pan: a wide low basin, on a substantial foot, with or without two handles, intended for ablutions.

Yi: a vessel resembling a sauce boat with a wide open or tubular spout, provided with a handle and sometimes four animal-shaped feet. Dated to the middle Zhou and later.

Jian: a massive basin on a low foot-ring, usually with four handles. It was either filled with water and used as a mirror, or filled with ice in which perishable foods were stored. Surviving examples all date from the 5th to 3rd centuries BC.   *M.M.*

Bronze bells

For ceremonies of many kinds music has an essential part in most cultures, and China is no exception. Such ceremonies as sacrifices and ritual dancing, as well as state receptions, were accompanied by the sound of chiming bells and the sets of bells, usually of the type named *zhong,* were hung on a low sturdy wooden frame and struck with a hammer by a man squatting on the ground. These bells were elliptical in section, narrowing a little towards the flat top, from the centre of which rose a shaft with a loop at the base for suspension, or a tall narrow loop, or a complex ornamental loop. Sets of up to 16 of such bells are known. When a very deep note was called for, a very large bell, up to 1m in height, was available, and this was hung separately.   *M.M.*

Stone-chimes

The music of bronze bells could be replaced, or perhaps supplemented, by sets of musical stones or jades. These were fairly thin flat stones of roughly L-shape suspended from a wooden frame by a cord which passed through a hole drilled at the angle of the two arms. Very large musical stones were hung alone. As with the bronze bells, the objects were struck with a hammer, to emit a very delicate and attractive sound.   *M.M.*

Ritual jades

The most important, and one of the two most ancient of the ritual jades, was the *bi,* a flat disc with a central aperture of about one third of the diameter. It was the symbol of the sky and hence of Heaven. The earliest examples seem to have been plain, but later, from about the 5th century BC they were often quite richly decorated with *taotie,* 'glutton masks' and elaborately intertwined serpentine bodies and/or with simple rice-grain patterns of small protuberances (*guwen*) equidistant from each other over the surface. The second most important was the *zong,* now datable to the third millennium BC, a cylindrical tube in a square section column, symbolic of the square Earth. The earliest examples were decorated with human masks at the angles. These masks later became abstract patterns, and by Zhou times the *zong* became quite plain. The *zong* then disappeared, to be survived by the *bi,* which in Han times acquired a decorative value in its own right.

M.M.

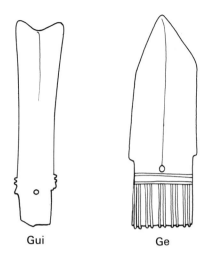

Gui   Ge

Jade insignia

These are mainly sceptres and halberds, *gui* and *ge*, and were marks of rank. One type of *gui* is an elongated flat tablet with a slight point at one end and a square cut base, and is sometimes decorated with rice grain pattern. Another type somewhat resembles the halberd, *ge*, but instead of a point has an arc cut out of the end. Both were emblems of office or of rank. The *ge* closely resembles the bronze form and the tang is often ornamented with narrow ridges or cross-hatchings. This became a badge of rank.

M.M.

Ceramics

In China the craft of the potter attained a high level of excellence at a much earlier period than in any other culture. One reason for this was undoubtedly the easy availability of good quality materials, but another reason may well have been related closely to the techniques associated with the bronze art, which during the Shang dynasty matured to a high degree and in which there was extensive use of the potters' skills in the preparation of moulds.

The actual methods of construction employed by the potters included hand building, throwing on the wheel, moulding and a primitive form of jolleying. One of the peculiar features of Chinese ceramics is the dichotomy in form. Either the shapes are of the simplest and most appropriate to the clay materials thrown on the wheel, or they are elaborate, sometimes almost achieving the improbable for the material, many parts having been made separately and then luted together to complete a single form. Such complex constructions are in fact a demonstration of a profound understanding of the materials allied to a great physical mastery of

them, and particularly there is an understanding of the shrinkage that takes place during drying and firing.

The earliest material consists of a wide range of hand built urns, amphorae, jugs, bowls, dishes, basins and tripod vessels of various kinds. They vary much in quality, from a coarse grey ware to a refined red bodied type in the Neolithic culture of Yangshao. In the apparently slightly later, or perhaps more prolonged culture of Longshan, much of the pottery is again handmade and of some-

Red earthenware amphora; hand built with a corded surface. Yangshao Neolithic culture from Banpo, Shaanxi Province.

what similar shapes, although there is a tripod jug not represented in the Yangshao repertory. The body also varies from coarse grey through a finer grey ware to a reddish type. It was, however, in the extremely fine black wares with burnished walls that Longshan differed significantly from Yangshao, for these often remarkable pieces were made on the wheel, an innovation that was to revolutionize ceramic form and introduce an elegance and exoticism previously unknown. The introduction of the potter's wheel involved an accelerated search for more suitable materials and better methods for their preparation. Even in late Neolithic times the potters had begun to look for white clays and these are seen in use on some pots at this time. Ultimately in medieval times the white kaolinic clays became the major material and led to the potters' success in evolving the pure white porcelain which in modern times has been especially associated with China. But between the late Neolithic earthenware and the pure white porcelain lies a long period of development during which many problems had to be resolved.

During the Bronze Age the earthenwares were somewhat variable, the coarse hand-built wares continuing to be made, but the best was a compact grey bodied ware to which a high-firing alkaline glaze was applied. This was the first stoneware and it was the foundation upon which the most important developments in Chinese ceramic history were established. It is interesting to note that high-fired glazes preceded the low-fired lead glazes in China, the reverse of the European experience. Lead-glazed wares only made their appearance in the 4th to 3rd century BC, and were used exclusively for burial wares for the next four or five hundred years, after which they seem to have declined, to be revived at intervals during the Northern and Southern Dynasties period, especially in the extreme north of China. The lead-glazed wares again achieved popularity in the Tang period both for burial and to some extent for domestic use. After the Tang dynasty during the 10th and 11th centuries they were ousted almost completely, except for tiles and facing bricks, by the stonewares, porcellanous wares and finally the true porcelain, which became dominant under the Yuan dynasty in the 14th century.

Decorative techniques

The earliest decoration consisted of cord marking, achieved by using a paddle bound round with cord. Such a tool imparts a texturing to the surface which may be sufficiently well ordered to produce a definite pattern. There are also examples of rather thin earthenwares decorated with woven silk texturing produced similarly by wrapping a paddle or stone with woven cloth, which is pressed firmly on to the wet surface of the pot. Incised linear decoration, either geometric or free-flowing was common, and on the dark grey earthenwares of late Shang and later the surfaces were

Red earthenware urn; hand built, painted in black and maroon slip colour. Yangshao type; Neolithic from Gansu Province, *c.* 2000 BC.

often burnished as well, so that the decoration stood out quite strongly. Small modelled elements were applied to pots at an early stage, and by about the 3rd century AD small moulded elements were being sprigged on to the surfaces. Rouletting as a rapid, repetitive form of impressing, seems to have been introduced at about the same time.

Painting with coloured slips occurred early in the Yangshao Neolithic culture, the colours deriving from iron and manganese, producing black, dark brown and maroon. A later addition was a white slip which heightened the decoration in a striking manner, and is best known in the eastern extension of the Yangshao culture in southern Shandong, Jiangsu and Anhui. After the Neolithic period the use of unfired colours lapsed until Han times when they were introduced once more, but now as unfired pigments that included red, blue, green, white and yellow, together with some use of black. Some of the pigments seem to have been combined with fairly thick clay slips, but this would seem to have varied from one place to another. After the Han the use of these colours persisted over a long period and were often elaborately used on a white slip ground, especially on the unglazed grey earthenware tomb figures. Figures painted in this way can be found as late as the Northern Song period.

Painting in dark brown or black slip on a white slip ground and then applying a transparent colourless glaze over the top was an important advance in the late Tang period in the latter part of the 9th century. This was a technique which developed to a high aesthetic level during the Song, and the glaze was sometimes coloured green or later still in the late 12th century, turquoise. Both colours are derived from copper, the former being incorporated in a lead glaze, and the latter in an alkaline, or lead-free glaze. In both cases it was necessary to biscuit-fire the stoneware bodies on which they and the slip painting were used. Related to this type of ware, and made at the same kilns were the *sgraffito* wares with the decoration scratched through the white slip to the raw greyish body beneath before the application of a transparent glaze. The technique began at the same time as the slip painting and at first was fairly simple. During the 10th and 11th centuries it was used extensively at a great number of kilns, and in the late 11th and 12th centuries became more complex with the use of two slips, one white and the other black, the latter applied over the former.

The earliest lead glazes were those used just before and during the Han dynasty. They were colourless, green, or occasionally brown. It should be noted that as the glaze was applied to a reddish earthenware body with a fairly high iron content, the colourless glaze always absorbed some of the iron from the body, causing it to turn a pleasing amber brown. The additional use of iron in the glaze to make a thick dark brown colour is relatively uncommon. It was much more usual to add copper to produce a pronounced green, which had the advantage of concealing the body colour. Polychrome lead glazing cannot be dated earlier than Eastern Han, to which period a few pieces can at present be dated. Other more securely dated examples are not earlier than the late 5th century. The real flowering of polychrome lead glazing came in the Tang dynasty in the 7th and first half of the 8th century. The clay bodies were usually slipped and the colours thus tended to be bright and clean. A colourless glaze was now used for white effects, with amber brown, green and, early in the 8th century, blue and yellow. Often the colours were splashed on rather carelessly, but there were also many examples of careful control of designs, the glaze being painted on.

During the Tang period interest seems to have developed in the possibilities of glaze transmutations and in the high-fired stonewares there are examples of pale bluish and grey splashings on a dark brown or black ground, and examples of delicate flecked effects resembling tea-dust and hare's fur. The Song saw the development of this aspect of decoration in the stonewares, alongside elaborate and accomplished carving and incising, which was confined to the transparent glazed wares such as Ding, Yue and the northern celadon, now often known as Yaozhou-type ware. The best known glaze transmutation types are Jun, in which suffusions

Green glazed jar and lid.

of copper were used to produce red or purple against a grey-blue ground using reduction firing, 'oil-spot' effects on a black glaze in the northern black stonewares, and 'hare's fur' effects in the Jian wares from Fujian. At the same time the use of two glazes, one dark applied first, and then a second, light coloured one splashed on the top, producing a 'tortoise shell' effect, was introduced at Jizhou in southern Jiangxi. It was at this group of kilns, too, that a series of novel techniques were developed among which were decorations produced by using wax resists and paper resists. These were paper-cut decorations, which involved sticking paper-cuts with light adhesive directly to the unfired body before glazing, so that in the firing the paper was destroyed leaving in its place a carbonaceous black pattern in a speckled light brown glaze. Even more unusual was the use of a leaf in a similar fashion in a black glaze, the trace of the leaf, high in silica, showing pale yellowish brown on the black ground.

If the southern potters were innovative in such a novel manner, the north had its own contributions to make. The introduction in the Cizhou type stonewares of polychrome overglaze enamelling, was an advance of considerable importance. The Cizhou type had a coloured body varying somewhat in quality, often being rather coarse, and it was the practice to cover it with a white slip, which provided a smooth surface suitable for painting, or as a step towards *sgraffito* decoration. The smooth white ground naturally invited decoration, but the new departure in the late 12th century

Porcelain vase painted in cobalt blue under the glaze depicting a drama scene. Mid-14th century.

was perfectly stable unless over-fired. The ultimate impact of this new technique was to be world wide, and in China it changed the whole direction of the ceramic art, opening the way to decoration on a grand scale, for while blue and white was to become universally popular, it was still possible to add the overglaze colours with dazzling effect, as they had already been applied to the stoneware pieces. It should be added that the lead fluxed colours could also be applied to the high-fired porcelain body provided this had first been fired to the high temperature required for porcelain, which is in excess of 1280°C. In fact this was frequently done from about the middle of the 15th century onward, when manganese purple was added to the palette of lead glazes. Until the 18th century all the overglaze colours in their varying shades, except black and red, were translucent. It was only in the 18th century, about 1716, that opaque colours were introduced from Europe with the so-called *famille rose* palette, a series of enamel colours made opaque by the addition of arsenical white and/or tin oxide. *M.M.*

White porcelain flask decorated in overglaze *famille rose* enamels. Yongzheng period, 1723–35.

or early 13th century was to fire a glazed, but undecorated piece to the stoneware temperature (1200°C–1300°C), and then when it had cooled, paint the surface with lead glazes of different colours, at first red, green, black and occasionally yellow, and fire the piece again in a muffle kiln to a temperature of about 900°C, high enough to fuse the lead fluxed colours, but still low enough not to upset the equilibrium of the high-firing glaze. The link between these polychrome enamelled stonewares of north China and the overglaze decorated porcelain of south China in the 15th century is not clear and at present there is little evidence available of any connection.

It was in south China that the next revolutionary step was taken, when sometime about the end of the first quarter of the 14th century cobalt blue was introduced from the Near East as a decorative pigment for use directly on the body before the application of the glaze. Copper had been tried in this way but was too unstable to be exploited at this point in time; cobalt blue on the other hand

Bronze

The founding of bronze dates in China from about the 18th or 17th century BC, the earliest material coming from Shang dynasty sites in north China. Smelting and casting were technically very advanced by the 14th century BC, with both *cire perdue* and piece moulding being used. Fragments of fine pottery moulds have been found on Shang sites such as those at Anyang and Zhengzhou. Parts of vessels, such as handles, were often pre-cast and 'cast in' with the whole body of the vessel. Early weapons were often cast with cells to permit inlay with turquoise or malachite. Even by the 4th century BC when the *cire perdue* method had become widely used for the more complicated forms common in the later period, the use of piece moulds was still quite usual, as is proved by the survival in excavations at Houma of carefully worked examples, not only of moulds, but of master models for impressing in the wet clay prepared for the piece moulds. During the Warring States period inlaying of bronze vessels and ornamental objects with gold and silver, copper, turquoise and malachite was generally practised. In the Han period, if not before, fire gilding was introduced, often with two colours of gold on the bronze ground to produce a pattern. After the Han dynasty the high standards of casting lapsed until Buddhism with its emphasis on icons led to the development of bronze sculpture on a large scale, with many complex figures and groups of figures, executed using *cire perdue*. Vessels, many of them of traditional and archaic shapes were cast from Song times on into modern times, the archaic and archaistic ones usually being ornamented in a manner similar to those of the Shang and Zhou periods.

M.M.

Gold

The use of gold by the Chinese was limited as compared with other cultures, the precious metal not having been accorded a comparable adulation. The earliest surviving gold, dating from the 8th to 6th centuries BC, is thin sheet with coarse traced details of coiling and interlacing dragons. The sheets, mostly circular, were glued to wooden vessels. In the later bronzes of the 5th to 4th centuries BC gold was frequently used alongside silver as inlay either as thick foil, or as fine threads. At about the same time repoussé was introduced for ornaments. A little later solid gold objects began to appear, the casting being executed by the *cire perdue* method as is proved by the intricate openwork designs of many pieces. Fire gilding seems to have been introduced in the Han period and was used mainly on bronze and silver. Granulation, almost certainly a technique brought in from the West, occurred

first in the Han period, and after this filigree developed. In the Tang came the use of gold foil for repoussé work on mirror backs and thin sheet cut-outs of birds and flowers with traced details were also used for mirror backs and other objects, the adhesive being a lacquer mastic. After the Tang dynasty there is little information about gold and its use until the Ming period, when relatively large beaten gold vessels occur, the earliest so far known being from the tomb of the Xuande Emperor (d. 1435) which were decorated with traced dragons and clouds, with precious stones scattered on the surface in beaten gold cups as settings. Later from the tomb of the Wanli Emperor, opened in 1955, came a headdress of woven wire and a large number of beaten gold dishes, basins and other vessels, some plain, others with filigree or traced and repoussé decoration. The Qing dynasty saw many small, rather elaborately decorated pieces of somewhat variable quality of craftsmanship.

M.M.

Silver

Except for use as inlay in bronze and iron, little or no silver has been found from before the 4th century BC. This may be partly due to poor resistance to corrosion, and partly to difficulties in purifying the metal. In the period preceding Han cast silver figures and belt hooks were not uncommon. During Han cast cups, bowls and boxes are occasionally found, but the great age for silver work was the Tang dynasty. The shapes of many vessels reflect the foreign influences, which were exceptionally strong in the Tang period. Some of the decorations, too, reflect alien influence. The silver, alloyed with a little tin and lead, was usually cast to shape and handles and feet soldered on. Decoration was traced and the background was frequently ring-punched to emphasize the designs. When the decoration showed through to the back too strongly, the vessel might be constructed with a smooth inner lining soldered at the lip. Engraving is rarely found. Relief ornaments, such as on sheet silver used for mirror backs, could be elab-

Beaten silver bowl in the shape of a lotus flower, with chased and gilt decoration. Early 8th century AD.

orate with additional traced detail and ring-punched backgrounds. Parcel gilding of designs was particularly common. The foreign influences that may be identified are Sassanian, Khorezmian, Central Asian and Indian, the last mentioned being rather remote. After Tang finds of silver have slightly increased in recent years, Deyang in Sichuan with early 12th-century material and Hefei in Anhui with material dated to 1333 being the two most important. Shapes and decorations follow very closely those of the contemporary ceramics, and from the 14th century on this kind of unity of form and decoration is a constant feature.   *M.M.*

Sculpture

In China the art and craft of sculpture in its broadest sense is not confined to stone and wood, but includes the casting of figures in bronze, the carving in ivory, and the working of jade. All have a history going back into antiquity and are both religious and secular in inspiration, although ivory and jade carving both tend more towards secular subjects than stone or bronze. Sculpture on a large scale, especially in stone, matured very slowly even under the influence of Buddhism, but in small-scale work, for instance in objects that could be held in the hand, the Chinese achieved very early a comprehension of volumes and articulation, and seem always to have been more comfortable working on a small scale.

Wood sculpture and carving

The perishable nature of wood has meant that little that is earlier than the Tang has survived. The earliest survivals are the rather flat doll-like figures recovered from tombs in the old state of Chu which were originally painted, sometimes in lacquer, and robed. In late Tang times large Buddhist figures were made, generally in several parts mortised and tenoned together. The wood was then covered with a thin plaster or gesso and painted, with some touches of gold. Such figures were often over life size and they continued to be made until well on into the Ming dynasty. In the Ming period running parallel with these devotional figures was secular carving in wood of a very different character. Small free-standing figures of immortals and secular portraits are fairly numerous, and most were painted or lacquered. In addition to these are the numerous small carvings for the scholar's desk and the collector, which include carvings of fruits, flowering plants, wrist rests and brush pots with a wide variety of decorations on the outside. The most

Wood figure of a man with ivory feet and head: traces of gold lacquer on the head and feet. Song dynasty, 12th–13th century.

Above: bamboo box in the shape of a mallow flower. Qing dynasty, 18th century. Left: bamboo brush pot, carved with pine branches and lichen. Early Ming dynasty.

appearance as decoration on the walls of tombs, but these are more closely related to painting in their pictorial inspiration than to the concepts of volume as implied in sculpture. The striking development in stone sculpture, using mallet and cold chisel to produce figures in the round, came under the inspiration of Buddhism. The visual expression of this inspiration came only in the 4th century, at least four centuries after the first official mention of the religion in AD 64. With the initiation of cave sculpture at Yungang in the far north, the beginnings of a sculptural style distinct from that of India and Afghanistan in the west can be discerned. In 494 when the Northern Wei moved the capital to Luoyang south of the Yellow River work was begun on another complex of cave temples at Longmen, and others soon followed at Gongxian, Tianlongshan and Maiqishan to name only a few centres. The early figures carved in high relief lack the sense of volume characteristic of a mature style, but they have a flowing rhythmic quality in relief that is impressive. The sculptors, bound by canons of which they understood little, worked as best they could and since heads and hands were iconographically important, they emphasized these at the expense of the rest of the figures, which were clothed in flowing robes. The robes reflected the artists' interest in linear patterning whether symmetrical or asymmetrical. Free-standing figures of the Buddha, Bodhisattvas and Maitreya were rare until the mid-6th

White marble sculpture of a roaring lion. Tang dynasty, early 8th century AD.

popular wood for such objects as wrist rests and brush pots was bamboo, which with age darkens to an attractive deep soft brown and has a wonderfully polished surface. These small pieces were usually exquisitely designed and executed with an eye for realism that is often surprising in the acuteness of the observation of detail.

Stone sculpture

Even in Shang times stone sculpture had an established place in artistic life. The earliest examples are small in size but of monumental bulk in character, comprising figures of tigers, buffaloes, owls and squatting human figures cut from white marble and ornamented on the surface with complex spiral designs echoing those of the contemporary bronzes. After Shang, in c. 1027, there is an apparent lapse in stone sculpture and it only comes once more to the fore in Han times (206 BC–AD 221) with some massive horses and lions, some winged, set up as figures in 'spirit ways', that is avenues leading to tombs. At the same time bas-reliefs made their

century, although these might appear on a stele with a large leaf-shaped mandorla behind, which was often elaborately decorated and embellished with flamiform motifs. In the course of the late 6th century the stylistic development towards a well proportioned and articulated figure, in which a sense of volume was clearly expressed, became rapid. At Longmen and Tianlongshan the fully matured art is seen at its best. After the suppression of Buddhism in 844–5, Buddhist sculpture in stone largely disappeared, but secular sculpture of figures for spirit ways to the imperial tombs continued, and those of the Ming tombs are among the best known. They are massive, not too well proportioned, but in detail very skilfully executed, and although not among the most accomplished sculptures, they remain impressive monuments. *M.M.*

Jade

For the Chinese jade is the most precious of all stones. Of no commercial value, it is esteemed for its hardness, texture and colour, and was used for sacred objects as well as for decoration. The Chinese word may mean a wide range of semi-precious stones, but nephrite and jadeite, two distinct minerals, are more usually intended. Nephrite, a silicate of calcium, magnesium and aluminium, belongs to the

Green jade (nephrite) *bi*-disc with four animal masks and a rice-grain pattern. Western Han dynasty, 2nd–1st century BC.

amphiboles and has a hardness on the Mohs' scale of 6.5, while jadeite, a silicate of sodium and aluminium, belongs to the pyroxenes and has a hardness of 6.75. The Chinese used nephrite at all times and the main sources have been Turkestan and Siberia, while jadeite, which was not used before the 18th century, came from Burma. Both materials are too hard to cut with steel and so cannot in the strict sense be carved, as it is necessary to work them with abrasive sands using drills, gouges, and later wheels and discs operated using cord or thong treadles. The abrasives in historical times have been quartz powder, crushed garnets, perhaps from Tang times, and corundum from about the 12th or 13th century. The working of jade goes back to Neolithic times when *zong* and axes were made in the 3rd and 2nd millennia BC. It was used in considerable quantities in Shang and Zhou times both for ceremonial tools, weapons, insignia and other sacred objects and for ornaments, sword fittings and small animal and human figures. Vessels do not appear to have been made much before the Han dynasty. The dating of jades after Han until the late 17th century is hazardous and depends largely on analogy with similar pieces in other materials such as ceramics and metalwork. The Song dynasty, however, saw the growth of antiquarian interests and it was during this period that archaisms began to appear not only in bronze but also in jade. A certain number of figures, human and animal can be attributed to the Yuan and Ming dynasties. While the Qing saw a growth of naturalism in the many examples of flowers and fruits, birds and small animals, it also saw an astonishing technical virtuosity with panels and brush pots carved with landscape scenes, immortals disporting themselves in the Isles of the Blest, elaborate vases with chain-link handles, and swing handles all worked in a single block of jade; even the lids of vases were cut continuously from the same piece of stone, as the veining of the stone often shows quite clearly. Whole 'moun-

Crouching, greyish-white jade bear with black flecks. Han dynasty, 1st–2nd century AD.

tains' with landscapes were also carved from large boulders over a foot wide at the base. One of the great skills of the jade carvers was in using the 'skin', or outside oxidized layer, artistically in their carving of animals and flower forms so that full advantage was taken of the variation in colour from outside to inside the stone, and adapting this economically to the design. *M.M.*

Siberian jade vase on a gilt stand. Vase, lid and the rings on the handles are carved from a single piece of stone. Qing dynasty, Qianlong (1736–95).

Ivory

The carving of ivory can be traced back to the Shang dynasty, when elephants were not unknown in China. The earliest examples reflect the artistic style of the contemporary bronzes. The later history is little charted until the Song to which a few small elegant figures may be assigned. It was mainly a material used for figure sculpture which varied in size from a few inches to between two and three feet. The very large pieces, mostly 18th and 19th century, display the natural curve of the tusk. In the Ming dynasty it was not uncommon for square seals surmounted by lions to be carved and this type has continued to the present day. In the late 17th century wrist rests and brush pots were added to the repertory. The soft material made it easy to carve intricate designs with much undercutting, and the best pieces are of extraordinary delicacy. It was probably not until the 19th century that the most intricate pieces like the revolving balls and delicate chess pieces were carved. *M.M.*

Ivory figure, with traces of gold lacquering, of Guanyin with a child. Late 16th century.

Symbolism in art

It is easy to suppose all forms and decorations in Chinese art have symbolic meaning, but it is much more difficult to identify and define these. Even when identifications and definitions are arrived at, the full force of some are only apparent in visual terms for limited periods. In time much that began as overtly symbolic became absorbed into the unconscious, and the use of many ultimately symbolic elements in later times was often an expression of the more generalized cultural background. In such instances stress on symbolism should not be over-emphasized. If too much is read into form or decoration the object becomes overloaded with symbolic meaning which may be inapplicable to what was properly a purely personal expression of emotion. Having said this, however, there is no doubt that the concept of *yin-yang* and the many numerical categories that are subsumed in it have been of overriding importance and became deeply embedded in the Chinese cultural tradition.

Yin and *yang*, resulting ultimately from the separation of Chaos in the creation of the world, are generally viewed as abstract cosmic forces. The mythological tradition on which the concept depends makes it clear that Chaos, which was like a hen's egg, gave birth to Pangu, and the parts of the egg separated, the heavy elements formed the Earth, the *yin* elements, and the light ones became the Sky or Heaven, the *yang* elements. Pangu grew and filled and enlarged the space between Earth and Heaven. Finally he died and the parts of his body became the mountains at the cardinal points, and his stomach the centre. This tradition gave rise early in the Han dynasty, or perhaps earlier, to the idea that everything light, south facing and male was *yang* and that everything dark, north facing and female was *yin*, while much that lay between partook in varying degrees of both elements. Linked to this were the Four (or Five) Directions, the Five Colours and the animals of the Four Quarters. These in turn became associated with the Four Seasons, and then came a series of numerical categories, and these, with their associated symbols, became recurring themes in the art of the Han period and have continued unabated to form a carefully organized cosmic diagram. Later in the course of the Northern and Southern dynasties the 12 animals of the Zodiac were added, together with the representation of such mythological figures as the Hare in the Moon pounding the Elixir of Life under the Cassia Tree, and the Three-legged Crow in the Sun. With such a rich foundation on which to build, the addition or multiplication of symbolic elements became an easy matter.

Ivory figure of hero Guan Yu (died AD 219) who becam Guandi, God of War. Ming dynasty, 15th century.

Marriage, a numerous progeny, wealth, honours and happiness were all given symbolic expression; even success in civil service examinations and in literature were provided with a symbolic representation in the theme *li hua long*, the carp passing through the Dragon Gate becomes a dragon. It was probably in the 13th century that the Four Seasons began to be represented by flowers, and soon after this the 12 months were similarly indicated. This does not mean that the earlier animal symbolism was abandoned, but in the decorative arts at least the floral symbols became more popular, as indeed they were better adapted to flowing rhythmic decoration. At about the same time emblems of immortality began to appear in great numbers accompanied by significant punning, the most obvious example being the bat, *fu*, the emblem of happiness, *fu*, while the *wu fu*, five happinesses, represented by five red bats

were symbolic of a happy marriage, a numerous progeny, wealth, honours and a good end. By combining these different symbolic elements in various ways a rebus could be created which would be flattering as well as auspicious for the owner. The trend in this direction began early, became more obvious in the Tang dynasty and was greatly developed in the Ming, to reach the height of complexity in the 18th century. At this late stage from Ming onwards it must be admitted that both the symbols and the symbolism were apt to become somewhat confused, especially when numerical categories were involved. For instance those relating to popular Daoism, which developed ultimately from the *yin-yang* tradition, often became mixed up with those of the Buddhist tradition, and so long as the number of elements was correct the artists appear not to have been disturbed.   *M.M.*

The Twelve Symbols

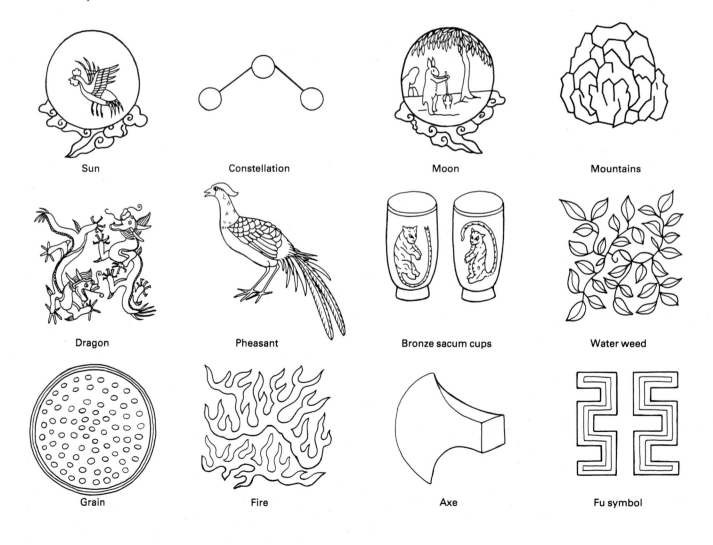

Sun Constellation Moon Mountains

Dragon Pheasant Bronze sacum cups Water weed

Grain Fire Axe Fu symbol

Pictorial references and emblems in Chinese art

Animals of the four directions

These are in common use in art from the Han dynasty onwards and there are correspondences associated with each, as indicated below, but it will be noted that there is a fifth, as the Chinese include the centre, the element Earth being allotted to this.

Animals	Directions	Seasons	Elements
Green Dragon	East	Spring	Wood
Scarlet Bird	South	Summer	Fire
Yellow Dragon	Centre		Earth
White Tiger	West	Autumn	Metal
Dark Warrior	North	Winter	Water

The Dark Warrior is represented in art by the tortoise with a serpent wrapped round it. The Four Animals, sometimes with the fifth, are frequently seen in the decoration of bronze mirror backs of the Eastern Han period.

Classic scroll

A formal linear scrolling pattern originating in the 9th century AD or earlier. It is used mainly as a decorative border or as a narrow band to separate rather strongly emphasized decorative themes that are unrelated to each other.

Cloud collar

An important decorative element of Mongol origin, it has been referred to in the past as an 'ogival panel' of 'lambrequins'. In its strict form it consists of four panels, each multilobed and ending in a point, the four organized round a central circular element so that each one is at right angles to the next. It is especially common in 14th-century decorative arts such as textiles and porcelain.

Cloud scroll

A motive showing great variation in the degree of abstraction of cloud forms, it is common to all the decorative arts, but is especially popular as a background in textiles.

Eight Buddhist emblems

These often appear in decorative arts from about the 13th century onwards. They are the chakra, or wheel, the conch shell, the umbrella, the canopy, the lotus, the vase, the paired fish and the endless knot.

Eight precious things (*Ba bao*)

These occur from the beginning of the Ming dynasty onwards, sometimes all together on an art object but also individually as a repeated theme or even as a mark. They are the jewel, the cash, the open lozenge and the solid lozenge, the musical stone, the pair of books, the pair of horns and the artemisia leaf; the last is particularly common as a mark on porcelain in the Kangxi period 1662–1722.

Eight Daoist emblems (*Ba'an xian*)

These occur in the decorative arts, especially textiles, ceramics and lacquer. They are: the fan carried by Zhongli Quan, the sword of Lü Dongbin, the gourd of Li Tieguai, the castanets of Cao Guoqin, the flower basket of Lan Caihe, the bamboo tube and rods of Zhang Guo Lao, the flute of Han Xiangzi, the lotus of He Xiangu.

Eight Buddhist Emblems

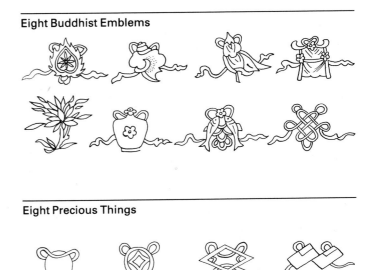

Eight Precious Things

Eight Daoist Emblems

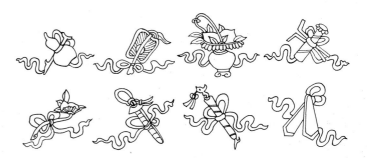

Huihuiwen

These are the so-called Mohammedan scrolls, which first occurred in the blue and white porcelain of the Zhengde period on ceramics made for the eunuchs in the imperial palace. The scrolls are recognizable by their outline and wash technique and their rather unvarying curvilinear flow. Often associated with the design are inscriptions in Arabic or Persian.

Leiwen

This is the so-called thunder pattern, a spiral filler pattern either round or squared, which is frequently used for backgrounds in the bronzes of the Shang and early Zhou periods.

Taotie

This is the glutton motif. The term occurs first in *Lü shih chun-qiu* (*Mr Lü's Spring and Autumn Annals*) in the 3rd century BC with reference to the animal mask, usually feline or bovine, which is a common feature of Shang and Zhou bronze decoration. It is a monster with a head, but no body, and is known in a great number of variations; it may even be composed of a series of detached elements, or of limbs of *kui*, an animal seen in profile with large head, eye and gaping jaw and with only one foreleg.

Flowers of the Four Seasons

These first became popular in the decorative arts in the late 14th century. They are usually:

Camellia	Winter
Peony	Spring
Lotus	Summer
Chrysanthemum	Autumn

In some instances the gardenia is substituted for the camellia.

Flowers of the 12 months

These were introduced into the repertory of decorative art early in the Ming dynasty.

1st month	Prunus	7th month	Lotus
2nd month	Magnolia	8th month	Pomegranate
3rd month	Peach	9th month	*Kuihua*
4th month	Rose	10th month	Chrysanthemum
5th month	Crab apple	11th month	Orchid
6th month	Peony	12th month	Narcissus

The *Kuihua* is usually to be identified as the mallow, but it is a name also used for the sunflower and the hibiscus. *M.M.*

Calligraphy

Calligraphy for the Chinese is an abstract art form of the highest order and ranks equal to, if not above, bamboo painting in the eye of the connoisseur. In calligraphy the importance of proper balance in a character cannot be overrated; it is essential that every stroke and dot should be correctly placed with a precisely measured intensity of the ink. The thick and thin must satisfy the most stringent judgement, for every stroke has both 'bones and flesh'. The 'bones' are the basic structure and 'flesh' the weight given to that structure. If the weight is too little, the structure appears weak and often emaciated; if too great the basic structure is concealed by the fat. Both flaws destroy the aesthetic impact, and underline the imbalance not only of an individual character, but also of the whole page. The respect in which the written word is held dates from an early period, even before the Han dynasty, a period when improvements were made in the brushes used. There are many different styles, each one with its own conventions, which make peculiar demands on the artist handling the brush.

The style generally associated with the Han period is the *lishu*, or clerical style, a bold somewhat severe style of writing in which there is strong emphasis on the horizontals and the sweeping downward strokes to the right, so that the characters have a rather squat appearance. It is a type of calligraphy which cannot be written at speed and so is suited to rather formal expression and is especially suitable for stone inscriptions. Hardly less formal in style but displaying pronounced verticality is the *kaishu*, or regular style in which the characters fit comfortably into a square frame, and are more closely linked on a page than the *lishu*. It became a standard script in the course of the 4th and 5th centuries and is the one normally taught in schools to the present day. Standing between *kaishu* and *lishu* on the one hand and the extreme fluency on the other is the running hand or *xingshu*. It developed out of the *lishu*, which was used for official documents and stone inscriptions, and seems to have been used for writing short notes and private letters of an informal and personal kind. It is a fairly fluent calligraphic style with a series of abbreviations which became standard in the course of the 4th century. The date of its development is uncertain, but it is traditionally thought to have been introduced by Wang Xizhi (321–79), who was closely associated with the rapid development of the scripts in the Eastern Jin period in the 4th century.

The most sophisticated calligraphic style, also associated with the name of Wang Xizhi is the *caoshu*, grass style, or cursive script, which is highly abstract. It is a style demanding great mastery of the brush and an intuitive understanding of the aesthetic, for here conventions are imposed, strokes omitted and characters abbreviated. It is less the character itself that is written than the idea of the character. It is a style which is impossible to write except at high speed, and is truly an example of what has been called 'the dance of the brush'. Very fluid as well as fluent in expression, it varies greatly from one artist to another, so individual is it. In some instances a complete line may be written without the tip of the brush actually leaving the surface, in others the line may be sketchy. The thick and thin of the strokes appear to follow no organized pattern as in the case of *kaishu*, and the frames of the individual characters are equally irregular; both are entirely dependent upon the expression which the artist seeks to impart. The visual, intellectual and emotional impact of a passage written by a great master such as Su Shi (1036–1101) or Mi Fu (1051–1107) is enormously impressive and the respect and admiration accorded to this unique abstract art form can well be understood.

Of a totally different nature are the passages written in the 'seal script', a very ancient form of writing for which the brush is but poorly adapted. In the late 17th century it achieved a popularity among certain calligraphers, and has remained relatively fashionable ever since, especially for writing commemorative couplets of a rather formal kind to be given as presents. In this style the conventions are at times arbitrary, so characters can be difficult to decipher. The strokes differ markedly from those of all other styles in that every one is given equal weight throughout. It is a solemn measured style that can be visually impressive. *M.M.*

HISTORICAL PHASES AND SCHOOLS

Perspective

The history of Chinese art is, like Chinese history itself, customarily divided chronologically by dynasty. This convention provides a convenient system by which to organize the study of Chinese art, although the developments of its various branches do not necessarily fit neatly into dynastic compartments.

Knowledge of the early pre-dynastic art of China depends upon the results of archaeological excavation. The study of Neolithic art, from the 5th millennium BC onwards, inevitably centres around ceramics and jade, durable objects of special importance in Neolithic society and mainly found in graves of the period. Among the various products of the Bronze Age Shang and Zhou dynasties, ritual bronze vessels claim the major attention. There are important parallels in the development of decoration on these ritual bronzes and on objects in other media, such as jade, ceramics and lacquer.

From early times the production of ceramics, bronzes, jade carvings, silk and lacquer was carried out in China at a level of perfection unsurpassed by the rest of the world. Highly organized groups of specialized artisans, frequently working together on the same object, were directed to the manufacture of these products.

While there was no concept of the individual artist-craftsman, excavations have shown that as early as the Neolithic period craftsman were accorded a special status, working in clearly defined areas and occupying relatively spacious houses. In more recent centuries the whole area around Jingdezhen, in Jiangxi Province, was organized as a large industrial complex coping virtually alone with the massive output required to satisfy imperial, domestic and foreign demand for porcelain, a Chinese invention.

Chinese bronze-casting was, similarly, the work of organized groups of craftsmen. Of special note is the use, unique to China, of ceramic piece-moulds rather than the 'lost wax' technique used elsewhere. This complicated method and the intricacy of the decoration on Chinese ritual bronzes required large reserves of skilled, coordinated labour concentrating on the production of prodigious quantities of these objects. In another medium something so apparently simple as a lacquer cup might pass through more than ten pairs of hands before completion.

Formidable as the Chinese achievements in these decorative arts may seem to Western eyes, the Chinese themselves have, at least from the Han period, regarded them as unimportant when compared with their great traditions of calligraphy and painting. Even sculpture, which in the West is not regarded as a medium inferior to painting, could not compete on the same level. It was never the vehicle, as calligraphy and painting often were, for the individual artist's feelings, impressions or ideas. Most surviving Chinese sculpture is Buddhist, and was produced to order by skilled craftsmen. Their patrons, whose names are often found on these images, believed that they would acquire merit by having them made and that they would be favoured in future incarnations. Few sculptors are identified, none is famous.

The names of painters, many of whom were members of the elite scholar-official class, rather than artisans, are recorded on their own paintings, as well as in the extensive Chinese literature on the history of art. Indeed, the names of some artists survive even when their work no longer exists. Chinese desire to seek perfection through emulation of the masters has meant that later generations had at least an idea of work otherwise lost or destroyed. In painting and especially in calligraphy, which was held in even higher esteem, a style once established was never lost, but remained as a possible vehicle for expression by later artists. This is still true today when traditional painting is once more gaining greater importance. *P.H-S.*

Neolithic period

Ceramics

The basic pottery of the Neolithic period was a coarse grey or brown earthenware with incised, cord-marked or basket-impressed decoration. Such pottery, intended for everyday use, was common to both the major Neolithic cultures, namely the Yangshao and the Longshan, of north China, although the finer pottery of these two cultures is quite different and is the main distinguishing feature between them.

The areas of the south and southeast had their own Neolithic culture. The best studied site is Dapenkeng in Taiwan. Its pottery jars and bowls are of clay ranging from buff to dark brown, decorated with impressed cord-markings and incised patterns.

Yangshao pottery is the red, painted pottery of the Yangshao culture, settled in the Yellow River basin, in Shaanxi, Henan, and later in Hebei, from about 5000 BC. Named after the site of Yangshao, where the characteristic red ware was first found, the culture as a whole is, in fact, better represented by vessels of an earlier

Earthenware jar. Banshan type; Neolithic from Gansu Province, c. 2500 BC.

phase found at Banpo, near Xi'an in Shaanxi. These include, besides a majority of bowls and jars of rough, sandy clay with incised and impressed decoration, a small number of fine bowls and cups of smooth, red burnished clay painted in black with fish motifs, sometimes with faces and masks, and geometric designs— predominantly of zigzags and triangles, which may possibly be derived from the fish and net motifs. Vessels from later sites in Shaanxi and Henan have abstract arc and dot designs or simple painted bands. The Yangshao culture was developed gradually into the Longshan culture which flourished in the east.

Gansu Yangshao pottery has similarities with that of some sites of the main Henan Yangshao culture, dating from the 5th millennium BC. But the vessels from the Majia site in Gansu (dating from the later part of the 4th millennium BC), for example, are painted in black with more linear designs and include different shapes, such as large jars. The patterns include spirals, dots surrounded by concentric circles, abstracted birds and eye-like dots. The famous jars from Banshan (3rd millennium BC), with their narrow necks and wide bellies with two handles, are decorated in red and black with bold spirals and cross-hatched shapes. Related to the Banshan vessels are those from Machang (first half of the 3rd millennium BC), which have a rougher, more rudimentary design often of anthropomorphic origin.

Longshan pottery is the black pottery of the so-called Longshan culture, named after the site where it was first found. Subsequent archaeological evidence has shown that this site represents a late phase, known as 'classic Longshan', in the development of the culture which stretched the length of the east coast of China. The earliest sites date from about 4000 BC. The 'classic' pottery is a lustrous black finely potted ware, turned on a wheel, with little or no surface decoration. Grey, red and white wares have also been found. Common shapes are tripods and delicate wine-cups with pierced stands, obviously for ceremonial use, and possibly the prototypes of later Shang ritual bronze forms. Some Jiangsu sites show a short period of Yangshao influence on their painted pottery, but the main cultural drift was westwards, creating the Henan and Shaanxi Longshan cultures as successors to the Yangshao.

Jade

By the Neolithic period jade had already assumed an important position in the values and beliefs of the Chinese. Jade axes and knives, similar to the contemporary stone weapons and tools, have been found in burial sites along with ritual pierced discs, called *bi*, plain rings, and *zong*—prisms pierced with a cylindrical hole down the long axis. The most important finds of Neolithic jades are associated with the sites at Hongshan and Liangzhu north of Shanghai, as well as others at Yangshao.

P.H-S., M.M.

Shang dynasty

Bronzes

Ritual bronzes of the Shang dynasty, in the form of wine, water and food vessels, are sophisticated both in technique and design. Their shapes, which are referred to by their Chinese type-names, reveal the influence of Neolithic Longshan ceramic forms and the hints of wrought metal prototypes. In contrast to the *cire perdue*, or 'lost wax', method used elsewhere, the Chinese built up ceramic piece-moulds around a central core, which partly accounts for the distinctive forms and designs of their bronzes. The decoration consists of numerous variations of a small number of components, the most common being the *taotie* (a sort of animal mask whose nature, origin or significance is not yet fully understood), the dragon, feather-like quills and a rectilinear spiral, called the *leiwen* or 'thunder pattern', which is commonly used as background pattern. Archaeological evidence seems to bear out the Five Styles enumerated by art historian Max Loehr as a guide to the evolution of Shang bronze decoration. The trend seems to be from thin

Bronze ritual vessel (*fangding*). Late Shang or early Western Zhou dynasty, 11th–10th century BC.

bands of abstract pattern in thread relief, easily produced by incising the ceramic moulds, thought the distinction of a main motif from a background of *leiwen*, to bold designs with the main motif raised in relief. Dating is complicated, however, by the use of several styles at once, and the existence and influence of provincial variants. Weapons were also produced in bronze.

Jade

In the Shang period jade was used primarily for ritual purposes, particularly those associated with the dead. Jade knives, axes and other ritual weapons had Neolithic prototypes, and had parallels in contemporary bronzes, with which there was a constant cross influence. The decoration is mostly in thread-relief, related to that of bronzes and marble sculpture. The Neolithic *bi*, or annular disc, recurs, but the *zong*, or pierced prism, is rare. Another important group of jades are realistic animal pendants or amulets, elaborated with surface decoration.

Ceramics

Shang pottery varies greatly in texture and ranges in colour from black and grey to red, pale yellow and white. Grey cord-marked and impressed wares predominate, made by hand, modelled, coiled or wheel-made. High-fired earthenware with a thin greenish-yellow glaze has also been found, indicating that the Chinese had already mastered the basic techniques for producing the green-glazed stonewares, a tradition that would last for centuries. The few hard white wares, with a high content of kaolin (one of the ingredients of porcelain), are decorated with elaborate designs similar to contemporary bronzes.

Sculpture

Mythical creatures, and recognizable animals were sculpted in the round in marble and limestone. Details were accentuated by surface detail, engraved or in thread-relief. Animal sculptures were also cast in bronze. Human figures were usually represented seated or kneeling. *P.H-S.*

Zhou dynasty

Bronzes

The bronze decoration of the early Western Zhou dynasty was a continuation of the late Shang style, mixed with elements of the pre-conquest Zhou regional style and earlier Shang styles. The trend of development, however, reversed that of the Shang period, tending to abstract designs rather than the clear delineation of specific motifs. The features of the *taotie* mask, dragons and birds were disjointed and arranged in bands or covered the whole vessel. Prominent hooked flanges and large animal-heads on the handles are features of some Zhou bronzes.

In the Eastern Zhou the trend towards abstraction continued, based on the interlace and repetition of designs. Notable developments are an emphasis on texture, including the use of studs, a group of bronzes with decoration depicting hunting scenes, and the practice of inlays of lacquer, copper, gold and silver. The effects achieved by inlay probably account for the general decline in the quality of casting. Cross-influence with jade-carving and lacquer-painting is evident.

One of a pair of ritual wine vessels (*hu*). Eastern Zhou period, 5th century BC.

Ceramics

Western Zhou ceramics were mainly grey wares, made by hand, wheel or mould, with impressed cord-marking or geometric designs. Glazed stoneware production centred in Anhui and Jiangsu. Brown glaze was applied with a brush and green glaze by dipping. In the Eastern Zhou ceramic shapes closely resemble those of bronzes, one aspect of their increased mortuary use. Vessels of inferior quality were increasingly made for this purpose, as were clay figurines. Soft, polished black wares and hard, pure white wares occur, and both the low-fired green lead glaze and a high-fired glaze were produced. Ceramic tiles and bricks were moulded with stamped or relief decoration.

Jade

Jade carving suffered a decline in the Western Zhou, but reached new heights in the Eastern Zhou especially in the Warring States period. Jade was now used for personal adornment, but still mainly served as offerings to the dead. Designs reflect influences from bronzes, in which jade was sometimes inlaid. Rounded animal silhouettes, notably of the dragon, contrast with earlier angular prototypes and there is attention to surface detail, noticeable too on the annular *pi* disc.

Sculpture

The Shang practice of human sacrifice at funerals was replaced by the Zhou with the provision of tomb objects, called *mingqi*, which were models of the things enjoyed by the deceased in life and were the forerunners of the advanced tomb art of the Han and Tang dynasties. Clay figurines of humans, horses and chariots, and animals have been unearthed. In Changsha, Hunan, stylized wooden human figures were found, as well as antlered guardian monsters with long protruding tongues, and fine bronze drum stands in the form of birds and animals.   *P.H-S.*

Han dynasty

Painting

Recent archaeological discoveries of Western Han date have included funeral banners on silk and many painted designs on lacquered wood (for example, the outer coffin with spirits gambolling among clouds), from Mawangdui near Changsha, and painted tiles from Luoyang with historical as well as legendary scenes. Surviving monuments from Eastern Han include many engraved slabs with similar subjects from Shandong Province, and scenes of daily life, both engraved and as wall paintings.   *R.W.*

Sculpture

Almost all surviving Han sculpture comes from tombs. Large, roughly carved stone figures and animals lined the *shendao* or 'spirit road' which led to the burial mound. Bas-reliefs, chiefly found in Shandong and Sichuan, decorated the walls of the tombs and ancestral temples near the mounds, depicting historical or mythological scenes, and scenes of everyday Han life. Sichuan tombs were also decorated with tiles of lively design in moulded relief. Tiles that have the decoration stamped into the clay have been found in Henan.

The most numerous and important group of Han funerary sculpture are the so-called *mingqi*. These are models, generally of pottery with a lead glaze or painted in unfired pigment over a layer of slip, in the form of figures, animals, buildings, boats and vehicles. They were either individually modelled or mass-produced in moulds, the centre of production being around the Eastern Han capital of Luoyang. Models made in Sichuan and Guangdong provide interesting variants, showing, for example, the different southern styles of architecture.

Bronzes

The ornate moulded designs of the Shang and Zhou periods gave way to the plain, incised, inlaid or gilt surfaces of the Han dynasty. Gold and silver could be inlaid in sheet form, but an easier, cheaper method was the use of parcel gilding, which had the disadvantage, however, of rubbing off easily. The designs were usually silver cloud scrolls on a gilt ground. The shapes of Han bronzes include *hu* vases, *lian* caskets and incense-burners with lids in the form of mountain peaks, supposed to represent the Daoist paradise.

Details from painting on pierced tiles, from a tomb of the Western Han dynasty, 1st century BC: (below left) bear with a jade *bi*-disc; (below right) rider on a dragon.

Earthenware model of a watchtower. Han dynasty, 1st–2nd century AD.

Bronze mirror with 'TLV' design. Han dynasty, 1st century BC.

Mirrors

The most significant advance in bronze casting during the Han was in the decoration of the backs of mirrors, notably in the so-called 'TLV' pattern. Concave bands in the form of these three letters were combined with balance and precision with the 12 zodiacal animals, Animals of the Four Directions, or Daoist deities. These elements together with the inscriptions, which appear on mirrors for the first time, indicate a connection with Han astronomical and cosmological beliefs.

Ceramics

Han ceramics are predominantly of red or grey ware with either a lead glaze or a high-fired glaze. The shapes closely resemble contemporary bronze forms, especially notable in the *hu* vase form, complete with *taotie* masks on the shoulder. Other vessels and many of the *mingqi*, or tomb objects, are thinly coated with slip and painted in unfired colours. In the north lead-glazed ceramics tended to be simply cheap substitutes for bronzes and intended for tombs, but in the south ceramics were developed more in their own right.

Lacquer

The production of lacquer wares was highly developed by the Han dynasty, being carried out by specialized artisans in factories, mainly in Sichuan and southern Henan. An inscribed, dated cup

in the British Museum records by name the several workers involved in the various processes of this manufacture. Like ceramics, lacquered vessels often imitate bronze forms. They are decorated in red and black, sometimes also in yellow, green and blue with variants of the swirling cloud scroll design, birds, animals and dragons. The most spectacular examples of Han lacquer are the perfectly preserved vessels excavated from the Mawangdui tomb, Changsha, Hunan Province. *P.H-S.*

Wei, Jin and Northern and Southern dynasties

Calligraphy

Numerous funerary tablets engraved on stone, and Northern Wei votive inscriptions in the Guyang cave at Longmen testify to a robust and angular script in north China. In the south more fluent styles were developed in the cultured circles of the southern courts, culminating in the unsurpassed achievements of Wang Xizhi (303?–61?) under the Eastern Jin.

Rubbing of a dedicatory inscription to an image of Maitreya from the Ku-yang cave, Longmen, Northern Wei dynasty, AD 502.

Painting

Also in the south, the Jin painter Gu Kaizhi (344?–406?) attained lasting fame. A handscroll, *Admonitions of the Instructress to the Court Ladies*, in the British Museum is attributed to him and the archaeological find of a painted screen from a tomb dated AD 484 at Datong confirms the antiquity of some of the scenes. Both feature a series of separate scenes, with passages of text. Brick reliefs from imperial tombs of the Southern dynasties near Nanjing, and wall-paintings from the tomb of a Northern Qi ruler near Taiyuan, throw light on the styles of other recorded masters such as Lu Tanwei (*c.* 440–500). At Dunhuang, in Gansu Province, narratives depicting the previous lives of Buddha appear in cave-wall paintings in horizontal registers, with the successive scenes connected by a continuous landscape. Critical theory of painting developed later than literary theory, but Xie He's *Liu fa* (*Six Methods*) (written *c.* AD 500) established certain fundamental principles for Chinese painting, such as the concern for 'spirit-consonance' and brush method. *R.W.*

Early Buddhist sculpture

The development of Chinese Buddhist art reflects periods of sinicization and Indian influence parallel to similar phases in the adoption of the religion itself. The earliest known Chinese Buddhist art is found in the decoration of mirrors of the 3rd and 4th centuries AD. The Buddhist deities represented show a strong similarity to their indigenous Daoist counterparts. Few bronze images are known to date before the 5th century, when images were still primitive and iconographically limited.

The Yungang cave temples built near Datong, Shanxi Province, the first capital of the Northern Wei dynasty, are representative of early, archaic Chinese Buddhist stone sculpture. They date from AD 460 until well into the 6th century, but mostly from before 494, when the capital was moved to Luoyang. These and other north Chinese cave temples have their cultural origins in India, transmitted along the Central Asian trade routes. Indian and Central Asian iconographic and stylistic influence is also evident at Yungang in the five huge sandstone images of the Buddha, representing the Buddha of the present age flanked by the two Buddhas of the past and the two of the future, and the surrounding carved decoration. In the earlier caves the faces are round with clear, sharp features. The fluid, linear folds of the thin robes, Western in style, follow the round contours of the body. However, images in later caves show a Chinese style, more rigid and flat with a more angular face, and heavier robes which conceal the narrow, sloping shoulders and body. The linear, geometric style folds are pulled out to an arranged pattern of pleats and points along the border.

The Longmen cave temples are carved in limestone cliffs near Luoyang and became the centre of Buddhist sculpture when the Northern Wei moved their capital there in AD 494. Here the flatter Chinese style became fully developed, more elegant and refined. Sculptures in bas-relief show the natural culmination of this style. Many of the images have dated inscriptions, with prayers to be reborn in the Western Paradise of Amitabha or the Pure Land of Maitreya, the Buddha of the Future. In the contemporary caves at Gongxian, near the Yellow River, the images show a slightly rounder treatment.

Gilt bronze figure of the Bodhisattva Guanyin inscribed with a date equivalent to AD 530.

The Tianlongshan and Xiangtangshan cave temples represent the 'transition' style that predominated in Chinese Buddhist sculpture between the fall of the Wei in the mid-6th century and the emergence of the fully fledged Tang style. The influence of Indian Gupta sculpture on the Northern Qi sculptors caused a return to rounder, more sensuous forms, with the robes again following the contours of the body. The ornament of lotuses and flying apsaras on the walls and ceilings also show Indian or Sassanian influence. However, the contemporary equivalents at Maijishan of the Northern Zhou show less of this influence.

The profusion of Buddhist sculpture in stone, marble, gilt bronze and other materials is accounted for by the Chinese preference for the Mahayana doctrine. This taught that one gained great merit by making a holy image and provided for salvation through the intercession of Bodhisattvas. Images of Buddha, Bodhisattvas such as Maitreya, and the layman Vimalakirti, and the later colossal statues of Buddha Vairocana indicate the aspects of Buddhism that most attracted the Chinese. The many dated examples provide documents for tracing the evolution of styles. By the end of the period Western influences appear to have been almost completely absorbed and the images have a more Chinese appearance.

Funerary sculpture

In spite of the influence of Buddhism during this period tomb sculpture continued to be produced. Objects similar to those of the earlier Han and following Tang dynasties have been found. Some also reflect the particularities of the northern barbarian rulers, such as their horses and their style of dress. Dynamic stone chimeras and winged lions lined the 'spirit road' to the tomb.

Green glazed stoneware bowl with animal head handles and three legs. Western Jin dynasty, 4th century AD.

Ceramics

Yue ware, a grey stoneware with an olive-green to grey-green refined glaze, produced since the Zhou period in the principality of Yue in Zhejiang Province, continued to be made. The bowls, jars and vases were decorated with bands of impressed geometric design, with animal masks in moulded relief. There are also small models of figures, animals and houses. *P.H-S., M.M.*

Tang dynasty

Calligraphy

Emperor Taizong was passionately interested in calligraphy and fervently collected and had copied every available work by the great Jin calligrapher, Wang Xizhi (303?–61?). Under Taizong, calligraphy almost became an instrument of government, as leading ministers were chosen for their handwriting style. Men like Ouyang Xun (557–641) and Chu Suiliang (596–658) established an elegant standard script which is still a model for calligraphers today.

Xingran tie, early Tang dynasty traced copy of a letter written by Wang Xizhi (?303–?361) in cursive script (*caoshu*). Marginal titles on this handscroll are by the Qing Emperor Qianlong.

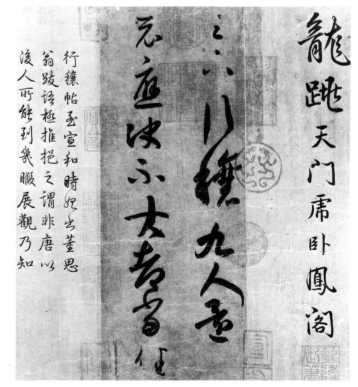

Wall painting

The principal pictorial medium was wall painting, but many of the most famous temple paintings were destroyed in Buddhist persecutions of AD 845. Many are recorded in Zhang Yanyuan's (9th century) *Lidai minghua ji* (*Record of Paintings of Successive Dynasties*) of AD 847. Those known today are either in the cave temples at Dunhuang, or in a small number of princely and aristocratic tombs excavated near Xi'an.

Figure paintings

The *Thirteen Emperors* handscroll attributed to Yan Liben (d. 673) (in the Boston Museum of Fine Arts) is one of the very few paintings to have been handed down through collections. Other painters, such as Wu Daozi (active *c.* 720–60) are known only through records: Wu's brush drawing was extremely vigorous. Many Buddhist votive and paradise paintings were preserved in a sealed cave library at Dunhuang and are now in collections in London, Paris, Leningrad, New Delhi, Japan and Korea; explorers in Central Asia early in the 20th century left few manuscripts and even fewer paintings to be preserved in China.

Court lady: detail from the engraved stone coffin shrine in the tomb of Princess Yongtai near Xi'an. Tang dynasty, AD 706.

Painting in the Five Dynasties

Important centres of painting during the Five Dynasties were in the kingdom of Shu in Sichuan Province and at Nanjing under Li Houzhu, ruler of the Southern Tang dynasty. Examples from these two centres are Huang Quan (d. 965), who attained special fame at Chengdu in the painting of flowers, and Zhou Wenju (10th century) at Nanjing, who was renowned for his figure paintings, especially of court ladies.

Landscape painting

Although usually still serving as a setting for figures or narrative,

Picture in ink and colours on silk of Avalokiteśvara as guide of Souls. Five dynasties, early 10th century AD.

Left: gilt bronze figure of Maitreya. Tang dynasty, inscribed with a date equivalent to AD 477.

Right: glazed earthenware Lokapala, or tomb guardian. Tang dynasty, 8th century AD; said to have come from the tomb of Liu Tingxun, who died in AD 728.

landscape was of increasing importance during the Tang. The poet Wang Wei (d. 761) is traditionally held to be the inventor of monochrome ink landscape painting, and Li Sixun (651–716) and his son Li Zhaodao (active *c*. 670–730) the exemplifiers of coloured landscape, a style later to be revived as the elaborate 'blue and green' tradition. Later theorists were to see these painters as the founders respectively of the Literati and the professional schools of painting, but there was no such distinction at the time.   *R.W.*

Buddhist sculpture

Almost all surviving Tang dynasty Buddhist sculpture is of stone. In Japan some contemporary pieces of bronze, wood, clay and dry lacquer are preserved. The images show the pronounced influence of the renewed contact with the West. The figures are more fleshy, sensuous and exotic. The thin, scant, more realistically flowing robes reveal the more relaxed, well-proportioned limbs. The faces are more naturalistic, with a serene expression replacing the stiff spirituality of the earlier images. The bejewelled Bodhisattvas have an almost secular appearance, and the muscular guardian figures affirm the renewed inspiration from the West.

This early Tang style is represented by the additions to the caves at Tianlongshan, now pillaged and parts of which are scattered all over the world. It is already well advanced from the stiffer, more solid and static images of the short-lived Sui dynasty. By the 8th century, however, Tang Buddhist sculpture had reached its peak, and was becoming increasingly stereotyped, before the Buddhist persecutions of the mid-9th century. The art declined with the religion, except in Sichuan, where the carving of cave temples continued into the Song dynasty.

Non-Buddhist sculpture

Daoist sculpture does not show the variety of the Buddhist pantheon. Images portray the mythical Yellow Emperor, or the philosopher Laozi with two attendants. Their inscriptions reveal borrowings of Buddhist terminology and expressions, thus indicating the prevailing supremacy of the Buddhist religion and its art.

Funerary sculpture

A notable exception to the vast majority of Chinese sculpture, designed and carved by anonymous artists, are the limestone panels from the tomb of the Tang emperor Taizong. They illustrate, life size and in relief, his six favourite horses, and are said to have been designed by the painter Yan Liben (d. 673). The monumental stone animal sculpture in the round of the later Tang emperors' tombs already shows the decline to the heavy, static forms of the Ming and Qing dynasties.

Sculptural objects placed inside the tombs, however, reached their highest stage of development in the Tang dynasty. The clay figures are painted or glazed with combinations of brown, green and cream or, more rarely, blue. The camels, horses, dancing-girls and musicians, and the bearded foreigners reflect the lively cosmopolitan character of the capital of Chang'an. The tombs of the upper classes also contained larger figures of monstrous guardian spirits, and tomb guardians resembling the Buddhist Lokapalas, or guardian deities, and sometimes, in spite of government proscriptions, tomb objects of more valuable materials. Vast quantities of lower quality figures were modelled or mass-produced in moulds. By the end of the Tang the practice of furnishing tombs declined, and tomb objects from later dynasties show far less vitality and sophistication.

Ceramics

Sancai, or 'three-colour' wares, are the ceramics most commonly associated with the Tang dynasty. The vessels, intended primarily for funerary purposes, like the tomb figures, are of pinkish white clay pottery, painted and unglazed, or decorated with one or a combination of the green, orange-brown, yellow, cream, blue or black glazes. The colours are separated by stamped incised lines or splashed on and allowed to run freely. The most common forms are lidded globular jars and offering trays with a horizontal rim and most often a stamped floral decoration in the centre. New, exotic shapes, however, reflect Western influence, such as the slim-necked vases with two dragon handles reminiscent of the Greek amphora, and the bird-headed ewers inspired by Sassanian metalwork. The rhyton, a horn-shaped drinking cup of Mesopotamian origin, was imitated in stoneware, porcelain and occasionally metalwork.

The Liao dynasty (AD 907–1125), based in Manchuria, continued to produce pottery with *sancai* glazes, notably a bright green and a new white glaze. Floral designs were often incised under the glaze and novel shapes include an imitation of a leather bottle.

Marbled pottery is another characteristic ware of the Tang dynasty. The marbled effect was achieved by mixing clays of different colours and firing under a transparent straw-coloured glaze.

Yue ware, the stoneware long produced in the old Yue principality in Zhejiang, in the area around Shanglinhu, was, during the Tang, completely covered by an olive-green glaze. The repertory of shapes broadened, the most common being vases and bowls, decorated with carved designs of lotus petals, phoenixes, dragons, wave patterns and flowers.

Porcelain seems to have been discovered in the Tang dynasty, although hard white wares with a content of kaolin had been known as early as the Shang dynasty. The secret of the technique was not discovered in the West until the 18th century.

Gold and silver

Smithing developed to a sudden flowering in the Tang dynasty, heavily influenced in technique and design by Sassanian metalwork. This was due to direct contact with Persian craftsmen, refugees to China after the fall of the Sassanid empire. Specimens of Tang work in gold are largely limited to hair ornaments, jewels and small boxes, especially reliquary caskets enshrined in the foundations of Buddhist pagodas. The most common forms of silverware are bowls, boxes, and stem-cups of beaten, and occasionally cast, silver, with chased and parcel-gilt designs of hunting scenes and floral or vine scrolls with animals and birds against a matt background of small rings. A few silver tomb objects have been found, but some show signs of use, indicating that they were not produced solely for burial.

Mirrors

The 'TLV' decoration on mirrors in the Han dynasty had by Sui and Tang times been modified to the extent that only the 'v' remained. Often the animal symbols for East and West were reversed because the mirrors were fixed to the ceilings of burial chambers. Seventh-century silvered mirrors have a fifth monster in place of the cord knob in the centre. The surrounding, elaborately intertwined design included grapevines and lions, both foreign to China. Wedding mirrors were often of foliate forms and decorated with auspicious bird symbols. Inlay of gold and silver in bronze was a Tang innovation.   *P.H-S.*

Song dynasty

Calligraphy

In the Song period the most important phenomenon was the appearance of distinctive individual hands in *xingshu* running script, freer than standard script but just as legible, unlike the wilder forms of cursive under the Tang. Great scholars such as Su Shi (1036–1101), Huang Tingjian (1045–1105), and Mi Fu (1051–1107) wrote in hands that were expressive of their own personality. The concept of calligraphy as a *xinyin*, or heart print, led to parallel ideas of self-expression in painting, notably in Literati painting.

Abundant harvest, letter by Mi Fu (1051–1107) in running script (*xingshu*), Northern Song dynasty.

Fishing in a mountain stream (detail), ink on silk by Xu Daoning (active 11th century AD), Northern Song dynasty.

Landscape painting

The 10th and 11th centuries were the age of the great landscape painters. Li Cheng (d. 967), Fan Kuan (early 11th century) and Guo Xi (later 11th century) painted the rocky mountains of north China; in the south Dong Yuan and Juran (both 10th century) painted landscapes no less awe-inspiring but with gentler contours, using long sweeping strokes of the brush that were to inspire the hermit painters of the late Yuan. Human figures are reduced to a minute scale in these landscapes of cosmic proportions; mists and dislocations of expected receding lines are used to enhance the effect of distance, together with sudden changes of scale.

Figure painting

Li Gonglin (*c.* 1040–1106) is the outstanding master of the Northern Song. He drew on a number of past masters—among them Gu Kaizhi, Wu Daozi and Wang Wei—to recreate a classical ideal.

Literati painting

The concept of calligraphy as expressive of the scholar's personality was extended in Literati art theory to painting as well. *Wenrenhua*, or literary men's painting, had its origins in the circle around Su Shi. Eventually, under the Yuan, *wenrenhua* was to extend beyond subjects with clear literary associations, such as plum blossom and bamboo, to landscape, which presented the greatest scope in recreating through brush and ink the hidden forces and visible appearance of the natural world.

Landscape with bare willows and distant mountains, silk fan painted in ink, mounted as a hanging scroll, by Ma Yuan (active *c.* 1190–1225), Southern Song dynasty.

Emperor Huizong

During his reign (1101–25) Huizong gathered artists from all over China to his court at Bianjing (modern Kaifeng). He was especially interested in the naturalistic depiction of flower and bird subjects, of which he was himself a distinguished practitioner. He invented his own style of calligraphy, known as Slender Gold, elegant and mannered; after the Jin invasion this style was adopted by Emperor Zhangzong of the Jin. Huizong's vast collections of calligraphy and painting were catalogued according to genre and published, forming a model for later catalogues of collections.

Southern Song Academy

With the retreat of the court to Hangzhou after the sack of Northern Song by the Jin, there came a change of mood in Song painting. The foremost painters at the court, such as Ma Yuan (active *c.* 1190–1225) and Xia Gui (active *c.* 1180–1224) no longer attempted to embrace the whole of creation in their landscapes. They and other painters of the Academy used ink washes to create mists and break up the component parts of the scene: the contours of rocks are echoed in the outlines of trees or distant mountains. The paintings are often more intimate in scale, with figures prominent as observers or part of the subject.

At the same time, Emperor Gaozong promoted the painting of a number of themes with associations of dynastic legitimacy in order to assert his right to rule in the whole of China, the north now being controlled by the Jin. Among these imperial commissions was a series of scrolls illustrating the classic *Book of Odes*, with the texts written by Gaozong himself, and paintings by the court artist Ma Hezhi (active mid-12th century).

Chan painting

The impressionistic effects of Southern Song painting reach an extreme in the works of Chan (Japanese: Zen) Buddhist painters such as Mu Qi and Ying Yujian (both active mid-13th century), long since almost exclusively preserved in Japan and almost unrecorded in China. Nevertheless, despite being ignored by later critics and connoisseurs, the wildly splashed ink and inspired effects of the Chan painters were firmly based in the Chinese tradition. They found an enthusiastic following in Japan.   *R.W.*

Ceramics

Although not considered by the Chinese themselves as an art form comparable to painting or calligraphy, Song ceramics reached a degree of perfection of technique and design scarcely rivalled in China or elsewhere, before or since. The beauty of the many types of Song stoneware and porcelain lies in the unity of the form, often simple, the decoration, if any—moulded, carved or incised—and the colour of the usually monochrome glaze. The names of the

Shrike on a branch in winter (detail), ink and colours on silk by Li Di (12th–13th century), Southern Song dynasty.

areas where the different types are known or believed to have been produced are often used for the type-name of the relevant ware.

Ding ware was produced in Hebei during the Northern Song. The thin, white porcelain with an ivory-coloured glaze was decorated with incised or moulded designs of ducks, lotus flowers or fish. The bowls and dishes were often fired upside-down and the unglazed rim would be bound in bronze. Ding ware is said to have been the official palace ware of the Northern Song emperors before it was replaced by Ru ware. Stoneware and porcelain imitations were made in the southern provinces.

Northern celadon ware was also made in the Northern Song, at kilns such as Yaozhou and Xunyi in Shaanxi Province. It is a grey stoneware, which burns red in the firing where not covered by the olive green to grey glaze. It was obviously influenced by the earlier Yue ware of the south.

Run ware was made in Runzhou south of the northern capital Kaifeng as well as at other centres. The buff stoneware has a thick opalescent lavender glaze, sometimes with a red or purple splashed blush. A green variety is rarer, and possibly earlier.

Ru ware, the rare imperial ware was produced at Qinglingsi Baofengsian in Henan until 1127, when the Song capital was moved to Hangzhou. It is a fine, undecorated ware with a pale grey-green glaze usually with a faint crackle.

The name Cizhou ware covers a wide variety of popular stoneware made in north China in the Song and later dynasties. The robust shapes were decorated with a design either painted in brown or black slip on a white slip under a clear glaze, or carved, incised and stamped through the slip to the darker ground, or with a technique known as *sgraffito*.

Jian ware, sometimes known by the Japanese name, *temmoku*, is a coarse-grained dark bodied ware made near Jianyang in Fujian. The shapes are limited to tea bowls. The glaze, varying from dark blue to brown, often has characteristic streaks or patches referred to as 'hare's fur', 'partridge feather' or 'oil spot'. The glaze is often thin at the rim, which may be bound in metal. This type was much appreciated and imitated by the Japanese.

Tea bowls were produced in Jizhou, Jiangxi in imitation of Jian ware. The brown speckled glaze of the bowls is decorated in black

Porcelain ewer and basin with *qingbai* (or *yingqing*) glaze. Song dynasty, 11th-12th century AD.

with designs including paper cut-out patterns, or with a mottled tortoise-shell effect in yellow. Other vessels painted in brown under the glaze, and green lead-glazed pieces have also been found at Jizhou kilns.

Other black wares were produced in Hebei and Henan, often at kilns making other wares, and consequently with similar shapes.

Guan ware or 'official' ware was the imperial ware of the Southern Song. The thin dark-bodied ware is covered with several layers of glaze. The colours of the glaze, which has a broad-veined crackle, range from a pale green through grey to lavender blue. The shapes are often imitative of ancient bronze or jade vessels.

Longquan celadons were one type of southern celadon made in the Southern Song and later dynasties. The thinly potted wares of the 12th and 13th centuries had a dense, pale blue-green glaze and were largely undecorated. Popular among the Japanese are mallet-shaped vases (*kinuta*) and wares with brown iron spots (*tobi*).

The *qingbai* or *yingqing*—the 'bluish white' or 'shadow blue'—wares produced in Jiangxi were of thin porcelain with a pale greenish-blue glaze. The finest early wares, some with foliated rims, were decorated with delicate freely carved and combed designs while inferior later wares had a crowded mould-impressed decoration.   *P.H-S.*

Yuan dynasty

Calligraphy and painting

The reunification of China under the Mongols had far-reaching consequences for art. Restored communication between north and south meant the rediscovery of northern painting for southerners such as Zhao Mengfu (1254–1322); reluctance to serve alien rulers ensured that brilliant talents, such as Huang Gongwang (1269–1354) and Wu Zhen (1280–1354), devoted themselves to the arts instead; the brush styles they created inspired painters for centuries.

As a central figure in this period, Zhao Mengfu chose to serve the Mongols despite having been an official under the Song; he was a brilliant calligrapher and established a new style, which was to remain a standard. In landscape painting, along with his older contemporary Qian Xuan (c. 1235–after 1300), he abandoned current trends and turned to the revival of archaic styles. The same attitude is seen in his figure and animal studies, for which his models were the paintings of the Tang dynasty when these subjects had been the chief genres, before the dominance of landscape painting that ensued in the Five Dynasties and Northern Song.

The Four Masters of Late Yuan—Huang Gongwang, Wu Zhen, Ni Zan (1301–74) and Wang Meng (c. 1309–85)—who were all forced by circumstances to forgo the normal expectation of an official career, painted landscapes of isolation in protest against

Above: *Sheep and goat*, handscroll, ink and colour on paper, by Zhao Mengfu (1254–1322), Yuan dynasty; inscribed by the artist. Below right: porcelain temple vases (known as the 'David vases', decorated in underglaze blue, Yuan dynasty, dated 1351.

Mongol rule. Using brush and ink on paper, they brought landscape painting fully within the scope of Literati painting (*wenrenhua*) so that it became the highest genre. They each painted in a distinctive personal style, but are linked in the achievement of a unified ground-plane and distance related scale, in place of the sharp contrasts in scale by which Song landscape attained its grandiose effects.   *R.W.*

Ceramics

In the early years of the Mongol Yuan dynasty some of the traditional Song wares continued to be produced. The forms later became heavier and cruder, with new shapes such as large dishes and bowls being introduced, and the glazes less brilliant and pure. However, surface decoration, whether painted or moulded in relief, became more dynamic and naturalistic and alongside the bluish *qingbai* glaze was developed a thicker more opaque glaze. This prepared the way for the famous 'blue and white' porcelain decorated with underglaze painting, the major innovation of Yuan ceramics.

Shufu, the only official ware of the Yuan, is white with an egg-white glaze, produced near Jingdezhen where ceramic production was henceforth to be concentrated. Some of the bowls and dishes are decorated with floral scrolls and characters including *shu* and *fu*, which together mean 'privy council'. The decoration is either incised under the glaze, or moulded.

Underglaze decoration was painted on porcelain in cobalt blue and copper red. The cobalt was imported from the Near East, the major market for the end product. By the mid-14th century the technique was fully mature. The dishes and vases are decorated with dragons, phoenixes, fish and flowers, painted in the blue or the less successful red, or occasionally left in white reverse on a coloured ground. Many of the wares, especially the foliated dishes, show the influence of Islamic designs.

Worked in green, red and yellow enamels, overglaze painting was an innovation of the 13th century, practised on small Cizhou pieces. This technique, however, did not become fully developed until the 15th century, when it was used on porcelain.

Other arts

Silver was worked to a high level, often in shapes inspired by ceramic forms. In lacquer, a Yuan development was the carved red lacquer technique. Finally, Buddhist sculpture, with the renewed patronage of the Mongol rulers, shows the influence of the Lamaistic art of Tibet and Nepal. An impressive example is the ornately carved stone gate, the Juyongguan, dated 1345, situated near Beijing.   *P.H.-S.*

Ming dynasty painting

In the early reigns of the Ming dynasty, Song dynasty styles of painting, especially grandiose landscapes, were revived. Court painters were given military ranks, but there was no academy as such. Rigid controls at court did not encourage artistic creativity. The foremost achievements under the Ming lie with the scholar-painters of the Wu school, the continuing professional tradition known as the Zhe school, and, late in the period, in a diversity of styles, with a reaction leading to a return to a classical canon.

Wu school

Named after Suzhou or Wu prefecture, these painters followed, although not by necessity, the example of the late Yuan masters in living in retirement, and used their different brush styles for the expression of different moods. The foremost master was Shen Zhou (1427–1509). His pupil Wen Zhengming (1470–1554), was equally brilliant as calligrapher and painter; nevertheless he spent many years in unsuccessful attempts at the official examinations.

Several generations of his descendants perpetuated his elegant style. Tang Yin (1470–1527), accused of cheating in the examinations, forfeited a brilliant career and found solace in painting instead. All painted for a circle of close friends with literary, antiquarian and artistic interests. Qiu Ying (*c.* 1494–1552) painted in a revived 'blue and green' style that attracted instant success and innumerable imitators throughout the Ming and Qing periods.

Zhe school

Named after Zhejiang Province, long a centre of professional Buddhist painting, the origins of the school lie with the Southern Song Academy tradition. The paintings, almost always on silk, feature bold brushwork and considerable use of ink-wash in contrast to the blunt calligraphic strokes on paper used by Shen Zhou and the Wu school.

Late Ming

Painting in the late Ming witnessed a number of eccentric developments: the inspired ink-wash flowers of Xu Wei (1520–93); the convoluted landscapes of Wu Bin (*c.* 1568–1626), and the archaistic figures of Chen Hongshou (1599–1652). Faced with a diversity of such narrow and independent views, there was a reaction in favour of a return to past values, led by theorists such as Dong Qichang.

Dong Qichang (1555–1636)

Dong was an official, painter and theorist who established a return to classical values in landscape painting through the study of surviving masterpieces by painters in the Literati tradition. Wang Shimin (1592–1680) was his pupil, and an album of

Above: Details from *Enjoying summer* (*c.* 1650), ink and colours on silk by Chen Hongshou (robes), Li Wansheng (faces), Yan Kan (setting). Late Ming–Early Qing dynasty.

Right: *Autumn landscape* (1666), ink and colours on paper by Kuncan.

Opposite: *Wintry trees* (after Li Cheng–10th century AD), hanging scroll in ink on paper, dated 1542, by Wen Zhengming (1470–1554), Ming dynasty.

Left: porcelain jar with *doucai* decoration. Ming dynasty, Chenghua (1465–87) mark and period. Above: tripod incense burner in cloisonné enamels, Ming dynasty, early 15th century.

Wang's reduced copies of ancient masterpieces, with inscriptions by Dong, is in the National Palace Museum, Taipei. Dong's influence was paramount in the early Qing. His own paintings include sketches of tree types (which can be seen in the Boston Museum of Fine Arts) and landscapes of almost abstract intellectuality. *R.W.*

Ming dynasty ceramics

The Ming dynasty witnessed the triumph of porcelain with underglaze decoration over pottery and stonewares with coloured glazes. Production was concentrated in huge industrial complexes around Jingdezhen, Jiangxi Province, where there were abundant deposits of kaolin and petuntse (from the Chinese, *baidunzi*), the essential ingredients for the porcelain body and the glaze. The following reigns are noted for important changes and developments in porcelain manufacture.

The appearance of reign marks on porcelain during the reign of the Yongle Emperor (1402–24) indicates the beginning of imperial supervision of production. Alongside blue and white, red monochromes and 'bodiless' white imperial wares were produced. The latter have a 'secret decoration', or *anhua*, incised in the body under the glaze, visible only when held up to the light.

The superb imperial pieces of the Xuande reign (1426–351) show improvements in the quality of the body, the thick 'orange skin' textured glaze, and the colour of the blue. On the now more sparsely decorated wares the blue was applied more thickly in places, giving a 'heaped-and-piled' effect. Yellow began to be used as a monochrome glaze or as background to underglaze blue decoration.

The imperial kilns reopened during the reign of Chenghua (1465–87) after closure during the interregnum. Often of elegant,

delicate shapes, imperial wares were decorated in a relatively pale blue, made with native cobalt. Polychrome decoration in overglaze enamels was developed. Green, red, turquoise and yellow enamels were used often in conjunction with underglaze blue, a technique known as *doucai*, meaning 'contrasting colours'.

Special blue and white pieces were made for the Mohammedan eunuch officials of the court of the Zhengde Emperor (1506–21). They mostly consist of writing accessories with Arabic and Persian inscriptions. Large vessels and garden stools were decorated with *san ts'ai*, or 'three colour', enamels. The turquoise, dark blue, purple and yellow glazes were separated by threads of slip, rather like cloisonné enamels on metal.

The blue and white wares of the reign of Jiajing (1522–67) are noted for the pure, deep blue of their decoration.

Imperial supervision of the kilns declined in the late 16th century. The best pieces were made for the private home market and for export. The blue and white wares of the so-called 'transitional' period in the 17th century, covering the end of the Ming to the reign of the Kangxi Emperor (1662–1722) are admired for the beauty and freedom of their painting.

Ming lacquer

The carving of red lacquer reached the peak of its artistic and technical development in the Ming dynasty. Inlay with different coloured lacquers and the technique of carving through layers of different colours satisfied the growing taste for polychrome effects, a tendency notable also in ceramics.

Ming cloisonné enamel

As a technique probably introduced to China during the Yuan dynasty, it became popular in the Ming. The decoration usually consists of flowers, birds or dragons on a blue ground. The classic pieces date from the Yongle and Xuande reigns. *P.H-S.*

Qing dynasty painting

During the 17th century the influence of the Ming theorist, calligrapher and painter Dong Qichang (1555–1636) was paramount, both in the work of his direct followers (Orthodox school) and in that of the Individualists, who were just as concerned with artistic structure and brushwork.

Orthodox school

The Four Wangs—Wang Shimin (1592–1680), Wang Jian (1598–1677), Wang Hui (1632–1717) and Wang Yuanqi (1642–1715)—with Wu Li (1632–1718) and Yun Shouping (1633–90) are the six 17th-century Orthodox masters. Their paintings are based on a creative re-interpretation of Song and particularly Yuan landscape painting, through calligraphic brushwork. Wang Hui, the most prolific and successful of the Wangs, did so to such an extent that his paintings were occasionally more acceptable to contemporary eyes than original Song or Yuan works. However, later followers in the mainstream tradition found themselves with little new to contribute.

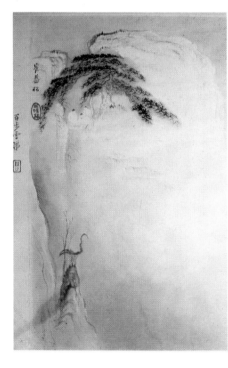

Orchids and bamboo, handscroll in ink on paper by Zheng Xie (1693–1765). The colophon in clerical script (*lishu*) and running script (*xingshu*) are by Chu Wenzhen (1718–*c*.1777).

The crane-sheltering pine, album leaf in ink and colours by Mei Qing (1623–97), Qing dynasty.

Individualists

A number of 17th-century artists painted in distinctive and original personal styles. Although they owed no allegiance to artists of the past, their attention to problems of brushwork and composition indicates a concern with the values of painting that is shared with the orthodox followers of Dong Qichang. Gong Xian (1617/18–89), Bada Shanren (1625–1705), Daoji (1641–*c*.1710), Kuncan (active second half 17th century) and others were to be immediately influential on the 18th-century Yangzhou eccentrics, and ultimately so in modern times in the work of Zhao Zhiqian (1829–84), Ren Yi (1840–96), Wu Changshi (1844–1927) and Qi Baishi (1863–1957).

Yangzhou eccentrics

Although usually referred to as 8 in number, the group numbered at least 11, each working with distinctive styles and subject-matter to satisfy the demand for painting from wealthy patrons in Yangzhou, a centre of culture since the 17th century when Daoji and others worked there.   *R.W.*

Qing dynasty ceramics

Qing ceramics show a striving for technical perfection and efficiency of production, often at the expense of aesthetic qualities. In the early reigns the imperial kilns of Jingdezhen were supervised by a succession of three rigorous and innovative superintendents. The huge export demand gradually diminished as European porcelain became more competitive. Blue and white porcelains, after a flowering in the reign of Kangxi (1661–1722), were ousted in popularity by polychrome enamelled wares.

Famille verte is the name of a group of enamelled wares on which the predominant colour is green. The enamels were applied over the glaze or as glazes on the 'biscuit'. Shapes and decoration vary widely, and the best pieces are considered to date from the early 18th century. *Famille noire* and *famille jaune* are related groups

Peach blossom water pot. Qing dynasty, Kangxi (1661–1722) period.

whose respective predominant colours of black and yellow were usually used as background.

From the Yongzheng reign (1723–35) onwards *famille rose* replaced the other groups of enamelled wares in popularity. The pink, from colloidal gold, was Europe's sole contribution to Chinese ceramics technology. The decorations of birds, flowers and figures were executed with minute attention to detail.

Experiments with monochrome glazes were made under the three great superintendents of the imperial kilns with glazes of all colours, giving rise to type-names such as *langyao* or *sang de boeuf*, peachbloom, *yuebai* or *clair de lune*, powder blue, iron rust, teadust and mirror black. A famous variety of white ware from Dehua in Fujian Province, called *blanc de Chine* or *Dehua*, consists mainly of modelled figurines.

Yixing ware is a reddish brown stoneware produced in Jiangsu Province since the 16th century. It is still being made—the most common forms are teapots, which often have decoration moulded in relief.

Guangdong ware—large vases and flower-pots of stoneware with flambé glazes—was possibly an attempt to imitate the Run ware of the Song. It was manufactured in the 18th and 19th centuries near Canton.

Snuff bottles

Snuff bottles were made in large quantities in the 18th and 19th centuries from glass, porcelain, jade, precious metals and stones, ivory and many other materials. The small phials have stoppers of jade, glass, coral and other substances, attached to which are tiny spoons of ivory, bone, silver, etc. Glass was the most common material used for the bottles, and was worked in different ways. For example, some were smooth and streaked in imitation of precious hardstones, others had relief carving in glass of a different colour, and those in a third group, dating from the late 19th to early 20th centuries, had minute landscapes and other scenes painted on the inside.

Qing dynasty jade

While most of the minor arts declined in quality during the Qing dynasty, jade carving revived after a lull of centuries which had been due probably to a scarcity of material. The technical virtuosity of the 18th-century carvers of jade, and especially jadeite (with a more oily or glassy appearance than the nephrite jade used since antiquity)—now imported in abundance from Burma—is seen in the ornate and intricate archaistic vessels, personal adornments and rock-like landscapes.   *P.H-S.*

Jade vase and cover with elephant head handles, carved with a design of quail beneath reeds on a river bank. Qing dynasty.

Porcelain vase with polychrome decoration in enamels. Hongxian mark, 1916.

The Republic

Hongxian porcelain

The notable achievement in the realm of the minor arts during the Republic was the porcelain made at Jingdezhen on order for Yuan Shikai, the president who proclaimed himself emperor in 1915, but died in 1916. The porcelains, delicately painted in enamels, have basemarks with the characters *Jurentang zhi* ('made for the hall where one dwells in benevolence'), or the reign mark *Hongxian nian zhi* ('made in the reign of Hongxian').

After Yuan's short reign, there being no reign mark to apply to their wares, potters used a variety of inscriptions, including *Jingdezhen zhi* ('made in Jingdezhen') and *Zhonghua minguo nian zhi* ('made in the years of the Chinese Republic'). *P.H-S.*

The People's Republic of China

Although one as yet can hardly speak of an artistic flowering under the People's Republic of China, many of the crafts have been encouraged, especially with regard to technical virtuosity and perfection. Fine porcelain is still being produced in Jingdezhen in traditional style. Other ceramic wares, such as Yixing teapots, are made, as well as export goods such as intricately carved jades, feather pictures and embroideries. *P.H-S.*

TECHNIQUES OF ART FORMS AND CRAFTS

Calligraphy and painting

Brush (*bi*)

Calligraphy and painting are practised with the same basic tools and materials. The Chinese brush is made of animal hair, selected and graded, carefully concentrically arranged in a bamboo holder. Different types of hair give the brush its resiliency or softness, and the construction, with the hair coming to a fine point, enables perfect control at all times of the breadth of the stroke. The brush is held vertically and movement comes from the wrist, the arm or indeed the whole body in the execution of larger strokes. The earliest brushes so far discovered date from the Han dynasty. At this time other instruments, such as a wooden or bamboo stylus, were also in use. Eventually, the superior qualities of the hair brush ensured its dominance over the rest.

Ink (*mo*)

Ink made from refined lampblack or pine soot has also been found dating from the Han dynasty. The soot was refined and solidified with animal glue into small sticks (often with impressed designs or legends). For use, the ink was prepared afresh each time by rubbing the inkstick on a smooth stone with a little water. The ink is intensely black, but capable of dilution down to the palest shade of grey for use as ink-washes in painting.

Paper and silk

The earliest paintings and manuscripts so far discovered, dating from the late Zhou and Western Han periods are on silk, but paper from the Han dynasty has been found. The use of silk permitted fine control over graded ink and colour washes, and remained standard for professional and court painters, while paper, with an immediate response to the touch of the brush, was the favourite medium for the scholar-painters. Both paper and silk required preparation by sizing (traditionally with alum and animal glue, but other sizes may have been used in Tang and earlier times) to ensure that the ink and colours would not spread.

Painting formats

Chinese calligraphy and painting are distinguished by the use of extreme formats: very long handscrolls and tall hanging scrolls. Both handscrolls and albums were intimate formats intended to be enjoyed at close quarters. Such works were very portable and passed freely from hand to hand.

A handscroll was a long roll in horizontal format, viewed from right to left by unrolling a short section at a time, as much as could be comfortably held between the hands, and then rolling on. An outer brocade cover, inner silk cover and title section generally preceded the painting or text. Inscriptions by the artist or later collectors could be added indefinitely at the end.

A roll in vertical format, the hanging scroll, was intended to be hung (using a two-pronged fork on a bamboo stick to hang the suspension loop) on a hook. Alternatively, an attendant might hold the stick with the painting suspended from the fork while it was unrolled, inspected and rolled up again. Chinese paintings were not usually left hanging for long periods.

Examples of calligraphy and smaller paintings up to about 300mm square were often mounted in accordion-leaf albums with wooden covers. Rubbings from stone inscriptions were cut into strips and similarly mounted so as to be read continuously in a convenient format. Early albums may have been collections of separate paintings, but from the Yuan dynasty subjects like plum blossom and bamboo were painted in series. Under the Qing, an album could serve as a summary of past styles (8, 10, 12 or more landscapes each in the style of a different master) or as a record of places visited.

Mounting techniques

Although paper and silk are fragile materials, proper attention to mounting and storage enables them to be conserved over centuries. Basically, the mounter constructs a thin laminate by pasting paper on the back of both the work of art and its borders of silk. Further thin backing papers are added to lock the complete assemble together. Each layer is dried flat on drying screens, on which the painting may remain for weeks or months until the mounter is satisfied that all tensions have been resolved. Equipped with top stave and bottom roller, the resulting scroll has to be capable of being unrolled to hang perfectly flat, and of being rerolled noiselessly in a closely-packed roll. The top border, always much longer than the bottom, gives several layers of protection against changes in temperature and humidity. The success of the mounting, and the length of time it will last before a new mounting is needed depend on the skill of the mounter and the care with which he selects and uses his materials. Among these, the paste is of crucial importance, for it must at all times over the life of the mount (up to about 200 years) remain flexible. It is prepared from wheat starch with the gluten removed (to prevent later embrittlement), and may be used either fresh or after ageing for a number of years (during which it loses some of its strength and can be used where a lesser degree of adhesive strength is required).

Inscriptions, seals and colophons

Until the Song, signatures of painters were generally small and often concealed in an inconspicuous part of the composition. From the Yuan dynasty onwards, especially in the works of Literati painters, inscriptions form an essential part of the painting. They may be by the artist or by others. Seals, carved in relief or intaglio, may be impressed on the painting using vermilion seal ink. They give the artist's personal or studio names or serve as a record of later ownership. Imperial seals are often larger and may be impressed in the centre instead of in the corners. Colophons may be written as marginal appreciations, or in the case of handscrolls, on extra sheets of paper following the work. The perusal of such additions serves both to enhance the viewer's enjoyment and to establish the collecting history of the work.

Imperial collections

The possession of works of art has always been an important aspect of the mandate to rule in China. Emperor Taizong's collection of the works of Wang Xizhi in the early Tang, and the vast collections of Emperor Huizong in the Northern Song, are prominent examples. The 18th-century Qianlong Emperor surpassed all his predecessors in the scope of the imperial collections; virtually all important paintings and calligraphy were absorbed into them. Since revival and reinterpretation of earlier styles was an essential feature of Chinese art, this had a stultifying effect on late Qing painting, an unforeseen consequence of imperial acquisitiveness. Since 1950 the presence of the greater part of the Qing imperial collections in Taiwan, and the care accorded to works of art and archaeological discoveries in the People's Republic, testify that the legacy of cultural and artistic works is still of outstanding political importance in China today. *R.W.*

Lacquer

Lacquer is the sap tapped from the lacquer tree, *Rhus verniciflua*, or *qishu*, which is grown and grows wild in southern and central China. Dried and kept in a humid atmosphere, it provides a hard, smooth, lustrous, protective and preservative coating, resistant to water, heat and acids. Colours include a range of reds (from cinnabar), black (from iron sulphate), various shades of brown, gold and silver. Lacquer can be applied to almost any material. Pinewood and hemp-cloth form the most usual bases, but others include metal, porcelain and basketware.

Painted lacquer

Lacquer was used as paint on carved wood in the Shang dynasty, sometimes with surface decoration in a different coloured lacquer. Han dynasty boxes, cups, etc. excavated near Changsha, Hunan, are painted in red on black and vice versa. Some also have white, yellow and green decoration. Made in factories, each piece was handled by many specialized workers. The painted basket, from a tomb in Lolang, Korea, is a famous example of Han painted lacquer. The technique was gradually superseded by carving and inlay, or was used in conjunction with them. Gold lacquer was used for painted decoration increasingly in the later dynasties, especially for furniture.

Carved lacquer

This was the most common technique used from the Yuan dynasty onwards. The lacquer was applied to the base in as many as 100 to 200 layers. As each coat took several days to dry, it could be years before the carving of the decoration could begin. Most carved lacquer is red, but black, buff, green and yellow pieces are also known. In 15th-century carved red lacquers a layer of black indicated to the carver when he was close to the base. In another Ming group, known by the Japanese term *guri* lacquer, or Garner's 'carved marbled lacquer', the lacquer was applied in layers of different colours and carved in scrolling or geometric designs to reveal the various strata. The most common combination is black-red-black, but more layers and colours could be used. Notable among the Qing carved lacquers are the so-called 'Coromandel' screens, exported to the West, whose designs were carved in relief and painted, or carved in intaglio.

Box made from red lacquer carved through to a yellow ground. Ming dynasty, Yongle (1403–24) mark and period.

Inlaid lacquer

Mother-of-pearl was the material most commonly inlaid in lacquer. Tang dynasty specimens survive in the Shōsōin Repository in Nara, Japan. The Yuan dynasty technique of surrounding the pieces of shell, by now thinner and sometimes tinted, with gilt wire to stop chipping was adopted from Korea. Gold and silver wire and foil were also often used for inlay. In the technique known as *qiangjin*, first made in the early 14th century, the decorations were etched with a needle and filled with gold. This technique was popular in the 15th century, but later, lacquers on which the designs were 'filled in' with lacquer of one or more different colours were preferred. 'Folk lacquer' of this type could be further decorated, and imprecision disguised with painting. Black lacquer inlaid with mother-of-pearl is known as *lac burgauté*. Other inlay materials include jade, soapstone, bone and ivory.

Dry lacquer

This technique is called *jiazhu* in Chinese. The figure or form required was shaped using cloth impregnated with lacquer. When this had dried and stiffened, additional coats of lacquer could then be applied. Large images could thus be made extremely light.

P.H-S.

Textiles

The materials

Silk cloth was woven in China in the Shang period, thousands of years before the secret was smuggled to the West in about the 6th century AD. Coarser, cheaper cloth was made from hemp. Cotton and wool were both found in the Dunhuang caves dating from the Tang dynasty, but there is no literary evidence for them until later dynasties.

The best silk is supposed to come from Zhejiang. It is also produced in Jiangsu and Anhui. Silkworms require careful raising, avoiding noise and extremes of temperature. They eat daily many times their own weight in fresh mulberry leaves. In north China tussore silk is produced from various species of moth, which in the worm stage feed on oak leaves.

Weaving

From the Han dynasty onwards the basic Chinese weaving techniques were those of warp-pattern silks, twills and gauze. Satin, velvet and brocade were also produced. For polychrome warp pattern silk about 3000 fine warp threads were used. To make the pattern, selected warps were tied together and drawn up with vertical strings in a predetermined sequence. Mistakes tended to be repeated the whole length of the cloth. Colours had to be limited for the clarity of outline and colour of the design.

Ming dynasty *kesi*, or type of tapestry.

The lacy effect of Chinese gauze is created by the warp threads being twisted and held in place by the weft threads.

Brocade

This is a polychrome fabric in which the pattern is created by coloured floating threads. The Chinese wove brocades from early times and often used gold and silver threads in the design. Indeed, the Chinese character for brocade, *jin*, consists of the metal radical and the phonetic element *bo*, which means 'silk' or 'cloth', thus establishing the importance of the metals. Strips of gold or silver foil backed with paper were most often used, but for large patterns the Chinese used gold foil wound round silk thread, which provided a more durable decoration.

Kesi

The most prized of Chinese weaves, *kesi* is a sort of tapestry. The Chinese word *kesi* has been written in different ways, meaning 'cross-threads', 'weft-woven threads' or 'weft-woven colours'. The characters now used mean 'cut threads'. They refer to the slits parallel with the warp threads, left where the weft threads stop at the edge of areas of a different colour, instead of running the width of the cloth. This technique may be Central Asian in origin, but was already perfected in China by the Song dynasty. The design was often enhanced by painting in the 18th century. In the Yuan dynasty a coarse form of *kesi* woven with gold became fashionable.

Embroidery

The Chinese recognize two main divisions of embroidery: one which uses satin stitch, or its variant, long-and-short stitch, and the other which uses Beijing stitch (the French knot). The other stitches used include stem stitch, chain stitch, split stitch and couching.

On gauzes, used for outer garments, *petit point* and Florentine stitch were the most common. Sometimes the Florentine stitch was used for the decorative motif and the background, giving the impression of solid weaving. The outlines of designs were usually couched. A peculiarly Chinese variant of couching consists of two threads twisted together and then couched down. A solid area in this stitch gives the effect of minutely sewn French knots. Knots of gold thread and the use of spun or couched peacock feathers are also characteristically Chinese. An entire robe might take as many as twelve workers as long as five years to embroider.

Dyeing

Dyeing techniques were passed down by word of mouth and, therefore, are mostly unrecorded. However, there is a section on dyes in the *Tiangong kaiwu*, an illustrated encyclopedia of the Ming dynasty.

Examples of Tang dynasty dyed patterned silk are found in the Shōsōin Repository in Nara, Japan. Two techniques are used. In one the silk is stretched between two boards perforated with the design. The other technique uses a wax-resist method similar to batik, or tie and dye.

Carpets

There are specimens of Tang dynasty felt rugs or mats in the Shōsōin Repository in Japan, which are made from pressed or beaten silk and wool. Felt rugs, used on the *kang*, or brick bed, in later dynasties were made of camel hair or sheep's wool and came from north China, Mongolia and Tibet. There were probably no wool carpet looms until the 18th century.   *P.H-S.*

Furniture

Carpentry

The finest Chinese furniture is remarkable for the ingenuity of its carpentry, which avoids the need for glue or metal nails, and permits disassembling and reassembling. Joints consist of variations of the mitre and mortise-and-tenon joints. Floating tongue-and-groove panels allow for the effects of climatic changes. Additional dovetailing and other interlocking devices secure the transverse braces and spandrels. Sometimes dowels were needed, and were often used in repair work. Doors could be made to swing on mortise-and-tenon pivots, but 19th-century doors tended to have fixed metal hinges. The central stile of a cupboard was usually removable, for easier access, and was often the essential part of the slide-lock mechanism.

Ming dynasty altar table .

Carved lacquer throne of the Qianlong Emperor (1736–96).

Carving

The round, curved members, like the arms and legs of chairs, were always carved and not turned on a lathe or steam-moulded. Apart from relatively simply carved 'aprons' and panels, carved decoration was often used for back splats and aprons. Surface and open-work carving of 19th-century pieces is highly elaborate, often to the detriment of the overall design. The carved red lacquer throne of Qianlong (1736–95) is a supreme example of a type reserved for palaces, temples and restaurants. In the late 17th and 18th centuries incised and painted lacquer furniture was exported to Europe in large quantities.

Wood

Hard, dark, finely grained, aromatic rosewoods were used for the best Chinese furniture. They are usually known by their Chinese trade names, such as the famous *zitan* and *huanghuali*, as they cannot all be botanically identified. The wood seems to have come from south China or to have been imported from India and Southeast Asia. A light-coloured satinwood, known as *jichimu*, was also prized, while cheaper furniture was made of pine, walnut, elm and fruit woods. Bamboo, boxwood and camphor all had specialized uses for light furniture, inlay and storage chests respectively.

Caning

Cane seats were made at least as early as the Wei, Jin and Northern and Southern dynasties period. Interwoven cords were threaded through holes in the wooden frame of the seat. Coarse webbing made from the bark of palm wood was overlaid with a fine cane matting, the ends of which were passed through the same holes as the webbing and tied on the underside. Supporting slats would be tenoned into the frame. Caned seats were sometimes replaced with wooden panels. The opposite conversion also occurred, often in the same piece.

Metal fittings

The corner pieces, handles, hinges and escutcheons of Ming and Qing furniture were usually of brass, varying in colour from yellow to the pale 'white brass' usually known as Paktong (*baitong*). The fittings were inlaid flush with the surface, or surface-mounted. A mount was secured by brass pins or straps driven through a hole in the mount with a brass wedge, which was then burnished flat. Straps attaching handles and parts of the slide-lock mechanism were driven through the wood, bent back and countersunk. Lacquer furniture often had chased and *cloisonné* mounts.   *P.H-S.*

Gold and silver

Casting

The techniques of bronze-casting, highly developed by the Shang dynasty, inevitably influenced casting in the rarer metals. Seams indicate the use of ceramic piece-moulds rather than the *cire perdue*, or 'lost wax' method. The scarcity of gold and silver in China made casting an extravagant and consequently a relatively rare technique compared with the working of sheet metal which would be much thinner. In the Tang dynasty a cheaper alloy of silver and tin was cast and covered with a coating of better quality silver. Bronze Age cast decoration was enhanced by a granular effect, produced by relief beading. Granulation was later developed in other techniques.

Sheet metal

Gold and silver beaten to sheets or foil of varying thicknesses could be used for inlay, as a covering for another material, or alone with surface or relief decoration. In the Tang dynasty the interior and exterior of a bowl or vessel were often of separate sheets soldered together, giving the impression of solid silver. Thin sheets could easily be decorated with openwork or with embossed designs chased from the reverse.

Silver stem-cup decorated with a hunting scene. Tang dynasty, 8th century AD.

Chasing and ring-matting

This combination of techniques for surface decoration was widely and most successfully used in the Tang dynasty, when gold- and silver-working reached their peak with the influence of Persian immigrant silversmiths. The floral scroll or other designs were chased on the metal and, if the metal was silver, sometimes gilded. The background was filled in with regular rows of tiny chased circles, 0.3 to 0.8mm in diameter, thus producing a so-called 'ring-matting' effect. Deeper impressions of the ring-matting tool gave a bead-like granular surface.

Granular work and filigree

Apart from granular effects achieved by casting and ring-matting, delicate granulation work was practised from early times by stringing minute beads on a gold wire, which was soldered to the piece, or by filling sunken lines or areas with the beads. Filigree jewellery of gold and silver wire, twisted, plaited, encrusted with jewels, metal foil or kingfisher feathers continued to develop after the Tang dynasty, while the general standards of the working of rare metals steadily declined.

Gilding

In the Han dynasty parcel gilding was used to decorate bronzes. This technique involved mixing gold or silver with mercury to form an amalgam or paste, which was painted on. The mercury was evaporated by heating, leaving the gold or silver on the surface. Gilding or silvering could also be achieved with a covering of thin foil. But with the large-scale production of small gilt bronze Buddhist figurines in the Wei, Jin and Northern and Southern Dynasties period fire-gilding became the usual practice.   *P.H-S.*

ARCHITECTURE

Archaeological evidence

The traditional Chinese building was timber-framed with wattle-and-daub walls and a heavy roof with overhanging eaves. The building was situated inside an enclosure and subordinate to its general layout. Some of the construction members changed, mainly in decorative emphasis, within the unitary technical tradition. Only a few old buildings are left, so the gradual development of Chinese building construction must be studied through archaeology, clay models of houses from tombs, murals and sculptural reliefs in combination with buildings.

Two characteristics are already evident in the earliest Neolithic sites, such as Banpo outside Xi'an. The village was surrounded by a moat; the houses, square or round, were 5m long on a central axis, had beaten earth floors and wattle-and-daub walls. The roof was carried by four wooden columns placed inside the house and the rafters were covered with a layer of clay mixed with straw. Short posts supported the eaves. The entrances to the houses were on their southern side. In a late stage in Banpo a long house, 20 x 12.5m, was built in the centre of the village.

Urban centres occurred during China's Bronze Age, the Shang dynasty. The different Shang capitals were located on level plains near waterways. Society had become stratified. The capitals had a walled nucleus divided into different sectors for the aristocracy, ceremonial buildings and different groups of craftsmen. These cities were orientated by the cardinal directions determined by the Polar Star and had emphasis on a south–north axis. The city wall was made of beaten earth and surrounded by a moat. Outside lived the peasantry, who provided the citizens with food.

Many Zhou cities have been excavated recently. All have some of the characteristics of Shang cities and, in fact, of later Chinese

cities up to modern times: a surrounding wall with a moat, subdivision into sectors for different workshops and trades, a grid of streets going south–north and east–west and an enclosure for a royal family or for the nobility. The royal enclosure can be located in the actual centre or north centre of the outer wall. Many Zhou cities consist of adjacent walled enclosures.   *E.G.*

Available materials

During the Western Zhou terracotta tiles came into use for covering roofs and during the Warring States period brick was fabricated. Although brick was available at an early date, it never became the primary building material. The timber-framed house

Above right: reed-thatch roofs and brick walls, near Kunming, 1944. Right: tiled roofs near Xi'an.

with wattle-and-daub walls and partitions had come to stay. Residential buildings were not intended to have permanence, but to be rebuilt. This and the evanescence of timber are reasons why so few old buildings are left and only a number of these have been preserved in their original state.

Brick and stone slabs were used for tombs, ceremonial buildings and sometimes bridges. Many details in these tombs are copies of carpentry carved in brick or stone. The technique of vault construction, common in tombs, is known from the Warring States period. A shortage of timber may be the reason why the fabrication of brick increased during Ming times, but it was mainly used to cover and protect city walls and fortifications made of beaten earth. Several wattle-and-daub walls were replaced by brick but these never had any load-carrying function.   *E.G., N.S.S.*

Structural methods

A traditional Chinese building rested on a platform of beaten earth, brick or stone slabs, according to its importance. The timber columns raised on the platform rested on stone bases. The heads of the columns were tied together by beams in both transverse and longitudinal directions. Additions of verandas made the floor plan more flexible. The roof construction was different from the rigid truss normally used in the West. In a Chinese roof a series of beams of diminishing length were placed one above the other, each resting on short posts raised on the beam below. The purlins were placed at the ends of these beams and the rafters went from purlin to purlin. This construction made it natural to curve the roof, but whether this was done for aesthetic or practical purposes is not

Detail of bracket sets supporting far projecting eaves of 'Frost Drifting Hall' in Xi'an, Shaanxi Province.

known. The roof was covered by semicircular tiles in two interlocking layers. This was usually the most impressive part of a building. Because a house usually had one storey and the overhanging eaves cast a shadow on the wall, the roof seemed to float in the air.

Traditionally, different roof shapes were used according to the importance of a building. Most important buildings had hipped roofs, next came hip-and-gable roofs, while unimportant buildings had simple gabled roofs. The most important buildings faced the south, and the outer walls to the north, east and west usually had no openings. The southern side was open, with doors, latticed windows covered with translucent paper and carved wooden panels. Partition walls were made of light material, easily built up or removed.

The overhanging eaves protected the light walls, let the winter sun in and kept the summer sun out. The eaves were carried by a series of bracket sets, situated on top of the columns or on the

Construction of bracket sets, Song dynasty.

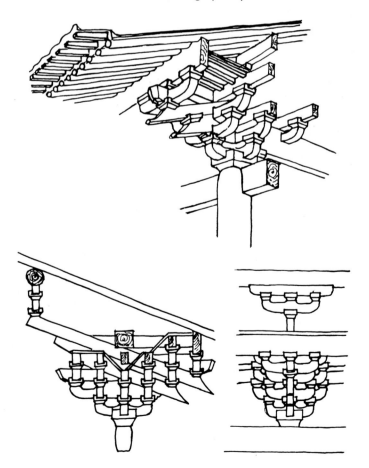

lintel. They consisted of bearing blocks which carried the bracket arms. The arms were intersected into the blocks and into each other at right angles. Series of arms and blocks placed one above the other at increasing widths transferred the weight of the roof to the columns. The most ingenious member of a bracket set was the lever, a pole placed obliquely over the column or lintel, the lower end of which carried the eave, the upper end abutting a purlin. All construction members were dovetailed into each other; nails were only used to fasten the rafters to the purlins. The members were meant to be visible from without and within and therefore were most important as decorative elements. There was a striking harmony between plan, section and elevation. The construction members were painted for their own protection as well as for decorative and symbolic reasons. The platform was white, the columns and walls red, beams and brackets were blue and green and the roof tiles yellow or green.

The use of bracket sets inside a building made a very flexible floor plan possible. When a building enshrined a big Buddha figure, bracket sets on top of the inside columns allowed wider spans and more space. However, this was exploited only before Ming times; after that columns were placed in a rigid grid. The complicated bracket construction is fully developed in one of the earliest remaining Chinese buildings, the main hall of Foguangsi in Wutaishan. It was built in AD 857 and has very deep eaves. All the possibilities of the bracket set were exploited in Song times. Surviving 11th-century buildings with Song characteristics are Holy Mother Hall at the Jin Shrines in Taiyuan, several halls at Longxing Monastery in Hebei Province, and the timber pagoda at Fogong Monastery south of Datong. From Ming times the lever lost its function and became merely a decorative member. The number of bracket sets in each bay increased for decorative purposes. Between the 8th and 14th centuries there would be one or two sets in each bay, but in Qing, 8 to 10. In Tang the height of the bracket set was half the height of the column, but this proportion decreased in Qing, when it was 1:10.

The cross section of the bracket arm continued to be the standard unit for measurements of the whole building. Each construction member was a multiple or division of this. Timber was cut in 8 to 11 different sizes and dried to be ready for use. When a carpenter was told how many bays long a building should be, he knew which size was demanded, and that was all the instruction needed. This modular standardization of 'prefabrication' was used in the earliest existing buildings from Tang times, so it must have been in use much earlier. *E.G., N.S.S.*

Traditional principles of layout and planning

The orientation of an enclosure, dwelling, temple, village or city, according to the cardinal directions with the main buildings placed on a south–north axis, south being the direction of superiority, goes back to the earliest days in Chinese history. In Chinese architecture space is as important as an individual building in the interaction between a courtyard and the buildings lining it, and between outside and inside.

A contemporary architect's example of how buildings can be integrated into the landscape.

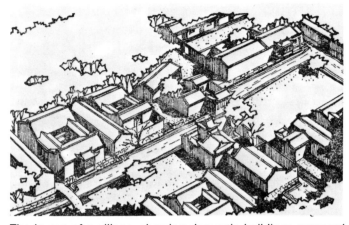

The layout of a village, showing domestic buildings arranged around their courtyards.

The Imperial Palace

The Imperial Palace, also known as the Forbidden City, in Beijing has all these features. Surrounded by a wall, it was originally situated inside the walled enclosure of the Imperial City. This was in its turn inside the city of Beijing, itself surrounded by the city walls of the so-called Inner City. The Outer City to the south was a self-grown suburb to each side of the south–north axis and was later enclosed by a wall. Tiananmen gate of the Imperial City and the wall around the Imperial Palace remain today.

The progression to the imperial audience hall leads through long, narrow and dark tunnels alternating with bright, open court-yards as a dramatic device to heighten the suspense of the visitor. The procession road from Tiananmen goes over a stream crossed by five marble bridges through one of the five openings in the thick wall. They lead into a bright, square courtyard and through an opening in a second wall into a second courtyard, at the end of which is the gate leading to the Imperial Palace. The passage under this is dark and followed by a front courtyard intersected by a stream that is crossed by marble bridges. At the northern end is a front building which finally leads into the courtyard of the imperial audience hall, the Taihedian. This is the most elaborate court-yard, with low side buildings emphasizing the magnificence of the hall. This is situated in a triple marble balustrade with two flights of marble steps and a central carved marble ramp over which the emperor's chair was carried.

The audience hall and two ceremonial halls behind it combine to form what is known as a *gong* plan, named for the Chinese character *gong* 工. This configuration is reserved for highest ranking Chinese building complexes. In the overall scheme the audience hall and the two ceremonial halls behind it constitute the climax. Behind the ceremonial halls are the living quarters of the imperial

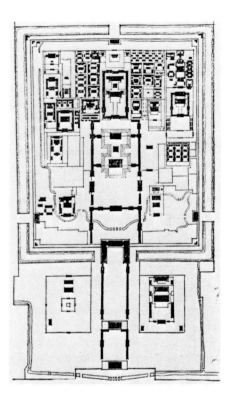

Plan of the Imperial Palace in Beijing, showing the formal layout of halls and courtyards with living quarters beyond.

family, ending with the northern gate of the Imperial Palace. Further north comes Coal Hill, then the Drum Tower and finally the Bell Tower. Here the axis ends, as there was no gate on it in the northern city wall.

The strict ceremonial layout of the palace is counterbalanced by the parks alongside three artificial lakes inside the former Imperial City. Their whole arrangement is deliberately irregular. Winding paths up and down artificial hills give new views of water, stones, vegetation and pavilions at each turn.   *E.G., N.S.S.*

Traditional building types

Domestic and agricultural

Most Chinese dwellings, rich or poor, in cities or in the country-side, were arranged according to the same pattern as the Imperial Palace, the number of courtyards decreasing according to the rank and wealth of the family. A high official lived in a big compound together with his whole family and servants. A main hall, the home of the head of the family, was situated to the north of a central south–north axis and facing south. The side buildings in the main courtyard were the homes of younger brothers and their families; cousins might occupy courtyards further south. The servants' quarters were along the southern wall near the entrance to the first courtyard. Inside the entrance was a screen for privacy. If the family was sufficiently wealthy, the enclosure would have a garden based on the same principles as the imperial parks and lakes in Beijing.

A craftsman lived in a single courtyard with one building to the north. Side buildings were for married children and for use as a workshop. Farmers in a village lived in the same way. In loess areas

The *kang* is the traditional means of heating in a Chinese house. The heated platform serves as a place to sit and sleep.

some people still live in barrel-vaulted caves carved into the loess. These are comfortably warm in winter and cool in summer.

Often, simple dwellings had no kitchen; food was cooked in the courtyard. Most houses are still heated by a *kang*, a raised platform of bricks with channels underneath. A *kang* is heated by a fire in a hearth, an opening in the outside wall of the house. Heat passes through the channels and smoke is let out through another exterior opening. The *kang* serves as a bed for the whole family and functions as the sitting place during the day.

Religious and ritual

Chinese civilization has always been secular. Temples were built with the same layout and the same constructions by the same craftsmen as all other buildings. There is no exterior architectural distinction between a Buddhist temple, *si*, a Daoist temple, *guan*, or a Confucian temple, *miao*. The Confucian temple often served as a local school and was called a *wenmiao*. Often a Buddhist temple was turned into a *wenmiao*.

Buddhism came to China from India during the first centuries AD, and brought a new building type, the pagoda. In India, where it originated, the pagoda was brick and was used to enshrine a sacred object. In China it served more often as a point of view in the landscape. The oldest surviving Chinese building is the brick pagoda at Songyuesi in Henan, built in AD 523. The timber pagoda at Fogong Monastery outside Datong is the most important monument in Chinese wooden architecture. It was built in 1056 in traditional timber construction.

Another Buddhist innovation was the cave temple. The caves housed Buddhist sculptures and their walls were richly decorated

A courtyard and garden in Shanghai. Traditionally, all Chinese dwellings were based on an arrangement of buildings around courtyards.

with reliefs and frescos. In Gansu on the pilgrimage road to India are the Dunhuang caves, hewn out between AD 366 and the 10th century. At that time there were more than 1000 caves; today about 475 have been preserved. The Yungang caves at Datong date from the 5th century and the Longmen caves at Luoyang from after 495.

Ritual buildings were used for imperial ceremonies for communication between Heaven and man, symbolized by the emperor. The *Book of Rites* from late Zhou stresses the importance of the *mingtang*, a special ceremonial building where the emperor performed ceremonies on behalf of the state. According to the texts, the building should be 'round above and square below', symbolizing the relation of Heaven and Earth, and consist of nine rooms, three to each side. The emperor should change his position in a circular movement around the centre to complete a rotation in the course of a year. No complete example of this enigmatic building exists today. Archaeological excavations at Xi'an have brought to light the foundation of a Han *mingtang*, but no evidence about the upper part of the building.

The Ming and Qing emperors offered their prayers to Heaven on the day of winter solstice at the Altar of Heaven in the Outer City of Beijing. The circular altar is a triple platform of marble. The enclosing wall is square. There is no building on the altar, no roof between Heaven and man. On the axis to the north are two circular buildings. The first is small and enclosed by a circular wall. It contained the ancestor tablets of the imperial house. The northern building is the Temple of Heaven, raised on a circular triple marble platform and situated in a square courtyard. The circular dome of the temple has an opening for an uninterrupted communication between Heaven and man.

Throughout Chinese history imperial tombs were subterranean and covered by a mound of earth. A procession way leading to the mound was flanked by stone statues of animals and officials. The Ming emperors erected surface buildings as an addition to the mound. These buildings, of enormous size, were used for sacrificial ceremonies. They are placed inside a courtyard with a gate and a front building in the traditional design. The northern wall of the courtyard is topped with a tower building, and immediately to the north of that is the circular mound. Along the axis of the excavated grave of the Wanli Emperor (reigned 1573–1619) is an entrance room, an antechamber, a sacrificial chamber and finally the burial room. To each side of the axis is a room for the coffin of each of the two empresses.

Bridges

From very early times waterways, natural or artificial, have been as important as or more important than roads for transportation in China. This created an early demand for bridges, and throughout

The Anji ('safe passage') bridge at Zhouxian, Hebei Province. Built during the Sui dynasty, it takes the form of a single flattened arch with spandrel arches at each end.

the country there remain bridges of all possible constructions, materials and ages. There are timber beam and cantilever constructions, suspension bridges and masonry bridges with stone arches in many forms. The simplest bridge consists of solid stone walls at right angles to the span, the sides are made of brick and the span of timber covered by beaten earth.

Most remarkable is the Anji Bridge at Zhaoxian, southwest of Beijing in Hebei Province. It is an open spandrel bridge built of stone slabs between AD 605 and 616. The bridge is 10m wide, the span is over 40m and the height of the curve is 8m. This low arch construction at such an early date is unique in world architecture. At each end are two segmental arches, which reduce the weight of the spandrel masonry and allow an overflow of water to pass through. The 1260 arch stones, cut to fit precisely, weigh more than one tonne each, but the two segmental arches at each end give an impression of weightlessness.

Fortification

China's most famous fortification is the Great Wall, which ran along the northern frontier of Zhou and Han China. The Zhou rulers built a series of walls along a line dividing farm land from steppe. The purpose of the wall was to keep the nomads out and the farmers in. Successive rulers connected most of the walls into one and maintained it. It was built of beaten earth but the Ming rulers had it faced with brick and stone. Approximately 4000km long and following the undulating form of the mountains, its average height is 8m, and its width is 7m at the base and 6m at the top. On the top are watchtowers 40m apart and fortresses at strategic points.

Cities were also fortified. The Chinese use the same term for a city as for a wall, *cheng*. City walls had the same functions as the Great Wall: to defend the population and to control it. Connected to the exterior of each city gate was a U-shaped enclosure with a barbican gate building, making unwanted passage in or out extremely difficult. Where the moats flowing through a city passed under a city wall there was a water gate locked by an iron grid. Nobody could sneak in or out that way.

20th-century construction in China

At the end of the last century the foreign concessions in Chinese ports were built up with Western buildings, factories, banks, hotels, consulates and dwelling quarters. During the early decades of this century young Chinese studied architecture at Western universities. Until then building had been regarded as anonymous craftsmanship; now it became one of the fine arts. Upon their return most of the Chinese architects worked for the *Guomindang* government in Nanjing, where they tried unsuccessfully to combine Western building techniques and materials with traditional Chinese architecture. Instead of transferring the flexibility of traditional Chinese building to new materials, the architects of the renaissance movement copied details such as bracket sets in concrete without giving them any structural function. Low, steel-framed roofs on high buildings were curved and covered with costly glazed tiles.

After 1949 the need for technical development and housing created great building activity. China was short of engineers and architects, so a number of Soviet specialists came to assist. The new monumental buildings from the 1950s show features of Soviet architecture as well as of the Chinese renaissance movement. The latter was severely criticized because it valued costly aesthetic decoration higher than practical function.

In the same period many dwelling quarters were built in the cities. Most were three-storeyed and built around green, tree-lined courtyards. Monumental buildings as well as dwellings show the uninterrupted high level of Chinese craftsmanship.

The withdrawal of the Soviet specialists in the early 1960s left the Chinese with a number of unfinished projects and no blueprints, slowing building activities considerably. The best Chinese architecture from the late 1960s and early 1970s are the many villages, rebuilt by the local population of local materials but with improved solidity and facilities.

During the 1970s and 1980s a number of skyscrapers were erected in Chinese cities for apartment buildings and hotels. The opening of China for tourism resulted in a flood of new construction. Some of the buildings exhibit a genuine appreciation for the interaction between structure and surroundings. *E.G., N.S.S.*

Garden architecture

The garden in China is a place to 'nourish the heart'. While the characteristic Chinese house with its progression of rectangular courtyards may be seen as a symbol of the Confucian desire to regulate human relationships, the Chinese garden—with its delicate balance between natural and man-made elements—mirrors the ancient Daoist principle of harmony with nature.

The ideal Chinese garden was recorded in a scroll painting of his country villa by the Tang poet Wang Wei (AD 699–761). A model of cultivated simplicity, it shows study pavilions set among

Below: Qichangyuan, the 17th-century garden at Wuxi, Jiangsu Province, said to be the inspiration for the 'garden of gardens' in the summer palace at Beijing. Bottom: the lake at Chengde, north of the Great Wall, the summer retreat created by the Qing emperors in the 18th century.

Pavilion on the famous West Lake at Hangzhou. The views here and at Suzhou gave rise to the saying: 'Above is Heaven, below is Suzhou and Hangzhou'.

Plum-blossom doorway in the Shizilin (the 'Stone Lion Grove'), one of the famous gardens of Suzhou.

rolling hills and apparently untouched valleys. The Chinese garden aims to be a three dimensional walk through such a landscape scroll, with calligraphic inscriptions and poems engraved on stone.

Broadly speaking, there are two main types of Chinese garden. One is the vast imperial park, its boundaries enclosing hills, lakes and islands liberally ornamented with loggias, arched bridges and little palace compounds. Today the Qianlong Emperor's retreat at Chengde (Jehol) beyond the Great Wall, the ruins of his Yuanmingyuan and the rebuilt summer palace near Beijing remain as echoes of these stupendous parks. Their origins go back to the hunting reserves of China's earliest kings. In the first century BC Emperor Qin Shihuang collected rare plants and beasts in these enclosures and those of the next dynasty became symbols of all the riches available in the empire. Imperial gardens are both an expression of conspicuous power and a microcosm of all the variety and beauty of the natural world.

The second kind of Chinese garden is the city retreat of the scholar-official. Like that of the country villa it sought to reproduce, it may be quite separate from the owner's house. And, like the imperial park, it aims not so much to imitate nature in miniature as to make possible, in a small space, all the emotions one might experience in the wild.

The most famous of these gardens are in Suzhou, where high white walls divide the peaceful heart from the busy world outside. Simple courtyards and passageways lead to central lotus lakes which wind out of sight behind billowing rockeries of rough stones piled up together to form peaks and caverns. These are 'miniature mountains', symbolic of the bony structure of the earth, and reminiscent of the magical homes of the Daoist Immortals. In Chinese terms the hard *yang* element of the rocks is balanced by the soft, reflective *yin* of the water, and the rest of the garden is also based on paired opposites: high leads to low, shade to sunlight, enclosed

to open spaces—all of them wound around by white-painted walls which undulate through the garden like regular waves. Shaped holes cut into these walls allow glimpses of what is to come: shadows on white walls; a pavement laid out in pebbles like a carpet; a huge standing stone, its flanks waterworn into strange hollows. Open-sided galleries also zigzag through the complex courtyard mazes of garden, leading to halls for entertaining, quiet study rooms and libraries and swoop-eaved pavilions set on stilts above water. Among them are placed pots of flowers, scented shrubs, and the 'three friends of winter'—pine, plum and bamboo.

Gardens in China were the settings for poetry competitions, for appreciating flowers, for contemplation, but also for enjoying children's pranks, festivals and parties and a little amorous dalliance. They were not solemn places, although in their joyous delight in nature, in their cultivated use of leisure, and in their intense appreciation of the passing moment, China's garden-makers reveal a deep understanding of philosophical truths. *M.K.*

SCIENCE AND TECHNOLOGY: HISTORICAL PERSPECTIVE

The Jinquan satellite-launching centre in west China.

AGRICULTURE AND BIOLOGICAL SCIENCES

Agriculture

Chinese agriculture depended in the main on the fertile areas close to the two main rivers, the Yellow River in the north and the Yangtze further south. The upper and northwestern areas, cradle of the Chinese civilization, consisted of fertile loess soil, dust blown ages ago from the Gobi desert. The lower northern area is largely silt carried down through geological ages by the Yellow River, and the resulting alluvial soil is very fertile. Given a good manuring, it supports intensive cultivation of crops which do not require artificial irrigation—wheat, millet and a wide variety of other plants such as barley, beans and hemp. In the south and west, centred on the Yangtze valley, climatic conditions are quite different. Constant irrigation is required, and the staple crop is rice, although there is subsidiary cultivation of mulberry trees and of cotton. In winter months, when the paddy-fields were dry, they were used for a second crop such as wheat, beans, rape-seed or barley.

Intensive cultivation

The Chinese practised a cereal agriculture, not a mixed pastoral and arable agriculture as found in Europe, and there was generally a constant struggle to raise enough food for a growing population. From at least the time of the Han dynasty the cultivation was of an intensity unknown in the West. It has been said that this cultivation was gardening rather than farming, and certainly the methods used, such as planting in rows, eased weeding and allowed plants to be given individual attention. Moreover, during the Han the seed-drill plough was invented and employed to drill a number of rows at a time. Seed-drilling had been known to the peoples of Mesopotamia in the 3rd millennium BC and it is possible that the Chinese learned of it from the Middle East. Its existence was not, however, known in Europe until the 16th century AD, and a practical drill did not appear until the 17th; even so it was not adopted widely for the next 200 years.

In south China intensive cultivation also led in the first or 2nd century AD to the practice of first sowing rice in seed-beds and then transplanting to the fields later. This was another way of increasing production, so that the yield per hectare in China was almost always in excess of what was achieved in the West.

Another example of intensive land use was to be found in the rice fields where the irrigation pools were also used for growing water-chestnuts and raising duck, while beans and cucumbers would be grown too. Mulberry trees were also cultivated on the banks of the irrigation channels; they were used for breeding silkworms and acted also as a shade for the water-buffalo, which tramped the area and so firmed up the channel bank.

Crop rotation

Chinese agriculturalists were well aware of the value of crop rotation and recycling. The first specific references to crop rotation are from the 6th century AD, but it seems that the practice may have been earlier than this. The Chinese also used fertilizers: mud dredged up from the canals of the Yangtze was used, while in both north and south it has been throughout the ages the practice to spread animal and human manure. This tied in with crop rotation, for early on the Chinese were aware that legumes enriched the soil but wheat weakened it. The use of 'green manure' thus started at an early date. In one sense crop rotation was nothing new; the Romans had practised a form of rotation by alternating a year of growing a particular crop with a year when the ground lay fallow. In most parts of China, however, fallowing was not carried out from Han time onwards, except as a last resort.

Terracing and land reclamation

Another practice was terracing. This was much in evidence during the Song dynasty and arose as a development of land reclamation which had begun in the 9th century AD and carried on well into the 12th and 13th centuries. Terraced mountain areas became a well-established feature. Besides the creation of terraced fields, lakes were drained and converted into poldered fields (i.e. fields

Modern terraced fields in Yunnan Province. Terracing has been practised in China from at least as far back as Song times.

with earth walls to keep out the water, as later to be found in Holland). Floating fields on bamboo rafts covered with water-weed and earth were another method of increasing areas for cultivation.

This all helped shift the economic balance from north to south. Originally taxes were paid in grain, as was natural for the Yellow River economy, and this method of payment continued when migration from the very fast growing population moved the economic centre to the Yangtze valley area. Here intensive farming developed, especially from the 11th century onwards when two crops were grown each year and land reclamation increased the area available for cultivation.

Agricultural implements

The Chinese developed many characteristic agricultural implements before the 9th century in the Tang dynasty, but from that time on things changed very little. The mould-board plough, which inverted the soil, was one such implement; it was superior to the scratch-plough then used in the West. There was a range of harrows, rollers, horse-hoes (hoes fixed to a framework and pulled between rows of crops) and the seed-drill plough. Since Chinese farmers were by and large smallholders, these implements were adequate and there was no call for further development. But in the Song dynasty (13th century) the rotary winnowing-fan was brought into general use, though not known in Europe till five centuries later. In the West farmers cultivated much larger areas and needed agricultural machinery on a larger scale. This was not easy to achieve with early technology and is, for instance, the reason why the West had to wait so long for an effective seed-drill plough. In China the methods adopted allowed full use to be made early on of comparatively simple aids.

Introduction of crops from abroad

From time to time crops were introduced into China from outside. In late Neolithic times wheat and barley came from western Asia, as many references to them in the Shang oracle-bones bear witness. Then, in the 6th to 8th centuries AD, cotton arrived from India, although the general production of cotton had to wait until the Mongol dynasty in the 12th and 13th centuries. Special strains of rice from the ancient Indochinese kingdom of Champa were introduced in the 11th century AD by the Chinese government in a campaign to introduce double cropping. Champa rice ripened quickly and by the 16th century Chinese farmers had developed a strain which would ripen in 50 to 60 days. Imported crops from America were beginning to be adopted in the 16th century: they comprised the sweet potato, maize, peanuts and tobacco. During the 17th century the Irish potato arrived in China.

The impact of these newly introduced crops on Chinese agriculture varied. Wheat and barley became important in the later Shang as winter crops, and while they were still a luxury in the Han, by the Song they were regularly accepted as alternating winter and summer crops. The chief effect of the American crops, except tobacco, was that they would all grow on poor soil unsuitable for the traditional Chinese crops. They were therefore cultivated on sandy river banks and on hilltops where, however, they led to some soil erosion.

J.N., C.A.R.

Botany

In its earliest phases botany was a purely descriptive science. Not until the 17th century did modern scientific botany begin, with the recognition of sex in plants, the development of plant physiology, morphology (the study of form and structure) and the foundation of taxonomy (classification based on scientifically related characteristics). Nevertheless the Chinese, like the Greeks, made headway in studying and describing plants two millennia and more before the advent of modern botany. But whereas in the West little was done after Greek times until the Renaissance, the Chinese had no such 'Dark Age', and continually developed their botanical studies from the time of the Warring States and the Qin and Han dynasties without a break down to modern times.

Chinese botany was helped by the fact that the variety of plants in China is incomparably greater than in Europe. In north Eurasian latitudes there is a belt of coniferous forest extending down

Botanical detail is excellent on this 12th-century handscroll, bird with lychee (*Litchi chinensis*), in ink and colours, attributed to the Song Emperor Huizong.

to about the northern frontier of the Manchurian provinces, but everywhere south of a line from Beijing and the Shandong peninsula to the borders of Indo-China and beyond, the land was originally deciduous forests and woodlands. In Shaanxi and Gansu there is grass and scrub-land, and Shaanxi was the cradle of the Qin and Han civilizations. There is desert or semi-desert in the Gobi and in Tibet, separated by the Persian grasslands from the lower-latitude deserts of Mesopotamia, Arabia and North Africa. The only omissions in the Chinese region are tundra and savannah areas.

Another factor helping botanical studies in China and leading to the beginnings of a basic study of geobotany was the central administration, which set great store by the correct use of land, and, in consequence, a proper knowledge of plants, trees and the environment in which different species flourished. This, in its turn, stimulated the study of soils. There was no equivalent of soil science in ancient Greece and its beginnings must be credited to the Chinese, who were writing specifically about the subject in the 4th century BC, although there is evidence indicating interest in the subject as far back as the 7th century. Later, the need to grow increasing amounts of food made it imperative to try the possibility of growing crops in regions outside their normal habitat, and this was explored with some success in Song and Yuan times.

Botanical linguistics

The study of plants calls immediately for descriptive terminology and classificatory nomenclature. Here the ideographic nature of the Chinese language brought certain advantages. Primitive pictographs lent themselves to the representation of stems and trunks, as also different sorts of leaves and fruit, and thus the beginnings of botanical language were available from the start. New characters were invented when necessary, for the Chinese had no 'dead language' to draw on such as was available in the West; there was no equivalent of botanical Latin for them.

By the 3rd century BC the Chinese were using binomes for plants, at least as a technical language, although there were common-or-garden names as well for many plants. Their names helped them to a clearly defined nomenclature for technical purposes and they had categories of plants which turn out to be 'natural families' somewhat similar to those of the West.

Botanical texts

There is a vast literature in Chinese on natural history. All through, there were many encyclopedias and dictionaries which contained botanical terms and they brought great order and stability to the botanical language. The first of all these dictionaries was the *Erya*

(*Literary Expositor*), prepared between the 4th and 2nd centuries BC, but containing material from the 6th. After the Han, these kinds of text branched out and there was a series of imperial 'florilegia', lists of plant names and descriptions prepared for the emperor and senior civil servants.

An even more important class of literature was known as *bencao*. These 'pharmaceutical natural histories' were practical books which assembled together the ever growing knowledge of the natural world of minerals, animals and plants. They began in the 2nd century BC, and while their later equivalents in the West were the lapidaries, bestiaries and herbals, the Chinese books contained less fabulous material and may be referred to collectively as the 'pandects' (i.e. treatises covering wide but specific subjects). These included, of course, the pharmacy of plants, though they also contained details of plants which had no medicinal use; in the 8th century, however, some were prepared listing only medicinal materials. In the same period, the lists began to include foreign plants. Printing, when it came, was widely used from the 10th century onwards, and when wood-block illustrations began to be usual in the 13th century these were accurately drawn so that plants could be recognized from them. This anticipated the work of the German 'fathers of botany' in the 16th century.

Fourteenth-century China saw a remarkable development, the 'esculentist movement', which lasted until the 17th century. As its name implies, this was a line of research with the object of identifying wild plants which could be used in times of famine and this produced masterpieces of applied botany, dealing with what to do in case of famine by listing and describing wild (emergency) food plants, so that it was in the vanguard of those who are today extending the sources of man's food supply.

Of all the writers of botanical texts the greatest was probably Li Shizhen (1518–93). Comparable with the best naturalists in Renaissance Europe, he read widely and in 1583, at the age of 65, completed a vast pharmaceutical natural history. All facts were critically presented and his choice of a preferred name for a plant followed by the other names in use was a forerunner of today's international nomenclature system. He also retained both natural and pharmaceutical classifications of plants.

A great number of monographs and tractates on particular species or genera were also produced in China in medieval times, especially on useful plants like the orange, and ornamental plants like the chrysanthemum, peony and rose. These were cultivated in Chinese gardens and later imported into Europe so that it has been said that most European garden plants are of Chinese origin. English gardens in the 18th century were much influenced by Chinese horticultural ideas, which avoided geometrical regularity and made the garden a more natural place for quiet and contemplation.

J.N., C.A.R.

Zoology

There are many interesting animals indigenous to China, and in ancient times these included the elephant and the rhinoceros, both of which were to be found north of the Yangtze River. But although a change of climate since then has made the country cooler, there is still a wide variety of wild life, including many remarkable animals such as the panda bear, Père David's deer (a rather rare species), the Yangtze dolphin, the gibbon monkey and the giant salamander.

Chinese zoological literature is large and comes from almost all periods of China's history. Zoological descriptions are incorporated in many works from the *Erya* (*Literary Expositor*) of the 4th century BC onwards, as well as in the *bencao* literature—those pharmaceutical natural histories assembling the ever-growing knowledge of the natural world, which began to appear in the 2nd century BC. Zoological monographs appeared from the Tang dynasty onwards, but were not so numerous as those on botany.

Much could be said of the varieties of animals which the Chinese developed by artificial selection. There was the water-buffalo, used for ploughing the rice fields, the Pekinese dog, kept as a pet, and many kinds of goldfish. Horses are another case in point, including the Mongolian pony and those from Ferghana in Central Asia.

A great speciality of the Chinese was the domestication of insects. They bred the silkworm from Shang times (*c.* 1500 BC) onwards, and in Sichuan the scale insect (*Ericerus sinensis*, growing on *Fraxinus*, a kind of ash) was cultivated commercially for its white wax, used medicinally and for candles. The lac, another scale insect, and insects equivalent to the cochineal (i.e. of the *Coccidae* family) were bred for the dyestuffs which could be produced from them. The cricket (family *Gryllidae*) was used for sport, being kept in small cages and then released to fight other crickets, much along the lines of Western cock-fighting. The Chinese kept bees from time immemorial and made use of their honey (largely as a vehicle in pharmacy, hence its presence to this day in apothecaries' shops). But a more remarkable development was the oldest known instance of biological plant protection. The *Nanfang caomu zhuan* (*Records of the Plants and Trees of the South*), written in the 3rd century AD, tells how the farmers who had citrus groves went to market to buy bags of ants, which they hung on the trees to protect them from aphids, mites, spiders, beetles and other pests. The species of ant used has been identified as *Oecophylla smaragdina*, since the practice continues to this day; and indeed at the present time biological plant protection is one of the most ingenious and flourishing aspects of the science in China.

There is so far no work in any Western language on Chinese zoology. Zoology was not recognized as a science in the modern sense but in the ancient and medieval literature there are many valuable accounts of animals and their behaviour. *J.N., C.A.R.*

PHYSICAL SCIENCES

Chemistry

Modern chemistry had its beginnings in the West in the 17th century and reached China in the 18th. Yet indigenous Chinese alchemy and proto-chemistry had made many contributions which found their way westwards over the Old Silk Road and reached Europe through the Arabs. Indeed it is possible that the words 'elixir' and 'chemistry' were derived originally from the Chinese.

In China alchemy was particularly the province of the Daoists who themselves conducted experiments, applying chemical and physical procedures in their quest for material immortality. For the Daoists, avoiding death was a very real aim, and though they never achieved it they made many discoveries by the way. Among other things they found out how to inhibit bodily decay, achieving this by keeping tombs airtight and establishing in them what we would now call anaerobic conditions. An example of this came to light during the excavation in 1972 of a tomb in Hunan Province in which was found the body of a woman, the Lady of Dai, who died in 168 BC. Astonishingly, the corpse was like that of a person who had died no more than a week or two before. Although the body had been dead for more than 2000 years a relatively perfect preservation had been achieved, yet neither embalming, mummification nor tanning had been used.

The Daoist alchemists coupled their advanced practical knowledge with religious ritual and incantation, since as has so often been the case, early science and magic ran side by side. The Chinese belief in the universe as an organism coloured the philosophy behind their researches, and led to correlations between mineral substances and the Five Elements (earth, wood, fire, metal and water), and the planets. The continuous rhythmic fluctuations of the *yin* and *yang* inspired the 'first law of traditional Chinese chemistry and physics', namely that any maximum state of a variable is inherently unstable since the process of going over to its opposite must necessarily begin.

Chemical equipment

For their experimental work ancient Chinese alchemists used a variety of equipment. They developed special ovens, stoves and furnaces, the design of which helped them to control temperatures with some precision. Special reaction-vessels were designed, often so that they could be completely sealed; and because of the pressures involved some were made strongly of metal, and even bound with wire. Although they lacked thermometers, the importance of temperature was fully recognized and much use was made of temperature stabilizers and water-baths. Ancillary apparatus comprised bamboo tubing for connecting one piece of equipment to another, steelyard balances for weighing, and sundials and water-clocks for timing operations.

As early as the Neolithic period (i.e. pre-1500 BC) the Chinese invented a peculiar vessel, the *li*, a cauldron or pot on three short hollow legs. This developed into a double-steaming vessel, the *zeng*, which had an upper compartment separated from the lower by a grating. Later on this was capped with a basin of cooling water so that the distillate dripped off into a cup placed upon the grating. Thus the East Asian type of still, which seems to have arisen independently of the Western Hellenistic design, came into existence. Distillation was practised by the Chinese alchemists certainly as early as the 7th century during the Tang dynasty although it may well go back to the 4th century or earlier.

Chemical knowledge and the discovery of gunpowder

The Chinese alchemists were primarily concerned with trying to find an elixir of immortality, but this brought them important results of quite a different kind. By Tang times they were distilling alcohol, a process that requires a still with a cooling system to condense the distillate so that the alcohol is not lost. Such a device was not available in the West until four or five centuries later. Moreover, literary references frequently speak of 'frozen-out wine'—a process in which all the water freezes first, leaving the alcohol behind. This technique, which may have been known in China by the 2nd century BC, also gives concentrated alcohol.

Chinese alchemists of the 8th century knew much about the salts of alkaline metals and were able to separate them out. In particular they could distinguish saltpetre (potassium nitrate), and this led them to discover gunpowder, that combination of saltpetre, charcoal and sulphur. Sulphur was, of course, well known in China, where it had been mined for centuries, charcoal was ubiquitous, available wherever trees were burned, and the discovery was presumably made while experimenting with various elixir reactions. The first military use of gunpowder occurred in the 10th century, and it became widespread in China during the next 200 years before reaching Islam in the 13th century and then Europe, where it came into general use in the 14th century. It can be shown that every stage in the development of firearms from the first gunpowder formula to the propellant metal-barrel cannon, can be found in China before the first European appearance of the latter in 1327.

The alchemists of China were also expert in the industrial extraction of copper by the 'wet method' in which an exchange of ions occurs; and they could get many very insoluble inorganic substances by the use of weak nitric acid formed from saltpetre by 'frozen-out' vinegar (60 per cent acetic acid). Chinese alchemy led also to a wide range of medical products, often of a mineral kind, such as calomel (mercurous chloride, $HgCl$) and arsenic sulphides, long before these were available in the West.

Theoretically the Chinese realized that reactions could provide totally new entities, not just simple mixtures, and tabulated categories of substances in a way which presaged the affinity theory of later scientific chemistry. They also made considerable use of quantitative methods, developing an insight into combining weights and proportions, a vital aspect of modern chemistry.

J.N., C.A.R.

Earth sciences

Meteorology

The Chinese were deeply interested in the weather and were long in advance of the West in certain methods of meteorological measurement, keeping records of a more complete nature over a longer time. Of course, weather forecasting in traditional China never became a modern science, although by the 2nd century BC it was the practice to weigh a hygroscopic material like elm charcoal to give a measure of atmospheric moisture and so obtain a guide to predicting rain. Thunderstorms and lightning were, of course, recorded. They were looked upon as a clash of *yin* and *yang*.

Records were kept of temperature, precipitation and wind, in the two latter at least as far back as 1216 BC. Rain and snow gauges were in common use and there seems to have been some attempt to measure wind-speed; indeed, during the Han dynasty, an anemometer with 'paddle wheel' arms was devised to do this—the precursor of modern instruments for wind-speed measurement. The circulation from land and sea to air and back by precipitation was expressly understood by the first century AD, although recognition of this water-cycle in Greece goes back to the 6th century BC. In China records were also kept of rainbows and parhelic phenomena ('mock suns'). The latter were described a thousand years earlier than in Europe.

Until modern times there was more interest in the tides in China too. Possibly this was stimulated by the impressive tidal bore of the Qiantang River. The Chinese recognized the coincidence of tides and phases of the Moon by the 2nd century BC, and three centuries later a causal connection between the two was formulated. Later on, in the 11th century, the delay in times between theoretical high tide and its actual occurrence, known now as 'the establishment of the port' and due to local effects of shore-line and other factors, was also recognized.

Geology and mineralogy

Geology is a post-Renaissance study and as a science it did not begin until the 17th century when folded strata, faulting, volcanic intrusions, etc. began to be described. Yet Chinese paintings and book illustrations show an early appreciation of geological features, and animal fossils were appreciated at their true value, whereas in Europe the accepted ideas of creation prevented such an understanding. China also contributed to the beginnings of palaeobotany with the recognition of the petrification of pine-trees perhaps as far back as the 3rd century AD and certainly by the 8th. In general, although Chinese appreciation of geological change was equalled by some Greek philosophers, after Hellenistic times Chinese understanding went ahead of that of the West until after the Renaissance.

Mineralogy goes back well before geology, because catalogues of different kinds of stones, ores and minerals were already being made in antiquity. The modern science of mineralogy is, however, a Western product of the 18th and 19th centuries.

The earliest Chinese ideas about the formation of minerals within the Earth appear contemporaneous with, and similar to, those in Greece, and it seems possible both were derived from earlier sources in Babylonia and Egypt. The Chinese, however, seem to have discovered quite independently in the first century BC that there were changes occurring underground in both minerals and ores. An independent mineral classification was also built up; based mainly on appearance, it nevertheless distinguished 'stones' from metals because the latter melted on heating. Clear factual descriptions of minerals are to be found in Chinese literature, many being listed in the pharmaceutical natural histories since they were used as drugs, and such descriptions often mention the crystal forms of the minerals, a characteristic that is the basis of modern classification. It is interesting that in China there was no prejudice against mineral drugs such as that which Galen established in the West.

In China minerals were connected with ideas of underground circulation of water, and by the 11th century AD great attention was paid to geological signs indicating the presence of ore beds, and to the types of plants which grew in areas of specific deposits. In this the Chinese were the forerunners of geological and geobotanical prospecting, which did not develop in Europe until the 18th century. Many specific minerals were widely used in China, especially alum, ammonium chloride (sal ammoniac), asbestos, borax, various precious stones and, above all, jade. Jade working early became a highly developed art. Rotary disc-knives were used, and

Illustration of northern Sichuan landscape from the *Tushu jicheng* (Imperial Encyclopedia) of 1726, showing geological features such as the U-shaped glacial valley in the background and dipping strata on the right.

although the first specific reference to them is of the 12th century, they were probably in common use long before that. Surprisingly, the Chinese were not acquainted with diamonds in cut and polished form.

Seismology

China is one of the world's greatest areas of seismic disturbance and it was natural, therefore, that the Chinese should have kept extensive records of earthquakes. Up to AD 1644 there were 908 shocks for which there are precise data, and from the records it emerges that there were 12 peaks of frequency between AD 479 and 1644. In explaining earthquakes Chinese ideas centred on the escape of *qi* (gas) from below the earth, not dissimilar to Greek theories of the escape of vapour.

It was in the recording of earthquakes that the Chinese excelled, and in the first century AD Zhang Heng (AD 78–139) invented the ancestor of all seismoscopes. Although some details of the mechanism of this first earthquake recorder are still uncertain, its general arrangement is known. Outwardly it appeared like a bronze wine-jar with a domed cover. Around it were eight dragon-heads, each holding a bronze ball in its mouth. On the ground round the vessel, which was some 2m in diameter, were placed eight bronze toads with their mouths open. When a distant earthquake occurred, a ball would be released from one of the dragon-heads and fall into the mouth of the appropriate toad. Thus the direction from which the shock came could be recorded. Internally the vessel contained a heavy inverted pendulum—the basis of many modern seismographs—and various levers to release the appropriate ball and set in place another. The instrument would record shocks too small to be felt by observers at the recording station. In Europe the first modern seismoscope was not set up until 1703.

J.N., C.A.R.

Mathematics

Numbers and arithmetic

Early Chinese mathematics showed some interesting facets when compared with developments elsewhere in this field. On the oracle bones of the 14th century BC a simple way of writing numbers is to be found, and as time passed this developed into a form of notation based on the use of counting-rods and counting-boards. By the 3rd century AD this system had stabilized as:

	1	2	3	4	5	6	7	8	9
Units, Hundreds, Ten thousands	I	II	III	IIII	IIIII	T	T	T	T
Tens, Thousands	—	=	≡	≡	≡	⊥	⊥	≟	≟

Thus the number 4716 would appear as ≡ T — T .The Chinese made use of counting boards in which the zero quantity was indicated by a blank space. They could thus do all calculations using only nine signs. The sign 0 for zero seems to have originated in the Chinese/Indian borderlands some time in the first decade of the 7th century AD.

As in the case of other civilizations, the Chinese were fascinated by numbers themselves and by number mysticism. This led in the 5th century BC to a legend about what was essentially a magic square—a collection of numbers arranged within a square which, when added, give the same total whichever way the addition is performed. Magic squares were mentioned most notably in the first

and 2nd centuries AD, although they did not become part of the main current of Chinese mathematical thought until the 13th century.

The Chinese made use of the four fundamental operations of arithmetic—addition, subtraction, multiplication and division. Multiplication was looked on as an abridgement of addition; their method did not resemble that generally used in Europe, but was similar to the modern Western method. There was no tendency to avoid fractions or irrational numbers as was the case in other civilizations. The Han mathematicians were adept at using the lowest common multiple and highest common denominator, factors which were not adopted in Europe until the 15th and 16th centuries. Decimal fractions were also used, and by the third century AD the Chinese had a notation equivalent to 10^{-1} for 0.1, 10^{-2} for 0.01, etc., and very large numbers expressed in the form Western mathematicians write as 10^4, 10^5, etc. were known and used in the 2nd century AD. Decimal measurement also dominated from the earliest times. Moreover, the Chinese found no difficulty in the concept of negative numbers as early as the 2nd century BC, whereas this concept did not arrive in Indian mathematics until the 7th century AD and the 16th in Europe. The Chinese were also adept at extracting square and cube roots, and roots of higher powers.

Calculating devices were used to assist computation, and the most famous is the abacus. This seems to have started in the form of balls threaded on wires carried over a board carved with divisions; such 'ball arithmetic' as it was called was probably in use in the 2nd century AD, and was certainly well known and used by the 6th.

Geometry

No geometry equivalent to the deductive Euclidean system of the Greeks with its axioms, theorems and proofs ever developed in China. Only the Mohists of the 4th century BC, who were contemporary with Euclid, tackled the subject using systematic definitions, but their work had little or no influence on later Chinese mathematics. Nevertheless, the Chinese knew of the relationships between the sides of right-angled triangles and had a proof of the theorem, different from the one derived by Pythagoras. They also worked out the most accurate value in early times for π (the ratio of the diameter to the circumference of the circle). In the 3rd century AD Liu Hui obtained 3.14159 and in the 5th a value of 3.14159 26 was obtained (modern value 3.14159 26536). In Europe it was not until about 1600 that a value approaching this in accuracy was reached.

The Chinese were also the founders of coordinate geometry (in which points, lines and curves are expressed by numbers or coordinates). By the 3rd century AD they had devised the square grid system of coordinates, probably from their map-making, tabulation of data and other activities, and realized that geometrical elements could be represented by numbers. In Europe coordinate geometry did not become fully developed and superior to the Chinese until the 17th century.

Algebra

The whole of Chinese mathematical thinking was essentially algebraic—they thought in terms of general relationships between quantities—in contrast with the Greeks whose outlook was fundamentally geometric, concerned with relationships between shapes. However, Chinese algebra was written out in words, not in symbols: this brought into play an abundance of abstract single syllable technical ideograms for indicating generalized quantities (rather than specific numbers) and for mathematical operations (multiplication, division and the like). The counting board was laid out so that certain positions were occupied by specific kinds of quantities (unknowns, powers, etc.).

The tendency to think in patterns gave rise in the Song dynasty to the use of a matrix or square of compartments filled by the terms of an equation. Several such matrix-boards could be used at the same time and the method was a great achievement. Yet no general theory of equations was evolved and from the time of the Song algebraists no further development was achieved.

To assist in solving equations, the algebraists of the Song needed what we call the Binomial Theorem. This theorem gives the coefficients for a binomial—i.e. a two-term expression, like $(x+1)$ for instance—raised to different powers. This can be demonstrated as follows:

		Power	Coefficients
$(x + 1)$	$= x + 1$	1	$1 + 1$
$(x + 1)^2$	$= x^2 + 2x + 1$	2	$1 + 2 + 1$
$(x + 1)^3$	$= x^3 + 3x^2 + 3x + 1$	3	$1 + 3 + 3 + 1$
$(x + 1)^4$	$= x^4 + 4x^3 + 6x^2 + 4x + 1$	4	$1 + 4 + 6 + 4 + 1$

The array on the right has been known in Europe as 'Pascal's Triangle' since the 17th century, when Blaise Pascal (1623–62) published it. But in China it had been understood and used from the 12th century at least, and it is likely that it originated in China.

The Chinese appear to have received little mathematical stimulation from Mesopotamia or Egypt. On the other hand a number of mathematical ideas seem to have radiated from China southwards and westwards, including the extraction of square and cube roots, expressing fractions in a vertical column, the use of negative numbers, an independent proof of Pythagoras' theorem, the foundations of coordinate geometry, geometrical questions like the areas of circles and volumes of some solid figures, a rule (the Rule of Three) for determining proportions, a rule (the Rule of False Position) for solving equations, and the Pascal Triangle. A symbol

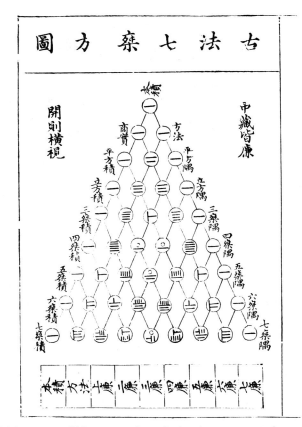

A 14th-century Chinese version of what later came to be called Pascal's Triangle. It tabulates the binomial coefficients up to the sixth power.

for zero came into China from outside, but even so it was from a mutual culture-area with India. Chinese mathematics was therefore quite comparable with pre-Renaissance achievements anywhere else in the Old World.   *J.N., C.A.R.*

Astronomy

Astronomy was of cardinal importance for a primarily agricultural people. The establishment of a dependable calendar by the emperor, and its acceptance by all who owed allegiance to him, brought astronomy and calendrical science into the realm of orthodox government. Astronomers were always government officials.

The belief that the heavens echoed the behaviour of the emperor and his government, so that administrative failures would be shown forth in celestial events, made it imperative that the heavens be carefully and regularly observed, and the evidence of any

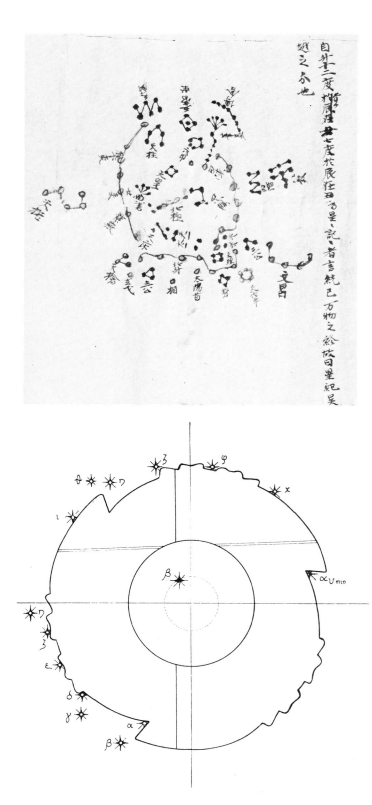

unusual events noted down. Thus it came about that Chinese astronomy has the oldest unbroken series of astronomical observations of any civilization. These go back to about 1300 BC and are still being used in current astronomical research. For instance, the *kexing*, or 'guest star', now known as the 'Crab Nebula' and recognized as having been a supernova explosion, was recorded in 11th century China; the observations are important for modern studies. Again, the earliest known appearances of Halley's comet can only be traced with the help of Chinese records. The Chinese also studied the Sun and recorded systematically the spots on it. Their recordings of eclipses of both Sun and Moon are also valuable.

Concepts of the universe

Three opinions about the nature of the universe were held in ancient and medieval China. The earliest seems to have been the *Gaitian* or Hemispherical Dome concept. This supposed the heavens to be an inverted bowl, with the constellation Ursa Major (The Great Bear) in the middle, while man's kingdom was in the centre of a square dome-shaped Earth lying beneath this. The Earth was surrounded by water—the Great Trench—into which the rains flowed. The view was closely similar to that held in ancient Mesopotamia.

The second view was that of the *Hun Tian* school, which taught that the heavens were a celestial sphere, not a hemisphere. The Greeks had a similar idea which originated about the same time (4th century BC). Its greatest Chinese exponent was Zhang Heng (AD 78–139), who realized that the conception of a spherical Earth arose out of it. He also thought of the heavens as infinite, a view associated especially with Qi Meng (flourished first century AD), possibly a younger contemporary. This, the *Xuan Ye* (Infinite Empty Space) theory, envisaged all celestial bodies floating in space at great distances.

The celestial pole in Chinese astronomy

Ancient and medieval Chinese astronomy was based on a system quite different from that of the West. The West measured celestial positions with respect to the ecliptic (the Sun's apparent path in the sky) and noted particularly the constellations of the Zodiac lying along it. The Chinese centred their attention on the celestial

Above left: section of a star-map of *c*. AD 940, showing the Purple Palace and Great Bear constellations. Left: diagram illustrating the use of the *xuanji*, the circumpolar constellation template. The Plough/Big Dipper is at the lower left-hand side. When the instrument was designed (*c*. 1250 BC) the star β Ursae Minoris was nearest to the pole; at present α Ursae Minoris is the Pole Star.

pole and the celestial equator (a system adopted in Europe in the late 16th century). They therefore concentrated not on the Zodiac but on the circumpolar stars which were always above the horizon; and the Great Bear became a key constellation. The sphere was divided into 365¼ degrees, and their key equatorial constellations were the 28 'lunar mansions' or 'lodges', *xiu*, the boundaries of which were determined from the meridian transits of specific circumpolar stars, often very dim ones. By the 4th century BC Chinese astronomers had drawn up catalogues of stars, and there is a long continuous tradition of Chinese celestial map-making.

Astronomical instruments

As elsewhere, the earliest instrument was the gnomon (a vertical pole in the ground) used for determining the Sun's shadow at midsummer and midwinter. In time this led to the development of sundials, both fixed and portable. In the 13th century the Chinese also adopted the Arabic-Indian practice of building large stone instruments for observing solar shadows and making other measurements; the errors in the making of the scales being proportionally reduced the larger the instrument on which they were carved. Much use was also made in China of water-clocks (*clepsydrae*), water flow being carefully regulated to constancy either by using a series of water tanks or by fitting an overflow (constant-level) tank, or by a combination of both.

For direct observation the Chinese, like the Babylonians, used a long empty tube or sighting tube; by excluding stray light this was useful in observing the circumpolar stars for determining the *xiu*. The most important instrument was the armillary sphere, consisting of a number of rings corresponding to the great circles on the celestial sphere such as the meridian, equator and ecliptic. Fitted with a sighting-tube it could be used for determining all visible celestial positions. Chinese armillary spheres concentrated on the celestial pole and the equator, and the simplest probably appeared about the 4th century BC. By the first century AD some may have been water-driven to depict the changing skies, and by the 8th century the invention of the first of all clock escapements meant that they could be used to compare with the motions of the heavens themselves, so that any discrepancies could readily be detected. The Chinese thus anticipated by some 11 centuries the automatically driven observing instruments of the West. Moreover, the Chinese concern with equatorial coordinates led to the construction of a sort of dissected armillary sphere which greatly facilitated positional observations of all celestial bodies, and anticipated by five centuries or so the introduction of the equatorial mounting of telescopes in the West. This was a notable achievement, because it enabled an observer to follow the apparent path of a celestial body across the sky with only one continuous movement, instead of the two previously necessary. The very real

The 'dissected' armillary sphere or 'Simplified Instrument' designed by Guo Shoujing in 1270. The first of all equatorial mountings, it allowed the curved apparent paths of celestial bodies across the sky to be followed by one motion only, by having one axis of rotation pointing to the celestial pole.

advantage this gave observational astronomers was the reason this mounting was adopted in the West.

It is not generally realized that the coordinates of star positions universally used today are the Chinese equatorial ones and not the ecliptic ones of the Greeks.

Calendar and calendar periods

In all civilizations the problem of making a calendar was the difficulty of trying to reconcile two incompatible periods, the lunar month of 29½ days and the solar year of 365¼ days. In China there was an ancient day count of 60 days (13th century BC), and from the first century BC this was extended to number the year in cycles. In the 11th century months of 30 and 31 days were introduced. The 7-day week was a late introduction from Central Asia; the Chinese week was 10 days.

The motions of the planets were observed, but no geometrical planetary theory was ever formulated, although by the 12th century it was realized that the short periods of backward motion by planets were a purely relative motion. The main Chinese interest in the planets was numerical, and they recognized Jupiter's 12-year orbital period, tying it in with the number of lunations in a year and with cycles of the five elements (earth, water, fire, wood and metal). They were interested, too, in other longer cycles of years when celestial phenomena were repeated.

The discovery of the magnetic compass

This was the most important of all Chinese discoveries in physics. Its origins lay in divination and divining boards, and their associated astronomical symbolism. The most significant of these was the *shi*, a double-decked board constituting a cosmical diagram in the form of a square 'Earth plate' surmounted by a rotatable disc-shaped 'Heaven plate', both marked with signs which included azimuth directions. Symbolic pieces were used on these boards, among them a spoon representing the Plough or Dipper, i.e. the Great Bear.

In either the first or 2nd century BC the spoon was carved from lodestone (magnetite) because of its unique magnetic properties, and so the 'south pointing spoon' was discovered. Between the first and 6th centuries AD it was found that the directive properties of the lodestone could be induced in small pieces of iron which were then floated on water and in the 7th or 8th century replaced by pivoted needles giving more accurate readings. Then by the 8th or 9th century, magnetic declination was discovered, i.e. the fact that the magnetic needle does not precisely indicate astronomical-geographical north–south. It has been said that the Chinese were worrying about the cause of the declination long before the Europeans knew even about the polarity.

The magnetic compass was employed in divination by measuring the layout of sites long before it was used in navigation. The first datable description (between AD 1111 and 1117) of its use in Chinese ships antedates its use in Europe by a century.

J.N., C.A.R.

TECHNOLOGY

Shipbuilding

Construction

From earliest times there was a stimulus to shipbuilding in China not only from its two very large waterways, the Yellow and the Yangtze Rivers, but also from its extensive 5000km coastline. Indeed the Chinese seem always to have enjoyed an abundance of water transport, due partly to the presence of an eminently suitable material in the giant bamboo (*Dendrocalamus giganteus*), which can grow to a height of some 24m. Its satisfactory nature is underlined by the fact that, even today, bamboo river rafts of Sichuan ply the 160km between Yazhou and Jiading, carrying seven tonnes of cargo with a draught of no more than 15cm, and can therefore navigate waters impassable to heavier vessels.

Although an apparently primitive boat-building material, bamboo was not confined to rafts, but was used in masts and sails for all shipping. The very nature of bamboo, with its short sections separated by septa looking like 'rings' on the outside, affected Chinese boat design, as can be seen in the junk, which is traditionally

a development of the raft. The Chinese junk has a flat or slightly curved bottom with no keel, and sides of planking which curve upwards; a shape very like half of a hollow cylinder. Unique are its square-ended bow and stern, without stem-post or stern-post. Unusual, too, is its construction, for instead of the skeletal ribs within a boat, the Chinese junk has solid partitions. These not only give immense strength but also provide the vessel with watertight compartments. They were remarked upon by Marco Polo (AD 1254–1324) but little notice was taken of what he wrote, and this valuable invention only became appreciated in the West in the 18th century.

Another Chinese invention was that of free-flooding compartments. Adopted at least as early as the 5th century AD, these were at bow and stern, perforated with holes purposely contrived in the planking. They were used especially in the salt boats which shot the rapids down from Ziliujing in Sichuan to cushion the shock from the water. Another remarkable vessel devised in China, probably in the 16th century, was the articulated junk. Working on the Grand Canal, it was a long narrow barge of shallow draught built in two separate sections which were detachable. The two halves could readily negotiate shallow winding channels where silting up had occurred, whereas a long vessel would have to await a rising water level.

Late 16th-century articulated barge being used as a minelayer. The loaded forward portion would remain by the target, while the aft part withdrew.

Propulsion

Wind power was the mainstay of the Chinese fresh-water junk and of all their ocean-going vessels, and here once again bamboo played an important part, for it was used to brace the sails. Because it is light for its strength, the Chinese were able to use it not only as the yards and booms of their great lugsails, but also to brace the sail at a number of intervals in between. Such mat-and-batten sails would not tear or blow away, and they were easier to furl, obviating the need to send men aloft in bad weather. But above all, this rig allowed fore-and-aft sailing, into or very near the wind. In the West it was impossible for the large square-rigged ships to do this; they could not tack, instead they had to 'wear about', travelling forward only slowly in a series of sideways loops, which meant much hard and time-consuming work. Chinese fore-and-aft sailing technique was known and practised in the 3rd century AD, but was not introduced to the West until the time of the Portuguese, 1300 years later.

Another form of propulsion invented by the Chinese somewhere towards the end of the 5th century AD, or a little earlier, was the man-powered treadle-operated paddle-wheel. This was developed especially for military use, and it came into its own during the Song dynasty, when ships 60 to 90m long might boast 20 or more paddle-wheels, and could carry 700 or 800 men.

Steering

Paddle-wheel ships were not suitable for long journeys across the seas; for this the sailing-ship had no equal. Yet that had to be guided through the sea, and this brought early shipbuilders face to face with the problem of how to steer. The earliest and most universal method was to use an oar or paddle, held at an angle on the aft quarter of a ship. Operated from the stern, a large steering-oar could be more effective.

But a far more efficient way was to use a rudder at the stern. The Chinese were the first to adopt this method and develop the central axial rudder. There are descriptions of such rudders in Chinese literature of the 5th and 6th centuries, but it is now established that these mentions are late. Pottery models of ships with axial rudders have been found in tombs of Later Han time, so that it is now clear that the invention goes back at least to the first century AD, thus antedating the Western use of it by 1100 years. The Chinese also developed balanced rudders and fenestrated rudders, again anticipating modern practices by many centuries.   *J.N., C.A.R.*

Above right: the fully set foresail of a Chinese junk, showing its characteristic shape and the way it is braced with bamboo battens, which facilitate immediate furling. Right: diagram of the central axial rudder and tiller of a Hangzhou Bay freighter.

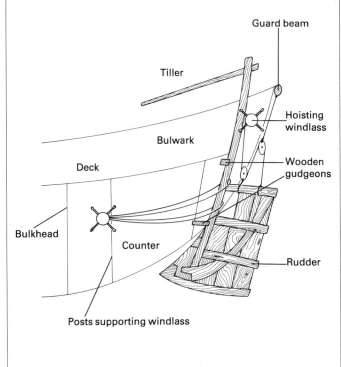

Salt industry and deep borehole drilling

The preparation in China of salt (sodium chloride) for human consumption goes back over 30 centuries, and mention of powdered salt in the 7th century BC attests the antiquity of a salt industry there. Vast subterranean deposits of brine in western China made the people of the Han dynasty the first people in the world to master deep borehole drilling, and to make use of the natural gas which they obtained as a by-product. Salt has also been linked with political power in China from the earliest times: the salt resources of Sichuan were in part responsible for its recurring independence whenever there were widespread disturbances in China, while various central governments nationalized the salt industry (known as the salt monopoly) from as early as the 2nd century BC, for it was a useful source of revenue.

Sources of common salt in China are sea salt (some 76 per cent), salt from lakes (5.4 per cent), borehole brine (16.5 per cent), rock salt (1 per cent) and salt as a by-product from gypsum mining (0.4 per cent).

Sea salt

Extraction of salt from seawater could follow a number of possible methods. If areas of land could be submerged by shallow water at high tide, and the brine then retained, direct evaporation in the sun was sufficient to allow the salt to be swept up and taken for refining. Salt was also retrieved from areas of foreshore well submerged at high tide by digging deep pits which were covered with reed mats with a layer of sand over them. When the tide was up seawater would drip through the mats, the sand acting as a filter, and the brine could then be taken up in buckets and poured out to evaporate in the sun. Seaweeds were also dried in the sun and their salt extracted with boiling water, or—the most primitive method—seawater was sprinkled on a wood fire then, after the fire was out, salt was recovered by the extraction of the ashes. Other, more elaborate, methods were used for dealing with areas covered with salt spray from the sea. On such land, above the high-tide mark, ashes of wheat stalks, reeds and rice were scattered over it so that heavy dew would draw up brine into the ashes, which could then be extracted.

The brine obtained needed refining. The simplest way was to dry the brine slowly in the sun whereby the large amounts of calcium sulphate present would be reduced by anaerobic bacteria to a black 'slush' (calcium sulphide) lying underneath the salt. It was then carefully separated from the salt, and in accordance with the Chinese practice of utilizing every by-product if possible, it was used as an emetic, as a protection against insect bites, for the sores of animals, and as a medicine for scabies and ringworm. Otherwise, refining was done by pouring brine through reed mats and then evaporating the product by boiling in large iron pans. During heating and before crystallization, soap-bean pods and millet chaff were added: this helped precipitate the salt and combined with the calcium sulphate impurity. Brine of low concentration was also sometimes cleaned by using the 'cleaver worm' (a small crustacean) which removes impurities by way of its digestive tract. The concentration was tested by seeing how many lotus seed pods would float in the brine, and this was used both in refining and in assessing salt tax.

Deep borehole drilling

For obtaining salt from underground in Sichuan recourse had to be made to boreholes. In the West in ancient times boreholes were known but they only reached depths of some 180m. In China the technique of deep borehole drilling, developed from the first century BC onwards, gave many borings twice this depth, while later the majority reached 850m and, on occasion, 1200m.

The Chinese drilling technique had many special features. The iron drilling bit was heavy—some 180kg—and was hung on a kind of cable carried over a pulley at the top of a drilling rig some 55m high. The cable was unique: made of strips of bamboo skin pressed into long pliable bands joined by strong hemp covered with rawhide, it was very flexible, non-elastic and immensely strong, much superior to the rods or poles used in Europe. Knowledge of this 'belt-cable' created a sensation when it reached there in 1823. The drill was operated from a drilling platform by two to six men standing on a long hardwood lever connected to the cable, and then suddenly jumping off to release the bit so that it fell to cut the rock. Spoil was withdrawn using long narrow bamboo 'buckets' each fitted with a valve, and the borehole was lined as work progressed.

Special tools were used for bringing up debris or repairing the walls of the hole and during the 17th or possibly the 16th century, the Chinese made the crucial invention of the 'jar'. This was a drilling bit in two separate parts linked by a tube. The cutting bit was at the bottom. When the whole bit was dropped, the cutting bit chipped the rock and then the upper half slid down the tube to give a second blow. Conversely, on withdrawing the bit, the upper half came first and when it reached the top of the tube it jerked the cutting bit upwards. Such a 'jarring' movement helped in releasing the cutting section.

Pipelines were often used to carry away the brine from the borehole heads. The pipes were made of bamboo, and the joints between the sections sealed with tung oil, lime and canvas. Such pipes were carried overland, on trestles where necessary, with intermediate pumps if required. Natural gas and artesian water were also extracted from boreholes from the 2nd century onwards, and the former was systematically used for heating the evaporation basins.

Salt production

Crystalline salt was refined by evaporating the brine in flat bowl-shaped pans. A soya bean suspension was put into the brine to help remove the calcium sulphate. Crystallization was induced at the appropriate moment by adding some salt as a nucleus. The whole process was somewhat complex and demanded expert knowledge. *J.N., C.A.R.*

Iron and steel technology

In China iron could be melted and cast almost as soon as it became known. This is in the sharpest contrast with the course of events in other parts of the Old World, where some 25 centuries elapsed between the first iron working and the first casting of iron. To appreciate what is involved in this difference, a few fundamental facts about iron must be recalled.

Iron is a metal the properties of which depend partly on small quantities of substances alloyed with it, and partly on the succession of treatments to which it has been subjected. Cast iron is formed from iron ore heated in a blast furnace where it melts and loses oxygen. With a carbon content of between 1.5 and 4.5 per cent, it is hard, brittle and suitable only for objects not likely to suffer shock or impact. Wrought iron is cast iron which has been purified and has a carbon content of no more than about 0.06 per cent; it is malleable, tough and fibrous, and is used for wire, nails, horseshoes and agricultural implements. Steel is intermediate, with carbon-content between that of cast iron and wrought iron, ranging from 0.1 up to 1.8 per cent; broadly speaking, the more the carbon, the harder the steel. Treatment is important: plunging the hot metal into a cold liquid (quenching) hardens the steel, annealing, or slow cooling, renders it more ductile, and tempering (i.e. raising to a moderate heat and then cooling) gives a combination of hardness and ductility.

Throughout antiquity and the Middle Ages down to the 14th century the extraction of iron in the West was carried out in small scale furnaces filled with alternate layers of iron ore and charcoal. The temperatures were such that nothing melted but the slag, which could be tapped off, the iron remaining as a pasty mass or 'bloom' needing much hammering on an anvil to free it from slag still embedded in it. Blast furnaces only appeared in the West about AD 1380. Steel was obtained from the wrought iron by packing it with charcoal and heating it for a long time at about 110°C, a temperature below the melting-point of iron.

Development in China

In the West the Iron Age began about 1300 BC, but in China metallic iron seems to have been known only from the 6th century BC onwards. The first products may have been blooms of carbon-free iron produced at comparatively low heat, as in the Western part of the Old World, but very little of this remains. Cast iron appears in the 4th century BC at latest, being used for agricultural implements, moulds for tools and implements, and for weapons of war. A number of factors were concerned with this early appearance in China of the fully liquid metal, some 17 centuries before it could be obtained at will in the West.

The first is that the blast furnaces either used ores rich in phosphorus or had phosphorus-rich material added, with the result that melting was possible at a somewhat lower temperature. Second, good refractory clays were readily available, and these allowed adequate though small blast furnaces to be built, as well as the efficient crucibles which were used in some parts of the country. With these coal could be used, and this permitted building very hot fires round crucibles to give true cast iron by another means. Third, certain technological developments helped: the invention of the double-acting single-cylinder piston-bellows to give a continuous blast, the application of water-power to these bellows, or perhaps to larger hinged types in the first century AD or earlier, and their provision with iron nozzles in the 3rd century AD. These all meant an abundance of cast iron in ancient and medieval China and constituted a radical difference from the civilizations in the West.

Correspondingly, the characteristic Chinese process of steel-making was the removal of carbon from cast iron, and was known as 'the hundred refinings'. It depended on the addition of oxygen by the direct use of a blast of cold air, and was fully in operation in the 2nd century BC. Moreover, later on, in the 17th century AD, this oxidizing process led Chinese and Japanese metallurgists to procedures whereby something like cast steel was produced, some two centuries before the similar Bessemer process was developed in the West.

From the 5th century AD onwards, however, most Chinese steel was made by the 'co-fusion' process, where billets of wrought iron were heated in a bath of cast iron, thus averaging the carbon content of the two. From a theoretical point of view this invention was the ancestor of the Siemens-Martin open-hearth process and other similar mid-19th century Western techniques.

The welding of hard and soft steels for weapon blades to give a good cutting edge, and at the same time a flexible resilient blade, was practised in China at least as early as the 3rd century AD, and transmitted to the Japanese in the 7th century. Since the process was also practised among some Western European peoples, the original focus of it may have been Central Asia, whence it spread both east and west from about the 2nd century AD. The 'Damascene' pattern of numerous veins to be found on Chinese steel blades, made either by welding or co-fusion, seems to have been derived both from the welding process itself and also, though less extensively, from the importation of 'wootz' crucible steel from India about the 6th century.

Once cast iron became available in Europe from about 1380 onwards, all these ways of using it appeared within about two centuries. If they and the blast furnaces had been, as previously thought, independent inventions, one would perhaps have expected a slower evolution.   *J.N., C.A.R.*

Mechanical engineering

The kind of mechanical engineering developed in traditional China was what is sometimes called 'eotechnic', where machinery was fashioned primarily from wood and bamboo, bronze and iron, i.e. materials used in that long period which lasted everywhere until the European Renaissance. But if materials were restricted, Chinese ingenuity and inventiveness were not.

The Chinese made good use of their inventions. Only after the Scientific Revolution of the 16th and 17th centuries in Europe did the West move ahead of China and begin that development of modern technology which, by its transmission outwards all over the world, is only now beginning to redress the balance of early Western indebtedness to the East. Of course, at the present time, with aerodynamics, space flight and rocket technology (but it was the Chinese who first made rockets fly), new and unheard-of alloys, telecommunications, computerization and nuclear technology, Europe and America have forged far ahead of China.

Exactly why the Scientific Revolution burgeoned in the West and not in the East is one of the most fundamental and intricate problems facing historians everywhere today. Intellectual, philosophical, even theological, factors, must assuredly be taken into account, but the fact is that China (and India) did not have aristocratic military feudalism, but rather a feudalism that was bureaucratic. The one could generate capitalism, the other could not. Unquestionably modern science grew up alongside capitalist enterprise, though whether it still needs it is another matter altogether. So the social and economic structure of society in East and West may have been at least as important as the intellectual differences between them.

Silk reeling

The manufacture of Chinese silk is very ancient. Remnants of silk have been found dating back before 1500 BC, although it seems

The classical Chinese silk-reeling machine, an illustration from a 19th-century treatise on sericulture. This type of machine was used from the 11th century onwards.

that it was not until the Zhou dynasty, or a little earlier, that organized sericulture began. But breeding silkworms is not enough; the fibre has to be processed. It must be wound from the cocoon before it can be woven, and a cocoon may contain anything up to 1km of silk. A winding or reeling machine would be a necessity, and although we have descriptions from the 11th century AD, it must have been used very much earlier. Mechanically it is important because it shows the first successful applications of a treadle to provide rotary motion, a belt-drive, and the use of a flyer to reel the thread evenly on the take-up spool.

Bellows and fans

Another important Chinese mechanical invention was the double-acting piston-bellows. Made of wood with a long rectangular chamber, the piston forced air out of the pump on both forward and backward strokes; giving, by the use of valves, a continuous blast of air. In using a single piston to achieve this it was a remarkable invention. It was used widely for metallurgy, and while the date of its appearance is uncertain, it may well go back to the 4th century BC. The West had no equivalent until the 17th century AD.

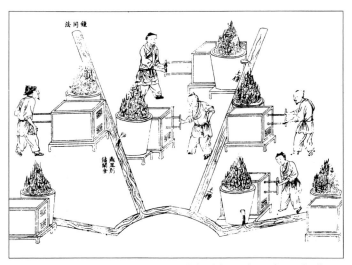

Bronze-founders using a battery of double-acting piston-bellows as depicted in a 17th-century woodcut.

The rotary-fan winnowing machine was another early Chinese invention involving a controllable current of air. Two types were used. One used a treadle-operated fan in an open framework machine, the other was hand-driven and totally enclosed and similar to those still in use on farms in China and the West. Both were early, the latter dating from the Han dynasty and the former earlier still. The device did not reach Europe until the 18th century AD.

Chinese knowledge of wind and draught is also seen in their kites, which seem to have appeared as early as the 4th century BC. They were used not only as toys but also for military purposes, yet remained unknown in the West until the 16th century AD. The helicopter with its revolving blades was referred to in China as early as the 4th century AD, when helicopter tops or 'bamboo dragonflies' were made. Both kites and tops exerted some influence on the beginnings of aeronautics in the West.

Mills

The longitudinal edge-runner mill, still in use in China, especially by pharmacists and metallurgists, is but little known in the West. It was developed probably before the Han and possibly as early as the Warring States period, but did not reach the West for some nine centuries. It was often to be found with two grinding wheels at opposite ends of a beam pivoted in the centre and working in a circle, a form which may in due course have given rise to the differential gear which was fitted to the 'south-pointing carriage'. This was a device to make a figure mounted on a vehicle always point in the same direction no matter which way the vehicle moved.

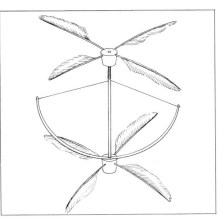

Above: the 'bamboo dragonfly' or Chinese helicopter top, which has been in use since the 4th century AD. Top: kiteflying at Haiguan: the Chinese brought their knowledge of wind pressure to this favourite pastime, which dates back to at least the 7th century AD.

The 'field-mill'—a mill on a vehicle drawn by horses and worked automatically as the cart moved along, grinding army provisions—is generally supposed to have been invented in the West in the 16th century. Yet during the 4th century AD the Chinese in north China were using 'pounding carts' with tilt-hammers and millstones that hulled rice and ground wheat while the carts were on the move.

The horse harness and other inventions

An invention of vital importance was an efficient harness for draught animals. In the West the throat-and-girth harness tended to choke the horses and severely limited the loads they could pull. To begin with the Chinese used the same harness, but they soon modified it to a breast-strap or 'trace' harness, which, completely developed by Han times, may go back as far as the 3rd century BC. This gave much greater efficiency. The Chinese in Central Asia also developed the padded horse-collar, adapted possibly from the padded saddle used on Bactrian camels. This was sometimes used with a framework attached to the shafts of the vehicle being drawn or else the shafts were fixed direct to the collar. In either case it came into general use in the 5th century AD, though it may conceivably have been used in Han times. These harness developments took at least 500 years to reach the West.

It is to the Chinese that the West also owes the invention of the wheel-barrow some time in the 3rd century AD or before, but whereas the Western wheel-barrow is ill-adapted for carrying heavy weights, the Chinese one can carry much freight and even as many as six adults. The difference arises because the wheel of the Chi-

The development of horse harness in China: (1) throat-and-girth harness, (2) breast-strap harness, (3) padded collar harness, (4) contemporary collar harness of north and north-west China.

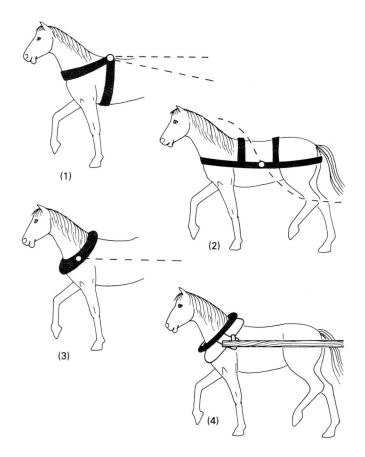

Above: hand-warming stove with 'Cardan suspension' made in the 13th century: the gimbal-mounted holder for the burning material is on the right. Top: the most characteristic type of Chinese wheelbarrow, with a central wheel protected by a housing above it; a most efficient form for carrying heavy loads and passengers.

nese wheel-barrow is central and so carries the load, whereas in the West the load is distributed between the wheel and the handles.

Another interesting device developed in China was what the West knows as the 'Cardan suspension', or gimbals mounting. In the 16th century Jerome Cardan described it as a chair on which an emperor could sit without being jolted, and said it had been used for suspending oil lamps: he did not claim the invention as his own. It had indeed been used by the Muslims for suspending lamps, but its origin is Chinese. Used for unspillable incense burners and bed-warmers it was known by AD 180, and probably came to the West by way of Persia.

The water-raising device known as the square-pallet chain-pump was another Chinese machine. It raised water by an endless chain of flat plates or pallets which drew the water along as they passed upwards through a flume or trough. Much used in China by the 2nd century AD, it may have been known as early as the 4th century BC.

The origin of the mechanical clock

The clock is the oldest and most important of complex scientific machines. It appeared quite suddenly in the West early in the 14th century AD, but we now know that its ancestor came from China. This was the astronomical clock-tower built by Su Song, or Su Zirong (flourished AD 1080), the basic drive of which was a water-wheel with scoops or buckets on its rim. Water poured into these from a constant-level tank, and an arrangement of linkwork operating each time a bucket was full brought the next bucket into place. This—the first of all escapements—was truly the essence of mechanical timekeeping, and the increasing accuracy of mechanical clocks achieved in the West in later centuries was primarily due to the refinement of the escapement mechanism and the increasing precision of the short intervals that measured the time. Yet even Su Song's clock was not completely novel—the escapement principle can be found in China at least as early as the 8th century AD in instruments demonstrating astronomical phenomena, some six centuries before any such device appeared in the West.

J.N., C.A.R.

Pictorial reconstruction of Su Song's astronomical clock tower at Kaifeng. It included an armillary sphere and a celestial globe, and was driven by a water-wheel escapement.

MINING AND CIVIL ENGINEERING

Mining and civil engineering before 1911

Hydraulic engineering has been central to the Chinese tradition of public works, providing irrigation, flood control and transport facilities at least from the 6th century BC. Tradition attributes the beginnings of water control to the Great Yu, but the earliest attested project was the Peony Dam at Shouxian in modern Anhui, constructed in the early 6th century BC. During the 4th and 3rd centuries BC many large-scale ventures were completed and were to remain central to the life of their region for more than two millennia. Most notable of these were the Zhengguo Canal, which used water from the River Jing to irrigate the area north of Chang'an (Xi'an), and Li Bing's (flourished 250 BC) scheme in Sichuan, which divided up the flow of the River Min to irrigate around 200 000 hectares; both these projects took place under the auspices of the state of Qin, and provided the material basis for its conquest and unification of China in 221 BC. During the Han, earlier projects were renovated and many others brought into operation, such as Xu Bo's (flourished 130 BC) canal between the Yellow River and Chang'an and the reconstruction of the Yellow River dikes under the Emperor Wudi.

Successive centuries saw the construction of innumerable hydraulic works of various sizes, generally centring on the regions of greatest economic importance to the reigning dynasty. Most famous were the two Grand Canals built by the Sui around AD 600 and by the Yuan around AD 1300 to transport tribute grain from the lower Yangtze to the respective capitals at Chang'an and Beijing. Each had to surmount major engineering problems, with the Yuan canal rising to as much as 42m (and with its destination, Beijing, being 36m) above the mean Yangtze level. Each needed vast investments of manpower and resources, and the suffering inflicted on the people in the course of the construction of the Sui canal was a major cause of the short duration of that dynasty. Another vast undertaking requiring central government control was the upkeep of the Yellow River dikes; a controversy raged throughout the imperial period as to whether these should be high and close together, hastening the flow of the river, or low and widely spaced to allow the river plenty of room. Indeed over the years the silt deposited by the river raised the level of its bed in places some 6m above the surrounding countryside. Such was the importance of the dikes that in the Qing dynasty their maintenance was the responsibility of an official only one rank below that of governor-general.

One point, however, should be stressed. The enumeration of the great projects wrought by the central government should not be allowed to obscure the fact that local and even private initiative was responsible for many more thousands of projects across China, which, while small in scope, provided the basis for the year to year operation of agriculture in many regions.

The construction of roads and their attendant bridges has also had a long history in China. The Han empire inherited a system of roads, which it extended to a length of perhaps 40 000km. (The Roman system was about 78 000km long.) While later transport relied more heavily on water, and the road system tended to atrophy, imperial roads were kept open for official couriers under all the dynasties. Bridge building technology was also highly advanced. The challenge of spanning the gorges of southwest China was met both by the construction of cantilever bridges from the 4th century AD and also by the use of suspension bridges at least from the first century AD; probably from the 6th century AD iron chains were used to build such bridges with spans of up to 100m. Arched bridges were probably used as early as the Zhou or even Shang; there remain many historic multi-arched bridges such as the Wannianqiao in Nancheng, Jiangxi, completed in 1647. Chinese use of the segmented arch predated its adoption in Europe by many centuries, as shown by the famous Anji bridge, with a span of 38m, built about AD 610 in Hebei.

The working of metals and therefore some sort of mining dates in China from the rather sudden onset of the Bronze Age in the mid-2nd millennium BC. Government interest in (and our information on) mining was greatest where the metal was to be used for weaponry, or—more important in the later period—for the currency. The great copper mines in Yunnan in the 18th century were operated privately, but with government rights of pre-emption at

Many bridges like this one span the canals of Jiangsu and Zhejiang Provinces.

a fixed price, and there were also many private mines across China which extracted metals or fuel for the populace. All mines, however, suffered the same problems of drainage and ventilation that plagued pre-modern European mining. Thus, they all remained on a small scale up to the beginning of modernization in the 1880s.

T.W.

Mining industry, 1911–49

With the partial exceptions of the coal and iron ore industries technology in mining remained primarily traditional in Republican China. While coal output did increase over the period, that of other minerals showed no clear trend; the major problems were those of distribution and demand.

Coal accounted for 60 per cent of the value of mining products (salt excluded) in the 1930s, and a much larger proportion of the labour force. Between 1913 and the Anti-Japanese War total output grew by 4 per cent per annum from 13 to 40 million tonnes; output from modern mines increased at 5.2 per cent per annum, from 5 to 29 million tonnes. The reduction of transport costs brought about by the construction of railways was crucial to the growth of the industry in the first two decades of the century, after which growth slowed, and became primarily a function of growing demand from modern industry. Over 70 per cent of output from modern mines came from mines with foreign connections, with the Sino-British Kailuan in northeast Hebei and the Japanese-run Fushun in Liaoning Province producing over 50 per cent of the total. After 1937 intensive efforts by the Japanese to increase production in north China ran into problems of labour supply, of capital shortage, and increasingly of the disruption of transport; in the unoccupied areas of the south and southwest the Nationalist government also tried to develop the much smaller deposits there. Output reached its pre-1949 peak of 68 million tonnes in 1942, after which the disruption caused by continuous wars took an increasing toll.

Modernization of the extraction of coal began around 1880, reaching the point where, by the mid-1930s, over 80 per cent of output came from so-called 'modern' mines. However the level of mechanization in such mines was very low. Manual methods of winning the coal were the rule; haulage mostly used human or animal power; modern winding engines were in fact the main criterion for designating a mine modern. Safety standards were low, and many serious mine accidents took place with heavy casualties.

In the case of iron ore foreign interests were even more paramount. The output of the Daye mine in Hubei, originally opened in 1891 to supply the first modern Chinese steelworks at Hanyang, soon became mortgaged to the Japanese, who wanted the iron for their state steelworks at Yawata. The other major mines, two in the northeast and one in Anhui, were also either completely owned by the Japanese or had Japanese participation. The overall pattern of iron ore output shows two periods of rapid growth—the First World War, a period of high prices, the main benefits of which went to Japan, and the 1930s, as Japan developed heavy industry in northeast China. As with coal, the wartime policies of the Japanese and of the Nationalists led to increased output up to a peak (in this case 1943), followed by a fall as the communications network ceased to function.

Other minerals were still mined almost entirely by traditional methods. In some of the rarer minerals China is very well endowed, with the world's largest reserves of tungsten and antimony, and during the First World War production and exports of these metals increased sharply to meet high world demand; but mining remained on the whole unmechanized and output declined with the fall in world prices when peace was restored. At Gejiu in Yunnan, where China's tin mining industry was centred, the extraction of the ore also remained decentralized, with little if any resort to machinery. From the mid-1930s the Nationalist government tried to extend control over and to modernize these industries, but these efforts were mainly concentrated on the refining stage, where some success was achieved; extraction of the ore from the ground still remained largely unmechanized.   *T.W.*

Mining industry and training, 1949 onwards

Output of minerals since 1949 has grown quite rapidly, particularly so in the first decade. Since the late 1960s a dualistic structure has emerged, with small-scale unmodernized mines supplementing the output of the large modern ones.

Up to 1952 the main concern in coal mining was the restoration of pre-war capacity, but a modernization and mechanization movement was begun which was to be strengthened in the succeeding period. The First Five-year Plan (1953–7) saw at once a major expansion of capacity—185 new mines were completed with a capacity of 61 million tonnes—and a modernization of technology. The major changes made in the technology of coal mining (by far the largest sector of the mining industry) were the adoption of long-wall working in place of the room-and-pillar which had been general before 1949, the replacement of the manual winning of coal by drilling and blasting or by mechanized extraction, and the reduction of manual haulage to a small part of the total. By 1957, while China's large coal mines were less mechanized than those of most developed countries, loading was the only operation still mainly done by hand.

After rapid growth and then decline during the Great Leap Forward (1958–60), the industry began to grow again, although more slowly. Since 1961 the task of loading has gradually been mechanized and blasting methods replaced by mechanized coal cutters. Another development, not without problems, has been the introduction of several hydraulic mines since the late 1950s. The main emphasis has been on the more intensive exploitation of existing mines and the opening of small mines, rather than on the heavy investment required to open large new mines.

As with much other local industry the rationale behind opening the small mines has been the saving of scarce capital and the desire not to overburden the transport system. Output from such mines increased at an annual average rate of 13.8 per cent in the decade following 1965, as against a growth rate of 5.1 per cent for modern mines. By 1986 mines operated by township or collective producers accounted for 33 per cent of total output, and the decontrol of prices of coal from the 50 000 mines run by peasants has greatly stimulated production. Nevertheless the limitations of this policy, which relies on the exploitation of easily available resources rather than on real increases in capacity, are now clear, and present policy also seeks to develop large mines.

Output grew more strongly than expected in the middle 1980s and reached 928 million tonnes in 1987. The target for the year 2000 is 1200 million tonnes, though the World Bank suggests that even 1400 million would barely meet likely demand. China is also using foreign capital to develop large projects, for instance the 15-million-tonne-capacity Antaibao mine in Shanxi, jointly run with Occidental Petroleum.

Much less is known about the other mining industries, but events probably followed a path similar to that of coal. In the case of iron ore, of which there are large reserves but of poor quality, investments have been insufficient to develop the resources to the extent needed.

The training of mining engineers and geologists has had a priority commensurate to that given to the industries themselves. The number of engineers and technicians working in coal mines increased from 12 000 in 1952 to 30 000 in 1956, while there was only a 20 per cent increase in the unskilled workforce. Around 45 000 of the 272 000 engineering graduates between 1953 and 1962 were in geology or mining. However, the stress in the late 1960s during the Cultural Revolution and in the early 1970s was away from specialized technical knowledge and towards reliance on the masses. The technological cost of this policy was high, though possibly less so than in other sectors. Since 1978 much emphasis has been put on technical education, with 11 colleges of coal mining under the jurisdiction of the Ministry and 100 coal mining technical schools. Increasing mechanization also requires a more highly trained workforce.   *T.W.*

Civil engineering, 1911–49

The disunity of China over most of the Republican period made giant projects of the traditional or post-1949 type impossible, and often made difficult even the maintenance of existing projects. With the important exception of the construction of an at least rudimentary road and rail network, the major achievements of the period were in or near major urban centres and in the earlier part of the period were often under foreign direction. In the rural areas, at best existing works were kept up and at worst the hydraulic works underpinning the agricultural sector fell into disrepair.

Despite the establishment of a National Conservancy and Irrigation Bureau in 1913 and the overall supervision of all hydraulic engineering by the National Economic Council in the 1930s, no major new projects were undertaken in this period. Plans were put forward for the control of major rivers, but except for some work begun in the 1930s on the Huai, it was all the authorities could do to respond to such major catastrophes as those in the Yangtze valley in 1931 and in the Yellow River in 1933 by repairing the dikes and defences. In 1938 the Yellow River dikes were intentionally destroyed to slow down the advance of the Japanese, flooding vast areas and costing countless lives, and in the late 1940s major projects were aimed at controlling that river, with the aid of the United Nations Relief and Rehabilitation Administration. In general, however, political divisions and a shortage of funds prevented all but the most local projects. The exceptions were those connected with navigation in the treaty ports where, as with the Haihe Conservancy in Tianjin, foreign interests ensured that sufficient work was carried out.

Some success was also achieved, even though limited again by lack of funds, in urban construction. New ports were opened at Huludao in the northeast and at Lianyungang in Jiangsu and in the major cities work proceeded on the paving of roads and in some cases, as in Qingdao, on the provision of a sewerage system. While some of this work was carried out by the foreign concessions, Chinese urban authorities were eager to provide similar facilities, and some success was achieved in building a modern city in Nanjing, though such efforts were largely ended by the war.

The other major achievement of the period was the construction of a transport network. While most of the railways were started in the last decade of the empire, many only came into operation around 1911. By 1937 a railway network of 21 000km connected at least the major cities of north and east-central China with single-track lines. While many had been built with foreign funds and techniques, the purely Chinese line from Beijing to Zhangjiakou, which included tunnels up to 1km long, aroused great national pride. The road network was a later development, dating from around 1920. Up to 1932 the roads, apart from a few kilometres around the national capital in Beijing, were mostly built by provincial or local governments or by bodies such as the International Famine Relief Commission. Most were at best tamped earth and sometimes merely levelled out or filled in to the level of the road and then left to the traffic to beat down. In the mid-1930s the Nanjing government began the construction of a network radiating from its centre of power in the lower Yangtze. By 1936 there were just over 100 000km of roads passable to motor vehicles for at least part of the year. During the Anti-Japanese and civil wars road building was primarily for military use, and the crowning achievement was the building of the Burma Road.   *T.W.*

Civil engineering and training, 1949 onwards

Since 1949 the government of the People's Republic of China has embarked on many huge civil engineering projects, encompassing both hydraulic and transport construction, and involving all levels of government and people.

The most spectacular projects have been hydraulic. Work has been carried out on the Huai River since the early 1950s, including a 190km canal from the Hongze Lake to the sea at Lianyungang. The problem of the Yellow River has been tackled by means of a 'staircase' of dams starting from above Guide in Qinghai and finishing near Zhengzhou in Henan. The biggest dam of all is at the Sanmen Gorge, built with Russian help to fulfil the three functions of flood control, irrigation and hydro-electricity. However, while some success has been achieved in reducing the danger of floods, silting still threatens the dams and reduces the yield of hydro-electricity. Even more ambitious is the giant Sanxia project on the Yangtze, which, however, seems unlikely to go beyond the already completed Gezhouba dam. In addition to major projects, innumerable small dams and canals have been and are being built on local initiative. The most famous local project is the Red Flag Canal, built through mountainous country almost entirely with manual methods to supply water to the dry county of Linxian in Henan. Although some projects, especially in the late 1950s, were built without regard for broader hydrological considerations, they nevertheless have succeeded in raising irrigated acreage from about 16 per cent of agricultural land in 1949 to 45 per cent in 1978. Since 1978, irrigated acreage has fallen slightly with the end of the collective system. However, the basic shortage of water in north China remains; the diversion of some of the waters of the Yangtze to north China, a massive project discussed sporadically over the years in China, would be one possible, though expensive, way of overcoming it.

Major efforts have also been made to develop the transport network, with road and rail systems both being extended, especially in the west because of its military and strategic importance and because of the government's policy of developing the inland regions. The rail network has expanded from around 23 000km to 53 000km route length, still not a very large system for a country of China's size. Great technical difficulties have had to be overcome in the construction of several lines, such as the spectacular mountain route between Chengdu in Sichuan and Kunming in Yunnan completed in 1970. Much effort has also been put into the expansion of the road system, around 100 000km in 1949, rising to 980 000km in 1987. While much of this increase is due to the building of local networks of roads suitable for motor transport, major strategic roads have been built over difficult terrain; the road through Aksai Chin, one of the causes of the Sino-Indian War of 1962, was only one of the more well-known. The construction of major bridges across the Yangtze at Wuhan and Nanjing were among the most notable achievements. The Nanjing bridge, completed in 1968, in particular had to overcome technical problems, such as the huge variation between the levels of the river, that had defeated Russian engineers. But transport capacity remains inadequate and construction of new facilities and more effective use of existing ones will continue to have a high priority.

The training of Chinese engineers which had been a priority from 1949 assumed even greater importance with the withdrawal of aid from the USSR in 1960. Engineering personnel in state enterprises rose from 164 000 in 1952 to 1.57 million in 1978 and 4 million in 1987. Following the disastrous fall in the number of properly trained engineers entering the labour force during the Cultural Revolution, the training of scientific personnel has been a major priority of the post-Mao government. *T.W.*

The construction of the road and rail bridge across the Yangtze at Nanjing had to overcome great obstacles; it is now a vital link in China's transport network.

APPENDICES

GUIDE FOR VISITORS

Common Chinese notices: basic recognition for foreigners

厕所	Lavatory
男厕	Men's Lavatory
女厕	Women's Lavatory
出口	Exit
入口	Entrance
银行	Bank
医院	Hospital
邮政局	Post Office
电报局	Telegraph Office
电话	Telephone
电话局	Telephone Office
禁止通行	It is forbidden to pass (this point)
禁止吸烟	Smoking prohibited
人行横道	Pedestrian crossing

Social and public manners

A most striking feature when adjusting to living in China is the difference in behaviour between Chinese who know each other, and Chinese who are total strangers. In Chinese society, people who are either colleagues, or friends or neighbours tend to show a great deal of courtesy towards each other, to the extent that one can almost become impatient with the endless 'disputing' over one person wishing to give precedence to the other, or tugs-of-war over suitcases, with the owner trying to keep hold of it, and his companion equally determined to relieve him of the burden. But in the realm of strangers, the foreigner is sometimes astonished by what would be considered to be downright bad manners in the West. In department stores people let doors swing in one another's faces; people elbow and push their way on to buses, in the sure knowledge that should they stand courteously on one side, then they would never manage to get on board. Within the traditional Confucian hierarchy of relationships there is no place for the stranger. Periodic attempts by the government to exhort people to demonstrate greater public awareness generally fail as revelations of high-level corruption have undermined the ideal of socialist morality. Many people worry that 'feudal' attitudes are being aggravated by the new get rich quick mentality of the economic reforms.

The visiting foreigner is generally appalled by the prevalence of hawking and spitting in China, and the Chinese themselves have developed a rather ambivalent attitude towards this habit. People are exhorted, in the name of public hygiene, not to spit, and yet the prevalence of spittoons indicates a degree of resignation to the habit. On the other hand, loud and obvious nose-blowing, especially during meals, is considered to be extremely bad-mannered, and if anyone is forced to blow his nose, he either does it as discreetly as possible, or even leaves the table to do so.

Visitors to China are frequently surprised by the amount of handshaking between the Chinese. Handshaking among Chinese communities in other parts of Asia is not seen to any great extent; it is a habit that seems to have increased in China during the past 30 years. Chinese never kiss each other in greeting or parting, although comradely hugging is seen. Young people, however, are now much more demonstrative in public and couples can be seen walking hand in hand or cuddling on park benches. With the over-crowding in cities, for many this may be their only time alone.

Parents seldom chastise their children in public. On the rare occasions that children are seen crying or whining in China, the adult accompanying the child is much more likely to soothe the child out of its tears rather than to chastise or speak sternly to it. In recent years there has been concern that the one child policy has prompted parents and grandparents to spoil their "little emperors". However, the majority of Chinese freely admit that their parents have hit them from time to time in the privacy of their home. This is the key to Chinese behaviour—emotions and private relationships should be kept private and not put on public display. Although this is the general rule, people are occasionally seen shouting at each other in the street, even coming to blows, but should bystanders notice that a foreigner is watching they hastily persuade the assailants to break up the dispute.

Another aspect of Chinese society which often surprises foreigners who come to China expecting to see egalitarianism in its purest form is the degree of hierarchy and rank-consciousness among the Chinese. It is quite common for an official to be addressed by his title, and frequently the most senior person in a group of Chinese is the one who sets the tone, with the more junior members not initiating any conversation unless he does so first. Equally, it is very seldom that one witnesses any controversial discussion in public among a group of Chinese, even a group of academics, which one would expect as commonplace in other countries. *E.W., N.M.*

East–West friction

As there is friction between countries with a similar historical and cultural background, it is not surprising that the friction and misunderstandings between cultures as far apart as those of China and the Western nations should be even greater. For the most part these misunderstandings and irritations arise through mutual ignorance and prejudice.

Until the 20th century (and even at various points during this century) China's policies were essentially introverted. The Chinese word for China—*Zhongguo*—means Middle Kingdom. The Chinese traditionally saw themselves as the centre of the universe, and from what they could see of the barbarian tribes living around the periphery of China, they felt no necessity to change this attitude.

On balance, China's early contacts with Europeans were inauspicious. Although some of the early Jesuit visitors to China in the 17th and 18th centuries were men of learning, much respected by the Chinese, the majority of early contacts were with traders, and, later, with missionaries. The brawling behaviour of the former, and the incomprehensible exclusiveness of the doctrines of the latter did nothing to convince the Chinese that European civilization had anything to offer China.

During the 19th century the attitudes of the Western powers towards China had changed. Under the influence of new materialistic and expansionist attitudes, the respect felt for Chinese culture and civilization during the 17th and 18th centuries gave way to disapproval of China's poverty and technical backwardness. In 1793 there had been a diplomatic disagreement when Lord Macartney refused to kneel and touch his forehead to the ground before the Qianlong Emperor. The Chinese had seen the Macartney mission as a mission from a tribute state, and not as a mission from an equal nation wishing to open trade links with China and had accordingly expected its leader to perform the kowtow. China was not accustomed to dealing with other nations as equals, and it was a severe blow to its pride to be subordinated, as a result of the Opium Wars of the 1840s and 1850s, to nations which it had previously regarded as inferior.

As the British, French, German, Belgian, American and, subsequently, the Russian and the Japanese presence and power increased in China, so too did mutual antagonisms. Although it could be argued that the foreign intentions behind railway building in China were sensible, the actual procedure for effecting the building process took little account of Chinese sensibilities, and violent protests arose over the routing of the railway through family graveyards, and areas traditionally sacred to the Chinese because of auspicious *fengshui* (literally 'wind-water'—a concept in geomancy). The teachings of the Christian missionaries were well-intentioned, but sometimes struck at the very foundations of Chinese society, and the Taiping Rebellion, which caused the death of millions in China in the mid-19th century, and was led by a fanatical Chinese Christian convert, served to reinforce the suspicion that Western ideas and the Western presence could only bring disaster.

The mutual suspicion and misunderstandings persisted through to the present century, and many still influence the attitudes of Chinese and Westerners when dealing with each other. Westerners persist in thinking of the Chinese as 'inscrutable', and one still frequently hears Chinese refer to Westerners as *yangguizi* (foreign devils). Understandably, as long as Chinese and Westerners find themselves in positions which are mutually beneficial, whether commercial, cultural, educational or scientific, there is generally mutual liking and admiration, but the moment that either side feels that it is being exploited, slighted or treated in a cavalier manner, old prejudices are apt to reassert themselves. Often the supposed slights are a result of linguistic misunderstandings—incorrect translations, or unfortunate choice of words. It will be a long time before prejudice and mistrust between East and West disappear, just as the historical prejudices between the various West European nations are slow to disappear, but increasing contact should help to bring about understanding, if not always acceptance, of the culture and ideas of these two different areas of the world.   *E.W.*

Do's and Don'ts in personal or commercial contact with individual Chinese

Although the Chinese are tolerant of cultural and national differences, they are acutely conscious of the 'host-guest' relationship, and expect foreigners who are visiting China to behave with courtesy and decorum. It is perfectly acceptable to discuss any subject that one wishes, but it is unwise to raise controversial or sensitive issues unless one is familiar with the character and degree of understanding of the Chinese with whom one is talking. While it is acceptable to behave naturally, the Chinese are embarrassed by an over-hearty, backslapping approach. Although physical contact between people of the same sex in China may be seen, there is little overt physical contact between people of the opposite sex, and the Chinese are embarrassed by displays of sexual attraction between visiting foreigners. The visiting foreign male should avoid even the most avuncular or platonic physical display towards a Chinese woman.

Punctuality is very important in China, and apart from causing inconvenience unpunctuality is regarded as impolite. The customary opener to almost any meeting is the serving of Chinese tea and the exchange of pleasantries. The hosts will then give their guests an introduction to the place they are visiting, often providing much statistical information. This also gives the visitor a chance to ask questions, which should be posed as politely as possible. It is not a good idea to press for an answer when one's hosts are evidently reluctant to respond.

During any visit to China one will probably participate in at least one banquet. The hosts will keep piling quantities of food on to the plate, but although the visitor should try everything, he is under no obligation to eat it all, and it is quite acceptable to decline second helpings, or leave food on the plate. Knives and forks are usually provided for foreigners, but it is much appreciated if one at least tries to master chopsticks. Each guest has three glasses in front of him, one for beer or mineral water, one for either grape wine, or hot rice wine, and the third for a powerful clear spirit, which varies from province to province, but the prince of which is generally considered to be the one called *maotai*. There is pressure from the government to curtail the lavishness of official entertaining and in particular the consumption of *maotai*. One is free to drink the beer or grape wine as one pleases, but the *maotai* is generally kept for toasts, when someone will propose a toast to health, friendship, or any number of things, and finish by saying *ganbei*. This literally means 'a dry (i.e. empty) glass', but there is no compulsion to drain the entire contents if one does not want to. It is generally expected that the leader of a foreign group will also give a short speech during a banquet, usually two or three courses after the host has made his.

Foreigners are sometimes irritated by the lack of stimulating or profound conversation at banquets in China, as the conversation often centres on the food, with lengthy disquisitions by the hosts on the different characteristics of the food of each province. However, after one has eaten with the same Chinese hosts on several occasions the conversation frequently becomes wider-ranging, and often very much to the point, although it is seldom that one encounters the sort of arguments on social, political or philosophical points which would be common in other countries.

A cardinal rule in China is to keep one's temper, no matter how trying the circumstances. Nothing is gained by losing it and, apart from embarrassing the Chinese, one goes down in their estimation. Care should be taken to avoid making a point at the public expense of any individual Chinese, as this will cause him or her to lose considerable 'face'. To the Chinese if a person does something that is socially unacceptable, or if a person is publicly humiliated by someone else, that person is said to 'lose face'. If, however, a person behaves 'correctly' according to society's definition, or if a person's status is raised, then that person is said to 'gain face'. One generally finds that in the long run nothing is gained by causing a Chinese to lose face however triumphant a release of frustration it might have seemed at the time.

Visits to China tend to be as a member of a group and, whether tourist or professional, the Chinese like to be able to identify one member of the group as the leader. On all subsequent occasions, both work and social, this person will be given first place in the protocol order. It is through this person, or through someone nominated as 'secretary' of the group that information, programme details, requests, etc. will be channelled. Many foreign groups, used to a much more democratic pattern of behaviour, have tried to change this, but attempts to have a different leader every day, or some such plan, simply confuse the Chinese and cause problems. Arrangements in China can be rather inflexible, and much depends on the personality of the guide/interpreter. But changes to the schedule can sometimes be made, especially if the request is presented in a reasonable manner, and with as much notice as possible.

A question which invariably arises for members of delegations or commercial missions is that of gifts for one's Chinese hosts. At one time it was wise to give nothing but the simplest of presents, such as dictionaries, technical books, pens, etc. However, Chinese delegations travelling abroad now tend to give gifts to anyone who acts as their host, and the gifts tend to take the form of typically Chinese artefacts, such as scrolls, silks, embroidery, books, etc. There is no reason why the visiting foreigner should not reciprocate with gifts representative of that which is most typical or best of his own country or line of commercial enterprise, within reason.

Although tipping is not officially encouraged in China some hotel staff and taxi drivers have taken to this foreign custom with alacrity. Guests may wish to thank interpreters and drivers who have been especially helpful; foreign books or cigarettes are particularly welcome.

In general, there is no problem about taking photographs in China. The exceptions are from aeroplane windows, from certain bridges, and from certain areas which guides will specify. It is a matter of common courtesy in any country not to take photographs of people without asking their permission, and China is no exception. One usually finds that parents are happy to have photographs of their children taken, as long as one asks. As a rule, it is not a good idea only to concentrate on the 'picturesque' in one's photography, as the Chinese are proud of their modern industrial achievements, and find it difficult to understand why foreigners find it more interesting to take photographs of old women with bound feet than of oil refineries.

Although each of the main cities open to tourists has a branch of the 'Friendship Store' where only foreigners, overseas Chinese and certain native Chinese may shop, foreigners are absolutely free to buy in any shop. Do not be surprised by the general apathy of some shop assistants. Except for those working in small privately-owned shops, staff occasionally appear to regard the customer as an inconvenience.

Although the extreme south of China is seldom really cold, the rest of China is cold in the winter, and in the summer can be very hot and humid. It is advisable to take a thick overcoat and sweaters for the winter, and cottons for the summer. The Chinese laundry service is quick and efficient, although do not entrust it with your favourite woollens.

The Chinese tend to dress comfortably and inconspicuously. In recent years the Western style suit has become very fashionable and has tended to replace the old 'Mao' jacket. The visitor should avoid dressing so as to draw too much attention. During the day dress can be informal, but men should wear a jacket and tie or suit for banquets. Evening wear or cocktail dresses are not expected.

Chinese Currency

Chinese currency is known as the *renminbi* (people's money or RMB). Visitors to China are initially bewildered by the existence of Foreign Exchange Certificates (FECs) which they receive when cashing travellers cheques. The FEC is denominated in the same way as the RMB and officially has the same value. In fact it is worth much more since only Foreign Exchange Certificates can be used to buy imported goods. A thriving blackmarket in FECs has developed and visitors are often approached to change money. This should be resisted not only because involvement breaks the law, but also because visitors will find themselves unable to spend much RMB as all hotels, restaurants and shops that cater to foreigners insist on payment in FECs. *E.W., N.M.*

Foreign Exchange Certificates.

SOURCES OF INFORMATION

The following is a selective list of organizations that supply English language information about China. Listings include academic institutes and research libraries, friendship associations, government bodies, trade organizations, Chinese embassies and bookshops.

AUSTRALIA

Chinese Embassy
247 Federal Highway
Watson, Canberra ACT 2602

friendship association

The Australia-China Friendship Society
4 Tattersalls Lane
Melbourne 3000

trade organizations

Australia-China Business Council
Confederation of Australian Industry
PO Box E14
Queen Victoria Terrace
Canberra, ACT 2600

Australia-China Chamber of Commerce and Industry
PO Box 2738
Sydney, NSW 2001

academic institutes

The Oriental Society of Australia
Department of Oriental Studies
University of Sydney, NSW 2006 (publishers of *The Journal of the Oriental Society of Australia*)

Contemporary China Centre
Australian National University
PO Box 4
Canberra, ACT 2600 (publishers of *Australian Journal of Chinese Affairs*)

National Library of Australia
Parkes Place
Canberra ACT 2600

Research School of Pacific Studies
Australian National University

Department of Far Eastern History
Australian National University (publishers of *Papers on Far Eastern History*)

Centre for the Study of Australian-Asia Relations
Griffith University
Nathan
Queensland 4111

CANADA

Chinese Embassy
411–415 St Andrew Street
Ottawa, Ontario K1N 5H3

friendship association

Federation of Canada-China Friendship Associations
Postal Station K
Toronto, Ontario M4P 2V3

trade organization

Department of Industry, Trade and Commerce
Pacific Bureau
235 Queen Street
Ottawa, Ontario

academic institutes

Institute of Asian Research
Department of Asian Studies
University of British Columbia
2075 Wesbrook Mall
Vancouver, British Columbia V6T 1W5
(publishers of *Pacific Affairs*)

Department of East Asian Studies
University of Toronto
Toronto, Ontario M5S 1A1

GREAT BRITAIN

Chinese Embassy
49–51 Portland Place
London W1N 3AH

Cultural Section
28 College Crescent
London NW3 5LH

Commercial Section
56–60 Lancaster Gate
London W2 3NG

Educational Section
51 Drayton Green
London W13 0JE

Visa Section
31 Portland Place
London W1N 3AG

friendship association

Society for Anglo-Chinese Understanding
(SACU)
c/o The Secretary
16 Portland Street
Cheltenham, Glos. GL52 2PB

trade organizations

China–Great Britain Trade Group
5th Floor, Abford House
15 Wilton Road
London SW1V 1LT

China Association
Regis House
43–46 King William Street
London EC4R 1BE

academic institutes

British Association for Chinese Studies
c/o The Secretary
[for address see current edition of *Directory of British Associations*]

British Library Oriental Collections
Orbit House
197 Blackfriars Road
London SE1 8NG

British Museum
Dept. of Oriental Antiquities
Great Russell Street
London WC1B 3DG

Needham Research Institute
East Asian History of Science Library
8 Sylvester Road
Cambridge CB3 9AF

Percival David Foundation of Chinese Art
53 Gordon Square
London WC1H 0PD

other

Great Britain-China Centre
15 Belgrave Square
London SW1X 8PG

British Council
10 Spring Gardens
London SW1A 2BN

China Society
31b Torrington Square
London WC1E 7JL

Xinhua News Agency, London Office
8 Swiss Terrace
Belsize Road
London NW6 4RR

HONG KONG

Hong Kong Government Office
6 Grafton Street
London W1X 3LB

academic institutes

Chinese University of Hong Kong
Shatin, New Territories:
Department of Chinese Language and Literature
New Asia Chinese Language Centre
Institute of Chinese Studies
Universities Service Centre

Contemporary China Research Collection
Hong Kong Baptist College Library
224 Waterloo Road
Kowloon

University of Hong Kong
Pokfulam Road:
Department of Chinese
Centre of Asian Studies

bookshops

Chung Hwa Book Company
450–2 Nathan Road
Kowloon

Commercial Press
9–15 Yee Wo Street
Causeway Bay

Cosmos Books Ltd
30 Johnston Road

Joint Publishing Company
9 Queen Victoria Street

Swindon Book Co. Ltd
13 Lock Road
Kowloon

other

China Travel Service (HK) Ltd
77 Queen's Road, Central

INDIA

academic institute

Centre for the Study of Developing Societies
Delhi
(publishers of *China Report*)

JAPAN

Chinese Embassy
4–33 Motoazabu 3-chome
Minato-ku, Tokyo 106

trade organization

JETRO
2–5 Toramomon 2-chome
Minato-ku, Tokyo 105

academic institute

Center for Modern Chinese Studies
c/o Toyo Bunka
28–21 Honkomagome 2-chome
Bunkyo-ku
Tokyo

research

Institute for Developing Economies
42 Ichigaya-hommura-cho
Shinjuku-ku, Tokyo 162

NEW ZEALAND

Chinese Embassy
2–6 Glenmore Street
Wellington

friendship association

New Zealand-China Friendship Society
52 Customs Street East
Auckland

trade organizations

New Zealand Chamber of Commerce
PO Box 1071
Wellington

New Zealand Institute of International Affairs
88 Fairlie Terrace
Kelburn
Wellington

PEOPLE'S REPUBLIC OF CHINA

friendship association

Chinese People's Association for Friendship with Foreign Countries
1 Taijichang Jie
Beijing

trade organization

China International Trust & Investment Corporation (CITIC)
19 Jianguomen Neidajie
Beijing

academic institutes

Chinese Academy of Sciences (Academia Sinica)
52 Sanlihelu
Beijing

Chinese Academy of Social Sciences
5 Jianguomen Waidajie
Beijing

National Library of China
39 Baishiqiao Lu
Haidian Qu, Beijing

book suppliers

China International Book Trading Corporation
(CIBTC)
21 Chegongzhuang Xilu
Beijing

China National Publishing Industry Trading
Corporation (CNPITC)
32 Bei Zongbu Hutong
Beijing

China National Publications Import & Export
Corporation (CNPIEC)
137 Chaoyangmen Neidajie
Beijing

TAIWAN

American Institute in Taiwan
Taipei Office
7 Lane 134
Hsinyi Road, Sec. 3
Taipei

Free Chinese Centre
4th Floor, Dorland House
14/16 Regent Street
London SW1Y 4PH

academic institutes

National Central Library
20 Chungshan South Road
Taipei

Institute of International Relations
64 Wan Shou Road
Mucha
Taipei

National Palace Museum
Wai-Shuang-Hsi
Shih-Lin
Taipei

UNITED NATIONS

International Labour Office Publications
CH-1211 Geneva 22
Switzerland

Publications Office
UN Research Institute for Special Development
Palais des Nations
CH-1211 Geneva 10
Switzerland

Distribution and Sales Section
Food and Agriculture Organization
Via delle Terme di Caracalla
00100 Rome
Italy

UNITED STATES

Chinese Embassy
2300 Connecticut Avenue NW
Washington, DC 20008

Visa Section
2310 Connecticut Avenue NW
Washington, DC 20008

friendship association

US–China Peoples' Friendship Association
Room 721
41 Union Square West
New York, NY 10003
(publishers of *New China*)

trade organization

National Council for US-China Trade
1050 17th Street NW
Washington, DC 20036
(publishers of *The China Business Review*)

academic institutes, libraries

East Coast

Fairbank Center for East Asian Research
Harvard University
1737 Cambridge Street
Cambridge, MA 02138

Harvard-Yenching Institute
2 Divinity Avenue
Cambridge, MA 02138

Institute for Sino-Soviet Studies
George Washington University
2130 H Street NW
Washington, DC 20052

Library of Congress
1st and Independence Streets SE
Washington, DC 20540

East Asian Collection
Yale University Library
New Haven, CT 06520

Wason Collection
Cornell University Library
Ithaca, NY 14853

East Asian Library
Columbia University
New York, NY 10027

Midwest

Association for Asian Studies
1 Lane Hall
University of Michigan
Ann Arbor, MI 48109
(publishers of *Journal of Asian Studies*)

Far Eastern Library
Joseph Regenstein Library
University of Chicago
Chicago, IL 60637

Asian Library
University of Illinois
Urbana, IL 61801

Asia Library
University of Michigan
Ann Arbor, MI 48109

West Coast

Center for Chinese Studies
University of California
2223 Fulton Street
Berkeley, CA 94720

Oriental Library
University of California at Los Angeles
Los Angeles, CA 90024

East Asiatic Library
University of California
Berkeley, CA 94720

East Asia Library
University of Washington
Seattle, WA 98195

East Asian Collection
Hoover Institution on War, Revolution
and Peace
Stanford University
Stanford, CA 94305

East-West Center Library
1777 East-West Road
Honolulu, HI 96848

other

Coordination Council for North American Affairs
Office in the United States of America
5161 River Road
Bethesda, MD 20816

National Committee on US-China Relations
777 UN Plaza
New York, NY 10017
(publishers of *Notes from the National
Committee*)

Committee on Scholarly Communication with
the People's Republic of China
National Academy of Sciences
2101 Constitution Avenue NW
Washington, DC 20418

National Technical Information Service (NTIS)
US Department of Commerce
Springfield, VA 22161
(US government press and radio translations
from China)

C.A.

Wade-Giles / Pinyin conversion tables

(a) WADE-GILES/PINYIN

W-G	Pinyin	W-G	Pinyin	W-G	Pinyin	W-G	Pinyin	W-G	Pinyin	W-G	Pinyin	W-G	Pinyin
a	a	chun	zhun	i	yi	lei	lei	nun	nen	shu	shu	ts'en	cen
ai	ai	ch'un	chun			leng	leng	nung	nong	shua	shua	tseng	zeng
an	an	chung	zhong	jan	ran	li	li	nü	nü	shuai	shuai	ts'eng	ceng
ang	ang	ch'ung	chong	jang	rang	lia	lia	nüeh	nüe	shuan	shuan	tso	zuo
ao	ao	chü	ju	jao	rao	liang	liang			shuang	shuang	ts'o	cuo
		ch'ü	qu	je	re	liao	liao	o	e	shui	shui	tsou	zou
cha	zha	chüan	juan	jen	ren	lieh	lie	ou	ou	shun	shun	ts'ou	cou
ch'a	cha	ch'üan	quan	jeng	reng	lien	lian			shuo	shuo	tsu	zu
chai	zhai	chüeh	jue	jih	ri	lin	lin	pa	ba	so	suo	ts'u	cu
ch'ai	chai	ch'üeh	que	jo	ruo	ling	ling	p'a	pa	sou	sou	tsuan	zuan
chan	zhan	chün	jun	jou	rou	liu	liu	pai	bai	ssu	si	ts'uan	cuan
ch'an	chan	ch'ün	qun	ju	ru	lo	luo	p'ai	pai	su	su	tsui	zui
chang	zhang			juan	ruan	lou	lou	pan	ban	suan	suan	ts'ui	cui
ch'ang	chang	en	en	jui	rui	lu	lu	p'an	pan	sui	sui	tsun	zun
chao	zhao	eng	eng	jun	run	luan	luan	pang	bang	sun	sun	ts'un	cun
ch'ao	chao	erh	er	jung	rong	lun	lun	p'ang	pang	sung	song	tsung	zong
che	zhe					lung	long	pao	bao			ts'ung	cong
ch'e	che	fa	fa	ka	ga	lü	lü	p'ao	pao	ta	da	tu	du
chei	zhei	fan	fan	k'a	ka	lüan	luan	pei	bei	t'a	ta	t'u	tu
chen	zhen	fang	fang	kai	gai	lüeh	lüe	p'ei	pei	tai	dai	tuan	duan
ch'en	chen	fei	fei	k'ai	kai			pen	ben	t'ai	tai	t'uan	tuan
cheng	zheng	fen	fen	kan	gan	ma	ma	p'en	pen	tan	dan	tui	dui
ch'eng	cheng	feng	feng	k'an	kan	mai	mai	peng	beng	t'an	tan	t'ui	tui
chi	ji	fo	fo	kang	gang	man	man	p'eng	peng	tang	dang	tun	dun
ch'i	qi	fou	fou	k'ang	kang	mang	mang	pi	bi	t'ang	tang	t'un	tun
chia	jia	fu	fu	kao	gao	mao	mao	p'i	pi	tao	dao	tung	dong
ch'ia	qia			k'ao	kao	mei	mei	piao	biao	t'ao	tao	t'ung	tong
chiang	jiang	ha	ha	kei	gei	men	men	p'iao	piao	te	de	tzu	zi
ch'iang	qiang	hai	hai	ken	gen	meng	meng	pieh	bie	t'e	te	tz'u	ci
chiao	jiao	han	han	k'en	ken	mi	mi	p'ieh	pie	tei	dei		
ch'iao	qiao	hang	hang	keng	geng	miao	miao	pien	bian	teng	deng	wa	wa
chieh	jie	hao	hao	k'eng	keng	mieh	mie	p'ien	pian	t'eng	teng	wai	wai
ch'ieh	qie	hei	hei	ko	ge	mien	mian	pin	bin	ti	di	wan	wan
chien	jian	hen	hen	k'o	ke	min	min	p'in	pin	t'i	ti	wang	wang
ch'ien	qian	heng	heng	kou	gou	ming	ming	ping	bing	tiao	diao	wei	wei
chih	zhi	ho	he	k'ou	kou	miu	miu	p'ing	ping	t'iao	tiao	wen	wen
ch'ih	chi	hou	hou	ku	gu	mo	mo	po	bo	tieh	die	weng	weng
chin	jin	hsi	xi	k'u	ku	mou	mou	p'o	po	t'ieh	tie	wo	wo
ch'in	qin	hsia	xia	kua	gua	mu	mu	p'ou	pou	tien	dian	wu	wu
ching	jing	hsiang	xiang	k'ua	kua			pu	bu	t'ien	tian		
ch'ing	qing	hsiao	xiao	kuai	guai	na	na	p'u	pu	ting	ding	ya	ya
chiu	jiu	hsieh	xie	k'uai	kuai	nai	nai			t'ing	ting	yai	yai
ch'iu	qiu	hsien	xian	kuan	guan	nan	nan	sa	sa	tiu	diu	yang	yang
chiung	jiong	hsin	xin	k'uan	kuan	nang	nang	sai	sai	to	duo	yao	yao
ch'iung	qiong	hsing	xing	kuang	guang	nao	nao	san	san	t'o	tuo	yeh	ye
cho	zhuo	hsiu	xiu	k'uang	kuang	ne	ne	sang	sang	tou	dou	yen	yan
ch'o	chuo	hsiung	xiong	kuei	gui	nei	nei	sao	sao	t'ou	tou	yin	yin
chou	zhou	hsü	xu	k'uei	kui	nen	nen	se	se	tsa	za	ying	ying
ch'ou	chou	hsüan	xuan	kun	gun	neng	neng	sen	sen	ts'a	ca	yu	you
chu	zhu	hsüeh	xue	k'un	kun	ni	ni	seng	seng	tsai	zai	yung	yong
ch'u	chu	hsün	xun	kung	gong	niang	niang	sha	sha	ts'ai	cai	yü	yu
chua	zhua	hu	hu	k'ung	kong	niao	niao	shai	shai	tsan	zan	yüan	yuan
ch'ua	chua	hua	hua	kuo	guo	nieh	nie	shan	shan	ts'an	can	yüeh	yue
chuai	zhuai	huai	huai	k'uo	kuo	nien	nian	shang	shang	tsang	zang	yün	yun
ch'uai	chuai	huan	huan			nin	nin	shao	shao	ts'ang	cang		
chuan	zhuan	huang	huang	la	la	ning	ning	she	she	tsao	zao		
ch'uan	chuan	hui	hui	lai	lai	niu	niu	shei	shei	ts'ao	cao		
chuang	zhuang	hun	hun	lan	lan	no	nuo	shen	shen	tse	ze		
ch'uang	chuang	hung	hong	lang	lang	nou	nou	sheng	sheng	ts'e	ce		
chui	zhui	huo	huo	lao	lao	nu	nu	shih	shi	tsei	zei		
ch'ui	chui			le	le	nuan	nuan	shou	shou	tsen	zen		

(b) PINYIN/WADE-GILES

Pinyin	W-G	Pinyin	W-G	Pinyin	W-G	Pinyin	W-G	Pinyin	W-G	Pinyin	W-G	Pinyin	W-G
a	a	dan	tan	hei	hei	lie	lieh	pan	p'an	shen	shen	xu	hsü
ai	ai	dang	tang	hen	hen	lin	lin	pang	p'ang	sheng	sheng	xuan	hsüan
an	an	dao	tao	heng	heng	ling	ling	pao	p'ao	shi	shih	xue	hsüeh
ang	ang	de	te	hong	hung	liu	liu	pei	p'ei	shou	shou	xun	hsün
ao	ao	dei	tei	hou	hou	long	lung	pen	p'en	shu	shu		
		deng	teng	hu	hu	lou	lou	peng	p'eng	shua	shua	ya	ya
ba	pa	di	ti	hua	hua	lu	lu	pi	p'i	shuai	shuai	yai	yai
bai	pai	dian	tien	huai	huai	lü	lü	pian	p'ien	shuan	shuan	yan	yen
ban	pan	diao	tiao	huan	huan	luan	luan/lüan	piao	p'iao	shuang	shuang	yang	yang
bang	pang	die	tieh	huang	huang	lüe	lüeh	pie	p'ieh	shui	shui	yao	yao
bao	pao	ding	ting	hui	hui	lun	lun	pin	p'in	shun	shun	ye	yeh
bei	pei	diu	tiu	hun	hun	luo	lo	ping	p'ing	shuo	shuo	yi	i
ben	pen	dong	tung	huo	huo			po	p'o	si	ssu	yin	yin
beng	peng	dou	tou			ma	ma	pou	p'ou	song	sung	ying	ying
bi	pi	du	tu	ji	chi	mai	mai	pu	p'u	sou	sou	yong	yung
bian	pien	duan	tuan	jia	chia	man	man			su	su	you	yu
biao	piao	dui	tui	jian	chien	mang	mang	qi	ch'i	suan	suan	yu	yü
bie	pieh	dun	tun	jiang	chiang	mao	mao	qia	ch'ia	sui	sui	yuan	yüan
bin	pin	duo	to	jiao	chiao	mei	mei	qian	ch'ien	sun	sun	yue	yüeh
bing	ping			jie	chieh	men	men	qiang	ch'iang	suo	so	yun	yün
bo	po	e	o	jin	chin	meng	meng	qiao	ch'iao				
bu	pu	en	en	jing	ching	mi	mi	qie	ch'ieh	ta	t'a	za	tsa
		eng	eng	jiong	chiung	mian	mien	qin	ch'in	tai	t'ai	zai	tsai
ca	ts'a	er	erh	jiu	chiu	miao	miao	qing	ch'ing	tan	t'an	zan	tsan
cai	ts'ai			ju	chü	mie	mieh	qiong	ch'iung	tang	t'ang	zang	tsang
can	ts'an	fa	fa	juan	chüan	min	min	qiu	ch'iu	tao	t'ao	zao	tsao
cang	ts'ang	fan	fan	jue	chüeh	ming	ming	qu	ch'ü	te	t'e	ze	tse
cao	ts'ao	fang	fang	jun	chün	miu	miu	quan	ch'üan	teng	t'eng	zei	tsei
ce	ts'e	fei	fei			mo	mo	que	ch'üeh	ti	t'i	zen	tsen
cen	ts'en	fen	fen	ka	k'a	mou	mou	qun	ch'ün	tian	t'ien	zeng	tseng
ceng	ts'eng	feng	feng	kai	k'ai	mu	mu			tiao	t'iao	zha	cha
cha	ch'a	fo	fo	kan	k'an			ran	jan	tie	t'ieh	zhai	chai
chai	ch'ai	fou	fou	kang	k'ang	na	na	rang	jang	ting	t'ing	zhan	chan
chan	ch'an	fu	fu	kao	k'ao	nai	nai	rao	jao	tong	t'ung	zhang	chang
chang	ch'ang			ke	k'o	nan	nan	re	je	tou	t'ou	zhao	chao
chao	ch'ao	ga	ka	ken	k'en	nang	nang	ren	jen	tu	t'u	zhe	che
che	ch'e	gai	kai	keng	k'eng	nao	nao	reng	jeng	tuan	t'uan	zhei	chei
chen	ch'en	gan	kan	kong	k'ung	ne	ne	ri	jih	tui	t'ui	zhen	chen
cheng	ch'eng	gang	kang	kou	k'ou	nei	nei	rong	jung	tun	t'un	zheng	cheng
chi	ch'ih	gao	kao	ku	k'u	nen	nen/nun	rou	jou	tuo	t'o	zhi	chih
chong	ch'ung	ge	ko	kua	k'ua	neng	neng	ru	ju			zhong	chung
chou	ch'ou	gei	kei	kuai	k'uai	ni	ni	ruan	juan	wa	wa	zhou	chou
chu	ch'u	gen	ken	kuan	k'uan	nian	nien	rui	jui	wai	wai	zhu	chu
chua	ch'ua	geng	keng	kuang	k'uang	niang	niang	run	jun	wan	wan	zhua	chua
chuai	ch'uai	gong	kung	kui	k'uei	niao	niao	ruo	jo	wang	wang	zhuai	chuai
chuan	ch'uan	gou	kou	kun	k'un	nie	nieh			wei	wei	zhuan	chuan
chuang	ch'uang	gu	ku	kuo	k'uo	nin	nin	sa	sa	wen	wen	zhuang	chuang
chui	ch'ui	gua	kua			ning	ning	sai	sai	weng	weng	zhui	chui
chun	ch'un	guai	kuai	la	la	niu	niu	san	san	wo	wo	zhun	chun
chuo	ch'o	guan	kuan	lai	lai	nong	nung	sang	sang	wu	wu	zhuo	cho
ci	tz'u	guang	kuang	lan	lan	nou	nou	sao	sao			zi	tzu
cong	ts'ung	gui	kuei	lang	lang	nu	nu	se	se	xi	hsi	zong	tsung
cou	ts'ou	gun	kun	lao	lao	nü	nü	sen	sen	xia	hsia	zou	tsou
cu	ts'u	guo	kuo	le	le	nuan	nuan	seng	seng	xian	hsien	zu	tsu
cuan	ts'uan			lei	lei	nüe	nüeh	sha	sha	xiang	hsiang	zuan	tsuan
cui	ts'ui	ha	ha	leng	leng	nuo	no	shai	shai	xiao	hsiao	zui	tsui
cun	ts'un	hai	hai	li	li			shan	shan	xie	hsieh	zun	tsun
cuo	ts'o	han	han	lia	lia	ou	ou	shang	shang	xin	hsin	zuo	tso
		hang	hang	lian	lien			shao	shao	xing	hsing		
da	ta	hao	hao	liang	liang	pa	p'a	she	she	xiong	hsiung		
dai	tai	he	ho	liao	liao	pai	p'ai	shei	shei	xiu	hsiu		

C.A.

Transcriptions of selected place names in three orthographies

(Alternative, obsolete and historical names are shown in brackets)

PINYIN	WADE-GILES	POST OFFICE	PINYIN	WADE-GILES	POST OFFICE
Anhui	An-hui	Anhwei	Liaoning	Liao-ning	Liaoning
Anqing	An-ch'ing	Anking	Nanchang	Nan-ch'ang	Nanchang
Aomen	Ao-men	Macao	Nanjing (Yingtian)	Nan-ching	Nanking
Beijing (Shuntian)	Pei-ching	Peking (Peiping)	Nanning	Nan-ning	Nanning
Changchun	Ch'ang-ch'un	Changchun (Hsinking)	Nei Menggu	Nei Meng-ku	Inner Mongolia
Changjiang	Ch'ang-chiang	(Yangtze kiang)	Ningbo	Ning-po	Ningpo
Changsha	Ch'ang-sha	Changsha	Ningxia	Ning-hsia	Ningsia, Ninghia
Chaozhou	Ch'ao-chou	Chaochow (Teochiu)	Qingdao	Ch'ing-tao	Tsingtao
Chengdu	Ch'eng-tu	Chengtu	Qinghai	Ch'ing-hai	Tsinghai
Chengte	Ch'eng-te	(Jehol)	Qiqihar	Ch'i-ch'i-ha-erh	Tsitsihar
Chongqing	Ch'ung-ch'ing	Chungking	Shaanxi	Shan-hsi	Shensi
Dalian (Lüda)	Ta-lien	(Dairen, Dalny)	Shandong	Shan-tung	Shantung
Fujian	Fu-chien	Fukien (Hokkien)	Shanghai	Shang-hai	Shanghai
Fuzhou	Fu-chou	Foochow	Shantou	Shan-t'ou	Swatow
Gansu	Kan-su	Kansu	Shanxi	Shan-hsi	Shansi
Guangdong	Kuang-tung	Kwangtung	Shaoxing	Shao-hsing	Shaohing
Guangxi	Kuang-hsi	Kwangsi	Shenyang	Shen-yang	(Mukden, Fengtien, Shengking)
Guangzhou	Kuang-chou	Canton	Shijiazhuang	Shih-chia-chuang	Shihchiachuang
Guilin	Kuei-lin	Kweilin	Sichuan	Ssu-ch'uan	Szechwan
Guiyang	Kuei-yang	Kweiyang	Suzhou	Su-chou	Soochow
Guizhou	Kuei-chou	Kweichow	Taibei	T'ai-pei	Taipeh
Haikou	Hai-k'ou	Hoihow (Kiungchow)	Taiwan	T'ai-wan	Taiwan (Formosa)
Hainan	Hai-nan	Hainan	Taiyuan	T'ai-yüan	Taiyuan
Hangzhou	Hang-chou	Hangchow	Tianjin	T'ien-chin	Tientsin
Harbin	Ha-erh-pin	Harbin	Ürümqi	Wu-lu-mu-ch'i	Urumchi (Tihwa)
Hebei	Ho-pei	Hopeh	Wuhan	Wu-han	(Wuchang, Hanyang, Hankow)
Hefei	Ho-fei	(Luchow)	Wuxi	Wu-hsi	Wusih
Heilongjiang	Hei-lung-chiang	Heilungkiang	Xi'an (Chang'an)	Hsi-an	Sian
Henan	Ho-nan	Honan	Xiamen	Hsia-men	Amoy
Hohhot	Hu-ho-hao-t'e	(Kweihwa, Suiyuan, Kweisui)	Xianggang	Hsiang-kang	Hong Kong
Huang He	Huang-ho	Hwang ho, Yellow River	Xigazê	Jih-k'a-tse	Shigatse
Hubei	Hu-pei	Hupeh	Xining	Hsi-ning	Sining
Hunan	Hu-nan	Hunan	Xinjiang	Hsin-chiang	Sinkiang
Jiangsu	Chiang-su	Kiangsu	Xizang	Hsi-tsang	Tibet
Jiangxi	Chiang-hsi	Kiangsi	Yan'an	Yen-an	Yenan
Jilin	Chi-lin	Kirin	Yantai	Yen-t'ai	(Chefoo, Tengchow)
Jinan	Chi-nan	Tsinan	Yinchuan	Yin-ch'uan	Yinchwan
Jiujiang	Chiu-chiang	Kiukiang	Yingkou	Ying-k'ou	(Newchwang)
Kaifeng (Bianjing)	K'ai-feng	Kaifeng	Yunnan	Yün-nan	Yunnan
Kashi	K'a-shih	Kashgar	Zhangjiakou	Chang-chia-k'ou	(Kalgan)
Kunming	K'un-ming	Kunming	Zhejiang	Che-chiang	Chekiang
Lüshun	Lü-shun	(Port Arthur)	Zhenjiang	Chen-chiang	Chinkiang
Lanzhou	Lan-chou	Lanchow	Zhengzhou	Cheng-chou	Chengchow
Lhasa	La-sa	Lhasa	Zunyi	Tsun-i	Tsunyi

C.A.

METHODS OF SIMPLIFYING CHARACTERS

Description	Examples
Reviving an ancient form	众(衆) crowd　　丰(豐) abundant　　尘(塵) dust
Standardizing variant forms	于(於) in; on; at　　斗(鬥、鬭、閗) fight　　亩(畝畆畮畂卧畞) (Chinese) acre

Normalizing non-standard forms

Cursive Script	专(專) specialize　　书(書) book　　为(為、爲) be; do
Running Script	学(學、斈) study　　会(會) assemble　　应(應) respond
Unorthodox Characters	听(聽) listen　　声(聲) sound　　旧(舊) old

Abbreviating components

Left	动(動) move　　龄(齡) age
Right	仅(僅) only　　协(協) accord
Left & right	归(歸) return　　临(臨) arrive
Bottom	仓(倉) warehouse　　枣(棗) dates
Overall	农(農、辳) agriculture　　齐(齊) uniform

Deleting

Left	务(務) affairs　　亏(虧) deficiency
Right	亲(親) relative　　类(類) category
Top	币(幣) currency　　电(電) electricity
Bottom	业(業) trade　　巩(鞏) consolidate
Middle	宁(寧、甯) peaceful　　奋(奮) impetuous
Substantial	厂(廠、厰) factory　　飞(飛) fly　　关(關、関) a frontier pass; shut

Assigning dual or triple roles

里 ⟨ 里 (Chinese) mile / 裏 inside

干 ⟨ 干 offend / 乾 dry / 幹 do; work

系 ⟨ 系 system / 係 be / 繫 fasten

New coinages

Compound Ideogram into Phonogram	艺(藝) art　　邮(郵) post
Phonogram into Compound Ideogram	泪(淚) tears　　卫(衛、衞) defend
Changing radical	脏(骯) dirty
Changing phonetic	忧(憂) worry　　拥(擁) support
Changing both radical & phonetic	惊(驚) startle　　护(護) protect
Others	历(厲) strict　　扰(擾) disturb　　穷(窮) poor

Chinese Communist Party Organizations

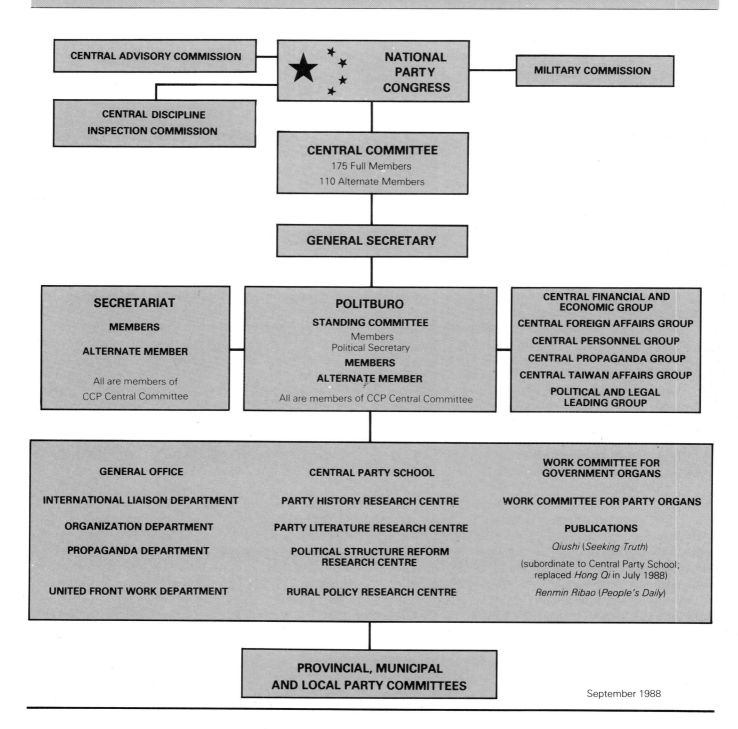

CENTRAL ADVISORY COMMISSION

NATIONAL PARTY CONGRESS

MILITARY COMMISSION

CENTRAL DISCIPLINE INSPECTION COMMISSION

CENTRAL COMMITTEE
175 Full Members
110 Alternate Members

GENERAL SECRETARY

SECRETARIAT

MEMBERS

ALTERNATE MEMBER

All are members of CCP Central Committee

POLITBURO
STANDING COMMITTEE
Members
Political Secretary
MEMBERS
ALTERNATE MEMBER

All are members of CCP Central Committee

CENTRAL FINANCIAL AND ECONOMIC GROUP

CENTRAL FOREIGN AFFAIRS GROUP

CENTRAL PERSONNEL GROUP

CENTRAL PROPAGANDA GROUP

CENTRAL TAIWAN AFFAIRS GROUP

POLITICAL AND LEGAL LEADING GROUP

GENERAL OFFICE

INTERNATIONAL LIAISON DEPARTMENT

ORGANIZATION DEPARTMENT

PROPAGANDA DEPARTMENT

UNITED FRONT WORK DEPARTMENT

CENTRAL PARTY SCHOOL

PARTY HISTORY RESEARCH CENTRE

PARTY LITERATURE RESEARCH CENTRE

POLITICAL STRUCTURE REFORM RESEARCH CENTRE

RURAL POLICY RESEARCH CENTRE

WORK COMMITTEE FOR GOVERNMENT ORGANS

WORK COMMITTEE FOR PARTY ORGANS

PUBLICATIONS

Qiushi (*Seeking Truth*)

(subordinate to Central Party School; replaced *Hong Qi* in July 1988)

Renmin Ribao (*People's Daily*)

PROVINCIAL, MUNICIPAL AND LOCAL PARTY COMMITTEES

September 1988

Government of the People's Republic of China

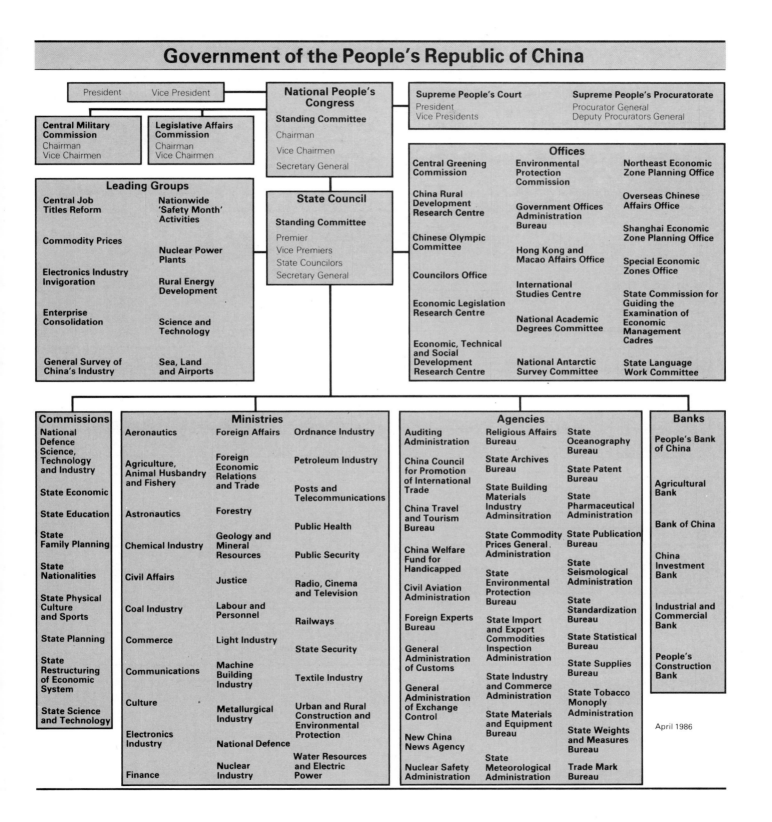

President | Vice President

National People's Congress
Standing Committee
Chairman
Vice Chairmen
Secretary General

Supreme People's Court
President
Vice Presidents

Supreme People's Procuratorate
Procurator General
Deputy Procurators General

Central Military Commission
Chairman
Vice Chairmen

Legislative Affairs Commission
Chairman
Vice Chairmen

Leading Groups

Central Job Titles Reform

Commodity Prices

Electronics Industry Invigoration

Enterprise Consolidation

General Survey of China's Industry

Nationwide 'Safety Month' Activities

Nuclear Power Plants

Rural Energy Development

Science and Technology

Sea, Land and Airports

State Council
Standing Committee
Premier
Vice Premiers
State Councilors
Secretary General

Offices

Central Greening Commission

China Rural Development Research Centre

Chinese Olympic Committee

Councilors Office

Economic Legislation Research Centre

Economic, Technical and Social Development Research Centre

Environmental Protection Commission

Government Offices Administration Bureau

Hong Kong and Macao Affairs Office

International Studies Centre

National Academic Degrees Committee

National Antarctic Survey Committee

Northeast Economic Zone Planning Office

Overseas Chinese Affairs Office

Shanghai Economic Zone Planning Office

Special Economic Zones Office

State Commission for Guiding the Examination of Economic Management Cadres

State Language Work Committee

Commissions

National Defence Science, Technology and Industry

State Economic

State Education

State Family Planning

State Nationalities

State Physical Culture and Sports

State Planning

State Restructuring of Economic System

State Science and Technology

Ministries

Aeronautics

Agriculture, Animal Husbandry and Fishery

Astronautics

Chemical Industry

Civil Affairs

Coal Industry

Commerce

Communications

Culture

Electronics Industry

Finance

Foreign Affairs

Foreign Economic Relations and Trade

Forestry

Geology and Mineral Resources

Justice

Labour and Personnel

Light Industry

Machine Building Industry

Metallurgical Industry

National Defence

Nuclear Industry

Ordnance Industry

Petroleum Industry

Posts and Telecommunications

Public Health

Public Security

Radio, Cinema and Television

Railways

State Security

Textile Industry

Urban and Rural Construction and Environmental Protection

Water Resources and Electric Power

Agencies

Auditing Administration

China Council for Promotion of International Trade

China Travel and Tourism Bureau

China Welfare Fund for Handicapped

Civil Aviation Administration

Foreign Experts Bureau

General Administration of Customs

General Administration of Exchange Control

New China News Agency

Nuclear Safety Administration

Religious Affairs Bureau

State Archives Bureau

State Building Materials Industry Adminsitration

State Commodity Prices General Administration

State Environmental Protection Bureau

State Import and Export Commodities Inspection Administration

State Industry and Commerce Administration

State Materials and Equipment Bureau

State Meteorological Administration

State Oceanography Bureau

State Patent Bureau

State Pharmaceutical Administration

State Publication Bureau

State Seismological Administration

State Standardization Bureau

State Statistical Bureau

State Supplies Bureau

State Tobacco Monoply Administration

State Weights and Measures Bureau

Trade Mark Bureau

Banks

People's Bank of China

Agricultural Bank

Bank of China

China Investment Bank

Industrial and Commercial Bank

People's Construction Bank

April 1986

Military Organizations of the People's Republic of China

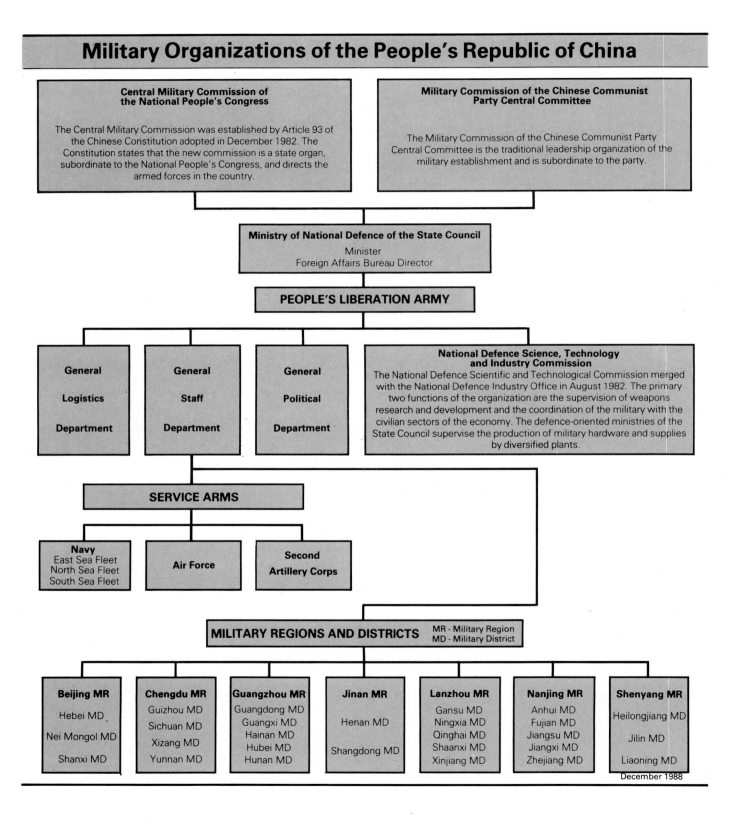

Central Military Commission of the National People's Congress

The Central Military Commission was established by Article 93 of the Chinese Constitution adopted in December 1982. The Constitution states that the new commission is a state organ, subordinate to the National People's Congress, and directs the armed forces in the country.

Military Commission of the Chinese Communist Party Central Committee

The Military Commission of the Chinese Communist Party Central Committee is the traditional leadership organization of the military establishment and is subordinate to the party.

Ministry of National Defence of the State Council
Minister
Foreign Affairs Bureau Director

PEOPLE'S LIBERATION ARMY

General Logistics Department

General Staff Department

General Political Department

National Defence Science, Technology and Industry Commission
The National Defence Scientific and Technological Commission merged with the National Defence Industry Office in August 1982. The primary two functions of the organization are the supervision of weapons research and development and the coordination of the military with the civilian sectors of the economy. The defence-oriented ministries of the State Council supervise the production of military hardware and supplies by diversified plants.

SERVICE ARMS

Navy
East Sea Fleet
North Sea Fleet
South Sea Fleet

Air Force

Second Artillery Corps

MILITARY REGIONS AND DISTRICTS   MR - Military Region
MD - Military District

Beijing MR
Hebei MD
Nei Mongol MD
Shanxi MD

Chengdu MR
Guizhou MD
Sichuan MD
Xizang MD
Yunnan MD

Guangzhou MR
Guangdong MD
Guangxi MD
Hainan MD
Hubei MD
Hunan MD

Jinan MR
Henan MD
Shangdong MD

Lanzhou MR
Gansu MD
Ningxia MD
Qinghai MD
Shaanxi MD
Xinjiang MD

Nanjing MR
Anhui MD
Fujian MD
Jiangsu MD
Jiangxi MD
Zhejiang MD

Shenyang MR
Heilongjiang MD
Jilin MD
Liaoning MD

December 1988

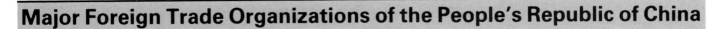

Major Foreign Trade Organizations of the People's Republic of China

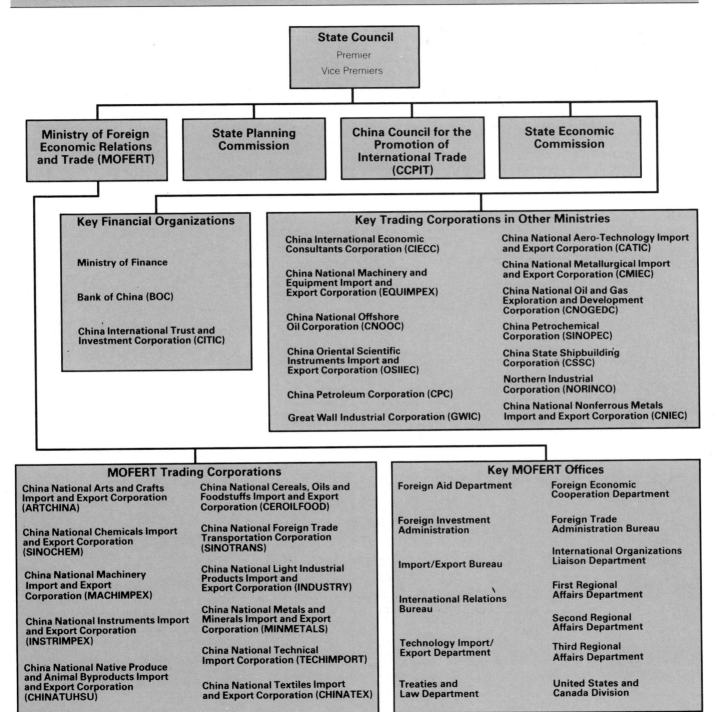

State Council
Premier
Vice Premiers

Ministry of Foreign Economic Relations and Trade (MOFERT)

State Planning Commission

China Council for the Promotion of International Trade (CCPIT)

State Economic Commission

Key Financial Organizations

Ministry of Finance

Bank of China (BOC)

China International Trust and Investment Corporation (CITIC)

Key Trading Corporations in Other Ministries

China International Economic Consultants Corporation (CIECC)

China National Machinery and Equipment Import and Export Corporation (EQUIMPEX)

China National Offshore Oil Corporation (CNOOC)

China Oriental Scientific Instruments Import and Export Corporation (OSIIEC)

China Petroleum Corporation (CPC)

Great Wall Industrial Corporation (GWIC)

China National Aero-Technology Import and Export Corporation (CATIC)

China National Metallurgical Import and Export Corporation (CMIEC)

China National Oil and Gas Exploration and Development Corporation (CNOGEDC)

China Petrochemical Corporation (SINOPEC)

China State Shipbuilding Corporation (CSSC)

Northern Industrial Corporation (NORINCO)

China National Nonferrous Metals Import and Export Corporation (CNIEC)

MOFERT Trading Corporations

China National Arts and Crafts Import and Export Corporation (ARTCHINA)

China National Chemicals Import and Export Corporation (SINOCHEM)

China National Machinery Import and Export Corporation (MACHIMPEX)

China National Instruments Import and Export Corporation (INSTRIMPEX)

China National Native Produce and Animal Byproducts Import and Export Corporation (CHINATUHSU)

China National Cereals, Oils and Foodstuffs Import and Export Corporation (CEROILFOOD)

China National Foreign Trade Transportation Corporation (SINOTRANS)

China National Light Industrial Products Import and Export Corporation (INDUSTRY)

China National Metals and Minerals Import and Export Corporation (MINMETALS)

China National Technical Import Corporation (TECHIMPORT)

China National Textiles Import and Export Corporation (CHINATEX)

Key MOFERT Offices

Foreign Aid Department

Foreign Investment Administration

Import/Export Bureau

International Relations Bureau

Technology Import/Export Department

Treaties and Law Department

Foreign Economic Cooperation Department

Foreign Trade Administration Bureau

International Organizations Liaison Department

First Regional Affairs Department

Second Regional Affairs Department

Third Regional Affairs Department

United States and Canada Division

FURTHER READING

LAND AND RESOURCES

Almanac of China's Foreign Economic Relations and Trade 1987, Beijing, 1987.

C. Blunden and M. Elvin, *Cultural Atlas of China*, New York, 1983.

China, State Statistical Bureau, *Statistical Yearbook of China*, annual.

F. Fesharaki and D. Fridley, *China's Petroleum Industry in the International Context*, London and Boulder, 1986.

S. Feuchtwang and A. Hussain (eds.), *The Chinese Ecomomic Reforms*, London, 1983.

H.G. Gloria, D.H. Harnisch and F. Braunann, *Die Energie und Rohstoffwirtschaft der Volksrepublik China*, Essen, 1985.

C. Howe, *China's Economy: A Basic Guide*, London, 1978.

Hsueh Mu-ch'iao et al., *Almanac of China's Economy*, annual.

R. Kirkby, *Urbanisation in China*, London, 1985.

F. Leeming, *Rural China Today*, London, 1985.

C.W. Pannell and L.J.C. Ma, *China: The Geography of Development and Modernization*, London, 1983.

C. Riskin, *China's Political Economy*, Oxford, 1987.

L. Ross, *Environmental Policy in China*, Bloomington, 1988.

V. Smil, *The Bad Earth: Environmental Degradation in China*, Armonk, 1984.

V. Smil, *Energy in China's Modernization: Advances and Limitations*, Armonk, 1988.

Sun Jingzhi (ed.), *The Economic Geography of China*, Hong Kong, 1986.

T.H. Tregear, *China: a Geographical Survey*, rev. edn, London, 1980.

Y-F. Tuan, *China*, Chicago, 1969.

US Congress, Joint Economic Committee, *China's Economy Looks Toward the Year 2000*, Washington D.C., 1987.

K.R. Walker, *Food Grain Procurement and Consumption in China*, Cambridge, 1984.

World Bank, *China: Long-term Development Issues and Options*, Washington D.C., 1985.

T. Wright, *Coal Mining in China's Economy and Society, 1895–1937*, Cambridge, 1984.

Zhao Songqiao, *Physical Geography of China*, Beijing, 1986; New York, 1987.

PEOPLES

G.T. Bowles, *The People of Asia*, London and New York, 1977.

L. P. Chia, The *Cave Home of Peking Man*, Beijing, 1975.

C.S. Coon, *The Living Races of Man*, New York, 1965.

J.W. Cushman and Wang Gungwu (eds.), *Changing Chinese Identities in Southeast Asia*, Hong Kong, 1988.

W.W. Howells, *Evolution of the Genus Homo*, Reading, Mass., 1973.

F. Ikawa-Smith (ed.), *Early Paleolithic in South and East Asia*, The Hague and Paris, 1978.

L.Y.C. Lim and L.A.P. Gosling (eds.), *The Chinese in Southeast Asia*, 2 vols., Singapore, 1983.

A.C. Moule, *Christians in China Before the Year 1550*, London, 1972.

Wang Gungwu, *Community and Nation, Essays on Southeast Asia and the Chinese*, Singapore and Sydney, 1981.

SOCIETY

J. Banister, *China's Changing Population*, Stanford, 1988.

T. Bernstein, *Up to the Mountains and Down to the Villages: The Transfer of Youth from Urban to Rural China*, New Haven, 1977.

D.F. Bodde and C. Morris, *Law in Imperial China*, Cambridge, Mass., 1967.

A. Chan, *Children of Mao: Personality Development and Political Activism in the Red Guard Generation*, Seattle, 1985.

T-T. Ch'u, *Law and Society in Traditional China*, The Hague and Paris, 1961.

J.A. Cohen, R.R. Edwards and F.C. Chen (eds.), *Essays on China's Legal Tradition*, Princeton, 1980.

J.M. Cole, *Shaohsing*, Tucson, 1986.

D. Davis-Friedmann, *Long Lives: Chinese Elderly and the Communist Revolution*, Cambridge, Mass., 1983

P.B. Ebrey and J.L. Watson (eds.), *Kinship Organization in Late Imperial China, 1000–1940*, Berkeley, 1986.

D. Faure, *The Structure of Chinese Rural Society*, Hong Kong, 1986.

M. Goldman, *China's Intellectuals and the State: In Search of a New Relationship*, Harvard, 1987.

R. Hayhoe and M. Bastid, *China's Education and the Industrialized World: Studies in Cultural Transfer*, New York and Toronto, 1987.

G.E. Henderson and M.S. Cohen, *The Chinese Hospital*, New Haven, 1984.

G. Hershatter, *The Workers of Tianjin, 1900–1949*, Stanford, 1986.

E. Hong, *Sisters and Strangers: Women in the Shanghai Cotton Mills, 1919–1949*, Stanford, 1986.

K.C. Hsiao, *Rural China: Imperial Control in the Nineteenth Century*, Seattle, 1960.

Leng Shao-Chuen, *Criminal Justice in Post-Mao China: Analysis and Documents*, Albany, 1985.

R. Madsen, *Morality and Power in a Chinese Village*, Berkeley, 1984.

J. Needham and Lu Gwei-djen, *Celestial Lancets*, Cambridge, 1980.

W.L. Parish and M.K. Whyte, *Village and Family in Contemporary China*, Chicago, 1978.

E.S. Rawski, *Education and Popular Literacy in Ch'ing China*, Ann Arbor, 1979.

G. Rozman, *The Chinese Debate About Soviet Socialism*, Princeton, 1987.

G. Rozman, *A Mirror for Socialism: Soviet Criticisms of China*, Princeton, 1985.

G.W. Skinner (ed.), *The City in Late Imperial China*, Stanford, 1977.

G.W. Skinner (ed.), *The Study of Chinese Society: Essays by Maurice Freedman*, Stanford, 1979.

J.D. Spence, *The Death of Woman Wang*, New York, 1978.

A.F. Thurston, *Enemies of the People: The Ordeal of the Intellectuals in China's Great Cultural Revolution*, Harvard, 1988.

J. Unger, *Education Under Mao: Class and Competition in Cantor Schools, 1960–1980*, New York, 1982.

P.U. Unschuld, *Introductory Readings in Classical Chinese Medicine*, Dordrecht, 1988.

P.U. Unschuld, *Medicine in China. A History of Ideas*, Berkeley, 1985.

A.G. Walder, *Communist Neo-Traditionalism: Work and Authority in Chinese Industry*, Berkeley, 1986.

M.K. Whyte and W.L. Parish, *Urban Life in Contemporary China*, Chicago, 1984.

M. Wright, *The Last Stand of Chinese Conservatism: The T'ung-Chih Restoration, 1862–1874*, Stanford, 1957, 1969.

A.P. Wolf and Chieh-shan Huang, *Marriage and Adoption in China, 1845–1945*, Stanford, 1980.

THE CONTINUITY OF CHINA

General

W. Eberhard, *A History of China*, Berkeley, 1977.

M. Elvin, *The Pattern of the Chinese Past*, Stanford, 1973.

J. Gernet, *A History of Chinese Civilization*, Cambridge, 1982.

R. Huang, *China: a Macrohistory*, New York, 1989.

C.O. Hucker, *China's Imperial Past: An Introduction to Chinese History and Culture*, Stanford, 1975.

F.A. Kierman, Jr. (ed.) *Chinese Ways in Warfare*, Harvard, 1974.

W. Rodzinski, *A History of China*, 2 vols., Oxford, 1979, 1983.

G. Rozman (ed.), *The Modernization of China*, Princeton, 1981.

D. Twitchett and J.K. Fairbank (eds.), *The Cambridge History of China*, Cambridge, 1986– (continuing series).

Prehistory, Legend and Archaeology

S. Allan, *The Heir and the Sage: Dynastic Legend in Early China*, San Francisco and Taipei, 1981.

K.C. Chang, *The Archaeology of Ancient China*, 4th edn, New Haven and London, 1986.

K.C. Chang, *Art, Myth, and Ritual: The Path to Authority in Ancient China*, Cambridge, Mass., 1983.

M. Granet, *Chinese Civilization*, London, 1957.

Institute of Vertebrate Paleontology and Paleoanthropology, *Atlas of Primitive Man in China*, Beijing, 1980.

D.N. Keightley (ed.), *The Origins of Chinese Civilization*, Berkeley, Los Angeles and London, 1983.

Qian H. et al., *Out of China's Earth*, New York, 1981.

W. Watson, *Cultural Frontiers in Ancient East Asia*, Edinburgh, 1971.

R. Wu and J.W. Olsen, *Palaeoanthropology and Palaeolithic Archaeology in the People's Republic of China*, Orlando, 1985.

The Shang Dynasty

N. Barnard and T. Sato, *Metallurgical Remains of Ancient China*, Tokyo, 1975.

K.C. Chang, *Shang Civilization*, New Haven and London, 1980.

K.C. Chang (ed.), *Studies of Shang Archaeology*, New Haven and London, 1986.

H.G. Creel, *The Birth of China: A Study of the Formative Period of Chinese Civilization*, New York, 1937.

D.N. Keightley, *Sources of Shang History: The Oracle-Bone Inscriptions of Bronze Age China*, Berkeley, Los Angeles and London, 1978.

Li Chi, *Anyang*, Seattle, 1977.

J. Rawson, *Ancient China: Art and Archaeology*, London 1980.

Wen Fong, *The Great Bronze Age of China*, New York, 1980.

The Zhou Dynasty

K. C. Chang, *Early Chinese Civiization: Anthropological Perspectives*, Cambridge, Mass., 1976.

H.G. Creel, *The Origins of Statecraft in China*, vol. 1: *The Western Chou Empire*, Chicago and London, 1970.

H. Fingarette, *Confucius: The Secular as Sacred*, New York, 1972.

W. Fong (ed.), *The Great Bronze Age of China*, New York, 1980.

D.L. Hall and R.T. Ames, *Thinking Through Confucius*, Albany, 1987.

K-C. Hsiao, *A History of Chinese Political Thought, vol. 1: From the Beginnings to the Sixth Century AD*, Princeton, 1979.

C.-Y. Hsu, *Ancient China in Transition*, Stanford, 1965.

C.-Y. Hsu and K. Linduff, *Western Zhou Civilization*, New Haven and London, 1988.

Li Xueqin, *Eastern Zhou and Qin Civilizations*, trans. K.C. Chang, New Haven and London, 1986.

H. Maspero, *China in Antiquity*, trans. F.A. Kierman, Jr., Folkestone, 1978.

F.W. Mote, *Intellectual Foundations of China*, New York, 1971.

L.A. Schneider, *Ku Chieh-kang and China's New History: Nationalism and the Quest for Alternative Traditions*, Berkeley, Los Angeles and London, 1971.

B. Schwartz, *The World of Thought in Ancient China*, Cambridge, Mass. and London, 1985.

P. Wheatley, *The Pivot of the Four Quarters: A Preliminary Inquiry into the Origins and Character of the Ancient Chinese City*, Chicago and Edinburgh, 1971.

The Qin Dynasty

D. Bodde, *China's First Unifier*, Hong Kong, 1967.

A.F.P. Hulsewé, *Remnants of Ch'in Law*, Leiden, 1985.

D. Twitchett and M. Loewe (eds.), *The Cambridge History of China, vol. 1: The Ch'in and Han Empires 221 BC–AD 220*, Cambridge, 1986.

A. Waldron, *On the Wall*, Cambridge, 1990.

The Han Dynasty

T.-T. Ch'ü, *Han Social Structure*, ed. J.L. Dull, Seattle, 1972.

R. de Crespigny, *The Last of the Han*, Canberra, 1969.

R. de Crespigny, *Northern Frontier: The Policies and Strategies of the Later Han Empire*, Canberra, 1984.

H.H. Dubs, *History of the Former Han Dynasty, Vols 1–3*, Baltimore, 1938–55.

A.F.P. Hulsewé, *Remnants of Han Law*, Leiden, 1955.

M. Loewe, *Chinese Ideas of Life and Death: Faith, Myth and Reason in the Han Period (202 BC–AD 220)*, London, 1982.

M. Loewe, *Crisis and Conflict in Han China*, London, 1974.

M. Loewe, *Everyday Life in Early Imperial China During the Han Period, 202 BC–AD 220*, London, 1968.

M. Pirazzoli-t'Serstevens, *The Han Civilization of China*, Oxford, 1982.

M. Pirazzoli-t'Serstevens, *The Han Dynasty*, New York, 1980.

Wang Zhongshu, *Han Civilization*, New Haven and London, 1982.

B.Watson, *Ssu-ma Ch'ien, Grand Historian of China*, New York, 1958.

Y.-S. Yu, *Trade and Expansion in Han China*, Berkeley and Los Angeles, 1967.

Three Kingdoms, Qin, Northern And Southern Dynasties

A. Fang, *The Chronicle of the Three Kingdoms (220–265)*, Cambridge, Mass., 1952.

W.J.F. Jenner, *Memories of Loyang*, Oxford, 1981.

D.G. Johnson, *The Medieval Chinese Oligarchy*, Boulder, 1977.

M.C. Rogers, *The Chronicle of Fu Chien: A Case of Exemplar History*, Berkeley and Los Angeles, 1968.

The Sui Dynasty

W. Bingham, *The Founding of the T'ang Dynasty: The Fall of Sui and the Rise of T'ang*, Baltimore, 1941.

D. Twitchett (ed.), *The Cambridge History of China, Vol. 3, Part 1: Sui and T'ang China*, Cambridge, 1979, pp. 589–906.

A.F. Wright, *The Sui Dynasty: The Unification of China, AD 581–617*, New York, 1978.

A.F. Wright (ed.), 'Sui Yang-ti: Personality and Stereotype', in *The Confucian Persuasion*, Stanford, 1960.

The Tang Dynasty

R.W.L. Guisso, *Wu Tse-t'ien and the Politics of Legitimation in T'ang China*, Bellingham, Wash., 1978.

D. Herbert, *Examine the Honest, Appraise the Able*, Canberra, 1989.

D. McMullen, *State and Scholars in T'ang China*, Cambridge, 1988.

J.C. Perry and B.L. Smith (eds.), *Essays on T'ang Society*, Leiden, 1976.

L.E.R. Picken (ed.), *Music from the Tang Court, Fascicle 1*, Oxford, 1981; Fascicle 2, Cambridge, 1985. Continuing series.

E.G. Pulleyblank, *Background to the Rebellion of An Lu-shan*, London, 1955.

D. Twitchett, *The Rise of the Meritocracy in China*, London, 1975. (Chinese Society Lecture).

D. Twitchett and A.F. Wright (eds.), *Perspectives on the T'ang*, New Haven, 1973.

Wang Gungwu, *The Structure of Power in North China During the Five Dynasties*, Kuala Lumpur, 1963; Stanford, 1967.

H. Wechsler, *Offerings of Jade and Silk*, New Haven and London, 1985.

S. Weinstein, *Buddhism Under the T'ang*, Cambridge, 1987.

H.A. Wittfogel and Feng Chia-sheng, *History of Chinese Society: Liao (907–1125)*, Philadelphia, 1949.

The Song Dynasty

J.W. Chaffee, *The Thorny Gates of Learning in Sung China*, Cambridge, 1985.

Chang Ch'un-shu and Joan Smythe (trans.), *South China in the Twelfth Century*, Hong Kong, 1981.

P.B. Ebrey, *Family and Property in Sung China: Yuan Ts'ai's Precepts for Social Life*, Princeton, 1984.

M. Elvin (trans.), *Commerce and Society in Sung China*, Ann Arbor, 1970.

J. Gernet, *Daily Life in China and the Eve of the Mongol Invasion, 1215–1276*, Stanford, 1962.

J.W. Haeger, *Crisis and Change in Sung China*, Tucson, 1975.

R.P. Hymes, *Statesmen and Gentlemen: the Elite of Fu-chou, Chiang-hsi, in Northern and Southern Sung China*, Cambridge, 1986.

E.A. Kracke, *Civil Service in Sung China 960–1067*, Cambridge, Mass., 1953.

Y.Lin, *The Gay Genius: The Life and Times of Su Tungpo*, New York, 1947.

J.T.C. Liu, *China Turning Inward: Intellectual–Political Changes in the Early Twelfth Century*, Cambridge, Mass., 1988.

J.T.C. Liu, *Reform in Sung China*, Cambridge, Mass., 1959.

W.W. Lo, *An Introduction to the Civil Service of Sung China*, Honolulu, 1987.

L.E.R. Picken, 'Music for a Lion-Dance of the Sung Dynasty', in *Musica Asiatica*, vol. 4, L.E.R. Picken (ed.), Cambridge, 1984.

The Yuan Dynasty

D.C. Twitchett and H. Franke (eds.), *The Cambridge History of China, Vol. 6: Alien Regions and Border States, 710–1368*, Cambridge, in press.

Ch'ang-ch'un, *The Travels of an Alchemist*, trans. A. Waley, London.

J.W. Dardess, *Conquerors and Confucians*, New York and London, 1973.

Hok-lam Chan and W.T. de Bary (eds.), *Yüan Thought*, New York, 1982.

J.D. Langlois, Jr. (ed.), *China Under Mongol Rule*, Princeton, 1981.

S.E. Lee and W-K. Ho, *Chinese Art under the Mongols*, Cleveland, Ohio, 1968.

I. de Rachewiltz, *Papal Envoys to the Great Khans*, London, 1971.

M. Rossabi, *Khubilai Khan: His Life and Times*, Berkeley and London, 1988.

M. Rossabi (ed.), *China among Equals: The Middle Kingdom and its Neighbours, 10th–11th Centuries*, Berkeley, 1983.

C.R. Bawden, *The Modern History of Mongolia*, London, 1968.

The Ming Dynasty

J. Dennerline, *The Chia-ting Loyalists: Confucian Leadership and Social Change in Seventeenth-Century China*, New Haven, 1981.

E.T. Dreyer, *Early Ming China: A Political History 1355–1435*, Stanford, 1982.

L.C. Goodrich and C. Fang (eds.), *Dictionary of Ming Biography*, 2 vols., New York and London, 1976.

R. Huang, *1587, A Year of No Significance: The Ming Dynasty in Decline*, New Haven and London, 1981.

F.W. Mote and D. Twitchett (eds.), *The Cambridge History of China, Vol. 7: The Ming Dynasty, 1368–1644, Part 1*, Cambridge, 1988; Part 2, Cambridge, in press!

A.H. Plaks, *The Four Masterworks of the Ming Novel, Ssu-ta ch'i-shu*, Princeton, 1987.

L. Struve, *The Southern Ming, 1644–1662*, New Haven, 1984.

The Qing Dynasty

C.R. Bawden, *The Modern History of Mongolia*, London 1968.

T-T. Ch'ü, *Local Government in China Under the Ch'ing*, Cambridge, Mass., 1962.

P.A. Cohen, *Between Tradition and Modernity: Wang T'ao and Reform in Late Ch'ing China*, Cambridge, Mass., 1958.

B. Elman, *From Philosophy to Philology: Intellectual and Social Aspects of Change in Late Imperial China*, Cambridge, Mass., 1984.

J.W. Esherick, *The Origins of The Boxer Uprising*, Berkeley, 1987.

J.K. Fairbank (ed.), *Cambridge History of China, Vol. 10: Late Ching, 1800–1911, Part 1*, Cambridge, 1978.

J.K. Fairbank (ed.), *The Chinese World Order: Traditional China's Foreign Relations*, Cambridge, Mass., 1968.

J.K. Fairbank and Kwang-Ching Liu, *Cambridge History of China, Vol. 11: Late Ching, 1800–1911*, Part 2, Cambridge, 1980.

A. Feuerwerker, *China's Early Industrialization*, Cambridge, Mass., 1958.

R. K. Guy, *The Emperor's Four Treasuries: Scholars and the State in the Late Ch'ien-lung Era*, Cambridge, Mass., 1987.

P.-T. Ho, *The Ladder of Success in Imperial China: Aspects of Social Mobility, 1368–1911*, New York, 1962.

I.C.Y. Hsu, *China's Entrance into the Family of Nations: The Diplomatic Phase, 1858–1880*, Cambridge, Mass., 1960.

I.C.Y. Hsu, *The Rise of Modern China*, 3rd edn, New York, 1983.

A. W. Hummel (ed.), *Eminent Chinese of the Ch'ing Period*, Washington, 1943–4.

H.L. Kahn, *Monarchy in the Emperor's Eyes: Image and Reality in the Ch'ien-lung Reign*, Cambridge, Mass., 1971.

R.H.G. Lee, *The Manchurian Frontier in Ch'ing History*, Cambridge, Mass., 1970.

M. Mancall, *Russia and China: Their Diplomatic Relations to 1728*, Cambridge, Mass., 1970.

S. Naquin, *Millenarian Rebellion in China: The Eight Trigrams Uprising of 1813*, New Haven, 1976.

S. Naquin and E. Rawski, *Chinese Society in the Eighteenth Century*, New Haven, 1987.

Pu Yi, *From Emperor to Citizen*, trans. W.J.F. Jenner, Oxford, 1988.

M. Rossabi, *China and Inner Asia from 1368 to the Present Day*, London, 1975.

W.T. Rowe, *Hankow: Commerce and Society in a Chinese City, 1796–1889*, Stanford, 1984.

W.D. Shakabpa, *Tibet: A Political History*, New Haven, 1967.

G.W. Skinner (ed.), *The City in Late Imperial China*, Stanford, 1977.

R.J. Smith, *China's Cultural Heritage: The Ch'ing Dynasty, 1644–1911*, Boulder, 1983.

J.D. Spence and J.E. Wills, Jr. (eds.), *From Ming to Ch'ing: Conquest, Region, and Continuity in Seventeenth-Century China*, New Haven and London, 1979.

F. Wakeman, Jr., *The Fall of Imperial China*, New York, 1975.

F. Wakeman, Jr., *The Great Enterprise: The Manchu Reconstruction of Imperial Order in Seventeenth-Century China*, 2 vols., Berkeley and Los Angeles, 1985.

F. Wakeman, Jr. and C. Grant, *Conflict and Control in Late Imperial China*, Berkeley, 1975.

P.-E. Will, *Bureaucratie et famine en Chine au 18e siècle*, Paris, 1980.

M. Zelin, *The Magistrate's Tael: Rationalizing Fiscal Reform in Eighteenth-Century Ch'ing China*, Berkeley, 1984.

The Republican Period

L. Bianco, *Origins of the Chinese Revolution, 1915–1949*, Stanford, 1971.

J. Ch'en, *Yuan Shih-k'ai, 1959-1916*, Stanford, 1972.

H.-S. Ch'i, *Nationalist China at War: Military Defeats and Political Collapse, 1937–1945*, Ann Arbor, 1982.

T.-T. Chow, *The May Fourth Movement: Intellectual Revolution in Modern China*, Cambridge, Mass., 1960.

A. Dirlik, *The Origins of Chinese Communism*, Oxford, 1989.

L.E. Eastman, *The Abortive Revolution: China Under Nationalist Rule, 1927–1937*, Cambridge, Mass., 1974.

L.E. Eastman, *Seeds of Destruction: Nationalist China in War and Revolution, 1937–1949*, Stanford, 1984.

J.K. Fairbank (ed.), *Cambridge History of China, Vol. 12: Republican China 1912–1949*, Part I, Cambridge, 1983.

J.K. Fairbank (ed.), *Cambridge History of China, Vol. 13: Republican China 1912–1949, Part 2*, Cambridge, 1986.

D.G. Gillin, *Warlord: Yen Hsi-shan in Shansi Province, 1911–1949*, Princeton, 1967.

J.B. Grieder, *Hu Shih and the Chinese Renaissance: Liberalism in the Chinese Revolution*, Cambridge, Mass., 1970.

J. Guillermaz, *A History of the Chinese Communist Party, 1921–1949*, London, 1972.

J.P. Harrison, *The Long March to Power: a History of the Chinese Communist Party, 1921–1972*, New York and Washington, 1972.

G. Hershatter, *The Workers of Tianjin, 1900–1949*, Stanford, 1986.

P.C. Huang, *The Peasant Economy and Social Change in North China*, Stanford, 1985.

D. Lary, *Region and Nation: the Kwangsi Clique in Chinese Politics, 1925–1937*, London, 1974.

G. McCormack, *Chang Tso-lin in Northeast China, 1911–1928: China, Japan and the Manchurian Idea*, Stanford, 1977.

S. Pepper, *Civil War in China: the Political Struggle, 1945–1949*, Berkeley, 1978.

J.E. Sheridan, *China in Disintegration: the Republican Era in Chinese History, 1912–1949*, London, 1975.

J.E. Sheridan, *Chinese Communism and the Rise of Mao*, Cambridge, Mass., 1951.

D.S. Sutton, *Provincial Militarism and the Chinese Republic: the Yunnan Army, 1905–1925*, Ann Arbor, 1979.

C.M. Wilbur, *The Nationalist Revolution in China, 1923–1928*, Cambridge, 1984.

C.M. Wilbur, *Sun Yat-sen: Frustrated Patriot*, New York, 1976.

E.P. Young, *The Presidency of Yuan Shih-k'ai: Liberalism and Dictatorship in Early Republican China*, Ann Arbor, 1977.

The People's Republic

R. Baum and L. Bennett (eds.), *China in Ferment*, Englewood Cliffs, N.J., 1971.

J.P. Burns and S. Rosen, *Policy Conflicts in Post-Mao China*, Armonk, 1986.

A.Chan, R. Madsen and J. Unger, *Chen Village: The Recent History of a Peasant Community in Mao's China*, Berkeley, 1984.

J. Ch'en, *Mao and the Chinese Revolution*, London, 1965.

L. Dittmer, *Liu Shao-ch'i and the Chinese Cultural Revolution*, Berkeley, 1974.

H. Harding, *China's Second Revolution: Reform After Mao*, Washington, D.C., 1987.

H. Harding, *Organizing China: Problems of Bureaucracy, 1949–1976*, Stanford, 1981.

J. Hawkins, *Education and Social Change in the People's Republic of China*, New York, 1983.

R. Hayhoe (ed.), *Contemporary Chinese Education*, London and New York, 1984.

T.C. Hsi-En, *Chinese Education Since 1949: Academic and Revolutionary Models*, New York, 1981.

E. Joffe, *The Chinese Army After Mao*, Cambridge, Mass., 1987.

S. Karnow, *Mao and China*, London, 1972.

D. M. Lampton, *Paths to Power: Elite Mobility in Contemporary China*, Ann Arbor, 1986.

D.M. Lampton (ed.), *Policy Implementation in Post-Mao China*, Berkeley, 1987.

J.W. Lewis and Xue Litai, *China Builds the Bomb*, Stanford, 1988.

K. Lieberthal and M. Oksenberg, *Policy-Making in China: Leaders, Structures and Processes*, Princeton, 1988.

R. MacFarquhar, *The Origins of the Cultural Revolution*, vol. 1, London, 1974; vol. 2, London, 1983.

R. MacFarquhar and J.K. Fairbank (eds.), *Cambridge History of China, Vol. 14: The People's Republic, Part 1: The Emergence of Revolutionary China 1949–1965*, Cambridge, 1987.

M.Meisner, *Mao's China and After: A History of the People's Republic*, New York, 1986.

L.W. Pye, *The Mandarin and the Cadre: China's Political Cultures*, Ann Arbor, 1988.

C.Riskin, *China's Political Economy: the Quest for Development Since 1949*, Oxford, 1988

W. Rodzinski, *The People's Republic of China: a Concise Political History*, London and new York, 1988.

S. Schram, *Mao Tse-tung*, Harmondsworth, 1967.

S. Schram, *The Thought of Mao Tse-Tung*, Cambridge, 1989.

S. Schram (ed.), *Mao Tse-tung Unrehearsed: Talks and Letters 1956–1971*, Harmondsworth, 1974.

D.L. Shambaugh, *The Making of a Premier: Zhao Ziyang's Provincial Career*, Boulder, 1984.

V. Shue, *Peasant China in Transition*, Berkeley, 1981.

F.C. Teiwes, *Politics and Purges in China*, Armonk, 1979.

J. Townsend and B. Womack, *Politics in China*, 3rd edn, Boston, 1986.

A.G. Walder, *Communist Neo-Traditionalism*, Berkeley, 1986.

D. Wilson (ed.), *Mao Tse-tung in the Scales of History*, Cambridge, 1977.

R. Witke, *Comrade Chiang Ch'ing*, Boston, 1977.

THE MIND AND SENSES OF CHINA

E.M. Ahern, *The Cult of the Dead in a Chinese Village*, Stanford, 1973.

G.S. Alitto, *The Last Confucian: Liang Shu-ming and the Chinese Dilemma of Modernity*, Berkeley, 1979.

E.N. Anderson, *The Food of China*, New Haven, 1988.

A.C. Barnes (trans.), *Sunrise*, Beijing, 1960.

C.H. Brewitt-Taylor (trans.), *Romance of the Three Kingdoms*, 2 vols, Shanghai, 1925; reprinted Rutland and Tokyo, 1959.

W.-T. Chan (ed.), *Chu Hsi and Neo-Confucianism*, Honolulu, 1986.

H. Chang, *Chinese Intellectuals in Crisis: the Search for Order and Meaning*, Berkeley, 1986.

H. Chang, *Liang Ch'i-ch'ao and Intellectual Transition in China, 1890–1907*, Cambridge, Mass., 1971.

H.C. Chang, *Chinese Literature, Popular Fiction and Drama*, Edinburgh, 1973.

K.C. Chang (ed.), *Food in Chinese Culture*, New Haven, 1977.

Y.R. Chao, *A Grammar of Spoken Chinese*, Berkeley, 1965.

S.-H. Chen and H. Acton (trans.), *The Peach Blossom Fan*, Berkeley, 1976.

K.K. Ch'en, *Buddhism in China*, Princeton, 1964.

L.L. Ch'en (trans.), *Master Tung's Western Chamber Romance, a Chinese Chantefable*, Cambridge, 1976.

T.-T. Chow, *The May Fourth Movement: Intellectual Revolution in Modern China*, Cambridge, Mass., 1960.

C. C.-H. Chu, *A Reference Grammar of Mandarin Chinese for English Speakers*, New York, 1983.

W.T. de Bary (ed.), *Neo-Confucian Orthodoxy and the Learning of Heart and Mind*, New York, 1983.

W.T. de Bary (ed.), *Sources of Chinese Tradition*, New York, 1960.

W.T. de Bary et al., (eds.), *The Unfolding of Neo-Confucianism*, New York, 1975.

J. de Francis, *The Chinese Language: Fact and Fantasy*, Honolulu, 1984.

J. de Francis, *Nationalism and Language Reform in China*, Princeton, 1950.

W. Dolby, *A History of Chinese Drama*, London, 1976.

M. Dolezelova-Velingerova and J.I. Crump, *Ballad of the Hidden Dragon*, Oxford, 1971.

J. Dreyer, *China's Forty Million*, Cambridge, Mass., 1974.

Y. Fung, *A History of Chinese Philosophy*, trans. D. Bodde, 2 vols., Princeton, 1952–3.

C. Furth (ed.), *The Limits of Change: Essays on Conservative Alternatives in Republican China*, Cambridge, Mass., 1976.

H.A. Giles, *Strange Stories from a Chinese Studio*, Shanghai, 1916; reprinted New York, 1969.

D. Hawkes, *Songs of the South*, Harmondsworth, 1985.

D. Hawkes and J. Minford (trans.), *The Story of the Stone*, 5 vols., Harmondsworth and Bloomington, 1973–82.

C.T. Hsia, *The Classic Chinese Novel, a Critical Introduction*, New York and London, 1968.

K.-C. Hsiao, *A Modern China and a New World: K'ang Yu-wei, Reformer and Utopian, 1858–1927*, Seattle, 1975.

K.-C. Hsiao and F.W. Mote, *A History of Chinese Political Thought*, vol. 1, Princeton, 1979.

S.I. Hsiung (trans.), *The Romance of the Western Chamber*, London, 1935, New York and London, 1968.

W.J.F. Jenner (trans.), *Journey to the West*, 3 vols., Peking, 1982–86.

D. Johnson, A.J. Nathan and E.S. Rawski (eds.), *Popular Culture in Late Imperial China*, Berkeley, 1985.

D.K. Jordan, *Gods, Ghosts and Ancestors: Folk Religion in a Taiwanese Village*, Berkeley, 1972.

M. Kaltenmark, *Lao-tzu and Taoism*, Stanford, 1969.

L.O.-F. Lee, *The Rotrantic Generation of Modern Chinese Writers*, Cambridge, Mass., 1973.

D.D. Leslie, *The Survival of the Chinese Jews*, Leiden, 1972.

J.H. Levis, *Foundations of Chinese Musical Art*, Beijing, 1936.

J. Leyda, *Dianying, Electric Shadows*, Cambridge, Mass., 1972.

C.N. Li and S.A. Thompson, *Mandarin Chinese: A Functional Reference Grammar*, Berkeley, 1981.

S.N.C. Lieu, *Manichaeism*, Manchester, 1985.

J.C. Lin, *Modern Chinese Poetry: an Introduction*, Seattle and London, 1972.

T-L. Liu (trans.), *Flowers in the Mirror*, Berkeley and Los Angeles, 1966.

M. Loewe, *Chinese Ideas of Life and Death*, London, 1982.

M. Loewe, *Ways to Paradise: The Chinese Quest for Immortality*, London, 1979.

B.S. McDougall, *The Introduction of Western Literary Theories into Modern China, 1919–1925*, Tokyo, 1971.

Y.W. Ma and J.S.M. Lau (eds.), *Traditional Chinese Stories: Themes and Variations*, New York, 1978.

C. Mackerras, *The Rise of the Peking Opera, 1770–1870*, Oxford, 1972.

N.G.D. Malmqvist (ed.), *A Selective Guide to Chinese Literature 1900–1949*, 4 vols., Leiden, 1988-90.

A.J. Nathan, *Chinese Democracy*, New York, 1985.

M.S. Ng, *The Russian Hero in Modern Chinese Fiction*, Hong Kong and New York, 1988.

W. H. Nienhauser (ed.), *The Indiana Companion to Traditional Chinese Literature*, Bloomington, 1986.

J. Norman, *Chinese*, Cambridge, 1988.

V. Schwarcz, *The Chinese Enlightenment: Intellectuals and the Legacy of the May Fourth Movement of 1919*, Berkeley, 1986.

B. Schwartz, *In Search of Wealth and Power: Yen Fu and the West*, Cambridge, Mass., 1964.

A.C. Scott, *The Classical Theatre of China*, London, 1957.

H. Shadick (trans.), *The Travels of Lao Ts'an*, Ithaca, 1952.

S. Shapiro, *Outlaws of the Marsh*, Beijing and Bloomington, 1981.

Shen Fu, *Six Chapters of a Floating Life*, (trans. L. Pratt and Chiang Su-hui), Harmondsworth, 1983.

J. Spence, *Gate of Heavenly Peace: Chinese and Their Revolution 1895–1980*, London, 1983.

F.P. Stuart, *Chinese Materia Medica*, Shanghai, 1911.

L. G. Thomson (trans.), *Ta T'ung Shu: The One World Philosophy of K'ang Yu-wei*, London, 1958.`

H.H.-Y. Tiee, *A Reference Grammar of Chinese Sentences*, Tuccson, 1986.

A.D. Waley, *Ballads and Stories from Tun-huang*, London, 1960.

A.D. Waley (trans.), *Monkey*, London, 1942; reprinted 1961, 1973.

A.D. Waley, *Yuan Mei: Eighteenth Century Poet*, New York, 1956; reprinted Stanford, 1970.

C.C. Wang, *Traditional Chinese Tales*, New York, 1944; reprinted 1968.

T.-L. Wang (trans.), *Thunderstorm*, Peking, 1958.

J.L. Watson and E.S. Rawski (eds.), *Death Ritual in Late Imperial and Modern China*, Berkeley, 1988.

H. Welch, *The Practice of Chinese Buddhism*, Cambridge, Mass., 1967.

R.O. Whyte, *Rural Nutrition in China*, Hong Kong, 1972.

H. Wilhelm, *Change, Eight Lectures on the I-ching*, trans. C.F. Baynes, London, 1961.

H. Wilhelm, *The I-ching or Book of Changes*, trans. C.F. Baynes, London, 1951.

A.P. Wolf (ed.) *Religion and Ritual in Chinese Society*, Stanford, 1974.

A.F. Wright, *Buddhism in Chinese History*, Stanford, 1959.

C.K. Yang, *Religion in Chinese Society*, Berkeley, 1971.

H.-S. and G. Yang (trans.), *A Dream of Red Mansions*, 3 vols., Beijing, 1978-9.

H.-S. and G. Yang (trans.), *The Scholars*, Beijing, 1957; reprinted 1973.

H.-S. and G. Yang (trans.), *The Palace of Eternal Youth*, Beijing, 1955.

H.-S. and G. Yang (trans.), *Selected Plays of Kuan Han-ch'ing*, Beijing, 1958.

H.-S. and G. Yang (trans.), *The White-Haired Girl*, Beijing, 1954.

A.C. Yu (trans.), *The Journey to the West*, 4 vols., Chicago, 1977–83.

E. Zürcher, *The Buddhist Conquest of China*, 2 vols., Leiden, 1959.

ART AND ARCHITECTURE

M. Beurdeley and G. Raindre, *Qing Porcelain: famille verte, famille rose*, New York, 1986.

A. Boyd, *Chinese Architecture and Town Planning, 1500 BC–AD 1911*, Chicago, 1962.

J. Cahill, *Chinese Painting*, Geneva, 1963; reprinted London, 1978.

J. Cahill, *Hills Beyond a River: Chinese Painting of the Yuan Dynasty 1279–1368*, New York, 1976.

J. Cahill, *Painting at the Shore: Chinese Painting of the Early and Middle Ming Dynasty, 1368–1580*, New York, 1978.

Y. Chiang, *Chinese Calligraphy*, London 1938 and 1954.

R.H. Ellsworth, *Chinese Furniture*, London, 1970; New York, 1971.

H. Garner, *Chinese and Japanese Cloisonné Enamels*, London, 1962.

H. Garner, *Oriental Blue and White*, rev. edn, London, 1970.

D. Goldschmidt, *Ming Porcelain*, London, 1979.

G.St.G.M. Goppertz, *Chinese Celadon Wares*, rev. edn, London, 1979.

B. Gyllensvard, *Chinese Gold and Silver in the Carl Kempe Collection*, Stockholm, 1953.

S.H. Hansford, *Chinese Carved Jade*, London, 1968.

K.G. Izikowitz (ed.), *The House in East and Southeast Asia*, Copenhagen, 1982.

R.S. Jenyns, *Ming Pottery and Porcelain*, rev. edn, London, 1988.

R.S. Jenyns and W. Watson, *Chinese Art: the Minor Arts*, New York, 1963.

B. Karlgren, *Catalogue of Bronzes in the Alfred P. Pillsbury Collection*, Minneapolis, 1952.

M. Keswick, *The Chinese Garden: Art, History, and Architecture*, London, 1978.

R. Knapp, *Chinese Traditional Rural Architecture*, Honolulu, 1986.

L. Ledderose, *Mi Fu and the Classical Tradition of Chinese Calligraphy*, Princeton, 1979.

M. Loehr, *Ancient Chinese Jades from the Grenville L. Winthrop Collection*, Cambridge, Mass., 1975.

M.Loehr, *Ritual Vessels of Bronze Age China*, New York, 1968.

M. Medley, *The Chinese Potter*, Oxford, 1976.

M. Medley, *Handbook of Chinese Art*, London, 1964 and 1979.

M. Medley, *T'ang Pottery and Porcelain*, London, 1981.

M. Medley, *Yuan Porcelain and Stoneware*, London, 1974.

H. Munsterberg, *Chinese Buddhist Bronzes*, Rutland and Tokyo, 1967.

M. Pirazzoli-t'Serstevens, *Living Architecture: China*, New York, 1971.

J.A. Pope, *Chinese Porcelains from the Ardebil Shrine*, Washington, 1956; rev. edn London, 1979.

J.A. Pope et al., *The Freer Chinese Bronzes*, 2 vols., Washington, 1967–9.

L. Sickman and A.C. Soper, *The Art and Architecture of China*, rev. edn Harmondsworth, 1971.

O. Siren, *Chinese Sculptures from the Fifth to the Fourteenth Century*, 4 vols., London, 1925.

D.L. Snellgrove (ed.), *The Image of the Buddha*, Paris, 1978.

N.S. Steinhardt, *Chinese Imperial City Planning*, Honolulu, 1990.

N.S. Steinhardt, *Chinese Traditional Architecture*, New York, 1984.

M. Tregear, *Sung Ceramics*, New York, 1985.

M. Sullivan, *The Arts of China*, London and Berkeley, 1973; rev. edn, 1984.

M. Sullivan, *The Meeting of Eastern and Western Art*, London and New York, 1973; rev. edn, Berkeley, 1989.

M. Sullivan, *Symbols of Eternity: The Art of Landscape Painting in China*, Oxford and Stanford, 1979.

W. Watson, *Ancient Chinese Bronzes*, rev. edn, London, 1977.

W. Watson, *Tang and Liao Ceramics*, London, 1984.

R. Whitfield, *In Pursuit of Antiquity*, Princeton, 1969.

C.A.S. Williams, *Outlines of Chinese Symbolism and Art Motives*, London 1976.

N.I. Wu, *Chinese and Indian Architecture*, New York, 1963.

SCIENCE AND TECHNOLOGY

P.M. Clark and F.R. Stephenson, *Applications of Early Astronomical Records*, Bristol, 1978.

L.-Y. Lam, *A Critical Study of the Yang Hin Suan Fa, a Thirteenth-Century Mathematical Treatise*, Singapore, 1977.

U. Libbrecht, *Chinese Mathematics in the Thirteenth Century: The Shu-Shu Chiu-chang of Ch'in Chiu-shao*, Cambridge, Mass., 1972.

J. Needham, *Clerks and Craftsmen in China and the West*, Cambridge, 1970.

J. Needham, *The Development of Iron and Steel Technology in China*, Cambridge, 1964.

J. Needham, *Science and Civilisation in China*, vol. 3, Cambridge, 1959; vol. 5, part 2, Cambridge, 1974, part 3, Cambridge, 1976, part 4, Cambridge 1981; vol. 6, part 2, Cambridge, 1984.

D. Perkins, *Agricultural Development in China*, 1368–1968, Chicago, 1969.

C.A. Ronan, *The Shorter Science and Civilisation in China*, vol. 2, Cambridge, 1981; vol. 3, Cambridge, 1986.

E.H. Schafer, *Pacing the Void, T'ang Approaches to the Stars*, Berkeley, 1977.

N. Sivin, *Traditional Medicine in Contemporary China*, Ann Arbor, 1987.

N. Sivin (ed.), *Science and Technology in East Asia*, New York, 1977.

Y.-H. Sung, *T'ien-kung k'ai-wu: Chinese Technology in the Seventeenth Century* (trans. E-tu Zen Sun and Shiou-chuan Sun), University Park, 1966.

P.U. Unschuld, *Medicine in China: A History of Pharmaceutics*, Berkeley, 1986.

S. Wittwer, Y. Youtai, S. Han and W. Lianzheng, *Feeding a Billion*, East Lansing, 1988.

G.R.G. Worcester, *The Junks and Sampans of the Yangtze: a Study in Chinese Nautical Research*, Shanghai, 1947.

G.R.G. Worcester, *The History and Development of the Chinese Junk as Illustrated by the Collection of Junk Models in the Science Museum*, London, 1966.

GUIDE FOR VISITORS

C.P. Fitzgerald, *The Chinese View of their Place in the World*, London, 1964; reprinted 1970.

S. Leys, *Chinese Shadows*, Harmondsworth, 1978.

L. Pan, *The New Chinese Revolution*, London, 1987.

M. Salzman, *Iron and Silk: Encounters with Martial Artists, Bureaucrats and other Citizens of Contemporary China*, London, 1987.

B. Whyte, *Unfinished Encounter: China and Christianity*, London, 1988.

Bibliographies, handbooks and guidebooks

Bibliography of Asian Studies (pub. annually by Association of Asian Studies, University of Michigan)

China: A Handbook, ed. Wu Yuan-li (Praeger Publishers, 1973)

China Directory (annual) (Radiopress, Inc., Tokyo)

The China Phone Book and Address Directory (annual) (The China Phone Book Co. Ltd., GPO Box 11581, Hong Kong)

China in Western Literature: A Continuation of Cordier's Bibliotheca Sinica, ed. Tung-li Yuan (Far Eastern Publications, 1958)

China (Les Guides Bleus) (Prentice Hall, 1988)

Chinese Collections in Western Europe, John T. Ma (Inter Documentation AG, 1985)

Communist China, Bibliographic Survey, 1971 (US Department of the Army, 1971)

Contemporary China: A Research Guide, ed. Peter Berton and Eugene Wu (Stanford; Hoover Institution, 1967)

Directory of Chinese Officials and Organizations (Central Intelligence Agency; updated regularly)

The History of Imperial China: A Research Guide, Endymion Wilkinson (Harvard University Press, 1973)

How to Tour China, ed. China National Tourism Administration (K.G. Saur, 1988)

Index Sinicus: A Catalogue of Articles Relating to China in Periodicals and Other Collective Publications, 1920–1955, ed. John Lust (Heffer, 1964)

Information China, ed. Chinese Academy of Social Sciences (Pergamon Press, 1988)

Modern China, 1840–1972: An Introduction to Sources and Research Aids, Andrew J. Nathan (University of Michigan Center for Chinese Studies, 1973)

Modern Chinese Society: An Analytical Bibliography, ed. G. William Skinner (Stanford University Press, 1973)

Nagel's Encyclopedia-Guide: China (Nagel, 1969)

The People's Republic of China, 1949–79: A Documentary Survey, ed. Harold C. Hinton (Scholarly Resources Inc., 1980)

Who's Who in China: Current Leaders (Foreign Languages Press, Beijing, 1989)

Serials: current affairs

A number of English-language periodicals on China are produced in China and made available through CIBTC: *China Pictorial*, *China Reconstructs*, *China's Foreign Trade*, *Chinese Literature*, *Chinese Medical Journal*, *Beijing Review*, *Science in China* and *Social Sciences in China*. There are also the English-language newspapers *China Daily* and *China Economic Weekly*.

Translations of Chinese broadcasts and press

BBC Summary of World Broadcasts, Part 3: *The Far East* (6 times a week, with weekly economic supplement)

US Foreign Broadcast Information Service (FBIS), Washington, DC, *Daily Report: People's Republic of China* (5 times a week); Index: *FBIS Daily Report: People's Republic of China* (New Canaan: NewsBank Inc.)

Translation journals

M.E. Sharpe Inc., 80 Business Park Drive, Armonk, NY 10504: *Chinese Economic Studies, Chinese Education, Chinese Law and Government, Chinese Sociology and Anthropology, Chinese Studies in History, Chinese Studies in Literature, Chinese Studies in Philosophy, Chinese Studies in Archaeology*

US Joint Publications Research Service (JPRS) (National Technical Information Service, 5285 Port Royal Road, Springfield, VA 22161): *JPRS Report : China; China Report : Agriculture; China Report : Science and Technology; China Report : 'Red Flag'; China Report : State Council Bulletin*

Serials: scholarly

Acta Asiatica
Institute of Eastern Culture, Toho Gakkai, 4–1 Nishi-Kanda 2-chome, Chiyoda-ku, Tokyo 101

Australian Journal of Chinese Affairs
Contemporary China Centre, Australian National University, GPO Box 4, Canberra, ACT 2601

Asian Survey
University of California Press, 2120 Berkeley Way, Berkeley, CA 94720

Bulletin of Concerned Asian Scholars
3239 9th Street, Boulder, CO 80302

Center for Chinese Research Materials Newsletter
Box 3090, Oakton, VA 22124

China News Analysis
GPO Box 3225, Hong Kong

The China Quarterly
School of Oriental & African Studies, Thornhaugh Street, London WC1H 0XG

Far Eastern Economic Review
GPO Box 160, Hong Kong

Issues and Studies
Institute of International Relations, 64 Wan Shou Road, Mucha, Taiwan

Journal of Asian Studies
Association for Asian Studies, One Lane Hall, University of Michigan, Ann Arbor, MI 48109

Journal of the Royal Asiatic Society, Hong Kong Branch
GPO Box 3864, Hong Kong

Modern Asian Studies
Cambridge University Press, Edinburgh Building, Shaftesbury Road, Cambridge CB2 2RU

Modern China
Sage Publications Inc., 2111 W. Hillcrest Drive, Newbury Park, CA 91320

Papers on Far Eastern History
Dept. of Far Eastern History, Australian National University, Canberra, ACT 2600

Problems of Communism
US Information Agency, 301 4th Street, Washington, DC 20547

Renditions
Research Centre for Translation, Chinese University of Hong Kong, Shatin, N.T., Hong Kong

C.A.

Select glossary

The glossary includes a selection of names and terms from the text in pinyin, followed by the Wade-Giles transliteration, English translations where applicable, and Chinese characters.

Abaoji (A-pao-chi) 阿保機

Ai Qing (Ai Ch'ing) 艾青

Ai Tian (Ai T'ien) 艾田

An Lushan (An Lu-shan) 安祿山

An Shigao (An Shih-kao) 安世高

Anhui (An-hui) 安徽

Anji (An-chi) bridge 安濟橋

Annan (An-nan) 安南

Anshan (An-shan) 鞍山

Anyang (An-yang) 安陽

Ba (Pa) state 巴

Ba Jin (Pa Chin) 巴金

ba (pa) (overlord) 霸

Bagua (Pa-kua) 八卦

Bai Chongxi (Pai Ch'ung-hsi) 白崇禧

Bai jia xing (Pai chia hsing) 百家姓

Baigepiao (Pai-ko-p'iao) 白鴿票

baihua (pai-hua) 白話

Ban Chao (Pan Ch'ao) 班超

Ban Gu (Pan Ku) 班固

Banpocun (Pan-p'o-ts'un) 半坡村

Banshan (Pan-shan) 半山

bao (pao) (household unit) 保

Bao'an (Pao-an) 保安

baojia (pao-chia) 保甲

Baopuzi (Pao-p'u-tzu) 抱朴子

Bei lin (Pei lin) 碑林

Beijing (Peking) 北京

Beiping (Pei-p'ing) 北平

Beiyang (Pei-yang) 北洋

Bencao gang mu (Pen-ts'ao kang mu) 本草綱目

bi (pi) (brush) 筆

bi (pi) (jade disc) 鄙

bi (pi) (jade) 璧

Bianjing (Pien-ching) 汴京

bianwan (pien-wen) 變文

Bo Juyi (Po Chü-i) 白居易

Bo Yibo (Po I-po) 薄一波

Bu po bu li (Pu p'o pu li) 不破不立

Cai Jing (Ts'ai Ching) 蔡京

Cai O (Ts'ai O) 蔡鍔

Cai Yuanpei (Ts'ai Yuan-p'ei) 蔡元培

Cantongqi (Ts'an-t'ung ch'i) 參同契

Cao Cao (Ts'ao Ts'ao) 曹操

Cao Guojiu (Ts'ao Kuo-chiu) 曹國舅

Cao Kun (Ts'ao K'un) 曹錕

Cao Xueqin (Ts'ao Hsueh-ch'in) 曹雪芹

Cao Yu (Ts'ao Yü) 曹禺

Cao Zhi (Ts'ao Chih) 曹植

Caodong (Ts'ao-tung) 曹洞

Cen Yuying (Ts'en Yü-ying) 岑毓英

Chai Rong (Ch'ai Jung) 柴榮

Chan (Ch'an) sect 禪

Chang'an (Ch'ang-an) 長安

Changchun (Ch'ang-ch'un) 長春

Changsha (Ch'ang-sha) 長沙

Chen (Ch'en) kingdom 陳

Chen Baxian (Ch'en Pa-hsien) 陳霸先

Chen Boda (Ch'en Po-ta) 陳伯達

Chen Cheng (Ch'en Ch'eng) 陳誠

Chen Duxiu (Ch'en Tu-hsiu) 陳獨秀

Chen Hongshou (Ch'en Hung-shou) 陳洪綬

Chen Jiongming (Ch'en Chiung-ming) 陳烔明

Chen Shaoyu (Ch'en Shao-yü) 陳紹禹

Chen Yi (Ch'en I) 陳儀

Chen Yonggui (Ch'en Yung-kuei) 陳永貴

Chen Youliang (Ch'en Yu-liang) 陳友諒

Chen Yucheng (Ch'en Yü-ch'eng) 陳玉成

Chen Yun (Ch'en Yun) 陳雲

Cheng Hao (Ch'eng Hao) 程顥

Cheng Hua (Ch'eng Hua) 成化

Cheng Miao (Ch'eng Miao) 程邈

Cheng Yi (Ch'eng I) 程頤

Cheng Zhanggeng (Ch'eng Chang-keng) 程長庚

Chengpu (Ch'eng-p'u) 城濮

chi (ch'ih) ('foot') 尺

Chiang Kai-shek 蔣介石

Chiyou (Ch'ih-yu) 蚩尤

Chongqing (Chungking) 重慶

Chongzhen (Ch'ung-chen) 崇禎

Chongzong (Ch'ung-tsung) 崇宗

Chu (Ch'u) state 楚

Chu ci (Ch'u tz'u) 楚辭

Chu Suiliang (Ch'u Sui-liang) 褚遂良

Chuanqi (Ch'uan-ch'i) 傳奇

Chunqiu (Ch'un-ch'iu) 春秋

475

ci (tz'u) 詞

Cian (Tz'u-an) 慈安

cihua (tz'u-hua) 詞話

Cixi (Tz'u-hsi) 慈禧

Cizhou (Tz'u-chou) 磁州

cun (ts'un) ('inch') 寸

Da Jitao (Tai Chi-t'ao) 戴季陶

Da Wangshu (Tai Wang-shu) 戴望舒

Da xue (Ta hsueh) 大學

da tong (ta t'ung) 大同

dan (tan) (pill) 丹

Dangxiang (Tang-hsiang) 黨項

Dao (Tao) 道

Daoan (Tao-an) 道安

Daochuo (Tao-ch'o) 道綽

Daode jing (Tao-te ching) 道德經

Daoguang (Tao-kuang) 道光

Daoji (Tao-chi) 道濟

Daoxuan (Tao-hsuan) 道宣

Daoxue (Tao-hsueh) 道學

Daozang (Tao-tsang) 道藏

Daozong (Tao-tsung) 道宗

Daqing (Ta-ch'ing) 大庆

Daxing cheng (Ta-hsing ch'eng) 大興城

Dazhai (Ta-chai) 大寨

Dehua (Te-hua) 德化

Deng Xiaoping (Teng Hsiao-p'ing) 鄧小平

Dezong (Te-tsung) 德宗

di (ti) (High God) 帝

di zhi (ti chih) ('earthly branches') 地支

Dilun (Ti-lun) sect 地論

Ding (Ting) ware 定

Ding Xilin (Ting Hsi-lin) 丁西林

ding (ting) vessel 鼎

diqu (ti-ch'ü) 地區

Dong Qichang (Tung Ch'i-ch'ang) 董其昌

Dong Yuan (Tung Yuan) 董源

Dong Zhongshu (Tung Chung-shu) 董仲舒

Donglin (Tung-lin) 東林

doucai (tou-ts'ai) 鬥彩

Du Fu (Tu Fu) 杜甫

Du Wenxiu (Tu Wen-hsiu) 杜文秀

Du Yuesheng (Tu Yueh-sheng) 杜月笙

Duan Qirui (Tuan Ch'i-jui) 段祺瑞

Dugu (Tu-ku) 獨孤

Dunhuang (Tun-huang) 敦煌

Erya (Erh Ya) 爾雅

Erzong jing (Erh-tsung ching) 二宗經

Eyuwan (O-yü-wan) 鄂豫皖

Fa jing (Fa-ching) 法經

Fan (Fan) tribes 蕃

Fan Chengda (Fan Ch'eng-ta) 范成大

Fan Kuan (Fan K'uan) 范寬

Faxiang (Fa-hsiang) sect 法相

Fazang (Fa-tsang) 法藏

Feidi (Fei-ti) 廢帝

Fen (Fen) river 汾

Feng Guifen (Feng Kuei-fen) 馮桂芬

Feng Guozhang (Feng Kuo-chang) 馮國璋

Feng Menglong (Feng Meng-lung) 馮夢龍

Feng Yunshan (Feng Yun-shan) 馮雲山

Feng Yuxiang (Feng Yü-hsiang) 馮玉祥

Feng Zhi (Feng Chih) 馮至

fengjian (feng-chien) 封建

Fengtai (Feng-t'ai) 豐臺

fu (fu) command 府

fu (happiness) 福

fu (rhyme-prose) 賦

fubing (fu-ping) 府兵

Fujian (Fu-chien) 福建

Fukien *see* Fujian

Fushun (Fu-shun) 撫順

Fuxi (Fu-hsi) 伏羲

Fuzhou (Fu-chou) 福州

Gan (Kan) dialects 贛

gan (kan) stems 干

Gansu (Kan-su) 甘肅

Gao Ming (Kao Ming) 高明

Gao Panlong (Kao P'an-lung) 高攀龍

Gao Qi (Kao Ch'i) 高啓

Gaozong (Kao-tsung) 高宗

Gaozu (Kao-tsu) 高祖

Ge Hong (Ko Hung) 葛洪

Geng Jingzhong (Keng Ching-chung) 耿精忠

Gong Xian (Kung Hsien) 龔賢

gong (kung) (egalitarian) 公

Gongan (Kung-an) school 公安

gongan (kung-an) 公案

Gongdi (Kung-ti) 恭帝

Gonggong (Kung-kung) 共工

Gongsun Long (Kung-sun Lung) 公孫龍

Gongxian (Kung-hsien) 鞏縣

Gongyang zhuan (Kung-yang chuan) 公羊傳

Gu Kaizhi (Ku K'ai-chih) 顧愷之

Gu wei jin yong, yang wei Zhong yong
   (Ku wei chin yung, yang wei Chung yung)
   古爲今用，洋爲中用

Gu Xiancheng (Ku Hsien-ch'eng) 顧憲成

Guan (Kuan) ware 官

Guan Yu (Kuan Yü) 關羽

guan (kuan) Daoist temple 觀

Guandu shangban (Kuan-tu shang-pan)
   官督商辦

Guangdong (Kuang-tung) 廣東

Guangxi (Kuang-hsi) 廣西

Guangxu (Kuang-hsü) 光緒

guanhua (Kuan-hua)　官話

Guanyin (Kuan-yin)　觀音

Guer jiu zu ji (Ku-erh chiu tsu chi)　孤兒救祖記

Guilin (Kuei-lin)　桂林

Guizhou (Kuei-chou)　貴州

Guliang Zhuan (Ku-liang chuan)　穀梁傳

Guo Moruo (Kuo Mo-jo)　郭沫若

Guo Wei (Kuo Wei)　郭威

Guo Xi (Kuo Hsi)　郭熙

Guo Zixing (Kuo Tzu-hsing)　郭子興

guoyu (kuo-yü)　國語

Guozi jian (Kuo-tzu chien)　國子監

Guwen (Ku-wen)　古文

Hai Rui (Hai Jui)　海瑞

Haihe (Hai-ho)　海河

Hainan (Hai-nan)　海南

Han dynasty　漢

Han Fei　韓非

Han Liner (Han Lin-erh)　韓林兒

Han state　韓

Han Xiangzi (Han Hsiang-tzu)　韓湘子

Han Yu (Han Yü)　韓愈

Handan (Han-tan)　邯鄲

Hangzhou (Hang-chou)　杭州

Hankou (Han-k'ou)　漢口

Hanyu pinyin (Han-yü p'in-yin)　漢語拼音

Hao (Zhao capital)　鎬

hao (hao) sobriquet　號

He Chun (Ho Ch'un)　和春

He Long (Ho Lung)　賀龍

He Xiangu (Ho Hsien-ku)　何仙姑

He Yingqin (Ho Ying-ch'in)　何應欽

Hebei (Ho-pei)　河北

Hefei (Ho-fei)　合肥

Heilongjiang (Hei-lung-chiang)　黑龍江

Henan (Ho-nan)　河南

Heshang da san, wufa wutian (Ho-shang ta san, wu-fa wu-t'ien)　和尚打傘, 無法無天

Heshen (Ho-shen)　和珅

Hong Pian (Hung P'ien)　洪楩

Hong Ren'gan (Hung Jen-kan)　洪仁玕

Hong Shen (Hung Shen)　洪深

Hong Sheng (Hung Sheng)　洪昇

Hong Xiuquan (Hung Hsiu-ch'üan)　洪秀全

Honglou meng (Hung-lou meng)　紅樓夢

Hongweibing (Hung-wei-ping)　红卫兵

Hongwu (Hung-wu)　洪武

Hongzhou (Hung-chou)　洪州

Hou Jing (Hou Ching)　候景

Houma (Hou-ma)　候馬

Hu Hanmin (Hu Han-min)　胡漢民

Hu Shi (Hu Shih)　胡適

Hu Weiyong (Hu Wei-yung)　胡惟庸

Hua Guofeng (Hua Kuo-feng)　華國鋒

Hua Tuo (Hua T'o)　華佗

Huai (Huai) river　淮

Huaihai (Huai-hai)　淮海

Huan, duke of Qi (Ch'i)　齊公桓

Huang Chao (Huang Ch'ao)　黃巢

Huang Gongwang (Huang Kung-wang)　黃公望

Huang Quan (Huang Ch'üan)　黃荃

Huang Tingjian (Huang T'ing-chien)　黃庭堅

Huang Zunxian (Huang Tsun-hsien)　黃遵憲

Huangdi (Huang-ti)　黃帝

Huanghe (Huang-ho)　黃河

Huanglao (Huang-lao)　黃老

Huanzong (Huan-tsung)　桓宗

Huayan (Hua-yen)　華嚴

Hubei (Hu-pei)　湖北

Hui Shi (Hui Shih)　惠施

Huidian (Hui-tien)　會典

Huineng (Hui-neng)　慧能

Huiyuan (Hui-yuan)　慧遠

Huizhou (Hui-chou)　徽州

Huizong (Hui-tsung) (Song)　徽宗

Huizong (Hui-tsung) (Xia)　惠宗

Hunan (Hu-nan)　湖南

Ji (Chi) clan　季

jia (chia) (family)　家

jia (chia) (household unit)　甲

Jiajing (Chia-ching)　嘉靖

Jiamusi (Chia-mu-ssu)　佳木斯

jian'ai (Chien ai)　兼愛

Jiang Qing (Chiang Ch'ing)　江青

Jiangdu (Chiang-tu)　江都

Jiangsu (Chiang-su)　江蘇

Jiangxi (Chiang-hsi)　江西

Jiankang (Chien-k'ang)　健康

Jiantizi (Chien-t'i-tzu)　簡體字（简体字）

Jianwen (Chien-wen)　建文

Jianyang (Chien-yang)　建陽

Jiaqing (Chia-ch'ing)　嘉慶

Jie (Chieh)　桀

Jili (Chi-li)　季歷

Jin (Chin) dynasty　金

Jin Ping Mei (Chin P'ing Mei)　金瓶梅

Jin Shengtan (Chin Sheng-t'an)　金聖歎

jin (chin) (catty)　斤

Jinan (Chi-nan)　濟南

Jing (Ching) river　涇

jing (ching) (classics, scriptures)　經

jing (ching) (painted face)　淨

jing (ching) (semen)　精

Jingdezhen (Ching-te-chen)　景德鎮

jingdu (ching-tu)　競度

jinghu (ching-hu)　京胡

Jinghua yuan (Ching-hua yuan)　鏡花緣

Jingnan (Ching-nan)　荆南

Jingshi daxue (Ching-shih ta-hsueh)　京師大學

Jingtu (Ching-t'u) sect　淨土

Jingzong (Ching-tsung) 景宗

Jingzong (Ching-tsung) (Tang) 敬宗

jinshi (chin-shih) 進士

jiu (chiu) (wine) 酒

Jiujiang (Chiu-chiang) 九江

Jiulianhuan (Chiu-lien-huan) 九連環

Jiusi (Chiu-ssu) 九寺

Jizhou (Chi-chou) 吉州

juan (chüan) scroll 卷

Jun (Chün) ware 鈞

jun (chün) commanderies 郡

juntian (chün-t'ien) 均田

junzi (chün-tzu) 君子

Juran (Chü-jan) 巨然

juren (chü-jen) 舉人

Juxian (Chü-hsien) 莒縣

Juxian (Kü-hsien) 莒縣

Juyan (Chü-yen) 居延

Juyongguan (Chü-yung-kuan) 居庸關

Kai Yuan (K'ai Yuan) era 開元

Kaifeng (K'ai-feng) 開封

Kailuan (K'ai-luan) 開灤

Kan Zegao (K'an Tse-kao) 闞澤高

Kang Youwei (K'ang Yu-wei) 康有爲

kang (k'ang) 炕

Kangda (K'ang-ta) 抗大

Kangxi zidian (K'ang-hsi tzu-tien) 康熙字典

kiang (Fuchow pron.) 驚

Kong Shangren (K'ung Shang-jen) 孔尚任

Kongfuzi (K'ung-fu-tzu) 孔夫子

Kuan Zhong (Kuan Chung) 管仲

Kuanzi (Kuan-tzu) 管子

Kui (K'uei) dragons 夔

Kuncan (K'un-ts'an) 髡殘

Kunming (K'un-ming) 昆明

Lai Wenguang (Lai Wen-kuang) 賴文光

lei (lei) 罍

Lan Caihe (Lan Ts'ai-ho) 蘭采和

Lanzhou (Lan-chou) 蘭州

Lao She (Lao She) 老舍

laosheng (lao-sheng) 老生

Laozi (Lao-tzu) 老子

leiwen (lei-wen) 雷紋

Li Bing (Li Ping) 李冰

Li Bo (Li Po) 李白

Li Cheng (Li Ch'eng) 李成

Li Dazhao (Li Ta-chao) 李大釗

Li Fuchun (Li Fu-ch'un) 李富春

Li Gonglin (Li Kung-lin) 李公麟

Li He (Li Ho) 李賀

Li Hongzhang (Li Hung-chang) 李洪章

Li Ji (Li Chi) 禮記

Li Jiancheng (Li Chien-ch'eng) 李建成

Li Jiqian (Li Chi-ch'ien) 李繼遷

Li Keyong (Li K'o-yung) 李克用

Li Linfu (Li Lin-fu) 李林甫

Li Lisan (Li Li-san) 李立三

Li Qingzhao (Li Ch'ing-chao) 李清照

Li Ruzhen (Li Ju-chen) 李汝珍

Li sao (Li sao) 离騷

Li Shangyin (Li Shang-yin) 李商隱

Li Shimin (Li Shih-min) 李世民

Li Shizhen (Li Shih-chen) 李時珍

Li Si (Li Ssu) 李斯

Li Sixun (Li Ssu-hsün) 李思訓

Li Tiekuai (Li T'ieh-k'uai) 李鐵枴

Li Wencheng (Li Wen-ch'eng) 李文成

Li Xian (Li Hsien) 李睍

Li Xiannian (Li Hsien-nien) 李先念

Li Xiucheng (Li Hsiu-ch'eng) 李秀成

Li Yuan (Li Yuan) 李淵

Li Yuanhao (Li Yuan-hao) 李元昊

Li Yuanhong (Li Yuan-hung) 李元洪

Li Zhaodao (Li Chao-tao) 李昭道

Li Zhi (Li Chih) 李贄

Li Zicheng (Li Tzu-ch'eng) 李自成

li ('manners') 禮

li (li) distance 里

li (li) principle 理

Liang (Liang) dynasty 梁

Liang Fa (Liang Fa) 梁發

Liang Qichao (Liang Ch'i-ch'ao) 梁啓超

Liang Shu-ming (Liang Shu-ming) 梁漱溟

Liang tiao tui zoulu

(*Liang t'iao t'ui tsou-lu*) 兩條腿走路

liang (liang) weight 兩

liangshuifa (liang-shui-fa) 兩稅法

liangzhi (liang-chih) 良智

Lianyungang (Lien-yün-kang) 連雲港

Liao zhai zhiyi (Liao-chai chih-i) 聊齋志異

Liaodong (Liao-tung) 遼東

Liaoning (Liao-ning) 遼寧

Lidai minghua ji

(*Li-tai ming-hua chi*) 歷代名畫記

Liexian zhuan (Lieh-hsien chuan) 列仙傳

Liezi (Lieh-tzu) 列子

lihualong (li-hua-lung) 鯉化龍

Lin Biao (Lin Piao) 林彪

Lin Shu (Lin Shu) 林紓

Lin Zexu (Lin Tse-hsü) 林則徐

Ling Lun (Ling Lun) 伶倫

Ling Mengchu (Ling Meng-ch'u) 凌濛初

Lingbao (Ling-pao) 靈寶

Lingnan (Ling-nan) 嶺南

Lingwu (Ling-wu) 靈武

Linji (Lin-chi) 臨濟

Liu Bei (Liu Pei) 劉備

Liu Desheng (Liu Te-sheng) 劉德昇

Liu E (Liu O) 劉鶚

Liu Hui 劉徽

Liu Jin (Liu Chin) 劉瑾

Liu Lichuan (Liu Li-ch'uan)　劉麗川

Liu Shaoqi (Liu Shao-ch'i)　劉少奇

Liu Xie (Liu Hsieh)　劉勰

Liu Yan (Liu Yen)　劉隱

Liu Yi (Liu I)　柳毅

Liu Yin (Liu Yin)　劉龑（巖）

Liu Yu (Liu Yü)　劉裕

Liu Zhixie (Liu Chih-hsieh)　劉之協

Liu Zhiyuan (Liu Chih-yuan)　劉知遠

Liu Zongyuan (Liu Tsung-yuan)　柳宗元

Liubu (Liu-pu)　六部

Liufa (Liu-fa)　六法

Liushu (Liu-shu)　六書

Lizong (Li-tsung)　理宗

Longmen (Lung-men)　龍門

Longquan (Lung-ch'üan) ware　龍泉

Longshan (Lung-shan)　龍山

Lü (Lü) sect　律

Lu (Lu) state　魯

Lü Dongbin (Lü Tung-pin)　呂洞賓

Lu Fayan (Lu Fa-yen)　陸法言

Lu Ji (Lu Chi)　陸機

Lü Shi Chunqiu (Lü Shih Ch'un-ch'iu)　呂氏春秋

Lu Xiangshan (Lu Hsiang-shan)　陸象山

Lu Xun (Lu Hsun)　魯迅

Lu You (Lu Yu)　陸游

Lunyu (Lun-yü)　論語

Luo Guanzhong (Lo Kuan-chung)　羅貫中

Luoyang (Lo-yang)　洛陽

Luoyi (Lo-i)　洛邑

Ma Dexin (Ma Te-hsin)　馬德新

Ma Hualong (Ma Hua-lung)　馬化瀧

Ma Rulong (Ma Ju-lung)　馬如龍

Ma Yuan　馬遠

Ma Zhiyuan (Ma Chih-yuan)　馬致遠

Maijishan (Mai-chi-shan)　麥積山

Majiang (Ma-chiang)　麻將

Majong see Majiang

Mao Dun (Mao Tun)　矛盾

Mao Gong Ding (Mao Kung Ting)　毛公鼎

Mao shi (Mao shih)　毛詩

Mao Zedong (Mao Tse-tung)　毛澤東

Mao Zonggang (Mao Tsung-kang)　毛宗崗

Maolin (Mao-lin)　茂林

Maoming (Mao-ming)　茂明

Mawangdui (Ma-wang-tui)　馬王堆

Mayi ken gutou (Ma-i k'en ku-t'ou)　螞蟻啃骨頭

Mei Lanfang (Mei Lan-fang)　梅蘭芳

Meng (Meng) clan　孟

Meng Zhixiang (Meng Chih-hsiang)　孟知祥

mengzhu (meng-chu)　盟主

Mengzi (Meng-tzu)　孟子

Menxia sheng (Men-hsia sheng)　門下省

Mi (Mi) sect　密

Mi Fu (Mi Fu)　米芾

miao (miao) (temple)　廟

Min (Min) kingdom　閩

Min (Min) river　閩

Min Bao (Min Pao)　民報

Min Guo (Min Kuo)　民國

Mindi (Min-ti)　閔帝

Ming (Ming) dynasty　明

ming (ming) (name)　名

Minghuang (Ming-huang)　明皇

Mingjiao (Ming-chiao)　明教

mingjing (ming-ching)　明經

Mingtang (Ming-t'ang)　明堂

Mingzong (Ming-tsung)　明宗

Minshu (Min-shu)　閩書

Mo Di (Mo Ti)　墨翟

mo (mo) (ink)　墨

Modi (Mo-ti) (Liang emperor)　末帝

Moni jiao (Mo-ni chiao)　摩尼敎

Mozi (Mo-tzu)　墨子

Mu Qi (Mu Ch'i)　牧溪

mu (mow) (land measure)　畝

Muzong (Mu-tsung)　穆宗

Nan Tang (Nan T'ang)　南唐

Nan Yue (Nan Yüeh)　南越

Nanchang (Nan-ch'ang)　南昌

Nanfang Caomu zhuang (Nan-fang Ts'ao-mu chuang)　南方草目狀

Nanjing (Nan-ching)　難經

Nanjing (Nanking)　南京

Nanzhao (Nan-chao)　南詔

neige (nei-ko)　內閣

Ni Zan (Ni Tsan)　倪瓚

Nian (Nien) movement　捻

nian hao (nien hao)　年號

Niepan (Nieh-p'an) sect　湼槃

Ningyuan (Ning-yuan)　寧遠

Nongjia (Nung-chia)　農家

Nügua (Nü-kua)　女媧

Ouyang Xiu (Ou-yang Hsiu)　歐陽修

Ouyang Yuqian (Ou-yang Yü-ch'ien)　歐陽予倩

pa (p'a) ('fear')　怕

pai (p'ai) (household unit)　牌

Pangu (P'an-ku)　盤古

Panlongcheng (P'an-lung-ch'eng)　盤龍城

Peng Dehuai (P'eng Teh-huai)　彭德懷

Peng Pai (P'eng P'ai)　彭湃

Peng Zhen (P'eng Chen)　彭眞

pinghua (p'ing-hua)　平話

Pitan (P'i-t'an) sect　毘曇

Pu ji (P'u chi)　普及

Pu Songling (P'u Sung-ling)　蒲松齡

putonghua (p'u-t'ung-hua) 普通話

Puyi (P'u-yi) 溥儀

Qi (Ch'i) state 齊

Qi Baishi (Ch'i Pai-shih) 齊白石

qi (ch'i) (gas) 氣

Qian Liu (Ch'ien Liu) 錢鏐

Qian Xuan (Ch'ien Hsuan) 錢選

Qian zi wen (Ch'ien tzu wen) 千字文

qian (ch'ien) (cash) 錢

Qiang (Ch'iang) tribes 羌

Qianlong (Ch'ien Lung) 乾隆

Qiaofu nan wei wu mi zhi chui (Ch'iao-fu nan wei wu mi chih ch'ui) 巧婦難爲無米之炊

Qidan (Ch'i-tan) 契丹

Qie yün (Ch'ieh yün) 切韻

Qin (Ch'in) state, dynasty 秦

Qin Bangxian (Ch'in Pang-hsien) 秦邦憲

Qin Gui (Ch'in Kuei) 秦檜

Qin Guli (Ch'in Ku-li) 禽滑釐

Qin Shihuangdi (Ch'in Shih-huang-ti) 秦始皇帝

qin (ch'in) (zither) 琴

Qing (Ch'ing) dynasty 清

Qing chuyü lan (Ch'ing ch'u-yü lan) 青出于藍

Qingbai (Ch'ing-pai) ware 青白

Qingdao (Ch'ing-tao) 青島

Qinghai (Ch'ing-hai) 青海

Qingliu (Ch'ing-liu) 清流

Qingming (Ch'ing Ming) 清明

qingyi (ch'ing-i) 清議

qingzhensi (ch'ing-chen-ssu) 清眞寺

Qinling (Ch'in-ling) 秦嶺

qinna (ch'in-na) 擒拿

Qinzong (Ch'in-tsung) 欽宗

Qiqiaotu (Ch'i-ch'iao-t'u) 七巧圖

Qiu Ying (Ch'iu Ying) 仇英

Qu Wuchen (Ch'ü Wu-ch'en) 屈巫臣

Qu Yuan (Ch'ü Yüan) 屈原

Ren Yi (Jen I) 任頤

ren (jen) goodness 仁

Renzong (Jen-tsung) 仁宗

Ru (Ju) ware 汝

Ruan Ji (Juan Chi) 阮籍

Ruanruan (Juan-juan) 蠕蠕

Ruizong (Jui-tsung) 睿宗

Rulin waishi (Ju-lin wai-shih) 儒林外史

san min zhuyi (san min chu-i) 三民主義

sancai (san-ts'ai) 三彩

Sanguo zhi yanyi (San-kuo chih yen-i) 三國志演義

Sanhuang wen (San-huang wen) 三皇文

Sanjie (San-chieh) sect 三階

Sanlun (San-lun) sect 三論

Sanmen (San-men) 三門

sansheng (san-sheng) 三省

Sanyuanli (San-yuan-li) 三元里

Sanzi jing (San-tzu ching) 三字經

Shandao (Shan-tao) 善導

Shandong (Shan-tung) 山東

Shang (Shang) dynasty 商

Shang Kexi (Shang K'o-hsi) 尚可喜

Shang shu (Shang shu) 尚書

Shang Yang 商鞅

Shangdu (Shang-tu) 上都

Shanghai (Shang-hai) 上海

Shanghan lun (Shang-han lun) 傷寒論

Shangqing (Shang-ch'ing) 上清

Shangshu sheng (Shang-shu sheng) 尚書省

Shangzi (Shang-tzu) 商子

Shanhaiguan (Shan-hai-kuan) 山海關

Shanxi (Shan-hsi) 山西

Shanxi (Shensi) 陝西

Shanxing (Shan-hsing) 擅興

Shaolin (Shao-lin) 少林

Shaoxing (Shao-hsing) 紹興

Shelun (She-lun) sect 攝論

Shen Buhai (Shen Pu-hai) 申不害

Shen Dao (Shen Tao) 愼到

Shen Dao (Shen Tao) (Spirit Road) 神道

Shen Fu 沈復

Shen Zhou (Shen Chou) 沈周

Sheng Xuanhuai (Sheng Hsuan-huai) 盛宣懷

sheng (sheng) (province) 省

Shengguantu (Sheng-kuan-t'u) 陞官圖

Shengzong (Sheng-tsung) 聖宗

shenjin (shen-chin) 紳衿

Shennong (Shen-nung) 神農

Shennong bencao jing (Shen-nung pen-ts'ao ching) 神農本草經

shenshi (shen-shih) 紳士

Shenxiu (Shen-hsiu) 神秀

Shenyang (Shen-yang) 瀋陽

Shenzong (Shen-tsung) 神宗

Shi Dakai (Shih Ta-k'ai) 石達開

Shi guan (Shih kuan) 史館

Shi Ji (Shih Chi) 史記

Shi jing (Shih ching) 詩經

Shi Jingtang (Shih Ching-t'ang) 石敬瑭

Shi Miyuan (Shih Mi-yuan) 史彌遠

Shi Naian (Shih Nai-an) 施耐庵

Shi Yousan (Shih Yu-san) 石友三

shi (shih) (class) 士

shi (shih) (poetry) 詩

Shiwu guan (Shih-wu kuan) 十五貫

Shizong (Shih-tsung) 世宗

Shizu (Shih-tsu) 世祖

Shouxian (Shou-hsien) 壽縣

Shu (Shu) clan 叔

Shu (Shu) states 蜀

Shu jing (Shu ching) 書經

shu (shu) ('techniques')　術

Shufu (Shu-fu) ware　樞府

Shuihu zhuan (Shui-hu chuan)　水滸傳

Shun (Shun)　舜

Shundi (Shun-ti)　順帝

Shuntian (Shun-t'ien) (Beijing)　順天

Shuo wen jie zi (Shuo wen chieh tzu)　說文解字

si (ssu) (temple)　寺

Si shu (Ssu shu)　四書

Sichuan (Ssu-ch'uan)　四川

Sima Guang (Ssu-ma Kuang)　司馬光

Sima Qian (Ssu-ma Ch'ien)　司馬遷

Sima Xiangru (Ssu-ma Hsiang-ju)　司馬相如

Song (Sung) dynasty　宋

Song Jiang (Sung Chiang)　宋江

Song Jiaoren (Sung Chiao-jen)　宋教仁

Song Zheyuan (Sung Che-yuan)　宋哲元

Songhuajiang

　(Sung-hua-chiang)　松花江

Su Dongpo (Su Tung-p'o)　蘇東坡

Su Shi (Su Shih)　蘇軾

Su Song (Su Sung)　蘇頌

Su Zhu (Su Chu)　蘇籀

Sui (Sui) dynasty　隋

Sun Chuanfang (Sun Ch'uan-fang)　孫傳芳

Sun Yat-sen　孫逸仙

Sunzi (Sun-tzu)　孫子

Sutizi (Su-t'i tzu)　俗體字

Suzhou (Su-chou)　蘇州

Suzong (Su-tsung)　肅宗

Tai xue (T'ai hsueh)　太學

Taihang (T'ai-hang)　太行

Taihe lü (T'ai-ho lü)　泰和律

taijiquan (t'ai-chi-ch'üan)　太極拳

Taiping (T'ai-p'ing) (princess)　太平

Taiping dao (T'ai-p'ing tao)　太平道

Taiping jing (T'ai-p'ing ching)　太平經

Taiping tianguo (T'ai-p'ing t'ien-kuo)　太平天國

Taiwan (T'ai-wan)　台灣

Taiyuan (T'ai-yuan)　太原

Taizong (T'ai-tsung)　太宗

Taizu (T'ai-tsu)　太祖

Tan Sitong (T'an Ssu-t'ung)　譚嗣同

Tan Xinpei (T'an Hsin-p'ei)　譚鑫培

Tan Yankai (T'an Yen'k'ai)　譚延闓

Tang (T'ang) dynasty　唐

Tang Jiyao (T'ang Chi-yao)　唐繼堯

Tang Xianzu (T'ang Hsien-tsu)　湯顯祖

Tang Yin (T'ang Yin)　唐寅

Tao Hongjing (T'ao Hung-ching)　陶弘景

Tao Qian (T'ao Ch'ien)　陶潛

Tao Yuanming (T'ao Yuan-ming)　陶淵明

taotie (t'ao-t'ieh)　饕餮

Ti gao (T'i kao)　提高

Tian Bao (T'ien Pao) era　天寶

Tian Han (T'ien Han)　田漢

Tian Jian (T'ien Chien)　田間

tian gan (t'ien kan)　天干

Tiananmen (T'ien An Men)　天安門

Tiandihui (T'ien-ti-hui)　天地會

Tiangong Kaiwu (T'ien-kung K'ai-wu)　天工開物

Tianjin (T'ien-chin)　天津

tianming (t'ien-ming)　天命

Tianqi (T'ien-ch'i)　天啓

Tianshi dao (T'ien-shih tao)　天師道

Tiantai (T'ien-t'ai)　天台

tianzi (t'ien-tzu)　天子

Tianzudi (T'ien-tsu-ti)　天祚帝

tianzun (t'ien-tsun)　天尊

tiyong (t'i yung)　體用

Tong Guan (T'ung Kuan) (Song eunuch)　童貫

Tongguan (T'ung-kuan)　潼關

Tongmenghui (T'ung-meng-hui)　同盟會

Tongwen guan (T'ung-wen kuan)　同文館

Tongzhi (T'ung-chih)　同治

Tujue (T'u-chüeh)　突厥

tuntian (t'un-t'ien)　屯田

Tuyuhun (T'u-yü-hun)　吐谷渾

Waiwu bu (Wai-wu pu)　外務部

Wang Anshi (Wang An-shih)　王安石

Wang Chongyang (Wang Ch'ung-yang)　王重陽

Wang Cizhong (Wang Tz'u-chung)　王次仲

Wang Gen (Wang Ken)　王艮

Wang Guangmei (Wang Kuang-mei)　王光美

Wang Guowei (Wang Kuo-wei)　王國維

Wang Hongwen (Wang Hung-wen)　王洪文

Wang Hui (Wang Hui)　王翬

Wang Ji (Wang Chi)　王畿

Wang Jian (Wang Chien) (late Tang)　王建

Wang Jian (Wang Chien) (painter)　王鑑

Wang Jingwei (Wang Ching-wei)　王精衞

Wang Mang (Wang Mang)　王莽

Wang Meng (Wang Meng)　王蒙

Wang Mian (Wang Mien)　王冕

Wang Ming (Wang Ming)　王明

Wang Shifu (Wang Shih-fu)　王實甫

Wang Shimin (Wang Shih-min)　王時敏

Wang Shouren (Wang Shou-jen)　王守仁

Wang Tao (Wang T'ao)　王韜

Wang Wei (Wang Wei)　王維

Wang Xizhi (Wang Hsi-chih)　王羲之

Wang Yangming (Wang Yang-ming)　王陽明

Wang Yuanqi (Wang Yuan-ch'i)　王原祁

Wang Zhen (Wang Chen) (Ming eunuch)　王振

Wang Zhi (Wang Chih)　王直

wang (king)　王

Wanli (Wan-li)　萬歷

Wannian Qiao (Wan-nien Ch'iao)　萬年橋

Wanping (Wan-p'ing)　宛平

Wei (Wei) kingdom　魏

Wei (Wei) river　渭

Wei Boyang (Wei Po-yang)　魏伯陽

Wei Changhui (Wei Ch'ang-hui)　韋昌輝

Wei Daoming (Wei Tao-ming)　魏道明

Wei Empress (Tang)　韋后

Wei Yuan (Wei Yuan)　魏源

Wei Zhongxian (Wei Chung-hsien)　魏忠賢

Wen miao (Wen miao)　文廟

Wen xin diao long

　(Wen hsin tiao lung)　文心雕龍

Wen xuan (Wen hsuan)　文選

Wen Yiduo (Wen I-to)　聞一多

Wen Zhengming

　(Wen Cheng-ming)　文徵明

Wendi (Wen-ti)　文帝

Weng wang (Wen wang)　文王

Wenrenhua (Wen-jen-hua)　文人畫

Wenxiang (Wen-hsiang)　文祥

wenyan (wen-yen)　文言

Wenzhou (Wen-chou)　溫州

Wenzong (Wen-tsung)　文宗

wonton　餛飩

Wu (Wu) school　吳

Wu (Wu) state　吳

Wu Bin (Wu Pin)　吳彬

Wu Changshi (Wu Ch'ang-shih)　吳昌碩

Wu Cheng'en (Wu Ch'eng-en)　吳承恩

Wu dai (Wu tai)　五代

Wu Daozi (Wu Tao-tzu)　吳道子

Wu Di (Wu Ti)　武帝

Wu Jingzi (Wu Ching-tzu)　吳敬梓

Wu Li (Wu Li)　吳歷

Wu Peifu (Wu P'ei-fu)　吳佩孚

Wu Sangui (Wu San-kuei)　吳三桂

Wu wang (Wu wang)　武王

Wu Xun zhuan (Wu Hsun chuan)　武訓傳

Wu Zhao (Wu Chao)　武曌

Wu Zhen (Wu Chen)　吳鎮

wu sheng (wu sheng)　五聲

wu wei (wu wei)　無爲

wufu (wu-fu)　五福

Wuhan (Wu-han)　武漢

Wuhuan (Wu-huan) tribes　烏桓

Wuman (Wu-man) tribe　烏蠻

Wushi bu xiao bai bu (Wu-shih

　pu hsiao pai pu)　五十步笑百步

wushu (wu-shu)　武術

Wutaishan (Wu-t'ai-shan)　五台山

wuxing (wu-hsing) ('five agencies')　五行

wuxing (wu-hsing) ('five punishments')　五刑

Wuyue (Wu Yueh)　吳越

Xi Kang (Hsi K'ang)　嵇康

Xi Kun (Hsi K'un)　西崑

Xi Xia (Hsi Hsia)　西夏

Xi'an (Hsi-an)　西安

Xia (Hsia) dynasty　夏

Xia Gui (Hsia Kuei)　夏珪

Xia Yan (Hsia Yen)　夏衍

Xiajiang (Hsia-chiang)　下江

Xiamen (Hsia-men)　廈門

Xian ru wei zhu

　(Hsien ju wei chu)　先入爲主

xian (hsien) county　縣

xian (hsien) immortal　仙

Xianbi (Hsien-pi)　鮮卑

Xianfeng (Hsien-feng)　咸豐

Xiang (Hsiang) dialects　湘

Xiang Rong (Hsiang Jung)　向榮

Xiang Ying (Hsiang Ying)　項英

Xianggang (Hsiang-kang)　香港

Xiangzong (Hsiang-tsung)　襄宗

Xianzong (Hsien-tsung) (Tang)　憲宗

Xianzong (Hsien-tsung) (Xia)　獻宗

Xiao jing (Hsiao ching)　孝經

Xiao Jun (Hsiao Chün)　蕭軍

Xiao Tong (Hsiao T'ung)　蕭統

Xiao Yan (Hsiao Yen)　蕭衍

xiao (hsiao)　孝

Xiaowendi (Hsiao-wen-ti)　孝文帝

Xiazi chi huntun, xinli youshu (Hsia-tzu ch'ih hun-

　t'un, hsin-li yu-shu)　瞎子吃餛飩, 心里有數

Xibo (Hsi-po)　西伯

Xie He (Hsieh Ho)　謝赫

Xie Lingyun (Hsieh Ling-yun)　謝靈運

Xijiang (Hsi-chiang)　西江

Ximen Qing (Hsi-men Ch'ing)　西門慶

Xin qingnian (Hsin ch'ing-nien)　新青年

xin (hsin) mind　心

xing (hsing) poet　興

xing (hsing) surname　姓

xing ming (hsing ming)　形名

Xingfa zhi (Hsing-fa chih)　刑法志

Xingzhonghui (Hsing-chung-hui)　興中會

Xingzong (Hsing-tsung)　興宗

Xining (Hsi-ning)　西寧

Xinxing (Hsin-hsing)　信行

Xiongnu (Hsiung-nu)　匈奴

Xixiang ji (Hsi-hsiang chi)　西廂記

Xiyou ji (Hsi-yu chi)　西遊記

Xiyu ji (Hsi-yü chi)　西域記

Xu Bo (Hsu Po)　徐伯

Xu Shen (Hsu Shen)　許慎

Xu Wei (Hsu Wei)　徐渭

Xu Xing (Hsu Hsing)　許行

Xu Zhimo (Hsu Chih-mo)　徐志摩

Xuande (Hsuan-te)　宣德

Xuantong (Hsuan-t'ung)　宣統

Xuanwu (Hsuan-wu) Gate　玄武門

Xuanzang (Hsuan-tsang)　玄奘

Xuanzong (Hsuan-tsung)　玄宗

Xuanzong (Hsuan-tsung)　宣宗

Xue Bu (Hsueh Pu)　學部

Xunzi (Hsun-tzu)　荀子

Yan (Yen) state　燕

Yan Fu (Yen Fu)　嚴復

Yan Hui (Yen Hui)　顏回

Yan Liben (Yen Li-pen)　閻立本

Yan Xishan (Yen Hsi-shan)　閻錫山

Yan'an (Yen-an)　延安

Yang Guang (Yang Kuang)　楊廣

Yang Guifei (Yang Kuei-fei)　楊貴妃

Yang Guozhong (Yang Kuo-chung)　楊國忠

Yang Jian (Yang Chien)　楊堅

Yang Xi (Yang Hsi)　楊羲

Yang Xiuqing (Yang Hsiu-ch'ing)　楊秀清

Yang Zhu (Yang Chu)　楊朱

Yangdi (Yang-ti)　煬帝

Yangshao (Yang-shao)　仰韶

Yangtze river　揚子

Yangwu (Yang-wu) movement　洋務

Yangzhou (Yang-chou)　揚州

Yanshi (Yen-shih)　偃師

Yao (Yao)　堯

Yao (Yao) tribes　猺

Yao Wenyuan (Yao Wen-yuan)　姚文元

Yaozhu (Yao-chou)　耀州

Yazi chi huanglian, you ku shuobuchu

　(Ya-tzu ch'ih huang-lien, yu k'u

　shuo-pu-ch'u)　啞子吃黃連，有苦說不出

Ye Mingchen (Yeh Ming-ch'en)　葉名琛

Ye Shi (Yeh Shih)　葉適

Ye Ting (Yeh T'ing)　葉挺

Yelang (Yeh-lang)　夜郎

Yelü Abaoji (Yeh-lü A-pao-chi)　耶律阿保機

Yi (I) (Archer)　羿

Yi ge bazhang paibuxiang (I ko pa-chang

　p'ai-pu-hsiang)　一个巴掌拍不响

Yi jing (I ching)　易經

Yi li (I li)　儀禮

Yi qiong er bai (I ch'iung erh pai)　一窮二白

Yi Yin (I Yin)　伊尹

Yi zhen jian xue (I chen chien hsueh)　一針見血

Yilin gaicuo (I-lin kai-ts'o)　醫林改錯

Yin (Yin) dynasty　殷

Yindi (Yin-ti)　隱帝

Ying Yujian (Ying Yü-chien)　瑩玉澗

Yingqing (Ying-ch'ing) ware　影青

Yingzong (Ying-tsung)　英宗

yinyang (yin-yang)　陰陽

Yixing (I-hsing) ware　宜興

Yizong (I-tsung) (Tang)　懿宗

Yizong (I-tsung) (Xia)　毅宗

Yongle (Yung-lo)　永樂

Yongle Dadian (Yung-lo Ta-tien)　永樂大典

Yongzheng (Yung-cheng)　雍正

Yu (Yü)　禹

Yu Dafu (Yü Ta-fu)　郁達夫

Yu Qiuli (Yü Ch'iu-li)　余秋里

Yu Xin (Yü Hsin)　庾信

yu (yü) (jade)　玉

Yuan (Yuan) dynasty　元

Yuan Haowen (Yuan Hao-wen)　元好問

Yuan Hongdao (Yuan Hung-tao)　袁宏道

Yuan Mei (Yuan Mei)　袁枚

Yuan Ming yuan (Yuan Ming yuan)　圓明園

Yuan Shikai (Yuan Shih-k'ai)　袁世凱

Yuan Zhen (Yuan Chen)　元稹

Yuan Zhongdao (Yuan Chung-tao)　袁中道

Yuan Zongdao (Yuan Tsung-tao)　袁宗道

Yue (Yueh) dialects　粵

Yue (Yueh) state　越

Yue (Yueh) ware　越

Yue Fei (Yueh Fei)　岳飛

yuebai (yueh-pai)　月白

Yueshi (Yueh-shih) tribe　月氏

Yuezhi (Yueh-chih)　月支

Yuman guan (Yü-men kuan)　玉門關

Yun Shouping (Yun Shou-p'ing)　惲壽平

Yunnan (Yun-nan)　雲南

Yuwen Kai (Yü-wen K'ai)　宇文愷

Yuwen Tai (Yü-wen T'ai)　宇文泰

Zaichun (Tsai-ch'un)　載淳

zaju (tsa-chü)　雜劇

Zeng Guofan (Tseng Kuo-fan)　曾國藩

Zeng Guoquan (Tseng Kuo-ch'üan)　曾國荃

Zeng Shen (Tseng Shen)　曾參

Zhan'guo ce (Chan-kuo ts'e)　戰國策

Zhang Chunqiao (Chang Ch'un-ch'iao)　張春橋

Zhang Daoling (Chang Tao-ling)　張道陵

Zhang Fei (Chang Fei)　張飛

Zhang Guolao (Chang Kuo-lao)　張果老

Zhang Guoliang (Chang Kuo-liang)　張國樑

Zhang Guotao (Chang Kuo-t'ao)　張國濤

Zhang Heng (Chang Heng)　張衡

Zhang Ji (Chang Chi)　張機

Zhang Jinghui (Chang Ching-hui)　張景惠

Zhang Juzheng (Chang Chü-cheng)　張居正

Zhang Lu (Chang Lu)　張魯

Zhang Luoxing (Chang Lo-hsing)　張洛行

Zhang Shicheng (Chang Shih-ch'eng)　張士誠

Zhang Wentian (Chang Wen-t'ien)　張聞天

Zhang Xueliang (Chang Hsueh-liang)　張學良

Zhang Xun (Chang Hsun)　張勳

Zhang Yanyuan (Chang Yen-yuan)　張彥遠

Zhang Zai (Chang Tsai)　張載

Zhang Zhidong (Chang Chih-tung)　張之洞

Zhang Zuolin (Chang Tso-lin)　張作霖

Zhangzong (Chang-tsung)　章宗

Zhao (Chao) state　趙

Zhao Kuangyi (Chao K'uang-i)　趙匡義

Zhao Kuangyin (Chao K'uang-yin)　趙匡胤

Zhao Mengfu (Chao Meng-fu)　趙孟頫

Zhao Tuo (Chao T'o)　趙佗

Zhao Yingcheng (Chao Ying-ch'eng)　趙映乘

Zhe (Che) (school)　浙

Zhejiang (Che-chiang) 浙江

zhen (chen) (truth) 眞

Zheng He (Cheng Ho) 鄭和

Zheng Xiaoxu (Cheng Hsiao-hsu) 鄭孝胥

Zhengde (Cheng-te) 正德

zhengfeng (cheng-feng) 整風

Zhengzhou (Cheng-chou) 鄭州

Zhenjiang (Chen-chiang) 鎭江

Zhi baobuzhu huo

    (Chih pao-pu-chu huo) 紙包不住火

Zhiyi (Chih-i) 智顗

Zhizhi (Chih-chih) 職制

Zhong yong (Chung yung) 中庸

Zhongguo (Chung-kuo) 中國

Zhongguo gemingdang (Chung-kuo
    ko-ming-tang) 中国革命党

Zhongguo gongchan dang (Chung-kuo
    kung-ch'an tang) 中国共产党

Zhongli Quan (Chung-li Ch'üan) 鐘離權

Zhongshu sheng (Chung-shu sheng) 中書省

Zhongzong (Chung-tsung) 中宗

Zhou (Chou) dynasty 周

Zhou (Chou) Shang king 紂

Zhou Dunyi (Chou Tun-i) 周敦頤

Zhou Enlai (Chou En-lai) 周恩來

Zhou guan (Chou kuan) 周官

Zhou li (Chou li) 周禮

Zhou Wenju (Chou Wen-chü) 周文矩

Zhou yi (Chou i) 周易

zhou (chou) (prefectures) 州

Zhougong (Chou-kung) 周公

Zhoukoudian (Chou-k'ou-tien) 周口店

Zhu Biao (Chu Piao) 朱標

Zhu Da (Chu Ta) 朱耷

Zhu De (Chu Te) 朱德

Zhu Di (Chu Ti) 朱棣

Zhu Wen (Chu Wen) 朱溫

Zhu Xi (Chu Hsi) 朱熹

Zhu Yougui (Chu Yu-kuei) 朱友珪

Zhu Yuanzhang (Chu Yuan-chang) 朱元璋

Zhu Yunwen (Chu Yun-wen) 朱允炆

Zhu Zaiyu (Chu Tsai-yü) 朱載堉

Zhuang (Chuang) tribes 僮

Zhuangzi (Chuang-tzu) 莊子

Zhuangzong (Chuang-tsung) 莊宗

Zhubing yuanhou lun (Chu-ping
    yuan-hou lun) 諸病源候論

Zhufu (Chu-fu) 祝福

Zhuge Liang (Chu-ko Liang) 諸葛亮

Zi Tan (Tzu T'an) 紫壇

Ziqiang (Tzu-ch'iang) 自强

ziran (tzu-jan) 自然

zong (tsung) (sect) 宗

Zongli yamen (Tsung-li ya-men) 總理衙門

Zou Yan (Tsou Yen) 鄒衍

zu (tsu) 族

zun (tsun) 尊

Zuo Qiuming (Tso Ch'iu-ming) 左丘明

Zuo zhuan (Tso chuan) 左傳

Zuo Zongtang (Tso Tsung-t'ang) 左宗堂

Index

Pages numbers in bold refer to main entries; those in italics refer to illustrations.

Achang people 78
abacus 440
Abahai 206, 208–9
acrobatics 361
actors 359, 360, 361
acupuncture *124*, 126, 129, *130*, 131, 288
administrative units 20–1, *22*, 30, 84
adoption, law of 105
Aeta people of Philippines 74
Afghanistan 76, 170, 269, 270
Africa 46, 51, 68, 71, 198–9
after-life 140, 144, 295, 297
agriculture **52, 53, 54–9, 434–5**; astronomy and 441; climate and 17, 19, 23; collectivization 52, 54–5, 58, 100, 257, 258, 261, 263; commercialization, (Song) 182, (PRC) 29, 45, 54, 56–8, 254, 263; communes 54–5; co-operatives **263–4**; crisis (1959–61) 258, 267–8; crop rotation **434**; draught animals 48, 58, 452; family *15*, 92, 100, 258, 268; foreign crops 368, 435; garden farming 29, 30; implements 182, 434, **435**; intensive cultivation **434**; invention of 71, 136; machinery 52, 54, *57*, 58, 60, 263, 434, **435**; modernization 26, 263, 279; multiple cropping 24, 27, 29, 30, *57*, 58, 182, 435; Neolithic 138–9, 435; planning 52, 54–5, 264; productivity 55, 56, 58–9, 100; responsibility system 100, 119, 280–1; shifting 76, 82, 84; soils and 20; terracing *24, 25, 434*; and village life 97; *see also*: fertilizers; fish; irrigation; land reclamation; livestock; *individual crops, and under individual dynasties and areas*
Aguda (Jurchen leader) 185
Ahongs (mullahs) 316
Ai Qing 356
Ai Tian 313
Aigun, Treaty of 221
Ainu people of Hokkaido 74
Aksai Jin plateau 268, 455
Albania 42
Albazin 212
alchemy 296, 299, 340, 437–8
alcohol 373–4, 438, 458
alfalfa in cuisine 368
'alienation' 281, 357
Allen, Young J. 225
almanacs 377, *378*
Altaic languages 78–9, 184
Altan Khan 210
altars *292, 423*
alum 439
aluminium 41

ambans (Qing commissioners) 210
amber 47
Amdo language 80
Amherst, 1st Earl of 217
Amur region 212, 220–2, 274, 285
An Lushan rebellion 108, **171–2**, 173, 314, 348
An Shigao 308
anarchism 236, 258, 321
ancestor cult **291–4**; and divination 288, 291; graves 94, 288, *289*, 291; halls 94, 96, *292*, 293–4; Rites Controversy and 210, 318; sacrifices *293*, 294, 342–3, 368; Shang 11, 144; tablets 293, 294, 302–3; Zhou 145, 147
Ancestral Admonition (Ming) 196
Anching 219
anemometer 438
Anhui Province 22, 25, 28; agriculture 55; crafts 391, 402, 422; dialect 327; drama 361; minerals 26, 38, 40, 43; population and administration 23; prehistory 69, 71; and Taiping rebellion 219
animals **32–3, 437**; draught 48, 58, 452; games of competition 133, 437; prehistoric 71, 138; *see also individual animals*
animism 79, 295
Anji Bridge, Hebei *430*, 452
Annam 46, 84, 176, 194, 226
Annan (Tonking) 173
Anshan, Liaoning 23, 38
Antaibao coal mine, Shanxi 453
antelopes 32
anthropology: early man **68–71**; Mongoloid family of peoples 72–4
Anti-Confucius Campaign **274**, 323
Anti-Japanese War 13, **246–7**, 248; arts during 355, 364, 365; Beijing occupied 137, 246; CCP in 246, 249, 250, 256; communications 452, 453, 454; Deng's rise 279; education 116; liberated areas 249, 256; Lin Biao in 273; Marco Polo Bridge Incident 246; mining 452; Nanjing government and 242; Zhao Ziyang in 280; Zhou Enlai in 260; *see also* United Front
Anti-Rightist Campaign 105, 250, **265**, 323
antimony 40, 453
Anyang, Henan 74, 162, 342, 390
aphrodisiacs 376
Arabs: conquest of Iran 313, 314; merchants 46, 47, 77, 168, 314; Ming expeditions 198–9; paper manufacture 340; sciences 194, 437, 438; soldiers in China 77
Aramaic script 82

archaeology **136–42**; *see also individual sites and cultures*
architecture **425–32**; *see also*: bridges; fortifications; housing; pagodas; *and under* Buddhism *and individual dynasties*
area of China, total 17
Arigh Böge 193
aristocracy 11, 12, 160, 181–2, 207, 301; Tang 76, 110, 170, 171, 173; *see also* elites
armies: banishment to 102; Black Flag 226; cavalry 157, 159, 160, 167; education 115, 285; eunuchs in 199; Hunan 224; Palace Corps 177, 178; New 234, 235; *see also* People's Liberation Army; Red Army; *and under individual dynasties*
armillary sphere *443*
Arrow War 208, **222–3**
arsenals 184, 223
asbestos 42, 439
Asia, Central 26; diet 368, 371; history 142, 157, 170, *191*, 193, 194; horses 147, 173, 185, *202*, 406, 437, 450; musical instruments 363; natural environment *27*; routeways 24, 153, 168, 185 (*see also* Silk Road); silver work 391
Asia, Southeast: Chinese communities 14, 29, 76, 84, 86, **87–9**; contact through Hong Kong 86; cuisine 368; Neolithic 139; Taiwanese investment 66; trade 43, 46, 175, 176, 198
Asian Games 134
astronomy 115, 194, 205, 318, 404, 437, **441–4**; *see also*: calendar; compasses
Atayal people 74
athletics 133
Atlantic Richfield 35
Australia 41, 86–7
Australo-Melanesian peoples 74
Australopithecines 68
Austrian Jews in China 314
Austro-Asiatic languages 80
autonomous regions 21, 30, 84
Avalokiteśvara *169*
aviation, civil 50–1, 242
Awakening Society, Tianjin 260

ba ('overlord') 147–8
Ba Jin 356, 367
Babao, Qinghai 42
Babylonian science 439, 443
badminton 134
bahe (tug of war) 133
Bai Chongxi 241
Bai Juyi 348–9

Bai people 78, 80
baigepiao (game) 133
Baijiaxing (primer) 112
Baiyin, Gansu 40
balance of payments 63, 64, 207, 216; Macao 66
Bali; overseas Chinese 90
ballads, religious 351
Baller, Frederick Williams 338
bamboo: in construction 33, 446; floating fields 435; furniture 423; games 132; plants 29, 30, 32, *33*; shipbuilding 444, 445; and writing and painting 30, 156, 340, 391, *392*, 398
Ban Biao 157
Ban Gu **157**, 309, 345, 347
Ban Zhao 157
Bandit Suppression Headquarters 253
bandits 92, 96, 173, 219, 243, 253
Bandung Conference (1955) 260
Bangkok, Thailand 87
Bangushan, Jiangxi 41
banishment 102
banking 66, 203, 379
bankruptcy law 63
banner system, Manchu 22, 209, 222
Banpo, Shaanxi; Neolithic culture 140, 141, 425; pottery *140*, 329, *386*, 400
banquets 371, 372, 458
Banshan culture 141, *400*
Baoan, Shaanxi 249
Baoding Military School 252
baojia system 97, 102, **200**
Baotou, Inner Mongolia 27, 38, 41
barley 268, 434, 435; Neolithic 139, 368, 435
barytes 42
basketball 133, 134
basketry, Neolithic 140, 141
bauxite reserves 41
Bayan Obo, Inner Mongolia 42
beans 27, 29, *57*, 368, 370, 434
bed, brick (*kang*) 423, *429*
bee-keeping 437
Bei Dao 357
Beijing *61, 97*; administration 21; Altar of Heaven *430*; Anglo-French attack (1860) 208, 221, 223; bishopric, medieval 317; Boxer Uprising 208, 229; canals 45, 451; as capital, (Liao) 185, (Ming) 108, 196, 198, (Qing) 205, (Yuan) 191; in civil war 251; climate 17, 19; Democracy Wall 281; dialect 326, 327, 329; Eight Trigrams Rebellion 215; Forbidden City *135*, 199, 215, 233, 259, *428*; games, (Asian) 134, (National) *134*; industry 35, 38, 39, 40, 42, 43; intellectual centre 236,

Beijing (*cont.*)
272; Japanese occupation (1937) 137, 246; Jews in medieval 313; Juyongguan gate 414; Legation Quarter 229; Matteo Ricci in 205, 318; population 23, 26; radio 51; State Academy Directorate *108*; Summer Palace 223, 432; *taijiquan 127*; Tiananmen gate 428; Tiananmen Square incidents, (1976) 261, **275–6**, 279, (1989) 106, 134, 270, 281, **282–4**, 285, 323, (aftermath) 85, 281, 364, 366; Tianningsi pagoda *308*; university 109, 115, 236, 339
Beijing, Conventions of (1860) 223, 225
Beijing, Treaty of 221–2, 274
Beijing Film Academy 365–6
Beilin (Forest of Stele, Xi'an) 345
Beixin culture 140, 141
Beiyang Fleet 223, 225
bellows 447, 448, *449*
bells, bronze 363, 385
belt-drives 446, 448
bencao literature 128, 130, *187*, 436, 437, 439; *Bencao gang mu* 128, *129*, **204**, 376
Beng Xian, Sichuan 42
Benxi, Liaoning 38
Bergson, Henri 321
Beringia land bridge 74
beryllium 40
beverages **373–4**, 458
Bi Sheng 341
Bianjing (Kaifeng) 184, 314, 411
Bible 219, 318
Bing Wang, King of Eastern Zhou 146, 147
biogas 35
biography 300, 306
birds, wild 33
birth control 20, 96, 97, 131
birthday celebrations 361, 359, 376
birthrate 53
bismuth 42
Blang people 78
Blucher, Vasily K. (Galin) 240
Blue Shirts 253
Boards, Six (*liu bu*) 167
Bodhidharma 127, 169, 307, 374
Bodhisattvas *304*, *306*, 392–3, 406, *408*
Bogorodsk; foundation 221
Bohai 42, 186
'Bolsheviks, 28' 244, 250
boluoqiu (polo) 133
Bon religion 307
Bonan people 78
bone carving 342
bones, oracle 120, *143*, 289, 333, 342–3, 363, 435, 440
Book of Changes 290, 302, 343
Book of Documents 147, 302, 343, 345
Book of Odes 301–2, 325, 343–4, **347**, 411
books; Burning of the 150, 151; in Cultural Revolution 272; early 340, 341
Books of Rites 430

borax 439
borehole drilling, deep **446–7**
Borneo 90
Borodin, Michael 237, *238*, 239, 240
botany 32–3, **435–6**, 439
Bouyei language 83
Bouyei people 78
Boxer Rebellion 99, 208, 225, *229*, 318, *319*
boxing 133; shadow 127, 133, 229
brass; furniture fittings 424
Brazil 34, 86
breathing exercises 127, 129, 296
Brecht, Berthold 364
bricks 402, 405, 425, 429, 430
bridges *50*, 426, *430*, **452**, *455*
brine, subterranean 446–7
Britain: and Anti-Japanese war (1939–45) 246; Boxer Indemnity Scholars 229; C19th relations 207, 208, 215–18, 219, 220, 221, 223, 226, 228; Chinese in 87; civil service examinations 111; concessions 222, 223, 231, 240 (*see also* treaty ports); 'coolies' in colonies 85; and Hong Kong 22, 65, 85–6; Japanese alliance (1902) 230; and Kailuan coal mine 452; literature 355, 356; railway construction 231; and Tibet 211; trade 40, 41, 43, 216–17; and Yuan Shikai 235
brocade 422
bronze **390**; bells 363, 385; caskets 403; casting 144, 390, 399, 401, 424; currency 193, 379; gilt 390, 403, *405*, *408*; ingots, as currency 379; inlaid 390, 402; inscriptions 329, 333, 343; ritual objects 144, *145*, *146*, 329, 343, **382–5**, 390, 398, 399, **401–2**; sculpture 390, 391, 401, *405*, 406, *408*
Bronze Age 74, 142, 387, 424, 425, 452; *see also* Shang *and* Zhou *dynasties*
Bruce, Frederick 223
Brunei 87, 90
brush pots 391, *392*, 393, 394
brushes 333, 398, 419
Buddha: Amitābha 169, 307, 309, 405; in art *304*, *306*, 392–3, 405, 406; Laozi and 298, 305
Buddhism 12, **304–9**; architecture 194, *308*, 429; biography 306; breathing techniques 127; Caodong school 169; Chan school 169, 307, 309, 411; charms 340; cuisine 370; and Daoism 297, 298, 305, 306, 309, 405, 408; during disunity after Han 157, 159, 405–6; Dzungar Mongols and 211; Eastern Jin 305; Esoteric school 171, 307; exegetical schools 306–7; and family 12; Han era 157, 340; Huan and 304; Indian contacts through 168; introduction and assimilation 47, 157, **304–6**; Japanese 169, 201, 340; Jurchen Jin 187; Khubilai Khan and 298; Lamaism 79, 194, 201, 210, 268, 307–8, 414, (*see also*

Dalai Lamas); Liao dynasty 177; literature 129, 168–9, 176, 299, 305, **308–9**, 351, (Canon) 306, 308, 309, 340, 341, (printing of) 188, 194; local gods and 295; Mahāyānā 303, 304, 307, 309, 406; Maitreya 195, 214, 215, 405; Mao on 323; medicine 122–3, 129; metaphysics 304; millenarianism 99, 193, 214; mirrors 405; monasticism 12, 162, 168, 194, 201, 268, 295–6, 305–6, 340; Mongols and 79, 192, 193, 194, 201, 210, 298, 308, 414; and Neo-Confucianism 190; persecutions 162, 306, 314, 407, 408; pilgrims 90, 430; popular 303; printing 188, 194; Pure Land 169, 307, 309, 405; Red Sect 210; rituals 297, 307; and Sanskrit loan-words 325; scholarship 306; schools 169, 171, **306–8**; symbolism in art 396, *397*; Theravāda 81, 309; Xixia 185; *see also under*: Confucianism; painting; sculpture; temples; translations; *and* Song, Sui *and* Tang *dynasties*
buildings, siting of 288, 289, 290–1
Bulgaria 40
bullfighting (*douniu*) 133
bureaucracy: in PRC 261–2, 264, 265; and technological stagnation 448; *see also* officials
burials 295–6; associations of enterprises and 98; banners 402; Buddhist 297, 306, 307; cremation 93; Daoist 297; Neolithic 140, 142; Rites Controversy 318; Shang dynasty 144; Tang 408–9; *see also*: tomb objects; tombs
Burma: boundary 269; Chinese community 84, 87, 89; history 47, 76, 173, 194, 248; jadeite 393, 418; languages 80, 82
Burma Road 48, 454
Byzantine Empire 168

cabbages 368, 370, 371, 376
cables, bamboo skin 446
Cai E 235
Cai Jing 179, 180
Cai Lun 156
Cai Yuanpei 115, *236*
caiquan (game) 133
Cairo Conference (1943) 248, 252, 253
calendar **377–8**, *443*; state control 155, 377, 441–2; *see also* festivals
calligraphy **333–4**, **398–9**, **419–21**; and examination system 110, 111; Literati painting and 409; Northern Wei *405*; printing of 341; Qianlong emperor 213; Su Dongpo 349; techniques 419–21; Yang Xi 300; Zhao Mengfu 412; *see also*: characters; writing; writing equipment
caltrop 139
Cambodia (Kampuchea) 87, 89, 139, 269, 270
camels 32, *47*
Campbell, James D. 226

Canada 40, 86–7
canals 45, **451**, *452*, 454; An Lushan rebellion and 172; Grand 25, *46*, 166, 184, 193, 218, 444, 451; North Jiangsu 25; Qing 207; Red Flag 454; Song 182; Tang 171; Zhengguo 451; *see also under* Han, Sui, Yuan *dynasties*
Canton *109*, *112*; administration 21; Anti-Japanese War 246; in Arrow War 223; British rights in 222, 225; Christianity 318; city walls razed 97; in civil war 251; climate 17, 19; dialect 326; emigration 86, 87, *88*; *Guomindang* in 233, 234, 239, 242, 252, 255; industry 29, 40, 203, 214; justice *104*; Muslims 314, *315*; Nationalist government (1931) 242; opium question 217; railways 49; Tang era 168, 313, 314; topography 29; trade; Canton system 215–16
Cantongqi (*The Kinship of the Three*) 299
Cao Cao 158, 352
Cao Kun 235
Cao Wei 158–9
Cao Xueqin 353–4
Cao Yu 357, 364
Cao Zhi 347
caravans *47*, 153, 168, 185, 193, 212
card games 132, 134
Cardan, Jerome 450
carpentry 423
carpets 423
Carpini, John of Plano 317
cartography *107*, *108*, 194, 318, **441**, 443
catalogues 411; Buddhist Canon 306, 309; of imperial library 345, 347
'Cathay' 177, 184, 318
Catholicism: missionaries 115, 194, 210, 317, 318; Philippines 89; Rites Controversy 205, 210; *see also* Jesuits
cattle; Neolithic 139, 368
Caucasian peoples 72, 77
cavalry 157, 159, 160, 167, 185
cave dwellings *249*, 429; *see also under* temples
cement 23, 42, **43–4**
Cen Yuying 220
censorship of media 361, 365, 366
censuses 77, 155, 192, 200
cerumen 73
Ceylon 47, 168
Chai Rong, Emperor 174, 175
Chaihe, Liaoning 40
chambers of commerce 98
Chamorros people 73
Champa 165, 194; rice 182, 368, 435
Chang, Carson (Zhang Junmai) 323
Chang Zhanggeng 361
Chang'an, Shaanxi: canals 45, 166, 451; city planning 155; Han 24, 151, 153, **155**, 156; location 149; Sui 24, 165, 166; Tang 24, 108, 168, 171, 173, 314, 340, 409; time, measurement of 377; Western Wei 162
Changchun, Manchuria 23, 243, 251

Changsha, Hunan; crafts 402, 404, 421; dialect 326, 327; fighting (1930) 244; industry 40; literacy scheme 113; Mao in 254; village 28

Changshan, Jiangsu 38

Changyang, Hubei 69, 71

'chanting fellows' 294, 295

characters, written 329–34; archaic 330; caoshu 330, 333–4, 398–9, 406; kaishu 329, 330, 334, 337, 398; lishu 330, 333, 398, 417; Modern Simplified (jiantizi) 330, 331, 334; number of 337, 341; Proto- 329, 330; reforms 113, 331–3; seal 330, 333, 399; Slender Gold 411; sutizi 330, 334; wenyan 327, 328; xingshu 330, 334, 398, 409, 410, 417; see also: calligraphy; writing

charcoal 438

chariots 142, 144, 146

charms, printed 340

chemical industry 42, 53; see also fertilizers

chemistry 300, 437–8; see also alchemy

Chen Baxian 164

Chen Boda 272

Chen Cheng 252

Chen Duxiu 236, 237, 238, 239, 241, 254

Chen Guofu 242

Chen Jiongming 237, 239

Chen Kaige 366

Chen Lifu 242

Chen Shaoyu (Wang Ming) 244, 250

Chen She, rebellion of 150

Chen Tingjing 337

Chen Yi 164, 252

Chen Youliang 195

Chen Yucheng 219

Chen Yun 250

Cheng Hao 190

Cheng Hongshou 415

Cheng Miao 333

Cheng Yi 190, 304, 319

Chengdi, Emperor 154

Chengdu, Sichuan 38, 49, 283; arts and crafts 188, 214, 340, 407; emperors' garden 431, 432

Chengpu, battle of 147

Chengua Emperor 195, 416

Chennault, Gen Claire 248

chess 132, 394

Chiang Ching-kuo 286

Chiang Kai-shek 252–3; at Cairo Conference 248, 253; China's Destiny 322; Christian 318; and civil war 251, 250; and Guomindang 236, 237, 252; heads Free China government 247–8; negotiations with Mao (1945) 250, 253, 257; in Nanjing government 241, 242, 253; and New Life Movement 116, 242, 253; and Northern Expedition 240, 252, 253; Shanghai coup 241, 252, 253, 255, 260, 356; in Taiwan 253, 285–6; and Tongmenghui 252; and United Front 239; Xi'an Incident 242, 246–7, 253, 256, 260

Chiang Kai-shek, Mme 242, 253

chickens 33, 368, 376

children 96, 96, 119, 133, 314; see also: birth control; education

Chile 40

chilli peppers 368, 370, 376

Chin dynasty see Jin

Ch'in dynasty see Qin

China Democratic League 260

China Inland Mission 318

China International Famine Relief Commission 48

China Merchants' Steam Navigation Company 223, 224

Chinese Communist Party: in Anti-Japanese war 246, 249, 250, 256; in Border Regions 118, 133, 249, 254, 262, 266 (see also Yan'an); and Chineseness 13–14; Congresses, (First) 255, (Eighth) 279, (Ninth) 270, 273–4, 276, 277, (Tenth) 259, 274–5, 277, (Eleventh) 280, (Twelfth) 281, (Thirteenth) 281; Constitution (1985) 281; education 113, 118, 249–50; European branch 260; and Guomindang 13–14, 240, 241, 250–1, 253, 285 (see also: civil war; United Front; May Fourth Movement and 236; military element 258, 273, 274, 285; Nanchang Uprising (1927) 285; organizations 470; Plena 280; pseudonyms 336; in Republican period 237–8 (see also Guomindang above); rural strategy 243, 244, 249, 255, 263; and secret societies 99; Soviets 243–4; strikes 241; urban and rural factions (1930s) 244; and USSR 245, 256; see also: Jiangxi Soviet; Long March; Marxism; Red Army; rectification; United Front; Yan'an

Chinese Nationalist Party see Guomindang

Chinese People's Political Consultative Conference 254, 261

Chinese Revolutionary Party 230, 237

Chineseness 11–14, 75

Ch'ing dynasty see Qing

Chongqing, Sichuan 21, 30, 251; Free China Government 246, 247–8, 252, 260; industry 30, 38, 40; Nationalist/Communist negotiations 250, 253, 257

Chongzhen Emperor 195, 205, 206

Chongzong (Tangut emperor) 176

chopsticks 368, 370, 373, 458

Chou dynasty see Zhou

Christianity 226, 317–19; Boxers and 229, 319; Russian Orthodox 318; Taipings and 218, 219, 318; see also: Catholicism; Jesuits; missionaries; Nestorianism

chromium 42

Chu, state of 75, 147, 148, 149, 347, 391

Chu, new state of 150, 152

Chu (Ten Kingdoms) 174, 175

Chu Suiliang 406

Chu Wuchen 148

chuanqi (dramatic form) 358

Chuansha, Shanghai 220

Chuanya 129

Chuci 347, 376

Chudi, Emperor (Jin) 174

Chuenpi (Chuanbi) Convention 218

Chunqiu 147, 302, 342, 344, 345

Cian, Empress 223, 227

cihua (verse tales) 351

cinema 365–7

cinnabar 296

cities 97–8, 300; administration 20, 21–2; choice of site 290–1; Shang 425; sieges 147; Song 188–9, 358, 359; town planning 97, 155, 157, 165, 425; walls 97, 425, 426, 428, 431; Yuan 193; Zhou 425

civil engineering 451–2, 454–5

civil service see officials

Civil War, Ming (1398–1402) 196, 198

civil war, Republican/Communist (1946–49/50) 250–1, 273, 279, 454

Cixi, Empress Dowager 223, 224, 225, 227; death 231, 233; and imperial succession 208, 227, 233; and Reform Movement (1898) 208, 228, 229; and Yuan Shikai 234, 235

clans 164, 301; see also lineages

clays: for iron founding 447; porcelain 43, 203, 387, 401, 416

climate: and agriculture 17, 19, 23; and flora and fauna 34, 437; precipitation 18; Shang dynasty 144; temperature 17, 18; for visitors 458; see also: disasters and under individual regions

clocks: mechanical 318, 443, 451; water- 377, 438, 443

coal 34, 35, 44, 63; development 52, 452, 453; fields 23, 25, 26, 29, 30, 52; transport 45, 46, 47, 49, 50

cobalt 41, 416

Cochin-China; overseas Chinese 87

cock fighting (douji) 133

coffee 374

coffin, Han painted lacquer 402

Cohong (guild) 215, 216, 218

coinage see under currency

collectivization 99–100, 266; coercion 264, 266–7; end 55, 58, 100; industry 27, 61; see also land allocation (PRC) and under agriculture

colonization 75–7, 202, 222; see also external China and under individual countries

colophons 417, 420

Comintern 237, 238, 239, 240, 256

commanderies 155

Commercial Press, Shanghai 114, 341

committees: revolutionary 21, 273; village 22

communes 54–5, 266–7, 268; Mao and 258, 265; Shanghai 258, 273; social aspects 92, 100

communications 45–51; Anti-Japanese War 452, 453; Nanjing government and 242; official 47, 51; satellite 51; see also individual areas and modes

Communism: and family 92–3, 94, 95; see also: Chinese Communist Party; Marxism

compasses 46, 289, 291, 443–4

concessions, foreign 241, 242, 431; 'scramble for' 227, 228, 230, 231; see also individual areas and Western countries

concubinage 105

Confucian classics 301–2, 343–5; commentaries 304, 319, 344–5; in examinations 110, 111; Neo-Confucianism and 304, 319, 345; printing of 114, 188, 190, 340; translation into Xixia 176; Wang Anshi and study of 184; Zhu Xi and 194; see also individual works

Confucianism 11, 12, 301–4; absorbs other philosophical schools (C5th–3rd BC) 309; anti-professionalism 131; and Buddhism 12, 190, 303–4, 306, 310, 344; and Daoism 190, 296, 344; Donglin Academy 205; emperors and 109, 209, 302; hierarchical view 94, 107, 109, 456; Jews assimilate 313; on li 312; on man's innate goodness 107, 109, 116; Mao on 323; May Fourth Movement and 321; metaphysics 304; and modernization (1920s) 13–14; mourning 310; and New Life Movement 242; 'new text' school 320; PRC anti-Confucian campaign 274; Qing 223; ritual 210, 301, 303, 321, 361–3; and social order 92, 94, 107, 109, 157, 301, 304, 321; Sui 164, 165; Yuan 195; Zhou 147; see also: Confucian classics; Confucius; and under: education; examination system; family; historiography; medicine; officials; temples; and individual dynasties

Confucius 302; and Chunqiu 147, 344; cult 107, 302; on food 368; Kang Youwei on 228; life and disciples 301–2; name 337; PRC discussion of 323; and Shijing 343–4, 347; Zhou Gong familiar spirit of 146; see also: Confucianism; Lunyu

Congregation for the Propagation of the Faith 318

consorts 154, 156, 170, 171

constitutions: Provisional Republican 235; PRC 105–6, 265, 273

Constitutional Movement 230–1, 232

consumerism 53, 63

contracts 62, 63, 104, 112

'coolies' 85, 86, 90

cooperatives 258, 263–4

copper 39–40; coinage 193, 201, 203, 207; import 40, 46; mining 39–40, 438, 452; objects 142, 183, 193, 402

corruption: and examinations 111; Ming 199, 201; Qing 207, 213, 220, 222, 227; PRC 261, 270; Socialist

corruption (*cont.*)
Education Movement and 270;
Tang 171
corvée: in disunity after Han 158,
159, 161; exemption 108, 109, 111,
162; Ming 203; Sui 165, 166, 167;
Yuan 193
cosmology **288**, 303, 311, 343, 362,
404
cotton 55, 56, 58, 59; in past 213,
422, 435; regions growing 24, 26,
27, 29, 434
counties (*xian*) 21–2, 84, 167
court, imperial: intrigue 154, 156,
170, 171, 172, (Cixi) 208, 227, 233;
Ming organization 199, 201
Courts, Nine (*Jiu si*) 167
craftsmen 94, 112, 399, 425, 429; *see
also individual crafts*
cricket fighting 133, 437
crossbow 147
Cuba 86
cuisine **368–77**; cooking and eating
outside *373*, 429; and health care
123, 373, 376; history 368–70;
ingredients, recipes and meals
372–3; nutrition 53, 58, 376
Cultural Revolution **270–3**;
anarchism 258; arts 267, 272, 357,
361, 364, 365; and Chineseness
14; Deng Xiaoping 275, 279; and
economy 50, 53, 63, 259; legal
system 105; Liu Shaoqi 270–1,
272; medicine 130; and overseas
Chinese 89; Peng Dehuai 267;
Peng Zhen 271–2; posters *60*;
railways 50; reasons for 269, 270;
rectification campaign 250; and
religion 268, 315–16, 319;
rehabilitation of victims 271, 272;
revolutionary committees 21, 273;
and social structure 92, 93, 94–5;
and Tibet 268; 'two lines' 258, 270;
and West 280; Wuhan Incident
272–3; Zhao Ziyang 280; *see also*:
January Storm; Red Guards; *and
under*: education; Mao Zedong;
Zhou Enlai
Cultural Revolution Group 272, 273
cup, Tang silver *424*
currency **379–80**, 459; coinage 153,
171, 289, 193, **379–80**, (copper)
193, 201, 203, 207; Foreign
Exchange Certificates 459; Jin
193; and mining 452; Nationalist
242, 251; paper 193, 242, 248, 251,
341, 379; spirit money 295; *see
also under* silver
Czechoslovakia 259, 269

Da Mingguo (Great Ming) 220
Da Xia *see* Xixia
Da Yi 144
Da Yue *see* Han, Southern
Dadiwan I culture 140, 141
Dadu (Beijing, Yuan) 191, 193, 194
Dagang, Shandong; oil 26, 35
'Dagu Repulse' 223
Dahecun culture 141
Dai, Lady of; tomb 437
Dai Jitao United Front 239
Dai language 80–1, 82

Dai people 78
Dai Wangshu 356
Dairen, Liaoning 254
Dajishan, Jiangxi 41
Dalai Lamas 210–11, 268, 307, 308
Dali, Shaanxi 69, 71
Dali, Yunnan 76, 80, 220
Dalian (Lüda), Liaoning 21, 35, 43
Damansky Island 274
dams 34, **451**, 454
dance; Tang dynasty 168, 171
Dangxiang *see* Tanguts
Danjiangkou, Hubei 36
Danshui (Tamsui), Guangdong 225
danwei (work unit) 93
Dao (the Way) 296, 301, 313
Daoan 305, 309
Daochuo 169
Daodejing 298, 299, 300
Daoguang Emperor 207, 215, 217
Daoism **12, 296–300**; absorbs other
philosophical schools 309;
alchemy and 296, 300, 437; artistic
symbolism 396, *397*, 403;
breathing exercises 296; and
Buddhism 297, 298, 305, 306, 309,
405, 408; C3rd revival 347–8;
charms 340; Chu 148; concepts
296–7; elite adopt, C5th 303;
Emperor Huan and 304; and
garden design 431; hagiography
340; and immortality 296–7, 300,
437; language 309, 312–13, 408;
literature 188, 299–300, 311,
340–1, 362; local gods and 295;
and magic 298; Manichaeism and
314; Mao on 323; Quanzhen
school 187, 299; rituals 295,
297–8, 300, 437; sages 298–9 (*see
also* Laozi); sculpture 408; and
secret societies 99; temples 429;
Yellow Turbans and 156; *yin* and
yang 288; *see also* Dao *and under*:
Confucianism; festivals;
medicine; *and* Han, Ming, Song,
Sui, Tang *and* Zhou *dynasties*
Daoji 417
Daoxuan 307
Daozang 299, 362
Dapenkeng, Taiwan 141, 400
Dapenkeng culture 139, 141
Daqin (Syria) 317
Daqing oilfield 23, 34, 35
daqiu (game) 133
Daquan (digests of learning) 197
darughachi (Mongol administrators)
192
Dashiqiao, Liaoning 41
Datong, Shanxi 405
Daur people 78
David (Nestorian metropolitan) 317
Dawenkou culture 140, 141, 142, 329
Daxi culture 140, 141
Daxingzheng (Chang'an, Sui) 166
Daxue 304, 344
Daya Bay, Guangdong *38*
Dayao, Yunnan 40
Daye, Hubei 38, 40, 452–3
Dazhai, Shanxi 25, 276
De'ang people 78
design 382–99
deer 33; Père David's 437

defence *see*: armies; military arts;
navies; nuclear weapons
defences, northern 150, 151, 153,
171, 197; *see also* walls (Great)
deforestation 33, 38
Dehua, Fujian 214, 418
demography *see*: birth control;
population
demonstrations, public 265, 268,
281; *see also* Beijing (Tiananmen
Square)
Deng Xiaoping 277, *278, 279*; and
agriculture 55, 56, 59; disgrace
and rehabilitation 274, 275, 276–7,
279, 280; and economy 53, 54,
281; and education 117, 118–19,
277, 279; and Hua Guofeng 280,
281; and Jiangxi Soviet 279; name
336; reforms 55, 59, 105, 117, 279,
280, 281, 323; religious toleration
under 316, 319; and Tiananmen
Square protests (1989) 282, 323;
and Zhao Ziyang 280
Denmark 44
deserts 24, 26, 32
Dewey, John 322
Dexing, Jianxi 40
Deyang, Sichuan 391
Dezong, Emperor (Tang) 172
Dharmapāla 307
Di (High God of Shang) 144
Di Xin 143
Di Yi 143
dialects 113, **326–8**, 367
diamonds 43
Dian kingdom, Yunnan 75
Dian kings of Qi 148
dice 132
dictionaries 205, 331, **337–9**, 340;
botanical 436; non-Han scripts 83;
rhyme 325; Xu Shen's 329, 337,
343
Diego antigen 73
diet *see* cuisine
dikes, river 207, 451, 454
Ding county, Hebei; literacy 113
Ding Zilin 357
Dingcun, Shanxi 69, 71, 138
Dingzhou commune *64*
diqu (prefectures) 21
Directions, Four (or Five) 395, 404
disasters, natural 207, 303; (1959–
61) 258, 266, 267, 268; Tang 167,
171, 172
distillation 438
disunity, period after fall of Han
157–64, 405–6; agriculture 157,
158; arts 157, 405–6; Buddhism
157, 159, 405–6; calligraphy 157,
404; city planning 165; education
108; historiography 345–6;
officials 109–10, 158, 159, 160;
sculpture 157, *305*, 405–6;
taxation 158, 159, 161; *see also
individual states*
divination 146, 147, **288–91**, 295,
296; *see also*: bones, oracle; *Book
of Changes*; geomancy;
hexagrams; milfoil;
plastromancy; scapulimancy
diving 134
divorce 93, 95, 104

Diyā 'al-Dīn 222
dogs 368, 370, 437; Neolithic 139,
140, 141, 368
dolls 133
dolomite processing plants 41
Dolonnur, Inner Mongolia 191
dolphin, Yangtze 437
Dominicans 210, 317
Dong, Master 354
Dong people 78
Dong Qichang 415–16, 417
Dong Yuan 410
Dong Zhongshu 151, 303
Dong-Shui language 80
Dongchuan, Yunnan 40
Donglin Academy 205
Dongxian people 78
Dorgon 205, 206, 209
Dōshō 169
douqu 133, 437
dragons' teeth (drugs) 68
drama 113, 357, **358–61, 364–5**;
Jurchen Jin 187; television and
367; *see also* opera *and under*
Ming, Song *and* Yuan *dynasties*
dramatic narratives 354
dream interpretation 340
Dream of the Red Chamber 353–4,
367
drought 19, 25, 26, 27, 167, 172, 207
drugs 148; *see also* pharmacology
drum stands, Zhou bronze 402
Drung people 78
Du Fu 348, 349
Du Wenxiu 220
Du Yuesheng 241
Duan Qirui 235, *235*
duck rearing 434
Dugu, Empress 165
Dugu clan 164
Dunhuang, Gansu; cave temples
422, 430; texts 300, 314, 317, 340,
351, 362, 407; wall paintings 363,
405, 407
Dushanzi, Gansu 35
dust-storms 19, 20
dyeing **422–3**, 437
Dzungaria 26, 76, 168, *206*, 210,
211–12, 222

E-Yu-Wan (Zhang Guotao) 244, 245
eagles 32
ear wax 73
earth sciences **438–40**
earthquakes 276, **439–40**
East India Company, British 216
eclipses 318, 442
economy **52–67**; PRC 253, 254, 259,
269, (under Deng) 55, 56, 279, 281;
*see also individual periods and
aspects*
Edjell, Seyyid 315
education **107–19**; Board of 133;
CCP 113, 118, 249–50; character
reform and 113; charitable
schools 108, 109, 112; Christian
missionaries and 114, 115, 225,
318; communes provide 100, 266;
Confucian based 107, 157, 304,
319; constitution of (1978) on 105;
in Cultural Revolution 117, 118,
272, 274, 453, 455; *Daquan* 197;

education (*cont.*)
  degree holders' role in village life 97; Deng's reforms 117, 118–19, 277, 279; family and 92; foreign languages 114–15, 223, 225; growth under PRC 92, 95, 106, 116, 118, 119; higher 114–16, 118, 119 (*see also* universities); indoctrination 116–17; lineage schools 112, 294; Maoist model 117–18, *119*; mass adult 113, 118; merchants and 98, 110, 112, 172; minority language policies 83; modernization 117; Nanjing government and 242; physical 133, 134; political 116–17; primers 112, 114, 133; private 108, 109; provincial schools 108, 109; radio and 367; rural part-time 112, 113, 119; State Academy Directorate *108*, 109, 345; technical and vocational 114, 119, 131, 453, 455; television and 367; temples used as schools 429; traditional system 107–9; tutors, private 112; USA and 115–16, 223, 225, 229; USSR and 117–18, 269; *wenmiao* schools 429; Westernized 98, 114–16, 118, 320; (students abroad) 119, 223, 229, 280, 320, 431; women 95–6, 111, 118; Xunzi on 303; *see also*: examination system; literacy; military arts; universities; *and under* Han, Ming, Qing, Song *and Sui dynasties, and* printing
Eight Princes, Troubles of the 159
Eight Trigrams Rebellion *214*, 215
elders, lineage 293
elections 235, 286
electricity 35, 41, *57*; *see also* hydro-electricity
Elements, Five 437, 443
elephants 33, 437
Elgin, 8th Earl of 223
elites 76, 93–4, 110, 172, 181–2; *see also*: aristocracy; officials
Elliot, Captain Charles 217, 218
embroidery 419, 422
emigration *see* external China
emperors: art collections 420–1; and calendar 155, 377, 441–2; edicts 116, 317; Han: role 155; killed by alchemy 296; loyalty towards (*zhong*) 12; personal power 13, 196, 225, 320; reign-periods 379; religious role 12, 109, 303, 320, 430; tombs 390, 408–9, 430; and weights and measures 380; *see also individual emperors and dynasties*
Emperors, Five 136
employment 62, 63, 92, 95, 99
enamelling *416*, 417, 418, 419
Encirclement Campaigns 242, *244*, 245
encyclopedias 310, 319, 362, 436; *see also: Tiangong kaiwu; Tushu jicheng*
energy resources 34–8; *see also individual types of energy*
engineering 115, 194, **448–55**

environment, natural 32–3, 38, 66; *see also* soils
Erlitou, Henan; Bronze Age 141, 142
Erya 344, 436, 437
Erzhu people 162
escapements 443, 451
esculentist movement 436
Eskimos 73
etiquette 456, 457–9
Eucken, Rudolf 320
eunuchs 154, 156, 172, 179, 215, 228; corruption 199, 227; Ming 197, 198, **199**, 201, 416
Europe, Eastern 42, 105, 284, 365; *see also individual countries*
Europe, Western: airlines 51; Chinese in 84, 86; early contacts 457; trade 63, 202, 203, 213, 220, 423, 457; and Taiwan 66; *see also individual countries*
evidentiary research, school of 319
Ewenki people 78
examination system, imperial **109–11, 200**; abolition 94, 115, 116, 320; calligraphy 111; Confucian basis 110, 111, 116, 190, 304, 344, 319; eight-legged essay 111, 197; 'facilitated examination' 181; games about 132, 133; Han 155; *jinshi* degree 108, 110, 111, 165, 181, 200, 224; printing and 114, 188; social composition of candidates 95, 110, 111, 172, 182, 359; Sui 110, 165; symbolic representation of success in 396; Taipings and 219; Wen Zhengming 414; *see also under* Ming, Qing, Song *and* Tang *dynasties*
exorcism 120, 128, 298
external China 14, **84–90**; cuisine 370; medicine 126; spoken language 338; Triad Societies 99; *see also*: Hong Kong; Macao

Fa jing (Canon of Laws) 101
'face' 458
family 12, 54, **92–3**; ancestor worship 291–2, 294; and commerce 92, 98; celebrations 359; collective punishment **102–3**, 196; Confucian ideal 92, 116; farming *15*, 92, 100, 258, 268; filial conduct 12, 102, 116; grandparents *67*, 93; law 92, 103; *li* and 301; Mohist disregard for 310; names 335–6; and responsibility system 100, 119, 280–1; women's role 95
famine 52, 258, 280–1, 314, 436
Fan Chengda 349
Fan Kuan 410
Fankuo mine, Guangdong 40
Far Eastern Championship Games 134
fauna, natural 32–3, 437
Fazang 307
feet, binding of 95
Fei River 160
Feidi, Emperor 173
Fen Valley 24
Feng, Dowager Empress 161

Feng Guifen 223
Feng Guozhang 235
Feng Menglong 351
Feng Yunshan 218
Feng Yuxiang 233, 236, 240, 242
Feng Zhi 356
Fengbitou culture 141
Fengman, Jilin 36
fengshui, see geomancy
Fengtian 220
Fengtongzhai Reserve, Sichuan 33
fertilizers 20, **44**, 58, 59; chemical 25, 26, 41, 44, 52, 57–8; natural 20, 27, 44, 58, 434
festivals 97, 98; Daoist 188, 297; folk religion 295; food for 371, 372, 376; Ghost *291*; *jiao* 297–8; by lunar calendar 378; New Year 98, 376, 378; Qingming 275; Song 188; winter solstice 430
feudalism 145–6, 149, 301, 448
'Feudatories, Three' 206, **210**
fiction 194, 350, 354–5, 355–6, 358
fiefs 192, 193, 196, 201
Fiji 87
fish and fisheries 33, 55, 58, 59; in cuisine 370, *371*, 376; Neolithic 139, 142, 368
Five Agencies 311
Five–Anti Campaign 261, 262
Five Classics 107, 112, 319, **343–4**
Five Dynasties 110, **173–4**, 180, 346, 407
Five Phases (*wu xing*) 121, 123
Five Year Plans **264**; First 52, 59, 257, 261, 263, 264, 453; Fourth 53
floods: control 37, 163, 179, 263, **451**; historical 163, 167, 172, 193, 207, 219, 313; present-day 19, 25, 28
flora, natural 32–3, 435–6
fluorspar 43
flutes 359, 361, 363
Fogong monastery, Datong 427, 429
Foguangsi, Wutaishan 427
Fong, Allen 367
Fontanier, Henri 226
food *see*: cuisine
football 133
foreign relations *see individual countries*, concessions; joint projects; loans; treaties; *and under individual countries and* education; railways
Foreign Exchange Certificates *459*
foreign language teaching 115, 117, 223, 225
forests 32, 33, 38
fortifications 426, **430–1**; *see also* walls
fortune cookies 375
fortune tellers 288, 296
Foshan, Guangdong 29
fossils 439; *see also: Homo erectus; Homo sapiens*
Four Books see *Sishu*
Four Modernizations 279
Framatone (company) 38
France: C19th relations 207, 208, 219, 220, 221, 223, 226–7, 230, 231, 252; Chinese in 113, 260, 277, (in colonies) 85, 87; joint project 44;

literature 355, 356, 357; Paris Commune 259, 266, 267
Franciscans 210, 317
Free China government, Chongqing 246, 247–8, 252, 260
fruit 59, 376, 437
fuels, traditional 38
Fugu plan for Manchuria 314
Fujian Province 29; agriculture 29; dialect 326; drama 358; energy *36*, 38; history 75, 76, 84, 174, 175, 202, 220, 231, 240, 242, 314; minerals 42, 43; minorities 78, 314; population and administration 23; prehistory 141, 142; printing 341; roads 49; and Taiwan 76, 286; topography 17, 29; wild environment 32
Fujiwara Sadatoshi 362
Fulin, Emperor 209
funerals *see* burials
fungi, cultivation of 33
furniture 423–4
fur trade 33, 47, 220
Fushun, Liaoning 23, 41, 452
Fusu, Prince of Qin 150
Fuxi (deity) *136*
Fuzhou, Fujian: Arsenal 115; dialect 327; Dockyard 223, 226; Min kingdom 174, 175; population 29; Song 188; treaty port 225

Galdan 210, 211
Galen 439
Galin (Vasily K. Blucher) 240
gambling 66, 132
games and sports **132–4**
gan stems, ten 144
Gandhi, Rajiv 269
'gang of four' 130, 259, 260, 274, **277**, 279, 280; fall 105, 276, 277, *278*; *see also individual names*
Gansu Province: Buddhist art 340; flora 436; geographical regions 24–5, 26; history 75, 76, 84, 220, 315; hydro-electricity 37; minerals 37, 39, 40–1, 42; Muslims 220, 315, 316; population and administration 23, 78; prehistory 140, 141, 400; soils and agriculture 20; *see also* Xixia
Gao family of Jingnan 174
Gao Gang 263
Gao Huan 162
Gao Ming 358
Gao Panlong 205
Gao Qi 350
Gao Xingjian 357, 364
Gao Yang 162
Gaodi, Emperor 150, **151–3**
Gaoshan people 78, 82
Gaozong, Emperor (Song) **179–80**, 188, 411
Gaozong, Emperor (Tang) 169–70
Gaozu, Emperor (Han) 174
Gaozu, Emperor (Jin) 174
Gaozu, Emperor (Tang) 166, 167
gardens 428, *429*, 431–2, 436
gas, natural 34, **35**, 36, 44, 446–7
Gaubil, Antoine 313
gazetteers, local 346
Ge Hong 299

dGe lugs pa ('Yellow Hats') school of Lamaism 307
Gejiu, Yunnan 40, 453
Gelo people 78
Geneva settlement (1954) 260
Geng Jingzhong 210
Genghis Khan 190, 191, 317
gentry **200**, 215, 230, 225, 226, 235
geography *16*, **17–22**, 205, 311
geology 17, 24, 25, **439**, 453
geomancy 288, 290–1, 340, 444, 457
George III, King of England 216
geothermal power 38
Gerbillon, Jean-François 212
gerbils 32
Germany: airlines 50; relations, (C19th) 227, 228, 229, 230, 231, 236, (C20th) 234, 243, 314; literature 356, 357; trade 40, 42, 43, 44
Gezhouba dam, Hubei 36, 454
ghosts *291*, 295, 297
Gigantopithecus blacki 68
gilding 390, 403, 409, 425
Giles, Herbert Allen 337, 338
ginseng 220
Giquel, Prosper 115
glaciations 69
Gladstone, W. E. *224*
glass; Qing snuff bottles 418
gnomon (astronomical instrument) 443
go (game) 132
Goa, India 205
goats 32, 368, 370
Gobi desert 32
gods, local 295, 297
Goes, Benedict de 318
gold **39**, 41, 379, 390, **424–5**; brocade 422; inlay 402, 403, 409, 424; lacquer 421; Macao 66; Manchurian; Qing monopoly 220; *see also* gilding
Golden Lotus 353, 354
goldfish 437
Goldi people *73*
Golovin, Fedor 212
Gong, Prince 114, 208, *223*, 225, 227
Gong Xian 417
gongan (paradoxical problems) 169
Gong'an school of poetry 350
Gongdi, Emperor (Sui) 165
Gongdi, Emperor (Zhou, Five Dynasties) 174
gongfu (kung-fu) 367, 368
Gonggong 136
Gongsun Long 311, 312
Gongxian cave temples 392, 405
Gongyangzhuan 344
Gongzui, Sichuan 36
Gorbachev, Mikhail 270, 274, 282
Gordon, Charles 219
grain: in diet 55, 56, 368, 370, 376; foreign trade (1980s) 59; growing regions 24, 27, 29; imperial tribute 45, 46, 220; Neolithic 140, 368; output 53, 55, 56, 100, 267; Qin and Sichuan 149; Sui 167; transport 46, 47, 49, 50, 171, 451
Grand Academy *see* Taixue
graves *see* tombs
Great Leap Forward 52, 59, **265–6**;

communes 100; Deng and 279; and education 118; failure 258, 259, 268, 270; Khrushchev on 269; and literature 357; Liu Shaoqi on 271; Mao and 258, 265; and mining 453; Peng Dehuai and 267; re-evaluation by Party (1981) 280; and social structure 94–5
Greece 438, 439, 440, 441, 442
Gros, Jean Baptiste, Baron 223
Gu Cheng 357
Gu Kaizhi 405, 410
Gu Xianzheng 205
Gu Yanwu 259
Guam 74
Guan Hanqing 350, 358
Guan Zhong (Guan Yiwu) 148
Guandi (God of War) *395*
Guandu Shangban enterprises 224
Guangdong Province 29; dialects 326; diet 58; energy 35, 37, 38; history 76, 174, 175–6, 220, 231, 239; incentive systems 280; industry 43; living standards 62; migration 87; minerals 37, 39, 40, 41, 42, 43; population 23, 29, 78; prehistory 71, 142; storytelling 354
Guangwudi, Emperor 156
Guangxi Province 29; administration 21, 23, *28*, 84; dialect 326; history 69, 74, 76, 174, 175–6, 208, 235, 241; hydro-electricity 37; minerals 39, 40, 41, 42, 43; minorities 21, *28*, 30, 78, 80, 84; population 23; railways 49
Guangxu Emperor 115, 208, 227, 228, 229
Guangzhou *see* Canton
Guanyin 169, *394*, *405*
Gugong Danfu 145
guilds 98, 103, 104, 113, 188, 203; Cohong 215, 216, 218
Guimeishan, Jiangxi 41
Guizhou Province 30; agriculture 30; dialect 327; grain consumption 55; history 71, 76, 84, 235; *Homo erectus* 71; minerals 39, 40, 41, 42, 43, 44; minorities 30, 78, 80, *81*; population 23, 30
Guliangzhuan 344
Gun (mythological figure) 136
gunpowder 194, 438
Guo Moruo 356
Guo Shoujing *443*
Guo Wei (Taizu) 174
Guo Xi 410
Guo Zixing 195
Guomindang 230, **236–7**, 239; army *244*; and Free China government 247–8; May Fourth Movement and 234, 236; and Nanjing government 241–2; and peasants 239, 242, 255; philosophy 322; radio 367; USSR assists 234, 237, 238, 252; Yuan Shikai and 234, 235; *see also*: Chiang Kai-shek; Chinese Communist Party (and *Guomindang*); civil war; Nationalist Army; Sun Yat-sen; Taiwan (Nationalist Government); Whampoa

Guominjun (National People's Army) 240
Guoyu Luomazi 337
Guozijian 108, 345
Guushi Khan 210
Guyana, Chinese in 87
Gwoyeu Romatzyh 337
gymnastics 127, 134, 361

Hai River; water control 25
Hai Rui 202, 267
Haifeng Peasants' Association 239
Haihe Conservancy, Tianjin 454
Hainan Island 29; aboriginals 72; dialect 326; environment 32, 38, 58; history 154, 246; minerals 39, 41, 42; natural gas 35; population and administration 21, 23, 29, 78, 80
Hakka languages 218
Hakka people *88*, 218, 326, 375
Hami, Turkestan 76, 211, 212
Han Chinese 17; expansion 74, 75–7
Han (Five Dynasties) 173, 174
Han (Warring States) 147, 148
Han, Northern (Ten Kingdoms) 173, 174, 178
Han, Southern (Ten Kingdoms) 174, 175–6
Han dynasty 147, 148, 149, **151–7**, **402–4**; agriculture 434, 435, 451; army 155; astronomy 404; Ban Gu 157; bronzes 390, 403; Buddhism 157; calligraphy 398; canals 45, 451; capitals 149, 155, 157; and Central Asia 75, 153, 154, **155**; Confucianism 157, 302, 303; court 154, 156; Daoism 151, 157, 403; economy 153; education 107–8, 157; Former 151–4; Great Wall 153, 155; historiography 155–6, 157, 345; institutions 155, 156, 167; jade *385*, *393*; and Korea 153; lacquer 404, 421; Later 156–7; mathematics 440; minorities 159; mirrors *404*; monopolies 153, 155; officials 109, 155, 156; painting 402, 420, 421; paper 156, 420; penal code 152, 155; poetry 347; pottery 387, 388, **404**; provincial system 152; roads 47; sculpture 392, 403; silver objects 390; taxation 152, 155; technology 38, 445, 446, 451; tiles *402*, 403; time, measurement of 377; tombs *132*, *403*, 437, 445; trade 47, 153, 176; and Vietnam 153; Western 151–4; and Xin 154, **156**; and Xiongnu 153, 154, **155**
Han Fei 149, 151, 312, 313
Han Liner 195
Han river 28
Han Yu 303
Handan, Hebei 26
Hangzhou, Zhejiang: Grand Canal 166; industry 29, 213; Jesuits 318; Jews 313; Lingyin temple *93*; Song 177, 179, 188, 341, 359; topography 29; West Lake *432*
Hangzhou Bay; shipbuilding *445*
Hani people 78
Hankou, Hubei 50, 225, 232, 240,

241, 246
Hanlin Academy 192, 224
Hanshu 157, 345
Hanyang, Hubei 240, 452
Hanyu da zidian 338
Hanyu pinyin, see pinyin
Hao (Zhou capital) 145, 146, 149
Harbin, Heilongjiang 21, 46, 313, 314
Hart, Robert 114
Hawaii 233, 236
He Chun 219
He Long 245
He Yingqin 240
health 100, 121, 131, 242, 252, 266; *see also* medicine
Hebei Province 25; dialect 326; history 17, 148, 167, 170, 171, 172, 184, 185, 251; industry 43; literacy 113; minerals 34, 38, 39, 42, 43, (coal) 26, 34, 50; population and administration 23, 78
Hefei, Anhui; C14th silver 391
Heilongjiang Province: agriculture 20, *55*, 58; climate 23; history 71, 220; minerals 23, 34, 35, 39; peat 38; population and administration 23, 78; wild environment 32
Hejin, Shanxi 41
hemp 140, 422, 434
Hemudu, Zhejiang 139, 141
Henan Province 25; administrative units 22; dialect 326; Han art 403, 404; history 142, 167, 172, 173, 214, 215, 251; industry 39, 40, 41, 43; mining 26, 39, 43, 50; natural gas 35; oil 35; population and administration 23; prehistory 17, 140, 141, 142; Sputnik commune 266
Hengyang, Hunan 40
herbalism 128, 130; *see also*; *bencao* literature
Heshen 213, 214–15
hexagrams 136, 289, *290*, 291, 343; Sixty-four 136
Hexian, Anhui 69, 71
Hezhen people 78
Hideyoshi Toyotomi 202
hierarchy-consciousness 93–5, 98, 107, 109, 456, 458
High Tide of Socialism (1955) 52
historiography 304, 346, **345–7**; *see also under* Han, Song, Yuan *and* Zhou *dynasties*
history, philosophy of 12, 322
Hoabinhian culture 138
Hokkien; emigration 86, 87, *88*
hominids, fossil 68
Homo erectus **68–71**, 73–4, 137–8
Homo sapiens 68, 71, 137, 138
Hong Kong 29; agriculture 29; British rule 65, 85, 218, (end of lease) 22, 65, 85–6, 106; Chinese in 14, 84, 85–6, 87, 104–5; cinema 366–7; economy 65; education 85, 233, 318; emigration 87; festivals *291*, 297; industry 29, 43, 44, 85; Jews 313; language 326, 337; law 65, 85, 104–5; medicine 126, 130; New Territories 85; population 29; technology 29, 85; trade 29, 34, 40, 43, 44, 63, 65, 86; Triad Societies

Hong Kong (*cont.*)
99; and Vietnam 86, 87; 'wind and water' disputes 288; *Xingzhonghui* 236
Hong Pian 351
Hong Ren'gan 219
Hong Shen 357, 364, 365
Hong Sheng 358
Hong Xiuquan 208, 218–19
Hongguang Emperor 195
Hongli *see* Qianlong Emperor
Hongshan culture 139, 140–1, 400
Hongwu emperor (Zhu Yuanzhang) 101, **196**, 199, 200, 201, 314, 350; rebellion 191, 193, 195
Hongxian porcelain *419*
Hongzhou 314
horses 32, 147, 173, 184, 185, 437; in art *202*, 406, 408; harness 449, *450*
hospitals 179, 225, *318*
hostages at court 168
Hou Hsiao-hsien 67
Hou Ji 136
Hou Jing 163–4
Hougang culture 141
Houma, Shanxi 390
housing 53, 55, 93, 98; Dai 81; traditional *425*, 426, 428–9
Hu, Count of Chong 146
Hu Hanmin 239, 322
Hu Shi 236, 322, 356
Hu Weiyong 196
Hu Yaobang 268, 280, 281, *282*, 323
Hua, Fujian 215
Hua Guofeng 53, 105, **276–7**, *279*, 280, 281; name 336
Hua Tuo 127
Huabei, Hebei 34, 35, 219
Huai river 454
Huai-Hai, battle of 251
Huainan, Anhui 175
Huan, Duke of Qi 147–8, 148
Huan, Emperor 304
Huan, king of Zhou 146
Huang Chao 173
Huang Di *see* Yellow Emperor
Huang Di neijing 124, 127–8
Huang Gongwang 412–13
Huang Jianxun 366
Huang Quan 407
Huang Tingjian 409
Huang Zhao's rebellion 173
Huang Zunxian 355
Huang-lao (Daoist deity) 304
Huangtingjing 299
Huanzong, Emperor 176
huaqiao (overseas Chinese) 84, 87
Huating, Gansu 74
Hubei Province 28; administration 21, 23; agriculture 29; dialect 327; history 214, 231, 240, 244; hydro-electricity 37; minerals 38, 39, 40, 42, 44; population 23; prehistory 71, 140, 141; wild environment 32
Huhai, Emperor of Qin 150
Hui, Ann 367
Hui, King of (Yuchen) 146, 147
Hui dian (legal text) 101
hui-kuan 98
Hui people 21, 77, 78, 316
Hui Shi 311
Huidi, Emperor (Han) 153

Huineng 169
Huiyuan 169
Huizhou merchants 202–3
Huizong, Emperor (Song) **179**, 180; and arts *179*, *182*, **411**, 420, *435*
Huizong, Emperor (Tangut) 176
Huludao, Liaoning 40, 454
Hunan Province 28; agriculture 29, *57*; cuisine 368, 375–6; dialect 326; geology 17; history 75, 76, 127, 143, 176, 231, 240; minerals 39, 40, 41, 42, 43; population and administration 23, 78; porcelain 43
Hunan Army 224
Hundred Flowers Campaign 105, 250, 257–8, 261, 264, **265**, 272, 323; and Islam 315, 317
Hungary 257, 260, 265
Hun Tian School of astronomy 442
hunting and gathering 71
hunting reserves, royal 432
Huo Guang 154
Huo Qubing 153
Hurley, Patrick 248, 260
Huxley, T. H. 320
Huzhou, Zhejiang 213
hydraulics 194, 450, 454–5
hydro-electricity 25, 28–9, **36–7** 41, 454

Iban people of Sarawak *73*
Ibn Battuta 313
Ibsen, Henrik 355, 357
Ice Ages 69, 73
Ichigo campaign 246, 248
Idealist school of philosophy 190, 319
idioms, newly coined 335
Ilkhan state 192
immortality 296–7, 300, 437
immunization 131
incense 295, 298; burners 403, 450
incentives 264, 266, 268, 280
incomes 62–3
indemnities 207, 208, 223, 227, 229
India: Anti-Japanese war 248; architecture 429; border conflict 53, 268–9, 285, 455; Buddhism 157, 168, 405; Chinese in 86, 87; cuisine 368, 370, 371; Islam 315; mathematics 440, 441; metallurgy 391, 447; Ming expeditions 198; opium 216; sculpture 405, 406; trade 46, 47, 168, 216, 435; Zhang Qian in 153
Indians, American 72, *73*, 74
Indo-China 260
Indo-European languages 80
indoctrination 114, 116–17
Indonesia: anthropology 69, 72, 73, 74; Chinese in 76, 86, 87, 90; trade, C18th 168
industry **59–64**; decentralization 62; Five-Anti campaign and 261–2; foreign involvement 63, 64, 263, 269 (*see also* joint projects); Great Leap Forward 266; growth rates 59, 264; heavy/light priorities 52, 59, 61, 264, 266; incomes 62–3; labour system 62–3; late Qing 52, 320; location 61–2; modernization

279; output 59; ownership 27, 52, 61, 94, 261; planning 62, 61; problems (1959–61) 267; railways and 50, 452; Republic 52; rural 37, *64*, 266; wages 62–3; Yuan 193; *see also individual industries and under individual regions*
infanticide, female 95
inflation: 1940s 65, 248, 251, *252*; 1950s 52, 253, 254; 1980s 53, 62, 98, 100; Qing 207; Taiwan 65; Yuan 193
inheritance 92, 105
inksticks 420
Inner Mongolia 26; administration 21, 23, 78, 84; agriculture 26; climate 26; history 76–7, 184; industry 41, 42; minerals 38, 39, 42; pastoralism 24; population 23; topography 26; wild environment 32
inquisition, literary 213
inscriptions **342–3**; Daoist 408; Neolithic 329, 343; *see also* bones, oracle *and under*: bronze; pottery; stone
insects 32, 33, 437
intellectuals 94, 95, 105, 117, 257–8, 260, 262, 265
Intelsat 367
International Famine Relief Commission 454
International Monetary Fund 280
investment 64, 266, 280
Iran 162, 194, 313, 314; Sassanian art 168, 391, 406, 409, 424
iridium 41
iron and steel **38–9**, **447–8**; Han 153, 155; location 23, 25, 27, 29, 30, 46, 452; ore 38, 452–3; Zhou 147
irrigation 36, 52, *57*, **58–9**, **451**, 454–5; cement for 43; collectivization and 263; hydro-electric schemes and 37; Yangtze 434; Yellow River 27
Islam **314–17**; assimilation 314, 315, 316; conquests 170, 313, 314; cuisine 368; Cultural Revolution and 315–16, 319; Hui people 77; Hundred Flowers and 315, 317; Indian C19th fundamentalism 315; Java 90; loyalty question 317; Muslim Rebellions 208, **220**, 315; New Teachings (*Xinjiao*) 220, 222, 315; overseas Chinese 86, 90; and porcelain design 414; sciences 194, 437; Sufism 211, 315; Tang dynasty 168, 314; Tungans 222, 316; Turkic peoples 79, 212; in Xinjiang 222, *316*; Yuan dynasty 194, 313, 315
Italy 39, 243, 368
ivory *391*, *394*, *395*, 418

jade 43
jade objects 342, 391, **393–4**, 401, 402; inscriptions 343; Neolithic 140, 142, *385*, 393, 399, **400**; PRC 419; Qing 393, *394*, 418, *419*; ritual objects, Zhou and Shang 144, 343, *385*, *386*, *393*, 400, 401, 402; specialization 399

jadeite 393, 418
Jahangir 222
Jalai Nur, Heilongjiang 69, 71
Jamaica 87
January Storm 272, 277
Japan: anthropology 72, 73, 74; Britain; alliance (1902) 230; Buddhism 169, 201, 340; Chinese in 86, 87, (political refugees) 85, 228, 230, 237, 259–60; coinage 201; concessions 52, 231, 236; drama 364; education 115, 116; folk religion 297; and Fujian 231; and Hong Kong 65; Jinan Incident 240; joint projects 44; and Korea 202; language 77, 325; law 101; and Liaoning 23, 452; Ming contacts 46, **201–2**, 203; New Village Movement 259–60; piracy 202; PRC relations 280; prehistoric 74, 139; printing 340; and Republic 234, 235, 240, 241; sculpture 408; shipping 46, 168; and Sui 165; and Taiwan 66, 252; and Tang trade 34, 40, 41, 42, 43, 44, 46, 63, 65, 201–2, 203, 213; and USSR 23, 233, 243; weapon blade manufacture 447; and Yuan 194; *see also*: Anti-Japanese War; Nara; Sino-Japanese War; Tokyo; *and under* Manchuria
Japano-Korean languages 77
Java 90, 138, 194
Jehol (Chengde) *431*, 432
Jesuits 115, 212, 362, 457; cultural accommodation 205, 210, 318; *see also* Ricci, Matteo
Jews 168, 194, **313–14**
Ji clan 147, 301
jia (traditional family) 92
Jia Di 153
Jiading; Small Sword Society Uprising 220
Jiajing Emperor 195, **202**, 416
Jiamusi, Heilongjiang 46
Jiang clan (kings of Qi) 148
Jiang Jia Liang *133*
Jiang Jieshi *see* Chiang Kai-shek
Jiang Kui 362
Jiang people 75, 76, 144
Jiang Qing (Madame Mao) *251*, 260, 272, 275, **277**, *278*
Jiang Zemin *284*, 285
Jiangdu (Yangzhou) 29, 165, 166
Jiangnan 220, 223, 224
Jiangsu Province 25; administration 20–1, 23; agriculture *57*; bridges *452*; crafts 402, 422; dialect 326, 327; energy 35, 38; incomes 62; industry 43, 402; minerals 41, 43; population 23; prehistory 141; Taiping rebellion 219
Jiangxi Province 28; agriculture 29; dialect 326; history 71, 75, 76, 176, 240, 242; minerals 37, 40, 41, 42, 43; population and administration 23, 29; porcelain 43; Soviet **243–4**, 245, 260, 279
Jiangyou, Sichuan 38
Jiankang (Nanjing) 160
Jianwen Emperor 195, 196
jianzi (shuttlecock) 133

jiao (festival) 297–8
Jiaozhou, Shandong 228, 229
Jiaqing Emperor 207, 214, 215
Jie, King of Xia 136
Jilin Province: climate 23; grain consumption 55; hydro-electricity 37; industry and minerals 39, 42; population and administration 23, 220; soils and agriculture 20; wild environment 32
Jilong (Keelung), Taiwan 226
Jin (Five Dynasties) 173, 174
Jin (Jurchen) **185–7**; arts 187, 404–6; law code 101, 186, 192; and Liao 179, 185, 186, 189–90; and Song 13, 177, 179–80, 184, 186, 187, 188, 190, 349; Yuan Haowen 350
Jin (Warring States) 75, **147–8**
Jin, Eastern 158, 160, 305; calligraphy 398, 405
Jin, Later 208
Jin, Western 158, *160*, 406
Jin Ping Mei 353, 354
Jin Shengtan 352
Jinan 26, 251; Incident 240
Jinchang, Gansu 39, 40–1
Jinduicheng, Shaanxi 42
Jing, Xinjiang 314
jing (primordial matter) 127
Jing people 78
Jing river 149, 451
Jingdezhen, Jiangxi; porcelain 43, **203**, 214, 399, 414, 416, 418, 419
Jingdi, Emperor 153
Jingnan (Ten Kingdoms) 174
Jingpo people 77, 78
Jingzong, Emperor (Tangut) 176, 177
Jinling (Nanjing) 175
Jinmen, Fujian 139
Jinniushan, Liaoning 69, 71
Jino people 78
Jiongzhou 225
jiu ('wine') 373–4
Jiu si (Nine Courts) 167
Jiujiang, Guangdong *29*, 45, 225, 240
jiulianhuan (puzzle) 132
Jiuquan space centre *433*
Joffe, Dr Adolf 237
John of Marignola 194
joint projects 64, 280; cement 44; civil aviation 50; fertilizer 44; law on 106; mining 35, 43, 452, 453; offshore oil 35; *see also under* railways
Jomon people of Japan 74
journalism 83, 225, 260, 281
Journey to the West see Xiyouji
judo 133
jujube 139, 341
Jung people 75
junks 45, 46, 444, *445*
juntian 161, 167, 172
Juran 410
Jurchens 13, 177, 185, 192; script 186, *187*; *see also* Jin (Jurchen)
justice *see* law

Kaifeng, Henan 313, 179, 184, 186, 190, *451*; *see also* Bianjing *and under* Song dynasty

Kailuan, Hebei 452
Kaiping, Hebei 34, 223
Kaiyang, Guizhou 41
Kalimantan, west 90
kang (brick bed) 423, *429*
Kang Sheng 256
Kang Youwei 114, 208, 225, **228**, 229, 304, **319–20**
Kangda Academy 249
Kangxi Emperor 207, 209–10, 213, 318
Kangxi zidian (dictionary) 337
kanhe (trade tally system) 202
Kaohsiung, Taiwan 29
Kara Khitai 177, 185
Kara-Khoto 185, *187*
Karamay (Kelamayi) oilfield 35
Karlgren, Bernhard 325, 338
Kashgar, Russian trading in 222
Kashi, Xinjiang 40
Kashmir 47, 269
Kazakhs 26, 78, 79, *206*, 211, 212, 222
Keelung (Jilong), Taiwan 226
Kehe, Shanxi; early man 69, 71
kesi (tapestry) *422*
Kexingzhuang culture 141
Khaidu 193
Khamba people 268
Kharakhula 211
Khitans 13, 167, 170, 174, 185, 192; in Jurchen state 186, 187; script 177, 185; *see also* Liao dynasty
Khojas, Black *and* White Mountain 211
Khrushchev, Nikita *258*, 267, 269; denounces Stalin 257, 260, 264, 265, 269
Khubilai Khan 190, *191*, 192, 193, 194; and religion 298, 308, 317
Khwarezm 190, 391
Kiakhta, Treaty of 212, 220
Kim Ok-kyun 227
kinship system 92, 143, 144, 291–4, 310; *see also*: family; lineages
Kirghiz people 78, 211, 222
kite flying 133, *449*
Koguryo 75, 166, 168, 185
Kokand, khanate of 222
Kong Ji 344
konghou (harp) 363
Kong Shangren 358
Kongfuzi *see* Confucius
kongzhong (diabolo) 133
Korea: Bronze Age 74; Chinese in 75, 84, 87; cuisine 374; and Han 75, 153, 421; Japanese and 202, 227, 230; and Jurchen state 187; Koguryo kingdom 75, 166, 168, 185; language 77, 82, 325; law 101; Liao dynasty and 177, 185; Min trades with 175; Ming trade 46, 203; nationals in China 78; Neolithic 139; people 72, 73; printing 341; Qing and 46, 209; shipping 168; Silla, state of 170; and Sui 165, 166; and Tang 168, 170; Tonghak Uprising 227; unification 76; Yuan Shikai in 234; *see also* Korean War
Korean War 256, **262**, 263, 267, 285, 286, 315
Kosygin, Alexei 274

Kowloon, Hong Kong 223, *291*
kowtow 216, 337, 457
Kropotkin, P. A. 320, 321
Kuan Chung 312
Kuiyang, Guizhou 41
Kumārajīva 305, 309
Kuncan *414*, 417
kung-fu 366, 367
Kunming, Yunnan 40, 49, *425*
Kunqu 358, 359, 362, 365
Kuwait 44

Labour Defence System 134
labour service *see* corvée
labour system 62–3, 85
lac (scale insect) 437
lacquer 399, 402, 404, 414, 416–17, **421**; furniture 423, 424
Lahu people 78
Lai Wenguang 219
Laibin, Guangxi 69
Laiyang, Shandong *60*
Lancang River 36
land allocation: imperial and Republican eras, (family/lineage and) 92, 93, 94, 96, (Han) 155, (in disunity after Han) 158, 161, 162, (Sui) 164, 167, (Tang) 172, (Song) 182, 184, (Ming) 200, (Taipings) 219, (Republic) 52, (Communist) 251, 254, 262, 263; PRC 93, 94, (1949–55) 52, 54, 99, 105, 253, 254, 261, **262–3**, (after 1955) 99–100, 263–4, (leasing) 93, 100, (private plots) 54, 55, 92, 93, 94–5, 99, 268; Taiwan 65–6
land reclamation 58, 179, 182, 268, **434–5**
landlords: imperial era 112, 182, 188; PRC 54, 94, 105, 262, 263; Taiwan 66
language, Han Chinese **324–9**; *baihua* (vernacular written) 321, 327, 328; Buddhism and 12; dialects 324, **326–8**; dictionaries 337–9; *guoyu* ('National Language') 329; ideographic nature 11, 324, 436; idioms 335; loan-words 325, 337; metaphors and allusions 334–5; Modern Standard 326, 327, 328–9; names 335–6, 337; origin 324–5; pronunciation, early 325–6; proverbial expressions 335; *putonghua* (Common Speech) 113, 329, 331; reform movements 113, 321, 327–8, 328–9; *wenyan* (classical written) 321, 327, 328, 349; as uniting factor 11, 324; Western influence 327–8; *xiehouyu* (aposiopesis) 335; *see also*: romanization; script, Han Chinese
languages, non-Han **77–84**; *see also individual languages and* scripts, non-Han
Lantian, Shaanxi 69–70, 138
Lanzhou 24, 25, 35, 37, 40, 41
Lao She 233, 356, 364, 365, 367
Laoguantai culture 140, 141
Laos 82, 87, 89
Laozi 168, 296, **298**, 305, 323, 408;

Daodejing 298, 299, 300
law **101–6**; bankruptcy 63; collective punishment 102–3; Communist 101, 105–6, 272; customary 103–5; education in 108, 110, 115, 184; family 92, 103, 105; foreign influence 101; Jin code 101, 186, 192; land reform 105, 263; Neo-Confucianism and 319; Northern Wei 161; penal system 101–2; Republic 105, 115; Sui 165; Tangut 176; *see also* constitutions *and under* Tang *and* Yuan *dynasties*
law, martial 106, 282, 285, 286
lead 40
League of Nations 243
Ledo Road 248
Legalism 121, 147, 149, 151, 157, 194, 303, **312–13**
legations, foreign 225, 228, 229
Lenin, V.I.; and Comintern 237, 238; theories 14, 238, 261, 266, 270, 321–2, 323
Lha-bza Khan 210
Lhasa, Tibet 210, 268
Lhoba people 78
Li (Confucian classic) 302, 344
Li (minority people) 78, 80
li (philosophical term) 205, 304, 312, 320
Li Bai 348
Li Bang *see* Gaodi
Li Bing 451
Li Cheng 410
Li Cunxu (Zhuxie Cunxu) 173
Li Dazhao 254, *237*, 238, 259–60, 321, 322
Li Di *411*
Li Gonglin 410
Li He 349
Li Hongzhang 114, 115, 223, **224–5**, 229; and foreign relations *224*, 225, 226, 227; on modernization 208, 223, 224–5; and rebellions 219, 224, 229
Li Houzhu (Southern Tang ruler) 407
Li Jianwu 357
Li Jianzheng (Sui prince) 167
Li Jinfa 356
Li Jing (Southern Tang ruler) 175
Li Jiquian 176
Li Keyong 173
Li Linfu 171
Li Lisan 244
Li Peng 281, 282, **284**
Li Qingzhao 349
Li Ruzhen 354
Li Shangyin 349
Li Sheng (Xu Zhigao) 175
Li Shimin *see* Taizong
Li Shizhen 128, 129, 204, 376, 436
Li Si 149–50, 151, 333
Li Sixun 408
Li Teng-hui 286
Li Wang, King of Zhou 146
Li Wansheng *415*
Li Wencheng 215
Li Xian, Emperor (Tangut) 176
Li Xiucheng 219
Li Yu 175, 349

Li Yuan *see* Gaozu, Emperor (Tang)
Li Yuanhao (ruler of Xixia) 185
Li Yuanhong 232
Li Zhaodao 408
Li Zhi 304, 350
Li Zicheng rebellion 205, 206
Lian Chengwu 362
Liancheng, Gansu 41
Liang (Five Dynasties) 158, 161, *163*, **173**
Liang, Later 165
Liang Fa 218
Liang Qichao 114, 208, 225, 235, 320, 322
Liang Shuming 320, 323
Liang Wudi (Xiao Yan) 163
Lianghekou conference 245
Liang-Huai Salt Administration 214
liangshuifo (tax system) 172
Liangzhou, Gansu 314
Liangzhu culture 141, 142, 400
Lianyungang, Jiangsu 454
Liao dynasty 76, 102, *177*, **184–5**, 409; external relations 173, 176, 177, 178, 179, 185, 186, 187, 189–90
Liao valley; Chinese pale 84
Liaodong Peninsula 227, 230
Liao-He oilfield, Liaoning 34, 35
Liaoning Province: administration 20–1, 23; agriculture 58; climate 23; gas 35; history 75, 77, 143; industry 23, 38, 40, 41, 42, 43; literacy 113; minerals 38, 39, 40, 41, 42, 43, (oil) 34, 35; population 23, 78; prehistory 71, 140, 141, 143
Liexianzhuan (Daoist text) 300
Liezi (Daoist text) 310
lijia system 200
Liji 344, 368
Lin Biao 105, 258, 267, **273–4**, 276, 285
Lin Qing 215
Lin Shu 350, 355
Lin Zexu *217*, 218
lineages 92, **94–5**, 96, 99, 113; ancestor cult 291, 292–4; judicial role 103; names 336; schools 112, 294
Ling, Empress Dowager 314
Ling Lun 362
Ling Menchu 351
Ling Qichao 228–9
Ling Zifeng 365
Lingbao (Daoist texts) 299
lingchi (death penalty) 102
Lingwu 171
Linqi (Buddhist school) 169
Lisu people 78, 83
literacy **111–13**, 118, 188, 205, 249, 319
literature **340–58**; alchemical 299; art history 399; botanical 436; Chu 148; dramatic narratives 354; in disunity after Han 157; Marxist influence 354–8; oral 112–13, 354; popular 112, 188, 194, 351–4; in PRC 265, 357–8; Taiwanese 358; Tangut 176; traditional 351–4; Western influences 350, 354–8; Yuan 194, 350; Zhou 147; *see also individual genres*, Confucian

classics, *and under*: Buddhism; Daoism; medicine
Liu Bang *see* Gaodi
liu bu (Six Boards) 167
Liu Desheng 334
Liu E 354
Liu Hui 440
Liu Jin 199
Liu Lichuan 220
Liu Pei (king of Shu) 159
Liu Shaoqi 249, 250, 258, 262, **270–1**, 272
Liu Song 214
Liu Tingxun, tomb of *408*
Liu Xie 348
Liu Xiu *see* Guangwudi
Liu Yan (Southern Han ruler) 176
Liu Yin 175–6
Liu Yu, Emperor (Liu-Song) 160
liubo (game) *132*
Liujiang county, Guangxi 69, 74
Liujia, Gansu 36
Liuqiu 227
liushu 329–31
Liu-Song state 158, 160, *162*
Liuzhiyuan 354
livestock farming *31*, 55, 56, 58; *see also individual animals and pastoralism*
living standards 53, 63, 100
Lizong, Emperor (Song) 180
Lokapalas (deities) *408*, 409
loans, foreign 235, 248, 280
loess region 20, *24*, 25, 429, 434
Lo-lang, Korea 421
London Missionary Society 318
Long March 133, **244–5**, 256, 263, 267, 273
longevity 127, 128
Longmen, Luoyang; cave temples 392, 393, 404, *405*, 430
Longshan cultures 140, 142, 386–7, 400, 401
Longtang Cave, Hexian 71
Longxing monastery, Hebei 427
Lü, Empress 153
Lu, state of *107*, 145, 146, 301; *see also Chunqiu*
Lu Dingyi 265
Lu Dongbin 299
Lu family (kings of Qi) 148
Lu Fayan; *Qieyun* 325
Lu Hsiang-shan 304
Lu Ji 348
Lu T'an-wei 405
Lu Xun 355, *356*, 365
Lu You 349
Lunyu 301, 302, 304, 322, 344
Luo Guanzhong 351–2
Luo Ruiqing 267
Luo Wenzau 318
Luo Zudao *117*
Luoyang, Henan **157**; Buddhism 157, 340; Cao Wei 158; education 108, 157; Grand Canal 166; Han 156, 157, 340, *402*, 403; Liang 163; measurement of time 377; modern industry 26, 40; Northern Wei 161–2, *405*; Sui 165; Tang 108, 168, 171, 314, 340; Western Jin 159; *see also* Longmen
Luoyi 145, 146

Lushan, Sichuan 258, 267
Lüshi chunqiu (encyclopedia) 310
Lytton, 2nd Earl of 243

Ma Dexin 220
Ma family (rulers of Chu) 174
Ma Hezi 411
Ma Hualong 220
Ma Rulong 220
Ma Yuan *401*, 411
Ma Zhiyuan 350
Maanshan, Anhui 38
Maba, Guangdong 69, 71
Macao *29*; Christianity 318; economy 29, 63, 66; government 22, 85; Matteo Ricci in 205; overseas Chinese 84, 85, 87; and Portugal 22, 202; Western merchants, C19th 215
Macartney, 1st Earl 207, **216**, 217, 457
Machang culture 141, 400
machinery: imports 63; manufacture 23, 25, 26, 27, 52; *see also under* agriculture
Madagascar 86
magic *122*, *126*, 127, 289, 298, 440
magnesium 41
mahjong (majiang) (game) 132
Maijishan 406
Maimonides 313
Maiqishan 392
Maitreya 392–3, 404, 405, 406, *408*
maize 26, 56, 82, 368, 435
Majia, Gansu 400
Majiabang culture 139, 141
Majiayao culture 141
Makassar (Sulawesi) 90
Malacca 89, 318
Malayo-Polynesian languages 82
Malaysia 46, 73, 139, 168; overseas Chinese 86, 87, 89–90, 104–5
man, origins of *68*, 69
Man (Manchu) people 23, 75, 76–7, 78, 82, 207, 308; *see also* Qing dynasty
Manchukuo (Manzhouguo) 23, 233, 243
Manchuria: Chinese settlers 19, 77, 84, 220, 222; in civil war 251, 273; industry, (Japanese development) 23, 52, 61, 243, 314, 452, (under PRC) 254, 262, 263, 61; Japan and, (gains concessions) 229, (occupation) 23, 52, 233, 242, 243, 244, 314, 452; Jurchens 185–6; and Korean War 262; under Liao 76, 177, 184; Parhae kingdom 76; Qing 220, 230; Russia and 212, **220–2**; Russo-Japanese War (1904–5) 229, 230; Tang influence 168; urbanization 97; Yuan postal service 193
Mandarin dialect 326, 327
manganese 41
Mangnai, Qinghai; asbestos 42
Manichaeism 168, 194, 195, 314
manners, social 456, 457–9
Mao, Madame *see* Jiang Qing
Mao, Mount, Jiangsu 299
Mao Dun 356

Mao Zedong **254–9**, *254*, *271*; assessment of achievement 259, 280; childhood 254, *255*; and civil war 250, 256, (Chongqing negotiations, 1945) 250, 253, *257*; and collectivization of agriculture 264; and communes 258, 265, 266, 267; and criticism 258, 265; and Cultural Revolution 117, 258, *259*, 269, 270; death 105, 269, 276; in early CCP 237; and economy 52, 53, 259; and education 113, 117–18, *119*, 254; and 'gang of four' 258, 259; and Great Leap Forward 258, 265–6; and High Tide of Socialism 52; and Hundred Flowers 265; and Jiangxi Soviet 243, 244; and land reform 262; and Lin Biao *273*; marriages *255*, (*see also* Jiang Qing); Marxism 249, 254, 255, 256, 321, 322, 323; and military 274; and modernization 279, 280; name 336; and New People's Study Society 260; Long March 245; and peasants 255, 259; and rectification campaigns 250; swim down Yangtze 134; and technology 258; in United Front 239; and USSR 254, 256, *258*, 266, 269, 270; writings and speeches 14, 114, 261, 265, 266, 272, 322, 335, 357; Yan'an period 245, *249*, *251*, *256*, 357
Mao Zonggang 351–2
Maogong ding (bronze vessel) 343
Maolin, Anhui 250
Maonan people 78
Maoshi see Book of Odes
maotai (alcoholic drink) 458
marble sculpture 401, 406
Marco Polo 34, 47, 188, 194, 313, 314, 368, 444
Marco Polo Bridge Incident 245–6
Marignolli, John 317
Maring, H. (Hendricus Sneevliet) 238
market economy 54, 63, 98, 100, 264, 281
markets, local 97, 98, 113, 165
marriage: arranged 95, 96, 97, 98, 259, 321; late 20; law 92, 95, 104–5, (Yuan) 313; rites 294; surname exogamy 94; widows' remarriage 95; work unit and permission for 93
Marshall, George Catlett 251, 260
martial arts 99, 133, 229, 366, 367
Martin, W. A. P. 225
Marxism: adaptation to China 249, 256, 322; Liang Qichaoon 229; and literature 354–8; May Fourth Movement and 229, 321; and medicine 129, 130, 131; as state ideology 116; theory of history 149; and Westernization 321; *see also under*: Lenin; Mao Zedong
Marxist Study Group 260
Masha, Fujian 341
masks, monster 142, *145*, *385*, *393*, 398, 401–2, 404, 406
Mass Education Movement 113
mass line 243, 244, 249, 250, 251, 257

massage 127
mathematics 108, 110, 115, 205, 318, **440–1**
Mathews, Robert Henry 338, *339*
Matsu island 286
Mauritius 85, 86, 87
Mawangdui tomb, Changsha 402, 404
May Fourth Movement 13, 115, **236**; and *Guomindang* 234, 236; leaders found CCP 236, 237, 321; literature and 355, 361, 364; New Life Movement and 242; Peng Pai in 239; philosophy 229, 321; 70th anniversary 282; Zhou Enlai and 260
McMahon Line 268
measurements 380, 438; *see also*: money; time
medicine **120–31**; alchemy and 438; anaesthesia 124, *130*, 131; anatomical knowledge 121, 122, 128; ancestral healing 120; blood, circulation of 121; body care, traditional 121, 127; breathing techniques 127, 129, 296; Buddhist 122–3, 129; college for 115; conduit therapies 123, 124, 125–6; Confucianism and 121, 125; Daoist 121, 124–5, 127, 300; demonic 120, 122, 123, 124, 127, 129, 130; diet and 123, 373, 376; face diagnosis 123; Five Agencies 124, 125–6; Five Phases (*wu xing*) 121, 123; 'gang of four' and 130; influences, flow of 121–2, 123, 127; Jin-Yuan 125; Legalism and 121; literature 127–9, 176, 194, 341; longevity 127, 128; missionaries and 131, 225, *318*; modernization 121, 129; popular, C18th 129; pragmatic drug 121–3, 129, 130; PRC medical services 131; pulse diagnosis *123*; *qi* 127; social and philosophical background 120–3; Song 122, 179; spell-drugs *122*, 129; systematic correspondence 121–3, 124, 125–6, 128, 130; Western 123, 129–31, 168; *yin* and *yang* 121, 123, 124, 125–6; *see also*: acupuncture; exorcism; health; hospitals; pharmacology
meditation 307, 374
mediums, spirit 296, 298
Mei Lanfang *360*, 361
Mei Qing *417*
Melanesians 74
Mencius (Mengzi) **303**, 310, 311, 319, 368; *Mengzi* **107**, 304, 344
Meng Chang (Later Shu ruler) 175
Meng Tian, General of Qin 150
Meng Zhixiang (Later Shu ruler) 175
mengzhu (league president) 148
Mengzi *see* Mencius
merchants 172, 193, 202–3, 214, 304, 314; literacy 112; social status 94, **98**, 110, 172; *see also under* Arabs
mercury 41
Mesopotamia 434, 442
Mesozoic era 17
metals and metallic ores 38–42; see

also individual types
metaphors and allusions 334–5
metaphysics 290, 304, 319, 320
meteorology 438–9
Mexico; overseas Chinese 86
Mi Fu 399, 409, *410*
Miao people 78, 81–2, 214
Miaodigou culture 140, 141
microlithic cultures 71, 138, 140
Micronesians 72, 73, 74
migration 92, 97; *see also*: colonization; coolies; external China
Mikhailovsk 221
military arts: education 110, 115, 235, 249, 252, 285; siegecraft 147; treatises 176, 299
military regions 253, 263, 285, 472
militia: past 165, 167, 184, 200, 215, 220; PRC 260, 266, 267
millenarianism 99, 193, 214, 215
Miller, Arthur 364
millet 26, 56, 144, 370, 434; Neolithic 139, 368
mills 449
Min (Ten Kingdoms) 174, 175
Min, river 451
Min dialects 326, 327
Min Bao (*The People's Journal*) 230
Mindi, Emperor (Tang) 173
minerals **38–43**, 439; *see also individual minerals*
Ming dynasty 13, **195–205**; architecture 426, 427; canals 45; capitals 196, 197–8, (*see also* Nanjing); Civil War (1398–1402) 196, 198; colonization 76, 196, 202; Confucianism 205, 209, 303; decline 202, 205; Daoism 202; drama 350, 358; economy 196; education 108–9, 116, 200, 205; emperors 195, 379 (*see also individual reigns*); eunuchs 197, 198, **199**, 201, 416; examination system 111, 200; expeditions 46, 198–9; fiefs 196, 201; gold objects 390; Great Wall 197, 198, 201, 430; institutions of state 196, 197, 199, 202; Islam 315; ivory *394, 395*; jade 393; and Japan 201–2; Jews 313; lacquer 416–17, *421*; law 101, 102; Li Zicheng rebellion 205, 206; literature 346, 350; Matteo Ricci 205; merchants 202–3; Mongol wars 199, 201, 202; music 362; officials 196, 202, 205; painting 414–16; philosophy 194, 204–5, 319; population 196; porcelain 201, 203, 416; printing 341; provincial government 196, 200; ritual 430; sculpture *287*, 391, *392*, 393, 409, 430; taxation 200, 203; technology *203*, **204**, 423; tombs, imperial 390, 430; trade 46, **200–2**; tribute system 196, 200–1; Wang Yangming 204–5
Minghuang, Emperor (Tang) 171
mingqi, see tomb objects
mingtang 430
Mingzong, Emperor (Tang, Five Dynasties) 173
mining 115, 231, 243, 439, 452–3;

see also individual minerals
ministers, chief 171, 180, 301
minorities, national **77–82**; administration 20, 21, 22, 26, 30, 84, 316; languages 77–82; official policies 77, 83–4, 105, 315–16; in past 158, 159, 220; scripts 82–4; statistics 78; *see also individual peoples and under individual areas*
Min-Yue, kingdom of 75
mirrors *404*, 405, 409
missionaries, Christian: Catholic 115, 194, 210, 317, 318 (*see also* Jesuits); and education 114, 115, 225, 318; and medicine 131; Nestorian 317; opposition to 225, 226, 229, 457; Protestant 115, 318–19; secularization of work 225
modernization 13–14, 323; agriculture 26, 263, 279; Nanjing government 242; PRC 106, 113, 117, 279, 281, 285; Qing dynasty 208, 223–4, 225, 227; railway and 231
Modi, Emperor (Liang) 173
Mohe, Heilongjiang 39
Mohism 310, 440; Later 312, 313
Moinba people 78
Moluccas 90
molybdenum 42
monasticism 103, 112, 133, 168, 317, 427; Daoist 194; tax exemption 162, 193, 306; *see also under* Buddhism
money *see* currency
Möngke (Mongol Khan) 193
Mongolia 49, 76–7, 138, 193, 269, 423; *see also* Inner Mongolia
Mongolic languages 78–9; Mongolian 82, 83, 192
Mongoloid peoples **72–4**, 77, 137
Mongols: conquests 11, 13, 76, 90, 176, 185, 186, 187, 190, *191*; cuisine 374; Dzungar 210, 211–12; government 192; language 82, 83, 192; law 101, 313; present-day minority 24, 26, 78; Qing campaigns 209; *see also* Yuan dynasty *and under*: Buddhism; Ming dynasty
monkeys 33, 437
Mon-Khmer languages 80, 82
monopolies, state 153, 155, 172, 446
Monte Corvino, John of 317
Morrison, Robert 318, 338, *339*
mother-of-pearl inlay 421
moths; tussore silk 422
mountaineering 134
mourning rites 295–6, 310
moxibustion 124
Mozi 310
Mu Qi 411
Mukden *see* Shenyang
Mulam people 78
mulberry cultivation 29, 422, 434
murals 405, 425; Buddhist cave temples *304*, 429–30, 363; Tang *381, 407*
Muraviev, Nikolai 220
music **361–3**; Cultural Revolution 272; in drama 358, 359, 361;

folksong 357, 361; instruments 359, 361, 362, 363, 385; Tang dynasty 168, 171; Western 363, 367
Muslim Rebellions 208, **220**, 315
Muzong, Emperor (Liao) 177
mythology 136, 395

Nagasaki, Japan 202
Nālandā, University of 168
names: personal **335–6**, 337; place 469
Nanchang, Jiangxi 240, 242, 314; Uprising (1927) 260, 284, 285
Nancheng, Jiangxi 246, 452
Nandan, Guanxi 40
Nanfang caomu zhuan 437
Nanjing, Jiangsu: Arsenal 223, 224; bridge *455*; building under Republic 454; coup against CCP (1927) 241; Eastern Jin 160; First National Athletics Meet (1910) 133; Imperial Naval Academy 115; Japanese occupation (1937–40) 246; Ming 108, 195, 198; Nationalist government (1945–9) 50, 241; and Northern Expedition (1926–8) 240; oil 35; Provisional Republic Government (1912) 230, 232; Qing textiles 213; Southern Dynasties tombs 405; Southern Tang painting 407; Taiping rebellion 208, 218, 219, 224; Treaty of (1842) 207, **218**, 225; university 115; *see also*: Jinling; Nanjing Government; Nanjing Incident
Nanjing (medical text) 127–8
Nanjing Government 48, 236, **241–2**, 246, 249, 253; roads 51, 242, 454
Nanjing Incident 241
Nanling mountains 40
Nanzhao, kingdom of 76, 168, 173
naphtha 44
Napier, 8th Baron 207, 216–17
Nara, Japan; Imperial Storehouse 363, 421
narratives: dramatic 354; popularized (*pinghua*) 351
National People's Congress, Fifth (1978) 105
National Revolutionary Army 234, 237, 239, 240, 246; *see also* Northern Expedition
nationalism 113, 230
Nationalist Army 242, *244*, 245, 247, 250, 260
Nationalist Government: (1927–37) *see* Nanjing Government; Free China (Chongqing) 246, 247–8, 252, 260; (1945–9) 50, 241; in Taiwan (post-1949) 46–7, 252, 253, 254, **285–6**
natural resources **34–44**
navies 115, 195, 223, 225, 269
Naxi people 78
Naxi script 82
Neo-Confucianism 13, 188, **190**, 194, 303, **304, 319**; commentaries 304, 319, 345; imperial adoption 12, 319; and medicine 122, 125; on social order 116

Neolithic era 74, **138–42, 400**; agriculture 435; architecture 425; jade objects 393, 399, **400**; pottery 138, 141, 142, 368, *382, 387*, 399, **400**, 438, (Longshan) 386–7, **400**, 401, (Yangshao) *140*, 142, 329, *386, 387*, 400; sculpture 140; writing 329, 343
Nepal 194, 211, 269, 414
nephrite 393
Nerchinsk, Treaty of *212*, 220, 318
Nestorianism 168, 194, 314, *317*
Netherlands; colonies 85
New Democracy 261
New Fourth Army Incident 247, 250, 260
New Life Movement 116, **242**, 253, 322
New Literature Movement 355
New People's Study Society 260
New Village Movement, Japan 259–60
New Year festival 98, 376, 378
New Youth Magazine 236, 321, 355
New Zealand; overseas Chinese 86
Ni Zan 194, 412–13
Nian rebellion 208, **219**
nickel 40–1
Nihewan, Shanxi 69, 137
Nikolaevsk 221
Ningbo, Zhejiang 225
Ningxia Province 26; administration 21, 23, 77, 78, 316; agriculture 27; minerals 39, 41, 43; population 23, 77; *see also*: Hui people; Xixia
Ningyuan, Hunan 208
Niuheliang 140
Niuzhuang, Liaoning 225
Nixon, Richard Milhouse 259, 280
nomadism 79, 84
Nongjia (Tillers) 310–11
noodles 368, *370*
North Korea 34
Northeast Frontier Agency 268
Northern dynasties **161–2**, *163*; arts 387, 395, 404–6; *see also*: Qi, Northern; Wei, Northern; Zhou, Northern
Northern Expedition **240**, 252, 253, 356
Norway 44
notices, public *112*, 456
Nu people 78
Nu River 36
nuclear power **37–8**
nuclear weapons 269, 285
Nügua (mythological figure) *136*
numerical notation 440
numerology 303, 440
Nurhachi 206, **208**

oases 26
observatory; Yuan, at Dadu 194
Occidental Petroleum 453
Oceania 84, 86, 87
Oceanic Negroid peoples 137
officials: Confucianism 110, 111, 116, 190, 301, 304; and eunuchs 172; family ties 92, 181; language 327; social origins 111, 150, 158, 170, 171, 172, 182, 301, 310, 359; *see also*: corruption; examination

system; *and under* disunity *and* Han, Ming, Qin, Qing, Song, Sui *and* Tang *dynasties*
oil (mineral) **34–5**; exports 34, 47, 63; fields 23, 26, 27, 30, **34–5**; offshore 34, 35; prices 57–8; refineries 27, 35
oil (vegetable) 57, 58, 59
Olympic Games 134
O'Neill, Eugene 357
'open door' policies 62, 66, 281
opera 358, 361, 362, 365; Peking 358, **360–1**, 362, 363, (revolutionary) 272, 357, 361
opium 216, *217*, 218, 223, 236; *see also* Opium War
Opium War 207, **218**, 220, 457
oral tradition 112–13, 354
oranges 29, 32, 436
Ordos microlithic culture 71, 138
Oroqen people 78
osmium reserves 41
Ouyang Xiu 190, 349
Ouyang Xun 406
Ouyang Yuqian 365
overseas Chinese *see* external China

pagodas *308*, 429
Pags pa (Dalai Lama) 308
Painbo Farm, Tibet *31*
painting: Buddhist 194, *304, 306*, 363, 405, 407, 411, 429–30; in disunity after Han 405; Five Dynasties 407; formats 398, 420; Jin 187; on lacquer 402, 421; Literati (*wenrenhua*) 408, 409, 410, 412–13; Ming 414–16; porcelain 203, 414; status 399; techniques 419–21; Wang Wei 431–2; Yuan 194, 410, **412–13**, 420; *see also* murals *and under* Han, Qing, Song *and* Tang *dynasties*
Pakhae 76, 168
Pakistan 68, 269
palaces 142, 165, 210, 432; *see also under* Beijing
Palaeolithic era 137–8
Palaeozoic era 17
palladium 41
Palmerston, 3rd Viscount 216
Pamirs 170
panda, giant *33*, 437
Pangu (deity) 136, 395
Panlongzheng, Hubei 143
Panthay rebellion 220
Panzhihua, Sichuan 38, 42
Papacy 210, 317
paper 30, 156, 203, **340**, 420; *see also under* currency
Papua New Guinea 40, 86
Paris Commune 259, 266, 267
Parkes, Harry 223
parliaments 231, **235**, 320
Pascal's Triangle *441*
pastoralism 24, 27, 31, 138, 142, 177, 185
Patriotic Christian Association 318
Peace and Alliance, Treaty of (1874) 226
Peace Protocol (1901) 225, 229, 245
peanuts 368, 435
pear trees 139, 341

Pearl River *29*, 46, 202
peasants 112, 144, 146, 184, 368; *Guomindang* and 239, 242, 255; Mao and 255, 259
peat 38
pedlars 113, 202–3
Peiligang, Henan 139, 140, 141
Peking Man 71, 73–4, 137–8
Peking opera *see under* opera
penal system **101–3**, *106*, 111, 192; Han 152, 155; Qin 149, 150, 152, 153
Peng Dehuai 243, 258, **267**, 274
Peng Pai 239, 259–60
Peng Zhen 271–2
People's Daily 265, 272
People's Liberation Army 49, 258, 268, 282, **285**; organization 269, 472; political power 258, 273, 274, 285
People's Republic of China **253–86**; *see also individual aspects*
peranakan (Indonesian Chinese) 90
Pereira, Tomas 212
Persian Gulf 46, 168, 198
Peru; overseas Chinese 87
Pescadores 227
pharmacology 120, 122, **124–6**, 127, 204; alchemy and 438; Daoist writings 300; honey in 437; mineral drugs 438, 439, 446; natural drugs 33, 68, 128, *129*, 130; pragmatic drug medicine 121–3, 129, 130; of systematic correspondence 123; *see also*: *bencao* literature
Philippines 34, 40, 74, 368; Chinese in 76, 84, 86, 87, 89; Ming and 46, 76, 202
philology 350–1
philosophy **309–13, 319–23**; on food 368, 376; Jin 187; Song 190; terminology 343; twentieth century 319–23; Western influence 319, 320–1, 323, 350; *see also*: Buddhism; Confucianism; Legalism; Mohism; *and under* Ming, Yuan *and* Zhou *dynasties*
phosphate deposits 44
pigs 27, 29, 33, 54, **58**; in cuisine 370, 371, 376; cycles 55, 58; Neolithic 139, 140, 141, 368
pilgrims 90, 168, 430
Pingcheng 161
pinghua (narratives) 351
Pinguo, Guanxi 41
Pingxing Pass 273
pinyin 331, **337**, 467–8, 469
pipelines 34, 35, 446
piracy 46, 201, 202
planning 52, 53, 54, 61, 263, 264; *see also* Five-Year Plans
plastromancy 120, 143, 289, 333, 342–3
platinum 39, 41
ploughs 434, 435
poetry 344, **347–51**, 355, 356–7, 358; evidence on pronunciation 325; celestial journeys 148, 347; on food 368; *fu* ('rhyme-prose') 347; *see also individual poets*, Book of Odes, *and under* Qing, Song *and*

Tang *dynasties*
Poland 40, 257, 260
polders 434
policing 181, 242, 282, 286; *baojia* system 97, 102, **200**
Polynesia, French 85, 86, 87
Polynesian people 72, 74
population **20**, 52, 96; density 17, 20, *21*, 23, 25, 26, 29, 52; historical 171, 182, 192, 196, 207; *see also* birth control *and under individual areas*
porcelain *see*: Jingdezhen; pottery
Port Arthur, Liaoning 230, 254
Ports, Three Northern 224
Portsmouth, Treaty of 230
Portugal 22, 66, 202
Post Office System 337, 469
postal service 51, 193
potassium deposits 44
potatoes 56, 368, 370, 435
potatoes, sweet 26, 56, 368, 370, 371, 376, 435
pottery **386–9**; Bronze Age 387; ceramic piece-moulds for metal casting 144, 390, 399, 401, 424; Dehua, Fujian 418; in disunity after Han 387, 406; *doucai* 416; enamelling 416, 418; glazes 387, 388, 402, 404; *Homo sapiens* and 71; Hongxian **419**; inscriptions 329, 333, 343; Jian ware 388, 412; Jun 388; Liao 409; Longquan 412; peachbloom *418*; porcelain introduced 409; *Tiangong kaiwu 203*; wheel introduced 387; Yixing ware 418, 419; Yue ware 388, *406*, 409, 411; *see also*: clays; Jingdezhen; tomb objects; *and under* Neolithic, *and* Han, Ming, Qing, Shang, Yuan *and* Zhou *dynasties*
Pottinger, Sir Henry 218
poultry 54, 370, 371, 376
Poyang Lake, battle of 195
precipitation 17, *18*, 19, 24, 25–6
prefectures 20–1, 167, 181
press 51, 83, 225, 230, 282, 320
printing **113–14, 340–2**; botanical *187*, 436; Buddhist 194; of Confucian classics 114, 188, 190, 340; and education 108, 110, 113–14, 188, 340; Jin 187; Ming 341; Tangut 194; *see also under* Song *and* Tang *dynasties*
private enterprise 34, 61, 92; 1950s 254, 261–2, 268; 1980s 93, 98, 106; land ownership 54, 55, 93, 94–5, 99, 268
production teams 93, 100, 266–7
progresses, imperial 143, 150, 213
pronunciation 325–6, 327
propaganda 51, 228, 364, 367
Propaganda Fide 318
proverbial expressions 335
provinces 21, 22; administration 150, 152, 171, 172, 174, 178, 181, 192, 196, 200, 222; law 101; schools 108, 109
Provisional Republic Government (1912) 230, 232, 234, 235
Pu Songling 350, 351

publishing 109, 113, 114, **340–2**
puji and *tigao* 133
Pumi people 78
pump, square pallet chain- 450
punctuation 346
puppet plays 189
Puyang oilfield, Henan 35
Puyi, Emperor 208, **232–3**, 235, 243
puzzles 132

Qaidam basin, Qinghai 44
Qamdo, Tibet 39
Qi (state) 147, **148**, 149
qi (natural energies) 127, 290, 296
Qi, Northern 158, 162, 405
Qi, Southern 158, *162*, 163
Qi Baishi 418
Qi Meng 442
Qian Lu (ruler of Wuyue) 175
Qian Xian, Shaanxi; tomb of Princess Yongtai *381, 407*
Qian Xuan 412
Qian Xuantong 331
Qianlong Emperor **207**, 209, 212, **213**, 214–15, 379; and arts 213, 361, *406*, 420–1, *423*, 432; Macartney embassy 207, **216**, 217, 457
Qiantang river; tidal bore 438
Qianziwen (primer) 112, 133
qiaopai (card game) 134
Qichangyuan (garden, Wuxi) *431*
Qijia 141, 142
Qin, Former 160, 161
Qin, Western 161
Qin Bangxian 244
Qin dynasty **149–51**; government 150, 155, 156; Great Wall 150, **151**, 153, 155; irrigation 451; penal system 149, 150, 152, 153; philosophy 303, 311, 312, 313; provinces 75, 150, 152; unifies China 12, 147, 148, 303; weights and measures 380; writing 333; and Xiongnu 75, 150; *see also* Shi Huangdi
Qin Gui 180
Qin Guli 310
Qincheng prison 271
Qing dynasty **206–33**; banner system 209; and Britain 215–18; climate 207, 219; Constitutional Movement 230–1; corruption 207, 213, 220, 222; economy 207, 223; education 109, 111, 112–13, 116, 214, 230, 235; elections 235; emperors 379 (*see also individual rulers*); establishment 205, 206, 209; eunuchs **215**, 228; examination system 111, 208, 209, 230; expansion 84, 207, 211–12; foreign relations 208, 212, 218, 220, 225, 318 (*see also under individual foreign powers*); gold objects 390; government 209, 223; Guandu Shangban enterprises 224; handicrafts 213–14; historical perspective 206–8; ivory 394; jade 393, 418, *419*; lacquer 421; law 101, 102, 103; literature 213, 346, 350; Manchus and 13, 23, 77, 209; Manchuria, Russia and 220–2;

ministers *see*: Li Hongzhang; Lin Zexu; Zeng Guofan; modernization 51, 208, 223–4, 227; officials 207, 213, 217, 220, 222, 228, 451; opium question 207, 216, 217, 218; painting 213, 417–18, 420–1; philosophy 319–21, 345; poetry 213, 350–1; population 207; porcelain 214, 418; provincial government 222; Railway Protection Movement 231, 232; rebellions *see under*: Boxer; Eight Trigrams; Muslim; Nian; Republican; Small Sword Society; Taiping; Three Feudatories; White Lotus; Wuchang; religions 225, 308, 313, 345, (Islam) 220, 222, 315, (Rites Controversy) 205, 210, 318; restoration attempt (1917) 228, 229, 233; ritual 430; roads 47; salt merchants 214; sculpture 409; snuff bottles 418; Taiwan 252; taxation 207, 222; Tianjin massacre 226; trade 46, 98, 203, 207, 213–14, 215–16, 220, 423; wars *see under*: Arrow; Opium; Russo-Japanese; Sino-French; Sino-Japanese; Yangwu Movement 224; *see also*: Self-Strengthening Movement; *Tongmenghui*
Qingdao, Shandong 454
Qingdongxia, Ningxia 41
Qinghai 23, 30, 49, 78, 140
Qinghua university 272
Qingliu ('Purists') 226
Qinglongquan culture 141
Qingming festival 275
Qingpu, Jiangsu 220
Qinhuangdao, Hebei 35
Qinling mountains 24, 30
qinna (martial art) 133
Qinsai (Hangzhou) 188
Qinshan, Zhejiang 38
Qinzong, Emperor (Song) 179
qiqiaoban (game) 132
Qiqihar, Heilongjiang 38, 46
Qiu Ying *200*, 415
Qu Wuchen 148
Qu Yuan 148, 347
quanfa (boxing) 133
Quanzhou (Zaitun) 313, 314, 317
Quemoy island 141, 286
Qufu, Shandong *107*
Qujialing culture 140, 141
Quxian, Shandong 329

radio 51, 134, 367
Railway Protection Movement **231**, 232
railways **49–50**; coal transport 34, 49, 50; construction (C19th) 49, 52, 231, 232, (Republic era) 23, 242, 243, 454, (PRC) 49, 254, 454, 455; crime *106*; foreign involvement, (to 1911), 49, **231**, 232, (Japanese, in Manchuria) 23, 243, (under PRC) 254, 454; and industrial development 50, 452; locomotives 50; and roads 48; in southwest 30, 49; Taiwan 66

Ramapithecus 68
Rao Shushi 263
rape-seed 434
rare-earth minerals 42
rationing (1980s) 93, 98
rattan factory *64*
rectification campaigns **249–50**, 256, 281
Red Army 243, 244, **245**, 249, 250
Red Eyebrows 155, 156
Red Guards 50, 131, 258, 270, *271*, **272**
Red River 30, 159, 226
Red Turban revolts 195
Reform Movement (1898) 208, **227–9**, 230, 320
refugees; Vietnamese, in Hong Kong 86
regions, geographical 17–33
reincarnation 102
religion: animism 79; Bon 307; in Chu 148; drama and 359; emperor's role 12, 109, 303, 320, 430; Indonesian Chinese 90; folk 294–6, 297, 298; *hui-kuan* and 98; national minorities' 79, 81; Neolithic 140; in PRC 265, 272; and secret societies 99; Taipings and 219; *see also*: ancestor cult; Buddhism; Christianity; Confucianism; Daoism; Islam; Manichaeism; sacrifices; shamanism; Zoroastrianism; *and under individual dynasties*
ren (virtue) 301, 320, 344
Ren Yi 418
Renqiu oilfield, Hebei 34, 35
Renzong, Emperor (Tangut) 176
Republican period 13, **233–53**; arts 355–6, 356–7, 419, 431; building 431, 454; communications 51; elections 235; industry 52, 452–3; Jiangxi Soviet **243–4**, 245, 260, 279; law 105; Marco Polo Bridge Incident 245–6; parliaments 231, **235**, 320; Peasants' Movement 239; rectification campaigns 249–50; Stilwell and 248; Taiwan 252; taxation 239; warlords 235–6; *see also*: Anti-Japanese War; civil war; Long March; Manchukuo; May Fourth; Nationalist Government; New Fourth Army; New Life; Northern Expedition; Provisional Republic Government; Sun Yat-sen; United Front; Yan'an; *and under*: Chinese Communist Party; *Guomindang*; Shanghai
Republican Revolution (1911) 109, **231–2**, 235, 252, 254, 318, 364
Réunion Island 86
rhodium 41
Riau-Lingga archipelago 90
Ricci, Matteo 205, 313, 318, 337
rice 56, *57, 95, 371*; canals and 166; Champa 182, 368, 435; in cuisine 368, 370, 371; dry-rice farming 80, 82; Neolithic 139, 141, 142, 368; paddy 20, 27, 29, 30, 76, 159, 166, 252, 434
Richard, Timothy 225

rights, human 105, 265, 268, 323
Rites Controversy 205, 210, 318
rituals 97, 110, 295–6, 310, 377; emperors' role 380, 430; *see also under individual religions*
roads 43, 47, **48–9**, 380, **452**, 455; pilgrimage 430; Republican 242, 454; Song 182; Sui 165; Taiwan 66; *see also*: Burma Road; Ledo Road; Silk Road
rodents, wild 32, 33
Roman empire 47, 157, 434, 452
Romania 44
romanization 205, **337**, **467–9**; *see also*: *pinyin*; Post Office System; Wade-Giles System
Roosevelt, Franklin D. 248, 253
Roosevelt, Theodore 230
Rouran, confederation of 162
Ruan Ji 348
Rubruck, William of 317
rudder, stern-post 46
Ruijin, Jiangxi 244
Ruizong, Emperor (Tang) 170, 171
Russell, Bertrand 322
Russia, pre-revolutionary: and Britain 211, 220; caravans 212; concessions 23, 223, 231, 236; and Japan 225, 229, *230*; Jews in Harbin 313; literature 355, 356; and Manchuria 49, 212, 229, 231; and Qing 109, **212**, **220–2**, 225; and Siberia 222; and Tang 170; trade 47, 212, 220, 222; Triple Intervention 227, 230; territorial disputes 17, 220–2, 212
Russian Orthodox Church 318
Russians in China 77, 78, 80
Russo-Japanese war (1904–5) 229, **230**

sacrifices 295, 297, 376, 430; ancestor cult *293*, 294, 342–3, 368; Shang 144, 342, (human) 402
Saigon-Cholon 87
salamander, giant 437
Salar people 78
salt **42–3**, **446–7**; boats 444; Chu 148; Han 153, 155; monopoly 155, 172, 219, 446, 235, 236; processing 44, 446, 447; Tang 172; tax 42, 155, 172, 446; Yangzhou merchants 214; Zhou 147
san shi ('three worms') 297
Sang Hongyang 153, 154
Sanguozhi yanyi 351–2
Sanhuangwu 299
Sanmen Gorge; dam 454
sanmin zhuyi ('Three Principles') 237
sansheng system 164
Sanskrit 80, 325
Sanxia project, Yangtze 34, 454
Sanyuanli incident 218
Sanzijing (primer) 112
Sarawak; Iban people *73*
Sassanian empire *see* Iran
Saudi Arabia, Chinese in 86
Sauma, Rabban 317
scale insect; domestication 437
scapulimancy; Neolithic 140, 142; *see also* bones, oracle
Schall von Bell, Adam 318

sciences **437–44**; Islamic 194, 437; PRC 118, 265, 269, 279; Western influence 205, 319–20, 350; *see also individual branches and technology*

scouts, boy 242

screens, 'Coromandel' 421

script, Han Chinese 11, 150, 168; algebraic 441; non-phonemic nature 51, 111, 324, 325; reform 113, 328; *see also*: calligraphy; romanization

scripts, non-Han **82–4**; *see also under*: Jurchens; Khitans; Xixia

scrolls 405, 420

sculpture **391–3**; Buddhist *305*, 306, 390, 391, 392–3, 399, 405–6, 408, 414, 425; Daoist 408; Neolithic 140; patronage 399; Qing 409; reliefs 392, 403, 405, 429–30; spirit ways *287*, 403, 430; status 399; Zhou 402; *see also under*: bronze; disunity; stone; tomb objects; wood; *and* Ming, Tang *and* Yuan *dynasties*

seals 340, 394, 420

secret societies **99**, 113, 314, 315; and rebellions 218, 220, 232, 233

seismology **439–40**

Self-strengthening Movement 208, **223–4**, 225, 226–7, 227–8, 319

semuren (Central Asians) 192, 193

service industries 29, 66, 188

sewage 35, 454

sexual practices 127, 128

sha (evil forces) 290

Sha Tin 85

Shaanxi Province 24–5, 28; agriculture 20, *25*; dialect 326; energy 25, 35; history 75, 76, 142, 220, 263; minerals 25, 39, 42; population and administration 23; prehistory 17, 71, 138, 140, 141, 142; railways 49; wild environment 32, 436

shadow boxing 127, 133, 229

shadow theatre 189

Shakespeare, William 364

shamanism 79, *122*, 307, 347

Shandao 169

Shandong Province 25; administration 23; dialect 326; energy 26, 34, 35; geology 17; German concessions 231, 236; Han art *402*, 403; history 148, 179, 187, 215, 229; industry 42, 43; migration from 77, 86; minerals 26, 35, 38, 39, 41, 42, 43; missionaries 115, *318*; population 23, 26; prehistory 17, 140–1, 142, 329

Shang dynasty 141, **142–5**; agriculture 144, 435; bronze **144–5**, 390, (ritual objects) *145*, 343, **382–5**, 390, 399, **401**; building 144, 426; chopsticks 368; cities 425; climate 144; economy 144; foundation 136, 142; inscriptions 343; ivory 394; medicine 120; mythology 136; pottery 144, 343, 401; religion 11, 143, 144; sculpture 144, 392, 401;

silk 422; state 11, 142–3, 149; taxation 143; time, measurement of 377; tombs 144; and Zhou 145, 146; *see also*: bones; masks; *and under*: jade objects; sacrifices; writing

Shang Jia 144

Shang Kexi 210

Shang Yang 151, 149, 312

Shang-Yin culture 329, 333

Shanghai *27, 91, 429*; administration 21, 23; agriculture 29, 59; cinema 365; drama 364; industry 27, 35, 38, 39, 40, 52, 61, 224; Jesuits 115, 318; Jews 313, 314; population 23, 27; under PRC 105, 272, 277, 280, 285, (Commune) 258, 273; printing 114, 341; under Qing 46, 213, 220, 225; radio 51; Republican period 237, 240, 241, 246, 252, 260, (May 30th and June 23rd incidents, 1925) 239, 255, (Chiang Kai-shek's coup, 1927) **241**, 252, 253, 255, 260, 356; telephones 51; transport 49, 50; universities 115, *117*

Shangshu 147, 302, 343, 345

shangtun (merchant colonies) 202

Shanhaiguan invasion 206, 209

Shantou (Swatow), Guangdong 29, 225

Shanxi Province 24–5; agriculture 20; dialect 326; diet 58; history 76, 142, 174, 202–3, 316; minerals 25, 34, 38, 39, 40, 41, 42; population and administration 23; prehistory 17, *70*, 71

Shanyuan, Treaty of 190

Shaoguan, Guangdong 40

Shaolin, monks of 133

Shaoshan, Hunan 254, 255

Shaoxing (Yue) 314

Shaw, George Bernard *356*

She people 78

sheep 32, 139, 145, 368, 370

Shen Buhai 312

Shen Dao 312

Shen Fu 350

Shen Zhou 414

sheng (provinces) 21

Sheng Xuanhuai 231

Shengli, Shandong 26, 34, 35

Shengzong, Emperor (Liao) 177

Shennong 123, 136, 310

Shennong bencaojing 128

shenshi, shenjin, see gentry

Shenxiu 169

Shenyang (Mukden), Liaoning 21, 23, 40, 43, 205

Shenzhen, Guangdong 29

Shenzong, Emperor (Song) 180, 183

Shenzong, Emperor (Tangut) 176

Shepherd, George 242

shi (administrative units) 21–2

shi (aristocrats) 301

Shi Dakai 219

Shi Huangdi (First Emperor, Qin) 147, **149–50**, 151, 259, 311, 333, 432

Shi Jing-tang (Gaozu) 174

Shi Miyuan 180

Shi Naian 352

Shi Yousan 242

Shibi (Eastern Turk Khan) 166

Shiguan (History Office) 346

Shiji 155–6, 374

Shijiazhuang, Hebei 26

Shijing see Book of Odes

Shilin guangji 362

Shimian, Sichuan 42

Shimonoseki, Treaty of 227, 252

shipbuilding 27, 46, 444–5

shipping 46–7; Arabs 168; C19th 52; coastal 34, 46–7; prehistoric 46, 74, 142; Tang 168; *see also* waterways, inland

Shixia, Guangdong 139, 142

Shiyu 69

Shizhuyuan, Hunan 42

Shizong, Emperor (Later Zhou) 174, 177

Shizong, Emperor (Liao) 177

Shizu *see* Khubilai Khan

shops *126, 371*

Shouxian, Anhui; Peony Dam 451

Shouxian, Anhui; Peony Dam 451

Shu (Three Kingdoms) 158, **159**, 352, 407

Shu, Former (Ten Kingdoms) 174, 175

Shu, Later (Ten Kingdoms) 174, 175

Shu Ting 357

shuaijiao (martial art) 133

Shuangmiaogou culture 141

Shufang, Fujian 341

Shu-Han, kingdom of 157

Shui people 78

Shuifeng, Liaoning 36

Shuihuzhuan 352, 354

Shuikoushan, Hunan; mines 40

Shujing see Book of Documents

Shun, Emperor 136

Shundi, Emperor 191

Shuntian (Beijing, Ming) 198

Shuowen jiezi 325, 326

Siberia 138, 212, 222, 393

Sichuan Province 30; administration 23, 30; agriculture 30, 149, 280–1; art 391, 403, 404, 408; climate 30; demonstrations (1989) 283; dialect 327; diet 58; energy 35; forests 38, 149; history 149, 173, 179, 408; industry 38, 42, 43; minerals 38, 39, 42, 43; minorities 30, 78, 316; population 23; printing 340, 341; salt 446–7; topography 17, 30; transport 49, 231, 232; wild environment 32

siegecraft 147

silk **422–3**; cultivation 27, 434, 437; Han 402; Neolithic 140; Qing 213; Shang 422, 437; Song 185; techniques 422–3, 448; trade 46, 47, 153, 168, 201 (*see also* Silk Road); tussore 422; writing on 156, 340, 420

Silk Road *47, 48*, 153, 157, 165, 168, 437

Silla, state of 170

silver 39, **390–1**, **424–5**; brocade 422; as currency 46, 185, 187, 193, 203, 207, 242, 379; reserves 39, 41; Song 183, 185, 187; Tang 390, 409, *424*; techniques 402, 403, 409, 424–5; trade 46, 202, 207, 216;

Yuan 193, 414; Zhou 402

Sima Guang 184, 190, 346

Sima Qian 147, 155–6, 345

Sima Xiangru 347

Sima Yan 159

Singapore 34, 86, 87, 89

sinification 161

Sino-French War (1884–5) 208, 226–7

Sino-Japanese War (1894–5) 208, 225, **226–7**, 228; settlement after 230, 227, 252

Sino-Tibetan languages *324*

Sishu 112, 304, 319, 344

Sivapithecus 68

slavery 102, 103, 149, 186

Small Sword Society Uprising 208, **220**

smuggling 202, 219

snakes 33, 368, 370

Sneevliet, Hendricus ('H. Maring') 238

snuff bottles, Qing 418

soapstone reserves 41

social order **92–100**; *see also*: aristocracy; collectivization; family; hierarchy; lineage; secret societies; villages; *and under* Confucianism

social security 98, 266, 269

Socialist Education Movement 53, 268, **270**

Socialist Realism 357

Socialist Youth Corps 237

soda industry 43

soils **19–20**, 182, 434, **436**; erosion *24*, 33, 435; *see also*: fertilizers; loess

Song dynasty **177–90**; agriculture 182, 183–4, 434, 435; alchemy 296; algebra 441; architecture 427; arts 13, 177, 393, 394, **409–12**, 422; Buddhism 188, 190, 408; calligraphy 178, 341, 409, 411; colonization 76; commerce 182–3, 379; Confucianism 180, 190, 344; Daoism 188, 299; death penalty 102; drama 189, 358, 359; economy 177, 182, 183–4; education 108, 112, 179, 184, 188; elite 181–2; examination system 110–11, 178, 181, 182, 184; government 178, *180*, 181–2; historiography 188, 190, 340, 346; Jews 313; Kaifeng 177, *183, 184*, 188, 341, 358, 359; land policy 182; law 101; and Liao 177, 178, 185; and Mongols 177, 190; music 362; Neo-Confucianism 13, 122, 116, 188, *190*, 303, 304; Northern 177–9, 352; officials 181, 183; painting 179, *182*, 190, 410, 411, *435*, (Zang Zeduan) *183, 184, 189*; poetry 188, 190, 349; pottery 387, 388–9, 411–12, 414; printing 110, 113, **187–8**, 340; shipbuilding 445; Southern 177, 179–80, 185, *186*, 187–8, 190, 411; and Southern Tang 173; subsidies 185, 187, 190; taxation 179, 181, 182–3, 184; trade 184, 187; unifies China 177, 178; wood carving *391*; and

Song dynasty (*cont.*)
Wuyue 178; and Xixia 176, 177, 190; Zoroastrianism 314; *see also* Hangzhou; Huizong; Taizong; Taizu; *and under*: cities; Jin (Jurchen); medicine
Song Jiaoren 235
Song Meiling (Mme Chiang Kai-shek) *253*
Song Qingling (Mme Sun Yat-sen) *258*
Song Yingxing 204
Song Zheyuan 246
Songhua River system 46
Songjiang, Shanghai 213
Songtao, Guizhou 41
Songyuesi, Henan 429
Songze culture 141
Sophists 311
sorghum 56, 368
South Africa 43, 86
South Korea 65, 86
Southern Dynasties 160, 387, 395, 405
Southern Song Academy 411
Sovereigns, Three 136
soviets 243–4, 263; Jiangxi Soviet **243–4**, 245, 260, 279
soya beans 56, 368, 370, 371
space technology 51, 285, 367, *433*, 448
Special Administrative Regions 22, 85, 106
Special Economic Zones 22, 29, 64, 280
spells 120, 127, 128
Spencer, Herbert 320
spirit ways *287*, 392, 393, 403, 406, 430
Spiritual Pollution Campaign 281, 357
sports 134, 437
Spring and Autumn Annals see *Chunqiu*
'Spring and Autumn' *see under* Zhou, Eastern
Sputnik Commune 266
St Petersburg, Treaty of 222
Stalin, Josef 240, 241, 256, 263, 266, 323; Khrushchev denounces 257, 260, 264, 265, 269; Mao and 256, 266
steel *see* iron and steel
steel-yard balances 438
Stein, Sir Aurel 340
stelai 345, 393
steppe, northern 24–5, 32
stills 438
Stilwell, Joseph Warren **248**
stone: chimes 363, 385; inscriptions 333, 340, 343, 398, 420; rubbings *302*, 404; sculpture *287*, **392–3**, 401, 403, 405, 408; tools, prehistoric *70*
stories, short 349, 351, 355
storytelling 113, 189, 194, 300, 354
strikes 241, 265
struggle, ideology of 94, 99, 100, 321
Su Dongpo 349
Su Shi 399, 409, 410
Su Song (Su Zirong) *451*

subsidies 185, 187, 190, 234
succession, law of 104–5
Sufism 211, 315
sugar 57, 58, 59, 252
Sui dynasty **164–6**; canals 45, 165, 166, 451; civil war at end of 166, 167; education 108, 110, 165; mirrors 409; officials 76, 110, 164, 165; religion 164, 165, 307; taxation 164, 167; *see also*: Jiangdu; Wendi
sulphur 201, 438
Sumatra, kingdom of 90
Sun Ce, King of Wu 159
Sun Chuanfang 240
Sun Quan (King of Wu) 159
Sun Yat-sen **233–4**, 236, 237; Christianity 225, 318; and Ling Qichao 228; name 337; opposition to Qing 227; in Provisional Republic Government 232–3, 234; PRC adopts policies 261; *Three People's Principles* 116, 237, 261, 322; and *Tongmenghui* 230; and United Front 238; wife (Song Qingling) *258*
Sun Yixian *see* Sun Yat-sen
Sundaland 74
sundials 438, 443
Sung dynasty *see* Song
Sunzi (military treatise) 299
Surinam 85, 87
surnames 92
suspension, Cardan *450*
Suzhou, Jiangsu 27, 195, 213, 222, 327, 358, *432*
Suzong, Emperor (Tang) 171
Sweet Dew Incident 172
swimming 133, 134
Switzerland 41
swords 201, 447–8
sylvite deposits 44
symbolism in art 395–8

table tennis *133*, 134
Tai, King (Gugong Danfu) 145
Tai Honjing 128
Taihang scarp 24
Taihe lü 101, 186, 192
taijiquan see shadow boxing
Tainan, Taiwan 225
Taipei, Taiwan 29, *126*, 252
Taiping, Princess 171
Taiping rebellion 20, 208, **218–19**, 224, 457; Black Flag Army 226; Christianity 219, 318; government 227; and Kaifeng Jews 313; Lin Zexu and 217; and Small Sword Society Uprising 220
Taipingdao *see* Yellow Turbans
Taiwan 29; aboriginals 72, 73, 74; administration 22; agriculture 29, 65, 252, 374; Chineseness 14; cinema 367; Daoism 296, 297, 300; defence 286; dialect 326; economy 65–6, 286; elections 286; energy 38; environment 66; gold mining 39; history 76, 84, 206, 226, 227, 252, 268; imperial collections 420–1; industry 29, 39, 66; land redistribution 65–6; language 337, 338; literature 358; Martial Law

286; medicine 126, 130; migration from 86, 87; minorities 78, 82; Nationalist government 22, 236, **285–6**, (establishment) 251, 252, 253, (legal status) 66, 254, (overseas Chinese loyalties) 86, 89, 90, (PRC relations with) 53, 285–6; and Olympic Games 134; philosophers 323; police 286; population 29; prehistory 141, 142, 400; railways 49; and Taiwan Strait 46–7; trade 65, 66, 286; and USA 66, 252, 253, 254; year-count 379
Taixue 107, 108, 345
Taiyuan, Shanxi 38, 39, 166, 314, 327, 427
Taizong, Emperor (Liao) 177
Taizong, Emperor (Song) 173, 178
Taizong, Emperor (Tang) 166, **167–8**, 168–9, 170; and arts 346, 406, 408, 420
Taizu, Emperor (Liang) 173
Taizu, Emperor (Liao) 177
Taizu, Emperor (Song) 174, 177–8
Taizu, Emperor (Zhou) 174
Tajiks 78, 80, 82
Taklamakan desert 153
talc 41, 43
talismans 120, 342
Tan Sitong 304, 320
Tan Xinpei 361
Tan Yankai 239
Tang (Five Dynasties) **173**
Tang, Southern (Ten Kingdoms) 173, 174, 175, 407
Tang Code 101, 165, 186
Tang dynasty **166–73, 406–9**; agriculture 435; armies 170, 171; Buddhism 12, **168, 169**, 306, 391, 408; Confucianism 190, 302; cosmopolitan nature 168, 313, 314; cuisine 368; Daoism 110, 111, 168, 296, 298, 299, 408; disasters, natural 167, 172; economy 172, 182, 379; education 108; eunuchs 172; examination system 108, 110, 170, 171, 172; foreign contacts 168, 313, 314, (religions) 168, 313, 314, 317; gardens 431–2; Huang Zhao's rebellion 173; institutions of state 167, 169–70; lacquer 421; law 103, 108, 110, 167, (Tang Code) 101, 165, 186; literature 346, 348–9, (poetry) 161, 178, 348–9; monopolies 155; mirrors 409; music 362; officials 167–8, 170, 171, 172; painting *381*, 407–8, 412, 431–2; paper 340; pottery 168, 387, 388, 409; printing *102*; provincial government 171, 172; sculpture *392*, 408–9; silver objects *390*, 409, 424; social structure 76, 110, 170, 171, 172, 173; taxation 171, 172, 340; textiles 422, 423; trade 13, 168, 175; women 170; *see also*: An Lushan; Taizong; Xuanzong; *and under*: aristocracy; Chang'an; Luoyang; tombs
Tang Jiyao 236
Tang the Victorious 136

Tang Xianju 358
Tang Yin 350, 415
Tangshan, Hebei 38, 276
Tanguts 13, 76, 167, 185, 194; *see also* Xixia
Tanluan 169
Tantrism 307
Tao Hongjing 299
Tao Xisheng 322
Tao Yuanming (Tao Qian) 348
taotie see masks
Taozong, Emperor (Liao) 177
Tarbagatai, Treaty of 222
Tarim Basin 26, 35, 44; in past 47, 75, 76, 155, 168, 173
Tartar people 77, 78
taxation 106, 119, 193, 239, 380; assessment units 97, 161; *liangshuifo* 172; *see also under*: disunity; monasticism; salt; *and* Han, Ming, Qing, Shang, Song, Sui *and* Tang *dynasties*
Taylor, James Hudson 318
tea *47*, 185, 216, 217, **374**; cultivation 29, 30, 32, 374
teahouses 113
technology **444–51**; foreign influence 29, 30, 53, 62, 114, 257, 279, 280; intermediate 266; PRC 41, 62, 258, 279, 280, 284; Song 177; Yuan 194; *see also under* education; Ming dynasty; *and individual branches*
telecommunications 51
television 51, 366, 367
temperature 17, *18*
temples: Buddhist 12, 165, 305, 429, (cave) *304*, 392, 393, 404, 405–6, 408, 429–30, (*see also*: Dunhuang); community 96, 295, 297; Confucian *93*, 302–3, 429; in Cultural Revolution 272; Daoist 429; Manichaean 314
Temür, Emperor (Yuan) 193
Ten Kingdoms 174–6
Ten Kings of Hell 102
tennis 133; table- *133*, 134
Teochiu emigrants 86, *88*
Tertiary period 32
Test-ban Treaty 269
textiles 25, 26, 52, 213–14; Neolithic 138, 140, 141; payment in 167, 185, 187; techniques 340, 422–3; trade 59, 63, 66; *see also individual fibres*
Thailand 82, 84, 85, 86, 87–8, 139
Thalweg Principle 274
'Third Front' areas 53
Three-Anti campaign 261–2
Three Kingdoms 157, 158, *159*
Three-Self Reform Movement 318
throne, lacquer *423*
thunder 298, 438
'thunder pattern' 398, 401
ti-yong dichotomy 114
Tian Han 364, 365
Tian Jian 356–7
Tian Zhuangzhuang 366
Tiangong kaiwu 203, **204**, 423
Tianjin: administration 21, 23; agriculture 58; history 223, 225, 226, 246, 251, 260; education 115;

Tianjin (*cont.*)
industry 38, 40, 42, 61, 223, 224, 454; population 23, 26, 314; Treaties of 223, 225
Tianlongshan cave temples 392, 393, 406, 408
tianming (Mandate of Heaven) 303
Tianningsi pagoda *308*
Tianqi Emperor 199, 205
Tianshidao (Daoist movement) 298–9
tianzi ('Son of Heaven') 12
Tianzun (Heavenly Honoured Ones) 297
Tianzuodi, Emperor (Liao) 177
Tibet 30; administration 21, 23, 84; agriculture and livestock 20, 31, 59, 268; climates 31; communications 31, *47*, 49; cuisine 374; felt rugs 423; flora 436; geothermal power 38; history 76–7, 194, 201, 210–11, 318, (kingdom) 76, 168, 170, 171, 173, (and Yuan) 192, 194, 414; industry 31; language 80, 82, 83, 300; literacy 113; minerals 39, 43; population 23, 31, 78; under PRC 77, 268, 285; topography 17; *see also*: Buddhism (Lamaism); Dalai Lamas
Tibeto-Burman languages 79, 80
tides 438–9
Tieling, Liaoning 40
tigao and *puji* 133
tigers 33, 145
tiles *402*, 403, 425, 426
Tillers (*Nongjia*) 310–11
timber 23, 29, 33, 46, 149; construction 425, *426*, 427, 429
time, measurement of **377–9**, 438; *see also*: calendar; clocks
Timor, overseas Chinese in 90
tin 30, 40, 453
titanium 42
toasts, drinking of 458
Toba people 76
tobacco 26, 55, 56, 58, 435
Toghon Temür (Shundi) 191
Tokharistan 314
Tokugawa Shogunate 202
Tokyo, Japan 228, 230, 233, 237
tomb objects: lacquer, Han 404; Neolithic 399; sculptures *132*, 402, *403*, 406, *408*, 409, 425, 445; silver, Tang 409
tombs: ancestral graves 94, 288, *289*, 291; building materials 426; choice of site 290–1; Han *132*, 437, 445; of Liu Tingxun *408*; Mawangdui, Changsha 404; Ming 390, 430; preservation of bodies 437; Northern and Southern Dynasties 405, 406; Shang 144; *see also*: spirit ways; tomb objects; *and under* Tang dynasty
Tong Guan 179
Tongguan Pass 166, 171
Tonghak Uprising, Korea 227
Tonghzi, Emperor 223, 227
Tongling, Anhui 40
Tongmenghui 208, **230**, 232, 233, 237, 252, 321

Tongren, Guizhou 41
Tongwen guan (foreign office language school) 114–15, 223, 225
Tongzhi Emperor 208
tools, prehistoric stone *70*, 71, 137, 138, 140, 142, 144
topography 17
totok (Indonesian Chinese) 90
tourism 51, 66, 431
townships (*xiang*) 22
trade, foreign 63–4; balance of 63, 64, 66, 207, 216; Canton system 215–16; external Chinese and 85; historic routes 47, 314; Java, medieval 90; PRC 53, 59, 63–4, 473; Republic 52; *see also*: caravans; guilds; merchants; *and under individual countries, commodities, dynasties and* Europe
trade corporations 64
trade unions 241, 254
translation 176, 194, 318, 355; Buddhist scriptures 168–9, 305, 306, 308–9; of Western works 320, 323, 350, 354–5, 364
transport *see individual modes*
travellers 153, 168, 313; *see also*: Marco Polo
treadle, invention of 448
treaties, unequal 207, 218, 223, 225, 248
treaty ports 98, **225**, *226*; creation 218, 220, 223, 225, *226*, 227; education in 98, 320; industry 61; postal services 51; under Republic 242, 454; and Western influence 133, 225, 320
Triad Societies 99, 220
tribute system 196, **200–1**, 451
Trigrams, Eight 136; Rebellion *214*, 215
Trinidad, Chinese in 87
Triple Intervention (1895) 227, 230
Truman, Harry S. 286
Tsewang Rabtan 210, 212
Tsong-kha-pa 210, 307
Tsuen Wan, Hong Kong 85
Tsurukhaitu, Manchuria 212
Tsushima, Battle of 230
Tu people 78
Tuen Mun 85
Tujia people 78
Tujue 166
Tumu, battle of 199
Tungans (Muslims) 222, 316
tungsten 41–2, 453
Tungusic peoples 77, 78–9; *see also* Jurchens
Tunisia 44
tuntian (farming projects) 158
Turanian people 77
Turfan *60*, 76, 211, 222
Turkestan *132*, **211–12**, 222, 393
Turkey, Chinese in 86
Turkic languages 78–9
Turks: Islam 79, 212; in north-east, C10th 76; Qing and 212; Shatuo 173, 174; Sui and 165, 166, 167; Tang and 68, 170, 171; Yuan and 192, 194
turtles 33, 289; *see also*

plastromancy
Tushu jicheng 341, *439*
tussore silk 422
tutanzhai (Daoist ritual) 297
tutors, private 112, 115
'two lines or roads' 258, 270
typhoons 19, 29
Tzang, O. Z. 338

Uighurs 26, 77, 78, 84, 316; cuisine 374; history 76, 168, 173, 192, 206, 211, 222; language 79, 300, (script) 82, 83; religion 314, 316
Union of Soviet Socialist Republics: advisers 118, 239, 240; aid (Republican era) 234, 237, 238, 239, 240, 246, 248, 252, (to PRC) 52, 256, 258, 267, 269, 455; airlines 51; architecture 431; borders 17, 26, 49, 212, 220–2, 269, 274, 285, 316; and CCP before Liberation 234, 237, 238, 245, 249, 254; cinema 365; and concessions in China 236; defence 267, 269; education 117–18, 269; and Japan 23, 233, 243; Jews in Harbin 313; Li Peng and 284; literature 355, 356, 357; and Manchuria 243, 254, 263, 269; Mao and 256, 266, 270; nuclear policy 269, 285; PRC uses Soviet models 52, 64, 93, 105, 256–7, 263, 264, 269; relations with PRC, (initial good) 254, 256, 261, 269, (breakdown) 14, 52, 53, 118, 258, 267, 269, 455, (conflict) 17, 212, 269–70, 274, 285, (summit, 1989) 270, 282; railways 49, 254; technical assistance 52, 257, 454; trade 40, 41, 44, 64; and USA 269; *see also*: Comintern; Russia
United Front, CCP/*Guomindang*: First (1920s) **238–9**, 250, 255, 260, 321; New (1937–41) **246–7**, 249, 250, 256, 260
United Nations 66, 85, 262, 286, 454
United States of America: C19th contacts 115, 207, 220, 223; and CCP in Yan'an 249; Chinese in 14, 86–7, (students) 119, 223, 229; cinema 365; and civil aviation 50, 51; civil service examinations 111; and civil war 250–1; and education 115–16, 223, 225, 229; and fertilizer industry 44; and Hong Kong 65; Jewish exodus to 314; and Korean War 262; literary influence 355, 356; military aid (1937–45) 246, 248; and Philippines 89; and PRC (official relations) 66, 254, 259, 269, 286; rapprochement (1970s) 134, 275, 280, 316, (1980s) 279; Reagan administration 269; and Russo-Japanese War 230; and Taiwan 66, 252, 253, 254, 286; and Tibet 268; trade 34, 40, 41, 42, 43, 63, 65, 220; in WWII 246, 248, 252; and USSR 269
Universal Postal Union 51
universe, concepts of 290, 437, 442
universities 116, 118, 119, 272;

foreign 119, 223, 229, 280, 431; Imperial (Peking) 109, 114–15, 236, 254, 339; missionary 114, 115, 318; National Defence 285; Qinghua 272; Shanghai 115, *117*; Tianjin 115
uranium, fissionable 37
Ürümqi, Xinjiang 37, 76, *316*
Ussuri Incident 212, 274, 285
Uzbek people 77, 78

Va (Wa) people 77, 78
vases 393, *394*, 403, 404, 409
vegetables 59, 139, 368, 370, 376; *see also individual vegetables*
vehicle building 23
Verbiest, Ferdinand 318
Versailles, Treaty of 236, 321
Vietnam: and Cambodia 269, 270; Chinese in 85, 86, 87, 89; Chinese invasion (1979) 285; cuisine 368; history 75, 76, 153, 165 (*see also* Annam); language 325; law 101; Miao-Yao people 82; migrants in China 78; prehistoric 68, 139, 141, 142; railways 49; refugees in Hong Kong 86; War (1960s) 53, 269, 280
villages 22, 25, 82; appearance *428*, 429, 431; society 93, 96–7, 103
Vimalakirti, statues of 406
Voitinsky, Gregory 237

Wade, Sir Thomas Francis 337, 338
Wade-Giles System 337, 338, 467–8, 469
wages 62–3
Walī Khan 222
walls, defensive 430; Great *24*, **430**, (Han) 155, (Jin) 174, (Ming) 198, 201, 430, (Qin) 150, 151, 153, 155, (Qing) 205, 209, (Sui) 145, (Zhou) 165, 430; Neolithic 142; settlements 92, 96, 97, 219, 425, 426, 428, 431
Wang, Empress (Tang dynasty) 170
Wang Anshi 179, 180, 190, 200, 349
Wang Chongyang 299
Wang Cizhong 334
Wang Faseng 214
Wang Fuzhi 259
Wang Guangmei 270, 271
Wang Guowei *350*, 351
Wang Hongwen 274, 277; *see also* 'gang of four'
Wang Hui 417
Wang Ji 304
Wang Jian (former Shu) 175
Wang Jian (painter) 417
Wang Jingwei 239, 240, 241, 242, 253
Wang Ken 304
Wang Mang 154, 156, 302
Wang Meng 412–13
Wang Ming (Chen Shaoyu) 250
Wang Shenzhi (King of Min) 175
Wang Shimin 415–16, 417
Wang Tao 225
Wang Wei 348, 410, 431–2
Wang Xizhi 398, 405, *406*
Wang Yangming **204–5**, 304, 319
Wang Yuanqi 417

Wang Zhen 199, 341
Wang Zhi 199
Wanli Emperor 195, **202**, 390, 430
Wannianqiao bridge, Nancheng 452
Wanshan, Guizhou 41
Wanyan clan 186
warlords 76, 99, 224; Republican period 232, 234, **235–6**, 241
Warring States period 75, **147**, *148*; bronzes 343, 382, 390; Confucianism 303; jade 402; northern defences 151; technology 425, 449
Waseda, Japan 259
water, artesian 446–7
water buffalo 139, 141, 145, 368, 434, 437
water-chestnuts 139, 434
water control 266, **454–5**; north China plain 25, 29; and paddy 20; in past 207, 454; Yangtze river 29, 454–5; Yellow River 24, 24–5, 25, 454; *see also*: hydro-electricity; irrigation
waterways, inland 37, **45–6**, 203, 444; importance 43, 49, 452; Song 182, *183*
water-wheel escapement *451*
weapons 438, 447–8, 452; ritual 400, 401
weaving *204*, **422**; Neolithic 138, 141
weddings 288, *293*, *294*, 359, 409; feasts 371, 376
Wedemeyer, Albert 248
Wei (Three Kingdoms, Cao Wei) 157, **158**, *159*
Wei (Warring States) 147, 148, 149
Wei, Eastern 162, *163*
Wei, Empress (Tang dynasty) 171
Wei, Northern 160, **161–2**, 163; arts **404–6**; Buddhist cave temples *304*, 392, 404, 405 (*see also*: Longmen; Yungang)
Wei, Western 162, *163*
Wei Boyang 299
Wei Changhui 219
Wei Daoming 252
Wei Jing-shen 281
Wei Qing 153
Wei Valley 24, 148–9
Wei Yuan 223
Wei Zhongxian 199, 205
weights and measures 150, **380**
welfare services 98, 266, 269
Wen, Duke of Jin 147–8
Wen Wang 145, 146
Wen Yiduo 356
Wen Zhengming 414, *415*
Wendi, Emperor (Han) 153
Wendi, Emperor (Sui) 162, *164*, 165, 166
wenmiao schools 429
Wenxiang 223, 225
Wenxuan anthology 340
Western influence *see under individual topics and countries*
Western Hills Clique 239
Western Jin **159–60**
Western Regions, Protectorate for 75
Whampoa Military Academy 234, 237, 252, 260

wheat: in cuisine 56, 368, 371; cultivation 26, 27, 29, 55, 56, 434, 435; Neolithic 139, 368, 435
wheel, potter's 387
wheelbarrow *450*
White Lotus Society 99, 219, 229; Rebellion 99, 207, 213, **214–15**, 229
wild environments **32–3**
'wind and water' 288, 291, 457
winds 17
wine (*jiu*) 33, 373–4; ritual vessels *383–4*
winnowing fan, rotary 435, 449
winter solstice 430
women **95–6**; and corvée 166; education 95–6, 111, 118; elderly 95; emancipation (Tang) 170, (PRC) 97, 105, 259, 321; literacy 111; and religion 295; and secret societies 99; suppression justified 288; in village society 95, 97; *see also* marriage
wood: fuel 38, 203; furniture 423; printing blocks *102*, 341; sculpture *391–2*, 402; writing on 156, 340
woollen fabrics 422, 423
Workers' Inspection Corps 241
World Bank 119, 280
World Economic Herald 285
World War, First 52, 235, 236, 321, 452
World War, Second 13, 113, 233, 248, 252; *see also* Anti-Japanese War
wrestling (*xianbu*) 133
wrist rests *391–2*, 394
writing **329–34**; basic strokes *332*; evolution 329, *330*; Neolithic 329, 343; numerical notation 440; Qin dynasty 333; reforms 113, 331–3, 334; Shang dynasty 142, *143*, 289, 329, 342–3, 435, 440; Shang-Yin period 333; talismans 342; as uniting factor 12; *wenyan* style 327; *Xingran tie 406*; Zhou period 12, 330; *see also*: calligraphy; characters
writing equipment 156, 202–3, *391–2*, 394, 416, 420; *see also*: brush pots; brushes; paper; wrist rests
Wu (Ten Kingdoms) 174, 175
Wu (Three Kingdoms) 157, 158–9
Wu (Warring States) 75, 148
Wu, Empress (Wu Zhao) 169, *170–1*
Wu Bin 415
Wu Changshi 418
Wu Cheng'en 352
Wu Daozi 407, 410
Wu Ding 143
Wu Han 267
Wu jing see Five Classics
Wu Jingzi 353
Wu Li 417
Wu Peifu 240
Wu Sangui, General 205, 209, 210
Wu Tianming 366
Wu Wang 145, 146
wu xing (Five Phases) 121
wu xing (five punishments) 101–2
Wu Zhen 412–13

Wu Ziniu 366
Wuchang, Hubei 115, 240; Uprising 208, 227, 230, **231–2**
Wucheng, Henan 43
Wuchuan, Guizhou 41
Wudi, Emperor (Han) 107, 153, 379, 451
Wudi, Emperor (Liang) 163–4
Wuhan: administration 21; bridge 455; climate 30; industry 29, 38, 40; Nationalist government (1920s) 240, 241; Wuhan Incident (1967) 272–3
Wuhu, Anwei *28*, 45
Wujiangdu, Guizhou 36
Wuwei (Liangzhou), Gansu 314
wuwei (non-activity) 296, 305, 313
Wuxi, Jiangsu 27, *46*, 205, *431*
Wuyue (Ten Kingdoms) 175, *175*, 178, 188

Xavier, St Francis 318
Xi Jiang 46
Xi Kang 348
Xia ('Chinese') 75
Xia dynasty 136, 141, 142, 147
Xia dynasty, new (An Lushan) 171
Xia Gui 411
Xia Yan 365
Xiachuan, Shanxi 69
Xiajiadian, Lower; culture 141
Xiajiang dialect subgroup 327
Xiamen (Amoy), Fujian 29, 220, 225, 327
Xi'an, Shanxi: administration 21; architecture *426*, 430; in Boxer Uprising 229, 230; Chiang Kai-shek's arrest 242, 246–7, 253, 256, 260; Forest of Stele 345; industry 25, 38; importance of area 145, 149; irrigation 451; Neolithic 329; royal tombs *381*, *407*
xian (counties) 21–2, 84, 167
Xianbei people 75, 76, 161
xianbu (wrestling) 133
Xiandi, Emperor (Han) 157
Xianfeng Emperor (Qing) 208, 227
xiang (townships) 22
Xiang river *28*
Xiang Rong 219
Xiang Ying 250
Xiang Yu 150, 151, 152
Xiangtan, Hunan 29
Xiangtangshan cave temples 406
Xiangzong, Emperor (Tangut) 176
Xianrendong, Jiangxi 69, 71, 139
Xianzong, Emperor (Tang) 172
Xianzong, Emperor (Tangut) 176
xiao (filial feeling) 12
Xiao He 152
Xiao Jun 356
Xiao Tong 348
Xiao Yan (Liang Wudi) 163
Xiaojiayingzi, Liaoning 42
Xiaojing 344
Xiaonanhai 69
Xiaotun, Henan 142, *143*
Xiaowendi, Emperor 161
Xibe people 78
Xibeigang, Henan; Shang tombs 144

Xie (Shang ancestor) 136
Xie He 405
Xie Lingyun 348
xiehouyu (aposiopesis) 335
Xihoudu, Shanxi 69, *70*
Xihuashan, Jiangxi 41
Xikuang, Hunan 40, 41
xin (philosophical term) 204
Xin dynasty 154, **156**
Xin'anjiang 36
Xing (Zhou vassal) 343
Xing fa zhi (legal text) 101
Xing tong (law code) 101
Xinglongzhuang, Shandong *34*
Xingran tie (letter) *406*
xingzai, Hangzhou 188
Xingzhonghui 236
Xingzong, Emperor (Liao) 177
Xinhua zidian 338
Xining, Qinghai 31, 38
Xinjiang Province 26; administration 21, 23, 84, 316; agriculture 58; Buddhism 340; history 76–7, 212, 222, 315, 318; Islam 222, 315; land reclamation 58; minerals 37, 39, 40, 44; minority population 77, 78, 80; oil 35; population 23; routes 49; topography 17, 26; USSR and 269, 274
Xinjing (Changchun), Manchukuo 243
Xinle culture 141
Xinxing 307
Xiongnu 75, 76, 150, 151, 153, 154, **155**, 159
Xixia (Tangut empire) 76, **176**, 185, *186*, 187; and Liao and Song 176, 177, 185, 189, 190; script *176*, 185
Xiyouji 168–9, 352, 367
Xu Bo 451
Xu Daoning *410*
Xu Shen 329, 337, 343
Xu Wei 415
Xu Wen 175
Xu Xing 311
Xu Zhigao (Li Sheng) 175
Xu Zhimo 356
Xuande Emperor (Ming) 195, 390, 416, 417
Xuandi, Emperor (Han) 154
Xuangzong, Emperor (Tang) 348
xuanji 442, 443
Xuantong Emperor *see* Puyi
Xuanwu Gate Incident 167
Xuanzang, Emperor (Tang) 168–9, 307, 352
Xuanzong, Emperor (Tang, Minghuang) 171, 354, 358, 379
Xuge, battle of (707 BC) 146
Xujiayao, Shanxi 69, *70*, 71
Xun Kuang 121
Xunyi, Shaanxi 411
Xunzi 303

Yale University 337, 338
Yan, state of 75, 147, 148, 149
Yan Fu 320, *350*
Yan Hui 302
Yan Kan *415*
Yan Liben 407, 408
Yan Xishan 236, 240, 242

Yan Yangchu (Jimmy Yen) 113
Yan'an period of CCP 247, **249**, 251, 258, 260, 263, 357; Mao at *249, 250, 251, 256*
Yang 314
Yang, Edward 367
Yang Guan *see* Yangdi
Yang Guifei 171, 358
Yang Guozhong 171
Yang Jian *see* Wendi
Yang Kaihui (Mme Mao) *255*
Yang Pu (ruler of Wu) 175
Yang Xi 299, 300
Yang Xingmi (ruler of Wu) 175
Yang Xiuqing 218, 219
Yang Zhu 310
Yangdi, Emperor (Sui) 165, 166
Yangism 310
Yangjiazhangzi, Liaoning 42
Yangshao culture 74, **140**, 141, 329, 400, 425; pottery 140, 142, 329, *386, 387,* 400
Yangtze region *27, 28–9*; agriculture 27, 28, 166, 434, 435; communications 45, 47, 48, 166; history 17, 75, 174, 175, 179, 182, 198, 208, 231; industry 27, 35, 43; minerals 39; Neolithic 140–1; *see also individual provinces*
Yangtze river 28; bridges 455; Gorges 30, 45; hydro-electricity 28–9, 36; navigation 45, 46, 444; water control 28, 29, 34, 434, 454–5
Yangwu Movement 224
Yangzhou, Jiangsu 175, 214, 327, 354; Tang 168, 314, 340; *see also* Jiangdu
Yanmen, Shanxi 166
Yanshi, Henan 143
Yao, Count of Zhi 147
Yao, Emperor 136
Yao people *33, 78,* 81–2
Yao Wenyuan 258, 277; *see also* 'gang of four'
Yarlung Zangbo River 36
Yayoi culture of Japan 74
Ye (Anyang, Henan) 162
Ye Mingchen 223
Ye Shi 190
Ye Ting 250
years, cycle of 378–9
Yellow Emperor 136, 336, 408
Yellow Hats 307
Yellow River 26, 41, 140, 434; water control 24–5, 27, 45, 451, 454
Yellow Turbans 156, 158, 298, 299
Yelü Abaoji 177, 184–5
Yen, Former 161
Yen, Jimmy (Yan Yangchu) 113
Yen, Later 161
Yen, Western 161
Yi people 75, 78, 82, *83*
Yi tiao bian (tax reform) 203
Yi Yin 144
Yijing 290, 343
Yijiu (Bing Wang) 146, 147
Yili (Confucian classic) 344
Yili Valley 26, 27, 222
Yimen, Yunnan 40
yin and *yang* 121, 125–6, 288; and arts 395, 432; and diet 376; and

folk religion 295; and Han political ideas 151; and medicine 123, 124; and sciences 437; thunder as clash of 438
Yin-Yang School of philosophy 311–12
Yindi, Emperor (Han) 174
Ying Yujian 411
Yingtian (Nanjing) 108, 195, 198
Yingzong Emperor 199
Yinzhen *see* Yongzheng Emperor
Yishan, Guangxi 221
Yixing, Jiangsu 214, 419
Yizhou 314
Yizong (Tangut emperor) 176
Yongle dadian 197
Yongle Emperor 195, **196–7**, 198, 199, 416, 417
Yongli Emperor 195
Yongtai, Princess; tomb *381, 407*
Yongzheng Emperor 116, 207, 210, 213
Yougui 173
Young Men's Christian Association 133
Younghusband, Colonel Francis 211
yttrium 42
Yu, Great 136, 451
Yu Dafu 355–6
Yu Wang (king of Zhou) 146
Yu Xin 348
Yuan dynasty 13, **191–4**, *412–14*; agriculture 192–3, 435; building 193; Buddhism 192, 193, 194, 210, 298, 308, 414; calligraphy 194, 412–13; canals 45, 193, 451; census 192; cuisine 368; Daoism 194, 195, 298; death penalty 102; drama 194, 350, 358; economy 192–3; education 108; emperors 191–2; examination system 111; factions and rebellions 193; fall 451; fiefs 192, 193; foreign relations 192, 194; government 192; historiography 192, 346; Islam 194, 313, 315; Jews 313; law 101, 102, 192; literature 194, 350; painting 408, 409, 410, 412–13, 420; philosophy 194; population 192; pottery 387, *413,* **414**; science 194; sculpture 194, 414; and Song dynasty 177; succession procedures 191; and Yunnan 76, 315
Yuan Haowen 187, 350
Yuan Hongdao 350
Yuan Mei 350
Yuan River 36
Yuan Shikai 114, 228, 230, 232–3, **234–5**; in Korea 227, 234; monarchical attempt 228–9, 235, 419
Yuan Songdao 350
Yuan Zhen 349
Yuan Zhongdao 350
Yuandi, Emperor (Han) 154
Yuanmingyuan (garden) 432
Yuanmou, Yunnan 69, 71, 138
Yuanqu, Shanxi 40
Yuanquxuan (drama) 194
Yuchen, King of Hui 146, 147
Yue, state of 46, 75, 148, 314

Yue Fei 180
Yuku people 78
Yun Shouping 417
Yungang, Shanxi *304,* 392, 405, 430
Yunnan Province 30; administration 21, 23; agriculture 30, 58, 80, 374, *434*; dialect 327; environment 32, 33, 38; geothermal power 38; history 75–6, 84, 168, 173, 196, 220, 235, 315; Islam 220, 315, 316; minerals 38, 39, 40, 42, 43, 44, 452, 453; minorities 30, 78, 80, 81; population 23, 30; prehistory 68, 71, 138; railways 49; trade route 47
Yuwen family (Northern Zhou) 162
Yuwen Kai 165, 166
Yuwen Tai 162

Zaichun (Tongzhi Emperor) 208
Zaitun 317
Zang Zeduan *183, 184*
Zeng Guofan 114, 208, 219, 223, 224, 226
Zeng Guoquan 219
Zeng Shen 344
Zengpiyan 139
zero symbol 440, 441
Zhang Chunqiao 258, 272, 273, 277; *see also* 'gang of four'
Zhang Daoling 298, 299
Zhang Guoliang 219
Zhang Guotao (E-Yu-Wan) 244, 245
Zhang Heng 347, 439–40, 442
Zhang Ji 128
Zhang Jinghui 243
Zhang Jue 156
Zhang Junmai (Carson Chang) 323
Zhang Juzheng 202
Zhang Lu 299
Zhang Luoxing 219
Zhang Qian 153
Zhang Shicheng 195
Zhang Wentian 244
Zhang Xueliang 242, 246–7, 253
Zhang Xun 228, 233
Zhang Yanyuan 407
Zhang Yimou 366
Zhang Yushu 337
Zhang Zai 190, 304
Zhang Zeduan *183, 189*
Zhang Zhidong 114, 231
Zhang Zhidong 114, 231
Zhangzai, Shandong 41
Zhangzong, Emperor 411
Zhanjiang (Song capital) 179, 188
Zhao, state of 147, 148, 149
Zhao, Later 160, 161
Zhao Gao 150
Zhao Kuangyin *see* Taizong, Emperor (Song)
Zhao Mengfu 194, 412, *413*
Zhao Yingcheng 313
Zhao Zhiqian 418
Zhao Ziyang 277, **280–1**, *282,* 284, 323
Zhaodi, Emperor (Han) 154
Zhaohui 212
Zhaoxian, Hebei *430,* 452
Zhaoyang Lake 25
Zhaoyuan Xian, Shandong 39
Zhejiang Province 29, *452;* dialect

326; drama 358, 365; history 141, 173, 179, 192–3, 219, 220; industry 42, 43, 422; minorities 78; nuclear power 38; population and administration 23
Zhenbao Island 274
Zheng, king of Qin *see* Shi Huangdi
Zheng He 46, *198*
Zheng Xiaoxu 243
Zheng Xie *417*
Zhengde Emperor 195, 199, 202, 416
Zhengdi, Emperor 154
Zhengguo Canal 451
Zhengzhou, Henan 26, 41, 143, 240, 390
Zhenjiang 225, 314
Zhi, Count of 148
Zhifu (Chefoo) 225
Zhili 215, 224, 229
Zhiyi 307
Zhongguo (China) 457
zhongguo (states of the centre) 145
Zhongyong 304, 344
Zhong yuan, Guangdong 35, 141
Zhongzong, Emperor 170, 171
Zhu Wen (Taizu, Liang emperor) 173
Zhou (court recorder) 333
zhou (administrative units) 21, 167
Zhou (Five Dynasties) 173, 174
Zhou, Duke of 302
Zhou, Northern 158, **162**, 164, 165, 406
Zhou Dunyi 304
Zhou dynasty **145–9**; alcoholism 374; army 145–6, 147; arts 398, 401–2, 420; bronze wares *146,* 329, 343, *382–5,* 398, **401–2**; building 425, 452; canals 166; Chineseness 11–12; cities 425; Daoism 147; divination 146; Eastern **146–7**, 343, *402;* economy 147; emblematic colour 311; feudalism 145–6, 147; Great Wall 165, 430; historiography 147, 342, 345; inscriptions 333, 343; jade carving *385,* 393; justification of accession 303; literature 147, 347; medicine 120; metallurgy 147; military art 147; money *379;* music 362; mythology 136; philosophy 107, 109, 120–1, 147, 311, (*see also* Confucius); pottery 333; religion 145, 146, 147, 377; silk 420, 448; society 145–6; 'Spring and Autumn' period 147, 343; Wen Wang 146; Western 145–6; Zhou Gong 145, 146
Zhou dynasty (Empress Wu) 170
Zhou Enlai **259–61**, *260, 271;* anti-Confucian campaign attacks 274; anti-miltarism 274; birth and education 259, 277; and Cultural Revolution 260, 272, 274, 275; death 275, (turmoil after) 105, 261, *275;* and economy 53; foreign policies 259, 269, 274; and Hundred Flowers 265; in Republican period 239, 241, 248; and Li Peng 284; and modernization 279, 280; name 336; personality 260–1
Zhou Gong 145, 146

Zhou Wenju 407
Zhouguan 344
Zhoukoudian 69, 71, 73–4, 137, *138*
Zhouli 219, 344, 368
Zhouyi 290, 302, 344
Zhu Biao 196
Zhu De 243, 245, 256
Zhu Di *see* Yongle Emperor
Zhu Xi 190, 194, 304, 319, 362
Zhu Xia ('Chinese') 75
Zhu Yuanzhang *see* Yellow Emperor

Zhu Yunwen *see* Jianwen Emperor
Zhu Zaiyu 362
Zhuang, Count of Zheng 146
Zhuang people 78, 84; script 82, 83
Zhuangzi 148, 298, 299, 323
Zhuangzi (Daoist text) 310, 311
Zhuangzong, Emperor 173
zhuanqu (prefectures) 21
Zhuge Liang 159, 352
zhugongdiao (narratives) 354
Zhuhai Special Economic Zone 29

Zhuxie Cunxu (Li Cunxu) 173
Zhuzhou, Hunan 40
zihua (game) 133
zinc 40
ziran 296
zizhiqu see autonomous regions
zong ('school' or 'sect') 306
Zongli Yamen (foreign office) 114, 223, 224, 225
Zongtiaoshen mine, Shanxi 40
zoology *129*, 437

Zoroastrianism 168, 314
Zou Yan 311
Zouxin (Shang king) 145, 146
zu (lineage) 94
Zu Jia (Shang king) 143
Zunyi Conference 245
Zuo Zongtang 219, 220, 223
Zuoqin Ming 344
Zuozhuan 147, 344, 345

Acknowledgements

Every effort has been made to obtain permission to use copyright materials; the publishers welcome any errors or omissions being brought to their attention.

15, 28*br*, 57*l*, 64*b*, 67, 91, 97, 119, 127, 249, 260, 283, 287, 372, 373, 425, 429*l*, 455, 459 Sally & Richard Greenhill; 24*l*, 27*b*, 28*bl, tr*, 29, 46, 57*t, c*, 271*r*, 305, 426*l*, 430 Vision International/Paolo Koch; 24*r*, 27*t*, 381 Vision International/Simon Holledge; 25, 33, 34, 53, 60*tl*, 95, 247, 248, 253, 271*l*, 278*b*, 297, 433 Camera Press Ltd; 28*tl* Catherine Sanders; 31, 50, 252, 236, 237, 245, 251, 252, 254, 262, 279, 308, 350, 356 courtesy of Xinhua News Agency; 33 John Mackinnon/Bruce Coleman Ltd; 36, 55, 256, 273 Society for Anglo-Chinese Understanding; 38 courtesy of the Hong Kong Nuclear Investment Co; 47, 104, 112, 247*b*, 257, 258, 278*l*, 315, 359, 452 Popperfoto; 60*b* Julia Wilkinson/Aspect Picture Library; 60*tr*, 61, 64 C.B. Howe; 73 Peabody Museum of Archaeology & Ethnology, Harvard University; 81 Sarah Errington/ Hutchison Library; 93 Ma Po Shum/Aspect Picture Library; 96 Martin Black/Camera Press; 102, 132, 306, 386, 400, 401, 402, 403, 404, 405, 407, 408*r*, 412, 414, 415*b*, 416, 421, 424, 435 reproduced by courtesy of the Trustees of the British Museum; 106 Rupert Harrison; 107, 300, 345 by permission of the Syndics of the Cambridge University Library; 109, 114, 319 London Missionary Society Archive, School of Oriental and African Studies; 110 Princeton University Gest Library; 117 courtesy of Xinhua News Agency/photo by Wang Zijin; 123, 124, 125, 126, 129, 130 Dr P.U. Unschuld; 133 courtesy of ETTA (English Table Tennis Association); 134 N. Menzies; 135 Marc Riboud/John Hillelson Agency Ltd; 143 Hopkins Collection, Cambridge University Library, reproduced by permission of the Syndics of the Cambridge University Library; 146, 390, 392*r*, 410*t* Nelson Gallery-Atkins Museum, Kansas City; 164, 179, 191, 196, 200, 213 Collection of the National Palace Museum, Taiwan; 182 History of Art Collection, Cornell University; 184, 189 Werner Forman Archive, 187*t* Prof. Dr. H. Franke; 187*b*, 325, 360*l* School of Oriental & African Studies; 202, 389*l*, 419, 422, 423 reproduced by permission of the Board of Trustees of the Victoria & Albert Museum; 223, 224, 227, 232 Hulton-Deutsch Collection; 234, 238, 244 Roger Violett; 247*t*, 370 Imperial War Museum, London; 255 Stuart Schram; 282 courtesy of David Shambaugh; 283 Associated Press; 284 courtesy of Xinhua News Agency/photo by Wang Xinqing; 289, 291*b*, 292, 293, 294, 295, 371 Dr. J.L. Watson; 291*t* Whipple Museum, Cambridge; 302, 388, 406*l* Ashmolean Museum, Oxford; 316 Hutchison Library; 363 Raymond Mann Chinese Instruments, London; 366 National Film Archive/Stills Library; 379 Gulbenkian Museum of Oriental Art, Durham; 387 Museum of Far Eastern Antiquities, Stockholm; 389*r*, 413, 418 Percival David Foundation of Chinese Art; 391 Cleveland Museum of Art, Ohio; 392*t* Philadelphia Museum of Art; 392*bl* Museum of Far Eastern Antiquities, Stockholm/Collection of HM King of Sweden; 393*l*, 408*l* Metropolitan Museum of Art, N.Y.; 393*r* Arthur M. Sackler Collection, N.Y.; 394*l* Merseyside County Art Galleries; 394*r* Allen Memorial Art Museum, Oberlin College, Ohio; 395 Asian Art Museum of San Francisco, the Avery Brundage Collection; 403, 407 Roderick Whitfield; 404 by permission of the British Library; 406*r*, 410*l*, 417*t* Princeton University Art Museum; 410*b* Boston Museum of Fine Art; 411, 417*b* Collection of the Shanghai Museum; 415*t, c* Collection of Suzhou Museum; 426, 427, 428 Prof. E. Glahn; 431, 432 Maggie Keswick; 433, 439, 441, 442, 444, 448, 449, 450, 451 by courtesy of the East Asian History of Science Library, Cambridge; 445*t* National Maritime Museum, London.